# Contemporary
# Literary Criticism

# Guide to Gale Literary Criticism Series

| For criticism on | Consult these Gale series |
|---|---|
| Authors now living or who died after December 31, 1999 | *CONTEMPORARY LITERARY CRITICISM (CLC)* |
| Authors who died between 1900 and 1999 | *TWENTIETH-CENTURY LITERARY CRITICISM (TCLC)* |
| Authors who died between 1800 and 1899 | *NINETEENTH-CENTURY LITERATURE CRITICISM (NCLC)* |
| Authors who died between 1400 and 1799 | *LITERATURE CRITICISM FROM 1400 TO 1800 (LC)* <br><br> *SHAKESPEAREAN CRITICISM (SC)* |
| Authors who died before 1400 | *CLASSICAL AND MEDIEVAL LITERATURE CRITICISM (CMLC)* |
| Authors of books for children and young adults | *CHILDREN'S LITERATURE REVIEW (CLR)* |
| Dramatists | *DRAMA CRITICISM (DC)* |
| Poets | *POETRY CRITICISM (PC)* |
| Short story writers | *SHORT STORY CRITICISM (SSC)* |
| Literary topics and movements | *HARLEM RENAISSANCE: A GALE CRITICAL COMPANION (HR)* <br><br> *THE BEAT GENERATION: A GALE CRITICAL COMPANION (BG)* |
| Asian American writers of the last two hundred years | *ASIAN AMERICAN LITERATURE (AAL)* |
| Black writers of the past two hundred years | *BLACK LITERATURE CRITICISM (BLC)* <br><br> *BLACK LITERATURE CRITICISM SUPPLEMENT (BLCS)* |
| Hispanic writers of the late nineteenth and twentieth centuries | *HISPANIC LITERATURE CRITICISM (HLC)* <br><br> *HISPANIC LITERATURE CRITICISM SUPPLEMENT (HLCS)* |
| Native North American writers and orators of the eighteenth, nineteenth, and twentieth centuries | *NATIVE NORTH AMERICAN LITERATURE (NNAL)* |
| Major authors from the Renaissance to the present | *WORLD LITERATURE CRITICISM, 1500 TO THE PRESENT (WLC)* <br><br> *WORLD LITERATURE CRITICISM SUPPLEMENT (WLCS)* |

ISSN 0091-3421

Volume 195

# Contemporary Literary Criticism

Criticism of the Works
of Today's Novelists, Poets, Playwrights,
Short Story Writers, Scriptwriters, and
Other Creative Writers

**Jeffrey W. Hunter**
PROJECT EDITOR

Detroit • New York • San Francisco • San Diego • New Haven, Conn. • Waterville, Maine • London • Munich

# Contemporary Literary Criticism, Vol. 195

**Project Editor**
Jeffrey W. Hunter

**Editorial**
Jessica Bomarito, Kathy D. Darrow, Jelena O. Krstović, Michelle Lee, Ellen McGeagh, Joseph Palmisano, Linda Pavlovski, Thomas J. Schoenberg, Lawrence J. Trudeau, Russel Whitaker

**Data Capture**
Francis Monroe, Gwen Tucker

**Indexing Services**
Laurie Andriot

**Rights and Acquisitions**
Margie Abendroth, Jacqueline Key, Mari Masalin-Cooper

**Imaging and Multimedia**
Dean Dauphinais, Leitha Etheridge-Sims, Lezlie Light, Mike Logusz, Dan Newell, Christine O'Bryan, Kelly A. Quin, Denay Wilding, Robyn Young

**Composition and Electronic Prepress**
Kathy Sauer

**Manufacturing**
Rhonda Williams

**Product Manager**
Janet Witalec

LIBRARY OF CONGRESS CATALOG CARD NUMBER 76-46132
ISBN 0-7876-7965-8
ISSN 0091-3421

Printed in the United States of America
10 9 8 7 6 5 4 3 2 1

# Contents

Preface vii

Acknowledgments xi

Literary Criticism Series Advisory Board xv

**Woody Allen 1935-** ...................................................................... 1
*American film director, screenwriter, actor, playwright, and humorist*

**Neil Gaiman 1960-** ...................................................................... 167
*English graphic novelist, novelist, short-story writer, editor,
children's writer, television writer, radio play writer, and
screenplay writer*

**Shena Mackay 1944-** ................................................................. 242
*Scottish novelist, short-story and novella writer, and editor*

**Susan Sontag 1933-** ................................................................... 282
*American essayist, novelist, short-story writer, critic, playwright,
screenplay writer, and film director*

Literary Criticism Series Cumulative Author Index 367

Literary Criticism Series Cumulative Topic Index 467

*CLC* Cumulative Nationality Index 479

*CLC*-195 Title Index 493

# Preface

Named "one of the twenty-five most distinguished reference titles published during the past twenty-five years" by *Reference Quarterly,* the *Contemporary Literary Criticism* (*CLC*) series provides readers with critical commentary and general information on more than 2,000 authors now living or who died after December 31, 1999. Volumes published from 1973 through 1999 include authors who died after December 31, 1959. Previous to the publication of the first volume of *CLC* in 1973, there was no ongoing digest monitoring scholarly and popular sources of critical opinion and explication of modern literature. *CLC,* therefore, has fulfilled an essential need, particularly since the complexity and variety of contemporary literature makes the function of criticism especially important to today's reader.

## Scope of the Series

*CLC* provides significant passages from published criticism of works by creative writers. Since many of the authors covered in *CLC* inspire continual critical commentary, writers are often represented in more than one volume. There is, of course, no duplication of reprinted criticism.

Authors are selected for inclusion for a variety of reasons, among them the publication or dramatic production of a critically acclaimed new work, the reception of a major literary award, revival of interest in past writings, or the adaptation of a literary work to film or television.

Attention is also given to several other groups of writers—authors of considerable public interest—about whose work criticism is often difficult to locate. These include mystery and science fiction writers, literary and social critics, foreign authors, and authors who represent particular ethnic groups.

Each *CLC* volume contains individual essays and reviews taken from hundreds of book review periodicals, general magazines, scholarly journals, monographs, and books. Entries include critical evaluations spanning from the beginning of an author's career to the most current commentary. Interviews, feature articles, and other published writings that offer insight into the author's works are also presented. Students, teachers, librarians, and researchers will find that the general critical and biographical material in *CLC* provides them with vital information required to write a term paper, analyze a poem, or lead a book discussion group. In addition, complete biographical citations note the original source and all of the information necessary for a term paper footnote or bibliography.

## Organization of the Book

A *CLC* entry consists of the following elements:

- The **Author Heading** cites the name under which the author most commonly wrote, followed by birth and death dates. Also located here are any name variations under which an author wrote, including transliterated forms for authors whose native languages use nonroman alphabets. If the author wrote consistently under a pseudonym, the pseudonym will be listed in the author heading and the author's actual name given in parenthesis on the first line of the biographical and critical information. Uncertain birth or death dates are indicated by question marks. Single-work entries are preceded by a heading that consists of the most common form of the title in English translation (if applicable) and the original date of composition.

- A **Portrait of the Author** is included when available.

- The **Introduction** contains background information that introduces the reader to the author, work, or topic that is the subject of the entry.

- The list of **Principal Works** is ordered chronologically by date of first publication and lists the most important works by the author. The genre and publication date of each work is given. In the case of foreign authors whose works have been translated into English, the English-language version of the title follows in brackets. Unless otherwise indicated, dramas are dated by first performance, not first publication.

- Reprinted **Criticism** is arranged chronologically in each entry to provide a useful perspective on changes in critical evaluation over time. The critic's name and the date of composition or publication of the critical work are given at the beginning of each piece of criticism. Unsigned criticism is preceded by the title of the source in which it appeared. All titles by the author featured in the text are printed in boldface type. Footnotes are reprinted at the end of each essay or excerpt. In the case of excerpted criticism, only those footnotes that pertain to the excerpted texts are included.

- A complete **Bibliographical Citation** of the original essay or book precedes each piece of criticism. Source citations in the Literary Criticism Series follow University of Chicago Press style, as outlined in *The Chicago Manual of Style,* 14th ed. (Chicago: The University of Chicago Press, 1993).

- Critical essays are prefaced by brief **Annotations** explicating each piece.

- Whenever possible, a recent **Author Interview** accompanies each entry.

- An annotated bibliography of **Further Reading** appears at the end of each entry and suggests resources for additional study. In some cases, significant essays for which the editors could not obtain reprint rights are included here. Boxed material following the further reading list provides references to other biographical and critical sources on the author in series published by Thomson Gale.

# Indexes

A **Cumulative Author Index** lists all of the authors that appear in a wide variety of reference sources published by Thomson Gale, including *CLC*. A complete list of these sources is found facing the first page of the Author Index. The index also includes birth and death dates and cross references between pseudonyms and actual names.

A **Cumulative Nationality Index** lists all authors featured in *CLC* by nationality, followed by the number of the *CLC* volume in which their entry appears.

A **Cumulative Topic Index** lists the literary themes and topics treated in the series as well as in *Literature Criticism from 1400 to 1800, Nineteenth-Century Literature Criticism, Twentieth-Century Literary Criticism,* and the *Contemporary Literary Criticism* Yearbook, which was discontinued in 1998.

An alphabetical **Title Index** accompanies each volume of *CLC*. Listings of titles by authors covered in the given volume are followed by the author's name and the corresponding page numbers where the titles are discussed. English translations of foreign titles and variations of titles are cross-referenced to the title under which a work was originally published. Titles of novels, dramas, nonfiction books, and poetry, short story, or essay collections are printed in italics, while individual poems, short stories, and essays are printed in roman type within quotation marks.

In response to numerous suggestions from librarians, Thomson Gale also produces an annual cumulative title index that alphabetically lists all titles reviewed in *CLC* and is available to all customers. Additional copies of this index are available upon request. Librarians and patrons will welcome this separate index; it saves shelf space, is easy to use, and is recyclable upon receipt of the next edition.

# Citing *Contemporary Literary Criticism*

When citing criticism reprinted in the Literary Criticism Series, students should provide complete bibliographic information so that the cited essay can be located in the original print or electronic source. Students who quote directly from reprinted criticism may use any accepted bibliographic format, such as University of Chicago Press style or Modern Language Association (MLA) style. Both the MLA and the University of Chicago formats are acceptable and recognized as being the current standards for citations. It is important, however, to choose one format for all citations; do not mix the two formats within a list of citations.

The examples below follow recommendations for preparing a bibliography set forth in *The Chicago Manual of Style,* 14th ed. (Chicago: The University of Chicago Press, 1993); the first example pertains to material drawn from periodicals, the second to material reprinted from books:

Morrison, Jago. "Narration and Unease in Ian McEwan's Later Fiction." *Critique* 42, no. 3 (spring 2001): 253-68. Reprinted in *Contemporary Literary Criticism.* Vol. 169, edited by Janet Witalec, 212-20. Detroit: Gale, 2003.

Brossard, Nicole. "Poetic Politics." In *The Politics of Poetic Form: Poetry and Public Policy,* edited by Charles Bernstein, 73-82. New York: Roof Books, 1990. Reprinted in *Contemporary Literary Criticism.* Vol. 169, edited by Janet Witalec, 3-8. Detroit: Gale, 2003.

The examples below follow recommendations for preparing a works cited list set forth in the *MLA Handbook for Writers of Research Papers,* 5th ed. (New York: The Modern Language Association of America, 1999); the first example pertains to material drawn from periodicals, the second to material reprinted from books:

Morrison, Jago. "Narration and Unease in Ian McEwan's Later Fiction." *Critique* 42.3 (spring 2001): 253-68. Reprinted in *Contemporary Literary Criticism.* Ed. Janet Witalec. Vol. 169. Detroit: Gale, 2003. 212-20.

Brossard, Nicole. "Poetic Politics." *The Politics of Poetic Form: Poetry and Public Policy.* Ed. Charles Bernstein. New York: Roof Books, 1990. 73-82. Reprinted in *Contemporary Literary Criticism.* Ed. Janet Witalec. Vol. 169. Detroit: Gale, 2003. 3-8.

## Suggestions are Welcome

Readers who wish to suggest new features, topics, or authors to appear in future volumes, or who have other suggestions or comments are cordially invited to call, write, or fax the Product Manager:

Product Manager, Literary Criticism Series
Thomson Gale
27500 Drake Road
Farmington Hills, MI 48331-3535
1-800-347-4253 (GALE)
Fax: 248-699-8054

# Acknowledgments

The editors wish to thank the copyright holders of the criticism included in this volume and the permissions managers of many book and magazine publishing companies for assisting us in securing reproduction rights. We are also grateful to the staffs of the Detroit Public Library, the Library of Congress, the University of Detroit Mercy Library, Wayne State University Purdy/Kresge Library Complex, and the University of Michigan Libraries for making their resources available to us. Following is a list of the copyright holders who have granted us permission to reproduce material in this volume of *CLC*. Every effort has been made to trace copyright, but if omissions have been made, please let us know.

## COPYRIGHTED MATERIAL IN *CLC*, VOLUME 195, WAS REPRODUCED FROM THE FOLLOWING PERIODICALS:

**COPYRIGHTED MATERIAL IN *CLC*, VOLUME 195, WAS REPRODUCED FROM THE FOLLOWING BOOKS:**

Pogel, Nancy. From *Woody Allen.* Twayne Publishers, 1987. Copyright © 1987 G. K. Hall & Co. All rights reserved. Reproduced by permission of The Gale Group. —Rauch, Stephen. From *Neil Gaiman's "The Sandman" and Joseph Campbell: In Search of the Modern Myth.* Wildside Press, 2003. Reproduced by permission.—Rollyson, Carl. From *Reading Susan Sontag: A Critical Introduction to Her Work.* Ivan R. Dee, 2001. Copyright © 2001 by Carl Rollyson. All rights reserved. Reproduced by the Courtesy of Ivan R. Dee, Publisher.

**PHOTOGRAPHS AND ILLUSTRATIONS APPEARING IN *CLC*, VOLUME 195, WERE RECEIVED FROM THE FOLLOWING SOURCES:**

Allen, Woody, photograph. The Kobal Collection/United Artists. Reproduced by permission.—Gaiman, Neil, photograph by Kelli Bickman. Copyright © Kelli Bickman. Reproduced by permission.—Sontag, Susan, photograph. AP/Wide World Photos. Reproduced by permission.

# Thomson Gale Literature Product Advisory Board

The members of the Thomson Gale Literature Product Advisory Board—reference librarians from public and academic library systems—represent a cross-section of our customer base and offer a variety of informed perspectives on both the presentation and content of our literature products. Advisory board members assess and define such quality issues as the relevance, currency, and usefulness of the author coverage, critical content, and literary topics included in our series; evaluate the layout, presentation, and general quality of our printed volumes; provide feedback on the criteria used for selecting authors and topics covered in our series; provide suggestions for potential enhancements to our series; identify any gaps in our coverage of authors or literary topics, recommending authors or topics for inclusion; analyze the appropriateness of our content and presentation for various user audiences, such as high school students, undergraduates, graduate students, librarians, and educators; and offer feedback on any proposed changes/enhancements to our series. We wish to thank the following advisors for their advice throughout the year.

# Woody Allen
## 1935-

(Born Allen Stewart Konigsberg; name legally changed to Heywood Allen) American film director, screenwriter, actor, playwright, and humorist.

The following entry provides criticism on Allen's career through 2003. For further information on his life and works, see *CLC*, Volumes 16 and 52.

## INTRODUCTION

Allen is a celebrated filmmaker, each of whose works bears the unmistakable signature of his unique style. His distinct screen persona has entered the cultural mainstream as an immediately recognizable type: an intellectual aesthete who is wracked by the multiple burdens of social insecurity, sexual neurosis, paranoia, existential angst, and chronic unhappiness. The writer, director, and star of the majority of his films, Allen may be the most prolific filmmaker of his generation, having released more than thirty-five films in thirty-eight years of filmmaking to date. His best-known and critically acclaimed films include *Annie Hall* (1977), *Manhattan* (1979), *Zelig* (1983), and *Hannah and Her Sisters* (1986).

## BIOGRAPHICAL INFORMATION

Allen was born December 1, 1935, in Brooklyn, New York, and was raised in a working-class Jewish neighborhood of Brooklyn. While in high school, Allen began writing and selling jokes for humor columnists and celebrity comedians. He became a staff writer for the National Broadcasting Corporation (NBC) in 1952, where he wrote jokes for such entertainers as Sid Caesar, Art Carney, Carol Channing, and others. Allen attended New York's City College in 1953 but dropped out. The following year, while still a teenager, Allen married his high school sweetheart, Harlene Rosen; the couple divorced in 1960. During the 1960s Allen worked as a stand-up comedian in cafes and nightclubs throughout New York City, and appeared as a guest on several television talk shows. During this period he developed his comic persona and changed his name to Heywood Allen, adopting the nickname "Woody." Allen began making movies in 1965, when he was asked by producer Charles Feldman to write the screenplay for *What's New, Pussycat?* (1965). His first Broadway play,

*Don't Drink the Water,* was produced in 1966. That same year he married actress Louise Lasser, who co-starred in several of his films, and whom he divorced in 1970. During the 1970s Allen was involved with actress Diane Keaton, who also co-starred with him in his movies. *Annie Hall* is generally considered to be a semi-autobiographical account of his relationship with Keaton. During the 1980s Allen was involved with actress Mia Farrow, another co-star, with whom he maintained a relationship until the early 1990s. Although Allen and Farrow lived in separate apartment buildings and never married, they had a son together, born in 1987, and co-adopted two children. In 1992 Allen's personal life became a major news item, as Farrow accused him of sexually molesting one of their adopted daughters. At the same time, the fifty-seven-year-old Allen became openly involved in a relationship with the college-aged Soon-Yi Previn, one of Farrow's adopted children from an earlier marriage. In a series of bitter court battles with Farrow, Allen was cleared of charges of child molestation, but continued to experience public disapproval. In 1997 Allen married Soon-Yi, with whom he adopted a daughter. In addition to his yearly fall film project, Allen has played jazz clarinet with his band in a hotel lounge in New York every Monday night for over twenty-five years.

## MAJOR WORKS

Allen's earliest films are madcap comedies, tending toward social satire, sexual farce, and genre-parody, heavily laden with one-liners and physical slapstick humor. *What's Up, Tiger Lily?* (1966), *Take the Money and Run* (1969), *Bananas* (1971), *Play It Again, Sam* (1972; originally produced as a stage play in 1969), *Sleeper* (1973), and other films of this period introduced Allen's comic persona to audiences and established him as a leading comedian of his generation.

*Love and Death* (1975), marks the beginning of a transition in Allen's career, toward deeper and more serious themes than those presented in his earlier films. A parody of nineteenth-century Russian literature, particularly Leo Tolstoy's *War and Peace,* the film features central characters who debate philosophical questions about the existence of God, the nature of morality, and the significance of death to the meaning of life, frequently citing and parodying famous philosophers. *Annie Hall* furthers Allen's movement away from madcap comedy. This bittersweet romantic comedy contains a more introspective exploration of male-female relationships and the nature of love in the modern world. Allen's most successful film, *Annie Hall* won Academy Awards for best picture, director, and screenplay in 1977. *Manhattan* is often discussed as a companion piece to *Annie Hall* as it explores similar themes, again within the genre of bittersweet romantic comedy. This period of Allen's career is also notable for two significant failures: *Interiors* (1978), Allen's first attempt at a completely serious film, and *Stardust Memories* (1980), which Allen himself has characterized as his least popular film. Both were critically and commercially unsuccessful.

In the 1980s Allen released several of his most critically admired films. In *Zelig* Allen plays the title character, who, because of insecurities about his identity, takes on the physical qualities of those he comes into contact with. Allen reproduced the quality of old black-and-white movie newsreels, utilized editing techniques to splice images of the protagonist into archival news footage, and used other devices to create the feel of an authentic documentary. *The Purple Rose of Cairo* (1985) highlights the role of spectatorship in the imagination of the film viewer. An abused New Jersey housewife struggling through the Depression years attends the movies seeking relief from the grim

circumstances of her life. When her favorite character steps off the screen and falls in love with her, she must face the conundrum of living with a fantasy that has come true. *Hannah and Her Sisters* and *Husbands and Wives* (1992) explore the complex interrelationships of Manhattan couples struggling with the trials of modern marriage. *Crimes and Misdemeanors* (1989) examines Allen's recurring preoccupation with moral and existential questioning, and the significance of the Holocaust to modern thought.

During the 1990s and the early part of the new millennium, Allen made a number of films explicitly designed to be light entertainment, eschewing his heavier themes. In these works Allen expresses a sense of nostalgia for classic Hollywood movies of the 1930s and 1940s: *Manhattan Murder Mystery* (1993), *Everyone Says I Love You* (1996), *Small Time Crooks* (2000), and *The Curse of the Jade Scorpion* (2001) each pay homage to such old movie genres as the mystery-thriller, musical, and screwball comedy. During this period Allen also made several films, including *Bullets over Broadway* (1994), *Celebrity* (1998), and *Sweet and Lowdown* (1999), that combine elements of comedy with more complex matters such as the challenges facing the creative artist who battles to maintain his integrity in a world of mass entertainment. Allen continued his exploration of a creator's struggles in a commercial society in his most recent films, *Hollywood Ending* (2002) and *Anything Else?* (2003).

Allen's theatrical productions include *Don't Drink the Water, Death* (1975), *God* (1975), *The Floating Lightbulb* (1981), *Death Defying Acts* (1995), and *Writer's Block* (2003). He has authored numerous satirical essays and short stories, many of them originally published in the *New Yorker,* and later collected in volumes such as *Getting Even* (1971), *Without Feathers* (1975), *Side Effects* (1980), and *The Complete Prose* (1991).

## CRITICAL RECEPTION

Critics of Allen's overall body of work have identified recurring thematic concerns throughout his films. Such themes focus on identity crises, the significance of artistic expression to the creative mind, the role of dreams, fantasies, and films in the psychology of the individual, chronic questioning about the meaning of life and death, and the nature of good and evil. Critics have also noted the influence of such filmmakers as Ingmar Bergman, Federico Fellini, and Jean-Luc Goddard, and have compared Allen's screen persona to the "tramp" figure created by Charlie Chaplin: a prototypical "little man," a lovable and charming social underdog whose motives remain sincere and heartfelt in a modern world of alienation and impersonal interactions. While Allen's persona also follows a heritage of Jewish comics such as the Marx Brothers—whom Allen has cited as a major influence on his work—the composite character is seen as Allen's unique creation.

Critics have generally agreed that Allen is at his best when working in the tragicomic vein, exploring serious themes of modern love and existential angst, balanced by a sense of the absurd. The films in which he intentionally withholds his penchant for comedy have generally been considered failures. *Annie Hall* is widely regarded as a perfect meshing of Allen's talents for comedy and absurdity with a sense of pathos that lends depth and complexity to his greatest films. With *Manhattan,* Allen was hailed as the consummate New York City filmmaker, celebrating the urban landscape with on-location cinematography, particularly favoring Manhattan's Central Park. However, with subsequent films shot in New York, some critics began to fault him for portraying a cleaned-up vision of the city, devoid of the poverty and crime typical of urban settings. Additionally, some criticized Allen for his failure to portray the racial and ethnic diversity of New York City, and while once praised for his knowing portraits of the social milieu of New York's cultural and intellectual elite, he was later faulted for expressing pretentious attitudes through his characters.

The public attention on Allen's personal life in 1992 marks a turning point in the tenor and focus critics have applied to the evaluation of his films. Many critics believe his relationship with Soon-Yi Previn and the accusations leveled at him have affected the critical appraisal for much of his subsequent work. Events from Allen's personal life have prompted reviewers to scrutinize his films for evidence of his psychological make-up and moral center. This tendency culminated in the critical reception for *Deconstructing Harry* (1997), which many viewed as a means by which Allen sought to justify his own questionable behavior by implying that the true artist is above morality. During the 1980s Allen was widely regarded as a writer of strong, intelligent, complex female characters. After 1992, however, critics began to note a tendency for Allen to cast himself in romantic lead roles coupled with women much younger than himself, which some found distasteful. Further, critics began to regard Allen's female characters and his representation of male-female relationships as an expression of a deep-seated misogyny, and asserted that he portrayed women as manipulative and controlling. Subsequently Allen began to write and direct more films in which he does not appear at all—such as *Bullets over Broadway* and *Celebrity.* Critics have noted, however, that, even when he does not appear as a protagonist in his own films, he usually chooses actors who embody the characteristic Woody Allen persona.

Allen's films of the 1990s marketed as light entertainment have been faulted by some reviewers, who assert these works do not live up to the standards Allen set for himself in earlier decades. Such critics found these films to be based on weak screenplays, lacking in humor, originality, or insight. Further, some reviewers noted that, while Allen's best films maintained a dark, edgy humor tempered by warmth and sincerity, more recent work expresses a cynicism devoid of humor or humanity. Others have disagreed, finding that Allen's latest films are successful purely as works of light comedy.

---

# PRINCIPAL WORKS

*From A to Z* [co-author] (play) 1960

*What's New, Pussycat?* [screenwriter] (film) 1965

*Don't Drink the Water* (play) 1966

*What's Up, Tiger Lily?* [co-screenwriter with Frank Buxton, Len Maxwell, Louise Lasser, and Mickey Rose] (film) 1966

*Play It Again, Sam* (play) 1969

*Take the Money and Run* [co-screenwriter with Rose and director] (film) 1969

*Bananas* [co-screenwriter with Rose; director] (film) 1971

*Getting Even* (essays and short stories) 1971

*Everything You Always Wanted to Know about Sex but Were Afraid to Ask* [screenwriter and director; based on the book by David Ruben] (film) 1972

*Play It Again, Sam* [screenwriter] (film) 1972

*Sleeper* [co-screenwriter with Marshall Brickman, and director] (film) 1973

*Death: A Comedy in One Act* (play) 1975

*God: A Comedy in One Act* (play) 1975

*Love and Death* [screenwriter and director] (film) 1975

*Without Feathers* (essays and short stories) 1975

*Annie Hall* [co-screenwriter with Brickman, and director] (film) 1977

*Interiors* [screenwriter and director] (film) 1978

*Non-Being and Somethingness* [collected from the comic strip *Inside Woody Allen*] (comic strips) 1978

*Manhattan* [co-screenwriter, with Brickman; director] (film) 1979

*Side Effects* (humor collection) 1980

*Stardust Memories* [screenwriter and director] (film) 1980

*The Floating Lightbulb* (play) 1981

*A Midsummer Night's Sex Comedy* [screenwriter and director] (film) 1982

*Zelig* [screenwriter and director] (film) 1983

*Broadway Danny Rose* [screenwriter and director] (film) 1984

*The Purple Rose of Cairo* [screenwriter and director] (film) 1985

*Hannah and Her Sisters* [screenwriter and director] (film) 1986

*Radio Days* [screenwriter and director] (film) 1987

*September* [screenwriter and director] (film) 1987

*Another Woman* [screenwriter and director] (film) 1988

*Crimes and Misdemeanors* [screenwriter and director] (film) 1989

*Oedipus Wrecks* [one of three films by various writer and directors in *New York Stories*] (film) 1989

*Alice* [screenwriter and director] (film) 1990

*The Complete Prose* (humor) 1991

*Husbands and Wives* [screenwriter and director] (film) 1992

*Shadows and Fog* [screenwriter and director] (film) 1992

*The Illustrated Woody Allen Reader* (humor) 1993

*Manhattan Murder Mystery* [screenwriter and director] (film) 1993

*Bullets over Broadway* [co-screenwriter and director] (film) 1994

*Death Defying Acts: Three One-Act Comedies* (play) 1995

*Mighty Aphrodite* [screenwriter and director] (film) 1995

*Woody Allen on Woody Allen: In Conversation with Stig Bjorkman* (interviews) 1995

*Everyone Says I Love You* [screenwriter and director] (film) 1996

*Deconstructing Harry* [screenwriter and director] (film) 1997

*Celebrity* [screenwriter and director] (film) 1998

*Sweet and Lowdown* [screenwriter and director] (film) 1999

*Small Time Crooks* [screenwriter and director] (film) 2000

*The Curse of the Jade Scorpion* [screenwriter and director] (film) 2001

*Hollywood Ending* [screenwriter and director] (film) 2002

*Anything Else?* [screenwriter and director] (film) 2003

*Writer's Block* [includes *Riverside Drive* and *Old Saybrook*] (plays) 2003

---

# CRITICISM

**Nancy Pogel (essay date 1987)**

SOURCE: Pogel, Nancy. "Humble Beginnings: The First 'Woody Allen' Films." In *Woody Allen*, pp. 33-54. Boston, Mass.: Twayne Publishers, 1987.

[*In the following essay, Pogel examines three of Allen's earliest films,* Take the Money and Run, Bananas, *and* Play It Again, Sam—*commenting on the films' inspirations and critical receptions.*]

The first three films that helped establish Woody Allen's reputation as a comic filmmaker, *Take the Money and Run* (1969), *Bananas* (1971), and *Play It Again, Sam* (1972), share several parallel patterns despite variations in narrative situation and setting. These films involve a meek central character, a reflexive context, and a dialogic, jokelike structure. The little man is tossed between two conflicting circumstances, the second of which often promises to be more rewarding than the first. Ultimately, however, neither situation proves satisfying; inevitably, the little man's encounter with a promising alternative only highlights its meaninglessness and the main character's foolishness and alienation—yet also, a third and more human possibility that he himself represents.[1]

Unlike the more complicated and self-conscious little men in several of Allen's later films, the figure in these early movies is an innocent and humble victim. He serves to expose the anxieties and absurdities of contemporary life, to examine the threat such a life poses to coherent identity, and to reveal the problems in attempting to live up to heroic images born out of Hollywood fantasy. While filmic allusions suggest how significant visual impressions have been in creating unreliable contemporary values and behavior patterns, those same images also contribute to the little man's survival. Like many modern examples of American humor and comic film, Allen's early work evokes skepticism, but it is not without hope; Allen explores a double-edged view of American dreams and false illusions in terms of his own language and medium. Even in his earliest films, he recognizes that film is part of the problem it describes, and even his earliest films are more inconclusive than they may first appear to be.

Although *Play It Again, Sam* has a tighter, more conventional narrative line than the other two early comedies, all three films are episodic and filled with slapstick, one-liners, and comic shtick transposed from nightclub performance and literary production to film. Always a remarkable mimic of visual as well as verbal styles, Allen used visual puns and relied heavily on reflexive allusions and references in his earliest films, but unlike the later films, his early efforts are not the work of a sophisticated visual artist. The jokes take precedence over composition, lighting, color, and carefully controlled mise-en-scène; and the films' overall coherence and depth appear to be secondary to entertaining dialogue and relatively simple comic effects.

"THE JUNGLE IS NO PLACE FOR A CELLIST":
*TAKE THE MONEY AND RUN*.

Neither the critics nor Woody Allen considered *What's New, Pussycat?* an artistically important movie, but it was such a commercial success that Allen's managers, Joffe and Rollins, were able to launch Allen as a director, actor, and writer of his own films. After a year and a half of looking for the right situation, Charles Joffe finally sold the script for *Take the Money and Run* to Palomar Pictures, who put up $1.6 million for its production and gave Allen the right to direct and star.[2] For his first film, Allen told Eric Lax, "I stayed with my safest stuff, which is the stuff I know: abject humility. I was very timid in that picture. But there was no way I could have been anything else. I had never made a film, I was never the star of a picture before."[3]

Allen, however, sought assistance. In addition to Joffe, who would produce, and Mickey Rose, who coauthored the script, Allen drew on the expertise of veteran cinematographer Lester Schorr, production manager Jack Grossberg, and Fred Gallo, who served as unit manager and right-hand man on this film. Allen also called upon editor Ralph Rosenblum, whose credits include *The Pawnbroker* (1965) and *Long Day's Journey into Night* (1962). Rosenblum, who would go on to edit *Bananas, Sleeper, Annie Hall,* and *Interiors,* was called in to save the film after screenings of a rough cut failed with trial audiences. Allen lacked confidence. As he put it later: "I had been too harsh on myself and lopped out gobs and gobs of material. His [Rosenblum's] big thing was to say, 'Put it back'"[4] Rosenblum believed the film's greatest problem was its uneven tone. He objected to the very combination of qualities that would characterize Allen's best films of the late seventies and eighties,—the pathos and seriousness that ran through what was supposed to be a comedy. Rosenblum especially disliked the ending, a bloody *Bonnie and Clyde* parody in which the little man was gunned down following a bank robbery. Rosenblum suggested a more upbeat conclusion.[5]

Allen claims to have thought seriously once about becoming a gangster. He said, "I never would have stopped trying to beat the law in the face of persistent defeat."[6] Before he began making *Take the Money and Run,* Allen had done a spoof of *Bonnie and Clyde* (1967) with Liza Minnelli on the "Kraft Music Hall Comedy Hour." Later he would write a piece on organized crime for *Getting Even,* his first collection of humorous essays.[7] Allen notes that he was thinking about Dillinger when he made the film, but Allen's little man, with the meek first name Virgil, takes his last name, Starkwell, from Charles Starkweather, a notorious 1950s killer. Virgil takes his story not only from the lives of real gangsters, but from countless moving pictures—from *Little Caesar* (1930) to *Bonnie and Clyde*—that created the gangster-hero myths so endemic to the American imagination.

*Take the Money and Run* is a genre fantasy involving all of the American gangster film conventions. Within a pseudodocumentary frame, Jackson Beck, the film's narrator, provides a Movietone-newsreel grittiness with his staccato voice-over that imitates the style of fifties films like *Walk East on Beacon* (1952). The narration, the newsreel-like footage, and the burlesque Pathe-style vignettes of Virgil's parents, his teacher, his cello instructor, his probation officer, and a fellow convict all spoof crime films' cinema verité techniques. Other moments in the film parody a variety of gangster genre paradigms. Represented are biographies of single criminals, the bad-kid-grows-up-to-be-a-gangster stories, the prison pictures, the organized crime movies, and the chain gang, big escape, and hostage films. In addition, *Take the Money* alludes to other films, such as *The Hustler* (1961) and *West Side Story* (1961), which lie on the outskirts of the genre.

But on each of the typical occasions drawn from gangster films, Virgil is far less than the macho masters of circumstances who have swaggered across American movie screens since James Cagney chucked his mother on the shoulder in *Public Enemy* (1931). Virgil Starkwell bungles one opportunity for stylish behavior after another. Virgil is no dapper young tough, who eludes the police and grows up to be a fearless criminal; he is a slight child with tousled red hair and freckles whose hands get stuck in the gumball machines he tries to rob. He violates all the old patterns: instead of being a Horatio Alger success, he fails as a young entrepreneur because he can't give a spit shoeshine without hitting his customer's trousers. He is not a frustrated artist led to crime, but a failure at mastering the cello—he blows into it. And he creates a classic moment of comic disorder when he attempts to perform sitting down in a marching band.

Unlike Paul Newman's Fast Eddy, Virgil plays an embarrassing game of pool. In a *West Side Story*-style street fight, Virgil's is the only switchblade that won't work. He is not the dapper, debonair hoodlum with a platinum blonde on his arm—he falls in love and marries a laundress, and on the day when he is preparing to rob a bank, squabbles with her over who has first rights to the bathroom. Even his bank robberies lack the élan of the classic robber: during his first attempt, the bank officials cannot read his holdup note. Appearing to say, "Apt natural I have a gub," the note highlights the little man's innocent use of language in contrast to sophisticated social protocol, and it leads to his imprisonment.

Neither of Virgil's options permits success or satisfies his desires. Attempting to be a criminal or attempting to go straight, Virgil's schlemiel persona is Allen's response to the romantic conventions of the classic American crime film. Virgil is victimized in prison by a treacherous shirt-folding machine in the laundry, by officials whose medical experiments turn him into a Hassidic rabbi, and by his fellow inmates, who don't bother to inform him that a planned escape is off and leave him outside the cell-block doors, banging to get back in. When he tries to be Cool Hand Luke and escapes from a work gang, he must do so in lockstep with five other prisoners to whom he is chained. Allen is also playing off such films as *20,000 Years in Sing-Sing* (1933), *The Big House* (1930), *I Was a Fugitive from a Chain Gang* (1932), *Dillinger* (1945), *The Asphalt Jungle* (1950), and *The Defiant Ones* (1958) in his depiction of Virgil's failures to live up to the heroic images of dashing gangster types.

*Take the Money and Run,* like other early Allen films, finds a humble little-man main character caught between two unsavory possibilities. He is no freer outside than inside prison, and his confinement becomes a representative contemporary predicament, and in comic form refers to greater modern paradoxes than innocent Virgil ever consciously considers. Virgil's confinement also involves a reflexive burlesque context, a comment on films and filmmaking.

Virgil is confined not merely by worlds inside and outside prison, but by the rigid demands of the genre he finds himself in; however, while he epitomizes our propensity to glorify false illusions, he also re-creates our impotence in a comic fashion and represents our hopes. His frustration in the face of everything from stubborn shirt machines to conscientious cops lies well within the conventions of twentieth-century literary and filmic humor, wherein mechanical contrivances of the smallest sort and authority of any sort are the stuff that nightmares are made of. But against the rigidities of bands marching in orderly formation, depressing domestic problems, the deadly routine of prison life, or the requirements of formulaic genres and their desensitizing macho codes, Virgil Starkwell's disorderly ineptitude signifies antistructure and makes us laugh at our reluctance to acknowledge our own very human flaws.

A more significant affirmation lies in Virgil's persistence, derived from his innocence and his unknowing attempts to imitate Hollywood images. The same illusions that entrap him encourage him to believe in love, freedom, and survival. Although later little men will be far more self-conscious about time and aging, Virgil has as little sense of time's tyranny as he has of the limits suggested by Allen's metaphors of place. Even though he has been sentenced to eight hundred years in jail, and even though life outside jail provides no haven from adversity, Virgil refuses to give up. Despite several earlier unsuccessful attempts, at the end of *Take the Money and Run,* he is planning to escape from prison again. Although he failed before when a gun carved out of soap and painted with shoe polish (à la Dillinger) turned to suds in a rainstorm, we see Virgil whittling away at yet another bar of soap. Just as in the movies, he has no doubt that his next attempt will succeed. Virgil's naïveté makes him a victim, but it also presumes a

creator behind the character who still toys with the idea of renewal. Although Virgil's persistence clearly has its pathetic side, we see him endure because, like Don Quixote, he believes and acts upon his faith. The film is inconclusive about whether we should value Virgil's innocence or reject his illusions.

In carrying on dialogues with the social codes that have become literary, political, or filmic conventions, Woody Allen reflects on the sophistication of his day—textbook history, the social fantasies that underlie the genre, his audience, and the customs of his medium. The parody and the self-reflexive comedy in this early Allen film are handled so gently and with such a sense of familiarity with filmic conventions, however, that Allen doesn't just expose our failures to ridicule and unsympathetic laughter. *Take the Money and Run,* like later films from *Play It Again, Sam* to *The Purple Rose of Cairo* (1985), implies that unrealistic figures created by the American film industry in complicity with an undiscerning audience may be damaging, but they are also woven into the American mythos as the fabric of hope. Paradoxically, they are related at once to our worst self-deceptions and to a modicum of genuine romantic faith that, like Jay Gatsby's dream, is difficult to abandon.

## MORE JUNGLES IN BANANAS

The 1960s were the politically intense years of Castro, revolts in South America, civil conflicts in the Dominican Republic, assassinations in the United States, and student unrest over civil rights and Vietnam. Woody Allen's second major film, *Bananas,* explores the issues of its times—politics, revolution, and violence—with surprising aggressiveness. In *Bananas,* the critical themes that are to interest Allen throughout his filmmaking career take on sharper definition. One of Woody Allen's major concerns is the individual's search for authenticity in the face of dehumanizing modern manners, ideologies, and technologies. Allen's film deals with contemporary living that fosters depersonalization, uniformity, alienation, and loneliness.

*Bananas*'s Fielding Mellish (Woody Allen), like Virgil Starkwell, is a humble little man. Like Virgil, he is interested in love, sex, and survival; however, the little soul's instinctive longing for an innocence that requires trust is in constant conflict with the painful realities of modern experience. Allen demands an open-eyed look at the world, a look that leads to doubt and militates against the modicum of faith that his main character unconsciously seeks to retain; but despite the odds against individual fulfillment, Fielding Mellish, like Allen's other littleman characters, is a reflection of his creator's best wishes. In *Bananas,* the media can desensitize and act as an analogue to both depersonalizing corporations that define the quality of work experience, and to power-hungry politicians who devalue life;

yet Fielding's comic struggle to win his girl stresses the quest for intimacy and the importance of personal relationships—the longing for a world where love may still triumph over death.

Although it contains a number of minor movements, *Bananas* is basically orchestrated into two major parts—the spatial pattern of the film sends Fielding Mellish away from a sophisticated American civilization and into a more primal setting where he tries to find greater satisfaction, but like the parallel worlds inside and outside prison in *Take the Money and Run,* the jungle in the banana republic is not unlike the urban jungle. The rebels are as egomaniacal and fascistic as the dictators they oppose; justice is expedient in both places; and for the little man, problems with machines, food, and women are common to both locations. As a result of his confrontation with two equally unsatisfying possibilities, the little man in *Bananas* becomes somewhat more self-aware and discerning. *Bananas* suggests that if meaning is to be found, it lies in a recovery of humane instincts and in close personal relationships rather than in political abstractions. But while Allen's film apparently denounces political approaches, it cannot escape some of its own political implications, and while the little man appears to achieve some success at the end of the film, like all Allen's endings, this one is not without its important qualifications.

The opening sequence explores the roles of television and Hollywood in desensitizing viewers to violence, and sets the tone for the remainder of the film. Wearing Sunday afternoon sports announcers' uniforms, complete with decals on their blazers, Howard Cosell and Don Dunphy provide a play-by-play description of political assassination in San Marcos, a banana republic. Without inflection, Dunphy reports that he has witnessed "many colorful riots . . . the traditional bombing of the U.S. Embassy," and the beating of a labor leader—one of "the most exciting spectacles [he] . . . has ever seen."

Visual allusions to violent moments from *Bonnie and Clyde* and *Potemkin* (1925) make the brutal assassination that follows a witty filmic ritual. While creating comic irony, the references suggest how quickly older films and the meaningful responses they originally evoked can become conventionalized. On the one hand, Allen's reflexive film appeals to a nostalgia for great film moments, and on the other, it demonstrates how even this film participates to some extent in the distancing and desensitization of an audience.

Following this prologue and the credits, set off by an appropriately ironic sound track—a happy Spanish love song and a barrage of machine-gun fire—the action moves to the Execuciser Corporation offices in New York, where Fielding Mellish is a products tester. The sequences's opening shot includes two profiles, one of the salesman and the other of the buyer, one on the far left and the other on the far right of the screen. The composition suggests that the seller and buyer are two parts of the same face and also emphasizes how corporate protocol encourages social distance. The stale discourse of this sequence is the sales pitch, but the nasal voice and rhythms resemble Cosell's.

The sales representative tries to sell a device that permits busy executives to exercise at their desks. One of the potential buyers, who looks remarkably like former vice president Spiro Agnew, supplies a connection between business and American politics. The irony is not only in the interchange that follows, but in the disparity between the businessmen's uninterested reactions and Mellish's predicament. The camera also emphasizes corporate power and expansionism by contrasting a tiny paperweight globe of the world with the huge execuciser desk on which it sits. A more important contrast finds small Fielding Mellish sprawled awkwardly on his hands and knees beside the orderly massive desk, as he tinkers with the execuciser apparatus. In addition, Mellish's costume emphasizes the lip service paid to individuality in the corporate setting; he wears a typical gray work uniform with a personalized touch: his given name, Fielding, embroidered over the pocket.

Initially, keeping time with the salesman's descriptions, Mellish confidently demonstrates the execuciser's bicycle and weight-lifting equipment. When Mellish's speed falls behind the pitch, however, the salesman fills in with gibberish until Mellish can catch up. The emptiness of the salesman's spiel is obvious from his syntax, as he announces that "basketballs as handled by Mr. Mellish develop reflexes." Indeed, as Fielding continues, the machinery, like Chaplin's assembly line or the eating machine in *Modern Times,* seems to come alive and outdistance him. The salesman and his customers are oblivious to Mellish as he is hit on the head with basketballs and pummeled by gadgets until he lies struggling on the floor. The proxemic contrast between Fielding alone at the big desk and the executives standing far across the room underlines the businessmen's ability to divorce themselves from the little man's misfortunes.

If Mellish is made to feel like a marshmallow at work, his personal life is no more satisfying. His fellow workers will not fix him up with a date, and the "easiest" woman in the office rejects him; so Fielding, like so many film spectators, is driven to voyeurism—in this case, to adult bookstores where he tries to hide a copy of *Orgasm* among *Time* and the *Saturday Review,* only to have the cashier broadcast his purchases. Mellish is reduced to mumbling transparent excuses for his natural desires: he says he is engaged in "a sociological study of aberrant sexuality."

Boarding a subway where commuters keep unneighborly distances from each other, Mellish soon runs into violence New York-style: two hoods taunt the passengers and attack a crippled old woman sitting next to him. Although Fielding tries to camouflage himself behind a copy of *Commentary*—and transcend the greasy punks—he cannot maintain intellectual distance. His better instincts lead him to attack the hoods—unsuccessfully, of course. A final irony occurs in the sequence's last shots; as Fielding runs away from his pursuers, the hoods' female victim enjoys his sexy magazine. Not only is Mellish a thwarted hero, but circumstances prevent him from having his orgasm, even as vicarious experience.

Fielding's home life is no more gratifying. Mellish battles not only with bullies, but with food. The choreography is related to the later lobster scene in *Annie Hall,* but instead of live lobsters, Mellish fights a slippery package of frozen spinach, which like twice-removed sexual experience or execucisers, further verifies the distance between life in a sophisticated society and people's basic needs.

Like little-men characters throughout Allen's collection, Fielding also has problems with romantic relationships. His love interest, Nancy (Louise Lasser), is a political activist who urges Fielding to sign a petition against General Vargas's dictatorship in San Marcos, but Fielding sees her as an answer to his loneliness. Despite the disparity between her activism and his lack of commitment, both Nancy and Fielding are more human than the sportscasters or executives in preceding scenes. Their fumbling attempts at communication stand in sharp contrast to the lack of communication in the porn shop and subway, and to glib sportscasting or sales jargon.

The little man is not experienced in political courtships, however. When he tries to join picket lines to please Nancy, Fielding only gets caught in the crossfire between police and demonstrators. Even ordinary romantic occasions are fraught with problems. So inept is Mellish as a romantic and political figure that Nancy eventually tells him that he is not enough of a "leader," and that "something is missing." This rejection scene, played in a pastoral setting with soft focus and sweeping camera movements, burlesques itself and frothy film love stores.

Cast off by Nancy and dissatisfied with his job, Mellish leaves the United States for San Marcos to see the revolution. He evades General Vargas's army and seeks asylum with the revolutionary opposition; however, Fielding finds no more satisfaction among the rebels than he found in New York.

The jokes about rebels in San Marcos grew out of a parody of popular revolutionary diaries as well as solemn films like *Viva Zapata!* (1952). Allen first wrote

**"Viva Vargas"** for the *Evergreen Review,* and it appeared later in **Getting Even.** Like the filmic allusions in **Take the Money and Run,** the references in **Bananas** involve a paradox. Allen's film parodies the false sentimentality film helps inspire for political solutions, while at the same time, heroic images bred by films such as *Viva Zapata!* inspire the innocent little man to achieve stature despite himself.

Fielding's first reaction to the rebels, conveyed in a wide-angle subjective shot that draws attention to the medium, makes them appear as disreputable as the New York subway hoods. Their leader, Esposito, speaks in high tones, telling Mellish, who has just escaped death at Vargas's hands, "You have a chance to die for freedom." But Esposito's attempts to evoke spirit with an unpoetic "Song of the Rebels" produce no reaction at all from his dirty, lethargic men.

Whatever romantic illusions Mellish retains about rebellion after this introduction are shattered further in a series of vignettes structurally paralleling an earlier montage in the "civilized" section of the film. Fielding naively orders a conventional breakfast, but receives a glutinous mash that turns out to be lizard. If New York is the home of overprocessed frozen spinach, then the San Marcos jungle is the home of food that is too primitive. Neither extreme is easy for Fielding to digest.

Mellish exchanges his gray work outfit for equally homogenizing rebel fatigues, but his failures at military maneuvers resemble his problems with the dehumanizing execuciser. Fielding can manage neither machetes nor more sophisticated technological weapons, and in an old Marx Brothers-type joke, Allen demonstrates Fielding's bad luck not only with military technology, but with politics—both right and left. When Fielding throws the pin and holds a grenade, the grenade detonates in his hand. His wound bandaged, he makes a second try; he pitches the grenade properly, but now the pin explodes in his other hand. The comic structure of the grenade episode replicates the form of Allen's early films and reminds us of a more profound joke about the absurdity of life in general.

Similarly, Fielding's attempt to avoid notice by camouflaging himself behind a copy of *Commentary* in the subway has its counterpart in Mellish's attempts to disguise himself as a tree in the jungle, only to have a rebel soldier urinate on him. When the rebels' trainer teaches new recruits to "suck out the poison" from snake bites, Fielding, using the kind of intellectual dodges he employed earlier in the adult bookstore, assumes an air of indignant propriety, insisting that "I cannot suck anybody's leg I am not engaged to." Yet when a female rebel runs through the camp with a snakebite on her breast, Mellish races to offer first aid.

Fielding's attempts to win women in San Marcos are also no more successful than they were in New York.

Imitating the flirtatious dinner sequence in *Tom Jones* (1963), Mellish only manages to drool water down his chin and get hit with a faceful of food. When he finally lures a reluctant woman to his cot, Allen burlesques love scenes just as he did in the first part of the film. The camera that so frequently leaves through a window or door to avoid showing love consummated in traditional Hollywood romances, searches hopelessly for an opening in the tent. After lovemaking, Fielding's romantic aspirations are depreciated further with a close shot of his lover's bored face; then, the camera pulls back to reveal that she is smoking and has worn her boots to bed. Here, even more than in Mellish's romance with Nancy, "something is missing."

After the rebels overthrow the government, the little man finds himself uncomfortably compromised by his political commitments, as he is forced to prepare the enemy for annihilation. When Esposito says that his own people are "too ignorant to vote," Fielding observes that the rebel leader, now as much a dictator as Vargas, looks "glassy eyed" with power. Esposito ignores Mellish's rejoinder, "But they [the people] have common sense," yet it marks an insight that separates Fielding Mellish from Virgil Starkwell, and it anticipates a developing self-awareness and concern for personal integrity in Allen's littleman characters.

Esposito's followers eventually depose him and select a reluctant Fielding to lead them, but Mellish's return to the United States to seek aid for San Marcos and his subsequent arrest and trial only further emphasize the universality of injustice. Where Esposito regularly eliminated the opposition by firing squad, in the United States, Fielding is hounded by the CIA and brought to trial for "subversive acts." The trial, made ludicrous by references to courtroom scenes in *Inherit the Wind* (1960), *Witness for the Prosecution* (1957), and *Duck Soup* (1933), also recalls the unreality of political trials of the 1960s. Fielding is decried as "a New York Jewish intellectual Communist crackpot" and condemned by a banal Miss America as "a traitor to this country because his views are different from the president and others of his kind." After such telling evidence, Fielding is, of course, convicted—but his sentence is suspended when he promises not to move into the judge's neighborhood. When the outcome of the trial is announced on a newscast sponsored by New Testament cigarettes, the film's suggestion that "The Word" is brought to us compliments of Wall Street, Washington, and the networks is hard to ignore.

Where, then, is Fielding Mellish to turn, and how is the film to end? Once more Ralph Rosenblum suggested a happy conclusion despite the odds stacked against the little-man antihero.[8] The finale offers a note of positive human communication even in the face of uninterested media hype, dehumanizing technology, and depersonalizing politics. However, the moment is a qualified one that does not violate the film's larger dialogic design, because the ending returns to a sequence reminiscent of the prologue. Surrounded by an audience, Howard Cosell calls the action during Fielding and Nancy Mellish's honeymoon night in bed. Lovemaking becomes a public sporting event, a TV spectacle, and Nancy is less than enthusiastic about Fielding's performance. Nevertheless, as Fielding tenderly kisses Nancy on the nose, he affirms a dimension of personal coming together that neither politics, big business, nor the media can thoroughly destroy. Allen's film depicts its main character as an innocent fool, but a fool whose priorities are humane, and whose sense of love is both affirmed and qualified by the constraints of the film's rules and the corresponding unreality of a world where images of experience and experience itself are too confused for comfort.

Neither the sophisticated United States nor the more primitive jungle, neither politics on the right nor politics on the left provide refuge from dehumanization, and the media finds its way even into the bedroom. The little man, in all his human clumsiness and his simple attempts to win his girl and do the right thing according to his best instincts, is still both a victim and the representative of an alternative sensibility in a comically senseless world. Fielding Mellish, however, is somewhat more aware and articulate than his counterpart in *Take the Money and Run,* and in this second major film Allen begins to stretch the significance of the oppositions that, like an ironic contemporary Colossus, the little man must straddle. Eventually, apparently conflicting values will become more difficult to distinguish and to assess. Allen uses the little-man protagonist as a focus through whom increasingly more complex and ambiguous social, moral, and philosophical issues can be explored.

### PLAY IT AGAIN, SAM

It is difficult to decide where to place *Play It Again, Sam* in any discussion of Allen's development, because the Broadway version was written before any of Allen's major films were produced. It is also the only major film that Allen wrote and in which he played the lead, but that someone else directed. In *Play It Again, Sam,* as in *Take the Money and Run* and *Bananas,* the little man is humble and less aggressive than in later films, torn between two conflicting points of view, and the ending of the film may appear to resolve itself more easily than is typical of Allen's later, most problematic comedies. In *Play It Again, Sam,* however, the little man's persona is complicated because of his developing self-awareness; as a film critic, he also alerts spectators to the film's reflexivity. Moreover, the little man's ability to betray a friend on one hand and fight for integrity on the other, and the stronger story line with more integrally related allusions are characteristics that anticipate later films.

Although time and memory are not such central issues as in the films beginning with *Annie Hall,* this is also the first film in which Allen's little-man hero tries consciously to come to terms with an event in his past. And, while Allen does not explore a concern with change and instability as fully in *Play It Again, Sam* as he will in later films, this film looks forward to such concerns, for it alludes to *Casablanca,* a movie that deals not only with heroic personal sacrifices and with romantic interludes, but with an attempt to understand and relive lost opportunities.

The joke about the confusion of artifice and life, so crucial to most of Allen's films, is also explored more frankly here than in *Take the Money and Run* and *Bananas,* and the little man deals with it more self-consciously. Like so many of Allen's little men (and women), the main character in *Play It Again, Sam* is a familiar figure in American humor, the greenhorn who has difficulty distinguishing between tall-tale lies and reality, between artifice and life. The little man's confusion is exacerbated because neither the tale-teller nor the audience can consistently determine where fiction ends and reality begins. Thus, even in this early Allen film, there are foreshadowings of the later films where filmmaker, audience, and characters will all be implicated more seriously in a modern viewpoint that permits no comforting certainties about what constitutes fiction.

Just as most of Allen's films are dialogic and open-ended, Allen seems to prefer that portions of his films remain open to shape themselves during production. According to director Herbert Ross, Allen did not want to direct *Sam* either as play or as film because he had structured it so carefully when he wrote it.[9] Ross helped to transform the play for the screen; he suggested using clips from *Casablanca* in the film's first sequence, modeling the final scene on *Casablanca*'s ending, setting the narrative in hilly San Francisco, and shooting characters as they moved from one place to another to accompany the dialogue.[10]

The film deals with little man Allan Felix's attempts to rebuild his shattered life after his divorce—to reintegrate his fragmented personality and to attain self-esteem in light of confusing options and models. Like the other early films, *Sam* portrays a main character caught between two unsatisfying extremes. Allan Felix is buffeted between a self-defeating underestimation of his potential, prompted by his ex-wife, Nancy, whom he cannot forget, and a romanticized self-image proposed by macho film hero Humphrey Bogart.

In this film, unlike the other early movies, one of the two possibilities is bifurcated even further to accentuate a familiar problem in Allen's films. Both Allan Felix's

most positive aspirations and his most self-deceiving illusions are embodied in his relationship to Bogart; as Maurice Yacowar puts it, Allen explores "the ambivalent effects of film upon our self-conception."[11] For a lonely Allan Felix, who longs for a woman to replace Nancy and to bolster his self-image, Bogart is the epitome of what a lover should be. He is a Hollywood ideal of toughguy style who prevents Felix from accepting his own more natural, fumbling self as worthwhile. At the same time, Bogey is a sympathetic mentor who gives Allan fortitude and hope.

From the film's outset, Bogart's self-possession contrasts with Allan's self-doubt. A film critic, Felix is an observer, not a doer like Bogey. As *Play It Again, Sam* begins, wide-eyed Felix watches the conclusion of *Casablanca,* where Bogart graciously renounces the woman he has loved for many years in the name of a greater political and social good. So engrossed is Allan Felix that for a moment before *Casablanca* ends, he affects Bogart's mannerisms. The little man's connection to the spectator is also accentuated, as *Casablanca* fills the frame we watch, and as we participate intimately in Allan's responses by means of close shots and reaction shots. When the lights go on in the theater, however, Allan looks to the vacant seats on either side of him. In these empty seats and in the emptying theater, an emblem of hard reality is set against the softer glow of the film's illusions; the distance between Allan's identification with heroic models and the limitations of his real world becomes an important part of *Play It Again, Sam*'s comic design. As Felix puts it while he is leaving the theater: "Who'm I kidding? I'm not like that. I never was. I never will be—strictly the movies."

Despite Allan's (and our) apparent understanding of the distinction between film and life as *Casablanca* ends, however, film has become a major part of his reality, and Ross does not permit us to forget that it is also a major part of ours. Allan's apartment is dominated by Bogart memorabilia; lying on his bed, Allan is dwarfed by a large Bogart poster above him, and instead of his own image, Bogart's photograph faces Allan in a dresser mirror. Allan's reliance on filmic models becomes still more obvious when Bogart appears to him periodically throughout the narrative. While Allan is having trouble getting over the loss of Nancy, he is reminded of *Casablanca* and Rick's tough-minded attitude toward the love he left in Berlin. On Bogart's first visit, Allan says: "I'm not like you. At the end of *Casablanca* when you lost Ingrid Bergman, weren't you crushed?" Bogey replies, "Nothin' a little bourbon and soda wouldn't fix." But Felix's "body will not tolerate alcohol," and when he tries Bogey's remedy, he gags and passes out.

As Felix contemplates his romantic hopes and his sexual frustrations, the film continues to exploit the comical disparity between the Bogart ideal he aspires to and the postdivorce self-conception that leaves him incompetent. He has difficulties with food (he eats TV dinners, but doesn't cook them—he sucks on them frozen). He talks about the risky swinging life he plans to lead, but wears a bathing cap in the shower. Ross captures the diminutive figure with a hat pulled down over his ears as he climbs a steep San Francisco hill to do his laundry; for Allan Felix, unlike Bogart, even the smallest domestic tasks resemble Sisyphus's trials. Ross uses those hills on several other occasions to suggest the ups and downs in Allan's moods, his fluctuating fortunes, and the antithetical patterns of both film and life.

While Allan welcomes Bogart because Bogey encourages him, he also has flashbacks of Nancy that shake his confidence. She tells him that she couldn't stand their marriage because he wasn't any fun, because he suffocated her, and because she didn't "dig" him physically. Then she admonishes him, "Oh, for God's sake, Allan, don't take it personal." Allan's view of himself is built on his past experience with what he regards as reality; it explains his need for Bogart. On one hand, the reality and the negative self-image are too depressing to bear, while on the other, Bogart as a representative film hero offers an aspiration impossible to obtain. Neither Allen's retreat into the past nor his attempts to become his romantic movie hero in the future promises to satisfy his needs.

Felix's best friends, Dick and Linda Christie, fix him up with women, but despite lessons Bogart gives him, he is no more adept at dating than other little men in Allen's early films. Preparing to go out, he is nearly propelled from the room by his own hairdryer; he overuses aftershave; and he frantically scatters evidence of his accomplishments about his apartment to make an impression. He is so nervous and inept, however, that one date thinks he "is on something," fakes a headache, and leaves him still poised for action as she slams her door in his face. Other attempts to win women are no more successful. Like Virgil Starkwell and Fielding Mellish, Allan is victimized by hoodlums and comes home battered, having given up his girl to a bunch of bullies at a bar. With deep focus, the camera highlights his loneliness as he enters an empty apartment, an echo of the emptying theater in the film's first sequence.

However, Allan and Linda Christie (Diane Keaton in her first film with Allen) are drawn together because their very human irregularities contrast with the dehumanizing and orderly rituals of the less-sensitive world around them. Linda shares insecurities with Allan. She is a model, surrounded like Allan by tantalizing images that promise intimacy in a society where such intimacy remains elusive. They both have analysts and get migraine headaches and cold sores; they both like to throw up at the Cleveland airport. As Dick says, "The two of you should get married and move into a hospital."

Dick is of the business world. He tells Allan that he won Linda because even though he loved her, he pretended to coolness. Like the execuciser people in **Bananas,** he is a creature of the corporate age—more involved in commercial dealings than in personal relationships. Dick continually interrupts social occasions as well as intimate moments to report his whereabouts to his answering service, and he talks about romance in business terms. When Allan says that he loved his former wife, Linda cries, but Dick says: "Why do you feel like crying? A man makes an investment, it doesn't pay off." It is the businessman's version of the protective distance Bogart-like heroes display in films. Neither Dick nor Bogey (as portrayed in this film) is able to expose his vulnerability, as Allan and Linda do.

Linda, on the other hand, comes to be another mentor for Allan, a friend who offers an alternative to the extremes represented by Bogart and Nancy. Linda tells Allan he doesn't need "an image." "You're bright—and you're funny and I think you're even romantic. . . . Why not just be yourself; the girl will fall in love with you." Later Allan meets Linda in a park, where they sit together amid long rows of empty park benches that recall again the empty theater seats in the film's first scene, but now Allan is with someone despite the emptiness around him. Once they plan to have dinner together, however, Allan fluctuates between anticipating the romance with Linda and feeling guilty because of his friendship with Dick. As he walks home, a row of parking meters dominates the lower-right-hand portion of the frame to suggest the regulations and social taboos he believes he is violating as he plans the rendezvous.

Bogey and Nancy appear to Allan together at a supermarket, where Bogey encourages Allan to court Linda, while Nancy plays on his guilt and tells him that Dick will beat him to a pulp. The two polarities do battle as his own growing self-esteem battles with his remaining false fears on the one hand and his inflated romantic ideals on the other. Allan calls on Bogey for help as he tries to make advances with Linda that night; but Nancy again confronts Bogart, and this time she shoots him, leaving Allan to seduce Linda all by himself.

He does it, but their successful romance causes Allan even greater guilt, and in a pair of additional filmic allusions, Allan experiences the various kinds of confrontations he might have if Dick discovered his deception. One scene, recalling *Separate Tables* (1958), presents a formal British dinner in which all conflict is translated into polite conversation, and the other imitates a much more passionate Vittorio De Sica neorealist drama. Like his experiences with Bogey and Nancy, the confrontation scenes suggest the extremes toward which Allan's mind moves in his anxiety. The contemporary little man stands caught within debates—between passion and indifference, between inflated dreams of perfection and nightmares of inadequacy, between civilization and natural instinct.

Bogart appears for the last time in the film's final airport sequence, where Allan sees off Dick and Linda, who have reunited. Although Linda has already made a choice to go with Dick, Allan's concluding gestures are significant. Echoing Bogey's last speech to Paul Henreid in *Casablanca*, Felix convinces Dick that his wife is guiltless and sends his friends on their way with grace and style. In doing so, Allan replays with dignity the renunciation he could not face in his divorce. At the end of ***Play It Again, Sam,*** Allan Felix is left with a self-conception that is on the mend, a more confident figure than he was when the film began. Although Allan has not become a macho hero, he has begun to deal both with fears of inadequacy on the one hand and with unattainable aspirations on the other. Despite dilemmas that cause anxiety, images that discourage naturalness, and countless other obstacles, the little man has acted, he has achieved a memorable moment of intimacy, and he has shown personal integrity.

But the film's ending also leaves unresolved problems. The confusion of art and life, already aggravated throughout the narrative by Ross's refusal to consistently mark Nancy's and Bogey's appearances with transitions that usually signal fantasy, is complicated further by the replication of *Casablanca*'s finale in the conclusion, now with Allan, Dick, and Linda as key players. At the very moment that Allan seems to choose reality over fiction, and the spectator decides that ***Play It Again, Sam*** demonstrates that film images can and should be distinguished from reality, the ending reemphasizes that real life remains more difficult to separate from fiction than we thought.

Bogey affirms Allan's growth when he wishes him goodbye, noting that Allan doesn't need the movie star anymore since he has developed his own style, and Allan acknowledges that "the secret's not being you; it's being me." But Ross saw some of the more problematic implications of Allen's play and accentuated them. The little man's growing autonomy in ***Play It Again, Sam*** is not merely lip service paid to the easy "'60's bromide" "just be yourself and the world will love you," nor is the film's denouement "unqualifiedly sanguine."[12] Even this early movie hints that Allen's is a more complicated vision, which insists on taking uncertainties into account and which acknowledges that all resolutions are conditional in a world where fiction and reality have begun to merge. Moreover, pain cannot be overlooked from the film's perspective. Allan is able to act more courageously, but unlike the little man in Allen's play, who was immediately provided with a new love interest, in Ross's film, Allan is left as lonely as Rick in *Casablanca,* and he acknowledges his sense of loss. In such a vein, Allan Felix admits that his is no easy world; he tells us that he is heartbroken even as he tells Bogart that he—Allan—is "short and ugly enough" to succeed on his own.

## Notes

1. See Ruth R. Wisse, *The Schlemiel as Modern Hero* (Chicago: University of Chicago Press, 1971) and Maurice Yacowar, *Loser Take All.*

2. Eric Lax, *On Being Funny,* 65.

3. Ibid., 70.

4. Ibid., 126.

5. Rosenblum and Karen, *When the Shooting Stops,* 245, 251.

6. Lee Guthrie, *Woody Allen, a Biography* (New York: Drake, 1978), 64.

7. Woody Allen, "A Look at Organized Crime," in *Getting Even* (New York: Warner, 1972), 16-20.

8. Rosenblum and Karen, *When the Shooting Stops,* 259.

9. Richard Anobile, ed., *Woody Allen's "Play It Again Sam"* (New York: Grosset & Dunlap, 1977), 7.

10. Ibid., 7.

11. Yacowar, *Loser Take all,* 52.

12. Diane Jacobs, *. . . but we need the eggs: The Magic of Woody Allen* (New York: St. Martin's Press, 1982), 46.

## Nancy Pogel (essay date 1987)

SOURCE: Pogel, Nancy. "The Little Man's Screwball Comedy." In *Woody Allen,* pp. 81-97. Boston, Mass.: Twayne Publishers, 1987.

[*In the following essay, Pogel explores how Allen both subverts and embraces the traditions of the screwball comedy genre in* Annie Hall.]

In his sixth major film, Allen begins in earnest his departure from predominantly funny filmmaking. Allen claims that with each of his successes, his greater command of technique, and the knowledge that he could survive as a filmmaker, he became more "bullish" about expressing his personal concerns.[1] Although Allen had always been moving toward a seriocomic perspective and he had always been an acute social satirist, one more immediate touchstone for the changing mood of his films after ***Love and Death*** was his acting role in Martin Ritt's *The Front* (1976).

Created by writers and actors blacklisted during the McCarthy era, *The Front* is a serious comedy that deals with problems of commitment and personal integrity during the Communist witch hunts of the 1950s. In Walter Bernstein's script, Allen plays an uncommitted little man, Howard Prince, who fronts for writers who are not allowed to work because of their leftist affiliations. Initially, like the little man of Allen's early films, Prince prefers to remain outside the controversy, but when he is also called to appear before the House Un-American Activities Committee, he finally takes a stand. "I don't recognize the right of this committee to ask me these kinds of questions," he says, and he adds, "Furthermore, you can go fuck yourselves."

Although Ritt's film comes to a happy resolution—the littleman asserts his integrity and wins the girl—the difficulties involved in adopting a clear position in less-clearly defined circumstances may have suggested a number of possibilities to Woody Allen. Allen's involvement in a serio-comic film dealing with the need for commitment and personal integrity, as well as with the human damage left in the wake of a too clearly committed, closed-minded fanaticism, heralds his more recent work. With *Annie Hall* he goes beyond laughs to accentuate a darker side of the dialogic imagination that had remained in the background of his earlier films.

For all their drift toward inconclusiveness, Allen's early films portray oppositions primarily between civilization's "junk" and the guilelessness of the little-man victim. His humility, anxiety, and confusion played their role in dialogues between disorder and the rigidity of closed systems. The little man was often the foolish object of laughter himself, but he also mediated among extremes to retrieve an alternative point of view and to preserve the possibility of escape from absurdity.

Gradually, the humble little man learned to be a more aggressive smart aleck, although he never lost all of his common sense, tentativeness, and innocence. With Allen's adoption of the first-person narrator and a retrospective attempt to understand the events that lead to his execution in *Love and Death,* the persona becomes increasingly more self-aware—a conscious questioner and a searcher—and his innocence becomes more difficult. In *Annie Hall* the narrator's self-consciousness is even more prominent; not just a film critic as in *Play It Again, Sam,* he is now a comic artist like the filmmaker himself, and the sophistication that was located primarily outside the narrator is internalized and has demoralized him to a greater extent than in earlier funnier films. The little man's angst is examined more closely, and it is no longer only funny.

Not only does the narrator become more self-conscious, but the film as a whole becomes more seriously reflexive. Maurice Yacowar acknowledges that the film's many parallels "relate to the idea that art and life are continuous, mutually feeding forces"; the film, he believes, "contemplates death and loss" but "reaffirms

the values of life, art, and love."[2] Like Yacowar, Thomas Schatz sees the film's obviously self-referential qualities—the ironic relationships between Allen and his little-man character, the confusions between text and reality underlined by the fact that Allen had been Keaton's lover and mentor in real life, the associative plot structure, and the repeated use of author interruptions and asides to the camera. Schatz concludes that *"Annie Hall . . .* is 'about' how we tell stories, how we remember relationships and our own past, how we impose our rational minds on the happenstance of experience. As such it is a film that virtually demands that the viewer adopt a modernist perspective, a self-conscious attitude toward Allen and his narrative."[3]

Not surprisingly, from Allen's dialogic angle of vision, in *Annie Hall* the nature of self-awareness itself becomes a more obvious part of the problem. The emotional distancing involved, both in the little man's increased self-awareness and its effects upon his search for love and fulfillment, and in the distances created for the spectator watching a defamiliarizing, modernistic self-reflexive film, rather than a classical movie, involve both gains and losses.

What happens in *Annie Hall* is that we experience, more than in earlier Allen films, a feeling for the burden of history, the sophisticated self-consciousness, and the accompanying anxiety that contemporary people carry into their search for love, integrity, and meaning. When, against the background of this self-conscious film and the corresponding pressures of modern-day life, Woody Allen creates a few meaningful human moments of even qualified hope or when he suggests that the searching little man's survival is grounds for some measure of faith, such images must be taken as solace in the face of a mighty fear. Such dread of transience and meaninglessness is the sort that has always frightened our greatest comic minds as they attempted to tear away layer after layer of inauthentic experience to discover something real.

At first viewing, *Annie Hall* may appear to be a departure from Allen's dependence on influences and from his customary densely intertextual and allusive style; however, this film, like all of Allen's work, is best approached along the reflexive lines that Schatz and Yacowar suggest, and as a series of dialogues among antithetical worldviews, set within an intersecting reflexive dialogue between films and about filmmaking. Like *Stardust Memories, Annie Hall* might well be approached through one major resonant allusion within which Allen develops a number of other intertextual dialogues. While romantic comedy generally may have inspired Allen's *Annie Hall,* screwball comedy, particularly, appears to be a focal reference for the film Allen made with Diane Keaton in mind.

Screwball comedies, very popular from the late Depression 1930s well through the years of World War II, are generally regarded as films that aimed at "reconciling the irreconcilable," that dealt with the battle of the sexes and cemented a country threatened by class antagonisms and social discontents. Screwball comedies "created an America of perfect unity: all classes as one, the rural-urban divide breached, love and decency and neighborliness ascendant."[4] While they were laced with snappy dialogue between conflicting personalities with differing lifestyles, and while they focused squarely on a new "consciousness of women,"[5] they ultimately reminded audiences that similarities transcend differences, that uppity women are cute but tameable, and that despite threats to the status quo, the world is a stable and orderly place where traditional values hold and individual integrity is rewarded. Women are temporarily dominant over men in such films as *Bringing Up Baby* (1938), *Adam's Rib* (1949), *Woman of the Year* (1940), and *His Girl Friday* (1940), but men get the edge in time for a conventional happy ending—marriage or reunion. Romances are tested, and despite obstacles, most relationships survive the trial; opposites are united. Of course, these post-1934 Production Code comedies also contain only the most wholesome references to physical sexuality. Couples have romantic or domestic skirmishes, but never discuss serious bedtime problems.

Wacky, chaotic situations characterize screwball comedies, but most of these films are classically structured to suggest an underlying harmony beneath temporary disruption. They follow conventional narrative and dramatic patterns to strict closure; typically, they are symmetrical and balanced, with parallel scenes and subplots; they often obey unities of time and place.

Screwball comedies frequently begin in the city, but couples often grow closer and explore their relationships in country settings, away from the distractions of modern urban life. Nature is regarded positively as a place for lovers to be "natural" and to get to know one another in a simpler, more authentic place.

Although most screwball comedies are primarily classic texts, a surprising number of these comedies contain reflexive references to performance and often spoof saccharine romances and action dramas and films, thereby attempting to offer a more realistic account of romance. These references, however, usually serve only as light puns or as means to render potentially controversial issues, such as changing sex roles, identity problems, disquieting cultural change, or significant individual difference, harmless by defamiliarizing the viewer from the film at crucial moments.[6]

Woody Allen's *Annie Hall* (1977), produced three or four decades after screwball comedy's heyday, echoes the older genre and deals with questions that surfaced in it, but also reflects an intensification of these issues. The older form becomes a backdrop against which to measure cultural change and to describe the contemporary world, where even "newer women" provide men with greater problems; where identities are more confused and lovers (who have histories) have become more neurotic and self-conscious than in a more innocent age; where differences are not always reconcilable; and where opposites cannot be united. The resumption of order after chaos, crucial to screwball comedy, is replaced in *Annie Hall* by such a tenuous resolution that we feel a far less comforting sense of closure. In Allen's dialogic film, human issues cannot be reduced to formula, fixed ideas do not hold, and meaning is found only in evanescent moments of experience. While *Annie Hall* mocks the older genre and the damaging romantic values it entails, however, it also evokes a sense of lost innocence and a longing for the playfulness and naturalness that a self-conscious contemporary perspective makes so difficult to recover. In *Annie Hall,* as in earlier Allen films, Alvy and Annie, as well as the spectators of Allen's film, are either caught in the false expectations aroused by our dreams and romantic film's illusions or are freed from them as we participate in our demystification. Conversely, the film may suggest that sophisticated demystification and a modernistic outlook can itself become a trap.

In *Annie Hall,* Alvy Singer (Woody Allen) sees much of the contemporary world as contradictory, transitory, and unreliable; he is restless, skeptical, and at times paranoid. In such a world, "love fades" or true passion and genuine human connection do not last, and as Alvy says, it is hard to get our heads around that. In this film, Allen's little man is a New York Jewish comedy writer approaching middle age; he is streetwise about urban sophistication, and Annie, his flaky lover from Chippewa Falls, Wisconsin, is a creative innocent. But the relationship has broken up when the story begins, and the film is both an autopsy and a reminiscence. Unlike screwball comedies before it, the film is not concerned with how opposites eventually unite, but with why this important love did not endure. Woven into Alvy's self-conscious quest for answers is a look at the stress that contemporary culture places on romance, and a reflexive examination of the relationship of art to life.

Alvy Singer is a far more self-conscious, complicated, and neurotic character than heroes in earlier screwball films. Originally *Annie Hall* was to be called "Anhedonia" (the inability to experience pleasure), referring to Alvy Singer's depression and his existential angst. Unlike predecessors in earlier screwball comedies, Alvy finds it hard to have fun or to believe in love.

In traditional screwball comedies, heroes seldom aged or had early histories, but we envision their having had secure Andy Hardy childhoods. Alvy's history, on the other hand, is an albatross. In his opening words, Alvy, at forty, reveals his fear of aging, change, and death; yet he tells us that his depression over Annie is unusual because he had a reasonably happy childhood. Alvy's entire narrative is enveloped in inconclusiveness, however, because he is only a partially reliable narrator. Following his references to his relatively happy childhood, we see him as a depressed child who grew up during World War II—this accounts in part for his personality, "which is a little nervous."

Alvy contradicts his initial self-analysis in several other childhood remembrances. He tracks an early depression to his personalizing the big bang theory that the universe is expanding and will someday break apart and "that would be the end of everything." Alvy won't do his homework because "What's the point?" Thus, Allen traces Alvy's concern with unreliability to the age of seven, when he experienced full-fledged existential dread. His innocence is compromised by self-consciousness from a very early age.

Alvy's is also not the mainstream American family that we imagine raised Adam Bonner in *Adam's Rib*. Alvy's emasculating, shrewish mother reduces carrots to shavings as she derides Alvy for distrusting everyone, and she dismisses Alvy's early anxieties about the cosmos by screaming in frustration, "What is that your business? . . . What has the universe got to do with it? You're here in Brooklyn! Brooklyn is not expanding!" She and Alvy's father reveal how moral ambiguity has crept into everyday life as they argue heatedly and comically about whether cleaning women should be allowed to steal. Frank Capra, George Cukor, and Howard Hawkes never gave their characters a family so colorful, so New York, so Jewish, or so confusing.

From Alvy's perspective, reemphasized as he interrupts his own recollections by making an adult appearance within the scene, days at school evoke further distrust. Incompetent cartoon teachers preside over rigid classrooms filled with dull or competitive schoolmates who soon lose their innocence, growing up to be methadone addicts and owners of a "profitable dress company." A rosy-colored filmland childhood is as far from Alvy's experience as Annie's rural Wisconsin is from his Coney Island home beneath a roller coaster that shakes his tomato soup each time it passes.

Adult Alvy's interruption of his own narrative not only emphasizes its subjectivity, but reminds us that we are watching a film. Moreover, his interruption and stream of early memories are only two in a long series of disruptions to classical narrative structure that also serve to violate conventional boundaries between fiction and reality, to indicate Alvy's confusion, and to contrast pointedly with the comforting architecture of traditional screwball film. As Alvy sifts through his associations,

so the audience must deal not only with the pieces into which his life has flown, but with Alvy's attempts to make sense of them. The emphasis on self-analysis in a subjective time frame also stresses the contemporary self-consciousness that creates additional pressures on human relationships.

Fragments from Alvy's and Annie's pasts also come to suggest reflexively how film and other media have an impact on modern identity and confusion. Alvy's memories are filled with media interruptions, feature films, cartoons, and references to media theory. Among Alvy's memories is a TV screen that fills the frame, and we see Woody Allen's appearance on the Dick Cavett show. In images drawn from the filmmaker's own history, Allen self-consciously reminds us that the images of experience are too easily confused with experience itself and media plays a more ambivalent role in constructing our hopes and dreams—our personalities—than earlier screwball comedies ever considered.

The influence of visual imagery on contemporary psychology is also highlighted, since Annie and Alvy often go to movies. Two overanxious autograph seekers (no charming locals, these) impose themselves on Alvy's private memories, reminding him of characters from *The Godfather*; they are played by actors who actually had bit parts in Coppola's film. The films Alvy likes are Ingmar Bergman's *Face to Face,* wherein a psychiatrist confronts her own emotional limitations and attempts suicide, and Marcel Ophüls's *The Sorrow and the Pity,* the four-and-a-half-hour documentary dealing with French complicity with Nazism during the Holocaust. These films, which describe contemporary doubts and deal with problems of identity and commitment, contribute to our understanding of Alvy's angst and further distinguish **Annie Hall** from lighthearted screwball romances. Although clearly Allen respects Bergman's and Ophüls's films, in Annie's reluctance to sit through yet another four-hour documentary about Nazism, we come to see that even as screwball comedies may have created overly optimistic illusions, more pessimistic films also reinforce Alvy's negativism. And while Allen's film mediates between the possibilities, it also participates in the very problem it describes.

Allen also analyzes his medium reflexively in a scene where he and Annie wait in line at the New Yorker theater. As Annie and Alvy quarrel, a "Film, T.V., and Media" teacher diverts their attention with a stock critique of Fellini that blames his "self-indulgence" on television. Alvy's sense of inadequacy as Annie grows away from him is counterpointed by the critic's false assurance. In his frustration, Alvy finally redresses the would-be critic for knowing nothing about Marshall McLuhan, who has played a large role in the critic's pontifications. Alvy even produces McLuhan to refute him, but McLuhan's refutation not only undermines the pompous professor, but reinforces the film's dialogic inconclusiveness. "You know nothing of my work," says McLuhan. "You mean, my whole fallacy is wrong." Alvy enjoys the moment of comeuppance with the deflation of the critic's false illusions, but like Allan Felix in **Play It Again, Sam,** he acknowledges the unreliability of his own illusions and once more ironically blurs the distinction between fiction and reality as he sighs, "Boy, if life were only like this."

References to other events from his past further describe Alvy's depressing outlook on life. In *Pursuits of Happiness* Stanley Cavell shows that screwball comedies are Shakespearean-style "old comedies" of remarriage and reunion, hopeful myths of rebirth and renewal.[7] Unlike his screwball relatives, Alvy has been married not once, but twice, and his story reveals not only why those unions remained broken, but the impact of their history on his relationship with Annie, a relationship that echoes the screwball paradigm of achieving one reconciliation, but a relationship that ultimately does not work.

Alvy's depression is also linked to a search for authenticity. Unlike Capra and Cukor heroes who are eventually rewarded for maintaining their integrity, Alvy is not. He remembers his refusal to leave New York and follow his friend Rob (Tony Roberts), who sells out Shakespeare in the Park to take a TV job in California. Beverly Hills is Alvy's idea of the mindless future-world in **Sleeper,** which suggests how far passivity and optimistic illusions can drive us. To Alvy, California is a metaphor for decadence; people there are "mellow," and Alvy observes that "if I get too mellow, I ripen and then rot." Unqualified by Alvy's sort of skepticism and conscience, the atmosphere in Hollywood (where glib, resolved films are made) is politically dangerous. There people talk about Charlie Chaplin's problems with McCarthyism as "his un-American thing" and they confer awards wholesale; Alvy imagines an award for "greatest fascist dictator, Adolf Hitler." Visiting California, Alvy reluctantly eats alfalfa sprouts and mashed yeast instead of hardshelled lobsters who fight to survive. New York, with all its difficulties, is reality rather than "munchkin land." In **Annie Hall,** as in older screwball comedies, civilization and eros may be antagonists, but in this later film, the lack of authenticity and integrity in contemporary culture has created greater obstacles to intimacy and happiness. And in such a world, Alvy is a malcontent who loses his lover because he cannot adapt to change, rather than a traditional screwball hero who gains a woman and public acclaim for sticking to his principles.

From the onset of their relationship, like screwball couples before them, Annie and Alvy are extreme opposites. Initially, Annie is a crazy, humanizing antitoxin for Alvy's seriousness, and he plays a slow-moving, cautious straight man to her disorderly, kinetic character, not unlike Cary Grant's anthropologist playing off Katharine Hepburn's flighty character in *Bringing Up Baby* (1938). On the way to the tennis court where they first meet, Alvy frets about anti-Semitism. In contrast, during the tennis match the camera catches Annie's spontaneity as she happily flails away at a tennis ball.

Annie is dressed in an unconventional tramplike costume that declares her creative individuality and her independence. The outfit is born out of traditional sex role mergers in earlier screwball situations and costuming; she reminds us of an updated version of Katharine Hepburn in slacks. Her fumbling mannerisms make her a relative of Allen's natural and innocent little men in earlier films, and she presents an androgynous picture that may suggest that despite her apparent lack of ease, she is authentic and complete at the core.

Like other screwball couples, Annie and Alvy come from different cultures and classes. In this case, however, differences are not eventually erased to verify the American melting-pot myth, but remain as an unresolved dialogue and a disquieting sign of our times. Annie's man's tie was a gift from her Grammy Hall in Chippewa Falls; Alvy observes that his Jewish Grammy was too busy getting raped by Cossacks to give him gifts. Annie does not fear death as he does, and she takes risks. She drives through town with an abandon reminiscent of Amanda Bonner's days at the wheel; he is too nervous to own a car. At an Easter dinner in Chippewa Falls with Annie's family, where they serve ham and talk about swap meets and boats, Alvy imagines himself a Hasidic rabbi among Midwestern Wasps. A split screen emphasizes the contrarieties to show Alvy's family at a holiday meal, arguing loudly, eating furiously, and discussing sickness.

Although Alvy's stream of memories destroys conventional chronology, Allen's film does contain a series of parallel scenes, an ironic reminder of the movie's ancestors. We see related sequences scattered about in these memories that indicate a rising and falling movement to the romance. At first Alvy and Annie complement one another. She helps him to rediscover spontaneity and love, and she appreciates his humor and his experienced advice about her singing career. Alvy feels compelled, however, to distrust her innocence as much as Allen's deconstructive film may at first appear to distrust the innocence of screwball comedy's romantic vision. While he admires her, he also eventually denies her "wholeness," her uniqueness. In attempting to change her, he divides her from herself. As screwball heroes often preferred one side of their lovers to another and lectured them on their imperfections, so he teaches Annie his view of reality. She becomes a "newer woman," more self-confident, more self-conscious, and more worldly, but like the absurd alternatives in earlier Allen films, neither Annie as innocent nor Annie as experienced is entirely compatible with her neurotic partner. Annie's very growth contains counterindications—the seeds of the relationships's eventual failure. She finally longs to escape from her reality instructor.

Some recollected moments clearly belong in the early, upward movement of their relationship. Like the screwball couples who disentangled their problems and nurtured their relationships away from the urban sophistication, Alvy and Annie find their way outside the city despite Alvy's doubts about the romance of rural life. He associates the country with dead moths on screens and cult murderers.

In the kitchen at the beachhouse retreat, Annie and Alvy illustrate their ability to transcend adulthood's sex-specific behavior, much as earlier screwball heroes and heroines demonstrated their kitchen compatibility in the face of changing gender roles. Recapturing a sense of childhood innocence and play, in a moment that appears to transcend the film's encapsulating dialogues and the determinate nature of the film as medium, they shoo their lobster dinners toward a pot. Cavell has observed that while screwball comedies seldom involve children or offspring, the characters themselves try to "make room for playfulness in the gravity of adulthood . . . in an attempt to recover innocence."[8]

Such moments are to remember, and Annie takes still photographs of Alvy as she also took photographs of her family to hang about her apartment. While the references to photography tend to defamiliarize and to remind us again that this is a film, and thus to qualify even the film's best moments, Annie's photography, about which she refuses to intellectualize, does not associate her with the slick images that confuse contemporary identity; rather, Annie's photography may also be seen as a contrast presented in the middle of a sophisticated motion picture, as a relatively innocent and human art meant to secure meaningful moments from time. During their first meeting, Alvy said to Annie, "Photography is interesting, you know. . . . The medium enters in as a condition of the art form itself." But Annie's innocence, like Pearl's in *Interiors,* is associated with her simple aesthetic. Annie says, "Well, to me it's all instinctive. I just try to feel it." What begins to emerge in the discussion of Annie's photography is a tenuous and dialogic view of imagery in its relation to the human condition. While Allen casts doubt on his own film and reveals his concern with the dangers inherent in manipulative imagery, he also simultaneously explores the positive possibilities in Annie's authentic kind of photography, which helps us remember good moments, which does battle with time, and which breaks with self-conscious conventions to reach us in a personal way as great "moving" pictures always have.

Later, Annie and Alvy leave the city again, but this time nature offers no escape, for the relationship is in trouble. Initially Annie and Alvy enjoyed making love. He found her "polymorphously perverse," for she responded so readily with every part of her body. In their second visit to the country, however, Alvy forbids Annie to smoke pot to relax, and she cannot achieve intimacy without it. Instead of pot, Alvy puts a corny red light bulb in their bedside lamp "for atmosphere," and in an echo of the earlier scenes, quips that he and Annie could also develop photographs. But in doing so, he comments not only on the state of his romance with Annie, but on the nature of his self-conscious narrative and on Allen's more sophisticated anti-illusionistic film, as opposed to earlier romantic comedy. He suggests reflexively that the emphasis has moved from the metaphor of taking photos like Annie's innocent, spontaneous ones in the early part of their relationship, to a later stage in the photographic process that is more technical and more self-conscious—less natural. *Annie Hall* deconstructs and demystifies the earlier classic romances, but in this dialogue Allen remains as uncertain as he was in his earliest comedies about whether self-conscious film-making, anti-illusionism, and demystification are not also part of a backfiring hand-grenade joke such as he made in *Bananas.*

In this second visit to the country, therefore, time and Alvy's tutoring Annie have intervened, and it is not surprising that Annie is as distanced or defamiliarized from Alvy as spectators can be from extremely self-conscious, anti-illusionistic films, and we observe her image leaving her body in the bed even as she and Alvy are going through the motions of making love. Unlike earlier screwball comedies, then, in Alvy's more self-conscious narrative, sexual issues are more complex and sexual intimacy has become a problem. By this time Annie is seeing a psychiatrist on Alvy's advice, and Annie's visit to her therapist is seen on a split screen with Alvy's visit to his therapist. When the therapists ask how often they have sex, Alvy tells his, "Hardly ever. Maybe three times a week," while Annie tells hers: "Constantly. I'd say three times a week."

Although Annie and Alvy break up temporarily when Annie is caught arm in arm with her adult-education professor, they come to miss each other, and like many divorced screwball comedy couples, they reconcile. The difference is that this reconciliation does not last. Annie's moodiness, seen in memories from the last part of their relationship, indicates that she has learned self-consciousness from Alvy and has come to experience his discontent. While she has learned from experience with reading, analysis, adult education, and the films Alvy took her to, her whole background urges escape from the depression that accompanies Alvy's anhedonia. Thus, following a polished nightclub performance, she is flattered by an invitation from Tony Lacey (Paul

Simon) to develop her career in California, and she and Alvy agree to end their relationship finally.

While older screwball heroes reestablished order with the authentication of marriage that follows from self-knowledge and change or creation,[9] the lessons the contemporary little man teaches his partner, and the self-knowledge each achieves, produce less satisfying results. Alvy misses Annie and travels to California to propose, but Annie refuses. Back in New York, Alvy tries to deal with his loss through art; he writes a play about his love affair, but adds a happy ending. Art, he observes, is always more perfect than life. But art holds no more lasting meaning than anything else in this film. Woody Allen's reflexive film comments once more on its own construction and depicts a less perfect world. The ending to *Annie Hall* goes well beyond the naïveté of first plays or earlier screwball comedies with happy resolutions.

The important thing about *Annie Hall* is that it is not like the traditional screwball film, which moves forward in a progressive manner to a conclusion that answers questions about disorder and about whether life had meaning with images of renewal and affirmation. After Alvy's long examination and his sifting through his recollections of the confusing affair with Annie, he has no more rational understanding of why the relationship didn't work than before. He lives in circumstances even more reduced than those that challenged his screwball ancestors in the 1930s and 1940s. Change is beyond his control; his world is indeterminate; each forward motion or intimation of progress may contain its own contrariety; and even his best impulses may produce results quite different from those he anticipated. He is just as caught within the world his pessimistic vision, his narrative, and Allen's contemporary self-conscious film have created as the passive spectator of optimistic classic screwball films is caught in the world he has based on traditional romantic illusions.

What, then, is to be saved from this film that duplicates the nervous state of contemporary relationships and reflects the unreal quality of an overly sophisticated world? The film concludes that there are no sure resolutions, no pat answers, just the ongoing process of life itself, some tenuous faith in our instinct to survive, and a filmmaker's refusal to accept either his most pessimistic visions or some easy bromides as an escape from the inconclusiveness of experience. If there is anything one can hold onto, it is the few remembered moments of tenderness, intimacy, and human connection that appear to, but never do quite entirely, escape the envelope of the medium. The conflicts between life's pleasure and pain, between Allen's comic and tragic visions, that have been a running tension throughout this film are perhaps best expressed in two ways at the end of *Annie Hall*: In the series of images recollecting An-

nie and Alvy's happiest moments together that survive in Alvy's memory and can be partially reexperienced through film, and in Alvy's closing joke, which provides a good picture of his bittersweet attitude toward life and loss.

A remarkable number of jail scenes occur in screwball comedies such as *Bringing Up Baby, Adam's Rib,* and *His Girl Friday,* but the stars never end up behind bars or even visiting jails in the finale. In his original script, the film was to end with Alvy commenting on life from a jail cell in California, but in an added ending, the imagery is more hopeful.

With the empty restaurant where he met Annie for lunch in the foreground and a busy New York street where life goes busily on seen through a window as the background, with Annie singing "Seems Like Old Times" behind his voice-over, Alvy has left the frame to generalize on his experience. Alvy remembers his good times with Annie in an anecdote. The pain he continues to endure from heartbreaks, he says, is as crazy as the fellow in the old joke who believes he is a chicken. But like the man's family, he observes that we don't alter the absurd situation because "we need the eggs" that love relationships provide.

The threat of time and change, the confusions and contradictions of modern life with its opposing sets of illusions, create far greater obstacles for lovers than they did in older screwball comedies. In an early description of Saul Bellow's work, Robert Alter wrote: "Reality is a multiverse, not a unified system in which fixed principles can be enunciated by those who know the system. . . . There is a tentativeness in the moral exploration of all [his] heroes. . . . [He is] anti-reducing human problems to a formula, a methodology, a technique."[10] So too, Woody Allen distrusts fixed principles, and Alvy's unreliable narrative deconstructs the pillars of his own medium's history, not simply out of disrespect, but out of a complex exploration of both the longing for romance and the dangers inherent in romantic illusions. At the same time, his self-conscious narrative—ultimately, the film itself—also deconstructs, so that we remain either caught or freed by our experience with it. For his ability to capture contemporary concerns in such well-selected detail and with such telling metaphors of meaning and meaninglessness, Woody Allen's *Annie Hall* received four Academy Awards and international critical recognition for being one of the best films of our times. In terms of his development as a filmmaker, this contemporary screwball film—with its reflexive, dialogic comedy and its pathos—is the gateway to Allen's later, most mature and significant work.

*Notes*

1. Michiko Kakutani, "How Woody Allen's *Zelig* Was Born in Anxiety and Grew into Comedy," *New York Times,* 18 July 1983, sec. C, p. 13.

2. Yacowar, *Loser Take All,* 177 and 180.

3. Thomas Schatz, *Old Hollywood/New Hollywood,* 225.

4. Andrew Bergman, *We're in the Money* (New York: Harper Colophon, 1972), 133.

5. Stanley Cavell, *Pursuits of Happiness* (Cambridge: Harvard Univ. Press, 1981), 17.

6. See especially the visual and verbal references to theater and performance in *Adam's Rib.*

7. Cavell, *Pursuits,* 1.

8. Ibid., 60.

9. Ibid., 56.

10. Robert Alter, *After the Tradition,* (New York: Dutton, 1969), 111.

**Stanley Kauffmann (review date 28 January 1991)**

SOURCE: Kauffmann, Stanley. "Troubles, Now and Then." *New Republic,* no. 3967 (28 January 1991): 24-5.

[*In the following review of* Alice, *Kauffmann asserts that Allen's direction is praiseworthy, but comments that the screenplay for the film is trite.*]

All the contributors to the Woody Allen Scholarship Fund can now feel satisfied. The man they have subsidized to learn film directing, which they did by attending the pictures he made while he was learning, is now expert. This has been increasingly evident in his last four or five films, and with his latest, his twentieth, he goes even further. *Alice* is very pleasant simply to watch.

See how Allen's camera sorts out people in a party scene; how he combines the movement of people on a large winding staircase with the flow of the camera; how he follows a couple from a crowded courtyard to isolation behind a wrought-iron railing. See how he frames a pair of lovers sitting on a bed under a huge skylight absolutely running with rain. (The room nicely designed by Santo Loquasto, acutely photographed by Carlo di Palma.) Once in a while Allen jars us with a close-up used for no reason, but on the whole, very much so, he has mastered his craft so well that it surpasses mere craft.

But those who supported his progress as a director may be less overjoyed by his screenwriting. Allen wrote *Alice* for his wife, Mia Farrow. (He doesn't appear in the film.) Once again he has treated a New York modus vivendi with hyper-realism, then added touches of the fantastic and supernatural (like the Jewish mother in the sky in his portion of *New York Stories*). Basically, *Alice* could hardly be more trite. Farrow, married for fifteen years to a very rich husband, mother of two children, is bored with her life, impatient with her lack of personal fulfillment. She becomes interested in another man—a musician who is, naturally, quite unlike her husband. To this hoary situation Allen adds an old Chinese doctor who, in Chinatown, dispenses herbs that have magical powers. Those herbs mark the only difference between *Alice* and the legion of prior plays and films about bored, rich wives who dally with men quite unlike their husbands.

The fantasy moments are the most interesting. My only quarrel with them is that they have more effect on the viewer than they do on the people in the film. These characters are filled to the brim with veristic details of the luxe life, yet they more or less blandly accept the fantastic when it happens. When Farrow becomes invisible for a while, when a long-dead boyfriend takes her on a flight over Manhattan, she resumes her life afterward as if she had gone on an amusement park ride—something out of the ordinary but quite comprehensible.

As with other Allen screenplays, he lavishes ingenuity and social satire on the story, he engenders conflict, only to settle everything at the end in swift, cobbled-up fashion. Once again the finish is a quick escape through an emergency exit, rather than a conclusion of what has gone before. But there's a lot of moderate entertainment along the way, mostly derived from the small vices of the plush Manhattan set—chic gossip, and chic chic.

Farrow is a touch too humdrum for the humdrum wife. We don't get much sense of wings beating frustratedly within her and even less sense of the attractiveness that men speak of. It's hard to believe that her ambitious, calculating husband would have chosen this woman. (William Hurt plays him with less than his usual pomposity.) Her sister, a lawyer, is done incisively by Blythe Danner. The picture would have been more amusing if—impossible dream—Danner and Farrow had exchanged roles.

Joe Mantegna plays the Other Man with grubby sexiness. In lesser roles Judy Davis is Mantegna's wife, Cybill Shepherd is a glitzy friend, Alec Baldwin the revenant sweetheart from the past. Judith Ivey has such a small part that she isn't even listed in the program. Apparently these prominent people, and others, are willing to work for Allen in lesser parts than they would accept elsewhere.

If only Screenwriter Allen would catch up with Director Allen.

## Richard A. Blake (review date 2 February 1991)

SOURCE: Blake, Richard A. "Wonderland." *America* 164, no. 4 (2 February 1991): 93-4.

[*In the following review, Blake describes* Alice *as a funny, charming, and thought-provoking minor work by a major director.*]

For years Woody Allen has been writing his artistic autobiography in films. His setting is the trendy West Side of New York, his ethnic environment is Jewish, and his persona is the beleaguered neurotic "little man," of the Chaplin mold, trying to survive in a hostile world.

*Alice* continues the story, with several surprises. The Woody Allen character does not appear in the film at all, none of the principal characters is Jewish and New York has been transformed from a menacing arena of competing neuroses to the springboard for gentle fantasy. *Alice,* despite its recognizable settings, is an urban fairy tale and must be disengaged from realism if its magic is to work.

Alice Tate (Mia Farrow), an aging waif, grows restless as her 16-year marriage to Doug Tate (William Hurt) settles into a routine of shopping, facials and pedicures. Doug comes from a Wasp family so wealthy that it does not "make" money, it "has" money. As an investment broker, however, Doug does not seem in danger of losing money either. Their apartment reflects good taste, expensive design and sterility. One of their favorite interior decorators actually tries to sell them a $9,000 wicker eel trap with the suggestion that they customize it into a lamp. Their two handsome children have no personalities in the film; they merely decorate the marriage and provide employment for their maids and nannies. As a sign of her discontent, Alice develops a backache and contemplates hiring "a Swede to walk on it." On the advice of both her personal trainer and her hair dresser, however, she sails her destroyer-sized limousine into the tiny canals of Chinatown to seek a cure from the famous herbalist Dr. Yang (Keye Luke).

Dr. Yang wisely perceives that her backache stems not from her spine but from her mind and heart. Under hypnosis Alice reveals that she feels remorse and guilt about her attraction to Joe Ruffalo (Joe Mantegna), a dark-eyed stranger she met as they both waited for their children at a nursery school that promises to improve their chances of getting into an Ivy League college. With the help of the doctor's magic potion, she overcomes her shyness and, dressed in her prim red schoolgirl hat, she engages him in a seductive dialogue that is one of the funniest moments in the story. If there remained any doubts, Mia Farrow once again proves herself a major comic actress. Joe, a divorced jazz saxophonist, is as amazed as she is at her smooth patter

and chemically induced knowledge of the workings of the instrument. They agree to meet at the Penguin House in Central Park, but, as the drug wears off, Alice changes her mind and her personality.

Another mysterious powder brings back Ed (Alec Baldwin), her first love, an artist and racing enthusiast who died years earlier in an automobile crash. Together they soar back over the skyscrapers of Manhattan like Superman and Lois Lane to the little dance hall on Long Island where she decided to reject his attentions for the promise of a career in fashion and a more conventional life.

Further adventures with Dr. Yang's magic herbs make her thoroughly invisible, which allows her to discover the truth about Joe, Doug and her women friends. A final potion makes her utterly irresistible to men, which causes some embarrassment when a cook accidentally drops the entire bag into the egg nog at a Christmas party.

\* \* \*

While the comedy and fantasy entertain, Woody Allen probes several of his usual themes. Alice, with her ethereal beauty, provides the image of the artist's ideal, torn between success and security with Doug and a second chance for excitement and adventure with Joe. By setting up this polarity Woody Allen asks himself whether he should stay with his proven formulas or branch off into unknown territories. More fundamentally, he asks whether the human condition finds happiness in security or in risk, in reason or in passion.

Since *Hannah and Her Sisters,* Woody Allen has been posing questions about the meaning of life in ever more religious terms. In *Hannah* he added the imagery of Catholicism to his usual Jewish cultural context, as his Jewish hero Mickey Sachs (Woody Allen) contemplates becoming a Catholic when he suspects that he has a fatal brain tumor. *Alice* pushes this evolution one step further. Alice Tate, the script explains, is a lapsed Catholic, a Sacred Heart girl, who used to pray in the convent chapel with her arms outstretched and thought of becoming a nun herself. At one point, her fantasies lead her back to an ornate confessional to confront her imaginary sins. Her well-intentioned friends assume that her Catholic upbringing lies at the heart of her unhappiness and repression. They encourage her to pursue her adultery with Joe, convinced that once she rejects her repressive Catholic scrupulosity, she will find freedom and happiness. When, for example, Alice tells the good Dr. Yang that she admires penguins because they mate for life, the normally laconic Doctor comments that she must think they are Catholics.

For the greater part of the story this pattern seems to be the tiresome line promulgated by anti-Catholic and ex-Catholic novelists and stand-up comics: "My life is a mess today because of what the nuns told me." Woody Allen is not tiresome. In the last few minutes of this moral tale he confounds Alice's friends and brings her to a new level of happiness by having her reject both her Wasp husband and her oriental herbalist and recover her Catholic past. Her fascination with Mother Teresa seems unrealistic, as of course it would be if the script called for reality rather than fantasy. *Alice,* however, is a fairy story with the requisite happy ending. Mother Teresa functions as the improbable fairy godmother. Who cares if the outcome stretches the boundaries of probability? For Alice Tate the happy ending demands a rediscovery of her real self, which happens to be resolutely Catholic. She can no more separate herself from her Catholic roots than Mickey Sachs could abandon his Judaism in the face of death.

* * *

Woody Allen suggests that at their worst Catholics may suffer from the effects of an overly rigid moral code, but at their best they know that happiness comes from serving rather than being served. In *Alice* he allows Mrs. Tate to outgrow the worst and mature into the best of her religious tradition. Little wonder then that the self-absorbed, neurotic Allen comic character, with his stutter and dark-rimmed glasses, has been put on sabbatical for this very funny, charming and thought-provoking minor work of America's major director.

## Richard Alleva (review date 8 March 1991)

SOURCE: Alleva, Richard. "Empty Houses." *Commonweal* 118, no. 5 (8 March 1991): 158-59.

[*In the following excerpt, Alleva asserts that Allen's directing in* Alice *is skillful, but that the characters are not well developed.*]

Woody Allen's *Alice* is an anomaly: a cleverly written, fluently directed bit of fluff about a woman's spiritual transformation. Allen has become a technician of suave, easygoing power. When he introduces us to the hyper-yuppie couple, Alice and Doug Tate, in their East Side New York apartment, he does so in a single shot that lasts about ninety seconds. And in that minute-and-a-half we see Alice greet and deal with her husband, children, physical trainer, decorator, cook, maid, and a member of a parent pool who has come to drive the kids to kindergarten. This single shot staging isn't just economical; it's meaningful and funny. As the camera pans back and forth in the huge, flesh-toned apartment (that has a hall as big as a hotel corridor) the employees and acquaintances seem to spring out of the woodwork. The place is infested with affluence and the mousy Alice can't really deal with such hectic comfort. She's

uneasy and there is an ache in her lower back that no expensive drug or massage can alleviate. She goes to a Dr. Yang of Chinatown who provides magic herbs that grant her, by turns, sexual boldness, invisibility, contact with the ghost of a former lover, advice from a literary muse, and (disastrously) the power to enthrall every single male at a cocktail party.

Much of the magical stuff is accomplished delightfully. When the ghostly lover, Ed, appears, he doesn't just crudely materialize à la *Topper.* Rather, his body seems to seep into a dimly lit room from some reality beyond our reality. When Dr. Yang has Alice relive her first encounter with her husband, there's no corny segue into flashback; Doug simply appears in Yang's office and the couple create the reality of the past with words and glances as the doctor looks on. Allen again demonstrates his flair for using familiar actors in slightly eccentric ways. Farrow has, as many have noticed, picked up some of her significant other's vocal patterns but these she uses with confidence and the sort of control that the more furtive Allen could never manage. She dominates the supernatural visitors and special effects by never seeming too surprised by them. Joe Mantegna brings to the part of Alice's musician-lover what he couldn't summon for his gangster in *The Godfather III*: a sustained, centered understanding of the man he plays. Mantegna's rough amiability suits well this role of a basically decent guy with strains of seediness and irresponsibility in his character. William Hurt has always had fatuousness as a color on his actor's palette. Appropriately, he dips his brush deeply into it for the part of Alice's heel of a husband. The late Keye Luke makes a great farewell appearance as Yang: he barks with unchallengeable authority.

If so much in the film is good, why doesn't it reverberate within me? The problem may be this: none of Alice's magical transformations revealed her past or her mental life for me, and, without such revelation, her final conversion carries little weight. For instance, that reenacted first date with her husband-to-be I have praised for its avoidance of the clichés of flashback. But that is, alas, its main virtue. At the conclusion of the scene, I knew no more of why Alice had been drawn to this particular man than before it started. The dialogue in it is nothing but generic courting conversation that could have been written by any apprentice playwright for any pair of cardboard lovers. The case is the same for Alice's scenes with her sister: generic sibling needling and reconciliation. (Contrast these scenes with the sisterly get-togethers in *Hannah and Her Sisters* where the siblings listen and don't listen to each other like particular women from a particular family.)

In fact, I'm stuck with the impression that Allen wrote this script very quickly and too enthusiastically, with great enthusiasm for its magical devices but little insight into his own characters. Allen the writer merely set Allen the director a series of technical tasks that the latter then dextrously fulfilled. But, at the film's conclusion, when Dr. Yang declares that Alice now has a better understanding of who she is, I'm afraid that I could only respond, "But I don't!" *Alice* has the strange distinction of being the least vivid good movie of the year.

## Anne Billson (review date 19 July 1991)

SOURCE: Billson, Anne. "*Alice in Wonderland.*" *New Statesman* 4, no. 160 (19 July 1991): 33.

[*In the following review, Billson describes* Alice *as whimsical and entertaining.*]

There are pros and cons to attending film previews. The major drawback is that you don't get a real-live audience reaction: a roomful of critics quietly sniggering or yawning behind their hands just doesn't match up to, say, a packed house at the Odeon Marble Arch bursting into spontaneous applause as Big Arnie rips someone's eyeballs out with a merry quip.

On the other hand, the major advantage of the preview is that you don't get a real-live audience. Critics, on the whole, don't rustle sweet-wrappers, guzzle foul-smelling popcorn, or give a stream-of-consciousness running commentary, counterpointing the action on the screen with *aperçus* along the lines of: "Ooh look, he's got a gun. I bet he's going to shoot him, ooh now he's dead." Punters are getting so used to watching films at home on video that they are now treating cinema auditoria like their own private living-rooms. The big plus about slam-bang Dolby-stereo gatta-gatta action movies is that the soundtrack usually drowns out these bone-heads.

Woody Allen films are quieter affairs, and they come with their own built-in hazard. This is the Woody Fan, who always sits behind you and brays with such hysterical laughter at the mildest of witticisms that you miss the next three lines of dialogue because your ears are still ringing. The Woody Fan is the main reason I maintained a rigid anti-Woody stance throughout the 1970s. Then I saw *Manhattan* and was forced to make a reassessment.

Woody Fans haven't gone away, though. They even sit in on his wannabee-Ingmar efforts such as *Another Woman,* slightly perplexed at the dearth of gags, but determined not to pass up on a single braying opportunity. Unfortunately, Woody Fans are not restricted to public screenings; they have infiltrated the private preview as well. As a consequence, a fair chunk of the dialogue in *Alice* was lost to me.

Whether or not this is a good thing is hard to decide. Allen's mighty misapprehension that in order to be serious you have to be po-faced and not make jokes has led to diminishing returns in his box-office as well as (in my view, anyway) his artistic credibility. Let us take a leaf out of Woody's book and drop a heavyweight cultural reference as an illustration of how-wrong-can-you-get. Ladies and gentlemen, I offer you an unbeatable combination of Verdi and Boito (with a little help from Shakespeare) rounding off the career-topping opera *Falstaff* with the fugue, "The whole world is but a joke, and man is born a clown." Take *that,* Mr Allen.

But back to *Alice.* This is Woody in whimsical, semi-funny mode. The film is a small but perfectly formed chamber-piece about a wealthy woman (Mia Farrow—who else?) from the Upper East Side (of Manhattan—where else?) who seeks a cure for niggling backache from a Chinese doctor. What she gets is a cure for her boring marriage to William Hurt and the chance to make something worthwhile out of her life, thanks to herbal remedies that remove inhibitions, confer invisibility, and conjure up an assortment of ghosts. After a brief affair with Joe Mantegna, she turns into a free spirit and flies to Calcutta to be with Mother Teresa. I don't *think* this last part was supposed to be a joke.

Among the pleasures to be had from *Alice,* there is a strong element of spot-the-star. Allen's films are getting to have more celebrity appearances than a 1970s Disaster Movie; Judy Davis, Alec Baldwin and Cybill Shepherd are among the famous names who pop up for a few lines here and there. Farrow, holding the whole thing together, is as excellent as ever, though the character she plays is somewhat tiresome, both before and after her self-discovery. The actress's collaborations with Allen might have transformed her career for the better, but isn't it time we saw her in a movie made by someone else?

But, as with most of this film-maker's work, there is pleasure to be had in the detailed perfectionism of the *mise en scène* (this is precisely the sort of hardcore cinéaste term that Allen's characters would use), the musings on life and love, and the roles for women that don't require them to teeter around in cha-cha heels before being taken hostage by a maniac with a Kalashnikov. This is thoughtful stuff, no question, but it is also perhaps a mite too refined for its own good.

Allen conveys the uselessness of Alice's life with a sure touch—so sure that one can't help wondering whether his own life isn't so far removed from the one on display; bulging with culture, perhaps, but sealed off in an ivory apartment block, many floors above pavement level. His New York City, a Wonderland of colour-coordinated knitwear and tasteful jazz, is certainly a welcome antidote to the poverty-racked, crack-crazed neo-Beirut now described in newspapers, but increasingly one gets the impression that he no longer has any idea of what lies in between.

## Aisling Foster (review date 19 July 1991)

SOURCE: Foster, Aisling. "Woody's Squeaky-Clean Manhattan." *Times Literary Supplement* (19 July 1991): 18.

[*In the following review, Foster emphasizes the elements of fantasy in* Alice.]

Woody Allen has always had a soft spot for fantasy. Most repeated is the one about his home town, which in *Alice* he describes once again with all the lush, squeaky-clean attraction of a grown-up Disneyland. A Manhattan swept clean of the mad, bad and homeless—or just the plain poor. As ever, his characters are rich and bored, real-life elements like work or children being glimpsed only as pleasant asides. Such romanticism has made Allen the George Cukor of our day, a maker of "women's movies" in a business where, we are told by a character in the film, "Blood and guts are what sells."

The eponymous heroine (Mia Farrow) has been married to the extremely rich Mr Tate (William Hurt) for almost sixteen years. She has two small children, an apartment opulent beyond the imagination of Tom Wolfe, and some unsatisfactory friendships with women. She is also a lapsed Catholic with an admiration for Mother Teresa and vague twinges of guilt. Sickened by years of serious shopping, she puts herself under the spell of a seedy herbalist. In line with all the men in this movie, this Oriental medicine man (Keye Luke) talks to her like an idiot child. As with another Alice, his magic potions are transforming, leading her ever deeper down life's little rabbit-holes. Unlike the original, though, this Alice never questions her orders. Why, we wonder, does she not ask herself: "Would you buy used herbs from this man?"

The answer is that this late twentieth-century Alice is pretty dim, surely a fatal flaw in a movie for modern female audiences? So, too, is the surprisingly dated notion that men are to blame for all of Alice's ills. Still, this is a Woody Allen fantasy, and as such it works pretty well. Each scene is played to merciless excess: there is something mesmeric about the first imbibing of herbs in the Valentino boutique, everything seductively black, lush, utterly tactile; then there is the haunting by a long dead lover who looks round her apartment ("Ah, a Steuben glass hippo—I always wondered who bought those"); and home time at the private kindergarten ("I want to arrange a play date for Tuesday. I'll have my chauffeur pick up the girls from school and drive them to the beach.").

Having swept the homeless out of the picture, Allen has to work pretty hard to underline the contradictions of Alice's life. For most of the film, poverty and hopelessness might be the sole problems of the Indian subcontinent. And only Woody Allen could make such blinkered perceptions funny, cutting from a Mother Teresa fundraising, filled with images of malnourished, sightless children and wet-eyed New Yorkers, to Alice's seduction by her tenor sax player (Joe Mantegna), her account of the event fading into a last murmur "I *am* going on a diet, you know."

At times like this, one realizes it will take more than a few mind-bending herbs or a shift of gear to change Alice Tate or Woody Allen. It becomes clear that the director's old tricks will not serve his heroine in this moral maze. Once upon a time, an Allen woman could write a brilliant poem and la-di-da it into a bright new world. But this is the 1990s, and the goodness straining beneath the buttons of her Chanel suit makes Alice the conscience of the new decade.

In the end, the Chinese herbs solve everything. When Alice announces that she is leaving her husband for Mother Teresa, is the slow fade from her face into an Air India jet the opening of a new, exciting chapter, or is it the last fantasy of a deranged housewife before the men in white coats come to take her away?

## Richard A. Blake (review date 21 March 1992)

SOURCE: Blake, Richard A. "Night Schtick." *America* 166, no. 10 (21 March 1992): 324.

[*In the following review, Blake asserts that* Shadows and Fog *is an entertaining comedy that also explores serious themes concerning God, evil, death, and the human soul.*]

*Shadows and Fog,* Woody Allen's new film, will not win enthusiastic responses from either critics or audiences. It is an extremely serious film, masquerading as a comedy. As a result, it suffers from an identity crisis. Some Allen fans, longing for a return to the vintage Allen with his outrageous one-liners, will find this new film tedious; the jokes are rare, and few of them rate with Allen's best. Others may wonder if Woody Allen has been able to continue his explorations of God, evil and death, concerns that have dominated his most recent films, *Crimes and Misdemeanors* and *Alice.* The answer is "yes," but with a comic style that lacks the poignancy of the first and the whimsy of the second. Even with those reservations. *Shadows and Fog* is a daring, complex and frequently very rewarding film.

The shadows and fog of the title provide, of course, a visual metaphor for human existence in Woody Allen's universe. The damp cobblestones, twisted alleys and dark passages provide a sense of menace. Light sources cast grotesque jagged shadows on gray walls in the manner of German Expressionism and the American films noirs. Friends and killers are indistinguishable in the dark. The brilliant black-and-white photography of Carlo Di Palma recreates the central Europe of *The Third Man* (Carol Reed, 1949). Woody Allen's world is as murky as Harry Lime's Vienna, but despair is the privilege of the arrogant. Allen exploits the darkness for its comic potential. For him, man is but a tiny, powerless creature, a plaything of fate, peering into a metaphysical void while trying to digest lunch.

As actor, Allen has frequently taken upon himself the twin roles of comic and tragic hero. He is the archetypal poor shnook. In the opening sequence of *Shadows and Fog,* a band of nameless vigilantes rouses Mr. Kleinman (Woody Allen) from his warm bed and drives him out into this threatening night. A killer prowls the shadows, and Kleinman cannot tell if he is a suspect. Everyone assumes he knows answers, but he has so little information that he cannot understand the simplest questions. His failure to explain himself only deepens suspicions that he is involved in some great evil. What is the evil? What should he do to save himself? Why are we, Kleinmans all, east into a damp night of unknowing to search for our salvation, with so few clues, so little light to guide us? Why is nature, or God, so cruel with us?

Kleinman's quest is spiritual. In contrast, a sinister and nameless Doctor (Donald Pleasence) performs endless autopsies in his search for the physical explanation of evil. Kleinman visits him in the hope of solving the mystery, but their conversation is futile. The Doctor sneers at his spiritual, even religious methods of inquiry, and Kleinman is revolted by the human refuse bottled and pickled in the laboratory. When the Doctor is murdered, Kleinman, as the last to have seen the Doctor alive, becomes the prime suspect.

Woody Allen has become consistently autobiographical in many of his recent films, and again in this film he explores his relationship to Mia Farrow. Another nameless character, the Clown (John Malkovich), has just left an unappreciative audience and fears that he has lost the ability to make people laugh. His lover, Irmy (Mia Farrow), a sword swallower, tries to console him. She expresses a longing for marriage and children, but he claims that a family would interfere with his creativity. They argue, and he seeks comfort with Marie (Madonna) a high-wire dancer, but their tryst is interrupted by Irmy, who decides to leave him and the circus forever. Throughout, the imagery and lighting show a strong debt to Ingmar Bergman's *The Naked Night* (also released under the title *Sawdust and Tinsel* [1953]).

Irmy trembles as she walks the dark streets alone and homeless. Eager to help her find shelter for the night, a streetwalker (Lily Tomlin) takes her to a local brothel, where the ladies-in-waiting, including Kathy Bates and Jodie Foster, explain their cynical views of men, money and survival. Irmy is warmed by wine and fascinated by their stories, but remains the emotionally distant observer, curious but innocent. After all, she represents the values of romantic love and family. A young customer (John Cusack) offers her $700 for her services; and after a moment of hesitation, she agrees. Arrested for practicing without a license, Irmy is taken away, fined and cast adrift once more on the cobblestone waves of her destiny.

Roaming streets in their parallel quests, Irmy and Kleinman meet and form an instant bond through their mutual despair. We assume the two will fall in love, but *Shadows and Fog* permits no such obvious plot devices. The would-be lovers continue their mad flight through the city. The Clown reappears, now ready to embrace family life. Kleinman is rescued from the mad strangler when a benevolent magician in the circus conjures up his most powerful illusions to save him.

The imagery again comes from Ingmar Bergman, whose film *The Magician* (also released as *The Face* [1958]) also extolled the artist's power to create illusion. The theme, however, is Allen's own. In *Hannah and Her Sisters* (1986), Mickey Sachs escapes from a despair that had led him to a suicide attempt by watching the Marx Brothers *Duck Soup.* In a world of bleak despair, art—entertainment, a joke, a song, illusions, light flashing from a projector in a dark room—are perhaps the surest way to find a path through the shadows and fog of life.

\* \* \*

This latest film is less explicit in its treatment of organized religions. Irmy's dressing table holds a small black and gold icon of Our Lady of Perpetual Help. The image points to the religious background of the character, but even more associates her with a woman's gift of life that transcends death. In a spasm of conscience, Irmy tries to donate her salary to a Catholic church, but in her guilt she cannot enter the church itself. Kleinman makes the offering for her. Yet when she sees an immediate need for the money, she asks Kleinman to take back half, which he does in a scene of great comedy and tension. Perhaps Allen finds a fissure in the religious sensibility. Churches deserve half an investment for their spiritual solace, but for immediate human needs, human energies work best when self-employed. As another autobiographical gloss on the script, Allen suggests that only Mia Farrow, his long-time companion and a woman of Catholic background, could force him to make even a half-hearted entry into the world of religion.

Woody Allen, the clown, need not worry that his audiences no longer laugh at his jokes as they once did. He has put his comedy at the service of other concerns. He still entertains, but the laughter is more restrained. He aims, not at the funny bone, but at the soul.

## Daniel Green (essay date 1991)

SOURCE: Green, Daniel. "The Comedian's Dilemma: Woody Allen's 'Serious' Comedy." *Literature/Film Quarterly* 19, no. 2 (1991): 70-6.

[*In the following essay, Green asserts that Allen's deeper themes are more effectively explored in his comic films than in his somber films. Green observes that Ze-lig represents a successful integration of Allen's skills as a comedian with his insightful treatment of serious themes.*]

Even though it is in many ways his worst film, *Interiors* may yet prove to be Woody Allen's most revealing. As his first "serious" film, it is ample evidence that Allen's forte is indeed the comic film; more importantly, it demonstrates convincingly that insofar as Allen is an artist of "ideas," those ideas are rather conventional. As cold and sterile as Eve's decorations, from which the film takes its title, *Interiors* nevertheless provides an opportunity to examine Allen's ideas laid bare, as it were, and to evaluate more clearly Allen's larger, and very real, achievements as a comic filmmaker.

Beginning with *Annie Hall,* and perhaps even earlier, reviewers and critics have helped to create an image of Woody Allen as the serious funnyman, a kind of comic guru/philosopher/sociologist/psychologist/literary critic. Richard Schickel's comments on *Manhattan* are typical:

> . . . a masterpiece that is that perfect blending of style and substance, humor and humanity that his friends and followers were convinced he would one day make. It is also a rare summarizing statement . . . in which an artist casts a selective eye over the fantastical life of his time and shapes his observations into an unsparing, compassionate, always witty and radically moral narra-tive. Tightly constructed, clearly focused intellectually, it is a prismatic portrait of a time and place that may be studied decades hence to see what kind of people we were.
>
> (63)

It is hard not to see such praise as overkill, notwithstand-ing *Manhattan*'s genuine merits. And Allen himself, of course, has seemed to encourage such grandiose interpretation, especially in *Interiors,* the film which immediately preceded *Manhattan.* Although *Interiors* received more negative reviews than any other Allen film, many critics took Allen seriously. Maurice Ya-cowar, writing one year after the release of *Interiors,* still maintained that the film was "a masterful harmoniz-

ing of form and content. Every nuance is expressive. In *Interiors* Allen achieves . . . a symbolic transcendence of 'the darkness and dread of the human condition,' as Becker puts it, only this time he worked without the safety net of comedy" (196).

Yacowar's comment about "the safety net of comedy" is particularly telling. The implication of both Yacowar and Schickel's commentary is that comedy is at best tangential to the art of Woody Allen. Indeed, it would seem that once Allen was able to achieve that "perfect blend of style and substance" (or "masterful harmoniz-ing of form and content"), he could dispense with comedy altogether. Why is it, one is led to ask, that in order to appreciate Woody Allen it is necessary to pretend that he isn't a comedian? Or that a comic film can't be "clearly focused intellectually"? Is comedy only a "safety net" in Allen's best films?

Allen has always acknowledged his debt to what Diane Jacobs calls "the comic film tradition." When asked about influences, he has cited film comics from Chaplin and Keaton to the Marx Brothers and Jacques Tati. Allen's films certainly show a variety of comic influ-ences: the Marx Brothers-inspired early films, the Keatonesque *Sleeper,* the social comedy of *Annie Hall* and *Manhattan,* the Chaplinesque *Broadway Danny Rose.* One of his best later films, *The Purple Rose of Cairo,* is a fascinating combination of Chaplin's comic pathos and Keaton's energetic self-reflexivity. But Allen has been equally free in his praise for filmmakers such as Bergman and Fellini, and critical opinion seems to accord more weight to these particular enthusiasms. And it was certainly to these "serious" directors that Allen turned in making *Interiors.*

That the critics received *Interiors* as badly as they did must have come as something of a shock to Allen, so universal had been the acclaim for *Annie Hall* as an intellectualized comedy. How better to follow it up than with a film which eliminates the comedy altogether, leaving only the intellectual message? Given the nature of the "message" in this case, one can hardly blame the reviewers for their reservations.

What is it that Allen seems to be trying "to say" in *Interiors*? In this movie, almost every character and every situation seem overdetermined, loaded with al-legorical significance, mainly through the obvious use of oppositions: Renata the successful artist vs. Joey the frustrated aspirant; the angry, cynical Frederick vs. the committed, understanding Mike; most of all, the cold, repressed Eve vs. the warm, unpretentious, and viva-cious Pearl. *Interiors* is a highly schematized movie, and none of the oppositions cries out so loudly as an artistic "statement" as the battle between the life force (Pearl) and the death force (Eve).

The contrasts between Eve and Pearl are obvious to the point of being belabored. Where Eve tends toward grays and other neutral colors, Pearl often dresses colorfully (we first see her in a red dress). Eve's preferences in art, as exemplified in her own interior decorations, are for the restrained and tasteful, whereas Pearl's, exemplified by her Trinidadian sculptures, are for the primitive and gaudy. Eve increasingly turns toward religion (in Renata's words, "Jesus Christ nonsense"), while Pearl believes in voodoo and fortune-telling. Everything about Eve suggests a life lived mainly inside—so much so that Arthur accuses her of constructing an "ice palace" around the family. Pearl, in Arthur's words, is "energetic, demonstrative, and open"; as she says of herself, she needs "pizzazz."

That we are to see Pearl as the necessary antidote to Eve—for Arthur, for his daughters—could not be more clear. Renata's comment at Pearl and Arthur's wedding party—"I've never seen him dance before in his life"—indicates the extent of Pearl's effect on her father. Renata herself reacts to Pearl in what seems her usual way: to avoid trouble, she puts on a sunny face. As she does with her husband and her mother, Renata refuses to say what she really thinks and feels. Like Eve, she lives an interior life, and over the course of the film she begins to act more and more like her mother—so much so that near the end of the movie death-obsessed Renata sits staring into the sea, clearly a foreshadowing of Eve's death. Renata seems beyond the reach of Pearl's salutary influence.

Joey, on the other hand, is clearly meant to be the character who benefits most from that influence. Even more than Renata, Joey becomes closely identified with Eve over the course of the film. It is Joey who cares for Eve after her breakdown and who defends Eve most vehemently against Pearl, ultimately making the pronouncement Renata will not: "she's a vulgarian." Joey is obviously the most in danger of becoming another Eve. Like her mother, she is repressed and tightly wound. Pale, gaunt, and unsmiling (with her spectacles, she even resembles Woody Allen), she seems the inevitable product of the "ice palace." And it is Joey who follows her mother into the sea and is on the verge of dying herself when Pearl, literally, breathes life back into her. We last see Joey taking the first tentative steps toward self-expression by writing down, in a diary, memories of her mother. Perhaps Eve's death will finally free Joey to find her own way.

It is fitting that the movie ends with Joey in the act of writing. Much of Joey's frustration in *Interiors* is a consequence of being a non-artist in a predominantly artistic milieu. She confesses to an artistic temperament without the necessary talent: "I feel a real need to express something, but I don't know what it is I want to express or how to express it." Yet, practically all of the artist characters are at least as unhappy as Joey. Renata is a successful poet, but suffers from writer's block

caused by death anxiety. Her husband, Frederick, is a once-promising novelist whose subsequent books have been received badly and who reacts by becoming bitter and cynical. Flynn is a successful actress, but realizes that she is not taken seriously and can only work on television because of her looks. Joey's lover, Mike, a political filmmaker, seems relatively well-adjusted, but is unable to affect Joey as Pearl does (and is a relatively blandly drawn character anyway). To a great degree, all of these characters are figures of accomplishment in their careers, but they remain unhappy and dissatisfied. The eternal lot of the artist? It would seem so.

It is surprising that Allen's idea of a "serious" movie is one which makes "statements" so banal: life is better than death; art is a poor substitute for life. They are, of course, the points Allen makes obsessively in many of his films, but never so singlemindedly, so lugubriously, or so unconvincingly, as in *Interiors*. Further, such "points" are never really *the point* of Allen's comedies, which leaven such bald thematic posturing with healthy portions of irony. In short, the all too obvious themes of *Interiors* are handled more adroitly in Allen's better films by playing them for laughs.

One could, perhaps, attempt to rescue *Interiors* by reading it as a parody of itself, as Ron Librach does in a recent article. Librach sees the film as an "experimental effort to let an ostensibly realistic drama gradually reveal the fallacies on which it is based." (177) In this view, the intellectual pretension of *Interiors* is the object of Allen's satire:

> Traditionally, comedy has been characterized as a celebrational response to experience, but many of its great theorists have long been at great pains to describe the mean-spiritedness to which its practitioners must momentarily commit themselves when they turn in the direction of satire or parody, for the purpose of these comic forms is frequently nothing less than the annihilation of an entire attitude towards life. What is annihilated is the *ridiculous* or the *ludicrous*.
>
> (177)

In this view, *both* the intellectual sterility of *Interior*'s characters, *as well as* the film's own sober mirroring of that sterility in its very tone and outlook, are targets for Allen's satiric deflation. The film cannibalizes itself.

This is an ingenious argument, but it fails to consider one of our primary expectations of comedy: that it make us laugh. Librach's twisting of the merely portentous into the comic assumes that the appeal of a comic film is largely intellectual—or at least that Allen is working a very narrow view of intellectual parody, a propensity for which there is little indication in Allen's previous films. (With the possible exception of *Love and Death*, although that film still has its share of belly laughs). Certainly such an approach is at least as guilty of what

Librach himself identifies as the "fallacy of believing that intellectual displacement is really a vicarious but valid way of striking a balance with oneself and with the world" (178), the mistaken notion which *Interiors* is supposedly attacking. Further, why attribute to Allen a more intricate conception than he himself would admit to? If, as Librach himself notes, Allen wanted to make a "serious" dramatic film, what purpose does it serve to deny the artist his premise because one doesn't want to believe Woody Allen capable of making a pretentious film? The warranted conclusion would seem to be that, despite Librach's rather tortured defense, Allen does not know how to handle "very heavy stuff" (166).

Librach's overly sophisticated argument is a natural consequence of his thesis that "Woody Allen's singularity as an important filmmaker results from his unique approach to philosophical problems" (165). While Librach is more clever than most who approach Allen from this angle, it remains a very oblique one by which to measure an artist whose chosen style is comedy. Although it is true that the great film comics (Keaton and Chaplin, e.g.) often dealt with subjects worthy of serious attention—another way of saying their films were not trivial—it seems needlessly contemptuous of Allen's comedic abilities to focus instead on his "unique approach to philosophical problems."

After *Interiors,* Allen's films fall more or less into a pattern which has persisted right up to *Crimes and Misdemeanors* (at this writing, his latest film). *Manhattan,* with its *Annie Hall*-like balance of comedy and moral inquiry, seemed to please everyone: the fans, the critics, and, presumably, Allen himself. *Hannah and Her Sisters* repeated this phenomenon eight years later. *Stardust Memories,* on the other hand, seemed to please no one. Critically panned and commercially disappointing, the film also seemed to embody Allen's annoyance at the demands his own insistence on being taken seriously had imposed. Although *Stardust Memories* avoids the leaden seriousness of *Interiors*—it contains, in fact, a number of comically ingenious moments Allen builds on further in *Zelig*—it still straddles uneasily the line between the comic exuberance of his "early, funny films" and the gloom of *Interiors* or *September. A Midsummer Night's Sex Comedy* is, like *Interiors,* an obvious imitation of a European art film (specifically, Bergman's *Smiles of a Summer Night*). However, since the film's tone seems simply flat—as if for Allen the attempt to make such a comedy of manners is just an exercise—we do not reach quite the depths of pretentiousness plumbed in *Interiors.* The film, like the later *Radio Days,* can only be seen as a trifle, lacking even the aura of Major Statement which emanates so clearly from Allen's earlier synthetic masterpiece.

The ambivalence and vacillation which mark this stage of Allen's career is seemingly confirmed with his next film, *Zelig,* but with a twist that makes all the difference. In *Zelig* Allen finally confronts this ambivalence head on. What better image of the conflicted artist Woody Allen than the "human chameleon," Leonard Zelig? In the same way that Zelig changes personalities according to his surroundings, Allen seems to be constantly in artistic metamorphosis, from slapstick comedian on the one hand to "serious artist" on the other. *Zelig* tells the tale of the self-reconciliation of the two sides of its maker, Woody Allen.

One of the most striking things about *Zelig,* which is beginning to look like one of Allen's most successful films, is the way in which Allen is able to use the medium itself to work out his artistic problem. He does so, however, while remaining faithful to the comic tradition exemplified by such films as *Never Give a Sucker an Even Break* or *Sherlock, Jr.,* films which amply illustrate the inherent self-reflexivity of the American comic film. Allen had first mined this territory in *Stardust Memories*; in *Zelig* he works out the implications of that film by taking its self-reflexive aspects a step further: where *Stardust Memories* is a film about filmmaking, *Zelig* is a film whose very existence is articulated through the self-conscious suturing and manipulation of filmed images which do not cloak their own artificiality. It is, in the most literal sense, a film about film.

*Zelig* is a fictional documentary, a form which Allen had used before in *Take the Money and Run.* The earlier film, however, was more truly a "mock" documentary, using staged simulations of documentary-like sequences, interspersing them with equally fictitious "conversations" with those close to Virgil Starkwell, the film's hero. *Take the Money and Run*'s documentary surface merely disguises, in other words, the otherwise straightforward narrative that is the vehicle for Allen's gags, much like the false nose-and-moustaches hide Virgil's parents' "real" identities—that is, very transparently. *Zelig,* on the other hand, could pass as an authentic documentary—if only, that is, Leonard Zelig had actually existed. Much of the newsreel footage included in *Zelig* is authentic, and the mock-footage is carefully designed and shot to look as "historical" as possible. We see nothing in *Zelig* that could not actually have been caught on film (or photograph), unlike many of the episodes in Virgil's life, for which it is difficult to imagine any camera could have been present.

*Zelig* is surely one of the most impressive technical achievements (in the more aesthetic sense of "style" rather than special effects) in recent American film. It is in many ways a *tour de force,* a triumph of both vision and execution.[1] Certainly one of the joys of *Zelig* for the viewer not emotionally tied to some exclusive preconception of a "Woody Allen film" is simple appreciation of its formal virtuosity. While this may seem a questionable virtue to *both* those who insist on the superiority of the "early, funny" films as well as those who take Allen seriously as a social observer, such an approach is perfectly in keeping with other, similarly "postmodern" developments in art and literature, and it is, at any rate, a much more fruitful avenue for Woody Allen's forays into art cinema than the leaden "drama" of *Interiors*. To some, self-reflexivity may be the last refuge of the desperate or the decadent, but it might also be seen as a way of examining the vital issues traditionally explored through art by simultaneously examining the ways in which art itself represents, or signifies, such issues. Thus, in *Zelig* Allen is able to integrate his "serious" and "funny" sides into a comic whole informed by a truly serious concern with the machinery by which the cinema creates its images.

Without diminishing the poignancy of his ostensible subject, Leonard Zelig, Allen is able to explore the supposed distinction between subject and medium and to indicate the extent to which the former is a function of the latter. Ultimately, Zelig the "human chameleon" is a unique creation of film, a character whose "life" is completely dependent on its manifestation in filmed images. We never actually experience Zelig's transformations; rather, we laugh at them as *fait accomplis* which have been caught by a camera. In a very real sense, we accept Leonard Zelig as an authentic subject for a documentary because of our willingness to accept the authenticity of the cinematic image itself.

Among the most interesting (and funny) sequences in the film are the so-called "White Room Sessions." Here we are able for the first time to see Leonard Zelig in the flesh, so to speak—previously we have seen and heard him only in still photographs and audio recordings, his elusiveness for the viewer mirroring the slipperiness of his identity as the "chameleon." But even here, of course, we are actually seeing Zelig secondhand. The White Room Sessions were filmed as a part of Zelig's therapy, and their existence is therefore merely fortuitous, a part of the residue left by the evolution of the technology of film and photography. The Sessions themselves, in fact, act as a kind of paradigm or recapitulation of the development of sound film. As a way of concealing the camera's presence, it is encased in a one-way glass booth. In addition, the camera's motor is muffled so that the hidden microphone does not pick up its whir. As anyone who has seen *Singin' in the Rain* (or read actual accounts of the period) is aware, this was the situation for filmmaking during the transition from silent to sound films. Further, the Sessions are filmed in a static, medium two-shot, representative of the limitations imposed by sound technology in its nascent state. These White Room Sessions, then, in which Leonard Zelig finally stumbles his way toward some firmer sense of himself, are presented as parallel with a similar groping for identity in the medium of filmmaking—and, most importantly, in the artistic development of Woody Allen. Perhaps Allen has in *Zelig* taken the advice given to him by the aliens in *Stardust Memories* and gone back to basics, using the Sessions as a metaphor for his own cinematic self-discovery. Through Leonard Zelig, the human chameleon, Woody Allen, the film chameleon, finally comes to terms with his influences. In a very real sense, *Zelig* is the first completely *whole* Allen film: by synthesizing his interests and influences—which results not in some derivative "outlook" on life, but a particular way of looking at film itself—and balancing his sincere desire to be serious with his manifest comic skills, Allen is able to "cure" his art (just as Eudora Fletcher is able to cure Leonard Zelig) of its incipient schizophrenia.

It is as if in *Zelig* Woody Allen has discovered that "serious" themes such as sex, death, or identity are made problematic by the artificial nature of all cinema, whether comedic *or* dramatic. Further, *Zelig* suggests that one way of approaching this dilemma is to expose the artifice deliberately, to explore the interplay of signifier and signified in the communication of "meaning." Thus, *Zelig* not only raises the "problem" of identity as we commonly think of it, it *enacts* the problem before our very eyes. It relates the fictional story of Leonard Zelig, a man in search of an identity, while also telling the story of a similar quest for identity in the medium itself. In addition to the White Room Sessions, such a device as the insertion of scenes from *The Chameleon Man,* Hollywood's reputed version of Zelig's story, acts as a commentary on the role of the Hollywood cinema's influence on our perceptions, as well as the role of the fiction film vs. the documentary, ultimately calling into question the claims of both as authentic versions of the truth. Ultimately the film also calls into question the viewer's own identity as moviegoer. Those scenes which feature Zelig appearing in historical film clips (the shot depicting Zelig "on deck" at Yankee Stadium, for example) require the viewer's active scrutiny of the mise-en-scene if he/she is to appreciate their humor and ingenuity. The passive spectator will be lost in the cinematic puzzle which is *Zelig.* The film asks implicitly that the viewer think about his/her own relationship to the movie-going experience, and such an activity, seriously pursued, leads inevitably to a consideration of nature and function of film. In short, *Zelig* encourages us to define and re-define our notions of what a movie properly *is*.

This readjustment of artistic priorities in *Zelig* seems to have a liberating effect on Woody Allen. The jokes and gags in the film are most reminiscent of the "early, funny" films such as *Bananas* or *Love and Death.* A few examples include the list of crimes with which Zelig is charged: "adultery, bigamy. . . . and performing unnecessary dental extractions"; Zelig's insistence that if he's late for his masturbation class "they'll start without me"; and the narrator's assertion that Zelig's transformation into a rabbi is so convincing that some Frenchmen request that he be sent to Devil's Island. The effect is that Allen seems to have renewed faith in his facility for joke-making and is able to integrate such jokes into the larger formal structure of *Zelig* with impunity. The canard with which Allen has long struggled is the assumption that comedy and seriousness are incompatible (an assumption which this essay has argued led Allen astray in *Interiors*). The unsettling resonances in the Devil's Island joke suggest the extent to which *Zelig* is able to set this canard aside. Like all of Allen's best jokes, it makes us laugh because of its cleverness, but also disturbs us because of its insight. The same could be said of *Zelig* itself.

*The Purple Rose of Cairo* continues the experiment in self-reflexivity begun in *Zelig* and although an analysis of this film is beyond the scope of the present essay, *Purple Rose* must be counted, with *Zelig*, as one of Allen's most impressive films of the 80s. Unfortunately, his subsequent films have not built on the promise fulfilled in these two films. Allen again seems to be in a period of artistic uncertainty, exemplified perhaps by *Crimes and Misdemeanors*, in which Allen's conflicting impulses, ostensibly allied, actually compete with each other rather uneasily. The film, although much more compelling than either *September* or *Another Woman*, derives much of its interest from the unresolved tensions between "comedy" and "drama" which again give the film a schizophrenic feeling. Further, while the film has a morbid fascination, in other ways it could be seen as merely another in the series of claustrophobic dramas Allen announced in interviews following the release of *Radio Days*, films predicated largely on ease and simplicity of production.[2] But Woody Allen has proven to be frustratingly unpredictable as a filmmaker and often circumspect in his comments on his work. We can surely still hope that he will once more make films worthy of the serious, probing, comic artist of *Zelig*.

### Notes

1. All due credit should go to cinematographer Gordon Willis and his associates, who were certainly indispensable in the task of creating such a film as *Zelig*.

2. William E. Geist, "*The Rolling Stone* Interview— Woody Allen," *Rolling Stone*, April 9, 1987: Tom Schales, "Woody: The First Hundred Years," *Esquire*. April 1987.

### Works Cited

Jacobs, Diane. . . . *but we need the eggs: The Magic of Woody Allen.* New York: St. Martin's Press, 1982.

Librach, Ronald S. "A Portrait of the Artist as a Neurotic: Studies in Interior Distancing in the Films of Woody Allen." *The Missouri Review* IX: 2 (1986): 165-184.

Schickel, Richard. "Woody Allen Comes of Age." *Time* 30 April 1979: 62-65.

Yacowar, Maurice. *Loser Take All: The Comic Art of Woody Allen.* New York: Frederick Ungar Publishing Co., 1979.

### Ralph Tutt (essay date 1991)

SOURCE: Tutt, Ralph. "Truth, Beauty and Travesty: Woody Allen's Well Wrought Urn." *Literature/Film Quarterly* 19, no. 2 (1991): 104-08.

[*In the following essay, Tutt discusses* Stardust Memories *in terms of Allen's increasing interest in making films that serve as commentary on filmmaking and the film industry.*]

Realism is incompatible with the democracy—and the implausibility—of popular film art. This point was easily grasped by Hollywood genre experts of the 30s and 40s negotiating the straits of realism and romance: De Mille, Hawks, Ford, Hitchcock—none recognized it more clearly than writer/director Preston Sturges in his 1941 film, *Sullivan's Travels*. King of Comedy John Lloyd Sullivan (Joel McCrea), in search of ultra verisimilitude for his first "serious" picture, *Brother, Where Art Thou?*, suffers with the masses in Depression American only to discover the obvious: the Depressed don't go to the movies seeking firsthand experience. Brotherly love, lacking in boxcars and flophouses, is found right under Sullivan's eyes in a Black church where convict spectators laugh together at a Mickey Mouse cartoon.

Sociological authenticity is lost on mass audiences in Disneyland America because it resists the encoding process by which genres, hit or miss, have been established. Conversely, the real world in hard times jeopardizes the stability of popular generic codes. This point is brought "touchingly" to life by the celluloid stick figures in Woody Allen's picture-within-a-picture of escapism in Depression America, *The Purple Rose of Cairo* (1985).

Like the Arcadian revelers on Keats's urn, the café socialites of Allen's antiquated genre piece are immutable figures of fun in a world of woe and change. Popular stereotypes of their day, they are also fixed points in eternity who periodically tease disconsolate dreamers out of thought. The rigid deportment preserved by Keats's band of Arcadians is more becoming of immortals than the spectator intercourse Allen permits his madcap crew—to be sure." But just as the characters on Allen's black-and-white screen converse with its color audience, so Keats's urn, personified as a Sylvan Historian, addresses the poet/speaker of "Ode on a Grecian Urn," informing him in the poem's concluding lines "Beauty is truth, truth beauty,—that is all / Ye know on earth, and all ye need to know." The noumenal experience is the same in each case, and the Keats/ Allen analogy is instructive on biographical and historical levels as well.

In a literary epoch dominated by realist Wordsworth, Keats, often inspired by works of art from the classical past, was caught in a time warp between the neo-classic and the romantic. His narrative, epic and dramatic ambitions were cut short by tuberculosis—also, according to popular myth, by critical ridicule of *Endymion,* his first attempt to extend his gifts beyond lyric to epic form. In a film epoch threatened by television, standup comic and skit artist Allen launched his professional writing career as parodist par excellence with Mel Brooks, Larry Gelbert, Carl Reiner, and Neil Simon on "Your Show of Shows." Allen's Golden Age in TV Comedy was soon eclipsed by more ambitious ventures acting, writing and directing for stage and screen. He was doing fine at the box office until he turned dead serious in 1978 with the Bergmanesque *Interiors.* Maybe *Blackwood's Magazine* critic John Lockhart in his notorious attack on the "Cockney School of Poetry" (October, 1817) did help to kill John Keats; it's certain that Allen followers, in their defection after *Interiors,* embittered the woe-begone clown.

Two years after *Interiors* fickle critics and fans were in for attack in Allen's *Stardust Memories* (1980), a mean-spirited project shunning fame and inviting comparison with *8½* (1963). Fellini's film was *about* a director bankrupt of new ideas, Roger Ebert quipped, while Allen's was *by* a director with no new ideas. Nimble line; but disregarding Allen's sour grapes we find in *Stardust Memories* as well as *8½,* which is widely regarded as Fellini's masterpiece, an energetic depiction of what Christian Metz calls the "cinema machine" and a clear indication of Allen's growing preoccupation with the possibilities of film aesthetics vis-a-vis the film industry as a subject for filmmaking.

Cinema, Metz writes, "is not just the cinema industry (which works to fill cinemas, not empty them), it is also the mental machinery—another industry—which spectators 'accustomed to the cinema' have internalised historically and which has adapted them to the consumption of films" (7). Genres are, of course, fundamental components of the cinema machine and shifting generic gears is risky business.

In the retread world of entertainment, reliable genres of the classical Hollywood period have faded out and in. Their sharpest signifiers, borrowed by couture and advertising, have been peddled in the nostalgia market. They have been crossbred with other genres, or temporarily shelved until the time was right to steal back into public favor. The frontier idealism of the Western waned, as everyone knows, long before its most enduring icon became a Green Beret in the late sixties. Drifting into noir territory in the fifties, the Western was so bogged in subjectivism and gloom by the 70s that audiences lost interest. Still it defied death. Indeed its own death warrant served in 1976 as the theme of John Wayne's valedictory, *The Shootist.* Its plot conventions have since been appropriated for fantasy, science fiction and urban police drama (*Star Wars, Blade Runner, Outland, Fort Apache, the Bronx*) while its mise-en-scene has informed promotional fantasies ranging from the dreary rites of breakfast cereal, coffee, cigarettes, and life insurance to the recherche outlands of Ralph Lauren and Calvin Klein. And just when we thought Michael Cimino, if not Mel Brooks, had given it the coup de grace, Dirty Harry and Shane were transfigured in Clint Eastwood's Fourth Horseman of the Apocalypse. *Pale Rider* grossed $28 million in its first 17 days. Fast on its heels came Laurence Kasdan's *Silverado* with reviewers shouting "Yippee!" and *Gentleman's Quarterly* featuring the "Silverado Look," a "high noon of men's fashion." Now we are back to the future with critics predicting a new wave of Westerns inspired by *Lonesome Dove, Young Guns* I and II, *Back to the Future* III, and *Dances with Wolves.*

In 1981 Kasdan's *Body Heat,* repeating the triumph of *Chinatown* (1974), reversed speculation that the American noir cycle ended in 1958 with Orson Welles's *Touch of Evil.* Carl Reiner's 1982 send-up, *Dead Men Don't Wear Plaid,* seemed sophomoric to noir fans whose infatuation with the genre had matured into a sober awareness that its morality play conflicts and doppelganger themes mirrored American anomie in the 80s just as accurately as they had in the 40s. *Body Heat* was followed by a steady flow of noir hits. *The Verdict* (1982), *Against All Odds* (1983—an updated remake of the 1947 classic, *Out of the Past*), *Tightrope* (1984), and, rounding out the 80s cycle, Kasdan's sequel to *Chinatown, The Two Jakes.*

In the forties, a decade notable for the first serious tremors of social conscience in Hollywood—Ford's *The Grapes of Wrath* (1940) and *Tobacco Road* (1941), Edward Dmytryk's *Crossfire* (1947), Elia Kazan's *Gentleman's Agreement* (1947) and *Pinky* (1949), Clarence Brown's *Intruder in the Dust* (1949), Mark Robson's *Home of the Brave* (1949), Alfred Werker's *Lost Boundaries* (1949)—the financial and critical success of Walt Disney's technicolor musical *Song of the South* (1946) was all the more remarkable. Notwithstanding the success of this Cloud-Cuckoo-Land throwback to the plantation rhythms of Shirley Temple and "Bojangles" Robinson in the mid-thirties, the antebellum plantation romance which whitewashed slavery, bigotry and despotism was distinctly passe in the mid-40s, and films about the plight of poor white farmers were eclipsed by those with the more pressing national concerns of racism and civil rights. The embellishments of plantation romance survived in major neo-abolitionist productions of the 50s, 60s and 70s: *Band of Angels* and *Raintree County* (1957); *Slaves* (1969); *Mandingo* (1975) and its sequel in 1976, *Drum.* By a simple reversal of the old codes conveying white benevolence and black docility, producers continued to market staples of Southern romance just as they continued to make Westerns with cowboys and Indians, revising codes, as in Ford's last Western, *Cheyenne Autumn* (1964), to show that all Indians were not like the beastly Comanches of his 1956 classic, *The Searchers.*

If unpredictable, fluctuations of genre cycles in the commercial cinema are nonetheless constant: one thing that never changes in the cinema machine is change itself. While parody such as Mel Brooks's, Carl Reiner's and Woody Allen's may seem to signal the end of a genre cycle, film history has shown this is seldom the case.

In the black-and-white film-within-a-film, ***The Purple Rose of Cairo,*** Allen shows that he hasn't lost the satiric touch that made him famous. He presents not only restrained parodies of 30s programmers—nightclub musicals such as RKO turned out by the score in the 30s and 40s; Universal's mummy's tomb cycle, which began in 1932 with Karl Freund's *The Mummy* starring Boris Karloff—but also a travesty of quest narratives popularized in comic strips and Saturday serials.

Tom Baxter, poet, adventurer, explorer, has come to Cairo in search of a legendary rose that has fascinated him for years. A pharaoh, the legend goes, once had a rose painted purple for his queen; now, it is said, purple roses grow wild at her tomb. Introduced in the pyramid sequence where Baxter bumps into bored Manhattanites, Henry, Jason and Rita, this motif assumes serious consequences in the film's realistic context. Once Baxter, in pith helmet and khaki, deserts his onscreen cohorts to seek the real world with Cecilia, Allen's hooked-on-the-movies waitress waif, the initial element of travesty subsides in a chilly Depression mood.

The central reality-and-artifice paradox in ***Purple Rose*** is spectators at the fictitious Jewel Theatre conversing with onscreen characters in the black-and-white film, which is credited as an "RKO Radio Picture." Beyond this audacious exchange is the further paradox of spectators who have paid real money in real theatres to watch. They are watching a film of the same title credited to writer/director Woody Allen and his producer, Orion Pictures corporation. When the frame-within-a-frame shows the familiar RKO logo—an antenna on top of a globe—we spectators of the Orion production (as well as the RKO production) are cued on our roles: we

constitute a third-dimensional frame encompassing both RKO and Orion frames. We are teased into the reminder that film consumers too are collaborators in the filmmaking process—all the crazy fluctuations of the cinema machine. Reporters interviewing an irate woman who demands her money back when Baxter deserts the screen in search of truth with Cecilia are told: "I saw the movie just last week. This is not what happens. I want what happened in the movie last week to happen this week. Otherwise what's life all about anyway?" Toying with the tried-and-true can get a pop artist in trouble. When romance courts realism, here as in *Sullivan's Travels,* the cinema machine goes haywire.

Collaborators in the filmmaking process are only as good as their last picture. Typecasting can grow tedious, however, and in the face of radical social change may prove as costly to career longevity as casting against type. Gil Shepherd (Jeff Daniels), tired of playing romantic adventurers like Tom Baxter, wants to stretch himself, tackling the role of a real-life hero in his next film, a bio-pic based on the life of Charles Lindbergh. While Tom and Cecilia hide out in New Jersey, panic strikes all echelons of the movie colony from projection booth to mogul office. While they exchange ingenuous bons mots about realism and romance, Shepherd flies east to recover Baxter, the bankable character he created, who in turn made him a star. It's tough living in the real world, Cecilia instructs Baxter, with wars and no jobs.

CECILIA

You, you probably never even heard of the Great War.

TOM

(Shaking his head) No, I'm sorry. I missed it.

CECILIA

Yeah, well (shaking her head) y-you, people, people get old, and sick, and never find true love.

TOM

(Sighing) Well, you know, where I come from, people, they don't disappoint. They're consistent. They're always reliable.

CECILIA

Y-you don't find that kind in real life.

The most cerebral of Allen's films to date, ***Purple Rose*** drew some confessions of bafflement from the press but generally received high marks and favorable comparisons with Buster Keaton's *Sherlock Jr.* and Pirandello's *Six Characters in Search of an Author*—no mention of *A Midsummer Night's Dream* or *Smiles of a Summer Night* and their influence on Allen's serio-comic development of a favorite theme, inconsistency and unrealiability in courtship, love and marriage. Once more he was in jeopardy with popular audiences still attuned to his earnest blend of comedy and romance in 70s hits *Annie Hall* (1977) and *Manhattan* (1979).

Each time a new Allen film appears, reviewers trot out the issue of his progress in the direction of serious comedy and tragedy. "Allen wouldn't be Allen," David Ansen commented in his *Newsweek* review of *Alice,* Allen's twentieth film, "if his earnest side didn't eventually pop up." *Alice* is "fluff," he writes, but fluff of a high order. "Yet the thematic links are there to his 'serious' movies" (61). A new Allen film is either a diversion, a regression or, as in the case of *Crimes and Misdemeanors* (1989), a serious step forward. Progression hounds have diverted attention from Allen's achievements in individual works and his considerable versatility in a filmmaking career spanning twenty-five years. The image persists of the standup comic-turned-auteur dangling in a Hollywood netherworld somewhere between mid and high cult, high and low comedy, with periodic pretensions to solemnity.

For Allen as for his dreamer, Cecilia, Hollywood icons like Fred Astaire and Ginger Rogers are reliable agents of escape from vicissitude. Objects of truth and beauty, they remain so for creator and beholder—but only on a temporal basis in the dream state to which Cecilia returns at the end of the film. Allen is conspicuously absent as an actor in *Purple Rose,* but it is the most autobiographical of his films about filmmaking (*The Front, Stardust Memories, Zelig,* and *Crimes and Misdemeanors*); in it he assumes three personae: Cecilia, worshiper of film romance, and Tom Baxter/Gil Shepherd, both seeking a change of pace in realism—all are Allen Stand-ins. They represent (to press the Keats/Allen analogy further) not only his enchantment with antique art objects but also a new authorial detachment, contentment and pleasure in "Negative Capability," the Keatsian attitude that "the sense of Beauty . . . obliterates all other consideration"; the ideal state for the artist is one of suspension when one is "capable of being in uncertainties, mysteries, doubts, without any irritable reaching after fact and reason" (Letter to George and Tom Keats, Dec. 1817).

In his characterization of another stand-in, Alvy Singer, the relentless quipster of *Annie Hall,* Allen confronts the limitations of the comic reflex. If the darkness of *Stardust Memories* marks the first sharp turning point in his comedic career, *Annie Hall, The Purple Rose of Cairo* and *Crimes and Misdemeanors* are giant steps forward in his steady move beyond parody, burlesque and travesty toward tragicomedy. The extended metaphor of watching—spectators watching backs of spectators watching frames-within-frames and the playful reversal of this order when Tom Baxter confronts the audience in *Purple Rose*—is carried to metaphysical

extremes in *Crimes and Misdemeanors,* Allen's most solemn film to date. Eye trouble, literally and figuratively, is pushed to such Sophoclean limits (ocular imagery ranges from eye glasses and automobile headlights to the eyes of a demon lover) that we are all but blinded by the symbolic overkill of the script.

With its obvious debts to *Diabolique* and *Fatal Attraction, Crimes and Misdemeanors* reminds us of Allen's eclecticism—other films, other genres; it reminds us of his homage to other authors, his efforts to satirize (or emulate) foreign directors Bergman, Kurosawa, Fellini, Bũnuel, Antonioni, and others. *Purple Rose,* however, transcends homage and genre. It gives us a bona fide auteur working independently in the serio-comic mode most congenial to his talent.

Keats's "Ode on a Grecian Urn," which glorifies the pastoral of classical antiquity, came in 1819 about forty years after Samuel Johnson had declared pastoral an obsolete genre. Personifying (and immortalizing) the urn, Keats revived pastoral, teasing himself (and us) out of thought in a museum setting. In *Purple Rose* Allen revives movie programmers of the 30s, teasing Cecilia out of thought while leading his contemporaries down memory lane as in *Radio Days* (1987).

Cecilia is watching a new film as *Purple Rose* ends: Astaire and Rogers in *Top Hat.* No silly programmer this. Astaire is singing, "Heaven, I'm in heaven / And my heart beats so that I can hardly speak. / And I seem to find the happiness I seek. . . ."

> Cecilia settles down in her seat as Astaire and Rogers do their spectacular graceful duet. They dance on, the music reaching a crescendo as Astaire twirls Rogers in his arms . . . she does a beautiful dip, almost to the floor.

> (467)

The film cuts to Cecilia, in color, watching the dancing couple. She is totally engrossed in the movie. The dance music plays on as she starts to smile, and the Orion production fades to black. This final fade is in effect a freeze frame evoking the dancers—and Keats's ode—beauty in motion frozen at the peak of perfection.

## *Works Cited*

Allen, Woody. *Three Films of Woody Allen: "Zelig," "Broadway Danny Rose," "The Purple Rose of Cairo."* New York: Vintage Books, 1987.

Ansen, David. "Woody Allen in a Most Fantastical Mood," *Newsweek,* Dec. 31, 1990.

Christian Metz. *The Imaginary Signifier: Psychoanalysis and the Cinema.* Bloomington: Indiana University Press, 1977.

## Stanley Kauffmann (review date 20 April 1992)

SOURCE: Kauffmann, Stanley. "Fun and Fumble." *New Republic,* no. 4031 (20 April 1992): 34-6.

[*In the following review, Kauffmann contends that* Shadows and Fog *is pointless and inconclusive.*]

Woody Allen's warmest admirers may be the ones who will want to forget his new film most quickly. *Shadows and Fog* is the flip side of creative freedom. All serious filmmakers want the power to make films as they choose; Allen is one of the few who have that power. *Shadows and Fog* exemplifies the worst that can happen when a good filmmaker (which Allen has become) gets his unsupervised way.

An unnamed country. At the beginning a dream, in fog-bound narrow nighttime streets, through which a strangler prowls. This dream, accompanied by tunes from *The Threepenny Opera,* sets the tone of what follows, in black and white. The dreamer is Allen, who wakes with a start as friends pound on his door and ask him to come and help them catch the strangler.

Into these streets, reminiscent of many Jack the Ripper films, goes Allen's sniveling Jewish schnook, here named Kleinman. (Little man, in case we're missing the point.) Various segments take place with and without him—in a circus, a brothel, a medical examiner's lab. The connection between the segments is thin, the point of the picture nonexistent. It doesn't even conclude: it merely stops on a note of pompous, because unearned, ambiguity.

I shudder to think of what film journals will publish about this unredeemed mess. Allen's stock character in this quasi-Victorian atmosphere signifies that murder threatened and still threatens Jews? Life is a circus? Life is a brothel? Life is a circus *and* a brothel, wrapped in the fog of mystery? I can hear the word processors humming in every college town in America. (They've already begun in France, where the film had its premiere.)

Allen has made better and better films in recent years, which are always improved when he isn't in them. But *Shadows and Fog,* a title too plainly meant to echo Resnais's *Night and Fog,* is a willful disaster.

## Richard Alleva (review date 8 May 1992)

SOURCE: Alleva, Richard. "Visibility Nil." *Commonweal* 119, no. 9 (8 May 1992): 19-21.

[*In the following review, Alleva finds that Allen's weakest films are those in which he tries to appropriate the styles of earlier filmmakers, asserting that* Shadows and Fog, *in which Allen mimics the style of Ingmar Bergman, is a poor imitation.*]

I'm beginning to understand why *Zelig* was one of Woody Allen's best movies. That witty fantasy dealt with a human chameleon, a man without a distinct personality who took on the characteristics of whatever milieu he encountered. As a moviemaker, Allen has that tendency himself. Every so often he tries to turn into Federico Fellini or Ingmar Bergman, and the results constitute about half—pretty much the weaker half—of the corpus of Allen's work: *Interiors, A Midsummer Night's Sex Comedy, September, Another Woman* (all in the Bergman mode); *Stardust Memories, Radio Days, Alice* (Fellini mode). I'm not here repeating the old canard about Allen being authentic only when he's funny, for he was capable of making the fine somber film, *Crimes and Misdemeanors.* But Woody is simply not a very good mimic. Once he abandons his own voice, he stutters.

With *Shadows and Fog,* Allen is back in his Bergman mode and he has never been so pathetically imitative. Like a weakling son who slouches and mumbles in the presence of a domineering parent, Allen is unnerved by the spiritual presence of the presiding genius that he himself has invoked. He has momentarily lost his sense of the way people talk and move and react. His comic timing, both as actor and as director, is absent, and he has let himself be dominated by his own cinematographer.

To be sure, that cameraman is the superb Carlo Di Palma, and thanks to him and to designer Santo Loquasto, this movie has a certain visual flair even if it is a nonstarter in every other respect. For this story of how certain citizens of a nameless Central European town in a period that may be the 1920s respond to the onslaught of a murderous psycho, Di Palma has rendered the ingredients of the title voluptuously, in delicious layers and various shades of grey, white, and black. How colorful black-and-white can be! But, paradoxically, Di Palma's skill emphasizes rather than mitigates the ineptitude of every other element in the movie. In each gorgeous frame everyone and everything is so swathed and nuanced by the most delicate use of light and shadow that you are constantly struck by the incongruity of the undergraduate script and acting. And, though the lighting is magisterial, the placement of the camera (ultimately, the director's responsibility) is not. One scene, in particular, may haunt me forever with its stupid, pointless virtuosity. A group of prostitutes discussing the clientele is seated roughly in a circle; the camera takes a 360 degree tour of the countenances of the women with the camera coming to rest in turn on the face of each whore just as she contributes her bit to the discussion. It's a photographic stunt that not only fails to illuminate the meaning of the scene but actually contradicts it. The women are supposed to be relating to each other with their complaints and mockery of the male sex but the panning camera instead isolates each female in space and turns her face into a monstrous portrait à la Diane Arbus. One might expect this from a student filmmaker drunk on the newly discovered resources of his medium but not from a seasoned director like Allen. But, as I have noted, in a figurative presence of a master like Bergman, Allen turns into a boy.

Actually, more than one master is evoked, for elements of the story are drawn from Kafka as well as Bergman. But Allen doesn't have the courage of his own thievery. Kafkaesque themes are introduced only to be dropped midway through in favor of other themes which are also dropped before the movie is over. Allen as a wormy little clerk named Kleinman (a K hero, get it?) is drafted into a vigilante organization trying to apprehend the killer and is told that he will receive his orders from an unknown superior quite soon. So, like Kafka's Joseph K., he awaits his charge and, as in a Kafka novel, it never comes. But, unlike Kafka, Allen doesn't explore the tensions of such a psychological purgatory; he just trades in his hero's situation for a more frenetic one when Kleinman is preposterously accused of being the killer. Similarly, in a subplot, a clown (John Malkovich) from a visiting circus troupe lives in a marital hell with his sword-swallowing wife (Mia Farrow)—a situation that recalls Bergman's *The Naked Night*. The differences between the couple seem irreconcilable until the woman discovers an orphaned baby and her husband immediately becomes a doting father. Thus, a Strindbergian couple is suddenly transformed into the holy family model out of *The Seventh Seal*. Pure cop-out.

The overall situation of the insane killer threatening a community seems meant to portray the condition of mankind living under the shadow of death. But Allen makes the killer such a specific psycho that, far from accepting him as a symbol or an elemental force, you merely want to see the nut locked up. When he is first magically disarmed by a magician (another steal from Bergman, this time *The Magician*) and then evaporates into thin air, you get the symbolic point: art can divert us from death but cannot defeat it. But again, that killer is too specific to haul such symbolic freight. You merely shudder to think whose throat he will be slitting next. (How wise Camus was to make the ubiquity of death a matter of microbes in *The Plague*.)

*Shadows and Fog* has an all-star cast: Mia Farrow, John Malkovich, John Cusack, Madonna, Jodie Foster, Kathy Bates, Lily Tomlin, Julie Kavner, Kate Nelligan, et. al. There's something distasteful about Allen's propensity for cramming as many hot properties as possible into one movie. It's as if the actors were being used not for their talents but just to show that the director can command their loyalty even when he casts them in small parts. Loyalty seems to be the only thing he has commanded from them. *Shadows and Fog* must be the worst acted American film of the last few years.

Jodie Foster working up a cackle that is supposed to be sensuously all-knowing and Julie Kavner, sawing the air and disobeying each of Hamlet's dicta to the players, are particularly revolting. John Malkovich is rather fascinating to watch because he is so bad that he comes across as mentally impaired. I detest the mousiness that Allen has imposed on Mia Farrow in their last few collaborations, and it is particularly out of place here since she is playing a circus performer used to working crowds. Allen himself dithers tiresomely. Only John Cusack, as a serenely self-absorbed rich kid, gives the audience something and someone interesting to watch.

## Leonard Quart (review date summer 1992)

SOURCE: Quart, Leonard. "Woody Allen's New York." *Cineaste* 19, nos. 2-3 (summer 1992): 16-19.

[*In the following review, Quart discusses the representation of New York City in a variety of Allen's films.*]

There was a time, not so long ago, when New York was less volatile and threatening, when its social desperation and agony seemed more manageable and avoidable. It was during that period—the Thirties through the Fifties—that Hollywood created a dream city both out of the iconography of New York's skyscrapers, penthouses, bridges, and neon lights, and out of the intense street rhythms and theatrics on the ground. Crime, poverty, and fear continued to exist on those celluloid streets (e.g., *Dead End* in the Thirties, the weariness and cynicism of the documentary-style *The Naked City* in the Forties), but the dominant tone inherent in Hollywood's depiction of the city was a buoyant one—cinematic New York, often even when it was corrupt, was a world of romantic possibility. And for decades that fiction about the city helped shape both its citizens, as well as a worldwide audience's vision of New York.

In Thirties' screwball comedies like *Easy Living* (1937), musicals like *On the Town* (1949) and *The Band Wagon* (1953), and romances like *The Clock* (1945), the mixture of carefully selected locations and artfully designed sets evoked an exhilarating and humane world. The city in *On the Town* could elicit the most exultant and joyous of responses from its central characters, three sailors played by Gene Kelly, Jules Munshin, and Frank Sinatra, inspiring them together with their female partners to lift their voices in song and kick up their heels in dance. In fact, the "helluva town" of historic landmarks and ethnic nightclubs that the three sailors giddily race about on their shore leave, the imaginatively designed 42nd street arcade in *The Band Wagon* where Fred Astaire dances with a shoeshine man, and *The Clock*'s wartime portrait of caring, earthy New York milkmen and idyllic nights in misty city parks along the

Hudson, were almost the visual equivalent of Thomas Wolfe's overripe paeans to a city which had moved him to "grow drunk with ecstasy" and to feel that he "can never die."

Obviously, these cinematic evocations of the city never pretended to social realism or criticism. They were mainly interested in stylizing and mythologizing the social universe so an audience could escape into a more radiant, romantic, or exciting world for a couple of hours. The films were so constructed that all those small town, middle Americans in the audience could identify with their counterparts in *On the Town* and *The Clock,* wandering around wide-eyed in the big city. Even in films which portrayed poverty in the New York slums and were genuinely concerned with social issues, class animosity, and injustice, like William Wyler's *Dead End* (1937), urban social problems unfolded on a meticulously and beautifully constructed stage set and were strikingly augmented by cinematographer Greg Toland's use of deep focus and light and shadow. In *Dead End* every fire escape, tenement stoop, roof, garbage can, and huddle of people conveyed more of a calibrated esthetic effect than a statement about urban entrapment. From the vantage point of the Nineties, life in *Dead End*'s New York slum, despite its poverty and violence, looks pretty good—a vital neighborhood with a river view which was ripe for the kind of gentrification the film depicts as already in process.

The movie industry repeatedly used New York to project an image of a city that would excite the collective imagination and fantasies of its audience, offering them either upper class glamor and success or working class warmth and folksiness. The cinematic city was centered in neighborhoods like a moneyed, chic Upper East Side, a charming, bohemian Greenwich Village, a communal but impoverished Lower East Side, and a daffy, distinctively accented Brooklyn, whose mere mention would elicit laughs from movie audiences throughout the country. For the moviegoing public of the time, Brooklyn was the apotheosis of all the kind-hearted, good-humored, raw, democratic virtues of America's urban, ethnic common man. And New York's fire escapes, pushcarts, town houses, elevated trains, office buildings, art galleries, night clubs, and quaint, checkerboard tableclothed Italian restaurants dominated Hollywood's vision of the city in films ranging from screwball comedies like *The Awful Truth* (1937) to *film noir* classics like Fritz Lang's *Scarlet Street* (1945). In the *noir* films the dark, shadowy, glistening wet streets of the studio back lots whetted the audience's appetite for fashionable corruption. For Hollywood, setting a film in a large city, more often than not, meant placing it in New York.

Since the mid-Sixties, however, as the city began to unravel—its social problems more insoluble, its middle class leaving for the suburbs, the underclass growing in numbers and menace—Hollywood's image of New York began to change. From *Midnight Cowboy* (1969) through Scorsese's *Taxi Driver* (1976) to Lumet's *Q & A* (1990), to countless, violent exploitation films, New York has been portrayed on the screen as a traumatized city overwhelmed by drug dealers, prostitutes, and street criminals, permeated with garbage-laden streets and graffiti-scarred buildings, and with a jarring symphony of sirens and alarms constantly playing as an accompaniment in the background. Even so, this cinematic nightmare vision of New York can still make the city seem seductive. Scorsese's city in *Taxi Driver* is perversely beautiful and galvanizing—a rancid night world of steam hissing from manhole covers, hydrants spouting streams of water, and ominous figures shimmering in the oppressive summer heat. It's an inversion of the dream city—a luminous portrait of urban rot and foreboding—and it's almost as phantasmagoric a view of the city as *On the Town*'s sanitized version of an earlier, more serene New York. *Taxi Driver* remains the hallucinatory vision of one singular director in collaboration with his scriptwriter, Paul Schrader, with both men more interested in projecting their personal obsessions and demons onto the New York urbanscape than in documenting its social breakdown.

Despite the film being conceived and shot from the point of view of Travis Bickle (Robert De Niro), a character who is a paranoid and a psychopath, Scorsese's New York remains touched with a great deal of gritty reality. Living in New York there is no avoiding the precariousness and edginess which suffuses a great many urban encounters and neighborhoods, and the film echoes that sense of public danger and decay. Still, even in the turbulent New York of the Nineties—a city in constant financial and social crisis—a dark, sinister film like *Taxi Driver* offers up only one of many possible, very different New Yorks.

Clearly there are other visions of New York that can be conjured up on the screen. A film like Nancy Savoca's *True Love* (1989) provides an unsentimentally realistic portrait of Bronx working class Italian-Americans who live in a coherent world whose public life is neither violent nor fragmented. In fact, in *True Love*'s Bronx, the characters' confusion and pain is not brought on by social desperation or alienation, but by the communal and familial pressure to conform to traditional codes of male and female behavior. In *Do the Right Thing* (1989), Spike Lee creates a Brooklyn block devoid of drugs or street violence and crime—a softened (artificially and radiantly lit), relatively benign version of an inner city street. It's a block whose sense of community owes more to Thirties films about white working class life, like Vidor's *Street Scene* (1931), than to inner city life in the Nineties. Other Hollywood films use Soho, the Upper East Side, and Wall Street to capture arty, stylish, and high living slices of the city, which, if neither spiritual sanctuaries nor totally cut off from the city's agony, are physically comfortable, livable, and, to many, desirable worlds.

The most powerful antidote in films to the nightmare vision of New York is conveyed by Woody Allen. From *Bananas* (1971) to *Alice* (1990), most of Allen's films use New York locations and treat the city as one of the prime subjects of his work. Allen's city is foregrounded, it's one more character in his films. It's never merely used as a visually interesting or picturesque background for the narrative to evolve in or to complement the interaction of his characters. His Manhattan is an extension of Allen's protagonist's personalities—its streets are places to walk in, hold conversations, have random and absurd encounters, reflect on both one's private angst and the city's plight, and mute or escape one's anxieties. New York is also a public projection of Allen's protagonists' generally best selves and moments—a city of infinite promise, possibility, and grandeur. It's a city where, in Allen's most famous image in *Manhattan* (1979), with Isaac (Allen) and Mary (Diane Keaton) romantically silhouetted, sitting on a bench in the beckoning shadows of the Queensborough Bridge at dawn, Isaac can unambiguously assert, "This is really a great city, I'm knocked out."

Allen's New York is the sum of the striking and chic neighborhoods and icons his camera focuses on either in glorious long shot or in more intimate tracking shots—Fifth and Madison Avenues, Central Park West, Bloomingdale's, Lincoln Center, the Hayden Planetarium, the Plaza, Zabar's, the Russian Tea Room, the Dakota, and so on. His city is basically limited to a large fragment of one borough, Manhattan—though both *Annie Hall* (1977) and *Radio Days* (1986) reconstruct scenes from his central characters' boyhoods in Brooklyn and Rockaway, the other boroughs are usually treated as if they have been severed from the city—an upscale section that runs from the Upper West Side through Central Park to the Village and Soho and from the East 80s to Gramercy Park. There are scenes set on the Columbia University campus with its grand McKim, Mead, and White buildings, but Harlem, Washington Heights, and even the Lower East Side barely make an appearance in his films.

Of course, Allen is no neorealist like early De Sica or a *cinéma-vérité* documentarian like Frederick Wiseman, who, in one of his recent works, exhaustively compiled footage of much of the daily activity which takes place in Central Park. Allen's films aren't interested in exploring urban problems like racial tensions, AIDS, or crime, nor does he have an interest in providing a composite, wide-ranging portrait of urban life. His New York has a narrow social and racial base, it's limited to an upper-middle class world of WASPs and Jews who are primarily artists, academics, or media people—people who share his world and values and are able to evoke some empathy from him. In this New York, the poor, Afro-Americans, and Hispanics play almost no role. In fact, they don't even have bit parts in Allen's films.

As one can see, Allen's vision of the city is a carefully selective one—a world where social pain and threat never intrude on the private lives and agonies of his characters. It's a city of dreams whose streets range from a cool, symmetrical Park Avenue with its groomed green medians to the raw, powerful, cast-iron building blocks of Soho. Allen's directorial eye doesn't look only at life on the streets, but also at the esthetics of the buildings themselves. As the architect David (Sam Waterston) says in *Hannah and Her Sisters* (1986), "People pass by vital structures in this city all the time, and they never take the trouble to appreciate them." Allen forces us to look closely at the peeling posters and classical pediments that adorn the Soho loft buildings, the terra cotta reliefs on the richly decorated Alwyn Court building on 58th Street and Seventh Avenue, and the grace and elegance of the tapering Art Deco towers and gargoyles on the Chrysler Building.

In *Manhattan,* Allen's protagonist is writing a novel about a hero who "thrived on the hustle and bustle of the crowds and the traffic." But the films keep the city's fever pitch, collective anxiety, and chaos under control. Allen's depiction of Central Park illustrates this perfectly. Allen is so urban-oriented and committed a director that he treats the natural world in his films as a comic antagonist—as a landscape in which his protagonists are totally ill at ease. The only natural space that he can tolerate and embrace in his films is Central Park, which he treats as both his backyard and version of the pastoral ideal, albeit an urbanized one, surrounded by magnificent edifices like the Beresford apartment building on its West Side and the Guggenheim on its East. And in his vision of the park, the litter, noise, homeless people, and crowds at mass events that are an integral part of its reality have been removed from view. What is left is a relatively quiet oasis—the ideal of its original nineteenth century designers, Olmstead and Vaux— where one can watch the change of seasons, count lovers in hansom carriages and boats on the lake, and play ball with one's son on the Great Lawn. One can even seek the meaning of life in a discussion with a Hare Krishna follower, in a luminous scene in *Hannah* . . . , where the screen is split into three bands—at the top a dusky blue sky, in the middle a delicately shadowed, glowing gold-green Sheep's Meadow where Hare Krishna followers are dancing, and, at the bottom of the frame, an anguish-ridden Mickey (Allen) in search of the meaning of life. The park here is transformed into a slice of paradise, providing a moment of utter relief for a man in emotional difficulty.

An image in *Manhattan* of Central Park enveloped in snow, harking back to nineteenth century Currier &

Ives prints, is also part of Allen's opening montage in homage to the city. This breathtaking montage and the film itself resurrects the New York of memory that Allen loves. It's a New York which is a fitting object of a grand passion—the city of Dixieland, Willie Mays, Cole Porter, and the Marx Brothers. The montage itself is built on voluptuous images of an incandescent Park Avenue in winter, Broadway's neon lights, a dramatic aerial view of Yankee Stadium at night, mixed with images catching the everyday vitality of the streets, culminating in a crescendo of fireworks lighting up the night sky over Central Park, all accompanied by Gershwin's pulsating "Rhapsody in Blue" on the soundtrack.

These are contemporary, familiar New York images, shot in a dazzling high contrast black and white rather than color, which Allen utilizes to project the city's continuity with, from his perspective, its more elegant and civilized past. These fabulistic images also act as a self-conscious reminder of the way many old Hollywood films once projected a portrait of a city that gleamed and soared. Of course, Allen's vision of New York is more deeply felt, personal, and knowing than Minnelli's in *The Band Wagon* or the coy portrait of supposedly 'liberated' Greenwich Village life in *My Sister Eileen* (1955). It's the city as seen by a man who, without too many illusions and full awareness of New York's social sores ("drugs, garbage, crime"), continues to love and burnish it ("New York was his town, and it always would be"), and steadfastly refuses to allow New York's real tawdriness to encroach on his vision of the heavenly city.

Allen is not uncritical of the city in *Manhattan,* but the brunt of his critique is cultural rather than social and political. In the opening voice-over in *Manhattan,* Isaac intones that his novel will be about "New York as a metaphor for the decay of contemporary culture." But it's not the city's gnawing poverty, the breakdown of its social services, its gratuitous violence, or its crumbling infrastructure that Allen is concerned with. The decay he inveighs against is his friends and social milieu's penchant for self-indulgently betraying their talents and relationships. It's that insecure, shallow, narcissistic, name-dropping world which the moralist in Allen is angered by. His character Isaac's prime insight is that "people in Manhattan are constantly creating these unnecessary neurotic problems for themselves because it keeps them from dealing with the terrible, unsolvable problems of the universe"—like death.

Taken as cultural analysis, Allen's attack on modern decadence is itself specious and shallow—a mixture of cafeteria existentialism and some genuine revulsion with a milieu of which he is a member in good standing. But nobody asks Allen to be a De Tocqueville, Marx, or even a Christopher Lasch—it's sufficient that his satirical thrusts at sophisticated Manhattan behavior often hit their mark.

Despite his censure, it's this same Manhattan which Allen's characters, like Alvy Singer in *Annie Hall,* trek over the Brooklyn Bridge to passionately embrace and defend. In *Radio Days,* Allen's skillfully crafted, nostalgic evocation of growing up in Rockaway in the late Thirties and the WWII years to old radio programs like *The Green Hornet* and pop songs like "Lay that Pistol Down," Manhattan is always there to provoke a boy's fantasies. In this sentimental film, built around a series of vignettes, lower-middle class Rockaway is not an oppressive world. It is remembered as an utterly domesticated, innocent neighborhood of teenage girls sitting in soda shops and sighing in unison while listening to crooners on the radio, a neighborhood where violence in school was no more than a spitball fight, and sex was just boys hungrily looking through binoculars at a nude, Rubenesque woman dancing in her apartment to the strains of "Babalu."

These Rockaway memories are filled with charm and warm feeling, Allen even granting the clamorous, insensitive family life of his young alter ego—a nearsighted, quietly irreverent boy named Joe—a semi-Edenic glow. All the family's abrasion—his uncle telling his aunt "to take the gaspipe"—is treated as a comic conceit, and the neighborhood cozily encompasses white beaches and piers to walk out to the ocean on. Still, underlying these soft-focused reminiscences is the strong feeling that neighborhood life is constricted and that home life is nothing more than a place where Joe's family settles down to tedious evenings of endless bickering, playing cards, washing the dishes, and listening to the radio. It is Manhattan, with its radio quiz shows, restaurants with cheek to cheek dancing, and a Radio City Music Hall with carpeted corridors and grand spaces, that Joe truly longs for.

It's Manhattan in *Radio Days,* both the real and the imagined one, which provides Allen's young protagonist with a sense of transcendence. The pleasure and excitement of his infrequent trips to Manhattan is reinforced by radio programs like the breakfast show over which 'Roger and Irene' preside. It is a show that conjures up images of sophisticated people living in glamorous Manhattan penthouses, spending their evenings at the Stork Club, formally dressed for dancing and engaging in civilized adultery and urbane chitchat with other radio celebrities. The film, however, does not romanticize the celebrities—they're unprepossessing, somewhat absurd figures. But for Allen, the high style and success that this Manhattan world provides is clearly preferable to the more prosaic virtues of Jewish, lower-middle class Rockaway. It's not that Allen repudiates his own ethnicity or roots: his persona, especially in the early films, is modeled after the classic Jewish victim-schlemiel; Alvy Singer is obsessed with anti-Semitism and jokes about his Jewish identity and past in *Annie Hall*; and *Broadway Danny Rose* (1984) is, on one level, a homage to Jewish Catskill comics. It's not, however, Jewish upper middle class suburban life young Joe dreams about, but a cosmopolitan Manhattan, with all its spiritual imperfections (and, given Allen's recent romantic revelations and travails, an emotionally more Dostoyevskian and anguished Manhattan than any of his films have conveyed) that the adult Allen now inhabits.

In a concluding voice-over in *Radio Days,* Allen speaks of these memories as growing dimmer with each passing year. But it's clear from Allen's films that the stylized memories of a magical Manhattan New Year's Eve in *Radio Days*—moonlit skies, gossamerlike snow flakes, and a large neon Camel sign blowing smoke— still vividly color and shape his vision of the New York present.

Allen's New York is very different from the city of streets filled with wandering, dispossessed souls, shards of broken glass, ruined buildings, and sporadic, murderous gunfire that characterizes the New York films of Scorsese and Lumet. He has consciously projected a city which may not be celestial, but comes as close as possible to a luminous "city on the hill." Obviously, that city is far removed from the daily reality of dire social and economic statistics and screaming headlines, but, in this city of continual flux, there are still neighborhoods, streets, and moments where the dreamscape is ascendant. Allen's indelible urban images offer consolation and hope for those who believe that the delicate balance between dream and nightmare in New York will be preserved into the next century.

### Richard A. Blake (review date 10 October 1992)

SOURCE: Blake, Richard A. "Love Amid the Ruins." *America* 167, no. 10 (10 October 1992): 255.

[*In the following review, Blake judges* Husbands and Wives *as a brilliant, superbly crafted, and innovative film.*]

Events of the last several months have changed forever the way we must look at Woody Allen's films. Before tabloid journalists went into a feeding frenzy about his private life, his admitted romantic involvement with the oldest adopted daughter of his long-time companion Mia Farrow and her allegations of sexual abuse involving her other children, one could understand his films as psycho-documentary.

Now a more psychoanalytic reading of the films seems more appropriate and more rewarding. Allen, the clown character, has been observing, not other people, but the varied dark sides of his own very complex personality.

His fictional characters desperately search for love in a tough world, imaged by the concrete canyons of Manhattan. In their quest, they become in turn pathetic and destructive of others as well as themselves. The genius of the artist is that the portrayal of moral ambiguity, sin and redemption in his own life, reflected in many of the less sympathetic figures in his films, says a lot about personal sin as it touches all of us.

*Husbands and Wives,* Woody Allen's brilliant new film, echoes with spooky references to the summer headlines. The autobiographical elements, though striking in the present context of sensational revelations and allegations, are no more revealing of the author than many of his earlier films. Allen once again segments his own personality, dividing the burden among several of his key characters and examining each one in turn. Gabe Roth (Woody Allen), a modestly prosperous novelist and professor of creative writing at Columbia, finds himself attracted to Rain (Juliette Lewis), a talented 20-year-old student in one of his classes. Her parents named her after the poet Rainer Maria Rilke, but Allen buffs recall Allen's use of the e. e. cummings line "nobody, not even the rain, has such small hands" as an expression of the romantic ideal in *Hannah and Her Sisters* (1986). His infatuation goes no further than an adult kiss at her 21st-birthday party.

As usual, the Allen protagonist searches for an ideal love, which, given the human condition, is simply unattainable. Gabe's wife Judy (Mia Farrow) needs to be needed and wants another child, but Gabe refuses, concerned with his work and the terrible state of the world. Their apparently happy marriage, long little more than a truce, inevitably slides into open hostility. The romance of unfilled promise leading to lowered expectations is the most universal theme in Allen's films. Happiness comes only from appreciation of the commonplace, like a walk in Central Park after a snowfall. When these simple joys become dusty memories, then the marriage is over.

The opening scene of *Husbands and Wives* offers fair warning that this film will be different and disturbing. In an unbearably long take, cinematographer Carlo Di Palma moves his restless camera from face to face in a cramped apartment as Sally (Judy Davis) and Jack (Sydney Pollack) explain to Gabe and Judy that they have decided to separate. The nervous movement of the camera makes us seasick watching this painful scene. This documentary quality, maintained throughout the film, creates the intimacy of home movies. At times the action stops, and the characters face the camera for a few moments of a television-style interview with an off-camera voice that approaches the self-revelation of a therapy session.

As Sally and Jack follow out their decision to separate, they reveal themselves as unpleasant facets of Allen's own personality. In the manner of all English teachers. Gabe is ever critical of people and their ideas. Like Allen, the meticulous director, Gabe pushes his charges to ever higher levels of performance. For this reason Judy cannot show her husband her poetry. Judy Davis brilliantly creates in Sally a nasty caricature of Allen's and Gabe's perfectionism. Chain-smoking and foul-mouthed, she rarely finds a positive word or thought about anything. Who could live with such a person? Certainly not her husband Jack, whose pathetic search for love leads him into a series of inept, transparent and ultimately unsatisfying adulteries. He may believe his adolescent behavior is a cry for help, but Sally hears it as a call to arms, preferably nuclear.

Sally and Jack experiment with different partners during their separation. Sally's outspoken and negative wit, once taken as a sign of delightful independent-mindedness, soon erodes her relationship with Michael (Liam Neeson), a charming editor she met through the aggressive matchmaking of Judy, who has her own unrecognized attraction for him. Freed from Sally's carping criticism and New York Times sophistication, Jack finds great delight in the company of Sam (Lysette Anthony), a simple young aerobics instructor. Soon, however, her mindless preoccupation with health foods and horoscopes drives him to the edge of violence. Perhaps Sally and Jack are not so bad for each other after all.

In an early bit of dialogue, Gabe accuses God of playing hide-and-seek with him, and without some awareness of a personal God and some criteria for morality, these affluent, talented Manhattanites stumble from one unsatisfying relationship to the next. What are they looking for? Allen offers little logical explanation for his characters' decisions. They plan no malice and sincerely want to hurt no one, but things happen to them. In affairs of the heart there is no logic, Allen maintains. As love works out its own cruel devices, the innocent become victims, and victims become assassins. In the end, the relationships sort themselves out, and only Gabe is left alone, with no companionship other than his work, another novel that he struggles to complete. Looking into the camera, he asks, "Is this over? Can I go now?"

\* \* \*

Is *Husbands and Wives* autobiography? Or apologia? Some of the screen portrayals certainly hit very close to the news stories. The Mia Farrow character, in earlier films presented as a personification of gentleness and compassion, emerges as grasping, confused and emotionally unstable in Judy. Rain's parents encourage her friendship with her professor, and at one point in their relationship they take in a Knicks game at Madison Square Garden.

Hunting for parallels between life and the film can be fun, but it can also be a distraction from a superbly crafted, imaginative and innovative film. Any artist, even one of great imagination like Woody Allen, has to base art to some extent on experience. As the most personal of American film-makers, Allen should not surprise us by his use of autobiographical images and situations. If, however, his relationship with Mia Farrow had remained stable and this were "just another" Woody Allen movie, *Husbands and Wives* would still be a splendid piece of art and a priceless comment on life and love in urban America at the end of this very tired, shopworn century.

## John Simon (review date 19 October 1992)

SOURCE: Simon, John. "The Road to Stockholm." *National Review* 44, no. 20 (19 October 1992): 57-60.

[*In the following review, Simon asserts that* Husbands and Wives *is superficial, far-fetched, and formulaic, with poorly developed characters, an inconsistent plot-line, and pretentious, predictable jokes.*]

Is there much point in reviewing *Husbands and Wives,* Woody Allen's latest? With the invaluable publicity the movie has been getting via Woody, Mia, their sundry daughters, and the media, breathes there anyone with soul so dead who to him or herself hasn't said, "I've got to check this one out"? It's open season for the hunting of clues, parallels, revelations, and, with a mere few dollars as the price of a license, who wouldn't join in the hunt?

But before you rush off to catch the movie, isn't it time for a little summing up of Allen's œuvre? It has become progressively clearer—though it was pretty clear a long time ago—that Allen is a gifted comedian and impassioned workaholic who, given the carte blanche withheld from less fortunate filmmakers, has turned out a number of funny film comedies and a number of terrible, almost equally funny, film dramas. And he has also scored successes with an in-between genre, e.g., *Hannah and Her Sisters,* meant to be both funny and serious, which, though a bit more fitfully, can match the serious efforts for badness.

*Husbands and Wives* belongs to this tertium quid, and if one had nothing better to do, one could speculate about whether it is a comedy with serious overtones or a drama with comic undertones. It concerns Gabe Roth (Woody Allen), a novelist who teaches creative writing at Barnard; his wife, Judy (Mia Farrow), an art-magazine editor; and their favorite fellow married couple: Jack (Sydney Pollack), a big businessman, and his wife, Sally (Judy Davis), who works in Landmarks

Preservation. (Typically for an Allen film, we do not see her preserve a single landmark.) While everyone here is, of course, a neurotic, Sally is an advanced neurotic, a ballbreaker but also a self-destroyer.

As the film begins, Jack and Sally arrive at the Roths to go out for dinner, and announce with somewhat studied casualness that they are divorcing. This sends the insecurely married Roths into a tailspin, and they try to talk them out of it—Judy even gets furious. All kinds of palaver crisscross the scene as the handheld camera flash-pans truculently from one character to the next. Meanwhile the characters themselves indulge in a frantic choreography through various rooms, with the camera sometimes hurtling after them, sometimes colliding with them, and sometimes cunningly lying in wait for them. Bits of Bergman, Godard, and even Cassavetes fly by; it feels like riding out a storm in a Piper Cub.

In the course of the movie, Jack will set out on some tawdry dalliances, presented as crosses between a sight gag and a vignette, until he comes to a halt at Sam (Lysette Anthony), a pretty, very young aerobics instructor who also dabbles in nutrition and astrology. When Gabe condescendingly refers to her as a cocktail waitress, Jack parries, "So she's not Simone de Beauvoir, but I can relax with her. . . . I was bored at the opera. . . . I want someone who digs her nails into my back and screams. . . ." I doubt whether businessman Jack, for whom even the operas Sally drags him to are too much, would so mundanely invoke Simone de Beauvoir—more likely it is Woody venting his everlasting erudition. But this is paradigmatic Allen stuff. Is Gabe proving his acuity by equating aerobics and waitressing? Or is this a dig at his snobbery? Is Beauvoirism a good or a bad thing? Is full-throttle sex with a dizzy young chick the best medicine for marital stalemate or just a middle-aged escapist's pathetic stratagem? Is being a cocktail waitress really worse than being a businessman?

Throughout, Allen depends on these kinds of ambiguities, this juggling with open questions made to look like the ultimate in sophistication, if not indeed profundity. An artist may, and very often does, use ambiguity creatively, but then not so glibly, casually, polysemously perversely, until everything becomes trickery. You might say that Allen makes fun of the superficiality of his characters. The old joke about Hollywood is that it is so much fake tinsel hiding the genuine tinsel. Could Allen's lampooned superficiality merely conceal the real one?

Consider another scene, in which Sally, who has predictably ended up enraged at Jack's defection, finally goes on a date of her own. The man is taking her to the opera: *Don Giovanni*. This enables the mentally hyper-ventilating Sally to draw parallels between Jack and Juan (clever!) and at the same time reveal that she knows little about *Don Giovanni* (funny!) and cares less. But how could any person who kept dragging her husband to the opera have escaped this one, whether she was a genuine opera lover or a fake? Clearly, Woody makes up his gags as he goes along, with little regard for consistency or dramatic logic.

Now take a still later scene, in which Michael (Liam Neeson), a handsome fellow editor of Judy's, takes out Sally on a date engineered by the matchmaking Judy. (Later, Judy, who herself secretly wants Michael—surprise!—will resent Sally's making out with him—surprise, surprise!) Anyway, Michael takes Sally to a concert featuring the Mahler Ninth. Afterward she tells him that it was divine, but that the last movement could have been cut a little bit. The audience laughs, yet what does this really mean? That Sally is a sickie who must spoil everything for everyone, herself included? Or that she is a fool who would criticize a masterpiece? Or does she merely find Mahler sometimes excessive, as some critics and connoisseurs do—even if Allen may not realize it? Ambiguity, intended and unintended, proliferates and leaves issues good and muddied.

Still, let us assume that Allen knows what he is doing, and that he is being satirical here. A true satirist, however, is a good hater or lover, or, better yet, both. Allen appears to be neither. If he has any feeling for his characters—other than his alter egos—it is patronization. With every scene and almost every one-liner, you can identify the intended audience by address: this is a bit for the Upper West Side crowd; this one is for the Upper East Siders; this is a sop to SoHo and Tribeca. Allen is an operator: things are geared to these enclaves, which are being massaged in their little prejudices, condescensions, foolishnesses. These scenes, these gags are expensively packaged cheap shots.

And something else: true humor always comes as a genuine surprise. Too many of Allen's ironies and witticisms, however, are predictable. Just as Judy resents Sally's short-lived success with Michael, and just as Sally resents Jack's adventures with other women, Jack goes to pieces the moment he hears about Sally and other men. I could cite other instances, but this movie cannot afford to have that much of its sparse plot given away. Totally unsurprising to Allen buffs, though, should be the casting, in the role of Judy's ex-husband of the in-the-news ex-president of Yale, Benno Schmidt. Having already embarked on a much-publicized but spurious venture, Schmidt must have felt right at home here. He typifies Allen's intellectual-cachet-mongering casting procedures, also represented here by the writers Bruce Jay Friedman and Jack Richardson in bit parts.

For similar prestige reasons, Juliette Lewis was cast as Rain, the supposedly brilliant twenty-year-old who is the brainy and sexy star of Gabe's writing course. The saving grace of Scorsese's rancid *Cape Fear,* she was snapped up when Emily Lloyd became unavailable. But Miss Lewis is neither sexy nor flaky, and it is hard to believe her as the sexpot who seduces, among others, her father's business partner and her own psychiatrist. Woody Allen doesn't quite know what to do with the character. He makes fun of her mother for naming her after her favorite poet, Rainer Maria Rilke (good thing Mom's favorite wasn't Odysseus Elytis); he makes fun of her fellow Barnard students who write papers on "The Orgasm in the Age of Deconstruction"; he makes fun of her middle-aged shrink who throws a jealous tantrum on her doorstep, where he lies in wait for her as Gabe brings her home one afternoon. But he treats her having had affairs with at least three middle-aged men as mere growing pains and an excuse for sallies such as "What the hell am I doing with the midlife-crisis set?" And her flirtation with Gabe remains platonic—perhaps because she represents Soon-Yi, who must not be besmirched.

But Allen is no better with the character of Michael, played by the current Hibernian heart-throb, the somewhat beefy, brogue-brandishing Liam Neeson. Michael is meant to be truly good, which Allen can't deal with. After all, it is his alter ego, Gabe, who, for all his flaws, must emerge as the battered existential hero. Michael must be subtly queered, lest he seem better than Gabe. So he is made to talk of "going to see [*sic*] Mahler's Ninth." So, too, he becomes the awkward *terzo incomodo* when Jack finds Sally *in flagrante* with him; and so, when he ends up ostensibly happily married to Judy—labeled a passive-aggressive type, and the film's least sympathetic character—he seems uncomfortable, unmanned. Gabe, in his final aloneness, is a Pyrrhic victor. True, he doesn't get Rain, but he does get rained on when Judy kicks him out in a downpour, and, thus cleansed, he wises up: "I realized that I really blew it," he says, sans wisecrack.

Even the nature of the jokes here is denatured—by pretentiousness, farfetchedness, and the formulaic. We are to laugh at "anyone who writes a paper saying the Sabine women had it coming to them," but we are to chuckle admiringly when Gabe (who speaks rather un-grammatically for a writer-professor) says to Rain: "Your line was great—about life doesn't imitate art, it imitates television," a case of Woody painting Wilde's lily. When, at her 21st-birthday party, Rain asks Gabe to kiss her on the mouth, he exclaims, "Why is it that I'm hearing fifty thousand dollars' worth of psycho-therapy dialing 911?" This is Woody with his hangups, but it's not integrated into Gabe and the movie. Similarly, "I always fall in love with kamikaze women" who "crash into you" is not Gabe but Woody in his self-pitying, or shell-shocked sex-war veteran, mode, laughing through his scars. And how is one to tell

whether a line like the quotation from Shelley, "I fall upon the thorns of life! I bleed!" is intended to be funny or to show off Woody's erudition? Quite often with Allen, art imitates the dictionary of quotations or the thesaurus.

The terrible thing is that this entire sorry mess is sup-posed to equal, if not surpass, Ingmar Bergman. Vin-cent Canby, who early on sealed Allen's doom by proclaiming him the American Bergman, is at it again in his review of *Husbands and Wives,* which, he says, "goes beneath the surface of things in a way few mov-ies ever do." It is "Mr. Allen's uproarious answer to In-gmar Bergman's . . . *Scenes from a Marriage.*" Answer? What was the question? We can't, of course, blame it all on Canby, and the only reason I won't say it takes two to tango is so as not to give anyone the idea of pronouncing Woody the American Borges.

The monstrous conceit of the man comes through in one of the filmmaker's conceits. Modeling himself on Bergman's *The Passion of Anna,* Allen introduces sequences in which the characters are interviewed about their lives. The offscreen voice of Jeffrey Kurland, the film's costume designer, drones out questions to which a given character, in tight closeup, spouts answers into a lavaliere microphone bemedaling his or her chest. Bergman himself has since repudiated this device as a mistake, but in his film, at any rate, the actors com-mented on their characters *qua* actors, by way of a Brechtian alienation effect. Here, however, the charac-ters remain in character and pontificate, either improvis-ing or mouthing the "improvisations" Allen has written for them. It makes no sense. Is this a TV talkshow host interviewing them? (Remember, life imitates television, or something.) But what TV show even is low enough to want to interview these characters about their dreary relationships? Well, you say, Woody thought them worthy of a whole movie about them. True, but that is *his* problem.

**Richard Alleva (review date 23 October 1992)**

SOURCE: Alleva, Richard. "Nouveau Allen." *Common-weal* 119, no. 18 (23 October 1992): 16-18.

[*In the following review, Alleva praises the cinema verité style used in* Husbands and Wives, *asserting that the film conveys the emotional chaos of real-life relationships, but is ultimately unsatisfying.*]

No Woody Allen film runs its course without at least one good quip on its sound track. Judy Davis gets to deliver a great one in *Husbands and Wives* when, as a middle-aged woman newly separated from her husband and trying to reenter the dating game, she fends off the advances of an aspiring lover with the plea that he's coming on to her too fast: "Metabolically, it's not my rhythm." And Davis's delivery is so cleverly shaded, so tremulous yet incisive, that Allen's mockery of listen-to-your-body newspeak seems as witty as a line from Congreve or Wilde.

Yet what's remarkable about Allen's latest effort is that so little of it depends upon his talent for such quips or for language in general. In fact, though the script tours familiar Allen territory—the anguished love lives of successful professionals living in or near Manhattan—its method is a true departure for Allen. In all his previous features, good or bad, the emotions of his characters registered primarily through the dialogue, and the dialogue was written and delivered in the basic theatrical mode that prevails both in plays and movies: linear, pregnant with meaning and wit, and necessarily more lucid and emphatic than 99.5 percent of the talk we hear in everyday life. And such dialogue, on screen or stage, is a major determinant of what the director does. In all previous Allen movies, the dialogue determined whether the camera should be near or far, still or mobile.

Not so in **Husbands and Wives.** First, despite the occasional witty exchange, most of the dialogue is loaded with the trivialities, the nonsequiturs, the fruitless excursions away from the main point, the interruptions and self-interruptions we hear in everyday life and in documentaries. The actors have been directed not only to overlap their lines but often to speak all at once, to trail off in midsentence, to take little pauses in unexpected places, to replace intended words with glances that preempt words. All this brings us much closer to the jagged discourse of *cinéma vérité* than to the lucid volleying of comedy. The *bon mot* and the riposte have been devalued; what counts in this movie is the tangle, the buzz, the blur of heated arguments in expensive apartments where nobody listens to anybody except to refute what's just been said. The camera isn't cued by words but by currents of feeling.

Second, much of the camerawork (by Carlo di Palma) is handheld, constantly mobile, deliberately shaky. Even if the acting and dialogue were more conventional, such photography would destabilize them.

Third, borrowing from Jean Luc-Goddard, Allen interrupts his narrative several times to have his characters interviewed by an unidentified interrogator on the other side of the camera. This strategy contributes to giving **Husbands and Wives** the texture of a case study, a documentary in the making.

Does the method match the matter? The story is a symmetrical one: one married pair, Sydney Pollack and Judy Davis, announce their separation to their friends, Mia Farrow and Woody Allen, a seemingly stable couple. By the end of the movie, Pollack and Davis have learned they can't live without each other while Farrow and Allen, their long-suppressed differences and hostilities shaken to the surface by the discord between their friends, divorce. Another director, Eric Rohmer, say, might have accentuated the formal simplicity of the story by shooting with an anchored, motionless camera and by employing unobtrusive cuts. Allen, however, isn't trying to choreograph an elegant dance of love and loss, but instead wants to plunge us into a free-for-all of the emotions in which lovers flail. His new filmic style conveys this emotional chaos well.

But he goes overboard. The nearly nonstop jitteriness (only the Goddardesque interviews and a couple of quiet scenes were shot with a steady camera) is applied even to scenes that might have benefited from a steadier approach. When we are being constantly hustled through the action (as if the director had us by the scruff of the neck), a sort of visual bullying seems to be going on. We are always being told where to look, never allowed to search the frame for whatever details we can pick up for ourselves. Of course, all good directors ultimately determine what we look at in each shot, but there is a difference between subtly guiding the eyes and taking onlookers by the throat.

Though Allen's own performance is a disaster (his voice has become unbearable in that he ends every other sentence on a screech or a whine), all the other actors respond beautifully to his direction. Juliette Lewis as a literary-minded postnymphet annoys initially by projecting solipsism that at first seems more the actress's than the character's. But gradually her performance blooms and fascinates, especially in a scene in which she picks her writing teacher's latest novel to pieces but prefaces each barb with an enchanting and self-enchanting smile. Liam Neeson, as Davis's prospective lover, seems at first nothing but a hunk with a good baritone voice but, by the end of the movie, has created a believable man so ridden with self-doubt that he is ready to acquiesce in a marriage that will bring him not joy but only a temporary equilibrium. Mia Farrow gives her rather mousy, self-pitying character interesting shades of unspoken fierceness that justify one character's description of her as "passive-aggressive." One gets a glimpse of the emotional buccaneer within the waif.

But Sydney Pollack and Judy Davis give the best performances, and their naturalism, leashed by crack timing and laced with wit, justify Allen's method. For instance, in a scene in which Pollack, having a verbal brawl with his wife and girlfriend, notices his wife's lover on the sidelines and invites him to join the fracas, Pollack gets a laugh not by inflecting a single word or phrase but simply by letting an extra burst of desperation and bewilderment infuse his entire body.

Davis's character is so self-dramatizing that Davis can be theatrical without detracting from the naturalism of the movie. And her theatricality is delicious. In a scene in which she systematically yet unself-consciously explains to Neeson that every single stage of their last date was considerably subpar, Davis makes us laugh at her cruelty, and pity her brittle misery all at once. Only a great comedienne could have brought this scene off.

Monotonous in visual style, predictable in its plot, catering too exclusively to urban sophisticates who want to laugh affectionately, too affectionately, at themselves, *Husbands and Wives* isn't satisfying. Yet Woody Allen has made an interesting movie that at least deserves to outlive the scandal-sheet headlines that now serve as its unofficial advertising.

## James Bowman (review date 30 October 1992)

SOURCE: Bowman, James. "Shrink Wrapped." *Times Literary Supplement*, no. 4674 (30 October 1992): 18.

[*In the following review, Bowman judges* Husbands and Wives *as a charming and funny movie that presents a bleak perspective on love, sex, and marriage in contemporary New York.*]

Say what you like about Woody Allen—and much has been said about him since last summer—his films reproduce brilliantly the conversational style that we might call New York-analytical. His latest, *Husbands and Wives,* is at times hilariously funny, but even when it is serious it has the charm of looking like what New Yorkers, at any rate, would call real life. Jerky, hand-held camera technique and quasi-documentary interviews of the main characters are reminiscent of the atmospheric, Bergmanian pictures into which Allen has unfortunately poured so much of his creative energy, but here he is on home ground.

The familiarity of the material—two New York marriages in different stages of dissolution—and the humor with which it is presented almost save the film from the leaden weight of philosophical reflection promised by the title and the scratchy old recording of "What Is This Thing Called Love?" which begins and ends it. But it would be unrealistic to expect Allen to be any more daunted by the question he has apparently taken it upon himself to answer than he has ever been by the risk of pretentiousness in his films.

Here, however, his own pretentiousness gets lost amid the pretentiousness of the New York intellectual world that he presents. Where it is natural for the characters to talk about Tolstoy and Dostoevsky, Mozart and Mahler, the Bauhaus and Einstein to no other apparent purpose

than to display their own intellectual bona fides, it hardly seems to signify that the director himself is playing philosopher; where everyone has Freud at his fingers' ends, it is only natural for the director, too, to turn psychologist.

And he is not unaware of the potential for irony. One of the funniest of the film's many funny scenes takes place when Judy Davis, as the manic Sally, comes home from a concert and launches an all-out assault on the attempts of her hapless date (Liam Neeson) to make polite, complimentary conversation by criticizing, in a superior way, Mahler's music, the chef's Alfredo sauce, his driving and her own furniture. As when she is later in bed with the same beau and whiles away the time classifying all her friends as foxes or hedgehogs, frustrated sexual energy turns itself into obsessive analysis.

The same could be said of the film itself. All the characters analyse one another and themselves in a constant stream of psychobabble that is facilitated by the interview-style speeches to camera. Strikingly, only Woody Allen's character, a teacher of creative writing at Barnard College, arrives at a self-assessment which the film itself seems to approve, while the others are either self-deceived or only present in order to throw some light on the nature of those self-deceptions. The result is a much bleaker picture of love, sex and marriage in contemporary New York than is at first apparent amid all the laughter.

Inevitably, the chief interest of the film on its release was the way in which it was thought to foreshadow its director's spectacularly public break-up with Mia Farrow, who also portrays his wife on screen. There are a few moments where the audience titters, as when Farrow says to Allen: "Do you ever hide things from me?" And he replies, with a stammer: "N-n-no. Do you?" She replies: "Sometimes." But it is a significant moment in the film because it forewarns us not of Woody Allen's alleged affair with his adopted stepdaughter and various legal actions still pending, but of what is going to be the tenor of the rest of the film.

Allen appears as a fallible, rather comic but ultimately honourable character who does *not* hide things, who does *not* have the affair with the twenty-year-old girl, who does *not* leave his wife for youth and freshness and novelty. Mia Farrow, as his fictional wife, is a sly, deceitful, ruthlessly selfish woman who decides what it is she wants and then proceeds to get it by what the other characters naturally call "passive aggression"— which is to say, by pretending to be utterly unselfish and helpless, thus effectively blackmailing all the sensitive males, of which modern-day New York is chock-full, into doing exactly what she wants of them.

In fact, all the women in this film are appalling. Farrow's character is the worst, but the others are not far behind. Judy Davis's character is full of sexual rage, for all the comedy with which she expresses it; Lysette Anthony portrays an aerobics instructor with a degree in (what else?) psychology, a passionate belief in astrology and absolutely nothing between her ears; and the nymphet called Rain (New York investment bankers probably really do name their children after Rilke), played by Juliette Lewis, has already, by the age of twenty, set herself up as an intellectual and learned how to use her sexual powers to manipulate men.

The real parallel between the film and Woody Allen's private life is not the dramatic situation—in which a very different sort of marriage undergoes a very different sort of break-up—but the anger it reveals towards New York women in general and Miss Farrow in particular.


**Jonathan Romney (review date November 1992)**

SOURCE: Romney, Jonathan. Review of *Husbands and Wives,* by Woody Allen. *Sight and Sound* 2, no. 7 (November 1992): 44.

[*In the following review, Romney contends that* Husbands and Wives *is insightful about relationships, but that it is also pretentious and snobby.*]

[In *Husbands and Wives,*] Gabe and Judy Roth, a New York couple, are visited for dinner by their friends Jack and Sally, who announce that they have decided to separate after a long marriage. Judy is deeply distraught, and starts to question the stability of her own marriage. Gabe explains the background to Jack and Sally's parting: Jack had started seeing a call-girl, on the prompting of a business partner. Gabe and Judy discuss the problems of their marriage: his unwillingness to have children, and the stress on their sex life caused by busy schedules.

During an evening with a prospective date, Sally telephones Jack, furious that he is living with someone new. Gabe is becoming attracted to Rain, a twenty-year-old student in the creative writing class he teaches. Walking in the street, Sally, Judy and Gabe meet Jack with his new girlfriend Sam, and Sally leaves in a rage. Later, Sally tells Judy she has come to enjoy being single, and explains Judy's distress at her splitting with Jack—it is because she too always dreamed of being single. Judy introduces Sally to a work colleague of hers, Michael. Gabe and Judy discuss their marriage; he now wants to talk about children, but she sees this as a sign of his discontent.

Sally and Michael date, but she is uncertain about accepting his advances. Rain introduces Gabe to her parents, and he has a run-in with her ex-boyfriend (and former therapist), one of a series of older men with whom she has had relationships. Judy's rapport with Michael grows over her poems, which she has shown to him but never to Gabe. At a party, Jack hears that Sally is seeing Michael, and this prompts a furious row with Sam; he drives to Sally's house and stages a confrontation, as Sam and Michael look on.

Rain has read Gabe's novel about relationships, but has left it in a taxi—en route to retrieve it, her criticism of it only fuels his growing infatuation with her. After a dinner with Jack and Sally, who are now reunited, Gabe and Judy split up, with her telling him she wants to explore her feelings for Michael. On the night of a rainstorm, Gabe and Rain kiss at her twenty-first birthday party; Judy and Michael quarrel; and Jack and Sally stay in bed together. A year and a half later, Judy and Michael are married, and Jack and Sally discuss their repaired marriage. Gabe explains that he decided not to get involved with Rain, and that he is currently single and working on a new novel.

\* \* \*

Rushed out by its British distributor to coincide with the showbiz shock-horror story of the year, *Husbands and Wives* is the first Woody Allen film in which the ironies are not strictly internal. However, those uncomfortable moments in which the film appears to comment on the headlines (as when Judy plaintively enquires, "You think we'd ever break up?", or Gabe admits, "I've learned nothing over the years") run out after some ten minutes as the film's own logic takes effect. In fact, those determined to read the film for signs that the eternal good guy Woody was a fool or a villain all along will find rather less convincing evidence here than they might in the temporarily shelved *Shadows and Fog* (its predecessor), in which Allen's persecuted Joseph K figure turns out to be guilty as sin.

*Husbands and Wives* returns to Allen's favourite question—"What is this thing called love?" Thematically and visually, it is a companion-piece to *Hannah and Her Sisters* and *Crimes and Misdemeanors,* set in the same urbane milieu. Formally, though, it adopts a quasi-documentary approach, with the story told partly in flashbacks, partly by characters offering testimony and commentary about themselves and others in interviews (complete with clip-on mike) with an unseen interlocutor. This interviewer might be pictured as a journalist trying to assemble a whole truth (extremely long takes with hand-held camera push the *vérité* aesthetic to its limit) out of a fragmented picture, *Kane*-style; or as an interrogating God, the deity who, says Gabe in the film's first one-liner, plays hide-and-seek rather than, as Einstein imagined, dice; or, since this is a Woody Allen film, as a therapist.

In the latter case, the film could be seen as a double therapy. On one level, its characters delve into their motives, learn to read through their own self-deceptions, and emerge wiser if not wholly repaired. Thus, Gabe ends up reconciled to solitude and able to embark on a new novel, "less confessional, more political"; thus, Jack and Sally accept that their sexual problems are to be lived with. On another level, the film could be read as being therapeutic for its writer-director in that it exorcises certain possibilities of life, rehearsing them and perhaps pre-empting them.

This is not to say that **Husbands and Wives** should be taken as being 'about' Allen's real-life complications; rather, those complications would have to be read as being partly 'about' the dilemmas reviewed by this film. That Gabe makes a decision *not* to go off with Rain in no way reflects on Woody Allen's own dealings with younger women. But it is clear that the film and the reality invite us to perceive parallels and divergences, because Allen has always used his films to make public certain questions of personal interest to him, and—more peculiarly—to display publicly those questions as being of interest to him. Seen in this way, the film acts as an added incentive to read the Allen-Farrow case in the same quasi-literary terms in which we read his films' narratives.

Curiously, though, in view of the fact that Allen's real life is currently being read as essentially a moral drama, **Husbands and Wives** is less to do with moral decisions (compared, say, with **Crimes and Misdemeanors**), than with people's self-deception and mutual dependence. As individuals, Jack and Sally are less than the totality they form as "Jack and Sally", but rather than being a paean to marriage, the film demonstrates that they need first to be separated before they can properly be together. As far as such observations go, much of the film outdoes Rohmer at his most acute, and is certainly more acerbic. Two exceptionally discomforting scenes involve Jack and Sally's respective rages when they discover that the person they want to be separate from is together with someone else.

**Husbands and Wives** is also acute about the way that these characters act out their dramas almost consciously, perhaps as stories to tell future therapists. The love scenes on the night of the thunderstorm are practically staged melodrama, with pathetic fallacy laid on *ad lib*. The messiness and multiplicity of life is also well caught, as different characters' memories and experiences bleed into each other. Gabe comes face to face with Rain's array of past lovers, and his own voracious but crazy ex-lover Harriet (a briefly glimpsed paradigm of all Allen's manifestly excessive fantasy women) is a figure against whom every other woman in his life must measure up.

But for all its insightfulness, the film reveals Allen's fatal flaw—a terrible snobbery, directed here with unwarranted cruelty at the astrology-obsessed Sam. She is shown up as the ridiculous object of Jack's regressive infatuation ("So she's not Simone de Beauvoir", he protests); she is made out to be a manifestly unworthy object of his attentions, as opposed to simply inadequate, as Rain is for Gabe. An aerobics instructor, she is mistaken for a cocktail waitress (both jobs are clearly considered equally contemptible); it is surely not just Gabe and Jack who look down on her, but the film itself. If only she were as naturally talented and—the ultimate saving grace for Allen—as *neurotic* as the clearly superior Rain. Perhaps an aerobics teacher is just too healthy to have a place in Allen's world.

This dead giveaway about Allen's values is perhaps an inevitable side product in a film which suggests that, despite illusion and equivocation, 'truth will out'. It is razor-sharp on slips—as in the taxi scene, when Rain inadvertently compares Gabe's novel to *Triumph of the Will*, and he retorts by calling her a "twenty-year-old twit". Characters end up saying what they really mean; in that light, one might read the film as a clue that, having indulged in enough self-exposure to last a lifetime, Allen may be moving on to other things. Gabe follows the news about his new novel with a phrase that makes one wonder whether Allen is finally ready to withdraw from play as a character in his own fiction: "Can I go—is this over?"

## Richard Combs (essay date July-August 1993)

SOURCE: Combs, Richard. "Little Man, What Now?" *Film Comment* 29, no. 4 (July-August 1993): 2-4.

[*In the following essay, Combs compares the on-screen persona of Woody Allen to that of Charlie Chaplin, in light of debates over events in Allen's personal life.*]

When the Woody Allen-Mia Farrow fracas was in its early stages last year, when the rallies of accusation and counter-accusation had just burst forth like some startling new summer sport, there was one charge that zipped by fairly quickly and unremarked. Allen, it was claimed, had hired a detective agency to keep a constant watch on his across-the-park partner. And not just any agency, but Manhattan's powerful Kroll Associates, which at one point had been hired by the government of Kuwait to find Saddam Hussein.

Nonsense, said someone for Woody's side, and the item disappeared. There's a connection in the story, though, that does ring true. Though perhaps not true of Woody's life, it does say something about his art. And it's the life-imitates-art aspect that has lent an extra frisson, another dimension, to the whole scandal. We are involved in a moral quandary, not as titilated newspaper readers but as viewers of Woody Allen's films. After the revelation of his affair with his stepdaughter, is it possible to go on admiring films like **Manhattan,** in which the director-star puts the make on a young girl? Wouldn't that be like admiring *Triumph of the Will* while despising the ideas behind it—which is how a similar art/life dilemma is turned into a very Woody gag in **Husbands and Wives.**

But the private detective story throws up a conjunction more extreme and more ludicrous than the sexual one; this is a story, after all, about one of the cinema's preeminent comedians. Woody Allen and Saddam Hussein. Tangential and fortuitous as it is, and in a story of doubtful authenticity, the pairing goes to the heart of Allen's comedy. It is one of those absurdities that has its own teasing logic. It is, in fact, a classic comedy act: little and large. The "little man" whose sense of inferiority is, he believes, making him ever smaller in the world's eyes, and the self-important blusterer whose very visible failings are turned into strengths by a triumph of the will.

Saddam Hussein hasn't actually put in an appearance in a Woody Allen film (*Hot Shots! Part Deux* nabbed him first), but the situation in which he might certainly has. The 1983 **Zelig** was the ultimate little-man comedy, whose hero becomes so little that he shrinks into negative space. He is not so much a nonbeing as an agonizingly embarrassed one, a merely potential person. Too unconfident to claim his own self, Leonard Zelig, human chameleon, turns into a duplicate of anybody who happens to be nearby. It is a brilliant conceit, the characteristically Allen figure of the self-doubter, stricken with fears of inadequacy, of not being accepted, in an irreducibly funny form.

To do his hero justice, Allen simply reduced the film around him, turning it into a gray pseudodocumentary about this pseudopersonality. Allen's own elusive appearances as Zelig were spliced into actuality footage of the 1930s, when Zelig enjoyed his non-heyday, turning into instant carbon copies of Scott Fitzgerald, Eugene O'Neill, or the Chinese man in the street. It's hard to imagine more extreme poles of little- and large-ism: the nonentity achieving the fame for which he feels completely unworthy by becoming an other-entity. In an equally absurd happy ending, Zelig does achieve fame in his own right—for being nobody, or for his potential to be everybody.

But fame comes in all forms, nice and not so nice. Unhinged by his notoriety as a freak, Zelig flees the good doctor (Mia Farrow) who has undertaken his self repair. He winds up blending with the crowd in Nazi Germany—and three guesses whom he is standing next to, and is in the process of turning into, when the doctor comes to his rescue. Does this mean that the little man of screen tradition is really a repressed fascist,

who dreams of squelching those he feels inferior to by becoming a dictator? There must be an element of this, though here the relationship of little to large becomes complex.

In Allen's case, it is inseparable from the Jewish experience and Jewish humor, which comes more to the fore in his little-man films than in the all-Manhattan-sophisticates-together variety of **Husbands and Wives.** The Leonard Zelig syndrome, we're told, is an extreme case of "assimilation anxiety," beginning in his childhood when he was bullied by anti-Semites—with whom his parents always sided. What could be more exquisitely Jewish than to push the comedy of self-abnegation so far that it mimics and mocks the mind that could practice this annihilation on others?

It's also exquisitely nervous: One could compile an anthology of Hitler and/or *Triumph of the Will* jokes from Allen's films. But the comedy embodies the logic that will lead us from Woody Allen to Saddam Hussein without the help of Kroll Associates. The tortuous self-doubts of the little man force him to identify with everybody else's viewpoint; ultimately, he identifies with a personality who ignores every viewpoint but his own. In another sphere, one that is culturally approved of, Allen has already achieved this: the benign dictatorship that allows him to exercise complete control over his films, to work in conditions of strictly maintained privacy, and even to recast and reshoot a large portion of a film (**September**) if he's dissatisfied.

\* \* \*

Extreme case that he is, Leonard Zelig—and Allen as a comic sensibility—does have his precedents. There's Charlie Chaplin, whose archetypal little man underwent his own form of Zeligism in *The Great Dictator.* As a shellshocked Jewish tailor, he is persuaded that his resemblance to his country's Hitler-like dictator means that he actually is Adenoid Hynkel. Richard Attenborough's recent biopic makes a great deal of this. Chaplin, *Chaplin* suggests, undertook his lampoon of the Führer not just because he saw it as a social duty, but because he felt that he and Hitler were somehow psychically matched. "I know you, you bastard," says Robert Downey Jr.'s Charlie, studying for his *Great Dictator* part by watching Hitler ranting, and his hordes goose-estepping, on a wall-sized screen. To his brother Sydney, Chaplin explains, "We were born the same year, four days apart," and then suggests, most mysteriously, what their real link is: "We're capable of anything." Hitler was capable of launching legions; perhaps Charlie, like Zelig, was capable of containing them.

And perhaps Attenborough's *Chaplin* is best understood as another study of the Zelig syndrome—quite a fascinating one, that delves perceptively into the psychology and mechanisms of Chaplin's comedy. The film's generally poor reception stems from a problem it partly creates for itself: *Chaplin* comes on like a conventional biopic, within which a subject as radical as *Zelig* is trying to get out, a subject who experiences himself as many "subjects." At the end of the film, Charlie muses on what motivated him, and what lies behind the vagueness and evasiveness that his editor finds in his autobiography. He talks of the effort to achieve perfection in his work, to get an effect, a sketch, a character absolutely right, and feeling that he never quite made it because he wasn't "complete enough."

The sense of incompleteness goes with the dazzling powers of mimicry, and is explored by the film through all his relationships, not just the putative one with Hitler. It begins with his first, lost love, the showgirl Hetty Kelly (Moira Kelly). In a scene in her dressing-room, Chaplin holds up a mirror, half-obscuring his own face, while she puts on her makeup, and for a moment their two faces are split and combined in an image from *Persona* via *Performance*. It may or may not be to *Chaplin*'s advantage that there's no suggestion of polymorphous sexuality to the theme. This is as "clean" and clinical a case study as *Zelig.* But there is a poignancy, a nonsexual yearning and regret, to Chaplin's idolizing of an amiable monster of self-confidence, Hitler's happy half, the action star Douglas Fairbanks (Kevin Kline).

If *Chaplin* often seems like a highly colored, epic version of *Zelig,* the debt may be two-way. Did Allen draw on Chaplin's life for some of his material? The showbiz scandals in which Zelig becomes involved have a familiar ring, especially the paternity suit brought against him for what one of his replica selves has done.

Little and large, nobody and everybody. The tension between the worm's-eye-view and the urge to achieve universality through their art—which leads to dissatisfaction with being "just" comics—is central to both men. There are also two ways of construing their achievement, two ways of understanding what they have to say about all human potential. There's the funny-pathetic diagnosis of the Zelig condition, which was said as well of Chaplin the entertainer: that someone who could display such an infinite number of selves must lack one of his own. Or there's Federico Fellini's estimation of Chaplin's appeal, and his place in the history of cinema, as "a sort of Adam, from who we are all descended."

### Richard A. Blake (review date 20 November 1993)

SOURCE: Blake, Richard A. "Aging Gracefully." *America* 169, no. 16 (20 November 1993): 22-3.

[*In the following review, Blake describes* Manhattan Murder Mystery *as a charming and funny comedy about middle-age.*]

When Woody Allen's latest film, **Manhattan Murder Mystery,** opened in New York in mid-August, the local critics greeted it with respect, but scarcely with enthusiasm. At least, they were able to conclude that the turmoil in his personal life over the past year had hobbled neither his comic wit nor his love for New York. Reunited with Diane Keaton for the first time since **Manhattan** (1979)—notwithstanding a song she sings in **Radio Days** (1987)—Allen rediscovers the magic that once made them the screen's funniest and most improbable couple. They were Burns and Allen, with both characters playing Gracie.

In **Manhattan Murder Mystery** the couple shows its age delightfully. Both actors have become too settled to engage in the frantic zaniness of their capers in **Sleeper** (1963) or **Love and Death** (1975). This latest film is middle-aged comedy. Larry (Woody Allen) and Carol (Diane Keaton) have grown comfortable in their marriage, and they have a son at Brown. Larry, like almost all previous Allen heroes, inhabits a threatening universe, but his work as a book editor at Harper's does not leave much time for endless neurotic reflections on the meaning of life or for hysterical contemplation of his imaginary symptoms, standard comic devices in the earlier films. Carol is not quite sure what she wants to do with the next phase of her life, but she is thinking of using her talent for gourmet cooking to open a restaurant. The Keaton character is still confused about life, but she has clearly outgrown the endearing ditziness of her Annie Hall (1977).

New York really functions as a central character and antagonist in many of Allen's films, and it does in this one. The camera opens on a beautiful nighttime helicopter shot of the Midtown skyline and slowly the lens settles on Madison Square Garden, while on the sound track Bobby Short sings a love song to the city lesser mortals love to hate. The lovely lyricism of the opening shot is broken by mindless violence, in the guise of a hockey game inside the arena. Larry has dragged Carol to the game, and in return he has promised to accompany her to a Wagner opera at Lincoln Center the next week. Clearly they have learned the art of accommodation, the key ingredient in any successful marriage. The shots of the Metropolitan Opera House with its huge Chagall murals restate Allen's romantic delight in New York architecture, but by this time the violence, once a spectator sport for them, has penetrated the stone walls of their apartment fortress. Allen's New York, his standard metaphor for the universe as he sees it, provides a fascinating mixture of beauty and danger.

On the night of the hockey game, the Liptons meet another couple on the elevator of their apartment building, and in an unthinkable transgression of the mores, if not the canons, of New York cliff-dwellers, they engage their long-time neighbors in conversation and even accept an invitation to join them for late-night coffee. Paul (Jerry Adler) and Lillian House (Lynn Cohen) appear even more settled in their marriage than the Liptons. Carol and Lillian trade diet strategies, while Paul drives Larry to the edge of insanity by showing off his stamp collection. The Houses are planning a vacation trip, and the prospect of future snapshots glazes Larry's eyes and mind.

The vacation never takes place. Lillian House apparently suffers a fatal heart attack, but Carol, her mind in overdrive even if the steering wheel is out, believes there may be foul play. Like any true New Yorker who wants to survive in the city without becoming a recluse, Larry simply denies the possibility that violence could ever touch their lives, especially on the Upper East Side. Carol gains support from a recently divorced friend, Ted (Alan Alda), a television writer whose encouragement and skill in fiction writing fuels her aspirations to solve her "crime." Still unconvinced that a crime has been committed, Larry works on a trashy novel with a famous author, the cool and sexy Marcia Fox (Anjelica Houston), and eventually she adds her sleuthing skills to the project as well. Is life in New York, or in the world for that matter, Allen asks, any stranger than pulp fiction or a television miniseries, or can anyone really tell the difference? In fact, these two mass production artists deal with life in New York more competently than Larry, the responsible and completely logical editor.

At the core of *Manhattan Murder Mystery* is a wildly improbable caper, in the best tradition of the Screwball Comedies of the 1930's and 1940's. The dialogue is fast and very funny. The Liptons represent different worlds: she the world of imagination, adventure and fantasy; he the workaday world of rationality. Still, their mutual love is undeniable. In the Screwball era, the couple would resolve their differences and marry, but that age has passed. This couple is already married, and although their adventures put pressures on their relationship their differences will be resolved. Keaton and Allen are Hepburn and Tracy, but they have lived in New York long enough to accept lunacy as a way of life. Appropriately, Larry's night table holds a copy of James Harvey's *Romantic Comedy* (1987), the definitive critical history of Screwball movies.

Allen also adds touches of the film noir tradition of the classic detective movies of the 1940's and 1950's. Most of the outdoor scenes are shot at night and a continual drizzle keeps the streets damp, and thus perfect for reflecting menacing headlights. The characters creep through the shadows in basements, elevator shafts and back stairways. As the narrative line unwinds, neither the ersatz detectives nor the audience has any idea what really happened. A climactic scene is a wonderful spoof of Orson Welles's *Lady from Shanghai* (1948), complete with a shoot-out in a hall of mirrors. The antagonists grope their way through a twisted, murky moral landscape, unable to distinguish fact from fancy, reality from reflection, good from evil.

Allen's films seldom resolve problems, and never does he try to explain the existence of evil in the world. He allows mystery to remain mystery, as vexatious as that strategy is. At the same time, he never allows his characters to bury themselves in self-pity or despair. They groan and kvetch, but in the end they find solace in the life of the imagination, especially the movies, or in memories of past happiness or, most frequently, in the love of a flawed but interesting partner. At the end of the film, as their adventures draw to a conclusion of sorts, Larry and Carol return to their apartment, enjoying a bit of banter to prove to themselves that their love is still very much alive despite the discovery of real differences in their view of life.

Technically, *Manhattan Murder Mystery* shows off the best of the Allen team. Santo Loquasto provides sets and costumes of rich reds and browns, autumn colors that provide a sense of warmth to the interiors. The exteriors, appropriately, are gray and black. Carlo Di Palma's camera is flawless, as usual when he works with Woody Allen. The actors all respond to the Allen touch, with the exception of Anjelica Huston, a splendid actress who seems wasted this time around. Allen and his co-writer Marshall Brickman have pointlessly made Marcia a poker expert, and one scene in which she allegedly tries to teach Larry some tricks of the game embarrasses both actors. Perhaps the device was a joking reference to her role in *The Grifters*, but it simply does not work.

Sadly, reviewers and even the public expect a director of Allen's talent to surpass his previous achievements with each new film. *Manhattan Murder Mystery* will not enter the Allen canon as a masterpiece, but it is a delightful, charming and thoroughly engaging comedy for adults about adults. What more can we ask of anyone?

## James M. Welsh (review date November-December 1993)

SOURCE: Welsh, James M. Review of *Manhattan Murder Mystery*, by Woody Allen. *Films in Review* 44, nos. 11-12 (November-December 1993): 413-14.

[*In the following review, Welsh compares* Manhattan Murder Mystery *to Alfred Hitchcock's* Rear Window, *asserting that Allen's film is entertaining, and may appeal to a broader audience than his previous films.*]

At first *Manhattan Murder Mystery* seems merely a throwback to an earlier phase of Woody's career, since the screenplay was co-authored with Marshall Brickman, who also collaborated with Allen on *Annie Hall* (1977) and *Manhattan* (1979), two pictures that showcased the talents of Diane Keaton. After what critic Nancy Pogel has called "Allen's Rose Period" (culminating in *Purple Rose of Cairo* in 1985 and the much neglected *Broadway Danny Rose* in 1984), *Manhattan Murder Mystery* seems to shift back into the mode of romantic comedy, as several reviewers noted, but this is a rather simplistic dismissal.

Though it was hard to take the comic gangsters of *Broadway Danny Rose* seriously, there was the (remote) chance that the plot of that comedy could take a nasty turn, and the same is true of *Manhattan Murder Mystery,* which, in a way, is *Manhattan* meets *Rear Window* and *The Lady from Shanghai*. In Hitchcock's *Rear Window,* Jimmy Stewart was certain that Raymond Burr, his neighbor across the courtyard, had murdered his wife. In *Manhattan Murder Mystery,* Carol Lipton (Diane Keaton) is convinced her neighbor Paul House (Jerry Adler) has murdered his wife. She becomes obsessed with this "mystery," and finds more support from her friend Ted (an oily Alan Alda, obviously on the make) than from her husband Larry (Woody Allen). The audience is soon convinced that she is merely a screwball, but she turns out to be right.

In *Rear Window* Jimmy Stewart, confined to his room with a broken leg in a cast, sent Grace Kelly to snoop into his neighbor's apartment. In *Manhattan Murder Mystery* Diane Keaton gets a key from Jack, the Super, and, like Grace Kelly, almost gets caught. Allen builds tension the same way Hitchcock did, but at that point the audience thinks the neighbor is probably innocent and that Keaton is merely addlepated.

Allen himself does a fine comic turn as the not-too-patient husband who tolerates his wife's eccentric mania, but one of his writers (the Allen character is a book editor in this film), Marcia Fox (Anjelica Huston) works out a plausible murder plot, and everyone starts to wonder if Carol is so crazy, after all. Huston, the Fox (in two senses), is flirting with Allen all the while, and Alda is flirting with Keaton, which recalls the romantic complications of Allen's later films; but this film stays on course as a romantic comedy, with Allen and Keaton doing a Nick and Nora number. Fox concocts a scheme to entrap the murderer. The murderer kidnaps Keaton and holds her captive. Woody Allen is forced to play the role of the unlikely hero.

The film reaches a smashing finale that recalls the famous Hall of Mirrors conclusion of Orson Welles's *The Lady from Shanghai* and also uses footage from the Welles film, brilliantly. This is Woody the auteur paying "hommage" to the Master. It's a derivative gimmick, but perfectly executed. There is not much more to this movie than meets the well trained eye, if the viewer is watching closely. But it has much more to offer than in-jokes for movie buffs, and it has wider appeal than the usual Allen film and should draw a wider audience. If not, well, Woody Allen seems to be covering his bets by planning to shoot his next film in France, in French. But will Paris satisfy him after all those years in New York?

One hopes that American viewers will support and embrace this entertaining film so that Allen may be persuaded to come back, soon. By now, it should be obvious that Woody Allen is a national treasure, not to be invested abroad.

## Jonathan Romney (interview date February 1994)

SOURCE: Romney, Jonathan. "Shelter from the Storm." *Sight and Sound* 4, no. 2 (February 1994): 6-9.

[*In the following interview, Romney discusses* Manhattan Murder Mystery *with Allen, who emphasizes the film's value as light entertainment, while Romney focuses on underlying themes of relationships and aging.*]

Why does interviewing Woody Allen feel like an experiment in virtual reality? I'm sitting in a London hotel room with this small, quiet-spoken, middle-aged man in a navy blazer and beige slacks, and we're talking civilly about films, as you might with any American director who's in town to promote new product.

Yet I'm half convinced that this cannot possibly be Woody Allen. It could be a hologram, or a well-schooled impersonator—although the familiar yammering verbal rhythms have given way to the formal composure of interview etiquette, he looks and sounds too uncannily like Woody Allen to be true. I'm about as persuaded of his reality as I would be if Groucho Marx were sitting there in coat-tails and painted-on moustache, or Michael Jackson in full regalia, or Roger Rabbit. I've seen his films, after all, and I *know* that Woody Allen is not real—he's a made-up character.

### A Golem out of control

Over the years Woody Allen has come to denote less a real person than an assemblage of ideas and images—a brand name that stands not just for a body of work, but for a stance, a style of humour and high seriousness. The name also implies a repertoire of characteristics that have been attached to fictional figures such as Alvy Singer, Sandy Bates, the protean Zelig. 'Woody Allen' the persona is as much a cartoon icon as Chaplin or

Groucho Marx, and like them he is easily identified by the physical 'props' that stand for the whole: the twitchy demeanour, the glasses, the washed-out beige wardrobe, the scraggy hair.

The difference is that no one would dream of identifying the 'Groucho' persona with Groucho Marx the man. With Woody Allen, however, not only are the physical characteristics unmistakably his own, but aspects of his supposedly secretive, yet in fact unusually well-publicised life (the reclusiveness, the psychoanalysis, the complex romantic history) crop up in his films with obsessive regularity, apparently all but untranslated. A simulacrum of himself, Woody Allen is, in the terms of Jewish myth, his own Golem: a construct brought into life through the Word, and become bigger than the real, effectively eclipsing it.

It may be that the Golem has got out of control. The blurring of Allen's real and fantasy selves was heightened by his split with Mia Farrow, followed by the revelations about his relationship with her adopted daughter Soon-Yi Previn and allegations of child abuse concerning Dylan Farrow. When the story broke, many commentators seemed to take for granted the conflation of Allen's life and art, while some expressed a feeling of betrayal at the realisation that the wise, sensitive, lovable figure depicted in the films may not have been real after all. The conflation remained so complete and unconscious that Woody-watchers could now scan the films for 'evidence', for lines which would yield the truth of the matter. At the first press screenings of *Husbands and Wives* (1992), a film generally interpreted as telling a version of the split, certain remarks elicited gales of laughter for their apparently revelatory aptness. When Allen's character Gabe Roth said, "I've learned nothing over the years," it was seen as a terrible admission. By a peculiar reversal, the real-life story was now being read as an extension of the films—Woody's latest scrape.

Though little could be known of the truth of the case, even sceptics wondered whether the Allen persona could survive the exposure unimpaired. As Adam Gopnik recently argued in the *New Yorker*, "What has really been put in doubt by Woody Allen's tribulations is his *judgement*, and with it, his place as an arbiter of manners—his ability to tell cool from un-cool, and make that distinction stick." Gopnik continues, "If you were susceptible, the discriminations were so inspiring that the resulting confusion between life and art wasn't just between Allen's life and his art. It was between *your* life and his art."

What was important to Allen's public was their own investment in his persona. His films, especially the New York comedies of manners *Annie Hall* (1977) and *Manhattan* (1979), provided a lifestyle template for a generation of would-be sophisticates. What was at stake was not only a set of supposedly unassailable high-culture values—most famously, the list of favourite things at the end of *Manhattan*—but also a comic attitude that made defensive hostility into a form of heroism. Watching the Allen anti-hero, you could believe that his anxiety, ineptitude and pusillanimity were simply the flipside of a sceptical stoicism in the face of the glitzier, shallower aspects of the world.

There may be a hidden agenda to Allen's current bout of promotion—to remind his public that he is not primarily a pilloried press bogeyman, but a purveyor of amusements with a new film, *Manhattan Murder Mystery,* to sell. He emphasises the 'entertainment' angle with unexpected zeal, possibly because he and/or his distributors Tri-Star—it's the last film of their deal before he departs for his friend Jean Doumanian's Sweetland Films—agree with the widely held view that the image of Woody Allen as an anguished moral philosopher won't wash right now. How does he feel, then, about his fans' need to invest his persona with so much 'reality'?

"I've had problems with that, I wish they would not do that. In the same sense that you can't identify Charlie Chaplin on screen with Charlie Chaplin off screen, or Buster Keaton or whoever else—they're not the same person. There are some little carry-overs, but I'm not the person on screen that I am in life. I'm a completely different person—or not *completely,* but certainly a different person, who makes those films. They're creations, they're acts of imagination.

"People have thought about me that I'm intellectual, I'm not; that I'm inept, that I'm too Jewish, that I'm not Jewish enough, considering I'm Jewish; that I'm a loser with women, always with women . . . They're all simplistic things that they come away with.

"And sometimes it costs me some affection or loyalty because after a picture like *Stardust Memories,* people come away thinking, 'Oh, it's Woody Allen saying he has contempt for his own audience.' But it wasn't me. I was making a fictional story about a director who is an artist—I happened to make him a director because I know about that—who is depressed because he has everything in life and is still miserably unhappy. When I was making that film, I didn't remember incidents that happened to me, and didn't reflect my feeling precisely. There'd be an overlap in one or two areas, but it was a complete work of fiction."

It seems a little disingenuous. By the very fact of playing the role and recognising the overlaps, surely he's openly rehearsing aspects of his life?

"Well, if I did then it was a mistake. Then I should have cast Dustin Hoffman. I played the role because I naturally played the roles I was writing. In retrospect, I should have had someone else play the part, then at least no matter how people responded to the film it would have toned down the notion that it was me. Or maybe I shouldn't have made him a film director, maybe that would have helped.

"People thought that ***Husbands and Wives*** was an autobiographical movie. They thought Mia was playing Mia, and I was playing me. The truth of the matter is, I finished the script, I gave it to Mia and I asked her which character she wanted to play. She was going to play the Judy Davis character, and then decided to play the other character because it would be shorter and left her more free time.

"It was not an autobiographical movie, I made up all those characters and all those things. It came out at a time when I was having a personal crisis that was reported in the newspapers, but there had been a million things printed in the press that were way off the mark, that were simply not true at all, and the fact that this was autobiographical was one of them."

Would he now be tempted to opt for anonymity, to try to disappear from his films altogether?

"I have certainly cooled it down at the moment. I'm not even in the movie I'm starting to shoot [reportedly titled ***Bullets over Broadway*** or *The Artist,* and starring John Cusack and Mary-Louise Parker]. If there's any way I can disabuse people of the notion that I'm the character in my movies I'll do it . . . On the other hand, I have a feeling I'm not going to be able to. I have a feeling I'll probably wind up just doing the ideas I think of, because I won't be able to do anything else. When a film is over and I have to get a new one, I'm thrilled to have an idea. And if the idea is about me, and I'm playing a writer in New York, and I get involved with a woman, and the audiences see it as my real life, then we'll both have to live with that."

### FRED ASTAIRE, NOT BERGMAN

Effectively a genre movie, ***Manhattan Murder Mystery*** certainly seems to keep the real at bay. "I wanted to do this murder mystery because I felt I had had such a painful year I was going to indulge myself and do it and have a good time." A diversion in many senses, ***Manhattan Murder Mystery*** will reassure anyone who, like the much-quoted aliens in ***Stardust Memories,*** preferred the early, funny films. A pure anachronism, it's a comedy thriller in the style of *The Thin Man* movies, with Allen and Diane Keaton bantering urbanely in the Nick and Nora Charles roles. It revives an idea originally intended for ***Annie Hall,*** but rejected by Allen as "too insubstantial". Now revamped in collaboration with his old writing partner Marshall Brickman, it features Allen in his familiar nice-guy nebbish role as a

book editor embroiled in a drama which, on the surface at least, is entirely someone else's—the possibility that the man across the hall is a wife murderer.

When Diane Keaton stepped into the co-star role originally earmarked for Mia Farrow, her presence gave the film a nostalgic twist, harking back to Allen's 70s urban box-office peak, and to a more innocent, utopian vision of city life—a feeling expressed immediately in the opening aerial shot of the city by night, set to an exuberant treatment of Cole Porter's 'I Happen to Like New York'. It's an affirmation of faith that, 17 years after ***Annie Hall,*** there *are* lobsters still for tea.

Allen insists that the film is *entertainment*—a term that seems to have become a bottom-line reference for him. It's unexpected to find the director of ***Interiors*** (1978) and ***Another Woman*** (1988) saying, as he did in *Rolling Stone* last year, "It's great when people can go into a movie house for an hour and a half and just see Fred Astaire or Abbott and Costello . . . They've had a breather from the storm—and *that* should be the function of films—not *Bicycle Thieves* or *Grand Illusion* or Bergman . . . You may really be serving people best by giving them a little light refreshment."

### KOOKINESS TURNED TETCHY

Allen insists that the new film is precisely that, although its numerous Hitchcock references underpin themes of guilt, paranoia and voyeurism that are straight out of *Rear Window.* "I don't agree with Truffaut that there's great meaning in Hitchcock. There are four or five of his films that I just love to see over and over again, but I see them as pure entertainment, pure airport reading. And I see this movie as pure airport reading. This is just the kind of movie I would have loved to go and see when I was younger. Just pure enjoyment, non-confrontational, non-riddled with exploration of character and psychology."

But what gives the story resonance is that the disturbance is not confined to what goes on next door. The murder mystery turns upside down the life of Larry and Carol Lipton (Allen and Keaton), whose apparently solid marriage is riddled with hairline fractures. It is part of the film's energy that it attempts to contain with jovial slapstick an altogether disturbing situation. The concluding 'up' note is characteristically ambivalent— the Liptons' staid existence has been given a lift, but perhaps no more than that.

"Right, they're not changed radically. It's just an experience for them—an ultimately funny experience when they look back on it, but harrowing while it's happening. A friend said to me, 'To keep this marriage together, they're going to have to have one of those murders every year,' and it's true. But I didn't want to get into the seriousness of what was afflicting them. I felt I could afflict them with a minor problem and it would be good enough for this story."

In a way, it's the very lightness of the film that strikes its most jarring note. When Woody Allen starts to talk, like any Hollywood box-office maven, about escapism, you're tempted to act the shrink and invoke ideas of resistance or denial. The all-out slapstick of some sequences in the film—of which only some work—seems like a hysterical denial of the story's more distressing strands. Partly because it evokes a recognisably everyday image of New York life, the film retains a strong sense of unease. It deals with worries that can't be brushed under the comic carpet—the tenuous bonds that keep couples together and that might easily turn to hostility or worse; the fear of ageing and losing touch with past energies (Allen and Keaton resemble their former selves, but they are frailer, their kookiness turned tetchy, and their characters live a boxed-in life that Alvy and Annie never did). Like *Rear Window,* it's also about the terrifying possibility that there might be no gap whatsoever between reality and your worst imaginings. The frantic energies the film devotes to seeming throwaway look like an exercise in damage limitation. Could it be that Allen is now simply reluctant to be perceived as serious?

If so, it may be because his seriousness has increasingly alienated his public. The spirit of high philosophical inquiry that reached its apogee in *Crimes and Misdemeanors* (1989) and *Shadows and Fog* (1991) seems something of an anachronism—a linchpin for Allen's idol Ingmar Bergman, but no longer a major preoccupation of contemporary cinema, even at its most serious. In *Manhattan,* Allen's character imagines a story about people "constantly creating these real unnecessary neurotic problems for themselves 'cause it keeps them from dealing with more unsolvable, terrifying problems about the universe." In this line, Allen seemed to upbraid himself for his preoccupation with the ephemera of his characters' romantic confusion (which is what his public likes) when he could have been dealing with weightier imponderables (which he did in *Shadows and Fog,* only to discover that his public didn't want to know). Perhaps the big metaphysical questions have little to do with most people's experience or interests, and when raised in cinema often come across as a purely academic distraction.

"No, I don't feel that way entirely, these questions have to do with the very fabric of everybody's life. That's what they are immersed in from the day they're born . . . I feel that in real life people do create all kinds of obsessive neurotic details so they don't have to confront larger issues. If your problem is getting food for the evening, you don't have time to sit around and reflect on the purpose of life and existential *ennui,* because

you have another more pressing problem. But when the pressing problems are solved, then you start to think, 'Gee, what does it all mean, what is the purpose of this? I've got it and then what? I'm older, life is short and it doesn't seem to have much purpose.' You start thinking about those things—and then if someone yells 'Fire!' and the building's on fire, it's all done. I think it's important for people in their daily denial, which they need for survival, to create stupid little problems so as not to have to confront the larger problems which are scary, unsolvable and make you depressed."

LAUGHTER IN THE DARK

Allen's films are generally least satisfying when they seem to be aiming for one of two poles—to be unequivocally funny or unequivocally serious. What most fascinates is the mercurial way they shift between sobriety and flippancy, between the transcendent imponderables and the nagging everyday kvetches. It's a cliché to say that his films, like his persona, are 'neurotic', but there is a particular neurosis about them that most reveals its discontents when it appears to be dismissing them, and vice versa.

This movement seems indissolubly linked to Allen's Jewishness. The great truism about Jewish humour is that it evolved as a mechanism for conjuring away anxieties that were too painful to address directly. But in Allen's films, this offhanded approach seems to be revealing agonies with increasing explicitness. Jewishness has become more and more prominent in his recent films—in the rabbinical moralists who haunt *Crimes and Misdemeanors,* in 'Oedipus Wrecks', the ultimate Jewish mother sketch from the *New York Stories* portmanteau (1989), and in the much maligned *Shadows and Fog,* an extended homage to Bergman, Kafka and German Expressionist cinema.

*Shadows and Fog* seemed confused—but, as Joyce would have said, it's natural that things look confused in the fog. Released out of sequence in Britain, after *Husbands and Wives,* it was generally written off as a naive folly which hugely overstated its themes. But *Shadows and Fog* is a *film maudit* in the best sense—not just because no one wanted to see it, but because in a fascinating way it doesn't *quite* make sense. True, the overstatement is flagrant—themes are both presented visually *and* debated verbally in a manner that combines Strindbergian dramaturgy with Talmudic dispute. Yet there is also a curious understatement, as if the film were afraid to say what it is really about.

What is never named, although it is alluded to obsessively, is Jewishness. There are references to the Holocaust, to pogrom-like round-ups, to a disappearing, scapegoated Jewish community. We can't help sympathising with the beleaguered hero Kleinman, but at the same time we wonder why Allen would want to revive such an extreme version of the 'little man' archetype, particularly when it embodies such a negative myth of the Jew as eternal victim. Literally a wandering Jew, Kleinman is abstracted from any Jewish community, though this is in any case doomed to invisibility. Jewishness, although the very basis of Kleinman's being, is represented in an entirely negative light, like a transcendental curse.

The most direct allusion comes in an altogether alarming one-liner. "My people pray in a different language," says Kleinman. "For all I know, they were requesting their own troubles." It's a remarkably loaded line—in the payoff, "*my* people" suddenly become "they", the verb moves to the past tense, and Kleinman covers his tracks with "For all I know". Triply dissociating himself from Jewish identity, Kleinman also perpetuates a myth of eternal Jewish masochism—a notion that finds a friendlier expression in Allen's usual self-tormenting *schlemihl* persona, but takes on a more threatening resonance in a film ostensibly about anti-semitism.

"It seems to me a completely accurate portrayal of standard feelings Jews have about Jews. Maybe other people have them too. But it's certainly a prevalent feeling that Jews have about Jews, that they have been a victimised people, which indeed they have been."

But surely the idea of calling down your own troubles seems a dangerous one in a film that evokes the ambience of pre-Nazi Germany?

"Right, but one cannot take a joke in a movie to mean that much. It's a line, it's a joke in a film, and to impute to it more meaning than it really has . . . What is the implication of people worrying about it? That there will be people massing, and isolating the line and putting it on slogans? These are jokes in movies.

"But it does express an American-Jewish feeling, where people have often been raised to pray in a language they have never understood a single word of, and here are these people being admonished by their parents to come to a synagogue when they have no religious feeling whatsoever. So in a certain sense I lump the Jewish religion in with all other religions as an organised religion and consequently baneful. I think all organised religions are not to the good of the human race. What could be more preposterous than taking a young boy and forcing him to go to a synagogue and pray to God in a language in which he has no idea what he's saying? He could just as easily *be* calling down his own troubles, he could be saying anything.

"Each religion has its great list of preposterous notions and even worse than preposterous, even quite harmful. That's as silly a notion as anything, to be praying, to be

allegedly speaking to God . . . The Jewish religious experience, the Christian religious experience, it's all guys in rooms writing rules for the propagation of their own security and power and peace of mind, it has no connection whatsoever with God, if he exists. If a God exists, these guys don't have the faintest idea what language you're supposed to speak to him in, they don't know where to begin.

"If anything, all the religions have demonstrated wasteful foolishness. They've earned scorn, not reverence. I'm not saying that a person cannot be personally religious and have real feelings, but as they are organised, that in itself is all the condemnation you need."

The surprising thing is to hear from Woody Allen the disclaimer, "It's just a joke." As a long-term analysand, he must surely be aware that jokes are precisely where you expect to see meaning revealed, and that exegeses of his work are invariably based on his casual one-liners.

"Right, but one still cannot take those things too seriously, they're still jokes. They're interesting from a Freudian point of view in that they may or may not reveal something, and that something they do reveal—if indeed they *do* reveal anything—is arguable as to what it is. But to put too much weight on jokes, or even art in general, has always been a mistake. I never thought art could change things. To the degree that it's entertaining, it's got a use, but that's not the thing that changes people or countries or political systems, that's usually done through political action.

"Someone can be cruel and terrible and vicious to you and you can go home and write a satire on him, it never means anything. But when you finally go and confront him and sue him or punch him on the nose, then you get something done."

If it really means nothing but escapism, you might well ask why Woody Allen makes films at all? *Shadows and Fog* seems to be largely about this question. Perhaps it's no accident when a director ends up making a film that no one wants to see—"Maybe it's too much of me to expect that an audience is going to be interested in an allegorical piece and a black and white piece and a period piece set in some anonymous European country," he shrugs. But it is precisely such films that allow filmmakers to comment, as in marginalia, on their work.

*Shadows and Fog* concludes for the necessity of illusion and distraction in the face of worldly woes (the day is saved by a droll Bergmanesque magician); but it also proves immensely revelatory about Allen's chronic outsider complex. The film explicitly sets him apart from the rest of contemporary cinema, art-house *and* mainstream, and allows him to claim a mythical black and white past as his own private ghetto. In Kleinman's isolation, Allen's fantasy of an ideal cinema is represented as a sort of transcendental Jewishness, an absolute apartness.

If Allen keeps making films, and returning habitually to something like mainstream expectations, it is also because of the basic requirement of all performers—the need to remain visible. But Woody Allen of all people should be aware of the perils of exposure, and throughout his work there is a concomitant urge to vanish that is itself no less exhibitionist; there's always the need to elicit the gasp that greets the conjurer's disappearing act. The last few films play constantly on this theme: **Crimes and Misdemeanors,** with the "eyes of God" hovering over the sinning ophthalmologist Judah; **Alice** (1990), with its skittish fantasy of invisibility; **'Oedipus Wrecks,'** with its monstrous mother exposing the hero's embarrassment to all Manhattan; and **Shadows and Fog,** in which Kleinman, lost in the night, ponders (both fearfully and hopefully), "Maybe they have me under surveillance." **Zelig** (1983) was a parable about social conformity and the perils of fame: the chameleon man may vanish in the crowd, but it doesn't take much scanning of the cleverly doctored newsreel footage to spot a familiar sheepish smile gleaming out like a beacon. All these films articulate the recurrent message: "Are you looking?"

## Does God get the jokes?

You could discern a religious aspect to this tendency, in keeping with the films' anxiety about the gaze of God. The overwhelming desire to be seen could be read as a need to know if God is looking, if God is reachable through any language. The misgivings Allen expresses about Judaism and prayer are an extension of a condition peculiar to the Jewish diaspora—to speak any language other than Hebrew is seen as an exile from one's own culture, but for non-Hebrew speakers, that language itself entails a further alienation. Jewish humour can be seen as responding to that very problem— it's a way of using whatever language is available to cut through the linguistic impasse and speak directly of one's condition. A surrogate holy language, the wisecrack becomes the authentic expression of the self—a hot line to the real. It's a common theological debate to wonder whether God gets jokes—Jewish humour stakes all on betting that he does.

In a more pragmatic sense, a film-maker has only one god to answer to, and that's the public. As frequently as Woody Allen turns his back on his public, he becomes aware of that deity's mounting ire and will pay it court. The most individualistic film-maker, roaming the art-house wilderness, may at times feel the need to follow that god's commands and accept a different set of priorities—and if Woody Allen should now, of all times,

choose to read as the First Commandment, "Thou shalt make entertainment", that is perhaps understandable. But the Golem which has trailed him throughout his career, and which is made of a more complex clay than mere celebrity, is going to be a lot harder to appease.

## Richard A. Blake (review date 14 January 1995)

SOURCE: Blake, Richard A. "Misfire." *America* 172, no. 1 (14 January 1995): 22-3.

[*In the following review, Blake suggests that the two central male characters in* Bullets over Broadway *represent two sides of Allen's personality, and contends that the film uses gangersterism as a metaphor for the arts industry in order to explore themes of artistic integrity and compromise.*]

When European directors were still making interesting films, some misguided critics explained that Americans only recycled old films, while across the Atlantic film makers embraced literature, theater and painting. Of course, they concluded, the foreign product had to be superior. Snobbery triumphant! With the infallible wisdom of hindsight, it soon became clear that the burst of creative activity that exploded and then immediately fizzled in Sweden, Italy, France and, to a lesser extent, in Spain and Germany could not sustain itself by poaching on the territory of the other arts.

The Americans were clearly on the right sound track. The new American movie makers—Spielberg, Lucas, Scorsese, for example—all received their education under a marquee rather than under an ivy-covered tower and did their advanced study in an editing room rather than a library carrel. When they reach into their cultural grab-bag to provide a historic allusion, it is likely that they will come out with Orson Welles rather than Walt Whitman. With delicious irony, it was the French critics of the 1960's who praised the Americans for their ability to stamp a commonly used film genre, like the Western or the musical, with originality and even genius. What Americans called imitation, the French were calling self-reflection: the genre reflects upon itself as it develops.

Woody Allen's last two ventures build on familiar genres. Is this a personal reworking of cinema history, or is it the last flicker of a fading talent? The use of awkward alliterative titles is not a good sign. **Manhattan Murder Mystery** (1993) was a detective caper with clear roots in the Thin Man series, and his latest **Bullets over Broadway,** is a zany tribute to the gangsters of the 1930's, like Paul Muni's *Scarface* (Hawks, 1931). Presumption of the audience's familiarity with the genre enables Allen and his co-writer Douglas McGrath to reinvent the style in a comic style.

* * *

In this latest film [**Bullets over Broadway**], Allen continues his cinema of narcissism, even down to the self-justifying line, "The artist creates his own moral universe," later repeated as "The superior intellect creates his own moral universe." Using his familiar technique, he dissects his own ego and assigns the fragments to different characters. The aspiring playwright Daniel Shayne (John Cusack) and Cheech (Chazz Palminteri), a hit man for the mob, represent two sides of Woody Allen.

Shayne wants to become another Chekhov and talks to his Greenwich Village friends about artistic integrity, but he discovers compromise as the primrose path to production. To get mob money for the work, he accepts moll-doll Olive Neal (Jennifer Tilly) to play the part of a psychiatrist. Helen Sinclair (Dianne Wiest) has long ago drowned her career in bathtub gin, but she does have name recognition, and by threat or seduction she can easily persuade Dan to rewrite scenes for her. With Cheech's muscular support, Olive, too, insists on a few "adjustments" to enhance her part. From the first moment artists talk to producers, who are little more than gangsters, Allen concludes, they begin an irreversible series of sell-outs.

Cheech does not sell out as easily as Shayne. As Olive's bodyguard, Cheech sits through the painful rehearsals. The abominable dialogue and improbable situations eventually get to him, and in desperation he begins offering suggestions. It is clear that he is a raw talent, with more experience of life (and its sudden termination) than the N.Y.U. anarchist-playwright who wrote this thing. Cheech soon takes over the rewrite and becomes so heavily invested in the project that he is willing to kill rather than see his work mutilated by amateurs. He does, and then he meets the end of all artists who value their integrity over the wishes of the producers.

For Allen gangland becomes an effective and very funny metaphor for the arts. The traditional gangster of the 1930's works his way up in the mob, consolidates his power by eliminating rivals and becomes boss. At the top of the world, he becomes too proud to deal with other mobs, the police or even his own henchmen, and as a result, in the last reel he must die in a spray of tommy-gun fire. Unlike Allen, Cheech failed to learn the lessons of his fathers in film.

* * *

Carlo Depalma's color camera and Santo Loquasto's design have provided the dark, brooding look of crime movies of the 1930's and 1940's, as they in turn once tried to recreate the midnight world of 1920's mobsters. As usual, the bouncy music provides ironic comment on the action. When Cheech, for example, takes his clients for a ride to the waterfront, the transaction is accompanied by "Up a Lazy River."

Ensemble acting has always been a virtue in Allen films, and here the cast is uniformly superb. Shayne is the Allen surrogate. He is the striving artist and lover, the little man trying to survive in a hostile universe. John Cusack becomes the familiar "nebbish" character, even down to the stammer and nervous gestures that became part of the Allen screen persona. Dianne Wiest's booze-pickled vocal chords register several octaves lower than Jennifer Tilly's nasal chirping, which leads Cheech to devise a strategy so that he "won't have to listen to her any more." Both are very funny. Chazz Palminteri's face is as craggy as his voice and his morals. He is the perfect contrast to Jim Broadbent's plumpish Warner Purcell, the actor whose appetite for Danish makes him a candidate for the Macy's Thanksgiving parade, and whose appetite for Olive makes him a candidate for a funeral procession.

What about Allen the artist? In this film, at any rate, the Cheech side of him is dead. This is no innovative **Crimes and Misdemeanors** or **Hannah and Her Sisters, Bullets over Broadway** marks a retreat into the safe and all-too-familiar corridors of the artist's psyche, and it may even provide a response to those critics who, Allen imagines, want him to go back to making funny movies the way he used to. The old neighborhood, unfortunately, has become a bit shabby over the years, nice to visit once in a while for nostalgia's sake, but scarcely a place anyone would want to stay for very long.

## Jonathan Romney (review date May 1995)

SOURCE: Romney, Jonathan. Review of *Bullets over Broadway,* by Woody Allen. *Sight and Sound* 5, no. 5 (May 1995): 40.

[*In the following review, Romney asserts that* Bullets over Broadway *is fresh, light entertainment that also explores the role of film as art in society.*]

New York, the 20s. David Shayne, an aspiring, idealistic young playwright, is determined to direct his new play himself [in **Bullets over Broadway**]. Unexpectedly, producer Julian Marx tells him that he has backing—from mobster Nick Valenti, whose volatile and talentless girlfriend Olive Neal has ambitions to be an actress; the only condition is that Olive must play a lead. David and Marx approach grandiose, heavy-drinking Broadway star Helen Sinclair for a role. Rehearsals start: among the cast are dapper English leading man Warner Purcell, a compulsive eater, and irrepressibly chirpy actress Eden Brent. Olive is accompanied by Cheech, whom Valenti has assigned as her bodyguard, and who makes his threatening presence felt from the stalls.

David increasingly spends time with Helen, who captivates him with her flamboyant thespian glamour. Cheech begins to offer his own suggestions for the play, to David's dismay and the cast's general approval. While Cheech's back is turned, Olive and Warner begin a furtive affair. At a speakeasy, David runs into Cheech; the two make peace and Cheech begins to take even more of a hand, effectively becoming David's mentor and suggesting further changes, which David now eagerly incorporates. David embarks on a full-blown affair with Helen. Cheech tells Warner to keep away from Olive and the actor responds by going on an eating binge.

As the play gets under way, prior to its New York run, Cheech, increasingly possessive of 'his' work, becomes enraged by Olive's hopeless acting; at one performance she is replaced by an understudy and the play improves. Valenti demands more lines for Olive; furious, Cheech takes her away and shoots her dead. David confronts him, but Cheech will brook no debate. David's girlfriend Ellen, who by now suspects his affair with Helen, reveals she has become involved with their bohemian friend Sheldon Flender—formerly David's guru. Valenti, suspecting Cheech of Olive's murder, has his men follow him to the play's Broadway opening; Cheech is killed, and the critics assume that the gunshots are a brilliant dramatic touch. David has showdown with Ellen and Flender; he tells her he knows he is no artist. She agrees to return to Pittsburgh and marry him.

* * *

The last two lines of *Bullets over Broadway* are a *reductio ad absurdum* of the eternal happy ending. The hero walks with his true love into a presumably duller but happier future: "Will you marry me?"—"Yes". However cynical we might expect Woody Allen to be about connubial bliss, this gentle up-turn seems unequivocal. Allen here seems to be celebrating his own reconciliation with the well-made play. Allen's lightest work for some time, *Bullets over Broadway* is an unabashed entertainment with few of those troubling speculations on mortality that marked even such gentle exercises as *The Purple Rose of Cairo* and *A Midsummer Night's Sex Comedy.* Fresher and funnier than *Manhattan Murder Mystery,* the film might not provide that much grist for Allen's auteurist constituency, but it's enormously winning.

As a spectacle this is something like a scaled-down version of *The Cotton Club,* with a touch of *Some Like It Hot* in its flipness about gangland. As a backstage comedy. *Bullets* is all about putting on a show. Where recent Allen films have been self-consciously concerned with the textures of film—the expressionist pastiche of *Shadows and Fog,* the *cinema vérité* wobble of *Husbands and Wives—Bullets* largely takes cinema for

granted, concentrating instead on stagecraft. Allen seems to be thinking theatrically these days: he recently directed a television version of his 1966 stage play *Don't Drink the Water*—an unsuccessful venture, by all accounts—as well as contributing a one-acter to a portmanteau off-Broadway show with David Mamet and Elaine May. But here we see a different kind of stagecraft. His cast is required not to underplay, but to let rip with fruity caricature. *Bullets* is peopled with comic ready-mades: Jim Broadbent's old-school British thesp, his gallantry hiding a core of bulimic hysteria; Tracey Ullman's frantically nice fusspot; and Jennifer Tilly's witless flapper, a role she makes work by turning up the screeching volume. It's a telling role, though, demonstrating how radically Allen's approach to acting is at odds with his hero's; Olive ruins the play by being intractably bigger-than-life, Tilly adds to the film by overdoing it.

Acting the part versus being it is the film's central opposition. Pittsburgh boy David yearns to be a New York playwright, but he's not sure what role suits him best. He is as much a fish out of water amid the uptown swank of Helen's world as he is in the boho circle where his mentor Sheldon pontificates about the artist making "his own moral universe". That the film is primarily about performance is exemplified by Dianne Wiest's wildly histrionic turn as the diva who saves her highest ham for offstage, constantly swooning with Sarah Bernhardt hauteur. Her refrain, "No! Don't speak!", gets funnier with further over-use.

There are some more traditional Allen obsessions at work too. *Bullets* is an inversion of *The Purple Rose of Cairo,* in which fiction stepped off the screen and into the real; here the real takes a hand and rewrites imagination. It's a fresh take also on *Amadeus:* an idealistic slogger who believes passionately in his calling is ignominiously upstaged by a hugely talented newcomer who couldn't give a toss for 'art', but can't help being himself.

In presenting Cheech's argument that artists should just "be themselves", Allen is acting out his own attempt to balance the requirements of working in genre against the imperative to be himself. David writes what he thinks is a Broadway play, something stilted and impersonal; Cheech proves that a work should thrive on the idiosyncratic rhythms that an artist can't help producing. Hence, at the end, the film ditches the Broadway stereotypes to round off with a consummate Allen moment—a showdown between thinking lovers, which suddenly sends us straight back to the twitchy, mock-learned disputations of *Shadows and Fog.*

*Bullets over Broadway* therefore engages in a commercial debate about what film should be doing, and whom it should be trying to please. David starts off trying to please the producers, then ends up having to do justice to the demands of art, even if it's someone else's. Cheech may be Mozart to his Salieri, but he's a killer, and becomes most fully evil the minute he becomes inspired by, and possessive of, his own writing. Sheldon, meanwhile, is a man of such integrity that none of his work ever gets produced; his posing is simply a pretext for moral slobbishness, but he's a sorry shadow of Cheech, who horrifically fulfils Sheldon's prescription for the artist forging his own ethical code.

Yet it's tempting to think that once David admits at last, "I'm not an artist", then he may yet get to be a playwright. There is, after all, more ambivalence in Allen's 'happily ever after' than is immediately apparent; this gentle farce may even be softening us up for stronger philosophical fare yet to come.


## David Sterritt (review date 3 November 1995)

SOURCE: Sterritt, David. "Allen's *Mighty Aphrodite* Takes Shallow Look at Love." *Christian Science Monitor* 87, no. 238 (3 November 1995): 12.

[*In the following review of* Mighty Aphrodite, *Sterritt contends that Allen uses the cliché concept of "love conquers all" as a justification for being self-indulgent in his personal life.*]

There he goes again. Woody Allen has long complained that moviegoers draw too many connections between him and the characters he plays.

If he's so peeved about this problem, though, one might ask why he keeps writing this character over and over—the reasonably brainy, moderately nerdy Jewish guy who's such an obsessive New Yorker that not even rocky love affairs (which he endures in film after film) can shake him out of Manhattan.

Allen might answer, as he did when I interviewed him years ago; that his narrow acting range requires an equally narrow assortment of roles. Still, he can't expect audiences to draw clear lines between his on-screen and off-screen personas as long as he patterns important aspects of his characters on traits, mannerisms, and idiosyncrasies that are part of his own personality.

And this is bound to lead to trouble. It did in 1980, when he starred in *Stardust Memories* as a filmmaker who despised his audience. And it's happening this year with his new comedy, *Mighty Aphrodite,* which leaves uncomfortably large openings for moviegoers to draw parallels—however strained or unfair these might be—between his cinematic work and the personal troubles that have made him a tabloid staple in recent years.

Allen plays a sportswriter whose wife talks him into adopting a baby. After a bit of initial terror, he falls goofily in love with the kid, but his affection takes a peculiar turn when he becomes fixated on locating the mother who gave the child up for adoption. She turns out to be a good-natured prostitute whose coarse exterior masks a diamond-in-the-rough inner self.

The plot takes many turns as our hero tries to help the prostitute improve her life, manage his own romantic feelings toward her, and hold his marriage together as he and his wife are both tempted by outside relationships.

Some observers have seized on a minor story point—the prostitute is younger than Allen's character—to accuse Allen of exploiting May-December romance in the wake of his own widely publicized involvement with a much younger woman. I think this is a cheap shot at Allen, given the vast differences between the fanciful screenplay and the facts of his real-life troubles.

Still, it seems clear that parts of *Mighty Aphrodite* are meant as self-justifications. Much of the opening portion shows Allen's character as an excellent adoptive dad, countering public charges that he badly failed in this department. The overall thrust of the narrative is to show him as a bumbling yet good-hearted man who may stumble into temptation but would never allow things to get too far out of hand.

The very title of the movie suggests that romantic attachment—here symbolized by Aphrodite, the Greek goddess of love—is a matter of destiny more than decision, and what's a poor guy to do when his emotions take over?

There's more than a trace of hypocrisy in this, of course. Allen has presented himself for decades as a hip intellectual with a healthy skepticism about bromides and platitudes. So it's hard not to cringe when he relies on an old saw like "love conquers all" to justify self-indulgences on or off the screen.

This aggressively shallow approach to life and love, coupled with a badly condescending attitude toward the story's working-class characters, makes *Mighty Aphrodite* one of Allen's least satisfactory films. This is too bad for the excellent cast, including Mira Sorvino as the prostitute, Helena Bonham Carter as the wife, and F. Murray Abraham as the leader of a Greek chorus that punctuates the action with hilarious commentary.


## Richard Alleva (review date 15 December 1995)

SOURCE: Alleva, Richard. "Two Smooth Characters." *Commonweal* 122, no. 22 (15 December 1995): 17-18.

[*In the following review, Alleva praises Allen's direction in* Mighty Aphrodite, *and finds the device of a modernized Greek chorus in the film to be interesting.*]

In one of his letters to Louis Untermeyer, Robert Frost insisted upon the essential cowardice of comedy, its function being not to confront harsh realities but to elude them with laughter. Comedy lovers like myself who believe that the form confronts truth in its own way may find Frost's notion perverse, but you can at least grasp his point by viewing *Mighty Aphrodite.* For Woody Allen's latest isn't just a comedy but an anti-tragedy. It celebrates the one thing tragedy always destroys: blissful ignorance.

At first, *Aphrodite*'s hero, Lenny (played by Allen), seems a shmuck version of a tragic hero as he pursues the truth regardless of the consequences. An adoring adoptive father, he becomes obsessed with finding the birth-mother of his child, partly for reassurance that there's nothing genetically wrong with the boy but mostly because Lenny feels he will know his son better if he understands the nature of the mother.

But when Linda Ash, a.k.a. Judy Cum, is tracked down, she turns out to be a genetic nightmare. The scion of a long line of idiots and criminals, she's a talentless would-be actress working as a hooker and porn performer. She's dumb and tasteless, feckless about health and morality, and phallically obsessed. (Her living room shows that she raids sex shops the way others do antique stores.) But she's also good-hearted, as emotionally fragile as she is physically robust, and, in her own way, honest. Feeling protective, Lenny attaches himself to Linda without telling her he's adopted her child, and he tries to get her out of the sex business and into a relationship with an equally good-hearted and dumb boxer. He even confronts her furious pimp. But, as his own marriage to an ambitious art galley manager, Amanda, deteriorates, Lenny seems headed for a fling with Linda and the sort of fate meted out to Emile Jannings in *The Blue Angel.* A Greek chorus, magically transported from ancient Greece to Lenny's consciousness, keeps warning our hero to beware, not to go too far, not to know too much. All the usual advice that Greek heroes ignore.

But not to worry. That's what the movie keeps telling us over and over. Not to worry. Lenny doesn't go too far. No one goes too far. When Lenny confronts the pimp, he doesn't dare physical heroics but simply pays off the bully with a season pass to the Knicks. He does sleep with Linda once but is glad to reconcile with his wife, who in turn has fended off an adulterous relationship with a business associate. Lenny never tells Linda that he's adopted her son and, when that one moment of carnality with our hero makes her pregnant, Linda never tells Lenny about it but finds a husband for herself (the boxer having retreated) who will accept her checkered past.

And fate proves benevolent, acting more like a celestial sitcom writer than the harsh taskmaster of the Greeks.

Happy coincidences abound. Lenny is able to bribe the pimp because the latter is a sports fan and our hero just happens to be a sports writer with access to season passes. Amanda decides to revive her marriage precisely on the day when her husband's fidelity is faltering. Linda's happiness drops out of the blue, a literal *deus ex machina.* It's all enough to make any self-respecting Greek chorus consider a career change. Who needs its dire warnings when the universe is so resolutely untragic?

Yet what a superbly slaphappy chorus it is. Its speeches and strophes bring out the old, sly *New Yorker* Woody Allen who once seemed the heir of S. J. Perelman and Robert Benchley. "Ah!" the masked figures intone, sinking to their knees. "Certain things are better left unthunk." And—in an inspired moment of lunacy that rivals the Marshall McLuhan episode in *Annie Hall*—when the chorus members raise their hands to the lord of Olympus and beseech his intervention, they are met with a distinctly modern response.

Less inspired, often pedestrian, is Allen's writing of the realistic passages, what Allen's idol, Ingmar Bergman, called the "dirt of life": marital quarrels, would-be seductions, everyday social encounters. I'm told that everything we hear in Woody Allen films is written by him and never improvised by the actors; yet much of the language might just as well be improvised since it lacks either hilarity or bite. The Lenny-Linda scenes come off best, kept afloat by Allen's confident direction and Mia Sorvino's piquant acting, but even they would have been better with fresher dialogue. The one conversation that contains something truly unexpected is a passage between Linda and her boxer-suitor. Asked to reveal one of his dreams to her, this knucklehead responds with a fantasy about being borne aloft in the talons of a giant hawk and dropped into a field of snow. It's an astonishing moment that believably prefigures how the boy's love of purity will lead him to reject Linda. Allen needs more surprises like this in his writing.

But Allen's overall plotting and his direction of camera and actors are deft. *Mighty Aphrodite* is, on the whole, a diverting testament to the mingy wisdom of keeping your secrets to yourself and sticking your neck out only so far.

### Andy Pawelczak (review date January-February 1996)

SOURCE: Pawelczak, Andy. Review of *Mighty Aphrodite,* by Woody Allen. *Films in Review* 47, nos. 1-2 (January-February 1996): 64-5.

[*In the following review, Pawelczak offers praise for* Mighty Aphrodite, *observing that it successfully integrates older and newer elements of Allen's cinematic oeuvre.*]

The joke begins with the clangy doggerel rhyme in *Mighty Aphrodite*'s title and continues with the Zorba bouzouki music which accompanies the opening credits. Woody Allen's new film is part throwback to the inspired sophomorism of *Bananas* and *Everything You Always Wanted to Know about Sex* and part continuation of the East Side saga of tangled relationships and upscale angst that we're accustomed to from Woody's later films. The good news is that the combination works: the two sides of Woody throw each other into high relief. Aristophanic it's not, but *Mighty Aphrodite* is full of funny literate conceits and uninhibited vulgarity, and Woody himself seems rejuvenated by this resurrection of an earlier self.

Lenny Winerib (Allen) is a sportswriter married to Amanda (Helena Bonham Carter), an ambitious fledgling art dealer too busy to have a child. Against Lenny's better judgment, they adopt (attention voyeurs: this is the only reference to the real-life Woody's problems) and six years later, when the marriage is foundering, Lenny becomes obsessed with finding his son's biological mother. She turns out to be a hooker and porn film actress and the rest of the movie is about Lenny's Pygmalion-like attempt to remake her into a lady and find her a husband.

The film's central scene is Lenny's first meeting with Linda (Mira Sorvino), a towering, dirty-mouthed but sweet-tempered Aphrodite whose apartment is filled with phallic tschokes. When she tells Lenny that her best film was "The Enchanted Pussy," he does a stuttering, embarrassed double take, as did some members of the audience in the Lincoln Plaza Cinema where I saw the picture. The joke here is on Woody's genteel, faintly snobbish persona, and if the lower class sex-goddess Linda is not quite Shaw's life force, by the end she does awaken something dormant in the repressed Lenny.

The picture's other major joke is the use of a campy Greek chorus that comments on the actions at vital moments. In some horrible space/time warp, Woody would be not altogether incapable of putting a chorus on stage for real—remember the Bergmanesque pretensions of *Interiors*—so the chorus here functions partly as an ironic commentary on Woody's own cultural propensities. Dressed in robes and masks and filmed in the ruins of a Greek amphitheater in Sicily, the chorus swings and sways, cries out oracular warnings, and at one point even croons a Cole Porter song. When Lenny decides to search for his son's mother, there's a crack of thunder and the chorus tells him not to be a schmuck. In addition to the chorus, there are also a Jocasta (played by Olympia Dukakis) and Oedipus about whom the chorus remarks that they started a whole new profession. As in Mel Brooks' *History of the World Part One*, the joke consists of the contrast between the archaic, portentous figures and the Borscht Belt wisecracks they utter.

As Lenny, Allen is the familiar neurotic but ineluctably charming denizen of New York's tonier neighborhoods. Lenny's profession of sportswriter makes him into a less rarefied Everyman than the usual Woody character, and it enables Allen to populate the film, as in *Broadway Danny Rose,* with a variety of Damon Runyon types. Helena Bonham Carter as Lenny's wife is a suitable foil to Sorvino's hooker: she's beautiful, cool, and inexorably upwardly mobile. Class is the great repressed in Allen's films, and in this picture it almost breaks through the screen fantasies in the contrast between the working class Sorvino and the WASPish Carter. Sorvino, the daughter of actor Paul Sorvino, dominates every scene she's in. Her alarming habit of talking dirty is rendered even funnier by her high piping voice and appealing innocence.

In the supporting cast, F. Murray Abraham makes periodic appearances as the chorus leader, Jack Warden is a very contemporary Tiresias, and Peter Weller, of *Robocop* and *Naked Lunch,* is a lecherous art dealer with designs on Lenny's wife. Michael Rapaport, who played an oily thug in the recent *Kiss of Death,* deserves special mention as Kevin, a prizefighter who falls for Linda and is so dumb that when Lenny says he feels superfluous Kevin asks if he's sick or something.

*Mighty Aphrodite* reminded me, more strongly than some other recent Allen movies, of where Allen comes from. His is a world where the Freudian demi-urge still reigns, where mothers and whores still bedevil the psyches of tottering, embattled males, and where a well aimed wise-crack can right the balance for at least a moment. In some ways, Allen's closest literary counterpart is Philip Roth. Both men come out of a tradition of Jewish humor, moral probity, and social striving, and both have outlasted their social contexts by reinventing themselves several times over. *Mighty Aphrodite* is a palimpsest of old and new Allen. It made me anxious to see where he will go in his next film, which he was already shooting the week *Aphrodite* opened in New York. Mighty Woody.

### Lizzie Francke (review date 12 April 1996)

SOURCE: Francke, Lizzie. "Woody Allen Can Give a Gal a Good Role." *New Statesman & Society* (12 April 1996): 33.

[*In the following review of* Mighty Aphrodite, *Francke maintains that Allen has written a strong female role in the character of brassy call-girl Linda Ash, played by Mira Sorvino.*]

Woody Allen might be in his autumnal years—and there is something very autumnal about his bark-brown demeanour in *Mighty Aphrodite*—but his latest film seems like something he might have produced when he was greener. It opens in a sun-dried amphitheatre where a Greek chorus—heavily robed and with pale, mugging faces—bemoan the fates of Oedipus, Jocasta and Co, only to turn their attention away from Thebes to Manhattan's Upper East Side, where the actions of one Lenny Weinrib are beginning to worry them a bit. And throughout the film, they are on hand to lend comment either in chunks of cod Sophocles or jaunty bursts of Cole Porter. Now, seeing a Greek chorus (courtesy of Dick Hyman and his orchestra) prance their way through "When You're Smiling" might not appeal to all. It tickled me, but the night I saw the film I was in a ticklish sort of mood where anything vaguely silly would prompt hysterics. Back at the word processor, I now recognise it as a jape that might pall for some. It is the kind of gag one might find in Allen's juvenilia files—but then Allen turns his films around with such mighty gusto that one can hardly blame him for dusting down an old idea. Remember over 20 years back to **Play It Again, Sam**—how the "Humphrey Bogart" was on hand to offer the nervy Allen advice on his love life. In the same way, the leader of the chorus (F Murray Abraham), flowing garb and all, strides incongruously through Manhattan offering occasional counsel—a weird flip in a film that is otherwise visually stylistically modest.

This light conceit with its highbrow leanings (which allows for jokes about what a partypooper that old moaning Cassandra can be), however, rather rattles **Mighty Aphrodite.** For when it comes down to it, the film pits Upper East Side erudition against downtown dumbness. The story follows Lenny (Allen, the familiar angsty persona), a whizz of a sports writer, and his art buyer wife Amanda (Helena Bonham Carter—breaking her fragile mould with a very neat performance as waspish chainsmoker that seems to owe a tad of homage to Mia Farrow), who are considering having a child. Not their own, mind you, for Amanda, who has designs on opening her own gallery, maintains that she couldn't possibly fit it into her schedule right now. So this well-heeled couple acquire a child in the same way that Amanda might get her hands on a rare object—she has a good contact at the right agency. The little bairn might as well have arrived giftwrapped (and one wonders if this is Allen's little dig at the child collector Farrow). Certainly, his parents seem more interested in the boy as a delightful accessory, particularly as young Max seems to be so clever, though he swiftly recedes from the view of the film as it shifts focus on to Lenny and Amanda's growing disaffection for each other.

Soon Lenny is musing as to who might be the real mother of his smart kid. He goes in search, hoping to find some latter-day oracle, only to discover to his horror that the prodigy springs from the loins of Linda Ash, a brassy hooker turned soft-porn star who delights

in the screen moniker of Judy Cum and whose apartment is chock-full with the kind of phallic objects that, had they been in Amanda's gallery, would prompt enthusiasm from the chattering classes, but here just look like cheap kitsch.

In Allen's last film, **Bullets over Broadway,** the playwright hero ended up being artistically aided—and ultimately outwitted—by a seemingly monosyllabic hood. In **Mighty Aphrodite,** there is the same edgy meeting between seemingly high and low lives. For the film pivots on Lenny's need, Professor Higgins-style, to overhaul Linda and turn her into the kind of mother he thinks his son should have and that might include paying off her pugnacious pimp while advising her to take up a respectable profession like hairdressing.

Linda might not prove to outwit him, but with Mira Sorvino in the role, she eclipses all expectations. The actress won her Oscar for best supporting actress on the strength of it. Best supporting actress is apt, for from the moment she appears she promptly carries the entire film, towering over the spindly Allen. In her flower-print capri pants and tight-knit sweaters that keep afloat a capacious bosom, Sorvino plays Linda—"the state of the art fellatrix"—with a touch of Marilyn Monroe or Judy Holliday. Indeed, at one point she is reading from the script of *The Philadelphia Story* to practise for an audition (Linda yearns to be taken seriously as an actress), while we know it is another George Cukor film that she should be considering: *Born Yesterday,* where Holliday plays the broad who gives the wise guys a run for their money. Her voice is helium high, but there's nothing cartoonish about her characterisation. Indeed, like Monroe or Holiday, she brings a pathos to the role that indemnifies it from a patronising stance while at the same time she has wonderful comic delivery. Allen is deft at writing roles for women—if you think back over his *oeuvre*—but more importantly he is shrewd about casting. Sorvino grabs the script and runs off with it, making something substantial out of its lightness. It may be green, but it puts a spring in the step.

## Jill Peláez Baumgaertner (review date 15 May 1996)

SOURCE: Baumgaertner, Jill Peláez. "*Crimes and Misdemeanors*: The Effects of Sin." *Christian Century* 113, no. 17 (15 May 1996): 550-51.

[*In the following review, Baumgaertner asserts that* Crimes and Misdemeanors *explores age-old theological questions regarding virtue, love, truth, sin, and God.*]

I can still feel the punch of Woody Allen's **Crimes and Misdemeanors.** Since the revelation of Allen's personal problems, in particular his liaison with the adopted daughter of Mia Farrow, the film has become for me an even more dramatic statement about the effects of sin, especially in a culture that encourages the deluded belief that humans are innately good creatures, their problems the result only of bad environment or deficient nutrition.

In one of the most dramatic scenes in the film a woman lies dead on her bedroom floor. Her lover, Judah Rosenthal (Martin Landau), a wealthy opthamologist, has arranged her murder and has returned to her apartment to retrieve letters which would reveal their affair. He looks into her open eyes and sits for a moment on the bed until he can compose himself. He knows what he has done. He also knows what he must do: erase from her apartment all signs of their relationship.

At a formal dinner honoring him for his philanthropy, Judah had sat with his family—devoted wife, admiring children, good friends. He had been distracted because just that afternoon he had intercepted a letter written by this former lover, an unstable and emotionally vulnerable woman, telling his wife of the affair.

Torn apart by the threats this woman has made, he also realizes how fragile and how dangerous she is. She has been driven to distraction by his desire to be free of her. When he meets with her, she reminds him of their clandestine moments of passion, their trips together, his gifts to her. Cautiously, he attempts to placate her.

During a family birthday celebration for him, she telephones and threatens to show up at his front door if he does not meet with her. He leaves the party and finds her in the pouring rain at a nearby gas station. The threat to his comfortable family life, the realization of how deeply he has betrayed his wife, his concern about his reputation as a good man, his fear of the power of the woman he has used and tossed away, intensify the claustrophobia of this scene inside the closed car, the relentless rain making the man and the woman an island of fear, betrayal and paralysis.

Judah confesses his problem to his close friend, a rabbi who because of retinal degeneration is losing his sight. Like the classic Greek blind seer, the one who sees the truth in spite of (or maybe because of) his separation from the world of images, the rabbi advises him to confess the affair to his wife.

Instead of confessing to his wife, Judah speaks with his brother, who is connected with the underworld of crime. To the doctor's professed shock, his brother says that there is an easy solution, that he can arrange the murder of the woman, that Judah can now relax and get on with his life.

And it is true. After the murder, his life returns to normal, his family is none the wiser, his practice continues to flourish, he is still honored as a good man. A several-time murderer is caught and sentenced for the crime. The doctor is never implicated.

At the wedding reception for the rabbi's daughter, the rabbi, now completely blind, dances with his daughter. The opthamologist ends up telling a story of a perfect crime (his own although he does not admit it) to another guest, played by Allen. Like the old sailor in "The Rime of the Ancient Mariner," the doctor seems destined to tell and retell the story to all who will hear. Like Coleridge's narrator, however, the doctor will discover that not many are interested. The world continues on its oblivious path, and on the surface at least he appears to have suffered no consequences at all from an act so horrible. Does he consider confession? No. Besides, who would believe him?

The questions this film raises are those that theologians, philosophers and prophets have always grappled with: What is virtue? What is love? What is truth? Where is God? Why do the good suffer? Why do the wicked prosper?

I remember sitting still in the theater after the credits rolled, realizing anew that in a fallen world there are no purely virtuous acts. The doctor was both a decent man and an evil man. It was easy to leap straight to Luther and the accompanying realization that I am both redeemed and sinful. How am I challenged by these contradictions inherent in my identity as a human being, grounded in the fallen world but reaching toward God? What does grace really mean to me? Does it make a difference in the way I live? All of this from a Woody Allen film.

**Christopher J. Knight (essay date 1996)**

SOURCE: Knight, Christopher J. "Woody Allen's *Hannah and Her Sisters*: Domesticity and Its Discontents." *Literature/Film Quarterly* 24, no. 4 (1996): 383-92.

[*In the following essay, Knight examines Allen's representation of domesticity and gendered identity in* Hannah and Her Sisters.]

"[A]ll really inhabited space bears the essence of the notion of home."

—Gaston Bachelard, *The Poetics of Space*

"It seems to me that a man must have faith, or must search for a faith, or his life will be empty, empty. . . . To live and not to know why the cranes fly, why babies are born, why there are stars in the sky. . . . Either you must know why you live, or everything is trivial, not worth a straw."

—Masha, in Anton Chekhov, *Three Sisters*

### THE GENDERING OF DOMESTICITY

In his well received essay, *Home,* Witold Rybczynski charts the history of the concept "home" and its offshoot "domesticity." Respecting the former, Rybczynski argues that home reflects the conflation of a state of consciousness with a physical condition. To this end, he quotes John Lukacs: "as the self-consciousness of medieval people was spare, the interiors of their houses were bare, including the halls of nobles and of kings. The interior furniture of houses appeared together with the interior furniture of minds" (36). A chicken and egg argument, it seems suasive enough, and I find myself accepting of Rybczynski's notion that home—intertwined with other notions such as consciousness, comfort, physical space, sanitation, etc.—is a relatively recent invention, at least as it projects a sense of private space which reaches beyond, even as it includes, family and hearth.

As for domesticity, Rybczynski conceives of it in both historical and gender terms. Particularly, he locates its irruption in the seventeenth-century Netherlands. Here, where favorable intellectual, political, and religious conditions combined with a sudden spurt in prosperity, the home became at once both more intimate and more feminine:

> not only was the house becoming more intimate, it was also, in the process, acquiring a special atmosphere. It was becoming a feminine place, or at least a place under feminine control. Thus control was tangible and real. It resulted in cleanliness, and in enforced rules, but it also introduced something to the house which had not existed before: domesticity.[1]

Part of Rybczynski's own achievement here is that he extols that (i.e., domesticity) which we, in twentieth-century North America, have come to take for granted and to be dismissive of. That is, Rybczynski reminds us of the value of that which we have almost ceased to value, not acknowledging that domesticity is a created value, and not yet ready to grant recognition to that work which remains identified as women's work. The long and short of this is that we are beginning to witness, at the end of the twentieth century, the demise of domesticity, as women, so instrumentally present at its creation, flee its confines for more culturally esteemed realms. Of course, the pity is not that women have sought value elsewhere, but that we—men and women—have yet to find a way to invigorate domesticity with new value. If we cannot reimagine domesticity as anything more than a female ghetto—the sort which left *Little Women*'s Jo March full of "disappointment in not being a boy" (3)—then we should do well to give the matter completely up. The hope remains, however, that domesticity has a future as well as a past.

### PAEAN AND LAMENT

All of this is meant to serve as an introduction to a discussion of ***Hannah and Her Sisters,*** for it seems to me that the Allen film is in many ways a paean to domesticity, even as it both acknowledges and offers evidence to the fact that domesticity is in decline. Certainly, there must be few narratives which foreground so many as three Thanksgiving dinners, as this film does, using the dinners both to open and close the story as well as to mark the passage of time within the story. Yet the dinners serve not simply to mark time. They are there primarily to celebrate a way of life, a way in which a great deal of importance is placed upon the larger family's ritual regathering in the same domestic space: Hannah's apartment. Hannah herself is the presiding grace here. (In Hebrew, the name "Hannah" means grace.) As played by Mia Farrow, she is perhaps too physically frail to be described as an earth mother, yet she is the gravitational force which, or who, holds everyone in orbit. All come to Hannah with their problems and all go away more or less satisfied: the improvident Holly is provided with a cash flow; the insecure Lee is given a role model; the boozy mother is helped back on the wagon; the bewildered father is reassured that he is loved; the wandering husband, like the adopted children, is given a place to call home, etc. Repeatedly, Hannah comes through for others, administering not only to their personal needs but also creating, in her Upper West Side apartment, a magnetic domestic space.

The Upper West Side apartment itself is, in fact, something of a leading character here; and if it is fair to call the film both a paean to, and a lament for, domesticity, it is probably necessary to locate more specifically its cultural matrix. ***Hannah and Her Sisters*** is not simply a New York film, or a Manhattan film though there are scenes placed throughout that borough (or more accurately, throughout the borough's bourgeois districts, for it never ventures, on the West Side, above Columbia University, nor on the East Side, above Mount Sinai Hospital). Rather, it is very much an Upper West Side film, a celebration of a way of life very much intertwined with the type of domestic space available. Of course, living space and human relations are rarely, if ever, separate matters, and the latter is often as much the consequence of the former, as vice versa. And with respect to the Upper West Side, there is the sense that the avenues (i.e., Central Park West, West End, Riverside, etc.) of twelve and fourteen story apartment houses, built during the luxury apartment building boom of the twenties and late thirties, very much molded the lives of their inhabitants.[2]

As originally designed, what was most notable about these apartment houses was both the level of craftsmanship (e.g., exterior stone work, ornamented lobbies, thick plaster walls, parquet flooring, omnipresent molding, etc.) and the capaciousness of the individual apartments, with their twelve foot ceilings and seven or eight rooms. These were apartment houses designed for families, and during the thirties and forties when so many people, particularly Jews, fearing Hitler's promise of a new world order, fled Middle Europe, quite a surprising number settled in these new dwellings.[3] The consequence was that for a series of decades the Upper West Side was synonymous with a kind of urban, middle-class domesticity which, though it was a familiar enough sight in pre- and post-war Europe, had hardly been seen before in the United States. Nor would it survive the middle class' flight to the suburbs which began in the early 1950s and did not abate until the late sixties, when "middle-class family" and "city dwellers" began antithetical terms. In a place such as Manhattan, and more particularly the Upper West Side, middle-class people would continue to reside, yet they would more often be singles, or couples without children, or if they were families, they would have a more than ordinary affluence. (See Robert Young's 1979 film *Rich Kids* about Upper West Side latch key kids.) Nor did the apartments themselves remain unchanged and acco-modating to middle-class families, for a majority of dwellings were subdivided up into smaller units.

By the mid-1980s, the moment of the film, the middle-class families which inhabited the Upper West Side at mid-century were becoming more and more a memory, even as they had made this district identifiable with themselves. It was still possible to see the Mr. Artur Sammler types, with their canes, weaving in and out of the shops on Broadway, or, as in Paul Mazursky's 1974 film *Harry and Tonto,* sunning themselves on the benches of the Broadway median divide. And yet for many a resident these elderly were little more than ei-dolons, deserted by their dead friends and spouses, and by children who had fled if not to the suburbs, then to cities such as Atlanta, Minneapolis, San Francisco, and Seattle.

Still, at this time, not every parent from this generation had passed away nor had every son or daughter left for elsewhere. Hannah's own family is a case in point. Her parents live on Central Park West, and the suggestion is that they have lived there, or in the neighborhood, for years. Their apartment is the family home, the place which Lee contemplates returning to when her relation-ship with Frederick, a SoHo painter, becomes too intolerable. Meanwhile, all three daughters remain in Manhattan (Holly lives downtown, in Chelsea), and Hannah herself, by choice, has inherited the responsibil-ity of making a family space. When we meet her, she is married to Elliot, her second husband, and has four children (through artificial insemination she has had twins fathered by her first husband Mickey's partner Norman, and she has also adopted two children).

Hannah's apartment is spacious and comfortable, and it has every appearance of being a home. That it does so follows not only from Hannah's genuine desire to make it so, but also from her financial good fortune. Though she works sporadically, she has made something of a name for herself as a stage actress, and as such is able to command both good parts and, it would seem, hand-some compensations. Also, in marrying Elliot, a prosperous financial adviser, she makes her economic position all that much more secure. And here economic power is not lightly dismissed. Without a large income, Hannah's domestic project would stand little chance of success; 1980s Manhattan living is a very expensive proposition.

Hannah herself has some rather definite ideas about domesticity. At times, in fact, she seems like the incarnation of another March sister, Meg, who at an early age decided that

> I should like a lovely house, full of all sorts of luxuri-ous things; nice food, pretty clothes, handsome furniture, pleasant people, and heaps of money. I am to be mistress of it, and manage it as I like, with plenty of servants, so I never need work a bit. How should I enjoy it! for I wouldn't be idle, but do good, and make every one love me dearly.
>
> (*Little Women,* 142)

Certainly, there are times when Elliot sees her this way, as for instance when, in a moment of pique, he tells her:

> You know, y-you have some very set plans on how your life should be structured. A-a house, uh, kids, certain schools, a h—, a home in Connecticut. I-it's all very preconceived.[4]

It is all "very . . . preconceived," and we might be tempted to judge Hannah harshly for this reason, or for the reason that the whole plan requires an almost im-moderate amount of money. And yet her motives are not only self-interested; she very much cares for her family—her parents, sisters, children, and husband. As she says to Elliot, in response: "Yeah, but I . . . uh—I thought you needed that. When-when-when we met, you said your life was chaos" (119). And she's right, as Elliot was right, for in a sense they are both right: Han-nah's domesticity can be coercive, though without the structuring it provides, Elliot's life would probably be a mess. That is, more of a mess, for with his philandering with Hannah's younger sister Lee, his life already has too many frayed edges to it. And while he risks being caught in his infidelity, there is also the sense that he takes the risk not because he actually wishes to terminate his marriage but because he is so secure in Hannah's affection that it does not altogether dawn on him that there is a risk. Simply, he takes advantage of Hannah, something that he at first acknowledges—see-ing his infidelity as an act of betrayal—yet to which he hesitates to put an end. And though he persists in the affair, one sees no reason to overthrow his first judg-ment made in the afterglow of his first tryst with Lee:

What passion today with Lee. She's a volcano. It was a totally fulfilling experience. . . . Just as I dreamed it would be. (Nodding slightly as he takes off his slippers) That's what it was. It was like living out a dream . . . a great dream. (Taking off his bathrobe) Now I feel very good and cozy being next to Hannah. There's something very lovely and real about Hannah. (Tossing his bathrobe aside and lying down on the bed next to Hannah, his hand crossed over his stomach) She gives me a very deep feeling of being part of something. She's a wonderful woman . . . and I betrayed her. She came into my empty life and changed it . . . and I paid her back by banging her sister in a hotel room.

(106)

## The Failures of Domesticity

Domesticity is not an ideal, though sometimes, as in *Hannah and Her Sisters,* it seems almost constructed this way. Hannah herself imagines it as something of an ideal, and her imagining has everything to do with what she is able to create. Yet whether it is an ideal or not, it remains a worthy value, capable of offering and nurturing some of our best and most generous impulses. And while in *Hannah and Her Sisters* it is a value that might seem less affirmed than denied—witness the things which afflict various members of the larger family: alcoholism, a cocaine habit, betrayal, divorce, infertility, philandering, etc.—it nevertheless offers itself as a standard by which the characters are judged, and to which they seek to return. That is, throughout the film, domesticity holds itself open as a possibility, and finds itself symbolized by the Thanksgiving reunions: the family—the parents, sisters, spouses, kids, relatives, and friends—gathered around the dinner table, bordered within a stage of intimate space.

But if the values of the home are to be given priority over those of the hotel room, the commitment will have to be more widely shared. One person cannot make domesticity work all by him- or herself, not even Hannah, nor should we want this. Yet throughout the film, we see the efforts on behalf of domesticity repeatedly undermined. Particularly, we find, as Rybczynski noted, that domesticity, even here in the 1980s, remains an emphatically gendered value. Repeatedly, we find the women more supportive than the men of domesticity. They more often speak of the desire for home and family:

HANNAH (to Elliot): "I want one [a child] with you."

(118)

. . . . .

LEE (to Frederick): "I want a husband, maybe even a child before it's too late."

(105)

. . . . .

HOLLY (to Mickey): "I'm pregnant."

(181)

The men, on the other hand, tend more to distance themselves from the same effort:

ELLIOT (to Hannah): "Because it's [a child] the last thing in the world we need right now."

. . . . .

FREDERICK (to Lee): "God! I should have married you years ago when you wanted to! I should have agreed."

(106)

. . . . .

MICKEY (to himself): "Gee, Hannah's sweet. Although, sometimes I still do get angry when I think of things. Oh, what the hell. At least, I'm not paying child support."

(36)

The men also tend to value the women less for their efforts on behalf of domesticity, or for their work in general, than for their beauty. David, the architect, wandering into the kitchen wherein Holly and April (Holly's business partner and friend) are busily preparing food for a large gathering, bluntly tells them: "Listen, you guys are too attractive to be caterers. Something's wrong" (46). Something's wrong, but David would need a mirror to see it. Until then, he'll remain something of a putz. And so will Elliot, the connoisseur of the male gaze:

ELLIOT'S VOICE-OVER: "God, she's beautiful."

(Lee glances over her should, then turns from the doorway and walks away. The camera follows her, moving across a book—and photograph filled bookshelf that obscures her from view as she walks into a crowded, comfortable vestibule. . . .)

ELLIOT'S VOICE-OVER: "She got the prettiest eyes, and she looks so sexy in that sweater."

ELLIOT'S VOICE-OVER: "I just want to be alone with her and hold her and kiss her."

ELLIOT'S VOICE-OVER: ". . . and tell her how much I love her and take care of her. Stop it, you idiot. She's your wife's sister. But I can't help it."

(The camera is still moving with Lee as she smiles and stops to chat with her mother. Elliot's voice, as well as the music ["You Made Me Love You"], continues over the low dim of warm conversation.)

(5-6)

Of course, as I've just suggested, this opening scene wherein both Elliot and the camera appear to leer at Lee, immediately raises the problem of "the male gaze," the now classic feminist formulation for that all too common situation in which the woman comes to stand, in Laura Mulvey's words, as a "signifier for the male other, bound by a symbolic order in which man can live out his fantasies and obsessions through a linguistic command, by imposing them on the silent image of woman still tied to her place as bearer of meaning, not maker of meaning" (7). The question for us is how should we read the camera's rapt attentiveness to Lee here? Does the camera merely say something about Elliot's lustful eye, or does it also say something larger about the way women are constructed in Allen's films? I think the answer is that it suggests both things, though, in fairness to Allen, more the former than the latter. That is, while the film seems to start as if it were an illustration of the male gaze, there are also important ways in which that gaze is deconstructed here. The sisters—Hannah, Lee, and Holly—have their say and carve out their own space. Yet before attending to how they do so, I should like to address a matter which is parallel to that of the male gaze: the Pygmalion motif.

Critics familiar with *Annie Hall* know how insistent can be the Allen hero's desire to mold and shape the heroine. There, one saw a likable enough hero, Alvy Singer, destroy a relationship with an equally likable heroine, Annie Hall, out of an inability to accept her as she was. Constantly judging her in terms of her preferences in books, magazines, mannerisms, diction, friends, etc., he finally gives her no choice but to fly away to Los Angeles, itself a frowned-upon city. The student, in effect, turned the tables on the teacher, judging as she had been judged. Which brings us back to *Hannah and Her Sisters* and particularly to the relationship of Frederick and Lee, for here again we find a man seeking to play Pygmalion to Lee's Galatea.

A successful painter, who seems to command impressive prices for his work, Frederick also uses his position to keep the considerably younger Lee somewhat hostage to his needs. While generally more learned and talented than the others (Lee: "It's such a treat to go through a museum with Frederick. I mean . . . you learn so much" [61]) he has, nevertheless, so positioned himself outside the circle of society that he becomes ensnared in his own aloofness and arrogance. Accordingly, Lee finds herself positioned as his bridge to the outside world (Frederick: "You are, you are my only connection to the world" [105]!), something that she comes to see as too onerous a responsibility: "Oh, God, that's too much responsibility for me. It's not fair!" (105). Yet before the relationship breaks down this way, it had been structured along the lines of teacher to indigent pupil. Frederick reminds Lee: "Well, there was a time . . . when you were very happy to be only with me. You wanted to learn everything about poetry, about music" (25). And when she threatens to move out, he also reminds her who provides for her: "What are you going to use for money" (103)?

Like Annie Hall, Lee leaves a relationship that has grown insidiously coercive, though (again like Annie Hall) freeing herself from one master/pupil relationship does not necessarily mean that she will not fall into the same pattern. As she tells Elliot, the man whom she, more or less, left Frederick for: "I want you to take care of me" (100). And then later, after she frees herself from this even more destructive relationship, she marries her college professor. Whatever the individual merits of this last relationship, it seems a pity that Lee once again finds herself thrust into a position of apparent dependency. Nor is the plight Lee's alone.

The general difficulty amounts to a question of who controls the purse strings. One does not have to be a cynic to acknowledge that money makes things possible, and that money itself is a symbol for power within the community. When one group—men, for instance—controls the money, it also ensures that its interests will be foregrounded. Meanwhile, though Hannah herself has money, a fact which makes all the difference in her general welfare, most of the other women here do not. Rather, Elliot, Frederick, Mickey, David, Doug (the professor) and Dusty (the rock star) control the purse strings; they make things happen. Holly, for example, is only able to get her scripts accepted because of Mickey. Whatever their merit (the suggestion is that they are good), we should be naive if we did not credit Mickey with opening the way toward their acceptance, something he is able to do because of his connections to the television business. Holly herself acknowledges this when she asks for his opinion: "No, the reason why I ask is I think it might make a great, uh, television script, and, you know, you're so active in television, so—" (163).

Mickey seems to be a genuinely good person, and, in his relationship to Holly, does not appear to use his power of the purse to unfair advantage. He feels less threatened than did Frederick, who felt that Lee's youth and beauty gave her an advantage that she would ultimately use against him: "I told you [Lee], one day you would leave me . . . for a younger man" (106). But if Mickey, unlike Frederick, is sympathetic this way, there is one who is his very opposite: David. With the story of David and his wife, the woman who "put him through architecture school" (123), we find ourselves very much in the terrain of the madwoman in the attic. David himself is the arch manipulator, if only evidenced by the way he plays Holly and April off one another, eventually breaking up their friendship. He is also married—to a woman, occasionally institutionalized, who suffers from schizophrenia. With her, he has a college age daughter, and once the daughter goes away to school, his plan is to permanently leave the wife, for he has already "really paid his dues" (123). That emotional obligations should be translated into economic metaphors seems not surprising, given everything we have said about the narrative. And whether he has truly "paid his dues" or not we really do not know, for we do not have enough information about David and his wife. Still, there is a sense in which

David's wife, like Rochester's wife in *Jane Eyre*, haunts the narrative. Hers is the muffled, silenced voice, which if it appears absent and unheard, it also appears present and very much heard. It is the voice which reminds us of just how exploitative male-female relations often are in this society, the voice which leaves us feeling most uneasy about so much that takes place in the film. If she has a kin in the film, it is probably that of the black maid Mavis, whose voice also remains unheard.

## WOMEN AS SUBJECTS

Yet if in *Hannah and Her Sisters* the women often find themselves objectified in familiar ways, this is not the only way that they are positioned. They, too, are subjects, and they disrupt the male gaze as often as they are its object. One sees this in their small acts of rebellion, for example, Holly's refusal to let Mickey identify her with her sisters:

> MICKEY: "I can't understand you. Your sisters, both sisters have such good taste in music. I don't know where you went, went wrong."
>
> HOLLY: (Gesturing) "Do you mind? I'm—I'm my own person."
>
> (113)

Or Lee's similar refusal to play the pupil to Frederick's teacher:

> FREDERICK: "I'm just trying to complete an education I started on you five years ago."
>
> LEE: "I'm not your pupil." (Sighing, her hands at her side) "I was, but I'm not."
>
> (103)

One also sees a disruption of the male gaze in those scenes wherein the sisters are simply left alone, with no Elliot, or Mickey or Frederick to badger them about how remiss they have been about this or that matter. Which is not to say that the sisters are above badgering one another or that they cannot be coercive, short, petty, envious or betraying with one another. They are human and their relations with one another are probably more similar than dissimilar to their relations with the men in their lives. At the same time, there is a difference, a difference which, as I say, comes out in the scenes wherein they are alone together, and perhaps most noticeably in the scene wherein they meet for lunch. For starters the scene is notable for the reason that we feel that as characters within a male author's (Allen's) text, Hannah, Lee, and Holly do not so much speak for him as for themselves. Such examples of independent voices are able, Mikhail Bakhtin tells us, "to break down the monologic unity of the artistic world—but only on condition that the hero, as self-consciousness, is really represented and not merely expressed, that is, does not fuse with the author, does not become the mouthpiece for his voice" (qtd. in Bauer 9).

And the sense that what we have on our hands is less an exercise in monologic closure than dialogic openness finds reinforcement in the extraordinary camera work here. For as the three sisters sit around the circular table, the camera slowly circles around them, sometimes framing one, more often two of the sisters, so that we have a combination of shots that include one sister (Holly) talking and another (Hannah) listening, or two sisters (Lee and Hannah) listening to the third (Holly) who speaks from outside the frame, or one sister (Lee) both listening and not listening as her own private thoughts pull her away, etc. But almost always, as the camera completes more than two full revolutions, what we witness is the simultaneous reciprocation of speaker and listener, the sense that though Holly is, in Lee's words, a bit "manic" (she has just been rejected at an audition), the sisters together evince a sympathetic intimacy which, even as their agendas conflict (Holly wants more money from Hannah; Lee's affair with Elliot is ongoing) and differences get aired, appears almost like a physical bond. And again, perhaps the camera is partly responsible for this, as it encircles them and reinforces the idea that they are grouped, even as it might, in another situation, accent something quite otherwise, as it does in the twice-referred to scene with Frederick and Lee, wherein Frederick (facing the camera) initially talks to the late returning Lee with his back to her, intent upon his sandwich and coffee, and intent upon offering a dissertation upon contemporary society culled from the evidence constituted by an evening's television offering, even as Lee (in the deep background) walks about with her own back to both Frederick and the camera. There is then the sense that, in *Hannah and Her Sisters,* the women, more or less, "assert their otherness not by surrendering, but by forcing their language into the context/contest of the dominant languages" (Bauer 10), by insisting that they be heard.

## MALE ANGST

Meanwhile, if Hannah, Lee, and Holly find themselves pitted against a stubborn patriarchy, Mickey's antagonist appears, perhaps, even more formidable. At least as he imagines it, for Mickey, anxious that his medical tests will confirm his worst fears (i.e. he has a brain tumor), experiences deep existential dread, a dread which is not relieved even when the tests prove negative. As he tells his assistant Gail:

> No, I'm not dying now, but . . . you know, when I ran out of the hospital, I, I was so thrilled because they told me I was going to be all right. And I'm running down the street, and suddenly I stop, 'cause it hit me, all right, so, you know, I'm not going to go today. I'm okay. I'm not going to go tomorrow. . . . But eventually, I'm going to be in that position.
>
> (96)

The end of a narrative reshapes everything which came before. And if the human end, death, be understood as utterly final, wherein no God comes to our rescue, then that sense of things will necessarily undermine the significance of everything which comes before. And this is where Mickey's understanding finds itself after his brush with death. Life for him has been robbed of its purposefulness, or if it has not, then he has to find out how things might be otherwise. So, believing, with Socrates, that "the unexamined life is not worth living," Mickey quits his job, determined to "get some answers" (98).

That the answers prove hard to come by will surprise only the most innocent viewer. Mickey experiments or, better, flirts with philosophy, Catholicism, Krishna, etc., but hardly finds himself nearer an answer. A major problem is that Mickey "want[s] certainty or nothing" (169), a demand which appears rather childish. And because certainty escapes him, Mickey moves to the serious contemplation of suicide, an act which here is comically undermined by a rifle barrel slipping off a perspiring forehead, dislodging a shell or two into the wall and causing general pandemonium. All of which leads Mickey, by way of escape, to a movie house, wherein the Marx Brothers' *Duck Soup* is in progress. And as these things sometimes work out, the movie proves a catalyst, offering Mickey a way to balance life's uncertainty with its possible pleasures:

> And I started to feel how can you even think of killing yourself? I mean, isn't it so stupid? I mean, I-look at all the people up there on the screen. You know, they're real funny, and, what if the worst is true? . . . What if there's no God, and you only go around once and that's it? Well, you know, don't you want to be part of the experience? You know, what the hell, it-i-it's not all a drag . . .

(172)

## GOOD NEWS

In a middle scene, wherein Mickey strolls before Columbia University's Low Library and a replica of Rodin's statue "The Thinker"—and wherein, launched upon his quest for answers, he finds himself frustrated by how far short the wisdom of Socrates ("You know, n-n-n—this guy used to kn-knock off little Greek boys" [109].), Nietzsche, and Freud takes one—he tosses off the comment, "Maybe the poets are right. Maybe love is the only answer" (109). The line is, as I say, buried among other things, jokes included, and my own sense of the film is that while we are not asked to give the line much heed at the time, we are asked to remember that it is there. The point is that the line does help to explain what the values of the larger narrative are. These values, as I have argued, are very much intertwined with domesticity, and domesticity, as I read it, has everything to do with the creation of not simply a comfortable space (its lesser function) but also of a nurturing space (its greater function). And this brings us back to love, for it is only in the context of loving others (or caring about ourselves as we see ourselves mirrored back by others) that we make the kinds of effort which domesticity requires.

Now clearly, Hannah has made the effort that I speak of. We already took note of Elliot's larger statement which includes the lines, "There's something very lovely and real about Hannah. She gives me a very deep feeling of being part of something" (106). That she does so follows from her affection for him, and this is linked with the expectation and hope that the affection and the effort are mutual. But she also senses that they are not, and this leads her to her own feelings of loneliness and dread, to the point wherein she turns one night in bed to Elliot and confesses, "I feel lost" (158). Yet it is also at a point when Elliot, despite his manifold weaknesses of character, has managed to put his transgressions behind him, and is able to sincerely respond, "You're not lost" (159). The suggestion is that Hannah is not lost because another person, Elliot, cares about her, and this makes her a part of something, a something which in itself is more than likely a part of something larger than itself. We complete and confirm one another's existence, and by symbolical or allegorical extension, we complete and confirm the existence of that Which or Who grounds the same. Or at least we hold that something—i.e. God—open as a possibility. "[W]ho knows?" says Mickey, "I mean, you know, maybe there is something. Nobody really knows, I know 'maybe' is a very slim reed to hang your whole life on, but that's the best we have" (172).

In the end, it seems that neither Mickey nor Hannah, neither Elliot nor Holly, is truly lost, for they are each part of a marriage, a family, a past and a future (symbolized by the children and the pregnant Holly), a domestic order of connectiveness which widens further and further. Still, to return to my opening remarks, if this order remains as it has been—an order built upon the backs of the nation's women—it is not only doomed to fail; it also deserves to fail. If, however, this order can garner not only the sympathies but the efforts of both women and men, then it has every chance of succeeding. And here the hope is that the film, directed by a man, presents itself not only as a lament for something passing but also as a commitment to something whose promise resides in the future. Meanwhile, it seems fitting that in the very last scene, when Holly tells Mickey her news, and Mickey bends over to kiss her, this is all synchronized with the punctuating lyric of "I'm in Love Again," which is "Good News!"

*Notes*

1. Rybczynski continues, saying:

To speak of domesticity is to describe a set of felt emotions, not a single attribute. Domesticity has to do with family, intimacy, and a devotion to the home, as well as with a sense of the house as embodying—not only harboring—the sentiments. It was the atmosphere of domesticity that permeated de Witte's and Vermeer's paintings. Not only was the interior a setting for domestic activity—as it had always been—but the rooms, and the objects that they contained, now acquired a life of their own. Thus life was not, of course, autonomous, but existed in the imagination of their owners, and so, paradoxically, homely domesticity depended on the development of a rich interior awareness, an awareness that was a result of the woman's role in the home. If domesticity was, as John Lukacs suggested, one of the principal achievements of the Bourgeois Age, it was, above all, a feminine achievement.

(74-75)

2. On the East Side's Fifth Avenue, a burst of these dozen-story luxury apartments began to rise up after the War, taking advantage of the zoning law which permitted residential buildings to rise to 150'. (Residential hotels could rise higher.) The new construction, however, produced a reaction, led by the Fifth Avenue Association, the City Club, and the Real Estate Board of New York, which caused the height limit on that avenue to be restricted to 75'. This, in turn, produced a counter-reaction, the result of which was that, in 1923, the restriction was set once more at 150'. The consequence of this change was that "[b]y 1931, forty-three new apartment houses had been built, radically transforming the avenue" (Stern 384). Meanwhile, what was happening on Fifth Avenue was also simultaneously happening on Manhattan's other grand avenues, including the Upper West Side's Riverside Avenue, West End Avenue, and Central Park West.

3. Writing in *Commentary* (April 1972) about the "Jewish romance with the American city," particularly New York City, Marshall Sklare argues that

> it is the apartment house that remains the emblem of the Jews' love affair with the city. Wherever Jews have formed an important segment of the urban American population, they have been the prime residents of apartment houses, especially of the so-called "elevator buildings," those bastions of the urban middle class. The phenomenon is best observed in New York City where this type of building has enjoyed its greatest vogue and where the Jewish preference for such housing was less influenced by non-Jewish tastes than elsewhere in the country. The elevator building was designed for people who had moved up from working class and the walk-up building, and who, though financially able to buy a one-family home in the suburbs, chose to remain in the city.

(72)

Sklare paints with a broad brush, as do I. The point I wish to make is simply that like "the great boulevards of Brooklyn, the Bronx, and . . . Queens—Eastern Parkway, Ocean Parkway, the Grand Concourse, and Queens Boulevard" (Sklare 72), the avenues of the Upper West Side attracted a large number of Jewish families, and hence contributed to the sense of the neighborhood as one identified with middle-class domesticity.

4. While I do not wish to confuse the film with its published script, I will, for the sake of convenience, mark quotations from the film with pagination in the latter (*Hannah and Her Sisters*), 119.

*Works Cited*

Allen, Woody. *Hannah and Her Sisters*. New York: Vintage, 1987.

Alcott, Louisa May. *Little Women*. New York: Penguin, 1989.

Bauer, Dale M. *Feminist Dialogics: A Theory of Failed Community*. Albany: State University of New York P, 1988.

Mulvey, Laura. "Visual Pleasure and Narrative Cinema." *Screen* 16. 3 (Autumn 1975).

Rybczynski, Witold. *Home*. New York: Viking, 1986.

Sklare, Marshall. "Jews, Ethnics, and the American City." *Commentary* (April 1972).

Stern, Robert A. M., Gregory Gilmartin, and Thomas Mellins. *New York 1930: Architecture and Urbanism Between the Two World Wars*. New York: Rizzoli, 1987.

**Suzanne Ferriss (essay date 1996)**

SOURCE: Ferriss, Suzanne. "The Other in Woody Allen's *Another Woman*." *Literature/Film Quarterly* 24, no. 4 (1996): 432-38.

[*In the following essay, Ferriss comments on Allen's exploration of personal identity in* Another Woman, *arguing that the filmmaker's underlying view of gender and identity is ultimately conventional, rigid, and simplistic.*]

Following his separation from Mia Farrow, Woody Allen's troubled romantic life came to dominate analyses of his films. Critics in the popular media turned to **Manhattan** to explain Allen's affair with Farrow's adopted daughter Soon-Yi Previn. Many read the more recent **Husbands and Wives** as a *roman à clef,* taking Farrow's turn as a beleaguered wife for a true-to-life portrait of her own discontent with the filmmaker. Allen's tendency to feature himself as the likeable schlemiel, paired with his companion of the moment (including Louise Lasser and Diane Keaton before Farrow), has only encouraged such reductive exercises in film criticism and biography.[1]

Films that do not feature Allen and his current companion, such as *Interiors* and *September,* resist simple biographical readings and, for the most part, have been rejected by popular audiences and reviewers. In fact, by their "seriousness" and Allen's absence, these films appear to offer more sophisticated studies of human relations that challenge tabloid-style readings. Allen's 1988 film, *Another Woman,* is exemplary. The film features a female protagonist (Gena Rowlands), a philosophy professor, who, on the cusp of fifty, experiences an identity crisis that hinges on her sexuality. It was roundly dismissed as too "serious."[2] Without Allen himself (or his current lover) as the central character, the film denied its critics easy biographical access. In fact, they characterized it as Allen's failed attempt to masquerade as Ingmar Bergman, as a denial of his Jewishness, in short, as un-Allen.[3]

The problem of identity, specifically its relation to sexuality, is precisely the film's focus. And, on one level, *Another Woman* does offer a far more complex exploration of the self than Allen's previous films. He uses his considerable cinematic talent to register visually a postmodern vision of the self as fragmented. Drawing on psychoanalytic ideas, the film charts the precariousness of personal identity in a female character, highlighting the specific problematic of femininity. Undergirding this analysis, however, is a rigid and simplistic dichotomy between masculine and feminine. Further, the protagonist's insight into the illusiveness and illusion of selfhood proves only temporary. Her crisis is resolved neatly by the film's end, as she squares her sense of self with that imposed by others, by accepting the "feminine" elements of her nature that she had once denied. Ultimately, the film disappoints, not because it is too serious, sophisticated, or complex, but because it is too simplistic. The film is divided against itself: beneath its cinematically arresting postmodern portrait of the unconscious and its persistent challenge to self-definition lies a rudimentary faith in a unified self and, more significantly, a crude belief in sexual determinacy.

The film's title plays on postmodern notions of the Other as well as the connectedness of sexuality and identity.[4] Reviewing her life at fifty, Marion Poste recognizes simultaneously that she is a woman who radically differs from her self-conception, and that her husband is having an affair with someone else. *Another Woman,* then, bears the trace of the clichéd term, "the other woman." As a result, at least part of Marion's self-recognition depends on accepting that she herself has been "the other woman" in this simple sense: Marion's relationship with her cardiologist husband, Ken (Ian Holm), began while he was still married to Kathy (Betty Buckley). Her estranged best friend, the actress Claire (Sandy Dennis), further accuses Marion of having tried to seduce Claire's boyfriend, David, in their youth, and charges that she has been flirting with Claire's current husband, Jack (Jacques Levy). Claire's accusations cause Marion to reevaluate her sexual relations. She asks Ken, for instance, "Did I seduce you away from your wife?" Questions about sexual deception are tied to self-deception.

In its confluence of sexuality and identity, the film allies itself with psychoanalysis.[5] I do not mean by this link to refer to the controversial and overused analogy between the cinematic apparatus and the psychoanalytic concept of the "male gaze."[6] Instead, the tie is far simpler here: the film itself stages the psychoanalytic scene. Marion overhears psychiatric sessions that initiate probing of her own psyche. Allen's film explores, as does psychoanalysis, how the unconscious challenges any sense we may have of a fixed, stable sense of self, in particular, our identity as man or woman. Jacqueline Rose explains:

> Freud's writing shows that sexual difference is . . . a hesitant and imperfect construction. Men and women take up positions of symbolic and polarised opposition against the grain of a multifarious and bisexual disposition. . . . The lines of that division are fragile in exact proportion to the rigid insistence with which our culture lays them down; they constantly converge and threaten to coalesce.
>
> (226-27)

Jacques Lacan, extending Freud's insights, argues that this division is enjoined on us by the symbolic, the structuring order of language and law. Juliet Mitchell argues that the goal of psychoanalysis is to reveal the illusory nature of this order:

> the analysand's unconscious reveals a fragmented subject of shifting and uncertain sexual identity. To be human is to be subjected to a law which decenters and divides: sexuality is created in a division, the subject is split; but an ideological world conceals this from the conscious subject who is supposed to feel whole and certain of a sexual identity. Psychoanalysis should aim at a destruction of this concealment and at a reconstruction of the subject's construction in all its splits.
>
> (26)

The unconscious, which according to Lacan is "structured in the most radical way like a language" (234), serves as a constant reminder within the psyche of the fragility of the symbolic order and exposes the fantasy of identity. While *Another Woman* stages a crisis of identity and pressures exerted by the unconscious, it ironically entrenches, rather than disturbs, the psychosocial lines of division between the sexes.

The film establishes this Lacanian division between the symbolic and the unconscious in the characters of Marion and Hope (Mia Farrow), equating the symbolic order with stereotypically masculine qualities—reason, ambition, and predatory sexuality—and the unconscious with equally stereotypically feminine qualities—emotion, maternity, and passivity. The wall separating Marion's office from the psychiatrist's marks the line dividing the two realms.

As a philosophy professor struggling to write a new book, Marion is engaged in a supremely rational pursuit. Furthermore, the film presents her pursuit of a career in philosophy as at once the source of her identity—she introduces herself in the voice-over narrative as "Marion Poste, director of undergraduate studies in philosophy at a women's college"—and as a "masculine" pursuit. Marion's professional choice allies her with her father (John Houseman), a historian, as opposed to her mother, for whom "nature, music and poetry" were her "whole existence." Marion at one time painted, like her artistic mother, but succumbed to her father's criticism that she could be someone if she would just stop daydreaming in the woods and doing watercolors. In heeding her father, she distances herself from her brother, Paul (Harris Yulin), whose writing she dismisses as "too emotional" and "embarrassing."

We further learn that she chose philosophy initially under the sway of identification with her first husband, the philosopher Sam (Philip Bosco), and that the demands of establishing herself as his equal, or even successor, in the field led her to reject being pregnant. Her first husband claimed that she made the decision to abort autocratically, incredulous that she could have been "capable of such a lack of feeling." His charge underscores her alliance with her father, who hopes to "build up an immunity" to love. Larry Lewis (Gene Hackman) similarly claims that her love for Ken is "all up here," gesturing to his head, that they are "two of a kind." The film highlights a pattern of professional egocentrism and emotional self-denial in Marion that she gradually acknowledges by identifying herself with Hope.

Hope's outpourings, which Marion overhears from her newly rented apartment, disturb her "life of the mind." In her emotionalism and extravagantly pregnant state, Hope appears as an obvious inverse of the "masculine" Marion. She gives vent to her sexual frustration, freely displays her sense of desperation and loneliness, and reveals her passivity in the face of her deteriorating marriage. In her encounters with the psychiatrist, Hope becomes aware of herself as Other. As their encounter in the liminal space between dream and wakefulness, between the professor's study and the psychiatrist's couch, indicates, Hope further serves as Marion's other. She stands simultaneously for everything that Marion has defined herself against and as the one person who can satisfy her desire for wholeness within herself.

The film presents the workings of the unconscious as the breaking down of the wall separating the two women, from themselves and from each other. The scenes in Marion's office become exercises in crossing borders, between her suite and the psychiatrist's, between sleep and wakefulness, between dream and philosophy. In the first scenes in her leased suite, Marion explains in her voiced-over narration that she is experiencing difficulty with her new book. As a release from the fatigue her struggle with writing produces, Marion finds herself taking uncharacteristic naps. She slips from the pressing demands of rationality, of philosophic argument, to the playground of unconscious desire, dreams. Through sleep, she further gains entrée to Hope's confessions in the psychoanalytic session.

As the receiver, albeit indirect, of Hope's outpourings, Marion steps into the analyst's role. In so doing, she complicates the workings of transference in the psychoanalytic session. The transference from analysand to analyst is bifurcated and deflected onto the unacknowledged listener, a process that brings with it a concomitantly complex effect: the transference between Hope and Marion doubles itself. Marion moves from simply commiserating with Hope in her suffering, to participating in it, and, finally, to reversing the direction of confession. This process is accompanied by a series of shifts in emotional reaction: from an initial desire to shut herself off from the voices of the patient and her analyst for fear of committing the aural equivalent of voyeurism, of transgressing the bounds of privacy, to a seemingly inexplicable identification with the young patient and need to participate in her recovery (a compulsion that leads Marion to initiate an "accidental" meeting outside the bounds of the two offices). That these shifts in emotion remain largely indecipherable to Marion is an index of the extent to which the unconscious is registering its effects: she cannot make sense of them in rational or symbolic terms.

Marion's immediate response on identifying the disembodied voices that fill her room on the first day of her work is to block the duct opening by which they are carried. Significantly, she initially overhears the "intimate revelations" of a man recounting his affair with another man. Her move to reinforce the wall mirrors her continuing investment in the edifice of the symbolic against the sexual disturbance of the unconscious. The chink in the wall that results when the pillow blocking the opening falls, notably during one of Marion's lapses into sleep, indicates that the unconscious has begun to seep through the edifice of rationality she has erected. Once the pillow has fallen, releasing a female voice this time, Marion finds herself unwilling or unable to replace it. This initial release from the law of the symbolic, the twin repressive urges of rationality (her desire for silence in which to pursue her philosophic project) and morality (her sense that eavesdropping should be prohibited) engenders an escalating play of the unconscious in the form of dreams. Hope's confessions spark a series of flashbacks and imaginings that trace the connections between the plights of the two women: Marion hears Hope speak of a dream so full of "deceptions" that she no longer knew who she was and her husband seemed a stranger. In later sessions, Hope expresses doubts about her marriage and reveals that she has had an affair with another man. The film charts their gradual identification not only through these obvious narrative links but spatially as Marion moves closer and closer to the opening, from removing the pillows entirely so she can hear Hope from her desk across the room, to sitting immediately before it, to dreaming of entering it.

When Marion entirely circumvents the wall, her action brings about the crisis of the film, a moment of recognition that shatters her self-image. Marion's surreptitious pursuit of Hope leads increasingly toward her recognition of the Other within herself. While following Hope home, she encounters her estranged friend, Claire, a meeting that later propels the most shocking, self-revelatory of her dreams: Marion is forced to watch the "drama" of her failing marriage to her second-husband, the cardiologist Ken, and her loss of Larry Lewis. Later, facing each other across the table at lunch, countertransference occurs as Marion replaces Hope as analysand by incessantly talking of herself under the influence of wine. This substitution, this recognition of herself in the other woman, as the other woman, coincides with the equally shocking revelation of her husband's relations with her best friend. The twinned pairings in the restaurant spatially echo Marion's dual recognition of the "other" woman, her husband's lover and herself.

The film highlights the split within Marion cinematically as a disjunction between the aural and the visual, between her voiced-over comments and abstract visual images. Her first-person voice-over—a linear narrative of events—belongs to the symbolic realm and is akin to her philosophic writing. Not surprisingly, Marion's musings are often highly literary. Critics have complained that Allen's dialogue is too "self-consciously 'literary,'" that his character's references to Rilke are self-indulgent displays of Allen's own erudition (Ansen 72). Such excesses, evident not only in Marion's voice-over but in the comments of her husband and friends, reveal their overwhelming attachment to the rational, an almost parodic investment in the symbolic. Ken's comment—"I accept your condemnation"—voiced twice, once to his ex-wife when she intrudes on the celebration of his upcoming marriage to Marion and again when Marion asks why he no longer sleeps with her—is later ridiculed by Larry Lewis as evidence of Ken's priggishness.

This highly self-conscious layer of language contrasts with an equally self-conscious visual one. Intruding on her first-person voice-over, just as Hope's words disturb

her writing, is a cinematic point of view allied with the unconscious. Marion's words are countered by her dreams, dreams that become increasingly non-mimetic. The first dreams are flashbacks, simply memories of childhood, her family's insistence on her education and her brother's resentment, progressing to her more immediate past, her relationship with her first husband, her abortion, and so on. But as the unconscious exerts increasing pressure on her conscious mind, her dreams become far less mimetic, culminating in a vision that displays the workings of dramatic creation. The staged scene dramatizing her love for Larry Lewis raises her dreams to the same level of self-reflexivity as her language, though here in reference to the visual arts. Abrupt cuts from scene to scene simultaneously defy the conventions of narrative and philosophic investigation and trace the workings of the unconscious.

The film creates significance not chronologically but accretively, by linking the threads of seemingly discontinuous segments through juxtaposition of repeated elements that mimic the associative qualities of dreams and other outlets for the unconscious. For example, Hope's revelation to her psychiatrist that there had once been "another man" in her life is followed by Marion's remembrance of the moment when the other man in *her* life tried to dissuade her from going through with her marriage to Ken. Marion's flashback to her childhood friend, Claire, prefigures their accidental meeting in the next scene. The scene in which Marion overhears her stepdaughter's charge that Marion is too judgmental, especially with respect to her brother, is followed by a scene in which he reminds Marion that she once told him his writing was too emotional, embarrassing, effectively quashing his ambitions.

The film's layering of scene upon scene in this manner mirrors the growth of the fissure within Marion. The most self-reflexive moments in the film, the acts of the drama-within-the-film, dovetail with Marion's psychic exploration: Marion's dreamed confrontation between Claire (portraying Marion) and Ken comes to fruition in the later scene in which Marion questions why they never spend time alone anymore. The disjunctive scenes recording Marion's climactic recognition most dramatically exploit this technique: Marion's wistful revelation to Hope at lunch, "Maybe it would be nice to have a child," sparks her recollection of arguing violently with Sam following her abortion. A cut takes us not back to the restaurant, but to Hope's account of their lunch in her session later that afternoon. Through the duct Marion hears Hope describe her: "She can't allow herself to feel. . . . She's pretended for so long everything is fine, but you can see clearly how lost she is." The revelation that Marion glimpsed her husband in a tête-à-tête with her best friend comes from her alter-ego and ushers in Marion's acknowledgment: the film flashes back to capture Marion's shocked, but guarded, reaction and forward again to record her anguished reaction.

In its most disjunctive, most cinematically self-reflexive moments, Allen's film introduces a series of stark images in quick succession: a panther pacing in its cage, a white mask against rain-covered pavement, and Klimt's painting of a pregnant woman, all allied with the unconscious and the feminine qualities Marion has denied. The panther evokes her earlier reading of Rilke: she revealed that his image of the panther staring out from its cage suggested death to her but then remembered that her mother's favorite poem, "Archaic Torso of Apollo," holds forth a contrary threat: "You must change your life." Both the mask and the Klimt painting suggest Marion's potential for fecundity. She had given the mask, from "La Giaconda," to her first husband, Sam, at a moment of great passion in their relationship, that is, before her abortion. Klimt's exaggerated portrait of pregnancy, "Hope," offers not only a condemnation of Marion for denying herself this experience but a reminder of her own painterly aspirations, similarly cast aside in pursuance of her "life of the mind."

The disjunctive elements representative of the unconscious can too easily be recuperated and shown to uphold a simplistic dichotomy between femininity and masculinity, between motherhood and career, between emotion and rationality, between art and philosophy. Marion resolves her crisis by accepting the "feminine" that was originally within herself. She cries, releasing her emotions. She voices her wish to have a child. But if, as characters repeatedly charge, she has been deluding herself by choosing the "masculine" pursuit of philosophy, by living out a predatory sexuality, by not having a child, her recognition of her feminine nature is itself an illusion. This can be seen in the climactic meeting that ushers in this newfound self-awareness. The meeting takes place in an emotional, maternal space: Marion and Hope meet in a "that great store" where she had purchased the mask from "La Giaconda" before she aborted Sam's child. She encounters Hope crying before the Klimt painting, which takes us back to earlier remembrances of Marion's own emotional, artistic mother whose tears spot the pages of Rilke. Marion recognizes herself in the excessively pregnant Hope as she faces the excessively pregnant "Hope," suggesting that she takes the painted image as the true image of herself: the promise or potential that she once had and to which she now returns: "Maybe it would be nice to have a child."

Allen's cinematic inscription of postmodern fragmentation challenges the audience to interpret the film aesthetically, to see meaning not simply in Marion's narrative but in the tension between the voice-over and the disjointed, self-consciously visual images. Marion's own reading of the aesthetic works undermines this lesson, however. For rather than accepting that she herself is split—between art and philosophy, masculine and feminine, self and Other—she embraces the dimension she has denied, accepting it as the "true" Marion. She disavows Otherness in herself, taking the other as herself: "Hope," the imagined rendering of promise and possibility is reduced to Hope, the pregnant woman, and finally equated with Marion's own need to have a child. "Hope" = Hope = motherhood. The same reductive logic obtains in Marion's interpretation of the mask. The mask can be taken as an image of Otherness: putting on the mask, Marion becomes something other than herself. It is also associated with masquerade, with acting, and, therefore, with the dramas of Marion's dreams that reveal her false image of herself. Rather than accepting the mask as an indicator of the illusory nature of identity, Marion equates it with Sam, with an earlier, pre-abortion, pre-philosophy, in short, presymbolic self. She takes refuge in an imaginary identification of herself with a pure self.

The film's ending only underscores the illusory nature of her new self-image. In the final scene, Marion turns to Larry Lewis's novel, reading about Helenka, the fictional character he claims he based on her. Her reading sparks a final flashback—purely mimetic, cinematically—in which she becomes the character in Larry's novel, fusing the fictional account with her memory of a walk with Larry, suddenly interrupted by a storm. Seeking shelter in a tunnel, Marion/Helenka and Larry share a kiss. Larry recounts that hers was "full of desire" but that "a wall went up and just as quickly I was screened out." He asserts, however, that she could be "capable of intense passion if she would one day just allow herself to feel." Taking herself as Helenka means believing that she has dismantled the "wall" preventing her from admitting her feminine desire.

The wall, however, remains. Marion once again reinforces the wall between her office and the psychiatrist's, belatedly informing him of the acoustic anomaly. At the same time she discovers Hope has ended her treatment, which is wholly appropriate if, as Marion believes, she is Hope/"Hope." She further reports that she is working well. Thus, she has resurrected the edifice of the symbolic. The only difference is that she now lines herself up on the feminine, as opposed to the masculine, side of the divide it enforces.

Marion closes the film with the words, "For the first time in a long time I felt at peace." Her sense of certainty and selfhood is the ultimate fantasy, an illusion the film itself upholds. Its narrative closure reduces the cinematically arresting images to temporary anomalies that disappear, along with Hope, once Marion has worked out her crisis. The tension between the aural and visual similarly appears to be a crisis requiring resolution rather than a sophisticated representation of postmodern identity. Hope's disruptive outpourings, which are heard but not seen, are blotted out as the visual level of the film is subsumed by the symbolic. Mia Farrow's convenient exit from the film means that it offers a reassuring and decidedly existentialist vision of the self as easily understood and within our control. Unfortunately for Woody Allen, this obtains only in the cinematic world of image and illusion.

### Notes

I would like to thank Steven Alford, Shari Benstock, and Ben Mulvey for their generous comments and suggestions on drafts of this essay.

1. For a critical analysis of such pairings, see Feldstein.

2. Reviews of *Another Woman* persist in setting up a dichotomy between the "funny" and "serious" Allen, a division that overlaps with a racist division between a Jewish and Waspish Allen. See Ansen, Denby, Kael, Kauffman, and Schickel. Schickel dismisses the film as Allen's pretention to "Bergmanesque seriousness" (70), while Kael moans, "If he could just stop dichotomizing himself between 'funny' Allen and 'serious' Allen" (83)!

3. Both Pauline Kael and David Ansen equate Allen's comedic talent with his Jewishness, and his serious bent with an inauthentic Waspishness. Ansen asks, "What does it mean (and what does it say about Allen) that his comedies are fundamentally Jewish, and his tragedies Gentile? . . . 'Wild Strawberries' is one thing; 'Wild Matzos' another" (72).

4. Shari Benstock argues that we should distinguish between the psychoanalytic notion of the Other and "existentialist notions of otherness, which presume an externality to difference and a complementarity of the sexes. . . . Lacan distinguishes between the Other, which structures subjectivity from its place in the unconscious, and other (lowercase *o*), which refers to objects and people through whom the subject tries to establish a relation of complementarity as a guarantee of identity" (10). In short, the Other stands for radical alterity within the psyche, and the other for the fantasy that another can fulfill one's desire for a unified self.

5. Others have commented on Allen's immersion in psychoanalysis on-screen and off. See Morris and Schapiro.

6. See Mulvey, Doane, Kaplan, Kuhn, and de Lauretis.

### Works Cited

Ansen, David. "A Serious Step Forward." *Newsweek* 24 October 1988: 72-73.

Benstock, Shari. *Textualizing the Feminine: On the Limits of Genre.* Norman: U of Oklahoma P, 1991.

de Lauretis, Teresa. *Alice Doesn't: Feminism, Semiotics and Cinema.* Bloomington: Indiana UP, 1984.

———. *Technologies of Gender: Essays on Theory, Film and Fiction.* Bloomington: Indiana UP, 1987.

Denby, David. "A Tale of Two Cities." *New York* 24 October 1988: 113-16.

Doane, Mary Ann. *The Desire to Desire: The Woman's Film of the 1940s.* Bloomington: Indiana UP, 1987.

Feldstein, Richard. "Displaced Feminine Representation in Woody Allen's Cinema." *Discontented Discourses: Feminism/Textual Intervention/Psychoanalysis.* Ed. Marleen S. Barr and Richard Feldstein. Urbana: U of Illinois P, 1989.

Kael, Pauline. "What's Wrong with This Picture?" *The New Yorker* 31 October 1988: 81-83.

Kaplan, E. Ann. *Women and Film: Both Sides of the Camera.* New York: Methuen, 1983.

Kauffmann, Stanley. "Double Meanings." *The New Republic* 21 November 1988: 30-31.

Kuhn, Annette. *The Power of the Image: Essays in Representation and Sexuality.* London: Routledge & Kegan Paul, 1985.

Lacan, Jacques. *Écrits.* Trans. Alan Sheridan. New York: Norton, 1977.

Mitchell, Juliet. Introduction I. *Feminine Sexuality: Jacques Lacan and the École Freudienne.* Ed. Juliet Mitchell and Jacqueline Rose. New York: Norton, 1977.

Morris, C. "Woody Allen's Comic Irony." *Literature/Film Quarterly* 15 (Fall 1987): 175-180.

Mulvey, Laura. "Visual Pleasure and Narrative Cinema." *Screen* 16 (Autumn 1975): 6-18.

Rose, Jacqueline. *Sexuality in the Field of Vision.* London: Verso, 1986.

Schapiro, Barbara. "Woody Allen's Search for Self." *Journal of Popular Culture* 19 (Spring 1986): 47-62.

Schickel, Richard. "Other Voices, Other Rooms." *Time* 17 October 1988: 70-71.

### Stanley Kauffmann (review date 11 November 1996)

SOURCE: Kauffmann, Stanley. "The Food of Love." *New Republic,* no. 4269 (11 November 1996): 40-1.

[*In the following review, Kauffmann finds that the songs from old Broadway and Hollywood musicals in* Everyone Says I Love You, *while dated, maintain a lasting appeal for young contemporary audiences.*]

Woody Allen's new film has charm. (I had to re-read that sentence. Yes, it's true.) *Everyone Says I Love You* is warm from its first moment, and, almost all the time thereafter, it glows. Why the difference from his past films? Look at this glittering roster of collaborators: Bert Kalmar and Harry Ruby, Walter Donaldson and Gus Kahn, Ray Henderson and Lew Brown and B. G. DeSylva, Richard Rodgers and Lorenz Hart, Cole Porter . . . others. They are some of the ace songwriters of the 1930s. Allen's new film is a musical, not with new songs but rich, very rich, with old ones. To cap it, Allen's music director was Dick Hyman, whose arrangements are the best kind of Broadway pulsing and caressing. And right alongside Hyman's scoring is the choreography of Graciela Daniele, brisk, electric dance of the 1930s.

Let's not shortchange Allen's own contribution—besides originating the idea. Allen's directing career is a prime instance of on-the-job training: he began directing before he really knew how, but now he's so at ease that his films seem to have been born the way they are. The maker's hand is almost invisible.

Here's the beginning of this picture. The first shot looks streetward through one of the fountains in front of the Metropolitan Museum at a young couple. First reaction: this is going to be another one of Allen's odes to the New York that he loves. True, but there's something else: he has to establish that this is a musical. He does it just by *doing* it. The Boy turns to the Girl and, instead of speaking, he starts to sing "Just You, Just Me." Right there in broad daylight on Fifth Avenue. It's Edward Norton singing, and it's Drew Barrymore responding. No dubbing of vocalists. (One of Allen's happiest ideas. All the principals do their own singing, which makes the songs pleasant enough and—forgive the term—more real.)

The song continues. We move along the street. A black nurse and her aged white charge sing a couple of lines. Then a panhandler. Norton and Barrymore stroll past a high-fashion shop; three mannequins in the window dance to the tune . . . and so on. Ernst Lubitsch, thou should'st be living at this hour. Allen is a bright disciple.

When Norton goes to Harry Winston to buy an engagement ring, the salesman shows him some expensive ones. Norton suddenly bursts into song, telling us "My baby don't care for rings / Or other expensive things. / My baby just cares for me." The salesman joins him, as do other customers, along with some slick tap dancers from God knows where. (Graciela Daniele knows, too.) Norton then buys a ring, which gets interestingly lost.

And that's how the film goes, suddenly blossoming from time to time into song and dance, sometimes frenetic, sometimes poignant, always enjoyable. There

are songs from Maurice Chevalier pictures and from Marx Brothers pictures. The film's title comes from a Marx Brothers number. The last sequence is a party in Paris at which everyone, male and female, wears a Groucho get-up, and we get "Hooray for Captain Spalding" in French.

This brings us to the story, or stories. They matter less than in most musicals. There's a glitch in the Boy-Girl relationship because of her brief excursion with a paroled convict brought into her life by her do-good mother, Goldie Hawn. (Who is also responsible for a surprise appearance of Itzhak Perlman and daughter.) Hawn's ex-husband is Allen, father of a daughter. Her present husband is Alan Alda, who brought along children of his own—including a politically conservative son who shocks his liberal father. (Ultimately the son is cured of his conservatism by surgery.) Also involved is an art historian played by Julia Roberts. (She sings "I'm a Dreamer, Aren't We All?") The plots exist only to provide rifts and reconciliations and changes of locale. Allen does plenty of New York adoration, but he also gives himself the chance to enjoy Venice and Paris. (He and Hawn do a dance on a Seine embankment that has some spiffy novelties.)

All the principals of the piece, except one, keep the film flying high—especially Hawn. Now that she has abandoned her giggling "Laugh-in" persona, she has become a sturdy comedienne. The exception is Allen himself. The trouble isn't that he's always the same—Alan Alda, for instance, is always the same—but Allen's sameness is uninviting; and it's dissonant. In his own ebullient picture, full of high spirits and high dudgeons, he snivels.

His performance doesn't even create self-parody. At one point in the picture, Julia Roberts has, for sufficient plot reasons, gone to bed with Allen and is in a semi-daze after his magnificent lovemaking. With a real comedian—say Robin Williams or Dustin Hoffman—this moment might be funny, a gorgeous woman reeling from an encounter with a shrimp. Here, however, all we can think of is that Allen, as director, is using his power to build himself up as a man.

Of course *Everyone* doesn't really take place in the three cities of its settings, least so in New York. Musically, for instance. The whole cast knows and sings these golden oldies. We keep wondering about this, especially with the younger ones. Where's the rock, the rap? One brief scene in a disco gives us a funny slice of a rap singer's version of one of the oldies, but rap is there just to be put down vis-à-vis the "straight" oldies. Otherwise, all these characters exist in a rockless, rapless world. And virtually everyone in the picture is well-off. A musical doesn't have to plumb social strata: money is an enablement for plot freedom. But this vision of Manhattan society has the same relation to the facts as Allen's carefully selected views of Manhattan's loveliness.

What's most curious in Allen is his nostalgia. He keeps trying to remake New York into what he imagines it was like about the time that he was born (1935), with music drawn from the Broadway and Hollywood hits of that decade. *Radio Days* was an overt attempt to go back there; *Bullets over Broadway* was a grab at Damon Runyon. Through many of Allen's films, despite their freight of topical reference, there's a hint that things used to be better, especially the music. (Remember how Gershwin on the sound track supported the up-to-date *Manhattan.*) Allen, full of postwar frankness about neuroses, yearns for what he feels was a pre-war Eden.

How will these old songs fare today? At Joseph Papp's production of *The Pirates of Penzance* in 1980 I was surrounded by young people who had clearly never heard a word or note of Gilbert and Sullivan and were there chiefly (they said) because Linda Ronstadt was in the cast. As the performance rolled on, I could see how they were being captivated by the piece. As they listened to the old, they were discovering, delighting in, something new. Maybe all those unfortunates who were born after World War Two will respond the same way to Allen's picture, to the Lubitsch *légèreté,* to those delectable old romantic songs. The opening line of *Twelfth Night*: "If music be the food of love, play on." What do you mean "if"?

## Bonnie Churchill (review date 24 January 1997)

SOURCE: Churchill, Bonnie. "Woody Allen's Musical Sings with Spontaneity." *Christian Science Monitor* 89, no. 41 (24 January 1997): 12.

[*In the following review, Churchill comments on the creation of* Everyone Says I Love You, *explaining how actors were signed to the film unaware that it was to be a musical.*]

Woody Allen, who is surprisingly shy in person, usually offers comments with the same ease as prying open an oyster shell. Not this time. When asked about his current film, *Everyone Says I Love You,* and his bold decision to ask actors in the musical (his first) to sing their own songs, he responds confidently.

"I didn't want slickly trained voices that hit the notes but not emotions," he says. "When I was a kid, I loved Jimmy Durante. It didn't matter to me if he croaked out the lyrics; he gave me feelings, not just words."

He continues: "I want people, particularly young people, to know there's a wonderful American heritage of Tin Pan Alley and Broadway songs."

Allen didn't tell co-stars Julia Roberts, Alan Alda, Goldie Hawn, Drew Barrymore, Tim Roth, or Edward Norton it was a musical until two weeks after they'd signed on. The surprise element is part of working for Allen. His actors never get the script in advance, they seldom know the name of the movie until it's ready for release, and he doesn't believe in rehearsals. "I prefer spontaneity," he says.

In *Everyone Says I Love You,* actors were given only the pages that included their dialogue. The one exception was Natasha Lyonne, the young Broadway actress who plays Allen's teenage daughter. She narrates the movie, so she had to see the completed script.

To reluctant actors, Allen said, "I'm singing, and if I can do it, anyone can." He adds, "I did have mercy on the audience, and only sang half a song."

Working for Allen has its compensations. Actors don't have to stick to a script; they can make up their own dialogue and even offer suggestions. And every Allen movie is conveniently shot in New York. (Most scenes for *Everyone Says I Love You* were filmed in the Big Apple, but it also includes scenes from his other favorite cities, Venice and Paris.)

Barrymore, who has seen each one of Allen's films "at least four times," is the only cast member who didn't sing—even after she'd heard Woody warble. As for working with him, Barrymore says, "If he doesn't say anything to you, it means you're doing OK. If he doesn't like what you're doing, without raising his voice, he offers suggestions."

Ed Norton plays Barrymore's love interest. "Ed had never sung or danced professionally," Allen says. "He just got with it and didn't mind at all." The filmmaker gave Norton this pep talk: "I remember as a kid watching my mom and dad in the living room dancing to the phonograph. They weren't Rogers and Astaire, but they just loved being together. That was the feeling I want for the movie."

Allen had a different problem with Goldie Hawn. "I knew her as a very funny actress," he began, "but I'd never met her. So when she started to sing and dance, she was a professional. Finally, I had to tell her, 'Can you sing a little less?'"

Allen selected all the songs from his own record collection. "I'd listen over and over, obsess over each decision, and finally decide I'd picked the right song for the right situation."

How does he test a film? "When it's completed, I get my sister [Letty Aronson] and a friend or two to come over. Letty is usually an executive producer on my movies. She's so honest, she'll say, 'I was bored stiff, I loved this, hated that.' I take it back to the editing room and obsess some more."

Allen is a walking encyclopedia of music and comedy. He'd rather play the clarinet on Monday nights than attend the Oscars. Ask which comedians influenced him, and without catching a breath, he says, "Groucho Marx. I got to meet Groucho the last 10 years of his life. He reminded me of every wisecracking Jewish uncle I'd ever known.

"The Marx Brothers' films were unsentimental, original, surreal, hilarious. Who can touch them? They are as good as you can get.

"Also Bob Hope was a big influence on me. I'm not bad at jokes, but I can't approximate Bob Hope in his prime."

Allen is well into his next comedy, **Deconstructing Harry,** with Demi Moore, Robin Williams, Amy Irving, and others. He'd hoped to cast Elliott Gould as the lead, but Gould was tied up with a stage contract. So he turned to his sister for advice. She told her little brother, Allen Stewart Konigsberg, "Woody, you play the role." He listens well.

## Richard A. Blake (review date 22 March 1997)

SOURCE: Blake, Richard A. "Uptown Melodies." *America* 176, no. 9 (22 March 1997): 25-6.

[*In the following review, Blake contends that* Everyone Says I Love You *is entertaining, holding that it invites viewers to appreciate the everyday world from a new perspective.*]

For several days now, a single raw potato has been sitting on the microwave in the kitchen. Who put it there, or for what purpose, no one seems to know. How long it will stay there, and who will move it to another site, no one dares imagine. It is a potato, and its biography is a mystery. For those with eyes to see, however, it is surely more than a misplaced vegetable. A philosopher might see it as a manifestation of the wonder of being, a theologian as a revelation of God's universe, a poet as an epiphany of beauty and a painter or photographer as an object of delight. Not for these capitulation to the tyranny of the commonplace.

Most of us mortals of lesser vision need artists to help us to savor the delights of the brute realities around us, from a simple thing like a potato to a sprawling reality like the Upper East Side of Manhattan. To look, to see, to be grateful for buildings, streets, parks, shops and

every possible form and hue of the human person is to profit from the toil of poets and painters and to become more human in the process.

***Everyone Says I Love You,*** Woody Allen's new musical film, invites this level of contemplation; and, as mystics testify, such activity brings unimagined delight. Lest this ponderous prologue mislead the unwary, it's also a very funny and hugely entertaining movie. Under the skilled direction of photographer Carlo Di Palma, the camera takes on the role of landscape painter of extraordinary delicacy. The opening shots present a portfolio of scenes from Central Park robed in all its glorious springtime finery. Muggers, jovial psychotics and litter have magically vanished from the scene, because, in the style of all musicals, the film presents an idealized version of the truth.

\* \* \*

Allen heightens the romantic atmosphere by having D. J.—the name is a trendy Eastside reworking of Djuna—(Natasha Lyonne), serve as off-camera narrator for much of the story. D. J. has enough sophistication in the ways of the world to know exactly what is happening in shifting relationships around her, but she remains enough of a young girl to bring a sense of wonder to her insights. For her, love is still, like, wonderful, you know, even if her parents and friends seem to make a botch of their romantic endeavors most of the time.

As the camera continues its scenic tour of the park, it rests on Holden (Edward Norton), who sings of love to his almost fiancée, Skylar (Drew Barrymore), both of whom are dressed like outtakes from a Lands' End catalogue, special preppie edition. The outfits and hair styles make it clear that they come from money, a lot of money, and are to the Eastside manor born. Holden breaks into song, protesting his love for Skylar. He doesn't sing very well, but that is part of the genius of the classic musicals. Fred Astaire didn't sing very well either. Every man in the audience believed he could sing (and if he had truly lost contact with reality, dance) just like Fred as he went dancing in the dark with Cyd Charisse. A bit later in the evolution of the genre, Howard Keel would make singing (and Gene Kelly dancing) a spectator sport. In musicals everyone can be as young, attractive, rich and idle as Holden and Skylar simply because we can sing like them. Or at least so we think. In this film all the actors sing except Drew Barrymore, and some of them can't carry a tune any better than we can. Woody Allen is truly awful, and thus ingratiating.

The musical reached its apogee in the 1950's at M.G.M., when Arthur Freed and his stable of great directors, like Vincente Minnelli, Stanley Donen and Gene Kelly created a total fantasy package by integrating narrative action and musical numbers into a cohesive whole. In keeping with the tradition, when Allen has his young lovers dance their way past the boutiques of Madison Avenue, even the mannequins in the windows join in their dance. A few scenes later, as Holden goes shopping for a ring at Harry Winston's, salespeople and customers—some of the tony ladies looking like refugees from a late Fellini film—burst into a song-and-dance routine. The ring is to be presented at Le Cirque that night. Skylar, unfortunately, attacks the whipped cream on the top of her desert with such bulimic frenzy that she fails to notice that Holden has replaced the customary cherry with Mr. Winston's diamonds. Gulp, and several thousands slip down the eager gullet. A quick trip to the emergency room at Lenox Hill Hospital leads into another lively dance number, featuring doctors, nurses, a lunatic in a straightjacket, a man in a body cast on a gurney and three huge, bathrobed mothers-to-be who refuse to let their delicate condition keep them from joining in the acrobatic fun.

Gradually, Allen introduces Skylar's family. Her mother Steffi (Goldie Hawn), ever guilty about her inherited wealth, espouses every liberal cause of the hour. Not one to let her money do all the talking, she delivers an impassioned plea to hire interior decorators to help convicts remodel their cells. The audience of uniformed New York City cops does not seem overly impressed. Bob (Alan Alda), Skylar's stepfather, is long-suffering; presiding as he does over a household of adolescent girls melded from two earlier marriages, he has to be. Fortunately for them and him, he never discovers that the girls' chief amusement involves spying on a psychiatrist and her patients in an adjacent apartment. Bob has enough trouble with his ne'er-do-well son Scott (Lukas Haas), who has begun reading The National Review and would like to execute all convicts before his mother has a chance to redecorate their cells. The eventual explanation for this morbid pathology draws the biggest laugh in the film.

Skylar's biological father, Joe Berlin (Woody Allen), lives in Paris; like many of the characters Allen has played in recent years, he is a writer and has no apparent worries about money. He is lonely, however, a condition his daughters hope to remedy by arranging a meeting with Von (Julia Roberts), armed with information about her private life they have gathered at the psychiatrist's knothole. In the meantime, Skylar interrupts her engagement to Holden to pursue Charles Ferry (Tim Roth), one of her mother's friends from the Big House on the Hudson. His rendition of "If I Had You" has a certain urgency to it that the songwriter might not have intended. Their romance can best be called an adventure.

\* \* \*

Von and Joe meet in Venice, where Di Palma's painterly camera captures the candle-lit gardens and luminous canals with reverence for their unimaginable beauty. During the Christmas holidays, the families converge in Paris, where Joe has taken an apartment in Montmartre in the shadow of the Sacre Coeur. Again the visual effect is breathtaking. On Christmas eve, they plan to attend a splendid party for the equally rich, and it appears that this will be the occasion for the final resolution of their various romantic escapades. Allen, however, will not let us take the denouement too seriously. All the guests at the party, men and women alike, wear Groucho Marx mustaches and brandish huge cigars. In a manic instant the ballroom turns into a stage filled with Groucho impersonators dancing and singing in French. It's all make-believe. Allen reminds us. His characters are fictions, actors playing roles in disguise.

Allen has one more trick lurking behind his Groucho disguise, however. Joe and Steffi leave the party, and as they walk along the Seine, they reminisce about their lives together and apart. The words lead into song and dance. Naturally. This is a musical. The choreography reflects their history with each other. It is the ultimate triumph of fantasy over reality. Even gravity exerts no control over them. They have loved and will love, and draw delight from the moments of happiness that love has given them.

Sometimes a potato is only a potato. Sometimes it is something much more. So is a musical. So is a love story.

**Jonathan Romney (review date April 1997)**

SOURCE: Romney, Jonathan. Review of *Everyone Says I Love You,* by Woody Allen. *Sight and Sound* 7, no. 4 (April 1997): 40-1.

[*In the following review, Romney asserts that* Everyone Says I Love You *is a glib, complacent film.*]

[In *Everyone Says I Love You,*] DJ, a young woman from New York's Upper East Side, narrates the story of her family. Her half-sister Skylar is in love with a young man named Holden and her mother Steffi, married to second husband Bob, organises prestigious charity events for liberal causes. DJ has another half-sister, Laura, and a half-brother Scott who, to Bob's dismay, is virulently conservative. Steffi's first husband Joe, lives in Paris and is very unlucky with women.

Holden buys Skylar an expensive engagement ring and hides it in her dessert at a restaurant, but she swallows it and has to have it removed. DJ goes on holiday with Joe to Venice, where she spots Von, a young woman from New York, DJ, Laura and her best friend, a psychotherapist's daughter, have eavesdropped on Von's therapy sessions, so DJ knows everything about her. DJ gives Joe advice on how to woo Von, and he arranges to meet her, using his inside knowledge to persuade her that he is her perfect match. Eventually, she leaves her husband to move in with him in Paris.

Steffi invites Charles Ferry to dinner, a young prisoner whose release she has successfully campaigned for; alarming the well-heeled guests, he romances Skylar. Later, however, her country drive with him turns out to be a part of a prison escape for two other convicts, and Skylar gets out of the car. Meanwhile, the family mourns the death of their confused Grandpa, and the flighty DJ continues to shift her romantic allegiances. Joe announces that Von has returned to her husband, and Scott's right-wing tendencies prove to have a purely physiological cause. Skylar returns to Holden. The family's year ends happily in Paris; Joe and Steffi step outside to reminisce and dance on the banks of the Seine.

\* \* \*

Woody Allen's apparently seamless career was marked by several simultaneous ruptures in 1992: the rift with Mia Farrow and ensuing accusations of private iniquity; the disappearance into *film maudit* status of his dark and distressing folly *Shadows and Fog*; the collapse of his distributor Orion followed by that of his production alliance with his long-time friend Jean Doumanian. Allen has emerged from this inferno smelling of roses, not just surviving but also going on to make his most confident and commercially successful films for some time.

But in many other ways, much has been lost. After years of silence, he became a professional interviewee on the promotion circuit, assiduously downplaying the themes of frustration and depression that had always fuelled his best work, and reinventing himself as a benign fabricator of feelgood divertissements. *Manhattan Murder Mystery* and *Bullets over Broadway,* agreeable throwaway farces, still hinted at subcurrents of moral horror and darkness, but with the social caricature of *Mighty Aphrodite,* and that film's one-gag twitting of classical culture and recourse to the appeal of a chirpy tune, Allen seemed to have plugged himself into the main artery of sitcom.

*Everyone Says I Love You*—named after the chipper Kalmar/Ruby song—causes concern the minute you read the director's statement recounted in the press notes. He set out, he says, "to make an amusing, entertaining confection." It's "a broad film, almost like a cartoon. These are characters that are fun and larger than life." It's always a bad sign when a film-maker starts sounding like his glibbest, most complacent reviewers, but then this is a glib, complacent film. It's family entertainment in more senses than one. Once again, this director with a famously sceptical, if not dysfunctional, relationship to families, presents an idealised image of the extended family as the seat of solid emotional values, although as usual he casts himself as a detached outsider. This is a film about generations and the getting of wisdom (touches of an uptown *Fanny and Alexander*), with the conventional message that wisdom and age do not always correspond.

The film sees us through a year, through love and its collapse, through hijinks, bereavement and Halloween, the continuous thread being Natasha Lyonne's sparky teenage narrator. DJ is a new figure in Allen's universe—the first of his teenage girls not to be either eroticised (although her own wayward passions are one of the film's running gags) or demonised, as was Juliette Lewis' precocious intellectual in *Husbands and Wives*. Engaging company as she is, the slackerish DJ looks like a rather contrived attempt by American cinema's most notorious mouldy fig to court younger audiences. The presence of vaguely hip names like Lukas Haas, Drew Barrymore, Natalie Portman and Tim Roth is a novel departure, and, unimaginably, Allen even manages a rap joke, although at the genre's expense. The film's musical leitmotif 'I'm Through with Love', is taken up by DJ's latest beau, who trounces the song's delicate lament into a bellow of generic pique: "I'm through with love, through with all you motherfuckers. . . ."

Never mind that this is the film's best joke, it's also typical of the snobbery that's been engulfing Allen's films of late. Roth's petty hood is a gruesome cartoon, a shabby shade of the genuinely menacing and contradictory figure of otherness that Chazz Palminteri embodied in *Bullets*. The joke of his arrival in Steffi's milieu is ostensibly on the snooty uptowners, but soon turns out to be on this shambling, lecherous, untrustworthy representative of the criminal class, whose presence is set up purely to be tossed away in a farcical chase sequence.

The film is equally unconvincing in its other attempts to engage with the big wild world outside Upper Manhattan. The rapper is one of a handful of black presences in the film, none of them actually characters. As for his much-vaunted geographical steps outside home base, location visits to Paris and Venice hardly constitute departures; Allen remoulds both towns as versions of his own terrain, inhabited primarily by Manhattanites. Would it have been too jarring for Allen to date a Parisienne in Venice, or for DJ's gondolier boyfriend to have a few lines to speak? The superficially Europhile Allen has never been so obviously close to the famous Saul Steinberg cartoon in which the world is merely a rudimentary fringe to Manhattan.

As for the use of musical standards—with the main characters' crooning accompanied by companies of jewellers, hospital staff and even phantoms—it doesn't seem that Allen has found a new solution to the problem of structuring a narrative around songs. For British viewers, and those few American ones who saw Herbert Ross' movie of *Pennies from Heaven,* these routines and their forced merriment will look uncomfortably close to Dennis Potter; but where Potter always used popular songs as the only appropriate expressible correlative of his characters' interiority, it doesn't work so well with Allen. Both Potter and his alter-egos dug Al Bowlly, but what do young things like Skylar and Holden have to do with the Gus Kahn songbook?

Allen is as much entitled as anyone else to make a gentle little *petit four* of a film, but this and **Mighty Aphrodite,** with its clowning Greek chorus, rather suffer in their attempts to puff up slight musical interventions into full-blown formal devices. Take away the songs and the Manhattan insularity, and you have got the sort of light moral comedy that the French old guard can still knock out on half the budget and rather less ceremony. *Everyone Says . . .* may be Allen's idea of a French twist, but despite his light fantastic on the Seine with a levitating Goldie Hawn, this *American in Paris* is less Gene Kelly, more a staid, toe-tapping Eric Rohmer.

## Mark Steyn (review date 12 April 1997)

SOURCE: Steyn, Mark. "Woody's Weedy Wobbly Warblers." *Spectator* (12 April 1997): 47-8.

[*In the following review, Steyn argues that Allen's choice to cast actors who are not professional singers in* Everyone Says I Love You *undermines the greatest strength of the musical genre.*]

He blew it. Woody Allen's first musical [*Everyone Says I Love You*] sings only of new inadequacies: not only is he no Ingmar Bergman, it turns out he's no Vincente Minnelli either. If his Bergmanesque outings are death by reverence, his attempt at musical comedy is a weird blend of cynicism, ignorance and cowardice. As his *oeuvre* demonstrates, Woody knows and loves music, but does he love *songs*—music with *words*—and does he know what they're meant to do in a musical? Even in his brilliant deployment of 'I've Heard That Song Before' throughout **Hannah and Her Sisters,** we never did actually hear the song: he went to extraordinary lengths to chisel the Helen Merrill vocal out of the middle of the Harry Jones recording and turn it into an instrumental.

The same awkwardness with sung sentiments disfigures **Everyone Says I Love You.** It's a good thing we've heard these songs before, because we certainly don't hear them here: Woody has chosen to cast non-singing actors—Julia Roberts, Tim Roth—on the grounds that this will make the songs truer and emotionally real. I can't wait for his next cinematic breakthrough; maybe a comedy, in which no one's funny, or *Terminator 5,* in which the action hero vaults over a wall but then feels a little tuckered out and has to lie down on the couch for 20 minutes while his wife calls the hernia specialist. Woody's weedy wobbly warblers deny his musical the form's greatest strength: the transformation of the prosaic into the magical. In *Top Hat,* Astaire and Rogers get caught in a shower in a London park and take shelter in a bandstand, where he sings 'Isn't This a Lovely Day (To Be Caught in the Rain)?' and charms her into dancing with him. The number is 'truer' than any of Woody's. From conversation to song to dance is ostensibly an escalation of unreality, but we accept it because situation, song and characters fit so snugly together it seems the most natural intensification of feeling. To sing the lyric indifferently and dance badly wouldn't make the number any more 'real', but it would miss the point: the potency of musicals is as aspirational romance; we'd all like to have a love worthy of a song like this.

For a couple of minutes, Allen takes the same line. He opens with his young lovers on the streets of Manhattan declaring 'Just You, Just Me'. Edward Norton has a boyish gaucheness and Drew Barrymore the same slightly common sexiness as Ginger Rogers (I mean that as a compliment). It's a chipper affirmation of musical comedy values, but it shrivels away to something grubby and joyless. Allen's film is set in three fabled musical comedy playgrounds—New York, Venice and Paris; his songs are from 70 years ago, give or take. But they're applied to modern characters with the usual Woody preoccupations—divorce, therapy, hot young babes who dig older guys—and they seem to have been parcelled out randomly. The stars who sing them look either sheepish or desperate, like tourist couples who've lost a bet in a piano bar. Instead of making the songs more real, these half-hearted versions constantly remind you that they're not expressions of character, just . . . songs. Everyone gets to sing 'I'm Through with Love', including one of Woody's daughter's many boyfriends, a gangsta rapper who renders it as 'Said I'm Through with Love / And All Them Muthafuckers!': this is the height of the film's musical inventiveness. Woody himself sings the song alone on his Venice balcony, in a thin little voice, in excruciating close-up yet avoiding all eye contact. It's as creepy as watching a cornered paedophile.

Back in the cutting-room, Woody seems to have chickened out. He's increasingly impatient during the vocal solos, cutting away at the first opportunity, flashing back, flashing forward, overlaying dialogue until the songs seem even more perfunctory. This film is tone-deaf in every sense: Allen has no feel whatsoever for the mood of these numbers, and has absolutely no understanding of the difference between the romantic impulse and the call of the one-eyed trouser-snake. If anything, he's even seedier than usual.

This time, he conscripts his daughter into passing on confidential psychotherapy records in order to seduce a married woman in her twenties—Julia Roberts. She, in turn, finds him 'sexy and magical'. When Astaire, pushing 60, romanced Cyd Charisse in *Silk Stockings,* he was, indeed, sexy and magical. Watching them dance, you understood why anyone would fall for him: in singing and dancing, he transcended age, looks and other earthbound considerations. Woody, though, doesn't want to work that hard.

In the finale, he and his ex, Goldie Hawn, come together *sous les ponts de Paris,* scene of Gene Kelly and Leslie Caron's lyrical *pas de deux.* Woody's too cool to learn how to dance but I've seen Miss Hawn in action and she's terrific. Here, alas, she's merely the butt of a lame-brain special effect: as she sings 'I'm Through with Love' (what else?), she begins to float up in the air. The point about musicals is that they're not *Independence Day* or *Twister*: song and dance are not special effects, but *human* effects. In *Hannah,* an exasperated Woody tells Dianne Wiest, 'You don't deserve Cole Porter.' He doesn't either.

## Bart Freundlich (essay date December 1997)

SOURCE: Freundlich, Bart. "Woody's Fingerprints." *Sight and Sound* 7, no. 12 (December 1997): 61.

[*In the following essay, director Freundlich comments on the making of his film,* The Myth of Fingerprints, *and explains the influence of Allen's* Hannah and Her Sisters *on this work.*]

I don't know if I would say that Woody Allen is my favourite film-maker, but I always enjoy seeing what he does even if I don't like it. My favourite is *Hannah and Her Sisters.* Although all Allen's films have a similar tone, he is constantly dealing with new things in them, in a new style. *Husbands and Wives* is like a documentary, *Bullets over Broadway* is a period-piece comedy, and then he does a slapstick comedy and then there is *Interiors* which he made during his 'Bergman period'. I would love my career to map out like that, where I could have total control over my films.

What struck me most about *Hannah and Her Sisters* was these eight or ten fully-defined characters in separate storylines with separate lives. They all intertwine in little ways, but they don't resolve everything together.

Someone passes someone in the hall but it's not the gimmick of the film, it's just about people. And oddly enough for a film that is mainly about emotional not narrative content, it uses those title cards with a line from the film. The first one is "God she's beautiful," which Michael Caine says about Barbara Hershey. It's amazing: you would think title cards would break up the flow of the film, but it works so beautifully. It's kind of literary.

Allen plays so much with point of view in this film. You don't see many other films that can skip around using different voiceovers from different characters so well. I think that this influenced my film *The Myth of Fingerprints* because it also has a lot of characters with their own storylines. I wanted to write eight fully-rounded characters that weren't just the stereotypical girlfriend, stereotypical father and so on. Although I didn't use voiceover in the film as Allen does in *Hannah and Her Sisters,* I played around with perspective, so just when you think you are following the children's perspective you see the father watching a home movie of his children and you feel you can't blame him for as much as you thought you could.

What I hope the film does, like *Hannah and Her Sisters,* is paint a portrait of these characters rather than pointing you to a place of judgment about them. In *Hannah and Her Sisters* you end up feeling some understanding for Michael Caine's character who is doing this awful thing, having sex with his wife's sister. I found it amazing that Allen was able to portray that dilemma so poignantly by using these internal monologues that tell you how these people feel. For *The Myth of Fingerprints* I relied more on the cinematography and the actors' ability just to express it in their faces, because *Myth* ends up being about what people don't say, not just what they do say.

At the end of *Hannah* Woody Allen has married another sister (Dianne Wiest), and it's Thanksgiving: he says, "Isn't this amazing, it would make a great story, a guy marries one sister, 10 years later marries another, completely in love, you know the heart is a very resilient little muscle." And she says, "Mickey, I'm pregnant". He couldn't get Mia Farrow's character pregnant at the beginning so there is a really nice resolution. It is a little bit self-referential obviously because he is saying, I've got a great story for you (he also does it in *Crimes and Misdemeanors* when Martin Landau is talking about the murder with Woody Allen on the bench). I think that *Myth* combines the feeling of *Hannah* with one of his darker movies, hopefully without being so directly referential to Bergman. It ends up being about this dark past that the family has, like the family that Allen depicts in *Interiors*—but *Interiors* is so committed to making you want to jump out the window. The good thing about a lot of his other films is that they combine humour with an element of drama.

I was extremely influenced by the way Allen shoots things. I think he has become more and more interested in getting to the crux of a scene. He sets up the camera and sometimes there is a little dolly involved or a zoom in or zoom out. Barbara Hershey walks in and out of the frame and is still talking to Mia Farrow, but you're on Farrow's face the whole time. Film-makers just don't do that enough because they're scared and feel that they have to feed the audience. The perfect example in *Hannah* is the shot at the beginning where the camera's above the table. Everyone is there and they're saying, "To her great success," meaning Hannah's great success in *A Doll's House,* and she says "Oh no no, I just want to be with my family." It's just one single shot from quite far away and you don't see anyone's face, but you do see all their relationships to one another.

I took a lot from that because in my movie I actually covered almost exactly the same angle but cut it up a bit more for pacing reasons, because Allen's scene was much more about comedy. In my 'table shot', where Margaret makes the toast, we had to get everybody's reactions. It was one of the first times the audience met everybody. I would love to be brave enough to let everything play out in single shots. *Manhattan* is the ultimate example, where there is literally something like 11 shots in the movie! A great example is when Woody is with Mariel Hemingway and he sees Diane Keaton and Michael Murphy, and he stops in mid-sentence looks offscreen and says, "God what are you doing here?" You don't see them and then they step into the shot. It doesn't feel like a gimmick, there is something very simple, utterly beautiful about it.

Although Woody Allen is known for improvising with his actors, apparently there was a finished version of *Hannah* written before they started shooting. I think when there are a lot of characters it is hard to improvise. Occasionally in *Myth* we would change a line here or there, but it was too hard because the balance with the characters was too delicate. We couldn't let one character shine too much, it was about trying to suppress everything until each character had its moment. The editor Kate Williams and I thought consistently about the rhythm within the scenes. The rhythm of the scenes next to each other is very fast, they cut back, they're not very long, the movie is not very long, only 90 minutes.

But all in all when it comes down to it, you end up having to shed your thoughts about other people's films and really understand what it is that is going to make your film your own. For me it was a tone to the movie that hopefully was in the script, and it was a rhythm so that you felt you had just experienced something but were really not explicitly told anything during the movie. It was a culmination of letting the actors govern the pace of the movie. And, of course, in the writing it was not resolving things in any way.

**Stanley Kauffmann (review date 19 January 1998)**

SOURCE: Kauffmann, Stanley. "New York Jews." *New Republic,* no. 4331 (19 January 1998): 24-5.

[*In the following review, Kauffmann argues that Allen's choice to cast himself in the lead role of* Deconstructing Harry *is effective, because the character serves as a vehicle for Allen to perform his "shtick."*]

At last Woody Allen's appearance in a leading role serves a purpose. Unintended, perhaps, but effective. In *Deconstructing Harry,* Allen's latest, his acting is, as always, coarse and repetitive, accompanied constantly by so much hand-wagging that he seems the victim of St. Vitus. But Harry, the Jewish New York novelist whom he plays, is such a despicable, exploitative, deceptive egotist that an authentic performance of the role—say, by Dustin Hoffman—would have made him unbearable. As we watch Allen we know that the part is not intended to be credible, like the other roles in the film: it's just an occasion for Allen's shtick. Harry is a convenience to make the film possible, as is the fact that so many women have been mad about him. Even the hooker we see is sympathetic to him.

Still, Allen's cartoon acting is all the more noticeable because he is surrounded by so many good actors. Or maybe, because Harry is so dreadful, Allen's cartoon acting now seems more egregious in these surroundings. Judy Davis has the opening scene with him, an ex-girlfriend who is murderously angry because Harry has utilized their relationship in his new novel; and Davis is excellent. Demi Moore, as a former wife who became devoutly Jewish, to Harry's discomfort, is funny. Kirstie Alley, as another former wife, very hostile, steams through her scenes. Other pleasing performances come from Caroline Aaron, Billy Crystal, and Elisabeth Shue. Richard Benjamin is at ease as one of Harry's autobiographical characters in a novel. Robin Williams amuses as a character in one of Harry's short stories that might have come from Ben Hecht.

These last two characters appear in some of the several episodes that are reenactments of Harry's fiction. Late in the film Harry confronts several of his characters in the, shall we say, flesh, but this is not a Pirandellian venture. It occurs simply because Allen needs more material to keep his film going.

All that really happens in the film's present tense is that Harry goes upstate to his university to be honored. He kidnaps his small son, who lives with the divorced mother, to accompany him on this trip. His affection for his son is Harry's one positive quality; yet he also pays a hooker in hot pants $500 to go along with them. (A great pal for his son, yes?) The university ceremony is stymied for various reasons, but Allen, perhaps touching his Fellini file, has it happen anyway in a dream sequence; the ceremony is held and all the people in his life, including his fictional characters, attend.

***Deconstructing Harry*** is really just a series of sketches, but many of them are amusing because this Manhattan Punchinello works with competent actors and because his dialogue is lithe and sometimes quotable. ("Tradition is the illusion of permanence.") The film shows yet again that Allen knows how to flatter his audience: Harry is a sexually busy, glib atheist, exploitative of women, whose continual patronage of hookers is clearly his ideal in man-woman relationships, which is why his marriages failed. Apparently audiences, American and otherwise, male and female, either identify with this character or are amused by his witty cynicism in a medium not especially noted for either quality.

Cinematic note: Allen and his editor, Susan E. Morse, use small jump cuts all through this picture, but they can't be called Godardian. They don't mirror any serious moral anarchism in the film itself. They're just décor.

### Ronald Goetz (review date 18 March 1998)

SOURCE: Goetz, Ronald. "Self-Justification." *Christian Century* 115, no. 9 (18 March 1998): 315-16.

[*In the following review, Goetz asserts that Allen fails to offer any new insight into his recurring themes of theological questioning in* Deconstructing Harry.]

It's hard to imagine a more autobiographical filmmaker than Woody Allen. Most of his movies feature a fictionalized, larger-than-life version of himself as a blundering, psychologically fragile victim of an existence that is almost too much for him. This persona survives by comic accident; his hilarious attempts to cope cost him dearly. What has previously made this persona so appealing is the sense that it is grounded in a fundamental decency and integrity.

The underlying seriousness of many of Allen's themes and his incapacity to leave the God question alone made one hope that his wrestling with the God of his forbears might one day lead him to some theologically penetrating resolution. But ***Deconstructing Harry*** is thoroughly disillusioning.

Allen plays Harry Block, a successful writer whose infinite capacity to rationalize his lack of self-control and whose duplicity in all things sexual render him incapable of marital fidelity. In a disturbing parallel to Allen's scandalous affair with Soon-Yi Previn, the adopted teenage daughter of Allen's former lover, Mia

Farrow, Block seduces one of his wife's psychiatric patients. The wife, fiercely played by Kirstie Alley, loathes him for violating what she considers a sacred trust—the relationship between a doctor and her patients.

Judy Davis is brilliant as Harry's brittle, neurotic sister-in-law, with whom he has an affair. He not only dumps her for a younger woman but makes her a thinly disguised character in his latest novel, thus destroying her marriage and her relationship with her sister.

Harry, who lives by impulse, is increasingly isolated but still desperate for approval. When the university that once expelled him decides to honor him for his literary achievements, he wants to be accompanied by an admiring coterie. He hires a smart, self-assured hooker (Hazel Goodman), prevails on one of his few remaining friends, and kidnaps his young son to go with him.

Though Harry is always willing to confess the pain, consternation and rage he causes in his relationships with women, he never really understands that he has harmed them. When his latest love (Elisabeth Shue) leaves him and marries one of his old friends (Billy Crystal), Harry cannot understand why she won't, on the day of her marriage, leave her husband-to-be and accept Harry's belated proposal. She has realized that—as Harry had warned her—he is concerned only with filling his immediate needs, and he mistakes his loneliness for a capacity for commitment.

Allen often seems to yearn to be able to make a faith commitment, a longing reflected in this film. In a dream sequence, Harry finds himself in a hell in which escaped war criminals and television evangelists share one of the lowest rungs. Descending to an even deeper pit, Harry meets the father who had despised him because his beloved wife died in giving him birth. Harry forgives him and pleads that his father be allowed to go to heaven. His father gruffly states that Jews don't believe in heaven.

Though probably more Jews believe in heaven than believe in hell, this scene demonstrates that for Allen life points more to the triumph of darkness than of light. His humor belongs more to the darkness of the gallows than to the gaiety of angels. In Harry, Allen seems to present himself as a reluctant but resolutely rationalistic atheist, contemptuous of religious Judaism. Harry's antipathy to his believing sister and her deeply religious husband borders on blind prejudice.

At the film's end, when Harry finds himself completely alone, he concludes that his life's justification is his writing—his powerful imagination and his art. Yet he is suffering writer's block. His "redemption" comes in a dream. His academic admirers lead him to a place where all the characters of his fiction await him. They offer him sincere and grateful applause for having created them. When he awakens, his writer's block is gone. He sits down to begin his next novel, about a writer whose purpose and justification lie in his art, despite his inability to live authentically. Art justifies Harry's cruelty and betrayal of his friends and lovers. If his victims understood the value of art, even they would praise him. So the film ends by celebrating a callous aesthetic elitism.

Some reviewers have regarded this film as a triumph of honesty. But confession without repentance is self-congratulatory exhibitionism.

## David Thomson (essay date March-April 1998)

SOURCE: Thomson, David. "Shoot the Actor." *Film Comment* 34, no. 2 (March-April 1998): 12-19.

[*In the following essay, Thomson argues that Allen is an important filmmaker who explores basic human concerns with comedy and pathos, focusing on* Deconstructing Harry, Bullets over Broadway, *and several other films by Allen.*]

What do you all expect of me? Woody Allen's Harry Block seems to be asking throughout *Deconstructing Harry.* And he brings a load of whiny lament to the line and its attitude, even if he isn't an actor—so much as a block, a feeling-blocker. He shapes the climate in which he's always there ready to make a last effort to meet anyone's (cockamamie) ideas; it's part of his dogged, weary calm—never losing control, never eating the scenery—no matter that lots of the women who brush up against him are, sooner or later, made into crimson harpies of wrath, helpless incoherence, and torrential other-ness; it's the credo that lets him think of himself as an endlessly patient, tolerant man, ready to talk about everything intelligently—especially the things that were most hurtful and irrational; and it's the mainstay of his self-pity, the way in which, whatever happens, whatever charges or bullets are hurled at him, whatever tirades slip like water from his sloped shoulders and elfin head, he's ready to be the sucker, the one who sits there and takes it, the victim.

And this works well enough until, at last, you get a chance to look at him straight on and you see the bleakest eyes on today's screen, the intransigent certainty that it's all about *him,* and the passive resistance that knows if he keeps on asking in his listless, plaintive way, "What do you expect of me?", he doesn't have to deal with the question himself. But what does Woody want or expect?

I must admit a few things straightaway: I don't like to look at Woody Allen; I don't like to listen to him; but I think he's getting better all the time at that thing called filmmaking. And by now I'm getting used to the realization that it's so hard to like filmmakers—as opposed to their work. By which I mean to suggest that while Woody Allen does not just like himself so much, but can hardly see anything else with the same intensity or respect, there is an extraordinary tension rising (in me) between hostility and fondness. But is there really another American filmmaker around worth wrestling with in the same way?

After all, what do we want from Woody? In the Christmas season of 1997, just about every critic observed that nearly every movie—the good, the bad, and the fatuous—was going on too long, and slowing down to accommodate that length. But *Deconstructing Harry* came in at 95 minutes, with twenty or so significant characters and four or five weaving storylines, with characters appearing as their real selves and as they figured in Harry's chronic fictions, and everything was clear and workable, the set-pieces and the segues, the funniest lines and situations of the season, self-loathing as sharp as fresh anchovy—time to look at Elisabeth Shue and see her odd, Novakian shyness, while seeing yet again that Billy Crystal (electric and beguiling on the Oscars or in Ken Burns's *Baseball*) is a terminally empty actor (does Woody see it in others? you bet he does), and time for that riveting thirty seconds of sprung rhythm and bravura editing from Susan Morse (the code gone wild), as Judy Davis gets out of her car, as if to say, Did you ever think that movies could look like this?, so your eye wakes up again—and I was reminded of David Hockney's observation, ten years or so ago, that he gave up movies because he knew what shot was coming next—and there's now an urge in Woody as there was once in Godard to find a new way of seeing—in short, whether you think it was funny or touching, or not, was there a movie last year that had more going on, and such assurance, such fucking facility, that the more was merrier, so that a little while into the picture you eased back into its serene momentum, knowing that it knew where it was going? Which is nowhere near the same as liking it or not.

I noticed in the year's roundup that several *Film Comment* writers had liked *My Best Friend's Wedding.* I was pleasantly surprised by it, too, but in the broad area of romantic comedy can anyone honestly claim that it rivaled the knowledge of people, the speed, the deftness, the formal daring, or the Parker-like (not Alan Parker) shifts of tone and voice in *Deconstructing Harry*? I mean, don't we need to admit some very basic facts of dramatic skill—like *Husbands and Wives,* 107 minutes; *Manhattan Murder Mystery,* 108; *Bullets over Broadway,* 99; *Mighty Aphrodite,* 93 . . . or *Radio Days,* 85; *The Purple Rose of Cairo,* 82?

And when I say dramatic skill, I'm really referring to the very subtle movements of different lines and impulses that go to make a sweet, harmonious whole. If you wonder any further what that means, I challenge you, here and now, to write down a halfway adequate synopsis of *The Purple Rose of Cairo,* say, or *Radio Days* or *Deconstructing Harry.* You won't be able to do it because, all of a sudden, you'll realize how rich, intricate, and tricky these pictures are, and how much what happens depends on how you're seeing it. Whereas, synopsize *Casino,* say, and you have to marvel that the thing itself got to be 182 minutes. Pure cinema for 182 minutes, of course. None of which, necessarily, gets close to whether we like *Casino* more or less than *Radio Days.*

But it does start you thinking, and swept along on that unruly river, you'll soon find yourself adding up some more numbers. And then you discover that, so far, Allen has directed 26.333 films—that third being his share of *New York Stories.* One does not automatically esteem a director because of productivity—Edward L. Cahn did over sixty between 1931 and 1963, and as yet few festivals have made a fuss over him as our forgotten man. But maybe festival fever does overlook fecundity sometimes; it can be its own smokescreen. So a Kubrick, only seven years older than Woody, is deemed grand just because he's in the process of evacuating his thirteenth film. Would some of us feel inclined to take Woody more seriously if he worked less often—if he was more measured, more blocked? But then think of Sydney Pollack, at 63, a year older than Allen and the director of sixteen films. (True, he has done more; he has produced and enabled, and he has acted—wasn't he that grave, vain idiot in *Husbands and Wives*? Why do people act in his films?) And *The Firm* was 154 minutes; *Out of Africa,* 161.

Still, if we ever again honor the notion that directing is an art or a craft or a trick that benefits from practice, we may regret that so many of our better directors work so sparingly (because they grow weary, or because they need too much time to make their deals first?). No one would argue that Allen has driven himself into poverty by disregarding his own deals. Still, he has done that thing most critics and teachers advise—just kept working, and never ended one project without having the next one lined up. And—whether you like the stuff or not—doesn't that steady application show? I mean: isn't he better than he was?

After all, no one gets all there is into *Deconstructing Harry* without having learned how quickly and lucidly you can show things. And just as Woody Allen went from being a kind of amateurish slapstick filmmaker (*Bananas, Love and Death, Sleeper*) to a sad impresario of the bitter comedy of emotional hope (*Stardust Memories, Manhattan, Hannah and Her Sisters*), and just as

he discovered the advantage and the film language in having Carlo Di Palma and Santo Loquasto as his regular collaborators, so the "visual" in his movies has relied increasingly on talking heads and the very complete spatial relationships in shifting group shots. The films have become much more engrossing as something to see. Minus the élan of camera movements—exhilaration is all on the soundtracks in Woody's films, in talk and music—he has come to look like Renoir of the late Thirties. Not that you have to take the films that seriously, if the comparison throws you. But why not look again?

It's not just that Allen keeps working away, as if only that regimen could keep him alive or fight back the depressions that prey on ease or inactivity. He goes so much further to meet the model of a modern film director as drawn up by the most liberal and humane film critics and commentators. He never yields to the great gambles of *Titanic* or *The Postman*; he would hardly know what to do with the creatures and the hardware in *Alien Resurrection* or *Starship Troopers*. *Zelig* aside—a rather large aside, let us say, years ahead of the rest of Hollywood in putting nonentities hand-in-hand with the great—you will not find special effects in Woody Allen movies. Rather, he insists that moviemaking is a matter of real places and natural light, with no drama more uplifting and no effect more special than the turmoil in a human face—whether it is Judy Davis struggling to hide blushing pride and self at being her sister's "other woman" in *Harry,* or the kid wisdom in Mariel Hemingway in *Manhattan* telling Woody, "Look, you have to have a little faith in people." Or is it faith in little people?

Woody Allen doesn't kid us, or himself, that he knows, understands, or is interested in real gangsters, say, or the Dalai Lama. Yet, time after time, he makes pictures about the people he knows, the city he has locked himself into, the very streets and apartments that are like his lovely life sentence. Ironically, more or less, that world is pretty close to ours, for just like Jules Feiffer in his cartoons, Woody Allen has regularly depicted his own audience—a world and wealth of people worried about being safe and adventurous at the same time, about being in love, being esteemed, being smart and hip and cool and warm in the late part of the 20th century. These people worry about their work, their integrity, their motives, their sincerity—and, increasingly, they have gone from worrying about Woody (or the Wood within) to being just a little restless and jittery about being near him, or near enough to become his creatures.

Call it selfconsciousness—which, surely, can as easily be stupid and vain as noble or touching. But who else in our panorama of moviemaking has had the wit, the accuracy, the lightness, and the indifference to human pain to make that uneasiness so profound a subject?

And don't we sigh with rapturous agreement when the very talented but surely out-on-a-limb James Cameron says that all he wants to do now is just two or three very small, intimate films—as if to urge him on, yes, yes, that's where art and depth lie, Jim, not just at the bottom of the sea. Study Bonnard and Monet until you've lost that young affection for comic book cutouts. And isn't that what Woody Allen has been doing for over twenty-five years, so that one scene from *Deconstructing Harry*—you can have Kirstie Alley's multiple explosions, the Richard Benjamin-Julia Louis-Dreyfus assignation, or the conversation between Davis and Amy Irving—is enough to let a *Titanic* fan know that, yes, there are quite different decks and classes of human talk, substance, and uptake, and some people have them and some don't. Woody can be smartass, facetious, too cute for his own good, nastier than he knows—he can be like Gore Vidal, so you can't quite judge where your respect for him and the loathing meet—but Woody Allen does think, does know, and can say things (even if you worry about the prowess) that so many other filmmakers are deaf to.

So all we have here, really, is just a 62-year-old guy who can't stop making movies, who makes them by old-fashioned precepts we prefer, who makes them modestly, using the camera and film as they were intended to be used, exposing us to ourselves, our foolishness and our dreams, more or less with comedy and pathos. And—let us not forget this—when he runs into the most notable "difficulty" his life has yet had; or, if you want to put it this way, when his cold, selfish manipulation of others is discovered; and when he is widely trashed, mocked, and abused by *his* people (because his people worry more than most others about whether you could and should fuck your stepchild), he does not falter or cave in, he does not "rest," he does not back down, or seem to immerse himself in extra therapy (surely, he is the great visionary and exponent of therapy sessions as just another name for story development or actors' improv). Instead, he digs in and makes not just one film a year, same as always, but makes *Husbands and Wives, Manhattan Murder Mystery, Bullets over Broadway, Mighty Aphrodite, Everyone Says I Love You,* and *Deconstructing Harry.*

As if to say, thanks skin bracer—I needed that!

Now, you don't have to *like* those films, you understand. No, all you need to do is show me anyone else in America who has come anywhere near that run of work. And sure, you can say it's just Woody being Woody, making the films so fast that he doesn't have to pause or think them through—that his "thinking" and "worrying" are just schtick. All right, I don't like him, either; I don't want to be with him or have to listen to his justifications in person. I wouldn't want to have to watch him and Soon-Yi under any circumstances. But

we see a country prepared to defy the character "thing," so long as Bill Clinton does such a terrific job playing that other character, the guy thing. Meanwhile, *Broadway Danny Rose, Hannah and Her Sisters, Radio Days, Husbands and Wives, Bullets over Broadway, Mighty Aphrodite, Everyone Says I Love You, Deconstructing Harry*—you don't have to please me by liking them, or working at liking them. But still, throw in *Annie Hall, Manhattan,* and *The Purple Rose of Cairo* and you've got eleven films that are. . . . Well, never mind what they are, can you really tell yourself that we're not in the presence of a major director?

Take *Bullets over Broadway,* and the moment when David (John Cusack), the playwright, realizes that Cheech (Chazz Palminteri) has killed Olive (Jennifer Tilly), the woman he was hired to protect. Olive was the gangster's moll and a showgirl with dreams of doing theater. So the gangster put up the money for David's play—*God of Our Fathers*—so long as Olive had a part in it.

I know, I'm talking about gangsters, and you're saying I told you before that Allen didn't use gangsters. What I said was, he didn't kid us, or himself, that he knew or understood or was interested in real gangsters. The Thirties hoodlums in *Bullets over Broadway* are the kind of figures that Allen's imagination has inherited from movies, and he's only interested in what he can imagine. They're play figures, as well as guys in a play, stooges that let him do the voices and hire some actors. But their presence immediately leaves some sense of a gap, an abyss, between reality and play. You get the same thing in Hawks, all the time, where the most consistent straightfaced joke was that Howard was a man of these real tough worlds—instead of a fantasist. The same gap exists in David, between the very forceful assertion that he's an artist and his real status as an opportunistic hack. Because he's all talk and no substance.

Olive can't act (though Jennifer Tilly handles that limitation very prettily, and got an Oscar nomination for it). Still, her role is small. She's getting along well enough in the rehearsals, and Cheech just sits there in the gloom of the theater waiting for her to finish. He's there because, whatever Allen knows about gangsters, the gangster boss knows show people are too tricky to leave anyone as dumb as Olive alone with them.

There comes a day at rehearsal when, out of the dark, Cheech, in fury and frustration, throws out an idea about fixing a dud moment in the play. This is delivered in longshot so that we see the stage, the front rows of the orchestra seats, and—with a swaying pan—the place where Cheech is sitting. There has been no one shot, let alone a soulful closeup, of Cheech listening to David's naïve, pretentious play, grinding his teeth. Allen hardly gives us a closeup in the entire elegance of the picture, preferring those tricky long-distance views where people struggle for position and we have to look and see. You can say that's because it's a movie about a stage play, but in fact Allen has always been drawn towards the detached, problematic point of view, and the crowded stage on which everyone has his reasons, and his chance.

He feels no need to reveal or underline the artist in Cheech, or to separate him from others in the story. But as soon as we hear the bored bodyguard's idea we know he's got genius in him, and the camera wavers—as if it needed a second to adjust to that—and then carries the idea back to the professionals as insight, answer. From that moment on, Cheech begins to be co-author of the play (whenever he can remember to be that polite to David).

So Cheech comes to the point of knowing that Olive is ruining the play—killing it. No, she's not that bad, says David; and anyway, it's a small part. She's a necessary compromise. Again, there is no closeup soliloquy to show Cheech's brooding: though worry is Allen's great subject, he is at his best when not isolating it (framing it in self-pity), but letting it air out in the weather of the ensemble. So Cheech just shoots Olive: which isn't what a gangster would do (and it surely means Cheech's demise); it's what an artist would do—because that kind of willfulness has no choice and no truck with compromise.

David guesses instantly what has happened, and he storms in on Cheech in a pool hall. The slam of the door opens the scene and sweeps David across the room to where Cheech stands. This is the master shot, and the only shot; the single setup looks at a receding diagonal, and it plays the splashes of orange light on the walls against the squashed pistachio rectangles of the tables. Without ever giving you a shot to knock your eyes out, Allen has become one of the most grace-ful, and spatially enquiring, composers in American film. It's a camera style such as one finds in the best of Preminger (a great arbiter of doubt)—and it's something that has received hardly any comment over the years.

The beauty of the image is utterly unspectacular and unshowy; it's just a way of keeping an open mind and making us address what people say. (Time and again, directors intent on talk make the best compositions.) David rants at the gangster for being so callous, as he defends himself as a way of measuring what has hap-pened—"I'm a decent, moral human being." Seen and heard at a distance, that's nothing but a bum line—one we flinch from, in the way Cheech might have done. And Cheech asks what sort of decency it is to be carry-ing on with the lead when David has a girl already. He knocks the "author" down and tells him, with an absolute severity, "Nobody is going to ruin my work."

*Bullets over Broadway* is a comedy. Its framework can-not help but see the sad irony in the meeting of an "art-ist" and a gangster that teaches both of them what fakes they are. David takes a lesson in playwriting and in basic modesty, and he goes back to his girl (why not? she's only been having sex, sensational sex, with Rob Reiner—nothing like love)—"I know I'm not an artist, and I know I love you." And Cheech is as dead as van Gogh or Schubert; his own last line is another knockout suggestion to fix the play's curtain line. The humor here is not a matter of Woody's one-liners—it's the line, the arc, that goes all through the film, and it's what genius is all about. It harks back to the chief gangster's knowledge—that show people are tricky; they fool themselves, for the sake of it; they play around. But that leaves an impulse, a commitment to perfection, quite ready to destroy itself if the play is improved in the process. Which only helps remind us what a serious business comedy is, and how it was always made and intended for the tougher, more painful lessons about emotional life, social order, and human ambition.

Somewhere along the line, Woody Allen is a David who has absorbed Cheech's lesson—and thus a New York showperson who has acquired the concentration, the cruelty, even, that may make a genius resemble a killer. If you doubt that progress, then look at *Crimes and Misdemeanors,* which comes just five years before *Bullets over Broadway,* and which stands as one of the most rigged, shitty, dankly sanctimonious of Woody's films.

*Crimes* was not shot by Di Palma. Its photographer is Sven Nykvist, which may mean just that Di Palma was busy elsewhere, or that Allen wanted to get himself in a Bergman-like moral trough. The results are horrible. A ponderous pan shot insists on linking a closeup of Judah (Martin Landau) with one of his dead girlfriend (Anjelica Huston) at his feet. The style is always look-ing to confront some of the most slippery and unlike-able of characters with Moral Dilemma. It's misanthropy with a vengeance. The group shots are filled with fussy irrelevance: the ensemble-ism this time degenerates into names like Claire Bloom, Sam Waterston, Joanna Glea-son—and, let us add, Mia Farrow—doing nothing (and Allen's big casts have always offered far too much of that—he doesn't so much showcase his guest stars as humble them and becalm them in their vanity).

But in some grim contest with himself, Woody has found Landau as the only other actor around as unworthy of a lead role as himself. Landau's self-regard is unctuous and unwholesome. The thought of his affair with Ms. Huston is preposterous—indeed, the posed love matches in Allen films are often offered without the least conviction or spark. Obsessed with sex, he is terrified of looking at it. Landau's self-justification is humorless, clammy, and revolting. And when he tells his brother Jack (Jerry Orbach doing *Outlaw and Order*), "I'm not going to let this neurotic woman destroy me!", we hear a line that was waiting to be traded back into Woody's real, ugly life with merciless ease. So Judah lets Jack—a mysteriously humdrum figure, with contacts—arrange for Huston to be offed. Orbach gives us maybe the only grownup or appealing figure in the film, a glum, practical man, oppressed by a lifetime of being the black-sheep brother, the dumb one and the failure. There's a great moment when, after the deed is done, as Judah is lamenting and stroking his bad feelings, Jack tells him curtly, "Be a man!" It's as if the line had slipped through the prevailing self-pity that leaves every other line cute and stuffed.

And if Woody is expecting us to sympathize with his moral refinement in seeing how Judah gets away with it all, and even feels better as time passes, so he throws in the most woeful and childlike of his own countenances at the end—that cringe-making stricken closeup as he realizes Mia Farrow has gone off with Alan Alda (at just the time, maybe, he was longing for the real woman to find someone else).

In other words, the determination about feeling bad overwhelms life or courage in *Crimes and Misdemeanors* (the more Woody's films hinge on men, the more likely this outcome—*Henry and His Brothers* would turn out an orgy of suicide). And the character Allen plays—the high-minded documentary filmmaker who can't stop taking his 12-year-old niece to the movies or see why his wife has given up sex—is creepier and more alarming than he ever seems to understand. (There are people in Allen films way past the need for therapy; only terrific drugs would help.) There is no more glaring proof of the self-destructiveness of Woody acting in his own movies than this film, and no more grisly moment than his monstrous reaction to the story his sister tells of the lover who defecated on her. He howls and covers his eyes—the exaggeration loses her experience. That's not just bad acting, it's a level of performance that derides the art and community of acting, and undermines the pretend reality of the work. It's what got Olive shot—and any one of us would be ready to squeeze the trigger. *Crimes and Misdemeanors* may be as bad as he got—we have to hope so—as a study of self-adoring cowardice dressed up as moral discrimination. Of course, it also got Oscar nominations for Best Director and Screenplay—so it's up to you about liking it.

Much as I like *Deconstructing Harry,* I don't support Allen playing Harry—nor do I really believe that he tried desperately hard to find someone else. (Though I can see a wonderful film about a director like Woody, going through actors endlessly, and being "dismayed" because in the end only Oscar Jaffe can play Oscar.)

Imagine Harry played by Richard Gere, say, or even Alan Alda (an actor who evidently holds a dreadful fascination for Allen), and the implicit poison would leap into view. Imagine Chazz Palminteri—he deserves more. Imagine Gore Vidal—he likes to act. But finally, Woody, just give us anyone but yourself now that you've found the hard, sure distance and the necessary resolve to stand back from human beings and just watch their tricks.

Of course, we don't have to like all these films (he makes enough for hits and misses), just as we don't have to forgive or forget what happened with Woody, over there . . . in life. Do we? As it is, in the last few years, the hero-worshiping stance has had to come to terms with the unequivocal report that Capra, Hawks, and Lang were all shits. The same sort of comeuppance may be on its way for Clint Eastwood and all the others. It's just possible one day that we'll grasp the need to be a pretty awful person if you want to be an artist. In which case, I'd propose, *Deconstructing Harry* is an indelible lesson along the way, with that shameless last view of the zealous clerk to his own imagination, typing up life as art.

There's stuff I haven't even mentioned that I never want to have to see again—*Interiors, Alice, Shadows and Fog, Another Woman,* and those early films where people said he was so funny. But I do want to say that I think Allen has grown up, devouring his own poison, and being tougher because of it (it seems clear now that the events of the early Nineties strengthened him— okay, left him no alternative but to be a bastard). He has found a deeply impressive style and the habit of making one adventurous film after another. I mean, we've hardly touched on *Everyone Says I Love You,* which came out of some side-pocket, filled with authentic whimsy, creating a race of song-snatched people, with Goldie Hawn never better, and with that odd, awful, sly trick about the secrets of therapy being used to advantage, so long as it's all for story.

I'm not sure what we should make of such numbers, but at the age of 62 Woody Allen has been nominated six times for Best Director and eleven for Best Screenplay—that's in the Billy Wilder class, and Wilder is an untouchable. More to the point, let us offer the thought that in *Bullets* and *Harry* there's a style and an intelligence akin to the way Renoir regards Jean Gabin's showman at the end of *French Cancan.* This is a filmmaker whose journey exceeds that of any American working today. His sense of the great untidy group of acquaintances is, at its best, a vision of great originality and importance. It makes his contemporaries seem narrow and old-fashioned; it lets you believe still that movies might address our modern-ness better than other arts. This is a great filmmaker. And if we've never liked "Woody" less, well maybe that tells us something about filmmaking and art that we are still too young to take hold of.

Still, I'd shoot the actor, given half a chance.

**Jonathan Romney (review date April 1998)**

SOURCE: Romney, Jonathan. "Scuzzballs Like Us." *Sight and Sound* 8, no. 4 (April 1998): 10-13.

[*In the following review, Romney compares* Deconstructing Harry *with* Wild Man Blues, *a documentary of Allen's European tour as a jazz clarinetist, directed by Barbara Kopple. Romney examines each in terms of their treatments of the relationship between Allen's on-screen and real-life personae.*]

In *Wild Man Blues,* Barbara Kopple's documentary about Woody Allen in Europe, New York's most famous recluse explains his reluctance to leave the city in which he is practically an official landmark. There's nowhere else in the world, he points out, where he could get duck wonton soup at 4.30 in the morning. But, he adds, "I *don't* get it, because who needs that at 4.30 in the morning?" This sublime paradox—with its image of the artist as spoiled, needy child—seems so neatly to encapsulate all our assumptions about Woody Allen's neurotic nature that it could be a gag from one of his fictions.

But this is not fiction—it's reality, or appears to be. Anyone who has followed the career of this incorrigible fabulist, whose films constantly seem to offer thinly disguised versions of himself, might well have tired by now of the question: what in Woody's work is self-portrait and what is fantasy? Enough already with the ontology! Still, it's a question Allen's films repeatedly nudge us to ask, and one his two latest features—*Wild Man Blues* and his own **Deconstructing Harry**—are fixated on. In *Wild Man Blues,* an off-screen voice, presumably Kopple's, asks, "Woody, is this reality?" He replies, "For me, this is a total digression from reality."

A loaded question and a loaded answer. Ostensibly, Kopple is asking whether the business of touring with a jazz band, being filmed by her, taking part in press conferences, photo opportunities, autograph signings, can be considered part of his real life. No, he replies, real life for him takes place only within the familiar limits of Manhattan, consists only of the private routine of his writing, his filmmaking, his notoriously fastidious habits. But beyond that, Kopple seems to be asking a more abstract question about the business of being

Woody Allen: about what it might mean to be exposed, identified as 'Woody Allen himself', in a documentary made by someone else, as opposed to hiding behind the personae of his own fictions. Allen's reply doesn't begin to answer this: for playing the improbable part of 'Woody On Tour' is as much a fictional role as any other.

Allen's most recent such persona is a novelist suffering from creative stasis—and named Harry Block. Harry's family, erstwhile friends and ex-lovers deeply resent the way he has used them, lightly modified and portrayed in wildly uncomplimentary fashion, as characters in his fictions, some of which are extracted as narratives within the film. This womanising, pill-popping, depressive narcissist kidnaps his son, and, in the company of his last remaining friend and a prostitute hired as an escort, drives to his old college where his literary achievements are to be honoured. En route, he is berated by his sister and receives visitations from his own characters, finally attaining cathartic enlightenment about the nature of his life as man and writer.

If this film, through Harry, seems to be indirectly about the honouring of Woody Allen as fabulist, then *Wild Man Blues* is entirely about Allen's honouring in real life. He and his then-partner, now wife—"the notorious Soon-Yi Previn", as he introduces her—are filmed touring Europe with his New Orleans jazz band. Allen clearly hates life on the road, but is apparently able to shed his angst, and his self, when blowing clarinet on stage: "There's nothing between you and the pure feeling of the playing," he says. "There's no cerebral element at all."

His life does indeed seem hellish, and not just because he's cranky to the point of neurasthenia—he hates dogs, can't stand on marble even in luxury showers, gets seasick on a Venice vaporetto, could maybe learn to love Bologna's medieval streets given a couple of Valium. He can't get time or space alone: hotel guests phone his room begging for a photo, crowds cluster for a glimpse. Kopple sets the throngs of rubberneckers and paparazzi to Nino Rota's music from *8½*—an over-obvious choice given the setting and the image Allen has cultivated as a Fellini-esque creator who would love to escape into his fictions but whose real self can't help attracting worldly attention. When Allen and Soon-Yi take a quiet, unaccompanied trip in a Venice gondola (unaccompanied, that is, except for Kopple's crew), people crowd the bridges to look. "That's right, it's me, I'm the guy," says Allen with undisguised ill grace. "They won't pay ten cents to see one of my movies, but in a gondola they love it."

His discontent might be justified, except that a star who has so marketed his image can hardly complain when he is conspicuous: Woody is as much a self-trademarked character as Chaplin or Groucho Marx. But Kopple shows him constantly griping about fame. He worries that people will come and see his band not for the music, but because it's him. He's right—why else would people fill out a Milan concert hall for what he describes as "hardcore New Orleans jazz, esoteric tunes"? It's likely that audiences will rush for much the same reason to *Wild Man Blues*, which stands every chance of being more successful than *Deconstructing Harry*: after all, you can catch a new Woody Allen movie every year, but how often do you get to see him in a gondola?

*Wild Man Blues* looks like a case of special pleading—both a plea to be left alone and a plea not to take your eyes off him for a second. And the pleading, it seems, is largely Allen's own. This may be Kopple's film, but it is produced by Jean Doumanian—Allen's producer since *Bullets over Broadway* (1994)—and could not have been made without its subject's co-operation. At one point the film was reportedly to have been directed by Terry Zwigoff, whose *Crumb* performed a painful psychological dissection of cartoonist Robert Crumb. Allen was apparently impressed by the film's uncompromising nature, but in the final instance it seems Zwigoff bowed out because he was unable to secure complete control. This suggests that Kopple—a left-wing documentarist best known for her Academy Award-winning *Harlan County USA* (1976)—had to settle for less, and that it was Allen's camp who called the shots. This is not to belittle Kopple's integrity—but the pleasures of *Wild Man Blues* lie not in its revelations but in the ways it confirms our preconception that Allen really is a spoilt, kvetching fusspot: in short that he really is just like his screen persona.

*Wild Man Blues* belongs to a particular documentary genre, the 'access all areas' backstage movie, other notable examples being Alek Keshishian's 1991 *In Bed with Madonna* and D. A. Pennebaker's Bob Dylan film *Don't Look Back* (1967). These films depict not just the stage performance, but also the space around the performance—the dressing room, the tour bus, the hotel room. The artists under scrutiny ultimately control their own image by the way they behave in supposedly intimate scenes. And the artist finally calls the shots in terms of allowing access: the Madonna film contains a scene in which the star flamboyantly shuts Keshishian out of her space, or feigns to. Such films offer us a very limited spectacle of reality—it's hard to imagine what sort of 'real' personality could manifest itself in these privileged backstage spaces, the ante-rooms of performance. And while pop stars might find the tour jet more of a 'natural' habitat than their own homes, the retiring Allen is clearly likely to appear far more 'himself' in one of his fictions than in an Italian hotel suite.

*Wild Man Blues* is an object lesson in the unreliability of documentary. Kopple's questions to the participants are few and come seemingly at random. We see only selected aspects of the tour: little of the security and publicity machine that presumably surrounds Woody and Soon-Yi, only glimpses of an unidentified Jean Doumanian and her husband John, the tour manager. There is very little of Allen's interaction with the other musicians and nothing to indicate how the concerts might have related to Allen's filming of *Everyone Says I Love You* in Paris and Venice at around the same time. In an interview in *Libération*, Kopple says that Allen gave her complete access and never attempted to instruct her in any way. But because Allen seems to be so consummately performing his own role throughout, *Wild Man Blues* finally comes across as a promotional movie—promoting Allen as a personality, suggesting that he is every bit as we assumed him to be, and that we can take him or leave him as such.

In fact, the film seems like the culmination of an extensive PR campaign that has been under way since Allen's break-up with Mia Farrow, his embarking on a 'scandalous' relationship with her adopted daughter Soon-Yi, and the ensuing court case. Since then Allen, previously reclusive in the extreme, has been assiduously making himself available to the media. Since *Manhattan Murder Mystery* (1993) he has regularly explained himself in interviews both personally and as a film-maker, insisting that his films are not soul-searching but simple entertainment and are emphatically not about his own life. After *Husbands and Wives* (1992), a film about marital break-up that felt uncomfortably close to home in the wake of the Farrow affair, he made a series of impersonal-seeming movies that recast his earlier moral wranglings in the most accessible light-comedy terms (*Bullets over Broadway*), or were structured around gimmicky comic conceits (a Greek chorus in *Mighty Aphrodite,* 1995, song-and-dance in *Everyone Says . . .* , 1996). And the latest stage in this normalisation process seems to be *Wild Man Blues,* which presents Woody and Soon-Yi as a charming, regular, if dippy, tourist couple: in a Milan suite, complete with pool, he remarks it's an odd place for "two scuzzballs like us . . . like two kids locked into FAO Schwartz overnight." It's a cute double act, even if a degree of tetchiness shows through: amazed that Soon-Yi has never seen *Annie Hall,* he suggests, "go with one of your teenage twitty friends."

If this is the culmination of Woody's repackaging as a showbiz good guy, how are we to take the altogether more troubling *Deconstructing Harry*? For the first time since *Husbands and Wives,* Allen has cast himself as a man neck-deep in trauma, and as a character who might, in superficial and profound ways, be read as a representation of Allen himself—or, at least, of ways in which Allen has been perceived.

Harry Block, it is clear from the start, is thoroughly disagreeable, misguided, even *bad*. He also shares a few superficial traits with Woody Allen—he likes jazz and baseball, has been through a number of marriages, and is in long-term psychoanalysis. Harry is as close as dammit to being *explicitly* the dark side of Woody, amplifying what might be considered the worst traits of his creator's screen persona—hypochondria, sexual obsession, insensitivity, narcissism, and a self-ironising attitude to his Jewishness that could almost be construed as anti-Semitic. Aspects of Harry's character even appear to respond indirectly to Mia Farrow's accusations of child abuse: his behaviour with his son includes teaching him such terms as "banging beaver" and discussing penis size and lingerie.

What causes most resentment among his intimates is Harry's tendency to use life as material for fiction. The film opens with his ex-sister-in-law Lucy (Judy Davis) arriving at his apartment, first suicidal then homicidal because she recognises herself as the basis for his character Leslie, seen in a moment of grotesque farce enjoying an adulterous quickie with Harry's novelistic alter ego Ken. "It was loosely based on us," pleads Harry. "I lived through it with you—I know how 'loosely based' it was," she replies, cursing his "exaggerations—or as the critics say, inspired comic flights."

With what looks like typical disingenuousness, Allen has taken pains to distance himself from his character. He told the *New York Times*, "People confuse the details of Harry's life with my life, when I'm nothing like Harry . . . I've never experienced writer's block, I've never used the lives of my friends in fiction, like Harry. I've done 27 films and never once has anyone complained." He added, however, "Harry's philosophy speaks to me—I feel the same way he feels about women, about science, about philosophy, religion and art. But he's got such a chaotic life. He's got six hundred crises coming in on him from all sides. I don't." This last remark is rich, coming from someone whose recent life featured one single crisis convoluted enough to match all of Harry's put together.

Rather than ask whether Harry is or isn't a version of Woody, it seems more pertinent to ask why we are so interested in this question—why the films encourage us to sniff out traces of the 'real' Woody Allen in his characters (never forgetting that 'Woody Allen' was in the first place the invention of a stand-up comic from Brooklyn). The simple fact about these characters who appear to be versions of Woody Allen is that Woody Allen has chosen to play them. At the very least, we can say that he has a compulsion to exhibit himself on screen, or that he is the only actor he can trust to play certain parts. The fact that in *Deconstructing Harry* he casts other actors—Tobey Maguire, Richard Benjamin—as Harry's fictional selves only reinforces his own identification with Harry's real-world self.

Conversely, if he had really wanted us to identify any of his characters with himself, he could have called

them 'Woody Allen'. After all, Nanni Moretti makes films—*Caro diario* (*Dear Diary,* 1994), the forthcoming *Aprile*—in which he plays a character called 'Nanni Moretti' and which, as far as we can tell, dramatise his own life. Philip Roth's 1993 novel *Operation Shylock: A Confession* is a first-person narration by a character called 'Philip Roth', author of novels including *Portnoy's Complaint,* whose circumstances are remarkably similar to the real Philip Roth's; like him, and like Harry, he is accused of sexual immoderation and of Jewish self-hatred. And like Harry too, the real-life Roth has been accused of recasting his own life in print.

One suspects that Allen might specifically be using Roth as a narrative model. Harry's alter ego Ken is played by Richard Benjamin, an actor who in late 60s US cinema was as prominent an archetype of East Coast Jewish intellectual agony as Allen himself, playing the lead in two adaptations of Roth stories—*Goodbye, Columbus* (Larry Peerce, 1969) and *Portnoy's Complaint* (Ernest Lehman, 1972). Roth's experiments with ambivalent self-portraiture certainly allow Allen a ready-made structure for his creation of a character who can be interpreted both as himself and not himself. But as his title suggests, Allen invites us not to psychoanalyse, but to deconstruct: where Harry's fictions are taken by his angry acquaintances to refer directly to his own life, the film must be read indirectly as a commentary on the workings of Allen's fiction and can be made to yield up a theory of what Woody Allen's fiction is *for.*

*Deconstructing Harry* is Allen's contribution to an established genre of self-referential fiction—fiction that questions the ways writers are responsible for their lives, their work and the relations between them. In many such narratives, authors are seen to be not entirely in control of their work—and the creative block is the archetypal signifier of the writer's impotence, as well as working as a device to produce stasis, a blank space in which the writer is free (or forced) to reappraise his or her position. It's the subject of *Operation Shylock*; of Proust's *Recherche* (the whole story is that of the narrator's failure to turn his life satisfactorily into writing); and in film of *8½,* a movie whose own genesis is enacted in the traumas of Fellini's director hero Guido.

Creative juices stalled, Harry reviews his back catalogue of stories. One resembles Allen's own *New Yorker* tales: an actor suddenly discovers he is in soft-focus. The story of Epstein, who marries his analyst only for her to turn Jewish on him, is pure Roth. And the old Jewish man with a horrific secret could be straight from Isaac Bashevis Singer.

As Harry's characters and their real-life models pile up, the effect of the various doublings becomes deeply confusing. Epstein's wife (Demi Moore) turns out to be an amalgam of Harry's analyst ex (Kirstie Alley) and his sister. There's a real-life Lucy and a fictional Leslie (Julia Louis-Dreyfus), while Harry's rival and satanic counterpart (Billy Crystal) is called Larry. The reflections also extend to other Allen films—Larry is another of those resented buddies turned rivals, as played in the past by Tony Roberts and Alan Alda, and Fay (Elisabeth Shue) is another incarnation of the elusive princess, like Mariel Hemingway in *Manhattan* (1979) or Juliette Lewis in *Husbands and Wives.* Several performers recur from other films by Allen, who has generally avoided Altman-style 'repertory' casting: Bob Balaban, Julie Kavner, Caroline Aaron, Judy Davis, Hemingway.

Harry finally learns a lesson and achieves his unblocking—rather too neatly, perhaps, as the characters line up to dispense wisdom in the final reel. But his education comes with a twist that seems a radical reversal of the customary Hollywood catharsis. His friend Richard (Balaban), reappearing from beyond the grave, advises, "Make peace with your demons and your block will pass. To be alive is to be happy." It's a banal lesson, and Harry knows it: "It sounds trite, I know," he ponders. In fact the lesson has, in the previous sequence, been taken quite literally. In a moment of self-awareness, Harry agonises, "I'm the worst person in the world—who's worse than me?", and then, in a new story, meets his counterpart—the Devil himself, played by Harry's rival Larry. They compare notes, and degrees of wickedness. Instead of denying his own evil side, Harry accepts it and learns a crucial lesson from Satan: "Life's like Vegas—the house always wins, but in the end you had fun."

*In the end you had fun.* It would be satisfying to close on this note, but one more lesson follows. The whole swarm of Harry's characters gather round to present their own homage to their creator, and he honours them in turn: "I love all of you—you've given me the happiest moments of my life." Who would have thought that Woody Allen would break the *Seinfeld* golden rule—"No lessons, no hugs"?

Embracing writing rather than the world as his *real* life, Harry can retreat again into fiction, embarking on another self-referential tale, this time about one Rifkin and his awareness of fragmentation. Here, in the closing moments, we at last have an explanation of the jump-cut editing style that runs through the film, disrupting its real-world sequences—which have the feel of a book someone is flicking through—but leaving the interpolated fictions intact. For Harry, it is life, not fiction, that is provisional, rearrangeable. Harry is faced with a choice—to function in life or in art; to visit the outer world, like Amazon traveller Larry, or to stay home and explore inner landscapes. He chooses the latter.

All of which begs the question: is that all there is? The idea for a character who can't function in life, but only in art? Harry's finishing point is in fact the starting point of much modernist fiction, generally regarded as an obstacle to overcome rather than the outcome of a moral/aesthetic quest. True, this ending seems an unimaginable heresy beside the average Hollywood finale, which finds in favour of the outside world (the 'curing' of Jack Nicholson's neurotic, closeted writer in the current *As Good As It Gets*). But in the context of modernist film, it has an obvious model: the merging of life and fiction in Harry's honour ceremony restages the dancing ronde of Guido's familiars at the end of *8½.* Allen's conclusion seems so much less satisfactory, however, in that Harry is finally reunited only with his characters while Guido enlists the cast of his life into his imaginary repertory company.

***Deconstructing Harry*** does finally offer some sort of key to Allen's fictions, and to what they might mean to him—if not as a person, then as an artist. The film's recycling of identities, themes and actors suggests that Allen has only a limited need of new stimuli. Just as Harry is finally able to pursue further variants on his writing, so Woody Allen need never fear creative exhaustion: delving into his own repertoire, he can go on generating new fictions forever.

The ending of Allen's meatiest, most deconstructible text for some time reassures fans that they should stick around for further developments. Yet there is also something dispiriting about the notion that he is reconciled to the outside world evading him. He has always admitted to having little understanding of the sphere outside his enchanted circle—claiming, for example, that his films lacked black characters because he didn't sufficiently know black people. At last—***Deconstructing Harry***'s most glaring flaw—he has a black character, and she proves to be a monstrous stereotype, a tart-with-a-heart called Cookie (Hazelle Goodman) who is as excruciating a figure of the 'other' that Allen cannot comprehend as Mira Sorvino's chipper tart in ***Mighty Aphrodite*** or Tim Roth's two-dimensional hood in ***Everyone Says. . . .***

And as we see in *Wild Man Blues,* Allen has also admitted defeat with place: his recent ventures beyond the gates of Manhattan show his myopia towards the outside world. In ***Everyone Says . . .*** his characters go to Venice and jog as if they were on Central Park West, while Paris is seen as an adjunct of movieland, with Fred-and-Ginger dance routines by the Seine. As much as ***Deconstructing Harry,*** his recent inferior films are a strong argument for staying in his uptown enclave, where he thrives.

So, with ***Deconstructing Harry*** and *Wild Man Blues* presenting a view from inside and outside, do we finally know Woody Allen any better? I think we do, if only in terms of understanding the problems of his fictional production and the limits of his relation to the world. Finally, only his fictions can comment authoritatively on where Woody's at, just as it is Harry's characters who provide true insight into Harry: Ken, Harry's fictional self, tells him, "I'm not like your shrink. He knows what you tell him. I know the truth."

If Harry's characters get the last word on him, in *Wild Man Blues* the last word on Woody is given to his mother. The film ends, against all expectations, with what seems an irreducible moment of truth—one that, if you wanted to be crassly psychoanalytical, might seem to explain all Woody's troubles from way back. Kopple accompanies him and Soon-Yi on a visit to his parents Nettie and Martin, aged 90 and 96 respectively. It turns out to be a "lunch from hell", as Allen puts it, as awful a parental nightmare as the one in *New York Stories* (1989), whose hero is plagued by a celestial scolding supermom. Woody comes laden with honours from abroad, but his father tells him he might have done more good as a pharmacist. "You did a lot of good things, but you never pursued them," laments Nettie, then delivers the killer punch. In earshot of Soon-Yi, she bemoans, "I would have liked him from the beginning to fall in love with a . . . [*whisper*] nice Jewish girl."

Has *this* been his problem all along: a man who's spent his whole life playing the guilt-ridden son to parents who still see him as a feckless adolescent—and he turns out to be just that? In a rare manipulative stroke, Kopple also gives his mother the final say on Woody's work. "Are Woody's films about his real life?" she asks. "Sometimes, but very seldom," Mrs Konigsberg replies. "He adds and subtracts from his life. He doesn't want to make a movie of his life." Then she makes an imperious gesture—"Now go" and dismisses the camera, guests and audience. And Woody and Soon-Yi presumably head off to unwind with that long-promised duck wonton.

### Kent Jones (essay date May-June 1998)

SOURCE: Jones, Kent. "Into the Woods." *Film Comment* 34, no. 3 (May-June 1998): 4-6.

[*In the following letter, written as a response to an article by David Thompson published in an earlier issue of* Film Comment, *Jones agrees with many of the points in Thompson's piece, but refutes and questions several key assertions made by Thompson about the quality of Allen's films.*]

Dear David [Thomson],

With respect for you and for your work (in your case I don't find it at all difficult to like the artist), I have a couple of problems with your assessment of Woody Allen in the last issue of *Film Comment.* I think you do a great job of detailing the drama of your own shifting feelings about Allen, but the films you describe don't quite conform to the ones I've seen. I'm not sure if you're as interested in the films as you are in the man, and the way that his presence provokes alternating feelings of goodwill and revulsion.

I'll start with a compliment: it's one of the more probing and intelligent pieces I've read about Allen, and I enthusiastically agree with most of the points you make. I too think *Deconstructing Harry* is a bold, bracing film. And while I feel that it's far from his worst, I would have to agree that *Crimes and Misdemeanors* is a pretentious, insanely overrated movie that imposes a WASPish solemnity on its predominantly Jewish milieu and betrays a profound moral confusion in its portrayal of Allen's own character (although given the fact that his subsequent films were so much better, the confusion seems to have been productive in the long run). I also agree that Allen has improved over the years, as he's been willing to forgo some of the many annoying constants of his cinema. And I also agree that he has a perfect right to deal with what he likes and imagines rather than what he thinks might interest others—I love the gangsters in *Bullets over Broadway,* and I love the ones in *Radio Days* and *Broadway Danny Rose* even more. And even though you don't deal with it directly, you manage to address the endlessly repeated complaints about Allen's blinkered vision of Manhattan, which I've never found convincing, even when making them myself—can anyone justifiably fault an artist for what he or she *doesn't* pay attention to?

I'll even go your qualified praise one better by repeating what has been said so often: that Woody Allen is a New York institution. I rejoice whenever one of his films opens. For the record, I think *Husbands and Wives* is close to a great film, and that *Manhattan Murder Mystery* is the genuine article. Finally, I agree that his personal life has no bearing on the value of his work, except to the extent that the turmoil of five years ago seems to have sharpened his powers as an artist. (On the other hand, I can't exactly share your amazement at the realization that most artists are assholes—is there anyone who ever even dreamed that Fritz Lang was a nice guy?)

In fact, David, I only have difficulty with two ideas in your piece, albeit pretty central ones. First of all, your contention that Allen has become "one of the most graceful, spatially enquiring composers in American film." And secondly, your confident declaration that "this is a great filmmaker." If you'll allow me to sum up your piece as a grudging but finally exalted cry from the rooftops of the maxim "Practice makes perfect," then imagine me as a shocked bystander looking up from the ground below and shouting in response: "Some people have it and some people don't."

Over the years, there has been more unreflectively worshipful prose written about Woody Allen than about any other American filmmaker. This is probably due to the fact that his admirers are so partisan: every film that comes out is first and foremost the latest model from the Woody Allen factory, secondly another installment in the ongoing saga of Allen's artistic growth, and only thirdly a film. In this sense Allen suffers from the same malady as Bergman and Godard, whose admirers have in some ways done them more damage than good by creating flawless, omniscient Idols in their image. Maybe it's just my imagination, but in Allen's case I sense a quiet satisfaction with such tripe, an artistic complacency that has ultimately led to movies like *Interiors* or *September.* Any other director would have been demolished for making such patently false and relentlessly sterile films, but for Woody's fans they were necessary steps in his evolution, as both a person and as an artist. I'm always amazed when Allen's alleged perfectionism is dramatized in hagiographic magazine profiles by the story about how he shot *September* two and a half times with three different casts before he felt he got it right. Surely the more astonishing fact is that he made such an idiotic movie in the first place.

The popular myth is that Allen came of artistic age with *Annie Hall* and has been growing steadily as a filmmaker ever since: we're constantly reminded of his ever-increasing maturity, which is starting to get a little tired now that he's in his mid-60s. Of course, this kind of cheerleading has less to do with Allen as an artist than as the purveyor of a smooth-sell urbanity liberally seasoned with infectious self-deprecation, brilliantly harnessed, streamlined, and toughened up in the Nineties by "Seinfeld," whose titanic popularity has imbued Woody's films with a quaint, homemade quality that suits his dotage well. The fact that *Manhattan* is a big mug full of Woody's Brew while *Alice* is a piddly little shot of it hardly matters—the important thing is that it's always slightly different yet fundamentally unchanged. Thus the astonishing sameness of his films from year to year, so that the pace (sprightly but measured and unvarying, like a song by the Boswell Sisters), tone (uniformly pleasant, discreetly uninquisitive, sweetly chaste), and sense of physicality (people either moving frantically in the midst of some private quest or nervous activity, or seated at a table confessing or listening to a confession) combine to create the effect of a comfy pair of old shoes. This has often been referred to as stylistic consistency. But I would call it an inventory, which also consists of visual tics (people framed through doorways as they purposefully walk to and fro, neutrally shaded color coordination that seems therapeutically designed not to hurt the eyes), relationships (Allen and an adoring young woman; Allen and a smooth friend, said smoothness inevitably revealed to be a sign of moral weakness; Allen and a child whom

he is gently instructing in the ways of the world), a careful balance of high- and low-cultural reference points (often stuffed into the dialogue like four pounds of candy into a three-pound bag, as in "Here, you dropped your book of Edna St. Vincent Millay poems"), seriocomic obsessions (the expansion of the universe, whether or not God is just), cinematic reference points (Bergman and Fellini), and locations around New York. See enough of his work and you'll eventually be struck with the remarkable, touching, and rather terrifying realization that each item on the inventory is carried into each film the way a child brings a teddy bear to bed.

And, of course, the final but most crucial item is Woody Allen, either in the flesh or not. As you point out so well, his is an aggressively inert presence that organizes the world around itself rather than gets up to meet it. Thus Allen's terrifying knack for getting actors of all shapes and levels of inspiration and experience to move and talk like himself. Never has a supposedly great director given more gifted actors less to do, and only tough, deep-dish talents like Dianne Wiest, Michael Caine, Blythe Danner, Martin Landau, or Judy Davis have the muscle to hack through the films' Teflon-coated tidiness (or else it melts in the heat of Allen's ardor for Diane Keaton).

\* \* \*

Another related byproduct of this extraordinary insularity is the oddly presentational sense of space that he's never shaken since his days as a sketch filmmaker. David, I have to admit that you lose me when you posit Allen as a "spatially enquiring" filmmaker. Maybe we just have vastly different ideas about what constitutes spatial enquiry in filmmaking, but it's hard for me to think of another filmmaker *less* interested in space— visual, narrative, psychological, or metaphorical—and the possibilities it offers. Allen always gets into a scene in the same fashion, with an apparently off-the-cuff establishing shot followed by a series of setups that feel like a succession of squares within squares. Even his closeups often seem like establishing shots, so pathologically constant is his superstitious lack of interest in specifics. Particularly during his endless Gordon Willis period, Allen's cinema played in the mind as a succession of "homely," semi-elegant camera placements to which the actors (and the director himself) seemed to be only partially privy. I also applaud the partnership with Carlo Di Palma for the warmth and relative spontaneity it has brought to Allen's cinema, but I can't agree that it adds up to a passionate spatial enquiry—it simply puts a little more spring in the step of an emotionally withholding camera.

The poolroom sequence you cite in *Bullets over Broadway,* one of Allen's prettiest films, is very handsome, but can it honestly be said that it's even close to the priceless habit of seizing on offhand details that makes Renoir's cinema so rapturously beautiful? To my eyes, it looks like nothing more than a nicely understated dramatic confrontation, made possible by a comfortable partnership between director, cinematographer, and set designer, and tonally indistinguishable from the rest of the movie. Unless he is isolating a woman in a warm glow of desire (Keaton at the microphone in *Annie Hall*, Wiest in the final shot of *Hannah and Her Sisters*), Allen always approaches his actors in the same polite, sidelong fashion, whereas Renoir seized on the individual magic of each actor and carved out a place for it, joyfully disrupting the narrative flow; think of Jouvet's walk in *Les Bas-fonds*, or the time and care taken to isolate the different styles of movement of the three girls in *The River*. When it comes to spatial enquiry in modern cinema, nothing Allen has ever done comes within hailing distance of the party scene in Assayas's *Cold Water*, the climax of Hartley's *Simple Men*, the hotel sequences in Jacquot's *La Fille seule*, or any given moment in the last two Tsai Ming-liang films. And is there anything in Allen's entire 26⅓-strong oeuvre that equals the excitement of a single shot from *Satyricon* or *Fanny and Alexander*, to name one movie each by the directors of whom he is most enamored?

If I'm being tough on Allen, it's because he's gotten such a free ride for so many years from people who confuse cultish self-deprecation with real artistry—was there ever another filmmaker whose personality was so integral to every single discussion of his work? I guess I feel that, despite your well-observed qualifications, you're waving him through the tollbooth one more time by coming to the conclusion that he is—let's face it—a "great filmmaker." In terms of sheer visibility and, yes, productivity, I can accept "major filmmaker." But great? Does Woody Allen really have to be compared to Jean Renoir to prove that he's not Edward L. Cahn? Moreover, what exactly is the intrinsic virtue of a short running time? I'd rather sit through a Val Lewton movie than almost anything, and the economy of the films he produced is certainly one of their pleasures, but I also get a lot of pleasure out of the time that Tarantino takes with *Jackie Brown* or, for that matter, that Kubrick takes with *Barry Lyndon*. I'm not so sure that the uneasiness and selfconsciousness of "the great untidy group of acquaintances" is Allen's true subject. And pardon me if I characterize your evocation of Renoir on this point as a sort of safety net. Aside from the fact that their films often feature large numbers of people interacting with one another, it's difficult for me to think of two artists more dissimilar than Jean Renoir and Woody Allen. The former makes films whose rough beauty flows directly from the reality of whatever is before his camera, while the latter makes films whose beauty often feels like it's been appliquéd over the image. The former stretches the shape of his scenes to accommodate the most wayward emotions and sensations, while the latter

always maintains the same discreet distance, the same dramatic tidiness and virtually the same pace from film to film. Which is why I must respectfully disagree with your thematic assessment of *Bullets over Broadway,* a hilarious and beautifully embroidered joke about the lure of artistic pretension that is about 10,000 light-years away from the profoundly human irony that closes *French Cancan*.

I don't think that Woody Allen makes films about the people he knows as much as the people he wants to know, or, to put it more exactly, the people he wants to have known, and among whom he wants to have grown up. The look of people in an Allen film is always valid and true; he knows the surfaces of affluent Manhattan unlike anyone else. But the minute a character opens his or her mouth it becomes clear that we're into something much stranger than a keen observation of the self consciousness of modern New Yorkers. Woody's "pictures" indeed—his secondary characters often leave me with the feeling that Allen spends his evenings hiding pods in the basements and cellars of upper Manhattan. The range of obsessions, conversational topics, phobias, neuroses, and even physical postures never changes, the cultural reference points are rarely if ever contemporary (jazz or pop standards from the Thirties through the Fifties, "intellectual" chatter that proves that Allen doesn't get out of the house much), and the overall ambience always strikes me as circa 1965. In other words, I think that in order to maintain his awestruck feelings about rich Manhattanites, he can't allow himself to dig too deeply beneath appearances. The fact that Allen never budges from his short range of private archetypes gives his films a charming coziness that makes them one of the small glories of modern cinema, but it's also what gives them their precious, faintly mildewed aroma, like an old lady's pantry.

I agree that the "events of 1993" proved to be a tonic for Allen's movies—after thirty years, he finally discovered both agitation and eroticism, which cross paths so brilliantly in that astonishing moment in *Husbands and Wives* when Judy Davis recites an obsessive-compulsive interior monologue as Liam Neeson goes down on her. But if the more apparently modest *Manhattan Murder Mystery* strikes me as the greater film, it's because it has a very unusual structure (for Allen) that plays on the insularity that runs through the rest of his movies as an unsettling subtext (he wants to stay home and ignore the signs that his neighbor is a murderer, while his wife wants to follow the adventure and reinvigorate her life). I think that the return of Diane Keaton liberates him and his camera, leading to a genuinely warm expression of marital fulfillment and an over-the-shoulder hymn to New York that has a much lighter and less compulsive feeling than usual. It's in this joyous and fundamentally honest movie that Woody finds a grace that has always eluded him. Renoir it ain't—but maybe it's Pagnol. Or maybe just Woody Allen, whose fear of the big wide world out there has allowed us to keep our dream of a glittering, vibrant Manhattan intact.

Best,

Kent

## Doug Sternberg (essay date 1998)

SOURCE: Sternberg, Doug. "Who Shot the Seagull? Anton Chekhov's Influence on Woody Allen's *Bullets over Broadway.*" *Literature/Film Quarterly* 26, no. 3 (1998): 204-13.

[*In the following essay, Sternberg discusses the influence of Anton Chekhov's play* The Seagull *on Allen's film* Bullets over Broadway.]

> I wasn't equal to it. But maybe next time I will be, or maybe it will take me five more tries. But it's the goal that's important. With these kinds of films you're talking about the highest kind of achievement—like that of O'Neill, Chekhov, Bergman . . . Maybe now that I've moved into my fifties and I am more confident, I can come up with a couple that are true literature.

> —Woody Allen (Lax 371-72)

Woody Allen, despite his lack of a formal education, has always seemed to be well-versed in Russian literature. There are, for example, numerous references to Tolstoy and Dostoevsky throughout his work. In *Bullets over Broadway,* he owes a special debt to Chekhov in terms of plot, characterization, and the creative life of the Russian writer and playwright that resonates throughout the film.

The infrastructure and themes of *Bullets* resemble most closely Chekhov's first major play, *The Seagull.* Prominent features of both are the struggles of young writers and actresses, numerous love triangles, debates about art and the artist, two writers with different talents and destinies who are in love with leading ladies,[1] an overbearing grande dame of the theater, a play within each work, concluding gun shots, and final revelations from those characters capable of seeing themselves and their circumstances for what they truly are. The theatrical spirit of the film is reinforced as well through "Allen's decision to frame most of his scenes in longshot (as if we are watching a play through a proscenium)."[2]

*Bullets* opens with David Shayne (John Cusack) declaring to his agent Julian Marx[3] (Jack Warden), "I'm an artist and I won't change a word of my play to pander to some commercial Broadway audience."[4] To Marx's

objections that he cannot afford another financial failure, David declares, "It's the theater's duty not just to entertain, but to transform men's souls." Chekhov's Treplev is just as earnest as he describes the open-air theater upon which his play involving the world soul will be staged: "There's a theatre for you! Just the curtain and the two wings and beyond it—open space. No scenery. You have an unimpeded view of the lake and the horizon. We'll raise the curtain at half past nine when the moon comes up."[5] Just as David pursues his mission by staging *God of Our Fathers,* Treplev's work is a challenge to his mother's theatrical world. He says:

> Moreover, she knows that I have no use for the theatre. She loves the theatre, she imagines that she's serving humanity, whereas in my opinion the theatre of today is in a rut, and full of prejudices and conventions. When I see the curtain rise on a room with three walls, when I watch these great and talented people, these high priests of a sacred art depicting the way people eat, drink, make love, walk about and wear their clothes, in the artificial light of the stage; when I hear them trying to squeeze a moral out of the tritest words and emptiest scenes—some petty little moral that's easy to understand and suitable for use in the home; when I'm presented with a thousand variations of the same old thing time, the same thing again and again—well, I just have to escape, I run away as Maupassant ran away from the Eiffel Tower which so oppressed him with its vulgarity.

> (123)

David begins his work on a hopeful note. He writes, "Monday, September 10. Today rehearsals began and I have decided to keep a journal. Perhaps my experience will be of value to others just as I have poured over with relish the notes of my idols, Chekhov and Strindberg." And in keeping with Treplev's need for Nina to be exactly on time and to deliver his lines on the makeshift stage, David initially is adamant about his casting choices. He calls the mob moll Olive (Jennifer Tilly) a "thing" and refuses to consider her for the role of the psychiatrist. When David does capitulate to guarantee funding for the production, he tries to set a professional tone at the first rehearsal when she is accompanied by Cheech the bodyguard (Chazz Palminteri): "I don't like other people watching rehearsals, generally as a rule, because the actors are very sensitive." Needless to say, Cheech stays put.

Both David and Treplev exit in agitation throughout both film and play respectively. Toward the end of his meeting with the mobster Nick Valenti (Joe Viterelli) and Olive, David admits, "I'm feeling a bit unstable. I think maybe I'll go and check into a sanitarium and get the help that I need. . . ." Later, when Cheech complains about David's writing in front of the cast by calling it "garbage" and announcing, "She's right, it stinks . . . It's a stupid way of talking and nobody talks like that," David storms out of the theater as Olive calls him "Mr. Temperamental." Treplev reacts in a similar way when his work is not appreciated:

> That's enough! Curtain! Let down the curtain! [*Stamping his foot.*] Curtain!
>
> [*The curtain drops.*]
>
> I apologize! I overlooked the fact that only a select few are permitted to write plays and act on the stage. I've encroached on the preserves of a monopoly! To me . . . I mean, I . . . . [*Tries to continue, then makes a resigned gesture and goes out to the left.*]
>
> (131)[6]

Valenti's gangster Cheech is called a "Neanderthal," a "strong-arm man with an IQ of minus fifty," a "goon," and a "gorilla." But according to Woody Allen,[7] Cheech is the true artist in ***Bullets***. Note how he continually emphasizes the need for simplicity and realism regarding David's writing. And Arkadina says of the writer Trigorin, "You musn't talk like that. When anyone talks high-flown language to him, he hasn't the least idea what to say" (134). Trigorin, like Cheech, is indifferent to fame as he asks, "What sort of feeling? Perhaps none. I've never thought about it. [*After a moment's thought.*] It's one thing or the other. Either you exaggerate the extent of my fame, or I'm quite insensitive to it" (146). Cheech will remain on the periphery, content to let David accept the acclaim.

Treplev is threatened by Trigorin as well in terms of his talent and manhood, especially since Nina and Arkadina praise the established writer's work and are romantically involved with him. Treplev tells Nina, "It started that evening when my play was such a stupid fiasco. Women don't forgive failure. I burnt it all, down to the last scrap . . . My play wasn't liked, you despise my kind of inspiration, and now you think I'm commonplace and insignificant, just like all the rest" (145-146). In ***Bullets*** Helen Sinclair (Dianne Wiest) refers to David's original draft as the "eunuch version," and the cast reacts to Cheech's rewrite with the very accolades David has desired: "brilliant," and "the whole thing . . . drives on." He is called "a major talent," "a major new voice in the theater," and a "genius." Eden Brent (Tracey Ullman) sums up the reactions with "Congratulations, it finally has balls."

The issue of men writing for women is discussed in both works. David's girlfriend Ellen (Mary-Louise Parker) thinks that Helen's Sylvia Poston is the best female character David has written in a long time. She says that he has "problems getting into the female mind" and continues with "All your friends are men. You've always had problems writing for women. Witness your relationship with your mother, your grandmother, your two aunts, your sister." David responds by saying that Ellen does not understand his work at all. Trigorin likewise admits to Nina that ". . . the girls in my novels and stories are usually so artificial. I wish I could exchange places with you, even if only for an hour, just to find out what your thoughts are . . ." (146).

After another episode David decides to apologize to the "big Gorgonzola," and admits that he overreacted as his ego got in the way of the work. Cheech then gives him advice which shows that there is little distinction between Helen and her character Sylvia: "She's too . . . on top of him all the time. That's not love. That's like keeping somebody in prison." David senses that Cheech is "talking about a whole different direction for the play." Cheech suggests monologues and opportunities for the suspension of disbelief which the younger writer has not considered. And David refers to himself as a "struggling writer." Note Trigorin's description of his creative beginnings which mirrors the difficulties faced by young David and Treplev:

> As for the years when I was starting—my younger, better years—in those days my writing used to be one continuous torment. A minor writer, especially if he hasn't had much luck, sees himself as clumsy, awkward, and unwanted. He gets nervous and overwrought, and feels irresistibly drawn towards people connected with literature, or art, but then he wanders among them unrecognized and unnoticed, unable to look them straight and courageously in the eye. . . .
>
> (148-49)

Later, David spends all night working on his third act, but nevertheless asks Cheech to read it. Cheech then insists on writing the script and demands that David shoot a rack of pool. He tells him: "You missed the idea . . . nobody talks like that. You really got that problem. You don't write like people talk . . . Poetic license bullshit. People believe what they see when the actors sound real . . . I know how people talk . . . I saw you playing the big shot. I know what it's all about. Where I come from nobody squeals."

During another session of collaborative work Cheech suggests that Sylvia have visions of her dead husband. David feels that the suggestion is "great" and then says that Cheech has "a huge [writing] gift . . . It's uncanny . . . your instincts . . . really enviable." Cheech reassures him with "Let me tell you something. Listen to me. Your play was very good. Your play was very good. You just didn't use your head. Sometimes people don't think." To David's statement that he has studied play writing with every teacher and read every book, Cheech responds, "Let me tell you something about teachers. I hate teachers. Those blue-haired bitches used to whack us with rulers. Forget teachers." David understands his own limitations in much the same way that Treplev realizes he cannot write like Trigorin:

> Trigorin has worked out his own methods—it comes easily to him. . . . He would just mention the neck of a broken bottle glistening on the dam and the black

shadow of a mill-wheel—and there you'd have a moonlit night. But I have to put in the tremulous light, the soft twinkling of the stars, and the distant sounds of a piano, dying away in the still, fragrant air. . . . It's excruciating!

(177)

Trigorin offers Treplev some false praise in Act IV. However, like David, who is not the true author of *God of Our Fathers,* no one knows the younger writer's real name because he always publishes under a pseudonym. He is ". . . as mysterious as the Man in the Iron Mask" (173). Trigorin's observations on Treplev's writing, though more severe, could sum up Cheech's commentaries regarding David's work: "He's unlucky. He still can't manage to strike the right note somehow. There's something strange and vague about his writing . . . not a single living character" (175)!

David will realize that the initial praise of his play is groundless ("thrilling," "turbulent," "a page turner," "It's a wonderful play, lovely speeches") and that positive reactions after Cheech's contributions should be directed toward the far more talented collaborator. He eventually walks away from the public accolades Cheech will never hear as Marx reads reviews which include praise for the misinterpreted gunshots that killed the true author: "A masterpiece. A theatrical stunner. A work of art of the highest quality . . . Writer-Director David Shayne is the find of the decade." Likewise, Treplev loses faith in his own work, though he has made a significant impression on Doctor Dorn. Dorn says that he believes in Treplev, is moved by his writing, and feels that he ". . . thinks in images, his stories are vivid, full of colour . . ." (176). In Act I, Dorn is the only character to engage the young man's play:

> I don't know, maybe I don't understand anything, maybe I've gone off my head, but I did like that play. There is something in it. When that child was holding forth about loneliness, and later when the devil's red eyes appeared, I was so moved that my hands were shaking. It was fresh, unaffected. . . . Ah! I think he's coming along now. I feel like telling him a lot of nice things about it.

(135)[8]

Cheech is ultimately far more passionate than Trigorin and as extreme as Treplev regarding his work. Despite the fact that Olive cannot act, David is willing to compromise, make concessions, and claims that her "notices were decent." Cheech is incensed and responds with "Decent? Is that what you want? Decent ain't good enough. She's killin my words . . . I can't have her ruining my show . . . I put a lot into this and it could have been perfect." Eventually Cheech murders Olive to save *his* play and then defends himself by asking, "You think it's right some tootsie walks in and messes up a beautiful thing like this, eh?" Cheech tells David

that nobody is going to ruin what he wrote before throwing the younger man on the floor. He then decides to attend the New York opening where he is gunned down by Valenti's men. And David tells him just before the shooting that he cannot forgive him for killing Olive: "I don't care what kind of a genius you are." Treplev will make a point of facetiously referring to Trigorin as a genius.

Olive[9] is a laughable counterpart to Chekhov's Nina; both women aspire to be actresses. Olive says, "I'm fed up. I'm fed up . . . I am not sharing a dressing room . . . Six months, six months, and I'm still stuck in this crummy rat trap . . . I came to New York to be an actress." She insists that she has experience, despite the fact that "she used to wiggle at this joint in Hoboken . . . pick up quarters off the tabletops with her. . . ." But Olive, who has some ideas to "goose up" David's play, claims that she had two songs ". . . in a musical review in Wichita . . . *Leave a Specimen.*" She did not come to New York just "to swing it around in a chorus line." Nina expresses the desire for "real, resounding fame" like that which David needs before his gradual corruption. Like David, she will learn more about the demands of art by not achieving her original goal.

Both women have problems on stage. Olive feels that everybody is "so stuck up," and reacts negatively to the expectation that she memorize lines. She says, "Imagine that director telling me I'm overacting in the first scene and I don't know what I'm saying." David writes in his diary regarding their Boston preview: "It went well, although my heart's in my mouth every time Olive speaks." In Act IV, Treplev claims that Nina ". . . would always take on big parts, but she acted them crudely, without distinction—with false intonations and violent gestures. There were moments when she showed talent—as when she uttered a cry, or died on the stage— but they were only moments" (171). Nina confirms that earlier she acted on the stage "stupidly" and "abominably," but she has since become a "real actress" who performs with "enthusiasm" and feels both "intoxicated" and "beautiful" on stage (181). Nina believes that she will become "a great actress." Olive, who initially told David that she is a "great actress," eventually is killed by Cheech because she is a "horrible actress."

Nina and Olive are critical of their respective playwrights. Olive ponderously delivers the line: "The heart is . . . a maze beset with brutal pitfalls and mean obstacles." David explains after she refuses to say it as written, "It's just a stylish way of expressing a particular idea." But Olive is unconvinced. She says, "It doesn't make sense. It's stupid. I don't get it," then mispronounces "gibberish" in reference to the line before declaring, "No, I'm not making a fool of myself." During a later rehearsal Eden feels that she is mouthing the playwright's philosophy, while Olive adds that it is "bad writing." Then Cheech offers a better plot twist which the company accepts, because the innovation is the way "it would happen in real life." David becomes nonplussed and is accused of being egotistical as he leaves with the declaration "I quit." Nina also makes her feelings known by saying that Treplev's play is "so uninteresting" (140). In this regard, Chekhov's earlier dialogue is especially revealing:

> Nina. It's difficult to act in your play. There are no real living characters in it.
>
> Treplev. Living characters! We don't have to depict life as it is, or as it ought to be, but as we see it in our dreams.[10]
>
> Nina. But there's hardly any action in your play, there are only speeches. And then I do think there ought to be love in a play.
>
> (126)

Nina's observations on famous people reflect the characters' behavior in ***Bullets*** and David's eventual understanding of New York's all-too-human theater world: "How strange it is to see a famous actress crying . . . and for such a trifling reason . . . I used to think that famous people were proud and inaccessible and that they despised the crowd; I thought that the glory and lustre of their names enabled them, as it were, to revenge themselves on people who put birth and wealth above everything else. But here they are, crying, fishing, playing cards, laughing and getting angry like anyone else" (144-145). Likewise, Nina's description of her home life in contrast to Arkadina's estate is like Ellen's situation in Pittsburgh before she follows David to Greenwich Village: "My father and stepmother won't let me come here. They say this place is Bohemian . . . they're afraid of my going on the stage. And I am drawn to this place, to this lake, as if I were a seagull" (125).

The similarities between Helen Sinclair and Arkadina are the most striking. Arkadina's first words to Treplev after her entrance (128) are from *Hamlet*: "'Oh, Hamlet, speak no more! / Thou turn'st mine eyes into my very soul; / And there I see such black and grained spots / As will not leave their tinct.'" They are in keeping with Helen's catch phrase throughout the film, "Don't speak," and her ode in the theater cut short by the barking of Eden's dachshund Woofles before the first rehearsal: "This old theater. This church, so replete with memories, so full of ghosts. Mrs. Alving. Uncle Vanya. There's Cordelia. There's Ophelia. Clytemnestra. Each performance a birth. Each curtain a death." Treplev's description of his mother could apply to Helen:

> . . . she leads such a fatuous life, for ever fussing around with this novelist of hers, her name always being bandied about in the papers. I find it all so fatiguing. And sometimes I simply regret, like the ordinary selfish mortal I am, that I have a famous actress for a mother, and I find myself imagining that if she were an ordinary woman I should have been happier.
>
> (123)[11]

Helen initially imitates the sceptical Arkadina in reacting to the work of "a novice" who is the author of "two flops." She throws the script downstairs and yells, "You must be joking. You want me to play some frumpy housewife who gets dumped for a flapper? Don't you know who I am? Don't you remember who you represent? I'm Helen Sinclair . . . My ex-husband used to say, 'If you're going to go down, go down with the best of them' . . . I don't know which ex-husband. The one with the mustache." Her agent Sid Loomis (Harvey Fierstein) reminds her that she is better known as an adulteress and a drunk who has not had a hit in a very long time.[12] Only when she receives flowers sent by David does she moderate her views. His card reads: "As a small artist to a greater one, that you merely consider my play is all the fulfillment I require." She is assured that her billing will be over the title and that David is ". . . terrific, a genius ready to emerge." Arkadina is also impressed with gifts as she talks of her reception in Kharkov and declares, "The students gave me a regular ovation. . . . Three baskets of flowers, two garlands, and this as well. . . . [*Unfastens a brooch on her throat and tosses it on to the table*]" (175).

One feels that Helen and Arkadina are always on stage.[13] Evidence of Arkadina's dissembling is her reaction to Trigorin's passivity: "Now he's mine! [*Affecting an easy manner as if nothing had happened.*] But, of course, you can stay if you want to" (162). She also masks her insecurity regarding the younger Nina with false praise: "Bravo! Bravo! We did admire you. You know, with your looks and your lovely voice, you really ought not to stay in the country! It's a sin. I'm sure you have a gift for acting. Listen to me! You must go on the stage" (133)!

Helen and Arkadina are extremely conscious of their aging. Arkadina's first line is especially ironic: "You're always inquiring about some old fossil or other" (128). Helen claims that there is no limit to her range and it is said she can still play "late twenties . . . thirty tops." Furthermore, Olive's understudy delivers a line from David's play to Sylvia which could not be more apt: ". . . a woman of your age should have leapt past the realm of such acute narcissism." According to Treplev, Arkadina wants to have love affairs and wear bright dresses. She opens Act II with the following:

ARKADINA.

. . . Stand by my side. You are twenty-two, and I'm nearly twice that. Yevgheniy Serghyeevich, which of us looks the younger?

DORN.

You, of course.

ARKADINA.

There you are! And why is it? Because I work, I care about things, I'm always on the go, while you stay in the same place all the time, you don't really live . . . I am as particular about myself as an Englishman. Yes, my dear, I keep myself in hand, as they say—I'm always properly dressed and have my hair done just *comme il faut*. Do you think I'd permit myself to come out of the house, even into the garden like this, in a dressing-gown or with my hair untidy? Never. That's why it is I've kept so young-looking—because I've never been a slattern or let myself go, as some women do. . . . [*Walks up and down the lawn, her hands on her hips.*] There! you see? I'm as brisk as a bird. Fit to take the part of a fifteen-year-old girl!

(138-139)

Arkadina's line "Am I really so old and ugly that you can talk to me about other women without embarrassment?" (161) is in keeping with Helen and Sylvia who asks, "Doctor, am I unattractive, worn-out, spent, broken, desiccated, old?" While Nina gives Trigorin a medallion with a telling line from his writing ("If ever you need my life, come and take it."), Helen presents a cigarette case from Cole Porter to David bearing the inscription: "To Helen. Let's do it." Helen's gesture has cost nothing. Arkadina likewise claims that she cannot afford a new suit for her son, gives the servants one ruble to be split three ways upon her Act III departure, and says, "I have no money. I'm an actress, not a banker" (157). Sorin nevertheless praises her as "a generous, noble-hearted woman" (156).[14]

Just as Arkadina is *comme il faut*, Helen's ". . . taste is superb [and] eyes are exquisite." But Helen is threatened by Eden in much the same way that Arkadina fears Nina. She cannot deliver a certain speech when Eden is "fidgeting." An eruption occurs when Helen comments, ". . . you're asking an audience to believe that my husband would leave me for this woman?" Later she poses another question: "What are we going to do about that canine-loving ingenue? Did you cast her because you thought she was attractive . . . She's perky all right. She makes you want to sneak up behind her with a pillow and suffocate her."

Helen and Arkadina flatter their writers for their own selfish reasons, and their maneuverings are virtually identical. Helen begins to seduce David when they have drinks after the first rehearsal. He senses that she will be brilliant based upon the day's reading. She feels that his play is wonderful and says "it's so rare that anything is really about something." Though Helen has been reluctant to play the part because the character is "colorless," she has since realized how "profound" and "complex her inner life really is." She is used to "playing more overtly heroic women, less tentative, more alluring, certainly not frigid . . . Who am I some vain Broadway legend? You, you're a budding Chekhov." David says that he is willing to make changes in the script since her "instincts as an actress are impeccable," while Helen keeps at it with "You're clever. You're brilliant. What insight into women. Don't deny it." The

scene ends with the concession that Sylvia no longer has to be frigid.

David will tell Helen that his play is not working and that perhaps it is a "turkey." She asks him to calm himself and her description of Central Park prompts David's declaration of love. She then responds with characteristic melodrama: "Oh, words. What are words?[15] David, everything meaningful is in some unexplainable form. It's more primordial than mere language." David says that he does not understand, though the overdone speech is characteristic of his own ponderous writing.

Chekhov provides his own commentary through Arkadina's reading of Maupassant's *Sur l'eau*: "'Thus, when a woman has chosen a writer whom she wishes to capture, she lays siege to him with the aid of compliments, flattery and favours'" (139). In the same spirit, Helen speaks to David about the new version of his play which has actually been rewritten by Cheech: "What dialogue. This is better than O'Neill. Max Anderson will never touch you . . . It's so full of passion. It's so full of life . . . What a difference between this and your first draft. You hadn't found yourself yet. The idea was there, but it hadn't crystallized. You needed to hear it on its feet and now this. It's no longer tepid and cerebral. It's full of life. It's full of passion. It reeks with human sexuality. It's carnivorous at last . . . I went back and reread your earlier plays. They suffered from the same problem. Good ideas, but too contrived, no real guts. It's like you finally happened . . . Dear, dear David, pungent seething artist . . . I would give my body freely to the man who wrote those words, those glorious, powerful words." David is seduced. Helen has offered him Broadway and in asking the naive young man "to create a vehicle" for her, she wins his dedication and becomes his "inspiration." Arkadina likewise temporarily ensnares Trigorin with:

> My darling reckless boy, you may want to behave as if you were mad, but I won't let you, I won't let you. . . . [*Laughs.*] You're mine . . . mine. . . . This forehead is mine, and these eyes, and this beautiful silky hair is mine too. . . .[16] All of you is mine. You're so gifted, so clever—you're the best of all modern writers, the only hope of Russia. . . . You have such sincerity, simplicity, freshness, stimulating humour. . . . With a stroke of your pen you can convey the whole essence of a character or a landscape; people in your books are so alive. It is impossible to read your work and not be delighted by it. Do you think this is just hero-worship? You think I'm flattering you? Come, look into my eyes . . . look. . . . Do I look like a liar? There! you see—I alone know how to appreciate you, I'm the one person who tells you the truth, my darling, my wonderful man. . . . Will you come? Yes? You'll not leave me? . . .

(161-162)

Trigorin anticipates a return with Arkadina to the sated complacency that characterizes Helen's life as well:

"More railway carriages, stations, refreshment bars, veal cutlets, conversations" (162). And Helen's alterego Sylvia has intoned, "I can't live like this. The same routine over and over and over. The days blend together like melted celluloid, like a film whose images become distorted and meaningless."

The most compelling feature of both comedies is the debate over art and artists. Chekhov offered a sober view in a letter to Ivan Leontyev of March 22, 1890: "As to the word 'artistic,' it frightens me the way brimstone frightens merchants' wives. When people speak to me of what is artistic and what anti-artistic, of what is dramatically effective, of tendentiousness and realism and the like, I am at an utter loss, I nod to everything uncertainly, and answer in banal half truths that aren't worth a brass farthing. I divide all works into two categories: those I like and those I don't" (*Life* 163). But as both the film and play show, artists themselves and those who admire them are willing to allow for much. Dorn says, "It's in the nature of things for people to admire artists and treat them differently from . . . well, let us say, tradesmen. It's a sort of idealism" (127). And Nina's adoration of the artist is evident not only in her awe of Trigorin but in the following reaction to a silly spat: "To refuse Irena Nikolayevna, the famous actress! Surely, any wish of hers, even a mere whim, is more important than your farming? It's simply incredible" (143). Arkadina is also quick to assert her importance. She tells Treplev that he is "incapable of writing even a couple of miserable scenes" (159), and behaves like Helen with regard to the rest of David's cast as she exclaims: "Mediocre people trying to make unjustifiable claims about themselves have to run down people with real talent" (158). And when David praises Helen, he is unknowingly revealing to us the shallowness of the "artist": "She's so charismatic and she's brilliant and beautiful and a real artist. And we speak the same language."

One of Treplev's tirades could pass for Flender's (Rob Reiner) self-justification about writing plays which are specifically intended never to be produced: "It's conventional, hide-bound people like you who have grabbed the best places in the arts today, who regard as genuine and legitimate only what you do yourselves. Everything else you have to smother and suppress! I refuse to accept you at your own valuation" (158-59)! However, Flender offers a scenario which anticipates Cheech's decision about Olive: "Let's say there was a burning building and you could rush in and you could save only one thing, either the last known copy of Shakespeare's plays or some anonymous human being . . . It's art. "Art is life, it lives."[17] With regard to questions of trust and fidelity, Flender believes that "the artist creates his own moral universe" which he reduces to

"You gotta do what you gotta do." And yet the world continues to foster the reverent attitudes evident in Dorn's speculation:

> I'm satisfied. But if it had ever been my lot to experience the exaltation an artist feels at the moment of creative achievement, I believe I should have come to despise this material body of mine and all that goes with it, and my soul would have taken wings and soared into the heights.
>
> (136)

The conclusions of ***Bullets*** and *The Seagull* are also similar. After David's successful New York opening and the death of Cheech, he stands beneath Flender's window and calls for Helen. Note that Treplev had pledged to stay in the garden all night watching Nina's window in Act I and confesses before his death, "I stood under your window like a beggar" (178). Ellen says from above, "I could love a man if he's not a real artist, but I couldn't love an artist if he's not a real man." David answers by admitting that he is certain of two things; he loves Ellen and he is not an artist. Through his confession David moves beyond the kinds of compromises Trigorin has made for success and the very inability to compromise which leads to Treplev's suicide. David has been willing to live with his concessions and falsehood until the ruse turns deadly.

David's decision to marry Ellen and leave his creative life behind in New York reflects Trigorin's earlier perspective: ". . . I begin to imagine that this attentiveness on the part of my friends, all this praise and admiration, is just a sham, that they are trying to deceive me just as if I were insane" (148). And Trigorin's subsequent confession to Nina is indicative of the way Treplev and David come to view their own work: ". . . in the end I feel that all I can do is to paint landscapes, and that everything else I write is a sham—false to the very core" (150). Like David, Treplev confesses to his beloved (". . . all the time I knew that I was bound to you heart and soul, and for ever! It's not in my power to stop loving you, Nina. Ever since I lost you, ever since I began to get my work published, my life's been intolerable. I'm wretched. . . ." 179-180). Once Treplev's creative disappointment is coupled with Nina's rejection, he spends two minutes tearing up his writing and remembers his mother before the fatal gun shot. Fortunately, David's love is requited.

Both Helen and Arkadina are amusing themselves in the end, oblivious to the real drama taking place beyond their sensibilities. Treplev's play lives on in Nina's memory just as Cheech's work will be staged after his death. And as the true artist in ***Bullets*** suffers death to witness his creation, the true artist in *The Seagull* takes on the hardships which her calling demands. Nina says:

> . . . what really matters is not fame, or glamour, not the things I used to dream about—but knowing how to

endure things. How to bear one's cross and have faith. I have faith now and I'm not suffering quite so much, and when I think of my vocation I'm not afraid of life.

(181)

Like Woody Allen, Chekhov began his career writing for laughs. Gradually, the art of the Russian writer matured. Nevertheless, Chekhov never lost his comic roots and called his final play *The Cherry Orchard* a "comedy." In this play, Stanislavsky preferred to emphasize the sadness associated with the death of an old world, the displacement of a family, memories of deceased relatives which bring characters to tears, and the destruction of an ancestral home and cherry orchard. Yet all this takes place in the midst of people falling down stairs, swallowing bottles of pills for a lark, getting hit on the head with billiard cues, and making orations to bookcases. ***Bullets over Broadway*** is as hilarious as film-making gets. Nevertheless, issues involving the commercialization of art, the corruption of artists, and lethal decisions regarding the artist's "moral universe" underlie the shenanigans and mayhem. While Chekhov's contributions to ***Bullets over Broadway*** are not as direct as Cheech's improvements on David Shayne's *God of Our Fathers,* the influence is nevertheless pervasive.

Chekhov wrote in 1889: "I'm not writing any plays and won't write any in the near future because I have neither the subject matter nor the desire. To write for the theater, you must love it; without love, nothing worthwhile will come of it. Without love even success has no appeal. Next season I'll start going to the theater regularly and try to educate myself in matters of the stage" (131). *The Seagull* as well as the other major plays resulted from such love and education. Woody Allen's ***Bullets over Broadway*** likewise reveals that an artist's greatest gifts are indeed eternal.

### Notes

1. Chekhov himself married one of the best actresses in the Moscow Art Theater, Olga Knipper.

2. William Arnold, "Allen takes aim at old Broadway comedy with *Bullets*," *Seattle Post-Intelligencer* (28 October 1994): "What's Happening": 3.

3. Ironically, Chekhov paid the German-Russian publisher Adolph Marx 75,000 rubles for the rights to everything he had written up to 1899. In a letter to Ivan Orlov of February 22, 1899, Chekhov wrote: "I've sold Marx everything—my past and future— and I've become a Marxist for the rest of my life." Heim and Karlinsky 340-43. This book will be referred to hereafter as *Life*. All dates are based on the Julian calendar.

4. The young Chekhov had very clear expectations regarding the staging of *Ivanov.* He wrote to Nikolai Leykin on November 15, 1887: "You write that the author only gets in the production's way, makes the actors uncomfortable, and more often than not contributes only the most inane comments. Let me answer you thusly: (1) the play is the author's property, not the actors'; (2) where the author is present, casting the play is his responsibility; (3) *all* my comments to date have improved the production, and they have all been put into practice . . . If you reduce author participation to a naught, what the hell will you come up with? Remember how Gogol raged when they put on his play" (*Life* 70)! David's attitude is similar as he tells Marx, ". . . you said you believed in my play . . . I'm directing this play . . . I won't see my work mangled again. I've been through this twice before. Two powerful scripts could have been tremendous successes, and I had to sit back and watch actors change my dialogue and directors misinterpret everything." What is more, in *The Seagull,* Trigorin admits that he was terrified whenever a new play of his was produced.

5. Anton Chekhov, *Anton Chekhov: Plays* (Middlesex, England: Penguin Books, Ltd., 1978): 121. All other page references are in the essay. Dialogue from the film has been transcribed.

6. David wakes up crying, "I've sold out. Oh, I've sold out. I've sold out. I'm a whore . . . Do I want success that badly? The answer's yes. The answer's yes . . . It's a deal with the devil . . . No, no more compromises. It is my play . . . I am not a whore."

7. Woody Allen says, "The character of Cheech . . . is the genuine artist . . . He is a perfectionist. He has a vision and he wants it exactly that way, and would even kill to have it that way. David, on the other hand . . . compromises all the way down the line from [the] start. In the first scene in the picture, he's carrying on about how he won't change a word of his play. But the truth of the matter is, he's ready to put the play on with this bad actress in it to get it on, and he's ready to make changes to suit Dianne Wiest when she's seducing him, and he's willing to settle for the good reviews he got out of town with Olive in the role. For him, that's good enough. Cheech is the artist; David is not." (*Press Notes* 3)

8. Helen reveals her true feelings about David's play only after she has compared it to Cheech's vastly improved version. Trigorin's assessment of Treplev's open-air effort is also muted to say the least. In response to Nina's comment that the play was "strange," Trigorin says, "I didn't understand it at all. But I watched it with pleasure, all the same. You acted with such sincerity. And the scenery was beautiful. [*Pause.*] There must be a lot of fish in this lake" (133). Both Helen and Arkadina obviously prefer to live in the city. Whereas the Russian actress describes life at the estate as "country boredom" (141), the "Broadway Legend" invites David to her house on the Vineyard where it is ". . . quiet . . . You can write. I'll bring you coffee . . . Fate has thrown us together."

9. Olive's use of triple repetitions when greeting people ("Olive, Olive, Olive" and "Charmed, charmed, charmed") also echoes features of Nina's monologue: "It is cold, cold, cold. . . . It is deserted, deserted, deserted. . . . It is terrifying, terrifying, terrifying" (129).

10. Both Treplev and Trigorin associate Nina with dreams as well. Olive provides a painful reading of David's line "Dreams are only disguised feelings. The more we bring these painful experiences to the fore. . . ." Note the spelling of Treplev in the Penguin text is Trepliov.

11. Just as David refers to Ellen's party as "a dream," Nina concludes her interaction alone with the "famous" Trigorin by saying, "It's a dream." Note that David is praised at Helen's gathering of "artists and writers," but Treplev's low self-esteem is applicable to David if one remembers that the unknown Cheech deserves credit for the play's success.

12. Chekhov's treatment of alcohol in *The Seagull* is expressed through Masha at the start of Act III who justifies her drinking with "Women drink more often than you imagine." Doctor Dorn also tells the pathetic Sorin, a sickly man with nothing left in life but his feeble appetites, "Wine and tobacco deprive you of your individuality" (141).

13. Treplev says with regard to Arkadina, "It makes her angry to think that it won't be she, but Zaryechnaia, who's going to make a success of it on this tiny stage! [*Glancing at his watch.*] A psychological oddity—that's my mother. Oh, there is no doubt about her being very gifted and intelligent: she's capable of weeping bitterly over a book, of reciting the whole of Nekrasov by heart, of nursing the sick with the patience of an angel. But just try and give a word of praise to Duse! Oh-ho-ho! You mustn't praise anybody but her, you mustn't write about anybody but her, you must acclaim her and go into raptures over her wonderful acting in *The Lady with the Camellias,* or *The Fumes of Life* . . . And she's close-fisted, too. She has seventy thousand in the bank, in Odessa—that I know for certain. But you try to borrow money from her, and she'll just burst into tears" (122).

14. The play within *Bullets* reflects both the film itself and features of *The Seagull*. Note this exchange which echoes Arkadina's conflict with Nina over Trigorin:

HELEN.

Take him. Take him. Let him leave me bereft without a penny. Go ahead and take him, but don't think it will last forever. The same thing will happen to you.

EDEN.

Sylvia, I don't know why you're so unhappy, why you're such a deeply unhappy person, but I want you to know . . .

HELEN.

Because you're taking my husband, my life, the very core of my being, you stupid idiot.

15. Treplev quotes Hamlet with "'Words, words, words'" before Trigorin talks with Nina in Act II.

16. Dianne Wiest makes a point of disheveling John Cusack's hair and appearance, even going so far as to dislodge his glasses as she pleads passionately "Don't speak."

17. This suggestion is reminiscent of Isaac's question in "Elaine's" at the opening of *Manhattan* regarding who would have the courage to save a drowning person. Other examples of Allen's recycling here are the gangsters' questions about what to eat after they murder bootleggers, which echo a debate about restaurants at the herring merchant's deathbed in *Love and Death,* Cheech's last words to David that Sylvia Poston should say she is pregnant as at the conclusion of *Hannah and Her Sisters,* and Allen's own willingness to look at his recent troubles in a comic light when Olive says, "The heart obeys its own rules."

## Works Cited

"*Bullets over Broadway* Press Notes." New York: Miramax Films, 1994.

Chekhov, Anton. *Anton Chekhov: Plays.* Middlesex, England: Penguin Books Ltd., 1978.

Heim, Michael Henry, and Simon Karlinsky. *Anton Chekhov's Life & Thought.* Berkeley: U of California P, 1975.

Lax, Eric. Woody Allen: *A Biography.* New York Alfred A. Knopf, 1991.

### Richard A. Blake (review date 19 December 1998)

SOURCE: Blake, Richard A. "The Blue Planet." *America* 179, no. 20 (19 December 1998): 17-19.

[*In the following review, Blake contends that* Celebrity *is an innovative film exploring themes of fame and celebrity.*]

"Calling earth. Come in, Blue Planet. Do you read me? Over."

"Er, I mean, I (cough) read you, Nebula Transhudsonia."

"What's your situation? We've been monitoring your transmissions from the past century. Age of stays and farthingales vanished like many of your past civilizations. First Watergate tapes. Now jokes about Viagra and the stains on Monica's blue dress. In public. On editorial pages as well as on late night comedy shows. Your females used to refer to their underwear as "unmentionables," but now they blister Little League umpires with gender-specific obscenities that would melt whalebone. Are you Earthlings so obsessed with procreation that you talk of nothing else and even use the language of procreation about everything from recalcitrant computers to enemy drivers? Are you suffering from a linguistic nervous breakdown. What the [expletive deleted] is happening to you [hyphenated noun deleted] on your [participial phrase deleted] planet?"

"Yeah. You, er, see, it's like, well, we're lonely. That's it. Yeah. Lonely, like, and sad. That's it, (cough) lonely and sad. It's like, you know we've got the, er, planetary blues."

*Celebrity* is Woody Allen's latest riff on his life's work, which is an ongoing fugue of planetary blues, arranged for solo whine and sexually mixed-up chorus. Some ungracious critics claim that his riparian solar system may be bounded by the Hudson, Harlem and East. Possibly, but this brick and asphalt aviary that stretches from Battery Park to the Cloisters continually yields fascinating, if grotesque specimens for cataloguing by its veteran ornithologist.

Allen's antiheroes, generally played by himself, search for love and community, which in Allen's world means a lasting and fulfilling sexual relationship with a beautiful, but apparently unattainable woman. These characters, however, gradually become pathetic in their quest. They stammer and fixate on their own physical and psychological problems, and they expect the world, including the idealized woman, to sympathize with their narcissism. When she leaves them, as any sane person must, they must console themselves with a memory of past happiness or a hope that things might be better in the future.

In *Celebrity* Allen adds a new ingredient. He examines the proposition that fame, based solely on the notion of being famous, provides the yellow brick road to fulfillment. He never denies the thesis. On the contrary, many of the characters in this highly intricate narrative do indeed find contentment in their passing moment of fame. He does, however, undercut his own eudaimonistic proposition by showing that celebrity and its attendant rewards are purely a matter of luck, and therefore must be suspect.

* * *

Lee Simon (Kenneth Branagh) is the Woody Allen antihero, even down to his stammer, baggy corduroy jacket and relentless pursuit of happiness, embodied in a succession of beautiful women. A writer of travel and celebrity pieces for mass circulation magazines and Sunday supplements, Lee merely wants to earn enough to see him through until he achieves fame as a novelist or screenwriter; he's not sure which. Before he appears on screen, the film opens as a sky-writer finishes the word "Help" over the Manhattan skyline. The word will provide the backdrop for a scene for a movie being shot on a plaza in front of one of those antiseptic office towers on Park Avenue. "Help" will also be Lee's personal statement throughout the film.

Lee watches the scene's star, Nicole Oliver (Melanie Griffith), hidden behind a head scarf, sunglasses and raincoat, get out of a car and run up the steps and across the plaza. Everyone praises the performance. She is a famous star. Who dares criticize her? Lee has to interrupt making his pass at Nola, a technician-actress-waitress (Winona Ryder), to interview Nicole in her childhood home in what looks suspiciously like Brooklyn. He enthusiastically transfers his attention to his subject, and Nicole provides a creative response to his inquiries.

* * *

These celebrities, Allen proposes, construct their own moral universe and live without fear of consequences, Brandon Darrow (Leonardo DiCaprio), a young movie-star thug high on cocaine, wrecks a hotel room and slaps around his girlfriend. Lee arrives to pitch a script idea to him, just as the police threaten to take Brandon to the station house. It's all a charade, however. Police, girlfriend and management alike choose not to prefer charges because, after all, Brandon is famous. Lee joins Brandon and his retinue for a trip to Atlantic City, but while the Famous People enjoy their rent-an-orgy dates with chemically assisted abandon, Lee listens to his assigned companion comparing her own writing to Chekhov.

Not only does he feel left out of all the carnal bliss that he believes celebrities enjoy; Lee must pay a terrible price for his own infidelities. His wife, Robin (Judy Davis), could swallow a Milltown factory and still make St. Vitus look comatose. Lee's asking her for a divorce is like parachuting into a live volcano without bothering to pull the ripcord. He has little luck with other women either. One of the sacrifices he must make for his work involves attending a fashion show to introduce a new line of lingerie. By a miracle of chance, he offers a ride to the gorgeous supermodel played by Charlize Theron, but as the introduces him to her chic, famous friends in the fast lane, he realizes that he is driving an avocado-colored Edsel with a cracked cylinder head. Predictably, the evening plunges to the earth in flames, like the Hindenburg in a Jersey cornfield.

After her initial eruption, Lee's wife, Robin, blames herself and her Catholic inhibitions for her failed marriage. She goes off to a retreat house in the country to try to put the lava back into the crater, but she finds as much tranquility as she would if her Bloomingdale's charge card had been canceled without advance notice. While she struggles for peace of soul, a celebrity priest, who has his own television show and line of self-help books arrives and basks in the adulation of the inmates. For him, recognition provides the serenity that Robin struggles to draw from quiet reflection in a religious environment.

At the suggestion of a friend, Lee thinks she might find more peace through plastic surgery than prayer. During her visit to the cellulite chop shop she accidentally meets a television director, Tony Gardella (Joe Mantegna), who is instrumental in starting a series of improbable events that lead to celebrity, and with celebrity the happiness and fulfillment that she could never achieve through her own efforts at spiritual and cosmetic makeovers.

For his part, Lee finally settles down to complete his novel. Still unlucky in love, one more failed romance and its harrowing aftermath rob him of his rise to fame as a bright young author. He has done all that he could to achieve celebrity, but circumstances beyond his understanding and control continue to conspire against him. He remains a competent hack on the fringes of Manhattan's incestuous literary cliques.

\* \* \*

*Celebrity* ends where it began. The film with the epigraph "Help" has its premier, and Lee, still the obscure freelance magazine writer, covers the event to add a final touch of color to his profile of Nicole. He seems oddly at peace with his lot in life, as though he has finally accepted himself as a mere pawn of destiny. As the lights in the cavernous Ziegfeld theater dim, "Help," written in smoke, appears on the screen. The camera cuts to the audience sitting in the dark mindlessly plunging oily fingers into tubs of overpriced popcorn. Some are rich and famous, others merely the munching, unwashed, ticket-buying multitude. In the dark they are indistinguishable, unknown to anyone or anything but fate. Who knows why some are famous and some obscure, some happy and some miserable?

*Celebrity* recycles many of the old Woody Allen themes and characters, but in its own way it is quite innovative. Shot in a grainy, documentary black-and-white by Sven Nykvist, its newsprint appearance reproduces the look of the tabloids that trade promiscuously in the reputations and lives of the famous and near-famous. It deals with frankly sexual material, but Allen has an extraordinary ability to be bawdy without being salacious. The vocabulary might wilt the wimple of Sister Wendy; but as that little green man—or rather person, since there is

no gender in Nebula Transhudsonia—has observed, Earthlings really do talk that way, especially when trying to cross the Triborough Bridge at rush hour.

\* \* \*

The ensemble cast is both brilliant and generous. Putting the neurotic Woody Allen persona into a robust, Irish actor makes the character's whining and fidgeting particularly obnoxious. Audiences could pity Allen because of his frail appearance, and to some extent could excuse his self-serving a-morality. Branagh makes him a tougher character whose moral myopia destroys those around him. Allen the director and writer is much harder on Branagh the actor than he could have been on Allen the actor. The change makes it a more powerful, if more disagreeable character.

"Jeez, What do you mean (cough) disagreeable? This is, you see, like on the blue planet. He's, you know, like what I said: lonely and sad."

"So are you, Earthling."

## Stanley Kauffmann (review date 21 December 1998)

SOURCE: Kauffmann, Stanley. "Doodling and Delving." *New Republic,* no. 4379 (21 December 1998): 26.

[*In the following review, Kauffmann asserts that the main character in* Celebrity *is not well developed.*]

Woody Allen's screenplay for *Celebrity* is an elaborated doodle. He seems to have lined up some reminiscences of past characters (a mixed-up writer, an unfulfilled woman) and of smart-set sterilities (parties, parties, parties), added a few jokes, not necessarily of the keenest (about a film critic: "He used to hate every movie; then he married a young woman with a big bosom and now he loves every movie"), seasoned with a few dabs of sex frankness, and then just switched the word processor on. This new picture looks as if Allen had tapped along hoping that the tapping would lead somewhere. It didn't, but he discovered that he had enough pages for a film anyway. (Including a few prestige-pumping quotes from Eliot and Tennessee Williams.)

This ad hokum script is the penalty that he and we must pay for his position. Allen is unique in American film, a writer-director who is in every creative sense independent and yet who in every industry sense is mainstream (glittery casts, first-rank technicians). Thus established, he can do virtually any project he conceives and can do it with topnotch colleagues—and his public will, in some measure, support him. (Especially abroad.) It would be easy to go through the Allen filmography and divide the list into those pictures that, whatever their defects, are memorable, and those that very probably would not have been made if they had originated with anyone else. High in this roster of non-existent yet existent films is *Celebrity.*

At least the leading male role, who is essentially the recently deconstructed Harry under another name, is not played by Allen himself. This is a plus, or anyway a helpful minus. But Allen has put Kenneth Branagh in the role. There's a difficulty here. The trouble is not that Branagh is a foreigner—his New York accent is passable. But the role is just a series of actions, mostly sexual in aim, with no realized person behind them; and Branagh is not an actor of strong personality. His Henry V, his Benedick, his Hamlet were all clear-cut, but in those cases the author gave him a good head-start. Branagh can fulfill what a good author gives him, but on his own, so to speak, he is pallid, almost transparent.

Branagh's wife here, from whom he separates at the start, is Judy Davis, an Australian who has played Americans before, for Allen and others. Davis is one of the best film actresses in the world, but it's discomfiting to see her in a female counterpart of Branagh's role—a series of sketches and incidents that pretend to delineate a human being. The woman had been a schoolteacher, and Allen contrives, not deftly, for her to become a TV personality under the auspices of a producer she meets who falls in love with her. She even takes a lesson in oral sex—from another woman and using two bananas—in order to please this new man more. (Allen, let's note, is not just being frantically up-to-date in sexual candor. He has been frank at least since *Everything You Always Wanted to Know about Sex* in 1972.)

Entwined with the adventures of the unyoked husband and wife are scenes in restaurants and at gallery openings and any other occasions that warrant the display of gorgeous women. A few of them Branagh pursues—in a manner apparently intended to suggest Allen's own jagged polygraph performing but that seems unattached to Branagh's body. Many of the scenes with women slog down in discussion, and the one point I really admired in the film was the fact that Allen dared to use a line that could be quoted against him. At one point a young woman says to Branagh, "Let's just stay in tonight and not over-analyze things." In this script, that was brave of Allen.

## Marcia Pally, Leonard Quart, Pat Dowell, Michael Kerbel, and Elayne Rapping (essay date 1998)

SOURCE: Pally, Marcia, Leonard Quart, Pat Dowell, Michael Kerbel, and Elayne Rapping. "Deconstructing Woody." *Cineaste* 23, no. 3 (1998): 32-8.

[*In the following essay, the critics discuss the relationship between Allen's on-screen persona and his real life, exploring Allen's representations of women, Jewish identity, New York City, psychotherapy, and mortality, as well as the role of art, fantasy, and the creative process in his films.*]

While Woody Allen's films have for years won great critical acclaim and delighted audiences worldwide, attention has rarely been focused on his patronizing treatment of female characters or on the angry and bilious man that sometimes coexisted with his comic, schlemiel persona. The public sordidness of the Mia Farrow/Soon-Yi scandal, however, which erupted in 1992, has changed all this, turning Allen into a controversial, even hated, figure. Indeed, since then each new film has become an occasion for venomous attacks and passionate defenses, a virtual Rorschach test for film critics, many of whom seem unable to separate the private man from the public artist. His latest film, *Deconstructing Harry,* has intensified and expanded the debate, with newspaper columnists and Op-Ed writers joining the fray.

But latter-day attacks by mainstream journalists on the suddenly apparent sexism or misanthropic tendencies of Allen's films overlook the expression of such views—perhaps more nuanced or comically veiled—in his earlier films, and the gradual transformation of his persona throughout a film career spanning more than three decades as the writer and/or director of thirty films. Many other themes must also be considered if we are to gain a more comprehensive view of Allen's work, including his relationship to Jewishness, New York City, psychotherapy, mortality, as well as the role that art, fantasy, and the creative process itself play in his films.

We've therefore invited a group of critics who have written regularly over the years about Allen's films, including three feminist critics, to contribute to a Critical Symposium which, in the process of "Deconstructing Woody," will hopefully contextualize his newest film, as well as provide a broader, more insightful, but no less partisan context for appreciating his work. He is clearly a complex artist who defies reductive interpretations or ad hominem put-downs and who is not served by simple-minded homages. Indeed, we believe that whether one hates or loves his films, Woody Allen is an artist and a cultural phenomenon who demands serious attention.

—The Editors

### "THE CINEMA AS SECULAR RELIGION," BY MARCIA PALLY

Woody Allen's *Deconstructing Harry* is one of the least subtle in a string of insistent films that began in 1992, after the dance of the hatchets with Mia Farrow. What is Allen insisting on? Is his subject masculinity? Is Allen, in his court-jester role, dramatizing the roving lusts of his gender? Is his subject Jews? Is he portraying the prideful self-mockery and fear of a Jewish community that is the most influential and yet most plagued by mass death since the Diaspora? Though Allen is doing some of both, his main interest is not so much sexual or Jewish neuroses as it is their relief through the imagination, however temporary that relief may be. Escape from life's durable woes lies in theater—on stage and screen, in jazz, and in religious myth—or so Allen suggests, apparently based on personal experience. Allen's films are autobiographical not because the filmmaker shares his characters' views on gender or Judaism, but because he shares their views on diversion. Life is broke, we can't fix it, except in fiction—or fixion. If Allen's movies have become insistent of late, it's because he has had a lot to get off his mind.

Over the course of his career, Allen has recommended fiction to his audiences in several ways, the most obvious being to suggest it straight out, as he does in *Harry.* A writer who regularly betrays both wives and lovers loses himself in his novels where he is better-looking and more successful than in life. The film's over-obvious coda announces the message—"How about a story about a writer who can't manage in life but manages in fiction?," the writer says. "Viewers angry with Allen have asked whether he thinks that acknowledging his younger-woman fetish—as he does in *Harry*—will earn him public forgiveness. This is not Allen's concern. He writes confessional movies not for absolution but for the fix.

*Deconstructing Harry* also looks at religious myth, or what some call faith. While the writer has made a hash of his life, his sister, an observant Jew, is happily married and content. Allen himself is agnostic; if this tortured world is God's way, then He surely is mysterious. Yet Allen recognizes that cynicism is too harsh a vision by which to live, agnosticism is insufficient, and so people construct fictions to soothe loss and doubt. The sister believes in God-in-Heaven and the writer believes in star(let)s. Who's to say that faith is a less legitimate fix than the movies?

Allen's exploration of fiction appears throughout his best and lesser works—most clearly in the triptych *Radio Days* (1987), *Broadway Danny Rose* (1984), and *The Purple Rose of Cairo* (1985)—which celebrate the palliative force of big-band jazz, stand-up comics and, of course, movies. In *Purple Rose,* an abused, Depression-era housewife escapes her misery at the pictures, where her favorite hero steps off the screen to rescue her—at least in the movie in her mind. In Allen's philosophy, her solution is not so different from the religious sister's in *Harry.* No wonder they called the chivalrous gents of the silver screen matinee "idols."

Almost as patently, *Bullets over Broadway* (1994) has the folks with unhappy lives (Mafia moll, thug, and aging actress) find refuge in the theater, but the playwright with the loving wife realizes he has nothing to say and goes off to the suburbs. The Kafkaesque terror in *Shadows and Fog* (1992) is dissipated first by the warm glow of a brothel—one of man's oldest fixes—and

finally by a circus where the hero escapes the bad guys through a magic trick involving a box of mirrors. If this is not a bow to the redemptive qualities of theater, nothing is. In *Another Woman* (1988), two women become foils—or 'films'—for each other, each one righting her life after hearing the other's story.

When Allen's films are not overtly about fiction, they are object lessons that recommend it. He scripts predicaments that would be disasters in life and gives them outrageously happy movie endings. *Mighty Aphrodite* (1995) is one such film, where a man's infidelities and bastard child by his mistress would make a muck of any marriage. But extraordinarily, ridiculously, it all works out on the screen. So, too, in *Manhattan Murder Mystery* (1993), where a nice old lady is murdered for her money. In Allen's hands, the tragedy turns into a Nancy Drew-like caper whose denouement—echoing *Shadows and Fog*—reels out behind a movie-theater screen. Just as improbably, a man has an affair with his wife's sister in *Hannah and Her Sisters* (1986), but instead of his losing both women in the course of a bloody divorce, it all pans out happily, with the guy marrying another sister in his ex-wife's family.

In his earliest work, Allen created happy endings by playing the buffoon. No matter how neurotic, insecure, or bumbling viewers may be, they have the satisfaction of feeling superior to Allen. While in films like *Purple Rose,* Allen told audiences outright that cinema was an opiate for life, the Seventies comedies simply were the opiate—and his films continue to be so whenever Allen's hang-ups are more over-the-top than those of the audience. *Zelig* was particularly clever in interposing the nebbishy Allen into the great photo-ops of the Twenties, which made not only Allen look like a fool but also the great men—Sigmund Freud, Eugene O'Neill, Babe Ruth, Scott Fitzgerald—with whom he posed. Audiences got to feel superior to them all.

*Stardust Memories* was famous for being the first film in which Allen put his nerdlike self in the role of glamorous star pursued by paparazzi and fans. When the film opened, viewers and the press laughed less at Allen's pose within the movie than at his chutzpah as director to cast himself as a glamor boy. In either case, Allen's gambit holds: folks feel better about themselves because at least they are not as gauche as he is. Nor as sexually outlandish. Beginning with *Manhattan*—Allen's first confession of his fetish for (much) younger women—and now in *Deconstructing Harry,* Allen allows viewers to feel that, no matter how embarrassing their sexual fantasies, they don't act out as flagrantly as he does.

Allen's fullest treatment of fiction is in *Crimes and Misdemeanors* (1989) which, like Harry, proposes film and faith as relief from life's injustice. Among those committing the crimes and misdemeanors in the movie, none comes to a happy end—from a man getting away with murdering his mistress, to a filmmaker cheating on his wife, to a wise, devout rabbi going blind. Characters roam the film looking for respite from meaninglessness, and they suggest two solutions. The rabbi looks to God, saying that faith in an overriding justice (a happy end, no matter how delayed) makes life joyous. The filmmaker relies on cinema, both as director and viewer. When the murderer suggests that the filmmaker make a movie about a fellow who gets away with murder, the filmmaker rejects the idea, insisting that, unless the murder exacts a cost, there is no story. He argues for a happy end where justice prevails—at least at the movies. Here, Allen most pointedly draws the congruence between film and religion. Neither can be proved to be true, but no matter. Going along with the story in movies or myth is already a leap into faith. Suspension of disbelief is belief nonetheless.

When Allen made *Crimes and Misdemeanors* he was recommending fiction to his viewers for their sakes. He had the equanimity to take care of us. It was before the hatchets, and at a time when he had enjoyed success for many years. Since then, his films have become more desperate. Rather than push fiction for our sakes, he now recommends it for his own.

### "WOODY ALLEN'S REFLEXIVE CRITICS," BY LEONARD QUART

In his last four films, Woody Allen coasted on his talent with small works like *Bullets over Broadway* (1994) and *Mighty Aphrodite* (1995) that are essentially pleasant and inoffensive but impersonal. The artistically ambitious Allen of *Annie Hall* (1977), *Manhattan* (1979), and *Hannah and Her Sisters* (1986) has resurfaced with *Deconstructing Harry,* but with a much rawer, raunchier, and actually hateful persona. This new image has evoked an entirely new level of rage among a number of critics and viewers. They are unable to look at an Allen film without confusing moral with esthetic judgment, the man with his work. Their enmity seems to blind them to the film's satirical wit, intelligence, and structural complexity, especially the imaginative transitions from Harry's life to its fictional representations. Such critics seem incapable of viewing Allen's work these days without thinking with revulsion about the Soon-Yi and Mia saga, and reflexively decrying the misogyny, physical ugliness (there is no suggestion in the films that it's his good looks that attract the women), self-indulgence, and amorality of Allen's protagonists. I doubt if any of these critics would inveigh, in a similar fashion, against the paranoid and animalistic Jake LaMotta in Scorsese's *Raging Bull* or Dostoyevsky's amoral Stavrogin. It's Allen who is their special poison.

The critics include satirical columnist Maureen Dowd, who took leave of her prime whipping boy Bill Clinton for one column to excoriate Allen as a "weaselly, overcivilized, undermoralized, terminally psychoanalyzed terminator." Dowd is no film critic and is obviously so blinded by her hatred of Allen and his persona that the virtues of this hilarious, inspired, and, at moments, poignant work are beyond her ken. In this blackest of comedies, Allen has dropped all the remnants of the victimized, insecure, endearing schlemiel of his earlier films, and instead created a character who is almost totally unsympathetic and repellent. He still whines, and is death-obsessed, and at odds with the natural world, as in *Annie Hall,* but he no longer is that 'superior' being who solemnly moralizes about other people's corrupt behavior (e.g., *Crimes and Misdemeanors* and *Manhattan*).

Allen displays greater honesty about himself than in past works. His Harry, though a successful writer, is an unloved, narcissistic, and callous womanizer who wants to fuck every woman he meets, and who gives no thought to the moral consequences of his behavior. It has to be said that Allen has a sufficient sense of fairness not to absolve himself, making justifiable the fury that a number of his female characters feel towards him. Though he does try to balance it somewhat by having two of the film's more understanding women (his smart half-sister and Allen's usual beautiful young mistress) speak sympathetically about him.

Still, none of their kind words can mute Allen's portrait of the out-of-focus Harry Block—a soulless man who pops pills, consorts with prostitutes (because these are women he doesn't have to talk to), and whose neuroses lack even a scintilla of charm. In Allen's own voice, he speaks of his emptiness and inability to have sexual pleasure, finding solace only in his art and love for his son. This may not be directly autobiographical (Allen too strenuously denies that it is), but Harry has Allen's barbed intelligence, his emotional remoteness, and his gift for one-liners. (For example, his half-sister angrily says that all Harry believes in is "nihilism, cynicism, sarcasm, and orgasm," to which he responds, "In France I could run on that slogan and win.")

Despite Harry being given few saving qualities, Allen does hedge a bit by granting him the same profound commitment to his art that Allen himself has. Still, if the film suggests that Harry's being a successful artist absolves him from ordinary moral standards (a sentiment echoed in other Allen works), it hesitates endorsing this megalomaniacal, self-justifying notion. Allen has Harry experience the melancholy self-knowledge that the only time people applaud him in the film occurs in his fantasy life. Consequently, the film's climax leaves Harry with nothing but his work—a far from triumphant image. He's only happy bent over his writing, which turns out to be his prime link to other people. The finale leaves Harry stripped down and alone—a direct admission of human failure.

If one compares Allen's Harry with the misanthropic, obsessive-compulsive neurotic that Jack Nicholson plays in James L. Brooks's commercially successful and Oscar nominated *As Good as It Gets,* one quickly sees the difference between a deeply felt creation and a canned one. The Nicholson character (Melvin), a successful writer, delivers some witty, sardonic remarks, but it's all fabricated—a skillful performance in a predictable sitcom that even throws in a happy ending in which the protagonist magically becomes humanized. In contrast, there is nothing synthetic and seamless about Allen's Harry. Allen invests him with a destructive, unredeemable personality, and a case of genuine despair; even though its full force is undermined by Allen being too light an actor and presence to project a profound sense of emotional loss.

In keeping with this dark vision, Allen also offers for the first time an astringent, satiric response to the whole question of his Jewish identity. In *Deconstructing Harry,* Allen provides send-ups of Jewish lower-middle-class behavior—expressing resentment of his parents by depicting an elderly Jewish storekeeper as a murderer and cannibal—and visual jokes about *nouveau riche* excess (e.g., the *Star Wars* themed bar mitzvah). He goes, however, well beyond this to a direct, serio-comic assault on Jewish religion, tribalism, and tradition. Harry displays contempt for his religious nationalist brother-in-law (a member of the Likud?), and those Jews who divide the world between themselves and the "other" whose humanity they barely recognize. He rejects "tradition as the illusion of permanence," has no use for "professional Jews," and he even has Demi Moore play a therapist in one of his stories that wickedly satirizes orthodox Jewish piety.

It's not that Allen rejects his Jewishness—that, like his being a committed New Yorker, has been a part of his comic persona since he began making films. His characters have often joked about their Jewish identity and fear of anti-Semitism. He has also cleverly juxtaposed WASP and Jewish life styles in a couple of films: the witty use of a split screen in *Annie Hall,* contrasting Annie's cool, gracious WASP family with his protagonist's turbulent, intrusive Jewish one; and the ambivalent depiction of his young alter-ego's lower-middle-class Jewish family in *Radio Days* (1987)—warm and crude—a narrow world that the young boy ultimately wants to escape from to WASP Manhattan. In *Crimes and Misdemeanors* (1989), interestingly, Allen links his own questions about morality to a Jewish tradition whose religion he rejects but whose moral and intellectual passions he takes seriously and admires.

Allen is no deracinated Jew. He doesn't, however, want it to define or circumscribe him politically, socially, or psychologically. For example, Harry emphatically asserts that he suffers from self-hatred, not *Jewish* self-

hatred. For Allen Jewishness is just one variable (albeit a significant one) among many that shape his identity, and *Deconstructing Harry* articulates his Jewish skeptic's stance with comic verve and intellectual authority.

*Deconstructing Harry* is a complex, bold film, though not one without flaws. Allen, however, has taken immense emotional risks here, deconstructing his persona and seemingly baring more of the baser, more pathological aspects of his psyche than he's ever done before. There are limits to his capacity for self-exposure, but these have much less to do with his penchant for rationalization and deflection (which he's skilled at) than with Allen's inability to go beyond the emotional constraints of his detached persona. As with Harry, the best of Allen goes into his art. If critics would stop reacting with antipathy to Allen the man, they would give a large, smart, and truly funny film like *Deconstructing Harry* the critical praise it deserves.

### "WOODY'S EFFORT TO RECONSTRUCT HIMSELF," BY PAT DOWELL

I read the other day that *Deconstructing Harry* is "one long diatribe against women, wives, and Jews." That's what Molly Haskell called it in an article in *The New York Times* taking Hollywood to task for its double standard in pairing elderly male performers with young female ones as believable romantic couples, while denying even middle-aged women the same age range of lovers.

Haskell, like many of Allen's erstwhile admirers, laments the decline of his films, although it's worth pointing out that Allen has cast very young women as his romantic admirers on screen for a long time, dating back at least to the teenage Mariel Hemingway in *Manhattan* (1979). "I'm dating a girl who has homework!," he whined in mock dismay (and thinly disguised pride) about his conquest.

Even then there was a tacit acknowledgment that Woody Allen wrote reflexively if not reflectively, but his transformation and display of his inner self was then considered a mark of his maturation as an artist, a certificate of graduation from silly farces to intelligent romantic comedy. That view of Allen has changed, but some things have not—the misogyny for one. Disparaging remarks about Others, made in a way that is also self-disparaging, pepper all his movies, but they reach raw, ugly dimensions in the new film, which makes their true nature impossible to ignore.

One aspect of Allen's movies has changed—the fictional disguise is wearing thin, so much so that the latest character he wrote and plays, novelist Harry Block, says near the end of *Deconstructing Harry,* "I don't even think I should disguise it any more. It's me." This may not be a disingenuous observation on Allen's part, but it does ring hollow.

And it is probably too little too late in Allen's attempt to reconstruct himself. The value of confessional candor is just about zilch in our society, where it can be purchased for a buck in any grocery checkout line. We expect to be told what kind of underwear the President wears, and movie stars routinely share every detail of decline, whether by wish or coercion. And Allen drags in others for his thinning disguises. *Deconstructing Harry* features a shrewish wife who becomes a fanatical mother once she and Harry have a son. There's an incidence of infidelity with a family member right under the family's nose (and literally blind eyes). A beautiful young woman played by Elisabeth Shue is very supportive to Harry and ardent to boot—a figure that echoes the role Juliette Lewis played in *Husbands and Wives,* not to mention a few more predecessors.

Furthermore, in a rather ominous development for Allen's notorious child-bride Soon-Yi, *Deconstructing Harry* exhibits a hard-featured Asian woman who is iconographically a dragon lady and narratively a prostitute. She appears in one of the episodes from Harry Block's fiction that pops up periodically on the screen. She is a whore servicing his youthful alter ego, his "Oriental passport to paradise." This conspicuous sexual exotic reappears among the adoring, applauding characters at the end of *Deconstructing Harry* who reassure the novelist that he brings "pleasure to millions." This kind of inflation is to be expected from the creator of a character who makes a living writing for *Film Quarterly* (in *Play It Again, Sam*)—Harry and Allen bring pleasure to thousands, maybe.

It was a long time ago that Allen began to use his movies to anticipate and undercut complaints about the evolution (or devolution) of his movie imagination. In *Stardust Memories* fans kept coming up to the film-maker Woody played to tell him how much they loved his movies—"Especially the early, funny ones." *Stardust Memories* remains the most underrated Allen comedy. Its hostile reception marked the first roar of a bear market in Allen's cultural stock. Nobody could have guessed how low it would go, but Haskell's assessment of *Deconstructing Harry* suggests we've found out.

Both movies are simultaneously self-deprecating and ego-aggrandizing exercises in fantasy. Both are clearly about Woody's own career and life. The Bergmanesque beginning of the earlier black-and-white film depicts with comic existential despair the start of a nightmare journey that surely comes to its bumpy end in *Deconstructing Harry.* The novelist Harry Block arrives after excruciating effort to receive an honor at the college in

upstate New York that once expelled him. He shows up with a corpse in the back seat, a gaudily dressed black hooker administering comfort, and accompanied by his young son, whom he has just kidnapped from school. His furious ex-wife has set the police on his trail; their Keystone Cops-style arrest of Harry completes the picture of unsurpassable personal chaos. The icing on the cake would be for somebody to call Woody "that little homunculus," the epithet he once used on a character portrayed by Wallace Shawn (now *there* are two careers and lives to compare and contrast).

In both movies the central characters, Woody's surrogates, are driven to display themselves in their work. Harry Block's psychiatrist takes it even further, insisting to Harry that his writing has saved his life—literally and figuratively stopping death. His is the story of a man who "can't function in life," the movie tells us, "but can in art." And this is probably where fantasy and ego take over once again. Allen saves a shred of illusion to hide his nakedness.

What he cannot hide is the most significant change in "Woody Allen"—the fact that he is no longer young, not even middle-aged. He is a senior citizen pushing sixty-three. For too many of his detractors, who frequently refer to him as a dirty old man, age is the real measure of his degradation. He is an old man with all the urges of a young one—all the bad habits, bitterness, mental stinginess, and prejudice that people coddled and admired for decades. Now he refuses to play *On Golden Pond* for his fans, and, just as in *Stardust Memories,* they hound him for refusing to pander to their fantasies instead of his.

Allen's last words in *Husbands and Wives* were said to an unseen interviewer who is essentially himself. "Can I go now?," he asked, no more impatient than many viewers, I suspect. "Is this over?" Not, it seems, until they pry his cold, dead fingers off the camera.

"The Redemptive Power of Art,"
by Michael Kerbel

*Deconstructing Harry* ends with Harry overcoming his creative block by writing about a man "who can't function well in life, but who can function in art." When Harry begins to create, he tells us that his fictional character's writing (and, by extension, his own, and, we must assume, Woody Allen's) "in more ways than one saved his life."

Harry's immersion in his writing is analogous to Allen's constantly working on one film after another. He states in his book-length interview with Stig Björkman that, "Making a film is a big struggle. But the fact that there's struggle helps me. I'd rather struggle with films than struggle with other things." As a way of avoiding those "other things," including the agonies of relationships and of honest self-confrontation, Allen's/Harry's solution provides an acceptable although simplistic conclusion.

Allen also implies, much more problematically, that even the most abhorrent individual (who proudly claims to be more evil than the Devil) is redeemed by being an artist. It takes a huge leap of faith to go along with the entire cast's applause for Harry in the film's penultimate scene. The same was true for the forgiveness Fellini benevolently bestowed upon Guido in *8½*, which has a strikingly similar finale, and—with its stream-of-consciousness structure that alternates among, and sometimes combines, present-tense events, flashbacks, and pieces of the central character's fiction—was clearly a model for *Deconstructing Harry.*

Like Fellini, Allen wants us to believe that the character is moving toward salvation, or at least toward happiness, despite the rest of the film's providing ample evidence of the contrary. This may be another *8½*, but it's much of Allen's career revisited as well. One overriding theme throughout his three decades of filmmaking has been that art, whether one's own or someone else's, can provide redemption or at least momentary respite, from the confusions, failures, or horrors of life.

Allen told Björkman, "It has been said, that if I have one big theme in my movies, it's got to do with the difference between reality and fantasy. It comes up very frequently in my films. I think what it boils down to, really, is that I hate reality. And, you know, unfortunately it's the only place where we can get a good steak dinner." His comments are prompted by a discussion of *Play It Again, Sam,* in which his character wills Bogart's Rick into existence to provide advice on making out with women. That the daydreams, at least briefly, ultimately lead to failure is not important—Allen suggests that they provide a gratifying escape. Many of his own characters are far from being artists, but they escape reality by acting out personae that confound their nebbishy personalities: thus whether through unconscious or artful role-playing, Allen's schlemiel transforms himself into a bank robber (*Take the Money and Run*), a revolutionary leader (*Bananas, Sleeper, Love and Death*), and a deceptively ideal lover for Julia Roberts (*Everyone Says I Love You*). The most extreme variation, of course, is *Zelig,* the human chameleon whose appearance and personality change depending upon whom he is with.

Allen's first artist roles—Alvy, a comedian, in *Annie Hall* and Isaac, a TV writer, in *Manhattan*—also brought his screen character closer to his own career. In both films, relationships are fraught with neuroses and irrationality and are infuriatingly impossible to control, but Allen's alter egos, like Harry Block, find an outlet

or inspiration in creative work. In *Annie Hall,* the ostensible purpose of Alvy's stream-of-consciousness narrative (which resembles that of *Deconstructing Harry*) is an exploration of his breakup with Annie, an attempt to understand and shape life through artistic creation. To underline the idea, Allen has Alvy write a play that reverses reality and unites the couple; as Alvy explains to us, "You know how you're always trying to get things to come out perfect in art because it's real difficult in life." Allen thus calls attention to the storytelling process itself, specifically the writer's ability to "save his life" through the alterations of fiction.

*Manhattan*'s central story (following Isaac's opening multiple-choice narration about New York, by which Allen once again reminds us of the storyteller's power to interpret reality) begins with the line, "I think the essence of art is to provide a kind of working through the situation for people, you know, so that you can get in touch with feelings that you didn't know you had." That the pretentious, would-be writer Yale says this seems to mark it as pseudointellectual drivel. The film ends, however, by validating Yale's point: Isaac "gets in touch with his feelings" by dictating ideas for a story into a tape recorder, inspiring him to attempt a reconciliation with the young woman he has betrayed. In *Manhattan* Allen takes his character beyond merely resuming work and moves him to try to behave more responsibly in relationships. *Deconstructing Harry* also concludes by dramatizing Yale's statement, but Allen isn't willing to translate Harry's involvement with art into even a tentative step toward functioning in the real world.

Allen has played film directors only twice—in *Stardust Memories* and *Crimes and Misdemeanors. Stardust,* which, in its structure, self-reflexiveness, and misanthropy is another warmup for *Deconstructing Harry,* indicates Allen's preference for the world of art by apparently staying entirely within Sandy Bates's (Allen's character) film and never entering the "real world." As Sandy says, "You can't control life. It doesn't wind up perfectly. Only art you can control. Art and masturbation. Two areas in which I am an absolute expert."

*Crimes and Misdemeanors* is arguably Allen's richest achievement, partly because, unlike *Deconstructing Harry,* it avoids the easy solution of finding satisfaction in art. Allen's character Cliff succeeds neither as a 'serious' documentarian (his subject, a life-affirming philosopher, commits suicide) nor as a public television director (Cliff self-destructively dooms the project to oblivion), nor even as someone who can learn from watching movies. Cliff's obsessive involvement in Hollywood movies blinds him to reality, so that when Judah tells his own story of getting away with murder, Cliff sees it only as a movie plot, and gives it a moral conclusion unavailable in the real world.

While powerfully making us aware of Cliff's self-delusion, Allen still suggests that imaginary worlds provide legitimate solace. Cliff is one of many major Allen characters who find comfort in other people's works of art. Most prominent is Cecilia (*The Purple Rose of Cairo*), for whom movies are the only escape from a world of drudgery and abuse. The final close-up of Cecilia, immersed in a scene from *Top Hat,* is repeated almost exactly in *Hannah and Her Sisters.* There, Allen's character, Mickey, who has driven himself to near-suicide, finds at least a slim reason to go on living by watching *Duck Soup.*

For Cecilia, movies are only a brief and ultimately not very comforting respite, especially considering the disappointments she has experienced through her involvement in Hollywood's fantasy world. In *Hannah,* Allen takes his character beyond the movies and endows him with a satisfactory romance and even the miracle of fathering a child. The suggestion is that art has done more than provide escape—it has truly redemptive powers. Still, Allen hints that we might view the happy ending ironically. Gazing with Holly into a mirror, Mickey suggests that their relationship would make "a great story"—the story, in fact, that we have been watching. Allen's uncharacteristic use of a mirror, suggesting the frame of the screen and the world of fantasy inside, coupled with the reference to storytelling, once again suggests that art is a comforting but possibly illusory way of cleaning up life's disorder.

Allen expresses this complex attitude about the world of art/fantasy/illusion most poignantly in *Shadows and Fog.* His tormented Kafkaesque character, Kleinman, decides to escape his terrifying world by joining a traveling circus as a magician's apprentice. As in *Hannah,* Allen's final shot has us looking into a mirror, more emphatically reminding us that we are watching an illusion because the characters are behind the mirror but remain visible. Kleinman, who, like Harry Block, looks forward to a revitalized existence, tells the magician, "What better way to spend the rest of my life than to help you with all those wonderful illusions of yours." An unseen man shouts, "It's true, everyone loves his illusions!" The magician responds with the final line, "Love them? They need them, like they need the air," and then makes himself and Kleinman disappear. Unlike the ending of *Deconstructing Harry,* this conclusion proclaims both the power and evanescence of our artistic creations.

### "A Feminist's Love/Hate Relationship with Woody," by Elayne Rapping

If the editors of this critical symposium were looking for a woman to admit, unequivocally, to feeling disgust, contempt, even nausea, at the way Woody Allen has conducted his private life (and one needn't be a compulsive reader of tabloids or a watcher of the E! Network to claim expertise in the matter), they lucked out with me. That's not because I'm one of those militant, man-hating feminists the media so love to caricature. No, my reasons for loathing the man, while certainly visceral, are far more personal. When my daughter was eight years old, I began living with a man twelve years my junior and as many years her senior. The relationship lasted many years, as I got older and she got sexier. So when I heard about the Woody/Mia/Soon-Yi affair, to say that I was outraged would have been putting it mildly. Had I been in Mia's place—and I could easily have imagined what that would have felt like—I would have been thumbing the Yellow Pages in search of a discreet, efficient, preferably female, contract killer.

So my first response to contribute to this symposium was, "No way!" Why go public with such embarrassingly intense emotions about a man I've never met? Worse yet, the issue at hand—the relationship between one's life and art—struck me as hopelessly banal, smacking vaguely of the kind of Stalinist, or ultrafeminist, esthetic reductivism that has always made me cringe. Of course one can't dismiss a work of art because its creator is flawed. In fact, in my own more banal moments of esthetic rumination, I tend toward the sappy notion that the greatest artists (as, ironically, Allen himself suggests in *Deconstructing Harry*) transcend and redeem their own flaws through their art. Think of Bertolt Brecht, sleazy womanizer par excellence, who fled the country after facing the HUAC hearings. Yet who would deny his immeasurable contribution to the theory and practice of political drama?

What finally did interest me about the topic at hand, however, was something that hadn't occurred to me at first: that my changing attitudes toward Allen's films, over the several decades I've followed his career, were directly related to my development as a feminist. In fact, counterintuitive as it may seem, I realized that it was actually *because* of my development as a feminist that I had, in recent years, found myself admiring and enjoying the creepy old misogynist's work more and more.

Let me try to untangle this admittedly odd statement. Before feminism, I loved Woody Allen's films innocently and uncritically. They were funny, sophisticated, and so wonderfully *Jewish* in a way that I could recognize, relate to, and love. His ambivalence about being a second-generation Jew in America mirrored mine exactly, and, since I lived in a city where Jewish culture was marginal at best, I adored him. It never occurred to me to analyze the gender relations portrayed in his films, or any other films for that matter. Allen's misanthropic portrayals of castrating female intellectuals, for example, merely echoed the clichés about gender with which I'd been brought up. Brainy women, 'pushy' women, women with ambition, were unlikely to 'catch' a man. We all knew the drill and feared its ramifications, should we make the mistakes Woody's brainy women kept making.

Then came the Second Wave and the wildly exhilarating and empowering period when I—and most of my women friends—began to see through and question such 'truisms,' and to feel an increasing rage at the cultural representations—among which Woody Allen movies certainly qualified—that inculcated and reinforced them. During those years, Allen suddenly appeared as the ultimate enemy—one of the army of cultural and political power brokers whose words and images were weapons in what we now understood to be a veritable war between the sexes. Allen's movies—as well as most Hollywood movies—were hard for feminists to sit through in those days, without cringing, muttering and, often as not, going home to knock-down, drag-out fights with the men who were unfortunate enough to share our lives. For the truth was that most of us were locked into relationships and psychological mind sets which—no matter how much 'consciousness raising' we engaged in—took a lot of time, work, and energy to fight. Our rage was rooted in a real sense of vulnerability and powerlessness. We saw what had happened to us, what we had put up with and suffered over, but we were still neck deep in the muck and mire of it, and the struggle to get free, emotionally much less politically, was tough and sometimes hopelessly discouraging.

But as time passed, and the personal, theoretical, and political work of feminists—perhaps especially feminist film theorists and critics—developed in power and sophistication, even gaining a significant amount of legitimacy and authority in public discourse and within social and political institutions and traditions, Woody Allen began to seem less important, less infuriating, less a figure to be reckoned with or taken seriously. What had been, for so long, a source of rage in Allen's films—his infuriating contempt for intelligent, mature women; his puerile lust for near children; his outrageous ability to spin his well publicized uses and abuses of women and girls into artistic and box-office gold—gradually dissipated, as the ideas and behaviors he represented and flaunted seemed—and feminism is wholly responsible for this change—more and more passé, less and less hegemonic and powerful.

As this process developed, personally and politically for more and more women, it suddenly became possible to enjoy Allen's movies—misogyny, hypocrisy, male arrogance, and all—as I had in the past. The misogyny has actually gotten worse, I think. But the days when it was necessary to focus single-mindedly on that aspect of his or any work of male culture—and during the early days of the Second Wave, it's important to remember, it really was *necessary,* because sexism was that powerful, that subconsciously internalized, that new to us as an idea—were clearly over, at least for many of us.

I realized all of this as I watched **Deconstructing Harry** and realized that I absolutely loved it. Weird as it seemed, despite the nastiness of the gender politics, I could appreciate the artistry, wit, charm, and style with which Allen manages to cop to, and then capitalize on, his near sociopathic ability to hurt and betray friends and lovers alike, to absorb the rage and scorn of all concerned, and come up smiling and unscathed. The coldblooded cynicism of the film was despicable on a human level, certainly. As a cinematic tour de force, however, it was difficult not to admire and enjoy it.

And enjoy it I did. Feminist that I am, I left the theater grinning, and not just because it's an intelligent, charming film. More importantly, it brought home to me—at a time when it's far from easy for Second Wave feminists to feel good about much of anything—what an enormous impact feminist film theory and criticism has really had. So, yeah, I know **Deconstructing Harry** is Woody Allen's most virulently mean-spirited treatment of women so far. And I know that for many women it must have been every bit as unbearable to watch as his earlier films had been for me. But because I no longer felt personally affected, personally vulnerable, I was free, once more, to take the pleasure in his work I had taken in more innocent days. After all, I don't have to live with the guy, or anyone even vaguely like him. Best of all—and, here again, I have feminism to thank—my daughter doesn't either. Of course, lots of women and their daughters still do, and will, for a long time to come.

But at a time when it's been harder and harder for feminists to believe this, Woody Allen, of all people, gave me renewed hope that progress in gender relations is actually still possible. It may be slow; it may be uneven; it make take a two-steps-forward, one-step-backward path. And it may—and certainly and unfortunately does—affect those of us who are more socially, racially, and economically privileged, long before it gets to others. But the news of its untimely death, Woody Allen of all people has reassured me, is greatly exaggerated.

### David Galef (review date spring 1999)

SOURCE: Galef, David. "Getting Even: Literary Posterity and the Case for Woody Allen." *South Atlantic Review* 64, no. 2 (spring 1999): 146-60.

[*In the following review, Galef addresses the question of whether Allen's written humor sketches will survive the test of time as vital works to be included in the canon of comic literature.*]

The subject of humor in canon formation is not a widely discussed topic, except in occasional hand-waving articles about timeless universals of human nature. What such an approach all too often reveals, however, is the dated quality of much comedy, dependent on contemporary references and mores.[1] Nonetheless, one can discuss the topic with some analytic rigor given restrictions in time, genre, and audience—necessary clarifications of what it means to be read with appreciation years after one's demise. Woody Allen makes for an interesting case in this regard, specifically the question of whether his humorous sketches will be around in the next century.

Such a test case starts with some general, if no longer quite valid, assumptions about art and audience. First is the matter of absolute high quality, long thought to be the key to literary longevity. Yet anyone versed in today's criticism must acknowledge the passing of such a standard. The study of popular culture long ago divorced Matthew Arnold's stamp of the Good from the right to be preserved. From a critical vantage, Barthes's semiotics legitimize the study of anything from a chair to a rock star. From a textual perspective, Derrida's deconstructive strategies balance Shakespeare with comic books on the grounds that both are textual artifacts contributing to an endless chain of signifiers. This means that Elvis may be more enduring than Melville, not just from popular response but also from an academic conviction that the King supplies excellent fodder for critical analysis. In any event, the Quality-Non Quality distinction has now entered semi-oblivion, open to charges of cultural elitism whenever it reappears. Woody Allen's blend of high and low cultural references make him somewhat immune to such criticism.

Another point about durability is T. S. Eliot's concern, amid changing sensibilities, about the importance of novelty that also heeds tradition. Eliot's "Tradition and the Individual Talent" stresses work that looks forward as well as backward. One could just as well quote Pound's dictum "Make it new" to note that good comedy renovates and remodels rather than rebuilding from the foundations.[2] From the outset, Allen's humor in all its zaniness exhibited a lineage stretching back to S. J. Perelman, Robert Benchley, and others.

A more current issue, seemingly extrinsic to the work yet crucial to its viability, is the sociopolitics that determine the work's audience. Quite simply (or complexly), a work's context has become as important as its text. Whether one embraces the holy trinity of race, gender, and class or subscribes to some other form of situating the work, continued attention to the work is predicated upon a case made for its relevant themes. Fortuitously, Allen has latched onto society's interest in victims by presenting himself as one of the disempowered, a helpless schlemiel.

Of course, underlying these quasi-epistemic concerns is the voice of Woody Allen, claiming, "So, then, to know a substance or an idea we must doubt it, and thus, doubting it, come to perceive the qualities it possesses in its finite state, which are truly 'in the thing itself,' or 'of the thing itself,' or of something or nothing" (**Getting Even** 29). The sentence is from the section "Critique of Pure Dread" in **"My Philosophy."** It is preceded by a more obvious tip-off: "Can we actually 'know' the universe? My God, it's hard enough finding your way around in Chinatown" (28). The perils of analyzing Allen should be obvious: academics who play around with him risk being played around with themselves.

In fact, the ground covered by Allen's sketches suggests a more relevant point for the future of his humor: the high-low blend of intellectual neurosis and frustrated carnality suits the taste of academics. And what do they like?—work that they feel reflects important concerns, such as their own. The significance of this appeal is obvious for anyone who has spent time in an institution. If people are what they learn, what's taught in the schools ensures a posterity predictable for at least a generation or two. Even after that, pieces migrate easily from current anthologies to historical surveys. In other words, if the academy still determines the canon, what we deem fit for inclusion all too often reflects us—in Allen's case, teasing and parodying but ultimately flattering our concept of ourselves as academics. Though by now Allen is better known for his films than for his prose pieces, this discussion focuses on one genre to render the topic manageable, and because the academy still enshrines text.

\* \* \*

Allen's first collection, **Getting Even,** spanned work from 1966 to 1971, just in time for the emergent generation of college professors to discover and embrace it wholeheartedly. It's no coincidence that much of Allen's humor appeals to the intellect even as it derides scholasticism. In fact, his early material is still loyally repeated at universities, where the apocryphal story of his expulsion from NYU has become a classic: "I cheated on my metaphysics final. I looked within the soul of the boy sitting next to me" (**Nightclub Years**). As Sanford Pinsker, Eric Lax, and others have noted, this was the apotheosis of the over-educated schlemiel. Never mind that, as John Lahr has recently pointed out, Allen himself is no schlemiel (68). As with Robert Benchley and other creators of feckless personae, the image is what counts.[3] Allen's image, it turns out, is quite carefully cultivated: straddling knowing and knowledgeable, hapless yet hip—in short, the impression of an academic manqué.

Proper venue is also important for posterity. In 1966 Allen broke into *The New Yorker,* once the vanguard of the cultural elite and still far less ephemeral than stand-up routines. Of the fifty-two pieces in his eventual three volumes, most appeared first in *The New Yorker,* with a smattering in *The New Republic, The New York Times, Esquire, Playboy,* and *The Kenyon Review.* The pieces have gone on to be anthologized in everything from the O. Henry award annuals to Irving Howe's *Jewish-American Stories.*[4]

In these sketches, Allen's *idée fixe* is the cerebral at war with itself, an intellectual attack on the overly intellectual. His first published piece, **"The Gossage-Vardebedian Papers,"** concerns a correspondence chess game carried on by two solipsistic brains:

> My Dear Vardebedian:
>
> I was more than a bit chagrined today, on going through the morning's mail, to find that my letter of September 16, containing my twenty-second move (knight to the king's fourth square), was returned unopened due to a small error in addressing—precisely, the omission of your name and residence (how Freudian can one get?), coupled with a failure to append postage.
>
> (*Getting Even* 57)

The style is a combination of Nabokov and Perelman, and the soon-vituperative exchange resembles nothing so much as an angry spate of letters in *The New York Review of Books,* with both correspondents ostensibly discussing the same topic, but as far apart as two oversized egos will allow. The parallel to certain infamous academic disputes is incontestable. Particularly noteworthy are the ruminations conflating literature and life, the typical academic predilection:

> Gossage:
>
> How curious your last letter was! Well-intended, concise, containing all the elements that would appear to make up what passes among certain reference groups as a communicative effect, yet tinged throughout by what Jean-Paul Sartre is so fond of referring to as "nothingness." One is immediately struck by a profound sense of despair, and reminded vividly of the diaries sometimes left by doomed explorers lost at the Pole, or the letters of German soldiers at Stalingrad. Fascinating how the senses disintegrate when faced with an occasional black truth, and scamper amuck, substantiating mirage and constructing a precarious buffer against the onslaught of all too terrifying existence!
>
> (62)

This tangled skein of text and reality is typical, almost stereotypical, of the academic *flâneur.* The purpose of such a Barthesian bricolage (to shift metaphors) is to erect a defense or, as Allen ventriloquizes through his epistolary mouthpiece, "a precarious buffer against the onslaught of all too terrifying existence." This is the ivory-tower refuge, where naked aggression is vented on paper, where mortal combat is rendered symbolic through a game of chess. In fact, the sketch itself isn't

so much about chess as about textual misprision, as both correspondents willfully misinterpret each other's missives. The piece ends in an absurd juxtaposition of words, aptly represented by a fixed game of Scrabble.

In keeping with the image of the scholar attuned to minutiae, the first piece in **Getting Even, "The Metterling Lists,"** pokes fun at academics who publish an author's letters, juvenilia, and anything else they can get their hands on. An out-take from the first paragraph says it all: "Venal & Sons has at last published the long-awaited first volume of Metterling's laundry lists (*The Collected Laundry Lists of Hans Metterling,* Vol. I, 437 pp., plus XXXII-page introduction; indexed; $18.75), with an erudite commentary by the noted Metterling scholar Gunther Eisenbud" (9). What follows is the kind of exegesis all too familiar to devotees of Bloomsbury or any other literary cottage industry, building annotation into a form of hagiography. The life of Metterling is treated from a psychoanalytic perspective—once *the* intellectual therapy (and to which Allen still subscribes).

In a sketch near the end of the collection, **"Conversations with Helmholtz,"** Allen turns his attention to the history of psycho-analysis itself, inventing a contemporary of Freud. Now supposedly in his nineties, Helmholtz is visited by a sycophantic scribe (an idolizer recognizable in a certain stripe of graduate student) who unknowingly illustrates just how neurotic the treaters of neurosis actually were: "Talk turned back to Freud, who seems to dominate Helmholtz's every thought, although the two men hated each other after an argument over some parsley" (86). "After dinner there were mints and Helmholtz brought out his collection of lacquered butterflies, which caused him to become petulant when he realized they would not fly" (88). Oral history, a medium for preserving authentic voices, has metamorphosed into farce.

Significantly, the *faux-académe* image that Allen projects has shifted along with the academy. As the field of cultural studies has increased in popularity, at times seeming even to swallow up the fields that spawned it, such as literary criticism and sociology, Allen's academic pastiches have reflected the new discourse. Specifically, the high-low culture game played by critics commenting on Madonna and Marxism, or juxtaposing Foucault and fashion, is evident in Allen's third volume.[5] In **"Fabrizio's: Criticism and Response,"** a restaurant write-up couched as an academic symposium, he parodies the new form precisely:

> Pasta as an expression of Italian Neo-Realistic starch is well understood by Mario Spinelli, the chef at Fabrizio's. Spinelli kneads his pasta slowly. He allows a buildup of tension by the customers as they sit salivat-

ing. His fettucine, though wry and puckish in an almost mischievous way, owes a lot to Barzino, whose use of fettucine as an instrument of social change is known to us all.

(*Side Effects* 173)

In academic criticism, such commentary serves as a way of validating learning while at the same time remaining grounded or "real." Subsequent scholars then attack the original criticism as being insensitive to a particular group or set of concerns (see the recent history of postcolonial criticism, for example). As the response letters fabricated by Allen indicate, indignant critics call into question everything from the review's small-minded outlook on family politics—"Fabrizio's relationships with his wife and son are capitalistic and peer-group oriented"—to the New Historicist approach espoused—"yet another shocking contemporary example of revisionist history" (176, 177).

As *interdisciplinary* became the academic buzz word of the 1970s, Allen produced a course listing in **"Spring Bulletin"** that included "*Yeats and Hygiene, A Comparative Study*: The poetry of William Butler Yeats is analyzed against a background of proper dental care" (*Getting Even* 51). To cite anecdotal evidence of canon-formation in its formative phase, one professor regularly assigned this piece in his advanced composition classes. Eventually, a former student of his got an instructorship and triumphantly wrote back to his old professor that he was teaching advanced composition. And what was he assigning?—Woody Allen's **"Spring Bulletin."** The irony of Allen's induction into the academy is evident in the preface to the piece: "Each time I read through the latest bulletin of extension courses, I make immediate plans to drop everything and return to school. (I was ejected from college many years ago . . .)" (47).

And what of the already extant canon, the pantheon that extends from the anthologies to the final exams? The truth is that Allen came late to the Great Works but reinvented them as most autodidacts do. Allen's **"A Twenties Memory,"** for instance, is a send-up of the pugilistic but arty Hemingway generation:

> We had great fun in Spain that year and we travelled and wrote and Hemingway took me tuna fishing and I caught four cans and we laughed and Alice Toklas asked me if I was in love with Gertrude Stein because I had dedicated a book of poems to her even though they were T. S. Eliot's and I said, yes, I loved her, but it could never work because she was far too intelligent for me and Alice Toklas agreed and then we put on some boxing gloves and Gertrude Stein broke my nose.
>
> (*Getting Even* 73)

More than a succession of dropped references, the prose provides an entire outlook—resembling the mixed dread and irreverence that the classic Modernists inspire in many college freshmen.

Yet if the ivory tower became a culturally besieged fortress while Allen wrote, it provided a touchstone, a *lingua franca* important to those who cared for more than sitting in front of a couple of beers and talking about the Mets. **"The Whore of Mensa,"** from Allen's 1975 collection, **Without Feathers,** perfectly sums up the angst of the bright adolescent, riddled with the social insecurity that arguably never leaves those in the academy. As the client Word Babcock explains to the Chandleresque detective in the story, "See, Kaiser, I'm basically an intellectual. Sure, a guy can meet all the bimbos he wants. But the really brainy women—they're not so easy to find on short notice" (33). Allen even provides an accurate backdrop for how many academic aspirants live. Sherry, the intellectual hooker in the story, explains in the face of the law: "I needed the money to complete my master's. I've been turned down for a grant. *Twice*. Oh, Christ" (36). Given the future of the academic job market, the spoof behind this piece may retain its eerie accuracy throughout the next century.

The Chandleresque touches, which Allen used in an earlier, eschatological detective tale called **"Mr. Big,"** are a double sign of high-low splicing, since Chandler himself gave his hard-boiled Marlowe metaphors worthy of Perelman. **"Mr. Big"** also pays lip service to the dream of many male academics when the female object of desire wheedles: "Oh, Kaiser, we could go away together. Just the two of us. We could forget about philosophy. Settle down and maybe get into semantics" (*Getting Even* 109). As it happens, he shoots her (to avoid her shooting him), and as she dies he recites Heideggerian philosophy.

This double-barreled technique relies on both high and low burlesque: high burlesque, in which a character suffers by comparison to a ridiculously high standard; and low burlesque, when a character is cramped by base comparisons. In other words, Allen's lower orders can talk of Proust while his intellectuals whine about carpeting. In **"Mr. Big,"** the mobster (and atheist) Chicago Phil tells the detective Kaiser Lupowitz, "Take it from me, Kaiser. There's no one out there. It's a void. I couldn't pass all those bad checks or screw society the way I do if for one second I was able to recognize any authentic sense of Being. The universe is strictly phenomenological" (105-6). The Pope, on the other hand, confesses, "Every morning I rise, put on this red suit, and suddenly I'm a big cheese. It's all in the suit. I mean, face it, if I went around in slacks and a sports jacket, I couldn't get arrested religion-wise" (108). The high-low contrasts in Allen's sketches thus form a splice that in ordinary discourse would be a gap, hence a seeming non sequitur.

Non sequiturs, as Maurice Charney has commented, are crucial to Allen's humor (339). Yet a real non sequitur is puzzling in its lack of connection, whereas Allen's non sequiturs depend on their own warped logic. In **"Selections from the Allen Notebooks,"** for instance, is a typical excerpt: "Should I marry W.? Not if she won't tell me the other letters in her name. And what about her career? How can I ask a woman of her beauty to give up the Roller Derby? Decisions . . ." (*Without Feathers* 4). The links and inversions are all there: a parody of the nineteenth-century novelists' discretion in mentioning certain towns and individuals only by initials, as well as the bathos of a femme fatale who battles other women on roller skates. Even when there appears to be genuine disjunction—"My room is damp and I have perpetual chills and palpitations of the heart. I noticed, too, that I am out of napkins" (3)—Freudian floating anxiety provides a certain connectivity: a fixation on whatever seems amiss. These preoccupying worries are partly a phenomenon of class: intellectuals are neurotic; others are merely complainers. Allen's real and imagined discomfitures, in his written material at least, are generally those with one foot fixed in higher culture.

Of course, some of Allen's juxtapositions defy easy analysis: "Idea for story: Some beavers take over Carnegie Hall and perform *Wozzeck*" (*Without Feathers* 4). Even here, however, the idea of animals as artists functions as high burlesque, with an additional payoff if the reader knows the opera based on Georg Büchner's 1830s play, about a philosophically inclined soldier who goes mad and kills his lover. Büchner's play prefigures the Theater of the Absurd—which is just what Allen is suggesting: an absurd connection. In this vein, Marc S. Reisch posits that Allen is an existentialist humorist (69), though this may simply be to claim him as a master of the absurd.[6] Since existentialism denies any causality or necessary connections, as Sartre's Roquentin discovers when touching a chestnut tree, existence itself becomes absurd—but it must be lived anyway. When Allen notes, "Of all the wonders of nature, a tree in summer is perhaps the most remarkable, with the possible exception of a moose singing 'Embraceable You'" (*Without Feathers* 101), he may be on to something similar. As more than one Marxist critic has observed, however, existentialism is an upper-class intellectual luxury—lowbrows being too focused on material culture and the poor too concerned for their very survival to agonize over the nature of existence. Ironically, Marxism nowadays has come under similar attack, yet the two philosophies continue to proliferate—where else?—in the academy. Allen takes potshots at both.

Reflecting the nagging academic worry over sterile cerebrality, much of Allen's absurdity resides in the mind-body problem, with the longings of both crossing each other up. Or as Sartre is claimed to have remarked, in a line that sounds as if it could have been written by Allen, "An intellectual is someone who's discovered a subject more interesting than sex." In **"The Kugelmass Episode,"** already well-anthologized,[7] Allen conflates both subjects, as a humanities professor at C.C.N.Y. named Kugelmass lives out his fantasy of sleeping with Emma Bovary. As the Brooklyn magician The Great Persky explains, "If I throw any novel into this cabinet with you, shut the doors, and tap it three times, you will find yourself projected into that book" (*Side Effects* 64). This prospect is the dream of endless academics, and Kugelmass is no exception.[8] Yet as Kugelmass finds out, not only does art reflect life, but Oscar Wilde's point that life reflects art holds sway, as well. Exposed to life outside the novel, Emma Bovary quickly adapts to New York, and Kugelmass cannot cope. After Emma returns to her novel, he ends up pursued by the verb *tener* in a remedial textbook, *Spanish Grammar*—symbolic of how language can turn on those who abuse it.

Of course, **"The Kugelmass Episode"** presumes some familiarity with Flaubert and more than a passing interest in the art-life distinction, and these connections beg another question about later generations who read Allen's work: will they appreciate the references to Immanuel Kant, Alfred Kazin, Emily Dickinson, Sigmund Freud, and others? The answer is probably yes, since, for better or worse, comedy that gets reread is generally prescribed by the academy, which also guards the List of Important Names. As the author of the *Woody Allen Encyclopedia* Mark Altman states, or perhaps overstates a bit: "**'The Kugelmass Episode'** . . . is read side by side in high schools today with *Madame Bovary*" (25).

Naturally, some rancor resides behind the wit. This is what Freud in *Jokes and Their Relation to the Unconscious* called tendentious humor (97), not innocent joking (if such a thing exists) but comedy with a target. Of the various meanings behind Allen's first title, *Getting Even,* one is surely paying back the academy that rejected him. Still, the academy so loves to be footnoted and cited that parody is an acceptable form of idolatry. And of course the parody is taken seriously: over eighty journal articles and books on Allen have accumulated in the MLA bibliography since 1983. In an essay devoted to the reception of *Madame Bovary,* Jonathan Culler glowingly describes the "post-modern *méta-récits*" "by that master of the post-modern, Woody Allen" (80). *The Collected Prose of Woody Allen* was published in 1992, providing a standard edition for more analysis and further enshrining the author's reputation.

To be fair: some of those learned essays strive to discover a more universal source of Allen's success. T. S. Eliot's theory of dramatic levels pertains here. Trying his hand at verse plays, Eliot wondered how Shakespeare acquired such an audience. He concluded that every public work of art must work on at least several discrete levels: crude action for some, pageantry for others, complex wordplay for a third group, and so on (154). It's also arguable that successful humor in a democracy must combine high and low, as Twain and others have historically shown. Karen C. Blansfield makes precisely this argument in her essay "Woody Allen and the Comic Tradition in America."[9]

Despite the academic interest, the broadest-based source of Allen's humor may stem from the Chaplinesque Little Man appeal. This sort of attraction derives less from Perelman than from Max Shulman—whom Allen also claims as an influence, along with Benchley (**"Art of Humor"** 203). Whether chronicling the antics of demobilized soldiers in *The Zebra Derby* or failed adolescent romances in the collection *I Was a Teen-Age Dwarf,* Shulman was definitely folksier than Perelman. Yet Shulman also featured intellectually aspiring heroes, and it's significant that what remains in humor anthologies is often Shulman's short story "Love Is a Fallacy," in which a young man attempts to teach logic to the woman he wants as his girlfriend—though eventually logic proves his undoing. In both writers, intellect is a form of power, but prone to unseating itself. Sensitivity is a gift, but likely to spill over into neurosis—as in Allen's **"If the Impressionists Had Been Dentists,"** whose subtitle, **"(A Fantasy Exploring the Transposition of Temperament),"** reveals the folly of neurasthenic overreaction.

Allen made his emerging reputation repeating these lessons. Paradoxically, one sign of posterity is often a halt in production. Some artists, like Beckett or Bergman, repeat and refine endlessly; others, like Joyce Carol Oates or John Updike, move around in style and genre. Allen turned out to be a repeater in prose (though not in his films). Why he eventually stopped writing his *New Yorker*-style casuals is partly answered in the preface to **"The Early Essays"**: *"Following are a few of the early essays of Woody Allen. There are no late essays, because he ran out of observations"* (**Without Feathers** 101). Or, as he remarked in Lax's biography *Woody Allen,* "I don't want to look up on the bookshelf one day and see ten collections of basically the same thing" (232). After his third collection, *Side Effects,* in 1981, he more or less stopped writing for the page, though he has hinted, intriguingly, at a novel in the wings (**"Art of Humor"** 206).

Just as writers like E. M. Forster and Sinclair Lewis seemed to shut down after their eras had passed, more is at work here than the fear of repetition. As Adam Gopnik noted in a post-Mia Farrow essay entitled "The Outsider," Allen's humor developed after the fault-line of the sexual revolution in American culture, "between what the fifties had taught you to say and the sixties and seventies allowed you to do" (88). In the current era, the academy's sober separation of sex and other offenses from comedy is a problem not just for Allen but for the realm of humor itself.[10]

In fact, the earnestness of political correctitude seems the one impediment to furthering Allen's writings posthumously. In the end, the professors may have the last word, if not the last laugh. After all, Stanley Fish's interpretive communities determine not only consensual validity but also whose work gets validated. Academics, particularly in the United States, have little power—a point that Allen's work often illustrates—but they do prescribe what is read in the schools. Assigned reading is often reread and analyzed in the classroom, and therefore often remembered for years afterwards. And in an era of declining interest in literature, what gets read only because it is assigned assumes ever-greater importance, especially since students are less and less likely to read other works outside of class.

The question begged is what posterity guarantees, after all. As Tom Stoppard, a sometimes-absurdist in another direction, once put in the mouth of a playwright on-stage: "I don't think writers are sacred, but words are. If you get the right ones in the right order, you can nudge the world a little or make a poem which children will speak for you when you're dead" (54). Allen does care about being read by future generations, but pretends to focus on more immediate concerns: "So you think to yourself, 'My work will live on.' As I've said many times, rather than live on in the hearts and minds of my fellow man, I'd rather live on in my apartment" (**"Art of Humor"** 216). Yet Allen is increasingly committed to an art beyond what he regards as his early, crude humor. Just as some of his last prose pieces, like **"The Shallowest Man"** and **"Retribution,"** began to forsake laughs for psychological depth, Allen's later films have dealt with patterns of love and infidelity that are hardly the stuff of *Everything You Always Wanted to Know about Sex but Were Afraid to Ask.* But whether the more sober truths that Allen evinces will be his enduring legacy depends again on what his audience chooses to embrace.

As for the authorities who judge, however, Allen may have the last comment: "What then is the function of the critic? Precisely to interpret the audio-visual electronic image and fragmentize individual coercive response against a background of selective subjectivity. He can do this either standing up or sitting . . ." (**"Woody"** 11). At the very least, Allen will stand up longer than his critics.

*Notes*

1. Though Aristotle's *Poetics* is quite prescriptive on how to bring about catharsis in an audience viewing a tragedy, his treatise on comedy remains a few tattered fragments of papyrus (see Richard Janko's attempted reconstruction of *Poetics* II, 47ff.). At least one sly critic has suggested that Aristotle never got beyond fragments in this area. Tragedy's easy—comedy's hard.

2. As Anatole Broyard once wrote, "If an experimental work is still called experimental after fifty years, then the experimental failed" (11). Successful humor looks inevitable in retrospect.

3. Though most audiences view Allen's persona as both true-to-life and static, Lax astutely reads it as a mask, as well as noting a shift in it over the years: "The Woody Allen character—initially an awkward fellow of dubious skills, none of which include successfully coping with daily life, more recently a stubbornly sane misfit who persists despite his fears and neuroses—is a hilarious creation concocted from a wildly exaggerated personal basis" (10-11).

4. See "No Kaddish for Weinstein" in *Jewish-American Stories,* ed. Irving Howe (New York: Mentor-Penguin, 1977). A full list of Allen's reprints is almost impossible to compile, but the range alone is impressive. To name just a few: "Count Dracula" in *Great Ghost Stories,* comp. Betty Ann Schwartz (New York: Julian Messner, 1985); "Mr. Big" in *Murder for Christmas,* ed. Thomas Godfrey (New York: Mysterious Press, 1982—a Book Club edition); and "The Diet" in *The Arbor House Celebrity Book of the Greatest Stories Ever Told,* comp. M. H. Greenberg and C. C. Waugh (New York: Arbor House, 1983). For the focus of this essay, academic recycling, even more significant are appearances in textbooks like *The Norton Reader,* 8th ed., ed. Arthur M. Eastman et al. (New York: Norton, 1992) and *The McGraw Hill Introduction to Literature,* ed. Gilbert H. Miller and John A. Williams (New York: McGraw Hill, 1995).

5. The high-low cultural seesaw was in fact a mark of modernism well before postmodernism—see the conjunction of high and low culture in a work like *Ulysses,* for example. This slightly belated aspect marks Allen even at his best. As Gopnik has pointed out (88-89), many parodists of Hemingway and belle lettrists preceded Allen, who simply went ahead and did it again, albeit with a self-conscious aspect that seems part of Allen's personality.

6. As Reisch claims, "Allen's nihilism consists in the denial of all given truth" (69), but the reader should be wary of confusing the author with his comic speakers. In any event, as Reisch admits near the end of his essay, "The world may seem *apparently* hopeless, but Allen's neurotic *personae* keep trying to make sense" (73, italics mine).

7. After its initial publication in *The New Yorker,* 2 May 1977, the story was reprinted in *The Year's Finest Fantasy,* ed. Terry Carr (New York: Berkeley-Putnam, 1978); *Prize Stories 1978: The O. Henry Awards,* ed. William Abrahams (Garden City, NY: Doubleday, 1978); *The Best of Modern Humor,* ed. Mordecai Richler (New York: Knopf, 1983); *The*

*Treasury of American Short Stories,* comp. Nancy Sullivan (Garden City, NY: Doubleday, 1981); and other volumes, all possible candidates for classroom use.

8. This is not to deny that people of all types daydream this way, but usually their romances and escapes are drawn from popular culture, not nineteenth-century French literature. In Allen's film *The Purple Rose of Cairo,* this kind of magic projection happens between reality and the silver screen, emphasizing the broader-based appeal of Allen's films, themselves part of a broader-based medium in this non-literary age.

9. As Blansfield observes: "for he is, in some respects, an intellectual comic, even though, like Shakespeare, he is also accessible to lesser educated audiences by virtue of his linguistic versatility and comic strokes" (150).

10. Cf. Tom Lehrer, who, as he said, stopped writing satirical songs when political realities grew too grim to parody. Lehrer also confessed that he was no longer so comfortable with his old liberal leanings, that if he saw a homeless person on his doorstep, for instance, he wouldn't know whether to invite him in or call the police. But Lehrer's audience has also changed, and the real problem is whether Lehrer's jabs would get laughs—or provoke the typical complaint, "That's not funny."

### Works Cited

Allen, Woody. "The Art of Humor" (I). *Paris Review* 136 (Fall 1995): 200-222.

———. *The Complete Prose of Woody Allen.* London: Picador, 1992.

———. *Getting Even.* 1971. New York: Warner, 1972.

———. *The Nightclub Years, 1964-1968.* 1972. EMI, 1990.

———. *Side Effects.* 1980. New York: Ballantine, 1981.

———. *Without Feathers.* New York: Random, 1975.

———. "Woody, the Would-Be Critic." *New York Times* 2 May 1971: sec. 2: 11.

Aristotle. Poetics *I, with The* Tractatus Coislinianus, *A Hypothetical Reconstruction of* Poetics *II, and The Fragment of the* On Poets. Trans. Richard Janko. Indianapolis: Hackett, 1987.

Blansfield, Karen C. "Woody Allen and the Comic Tradition in America." *Studies in American Humor* 6 (1988): 142-53.

Broyard, Anatole. "About Books." *New York Times Book Review* 24 Aug. 1986: 11.

Charney, Maurice. "Woody Allen's Non Sequiturs." *Humor* 8.4 (1995): 339-48.

Eliot, T. S. *The Use of Poetry and the Use of Criticism.* London: Faber and Faber, 1950.

Freud, Sigmund. *Jokes and Their Relation to the Unconscious.* 1905. *The Standard Edition of the Complete Psychological Works of Sigmund Freud.* Vol. 8. Trans. James Strachey. London: Hogarth, 1960.

Gopnik, Adam. "The Outsider." *New Yorker* 25 Oct. 1993: 86-93.

Lahr, John. "The Imperfectionist." *New Yorker* 9 Dec. 1996: 68-83.

Lax, Eric. *Woody Allen: A Biography.* New York: Knopf, 1991.

Pinsker, Sanford. "Woody Allen's Lovably Anxious *Schlemiels.*" *Studies in American Humor* 5.2-3 (Summer-Fall 1986): 177-89.

Reisch, Marc S. "Woody Allen: American Prose Humorist." *Journal of Popular Culture* 17.3 (Winter 1983): 68-74.

Stoppard, Tom. *The Real Thing.* London: Faber and Faber, 1983.

## Jonathan Romney (review date 21 June 1999)

SOURCE: Romney, Jonathan. "The Fame Game." *New Statesman* (21 June 1999): 38-9.

[*In the following review, Romney describes* Celebrity *as disappointing and overlong, and believes that Allen fails to offer any new insight into the issues concerning celebrity and the media.*]

Everything you really need to know about Woody Allen and celebrity you can get from Barbara Kopple's recent documentary *Wild Man Blues,* which followed Allen as he reluctantly toured the world with his jazz band. Allen *kvetched* about the showers and the sandwiches, grimaced behind the backs of adoring Venetian matrons and then returned to New York, where his nonagenarian parents put him firmly in his place. He'd have done better, they carp, if he'd become a pharmacist. Allen himself couldn't have devised a more deflating portrait of a star cushioned by fame, sneering defensively at his admirers, but finally humbled by a different kind of infantilisation. *Wild Man Blues* was all the more telling in that it coincided with *Deconstructing Harry,* Allen's own scathing picture of the kind of person we imagine him to be—a writer in the Philip Roth mould, recruiting people from his own life as characters for his novels but signally lacking insight into his own nature.

These two films offer such a comprehensive impression of Allen's attitudes to public life and the media that his latest, entitled *Celebrity,* looked certain to be anti-climactic. It's worse than that. For a start, you could always count on an Allen film clocking in neatly around the 100-minute mark. This one runs to 113; that may seem a niggling complaint, but it's a sign that he's not pulling his strokes with quality control. This is the first Woody Allen film that's made me check my watch throughout.

*Celebrity* reeks of world-loathing as much as—but not nearly as compellingly as—the bilious *Stardust Memories* (1980). It's a journey through a bright, noisy funfair of worldliness, undertaken in parallel by a divorced couple, Lee (Kenneth Branagh), a writer, and the lapsed academic Robin (Judy Davis). Lee wants to be a serious writer but spends his time writing intimate personality profiles of the *Vanity Fair* ilk. He gets closer to the stars than most European profile-writers, allotted their 60 minutes, might find credible. He falls into bed with the actress Nicole (Melanie Griffith), has a wretched night out with a supermodel (Charlize Theron), then crashes his implausibly flashy car into a shop window and resists being inveigled into several-way sex by the star brat Brandon (the film's scoop—Leonardo DiCaprio parodying his spoilt-puppy image). Meanwhile, Robin (Davis mangling herself into her inimitable angst-knots) passes through several shades of torment before reinventing herself as a glib daytime TV personality reporting on Donald Trump's dining habits.

What are *Celebrity*'s great revelations? Only that Allen can still be unpleasantly dyspeptic, is still seriously hung up on Fellini's *La Dolce Vita* and is pretty much a write-off as a social satirist. Branagh's Lee, blabbering and twitching in a grotesque and distracting impersonation of Allen himself, gets sucked into the whirlpool of glitz in too many repetitive sequences. Allen has nothing to say about the shallow and famous, other than: "So beautiful, so rich—yet look how they waste their time!" He doesn't present their world as anything genuinely novel or seductive—it's all shorthand to justify the morally instructive spectacle of smart people such as Lee and Robin frittering away their talent.

Allen is no more optimistic or insightful about contemporary appetites for culture and spirit—religion, therapy and the literary world all get carved up in mechanical fashion. Lee is made to look as dopey in his airier aspirations as he is when drawn to the carnival. He falls for a bohemian princess—Winona Ryder, who must get sick of being cast as wafty and vaguely cerebral. She's another version of Allen's precocious, brainy dream-girls who are best left alone, like Rain in *Husbands and Wives.* Then there's the novel that Lee finally writes, which his angry girlfriend (an incisive Famke Janssen) throws off the back of a boat. The old paper-fluttering-in-the-wind routine—can this wash any more? Is it pedantic to object that no sane writer today has only one draft of a novel? Lee can surely afford a laptop, or did he file all those profile pieces by carrier pigeon? The scene is a romantic cliché exposed by sloppy elderly thinking.

This impression of half-baked thought comes across in a formless succession of ugly routines that are less trenchant about fashionable emptiness than Brett Easton Ellis's *Glamorama* (which at least tackles the abyss from the inside) and less energetically silly than Robert Altman's much-maligned *Prêt à Porter.* Some sequences—at a cosmetician's, at various media bean-feasts—strain for a busy simultaneity of impressions in the manner of Fellini and Altman, but they're just blustery, as if Allen can't really stand the noise. Little is really said about the media other than that things get jumbled up in frivolous promiscuity. The single good gag is a TV chat show that programmes rabbis, Nazis and gangsters together—"Where are the bagels? The skinheads ate all the bagels already?"

Most of this is just deadening but the film becomes objectionable in its peevish handling of ordinary people. Lee attends a class reunion—that stalest chestnut of American social insight—and is shocked to see how staid and middle-aged everyone seems. Look, there's even a pony-tailed goon singing "The Impossible Dream"! It's meant to be Lee's moment of self-knowledge, as he realises that he's no spring chicken to be running around with club kids. But the scene reeks of distaste for the everybody.

If all you find is bourgeois stagnation on the one hand and tinselly neurosis on the other, what's there to do but retreat into contemplation of your own inner depths (which is more or less what the writer ends up doing in *Deconstructing Harry*)? You can only hope that the older and wiser Lee succeeds in this better than his creator, because Allen's creative depths seem to have dried up for the moment.

## Dave Kehr (review date November-December 1999)

SOURCE: Kehr, Dave. Review of *Sweet and Lowdown,* by Woody Allen. *Film Comment* 35, no. 6 (November-December 1999): 76.

[*In the following review, Kehr provides a favorable assessment of* Sweet and Lowdown. *Kehr praises the structure of the film and finds the anecdotes about entertainers from the past interesting.*]

*Sweet and Lowdown* finds Woody Allen indulging two of his great interests in life: jazz of the early swing era, and himself.

Allen's 1997 *Deconstructing Harry* made explicit what was implicit in most of his work: that his films are tightly, compulsively, unabashedly autobiographical.

Barely disguised, entire episodes of his life are re-created in his films, including his romantic confusions (*Annie Hall*), raging self-doubts (*Zelig*), triumphant ego (*Everyone Says I Love You*), and slavish devotion to the work of Federico Fellini (*Stardust Memories, Purple Rose of Cairo*) and Ingmar Bergman (*September, Another Woman*).

Within that range, Allen's work falls into two broad categories: those films in which he stars, and those in which he doesn't. The films in the first category tend to be warmly affectionate, self-regarding, Felliniesque—whimsical comedy dramas in which the Allen character, though assaulted by intellectual phonies and moral hypocrites from all sides, manages to remain true to his fundamentally sweet, romantic nature and (not incidentally) triumph over his enemies (*Manhattan* remains the archetype here, though *Broadway Danny Rose* is the most subtly vengeful). The films of the second group find Allen drafting substitutes for himself—Sam Waterston in *September,* John Cusack in *Bullets over Broadway,* Kenneth Branagh in *Celebrity*—who assume his posture and speaking patterns but display significant flaws of callowness, thoughtlessness, or naïveté (another, related subgroup are the anti-Allens in films in which Woody himself holds the moral center: Michael Caine in *Hannah and Her Sisters,* Martin Landau in *Crimes and Misdemeanors,* Sydney Pollack in *Husbands and Wives,* Tony Roberts in anything). With the distance provided by casting another performer as himself, Allen can tolerate a degree of self-criticism. Even so, his characters' *péchés* are apt to remain *mignons,* his acts of thoughtlessness more childlike than monstrous, his cruelty more incidental than intentional.

The project of the loose, amiable *Sweet and Lowdown* is to establish such faults as belonging to the rights and nature of the artist—the "dark side of genius" as it were, though this dark side is at most light gray. Playing a cartoon hipster—the sort of hop-headed, pencil-mustached musician who would fit right in on the bandstand of an early-Thirties Warner Bros. speakeasy—Sean Penn is quite entertaining as Emmett Ray, a pioneering, wholly fictional swing guitarist who is said by himself and others to be the second best performer on his instrument in the world. The first, of course, is the eminently nonfictional Django Reinhardt, a legendary guitarist who remains Emmett's distant, untouchable ideal—a godlike figure to whom he refers as "that gypsy in France."

Is it too much to see, behind the figure of a native American artist who feels overshadowed and outdone by a legendary European counterpart, a parallel to Allen's own relationship with some of his arthouse heroes? That gypsy in France could also be that philosopher in Sweden or that cartoonist in Rome—a comparison that seems a nice enough way of paying homage to one's masters, if it weren't so subtly self-flattering as well. (Does anyone really believe that Allen inherited Fellini's mantle when he died—apart from Allen, that is?) Both jazz and the movies are strongly (if not accurately) identified as quintessentially American artforms; Allen is perhaps protesting that our native arts have been hijacked by foreign interlopers, or at least that we are willing to give more credit and prestige to outlanders while overlooking the accomplishments of our homegrown geniuses (anyone in mind?).

The most engaging aspects of *Sweet and Lowdown* are the reenactments of old showbiz anecdotes, a format that has already served Allen well with *Broadway Danny Rose.* The stories, related *Reds*-style, by various expert witnesses (critic Nat Hentoff and others), are drawn from the lives of Bix Beiderbecke, Miles Davis, Louis Armstrong, Hoagy Carmichael, and others; they all have the perfect, polished forms of stories often told and improved with each telling. Emmett is at once impossibly arrogant and impossibly insecure (not an uncommon combination in the art world); his ego demands that he make his entrance on stage descending from a grinning, gilded crescent moon, his anxiety makes him so shaky that he falls out and plunges to the floor. For once, Allen assembles his anecdotes with rhythm and effective tonal variations: it's perhaps his most smoothly structured, most fleet-footed film.

For Allen, Emmett represents a paradox: the ignorant, insensitive slob (his favorite pastime is shooting rats at the city dump) who is nevertheless an artist of sublime, god-sent gifts. (There is a touch of *Amadeus* in the concept, as well as of such cautionary musical dramas as *Young Man with a Horn*). He has a gift he doesn't deserve, which makes him the representative of a certain kind of grace. That grace is embodied by Gracie (the greatly gifted young British actress Samantha Morton), a mute laundry girl whom Emmett picks up at an amusement pier and takes into his life. As her name suggests, Gracie is a fairly abstract character; her pulled-down cap and wistful half-smile seem to have been directly inspired by the Giulietta Masina character in Fellini's *La Strada,* as has her saintly forbearance. The latter, more turgid passages of *Sweet and Lowdown* have to do with Emmett's need, as a fully licensed, self-destructive genius, to mess up his relationship with this innocent, perfectly adoring, very much younger woman. Allen presents this development as tragic but inevitable—as if loneliness were the price of greatness and infidelity the curse of genius. Such things might bode ill for any innocent, perfectly adoring, very much younger women in Woody Allen's life, if there happen to be any.

## Richard A. Blake (review date 11 March 2000)

SOURCE: Blake, Richard A. "Allusions of Grandeur." *America* 182, no. 8 (11 March 2000): 15-17.

[*In the following review, Blake compares Allen's* Sweet and Lowdown *with* La Strada, *an Italian film directed by Federico Fellini.*]

When an art form starts to reflect upon itself, does the borrowing indicate maturity or senescence? I don't know. Film artists have copied one another since the very earliest comics in the silents realized that audiences loved chase scenes and so tried to outdo their rivals with ever more frantic eruptions of mayhem. Today's directors, many of them coming out of film schools, are self-conscious historians of cinema. Their hommages deliberately pay tribute to giants of the past. Like true postmodern artists, they rely upon earlier works as much as "reality" for their self-expression. Audiences then become unwitting players in the game. Recognizing familiar shots and scenes can be a distraction, but when such scenes are woven skillfully into the text of a film, they can add appreciably to one's enjoyment. To cite one obvious example, *Love and Death* (1975), Woody Allen's parody of Tolstoy's War and Peace, ends with Death leading the cast in a dance in imitation of Ingmar Bergman's *The Seventh Seal* (1956). Viewers unfamiliar with Bergman would miss the joke and the point of the scene.

In his most recent movie, *Sweet and Lowdown,* Woody Allen turns from the work of his earlier icon, Bergman, to *La Strada* (*The Road,* 1954), a masterpiece of the late Federico Fellini. Allen's transformation of the source material reveals a great deal about both filmmakers. In the earlier film, Zampano (Anthony Quinn) is an itinerant strongman, a brute of a man who travels through the back roads of postwar Italy on his motorcycle and trailer. He stops at crossroads, gathers what audiences he can and with his "lungs of steel" pops open a chain wrapped around his chest. Road and chain provide the defining images for him. He must continue his journey, while trying to reach beyond the chains that bind him in the tight circle of his own ego.

Early in the film, Zampano stops at a seaside village to secure for a modest price a traveling companion, Gelsomina (Giulietta Masina). This simpleminded, large-hearted mute girl will travel with him as a replacement for her older sister, who has died. The family needs the money. While the road and his chains define the strongman, the sea with its open horizons and infinite fertility mirror Gelsomina. At one point in their journey together, Zampano parks his bike at the edge of the beach and urinates in the water as a sign of his rejection of Gelsomina's world. Only at the end of the film, when he learns of her death, does Zampano realize the saving power of her love. Once again he wades into the waves, but this time he bathes his face in its baptismal waters and weeps in recognition of his lost love. In this final scene, Fellini holds out the hope that this brutal, unloving man has at last found redemption.

Woody Allen tells the same story, but with a very different intent. Employing a documentary style complete with talking-head commentators, one of whom is the filmmaker himself, Allen tells the "true" story of Emmet Ray (Sean Penn), a fictitious jazz guitarist of the 1930's. While playing a gig on the Jersey shore, Emmet and his friend try to pick up girls on the boardwalk. As it turns out, Emmet's date Hattie (Samantha Morton) has lost her speech because of a childhood illness. After their first awkward date, she discovers that she adores Emmet, and she has the added quality of not being able to interrupt him when he boasts about being the second greatest guitarist in the world.

It seems to be a match made in central casting. Emmet explains that he cannot tie himself down by marriage, but such a detail scarcely challenges her devotion and determination to stay with him through thin and thinner. She even takes in laundry to help pay the bills. They take off in his convertible roadster, stopping off for occasional amateur shows in farm country on their way to the big time in Hollywood.

Gelsomina endures and even takes perverse pride in Zampano's success with his female fans, but he needs freedom as much as she needs love. Eventually Zampano drives off without her. Emmet similarly dumps Hattie and marries a glamorous socialite and would-be author (Uma Thurman), who finds Emmet fascinating material for a book. She soon finds a gangster even more fascinating, however, so their marriage ends as quickly as one can say, "Cheese it! The cops." In time Emmet's travels bring him back to the Jersey shore, where he finds Hattie sitting quietly on the boardwalk eating her lunch. This time he is terribly alone, and almost aware of his loneliness. Of course, he cannot admit his need to Hattie or to anyone else.

At this point, Allen takes the material in a direction radically different from Fellini. The expected reconciliation between the one-time lovers and the consequent redemption for Emmet never take place. Without apology Emmet merely explains his need to keep moving and to remain faithful to his art. Allen, as the commentator, tells us that Emmet simply disappeared from the scene, leaving behind a few recordings that allow us to remember his great talent.

While Fellini was interested in a Catholic story of redemption through love, Allen turns the material into another chapter of his autobiography. As he has argued so often before, the artist creates his own moral universe and has no obligations to anyone or anything beyond his art. Who dares to judge him? Since there is no afterlife to make self-sacrifice, generosity or even kindness meaningful, the best the artist can hope for is the ability to leave a few works behind. In this alone resides immortality.

While Allen remains chained to his own ego and his own peculiar moral concerns, just like Zampano (the weakness of the film), he has had the good artistic judgment to allow the edgy character of Sean Penn to create his own version of the Allen surrogate (its undeniable strength). Emmet neither stammers nor frets about the usual Allen library of neuroses. He thrives in his simple world of wine, women and jazz, and although he feels a certain amount of Manhattan angst at the realization that another guitarist in Europe has a reputation as "the best," Emmet never doubts his own abilities. Allen allows us to enjoy his brash self-confidence, while suggesting that it all may be a cover for some vulnerabilities that he cannot bother exploring. Emmet is even less likely to hit a psychiatrist's couch than to jam with Lawrence Welk and the Champagne Lady.

Emmet may have problems, but he is too busy living his life to reflect upon them. In addition to his love of cars and travel, Emmet likes to visit freight yards at night. These giant engines rumble to some unknown but exotic destination, but Emmet never realizes that their journey follows iron rails that determine their route into the future. Such limits scarcely exist for a free spirit like Emmet Ray. He carries a huge, nickel-plated .45, which he uses to shoot at rats in any nearby dump. Crudely, he tosses the carcasses toward his girlfriends, perhaps as an unconscious suggestion of his association with the animal, or a promise that he continues to try to kill the rat that he has become. In any event, this pointless cruelty suggests a streak of hostility toward the world and toward those who might love him.

No one suffers more because of Emmet than Hattie. Samantha Morton, however, brilliantly makes her a survivor rather than a victim. She neither dies, like the original Gelsomina, nor does she become a whimpering neurotic, like so many of the characters Mia Farrow created in earlier Allen films. Gelsomina learns to play the drums and trumpet for her sidekick part in Zampano's threadbare act, but Hattie refuses to transform herself into something she is not in order to enter Emmet's world and earn his love. Silent she is, and silent she will remain, while Emmet as a musician lives in a world of sound. She lands a non-speaking bit part in a Hollywood movie simply because she looks like the kid sister of the star, but realizing that she is no actress, she leaves the studio after one day of shooting. When she finally understands that Emmet is impervious to her love, she simply gets another job in a laundry, knowing quite well that even in the Depression, people still need clean clothes.

A petite woman with an angelic smile to rival Giulietta Masina's, Samantha Morton's Hattie eats like a linebacker. This waif with the golden metabolism can devour a dessert cart while listening to Emmet play, and when her life with him finally falls apart, she wisely opens her sandwich bag and has lunch as she looks out over the surf. In contrast, Gelsomina refuses to eat whenever she realizes that Zampano does not love her. With her perky peach basket hat plopped on her head, Hattie will march through life, preferably with Emmet; but if that doesn't work out, march she will, one way or another. And she'll make sure to pack a lunch for herself.

Preoccupied as he is with self-justification—all the while arguing that the artist needs no justification—Woody Allen seems to suggest here that artists quite possibly hurt those who love them, but their victims can get over it. Life goes on. True artists can create more works of art as their purchase on immortality; their women can always take in laundry and eat lunch.

Like most of Woody Allen's films, *Sweet and Lowdown* explores serious moral and artistic questions in a setting that is both lovely and very funny. The jazz guitar numbers, played by Howard Alden and Bucky Pizzarelli, could stand alone as delightful moments of entertainment that in the context of the film offer some justification to Emmet's claim of great musicianship. The entire film is beautifully photographed in faded color and sepia tones by the great Chinese cinematographer Zhao Fei. The misty camera work suggests a scrapbook, in which these vivid, painful memories have somehow grown softer through time's relentless passage.

In one delicious moment of self-revelation, Emmet decides that he towers so far above his fellow musicians that he should be lowered from the ceiling of the nightclub on a plywood and tinsel half-moon, while they labor on the floor of the stage. Of course, he is so drunk (on his own ego as much as on bourbon) that he falls out of his perch, and the contraption nearly kills him when it comes crashing down behind him. Lesson in point: Beware the dangers of raising yourself above the realm of common mortals, even though you consider yourself a great artist surrounded by snails. If the fall doesn't get you, the artifice might. Did Woody Allen recognize the supreme irony here?

### Stuart Klawans (review date 19 June 2000)

SOURCE: Klawans, Stuart. "To Catch a Thief." *Nation* (19 June 2000): 35-6.

[*In the following excerpt, Klawans deems* Small Time Crooks *to be a warm and funny movie, reminiscent of the television series "The Honeymooners."*]

As Woody Allen awoke one morning from uneasy dreams, he found himself transformed in his bed into Jackie Gleason. The covers had slipped off his belly, so that he looked down from the freshly Brylcreemed pillow upon a hemisphere of flesh, which already was quivering with babyish violence.

What about sleeping a little longer and forgetting this nonsense, he thought. Only six months had passed since *Sweet and Lowdown,* and Mother and Father were dead. Yet his unaccustomed bulk had begun to intrigue Woody Allen, who wondered at how The Great One used to slide about in this body. Could he, too, move in rolls and waves? With firm resolution, he pushed himself off the bed.

"What's that?" someone cried, as he hit the floor. Although the bedroom door was locked, Woody Allen knew at once this was Tracey Ullman's voice. Something in her tone—or perhaps in this apartment, which he now perceived to be cramped and dingy—put him in mind of Audrey Meadows. At once, his limbs began to flail in self-contradiction, one arm stretching greedily as if to enclose his fictional wife, the other cocking back in mimed assault. "Wait, and I'll let you in!" he called, though she had neither asked for admission nor threatened to leave. Was this what it meant to speak like Jackie Gleason in *The Honeymooners*—to miss the point, to babble and fume? He suddenly realized that Tracey Ullman would snap all the wisecracks, while he would be reduced to empty threats and nonsense syllables. All his life, Woody Allen had stammered, as too many ideas fought to reach his tongue. Now he would stammer for want of words.

There, in spirit, you have the premise of *Small Time Crooks,* one of those comic miniatures that are a particular glory of Allen's career. I can't guess what uneasy dream might have inspired him to take on Gleason's persona, in the way he's previously emulated Bob Hope. All I know is that a supposedly stable commodity, "the Woody Allen movie," has somehow retained its identity while morphing into a feature-length version of *The Honeymooners,* complete with dumb pals, a cockamamie get-rich-quick scheme and the final "Baby, you're the greatest."

Of course, when you move from spirit to flesh, you find that Allen is hilariously out of proportion to the role he's assumed. As Ray Winkler, an ex-con who is currently working as a dishwasher, he first shows up in midstride on the streets of Manhattan, a copy of the *Daily News* tucked under one arm, his hands stuck deep into the pockets of his walking shorts. The gait is energetic, but the body's missing; the famous eyeglasses and nose seem to be bouncing on an armature composed solely of elbows and knees. Yet this is the corpus with which he claims to menace his wife, Frenchy (Ullman): a trim woman of middling size, with hair that must outweigh Ray by five pounds. "Get me my dinner!" Ray bellows; and for some reason, perhaps boredom, Frenchy rolls her toreador slacks off the bed on which she's been reposing, watching yet another TV show about Princess Di. She's as big as her husband and has him intellectually overmatched. But it seems that Frenchy has weaknesses. First, she actually loves the shnook she married. Second, as the Princess Di fixation suggests, she longs for respectability, and does so with all the fervor of a onetime stripper. It's this second vulnerability that leads to a quick, rough education for Frenchy and Ray, after they strike it rich.

Although Ray's initial criminal scheme is a bust, it launches Frenchy on an unexpected career in the cookie business, in which there's money galore. Yet when Frenchy, now dressed in much pricier leopard-skin outfits, attempts to follow Di's example and become a patron of the arts, she learns that her talent for things that taste good has not translated into good taste. "Show them your collection of leather pigs," Ray says encouragingly, as Frenchy gives a cluster of appalled socialites the tour of her new, gilt nightmare on Park Avenue. (The shrieks and giggles of the film's production designer, Santo Loquasto, are now reputed to echo from a refuge upstate.) And so, with admirable though fatal determination, Frenchy vows to improve herself. Her chosen instructor: Hugh Grant, here cast as a perfectly hugh-grantlike art dealer named David, whose savoir-faire and pheromones must surely rub off on Frenchy.

Ray, being incapable of improvement, sulks off into the company of someone who is as contentedly low-class as himself, and even dumber: Frenchy's cousin, who smiles as if recently struck on the head and snuffles the dialogue up her nose. To improve the joke, this logic-frazzler is played by one of the world's most terrifyingly brilliant people, Elaine May. Seeing her with Woody Allen is a joy comparable only to the meeting of Chaplin and Keaton in *Limelight*. With what sweet patience she endures Ray's sputterings! And with what joy he badgers her! At last, a woman who won't talk back. Sideways, he can deal with.

In the past, when mocking the stupidities of working-class people, Allen has sometimes vented a rancor beyond his anger at rich and middle-class idiots. *Mighty Aphrodite* provides one example of the trait, with a walloping does of misogyny thrown in. *Small Time Crooks* offers the redemptive sight of Allen's biases running the other way. This, too, may be to the credit of *The Honeymooners*. It was the show with the grimmest-looking set on television, where wife and husband, though locked into the strains of lifelong penury, kept rediscovering their mutual affection. *Small Time Crooks* has none of *The Honeymooners*' old-neighborhood sentimentality (just as Allen lacks The Great One's

bulk). And yet loyalty and lack of pretense count as overriding virtues here, as they did on Gleason's show, lending a surprising warmth to the humor of *Small Time Crooks.*

The visual equivalent would be the rooftop sunset that cinematographer Zhao Fei renders, with magical skill, toward the beginning of the film. It's one of those views of urban prettiness for which Allen has always been a sucker. Maybe it's also the sign of a late-career glow.

## Bert Cardullo (essay date fall 2000)

SOURCE: Cardullo, Bert. "Autumn Interiors, or The Ladies Eve: Woody Allen's Ingmar Bergman Complex." *Antioch Review* 58, no. 4 (fall 2000): 428-40.

[*In the following essay, Cardullo discusses the influence of Ingmar Bergman's film* Autumn Sonata *on Allen's* Interiors.]

If, without knowing anything whatsoever about the work of either director, one had seen Ingmar Bergman's *Autumn Sonata* right after Woody Allen's *Interiors,* one might easily have concluded that the Swedish film-maker had attempted to imitate the American. For these works share the same cinematographic and editing style, the same concentration on a handful of overwrought characters, and the very same subject—namely, maternal domination. Of course, the reverse sequence is the correct one: since 1971, if no farther back, Woody Allen had yearned to make what he thought of as a "European" film, preferably in the monastic style of Ingmar Bergman. Finally, in 1978 with *Interiors,* he made it, and fortuitously if not felicitously it resembles (at least in outline) the particular Bergman number that happened to be released in America at almost the same time. Since our view of the film Allen made depends to a great extent on the model he employed (the quintessential Bergman movie), we would do well to ask ourselves of what that model consists, before judging the carbon copy.

Among the many obsessions of Ingmar Bergman that American critics have failed to note, or failed to question closely, is his pervasive resentment in his art of the achieved man and occasionally the career woman—doctor, lawyer, professor, business executive. From the evidence of his numerous films, Bergman hates every professional except the artist. Predictably, since he is a puritan, his defense of the artist as somehow sacrosanct has engendered a feedback of guilt: periodically, having enshrined the creative personality in one context or another, he seems driven to follow up with a thumping self-accusation of the artist as charlatan or as detached and inhuman being. You may be sure that Bergman in his heart does not believe this, but he needs to hear an answering echo that absolves him of his own accusation.

Thus *Autumn Sonata* is characterized by the same kind of ambivalence that undermined the artistic veracity of *Wild Strawberries* in 1957. In the earlier film, Bergman's portrait of an old professor, whose egoistic frigidity lost him an idyllic sweetheart and produced an impotent son, was at odds with the visibly sympathetic performance of Victor Sjöström. Just as Bergman was reluctant in *Wild Strawberries* to follow the implications of his own scenario by destroying the professor-figure entirely, so in *Autumn Sonata* he sets up Ingrid Bergman as a concert pianist-cum-mother who is supposed to have crippled her two daughters (one child being insufficient for the force of his accusation); then the auteur becomes so enamored of the personality he has given his character that he is hard put to convince us she could possibly be either as indifferent or as ruthless as her articulate daughter maintains.

To synopsize this picture accurately for anyone who has not seen it is almost impossible, since what takes place in *Autumn Sonata* beyond the severely limited action is completely a matter of individual interpretation. Every statement made by the characters is open to question, and the whole moral issue on which the film hinges is never depicted. The damaging relationship of which this mother-daughter confrontation is supposed to be the climax is not visualized in flashbacks, so that viewers can judge for themselves; it is, rather, wholly summarized in verbal terms through the daughter Eva's accusatory retrospect.

At the beginning, reading her diary while she awaits the visit of her celebrated mother, Liv Ullmann-as-Eva seems pretty clearly, in her spinsterish appearance and manner, to be a manic-depressive type, melancholy and retentive but prone to fitfulness as well. We glimpse her husband hovering in the background, from which he scarcely emerges during the subsequent encounter; and we learn that since her son, aged fourteen, drowned some years ago, Eva has kept his room as it was when he died and moons over photographs of him. This morbid devotion to the irretrievable contradicts the leading statement she reads from her diary: "One must learn how to live. I work at it every day." We further discover that, before her marriage, Eva had lived with a doctor, and that she had once had tuberculosis. Not until later in the film do we become aware that she is looking after her bedridden sister, who suffers from a degenerative disease that has affected her speech and movement, and whom her mother believes to be in a nursing home.

When Mother arrives at this outpost of Ibsenism (Bergman's setting, for a change, is among the Norwegian fjords), it is not too surprising that, after the first affectionate exchanges are over, as Eva listens obediently to her parent's necessarily self-absorbed chatter (she has come, after all, from the world of professional music as practiced in European capitals), the daughter all the while regards her with mingled amusement and suspicion. In no time at all, suspicion has become hostility; and step by step Eva rebukes her mother's self-secured authority in a crescendo of bitter reproaches that mounts steadily into the realm of hysteria. The younger woman makes the distressed elder responsible for all the ills of her life and blames her, besides, for the condition of the drooling sister upstairs, whose presence in the house is an unwelcome shock to the fastidious visitor.

Following a long sequence of passionate denunciation by her daughter, which she stems only at momentary intervals, the mother, inwardly shaken but outwardly collected, leaves to fulfill another musical engagement. Then after a few solicitous suggestions from her husband—who, again, has passively remained on the sidelines of this internecine struggle being waged under his roof—Eva writes a letter to the departed woman in which she retracts the burden of the accusation she had hurled and makes a pathetic bid for love. This letter is in part read over the image of the mother, traveling south for her next concert.

Critics have generally received this film as if it were indeed a straightforward indictment by the neglected daughter of a selfish parent, which means that they accept at face value the allegations of the girl and pay no attention either to the personality or the remonstrance of the mother. In fact, we have only the daughter's word that her mother's inattention drove her into a messy relationship with that "doctor" who is briefly mentioned. What part any of this played in her contracting of tuberculosis is never clarified. One is left to infer how satisfactory or unsatisfactory her present marriage is. Whether her mother had an affair with someone named Marten without telling her husband, Josef, depends on which of the two women you believe; and what bearing this has on anything else is never made clear. One is also left to decide whether the mother's absence at a crucial hour was the impelling cause of the sister's disabling condition.

It is possible to take the other view, that Bergman intended the Liv Ullmann character to reveal herself unmistakably as a self-pitying neurotic, whose charges are patently cancelled by the clearly delineated superiority of the mother. (One of the most telling moments in the film would then be Ingrid Bergman's correction, at the piano, of her daughter's playing of a Chopin sonata: if the girl is to give the piece an authentic interpretation, declares the mother, she must avoid sentimentality and understand that the music should express *"pain, not reverie."*) However, even this view of Bergman's strategy may be ingenuous; it is much more in his line to establish an impeccably distinguished persona, poised against an unattractive spinster who is nonetheless married, in order to make the latter's accusations appear at first unlikely, then the more convincing, precisely because the accused has the more sovereign air. (This mechanism was invented by Strindberg in his play *The Stronger* [1889].)

In truth, near the end of *Autumn Sonata,* Bergman loses confidence in his own gambit. He cuts, in the most excruciatingly obvious way, from the sick daughter writhing helplessly on the floor, to the entrained mother coolly informing her agent that her visit home had been "most unpleasant": in other words, she shrugs it off. Unless we are to suppose she is acting, this is outrageously unbelievable; it totally contradicts the character of the woman we have witnessed, in merciless close-up, for the preceding hour. Evasive or hesitant she may have been when justifying a given response or action recounted by the vindictive Eva, but never for a moment did one feel that she was radically false. Equally unacceptable, as the film ends, is the abrupt change of heart that dictates Eva's remorse for the vehemence with which she has been arraigning her mother—thereby canceling, at the last minute, the substance of the movie's unrelenting inquisition.

Critics in America consistently underrate this Swedish inability of Bergman's to commit himself to the terms of a moral choice he has ostensibly initiated—unless, that is, he knows for certain he has a target to which absolutely no one will object. There is small point in trying to weight truth in the antithesis he has contrived for *Autumn Sonata.* At *any* latter-day Bergman movie, including the slightly earlier *Serpent's Egg* and the subsequent, aptly titled *From the Life of the Marionettes,* one cannot be sure whether this director-screenwriter is unaware of the dramatic incongruities that he creates through poor motivation or whether he doesn't really care. He seems indifferent to plot because a plot is an action consistent with the revealed nature of its characters, and Bergman seems unable to perceive consistency; his characters say what he wants them to say, to an end he alone has chosen, as opposed to what they would say if allowed to speak for themselves.

He used to be a master of comedy, as in his gloss on Renoir's *Rules of the Game* (1939), *Smiles of a Summer Night*—itself more or less remade by a spent Woody Allen as **A Midsummer Night's Sex Comedy** in 1982. For in secular, and even more so divine comedy you can give full rein to the improbable, just as you can in a religious allegory like Bergman's *Seventh Seal* (if not in existential meditations of the kind exemplified by his "faith" trilogy of *Through a Glass Darkly, Winter Light,* and *The Silence,* which secured the reputation of Ingmar Bergman in America in the early-to-mid-1960s). Lately, in 1992's *The Best Intentions* and *Sunday's Children,* both of which he wrote if not directed—actually, even before them in *Fanny and Alexander*—Bergman has become a purveyor of the probable or the consistent only through the form of self-absorbing autobiography.

With all this in mind, we should not expect the mundane inventions of *Autumn Sonata* to have objective credibility; the characters' motives are flimsily explored, the actualities of their lives not dramatized but reported after the fact. If Eva knew so much about her mother's devices of evasion, for example, as well as about her own victimization at her parent's hands, she would long since have ceased to be a victim—or at the very least she would have remedied those absurd outer signs of her condition thrust upon her by Bergman via his wardrobe department: I mean the old-maid's provincial hair bun and the disfiguring eyeglasses. Women's faces, preferably under stress, are what Ingmar Bergman likes to photograph; objective coherence he no longer cares to cultivate. Like many other films in his canon, *Autumn Sonata* is a private tribunal. Bergman himself is the confessor, prosecutor, plaintiff, and as neutral or uncommitted a judge as he can risk being.

Which brings us to Woody Allen and his perplexing, abject desire to make a film in emulation of the remote Swede, even to the point of using the archetypal Bergman actor, Max von Sydow, to confer legitimacy on his work. Impressed by the austerity of Bergman's style and by what he reads as the master's tragic view of life, Allen was faced at the outset with the dangerous problem of imposing a stark Swedish ethos on urban American material. Ever since *The Virgin Spring* in 1960, Bergman has as often as possible shut out not only the world of nature but also the world of people and things, of society at large, so that his agonists can battle nakedly with each other (or with a surrogate God), undistracted by the alternative points of view, the cultural frivolities, or even the earthly vistas that tempt the commonality of mankind. Allen's **Interiors** is far more populous than *Autumn Sonata* or any other late film of Bergman, so our comprehension of it is not delayed or derailed by a ground-level of universal, symbolic reference; it can be summarized as a storyline that holds together. Motivation or inducement, however, is another matter.

If *Autumn Sonata* is ambivalent because Bergman is playing a game with appearances, **Interiors** is eventually ambiguous because the calamities represented are in excess of the cause alleged. **Interiors** should have been the tragedy (or even the comedy) of a man's attempt, alternately assisted or opposed by his three daughters, to win his own soul by ridding himself of their mother, his wife. I say "should have been" because Allen's conception of that man is so feeble (in the Bergman tradition of the ineffectual male), and the performance of E. G. Marshall is so uninflected, that he emerges as a far less sympathetic character than the compulsively meticulous wife played with twitchy naturalism by Geraldine Page.

Arthur, as he's called, persists in his bid for freedom—he wants to go to the Mediterranean, presumably to be reborn—against the warnings of his plaintive wife, who threatens suicide before actually attempting it, and against the querulous protests of his daughter Joey, more closely identified with her mother than her sisters are, probably because her own identity is insecure (as yours might be, too, if you were burdened with a name normally reserved for the opposite sex). The father-husband returns from Greece uttering the same banalities as before—nothing about him has changed, not even his ties—together with a personable if clownish woman whom Joey indignantly and correctly describes as vulgar. When Arthur marries the creature, Mother, sure enough, walks into the sea. Loyal Joey is all but drowned in a vain attempt to save her, and she in turn is resuscitated by the unrefined stepmother: which proves that this name-flashing tourist may be an ox in the drawing room, but when it comes to fundamentals she is the pragmatist who saves the day.

Implicitly, Eve the mother deserves her fate, for in the explanation given her (too late) by Joey, she felt herself too good for this world and so created another, of interiors—of décor and decorum—which had demanded, from those around her, responses too strict for any of them to meet. Yet it is difficult to imagine that everyone around Eve is as derailed as they all seem to be by an excess of good taste; to repeat, the calamities represented are in excess of the cause alleged. (No one suggests, incidentally, that an exquisitely dictatorial mother might have been the answer to a visibly bland father.) The articulated miseries of the daughters and their men are strenuously reached for, hence appear contrived. They are phony excavations of the interior—of interior life—whereas Allen's specialty has always been the humorously objective observation of exteriors, the coolly comic send-up of surfaces. Diane Keaton plays intelligently an unintelligent poet whose self-contempt is fairly inexplicable, since her ignorance should be her bliss. Similarly, her husband, a churlish literary genius who's fearful that he is not as good as the critics say, decides to assert his misgivings by trying to rape his sister-in-law, a television actress given to drug addiction.

As I suggested earlier, the whole embroilment is distorted by Allen's insistence on telling his story in a style alien to the milieu he provides, a style that transposes the tenor of an American metropolitan setting into the hushed and claustrophobic atmosphere of Bergman's Baltic. He opens *Interiors* with unornamented credits, no simultaneous visuals behind them, no music. The exposition features single-shot close-ups of two sisters, each looking out a different window, followed by a medium shot of a male who, gazing at an urban panorama, commences a narration to himself and to the audience—a familiar Bergman beginning. Allen's

man has his back to the camera, perhaps to alleviate the shock of our eventual recognition that he is none other than the tepid Marshall, informing us, in an unlikely outburst of rhetoric, that suddenly in the course of his contented marriage he "found an enormous abyss opening at [his] feet." Too much of the dialogue thereafter is like this, the sort of talk which, in earlier Woody Allen vehicles, would have speedily led to a verbal pratfall, but here only makes for tragicomedy of the unintentional kind.

Allen tries hard—perhaps too hard—to keep his settings from becoming as cluttered or static as his language, staging crucial scenes at the dining table and in the bedroom, then in an empty church and at a beach house in an attempt to exile the everyday domestic world. Self-consciously he employs a camera at rest, passively framing close-ups of faces or middle-distance shots of a stationary group, except for moments when he is recalling other Bergman strategies. The most conspicuous of these is the tracking shot of two sisters conversing as they walk along the beach, which sententiously evokes the world of *Persona*. With every sequence Allen thus appears to have asked himself, not "How can I best shoot this?" but "How would Bergman shoot it?"

Moreover, he ends his film with a strict reversion to the Bergman format that, at the same time, summons a whole repertory of understated curtain tableaux from post-Ibsenian drama. After church and the business with the white roses and the coffin, the three sisters are aligned in profile (a reminder of the opening shots, as well as of Chekhov's greatest play), staring at the sea. One says, "The water is calm," and another solemnly replies, "Yes, it's very peaceful." That Allen should have been trapped by so obvious an error as to believe that you can depict tragedy by imitating the surface of it from someone else's (already superficial) version—this, I must say, is truly amazing.

He was less gullible when less assured as a director. According to Lee Guthrie's 1978 biography of Allen (which, significantly, was withdrawn from distribution shortly after the opening of *Interiors*), the comedian once admitted that, although he admired the films of Bergman, they could only be a bad influence on his work, "because they're so antithetical to comedy." He went on to explain that Bergman interested him more than any other filmmaker, owing to "the consummate marriage of technique, theatricality and themes that are both personally important to me and that have gigantic size—death, the meaning of life, the question of religious faith."

In a later declaration, Allen was prepared to throw previous caution to the wind and reach for just those "gigantic" themes, which he was now translating as "more personal" than those of his contemporaries. From the same source, we get the following statement: "I'm not sure any American film maker makes the kind of movie I want to make. I don't want to do films like *Bonnie and Clyde* or *Mean Streets* or *Badlands.* . . . To me, serious American movies always have one foot in entertainment—and I like more personal drama, though there may not be a market for it. The drama I like is what you see in the plays of O'Neill and Strindberg and Ibsen—and in foreign films."

God forbid that a "serious" movie should have one foot in the swamp of entertainment! And as if **Annie Hall** and **Crimes and Misdemeanors,** to name only two of Allen's seriocomic films, don't try to entertain at the same time as they confront—however lamely or indecisively—significant themes. But there you have it: the puritanical hunger for the High Serious, the discontent with authentic veins of American subject matter. Such material may not be shot through with the subtle values of living to be found in European movies—you know, all that wisdom, refinement, and *tendresse*—but it is nonetheless vital in its consideration of the harsh characteristics of so much of American life: baseness, greed, and brutality.

Incidentally, this coupling of O'Neill and Strindberg on the part of Allen is meaningful. Strindberg was the artistic stepfather of Eugene O'Neill, who successfully transplanted the Swede's suffocating ethos into American settings, and who, for his part, like the Bergman of *Smiles of a Summer Night,* managed to write only one comedy (*Ah, Wilderness!* [1932]) among his many works for the theatre. The Swedes flattered O'Neill and his solemn sensibility by staging all his plays at Stockholm's Dramaten in addition to awarding him the Nobel Prize in 1932 (before he had written his great naturalistic dramas, I might add). Strindberg is also, of course, the single most influential figure behind all Bergman's work, although the filmmaker seems to substitute excessive love for women for the dramatist's extreme antipathy toward them.

Indeed, the "rehearsal" in *After the Rehearsal* is of one of Strindberg's plays, a number of which Bergman himself has directed for the theatre; *Autumn Sonata* may derive its inspiration from that mad master's chamber drama titled *The Ghost Sonata* (1907). For all its avant-garde theatrical devices, this early-twentieth-century work is not unrelated in theme either to its Bergmanian namesake or to Allen's **Interiors,** for Strindberg attempts in his autumnal *Ghost Sonata* to penetrate the naturally deceptive or mediating façade of verbal language, as well as of bourgeois exteriors—not only through the visual eloquence of scenic design, but also through the abstract purity of musical form.

The sympathetic link between these Swedes and the Americans is the fundamental puritanism they culturally share. (Bergman's Nordic damnations are taken far less seriously, for example, by the English, the Italians, or the French.) It has been said that the smothering family atmosphere in certain Bergman films, even as in Strindberg's naturalistic *The Father* (1887) and O'Neill's *Long Day's Journey into Night* (1940), appealed to Allen by reason of his special Jewish vulnerability to comparably oppressive parents in his own environment. I would not wish to pronounce on this probability, if probability it is, but I suspect that the driving force behind Allen's wistful Bergman-worship is rather an aspiring intellectual's love of conceptual perfection and a confusion of it with the Less-Is-More aesthetic of Scandinavian reductionism, together with an obsessive love for women that Allen confuses with a desperate need to validate his narcissistic love for himself.

Be that as it may, the truth is that it takes more independent imagination, greater cinematic scope, and a richer sense of life's poetry to make *Bonnie and Clyde* (1967), *Mean Streets* (1973), or *Badlands* (1973), *Midnight Cowboy* (1969), *The Wild Bunch* (1969), or *Chinatown* (1974), *Raging Bull* (1980), *House of Games* (1987), or *Tender Mercies* (1983), than it does to make **Interiors.** Unlike a host of American movies in which the citizenry's blindest self-satisfactions with the status quo are upheld, or in which the most immoral and fantastic projections of callow romanticism, spurious religiosity, or miserable sentimentality are indulged, these films insist on writing down contemporary American society as they see it: a society alarmingly animated by powerful minority factions that are debased and selfish when they are not downright criminal; that is grotesquely peopled by a fringe of parasites surrendered to listless perversions or violent exploitations, or alternatively populated by a growing number of decent yet subsocial creatures who lead unexamined if not unworthy lives; that is forever encumbered by a floating majority, pitifully bewildered, vulgarized, and juvenile, which is sadomasochistic at its core, hence wanting in all resolution, guidance, and dignity except perhaps in time of war. If this is not the whole truth about the American experience, it is that part of the truth most commonly suppressed for public consumption.

What, by contrast, is Woody Allen's **Interiors** centrally about? Certainly not "the meaning of life"—a silly predication for any work of art, just as it would be silly to argue that *Autumn Sonata* is really about the nonexistence of objective truth. And though the rejected wife and mother kills herself, **Interiors** is in no awesome way about death. The people involved are not tragic, although some of them would like to be; they tend instead to be hysterical, obtuse, or pathetically abusive. Their behavior more closely resembles that of the pseudo-intellectual New Yorkers of Paul Mazursky's films, who simultaneously know too much about one another and bitch all the time at their own limitations. Is this quality what makes the movie, for Allen, "more personal"? Is this the quality that he admires in *Scenes from a Mall* (1980), Mazursky's absurd take, starring Allen himself, on Bergman's *Scenes from a Marriage*?

As his first screen "drama," then, *Interiors* is an embarrassing episode in Woody Allen's career, to be followed by such others as *September, Another Woman,* and *Alice.* It represents a feeble struggle to escape from his more authentic self, an incredible concession to the snobbish misgiving that comedy is an inferior art—something that doubtless would be news to figures as diverse as Aristophanes and Molière, Charlie Chaplin and Billy Wilder. *Interiors* additionally reveals a filmmaker's mistaken assumption that one can create great art by consciously setting out to do so, according to this or that recipe, instead of intuitively using artistic means to capture for all eternity an image or idea of humanity.

Allen used to be a funny guy, heretofore having exercised a welcome talent for parody and a shrewd recognition of the clichés by which many American urbanites live, if he has not allowed his comedic talent to develop much beyond the gag-and-skit stage of *Take the Money and Run, Bananas, Everything You Always Wanted to Know about Sex, Sleeper,* and *Love and Death* (which is the stage where he began as a writer for television in the 1950s). As a *showman,* he has developed a professional eye when choosing a cinematographer, a lively ear for the musical score, and a refined taste in actresses. (Although not in actors: witness his casting of himself in the leading roles of his comic and semi-comic films, which a better actor [such as Dustin Hoffman] would make even wittier, yet his exclusion of himself from his utterly serious movies, where he could perhaps do some humorous good!)

What on earth compelled, indeed continues to compel, Allen to settle for less and sell his art short by aping a mode of cinema in which he has had to inhibit himself, instead of releasing his better inspiration or instinct, is a problem for him to resolve; the movies may be the last place in which he can do so. He certainly didn't help his cause with such a narcissistic meditation on the filmmaking experience as *Stardust Memories,* itself a rip-off of Fellini's *8½* (1963), even as the comic fantasy of the vastly overrated *Purple Rose of Cairo* is lifted in reverse form from Buster Keaton's *Sherlock, Jr.* (1924).

And to say that he has resolved his artistic dilemma by striking a balance between the solemn and the funny in movies like *Annie Hall, Manhattan, Hannah and Her Sisters,* even *Crimes and Misdemeanors* and *Husbands and Wives,* is to miss the extent to which such pictures fail as genuine—dare I say Chekhovian?—tragicomedy. Rather than combining the serious and the comic into a unique new form, they just irresolutely lay the two elements side by side, or overemphasize one at the expense of the other, against the backdrop of culturally rich, culturally hip, psychically neurotic New York, which these films expect to do the real work of "meaning" for them. In movies like these, Allen is continually sending love letters to himself and to that province of provinces, Manhattan, and I for one don't enjoy reading other people's mail. A woman once told me that I should see *Hannah and Her Sisters* with someone I love. I don't know what she could have meant by this exhortation, given the film's solipsism, and I'm glad I didn't see it with her!

But, some people will say, those artsy Europeans, especially the French, love Woody Allen. Yes, well, they loved Samuel Fuller and Don Siegel not so long ago, and look where that got us. Europeans think that Americans (read: New Yorkers) are fabulously nutty at the same time that they believe America (read: New York) is wonderfully glamorous. *That's* why they love Woody Allen, Manhattan diarist. New Yorkers and all who aspire to be New Yorkers like *Annie Hall, Manhattan,* and *Hannah and Her Sisters* (among other Woody vehicles) because these films congratulate them on their choice of city in which to live, and because these people think that Allen is the cinema's answer to drama's Chekhov: serious, comic, and deliciously melancholy, all wrapped up in the same tidy little package. One, just one, difference between Allen and Chekhov (it's difficult to join their names in the same sentence) is that the latter had some distance on himself and life, to put it mildly. Irony played a large part in his art, as did his knowledge of the theatrical tradition that had immediately preceded him. Allen loves himself and New York so much, he's nostalgic about both before the fact, to the point of making it and his own person the real subject of his movies.

Penultimately, it may be worth remarking that while Bergman's *Autumn Sonata* and Allen's *Interiors* alike are postulating the destructive consequences of perfectionism in life as in art, each film's director has, in his own way, been aesthetically pursuing the absolute or the ideal like mad: Bergman, the recreant preacher, with immaculate cinematic compositions that achieve their immaculateness at the expense of worldly or natural conception; Allen, the derelict stand-up comic, by aspiring to place himself among the most mirthless geniuses of our era. And both men, in the case of *Autumn Sonata* and *Interiors,* by not-so-coincidentally choosing central characters with the primal name of Eve.

Allen has said that such recent films of his as *Manhattan Murder Mystery* and *Mighty Aphrodite*—itself a parody of the original murder mystery, *Oedipus the King* (430 B.C.)—mark a return to his "earlier, funnier" brand of filmmaking, to which I can only respond, "too little, too late." So desperate is he to return to previous form or prior success that his newly released *Everyone Says I Love You* nearly abandons reality altogether for the childish world of musical comedy, a world toward which Allen's Gershwin-and-Porter-driven soundtracks have been moving for some time. (Allen himself plays the clarinet, some times professionally, which tells me he may have missed his true vocation.) Except that "real" New York, in the form of carefully selected views of Manhattan's loveliness, is still on hand in this movie to be adored and to provide the action with a backdrop—ironically, the best word to describe the direction Woody Allen's career has taken since he went "deep" almost twenty years ago and made the fateful *Interiors.* As for the oft-made, desperate-seeming remark about what a competent *director* Allen has become, all that I can say is, with his bankroll and artistic support-system, I too could become a competent director after so many pictures. To echo André Bazin on auteurs, competent director, yes, but *of what*?

## Joseph Mills (review date 2001)

SOURCE: Mills, Joseph. "Roller Coasters, Aristotle, and the Films of Woody Allen." *Literature/Film Quarterly* 29, no. 1 (2001): 37-42.

[*In the following review, Mills examines the motif of the roller coaster in* Annie Hall *and* The Purple Rose of Cairo *as a metaphor for exploring metaphysical questions regarding the existence of God and the meaning of life.*]

> Understand you are dealing with a man who knocked off *Finnegans Wake* on the roller coaster at Coney Island, penetrating the abstruse Joycean arcana with ease, despite enough violent lurching to shake loose my silver fillings.
>
> —"A Little Louder, Please"

Early in Woody Allen's *Annie Hall,* Alvy Singer remarks, "My analyst says I exaggerate my childhood memories, but I swear I was brought up underneath the roller coaster in the Coney Island section. . . . Maybe that explains my disposition which is a bit nervous I guess." As Alvy narrates, the camera shows a white house under a roller coaster. It then cuts to a young Alvy trying to eat as the cars rumble by overhead.

Why does this image dominate Alvy's memory and his sense of self? Although it's funny for us to see the serious-minded child intent on his lunch while the world around him shakes, the image also offers a number of metaphorical possibilities. The roller coaster may be a simple cliché. Life has its ups and downs. If that's the case, however, why isn't Alvy riding?

Perhaps the roller coaster symbolizes the mechanistic world. Allen explores this theme in a number of movies, such as *Sleeper,* and in his night club material. He explains in his stand-up act, "I have never in my life had good relations with mechanical objects." (*The Nightclub Years*), and he tells a story about being insulted by an elevator, calling a meeting of his household appliances, and beating up a t.v. Or, does the roller coaster show that the Singer household is underneath or apart from the "fun" and entertainment the rest of society enjoys? The movie's working title was *Anhedonia,* and Alvy doesn't derive pleasure like others. He eats and reads alone while people joy-ride by him. As an adult, he stays in New York, set in his life, while Annie changes and moves around him. He apologizes for not being able to "mellow"; as he puts it, "if I get too mellow, I ripen and then rot." Change leads to decay. The young Alvy refuses to do his school work when he learns the universe is expanding and may fall apart because "what's the point?"

Allen's work is devoted to trying to answer "what's the point?" He insists, "The only questions of real interest are the ultimate questions, otherwise who cares about anything else" (Lax 183). In his films and writings, he explores the nature of a person's place in the universe, and, in doing so, he frequently utilizes imagery of rides, roller coasters, and carnivals. In *Purple Rose of Cairo,* the "fictional" character, Tom Baxter, steps down from a movie screen to meet Cecilia, a fan who has sat through several showings of the film. Deciding to stay in the "real world," he asks Cecilia to hide him, and they go to an amusement park which is closed for the season. As he walks among the rides, he becomes excited, saying, "I know where we are. I know what this is. It's written into my character." Like Alvy, roller coasters form an integral part of who Tom Baxter is. As he puts it, "it's in me." Later, as Tom waits for Cecilia and wanders around the park, he climbs into one of the roller coaster cars and sits there waiting for it to go. He is surprised that he cannot will it into motion.

*The Purple Rose of Cairo* explores questions of free will and responsibility. Is it possible to step out of an assigned role? Who created Tom Baxter, and who is responsible for him? Is it Gil Shepherd, the actor who plays Tom Baxter? Shepherd feels threatened by this idea; he wants Baxter captured and put back into the set narrative. Is it the screenwriter? When Cecilia questions Tom about his knowledge of a divine creator or "the reason for everything, the world, the universe," he says, "Oh I think I know what you mean, the two men who wrote the *Purple Rose of Cairo.* Irving Sacks and R. H. Levine. They're writers who collaborate on films." Cecilia tries to correct him, but in doing so she adopts his metaphor of the universe as a film. God gives it a purpose because "otherwise it would be a movie with no point and no happy ending." God authors our stories, but do we have the freedom to alter our assigned narratives?

Even though the characters in the movie that Tom has left regard him as a minor character, they cannot continue. They must wait until he returns to the screen. He has interrupted the narrative, stopped the ride in the middle, and gotten off, and everything is thrown into chaos as a result.

*Annie Hall* offers a reversal of this structure. Significantly, Alvy remembers the roller coaster during a time in which he is trying to sort through his relationship with Annie, and when he and Annie reconcile after a breakup, they make a trip back to the Coney Island house. As a ride, not only does a roller coaster suggest the ups and downs, the twists and turns, involved in a relationship, but it serves as an organizing device. It imposes a narrative and a structure. In "*Annie Hall* and the Issue of Modernism," Thomas Schatz notes that the relationship of Annie and Alvy can be considered as "a classical text imbedded within a primarily modernist one" (185). The relationship, itself, is told in a straightforward fashion without self-reflexiveness. When the couple begins to have problems, Alvy returns to the technique of directly addressing the audience. Schatz argues that "During the courtship narrative, Alvy is in a state of mental and emotional security, his disposition is determined by his relationship with Annie, and he—like the narrative itself, which is an extension of his own psyche—enjoys the only period of sustained unselfconsciousness in the film" (185). Schatz's comments have metaphorical implications that reverberate at the film's ending when Allen speculates about why we continually initiate relationships. Relationships, themselves, are a way of organizing our lives. Perhaps we are confused about what to do before and after them, but once we begin one, for a while, we no longer have to worry about the narrative. The bar comes down, the cars pull away, and we are along for the ride. Allen certainly suggests this in his movie *Alice.*

In *Alice,* a dissatisfied Alice Tate goes to Dr. Yang, an exotic herbalist, for treatment. He hypnotizes her, and she remembers when she first met her husband. It was at an amusement park. As she thinks back, a red neon sign saying "Rides" starts to flash outside the window. It dominates the scene. Her husband appears, and they act out the conversation that they had on their first date. It becomes clear that she must choose between marriage and a career as a costume designer. She chooses marriage, and once she has done so, her life seems to be plotted out. She has selected her ride.

Once you get on a roller coaster, you have exercised the extent of your will. There are no more decisions to be made until the ride ends. This contrasts markedly to driving a car. A driver exercises a certain amount of individual control and can choose a path or change destinations. Alvy Singer doesn't drive; Annie Hall does. In fact, Annie has a great deal of confidence in her abilities, insisting that she's an excellent driver as she weaves through traffic, narrowly misses trucks, looks for gum, and talks to Alvy. (Of course, we have to keep in mind that this is Alvy's memory of her driving, and he does exaggerate.) Annie drives dangerously, carelessly, but there's no indication that she has ever been in an accident. Her nonchalant recklessness is part of her appeal. Alvy, on the other hand, drives once during the movie, gets in a wreck, and ends up in jail.

In Alvy's flashback to childhood, he remembers two main things: the location of the house under the roller coaster and the bumper cars. He says, "I used to get my aggressions out in the bumper cars." However, the visual action undercuts the narration. Alvy's car has no forward momentum. He is being smashed by everyone else, and his car is pushed to the corner of the screen.

Alvy's driving in California is the one time when he tries to take charge. Throughout the relationship, he is passive. Annie makes decisions. She suggests moving in with him. She plans the trips and she instigates the reconciliation after the initial breakup. Although Alvy supports her in her singing career, she has already taken the step to pursue it. As the title suggests, it is her movie. When Alvy attempts to act, he crashes. His accident in the parking lot of the health food restaurant is interspersed with images of him as a child being hit by the other bumper cars. Alvy, a person dominated by the idea of the roller coaster rumbling along on a fixed track, cannot stake out an independent path.

In contrast to Alvy, Annie's brother Wayne has an obsession with cars. He sees driving as a spiritual experience. For him, the car has both religious and artistic implications. Wayne has one scene in the film. In it, he asks Alvy, "Can I confess something to you?" He then says, "I tell you this because as an artist I know you'll understand. . . ." He has fantasies about driving down the road and turning into the headlights of an oncoming car. He imagines the crash, the explosion, the flames. For Wayne, the car provides possibilities for a personal apocalypse. He can take control of the ultimate moment, his own death. This, to Alvy, is true craziness.

In her apartment Annie has photo montages of Wayne and Alvy on opposite walls. She represents the synthesis of their different sensibilities, balancing Alvy's inertia and Wayne's suicidal recklessness.

Alvy says that he doesn't drive because he has too much hostility. For him, the car is a tool of aggression. After all, the bumper cars in which Alvy learned to drive are designed for the sole purpose of smashing into one another. Free will and control involve not only individualism, but competition and antagonism. The roller coaster, however, takes everyone on the same ride. The entity is the group rather than the individual. In personal remarks, Allen has said, "It's very important to realize that we're up against an evil, insidious, hostile universe. It'll make you ill and age you and kill you. And there's somebody—or something—out there who for some irrational, unexplainable reason is killing us" (Lax 183). Allen's use of "we" and "us" shows an identification with people as a whole, a group grappling with the same problems, and in both movie theaters and on roller coasters, everyone faces the same way to share the experience together.

Like Alvy, Alice Tate suffers from excessive passivity, and both of them have a difficult time when they try to take control. In an effort to give Alice a type of control, Dr. Yang gives her a variety of herbs. Yet just as Alvy's trip to California ends in arrest, Dr. Yang's herbs backfire. When Alice is invisible, she learns that her husband is an adulterer. When she shares her invisible powder with her lover, he finds out that his ex-wife still desires him and he decides to go back to her. A love potion ends up in a communal punch bowl at a party, so that everyone, rather than her husband or lover, is attracted to her. However, regardless of these setbacks, Alice refuses to return to her passive role. At the end of *Annie Hall* Alvy is still living in New York and going to *The Sorrow and the Pity,* but Alice changes her life and finds fulfillment and a sense of purpose.

In their quests for control, both Alvy and Annie try to transmute their lives into art. Alvy writes a play about the breakup in LA; Alice suggests aspects of her life as storylines to a friend who works as a studio executive. They try to impose a narrative on their lives. In his play, Alvy changes the storyline so that Annie doesn't leave him. He explains that a person tries to get things to work out in art since they so rarely do in real life. The person, who sees his childhood as spent under a roller coaster, becomes a writer trying to recast his life into a stable, meaningful form. The progression is natural. After all, the roller coaster represents the perfect Aristotelian device. It has a beginning, middle, and end, rising and falling action, twists and reversals. It is constructed exactly like a conventional narrative.

Almost all of Allen's work deals self-consciously with form and genre. In addition to his films, he has written parodies of tough guy detective fiction with **"Mr. Big"** and **"The Whore of Mensa,"** historical scholarship with **"Slang Origins"** and **"The Discovery and Use of the Fake Ink Blot,"** epistolary works such as **"The Gossage-Vardebedian Papers,"** and several other forms, such as personal memoirs, food reviews, and graduation speeches. Allen utilizes genre conventions to

invoke certain audience expectations which he then refuses to satisfy. The joke stems from the resulting dislocation. For example, **"Match Wits with Inspector Ford"** recounts a number of crimes that Inspector Ford has solved. However, "clues" are withheld, and the reader cannot logically figure out the ridiculous solutions. In a case titled "The Macabre Accident," a man has been killed while hunting. Although his wife claims to have shot him accidentally, Inspector Ford deduces that it was murder. The answer key explains,

> An experienced hunter like Quincy Freem would never have stalked deer in his underwear. Actually Ms. Freem had bludgeoned him to death at home while he was playing the spoons and had tried to make it look like a hunting accident by dragging his body to the woods and leaving a copy of *Field and Stream* nearby. In her haste, she had forgotten to dress him.

> (*Without Feathers* 119-20)

None of these details were included in the original crime scene description. The humor comes from recognizing how Allen manipulates and mocks the genre. (It also assumes a literate reader. A person unfamiliar with books like *Encyclopedia Brown* or *Two Minute Mysteries* would simply be puzzled by the apparent non-sequiturs.)

Like Alvy living at Coney Island, Allen is intimately familiar with narrative forms, but is not bound by them. In a discussion about how he learned to write comic sketches, Allen emphasizes the importance of learning specific rules. He then says, "Now, later in life you wind up breaking those rules, but you break them in the same way an abstract artist does, who learns all the rules and then doesn't draw representationally; once you know what you're doing, you break those rules consciously, not mistakenly" (Lax 97). His films demonstrate such a progression. His early work, such as *Bananas Take the Money and Run* and *Sleeper,* although full of absurdist humor, rely on relatively traditional narrative structures. With *Annie Hall,* Allen begins to play with the narrative itself. He becomes self-reflexive, interrupting scenes and talking directly at the camera and the audience. The camera shots become more complex. Subjects talk off-screen. In *Manhattan,* he revises the introduction several times. In *Radio Days,* the narrator apologizes for the rain, saying "that's how I remember it." The viewer is always aware that a story is being told.

Allen explicitly explores the formal problems of storytelling in **"God (A Play)."** A precursor to *The Purple Rose of Cairo,* "God" examines the dictates set forth in Aristotle's *Poetics.* The play opens with a writer discussing with an actor possible endings for his new work.

ACTOR:

> Every play must have a beginning, middle, and end.

WRITER:

Why?

ACTOR (CONFIDENTLY):

Because everything in nature has a beginning, middle and end.

WRITER:

What about a circle?

ACTOR (THINKS):

Okay . . . A circle has no beginning, middle, or end—but they're not much fun either.

(*Without Feathers* 132)

Issues of narrative form intertwine with questions of authorship and, on a larger level, the question of the natural order. Tom Baxter in *Purple Rose* believes the screenwriters are "the reason for everything." In **"God,"** however, the characters are uneasy about the implications of the relationship between narrative, free will, and divinity.

Actor: . . . What if the universe is not rational and people are not set things? Then we could change the ending and it wouldn't have to conform to any fixed notions. You follow me?

Writer: Of course not. (*To the audience*) You follow him? He's an actor. Eats at Sardi's.

Actor: Play characters would have not determined traits and could choose their own characters. I wouldn't have to be the slave just because you wrote it that way. I could choose to become a hero.

(*Without Feathers* 137)

The writer argues that this would lead to chaos, and the actor asks "is freedom chaos?" At this point the "fourth wall" breaks down, and a woman from the audience, a philosophy major from Brooklyn College, comes onto the stage and enters the play. The action becomes increasingly absurd, and the actor calls the "real" playwright, Woody Allen, for advice. Similarly, when Tom Baxter wants to have his "freedom," the result is chaos. After Cecilia has literally come into the on-screen film, the maitre'd is ecstatic to find out the script has "been thrown out the window." He signals the band to play and begins to tap dance for the crowd.

Such challenge of narrative forms is subversive. It contains an implicit attack on an established order. When Tom Baxter stepped down from the screen, it causes panic. The people in power, the studio executives, regard his actions as catastrophic, and the FBI and the police are called in to control the characters. When another character wants to follow Tom and be free, he's warned, "that's communist talk." Some moviegoers leave when they find out what has hap-

pened to the on-screen film. One woman explains, "I want what happened in the movie last week to happen this week. Otherwise what's the point?" The stability of a defined story provides meaning.

In **"God,"** a character named Trichinosis suggests that the playwright use a machine that he's just designed as a way to end the play. Zeus will descend from the sky, hurl thunderbolts, and resolve all the problems. Although this *deux ex machina* would have audience appeal, the writer finds its implications disturbing.

WRITER:

But you're saying God comes in at the end and saves everything.

ACTOR:

I love it! It gives the people their money's worth!

DORIS:

He's right. It's like those Hollywood Bible movies.

WRITER (TAKING CENTER STAGE A LITTLE TOO DRAMATICALLY):

But if God saves everything, man is not responsible for his actions.

ACTOR:

You wonder why you're not invited to more parties . . .

DORIS:

But without God, the universe is meaningless. Life is meaningless. We're meaningless. (*Deadly pause*) I have a sudden and overpowering urge to get laid.

(*Without Feathers* 150)

It's a double-bind. With a god, there seems to be no free will; without a god, life is without purpose. *The Purple Rose of Cairo* focuses on choice. Tom wants "to be free to make my own choices," and Cecilia has to choose between Tom, who represents the perfection of Art, and Gil, the actor who plays Tom. As one character says, "Being human is the ability to choose," yet if, as Cecilia says, "I have to choose the real world," then it isn't a choice at all. She doesn't have freedom. It's not surprising then that when Tom and Cecilia's husband fight, it is at the front of a church.

In **"God,"** the writer decides to use the machine. The play within a play begins and with the stabilizing influence of yet another layer of narrative the characters stop self-reflexively addressing the audience, but at the end something goes wrong. At the crucial moment, "ZEUS is lowered very clumsily and he jerks around until we see the lowering wire has strangled him." God is dead. A Western Union message confirms it. After God dies, the narrative breaks down again, and the play becomes a chaotic free-for-all. Characters from other stories enter, such as Stanley Kowalski and Groucho Marx. The lack of order leads to violence. No longer pacified by the narrative, an audience member "Grabs a woman in the audience. Rips her blouse off, chases her up the aisle" (**Without Feathers** 189).

The play ends with the writer and the actor repeating the dialogue from the opening. This conclusion makes the work a circle, and thus solves the paradox set forth at the play's opening. Ending up where it began, the play offers a narrative roller coaster. Both have beginnings, middles and ends, yet also are circular. In a similar fashion, the multiple showings of a movie offer a type of circularity. One can see the same film several times a day all week long.

**"God"** begins with the word "nothing" and ends with the word "absurd." In the search for "what's the point?" Allen repeatedly returns to the idea that "art" is the point. We get on a ride wanting to be scared and allowing ourselves to be scared because we know that we're safe. We see a movie or read a book knowing that it is "artifice" and "unreal," yet allowing ourselves to be taken along the narrative. Cecilia chooses "reality" over "art," and it's a poor choice. It's reality, the Gil Shepherd who abandons her, that's deceitful. The movie ends with Cecilia back in the movie theater, her face turned up toward the screen. At the end of **Annie Hall**, Alvy compares relationships to an old joke about a relative who thinks he's a chicken. The family refuses to take him to a doctor because they "need the eggs." He notes relationships are similar. Roller coasters, rides, films, and narratives, are similar, too. We need them. They provide structure and meaning to our lives, if only temporarily.

*Works Cited*

*Alice.* Written and Directed by Woody Allen. Produced by Charles Joffe and Jack Rollins.

*Annie Hall.* Written by Woody Allen and Marshall Brickman. Directed by Woody Allen. Produced by Charles Joffe and Jack Rollins.

*Purple Rose of Cairo.* Written and Directed by Woody Allen. Produced by Charles Joffe and Jack Rollins.

*Radio Days.* Written and Directed by Woody Allen. Produced by Charles Joffe and Jack Rollins.

Allen, Woody. "God (A Play)" *Without Feathers.* New York: Warner Books, 1976. 129-90.

———. "Match Wits with Inspector Ford" *Without Feathers.* New York: Warner Books, 1976.

———. *Woody Allen: The Nightclub Years 1964-1968.* Los Angeles: United Artists Records.

Lax, Eric. *Woody Allen: A Biography.* New York: Knopf, 1991.

Schatz, Thomas. "*Annie Hall* and the Issue of Modernism." *Literature/Film Quarterly* 10:4 (1982): 180-87.

## Bonnie Churchill (essay date 17 August 2001)

SOURCE: Bonnie Churchill. "Writer Keeps the Well of Ideas Flowing." *Christian Science Monitor* (17 August 2001): 18.

[*In the following essay, Churchill discusses how Allen views his filmmaking process.*]

Woody Allen recalls walking down Lexington Avenue in Manhattan when he suddenly got an idea for a screenplay.

"I always write things down," Mr. Allen explains. "The only thing handy was a discarded matchbook cover." So he scribbled down a few words before joining some friends for an early dinner. He then headed over to Madison Square Garden for a New York Knick's game—an event he seldom misses.

"When I came home," he continues, "I went right to my idea drawer and dropped it on top. It's full of scraps of paper, backs of menus, corners of theater programs. All have a capsule idea for a movie."

Every time Allen plans a new film that he writes, directs, and usually stars in, he goes to the "well"—the idea drawer. "The only problem was I found two pieces of paper, plus the matchbook cover—with three ideas I really liked." The solution? He made all of them.

Last year, it was **Small Time Crooks** with Tracey Ullman. This year, it's **The Curse of the Jade Scorpion** with Helen Hunt, and next year we'll see **Hollywood Ending,** starring Allen, Debra Messing (*Will & Grace*), and Téa Leoni.

Lately, Allen has been getting some flack from critics who question his frequent role as leading man. His answer? "Often I can't get the actor I want because of scheduling. I'm available, so I adjust the script to my limitations, and start filming.

Also, there's the matter of star salaries. Some actors would rather miss a meal than cut their salaries. "But," Allen pointed out, "there are some great ones [like Sean Penn, Kenneth Branagh, and Judy Davis] where money isn't factor. Those are the ones I ask."

Allen shrugged his small frame and confessed. "I never asked anyone about starring as the male lead in **Hollywood Ending,** which I just finished. I was perfect for the part—a neurotic New York filmmaker," says Allen, who recently signed a three-movie deal with DreamWorks.

The second under that deal is *The Curse of the Jade Scorpion,* a 1940s crime caper. It concerns two office workers, Helen Hunt and Allen. She is a hard-as-nails efficiency expert, he an experienced insurance investigator. Both are hypnotized at an office party. The plot heats up when the evil hypnotist calls them days later and puts each into a trance, instructing them to steal some jewelry.

"When I was growing up, there were hypnotists in vaudeville," says Allen. "They always seemed entertaining—half comic, half sinister. I've never been hypnotized and don't think I could be, for I'd giggle."

Once Allen had completed the script for *Scorpion,* he and his staff started suggesting actors. "The second I heard Helen Hunt's name, that was it. She is the character. She projects intelligence and authority, and has a cutting sense of humor."

Allen says his favorite movies were made in the 1920s, '30s, and '40s. "That was such a romantic era, those wonderful pictures made by Billy Wilder and Ernst Lubitsch. The music, the visuals, the women in white satin, the gangsters carrying violin cases that housed machine guns, the soldiers and sailors kissing their girlfriends goodbye—teams like Cary Grant and Rosalind Russell, or [Spencer] Tracy and [Audrey] Hepburn. Their characters always seemed to hate each other, always insulted each other, but you knew somehow they'd get together."

As a kid, Allen managed to go to the movies even though money was tight. "My father drove a New York cab and brought home $50 a week. My mom worked at a florist and had a paycheck of $40.

"I never thought I was poor, for my sister, Letty, and I never missed a meal or didn't have clothing."

When Allen turned 16, he started writing jokes for comics for $50 a week, and then bigger jobs came along that paid $175 a week. By the time he was in his late teens, he made $1,000 weekly. "Show-business salaries are so undeservedly exaggerated that you just have to succeed a little and you are making more money than a much more deserving school teacher."

With all his hats—writing, directing, casting, and starring—he's left producing to his sister. Letty Aronson.

"I know when actors first come to the set, they think we look disorganized," says Allen. "I go home early, only work until 5:30 or 6 p.m., never work nights. The film is never my first priority. It's either family or going home on time, or going to the Knicks game, or getting to my clarinet practice.

"They soon realize that the movie is just part of my life. I'm not a perfectionist. I don't like to rehearse because it bores me. If I shoot a scene, and there's a mistake in it, I don't do another take unless it's major. I don't have the patience.

"After [actors have] learned to relax with my system, they tell me of directors who yell and pound their fists to get a performance out of a star. I never got a performance from anyone that wasn't there before I met them. I hire top people as actors, and then I get out of their way. I tell them if you want to change the script, change it; if you want to say these lines, say them; if you don't, make up your own—as long as they are in character."

Suddenly, Allen looked up over his horn-rimmed glasses and smiled, "I didn't mean to get on a soap box."

### Stanley Kauffmann (review date 10 September 2001)

SOURCE: Kauffmann, Stanley. "The Passing of the Past." *New Republic,* no. 4521 (10 September 2001): 28-9.

[*In the following excerpt, Kauffmann asserts that* The Curse of the Jade Scorpion *is lacking in humor and derides the film along with many of Allen's other movies.*]

Whatever one's opinion of Woody Allen—and mine is wary—no one can deny that he has reached a privileged situation in the film world. No other American writer-director today could present a new feature with a plot that would have fit a two-reel comedy of 1920, with himself grindingly inadequate in the leading role. *The Curse of the Jade Scorpion* confirms Allen's unique position. In fact, about all I could feel while watching it was amazement that he had been allowed to make it. But that amazement cooled when I remembered that, along with the few Allen works I have enjoyed, he has built much of his career with films that were well worth not making.

The year is 1940. People smoke a great deal, and Santo Loquasto's chief setting—a suite of insurance offices in New York—has the familiar soul-deadening effect of linoleum floors and office furniture that looked boring when it was new. Allen plays an investigator for this firm, though how this man who is a prime schnook had the brains to find a stolen Picasso is only the first of the questions that do not need to be answered.

The firm has acquired an efficiency expert—an attractive woman—who wants to get rid of Allen. At an office party in a nightclub, both he and she are hypnotized by a wizard using a small jade scorpion. Allen and the woman fall into trances and are brought out of them, but they remain susceptible to the wizard's commands. That's enough of the plot, except to say that one of the insurance firm's rich clients has a sensational blonde daughter who lusts after Allen. (Frank Sinatra, a slight man, often had scenes in his pictures in which he beat up big men. Allen, not exactly an Adonis, writes scripts in which beauties pant for him.)

*Curse* is apparently supposed to be seen as the divertissement of a large mind. I cannot agree with either part of that idea. The dialogue in Allen's screenplay struggles as hard to be funny as he does in his performance. No, the dialogue is a bit better: he has some talent in that area. Helen Hunt, the efficiency expert, acts with intelligence if not much appeal. Charlize Theron is burdened with the role of the blonde. Wallace Shawn, one of our best playwrights, loiters on the edges of the film as an office colleague. I hope that, to occupy his mind while he was loitering, Shawn was thinking about a new play of his own.

### Richard A. Blake (review date 3 December 2001)

SOURCE: Blake, Richard A. "Jaded and Grumpy." *America* 185, no. 18 (3 December 2001): 22-3.

[*In the following review, Blake discusses* The Curse of the Jade Scorpion *as a satire of classic Hollywood genre films of the 1930s and 1940s.*]

Even by the generous criteria generally applied to summer films, last summer was a particularly disappointing season. Vacation movies target young audiences with young themes, and, as a result, they emerge half-baked from the minds of young, or wannabe young, filmmakers. Okay, I plead *nolo contendere* to the obvious charge of senescent grumpiness, but read another paragraph or two, just in case I may have a point to help put my remarks about Woody Allen's latest offering into a wider cultural context.

The new film-school graduates cut their visual teeth on MTV and computer games. They revel in the optical capabilities of their medium, and so do their audiences. (Students I interview for the film program at Boston College inevitably want to get right to the digital editing equipment. Literature, history and art strike many as useless hurdles to get over before they can get into "film.") In addition, this generation of younger filmmakers inhabits a dot-com universe of quick fortunes made from brilliant marketing of disposable products. Make a box office killing the first weekend and then move on to the next potential blockbuster.

Drop 66-year-old Woody Allen into this milieu and "grumpy" seems not only understandable but admirable. After turning out roughly a film a year for the past 35

years, and presumably being financially secure by this time, Allen has earned freedom from both reviewers and audiences. As a result, he has become both a solipsist and an artistic reactionary. That is, he makes films for himself, not the mass market. Rather than push the limits of the new technology, like his market-conscious younger colleagues, he has progressively retreated into his vast mental archive of film history. Woody Allen doing computer-generated robots would be as likely as George Lucas filming Strindberg on a bare stage. Over the past 15 years, Woody Allen has examined the classic Hollywood genre films, often presenting his own quirky comment on them. Reactionary creativity. I like that. Perhaps we are brothers in grumpiness.

*The Curse of the Jade Scorpion,* his latest, follows this pattern. It pays tribute to the glorious screwball comedies and hardboiled detective yarns of the late 1930's and early 1940's, but with a decidedly postmodern wink at deconstructing them. The campy title, sounding much like a Saturday matinee serial, hints at his devious, satirical purposes. Allen looks back with misty-eyed nostalgia on these lovable old films of his childhood, but he also sees them with the clear-eyed, adult perspective of a major film artist. He's like a relative at an Irish wake, whose highly embellished stories of the deceased sparkle with affection and humor and yet at the same time carry the sting of unflattering truth: "Ah sure, he was a fine man . . . when he was sober." What Allen tries to accomplish then is quite a bit more subtle than appears on the surface of this ostensibly minor comic work. It's comedy, but more than that. It's also a very pointed reflection on two classic Hollywood film genres.

In the time-honored tradition, screwball comedy set a glamorous couple at each other's throats. They think they hate each other, but the audience knows that they will eventually realize that they are in love. In *Scorpion* Allen casts himself as the romantic lead, ace insurance investigator C. W. Briggs. No Clark Gable, Spencer Tracy or Humphrey Bogart he.

Briggs's romantic partner is Betty Ann Fitzgerald, or Fitz (Helen Hunt), who can surely stand in the company of Carole Lombard, Katherine Hepburn or Lauren Bacall, but she is different. Like them, she is quick-witted, independent and spunky, but beneath her stiff tailored business suit dwells a modern liberated woman. She graduated from Vassar and joined the firm as an efficiency expert, a shrewd, tough executive who might efficiency Briggs's job into oblivion. Not burdened with the ladylike polish of finishing school, she continually refers to Briggs with terms of endearment like "scurvy little rat." Her own job security rests on her torrid affair with her married boss, Chris Magruder (Dan Ackroyd).

The hardboiled detective, like Bogart's Sam Spade in *The Maltese Falcon,* wears a rumpled suit, lives by himself in a grubby apartment and works alone. Briggs has Bogie's wardrobe and vocabulary, but Allen's tough-guy posturing makes Briggs soft-boiled at best. Skinny and sixty-ish, he embodies that hidden vulnerability that made Bogie irresistible to Bacall and other sultry sirens of the films noirs. The tough shell is only a ruse, and a pretty funny one at that. Allen's playing Bogart playing Spade points out the artificiality and the fun of the detective icon.

The third classic character is the beautiful but bad-girl heiress, Laura Kensington (Charlize Theron). Her godmothers of the genre, Barbara Stanwyck, Gloria Grahame, Joan Crawford and their generation of conniving vixens used their charms to manipulate and betray their prey, proving time and time again that agitated hormones immediately and invariably strike directly at the male brainstem. In their day, we thought their seductions were pretty steamy stuff, but looking back on them now, they were really quite innocent and unconsciously funny. Laura simmers under a Veronica Lake cascade of blonde curls, and practices her trade with the breathy subtlety of Mae West. Since the object of her artfully fabricated affection is a very flustered Woody Allen pretending to be Bogie, her deadpan vamping unmasks the mock seriousness of the old seduction scenes.

Vintage detectives had to deal with sinister masterminds, like Sydney Greenstreet, and as they pursue the case, they become criminal suspects themselves. Voltan (David Ogden Stiers), the criminal genius behind Briggs's troubles, doubles as a professional magician and hypnotist. Rather than cajole Briggs and Fitz into his scheme with his lies, like a classic villain, he simply hypnotizes them. Allen underlines the comic side of Voltan's knavery by scoring his scenes with the same music that he used for the bumbling hypnotist in **"Oedipus Wrecks"** (1989). Today the suave schemers of the old films noirs provoke the same amusement we once found in the moustache-twirling dastardly villains of the 19th-century stage.

Old-time private eyes also had to contend with the upright but dimwitted detectives of the city police force. The cops have an unfair advantage. They have political connections, and they are not involved financially or romantically with the alleged perpetrators. They have to arrest somebody, and nabbing a smart aleck gumshoe would polish their badges as much as bagging the actual criminal. Instead of city cops, Briggs, the in-house insurance company investigator, runs afoul of two detectives from an outside agency. With their fedoras welded down over their ears, this pair of yoked human zeppelins makes the diminutive Briggs seem even more fragile than he is.

The designer Santo Loquasto and the cinematographer Zhao Fei have beautifully recreated the dark look of the black-and-white film noir in color. The seedy apartments, cluttered offices, grimy police station, dark alleys and subway stations seem coated with an amber varnish. The result is a moody sepia tone that adds temporal distance to the film. It's a subconscious reminder that we are looking at something from the past, like old photos in a family album.

Much of the dialogue in Allen's script seems stilted and awkward. This should strike us as odd. Even those who cannot stand Woody Allen—and there is a lot of America outside New York—admit grudgingly that he is a master of the snappy one-liner. Has his Muse entered the age of hot flashes? Again, I think the effect is deliberate. The old screwball comedies and hardboiled detective movies reveled in verbal sparring. Howard Hawks and Billy Wilder had their extremely witty, articulate lovers fire zingers at each other like duelists using Gatling guns at short range. Every movie detective tried to sound like Dashiell Hammett and every *femme noire* like Dorothy Parker. The dialogue was often sharp and funny, but as we look back on it now, it was also frequently overblown, stilted and awkward. At times the writers simply tried too hard. Maybe the lightening-fast repartee wasn't always as glib or as funny as we seem to remember it.

Does **The Curse of the Jade Scorpion** work? In part, yes. It's very funny in places. In part, no. The satire is clever, but the concept outreaches the execution. I'm fairly confident that I understand what he was trying to do, but the ends don't really justify the means this time. Broad satire of the Mel Brooks variety is difficult enough, but subtle, sophisticated satire, which presumes a great deal of knowledge on the part of the audience, offers almost insurmountable challenges. In this film, Woody Allen has provided a pleasant little comedy weighed down by his own artistic aspirations. In the end, it's not as funny as it might have been, nor as profound as it tries to be.

**Stanley Kauffmann (review date 27 May 2002)**

SOURCE: Kauffmann, Stanley. "Frenzy and Finesse." *New Republic,* no. 4558 (27 May 2002): 24.

[*In the following excerpt, Kauffmann asserts that Woody Allen is a poor actor, and that his performance as the lead character in* Hollywood Ending *ruins the film.*]

Woody Allen makes me dizzy. It's not his directing, which has become orderly and sometimes deft, nor the editing, which is not slam-bang; it's his acting. No, not even his acting: it's his arms. Every moment that he is on screen, and he is rarely off it in *Hollywood Ending* (Dream Works), both his arms are flailing away in simultaneous gestures. Very soon he makes us think of a sailor semaphoring wildly on a sinking ship.

From out of this frenzy, which is bad enough, a desperation winds its way into view. Allen's semaphoring is painful not because it violates any great precept of acting, although I have never seen a professional actor, serious or comic, indulge so insistently in Allen's gymnastics. It's worse. The real trouble is that all this grabbing of air, this gesticulating, this repetitive physical emphasis of matters that do not need it, is apparently a function of fear. Somewhere in his (certainly bright) mind, he knows that he is a feeble actor, and he keeps those arms going, going, going as if he were trying to claw his way to authenticity.

His feebleness is so manifest that it moves us past dislike into pathos. We begin to feel sorry for an actor who, when called on to manifest any emotion or reaction or combination of them, does a splitsecond search of his resources, finds that the cupboard is bare, and tries to manufacture the necessary response—with, as he thinks, the aid of those waving arms. He has the central role in his new film, and, whatever its plentiful faults, it is scuttled even before it leaves port by his performance. Imagine Robin Williams or Danny De Vito in the role, and *Hollywood Ending,* despite its script, ascends to a different life.

Here, I'd guess, is the order of creation of this screenplay—written by Allen, of course. What, he wondered, is the most farcical situation that could occur in the shooting of a film? Answer: the director is blind. And nobody knows it. Once that premise was in place, all that was necessary was to devise the way he gets the job, maintains it for the duration, and finishes up. Allen's solutions: a director with normal vision develops psychosomatic blindness just as the picture starts (a psychological cause is cooked up). He keeps his blindness secret because he frantically needs the job. He finds a trustworthy stooge to help him on the set, and a small crisis is then contrived when the stooge has to be replaced. When the film is finished, it is a cataclysmic mess. The producers are aghast. But though the picture is panned in the United States, it is hailed in France as an avant-garde marvel. (I thought of *Once in a Lifetime,* the Moss Hart-George S. Kaufman comedy of 1932, in which a dumbbell is put in charge of a Hollywood production. The result is a misery to his colleagues, yet the press calls the dumbbell an innovative genius.)

Allen's plot is incredible long before the blindness sets in. This director, who has been unemployable for ten years, is put in charge of a $60 million production—at the insistence of his ex-wife, who now works for the producer—after an initial meeting in which the director behaves like an advanced neurotic on leave from an institution. This early scene warns us to forget about credibility and just hope for some laughs. Indeed, there are a few, but not nearly enough to compensate for the plot and Allen's performance. (Incidentally, the director's first name is Val; his agent is Al; his producer is Hal. Is some Eleusinian mystery implied here?)

Still, despite all the above, we leave with a debt to Allen. He gave the leading female role, his ex-wife, to Téa Leoni. This is not Leoni's first film and she has also done much television, but here she has a truly prominent role, and she sparkles. She is tall, blonde, and highly attractive, and these qualities quickly become additions to the fact that she can act. What's more, she can play farce, one of the most difficult kinds of acting. She never seems merely to be supplying, or trying to supply, what the director wants at the moment. She never "acts": she is always the ex-wife who is unaware that she is in a farce, at the same time that she is Leoni who does know and who maneuvers this woman's way through the chaos.

More Leoni, please.

### Richard A. Blake (review date 3 June 2002)

SOURCE: Blake, Richard A. "The End of Hollywood." *America* 186, no. 19 (3 June 2002): 23-4.

[*In the following review, Blake concludes that* Hollywood Ending *offers humorous dialogue and effective satire, but that the storyline is unfeasible and the sight gags are predictable.*]

That delightful lull between the end of classes and the beginning of exams provided the perfect opportunity to catch up on movies missed during the last several months. As it turns out, I—and thus regular readers of this column—have missed little. Two walls of the neighborhood video shop feature "new releases," almost all of them targeted to audiences below the age of 21, or maybe 14. The action-adventures tend to include at least enough fantasy or science fiction to justify the computer-generated graphics that make them look like a wide-screen video game. The comedies generally seem to feature some dopey guy with his fat sidekick concocting some preposterous scheme to seduce a voluptuous but equally dopey cheerleader during spring break.

Discouraged but not deterred, I picked up DVD versions of *Sexy Beast,* a pedestrian British crime caper with a spectacular secondary character played by Ben

Kingsley; *Moulin Rouge,* a gaudy rock-opera with marvelous visual effects; and *Mulholland Drive,* David Lynch's enigmatic yet hypnotic murder mystery that may be a prolonged dream sequence, or science fiction or a ghost story. Like *Memento,* which tells its story backwards, with each scene progressively filling in enough background to make the story nearly intelligible, *Mulholland Drive* rejects the linear narrative. *Moulin Rouge* doesn't have enough narrative to reject. This new style of anti-narrative mimics the viewing habits of contemporary television users, who surf channels with their remotes, settle on interesting scenes for a few moments and then move on with little concern for coherence or closure. So much for a beginning, middle and end. So much for my catching up.

*Hollywood Ending* leads me to believe that Woody Allen shares my discomfort with the new directions of the film industry. The title is both pun and a thesis statement. Yes, in keeping with the literal title, the final sequence provided the happy Hollywood ending that classical film narrative technique requires. At the same time, the film also offers a portrait of an industry weakened through generations of inbreeding, twitching in commercial straightjackets and now gasping for its final breaths amid a miasma of artistic narcissism. Never a friend of the Hollywood side of the industry, Doctor Allen may have reached an overly grim diagnosis, and maybe not. Ever the grinning vivisectionist, Allen keeps his colleagues and cadaver laughing until the dismemberment is complete. Victor Frankenstein with schtick.

On its surface, the story appears to be another typical Allen comedy about the talented and hopelessly neurotic cave dwellers of Manhattan. Val Waxman (Woody Allen) first appears in a hooded parka, calling from Arctic Canada where he is on location filming a deodorant commercial. He's on his way back to New York and his live-in girlfriend, Lori (Debra Messing), an aspiring actor who could pass as his granddaughter. He's been fired. He's always fired. Once a successful director, he has not had a winner in a dozen years. To the power brokers in Hollywood, he's poison. They admit his talent, but with his bundle of neuroses and compulsions, he cannot complete a project. No one will work with him. For some inexplicable reason, his former wife, Ellie (Téa Leoni), a studio executive, argues that as the quintessential New York director, he would be perfect for "The City That Never Sleeps." In creating Val Waxman, Woody Allen cuts very close to the autobiographical bone.

With the help of his oily, ever-grinning-through-expensive-bridgework agent, Al Hack (Mark Rydell), Waxman gets the assignment. One problem arises almost immediately. As the cast gathers for the first day of shooting, Waxman suddenly goes blind. No problem, explains the specialists. The condition is only psychosomatic and could go away at any time. Nonetheless, Waxman can't see Central Park. No problem, argues Hack. They can fake it. The shooting goes ahead with a blind director, which according to Allen is typical of many Hollywood films. Ellie comes back into Waxman's life as a faithful assistant to help him hide his problem and finish the picture. After all, she has her own job to worry about. She insisted on hiring this hysterical nut-case in the first place. Their collusion leads to the inevitable romantic-comedy complications.

That's the story line, but it doesn't work. The concept of a blind film director makes a brilliant satirical point, but the comic turns on blindness were exhausted in vaudeville seventy years ago. Waxman looks in the wrong direction during conversations, resorts to double-talk to avoid making decisions on props, costumes and set decoration, stumbles over furniture and fails to perceive a bare-faced (and bare almost everything else) seduction from his leading lady. Most of the time the sight gags are sadly predictable. Pun intended.

The script lacks the usual Allen tautness. Waxman accidently reveals his scheme to a sleazy journalist, Andrea Ford (Jodie Markell), but nothing comes of his revelations. Does she publish her story or not? Allen never tells us. Waxman's analyst brings up his relationship with his estranged son, Tony (Mark Webber), a punk rocker who eats live rats as part of his act. In a reconciliation meeting, they talk about "seeing" one another's values. To his credit Allen backs away from the miraculous psychiatric cure of Hollywood cliché. He backs away from any other connection to the story as well. The son simply vanishes from the story. Why bring him in at all? And unless New York weather patterns have changed in the last few years, how is it possible for Al Hack to leave a Passover seder and arrive at Waxman's home on a beautiful summer evening?

For all its disappointment, *Hollywood Ending* offers its own quirky delights. The Allen one-liners sparkle through the dialogue, and that alone is worth the outrageous price of a ticket. The satire is deliciously venomous, especially when it sinks its fangs into the Hollywood power brokers. Hal (Treat Williams) runs the studio, but he can't pronounce "auteur," and when Waxman worries if Hal will hang around the set all day, Ellie says his attention span lasts only about a half hour. Surely the name invokes the memory of the computer in *2001: A Space Odyssey.* Ed (George Hamilton) attends all the high-level meetings, with no apparent qualifications other than his suntan. Elio Sebastian (the fashion designer, Isaac Mizrahi), the production designer sent by Hollywood to recreate authentic New York sets, finds Central Park unacceptable and plans to rebuild it, along with Harlem and Times Square, on the studio back lot, just to make it look more realistic. Like her male counterparts, Ellie looks great, as though she has spent more of her life in California health clubs than in the archives of the New York Public Library.

New Yorkers also get the Allen treatment. Lori, Waxman's girlfriend, is such a bubble-brain that one is astonished that she was able to find the set, let alone memorize several highly forgettable lines. Andrea, the reptilian journalist, has been lined up by studio publicity to do a cover piece on the film, but her knowledge of movies seems limited to the boudoir escapades of stars and directors. Allen's feelings about this type of journalism have been well documented. Even though he has furnished a mother lode of material for the tabloids himself, he can't resist killing the messenger one more time.

Waxman insists on hiring a foreign camera operator to give the film an authentic New York feel. His choice (Lu Yu), however, is Chinese and speaks not a word of English. What's more, he seems to be just as crazy, temperamental and incompetent as Waxman, the blind director. His translator (Barney Cheng), a business major from N.Y.U., is hopelessly confused by these artsy types, like Margaret Dumont lost amid the Marx Brothers. Allen never fully cashes in on the comic potential of the situation.

Despite its slipshod script and squandered possibilities, **Hollywood Ending** has its moments. The whole is much less than the sum of the parts, it's true, but some of the parts are quite entertaining. In addition, the sustained satire keeps its focus clearly in place throughout the meanderings of the narrative. At the end, Waxman/Allen seems to reject the American film industry, even in its New York incarnation, no more on that. The final sequence holds one last ironic surprise.

Perhaps this review is overly gentle with a clearly disappointing effort. Despite Woody Allen's legendary contempt for critics, reviewers like me still treat him gently, and with good reason. What other filmmaker has so definitively rejected the computer-generated flash and glitter of action-adventure comic books and gross-out sex comedies aimed at 12-year olds? Who else provides adults with consistently funny, yet thought-provoking films on a yearly basis?

Follow my example. Take a tour of your own video shop in search of a new release that does not assault your senses and insult your intelligence. You will find very few. We should be grateful for a second- or even third-rate Woody Allen film, since it's a good deal better than just about anything else you'll find in multiplex or video stores these days. I'm disappointed. I'm grateful. I'm neurotic. I'm a New Yorker. You wanna make something out of it?

## Simon Louvish (review date January 2003)

SOURCE: Louvish, Simon. Review of *The Curse of the Jade Scorpion,* by Woody Allen. *Sight and Sound* 13, no. 1 (January 2003): 39-40.

[*In the following review, Louvish asserts that* The Curse of the Jade Scorpion *is amusing as light entertainment, but feels that Allen is inappropriately cast in the lead role due to his age.*]

In a 1940s-era insurance office C. W. Briggs prides himself on being the top investigator in his field, with a knack for reading a criminal's mind. His methods are old-fashioned both in filing and dating, and when the boss appoints female efficiency expert Betty Ann Fitzgerald to modernise the office Briggs develops an immediate hostility to her. During an office night out Briggs and Fitzgerald are put under the influence by stage hypnotist Voltan, who makes them believe they're in love with each other until they snap out of the trance. Unknown to either, Voltan has also set up a long-range influence by which he can order Briggs to rob his firm's clients and then wipe his memory of the thefts.

Rival detectives, however, are soon on Briggs' trail, and when he's put into a trance and walks out in the middle of a dalliance with a spectacular blonde suspicion grows even stronger. Fitzgerald becomes convinced he's the thief, until she too is put under the influence. Briggs is arrested, escapes and eventually triumphs in thwarting Voltan's plans, but the underlying attraction with Betty Ann enables them to walk off in love.

\* \* \*

Woody Allen has gone on record as saying that he wished to make this [**The Curse of the Jade Scorpion**] "a romantic bantering picture" akin to the classic Hollywood Cary Grant-Rosalind Russell or Tracy-Hepburn vehicles. It bears more resemblance, however, to those old Charlie Chan movies in which the Swedish Warner Oland invoked the wisdom of the orient to solve occidental crimes. The 1940s evoke for Allen the hypnotism craze and the malign influence of a small-time jewel thief rather than that other hypnotism occurring on a much grander scale in Nazi Germany. More and more the model for Allen's movies is other movies as he flirts with the danger of having his craft compared to that of directors like Howard Hawks or screenwriters like Ben Hecht and Charles MacArthur. Truth be said, it's as a writer that Allen's contribution to movies is most significant. At a time when Hollywood cinema comedy was practically moribund, veterans such as Groucho Marx anointed Allen as America's new court jester. The irreverent, politically anarchic babblings of the little New York Jewish hyper-neurotic were perfect for the age of Lyndon Johnson and Richard Nixon. Later on Allen's digressions into serious drama begged his own comparison with his adored Ingmar Bergman, yet the first of these, *Interiors* (1978), was finely crafted and the semi-serious *Hannah and Her Sisters* (1986) and *Crimes and Misdemeanours* (1989) were small American classics. Other maverick films, such as *Zelig* (1983), stand on their own as mutated fool's gold.

Allen's great triumph has been, against the odds, to continue creating on a regular basis, and if one year's film was off beam, the next, or next again, would pick up and keep alive a tradition of independent film-making more cherished in Europe than in its home. Allen appears to have become an actor in his own movies almost by default, since it's cheaper to cast yourself in the lead and, in any case, the basic character was test-run as a cabaret stand-up act in which the quick-fire delivery was honed and perfected. Allen admits, in the interview quoted above, that "I'm not an actor really. I can play a few things; I've very, very limited." But the Hanks and Cruises were not available for the present work, and so we have Woody again.

This highlights the ironic problem of [*The Curse of the Jade Scorpion*]: the central role is simply miscast. Allen is too old for the character he's supposed to be playing—the usual belief-deficit kicks in when Charlize Theron's stunning blonde Laura begs him to bed her. The star performance is wooden, good actors such as Wallace Shawn have little to do, the lines, nice as many of them are, are hardly delivered with the confidence of yesteryear and the whole romantic premise appears embarrassing. The direction is workmanlike, Zhao Fei's photography crisp and efficient. But even at the basic level of recapturing the 1940s ambience for which Allen has so often expressed his affection, there's not a great deal on offer. A few street scenes and a denouement in Chinatown are practically the movie's only digressions from the insurance-office and apartment interiors. Once upon a time the Woody character set his individual neurotic desires against the absurdities of a mad society. Today the surrounding society has dwindled to a nostalgically contrived virtual reality consisting of surfaces, sounds and floating ephemera, Jade Scorpions that, in the end, signify nothing.

Having said all this, the story is still amusing, the plot rattles along, the music pumps nicely, the hypnotist hypnotises, the misunderstandings mount, and a legion of Woody Allen fans will most likely count themselves happy. The early loser Woody has segued into the successful professional who remains the same schmo, but will get the girl in the end. And who else makes small, well-formed, easy-to-digest entertainments nowadays rather than overblown, sagging corporate sagas? So Woody Allen's audiences will most probably ignore the carping critic and hearken more to the adage of the old maestro Charlie Chan: "Theory like mist on eyeglasses—obscure vision."

## Philip Kerr (review date 6 January 2003)

SOURCE: Kerr, Philip. "Curse of the Ageing Little Schnook." *New Statesman* 132, no. 4619 (6 January 2003): 30.

[*In the following review, Kerr asserts that* Hollywood Ending *is a fairly amusing light comedy with a few good one-liners.*]

What with the vagaries of film distribution in Britain, Woody Allen's "latest" film, *The Curse of the Jade Scorpion,* is now almost two years old; and since making it, Allen has made and released yet another, titled *Hollywood Ending.* Just to let you know exactly how long it is since *The Curse of the Jade Scorpion* was released in America, I saw it at a New York cinema where *Captain Corelli's Mandolin* was also opening.

Given that most modern video players in this country can now accommodate the American NTSC format, you would be well advised—should you wish to see *The Curse of the Jade Scorpion*—not to go to a cinema at all, but to order up a VHS copy from Amazon, for about two quid. That's right, two quid. At a central London cinema, you couldn't buy Coke and popcorn for two quid. And although it may not be one of Woody Allen's best films, it's by no means his worst, and is certainly worth a couple of quid, plus postage.

Allen returns to the 1940s, to play an insurance investigator in a romantic comedy that matches him against Helen Hunt, playing a humourless efficiency expert. The two hate each other with venom until, under the influence of a stage hypnotist wielding a trance-inducing jade scorpion at an office party, they both reveal hidden desires for each other, at the same time as being set up to commit a series of jewel robberies. It's light, Bob Hope kind of stuff (*My Favorite Brunette*), intermittently amusing with a few good one-liners, and nicely shot, too.

Woody Allen has always specialised in the improbable romance, as, over the years, we were asked to believe that some of Hollywood's most attractive women could fall for a little schnook like him. But he is now 67 years old and it seems just as preposterous to me that someone as lovely as Helen Hunt could ever fall for a character played by Allen. Watching the then 39-year-old Hunt kissing a man as old and small as Woody Allen struck me as more than a little indecent, like Humbert Humbert bouncing Dolores Haze on his pyjama'd lap. Think about it—I bet Allen did—when *Love and Death* (my own Woody Allen favourite) was released back in 1975, Hunt would have been just 12 years old.

Was Allen damaged by his very messy falling out with Mia Farrow? Certainly, there's not much trace of this in any of the New York reviews of *Jade Scorpion,* or, for that matter, **Hollywood Ending.** But elsewhere in the world, I detect a certain cooling. Allen's audiences have never been large, but, given his incredible productivity (in the past 30 years, he has written and directed 29 pictures), people have stopped looking forward to his movies and learnt to expect them, with the same enthusiasm they might evince toward some neurotic, angst-ridden relation who was threatening to come and visit them. What's even worse is that Allen's movies have become much more expensive to make at about the same time as they have stopped making money. For example, **The Curse of the Jade Scorpion** cost $26m to make, while worldwide grosses have been just $16m. **Hollywood Ending,** released in the US in May 2002, cost $16m to make and took 36 per cent less in US domestic gross than **Jade Scorpion.**

But while it is clear to the rest of the world that the box office cannot continue to accommodate Allen's prolific level of movie production, it's perhaps not so obvious to him. A while ago, at Elton John's house in the south of France, I had dinner with Jean Doumanian. Doumanian is the producer of eight of Allen's most recent films and the woman who stood by him, continuing to finance his movies after his long-time studio, TriStar, got cold feet in the wake of the scandal over Allen's break-up with Farrow and his affair with her daughter, now his wife. I remember being struck by Doumanian's loyalty to Allen, and her obvious affection for the man and his films, and thinking how lucky Allen was to have a producer like her. The following year, Allen sued Doumanian, alleging she had cheated him out of $14m.

At the time of writing, the legal proceedings have just ended, with the parties settling out of court. I imagine most people would think it rather strange to hope to remain friends with someone you were suing for $14m. But Allen clearly did. That's what I call a real Hollywood ending.

By all accounts, the nine-day trial was a lot like one of Allen's more recent films: shrill, frivolous, with an improbable plot—Allen wrote Doumanian a note saying: "This was supposed to be amusing, like a Tracy-Hepburn movie, in court by day, friends by night"—and a few good one-liners, mostly from the judge; but, again just like one of his movies, despite much media attention, it was not well attended by the public. In the days of Tracy and Hepburn, Hollywood endings looked a little different.

## Charles Isherwood (review date 19 May 2003)

SOURCE: Isherwood, Charles. "Familiar Looks at Love in Allen's Stage Return." *Variety* 391, no. 1 (19 May 2003): 35.

[*In the following review, Isherwood comments on Allen's double-bill titled* Writer's Block, *comprised of*

*two plays,* Riverside Drive *and* Old Saybrook. *Isherwood observes that both plays explore Allen's recurring subject of sexual infidelity.*]

Woody Allen, a man not exactly known for his cinematic celebrations of wedded bliss, takes yet another dim view of matrimonial contentment in [**Writer's Block,** a] new pair of one-act plays staged by the author for the Atlantic Theater Co. These minor works [**Riverside Drive** and **Old Saybrook**] are united under an umbrella title suggesting their central theme is literary constipation, but it's really Allen's familiar—and increasingly belabored—preoccupation with sexual infidelity that takes center stage here. A bright cast made up almost exclusively of ex-sitcom stars works amiably to enliven the modestly funny if somewhat sour proceedings.

The first item, a seriously overextended sketch that suggests Albee's *Zoo Story* rewritten as a sitcom, finds screenwriter Jim (*Mad About You*'s Paul Reiser) locked in an increasingly deranged battle of wills with a mentally disturbed homeless man. The philandering Jim has made a date with his girlfriend on a lonely stretch of Riverside Drive. Before she arrives, he's accosted by a grubby character calling himself Fred Savage (Skip Sudduth) who reveals surprisingly intimate knowledge of Jim's life—his "rodentine" wife Lola, his g.f. Barbara, etc. He's convinced that Jim stole the idea for his hit movie from him, and he wants payback.

Although he's dressed in greasy tatters, Fred reveals a talent for elegant comic phrasing and a philosophical bent, even as he claims to be receiving transmissions from the top of the Empire State Building. Jim, who's merely neurotic ("I'm psychotic," offers Fred, "I could teach you a lot."), also knows his way around a punchline, even if some are a bit worn. When they begin sparring over Jim's infidelity, Jim allows that his shrink told him to stop. "So I stopped seeing the psychiatrist," he adds.

The improbability of this encounter is underlined by Jim's endless reiterations of annoyance, which the likably understated playing of Reiser can't save from sounding forced. Armed with a cell phone to cancel or postpone his assignation, who would stick around to take abuse from an obviously disturbed and possibly violent man? And the play takes a still more preposterous—not to mention distasteful—turn when Jim and Fred begin plotting to kill Barbara (Kate Blumberg), who threatens Jim with blackmail when he tries to give her the brushoff.

The second offering is livelier and funnier, although with a larger east on hand it also reveals Allen's rusty technique in writing and directing for the stage. It takes place in the roomy living room of a house in Old Saybrook, rendered with inviting warmth by Santo Loquasto.

Sheila (Bebe Neuwirth) and Norman (Jay Thomas) are playing host to her sister Jenny (Heather Burns) and Jenny's husband, David (Grant Shaud). The cocktail hour is interrupted by the arrival of another couple—there's an Albee-esque quality to this setup, too; think *Who's Afraid of Virginia Woolf?* meets *A Delicate Balance.* They are Hal (Christopher Evan Welch) and Sandy (Clea Lewis), who once owned the house and have stopped by to take a look.

When Hal points out a secret compartment in the fireplace to Sheila, she discovers a diary Norman has been keeping of his rampaging sexual affair with Jenny. Outraged comic sniping ensues, with Hal and Sandy revealing fissures in their own marriage—ultimately announcing that they, too, have both conducted extramarital affairs.

There are some juicy laughs, mostly from the appealingly daffy Lewis and Welch, who take casual glee in watching the fireworks until things cut too close to home. But a lot of the jokes sound either familiar or forced. When one of the women tosses off the phrase "over my dead body," you can predict her husband will say, "I'm not discussing our love life." And the gag about. David's obtuse inability to comprehend that his wife and her brother-in-law are getting it on—despite photographic evidence—is stretched well past the point of amusement. This play, too, takes an unpleasantly violent turn before a late twist borrowed from Pirandello.

And superior though it is to *Riverside Drive,* it also represents Allen in less than top form. For one thing, it's clear he's used to writing for the movies, where the camera frame usually focuses on one or two people. The dialogue here tends to keep breaking down into one-on-one confrontations that leave the rest of the characters onstage stranded. And Allen the director is clearly at a loss when this occurs: The characters not involved in these exchanges often sit frozen in artificial attitudes of anguish or annoyance before the camera, as it were, pans back to them and they spring back to life.

**Jeffrey Rubin-Dorsky (essay date summer 2003)**

SOURCE: Rubin-Dorsky, Jeffrey. "The Catskills Reinvented (and Redeemed): Woody Allen's *Broadway Danny Rose.*" *Kenyon Review* 25, nos. 3-4 (summer 2003): 264-81.

*[In the following essay, Rubin-Dorsky discusses Allen's portrayal of the Catskills and comedians from the past in* Broadway Danny Rose.*]*

Woody Allen, most especially in his early films, but extending through the middle period of his career (from *Annie Hall* in 1977 to *Crimes and Misdemeanors* in 1989), fashioned a persona built upon what Vivian Gornick labeled a "rich and potent outsider's anxiety," combining it with a wild, risky inventiveness that also defined his own generation of comics such as Mort Sahl, Mike Nichols and Elaine May, and Lenny Bruce ("Face It" 9). Like his predecessors, he created comic foils, objects of ridicule, to act out a sense of deprivation and humiliation he felt at being Jewish, and thus his work embodies an anger and hostility (usually expressed in the form of passive-aggressiveness), as well as a self-mocking view of Jewishness, often associated with the Borscht Belt comedians. Yet, interestingly, the one film among the thirty or so he has made that actually envisions a harmonious community (rather than the loneliness of the isolated spiritual seeker) is based on his memories of the Catskills, especially his appreciation of the entertainers and comics whose hand gestures and voice intonations his character, theatrical agent Danny Rose, so perfectly imitates. (He also replicates their comic style, the epitome of one-liner lounge acts and the vaudevillian tradition of ethnic mockery.) *Broadway Danny Rose* (1984) is neither a nostalgic overture toward the past nor an attempt to preserve it as a cultural artifact; rather, the film seeks to animate the past by giving it a living presence within Danny's psyche.

Signs of the Catskills abound in *Danny Rose.* Of the seven people sitting around the table at the Carnegie Delicatessen as the film opens, six are comedians who, at one time or another, have played the Catskills: Sandy Baron, Jackie Gale, Corbett Monica, Howie Storm, Will Jordan, and Morty Gunty. (The seventh is Allen's longtime producer, Jack Rollins.) In his days as an entertainer, Danny Rose also made the Borsht Belt scene, and as the comics reminisce about his career, we see that Danny, indeed, did the *shtick* (the routines and jokes) we associate with those performers. "He did all the old jokes," says one of the comics, "and stole from everybody" (much like Milton Berle, who has a key role in the film). In addition, Danny's acts—a one-armed juggler, a one-legged tap dancer, a blind xylophone player, a ventriloquist who stutters, a husband-and-wife balloon-folding team, a penguin that skates across the stage dressed as a rabbi, a parrot that sings "I Gotta Be Me"—are comic exaggerations of Catskills entertainment, but not so far removed from reality. (In fact, according to John Baxter, they are all "authentic club performers" [321-22].) In her memoir of her early years in the Catskills, *Enter Talking,* Joan Rivers remembers transporting various acts with her from one hotel to another: "I taxied men with barking suitcases, ventriloquists whose lips moved even when they were silent, and a trainer with three tap-dancing chickens who kept telling me his ambition was to have a line of chickens equal to the Rockettes" (Kanfer 230-31). Danny even tries to book his blind xylophone player and his one-legged tap dancer into Weinstein's

Majestic Bungalow Colony, the same Catskill resort in Accord, New York, where Woody Allen began his career as a stage magician (Baxter 34-35). Allen apparently bombed, and Danny has no better luck, since Weinstein's audience of "old Jewish people," says owner Philly Weinstein, are "mostly blind and crippled themselves."

Moreover, it might easily be argued that the spirit of one of the greatest (if not *the* greatest) of the Catskill comedians, Milton Berle, presides over the film's action, since, in addition to his name being evoked almost reverentially, Berle actually appears as the promoter of an "oldies" show exploiting the contemporary nostalgia craze. If Danny can convince him to include his Italian crooner (whom Phil Weinstein describes as "a dumb, fat, temperamental, has-been Italian singer with a drinking problem") in his upcoming TV special, Lou Canova's comeback will be complete, and Danny will finally capture the managerial success that so far has eluded him. Allen has acknowledged how "gifted" and "personally very funny" Berle was in his nightclub act, doing the famous Catskills routines from the thirties (which he then reprised in the fifties). This is despite the fact that Allen does not count Berle as one of his mentors ("he was never an influence on me," he told Stig Bjorkman [145]), and that he found "Uncle Miltie" (Berle's own sardonic coinage) "too broad on television" ("baggy pants, clownish, lets his teeth fall out"). Remarkably, this is also despite the fact that Berle's crude and misogynistic one-liners, such as—

> "A man took his wife to a psychiatrist and said, 'What's-her-name here complains that I don't give her enough attention.'"
>
> "Some airlines have a mother-in-law flight. It's nonstop!"
>
> "If she sued her face for slander, she could collect!"
>
> "I'll show you a lucky man—his secretary's lipstick is the same color as his wife's!"
>
> (Berle 27 ff.)

—were the farthest thing from his own intellectual monologues. Nonetheless, to Allen, and to Danny, Berle is a "giant in American comedy," an "immortal." "If it's old-fashioned to like Mr. Danny Kaye, Mr. Bob Hope, or Mr. Milton Berle," Danny Rose says respectfully, "then I'm old fashioned!"

In spite of its insularity and materialism, what Allen locates in the Jewish world of the Catskills, and what Danny Rose recreates with his ragtag band of odd "acts," is the sense of unforced community that existed among a people gathered together to share a culture that would inevitably disappear in the process of Americanization. The extent to which Jews have preserved "Jewishness" in the succeeding years is debatable, but the

first generations of twentieth-century American Jews created in the Catskills a collective enterprise that, above all, through its humor and entertainment, kept *Yiddishkeit*—the culture, traditions, and customs of the Eastern European Jews that would soon vanish—alive. Allen, whose popular film personae often embody the torturous search for values and meaning amidst the egocentrism of contemporary American life, for one moment in **Broadway Danny Rose** finds a nurturing spiritual connection to the Jewish past, thus assuring the film of a special place in his body of work as well as in his viewers' affection.

## MY CATSKILLS

I begin this section with an anecdote and a joke which, taken together, reveal something important about the shared Jewish experience of the Catskills that I personally witnessed. First, the anecdote:

> The comedian Joey Adams (born Joseph Abramowitz), who got his start in the mountains and later wrote a book on the Borscht Belt, was playing an upscale club in Boston. In the audience sat Wendell Adams, a member of the old New England family that included among its patriarchs John Adams, the second president of the United States; his son, John Quincy Adams, the sixth president of the United States; his son, Charles Francis Adams, the American minister to Great Britain from 1861-68; and his son, Henry Adams, the renowned American historian and author of the classic autobiography, *The Education of Henry Adams*. At the end of the performance, Wendell Adams approached Joey and jokingly inquired if they might be related. "I don't know," Joey replied, "what was your name before you changed it?"

Second, the joke (which I myself heard as a boy in the Catskills in the mid-1950s):

> After many years in New York, a man returns to the old country where his mother is still living. Staring at her clean-shaven son in his Brooks Brothers suit (when Brooks Brothers signified WASP conservatism), she's aghast. "Nu?" Mama asks. "What happened to your beard?"
>
> "Mama, nobody wears a beard in America."
>
> "But you continue to observe the Sabbath, of course."
>
> "Mama, in America almost everybody works on the Sabbath."
>
> She sighs heavily. "Well at least you keep kosher."
>
> "I . . . eat out a lot."
>
> The old lady motions to her son to come closer and whispers: "Yussele, tell mama, my boy. Are you still circumcised?"
>
> (Kanfer 144)

These bits of lore point to the complex—indeed, perplexed—condition of second-generation Jews desperately wanting and famously achieving middle-class American status: materially comfortable, economically stable (and in many cases, prosperous and successful) American Jews willingly transforming themselves into Jewish Americans, who nevertheless were burdened with and by residual uncertainty, latent tension, and veiled, often unacknowledged, hostility (which can be heard in Joey Adams's edgy reply). Here was a people joyously (or so it seemed) letting go of the old ways, the old customs, and (most important) the old prohibitions, yet still wary of the larger world around them, creating protective, monolithic communities even as they ventured farther into the fleshpots of America. The paradoxes of their lives were embodied in the Catskill enclaves they populated—the bungalow colonies, lodges, and hotels of upstate New York to which Jews began coming in earnest in the early twentieth century and which, in its heyday from the end of World War II through the 1960s (the era Phil Brown, in *Catskill Culture,* calls the "Golden Age of the Catskills" [41]), grew to accommodate a million vacationers each summer—communities that were, therefore and above all else, sites where Jews acted out the complicated (at times even torturous) process of acculturation (which, some sages bemoan, eventually became assimilation) to American society. Emulating the gentile ritual of the summer vacation, Jews mostly from New York made their way to the mountain resorts where they fashioned not a world of refinement and elegance, but one dominated by a pervasive Jewishness in speech, manners, cuisine, and, famously, in entertainment. Despite the diminishment of anti-Semitism, Jews still wanted to live enclosed in these mountain resorts, reinforcing their Jewishness, their self-awareness (and self-consciousness), while pursuing modern means of affluence and pleasure.

I was born in early June, 1947, and before the month was out I had been whisked off by my mother to spend the first of sixteen summers in the Catskills, initially at a *kuchalayn* (a central house with a common kitchen where renters cooked for themselves, often surrounded by bungalows or cottages) just outside of Monticello and then, for the bulk of my time in the mountains, at a modest bungalow colony in an exceedingly small town called Ferndale, not far from Old Liberty. In June of 1963, when I turned sixteen, I refused to return for even one more season. (Though only a few summers later, as a college student needing money, I did return to work at several well-known hotels, first as a busboy and then as a waiter.) Thus, a brief historical overview on my time in the Catskills looks like this: the summer I arrived in the mountains Eddie Fisher, then about twenty-one years old, had been "discovered" at Grossinger's, the most famous and popular of the (kosher) Jewish pleasure palaces in the thirties and forties, by Eddie Cantor, who was the starring attraction on the entertainment bill of fare. (Fisher would later marry both Debbie Reynolds and Elizabeth Taylor right

there on the premises.) The resort business, which had grown robustly between the two wars, underwent something of a renaissance during the fifties. The chief obstacle to increased patronage, the long, arduous drive from the city, was removed with the opening of the New York State Thruway, and then the building of the new Route 17, the four-lane so-called "Quickway" through Sullivan County; once the latter was completed, the mountains were, as Kanfer points out, "only ninety minutes away from Manhattan by car, without a single toll after the George Washington Bridge" (233). Some of the greatest Catskill performers of the thirties and forties made their way back to the hotel stages, including Milton Berle, George Jessel, Jerry Lewis, and the opera singer Robert Merrill. Georgia Gibbs, by then a successful recording star, and the young and exceedingly popular Sammy Davis, Jr., appeared on the circuit; so did Tony Martin, Red Buttons, and Joey Adams. Richard Tucker sang at Saturday night services. The dialect comedian Myron Cohen played the resort nightclubs, as did those comics who had gotten their start in the mountains, among them Buddy Hackett, Alan King, and Jackie Mason (Kanfer 233-34). When my parents knew someone staying at one of the hotels, they took me to see a few of these acts; later, with friends and dates, I snuck past security to see several others.

I have many vivid memories, but I have no nostalgia for the Catskills—neither my own nor my father's. Donald Weber quotes Leon Wieseltier's (sarcastic) comment that "Jewish sons have always been nostalgic for the nostalgia of Jewish fathers," and despite Wieseltier's tone, Weber finds himself "affected by the deep truths inscribed in this particular maxim," and confesses that a "yearning" or "fascination" for "such a long-departed time and place [his family's movements across the Bronx in the 1930s and 1940s] inform[s] [his] current study of Jewish American culture, popular and literary" (124-25). (Weber justifies his passion for recovery by producing a fine essay on the "Yinglish worlds of Gertrude Berg, Milton Berle, and Mickey Katz.") I, however, share the viewpoint of Daniel Boyarin and Chana Kronfeld, who have stamped each volume in the Jewish studies series they edit for Stanford University Press with a quotation from the Yiddish poet J. Gladstein: "Nostalgia Jewishness is a lullaby for old men / gumming soaked white bread." None of my recollections, summarized below, are based in nostalgia, which in fact mars the leading memoirs/celebrations of the Catskills: Myrna and Harvey Frommer's *It Happened in the Catskills* (1991), Irwin Richman's *Borscht Belt Bungalows* (1998), and Phil Brown's *Catskill Culture* (1998). Even the best and most historical study of the Jewish presence in the mountains, Stefan Kanfer's *A Summer World* (1989), fails to offer a critical analysis of the "culture" it studies.

I loved the Catskills as a boy, and I remember the feelings of elation when each June we would leave Brooklyn, head up the West Side Highway toward the Washington Bridge, and escape the city. My summer experiences were strongly marked by kinship ties within miniature societies, extended families sharing energies and resources, thus creating a feeling of abundance (though they were not yet economically prosperous) as well as fostering a sense of security. During the week it was an entire world of women, maternally loving and nurturing, and in addition to my grandmother, my great-aunt, my aunt, and my mother, there were all the other mothers to look after you and see to your needs. On the weekends my father and the other men arrived, and they were never more relaxed and available than during those summer respites from work. I remember my parents and their friends as vital, exuberant, even feisty people, living what seemed to me to be active, engaged American lives, and yet this was also a *haimish* (unpretentious, friendly) life, where *Yiddishkeit* was still available. "Everybody . . . was Jewish," says one of Phil Brown's interviewees, "enmeshed" in the "milieu" of Jewish experience (as Brown himself indicates), and this accords with my boyhood memories (200).

The Jews of my parents' generation had seemingly created a safe summer world in the Catskills, and yet as I grew older I realized that they lived with some undefined fear, and what at first felt like comfort began to seem like overprotectiveness. It wasn't anti-Semitism that they sought to keep at bay, and from which they wanted to shield their children; rather, it had more to do with a sense of contamination by the "other." While I can't remember the colony ever being penetrated by gentiles, apparently they were everywhere surrounding us, and even my "worldly" parents and their friends were worried about their harmful influence. Exactly how they were going to corrupt us was never made clear, since by the fifties—and surely by the sixties—an overwhelming number of Jewish Catskill families had already fallen away from traditional religious and culinary practices. Nevertheless, we were cautioned and forewarned, with the ironic result that the "safe" world became narrow, circumscribed and diminished not by threats from the outside, but by admonitions from within. By the time I and the rest of the boys and girls in our little resort were ready to venture forth into the surrounding towns, for shopping or entertainment or just plain exploration, the trip was as much of an escape as an adventure. As our adolescent horizons expanded, the life within the colony shrank: virtually unchanged since my childhood, it had become claustrophobic, stifling, parochial.

I hated the Catskills as a teenager and young adult, precisely because its chief aim was to perpetuate and inflate itself without ever diversifying the life inside it. Phil Brown quotes approvingly the comment of one vacationer on the demise of the mountain resorts: "It's really sad that those places are gone. I think it's a loss to Jewish culture. Where else are a group of Jewish people going to get together and feel comfortable and play cards and mah-jongg and have political discussion and can feel as relaxed that they could say anything they wanted to a fellow Jew that they would not say if there were a gentile sitting there?" (225). Nowhere else, one would hope: self-conscious but unreflective, the speaker highlights an increasing and intolerable provincialism that (for me) came to define the Catskill Jews. There were other problems: the wretched excess and self-indulgence that one hotel owner's son deliriously termed a "celebration of abundance" (Brown, 189); the crass materialism that grew rampantly in proportion to wealth; the arrogance of arrival and ownership that superseded the humility of struggle and apprenticeship. Moreover, where in Sullivan and Ulster counties was there a "Jewish culture" worth preserving?

## UNCLE MILTIE AND THE JEWS

The answer is: the Jewish humor abundantly on display in hotel clubs and auditoriums was the major cultural contribution of the mountains to American life. The Catskills became the spawning ground of the few great—and the many mediocre—(primarily male) Jewish comics of the forties and fifties, whose harsh, rasping, aggressive, cutting comedy, "rooted," according to Vivian Gornick, "in outsiderness and the pains of assimilation," was nevertheless turned self-mockingly inward on everything Jewish, from retrograde old-country customs to invasive mothers to the very excesses of the Catskills themselves. Their humor had, in Gornick's stunning metaphor, the "paradoxical healing powers of a knife point pressed to an open wound" ("Face It" 10). And no Jewish comic expressed what elsewhere Gornick described as "rage, resentment, and hunger" ("Twice an Outsider" 29) better than Milton Berle, who could trace his roots back to the Catskills, and specifically to Grossinger's where his mother, Sandra Berlinger, as a guest in the early thirties, had without being asked "organized an amateur show, worked out the choreography, rehearsed dancers in the dining room between meals, and badgered guests to participate" (Kanfer 145). Whether Berle's *chutzpah,* his audacity and brazenness, derived directly from mama is debatable, but Sandra's son was the most brash and impudent of the Catskill comics, willing to do anything for a laugh, and, as Gilbert Seldes first observed, "apparently committed to the technique of contagion because he always laughed first—and loudest—himself" (141).

The one-liners, the physical comedy, the sight gags, the non sequiturs, the nuttiness for no apparent reason, the incredibly fast-talking and slippery characters—Berle invented none of these; in fact, he never wrote his own material, and often bragged about his lack of originality and thus his thievery of others' material. What distinguished Berle from his predecessors was his loud voice, his big leer, his bared teeth, his broad gestures, and his willingness to pander to the crudest tastes of his audience. Berle wasn't just aggressive, he was unruly; he not only lacked reserve, he eschewed decorum of any sort, which was especially shocking on fifties television. He thought nothing of interrupting the routines of his guests, as if he feared they might show him up or "get the better of him" (144). If this interfered with his audiences' appreciation or enjoyment of their performance, Berle didn't seem to mind at all. As Seldes noted, "Instead of putting on the women's hats after dinner, he put on lace panties in public, and his whole career seemed a huge practical joke" (143). But not to everyone: my grandmother, for example, despised Berle, and called him, at least once in my hearing, "a shonda fur de goyim," someone who brought shame to the Jews in front of the gentiles, the worst of sins for an aspiring but tentative people. Like Vivian Gornick's mother, my own thought Berle was ugly, "coarse and vulgar," and turned her eyes away whenever he appeared on the screen. Dressed, as Kanfer says, in "outrageous drag complete with girdle and lipstick, firing dozens of one-liners at the audience," and then, breathless and sweaty, "baying" for their approval, Berle didn't just repulse my mother, he horrified her (224). How could he abandon all vestiges of civility, she wanted to know. Gornick's mother was also repelled by the "wildness of his humor and the no-holds-barred atmosphere that it generated"; Berle was "fast and furious, frightening in the speed of his cunning and his rage." For Mrs. Gornick, says her daughter, "this was Jewish self-hatred at its most vicious" ("Twice an Outsider" 30).

Offstage as well as on, Berle was unadulterated ego, taking credit, for example, for just about every innovation that made the Texaco Star Theatre such a hit TV show in the early fifties, even claiming to have "come up with" the idea for (and the title of) the show's famous theme song, "We Are the Men of Texaco" (Du Brow 30). "I produced the show, I directed it, and I appeared in it," Berle told his interviewer in 1985, and "there are quite a few firsts that I'd like to take credit for," which included developing the "isolated camera" (32). By his own admission he was aggressively egomaniacal, demanding greater and greater attention; in fact, Larry Gelbart claims, "*Berle* was the script; . . . whatever character he played, whatever the situation, he was always Milton Berle, the epitome of the brash, fast-talking, hip, flip urban wiseguy" (7). Interestingly, while Allen's Danny Rose failed as a Berle-type stand-up comic, which may be one reason for his professed admiration of Uncle Miltie, he couldn't be more opposite as a theatrical manager: as much as Berle appropriated everything and everyone around him for his comic skits, Danny sacrifices himself for his acts; he is a true agent for others. To the extent that Berle flaunted

his personality, Danny nurtures others, trying his best to raise them in stature and esteem. Berle soared to the top of the entertainment world on the strength of his self-projection; Danny hits financial bottom through the generosity of his self-abnegation.

Although Don Weber remembers his aunts liking Berle (his Aunt Tiny says that "we just knew that he was one of us" [135]), perhaps, generally speaking, the response to him breaks along gender lines; my father and my own Uncle Miltie loved his performances, roared with laughter at his crude antics and *tummler*-style gestures, and while both knew Yiddish but rarely spoke it, they seemed to derive great pleasure from Berle's occasional use of Yiddish words and phrasings, what Albert Goldman calls the "sly insertion of Jewishness in his skits" (84; a *tummler* is a noisy, lively entertainer, the proverbial "life of the party," often the social director of a Catskills resort). (When they took me to see Berle one summer—a memorable experience of my adolescence—both my mother and my Aunt Harriet refused to go with us.) According to Kanfer, the early Catskill comedians were "articulating a fluent Yiddish," though it was more a "Yiddish of the body and the idea, not the word" (224). And Weber is undoubtedly right when he claims that Berle's "particular comic style touched spaces of (repressed) Jewish memory in his audience; indeed, the knowing, insider laugh is itself the expressive sign of release, through recognition" (136). Gornick herself insists that she could see in Berle's performances "the idiom of [her] life coming back at [her], shaped and enlarged by a line of humorous intelligence as compelling as a poem in the sustained nature of its thesis and context. . . . When that famous chord of recognition strikes it is healing—illuminating and healing" ("Twice an Outsider" 30).

But I believe that for men like my father and my uncles—and for the countless Jewish fathers and uncles of their generation—Berle provided something more than "recognition." Whether the *goyim,* the non-Jews, were present (Berle on television) or not (Berle in the Catskills), Uncle Miltie created the space—sanctioned and safe—for liberation, provided the secret pleasure of "acting out" in front of the gentiles without any consequences. Albert Goldman beautifully articulated this dynamic when he wrote that "Jewish humor in mid-twentieth-century America . . . was not a gentle, ironic, Sholum Aleichem folksiness. . . . It was the plaint of a people who were highly successful in countless ways, yet who still felt inferior, tainted, outcast." To be sure, this "potent, explosive" humor released a "cathartic laughter" (83, 84), but beyond the self-directed anger and the self-mockery, and in spite of its *apparent* self-hatred, Berle's comedy allowed a generation of (perhaps mostly male) Jews to say, silently and in code, "up yours" to a society and a culture they were ambivalently entering, desiring its rewards yet fearing its rejection, suspicious of its mores while loathing its power of humiliation. Within the space of his performances, Berle licensed anarchy, attacking, through his wildness, his boorishness and his *in*civility, the forces of repression and control that my father and others publicly obeyed, because not to meant exclusion from America's rewards—the fruits of the golden *medine,* the promised land they had been raised to seek and acquire. In other words, if only for a brief moment, Berle authorized their private revolt against being "good Jewish boys." Though Allen fiercely eschewed Berle's outrageous clowning, his *shtick,* developing a far more psychologically oriented and self-analytical brand of humor, nevertheless this is the Berle to whom he pays homage in **Broadway Danny Rose.** Still, if Allen (and Danny) hated working the Catskills, and if, as I have asserted, they are so culturally forgettable (except as a site for the development of Jewish humor), and if Berle's primal, often frantic comedy is so utterly different in tone and style from Allen's more sophisticated manner, what are both doing in his most sweet and gentle film?

## DANNY ROSE AND HIS ACTS

The answer is: Berle represents the unregenerate Catskills, the raw, unsophisticated, self-enclosed community of my own later memory that drove me as far away from Jewish solidarity as I could get. **Broadway Danny Rose** redeems that community (at least for me) by finding within it the spiritual component that all the nostalgia in the world could not recover. The men and women of my youth who populated those bungalow colonies and resorts were united, not only by a common background and heritage, but also by a shared aspiration to make America work for them, to possess its material splendor. The vacation world they created embodied the central paradox of their lives: at the same time that they adapted and adopted gentile mores, they huddled together to protect themselves from gentile influence and judgment. The time was filled with both a carefree joy and a burdensome obligation—joyous because within their familiar enclave they were free to be their unpolished but unguarded selves, burdensome because of the inescapable recognition that beyond its boundaries lay an alien terrain that had to be mapped and, if not quite conquered, then at least appropriated. What the *landslayt* (the landsmen, fellow townsmen or countrymen) of this generation seemed to share above all else was an abiding belief that they could succeed in negotiating the passage from one to the other, and, mutually caring and supportive, they sustained their faith and optimism through the inevitable disappointments, rebuffs, sorrows, and losses that marked Jewish life in the diaspora. Although Allen doesn't directly examine this experience, **Broadway Danny Rose** conveys the sense of what it meant to belong to a community guided by such a faith.

The saintly Danny Rose, whose codes of loyalty and conduct (according to his Uncle Sidney, "acceptance, forgiveness, and love") have been transmitted to him from beloved relatives and spiritual advisers, watches over his "stable" of sweetly pathetic acts, Jack Kroll wrote in *Newsweek,* "like St. Francis over the animals" (Brode 227). Indeed, like Saint Francis, Danny does his utmost to shield the weak and the lame from the world's cruelties, here envisioned as the harsh, cutthroat business of New York entertainment, as brutal, in its way, as the cold and indifferent universe of Hollywood, characterized by Allen in **Annie Hall** not as a "dog-eat-dog" world, but as a place "where dog doesn't return other dog's phone calls." (Which makes Richard Blake's description of Danny as "no longer the perpetual underdog," but rather "the guardian angel of underdogs" so apt [Brode 230].) But Danny is a Jewish saint, and his Jewishness—outwardly signaled by his hand gestures, his use of Yiddish expressions and rhythms, his evocation of family ties, and (not least) by the *chai,* the Hebrew letter signaling good luck that he wears around his neck—provides the structure for his moral philosophy, the foundation of which is his abiding belief in the value of guilt.

By guilt Danny does not mean feelings of inadequacy or unworthiness or even sorrow resulting from one's failings, and he certainly does not mean the feeling of disappointment engendered by a loved one whose expectations and/or needs one has failed to meet and/or satisfy. What Danny has in mind is something related to "conscience," the internalization of right and wrong, especially where behavior toward other people is concerned. "It's important to feel guilty," Danny tells Mia Farrow's Tina, "otherwise you're capable of terrible things." Allen doesn't get the theology quite right (and Danny will also joke that "I feel guilty all the time, and I never did anything"), but he's after a moral value which Tina rejects without fully understanding it, but one which she will come to embrace eventually. For Danny, and for his Jewish forebears, it involves the respect and acknowledgment that we owe each other—as well as the responsibility we all bear to each other—by virtue of our shared humanity. Which is why when Danny learns that the mob goons have beaten up Barney Dunn, the ventriloquist whose name he offered up as Tina's lover to avoid being mauled himself (thinking that Barney was working out of town), he is both shocked by the cruel deed and instantly aware of his culpability. Chagrined and remorseful, Danny rushes to Barney's hospital bed to soothe and comfort him, insisting as well on paying all the medical bills, even though he can ill afford the expense.

Whenever Danny's acts become successful they leave him, forgetting what they owe to his devotion. Even Lou Canova, to whom Danny was "everything—his manager, his friend, his father-confessor"—betrays his faith. "I find them, I discover them, I breathe life into them, and then they go," Danny tells Phil Weinstein; and, moreover, they have no guilt about it. The father-creator, abandoned by his offspring-creations, suffers their rejection. In fact, when Danny tells Tina that while "it's important to have some laughs, but you've got to suffer a little too, otherwise you miss the whole point of life," she also rejects him, offering instead her own bankrupt credo, "It's over quick, so have a good time." Espousing a hedonistic, self-centered philosophy, embodied in such phrases as "You gotta do what you gotta do," or "Do it to the other guy first, 'cause if you don't, he'll do it to you," or "You see what you want, you go for it; don't pay any attention to anybody else," Tina perfectly articulates a contemporary attitude that Danny finds appalling: "That sounds like the screenplay of *Murder Incorporated*," he tells her, which is also an allusion to her Mafia connections, the community from which she will have to be weaned. "You don't get any medals for being a boy scout," Tina says derisively, a point of view in stark contrast with Danny's belief in duty and commitment to those who depend on him. As Allen sees it, there is redemption in this belief.

In a famous monograph called *The Lonely Man of Faith*, Rabbi Joseph Soloveitchik had a vision of a "faith community," drawn together, in defeat and through sacrifice, and with humility, toward the possibility of a redemptive life (which he did not equate with a humanly digni-fied life). In contrast to dignity, attained through man's control over his environment, what Soloveitchik called "cathartic redemptiveness" could only be achieved through man's control over himself (35). To participate, then, in a genuine community, defined foremost by com-munion—that is, by compassion, caring, and com-municating—man must make a "sacrificial gesture." (Communicating itself may be considered a redemptive sacrificial gesture.) Thus, companionship within this community cannot be attained through conquest, but through mutual "surrender and retreat." "In crisis and distress," says Soloveitchik, "there was planted the seed of a new type of community—the faith community" (39).

"Dignity is acquired by man whenever he triumphs over nature. Man finds redemption whenever he is overpowered by the Creator of nature. Dignity is discovered at the summit of success; redemption in the depth of crisis and failure" (36). The medium of attain-ing full redemption, according to Soloveitchik, is defeat. Clearly, by the end of *Broadway Danny Rose* the world has overwhelmed Danny: he's broke, he's lost his best act, he's without prospects. While Lou, now under the powerful Sid Bacharach's management, has gone on to success, Danny has suffered defeat, and it appears as if Tina was right in her assessment of him as a "loser." But as he says in his own defense, he's not. His more successful acts may leave him, but that's because they

are self-aggrandizing, too selfish to appreciate the car-ing and nurturing—the "personal" management—he of-fers them. They live in and for the moment, seeking positions of advantage and power, but Danny, because he feels responsibility to and connection with other hu-man beings, lives in history and tradition. By accepting the past as a source of wisdom to which he is indebted, and by acknowledging the future as a reality that he is obliged to create, and by sharing and experiencing the "travail and suffering" of others, Danny participates in the covenantal community. ("The individual member of the covenantal faith community," writes Soloveitchik, "feels rooted in the past and related to the future" [72]). Thus, unlike Tina after she encourages Lou to cast him aside, and in spite of all his worry and aggravation, his *tsuris*, Danny is neither alone nor, ultimately, lonely. All of his firmly held codes have brought him to this juncture in his life—he may not get to know God (the reward Soloveitchik envisions), but he does achieve an honor bestowed only on the chosen: the Carnegie Deli names a sandwich for him, the "Danny Rose Special" ("probably a bagel and cream cheese with marinara sauce," jokes one of the comedians), a compliment they have also paid to Woody Allen (a huge sandwich of corned beef piled on top of pastrami [Baxter 317]).

At the film's conclusion, Danny gathers his offspring together for a ritual Thanksgiving celebration (a secular feast that Allen has used to mark significant and meaningful moments in other films, most memorably *Hannah and Her Sisters*). Of course, Allen being Allen, he also makes fun of the occasion by having Danny serve frozen turkey dinners. Nevertheless, his purpose is a serious one: to reaffirm the familial values Danny has espoused, especially in his time of trial. It is important that Tina returns to ask for forgiveness at just this moment; she has repented, and is now ready to join the community. While Danny first rejects her, he then performs the duty expected of a man of faith (a duty also borne by the father of his family) by retrieving her and bringing her into the fold, finally modifying her fierce individualism with his spirit of unity.

For Soloveitchik, the way to maintain connection to a spiritual community is through memory. Throughout the film, Danny remembers the ethical principles which ought to guide his life, principles that he was taught by his relatives, by his teachers, even his rabbi. While at times Allen presents this idea through Danny's humor-ous riffs on family (like his digressive and largely ir-relevant story about his Uncle Meyer who sold apples), and while he occasionally turns Danny into a parodic character through his exaggerated hand and facial gestures, the point is nevertheless clear: those characters who have forgotten or who have never learned, or worse, who know but reject the lessons from the past, perpetuate the film's greatest sin; like Lou, who leaves Danny because he's "gotta do what's right for [his] career," and like Tina, who encourages and abets his apostasy (before she is redeemed), they think only of themselves. Bound to no one, they float free of meaningful relationships; anchored by no greater aspiration than self-gratification, they lead spiritually debased lives. But Danny and his acts are a community of commitment, not a group of isolated individuals who perform separate tasks in the world; thus, a spiritually enriching life is possible here, if not a worldly successful one.

Retrospectively, this is Allen's sense of the Catskills as, despite all of its grossness and insularity, a "faith community." For Soloveitchik, a learned, pious man, faith means—indeed, necessitates—a fundamental and absolute belief in God. Danny's acts of spiritual solidarity are, on the other hand, appropriately grounded in secular Jewish values, one component (as I certainly remember it) of the dual orientation of the American Jews of my parents' generation. (The other, equally strong, was their trust in America as a plural society, open and welcoming.) "In film after film," says Kathryn Bernheimer, "Allen has asserted his conviction that a secular Jew is still very much a Jew," but, significantly, **Broadway Danny Rose** may be his boldest declaration of the authenticity of secular Jewish identity (137). Unlike his other alter egos, Alvy Singer in **Annie Hall** (1977), Isaac Davis in **Manhattan** (1979), Sandy Bates in **Stardust Memories** (1980), and Cliff Stern in **Crimes and Misdemeanors** (1989), Danny Rose has no ambivalence about being a Jew. Yet ironically, at the time of the film's appearance, and well after the decline of the Borscht Belt, the Catskills were being transformed into a different sort of faith community, as Orthodox Hasidic Jews were resettling and refurbishing the old Catskill colonies and resorts, turning them into centers, camps, and retreats for religious education and study (Brown 227-28). Far less worldly and even more self-contained, these new pioneer Jews may indeed be "recycling the Catskills" (as Brown nicely puts it [229]), but they will never replace the originals, who managed, as best they could, to keep faith with their ancestors as they embarked upon that strenuous but exhilarating voyage into America, a journey facilitated and mediated by the great Catskill comedians.

## Works Cited

Berle, Milton. *Milton Berle's Private Joke File: Over 10,000 of His Best Gags, Anecdotes, and One-liners.* New York: Crown, 1989.

Baxter, John. *Woody Allen: A Biography.* 1998; New York: Carroll & Graf, 1999.

Bernheimer, Kathryn. *The 50 Greatest Jewish Movies: A Critic's Ranking of the Very Best.* New York: Birch Lane/Carol Publishing Group, 1998.

Bjorkman, Stig, ed. *Woody Allen on Woody Allen. In Conversation with Stig Bjorkman.* New York: Grove, 1995.

Brode, Douglas. *The Films of Woody Allen.* Rev. ed., 1991. New York: Citadel/Carol Publishing Group, 1992.

Brown, Phil. *Catskill Culture: A Mountain Rat's Memories of the Great Jewish Resort Area.* Philadelphia: Temple UP, 1998.

Du Brow, Rick. "An Interview with Milton Berle." *Milton Berle: Mr. Television.* New York: Museum of Broadcasting, 1985. 27-35.

Gelbart, Larry. "An Introduction." *Milton Berle: Mr. Television.* 4-7.

Goldman, Albert. "Laughtermakers." *Jewish Wry: Essays on Jewish Humor.* Ed. Sarah Blacher Cohen. Bloomington: Indiana UP, 1987. 80-88.

Gornick, Vivian. "Face It, Woody Allen, You're Not a Schlep Anymore." *Village Voice* 5 Jan. 1976: 9-11.

———. "Twice an Outsider: On Being Jewish and a Woman." *Tikkun* Mar./Apr. 1989: 29-31, 123-25.

Kanfer, Stefan. *A Summer World: The Attempt to Build a Jewish Eden in the Catskills, from the Days of the Ghetto to the Rise and Decline of the Borscht Belt.* New York: Farrar, 1989.

Seldes, Gilbert. "The Good-Bad Berle." *The Public Arts.* New York: Simon and Schuster, 1956. 141-46.

Soloveitchik, Joseph. *The Lonely Man of Faith.* 1965; New York: Doubleday, 1992.

Weber, Donald. "Taking Jewish American Popular Culture Seriously: The Yinglish Worlds of Gertrude Berg, Milton Berle, and Mickey Katz." *Jewish Social Studies* 5 (Fall 1998/Winter 1999): 124-53.

## Stephen Hunter (review date 19 September 2003)

SOURCE: Hunter, Stephen. "There's Not Much 'Else' Like the Real Woody." *Washington Post* (19 September 2003): C1.

[*In the following review of* Anything Else, *Hunter suggests that the character of Dobel could be merely a figment of the protagonist's imagination.*]

**Anything Else** poses a philosophical question: How many Woody Allens can dance on the head of a pin?

It answers: Two.

Incorrecto-mundo!

Wrongarooni!

Does Not Compute!

In actual fact, a head of a pin or a single movie may sustain only one Woody Allen. *Anything Else* attempts to accommodate two—Allen himself, plus a thin parody of young-Allen, played by *American Pie* alum Jason Biggs—and it doesn't quite work. The movie cannot contain multitudes. One Woody Allen is fabulous, and Allen is fabulous in the movie, playing an older, wiser but crazier version of himself. Is there anybody who doesn't love Woody Allen, other than exes of one sort or other? Off with their heads!

But two Woody Allens, two kvetching, whining, neurotic incompetents bungling their lives, being taken advantage of, furiously resenting the universe, which will not notice them until it decides to kill them . . . that's one too many Woody Allens.

Another way of saying the same thing: Biggs, as Jerry Falk, comedy-writer wannabe prowling the environs of New York showbiz while trying to sort out a hopelessly mangled romantic life, isn't particularly interesting or compelling. And he's not very funny at all.

Falk is a kind of eternal victim; his pathology is that he allows his intimates to take control of his life and, crippled by self-doubt, he is unable to assert himself or defend his best interests. Thus he is professionally represented by incompetent agent Danny DeVito (who may be a third Woody Allen, because he's close to Allen's *Broadway Danny Rose*). Falk is living with and in love with A Girl From Hell, who laughingly abuses him every step of the way yet worms her smarmy way back into bed (though never back into his arms; the relationship is now without sex). She also moves her semi-alcoholic mother into his office, and the mother is soon renting a piano and rehearsing her nightclub act in the living room and dating a dope dealer. Falk's psychiatrist never responds to him, possibly because he finds him so hopeless. In the miasma of his life, only one person doesn't exploit him: the older writer David Dobel, who is constantly expounding and giving Falk advice that he doesn't want to hear and, if he hears, cannot act upon.

As Dobel, Allen is so good and so funny that you wish the movie were about him. Every time it focuses on the hapless, pathetic and uninteresting Biggs, the air just goes out of it. Possibly Allen has been oversensitive to complaints that in his sixties, he was far too old to get the girl (and watching him kiss Tea Leoni in *Hollywood Ending* was revolting), but he's totally removed himself from the romantic tensions of the story, and it debilitates the movie.

He also makes mistakes as director-writer that he doesn't make as star. For one thing, if we are to be interested in young Jerry Falk, Allen has to establish him as uniquely talented, a Woody Allen in training, with a unique vision and boundless possibilities. He never does. Falk just seems like an ill-adjusted poseur with vague plans of "being a writer" who is writing what appears to be the most amateurish first novel in history. We need to see him do something to feel him worthy of our empathy. We also have to know how he can afford an apartment that nice in Manhattan.

Worse, in the opening half-hour, we see him dump one woman (cute Kadee Strickland) for the aforementioned mythic Girl From Hell (Christina Ricci), after a series of unconvincing, annoying lies that alienate us even further. So who in the end cares whether Falk follows the wiser Dobel's advice and extricates himself from the mess he's invented for himself? I certainly don't.

One can feel the black comic impulses (and the misogyny) in Allen's portrayal of Falk's relationship with GFH, also known as Amanda. The relationship makes the one between Oed and his ma look healthy: Amanda is manipulative, clever, treacherous, dismissive, beautiful, dishonest, and with Ricci's big forehead and luminous eyes, she seems from another planet. Unfortunately she and Biggs have almost no chemistry, and it seems a waste of this actress's powerful gift for projecting magnum levels of femme fatale energy that it's used on this dim whelp.

There's also some odd irony at play in Allen's portrayal of David Dobel that is worthy of mention. That is, decoded, his message to a younger generation: Don't be Woody Allen. He seems to be addressing at least three of my four friends, who have made such an icon of Allen that they imitate him down to the last unfetching dither and stammer and the weird little squeaks that tweak his voice when he becomes anxious, which is all the time. In other words, Dobel keeps trying to get Falk out of the kind of behavior patterns that he learned from seeing too many Woody Allen movies. He's actually more like John Wayne than he is Woody Allen in his program: Buy a gun. Be self-reliant. Don't take guff. Stand up for yourself. Don't let people use you. Get revenge. Dump all losers.

It's also possible that Dobel is meant to be a figment of Falk's imagination, for he has odd ways of coming and going. We never see his "real" life; he's only there when Falk is there. Plus, he drives a car, a red sports car. Everybody knows Allen wouldn't be caught dead in a red sports car; that seems a signifier of fantasy. The mechanism here may be taken as similar to the one at the heart of *Fight Club,* in which a repressed young man befriends a much tougher fellow who does the things he could never do; then he learns, at movie end, that the friend is himself. Whatever, Dobel represents the part of the young man's mind that still adores the old forms of masculinity, before feminism and PC made them difficult to express in public. He also stands for a certain strain of Jewishness favored by Bugsy Siegel, Barney Ross and the commandos of Israel: Strike first, strike hard, and win.

These may be ideals that Allen is uncomfortable espousing in any form except as a mad old man in a possibly fantasical movie, but he's so convincing that you wonder whether he hasn't at last found a way to express something he's never expressed before.

## Jeffrey Rubin-Dorsky (essay date fall 2003)

SOURCE: Rubin-Dorsky, Jeffrey. "Woody Allen after the Fall: Literary Gold from Amoral Alchemy." *Shofar: An Interdisciplinary Journal of Jewish Studies* 22, no. 1 (fall 2003): 5-28.

[*In the following essay, Rubin-Dorsky creates parallels between Allen's divorce from actress Mia Farrow and the portrayal of the dilemmas facing the artists in* Husbands and Wives, Bullets over Broadway, *and* Deconstructing Harry.]

Over the past ten years, Woody Allen has responded to exigency and circumstance—some, of course, of his own making—by replenishing and renewing his fundamental commitment to his art. Because he has refused to remain static or complacent in the face of popular recognition and critical acclaim, he has taken great risks in his desire to expand his talents and enlarge his vision.[1] Radical changes in his private life have served as a trigger for his growth as a director. In an earlier period, a split with Diane Keaton marked the end of his physical comedy (his "funny movies" with caricatured Jews) and generated the development, beginning with *Annie Hall* (1977), of personae who are sincere if unsuccessful, though still lovable, seekers after romance and meaning, who muddle through moral conundrums while striving to make the right choices. The break with Mia Farrow engendered a search for a new artistic direction (and a new persona), signaled by the unsettling film *Husbands and Wives* (1992) and followed by two extraordinary views on the moral dilemmas and personal sacrifices of and within a life in art, *Bullets over Broadway* (1994) and *Deconstructing Harry* (1997).

The affair with (and subsequent marriage to) Soon-Yi Farrow Previn distanced Allen from his admirers, since he was both negating their veneration and rejecting their outrage, instead challenging them to relinquish expectations of consistency and uniformity. That is, the scandal finally forced his audience to separate the artist from the man, while at the same time for Allen it obliterated an outworn self-image. The best of his recent work (i.e., the three films studied in this essay, *Hus-*

*bands and Wives, Bullets over Broadway,* and *Deconstructing Harry*) demonstrates a deeply reflective, and self-reflexive, mood and mode as the director meditates on the modernist issues of the autonomy of the artist and the salvation of art, simultaneously transforming the image of his lead actor from a caring, concerned individual into a rapacious, unresponsive one. Indeed, what may be hardest of all for his audience to accept about these three films is that they embrace a vision of the artist/writer as a carnivorous creator of beauty and form, completely indifferent to offending the moral sensitivities or violating the personal sensibilities of family, friends, and lovers, whose lives nurture, sustain, and, literally in *Deconstructing Harry,* feed his talent.

The danger for Allen at this juncture in his career is that as he narrows his thematic focus and—if such a thing were possible—further shrinks his subject range, he will lose even the loyalty of those fans who have always appreciated the deeply personal nature of his work. Allen concedes that his base has already diminished, though he refuses to believe that the controversy surrounding his courtship of Soon-Yi is responsible, claiming instead that "inaccessible" and "foreign feeling" pictures such as *Interiors* (1978) and *Stardust Memories* (1980) had already driven audiences away. All the affair did "for these people," Allen told an interviewer upon the release of *Sweet and Lowdown* (1999), was to confirm "everything they had been thinking about my work."[2] As he configures the story, he was the one who "betrayed the [implicit] contract" with moviegoers who enjoyed his early, "funny" films. He entertained them, he made them laugh, and then he abandoned them by switching styles. In response, they began to complain: "This guy doesn't like God. He doesn't like the country. He doesn't like relationships. He's cynical and thinks life is difficult." In other words, the "audience didn't leave me; I left them."

Unfortunately, by donning this defensive posture, Allen underestimates his audience's tolerance for the narrative innovation, and their appreciation of the social realism, of films like *Annie Hall* and *Manhattan* (1979), which were popular as well as critical successes. Moreover, his biggest box-office hit, *Hannah and Her Sisters* (1986), appeared well after (according to the above scenario) sizeable numbers of his fans "drifted" from him. In fact, the opposite is true, and sadly so: the films from the mid-nineties confirm everything people were thinking about him after the affair. Since Allen refuses (as he put it) "to curry favor" with these former fans, the problem is not that producers have gone running, for thanks to profitable European distribution his movies have managed to break even (so far at least). Rather, the real threat is to Allen's individuality and integrity as a writer/director, and, in spite of his claim, he may no longer be able to craft complex and disturbing films for fear of no one showing up to watch them. It appears that even the most notoriously disciplined of isolationists cannot continue to create masterworks that disappear into the void.

## I.

What is genuinely disturbing about **Husbands and Wives** is the disappearance of the angst-ridden Woody Allen persona; while he may in the past have been nothing more than a marvelously successful invention, even that fiction could no longer be sustained. The emotional gap Allen the artist created between himself and his public is deliberately reflected in the withdrawal of the Woody figure. One of the hallmarks of Allen's films in which he appears, from **Annie Hall** through **Crimes and Misdemeanors** (1989), is his role as moral center, the person on whom the audience could rely, in the midst of uncertainty and confusion, to articulate the ethical issues and problems, if not actually solve them.[3] But in **Husbands and Wives** his character, Gabe Roth, is stuck in malaise just like everyone else, providing no clue or clarity, with barely an observation worth remembering. Remote and unembraceable, he is neither the anxious quester after certainty nor the besieged defender of veracity. Amidst the twisted and unsatisfied lives, his is as unfulfilled as any, perhaps even more so, since he winds up alone, yet unaccountably thinking that he "really blew it" with his wife, Judy, a relationship marked by unexamined resentment, full of deceit and dishonesty, one that we understand to have died before the film began. (We know, too, from her first husband's interviews, that she can be manipulative and duplicitous; hence the name Judy, suggesting Judas the betrayer.) In scenes with Farrow's Judy and elsewhere, Gabe's responses have no authenticity to them. We can't fathom Gabe Roth: for the first time in an Allen film, his character is self-absorbed (exactly, by the way, what New York State Supreme Court Justice Wilk said of Allen as father in his child custody battle with Farrow[4]) to the point of vanishing, like an imploding star. He is truly unavailable to us.

In his *New Yorker* review of **Husbands and Wives,** Terrence Rafferty called Gabe the "man without illusions," his solitude at the end a "token of his newfound honesty and philosophical rigor," and claimed that Allen confers on his protagonist "a sort of alienated-hero stature."[5] Nothing could be further from the truth—or rather the truthful experience of this film. Allen's characters have always been flawed, which has been part of their charm, but none quite like Gabe, who is utterly uncharismatic. Without self-knowledge, indulging in avoidance and denial, or perhaps just attempting to hide his complaints and longings, he is unable or unwilling to say what he feels. Like one of the sperm in the novel he has written, Gabe is minuscule and unformed, embryonic and voiceless. His acts seem motivated not by any guiding principle or belief—and surely by nothing like Isaac

Davis's plea in **Manhattan** for personal integrity—but rather by a spontaneous intuition for what the moment demands.

His most important sequence in the film, his pursuit of his student Rain, climaxing in a romantic kiss, and then his refusal to follow through with the affair, gives rise to no serious reflection, yields no larger meaning about either morality or maturity, or even motivation. When asked by the interviewer (or the therapist, or the director of the film-within-the-film) why he is drawn to Rain, he offers a superficial response that a vague something within him is unfulfilled in his marriage. Finally, all Gabe can mutter is a version of Allen's infamous remark about the obstinacy of eros (when asked about his relationship to Mia Farrow's adopted daughter Soon-Yi): "My heart does not know from logic."[6] His most oft-repeated phrase in the film (which other characters also mouth) echoes the evasions of his "60 Minutes" interview (where he could not explain why he kept "embarrassing pictures" of Soon-Yi on his mantel, subsequently found by Farrow): "I don't know; I don't know."[7] This may be Rafferty's idea of "lofty indifference," but it sounds to me like willful ignorance. Or determined withdrawal. (Where is the integrity, either personal or philosophical, in "I don't know"?) At best, it's the response of a puzzled man desperately in need of intensive psychotherapy.

All the characters' lives, including Gabe's, are marked by failures of self-knowledge and self-analysis. By listening carefully to their conversations you can hear the discordances underneath the smooth verbal surfaces, and when you juxtapose earlier statements with later ones, you realize how, even when they believe they are in agreement, they contradict one another—and themselves. Sally, for example, who is the most intellectual spouse in the two couples, after splitting up with Jack, tells Judy that she likes being single, especially because the "resentments of the marriage are gone." After a Mahler concert with Michael (he's ecstatic; she's bored), she says again, "I love being single," yet only minutes later, after seething resentment over Jack's infidelity, admits, without the slightest bit of self-awareness, that she's "one of those people who needs to be married." The truth, of course, is that she craves the security, and this becomes fully evident when she confesses to Jack upon their reuniting, again without quite realizing what she's saying, that "I was scared enough sleeping alone." In their final interview, Sally and Jack, supposedly having "learn[ed] to deal with problems," speak over and around their (sexual) difficulties, betray their true feelings through facial expressions, and thus convince no one but themselves that "we're doing fine."

While you might expect Gabe (as Rafferty obviously does) to transcend the blindness and insincerity that befall others, Allen makes him into one of the worst offenders. In fact, his responses match Judy's for emotional evasiveness. He justifies his refusal to have children on the most tenuous (actually banal) of "philosophical" grounds, arguing that "it's cruel to bring life into this terrible world." When Judy complains that they make love "less and less," Gabe blames it on their "schedules," which are "not exactly conducive." (Judy's response—"that's just bullshit"—is the right one.) He refuses to acknowledge that he's attracted to other women and denies that he finds his "talented" students alluring, even though Rain has already become an object of his desire. In the one passionate moment he shares with Judy, he tells her that he wants to have sex without her diaphragm because he's "resisted having a child too strenuously," but as they begin arguing over the implications of his decision, he shifts ground dramatically. "This is crazy," he says angrily. "I'm begging you to have a baby I don't even want."

Finally, in the midst of their devastating break-up, Gabe declares that he hates change because "change equals death." (People change, and "that's why relationships go sour.") Again, Judy has it exactly right when she tells him, "That's just a bullshit line . . . Change is what life is made of. If you don't change you don't grow." Clearly, Allen does not intend Gabe to be a fuzzy, sympathetic, and knowing character, and if you contrast Tracy's gently chiding the distrustful Isaac (at the end of *Manhattan*) that he has to "have a little faith in people" with Rain's critique of Gabe's "shallow" and "retrograde" attitudes toward women, you see how wide the gap is between protagonists, and thus how far the director has receded from his audience.

*Husbands and Wives* intends, therefore, to decenter its viewers. Instead of being aligned with the Allen persona, pondering the universe of the film from his point of view, we are pushed to its periphery, stranded in disconnection. The book-lined studies and work spaces we see throughout Gabe's apartment signal not a safe world, but an enclosed one; there is no opening through which we can enter. The unsteadiness of the hand-held camera (criticized unfairly by reviewers as little more than an empty imitation of *cinema verité* technique), the nervous, edgy, unsettled quality it brings to the picture, not only mirrors the ragged lives of its characters, but also unmoors the viewer, deliberately so; and the director refuses to stabilize the turbulence. The jump-cutting that frequently interrupts the actors' testimony (shot in close-ups) eliminates the "repetitions and non-essential information," says Vincent Canby, but more significantly it precludes character introspection (the interviews provide only the *illusion* of self-analysis) and audience involvement.[8] And what little humor the film possesses (Canby and others mysteriously label it "uproarious" and "hilarious") is so deeply rooted in the blindness of the characters, who ironically, and pathetically, gloat in what they believe is their self-awareness,

that laughter seems more like an act of cruelty than a sharing of foibles. The one genuine self-mocking line in the film, uttered by the fifty-year-old Gabe just as he is about to embrace the twenty-one-year-old Rain in spite of danger signals—"Why do I hear fifty thousand dollars worth of psychotherapy dialing 911?"—stands out because of its singularity. There can be no self-mockery where there is no self-knowledge.

Canby wonders whether the form of *Husbands and Wives,* producing the sense that we are watching a narrative in which the characters are reticent participant-actors (a feeling intensified by the jerky, hand-held camera, giving the effect of an impromptu home movie that no one wants to be in), shows Allen to be working in a "post-modern mode," and the question is an important one. For all of its assault on the possibility of shared reality, on absolute truth—there are many realities here and no central truth—and for all of its undermining of belief in the stable and knowable self, the film as text shies away from regarding itself as the source of experience rather than its reflection. Though the film-within-the-film's camera may bully the actors and intrude into the characters' lives, it does not create those lives; reality, fragmented and in shards though it may be, is not, as it would be in an early Bergman film, an artifact of imagination. That is because, for Allen, social justice and righteous action in the world still matter, and qualities such as honesty, loyalty, and generosity still define personal success. They're just harder to find.

By the end of *Husbands and Wives* Allen had not abandoned the search for a meaningful life in the world, had not given up his faith in people's ability to grow in moral stature. Rather, what he articulates at the film's conclusion is a desire to be liberated from the contours of an old mask, one that had outlived its usefulness. Gabe's final, self-reflexive words ("Can I go? Is this over?"), signaling the story's end, indicate his reluctance to reveal more of himself while at the same time showing the filmmaker's spirit rebelling against the frame of the film, just as Allen the man attempted to escape (albeit somewhat clumsily in his affair with Soon-Yi) from the narrative of the twelve years of his life with Mia Farrow. A newer version of his persona was already taking shape in what would be yet another cinematic form, for as we can see from his films during that period, Allen has found what Philip Roth calls the "disguise of me" (see his novel *Operation Shylock* [1993], where the author is impersonated by a man purporting to be "Philip Roth") enormously energizing and, in spite of his pronouncements to the contrary, a means of exploring, and transcending the intractability of, selfhood.

*Husbands and Wives* brilliantly encodes artistic restlessness, and in this respect it most closely resembles another of Allen's troubling films (also greeted with some dismay), *Stardust Memories.* Critics and fans alike have linked *Husbands and Wives* to *Manhattan* because both portray an older man/younger woman liaison; supposedly Gabe's flirtation with Rain replays Isaac's romance with Tracy—and both reflect on Allen's courting of Soon-Yi (the latter obviously retrospectively)—but in truth the likeness is a shallow one, since the women are far from similar and the relationships serve quite different needs. *Stardust Memories,* on the other hand, with its grotesque view of Sandy Bates's audience, and its sarcastic, hostile portrait of fans unwilling to grant him artistic privilege or allow him to progress beyond his earlier, "funnier movies," offers a much deeper connection to *Husbands and Wives* since it, too, concerns a revision in Allen's screen persona. *Stardust Memories* closed off the first phase of Allen's film career, just as *Husbands and Wives* marks the end of the second.

Unlike Alvy Singer in *Annie Hall* or Isaac Davis in *Manhattan,* but very much like Gabe Roth the creative writer, Sandy Bates the filmmaker perversely keeps his audience at an emotional distance, showing little or no appreciation of the investment they have made in his work. Moreover, like Gabe, who is trying to finish an (autobiographical) novel that receives some harsh criticism in manuscript, Sandy has completed a new (autobiographical) movie that his producers despise and want to change without his permission. Issues of art and autonomy are thus foregrounded, issues that had always been linked for Allen the director, and ones that would, in fact, become the focus of the later films *Bullets over Broadway* and *Deconstructing Harry.* Both *Stardust Memories* and *Husbands and Wives* are meta-cinema—both embed references to the making of art (films and books), as well as containing a film-within-the-film, calling attention to themselves as aesthetic constructs—and insist on their creator's right to leave old modes behind, to shatter an audience's expectations for the sake of creative renewal, even when this process involves killing off a beloved persona.

Both *Stardust Memories* and *Husbands and Wives* are formally bold in the way that T. S. Eliot and Ezra Pound insist modern innovation occurs. That is, they "make it new," they revise and reinvent traditional techniques. In *Stardust Memories,* Allen incorporates Felliniesque hallucinations and memory passages (with pervasive cinematic allusions to 8½) to underscore Sandy's fragile psychological balance. In *Husbands and Wives,* he borrows documentary devices and the on-screen interview (as well as the aforementioned jump-cutting effect developed by Jean-Luc Godard) to illuminate Gabe's marital confusion and emotional unavailability. In both instances, Allen the director enlivens a film in which his own character remains cold and distant, a figure of perplexity rather than an icon of clarity.

After *Stardust Memories* Allen's films become bleaker, far more pessimistic that a romantic, hopeful vision could be sustained (except for *Hannah,* whose upbeat, fairy tale ending is false and unearned). In fact, nothing so much signals the last gasp of this outlook as the way in which, twelve years later (coinciding exactly with the twelve years of the Allen-Farrow non-marriage), *Husbands and Wives* reinvents two scenes from *Stardust Memories,* scenes meant to be comic and uplifting in the earlier film but which are melancholy and depressing in the later one. The first embodies and reflects the dichotomy of the Isobel/Judy and Dorrie/Rain characters—which in turn represents the psychic split in both Sandy and Gabe—between the domestic, stable and sane (and thus safe) but sexually uninspired light-haired sweethearts and the adventurous, tempestuous, and unpredictable (and thus dangerous) but passionately uninhibited dark-haired temptresses. (Though Gabe discovers over time that Judy, too, can be willful, difficult and unreasonable.) In *Stardust Memories,* Sandy projects this dilemma into a film where he plays a doctor intent upon creating the "perfect woman" by surgically implanting the brain of Doris, the sweet blonde with the great personality (but who turns him off sexually), into the body of Rita, the nasty brunette with the animal instincts (but who arouses his carnal desire). After the successful operation, in which he switches personalities, Rita (Dorrie's double) becomes a "warm, wonderful, charming, sexy, sweet, giving, mature woman," whereupon he falls in love with Doris (Isobel's substitute). The audience, watching the film at the Stardust retrospective of Sandy's oeuvre, laughs joyfully, underscoring not only the comic absurdity of the scene, but also Sandy's ability to transform his obsessions into pleasing self-mockery.

In the complementary scene in *Husbands and Wives,* Gabe bifurcates himself into two fictional characters, Pepkin and Knapp, the former a faithful husband and loving father whose domestic life is placid but dull, the latter a swinging bachelor and uncommitted lover whose playboy existence is tumultuous but empty. Ironically, writes Gabe, "Pepkin, from the calm of his fidelity, envied Knapp; Knapp, lonely beyond belief, envied Pepkin," and then, after a few sour observations in another story on the myths of "deepening romance" and "simultaneous orgasm" ("the only time Rifkin and his wife experienced a simultaneous orgasm was when the judge handed them their divorce"), concludes rather sadly that "in the end, the idea was not to expect too much out of life." Rain, who's been reading the novel (and thus serves as its audience), and who finds it generally "entertaining and imaginative," nevertheless criticizes its "ideas toward life." "Are our choices really between chronic dissatisfaction and suburban drudgery?," she asks skeptically. Whether Gabe has "trivialized" his view of relationships, as Rain charges, or deliberately distorted it to show "how hard it is to be married," as he claims, the fact is that their exchange is rather an unpleasant one: Rain, insisting that she's "competitive by nature," triumphantly smiles in the realization that she's "hit a nerve"; Gabe, wanting approval, angrily accuses her of "turning on" him. "I don't need a lecture on maturity or writing from a twenty-year-old twit," he says nastily. Unlike the earlier film, there is no comedy, and no laughter, and no joy.

The second set of parallel scenes involves the memories to which the Allen character fondly clings in the face of disappointment and loss—a version of Isaac Davis's list at the end of **Manhattan** of the few things that make life worth living. In one of the film-within-the-film sequences in **Stardust Memories,** Sandy, addressing the audience, says that when he was on his death-bed and "reaching for something to give [his] life meaning," he recalled a warm spring Sunday when he and Dorrie were together in his apartment, the sun shining through the tall windows, a Louis Armstrong recording of "Stardust" playing in the background. As he glances at Dorrie lying on the floor unselfconsciously reading the *New York Times,* then lifting her head and smiling up at him, he thinks to himself how beautiful she looks, how much he loves her—and he remembers that, in the peacefulness and perfection of the moment, he felt deliriously happy, "almost indestructible." That "simple little moment of contact," he says by way of commentary, "moved me in a very, very profound way." Even though the listeners react contradictorily—one man calls him a "cop out artist," another a "sentimental bore," though a woman says, "That was so beautiful"—the stillness of the setting, the sincerity in Sandy's voice, the sweetness of Dorrie's smile, all push us toward the possibility that such moments, and the memories they provide, are indeed "profound." If nothing else, they have an undeniable significance in the ethos of the film.

The replay in **Husbands and Wives** occurs near its climax, after a brutal argument between Gabe and Judy has left them both physically spent and emotionally separated. (Shot by jump-cutting from explosion to explosion, thus eliminating the pauses within the verbal combat, this scene is by far the most tense one in the film; neither Allen nor Farrow in any of their roles together had ever expressed such scorching anger and hostility.) In the aftermath of the battle, and the unraveling of their marriage, Gabe seeks a point of connection by reminding Judy of two luminous events from their past: first, one night when they both couldn't sleep, he found Bergman's *Wild Strawberries* on the cable station and they stayed up all night watching the movie (it was a "great moment for me," Gabe says); and second, on an "icy black" though very beautiful night, they were on Fifth Avenue headed downtown for a faculty dinner, when suddenly they turned around and instead walked into Central Park under a sky where every star was visible ("I'll never forget this," Gabe tells her). As he

reaches tenderly for her, he whispers, "you were so beautiful in that black dress," but Judy pushes him away, saying "Don't do that . . . it's over and we both know it." And then she utters the words that not only kill the mood, but also destroy one of the hallmark beliefs of Allen's persona, the sacred trust in the possibility that a perfect though evanescent human experience in the "real world" can be memorialized into a lastingly beautiful, transcendent image in the imagination—an image, moreover, replete with healing powers. "Those memories [are] just memories," she says, "they're just isolated moments. They don't tell the whole story." Although Judy speaks quietly, almost matter-of-factly, it is nevertheless the most painful utterance in the film, and Gabe is devastated.

## II.

**Husbands and Wives** also foreshadows the questioning spirit of **Bullets over Broadway,** where a much younger actor (John Cusack, substituting for Allen in a role the director might once have given himself) plays an inexperienced, idealistic playwright struggling with the ethics of Broadway, the purity of Art, and the morality of sexuality fidelity—all issues of paramount importance in both the real and imagined worlds of Woody Allen. Using a period piece and the added device of a play within the film (Jewishly titled *God of Our Fathers*) to camouflage, and psychologically distance himself from, the personal, Allen examines the problem of whether an "artist creates his own moral universe," words spoken in the film, interestingly enough, by an untrustworthy figure named Flender (sounds like philanderer, which he is). Yet this idea was championed by Allen himself during his crisis with Mia Farrow; and in **Bullets over Broadway** the true wordsmith is also a gangster and a murderer. A ruthless Nietzchean monster/hero, Cheech prizes direct, vital language above everything, and the contradictions of his character force us to ask such questions as, Who is an artist, and can you really, as Allen insisted, separate the artist from the man? How can a moral reprobate create significant art; how, in fact, can this unrepentant murderer be a good dramatist? What sacrifices does art demand, and what compromises, if any, must the artist make with his society? Moreover, in **Bullets over Broadway** Allen also ponders the problem of what happens when Art supersedes humanity, when in the modern world (the film is set in the 1920s, the era of Joyce and Hemingway) the all-knowing, all-seeing Artist becomes the repository of truth, replacing the (Hebrew) God of our Fathers.

The genuine artist loves language, and Cheech, whose name suggests "speech," and whose own New York gangster lingo is intense and forceful, points us toward the truths of art, primarily that the language of the theater—and by extension, that of all artistic endeavor, including film—cannot merely approximate the language of experience, but must actually *be* the language of experience. "You don't write the way people talk," Cheech tells David Shayne, the naive artist-*manqué*. (Shayne sounds like "sham," or "shame," or even *shonda*.) "People believe what's real." Untrained in the ways of craftsmanship—he is the product of the streets rather than a creative writing class—Cheech instead possesses natural talent and perfect instincts, which David recognizes as a huge gift. Moreover, and equally as important, he will do anything, even commit murder, to protect the integrity of his words. Midway through the film Cheech tells his girlfriend to "shut up" and "don't interrupt me" (he won't have the flow of his sentences disrupted), and this act of verbal violence foreshadows the physically brutal one at the end when he bumps off Olive because, as he says, "she's killing my words." (He was ordered by the Mafia boss to take care of his girl and, indeed, he does "take care of" her.) Having commandeered the script, Cheech can't "turn a blind eye" to anyone who's less than perfect in his/her role; thus, when David tries to protect Olive by protesting that they're getting "decent notices" with her, Cheech responds, "decent isn't good enough." To David's plea of "We could have survived [her performance]," Cheech the perfectionist sneeringly responds, "Is *that* what you want?"

From the beginning, the word that David Shayne uses to explain and justify his artistic choices is "compromise." But Allen understands that while life is full of such things, art does not have to be. David's first words in the film are "I'm an artist," and soon after he insists that he won't change a word of his play to pander to commercial tastes, uttering idealistic but banal phrases about the purpose of art being to transform men's souls. Yet when the moment of truth arises, and David has the opportunity of having his work produced on Broadway if he accepts a woeful amateur (Olive) in an important role, he willingly accommodates himself to the demands of his financial backers. "I sold out," he says as he awakes from a nightmare. "I sold out my art and my work." "Do I want success that badly?" he asks himself. "The answer is yes," he says emphatically. Which is why, even though he knows that the play is far more alive with Olive's understudy in the role, he declares "Olive is a compromise I have to live with."

But not Cheech, because in **Bullets over Broadway** the real artist refuses to make concessions. "No one's gonna ruin my play," Cheech says. "Nobody." Just as his father once killed a singer who was mangling one of his favorite operas, Cheech disposes of Olive for destroying (as he puts it) a "thing of beauty." David, on the other hand, doesn't have the will to (artistic) triumph—or the stomach for violence. (Shayne is close to the Yiddish word for beautiful, *sheyn,* and ironically, while David recognizes the beauty of language and form, he can neither create, preserve, nor protect it.[9])

Thus, in the film's penultimate scene, when Cheech arrives at the play's opening, David says, "What do you want? You killed Olive. I don't care what kind of genius you are." Ever the moralist, David cannot "forgive" Cheech's deed, but Cheech is beyond such judgments. With his dying words he seeks not to save his soul, but to improve the play, revising it one more time by adding the final element that will bring dramatic closure. "Tell Sylvia Postum to say she's pregnant," Cheech tells David. "It'll be a great finish." And indeed it is, as Cheech has completely transformed Sylvia from the "frigid" (and enervated) character of David's early conception to the passionate (and vital) being of his own. In fact, Cheech's ending works much better in *God of Our Father* than it did when Allen used it in **Hannah and Her Sisters,** where Holly's revelation to Mickey that she's going to have a baby tags a "happy" coda onto the film's fundamentally bleak narrative (while also contradicting the little detail of Mickey's infertility). Unlike Allen, who violated his own point of view by imposing a "satisfying resolution" on the story of Hannah's cruel betrayal by her envious sisters, Cheech remains faithful to his vision of Sylvia's triumph over her rival by shifting the play's direction to reach the affirming conclusion it rightly deserves.[10]

Finally, the film wants to know, what sacrifices will you make for art? Perhaps for Allen at the time of the script's genesis, it meant, however cruelly, jettisoning Mia Farrow for a younger muse named Soon-Yi. (In **Bullets** David dumps a fiancee his own age for an *older* lover, Helen Sinclair, whom he imagines as his inspiration, though in the end he will leave her and return to his beloved for a life of domesticity.) Two questions arise within the film concerning the artist, and divergent answers are offered to both. "Do you love the artist or the man" (or, again, "can you separate the artist from the man") is one. Helen Sinclair, the great Broadway actress (brilliantly portrayed by Dianne Wiest), and the other true artist in the film, says she loves both and doesn't see a difference between them, primarily because she has fused the two in her own life—which is why she delivers every line, and makes every move and gesture, both inside and outside the play, with dramatic flair. Moreover, she appreciates forceful, arresting language as much as Cheech, and doubtlessly utters the most memorable lines in the film when she tells David on the eve of opening night that "the world will open to you like an oyster"; and then like a dramatist rewriting, "No, not like an oyster; the world will open to you like a magnificent vagina." (The image overwhelms David, and he feels a bit faint.) Completely defined by the roles she has played, the characters she has brought to life, Helen gives a magnificent performance when she first enters the theater, majestically recalling her triumphs, from Cordelia to Ophelia to Clytemnestra, as if she were memorializing loved ones. Indeed, as Helen experiences it, within the sacred space of the theater (she refers to it as a "church") the miracle of creation occurs, with "each performance a birth, each curtain a death." Fully inhabiting her parts, and just as fully aware of her grandeur, she requires "heroic" women and manipulates David into enlarging and enlivening the character of Sylvia, whom she initially (and correctly) sees as insipid. But acute theatrical instincts do not necessarily translate into worldly perceptiveness; someone so immersed in and absorbed by her career can easily be misled, at times willfully so. Thus, while she celebrates the transformation of David's "tepid," "cerebral" play into a "carnivorous" one, she fails to identify Cheech as the authentic writer responsible for the metamorphosis, instead giving herself to the fraudulent author of the "eunuch version."

David's girlfriend, Ellen, however, loves the man, and at the café discussion near the opening of the film she declares that "as long as he's a good man, keep him." At its conclusion, when David asks her, "Did you love me as the artist or the man?" she responds, consistently, "I could love a real man if he weren't an artist, but I couldn't love an artist if he weren't a real man." David isn't a real artist, but in the end he at least becomes an honest man, confessing his foibles and follies, and then choosing a conventional relationship and a thoroughly middle-class existence—which Allen seemingly mocks by comparing it to the charged and dangerous world of the artist, but actually uses to underscore the risks inherent in inhabiting the latter. Yet at the same time he achieves a delicious dramatic irony since his character's choice in the film is the polar opposite of the director's in the world.

The second question, occurring early in the action and thus lurking behind every scene, although on a literal level absurd, metaphorically underscores Allen's point about the fierceness (emotionally speaking) of a life committed to the making of art. Which would you save from a burning building: the last known copy of Shakespeare's plays or an anonymous person? David Shayne claims he would save the plays, but his choices throughout the film, and his horror at Olive's removal (which insures a successful production), show him again to be false. His friend Sheldon Flender also insists on the purity of his devotion to art, but never has to test it because he does not live an engaged artistic life. A self-deluded philosopher as well, he declares that "My plays are art," "I write to go unpublished," a statement and an attitude Allen obviously considers phony and pretentious. ("No truly great artist," Flender pontificates, "has ever been appreciated in his lifetime.") Both David and Sheldon would claim that art *is* life, but Cheech wholly embodies this idea, the only character for whom it becomes a living principle. Although he never verbally addresses the question, his deeds represent his response, since the true artist acts unilaterally and authoritatively. He makes no pronouncements, but rather, like the

writer/director of *Bullets over Broadway,* he produces art. He even dies for it, wiped out by the mob goons for eliminating Olive (talk about sacrifice!), and while one could argue that Cheech's death is a form of punishment and thus illustrates the "morality" for which Allen's films from the late seventies through the eighties were acclaimed, this would be imposing a sentimental reading on a decidedly unsentimental film.[11] Cheech dies because he lived daringly in a brutal world, a harsh—and, to be sure, an occasionally just—one suggested by the play's title; our fathers' God could be, and often was, angry and vindictive. Allen himself felt the wrathful condemnation of that world, and while his public crucifixion did not end in demise, he suffered deep wounds. Still, he has always been and continues to remain unrepentant, insisting that the only expectations and judgments that matter are his own.

Interestingly, the question *Bullets over Broadway* asks only indirectly, forcing viewers to confront by implication, is the one that speaks directly to this issue: What is the responsibility of the artist to his/her audience? In *Shadows and Fog* (1992), the film that immediately preceded *Husbands and Wives,* Allen had meditated briefly on this dilemma when, near the beginning, the clown declares that artists are "not like other people," and thus "with great talent comes responsibility." Allen himself rejects the idea of the superiority of the artist inherent in this statement, nor does he consider possessing talent to be an "achievement"; rather, he sees it as a "gift," and if one is "lucky" enough to have it, then "with that comes a certain responsibility."[12] But in 1992 and after, that sense of accommodation does not mean infusing his films with obvious life lessons or incorporating recognizable moral messages. "I feel no obligation to the press or the public," he told an interviewer on the eve of the London opening of *Bullets over Broadway,* "except to try and do good work." And while "good work" could include any number of qualities, Allen (like Cheech) clearly had something in mind beyond communal definition—and, for that matter, communal morality (i.e., living a good life). Filmmaking is "one person's vision," he insisted; the *sine qua non* for the filmmaker is "artistic freedom."[13]

### III.

Another artist-monster figure, though hardly a heroic one—not even an anti-heroic one—dominates *Deconstructing Harry*; in fact, Harry may very well be the most uncompromising, unyielding, unfeeling character Allen has ever created. Neither in life nor in art does he display any signs of compassion. Moreover, his behavior follows no principles or scruples; he doesn't care whom he hurts or kills off through his fiction, be it friend, sister, or parents. His world, in effect, is a moral vacuum. (Even Cheech has his codes of conduct, his sense of justice: as he tells David while supplying words for the play, he won't say anything about being the ghost writer because "where I come from nobody squeals.") A man who can only live successfully in and through his autobiographical creations, Harry has pillaged his life for his art, turning the suffering of wives and lovers into beautifully wrought, highly amusing and entertaining stories—"literary gold," as one of his "victims" describes the output, manufactured through a process of "amoral alchemy." To her, Harry is the "black magician," marvelously talented but without either scruples or remorse. Thus, while his existence is fragmented and full of mayhem (signaled by the director's use of jump cuts throughout the telling of his tale, and especially in his memory sequences—but not in the visual passages and episodes from his fiction), his stories and novels are tightly woven, unified pieces.

*Deconstructing Harry* abounds with references and allusions to Allen's earlier films, including the reappearance of actors (Judy Davis, from *Husbands and Wives,* and Julie Kavner, from *Hannah, Radio Days,* and *Oedipus Wrecks,* are only two of many), and the repetition of scenes (most memorably the Seder dinner from *Crimes and Misdemeanors*), underscoring its self-reflexivity. Although the film has its parodic moments, and a vengeful attitude toward critics, it is nevertheless first and foremost an "apologia"—not outright apology for misdeeds and appropriations, but rather a deeper understanding of a life and career devoted to, indeed subsumed by, creative endeavor. That is why, despite the fact that throughout the film Allen the director uses Allen the actor to portray Harry harshly and unsparingly, in the end he adopts a forgiving (self-forgiving?) tone toward his wayward character. Harry may not be redeemed (he is delivered from neither sin nor guilt), but he is saved (his psychological life is intact).

Harry's novels and stories can be deliciously and devilishly playful, and the sexuality within them daring and provocative (especially for a Woody Allen piece), but the real-life scenes upon which they are based are often brutal, full of Harry's misogynistic tendencies and his penchant for inflicting cruelty, especially by cheating on his wives in the most humiliating ways. (He betrays one with her sister and another, a psychoanalyst, with her patient.) Harry's vulgarity and violence also manifest themselves in language, and if, as John Baxter reports, the actors and actresses in *Husbands and Wives* "were surprised by the script's combativeness and abrasive language," then what must their counterparts in *Deconstructing Harry* have made of the coarse and derogatory exchanges between Harry and the women in his life?[14] Only minutes after the film begins, the frenzied and nearly deranged Lucy (Judy Davis), shouting "you shmuck, you bastard," "I'd like to cut your fucking head off," you "prick," and finally, you "motherfucker," tries to shoot Harry, who fires back with the shocking (and certainly unexpected) retort, "world class

*meshugene* cunt." Later, when Harry visits his son's school, he has a conversation with Hilly, overheard by Beth Kramer (Mariel Hemingway), a classmate's mother, on the appropriate name for his penis. (The kid decides on Dillinger, much to Harry's delight.) When confronted by his ex-wife, Joan (Kirstie Alley), to whom Beth has obviously revealed this travesty, Harry flies into a rage, calling Beth an "aggressive, tight-ass, busy-body cunt," while insisting that "it's not her business how I speak to my son," as if that claim justified his outburst. Joan will subsequently have her own tirade upon discovering Harry's infidelity, a screed remarkable for its abiding and explosive anger as well as its virulent vocabulary. In fact, the level of hostility here far exceeds anything in *Husbands and Wives,* with Joan's furious response to Harry ("you fucking asshole") making Judy's severest one to Gabe ("that's just bullshit") seem rather mild by comparison. Moreover, while the camera in the earlier film often treated Farrow unkindly—she looked hunched and haggard, even at times dowdy and cow-like—it acted downright nastily to Alley, who in her enraged state appears bloated and apoplectic. Only Elisabeth Shue as Fay, the younger woman for whom Harry feels affection and appreciation (and in a moment of duress confesses love), escapes the camera's scornful gaze—and his own acerbic pen.

Harry's "morally reprehensible" (in Joan's words) views of women are matched by his noxious images of Jews and Jewishness. As he sees it, Judaism equals "superstition" and, like other denominations, it is no more than an "exclusionary" "club" that "foster[s] the concept of the 'other' so you know clearly who [sic] you should hate." In one of the film's real-life episodes, Harry visits his sister Doris, and through their conversation we learn not only of his contempt for her return to "roots" (he sarcastically refers to her as "professionally Jewish"), but also of his having caricatured her "religious dedication" in one of his novels, attributing it to the character representing his ex-wife, who (as we see in a fictional sequence) blesses everything before she touches or eats it, including Harry's member. The mockery may be amusing, though it becomes harder to laugh at his story about a secret that Max Pinkus has kept from his wife, Dolly, for thirty years, but which she discovers through a conversation at a Bar Mitzvah (a Bar Mitzvah with a Star Wars theme, no less). It seems Max had been married before to a woman with two children, and one night, after killing all three (plus his mistress) with an axe, he disposed of the bodies by eating them. "So what are you making a fuss," Max says (using a Yiddish intonation) to Dolly as he finally confesses, "some bury, some burn, I ate." Whether or not this story embodies Harry's "sick view of our parents," as Doris insists, Jewish primitivism is a bit hard to take. It's one thing for Harry to reject his heritage, to believe that "tradition" is nothing but the "illusion of permanence," quite another to depict Jews, as Doris's husband Burt accuses him of doing, as "homicidal cannibals." Even though Harry considers Burt a Zionist "fanatic" and a religious "zealot" (and Eric Bogosian plays him as a self-righteous moralist), he may very well be right that "Max Pinkus's Dark Secret" is a "disrespectful, shameful" story.

While we should never make the mistake of oversimplifying the director/author-actor/character relationship, believing that a one-to-one correspondence exists between Allen and his fictional creation, it's almost impossible not to be disappointed at the simplistic Jewish portraits that emerge here, especially after the complexities of *Zelig* (1983), *Broadway Danny Rose* (1984), *Crimes and Misdemeanors,* and *Shadows and Fog.* Allen himself would no doubt remind us that they are *Harry's* portraits, and that Harry's biases are not to be equated with his own, that they are intended to reveal his disturbed and unbalanced character; and that, moreover, Harry's negative attitudes toward his own people—indeed, his outright rejection of Jewish identity—illustrate and support his frank self-condemnation: "I'm spiritually bankrupt, I'm empty, I've got no soul."[15] In fact, far from admitting that Harry bears any resemblance to Woody, Allen (according to Baxter) has stated that Philip Roth provided the model for his Jewishly-challenged writer, and indeed some of the criticisms directed at Harry (both Doris and Burt believe he's a "self-hating Jew") were also leveled at the younger Roth by various segments of the Jewish community.[16]

But despite their satiric edge and ironic bite, none of Roth's early stories that antagonized Jewish readers (most notoriously, "The Conversion of the Jews" and "Defender of the Faith") were so unflatteringly reductionist or so blatantly caricaturist as "Max Pinkus's Dark Secret." (Not even Nathan Zuckerman's recreation of this fiction in *The Ghost Writer,* a story called "Higher Education," dared to envision such a violation of Jewish dietary prohibitions.) And while Roth irreverently—and brazenly—imagined the great icon of Jewish victimization, Anne Frank, returned to life as Zuckerman's love interest (also in *The Ghost Writer*), he never crossed over into arrogance, as Harry seemingly does when he responds to Burt's hostile question, "Do you care even about the Holocaust or do you think it never happened?," with a line meant to be witty but which is no more than flippant: "Not only do I know that we lost six million, but the scary thing is records are made to be broken." The sports metaphor is not just inappropriate; it's offensive.

No Woody Allen film has ever exhibited such a rough and inescapably unpleasant exterior; nevertheless, in spite of this visual and verbal assault on the viewer, *Deconstructing Harry*'s ultimate reality is interior (i.e., fictional), and in this respect it is the most self-conscious piece in Woody Allen's canon. From beginning to end it continually refers to itself as film, that is, as an artistic construct rather than the pretense of realism. It opens with four takes of the same scene—Lucy getting out of a taxi and walking up to Harry's front door to confront him about the embarrassingly autobiographical novel he's just published. Clearly, the emphasis here is on composition, and the point is that it took four takes to get it right. Immediately, the viewer is forced into an awareness of film as medium. It closes with Harry sitting at a typewriter, making notes for a new story based on a writer (called Rifkin) who can only live harmoniously in his fiction and intimately with his characters. Although his role in the real world may be a chaotic and disjointed one—"our lives," Rifkin has concluded, "consist of how we choose to distort [them]"—and an utter failure in human terms, in his art he achieves something like wholeness.[17] "Only his writing was calm," Harry says of Rifkin, "[it] saved his life." (These are almost precisely the words Woody Allen used to describe the meaning of his own work during the turmoil of the Soon-Yi affair.) This is, in fact, the story we've just seen, making *Deconstructing Harry* a self-referential narrative in the modernist vein. And like so many modernist texts, the primary dilemma of the film is resolved as the circle closes: the artistically blocked Harry Block is able to write again because his life once more has become the subject of his fiction. But unlike most modernist literature, *Deconstructing Harry* does not view this state of utter interiority as a moral dilemma for its protagonist; rather than an emotional obstacle to overcome, it is an aesthetic victory to be celebrated.

Since fiction/cinema is the true reality, being a protagonist in a story/film is the ultimate form of being. In one of the best sequences in *Deconstructing Harry,* Robin Williams plays a character in one of Harry's tales named Mel, an actor who is "out of focus" and thus cannot be filmed. His blurry condition reflects Harry's feelings of instability, as well as his growing insecurity, which intensify to the point of breakdown. (Later Harry will actually suffer a similar fate when he cannot face the audience gathered to honor him at his old alma mater.) For an actor to be out of focus is (in filmspeak) to be "soft," that is, undefined, not having made himself sufficiently real to viewers. Or, from the perspective of his creator, he is unformed, not yet alchemically transmuted from life into art. A character can be in no worse state: if he cannot be seen clearly, he simply does not exist within the picture. As Henri Bergson and Samuel Beckett have taught us, to be is to be seen.

In Harry's moment of crisis he becomes like Mel: he is out of focus because he does not want to be seen by his admirers. His softness also indicates his emotional collapse—as he puts it, "I'm ODing on myself"—a condition from which he will recover through a series of imagined conversations with both his real-life friends and his fictional creations. (Initially, he is calmed by Cookie, the black prostitute.) Here, in effect, he becomes one of his characters. Thus, his life, as he experiences it, is a fiction, and since it is not real, he gives himself license to behave at best amorally, though many see him as immoral. All his relationships are strained and tense, except the one with Cookie, and that's because he pays her to perform; in a sense, he creates her. Which is why, in a dream sequence near the end of the film, speaking to the college students gathered to honor him, he says that the main character in a new story he is writing is a "thinly disguised version" of himself. Then he adds, dropping the pretense, "No, it is me." And suddenly we see Harry himself—and not simply a character based on him—inside a fictional landscape, a scene set in Hell. It's the final indication, so powerfully evoked that it comes as something of a revelation, à la Philip Roth (and here the comparison *is* apt, especially to the Roth of *Operation Shylock*), that Harry understands himself only in relation to his created world. But through this understanding comes acceptance, even self-embrace, which allows him to pursue still more variations on the essential theme of his writing—just as Woody Allen has retrieved, recycled, and reanimated scenes, settings, and characters from his film oeuvre, generating still more fictions and fictional self-representations.

Harry's descent into Hell, with its glowing landscape of writhing, tortured, naked bodies, provides the viewer with an evocative visual metaphor for his troubled psyche. An old literary technique buffed into new brilliance, the journey down to the lowest level of consciousness reveals the depth of Harry's depravity, the bottomlessness of his self-loathing. His foul deeds, he claims, match the Devil's: cheating on his wives, sleeping with whores, drinking to excess, popping pills, lying, committing violent acts. He even has the *chutzpah* to boast that, of the two, he's the greater sinner, since the Devil, after all, is a "fallen angel," whereas Harry "never believed in God." On the contrary, he embraces the fictions of modern physics, "quarks and particles and black holes"; to him, "all the other stuff is junk." But the Devil (in the guise of Larry, who's stolen Fay) is unfazed: he knows Harry will never triumph, because, "like Vegas . . . the house always wins." His advice, therefore, is to stop being so "angry at life," to "back off" and "have [some] fun." Harry acknowledges the Devil's superiority by commenting on the majesty of his kingdom: "It's better to rule down here than to serve in Heaven," and the allusion to *Paradise Lost* points toward the lasting lesson of this fictional episode. Like Milton's Satan, Harry learns that wherever he is, there lies Hell, which is only another way of saying that hell exists within. But then so, too, does heaven.

In the end, Harry is isolated, bereft of any human (read: female) connection, meaningful or otherwise: no ex-wife to abuse with his foul language, no current wife to betray with his sexual misdeeds, no girlfriend to seduce with his verbal brilliance, no hooker to debase with his perverted erotic needs. (Not even a shrink to complain to at $175 an hour.) Like Gabe, who tells the interviewer that he's working on a new novel when last we hear from him, and like Cheech, who rescripts the play's last lines as he expires, Harry is alone with his creations, turned inward to the only (mental) space where he's ever been at home, the only (emotional) place where he's ever felt contentment. Formally, aesthetically, these final scenes make beautiful sense, convincing us momentarily, if not ultimately, that creative intensity and artistic satisfaction may truly compensate for the turbulent, incoherent events of a life. In fact, by examining the progression (or perhaps, from another point of view, the regression) of these three films one notices that the more unruly each protagonist's world becomes, the more he withdraws into his work, and the more he depends upon fiction to displace reality—until, finally, there is no reality, no there there. Working, Allen has said, is a way of "taking control over the chaos of life. . . . The problems of theatre or film are stimulating and difficult, but at least you can cope with them; and they keep your mind off those problems you can't cope with."[18]

Yet you have to wonder how Allen's imagination, perhaps the richest and most fertile of any contemporary director, arrived at this extreme point of withdrawal, a position from which there is no apparent return. Since Allen has reconstructed his domestic life, complete with marriage to Soon-Yi, upper-east-side townhouse, and two adopted children, he cannot have meant Harry's situation to mirror his own. But understood metaphorically, Harry's absorption into his fiction becomes an emblem of Allen's commitment to writing—writing as a life-defining activity, writing as a means of self-discovery, writing as a form of spiritual sustenance. "I wanted to be a writer," Allen told an interviewer when **Bullets** was about to open in London, "I [only] directed my films in order to get them done properly." Indeed, he said, "If I had my life to live over, knowing what I know now, I might not go into film-making. . . . I could have been more productive if I'd just written books, because you finish writing then write again, and write again."[19] How much more productive can a man who has done thirty-odd films in thirty years be? But, despite Allen's claim, that is not the point. The true goal is to sustain the inner life, and to accomplish this you must write, and write, and write until the outer disappears; or, to paraphrase a famous about line about winning attributed to the immortal Green Bay Packers coach Vince Lombardi, "Writing isn't everything; it's the only thing."

After so much dubious (and in Harry's case, obnoxious and repellent) behavior on the part of Allen's protagonists, including their retreat into solipsism and their seeming indifference to other people's welfare, one has a right to ask, What happened to such Jewish themes as the desire for an honest life, free from duplicity and prevarication, that was a hallmark of *Broadway Danny Rose*? What happened to the search for *mentshlekhkayt*, to the longing for wisdom and worthiness, that distinguished *Crimes and Misdemeanors*? One answer would replicate Aunt May's response to her brother Sol (Judah's father) during their heated argument about crime and punishment at the Seder table in *Crimes.* "Is there no morality?" the pious believer asks the alienated intellectual, meaning (among other things) aren't human being responsible to a higher order? To which she replies, ironically, "For those who want morality there's morality." Similarly, for those who need uplifting moments in these later Allen films there are uplifting moments: there's Gabe's willingness at the end of *Husbands* to turn away from an alluring (albeit destructive) relationship with another "kamikaze" woman and head home to an empty, lonely apartment; there's David's realization at the conclusion of *Bullets* that whether or not he is equipped to lead the artist's life, he would prefer a decent middle-class one, filled with the pains and joys of real world experience; and there's Harry's generosity both to his ex-lover Fay and his friend Larry (Billy Crystal), and finally to his father, giving his blessing to the former upon their marriage and his forgiveness to the latter when he encounters him in the underworld. Yet such gestures, however sincerely intended by the writer/director, when set against the artist's dominating amorality—that is, his ruthless quest for aesthetic fulfillment and his devouring hunger for artistic integrity—can hardly support an optimistic, joyous, message-laden interpretation of these films. The truth is that Allen has turned away from his past pursuits and offered a version of the old W. B. Yeats adage about the artist choosing between "perfection of life, or of the work," only in Allen's case there's no romantic suggestion about the worldly sacrifice necessitated by a higher calling.[20] The writer may transmute mundane experience into golden images, but doing so brings him no greater spiritual reward and no hope for happiness. Allen refuses to glamorize or valorize obsession; in the end what the artist has to show for his labor is his art, not the rehabilitation of his life, or for that matter, necessarily of his career.

Previously, I mentioned the questions that Gabe Roth asks the interlocutor at the end of *Husbands and Wives*: "Can I go? Is this over?" The film supplies no answers, but here they are: Yes and No. Complaining that *Husbands and Wives* was a self-enclosed film, Stuart Klawans insisted that Allen had to enlarge his view of the world and find "a riskier way of making pictures about it." The time has come, he said, "for those of us who

love him to let the old Woody go."[21] This was true in 1992, and still is true—again. Several years ago we had to relinquish the Woody Allen who, in Sandy Bates's words from *Stardust Memories* about his own earlier films, "was just trying to be funny." In the more recent past we've had to say goodbye to the Woody Allen who claimed in *Manhattan,* in the guise of Isaac Davis, that honesty and forthrightness are the highest achievements. Indeed, as I have argued, Allen has abandoned that persona for an unapproachable, uncompromising, and, as in *Deconstructing Harry* (and in both *Celebrity* [1998] and *Sweet and Lowdown* [1999], where Kenneth Branagh and Sean Penn, respectively, stand in for him), an unregenerate one. And he has turned at least part of Klawans's plea on its head, narrowing rather than enlarging the scope of his concerns to the realm of art and the writerly life. In the process, he seems to have disappointed many of his critics, even those who had previously championed him, and upset a large part of his audience, whose faithfulness has been tested by the absence of a character with whom they could identify. Nevertheless, after his fall from grace he has in fact satisfied Klawans's other desire: in the mid-nineties, at least, he became the riskiest of filmmakers, one who was not afraid to turn an unfriendly lens on his own (inner) being, revealing through new incarnations of his persona a harsh and icy self he had previously kept hidden.

Earlier, I also raised the issue that, after *Deconstructing Harry,* Allen again may be accused of Jewish self-hatred or, less severely, indifference to his Jewish identity. Should Allen's Jewish viewers, then, many of whom are fiercely loyal to their Jewish background and heritage—and many of whom, in the process of reclaiming their own identities as Jews, resonated with his exploration of Jewishness in previous films—now give up on an apparently wayward and disloyal son? To repeat: the answer is Yes and No. If we demand consistently flattering representations of Jews and Jewishness, and if we insist that each succeeding film pursue a deeper and more meaningful (self-)identification with the Jewish people, then we might as well delete Allen's name from the list of approved filmmakers. Like his counterpart in the world of fiction, Philip Roth, Allen has proven to be the most intractable and unpredictable of artists, immune (or nearly so) to the demands of his audience for a recognizably particular (Jewish) performance, for the adherence to a linear form of (Jewish) development. If, however, we are cheered by a writer/director "freed from predictive forces" (as Cynthia Ozick has described Saul Bellow), be they exerted through family, community, or environment, and thrilled to be in the presence of invention "true to its own stirrings" (Ozick again), and if we are prepared to grant the gifted imagination liberty to roam where it may, then we ought to accept Allen's waywardness (while forgiving, or at least overlooking, his "disloyalty") as the result of an artist committed, above all, to his art.[22] This could mean that another return is possible, though who can say whether our faith in such an outcome will be rewarded. On the other hand, Allen's immense talent, coupled with his desire to grow artistically while remaining fiercely independent of the studio system, will surely produce new and surprising personal incarnations.

*Notes*

1. Arguably, there are a few exceptions to this statement in Allen's recent canon, most notably *Manhattan Murder Mystery* (1993) and *Small Time Crooks* (2000), both of which reprise an earlier persona and rely for much of their humor on physical comedy (more so in the latter). In both films, Allen looks uncomfortable in his roles, and both lack the wit and verbal panache that distinguish his best work. Allen himself referred to *Manhattan Murder Mystery* as an "indulgence," an "escapist movie," a "trivial picture" (*Woody Allen on Woody Allen: In Conversation with Stig Bjorkman* [New York: Grove, 1993], pp. 192, 255). *Small Time Crooks* is even weaker and more "unambitious" because its plot is worn and cliched. Sadly, his newest films, *The Curse of the Jade Scorpion* (2001) and *Hollywood Ending* (2002) are equally disappointing efforts.

2. Barry Koltnow, "Woody: I Left Audience Behind," *Denver Post,* January 28, 2000: 5C. Interestingly, a previous interview, containing much of the same language and sentiment, appeared in the *London Free Press.* Apparently Allen had anticipated the questions and had already prepared his answers.

3. I have argued elsewhere that the films in this middle phase of Allen's career demonstrate his fictional alter egos' desire to achieve *mentshlekhkayt,* a vision or state of wisdom and worthiness ("Perversion or Perversity? Woody and Me," in *People of the Book: Thirty Scholars Reflect on Their Jewish Identity,* ed. Jeffrey Rubin-Dorsky and Shelley Fisher Fishkin [Madison: U. of Wisconsin P., 1996], pp. 456-71).

4. See Peter Marks, "Allen Loses to Farrow in Bitter Custody Battle," *New York Times,* June 8, 1993: A1, B16. Where Mia Farrow was loving and protective toward their children, Justice Wilk declared, Allen was "self-absorbed, untrustworthy and insensitive."

5. Rafferty, "Getting Old," *The New Yorker,* September 21, 1992: 102.

6. In an interview with Walter Isaacson, Allen justified his behavior with Soon-Yi by declaring "the heart wants what it wants" ("'The Heart Wants What It Wants,'" *Time,* August 31, 1992: 61).

7. Allen appeared on "60 Minutes" on November 22, 1992, three months after the Soon-Yi scandal broke. In the interview he claimed that he "never really thought" about the consequences, or even the pos-

sibility, of Farrow's discovering the easily accessible nude photographs. Incredibly, all he could muster by way of a response were the words, "I don't know—I don't really know."

8. Canby, "Is Life Following Art? It Doesn't Matter," *New York Times,* September 18, 1992: B4. Allen himself said the purpose of the jump-cutting technique was to make the feeling of certain scenes "more disturbing" and "more dissonant" because "the internal, emotional and mental states of the characters are dissonant" (*Woody Allen on Woody Allen,* p. 252).

9. I am indebted to Prof. Stephen Whitfield of Brandeis University for the Shayne=*sheyn* observation.

10. Allen subsequently realized that he had "backed out" at the end of *Hannah,* turning away from, among other themes, the sense of futility in human relationships. As he put it, "I copped out a little on the film" (*Woody Allen on Woody Allen,* p. 156). Since Allen is, of course, the controlling mind behind Cheech, one can say that in *Bullets over Broadway* he redeems the artistic blunder in *Hannah and Her Sisters.* It's also interesting to note that in *Hannah* a younger Dianne Wiest played the role of Holly (just as in *Bullets* an older Dianne Wiest plays the role of the actress Helen, who plays the role of Sylvia).

11. In *Reconstructing Woody: Art, Love, and Life in the Films of Woody Allen* (Lanham, Md.: Rowman & Littlefield, 1998), Mary P. Nichols tries desperately to find moral significance in Cheech's death. But in order to accomplish this, she distorts the meaning of his final words to David, "Don't speak!," reading them as a refusal to acknowledge and experience the moment, rather than realizing that they are intended comically (just as they were when Helen Sinclair used them) to silence David because he mangles language, ruining the emotional resonance of a scene (in reality as in the play) with his inadequate words. In addition, she elevates David's recognition of his authorial deficiencies and his choice of marriage and children into an act of "moral integrity" when all his new-found certainty—that he loves Ellen and that he is not an artist—indicates is that he has finally found his proper role in life (pp. 189-93). Like others, Nichols wants to see a seamless continuity in Allen's career, rather than appreciating that the director's development has been disjointed and at times discordant. Thus, she concludes her study of his major films with an utterly sentimental and banal observation: "They are good, most importantly, because they reveal what is good in the reality they reflect" (p. 221). Arriving at such a position requires that you not only overlook their deeper meanings, but also ignore their actual content.

12. *Woody Allen on Woody Allen,* p. 242.

13. Geoff Andrew, "Biting the Bullets" (interview with Woody Allen), *Time Out,* April 5-12, 1995: 22. When the interviewer asked Allen if people were angry

with him (during the Soon-Yi affair) because he "refused to play the game of parading the usual emotions," because he seemed "detached" instead of repentant, he responded, "I didn't feel I should be repentant for anything; it was the outside world that should be repentant to me" (p. 21).

14. John Baxter, *Woody Allen: A Biography* (New York: Carroll & Graf, 1998), p. 396. One particular moment in *Husbands and Wives* shocked the entire crew: after Jack (Sydney Pollack) drags Sam (Lysette Anthony) away from a party where she has embarrassed him in front of his friends by insisting on the truthfulness of astrology, he angrily wrestles her into a car as she screams for help. According to Anthony, "There were people with their mouths open, going, 'My God, I've never seen this much violence in a Woody Allen movie.'"

15. Not surprisingly, Allen has denied any connection between his life and Harry's, pointing out that, unlike his character, he's disciplined, he has a "number of good relationships," and most importantly, he functions quite well in the world (Denis Hamill, "Deconstructing Woody," *Daily News* [Sunday Extra], October 5, 1997: 4). In another interview prompted by the film, he put it more broadly, though no less emphatically: "I really do make up my stories. People think I take them from my life, but of course I don't. If I did—I've made 27 movies now—my life would be this rich adventure of fascinating women and strange relationships. . . . But it's not" (Aaron Gell, "Go Where the Good Laugh Is—Regardless," *Time Out New York,* December 4-11, 1997: 8).

On the other hand, Harry's comment about Judaism "foster[ing] the concept of the 'other'" echoes an idea Allen expressed about a year before the film opened: "I wish the stress was on the togetherness—similarity of people, not on separateness. Against what the world's religions, the organized religion, have done to keep people apart." As Allen sees it, all religions, but especially Judaism, promote "otherness"—and it's a bad thing (*New York,* September 9, 1996: 38).

16. Baxter, *Woody Allen: A Biography,* p. 436. Baxter provides no source for this reference, and I have not come across such a statement in any published Allen interview. However, at least two commentators have argued for the likeness to Roth, noting especially that the acclaimed novelist has exploited his closest relationships for fictional gain. See Adam Carl, "That's Not Woody in *Harry,* It's Philip," *Los Angeles Times,* December 22, 1997: F3, and Robert Sklar, "Woody Allen, Unbound, Takes a Page from Roth," *Forward,* November 25, 1997: 11.

17. Prof. Lawrence Baron, the editor of this special issue of *Shofar,* pointed out that Harry's negative (self-) reflection here dramatically contrasts with Professor Louis Levy's elevated idea at the end of *Crimes and Misdemeanors* that through choice we invest meaning into the little aspects of life.

In "Woody Allen, 'the Artist,' and 'the Little Girl,'" (in Jon Lewis, ed., *The End of Cinema as We Know It: American Film in the Nineties* [New York: New York University Press, 2001], pp. 195-202), David R. Shumway looks at the "artist" in *Husbands and Wives* and *Deconstructing Harry,* especially in terms of his "pedagogical relationship" to a younger woman, and while some of our observations overlap, he does not develop a sustained argument about either Allen's attitude toward this figure or the shift in his persona in these films. Moreover, I disagree with some of his pronouncements—for example, that *Husbands and Wives* "has depicted the relationship between Gabe and Rain in an idealized way" (p. 200) and that *Deconstructing Harry* presents Fay as the "woman who should have been Harry's salvation" (p. 201)—because, from my point of view, they are based on misreadings of the films' fundamental meanings and intentions.

18. "Biting the Bullets," p. 21.

19. "Biting the Bullets," p. 22.

20. Yeats quoted in Joseph J. Ellis, "Exploring the Morning of a Long Day's Journey" (review of *O'Neill: Life with Monte Cristo,* by Arthur and Barbara Gelb), *New York Times Book Review,* May 19, 2000: B43. Like Harry, Eugene O'Neill clearly chose work over life, and also seemed determined, says Ellis, to "make his personal life into a series of painful imperfections that then became the creative material for his most enduring work." In fact, rather than "conceal[ing] his private sins, personal obsessions or domestic catastrophes," O'Neill "put them on the stage for all the world to see." Whether or not Allen may have had O'Neill in mind as a model for his driven writer, Harry exhibits similar neurotic traits and self-destructive tendencies, as well as an all-encompassing devotion to artistic fulfillment.

21. Klawans, "Husbands and Wives," *The Nation,* October 19, 1992: 447.

22. Ozick, "Throwing Away the Clef" (review of *Ravelstein,* by Saul Bellow), *The New Republic,* May 22, 2000: 27, 28.

**Ethan Alter (review date October 2003)**

SOURCE: Alter, Ethan. Review of *Anything Else,* by Woody Allen. *Film Journal International* 106, no. 10 (October 2003): 104.

[*In the following review, Alter comments that* Anything Else *is significantly better than several of Allen's recent films, but is not on par with his best work.*]

Quick, which of the following moments in *Anything Else* do you recognize from previous Woody Allen films?

A) An old joke is treated as a metaphor for the main character's life.

B) One-liners about the joys of masturbation.

C) A possible misunderstanding involving the word "Jew."

D) All of the above.

If you correctly answered D, you're obviously a big Woody Allen fan. In that case, you probably also realize that all of these bits come from the same movie, his seminal romantic comedy *Annie Hall.* This sort of blatant cannibalizing shouldn't be a surprise for anyone who has suffered through Allen's recent films, the bland *Hollywood Ending* and the dismal *Curse of the Jade Scorpion.* It's just disappointing to discover—yet again—that this once innovative writer-director now seems completely bankrupt of fresh ideas. Against the odds, however, *Anything Else* turns out to be a modestly entertaining comedy. It's no *Manhattan*—hell, it's not even *Manhattan Murder Mystery*—but Allen has certainly made worse movies. (*Celebrity,* anyone?)

Jason Biggs stars as Alvy Sing . . . excuse me, Jerry Falk, a would-be novelist who makes his living writing jokes for stand-up comics (again, shades of *Annie Hall*). Like almost every lead character in an Allen film, Jerry is a neurotic quipster with a bad case of the relationship blues. See, his gorgeous but high-strung girlfriend Amanda (Christina Ricci) has grown tired of their romance, to the point where she can't be "intimate" with him anymore. The arrival of her estranged mother (a nice supporting turn by Stockard Channing) puts further strain on the couple, and Amanda—who has a history of leaving heartbroken men behind—suddenly appears more than ready to move on. If that's not enough, Jerry is also facing problems in his professional life; his bumbling agent (amusingly played by Danny DeVito) wants him to sign a new seven-year contract and his novel is going nowhere fast. Fortunately, the young man finds a friend in David Dobel (Allen), a fellow gag writer-for-hire who, through a series of bizarre circumstances, teaches Jerry how to grow up and start making decisions for himself.

*Anything Else* is really two movies in one. The first follows the inevitable dissolution of Jerry and Amanda's relationship, while the second tracks Jerry's transformation into a confident adult with a little help from David. Only one of these storylines carries any dramatic weight, however, and it's not the one that's being featured in the film's trailer and posters. Based on DreamWorks' Biggs and Ricci-centric ad campaign, you'd never know that Allen even appears in the movie. That's a shame, because he gives one of his loosest and funniest performances in ages. If it wasn't clear before now, *Anything Else* proves that Allen should really consider relegating himself to supporting roles from here on out. At the same time, he needs to take more care choosing his stand-in. Biggs isn't a complete washout, but it's hard to buy him as a Sartre-reading intellectual. It doesn't help that the actor appears distracted much of the time, as if he's constantly looking off-camera for Allen's approval. He does gain confidence whenever he shares the screen with his director, and their scenes together are what make the movie work. That's not to completely dismiss Ricci, who does what she can in an oddly written role. She's certainly well-cast as a dark-eyed temptress, but Amanda is a somewhat unpleasant character—think Annie Hall without the charm—whose constant whining grates after a while. Furthermore, Ricci and Biggs aren't remotely believable as this type of couple; Allen's standard relationship banter doesn't sound at all natural coming out of their mouths. As a result, they often seem like teenagers playacting as adults.

Ultimately, the only audiences likely to be entertained by *Anything Else* are die-hard Allen fans who unfailingly attend each of his new releases in the hope that he'll recapture his former glory. This effort can't really be called a success, but it does have several funny and charming moments. And if nothing else, it shows that Allen may have finally learned to act his age.

---

# FURTHER READING

### Biography

Meade, Marion. *The Unruly Life of Woody Allen: A Biography,* New York: Scribner, 2000, 384 p.
    A biography of Woody Allen.

### Criticism

Blake, Richard A. *Woody Allen* Lanham, Md.: Rowman and Littlefield, 1995, 235 p.
    Provides a discussion of humor and religious references in Allen's films.

Bray, Christopher. "Woody's Genuine Froth." *Times Literary Supplement,* (28 January 1994): 16.
    Review of *Manhattan Murder Mystery,* faulting it for a stereotypically happy ending, and proposing an alternate conclusion and suggestions for treating darker themes left unexplored in the film.

Fox, Julian. *Woody: Movies from Manhattan,* Woodstock: Overlook Press, 1996, 288 p.

Provides an examination of Allen's representations of New York City in his films.

Felperin, Leslie. "Ms. Tough." *Sight and Sound* 9, no. 6 (June 1999): 10-12.

Presents in-depth discussion of actress Judy Davis's roles in Allen's films, particularly in *Husbands and Wives* and *Celebrity.*

Francke, Lizzie. Review of *Shadows and Fog,* written and directed by Woody Allen. *Sight & Sound* 3, no. 4 (April 1993): 56-7.

Review of *Shadows and Fog.*

King, Kimball. *Woody Allen: A Casebook,* New York: Routledge, 2001, 158 p.

Presents a collection of essays by various authors discussing Allen's films.

Lee, Sander H. *Woody Allen's Angst: Philosophical Commentaries on His Serious Films,* Jefferson, N.C.: McFarland & Co., 1996, 402 p.

Provides critical analysis of the themes of angst, faith, and existentialism in Allen's films.

Romney, Jonathan. "Circus of Deceit." *New Statesman & Society* (January 1993): 43-5.

Review of *Shadows and Fog,* faulting the film for treating familiar themes from earlier movies.

Schickel, Richard. *Woody Allen: A Life in Film,* Chicago: Ivan R. Dee, 2003, 224 p.

Provides discussion of the autobiographical elements in Allen's films, and his views on his work. Based on a four-hour interview conducted by Schickel to produce a 90-minute television documentary.

Schwartz, Richard A. *Woody from Antz to Zelig: A Reference Guide to Woody Allen's Creative Work, 1964-1998,* Westport, Conn.: Greenwood Press, 2000, 336 p.

A reference guide to Allen's films, providing production information, literary analysis of the works, discussion of major themes, relationships, and influences in Allen's movies.

---

**Additional coverage of Allen's life and career is contained in the following sources published by Thomson Gale:** *Authors and Artists for Young Adults,* **Vols. 10, 51;** *Contemporary Authors,* **Vols. 33-36R;** *Contemporary Authors New Revision Series,* **Vols. 27, 38, 63, 128;** *Contemporary Literary Criticism,* **Vols. 16, 52;** *Dictionary of Literary Biography,* **Vol. 44;** *DISCovering Authors Modules, Popular Fiction and Genre Authors*; *Literature Resource Center*; **and** *Major 20th-Century Writers,* **Ed. 1.**

# Neil Gaiman
## 1960-

(Full name Neil Richard Gaiman) English graphic novelist, novelist, short-story writer, editor, children's writer, television writer, radio play writer, and screenplay writer.

The following entry presents an overview of Gaiman's career through 2004.

## INTRODUCTION

Gaiman is a central figure in the emergence of the "graphic novel," a genre which combines novelistic storylines with comic-book graphics. Gaiman has won numerous awards for his bestselling, critically acclaimed graphic novels and illustrated prose novels that combine elements of science fiction, Gothic horror, dark fantasy, age-old legend, ancient mythology, and biblical allegory in modern-day settings. His stories have been hailed as myths for the modern world, exploring with sophistication, complexity, and a postmodern sensibility the enduring power of dreams, storytelling, and the imagination in life at the turn of the millennium. Gaiman is best known for his epic graphic novel series *The Sandman* (1990-97), depicting episodes in the adventures of Morpheus, the Dream Lord, a mythical character who rules over the realm of human dreams and nightmares. The immense popularity of Gaiman's works has earned him a cult-like celebrity status among his many adoring and enthusiastic fans and spawned a host of product tie-ins, such as T-shirts, posters, calendars, and toys. Jeff Zeleski quotes Gaiman's film agent, Jon Levin, as saying that Gaiman "is able to synthesize ancient mythology with the current zeitgeist. His characters, no matter how fantastical the world, are essentially human."

## BIOGRAPHICAL INFORMATION

Gaiman was born November 10, 1960, in Portchester, England. His father owned a vitamin-pill factory and his mother was a pharmacist. As a child, Gaiman was a voracious reader. "I loved comics when I was growing up," he told novelist Steve Erickson in an interview, "and I never saw any reason why they should be considered inferior. I thought they could have as much power and passion and elegance as any other medium." While influenced by British fantasy novelists such as J.

R. R. Tolkein and C. S. Lewis, Gaiman found American comic books more compelling than their British counterparts. As a teenager, he became disillusioned with the comic book medium as a whole, feeling it had nothing new to offer. However, with the emergence of the graphic novel form in the late 1970s and early 1980s, Gaiman was inspired by the possibilities of this new development in the comic book genre. He was especially influenced by the comic book series *The Swamp Thing,* written by Alan Moore and published during the mid-1980s. Gaiman graduated from Whitgift School in 1977, at age sixteen. Intending to one day become a comic book writer, he decided to work first as a journalist, in order to learn more about the publishing industry. During the 1980s, he lived in London and worked as a freelance journalist and editor. Before making a name for himself as a graphic novelist, Gaiman wrote several nonfiction books on commission, such as *Duran, Duran* (1984), a history of the popular rock band of the same name, and *Don't Panic* (1987), a companion guide to the satirical science fiction novel

*The Hitchhiker's Guide to the Galaxy* by Douglas Adams. He collaborated with his friend Dave McKean, an artist, on *Violent Cases* (1987), his first comic book publication. *Violent Cases* was soon published as a graphic novel, and Gaiman was invited by DC Comics, the purveyor of many of the twentieth-century's classic comic book heroes, to write a comic book based on one of their already-created superheroes from the 1940s. Gaiman thus wrote an updated story based on the classic comic book heroine Black Orchid. He next turned to the little-known DC Comics character of the Sandman, completely reinventing this classic superhero on his own terms. Gaiman has since authored numerous graphic novels, short stories, prose novels, and children's books. He served as Chair of the Society of Comic Strip Illustrators from 1988 to 1990 and sits on the advisory board of the International Museum of Cartoon Art. He is a major contributor and active fund-raiser for the Comic Legal Defense Fund, an anti-censorship lobbying organization. Gaiman lives in Minnesota with his American-born wife and their three children.

## MAJOR WORKS

The *Sandman* series comprises seventy-five volumes, totaling over a million words of text, which were originally published as individual comic books between 1988 and 1996 and republished in ten multi-volume hardcover books. The eponymous hero of the *Sandman* series, who is also called Morpheus, the Lord of the Dreaming and the Prince of Stories, is a member of a family of seven supernatural beings, known collectively as the Endless, each one representing different states of mind: Death, Delirium, Desire, Destruction, Despair, Destiny, and Dream. The figure of Death is depicted as a good-natured young woman dressed in the fashion of punk-rock, while Delirium is depicted as a loquacious girl with green and pink hair who walks around with a pet fish on a leash. The Sandman himself, called Dream, is depicted as a scrawny, sallow man with deep sunken eyes and a shock of black hair. Dream rules over The Dreaming, a fantastical realm which humans can enter only when they sleep. The accoutrements necessary to his powers include a pouch of magical sand, a helmet, and a ruby dream jewel. Gaiman informed DC Comics that he wished to end the *Sandman* series while it was at its height, rather than continuing it indefinitely. He thus describes the death of the Sandman in issue sixty-nine, although the series continued for six more issues before the epic tale was complete. Gaiman has since published several spin-off graphic novels that feature the Sandman but are separate from the storyline of the original series. One such spin-off is *Sandman: The Dream Hunters* (1999), which is based on a Japanese folk tale and features a badger, a monk, and a female fox. The fox falls in love with the gentle monk, and she

enters the realm of the Dreaming ruled by the Sandman in an attempt to save the monk from harm. *Sandman: Endless Nights* (2003), another *Sandman* spin-off graphic novel, comprises seven tales, each focused on one of the seven siblings in the Endless family, with each tale illustrated by a different artist. In addition to the *Sandman* opus, Gaiman has authored numerous other graphic novels. *Violent Cases* chronicles episodes from the nightmares of a young boy and is based on tales he heard of the Depression-era gangster Al Capone. The adult narrator of *Violent Cases* looks back on these childhood dreams in an attempt to make sense of the adult he has become. Gaiman won the 1988 Eagle Award for best graphic novel for *Violent Cases*. *The Tragical Comedy or Comical Tragedy of Mr. Punch* (1994), another stand-alone graphic novel not part of the *Sandman* opus, is the coming-of-age story of a young boy, chronicling his encounters with a mean-spirited puppeteer of the classic Punch & Judy puppet shows and a woman costumed as a mermaid. *1602* (2003), planned as an eight-issue graphic novel published by Marvel Comics, is a science fiction story about mutants living in Elizabethan England.

Gaiman has authored a number of fantasy/science-fiction/horror novels that place mythological characters and stories in settings familiar to contemporary life. Some of these works, though written in the prose form of the novel, are accompanied by extensive illustrations by some of the same artists with whom he has collaborated on his graphic novels. *Good Omens* (1990), co-authored with Terry Pratchett, is a satire based on the biblical prophecy of Armageddon, the apocalyptic battle described in Revelation, the final book of the Bible. Gaiman's story concerns the fate of a reluctant child Antichrist at the hands of Aziraphale, an angel, and Crowley, a demonic serpent, who battle over his soul. Gaiman offers humorous juxtapositions of biblical mythology and modern society in *Good Omens,* with such elements as the Four Bikepersons of the Apocalypse, a riff on the biblical figures of the Four Horsemen of the Apocalypse. Gaiman's novel *Neverwhere* (1996), adapted from his teleplay for the British Broadcasting Corporation (BBC) television miniseries, concerns the adventures of Richard Mayhew, a young businessman who helps a bizarre homeless girl and is subsequently drawn into "London Below," a fantastical underworld that exists beneath the city of London. *Stardust* (1998), written by Gaiman and illustrated by Charles Vess, is an adult fairy tale narrated in the manner of British children's stories published during the 1920s. Set in Victorian England, *Stardust* follows the adventures of seventeen-year-old Tristran Thorn, who journeys to Faerieland on a quest for a fallen star which he hopes to bring back to Victoria, the girl he is in love with. Gaiman received the 1999 Mythopoetic Award for best novel for adults for *Stardust*. *American Gods* (2001)—at some 450 pages Gaiman's longest and most novelistic prose novel—follows the adventures of Shadow, a man who is released from prison only to find that his wife has died in a car accident. Shadow aimlessly takes a job as a bodyguard to Mr. Wednesday with whom he sets out on a road trip across the American Midwest. Mr. Wednesday eventually reveals himself to be the Norse god Odin, while his companion Nancy is revealed to be Anansi, a trickster spider from African mythology. In their company, Shadow finds himself in an alternate reality where he is drawn into a war between the old gods of mythology and religion and the modern gods of technology and mass media. Gaiman's American Gods was the first work ever to win all four of the major "speculative fiction" awards for best novel: the Hugo Award, the Bram Stoker Award, the Nebula Award, and the World Fantasy Award.

Gaiman has published several picture books for young children, such as *The Day I Swapped My Dad for Two Goldfish* (1996), *The Wolves in the Walls* (2003), and a short illustrated novel *Coraline* (2002), aimed at young adult readers. *Coraline* has been compared to the classic children's story *Alice in Wonderland* by Lewis Carroll and relates the adventures of a girl who discovers a magic door in her house, which at first opens onto a bricked-up wall but later allows her to step across its threshold into an alternate reality. In the world inside the door, Coraline finds that she has two creepy alternate parents, with pale complexions and black button eyes, who wish to keep her. She struggles to escape back through the door and into her house but finds that her real parents have been taken into the alternate world, and she must go back in to save them from the nefarious alternate parents. Gaiman received the 2002 World Science Fiction Society Bram Stoker Award for best work for young readers and the 2003 Hugo Award for best novella, both for *Coraline*.

## CRITICAL RECEPTION

Gaiman's graphic novels and prose novels have been almost universally acclaimed. Many reviewers applauded Gaiman's inventiveness as well as his skill at maintaining complex, multi-layered storylines throughout the *Sandman* series. Gaiman is further credited as having a significant impact on the elevation of the comic book genre to the status of serious literature. As Frank McConnell noted, "What [Gaiman] has done with *Sandman* is establish the fact that a comic book can be a work of high and very serious art—a story that other storytellers, in whatever medium they work, will have to take into account as an exploration of what stories can do and what stories are for." Steve Erickson noted that Sandman is "literate and sophisticated by any measure, let alone that of comic books," as well as being "complex to the point of labyrinthine, non-linear to

the point of vertiginous." In portraying the narrative breadth and wide-ranging complexity of Gaiman's tale, Erickson described the Sandman series as "an open-ended epic[;] the narrative, and the stories within it, and the stories within the stories, move from the atriums of ancient Greek myth to the veldt of African folklore, from the French Revolution to modern-day Manhattan, from the tale of a man who has decided never to die to the bodiless head of Orpheus begging someone to kill him, from Shakespeare making the terrible bargain that will transform him from hack to genius, to Thomas Paine muttering in his jail cell about the ideal that betrayed him, from a novelist who locks his muse in his attic, defiling her for black inspiration, to a convention of serial killers in the American South with a guest of honor who swallows peoples' eyes." In his book *Neil Gaiman's "The Sandman" and Joseph Campbell* (2003), Stephen Rauch drew on the theories of mythical archetypes put forth by Joseph Campbell (in his 1949 study *The Hero with a Thousand Faces*) to demonstrate the ways in which the *Sandman* series is a work of modern mythology. Rauch argued that in *Sandman* Gaiman draws on existing mythological concepts to create a new mythology which speaks to modern experience. Rauch asserted that the *Sandman* series ultimately fulfills Joseph Campbell's definition of myth as serving four main functions: "First, *Sandman* is full of wonder, both overt and subtle. Second, it tells us about the structure of the macrocosm, what the universe is like and who rules it. Third, it provides a sociology, telling us how to be good, or human, to each other. Finally, fourth, it tells us how to move through the stages of our lives, from birth to the various rites of passage of puberty, marriage, and old age, and finally death." Gaiman's construction of *The Sandman* as a meta-narrative, commenting on the role of storytelling in modern society, has also been widely praised. McConnell observed that the *Sandman* series as a whole represents "the history of western storytelling altogether, and especially of the stories we like to call 'modern,'" adding, "it is simply magnificent metafiction, a story about story."

---

# PRINCIPAL WORKS

*Duran, Duran: The First Four Years of the Fab Five* (nonfiction) 1984

*Violent Cases* [illustrated by Dave McKean] (graphic novel) 1987

*Don't Panic: The Official "Hitchhiker's Guide to the Galaxy" Companion* [revised with David K. Dickson and republished as *Don't Panic: Douglas Adams & "The Hitchhiker's Guide to the Galaxy,"* 1993] (nonfiction) 1988

*Good Omens: The Nice and Accurate Prophecies of Agnes Nutter, Witch* [with Terry Pratchett] (novel) 1990

*The Sandman: Preludes and Nocturnes* [illustrated by Sam Keith and Mike Dringenberg; originally published in *The Sandman,* issues 1-8 in 1988-1989] (graphic novel) 1990

*The Sandman: The Doll's House* [illustrated by Dringenberg; originally published in *The Sandman,* issues 8-16 in 1989-1990] (graphic novel) 1990

*Black Orchid* [4 vols.; illustrated by McKean] (graphic novel) 1991

*The Sandman: Dream Country* [illustrated by Kelley Jones; originally published in *The Sandman,* issues 17-20 in 1990] (graphic novel) 1991

*The Sandman: Season of Mists* [illustrated by Kelley Jones; originally published in *The Sandman,* issues 21-28 in 1990-1991] (graphic novel) 1992

*Signal to Noise* [illustrated by McKean; adapted as a radio play, 1996] (graphic novel) 1992

*\*Angels and Visitations: A Miscellany* (short stories) 1993

*The Books of Magic* [4 vols.; illustrated by John Bolton] (graphic novel) 1993

*The Sandman: Fables and Reflections* [illustrated by Bryan Talbot; originally published in *The Sandman,* issues 29-31, 38-40, 50 in 1991, 1992, and 1993] (graphic novel) 1993

*The Sandman: A Game of You* [illustrated by Shawn McManus; originally published in *The Sandman,* issues 32-37 in 1991-1992] (graphic novel) 1993

*Miracleman: Book 4: The Golden Age* [illustrated by Mark Buckingham] (graphic novel) 1993

*The Children's Crusade* [illustrated by Chris Bachalo] (graphic novel) 1993-94

*Death: The High Cost of Living* [3 issues; illustrated by Chris Bachalo, Buckingham, and McKean; introduction by Tori Amos] (graphic novel) 1994

*The Sandman: Brief Lives* [illustrated by Jill Thompson; originally published in *The Sandman,* issues 41-49 in 1992-1993] (graphic novel) 1994

"Snow, Glass, Apples" [revised as *Snow Glass Apples: A Play for Voices,* 2002] (radio play) 1994

*The Tragical Comedy or Comical Tragedy of Mr. Punch: A Romance* [illustrated by McKean] (graphic novel) 1994

*WitchCraft* [3 isssues; illustrated by James Robinson, Peter Snejbjerg, and Teddy Kristiansen] (graphic novel) 1994

*The Complete Alice Cooper: Incorporating the Three Acts of Alice Cooper's The Last Temptation* [co-author, with Alice Cooper; illustrated by Zulli; republished as *The Last Temptation,* 2000] (graphic novel) 1995

*The Sandman: World's End* [illustrated by D. Giordano, Vince Locke, and McKean; originally published in *The Sandman,* issues 51-56 in 1993] (graphic novel) 1995

*The Sandman Midnight Theatre* [co-author, with Wagner; illustrated by Kristiansen] (graphic novel) 1995

*Warning: Contains Language* [readings by Gaiman, music by McKean and the Flash Girls] (sound recording) 1995

*The Day I Swapped My Dad for Two Goldfish* [illustrated by McKean] (picture book) 1996

*Neverwhere* [co-author, with Lenny Henry; adapted as a novel, 1996] (teleplay) 1996

*The Sandman: Book of Dreams* [editor; with Edward E. Kramer] (short stories) 1996

*The Sandman: The Kindly Ones* [illustrated by Marc Hempel, Richard Case, D'Israeli, Kristiansen, Blyn Dillon, Charles Vess, Dean Ormston, and Devin Nowlan; originally published in *The Sandman,* issues 57-69 in 1993-1995] (graphic novel) 1996

*The Tempest* [additional volume of *The Sandman*] (graphic novel) 1996

*Death: The Time of Your Life* [part of *The Sandman* series] (graphic novel) 1997

*The Sandman: The Wake* [illustrated by Zulli, Jon J. Muth, and Vess; originally published in *The Sandman,* issues 70-75 in 1995-1996] (graphic novel) 1997

*The Dreaming: Beyond the Shores of Night* [co-illustrator] (graphic novel) 1998

*Smoke and Mirrors: Short Fictions and Illusions* (short stories) 1998

*Stardust: Being a Romance within the Realms of Faerie* [illustrated by Vess; republished as *Stardust,* 1999] (graphic novel) 1998

*Princess Mononoke* [English-language adaptation of the Japanese animated movie *Hayao Miyazaki*] (screenplay dialogue) 1999

*The Dreaming: Through the Gates of Horn and Ivory* (graphic novel) 1999

*Sandman: The Dream Hunters* [illustrated by Yoshitaka Amano] (graphic novel) 1999

*The Quotable Sandman: Memorable Lines from the Acclaimed Series* (quotations) 2000

*American Gods* (novel) 2001

*Harlequin Valentine* [illustrated by Bolton] (comics) 2001

*Coraline* [illustrated by McKean] (juvenile novel) 2002

*Murder Mysteries* [illustrated by P. Craig Russell; adaptation of radio play] (graphic novel) 2002

*The Sandman: Endless Nights* [illustrated by Glenn Fabry, Milo Manara, Miguelanxo Prado, Frank Quitely, P. Craig Russell, Bill Sienkiewicz, and Barron Storey] (graphic novel) 2003

*The Wolves in the Walls* [illustrated by McKean] (picture book) 2003

*1602* [illustrated by Andy Kubert; originally published in seven issues in 2003-2004] (graphic novel) 2004

*This work was later expanded and republished as *Smoke and Mirrors: Short Fictions and Illusions* in 1998.

# CRITICISM

## Steve Erickson (essay date 3 September 1995)

SOURCE: Erickson, Steve. "Dreamland." *Los Angeles Times* (3 September 1995): 14.

[*In the following essay, Erickson discusses Gaiman's career as a graphic novelist and the development of the* Sandman *series.*]

Neil Gaiman never remembers his dreams. They are devoured by his imagination before consciousness can reach them. If he has one recurring dream, it's of a house. "I think it's always the same house," he says, "but I don't think I've ever visited the same room twice. And the house continues for practically forever, and it's, you know, not really a house at all—it's a life." It doesn't seem to be the house of Gaiman's childhood in England, or the house he lived in outside London before he moved to the United States, or even the old red-brick Victorian house he lives in now, an hour outside Minneapolis, that looks like it could be from a dream. The glass gazebo in back, where the hill begins to slope into the woods, could be from a dream as well. Isolated, incommunicado, there Gaiman writes about dreams all the time—not his, because he doesn't remember his, but yours, because yours he remembers before you have them.

He writes about them in a comic book. *The Sandman,* published by DC Comics, is Gaiman's rapid-eye almanac of a "place" called The Dreaming. This is a landscape of psychic rather than physical borders, with a topography as amorphous as mist. It's a little like a five-dimensional chessboard, time being the fourth dimension and memory the fifth, over and across which all of us move every night. Every night each of us returns to the Dreaming in our most primal form, perhaps as the little boy or girl we once were and never completely left behind, perhaps as a cat we once held or a raven that once perched outside our window, perhaps not as an animate object at all but a particularly lovely knoll, green and shady, that we saw as a child for only a few moments. Perhaps as a long-buried secret about ourselves that we never knew or wanted to know. But sooner or later in The Dreaming, we bump into him. He's never actually called the Sandman. The more classically bent would prefer to know him as Morpheus; to the populists among us, his name is just Dream. At any rate, he runs the joint.

Well, not really. Neil Gaiman runs the joint, and over seven years and nearly 2,000 pages he has moved over and across The Dreaming in seemingly every direction at once, teetering on occasion but never toppling. An open-ended epic, the narrative, and the stories within it, and the stories within the stories, move from the atriums of ancient Greek myth to the veldt of African folklore, from the French Revolution to modern-day Manhattan, from the tale of a man who has decided never to die to the bodiless head of Orpheus begging someone to kill him, from Shakespeare making the terrible bargain that will transform him from hack to genius, to Thomas Paine muttering in his jail cell about the ideal that betrayed him, from a novelist who locks his muse in his attic, defiling her for black inspiration, to a convention of serial killers in the American South with a guest of honor who swallows people's eyes. Literate and sophisticated by any measure, let alone that of comic books, *The Sandman* is complex to the point of labyrinthine, non-linear to the point of vertiginous. Reading the whole thing, the reader wants to lay out all the pages in a field somewhere, and look at it from the vantage point of a bird circling overhead.

Besides being the best monthly comic book in the world, *The Sandman* is also one of the most popular. Many of its most devoted fans are people who don't otherwise read comics, and it has won not only the praise of literary big shots ("A comic strip for intellectuals," Norman Mailer declared a few years back, "and I say it's about time") but more prizes than Gaiman can find room for in his house, including four straight Eisner awards—the comic book Oscar—and the World Fantasy Award, the only time this has gone to a comic. Immediately afterward, the World Fantasy people changed the rules so such an outrage could never happen again. *Sandman* has inspired college doctorates and songs by Metallica and Tori Amos, it is the primary text for classes on myth at the University of California, and a film is in the works to which Gaiman has offered his blessing though nothing else. Gaiman claims, and DC does not dispute, that the Sandman is the company's third-most popular character after Batman and Superman, and at L.A.'s Golden Apple store it is consistently DC's best seller; in college towns it sometimes outsells "X-Men," published by DC rival Marvel Comics and the single biggest title of the last 20 years. The entire run of *Sandman* has been collected in deluxe bound volumes (start with *Preludes & Nocturnes* and *The Doll's House*), with comments by Stephen King, Clive Barker, Mikal Gilmore, Peter Straub and Gene Wolfe genuflecting before Gaiman's brilliance. . . .

Enough, you must be saying at this point. Enough, Gaiman may well agree. Because this fall, with issue number 75, he is quitting the magazine that he has written since December, 1988. This happens all the time in comics, blazingly successful writers burning out on a book and handing it off to someone else. Except this isn't the case. Gaiman isn't burning out, and he isn't handing the book off to anyone, and in defiance of the universal corporate law that says no one is irreplaceable, DC has made a creative decision flatly in conflict with its profits. It is killing *The Sandman* off and closing The Dreaming down.

\* \* \*

Like many people who live in the world of their imaginations, Neil Gaiman doesn't quite seem to belong in the real one. A little lost in his big red-brick Midwest house, still sleep-disheveled at noon and tending the baby until his wife Mary gets home, he yearns for England "only about 90% of the time." The first thing he wants to show you is the garden in back, recounting its various vegetables with that inexplicable enthusiasm for gardens to which the English must be genetically disposed. More dishevelment abounds. Shambling around the house, he knocks over stacks of old comics looking for one in particular; upstairs in the TV room, he rummages among the rubble of videos for an obscure Czech fantasy to put in the VCR. "Lorraine will kill me," he shrugs, surveying the new mess. Lorraine Garland has graduated from being Neil's assistant to serving as the all-purpose Gaiman family assistant, managing the schedule and answering the telephone and returning messages and helping to tend the three children. Picking up everyone's comic books.

Watch Gaiman long enough and you'll notice he reminds you of someone, and then of course you realize it's the Sandman himself, allowing for the liberties taken by the 33 artists who have visually interpreted the character over the years. On the Sandman, for instance, Gaiman's dark unruly hair is a detonation of black smoke that makes him look like that guy who sings for the Cure; but then Gaiman cultivates a rock-star persona of his own, always dressed in black and never appearing in public without a leather jacket and sunglasses. He's a lot funnier than the Sandman, but then everyone's funnier than the Sandman. Charming and charismatic, affable and gracious, at once warmly empathetic and distantly ironic, Gaiman can also seem a little full of himself at first; when his celebrity suddenly rose five years ago, he came to Los Angeles on a promotional tour and brashly held court for a bunch of sullen journalists at a restaurant on Melrose shaped like a hamburger. In fairness, it wasn't his idea. One doesn't write something as absurdly ambitious as *The Sandman* without at the very least a sense of mission. He's cheeky without ever being brash, and eventually the cheek gives way to a more nuanced sense of proportion about his life and work, inevitably followed by an outburst of outright self-deprecation: "Remember," he reminds you when the discussion gets a little inflated, "I write comics.

"I remember once at a party running into the editor of the literary page of a major newspaper." You can already tell that, pushing back in his chair behind the desk of his office, he really likes telling this story. "And he was asking me what I did, and I said, 'I write comics.' And I could see him turn off—it was like, This is somebody beneath my nose. 'Well,' he said, 'which comics do you write?' and I told him this and that, and then I said, 'I also do this thing called *Sandman,* and he went, 'Wait, hang on, you're Neil Gaiman!' He said, 'My God, man, you don't write comics, you write graphic novels.' And I suddenly felt like someone who had been informed that she wasn't a hooker, that in fact she was a lady of the evening.

"I loved comics when I was growing up," Gaiman says, "and I never saw any reason why they should be considered inferior. I thought they could have as much power and passion and elegance as any other medium." At the age of 9 he read his way through the entire children's section of the Sussex library where his mother, a pharmacist, and his father, the owner of a vitamin company, would drop him off on their way to work. "When I finished the children's library," he remembers, "I moved on to the adult's library. I started at A." Some of his favorite authors were C. S. Lewis, Michael Moorcock and a Virginia writer named James Branch Cabell, whose strange oeuvre presently occupies three shelves in Gaiman's office. "Ghosts, space," Gaiman sums up his childhood interests, "anything indicating the imagination," and when his teen years coincided with a new wave of science-fiction writers as incorrigible as they were literary, Gaiman's own sensibilities crystallized. His heroes included Samuel R. Delany, Harlan Ellison and Roger Zelazny, all of whom went on to become Neil Gaiman fans, sometimes littering the covers of *Sandman* books with blurbs or composing those effusive introductions.

The first stories Gaiman wrote, around the same time he was at the local library lost between A and Z, were about a day in the life of a penny; a professor, his young assistant and their pet white mountain lion; and an alien Gaiman distinctly remembers looking like a frog, with a spaceship he distinctly remembers looking like a football. At the age of 20 he sold his first article to a small newspaper—a review of a 10cc concert—stepping in for a rock-journalist friend who couldn't make the gig. Over the following years he wrote features about science-fiction for *Time Out, Punch* and *Penthouse,* while submitting short stories to anyone and everyone. Waiting for success, it crossed his mind that perhaps he had no talent, "a conclusion which," he says, "for reasons of arrogance I declined to believe though, looking back, it now occurs to me there may have been more to it than I thought."

He really didn't have so long to wait: Within a few years he was writing comics on both sides of the Atlantic. If part of success' secret is timing, Gaiman's was about to prove perfect. He came along just as

American popular culture was mid-whiplash on the subject of comics. While in Europe and Japan comics have long been read by everyone from proles riding the Metro to intellectuals in cafes, in the United States the form had been mired for 50 years in the adolescence of its audience, and the not-entirely unfounded biases of grown-ups who think nothing of watching one inane TV sitcom after another but assume that comics are beneath them. Then in the early '80s appeared a book called *American Flagg!* written and drawn by Howard Chaykin. Set in a future bluntly polarized between authoritarianism and anarchy, *American Flagg!* was comic-strip Godard in its visual density, frantic energy, jagged jump-cuts and subliminal story logic. For the next several years there was a renaissance in American comics, led by hip, smart writers and artists usually from England or the more disenfranchised pockets of American society, who had come of age with comics but brought along with them everything else they had come of age with as well—the excitement of movies and the passion of rock 'n' roll and the influences of novelists from Dostoyevsky to Orwell to Chandler to Pynchon.

"We were suddenly in a world," recalls Gaiman, "where comics could be as good as anything. It was simply another medium with its own set of strengths and its own set of weaknesses. You could have words and pictures counterpointing each other, and you could get to a level of complexity that might be difficult in a film, for instance, because in a film you have no control over time, whereas in a comic you can go backwards and forwards" In a blur rushed one landmark after another: Alan Moore's *Swamp Thing*; Jaime and Gilbert Hernandez's *Love and Rockets*; Art Spiegelman's Pulitzer Prize-winning *Maus*; Jamie Delano's *Hellblazer*; Frank Miller's *The Dark Knight Returns,* which resurrected Batman from camp and turned him into a multizillion-dollar phenomenon; and Alan Moore and Dave Gibbons' epochal *Watchmen,* with its not-very-pretty conclusions about why we need supermen, and how the childish innocence of that need curdles to something pathetic and fascist.

Then the renaissance ended. Looking back, it's surprising how abruptly it ended. Inspiration gave way to the frustration and fury that the best writers and artists felt from dealing with the creative limitations, commercial demands and corporate bureaucracy of the mainstream—which is to say DC and especially Marvel, the monster of the business. Most notably Miller and Moore veered sharply toward the margins, where they would not have to accommodate a market still driven by 14-year-old boys, and where other gonzo geniuses, led principally by the Hernandez Brothers, were waiting. The work they have done there, like Miller's noir *Sin City* and Moore's Jack-the-Ripper saga *From Hell,* has been as exhilarating as it is subversive. But on the margins of the business it remains.

In the late '80s, after other people kicked down the doors, Neil Gaiman happened to wander through. He found he practically had the mainstream to himself, as well as a new market created over the preceding few years that wasn't just 14-year-old boys. The first project that got him attention in America was **Black Orchid,** a bold if not entirely successful metaphysical title influenced by *Swamp Thing.* After that he went on to **Miracleman** and **Books of Magic,** the graphic novels **Violent Cases** and **Mr. Punch,** and the particularly fine **Signal to Noise,** about a dying filmmaker. As well, he co-authored **Good Omens,** one of those novels published from time to time with lots of words and no pictures whatsoever. No one, however, including Gaiman, would contest that **The Sandman** is his masterpiece, and almost immediately he began testing the boundaries of what he could get away with.

"You can sort of see in the earliest stories," points out artist Dave McKean, who has done the fabulously spooky, id-wracked covers for every issue of **Sandman,** "that when he first started out there was just this expectation of, Well, I'm doing this thing for this huge company, and this is the sort of thing they usually do, and you can only go so far. And then I think very quickly Neil decided, Well, why? Why shouldn't I just do what I want?"

\* \* \*

He did what he wanted. If at first Gaiman didn't know exactly what that was, within a year he knew in meticulous detail. A comic book script is not unlike a movie script, except that the writer is also the director, giving directions to the artist that may be loose or specific, depending on the comic and the writer and the artist. Gaiman's scripts, which often run 40 pages or more for a 24-page, 135-panel story, are precise down to describing not just the action in every panel but often how large and dominant the panels are, what's in the foreground and what's in the back, what the overall visual tone of the page is, what the characters look like, and what the juxtapositions are between image and dialogue.

While he has breezily broken comic book traditions right and left, writing narratives that spiral back into each other from the proximity of years apart (the seed for the upcoming final issue, number 75, was laid back in number 19), it may be that Gaiman's most daring creation has been the main character himself. Dream is a willfully unlikable master of ceremonies. His brooding mystique not withstanding, he is pompous and morose, harsh and utterly self-absorbed, bound to a code of honor ("the rules," he calls them) as capricious as it is mysterious, and he has all the social tact of the Velvet Underground's "Sister Ray" cranked to maximum volume at a baby shower. His conduct tends toward the extreme. Having banished the love of his life to eternal torment in Hell for nothing worse than simply being wiser than he, he never considered the malice and injustice of his action until thousands of years later, when his sister finally pointed out how rather horrid it all was; at that point he turned the waking and dreaming universe upside down to rectify the matter. Hell, Heaven and everything in between are still sorting out the mess. He has no sense of humor whatsoever; in 69 issues, unless it was with a subtlety that would make Noel Coward look like Sam Kinison, he has never made a joke, let alone a witticism or an aside that might be considered vaguely sardonic.

Of course, he did have a rather lousy stretch there for the first 90 years or so of the 20th Century. An Aleister Crowley sort, trying to conjure and trap Death in his cellar in 1916 England through black magic, got his spells crossed and snared Dream instead. This happened in *Sandman* No. 1. There in that basement, Dream waited, a prisoner for decade after decade while all over the world people slipped into a dreamless sleep, sometimes for their whole lives; the evidence of the 20th Century, from human lampshades and the Cultural Revolution to Richard Nixon's presidency and Michael Jackson's new CD, is that the collective subconscious has been out of whack ever since. No sooner did Dream escape his predicament than he ran into its intended captive, Death, who happens to be Dream's big sister, the one with all the free advice on how her brother should conduct his affairs. Lively and level-headed, in her tight black leotards with her pixie mouth and wanton hair, Death is as unsettlingly appealing as Dream is a pill, not a god or a ghost or a demon but, like her brother, an Endless, one of seven siblings—along with Destiny and Destruction and Desire and Despair—in eternity's most dysfunctional family.

From her first appearance in *Sandman* No. 8, Death threatened to run away with the comic. She became so popular that not only did she make frequent return appearances but even had her own graphic novel, *The High Cost of Living* (with another, *The Time of Your Life,* to come next year). Gaiman immediately understood that Death was a creation he had to make discriminating use of: "I've always tried to treat most of my characters as though I'm paying them," he notes. "Death is a superstar. She costs a lot." Soon enough, however, the spotlight was stolen from both Dream and Death by their littlest sister, Delirium, a cloud-addled punkette with green and pink hair who walks an airborne goldfish on a leash and is accompanied by a yammering dog named Barnabas—"George Burns," as Gaiman says, "to Delirium's Gracie Allen." Delirium

trills on and on in musical non sequiturs that, in the midst of all their surreal nonsense, contain unexpected bits of poetry and revelation.

Death and Delirium only partly account for the extraordinary appeal of *The Sandman* to female readers. In a market that is 90% male, Martha Thomases, DC's publicity manager, guesses that nearly half of the book's readership is female, something that Golden Apple's manager Tony Edwards confirms. To some extent this is a function of age: 18 years, when kids start to outgrow other comics, is about when Gaiman's readership starts; and the maturity of the comic, as well as the emphasis on fantasy rather than fistfights, particularly appeals to young women on the cusp between adolescence and adulthood. Distinctly adult not so much for its sexuality and violence, though there is some from time to time, but for what it demands of the reader, *Sandman* portrays adult matters (such as sex and violence) in a fashion as unsensational as it is unsentimental, with sometimes ruthless consequences. All of this speaks to female readers and more mature male readers who are drawn to the moodiness of the stories as well as the insight Gaiman invests in all his characters, so many of whom, along with Death and Delirium, are young women, or girls aging faster than they want to. Among male writers in comics, only the Hernandez brothers write women as well.

Gaiman plainly values and believes in the archetypal myths that Frank Miller and Alan Moore smashed in the late '80s. "That's the reason," suggests rock 'n' roll singer Tori Amos, who wrote the songs "Precious Things" and "Tear in Your Hand" after reading *Sandman,* "that people are waiting for the next issue. Neil is giving myth back to them. Some of them know it, some of them don't." Amos discovered Gaiman five years ago when she stumbled on **"Calliope,"** the story of a Greek muse abducted from Mount Helicon in the 1920s and locked in a room by a desperate, washed-up writer. For years, used and deceived and lonely, Calliope waits heartbroken for the freedom that has been promised to her and which, she finally realizes, will never be delivered. "Writers are liars, my dear," her captor finally explains. "Surely you have realized that by now?"

"We don't remember our myth anymore," Amos says. "And what is myth? It's just truth that has happened and that we've forgotten, but that's still happening now." Gaiman's reconstruction of comic book myths has wound up something very different from Batman or Superman. Dream may be the most morally neutral comic book hero ever, defined not by righteous revenge or nihilistic fury or messianic purpose, creating nightmares as easily as reveries because, in the Dreaming, there has to be both. *The Sandman* is not about heroism or justice or redemption; Amos thinks it's about "wholeness," about fragmented, busted-up people finding their common bond and becoming cohesive. But given the melancholy that pervades the book, it is also about loss. A sense of loss has gripped the comic from the beginning, when Dream lost his freedom within the prison of that English cellar. Ever since, it's been one loss after another: loss of faith, loss of friendship, loss of love, loss of innocence, loss of certainty, loss of identity, loss of the past, loss of the soul, loss of our dreams every time we wake, with Dream the agent of all our life's losses, until Death transacts the last and greatest loss of all.

\* \* \*

Almost from the beginning of *The Sandman,* there were rumors the end was near. By issue 20 Gaiman began suggesting in interviews that he would be finished with the story by issue 40, "and then as I got on I said, 'Well, it isn't going to be done by 40,' and then I said, 'Well, probably 50.' And then, when we got into the early 50s, I started saying, 'Well, if we're still going by issue 70, I'll be very surprised.'"

He finally killed Dream in issue 69, with so little theatrics one had to read it twice to realize it happened. "I think I knew all along I was going to kill him off, but I didn't know if I would have the guts when I got there. So I built escape holes and trap doors. All through the structure of *Sandman* there are dozens of trap doors, to get me out of it if that really wasn't where I wanted to be when I got there." It was Gaiman's idea that DC Comics simply discontinue *The Sandman* when he was finished. Gaiman doesn't legally own the character; some version or other of the Sandman dates back to the 1940s, having gone through three or four incarnations before Gaiman created his. At first the company flatly rejected the proposal, before acceding to Gaiman's wishes. No one in the business can recall something like this ever happening: a major company making a purely artistic decision that will lose it money. "When someone has created such an outstanding and phenomenal piece of work as Neil," says DC executive editor Karen Berger, "it would be counterproductive for us to just say the hell with you and we're going to do whatever we want."

In other words, it apparently occurred to DC that Gaiman himself is a potentially more valuable commodity than *The Sandman* will ever be. At the annual Comics Convention in San Diego in July, the line of people who brought their posters and books and comics for him to sign snaked through the cavernous convention hall out into the lobby; scheduled to last an hour, the signing was still going on after two, when Gaiman finally had to tear himself away for another commitment. At an event called "Spotlight on Neil Gaiman," with the aplomb and command of a brilliant monologuist, he regaled a standing-room-only, turn-away crowd

for 90 minutes with Tales of Gaiman. These included the story of his first comics job, offered him by a guy in a bar who claimed to own a company that Gaiman finally discovered months later didn't exist; and his encounter, at the age of 15, with the stunned school career counselor who could only greet the boy's announcement that he wanted to write comics with the reply: "Have you ever considered accountancy?" For his convention performance Gaiman dressed in his customary black, though the leather jacket and the shades came off soon enough, and he laughed as much as everyone else when the first question from the audience was, "When you look in your closet in the morning, how many colors do you see?"

This year's comic convention came in on the heels of the outgoing Harley-Davidson convention, whose attendees hadn't yet all roared out of town. At the hotel next door, comic conventioneers mingled with Harley conventioneers, and you didn't have a lot of trouble telling which were which; the comic people were the geeky teen-age boys in shorts and backpacks. Inside the convention hall, aisles and aisles of booths and booths selling and buying and promoting comics were overrun with costumed superheroes and superheroines, some of them fans and some bountiful models hired to tuck themselves into flimsy red Vampirella outfits and hope that with one wrong move they didn't come spilling out, an epiphany the geeks awaited rapturously. The comic convention also had a startling and inordinate number of people in wheelchairs, for whom flight into a comic book world of the physically superempowered might be more than just a diversionary escape. In contrast to the rest of the convention, Gaiman's fans were older and punkier—painfully shy college girls dressed in Death clothes who silently thrusted their books in front of the author for a signature and perhaps a heart-fluttering word or two. Gaiman's star status as he walked through the hall was obvious even to those few who had no idea who he was. "Are you Tim Burton?" someone wanted to know.

In a medium where the story inside has always been written around the cover that sells the magazine, and where the superstars have always been illustrators (or illustrators who incidentally happen to be writers, too), Gaiman's superstardom is anomalous. The only other name comparable—besides Stan Lee, who revolutionized the business at Marvel around the time Gaiman was born—is that of fellow Brit and mentor Alan Moore. Ten years ago Moore was in a position similar to Gaiman's before the business made him nuts, or at any rate nuttier than he already was, which is reportedly pretty nutty. If Gaiman is in danger of anything, it's a marketplace that's willing to turn his endless creative energy into a brand name; like Stephen King or Clive Barker, he's already plastered across the covers of other companies' comics, such as "Neil Gaiman's

Lady Justice," "Neil Gaiman's Mr. Hero" and "Neil Gaiman's Teknophage," with the truth of Neil Gaiman's actual involvement to be found in the credit box inside, which reads, "Based on a Concept Created by Neil Gaiman." Soon it will be, "Based on a Fleeting Notion Neil Had One Day Sitting Around His Gazebo Watching the Squirrels Frolic in the Woods," or "Based on a Whimsy Neil Himself Didn't Take Particularly Seriously for More Than Two or Three Seconds."

When someone at the convention asked if he ever finds himself writing "for the wrong reasons," Gaiman could still truthfully answer, "Not yet." But he would be the first to admit that none of his upcoming comic projects suggest a passionate purpose on the order of *Sandman,* and most are, rather conspicuously, *Sandman* offshoots: the second Death novel, a Delirium miniseries, a series called "The Dreaming" that will be another of those things Gaiman "conceives" without actually writing. Beyond the comics, spoken-word CDs and songs for a local folk group and a TV series for the BBC, which currently absorbs most of his effort and enthusiasm, as well as all the admirable time and money he contributes to the Comic Book Legal Defense Fund for fighting censorship. By his own admission, a passionate purpose isn't what he's looking for at the moment: "Something I can finish by tea time" is the way he puts it. Gaiman's future is now as open and invisible as the Midwest night, with its fleeting fireflies providing the only glimmer; and lately, talking on the telephone with his 1-year-old daughter in his arms, he almost sounds weary—a little at loose ends perhaps, and depressed by the recent death of his early science-fiction idol Roger Zelazny. He is intelligent and insightful enough to suspect that, whatever the triumphs of the future, he will probably never have more fun than he's had the last seven years; he will probably never have a better dream.

Counting off the latitudes and longitudes, stranding himself smack in the middle of the New World, Neil Gaiman hides out there. Whether he hides not only from the loopy past and the frenzied present, represented by tremulous teen-age girls dressed in black with Delirious hair, but also from the insomnia of the future, where there is no more dreaming and one writes for the wrong reasons, only he can say. Yearning for England as he does only 90% of the time, he misses the Old World's layers of age and meaning, forced on top of one another by the constraints of space. "In America," he says, "if you want to find something, you get in a car and drive. In England, you go down into the ground, through a thousand years." His new series for the BBC, *Neverwhere,* takes place in two Londons: one the London of daylight and wakefulness, the other a shadow London that exists underground, under the feet of all the somnambulists above. So in a sense nothing has changed; going down into the ground, going down into a thousand years of dreams, Gaiman is still exploring the subterranean side of consciousness, and the Sandman isn't dead after all. But now, having finally awakened from your dream, he is left to dream his own.

## Frank McConnell (essay date 20 October 1995)

SOURCE: McConnell, Frank. "Epic Comics: Neil Gaiman's *Sandman.*" *Commonweal* 122, no. 18 (20 October 1995): 21-2.

[*In the following essay, McConnell assesses the* Sandman *series as a whole and discusses Gaiman's central thematic concern with myth and storytelling.*]

A few years ago I wrote a column for *Commonweal* (February 28, 1992) on comic books and how they had become a refuge for some very fine, and very serious, storytellers. And I signaled that *Sandman,* written by Neil Gaiman, was not only a wonderful comic but one of the best bits of fiction altogether being produced these days.

Now I have to make a correction. *Sandman* is not one of the best pieces of fiction being done these days: as it approaches its conclusion, it emerges as *the* best piece of fiction being done these days. And that, not just because of the brilliance and intricacy of its storytelling—and I know few stories, outside the best of Joyce, Faulkner, and Pynchon, that are more intricate—but also because it tells its wonderful and humanizing tale in a medium, comic books, still largely considered *demimonde* by the tenured zombies of the academic establishment.

And never mind also that Gaiman has won awards and admiration and, most important for a writer, envy, from the whole civilized world. What he has done with *Sandman* is establish the fact that a *comic book* can be a work of high and very serious art—a story that other storytellers, in whatever medium they work, will have to take into account as an exploration of what stories can do and what stories are for.

Not that he doesn't have antecedents, and not that he doesn't acknowledge them. Will Eisner and Jack Kirby in the forties, Wally Wood and Carmine Infantino in the fifties, and lately Frank Miller and the superbly gifted Alan Moore—all of whom have been demonstrating that comics are a legitimate fictive mode—or, in Gaiman's simpler, better phrase, a machine for storytelling, no less rich, and no less exciting, than any other.

There are nods, throughout the issues of *Sandman,* toward all of those strong precursors: Gaiman is not the sort to forget or pretend to forget his guildmasters.

Nevertheless, with some excitement, I have to announce that *Sandman,* at issue number 71 as I write this in September, and with maybe three or four more issues to go, is a new thing. With the conclusion of the series, which began on a monthly basis in 1988, Gaiman will have created a single, massive tale—as long as a Henry James novel—which works both as an allegory of the storytelling imagination (a "metafiction," if we must use the word) and as—a term I do not use frivolously—a tragedy. And when I say "tragedy," I am thinking of *Lord Jim* and *Lear* and *Gilgamesh*: stories that exist to remind us of the terrible cost of being human.

Here's what happened. In 1987, DC Comics approached Gaiman to revive, with changes, an old DC character from the forties. Gaiman chose a relatively obscure character, the Sandman, who in the forties was a guy who would dress up at night in a gas mask, zap bad guys with his gas gun, and leave them to sleep it off until the cops came to pick them up next morning.

All Gaiman used was the name: "Sandman." The master of dreams; the master of stories; Morpheus, whose name means both "god of sleep" and "shaper of form" (make no mistake, when it comes to recondite allusions, nobody has a patch upon our scarily well-read lad). So he invented a theogony—a Family of more-than, less-than gods, the Endless as he calls them, anthropomorphic projections of fundamental human perceptions. In order of age, the family includes Destiny, Death, Dream, Destruction, Desire, Despair, and Delirium (who was once Delight).

The point of this psychic genealogy, is that Dream is at its center. We tell stories, create myths, write gospels of every sort, because we cannot tolerate the irrational. Absurdity offends us, as Norman Mailer says in *Oswald's Tale,* just because it attacks our sense that there is a reason for our pain. Is all this sadness for *nothing?* we ask. And the human answer comes back, again and again, no: it's for something but it may be for a little bit more than what you were expecting.

*Sandman,* in other words, is about failure: about the failure of the imagination successfully to encompass the chaos of ordinary human life, about the failure of all our stories to explain to us why we are such an unhappy people. Some critics—those at least smart enough to recognize the fineness of Gaiman's work—have described him as a "postmodern" writer, and that phrase, stupid as it innately is, may begin to catch the special quality of his work; but only glancingly.

I won't detail for you the plots, subplots, and skerries-within-subplots that are the tapestry of the work: like the best of Dickens, this is serial storytelling, and part of the fun of the thing is seeing how many more balls the author tosses into the air each month, and whether he can keep them all aloft. He (Charles and Neil) does.

But I will—and now, with the series approaching its end, I can—give you a sense of its grand design.

Dream of the Endless, the Lord of Stories, is imprisoned in 1916, by a necromancer in England. He frees himself in 1988 (coincidentally the year of the series' beginning) and regains his kingdom, only to find that he has become somehow tainted—spoiled—altered—by his captivity. Humanized, in fact. From that beginning, the rest of this great and discursive series of tales is all about Dream—Story—discovering that he is intimately involved with the fate of human beings, and can in fact not exist without them.

I don't want to belabor this but in fact *Sandman* fascinates us so just because it is a parable of the epochal transformation of the human imagination that began right around the time of the Renaissance. In that age, our myths began to be humanized: beginning, say, with Shakespeare, we began to realize that the gods had not invented us, but that we were in the process of inventing our gods. By now in the series Dream of the Endless has died—or committed suicide—but since stories cannot cease, anymore than the mind can stop thinking, Dream of the Endless has also been reborn— but this time as the exaltation of a *human* child, rather than as an anthropomorphic configuration. Gaiman is too subtle to say it, but I'm not: as the series ends, the Word is made Flesh, and from now on our stories will be the stories of the gods among us, rather than the gods whose chief characteristic is their apartness.

It is the history of Western storytelling altogether, and especially of the stories we like to call "modern." It is profoundly incarnational but also—Gaiman is very learnedly Jewish—wisely melancholy about the giant cost of moving from the transcendent to the immanent. If you can really read, it is simply magnificent metafiction, a story about story.

I hope DC will have the good sense to publish the entire run, but they probably won't. I know of nothing quite like it, and I don't expect there will be anything quite like it for some time. How often is a new, and deeply human, art form born? (How often do we invent a new—a really new—sin?)

If *Sandman* is a "comic," then *The Magic Flute* is a "musical" and *A Midsummer Night's Dream* is a skit. *Read* the damn thing: it's important.

### Sybil S. Steinberg (review date 22 July 1996)

SOURCE: Steinberg, Sybil S. Review of *Sandman: Book of Dreams,* edited by Neil Gaiman and Edward E. Kramer. *Publishers Weekly* 243, no. 30 (22 July 1996): 231-32.

[*In the following review of* Sandman: Book of Dreams, *a collection of short stories by various authors inspired by the* Sandman *series, edited by Gaiman and Edward*

*E. Kramer, Steinberg asserts that the book includes some powerful writing about the realm of dreams, but that the quality of the collection as a whole is uneven.*]

Though he won the World Fantasy Award for Short Fiction in 1991, Gaiman is best known as the writer who transformed the WWII-era DC Comics character the Sandman from a Batman-style detective/vigilante into the much darker Morpheus, aka Dream, the being who presides over the realm of Dreaming. One of seven siblings who represent various states of consciousness— Destiny, Death, Destruction, Desire, Despair, Dream and Delirium—Morpheus is head of the allegorical family called the Endless. Here [in **Sandman: Book of Dreams**], popular fantasy writers expand upon Gaiman's original concepts, with mixed results. Colin Greenland's bittersweet "Masquerade and High Water" and Barbara Hambly's "Each Damp Thing" provide insights into the backstage workings of the Endless. Tad Williams's "The Writer's Child" is a finely crafted story about loyalty and the value of innocence. Weak spots include George Alec Effinger's resurrection of a saccharine Little Nemo for "Seven Nights in Slumberland," Lisa Goldstein's bland "Stronger Than Desire" and B. W. Clough's vignette "The Birth Day." Susanna Clarke's "Stopp't-Clock Yard" and a lyrical meditation on Death by songwriter Tori Amos close the anthology on a strong note; a b&w drawing by Clive Barker opens it on a garish one. Though perhaps most interesting as an example of media-crossover, this collection presents some powerful writing about, and memorable images of, the other reality wherein we while away a third of our lives.

### Charles De Lint (review date April 2000)

SOURCE: De Lint, Charles. Review of *Sandman: The Dream Hunters*, by Neil Gaiman and Yoshitaka Amano. *Fantasy & Science Fiction* 98, no. 4 (April 2000): 32-3.

[*In the following review, De Lint asserts that the graphic novel* Sandman: The Dream Hunters *is an exquisite and evocative story by Gaiman which meshes perfectly with the illustrations by Yoshitaka Amano.*]

It strikes me that writing an illustrated book presents a real risk for the author, something that requires a certain measure of bravery to undertake. The reason for that is simple.

The illustrations have the potential to undo the compact between author and reader inherent in a book, intruding into that no man's land between the page and the eye where the imaginations of the participants meet to create a greater whole. As readers we make movies in our heads from the raw data of the words on the page, and

there's really nothing that can compare to that magic. It's why the movies based on our favorite books often fall flat: they simply don't—*can't*—match the pictures we call up in our own heads as we're reading.

Now, sometimes the illustrations and text are so entwined in our consideration of the experience that we can't imagine the one without the other. Ernest Shepherd's drawings for *The Wind in the Willows* and the Pooh books are like that for me. But mostly illustrations tread that same uneasy path as do film adaptations.

When they work, they enhance the experience. When they don't, nothing can bring the words to life. And the sad truth is—readers on a whole being so subjective in their likes and dislikes—what works and doesn't work is different for each one of us. So I'd think a writer would be cautious entering into such a project.

Neil Gaiman doesn't seem to worry overmuch about it. I suppose his bravery comes from his long association with the comics field. Having written scripts for so many years, the combination of pictures and words must seem completely natural to him. And even in regular books, his collaborators have certainly been high-end: British artist Dave McKean on any number of projects, World Fantasy Award-winning artist Charles Vess on **Stardust,** and now the evocative work of Japanese artist Yoshitaka Amano for the book in hand [**The Dream Hunters**].

**The Dream Hunters** is Gaiman's first visit back to the **Sandman** mythos in many years and doesn't require any familiarity with that long-running comic book series to work. The story is based on the Japanese folktale "The Fox, the Monk, and the Mikado of All Night's Dreaming"—something Gaiman discovered while researching Japanese history and mythology in preparation for the work he did on the English dialogue for the film **Princess Mononoke.** In his afterword to **The Dream Hunters,** Gaiman remarks on the similarity between the folktale and the **Sandman** series, and it really is eerie how well the folktale fits in.

It begins with a wager between a badger and a fox, the prize being the monk's temple that the winner will use as a den. But the fox falls in love with the monk and later, when she discovers that a lord of a nearby estate means him ill, she goes into the land of dreams and strikes a bargain with the Japanese counterpart of Morpheus to save the monk's life. How it all works out is for you to discover, but I will say that this is one of Gaiman's most exquisite and evocative stories to date.

Equal praise must go to Yoshitaka Amano's artwork. Profusely and gorgeously illustrated throughout—in many styles, but always with a stunning sense of design and rendering—this slender volume is as much of a delight for its art as for its words. The two mesh as perfectly with each other as did Gaiman's prose with Vess's art on **Stardust.** But that reminds me of something else. We can only hope that, down the road, Gaiman won't market a prose-only version of **The Dream Hunters** the way he did with **Stardust.** In a case such as this, it's just not necessary.

## Kurt Lancaster (essay date fall 2000)

SOURCE: Lancaster, Kurt. "Neil Gaiman's '*A Midsummer Night's Dream*': Shakespeare Integrated into Popular Culture." *Journal of American & Comparative Cultures* 23, no. 3 (fall 2000): 69-77.

[*In the following essay, Lancaster discusses Gaiman's award-winning story "A Midsummer's Night Dream," based on the play by William Shakespeare, in terms of cultural divisions between "high" and "low" art. Lancaster asserts that Gaiman's story successfully integrates the mythic qualities of Shakespeare into a popular modern medium.*]

> How this particular man produced the works that dominate the cultures of much of the world almost four hundred years after his death is one of life's mysteries—and one that will continue to tease our imaginations as we continue to delight in his plays and poems.
>
> (Mowat and Werstine 1993: xxxv)

[BILL MOYERS:]

> But, Shakespeare has no audience, today, to speak of. He really doesn't.

[PETER SELLARS:]

> Well, our audience has been taught that Shakespeare is not theirs. Our audience has been taught that Shakespeare belongs to the British and to the Royal Shakespeare Company [. . .]. What is maddening in America is most people have been separated from their culture. They've been told there's a special privileged class of artists—they have a special insight. A normal person doesn't have this insight and is not on the inside track of this work. That is a monstrous lie and it is hideous, because it is taught to us early on as we grow up in this system.
>
> (Moyers 1990)

The twentieth century saw about three hundred and eighty-five film and television adaptations of Shakespeare's plays—two hundred and thirty-four for film and one hundred and fifty-one for television (IMDB). Thirty-six of these films were made in the 1990s, the largest amount in any decade, except for the 1910s, when fifty-two of Shakespeare's plays were adapted to film. The most popular Shakespearean films of the

1990s in America most notably correspond with Kenneth Branagh's *Henry V* (1989), which led a Branagh-Shakespearian renaissance through such films as *Much Ado about Nothing* (1993), *Othello* (1995), and *Hamlet* (1996), all of which (except *Othello*) he directed. This popular British resurgence of Shakespeare on film also included Ian McKellen's adaptation and lead role in *Richard III* (1995) and Trevor Nunn's *Twelfth Night* (1996). Also, other popularizations of Shakespeare's plays adapted to film in the 1990s revolved around the popularity of movie stars, beginning most strikingly with action movie star Mel Gibson's appearance in the title role of Franco Zeffirelli's *Hamlet* (1990), as well as Leonardo DiCaprio and Clair Danes in Baz Luhrmann's *William Shakespeare's Romeo and Juliet* (1996), Al Pacino's documentary-postmodern rendition of *Richard III* in *Looking for Richard* (1996), and Calista Flockhart's, Kevin Kline's, and Michelle Pfeiffer's appearances in *A Midsummer Night's Dream* (1999). The 1990s Shakespearean film renaissance seemed to peak with *Shakespeare in Love* (1998), which earned an Academy Award for best picture in 1999, indicating not only the "high brow" sensibility of the Academy, but also the film's popularity in the larger public, a popularity not seen in America since the first half of the nineteenth century.

Interviewer Bill Moyers, talking to theater director Peter Sellars, mused about how he was fascinated to learn that "in the nineteenth century, great American actors would roam the countryside in the small towns. In Marshall, Texas, they would get off the railroad and they would perform Shakespeare for mill workers, for saloons, in mining camps, and they were speaking to an untutored, but appreciative audience" (1990). In fact, researching popular novels, playbills, and newspapers of the nineteenth century, historian Lawrence Levine discovered that Shakespeare's works were so integrated into American culture during the time period Moyers speaks of that he drew the following conclusion: "Shakespeare was popular entertainment in nineteenth century America" (Levine 21)—a view lost to most of the twentieth century, as Sellars bemoaned in the interview opening this essay.

During the first half of the nineteenth century, the plays of Shakespeare, Levine observes, were "presented as part of the same milieu inhabited by magicians, dancers, singers, acrobats, minstrels, and comics. [His works] appeared on the same playbills and was advertised in the same spirit" (23). Spectators didn't see Shakespeare as someone to revere, but as "part of the culture they enjoyed, a Shakespeare rendered familiar and intimate by virtue of his context" (23). Indeed, Richard Penn Smith even wrote a play, which, like the recent film, was also called *Shakespeare in Love*—about a "poor, worried, stumbling young man in love with a woman of whose feelings he is not yet certain" (23). A vaguely similar plot occurred in the 1998 film, in which we see Shakespeare getting the inspiration for his stories from the life he lives as he falls in love with a royal woman who wants to be an actor, which, at the same time, allows for the development of a parallel plot line with *Romeo and Juliet,* and, to some extent, *Twelfth Night.* The fact that both of these stories, focusing on the historical figure of Shakespeare, occurred during the height of Shakespearean popularity in their respective time periods cannot be understated.

If the late twentieth and early twenty-first centuries are on the tip of a new Shakespearean popularity wave—which the evidence of these Shakespeare films seem to suggest—then it is important to note how Shakespeare lost his popularity during the second half of the nineteenth century. During this period, Levine observes, Shakespeare evolved into a figure of "high brow" culture, and because of this *cultural invention* that the twentieth century inherited, Shakespeare lost his status as a figure of popular culture—the consequences of which I will state in the conclusion. However, suffice to say, as Levine contends, when Shakespeare remained a part of "free exchange" and was assimilated in popular culture, this process reflected the values and tastes of a "heterogeneous audience," but when cultural elitism removed Shakespeare from an atmosphere of "shared culture"—from a "mixed audience and from the presence of other cultural genres" (popular culture)—and as Shakespeare and his works were "removed from the pressures of everyday economic and social life" and placed within elite "cultural institutions," then that was when Americans were "taught to observe" Shakespeare "with reverent, informed, disciplined seriousness" (229-30), a view that most Americans, today, still share. Shakespeare and his works, according to the cultural elite, are essentially meant to be worshiped in a special place, cut off from the practice of everyday life that other works of popular culture seem to enjoy.

Such directors as Sellars, as well as the filmmakers mentioned above, have tried to make Shakespeare popular again at the end of the twentieth century. And that is why Sellars, in a 1990 interview with Bill Moyers, called Shakespeare the "great American playwright."[1] Even more telling was Moyers's response, who, usually cool, could not help being taken aback by Sellars's arresting statement, and blurted out, "The great what?—wait a minute" (Moyers). And this reaction reveals the bifurcation of Shakespeare in America at the beginning of the twenty-first century: one that places him on a pedestal, as a man of genius whose works must be revered with awe; and another that integrates Shakespeare into American popular culture. However, in the nineteenth century, a person making such a statement would not have received the same kind of reaction, as noted in James Fenimore Cooper's declaration—more than one hundred and sixty years before

Sellars's claim—that Shakespeare was "'the great author of America' and insisted that Americans had 'just a good a right' as Englishmen to claim Shakespeare as their countryman," because there was not the same level of cultural bifurcation (Levine 20). Although the late twentieth century is nothing like the first half of the nineteenth century—especially in regards as to how we view and consume Shakespeare in our culture and society—we do find a similar parallel, one that marks a small resurgence of Shakespeare being re-integrated into 1990s popular culture. We see evidence for this not just in the medium of film, the desire to see the historical figure of Shakespeare performed, and artists declaring Shakespeare as an American playwright, but we also see an integration of Shakespeare in the popular culture form of the comic book.

Neil Gaiman's graphic novel series ***The Sandman*** is one of the most important works of fiction written in that medium. Born in England and now living in Minnesota, Gaiman's seventy-five monthly graphic-novel stories were published between 1988 and 1996, selling over a million copies per year (Heidel 1).[2] However, as Shakespeare is looked up to by the cultural elite as a genius and high brow author, many look down on the comic book form as "low art" popular culture. But, by doing so, we are giving in to the logo-centric belief that the written word and only the written word is the best way to convey ideals of humanity through art. There are many different ways to enter an author's imaginary environment: through text, image, aurally, moving pictures, and a combination of these. Each one takes the participant into that imaginary universe in a different way, from a different perspective. And by privileging one form (text) over another betrays a gross ignorance about the nature of art and culture itself. Is the written word more "artistic," more superior than image art or a combination of image and text, as we find in the medium of comic books? The following event is revealing: In 1991, Gaiman's **"A Midsummer Night's Dream"** earned the World Fantasy Award for best short story, making it the first (and only) comic book ever to be awarded a literary award (Heidel 1). However, the following year members of the rules committee responsible for establishing the procedures on voting—apparently shocked that a "comic book" could win a literary award—changed the rules so only "literature" (text-only short stories) could be nominated. This kind of reaction reflects similar attitudes towards Shakespeare found at the end of the nineteenth century, but it certainly doesn't reflect the quality of alternative cultural creations found in diverse forms usually beyond the cultural elite's attention or understanding.

Because of this, as Shakespeare became relegated to "High Art" status and therefore "less accessible to large segments of the American people" by the end of the nineteenth century, most people had to satisfy "their aesthetic cravings through a number of new forms of expressive culture that were barred from high culture," Levine contends, which included such accessible forms as "the blues, jazz or jazz-derived music, musical comedy, photography, comic strips, movies, radio, popular comedians"—and it was these forms which "contained much that was fresh, exciting, innovative, intellectually challenging, and highly imaginative" (232). All of these qualities are reflected in Gaiman's work, despite the gatekeepers of literary awards and other elitists who would never examine works of art outside conventional literary forms.

Within his overall opus, Gaiman created a mythology that includes the seven sibling Ds: Death, Dream, Desire, Delirium, Despair, Destruction, and Destiny, who evoke in a palpable way the eternal nature of what it means to be human. Gaiman physicalizes these eternal forces of humanity and gives them personified weight, embodying in the character of the Dream Lord, for example, humanity's desire for dreams and the cost of attaining that desire. This is seen clearly in Gaiman's **"Men of Good Fortune,"** issue twelve of the series. Here, we see Shakespeare at the start of his playwriting career talking to Christopher Marlowe: "I would give anything to have your gifts. Or more than anything to give men dreams, that would live on long after I am dead. I'd bargain like your Faustus for that boon" (12). The character of the Dream Lord, overhearing Shakespeare's conversation with Marlowe, comes up to him: "I heard your talk, Will. Would you write great plays? Create new dreams to spur the minds of men?" and Shakespeare replies, "It is." "Then let us talk," is the reply of Morpheus, the Dream Lord (13). We would not see the use of Shakespeare in Gaiman's stories again until **"A Midsummer Night's Dream,"** issue number nineteen, which takes place four years after the "bargain" insinuated in **"Men of Good Fortune."**

In Gaiman's **"A Midsummer Night's Dream"** he not only weaves his mythology through the historical figure of Shakespeare, but also through his play, *A Midsummer Night's Dream* (c.1590s). In brief, Shakespeare's story is set in the world of Athens, containing English tropes, including European fairy myth, and contains four plots: the Athenian Lord Theseus's marriage to the Amazon, Hippolyta; the love triangle among the lovers Lysander-Hermia and Demetrius-Helena; the argument between the Fairy King and Queen, Oberon and Titania (who wants to keep an Indian boy that Oberon desires); and the Athenian workers who practice and put on a poorly performed play for Theseus's upcoming wedding.

In Gaiman's story—a work richly layered with a plethora of meaning on art, beauty, family, and other-worldliness—he provides a parallel meta-commentary on the action and plot of Shakespeare's play and his personal life. It opens with a troupe of actors, including Shakespeare and his eight-year-old son, Hamnet, traveling along the rolling countryside of England on June 23, 1593. We see an energetic and curious Hamnet asking his father where they will be performing "the new play tonight," "if not at an inn?" His father annoyingly replies that he has "no idea" and tells his son to "keep your eyes on the road ahead" (**"Midsummer"** 1).

As his son is about to ask him another question, one of his actors, Will Kemp, requests that Shakespeare consider allowing him to put in a new bit of stage business in the play. As Shakespeare refuses this request, Hamnet notices a figure standing on a hill: "Look. Will he be our audience?" Shakespeare asks Hamnet to "go and wait with Condell and the other boys" as he goes alone and speaks with this mysterious figure. In the second panel on page two, we see a close-up of a sad and dejected Hamnet in the foreground as his father, in the background, walks away, his back to Hamnet—a telling image that connects the reader to Hamnet's plight, and concretely conveys the theme of Gaiman's story.

As Shakespeare talks to the Dream Lord, the players and Hamnet get ready to put on their play, which will be performed "on the downs of Sussex" (Gaiman 3). For the audience, Morpheus has invited the *real* fairies depicted in Shakespeare's *A Midsummer Night's Dream* to watch the first performance of that play. Gaiman intercuts between the fairies watching and commenting on the performance, the performance itself (which draws on text from Shakespeare's play), and the actors backstage. For example, one of the fey spectators, comments: "What's this? What means this prancing, chattering mortal flesh? Methinks perhaps the Dream-Lord brought us here to feed?" Another larger fairy, looking like a blue potato-head figure, humorously replies: "Nar. Issa Wossname. You know. Thingie. A play. They're pretending things. . . . Issa love story. Not dinner" (8).

One of the backstage scenes reveal a quaking actor (playing Hermia), talking to Shakespeare (who plays Theseus): "But Master Will, they are not human! I saw boggarts, and trolls, and, and nixies, and things of every manner and kind"—to which Shakespeare replies: "Aye, and they are also our audience, Tommy. Calm yourself" (9). Gaiman's tale focuses on several characters, such as the comic-relief faeries, the Dream Lord's conversation with the "real" Queen Titania and King Auberon (as Gaiman spells the name of this character), as well as Auberon's interactions with the "real" Robin Goodfellow, also known as Puck: "Ohh. . . . How I do ache to make sport of them" (9).

In a telling moment, we see a conversation between Titania and the Dream Lord. As she watches the play, she notices Hamnet, who happens to be playing the orphaned Indian boy. This is the character that Oberon wants from Titania: "I do beg a little changeling boy / To be my henchman" (2.1.123-24). To which Titania replies: "[The mother], being mortal, of that boy did die, / And for her sake I rear up her boy / And for her sake I will not part with him" (140-42). In Shakespeare's text, the Indian boy never appears as a part in the play. However, Gaiman weaves the character in as a device to parallel the desire between the "fictional" Titania of the play and the "real" one watching the performance: "That child—the one playing the Indian boy. Who is he?" The Dream Lord replies, "He is the son of Will Shekespear,[3] the author of this play." Titania: "A beautiful child. Most pleasant. Will I meet him?" (Gaiman, **"Midsummer"** 11). And in these lines, we see the regard the Fairy Queen gives the boy, which contrasts with Shakespeare's unwillingness to give any attention to Hamnet.

Just before Titania meets Hamnet, we see a backstage conversation between Hamnet and Tommy (the actor afraid of the fairies). In this conversation, we see the history of the strained relationship between a father and his son, through Hamnet's eyes. In fact, we learn that "Mother ordered him to have me for this summer. It's the first time I've seen him for more than a week at a time" (Gaiman 13). The scene opens with Tommy stating, "You must be very proud of your father, Hamnet" (13). But Hamnet complains that his father is "very distant, Tommy. He doesn't seem like he's really there any more. . . . I'm less real to him than any of the characters in his plays. Mother says he's changed in the last five years. . . . All that matters is the stories" (13). And here we see how Gaiman wields dialogue with a brevity that yields deep characterizations. According to writer Joe Straczynski (the creator of the television series, *Babylon 5*), Gaiman, who wrote an episode of the series, "does things with words, simple yet elegant tricks that can explain an entire character in a few carefully selected words" (Straczynski, "Introduction" v). With these lines from Hamnet, "All that matters is the stories," we begin to see the Faustian cost Shakespeare has paid in attaining his dream.

In history, Shakespeare married Anne Hathaway when he was eighteen, after she became pregnant, and, according to biographer Park Honan, Shakespeare's "mother, no doubt, wished him to acquit himself well," and Shakespeare "had no choice *but* to take on abrupt responsibility—to be a husband, a father" (Honan 82). Gaiman seems to tease out the fact that Shakespeare sacrificed his entire family for the dream of attaining immortality through his plays: "I'd bargain like your Faustus for that boon," is the desire Shakespeare expresses to Marlowe in Gaiman's **"Men of Good Fortune"** (12). By having Titania speak to the Dream Lord about the "beautiful child," Gaiman sets up a two-edged tension of subtle horror in the reader: the cost ac-

crued to Shakespeare in attaining "a wonderful play, . . . Most enchanting and fine," as Titania exclaims to the Dream Lord (**"Midsummer"** 19); and the consequences of letting this happen. We know that Hamnet dies when he is eleven, and, within the fictional setting of Gaiman's story, we see the Fairy Queen—who in Shakespeare's tale takes an orphaned Indian boy—play out the desire to take Hamnet for herself, giving him the attention that Shakespeare neglects, who, in a sense, orphaned[4] his son to her charms.

So, when the "real" Titania speaks to Hamnet during the intermission, it is through the wonder of a surrogate father's full attention—an attention Shakespeare sacrifices in order to create plays "that would live on long after I am dead" (Gaiman, **"Men"** 12). For Hamnet desires only the attention of his father, and the Fairy Queen, Titania, supplies this hope through a surrogate promise, holding out a fairy wish through a seduction of the young Hamnet: "and bonny dragons that will come when you do call them and fly you through the honeyed amber skies. There is no night in my land, pretty boy, and it is forever summer's twilight" (16). What eight year-old boy would not want to attain such a dream,[5] where he can become a dragon-rider (all dragon-like fears tamed and attaining more wonders than his father could ever give him) in a land without darkness, death, or night—just the warm evening air of "summer's twilight," a forever Bradburian *Dandelion Wine,* a summer of "June dawns, July noons. August evenings" (Bradbury 239)?

The childhood desire for summer's twilight is also seen in Lord Dunsany's *The King of Elfland's Daughter* (1924). Here, the fairy twilight represents the past, the wonders and magic of lost childhood memories. The mortal Alveric wins the hand of the Elf King's daughter, Lirazel. However, after giving birth to their child, Orion, she misses her immortal home, and returns to her father. When that occurs, the Elf king, not wanting Alveric to pursue Lirazel, pulls the borders of Elfland away from Earth, leaving behind a desolate rocky plain in places where the two borders previously met. Alveric, on his quest to find his wife, comes across these abandoned fields that once caressed Elfland. While there, he finds an old toy of his, cast aside when he grew up. He "saw again and again those little forsaken things that had been lost from his childhood. . . . Old tunes, old songs, old voices, hummed there too, growing fainter and fainter" (68). Unlike Alveric, Shakespeare's son, Hamnet, in Gaiman's story, has yet to create any significant memories with his father, other than observing him work: "I'm less real to him than any of the characters in his plays. . . . I don't remember him any other way" (Gaiman, **"Midsummer"** 13). And thus it is Titania's promise of the creation of such memories that enamors Hamnet so. By making that seduction occur through a fairy-tale type setting, Gaiman ironically and metatextually juxtaposes Hamnet's desire against Shakespeare's concerns for his own stories.

For example, during the intermission, the "real" Puck has caused Dick Cowley, the actor portraying Puck, to fall asleep. He steals the actor's mask and Puck portrays Puck onstage. Shakespeare watching who he thinks is the actor in a scene between Puck and Oberon, comments almost to himself: "Dick Cowley acts well tonight. I have never seen him feign a finer Puck. He seems almost two-thirds hobgoblin" (Gaiman, **"Midsummer"** 17). As he muses in wonder, Hamnet approaches: "Father?" Shakespeare replies: "Not now, child. I must see this." Shakespeare's character, Puck, amazes him more than his son—which is the danger of the fey—luring mortals to pursue desires that they would normally fear. And as Shakespeare looks at the events unfolding on stage, we see Hamnet, sad of face, talk quietly to his father, who ignores him: "She was such a pretty lady, father, and she said such things to me" (17). Shakespeare doesn't realize the danger, and his ignorance furthers the subtle horror, when we discover Hamnet's early death linked with Titania's seductive promise.

The panel following immediately this image of Shakespeare ignoring his son once again reveals Puck playing Puck, stating Shakespeare's lines from the play: "Lord, what fools these mortals be!" (Gaiman, **"Midsummer"** 17). Through montage, Gaiman's scene juxtaposes with Shakespeare's, and a new meaning arises. Puck's lines now represent a comment on the foolishness of Shakespeare for failing to give attention to his son who needs the dreams of a father before the dreams of the fey. So, Hamnet's dreams—as portrayed through the regard Titania pays to Hamnet, parallels the Titania of Shakespeare's *A Midsummer Night's Dream,* in which we hear about her "rescue" of a motherless child from mortality. Because of this, the question naturally arises: Will Gaiman's Titania take Hamnet away from Shakespeare?

Gaiman seems to carry this concern a step further when he depicts the Dream Lord wondering if he had done the right thing in allowing Shakespeare to make this kind of sacrifice: "his words will echo down through time. It is what he wanted. But he did not understand the price. Mortals never do. They only see the prize, their heart's desire, their dream. . . . But the price of getting what you want, is getting what you once wanted" (Gaiman, **"Midsummer"** 19). In this instance, the Dream Lord—as an anthropomorphic representation of the dreams of humanity, becomes Shakespeare's conscience. The desire of the poet's dream, however, wins out over familial responsibility. For Shakespeare's words live on, and Hamnet's memory of his relationship to his father is forever lost,[6] only to be depicted through a historical mythology within Gaiman's

story—a far more powerful tale than the Academy Award winning film, *Shakespeare in Love.* We see this crisis represented when Hamnet watches his father perform Theseus in the famous monologue about the similarity between lovers, madmen, and poets—"and, as imagination bodies forth the forms of things unknown the poet's pen turns them to shapes, and gives to airy nothing a local habitation and a name." In an image drawn by artist Charles Vess and colored by Steve Oliff, we see young Hamnet looking on with adoration, a heart-rending image more powerful than text only could convey (20).

The actors finish their play and the fairies return to their world and the Dream Lord exits, with a promise from Shakespeare that he will give him one more tale "celebrating dreams" at the end of his career (which becomes **"The Tempest"** in Gaiman's final work of his opus fifty-six issues later in issue number seventy-five). Only Robin Goodfellow, Puck, has stayed behind to "confusticate and vex" mortals (Gaiman, **"Midsummer"** 22). The day dawns and the troupe wakes up from a disturbed slumber. Hamnet entreats his father: "I had such a strange dream. There was a great lady, who wanted me to go with her to a distant land." Shakespeare, still not appreciating the dream-memories of his son, behaves as a typical father not wanting to be disturbed and rebukes him: "Foolish fancies, boy. On the cart today, you must practice your handwriting. Perhaps you could write a letter to your mother, or to Judith" (24). Shakespeare is too busy to give his son the attention he needs, and the words of actor Richard Burbage stirs on the work ethic of the creative Shakespeare: "Come on, you vagabonds! Stir yourselves! We can be in Lewes by late afternoon, and there's an inn I know will be glad of a troupe of actors with a new comedy to show" (24). The final panel, colored in the honeyed amber color of fairy twilight contains the following words: "Hamnet Shakespeare died in 1596, aged eleven. Robin Goodfellow's present whereabouts are unknown." Here, through a semiotic code of color, fairy-dreams and death intermix, capping the story with gaunt sorrow and the realization that dreams—the magic of the fey—has a price beyond mortal understanding.

As a side note, Gaiman thematically ties this story with his work, **"The Tempest,"** in which he tells the story of Shakespeare writing his final play (solo) in 1610, while his twenty-five year old daughter, Judith—Hamnet's twin sister—looks on. Shakespeare pays attention to her, perhaps repentant for not giving Hamnet similar affections: "And will you read it to me, father, when it is done? And make the voices also?" Her father replies, "Aye. When 'tis done" (Gaiman, **"Tempest"** 2-3). Later in the story, Judith tells her father how envious she was when Hamnet "went with you that summer. He wrote letters home, and mother, or Susanne, would read to me what he said, and I would weep, for I could not be there with you. And mother also would weep. Mother wept most of all. Did you not think? Did you not care?" Her father replies: "I . . . followed a dream. I did as I saw best, at the time" (18). Although Gaiman's **"The Tempest"** deserves a fuller analysis, it can be said in this space how Gaiman ties his two stories together, bringing closure to the familial myth of belonging and sharing.

Throughout his tale, Gaiman blends the imaginary universe of his mythology with that of the Shakespearean imaginary universe of *A Midsummer Night's Dream* and a historical mythology of Shakespeare's life. By means of this, Gaiman is able to posit the same themes as Shakespeare does, who essentially asks, "What desires do we dream?" However, Gaiman carries the question one step further: "What is the cost of attaining that desire?" And Gaiman's answer—presented in the prophecy of the Dream Lord speaking to Titania—contains as sharp a truth as that of any written by Shakespeare: "The price of getting what you want, is getting what you once wanted" (Gaiman, **"Midsummer"** 19). In Shakespeare's play, we never discover the consequences of attaining the love that the lovers desire: the creation of children and the responsibilities that go with it.

In this way, Gaiman, through his mythic tale, creates anew what scholar Joseph Campbell says has been lost in the classical myths, which used to be "in the minds of people,"[7] allowing them to "see its relevance to something happening in [their] life," giving them a sense of "perspective" on what is occurring in their lives (Campbell 2). Campbell identifies four functions of myth:

• mystical—"realizing what a wonder the universe is, and what a wonder you are, and experiencing awe before this mystery";

• cosmological—science "showing you what the shape of the universe is";

• sociological—"supporting and validating a certain social order"; and the

• pedagogical—"how to live a human lifetime under any circumstances."

Gaiman layers this story with these four functions of myth by revolving them around four layers of fiction that continually shift through the work: the mystical is represented as the otherworldliness of European Fairy and Gaiman's own mythology through the character of the Dream Lord; the cosmological is represented through the historical world of Shakespeare, his contemporaries and Hamnet; the sociological is found in the European world-view as projected through the Athenian characters in Shakespeare's *A Midsummer Night's Dream*; and the pedagogical weaves itself throughout the themes of love conveyed in both stories.

In fact, Gaiman provides the reader a new kind of myth for the Western European and American contemporary, one that attempts to reveal and, perhaps, challenge how many people today sacrifice their families for work-day life (a system needed to generate money in order for many to survive)—and not, as in Shakespeare's case, for a work of art that will live on for ages of humanity. Gaiman's tale provides—in a popular mode—the artistic depth and mythic function which "high art" cannot instill, for, if Shakespeare, for example, remains ensconced away in "cultural institutions"—cut off from everyday practice—where audiences are, instead, "taught to observe" Shakespeare "with reverent, informed, disciplined seriousness" (Levine 229-30), then such an aesthetic placement of art can never provide for a people what art is supposed to instill: an integration of the visionary ideals of an artist into a person's everyday life.

Scholar Daniel Mackay contends that, like Greek myths, the medieval Christian church provided an integrated social and cultural praxis where a unified belief system structured not only the daily praxis of its followers, but even their art and entertainment were an extension of that unified belief system. Art and culture, he notes, were "wedded" to a "religious/efficacious mythology" (146). But, beginning with the Renaissance, Mackay believes, there was a "divorce of the self-evident *presence* of a single, collective, cultural imagination from the daily lives, practices, and structures of people" (145). In other words, if art is to be found only within the cultural elite's narrow definition and delineation of where and how to experience art, then people could never experience what both Campbell and Mackay believe has been lost in contemporary society—the mythic function of art, which requires integration into a daily praxis.

Instead, as anthropologist Victor Turner has noted, theater is, today, "set in the liminoid time of leisure between the role-playing times of 'work.' It is, in a way, 'play' or 'entertainment,'" (114). However, as Turner correctly ascertains, theater "is one of the abstractions from the original pansocietal 'ritual' which was part of the 'work' as well as the 'play' of the whole society before the division of labor and specialization split that great ensemble or gestalt into special professions and vocations" (114). So, when theater was integrated into the social fabric—and not institutionalized as the cultural elite did to Shakespeare in America by the end of the nineteenth century—it had the power to resolve "crises affecting everyone," Turner contends, and assigned *"meaning"* to "events following personal or social conflicts" (114)—a lived practice that many audience members experienced with Shakespeare's works during the first half of the nineteenth century in America.

Shakespeare was not just popular culture for many nineteenth century Americans—he was mythology. His art provided ideals that were socially and culturally integrated into everyday life.[8] Today, however, as Levine contends, we can only find the mythic function of art within works of popular culture. And when we see the "high art" of Shakespeare brought down to the level of popular culture, then Shakespeare, once again (as in the nineteenth century), has the potential to be seen and practiced as he was *really* meant to be—his artistic ideals breathing through the daily praxis of everyday life. For example, in an October 19, 1999, newspaper clipping we find a sports article comparing game five of the 1999 National League baseball play-off series between The New York Mets and Atlanta Braves at Shea Stadium to "the soggy battlefield of Agincourt in Shakespeare's *Henry V*" (Bruinius). During the fifteen-inning game (spanning five hours and forty-six minutes)—aside from the "steady drizzle"—Robin Ventura of the New York Mets hit a grand slam in the fifteenth inning. However, as he neared second base, his fellow players "mobbed" him, so he never reached home plate and his grand slam was "ruled a single" by the technically-minded referees. Bruinius, marking the game "legendary," closed the newspaper story with an altered line from *Henry V* (similar to how nineteenth century Americans shaped Shakespeare to fit their own needs), including a "politically correct" re-phrasing of the masculine article: "will gentlemen and women, now a-bed, think themselves accurs'd they were not here, when Ventura's slam became a single?" (Bruinius). The year 1999 also saw the publication of *Shakespeare on Management* (HarperBusiness) and *Shakespeare in Charge: The Bard's Guide to Leading and Succeeding on the Business Stage* (Hyperion), works which are marketed to business managers.

Similarly, in Gaiman's **"A Midsummer Night's Dream,"** we find Shakespeare palpably integrated into a popular medium for today's fiction, a work that instills Shakespearean themes by evoking wonder not because it is popular—which just means that a work is widely disseminated and appreciated—but because the artist has tapped into contemporary concerns and metaphorically provides answers to deep mythological questions still haunting the lives of humanity: What does it mean to love? How do we attain it? And what are the consequences of attaining it? The search for answers to such questions discloses the mythic function of art that needs to be practiced in everyday life.

As Straczynski wrote in the television series *Babylon 5* (1993-1998), truth is a three-edged sword: your side, my side, and the truth. As resolved through the high art and low art debate, we have on one side the elite high art world of Shakespeare; on the other side lies the popular/low art world of Gaiman's comic books; and on the third side is edged the truth an artist creates (as

revealed in both Gaiman and Shakespeare), who write from their own perspectives on life in the medium that affords them the best tools to create artistic truth irrespective of what other people may think. For, like Puck, the truth behind the theme of love and how this theme is played out in art and culture continues to confusticate and vex mortals. Thus, in that last panel of Gaiman's story, the dreams of Hamnet get encapsulated in a dry text recording his death set against the promise of a "forever summer's twilight" of a "honeyed amber sky" in the otherworldliness of fey, a mythological promise for the eternal paradise of childhood innocence sacrificed for the eternal words of the mighty Bard.

*Notes*

1. Shakespeare "wrote all about America," Sellars contends, because he "wrote about a country that was a world power that was in charge of commerce and that the grip was slipping. . . . America is the adolescent that Elizabethan England was." Sellars believes that many of Shakespeare's plays were "addressed to a nation to provoke the question of, How do you want to grow up, now?" (Moyers 1990).

2. On the bottom page of the last work of this series, "The Tempest," Gaiman indicates that he wrote *The Sandman* between October 1987 and January 1996 (38).

3. Reflecting, perhaps, the historical record of the many versions of how Shakespeare spelled his name, Gaiman uses both Shaxberd in "Men of Good Fortune" (13) and Shekespear, here.

4. The idea that Shakespeare orphaned his son came from one of my students, Dara Jeffries, in my MIT Shakespeare class on October 27, 1999.

5. Thanks to my friend, Earl Cookson, for this insight during a conversation on October 27, 1999.

6. Hamnet mentions how his sister Judith told him, that, if Hamnet died, his father would "just write a play about it. 'Hamnet'" (Gaiman, "Midsummer" 13), yet *Hamlet* is not the memory of Hamnet.

7. For example, in the plays and tales of ancient Greece, the stories of Odysseus, Hercules, and the Greek gods were so integrated into daily life that they became mythologies—ideas structuring, defining, and unifying, within the minds of a people, a cultural and social polis.

8. This kind of integration into the daily practice of nineteenth century Americans included Jim Bridger, an illiterate Rocky Mountain explorer, "hiring someone to read the plays to him" so he could "recite long passages from Shakespeare." Further, the teenager William Dean Howells "memorized great chunks of Shakespeare while working as an apprentice printer in his father's newspaper office." And steamboat pilot George Ealer would spend hours

reading Shakespeare to his apprentice, Mark Twain, who noted that Ealer "did not use the book, and did not need to." Further, politicians would quote Shakespeare as a part of "political discourse" (Levine 18, 36, 37).

## Works Cited

Bradbury, Ray. *Dandelion Wine.* New York: Bantam Books, 1976 [1957].

Bruinius, Harry. "Amid the Mist, Mets and Braves Craft a Hardball Legend." *The Christian Science Monitor* 19 Oct. 1999.

Campbell, Joseph. *The Power of Myth. With Bill Moyers.* Ed. Betty Sue Flowers. NY: Doubleday, 1991 [1988].

Dunsany, Lord. *The King of Elfland's Daughter.* New York: Ballantine, 1999 [1924].

Gaiman, Neil. "Men of Good Fortune." *The Sandman: The Doll's House.* New York: DC Comics, 1990.

———. "A Midsummer Night's Dream." *The Sandman: Dream Country.* New York: DC Comics, 1991.

———. "The Tempest." New York: DC Comics, 1996. Collected in *The Sandman: The Wake,* 1997.

Heidel, Andy. Press release to *Stardust.* New York: Avon Books, 1999.

Honan, Park. *Shakespeare: A Life.* Oxford: Oxford UP, 1998.

Internet Movie Data Base (imdb.com). Accessed under the search heading of "people: Shakespeare," subheading, "author," 2 Nov. 1999.

Levine, Lawrence. *Highbrow/Lowbrow: The Emergence of Cultural Hierarchy in America.* Cambridge: Harvard UP, 1988.

Mackay, Daniel. *The Fantasy Role-Playing Game: A New Performing Art.* Jefferson, NC: McFarland, 2001.

Mowat, Barbara A., and Paul Werstine, eds. *A Midsummer Night's Dream.* NY: Washington Square Press New Folger Edition, 1993.

Moyers, Bill. "Peter Sellars: Exploring the Avant-Garde." Video. *World of Ideas with Bill Moyers.* Princeton: Films for the Humanities and the Sciences, 1994 [1990].

Shakespeare, William. *A Midsummer Night's Dream.* Ed. Barbara A. Mowat and Paul Werstine. New York: Pocket Books, 1993.

Straczynski, J. Michael. *Babylon 5.* Television series, 1993-1998. Warner Brothers.

———. "Introduction." *Day of the Dead.* Neil Gaiman. Minneapolis: DreamHaven Books, 1998.

Turner, Victor. *From Ritual to Theater: The Human Seriousness of Play.* New York: PAJ Publications, 1982.

## Kera Bolonik (review date 29 July 2001)

SOURCE: Bolonik, Kera. Review of *American Gods,* by Neil Gaiman. *New York Times Book Review* (29 July 2001): 16.

[*In the following review of* American Gods, *Bolonik asserts that Gaiman is a masterful storyteller.*]

Neil Gaiman's new book is a noirish sci-fi road trip novel in which the melting pot of the United States extends not merely to mortals but to a motley assortment of disgruntled gods and deities. Early in ***American Gods*** we are introduced to Shadow, a man who has been released from prison only to learn that his wife has died in a car crash. With nothing to return home to, Shadow accepts a job protecting Mr. Wednesday, an omniscient one-eyed grifter. Then the going really gets strange. Soon the ex-convict finds himself in an alternate universe, where he is haunted by prophetic nightmares and visited by his dead wife. As he cruises the country with Mr. Wednesday, Shadow begins to realize that he is not dealing with ordinary oddballs: Mr. Wednesday reveals himself to be Odin, the chief Scandinavian god, for example, and Mr. Nancy, one of Mr. Wednesday's sidekicks, turns out to be Anansi, the African spider trickster. Americans, it seems, have been trading in these legends for newer deities—"gods of credit card and freeway, of Internet and telephone . . . gods of plastic and of beeper and of neon," who are "puffed up with their own newness and importance." Shadow's comrades are terrified that "unless they remade and redrew and rebuilt the world in their image, their time would already be over." Mr. Wednesday and his legions wage an underworld-wide war against the new regime. This might all sound like a bit much. But Gaiman—who is best known as the creator of the respected DC Comics ***Sandman*** series—has a deft hand with the mythologies he tinkers with here; even better, he's a fine, droll storyteller.

## Neil Gaiman and Linda Richards (interview date August 2001)

SOURCE: Gaiman, Neil, and Linda Richards. "January Interview: Neil Gaiman." *January Magazine* (online magazine) wysiwyg://119/http://www.januarymagazine.com/profiles/gaiman.html (August 2001).

[*In the following interview, Gaiman discusses the comic book industry, his development as a writer, and the significance of the* Sandman *series to his career as a whole.*]

There's a boyishness about Neil Gaiman that makes you doubt the 40 years he claims. A *bad* boyishness, complete with a mop of unruly dark hair and—on the day I met with him—a black leather jacket. He wears sunglasses the whole time we speak: modishly pale ones that only just mask the intense green of his eyes. He is, he tells me at one point, the father of three: an 18-year-old, a 16-year-old and a seven-year-old. And so 40 makes more sense but, even so, you wonder at the magic he's woven to maintain his youthful mien. On the other hand, consider the work: the fantastic worlds he's created that surely require the outlook of someone who sees a universe filled with wonder everywhere he looks.

And there are compensations for 40. For one thing, he is the author of an impressive body of work, the seminal **Sandman** series of graphic novels chief among them. But there is more: much more. The novel **Good Omens,** co-written with Terry Pratchett that is now being made into a movie to be written and directed by Terry Gilliam whose screen credits include darkly comic classics like *12 Monkeys* and *Brazil.* There are the novels **Neverwhere** and **Stardust** and even children's books. Most recently, however, Gaiman penned the epic novel that will most likely place him even more highly in the ranks of serious novelists. **American Gods** has been well received by critics. *January Magazine* reviewer, David Dalgliesh, called the book Gaiman's "best and most ambitious work since **The Sandman.**"

Born in the United Kingdom, Gaiman has made his home in the United States for the last nine years. In Minneapolis, the Midwest he draws so skillfully in **American Gods,** near his wife's family, where the couple's children could be near their grandparents and where Gaiman could satisfy one of his American dreams: "I thought," says Gaiman, "you know, if I'm going to leave England and go to America, I want one of those things that only America can provide and one of those things is *Addams Family* houses."

At present, Gaiman is looking forward to the publication of **Coraline,** a children's book expected in mid-2002 and the film version of **Good Omens.**

[Richards]: *There's been a lot of muttering in the UK press about J. K. Rowling "borrowing" ideas for her* Harry Potter *books from you. Would you care to comment on that?*

[Gaiman]: Last year, initially *The Scotsman* newspaper—being Scottish and J. K. Rowling being Scottish—and because of the English tendency to try and tear down their idols, they kept trying to build stories which said J. K. Rowling ripped off Neil Gaiman. They kept getting in touch with me and I kept declining to play because I thought it was silly. And then *The Daily Mirror* in England ran an article about that mad woman who was trying to sue J. K. Rowling over having stolen muggles from her. And they finished off with a line saying [something like]: And Neil Gaiman has accused her of stealing.

Luckily I found this online and I found it the night it came out by pure coincidence and the reporter's e-mail address was at the bottom of the thing so I fired off an e-mail saying: This is *not* true, I never said this. You are making this up. I got an apologetic e-mail back, but by the time I'd gotten the apologetic e-mail back it was already in *The Daily Mail* the following morning and it was very obvious that *The Daily Mail's* research [had] consisted of reading *The Daily Mirror.* And you're going: journalists are so lazy.

*What was it of yours they were accusing her of stealing from you?*

My character Tim Hunter from **Books of Magic** who came out in 1990 was a small dark-haired boy with big round spectacles—a 12-year-old English boy—who has the potential to be the most powerful wizard in the world and has a little barn owl.

*So there* were *commonalties, for sure.*

Well, yes and as I finally, pissed off, pointed out to an English reviewer who tried to start this again, I said: Look, all of the things that they actually have in common are such incredibly obvious, surface things that, had she actually been stealing, they were the things that would be first to be changed. Change hair color from brown to fair, you lose the glasses, you know: that kind of thing.

*Change the owl to a gecko.*

Yes. Or to a peregrine falcon. And I said to her that I thought we were both just stealing from T. H. White: very straightforward. But then I saw an online interview with the mad muggles lady where they were asking her about me and they said: what about Neil Gaiman? And she said: Well, he's been gotten to. [Laughs]

*By the Harry Potter conspiracy? [Laughs]*

I guess, yes.

*Where do you live now?*

In Minneapolis.

*Why?*

I have an American wife whose family all live in Minneapolis. We decided that it was time to move over so that her family could meet the kids and that was where we went. And also because I really wanted an *Addams Family* house. I thought, you know, if I'm going to leave England and go to America, I want one of those things that only America can provide and one of those things is *Addams Family* houses.

*And so you have one?*

I do. Yes: with the big pointy tower and wrap-around porch. It's fun. The only thing that's weird is kids do not come trick or treating at Halloween. Every year we used to buy the candy and stuff like that and we'd wait, but they'd never come.

*Does it have a reputation as a haunted house?*

I don't know. Somebody once told me that somebody had actually hung themselves in the tower but I've never been able to find anything about that anywhere else so I suspect they probably didn't.

*How long have you been there?*

About nine years now.

*So it has affected your writing. It gave birth to* **American Gods,** *I would think.*

Completely. It was what **American Gods** came from: discovering that America was a much more complex place than I thought it was and that the Midwest was a much more complex place. There was a review that came in from a Seattle paper that said how strange it was that the Midwest was much better drawn than the scenes in L.A. and New York in the novel. Which is probably because there's 500 pages of the Midwest and about 80 New York and probably about 80 L.A. But it's also because I figure everybody knows New York. Everybody knows L.A. There's not an awful lot of painting that one needs to do. Whereas nobody has ever written about [some of these] weird Midwesterny places. So that was part of the fun.

*Were Americans more than you expected? Were you surprised?*

It took me a couple of years. There were really interesting things going on under the surface. You wind up having to understand history and then come forward, to figure out who came where and what they did and what was going on economically and what the cultural patterns were and then you come back forward. Which again was stuff that I tried to get into the novel.

*How many kids do you have?*

Three. One just turned 18, one 16 and one seven.

*The older two are Brits?*

Well, yes. But they all have dual nationality. Two sets of passports.

**Sandman** *was, I think, life changing for its genre. Or even perhaps created its own genre. It's been very important, anyway.*

I don't know to what extent. At the time that I was doing it, I was very much hoping that it would change things for the medium of comics. Looking back on it, I don't think an awful lot. It did an awful lot for **Sandman** in that graphic novels are still out there, they still sell 80,000-odd a year, year in, year out in America alone. But what I was definitely hoping would happen was the same kind of thing that happened when I read Alan Moore was doing on *The Swamp Thing.* I went: Well, hang on. Here is someone writing stuff for adults and writing stuff with as much imagination and verve and depth as anything else out there: any other medium out there. I wasn't going: Oh, I want to write *Swamp Thing.* I was going: Oh, I want to create my own one of these. It will be interesting to see if in a few years time, the generation that was raised on **Sandman** do actually start creating more literary and more interesting comics.

*I think it's happening.*

Oh good.

*I mean, it seems that every time a new prominent graphic novel comes out,* **The Sandman** *is what is referenced.*

I think it's good. It's going to be very interesting to see where comics go over the next couple of decades. And the success of the *Jimmy Corrigan* book heartened me enormously and the fact that it's a book that simply got reviewed as itself. And nobody obviously went: Oh, we've already reviewed comics two years ago, we don't need to review this. I thought [that] was really good and really important.

As far as I'm concerned, comics are a medium. That really is the most important side of them.

*Where would you like to see the medium go?*

I just want it to be one medium amongst many. I would like it to be a commercially viable medium in that I worry a lot that comics has the potential to go the way of poetry. If it keeps shrinking commercially . . . I'm talking about poetry in terms of, you know, Byron used to bring out a poem and everybody read it. Kipling would bring out a book of poetry and everybody read the book, read the poems and quoted them to each other and knew them and these things were read. These days, poetry gets written by a very few people who are fundamentally hobbyists, for a very few people, who are fundamentally also hobbyists who want to see what the other people are doing. And I doubt there's a poetry book written more than once a decade that could financially sustain its author despite Guggenheims, Pulitzers and what have you. And there are some brilliant poets out there but, at the end of the day, it's become hobbyists exchanging [poetry] and little poetry magazines exist for other poets to buy and hope that their poems can be in them. I really hope that comics do not go that way. I think it [would] be very sad if comics did go that way. And I can see that happening. If the readership base gets small enough, if you get to the point where comics are things created by people who do comics for people who do comics . . . and I think that would be sad.

**Sandman** *is your benchmark. Everything you've done since, people always compare to* **The Sandman.** *How do you feel about* **Sandman** *all this time later?*

It's the biggest thing I've ever done. People would say—like with *Stardust*—Well, it's great, but it's not *Sandman*. And I'd say: Well, *Sandman* took me seven years to write, it's 2000 pages long, over 10 volumes, it's enormous. It's impossible, as far as we can tell, to try and bind the complete *Sandman* as one book because it would be the size of a family Bible and impossible to read and bind. *Stardust* was barely 60,000 words. Why are you comparing these two? [Laughs]

I'm pleased with *American Gods*. It's not as big and it's not as complex as *Sandman* partly because it took me two years to write rather than seven going on eight. But I think it's the first thing I've done that could actually spare to stand up against *Sandman*.

*It's a whole different thing. It's a big ol' novel. How many words?*

187,000 words.

*Do you think it's your most important work to date?*

I'm never quite sure what's important and I'm not sure that authors are meant to know what's important. And I'm not sure that anybody gets to make the call on the whole importance thing until a long time afterwards.

1930. Probably the most prominent English essayist was A. A. Milne. The editor of *Punch,* famed for his comedic essays and a man with several plays running in the West End concurrently. A man who had bestselling books with titles like *The Daily Round* and hilarious collections of essays and sketches. One of the funniest writers of his generation and an accomplished playwright. I did an *Amazon* search several months ago just out of interest to see just what of his was actually in print. And it listed 700 books: all of which, as I went

down page after page, were variant editions of the two *Winnie the Pooh* books and the two books of comic verse for children that he wrote. And that's all that we have left of A. A. Milne *and* he's in better shape than most of his contemporaries whose names we do not remember at all. I can't point to the other guy who was the biggest playwright in the 1930s because we don't know who that was and if I said his name, you'd be blank. The fact is, those two books of children's stories and two volumes of children's verse are what posterity, rightly or wrongly, has deemed the important thing to remember about what A. A. Milne did.

Actually, that's not true: there's one other thing we remember him for. His attempt to revive something forgotten which, again, worked brilliantly. To the point now where we didn't even know that it ever was forgotten. He wrote *Toad of Toad Hall* as a stage play, because he loved [it] and was furious that it had been forgotten—*The Wind in the Willows* [which was written by Kenneth Grahame]. And Kenneth Grahame's book came out and was a huge dud. Kenneth Grahame's other two books—*Dream Days* and *The Golden Age*—now completely forgotten. Portraits of sort of being a child in early Edwardian, early Victorian days—were seized on and loved by the Edwardians as these beautiful, sentimental portraits of childhood. These were Grahame's bestselling books. And the *Wind in the Willows* was a dud: it was completely forgotten to the point where A. A. Milne wound up writing an essay in the 1920s saying: Let me tell you about one of the best books in the world and you have never heard of it. It was called the *Wind in the Willows* and [A. A. Milne] went on and did *Toad of Toad Hall,* the theatrical adaptation, which then revived the book to the point where it's now considered one of the great children's classics. And if I'm burbling on about this stuff, I'm also burbling to point out that if Milne had not been a huge fan of this one book, there is no particular reason to think that *The Wind in the Willows* would have gone on to become the classic that it is.

It's quite possible that in 100 years time, people will say: You know that guy who wrote the book ***The Day I Swapped My Dad for Two Goldfish***? He did all this other stuff too? And people will say: *No.*

*And the guy who did the biography of Duran Duran.*

[Laughs] I can't see that one ever getting . . .

*But you* did *do a biography on the group?*

Yes, yes. That's the kind of thing you do when you're a 22-year-old journalist and somebody offers you money. It was great. Not only did I pay the rent, but that biography bought me an electric typewriter.

*When was it?*

I think it was written in 1984 and published in 1985. What was funny about that, of course, was the fact that it came out at a point where they were still hugely hot and promptly became an instant little minor bestseller. The first printing sold out in days.

*Fun. So you did more than buy an electric typewriter. You bought linoleum as well.*

No. I didn't. Because, what happened then was the publisher, before they could go back for the second printing, was taken into involuntary bankruptcy. Proteus Books. And that was that. And that was a really good thing, actually. I look back on it, because I got the advance. I got my 2000 pounds up front. But I never got any of the royalties I should have gotten and it never went on to make me any money which meant that I sort of got to stop and take stock. And I went: OK, so here am I and I spent several months writing a book that I wouldn't have wanted to read. I don't think I'll ever do that again. And I learned a lesson that every now and then the universe conspires to remind me of. It's like my one lesson and if somebody, while writing my life as one of these comedic tragedies, people would point to it as one of those recurring themes that he's needs to be every now and again retaught this one, which is: Whenever I do things for the money . . .

Whenever I do things because I want to do it and because it seems fun or interesting and so on and so forth, it almost always works. And it almost always winds up more than paying for itself. Whenever I do things for the money, not only does it prove a headache and a pain in the neck and come with all sorts of awful things attached, but I normally don't wind up getting the money, either. So, after a while, you do sort of start to learn [to] just forget about the things where people come to you and dangle huge wads of cash in front of you. Go for the one that seems interesting because, even if it all falls apart, you've got something interesting out of it. Whereas, the other way, you normally wind up getting absolutely nothing out of it.

The best thing about the Duran Duran book was, because I own the copyright on it and because the company went bankrupt, later they were actually taken over by somebody else who wrote me a letter saying: We want to bring it back into print. I got to say: No thank you.

*You were a rock journalist?*

No, I was a journalist. The rock bit simply happened because I had a friend named Kim Newman, with whom I was already writing a book called **Ghastly beyond Belief**. And Kim was writing a book called *Nightmare*

*Movies* for these people and he mentioned me as somebody who could write. I got a phone call from Proteus saying: OK, we have three books that need to be written very, very urgently. Pick one. I said: Great. Who are they? And they said: Duran Duran, Barry Manilow and Def Leppard. I figured Duran Duran had done much less. Barry Manilow I figured I was going to have to listen to, you know, 40 Barry Manilow albums.

I still leave the Duran Duran book off of biographies, more for fun than anything else, but one day in 1996 I was—due to a series of strange coincidences—on a yacht in the Mediterranean with Simon LeBon as part of the crew. Simon loves to sail. He's a big 'round the world yacht guy and stuff like that. He'd come out to crew the yacht for a week and I was there as a land loving passenger and we were friendly, we were chatting and about day three I thought: I can not keep this one, I have to say it. And I said: Look, I have to tell you. I wrote a Duran Duran biography once. And he said: Which one? And I said: The Proteus one. And he said: The one with the gray cover? We liked that one, it was great.

*So you hadn't met him? It wasn't the kind of biography where you tour with the band for half a year or anything?*

No. It was the kind of biography where you go down to the BBC and you say: Hello, BBC press cuttings library? I would like to buy everything you have with the words "Duran Duran" in it. And you pay 150 pounds for all their photocopying and you take it away and you take all of these press clippings and you write it into a book. And you listen to the albums.

The other thing that I learned at the same time was, lots and lots of my friends were writers in London. Writers may be solitary but they also tend to flock together: they like being solitary together. I knew a lot of writers in London and many of them were award-winning writers and many of them were award-winning, respectable writers. And the trouble with being an award-winning, respectable writer is that you probably are not making a living.

If you write one well-reviewed, well-respected, not bad selling, but not a bestseller list book every three years, which you sell for a whopping 30,000 pounds, that's still going to average out to 10,000 pounds a year and you will make more managing a McDonald's. With overtime you'd probably make more working in a McDonald's. So there were incredibly well-respected, award-winning senior writers who, to make ends meet, were writing film novelizations and TV novelizations under pen names that they were desperately embarrassed about and didn't want anybody to know about.

You know, the sort of secret knowledge that was passed on: Did you know that so-and-so wrote that casualty book? It's actually by such-and-such, you know? And, the thing that became very apparent as I became a writer was these people were selling out—and I do think of that as selling out, because they'd put pen names on because they didn't want to acknowledge them—for 1800 pounds a book. 2000 pounds a book. 2500 pounds a book. And I thought, then: It's not the selling out that's bad. It's that these people are selling out for absolutely nothing. You know, if you're going to sell out, sell out for a million dollars. Sell out for 10 million. Don't sell out to the point where you look at yourself in the mirror going: Oh my God, I'm a hack. Why am I doing this for 2000? For 1500? For heaven's sake!

There's a strange and wonderful alternate history of the London literary world of the 1970s and 80s and for all I know 90s, where you'd go and say: This famous writer wrote this episode of a novelization or this person wrote *Highlander III* and you could go and figure it all out.

*Speaking of selling out, I hear that* **Good Omens** *is being turned into a movie. [Laughs] Isn't that an awful way of putting it? But I wanted a sellout segue.*

I think it's a lovely sellout segue. What makes it a lovely sellout segue is that for 10 years, Terry Pratchett and I had a bad experience right at the beginning with that film. And then we spent eight years, nine years simply saying no. Every two or three months another major Hollywood entity would come along, clear its throat and say: We'd like to buy *Good Omens.* Expecting us to say: All hail! Give us money. And we would say: No thank you. And they would say: No, really. We mean it. We actually want to buy *Good Omens* and give you money and we would say: Please go away.

That went on for a long time until the Samuelsons came along and said: Look, we want to make *Good Omens* because this is what we feel it's about and furthermore we're talking to Terry Gilliam and we want Gilliam to write and direct it. At which point, Terry [Pratchett] and I said: Absolutely. Go with it. We took significantly less than we had been offered by many of the people to whom we'd said no because we liked the idea of Terry Gilliam doing it. If anybody is going to do *Good Omens,* I want it to be Gilliam. And then people say: Are you and Terry [Pratchett] involved [with the project]? And we say: No! Because we want to see what Terry Gilliam is going to do. We wrote the book. It's Terry Gilliam. I'm very happy to see whatever he does.

*What was the bad experience you had at first with the film version of the book?*

Terry and I were approached by these Hollywood people. They phoned us up and told us that they loved us. We went out to Hollywood and we had the kind of Hollywood experience that people joke about. I wound up transmogrifying our Hollywood experience into a short story in the *Smoke and Mirrors* collection called **"The Goldfish Bowl and Other Stories"** much of which was taken from literal things that were happening back then, Terry and I sort of watching this with horror.

Essentially what happened is we went out there, we spent a week going in for meetings around a big table, while people who couldn't write told us what they thought the movie should be. We'd go away and do an outline and hand it in the next day and nobody would have read it and we'd go in for another meeting and they'd tell us a whole bunch of different things and we'd say: That's essentially in the outline. And they'd say: Well, we haven't read the outline.

We went away and we wrote to script and we handed it in and they said: It's too much like the book. At which point Terry Pratchett very wisely said: I've had enough. I'm quitting. I'm off. And he quit. I said: I want to see what happens next. So I didn't quit and they said: This is what we want in the story. So I wrote a story that was what they said they wanted, wrote a script—actually, a very nice script. I'm still proud of it. It was very much what they said they wanted. And I handed it in. And they read it. And they said: Well, it's not like the book, is it?

I actually didn't get the pleasure of quitting because the day after that they went bankrupt. So that was one of those moments again when not only was it this strange sort of weird sellout, but I also didn't get paid.

*Are you working on something now?*

The next thing that will actually happen which should be fun is a children's book called *Coraline* and that's the next book to come out.

**Coraline?**

As in made of coral and as in Caroline, spelled wrong. For years I thought it was a name I'd made up and then I've actually discovered now that it's a real name. Which is always what happens when you make up a really good name. [Laughs] You discover other people made it up too.

**Charles De Lint (review date September 2001)**

SOURCE: De Lint, Charles. Review of *American Gods,* by Neil Gaiman. *Fantasy & Science Fiction* 101, no. 3 (September 2001): 97-8.

*[In the following review, De Lint offers high praise for Gaiman's* American Gods, *calling it a wonderful, superbly written novel that effectively balances the light and dark elements of the story.]*

Let's get this out of the way first: I'm sure a large number of Gaiman's fans (who came to his prose by way of his excellent work on *The Sandman* and other comic book projects) are otherwise unfamiliar with the fantasy field. They'll think that the underlying conceit of *American Gods*—that immigrants, however unknowingly, brought over with them the beings from folklore and myth who are now living hidden amongst us in North America—is terribly original. But it's not. We've seen it many times before, admirably handled by everyone from Roger Zelazny to, well, Mark Wagner, creator of the comic *Mage*.

Now before anyone protests, I know that Gaiman is aware of this as well. One of his characters even talks about something very like it in the book itself, though that character is referring to peoples' lives when he talks about ". . . the repetitive shape and form of the stories. The shape does not change: there was a human being who was born, lived, and then, by some means or another, died. There. You may fill in the details from your own experience. As unoriginal as any other tale, as unique as any other life."

Fantasy, though older, is often considered to be the mentally disadvantaged younger sibling of science fiction, which prides itself on being "the fiction of ideas." But let's face it, new ideas are far and few between in any sort of fiction these days. The thing that's important is what the author does with an idea, and in that sense Gaiman has done a superb job, proving in the process (if it should be required after such successful books as *Neverwhere*) that he doesn't need an illustrator to bring his fascinating characters and stories to life.

*American Gods* is a big, sprawling book that seems to take forever to get to its point, but what a wonderful journey it is to get there. We enter the hidden world of forgotten gods through the viewpoint of a character named Shadow whose life, after three years in prison, seems about to take an upturn. But that wouldn't make much of a story. So in short order, he's released a day or so early from prison because his wife has died, while cuckolding Shadow with his own best friend. The job he was supposed to have (as fitness trainer with said best friend) is now also gone.

Enter Wednesday, a rather enigmatic figure whose true nature we figure out before Shadow, and all too soon poor Shadow is drawn into a struggle between the forgotten gods (brought over to North America by their believers and then abandoned) and the new gods: the gods of technology, of cell phones and the Internet and every other modern contrivance. And along the way he needs to find some meaning and balance to his own life, one that for all its emotional ups and downs it seems he's been living by rote up to this point.

There are few authors who can manage to balance the light and dark aspects of a storyline as effectively as

Gaiman does. There are charming, utterly whimsical moments here, and others filled with doom and dread. The mythic characters are earthy and accessible without losing their godlike stature. The plot, while rambling, never strays into uninteresting territories and, more to the point, most of the seeming asides and subplots prove, once we reach the conclusion, to have been necessary to the principal storyline after all.

Another pleasure of reading Gaiman is that he has such a light touch with his prose. One gets the impression that it simply flowed effortlessly from his mind to the book we hold in hand, though that, of course, is one of the hardest tricks to pull off in the business of writing.

It's still early as I write this (the beginning of April), but it wouldn't surprise me if *American Gods* proves to be the Big Book of this year. It'll certainly be difficult to match in its paradoxical mix of broad scope and small intimacies.

## Neil Gaiman and Ray Olson (interview date August 2002)

SOURCE: Gaiman, Neil, and Ray Olson. "The Booklist Interview: Neil Gaiman." *Booklist* 98, no. 22 (August 2002): 1949.

[*In the following brief interview, Gaiman discusses whether his stories may accurately be categorized as horror fiction.*]

English fantasist Neil Gaiman's big breakthrough was the spooky graphic novel series *Sandman,* one of the most lauded works of its kind. He spent eight years writing it, and it keeps on selling—all 10 volumes' worth. It often looks like horror fiction, and so, at times, do Gaiman's novels *Neverwhere, Stardust,* and *American Gods.* His new book, *Coraline,* is a children's novel about a girl who visits an eerie parallel world in which she meets a sinister alternative mother. Still, debate persists as to whether Gaiman really is a horror author. At the delightful April 2002 World Horror Convention in Chicago—within relatively easy reach of his home in western Wisconsin—Gaiman reflected on that issue and expanded on it later in conversation with *Booklist.*

[*Booklist*]: *So, what's the answer to that nagging question—is Neil Gaiman a horror writer?*

[Gaiman]: Every now and then I get these horror awards. The first one was when [the story collection] *Angels and Visitations* won the International Horror Guild Award, the most recent last Saturday night [June 8] when *American Gods* walked away with the Bram Stoker Award from the Horror Writers of America. Do I think of myself as a horror writer? No. I don't, except that I love horror. I think of horror as a condiment rather than as a meal. I run into people who consider *Neverwhere* a horror novel. Obviously there are ways in which *American Gods* could be read as a horror novel. It has sequences [that] are viewed by horror people as proper horror. It gives them the buzz that they get from horror. Well, they gave it the award. . . . On the other hand, it's also nominated for [an award] for mythopoeic fantasy, and for a Hugo award for best sf novel. I love to put more, to put everything, in the pot. I cook rather like those nice people in New Orleans. You want the tastes *not* to mingle.

*Coraline* is the nearest to a horror novel in the conventional sense of anything you've written.

I agree.

*Might* Alice in Wonderland *have been in mind as you wrote* Coraline?

*Alice* I read first when I was 5, maybe, and always kept around as default reading between the ages of 5 and 12, and occasionally picked up and reread since. There are things Lewis Carroll did in *Alice* that are etched onto my circuitry. *Coraline* isn't *Alice in Wonderland,* which is fundamentally formless, as plotless as any dream. . . . In *Coraline,* I'm taking some of what I got from *Alice,* but form-wise, there are other very odd influences. The most forgotten is a lady named Lucy Clifford. . . . One [of her stories], "The New Mother," [is] about these children who are evil. They behave badly because they want something another kid has, this pear drop. Their mother keeps saying, "Please, please, please, don't misbehave, or I'll have to go away, and your new mother will have to come." And they do misbehave, and when they go home, their mother's not there. But they look down at the end of the road, in the dark, where they see coming toward them the flames of their new mother's eyes and hear the swish, swish, swishing of her wooden tail. That definitely stuck with me. Here was somebody writing children's fiction, at the same time *Alice* was written, who was willing to go all the way, into something really disturbing and primal.

*Does horror need a supernatural element?*

No, not particularly.

*Or a magical element?*

No. . . . [though] in *my* fiction it tends to.

*Sandman* is a serial, but, unlike so many fantasy writers, you haven't spun off sequels since.

I have too many things in my head and only a limited amount of time to get them down. I have one other story with the *Stardust* characters. I have a sequel that

hasn't finished gelling to *Neverwhere.* I could write a story about Mr. Nancy from *American Gods* tomorrow. But it's much more likely that when I start the next novel, it will be something else again. I suppose in some ways it's very perverse of me. . . . The joy of *Sandman* was, because I was doing a comic, and comics are their own little ghetto, nobody minded that I moved through every single variant of the horror genre, and pretty much every variant of the fantasy genre, and a number of mainstream genres on the way just because I wanted to, because I enjoyed it. Nobody ever said, "You can't do that cuz that's not a *Sandman* story." When I decided I wanted to do a political commentary in the form of a synoptic gospel, well, I did. You get that freedom, but I also knew that it was going to be difficult to transfer that to book publishing.

### Tom Easton (review date October 2002)

SOURCE: Easton, Tom. "The Reference Library." *Analog Science Fiction & Fact* 122, no. 10 (October 2002): 130-35.

[*In the following excerpt, Easton provides a brief overview of* Adventures in the Dream Trade, *a volume of miscellaneous writings by Gaiman.*]

Neil Gaiman established himself with remarkable graphic novels (*Sandman*). In February 1991, I reviewed favorably his collaboration with Terry Pratchett, *Good Omens: The Nice and Accurate Prophecies of Agnes Nutter, Witch.* Last year, he published *American Gods* to an excellent reception, and this year he was guest of honor at Boskone, the Boston-area SF con. To honor the occasion, NESFA brought out *Adventures in the Dream Trade,* a major part of which is Gaiman's "blog" (weblog) chronicling the proofreading, touring, and autographing chores that went with *Gods.*

That is perhaps enough for Gaiman fans or would-be Famous Writers. For the rest of the world, Gaiman includes a number of poems, song lyrics, short stories, and essays (most written as introductions to other folks' books). The overall flavor is quite charming, for Gaiman is witty, inventive, congenial, and fond of making things "story-shaped"—and nowhere more so than in a poem he did *not* include here.

Last winter, I heard him recite **"Crazy Hair"** at a performance at MIT, where Gaiman, Harlan Ellison, and Peter David entertained a large audience for hours. He wrote it, he said, for his daughter, and it was astonishingly full of fancies about what lives or nests in, visits, tours, and adventures in his expansive hair.

Maybe in his next book . . .

**Neil Gaiman and Joseph McCabe (interview date October 2002)**

SOURCE: Gaiman, Neil, and Joseph McCabe. "Hanging Out with the Dream King: Neil Gaiman on Comics and Collaborating." *Science Fiction Chronicle* 24, no. 10 (October 2002): 42-6.

[*In the following interview, Gaiman discusses the process of collaborating with other artists and writers on his graphic novels and illustrated novels.*]

[*McCabe*]: *I'd like to talk a little bit about your collaborations. You've worked with numerous individuals over the years, and the breadth of your collaborations is very impressive: artists, writers, musicians, and even, with the film* **Princess Mononoke,** *animator Hayao Miyazaki. I'd like to begin by just naming some of your collaborators, and getting your thoughts on working with them. Let's begin with some of the artists you worked with on* **The Sandman,** *starting with Dave McKean, who did the cover of every issue of the comic.*

[Gaiman]: Well, Dave was one of my first collaborators, and he's still the one who is most exciting for me to work with. I think I said yesterday on the panel interview that the thing about Dave is that I never know what I'm going to get. But it's always cool, and it's always different than whatever I imagined. A Charlie Vess ["**A Mid-Summer Night's Dream," "The Tempest"**] or a Craig Russell ["**Ramadan"**] are lovely examples of people who are brilliant and they will give you something that's like the kind of thing you thought they might do only it's better, but what Dave gives you is something that's nothing like what you had in your head, but it's still cool. In fact often it's cooler than the thing you had in your head. So I'm always fascinated by that. But I think very often there's a sort of creative tension with Dave that I don't necessarily get with other people because he's not doing it in the way that I expected it to be done, or would have done or just naturally have assumed he would have done it. It's always done off of this sort of ninety degrees in Dave World, which gives you a weird kind of stretch.

*Charles Vess.*

Charlie's brilliant. Charlie's just fun. I mean for me Charlie's a lot like getting to collaborate with Arthur Rackham or somebody. There is this delight to dealing with Charlie as a creator, as an artist, and as a thinker. Because I know what his influences are and I know where he's coming from, a wonderful sort of Heath Robinson, Brandywine, Rackhamesque tradition. What was actually fun with Charlie was when we collaborated on the comic mini-series ***Books of Magic.*** He was throwing in much stuff in musical terms. He put together a tape for me of music he thought I should hear, all this

English folk music that I didn't know, which I thought was lovely, a feeling of informing the thing. And that's with all of the collaborations with Charlie. I'd write something for him, he'd do something, and I'd say, "Oh, that's cool, I have to do more of that." The little hairy man was just meant to come on and go off, and I saw the drawing Charlie did of him in the first issue of **Stardust,** and it's like "Oh, great, we need more of him."

*Artist Marc Hempel* [**The Kindly Ones**].

Marc was lovely. Marc was my second choice for **The Kindly Ones.** My first was Mike Mignola, and when it became apparent we weren't going to get Mike I said, "Well, Marc Hempel." I wanted a sense of form. I wanted a sense of everything reducing to light and shadow, of everything reducing to simple shape.

*His work almost looks like stained-glass windows.*

And what is interesting is that, as a monthly comic, it didn't work at all. Because as a monthly comic coming out over a period of about sixteen months, you have a month to read a bunch of other stuff, and then you pick up the Hempel and the artificiality of it—not that other styles aren't artificial—people would find it distancing. With the **Kindly Ones** story collected in a book, you're in there and it may be distancing for the first couple of pages but as it goes on, you are in *that world.* Everything becomes form, everything becomes shape. It becomes these stained-glass windows.

*It's beautiful work. How about Jill Thompson* [**Brief Lives**]*?*

Jill was just so much fun. Jill may well have been my favorite collaborator on **The Sandman.**

*Really?*

Just from a personal point of view, the sheer amount of fun and delight we had working together. It was enormous fun. She'd send me these great little faxes. At one point—it was actually the only time this happened on **Sandman**—but she came and stayed with my family. And at one point *she was drawing on one end of the sofa and I was writing several pages ahead on the other end of the sofa.* Incredibly fun. And she brought a lot of herself to it, which I loved. And I also loved the fact that, when she began, nobody knew how good she was. She was sort of considered a minor *Wonder Woman* artist, and I just saw some of her stuff and I saw so much potential and so much that was interesting about what she was doing and what she could do. And I feel like we got a lot out of the work we did together. I think, these days, her talent really has flowered completely. With things like her children's book, *Scary Godmother,* people can see for themselves what she does and how good she is. I loved working with her. She drew me women who looked like women, which made me very happy.

*Yes, it was exciting to watch her find herself in* **Brief Lives.** *Whenever I think of Delirium, Jill Thompson jumps into my head.*

Jill put a lot of herself into the character.

*With all the praise that's been given it, do you feel you achieved everything you wanted to with* **The Sandman***?*

Well, you never achieve everything you wanted to. It's the simple act of writing. You begin with a platonic ideal that is a shimmering tower carved out of pure diamond, that is this perfect thing that stands there unfouled by gravity and the weather. And then, the thing that you build is this thing that you have to build out of whatever is to hand and you use empty sushi boxes and chairs and get friends to hold it up and try to make it look like it's standing. And at the end of it, people look at it and they say, "It's amazing." And you say, "Yes, but if only I could have done the thing that is in my head."

*What makes a good comic book collaborative team work?*

In terms of comics, the joy for me is always looking at an artist, looking at what they do, what they do best, and what they don't do very well, and how I can write best to play to their strengths and minimize their weaknesses. For me, the perfect example of that would be Alan Moore writing his story "Pog" with Shawn Mac-Manus [*A Game of You*].

*That story was in* Swamp Thing.

Yes. Shawn, at that time, couldn't draw very good people. They looked kind of lumpy and cartoonish. There was a lot of stuff he couldn't do terribly well. But Alan got Shawn to write a story that would break your heart. It's his *Pogo* story.

*With beautiful lumpy people.*

But rather than beautiful lumpy people, what you got was cartoon animals. It was a tale of these cartoon spacemen based on *Pogo*. And Alan completely avoided the issue of *the standards of realism to which Shawn was working at the time.* I still think it may well have been Alan's best-ever *Swamp Thing,* a remarkable piece of work. I always bore that in mind, that the smartest thing to do was to make an artist look good. To make them look good, because that would make you look

good. To look at what they did. What do they do well? What can they do? And sometimes you'd do odd sorts of little extrapolative things. Looking at Michael Zulli [*The Wake*], who sprang to fame drawing animals in *Puma Blues,* and thinking, what is important about Michael is not that he draws animals but that he draws what he sees. He's actually coming from a different artistic tradition than most people doing comics. Because they learned how to draw comics from drawing comics, and Michael came from a fine arts background combined with a sort of weird, wonderful bohemian-going-from-town-to-town-painting-things-for-people background. Which made me think, I can do a historical story with him. He would be amazing at that kind of stuff. Just that sense of realism, the sense that somebody's there drawing what he sees, that became useful. With Kelley Jones [*Season of Mists*], Kelley's a brilliant artist, but there is this wonderful wayward streak to Kelley, which could work against him in comics, where each drawing exists almost separate from any other. Not in terms of not moving—the flow of the comic moves fine—but he was much less concerned about making sure that a character looked like the same character from one panel to another. So in *Season of Mists* I made damn sure that while the angel might not have looked the same from one panel to another, you were always sure that was the angel. Thor's beard may have changed between one panel and the next, but it was only one huge, over-muscled Thor.

*How about writers collaborating with other writers?*

Well, many of the great collaborative teams have been comedians, comic writers, which is because the hardest thing to know in comedy is whether or not something's funny. The joy of writing **Good Omens** was we were two guys writing it and you knew, if you could make the other one laugh, it worked. It was that simple. There are so many, many great comedy-writing teams, particularly in the UK. Going back to Frank Muir and Denis Norden; George and Weedon Grossmith, who wrote *The Diary of a Nobody,* an incredibly funny book; Sellar and Yeatman, who did *1066 and All That*; Arthur Mathews and Graham Linehan, who wrote *Father Ted,* a British TV series; and, of course, Galton and Simpson who, again, were English comedy writers who wrote *Steptoe and Son* and all the great episodes of *Hancock.* Comedy teams—Marty Feldman and Barry Took, who wrote an English comedy show called *Round the Horne,* which, as soon as Marty Feldman left, stopped working, although a lot of the funniest bits may well have been written by Barry Took. But it was the combination of sensibilities that worked. Even in *Monty Python,* you had two writing teams, because you had Palin and Jones as a writing team and you had Chapman and Cleese as a writing team, and then Eric Idle off on his own. *Fawlty Towers* was written by Cleese and Connie Booth. This isn't just meant to be a reductive list of names. My point is, particularly in comedy, collaborations are successful and easy because you're in a room with somebody and you can tell if the joke is funny or not. If the other guy laughs, it stays in. It's nice and easy. In novels, I'd be much harder put to find successful collaborations. A nice example of where a collaboration works is in *The Talisman* and *Black House,* by King and Straub. Where it works, it works because it is not written by two people, it is written by one two-headed person. *Black House* was not written by Stephen King and Peter Straub, it was written by Stephen King-and-Peter Straub, who together have written a book that neither of them could or would have written. Not that way.

*The whole is greater than the sum of its parts?*

No, the whole is not greater than the sum, the whole is *different* than the sum. The whole is a new person. The whole is a different entity. And it has written a different book. Could Stephen King have written *Black House*? Yes. Could Peter Straub have written *Black House*? Yes. Would it have been that book? No. Why not? Well, partly because the act of collaborating gives you a specific audience. A lot of the time when you're writing your audience is either you or some kind of notion of the reader. The joy of collaboration is it's no longer you and it's no longer the reader, it is—in Stephen King's case—Peter Straub, and in Pete's case—Steve King. So all of the sudden, Steve is going to be sticking in jazz references to make Pete laugh. Pete will be doing some splattery stuff and he'll say, "Ah, Steve will like this." My favorite moment in writing *Good Omens* was a bit where Terry Pratchett had written the first scene where Adam met Anathema. Terry sent it in, I read that scene, and I looked at it. He had just a line where Anathema mentions a book and I said, "My God, he missed the ultimate opportunity." And I just went in and wrote a paragraph where Adam says something like, "I wrote a book once. It was really good, especially when the dinosaur came out and fought the cowboys." I just stuck in a paragraph in the middle of something Terry had written, and I sent it back to him and he phoned me up and he said, "I nearly pissed myself laughing." It was one of those perfect moments because I just wrote it to make him laugh in his bit.

*What was it like collaborating with Terry Pratchett?*

People arguing about and discussing *Good Omens* tend to pick the wrong thing to argue about and discuss, which is who wrote what and how much of us wrote which. Which tends to miss the point. The answer is of course that I actually wrote—and not a lot of people know this—ninety percent of *Good Omens.* But the trouble is that Terry wrote the other ninety percent. But what was it like for me, that particular collaboration? It was like going to college. Even at that point Terry was

a master craftsman, like a Wedgewood chairmaker or whatever. He could do it. And I had never made a chair before, but I had some ability as a woodworker. So there was a lot of Terry and I talking about this thing that we were building, and Terry would send me off and I'd do my bits, and we'd talk about it. But it was very much a fifty-fifty collaboration between a journeyman and a master craftsman and that's very much how I viewed, and still view, *Good Omens.* It's not that it was my idea—at least fifty percent of it is mine—but for me it was an amazing learning experience: working with Terry, and the way that Terry worked, having no idea where the characters were going to go, stitching it together at the end. And it's not necessarily a method that I would ordinarily use. My tendency is to start at the beginning and then keep writing until I get to the end and then stop. Although it was fun with *American Gods* to have my little short stories on the side so I could go off and do something different.

*Let's switch gears for a second and talk about an entirely different collaboration. I'm curious about the work you did with Japanese filmmaker Hayao Miyazaki. You wrote the English-language script translation of his animated epic* **Princess Mononoke,** *and, in a way, you were presenting his work to America, yet there's a lot of* you *in that version of the film.*

One of the joys of collaboration is knowing when to shut up and let someone else shine. The most important thing in collaboration is not standing in the middle of the stage, showing off. With Miyazaki, I figured that my role was to try and take the subtitles and the literal translation and turn it into dialog that people could say. The thing that always hurts in watching dubbings of foreign movies is when, all of the sudden, characters are trying to say things that sound stupid. Somebody's done some literal translation and you know, immediately, if you're listening to something or watching something that's been translated because characters are going to say something like, "Look! Watch! Over there! The things come! Their spears are raised!" You scratch your head and say, "What was that? What did he say?" A lot of what I was trying to do was twofold. One of which was just dialog that people could say, and the other was to try and fold in enough background surreptitiously. Like the moment when Ashitaka cuts his hair. For an American audience, that only meant one thing which is "He's leaving and he's thinking long hair will get in the way." They completely miss that this is something a samurai does when he becomes a monk. This is an act that literally means: "Once I cut my hair, I am dead. I am no longer." Which, when you understand that he is literally dead to the village, tells you why he doesn't come back to it at the end of the film. So I tried to fold in a little bit of dialog about "You will cut your hair and become dead to us" and stuff. Just little bits that Miyazaki wouldn't have thought necessary for a Japanese audience, but that I could slide in for an American audience.

*Had you ever done any work like that before?*

No.

*It must have been a pretty interesting experience for you.*

It was a hugely frustrating, enormously fun learning experience. The frustrating side of it was I'd keep coming up with lines of amazing beauty and subtlety and tenderness and brilliance and grace and poetry, and if only the characters had opened their mouths one more time I could have used them. You were sort of limited to lip flaps.

*But you were obviously very successful. Roger Ebert, after seeing **Princess Mononoke**, said it was one of the ten best films of 1999. I don't know of too many dubbed films that get that kind of praise in this country.*

It was very nice, having Ebert and having Janet Maslin of *The New York Times* singling out the script translation. It was very lovely.

*We've talked about books, comics, and movies, but you've also written songs for the goth-folk music duo the Flash Girls. How did that collaboration come about?*

Well, I've known Emma Bull about fifteen years. I met her and Will Shetterly when they came to the UK for a convention. I first met Lorraine Garland in about 1991 at a convention in Amherst. The two of them came out to my very first-ever Guy Fawkes party, when I moved to America. A lot of people had brought guitars and violins along and had come out to the Twin Cities and were playing music, and I hesitantly said, "Well, I occasionally write songs. Here's one." And I played them the song that they call **"Tea and Corpses,"** but that I still call **"The Tea Song."** It was at that party that we tried to get a fire going. The fire didn't actually get going—I didn't know much about lighting fires at that point—and Will and Emma and Lorraine were sitting around playing music. Emma and Lorraine had already played together in Renaissance festivals and stuff, and somehow by the end of that evening Emma and Lorraine had formed a band. I said blithely, "Oh, you can have that song that I did." After that I remember giving Lorraine some lyrics, and saying, "Here's a couple of things that I've written that I don't have tunes for." And she went off. And some of the time, I'd write music myself, and sometimes it would be Lorraine, or Lorraine and Emma, doing it. The **"All Purpose Folk Song,"** for example, was just written because I was listening to them play one day at a Renaissance festival

and I thought, they need a song that does this, this, this, and this, so I just wrote one, wrote the lyrics, handed it over to them and said, "Here you go." And two days later it was already in the act. You'll have to ask them what it's like to work with me as a songwriter because, from my perspective, I'm easy-going and a delight to work with.

*Utterly charming?*

Absolutely. In every possible way. [Laughs.] And they, of course, would say, "Okay is this on or off the record? He's a monster."

*We're talking about collaborations. And, in a broad sense, every written story is a collaboration between the writer and the reader. And, I suppose, every reading is a collaboration between the reader and the listener. How important is the connection with the audience to you?*

It's all-important, because if it's not there you're masturbating. There are writers out there who write for themselves. And while I write for myself in some sense—I get to be the first reader and I don't like writing things I don't enjoy—the audience and the existence of the audience is the most important thing for me. I am happier with a poem that gets printed in one of the Windling-Datlow anthologies and that 10,000 people will read than with a movie script that I'll get paid five-hundred times the amount that I get paid the poem for, but which will be read by three film executives and nobody else. It's always fun when it's read and there's that wonderful feeling of interaction, which does change what you're doing. It's fascinating for me doing any kind of live panel or live event or whatever, especially the ones where you just sit up there and you have no idea what's going to happen—you just do it. Because it is a collaboration with the audience. I did a question-and-answer last night, and it was completely a collaboration—you never knew where it was going to go.

*As you become more and more successful you draw larger audiences and bigger crowds to your readings, and to conventions such as this one. Does that fire you up? Does it give you more inspiration when you're doing a reading?*

No, it's much more fun when you're doing it out on your own and nobody knows you exist. This has been a very odd convention for me. On the one hand, Boskone is a lovely convention—great con, lovely people, well-run, a good convention—but on the other hand, it's very odd because I'm here but I'm thinking, I am not at this convention. Normally, if you come to a convention as a writer, you're *at* the convention. And I'm having to come to terms with the fact that "Okay, it's a convention I would love to be at, but I'm not here." I'm working the whole time. If I wander into a room party, I'm not wandering into the room party as some guy wandering into the room party. I'm wandering into the "Hey, look over there . . . [mock-whispers behind his hand]" And I'm sort of thinking, well, okay fine, and having to come to terms with the fact that I will probably have to rethink how and when I do conventions in the future—this *kind* of SF convention. I figured I would have one kind of convention and I'm thinking, it's not working. If I'm going to do this kind of convention in the future, I may as well just do the equivalent of a World Horror or a World Fantasy, and then do things like the International Conference for the Fantastic in the Arts on my own time, where it's just academics and writers, and I can actually meet new people and have conversations in hallways without suddenly realizing that I'm drawing crowds. It's very odd. And not necessarily odd-bad, but odd in the sense of having to think, I can't do this anymore. I'm no longer one of the attendees. You know, Charlie Vess is having a wonderful convention. He's either at the bar or he's over at the art show or he wanders around the dealers room.

*Or he's back at the bar.*

Or he's back at the bar. [Laughs.] He's having the kind of convention that I used to have, and can no longer have. So I'm starting to think, okay, I might just have to rethink this one.

*I heard Stephen King had similar experiences in the late seventies and early eighties.*

I remember Steve telling me the deciding thing about him not going to conventions any longer. He was actually sitting on a toilet and somebody pushed books under the door for him to sign. In the men's room. I think, certainly for him, that was the deciding factor.

*If someone told you that you could only work in one medium—comics, prose, screenwriting, poetry, music—what would it be?*

Is physical survival an option? By which I mean, does it have to be something that will at least pay my mortgage, or can I work in anything? Because if paying the mortgage were not an option, it would probably be radio plays. I'd go straight over to radio drama. I would, of course, have to send the children out in the streets to dance for pennies.

*Lemonade stands would probably be in order.*

Absolutely. But I love the fact that in many ways you're moviemaking, but you can make a movie in a weekend. You get to fuck with the inside of people's heads just like you do in a novel, you get immediacy, the kind of immediacy you can only get with a comic normally.

And it's fast and it's fun and it moves in real time. And it's evocative. And your special-effects budget *is* unlimited. For me the greatest line ever uttered in radio is in *The Hitch-Hiker's Guide to the Galaxy,* where Arthur Dent says to Ford Prefect, "Ford, you're turning into an infinite number of penguins." But this is not a line that could or should ever be seen. They tried on the TV show. Suddenly the screen gets covered with penguins. It's like, "You know, that was stupid." If I were directing it, I probably would have just had strange sort of blotchy, smudgy colors going on and close-ups of people's mouths.

*You've mentioned numerous times that you love reading stories to your daughter. Do think this hones your ability to do public readings, for which you're quite well-known?*

I don't know. It certainly keeps a hand in. But the weird thing is, an awful lot of what people, I suppose, think is charisma is in some ways confidence. And in some ways is the confidence of knowing that you haven't fucked up too badly in the past when you've done it. You can stick me up on a stage in front of five-thousand people and I will be nervous for the first thirty-five to forty seconds, and then it all comes back. And I can do it. And I don't know how I do it, particularly. I didn't do it this well fifteen years ago, I didn't do it this well *ten* years ago. A lot of it actually came from doing the Guardian Angel Tour stuff for the Comic Book Legal Defense Fund. Actually having to get out there and fill up the air time on my own, and read stories to a theater full of people who had come there to see me and nothing else and it's like, "Wow!" And then doing question-and-answers with an audience and discovering that, on the whole, I could do it.

There are different kinds of panels. This morning's panel was great fun—me, Bob Sheckley, Emma Bull, and Ginger Buchanan trying to discuss the subject with not really a wish to reach a conclusion, although I think some conclusions were reached, but much more from a point of view of "There is a bunch of opinions from people who've done some of this and have something to say." Which is different from "Get up there and talk about stuff." Can I keep an audience entertained for several hours? Sure. How? I don't know. I've been doing it long enough now that the idea of doing it doesn't scare me.

But I like them, and the audience likes me. When I was sixteen, I was in a punk band and I remember once getting a beer can in the chin—I still have a little scar under there—and being dragged off to a hospital to have my face stitched up. And I thought, you know, it's never going to be that bad again. A lot of it for me is wanting to treat people as I would like to be treated. Some of this goes back to me saying some of the stuff about this convention that I'm not comfortable with. Alan Moore was always my standard to "How do you behave towards fans? How do you behave toward the professionals? How do you behave towards people?" And one of the things I always like about Alan was he didn't have one head for fans and one head for writers and one head for famous people. He just treated everybody the same, which was with kindness, politeness, and grace, believing very much that a cult of celebrity had some kind of elevation of status that was fundamentally wrong and fundamentally a lie. Which I think is true, and which is how I've always tried to behave. It's like, "Everybody's here at the convention." I'm always very flattered when anybody wants to get in line and stand there for several hours to see Neil and get something signed, because there's nobody I would stand in line for five hours to see. God could return, and I'd say, "What? Stand in line for five hours?" So I always think it's terribly kind of people, terribly sweet and terribly nice. What I'm starting to figure out though is that there is a weirdness whereby sometimes it's not necessarily up to you whether or not that sort of status thing is there. Alan's line, which I always thought was fascinating, was "Communication is only possible between equals."

And what I've always tried to do is maintain an equality because that's where you get the communication. What I have misgivings about is if you get to the point where you have difficulty maintaining equality not because you're not trying to do it, but because people won't let you and they're not comfortable if you do. If you're sitting in a room party, *they* are not comfortable. Then it gets weird. Somebody sent me an e-mail to the website, to the journal, about AggieCon, saying, "Is there some sort of secret wave we could do to let you know that we think you're keen, and slip it in without bothering you?" "Well, actually," I said, "the best way is to just come over and say 'I think what you do is really cool and keen and neat and thank you very much.' Then if you say, 'Gee, what rotten weather we're having!' you might actually get a conversation out of it." [Laughs.]

*Darrell Schweitzer commented that, upon hearing you read your book* **Coraline** *at the 2000 World Horror Convention to an audience, he felt you could become one of this country's truly beloved storytellers. It was that powerful for the audience.*

They were such a nice audience. I started at eleven o'clock at night, and I said, "Look, I'm going to read the whole book to you." And, bless them, they stayed until two o'clock in the morning. They were still there—well, one guy fell asleep—and Darrell was one of them. I just thought they were very brave and very sweet because I got to stand there and find out what my book sounded like if you read it all through.

*Who are your favorite live speakers? What storytellers do you enjoy, and what do you think made them connect with an audience?*

I love Alan Bennett, who, interestingly, is not a live speaker. He does his stuff in studios mostly. I love poetry read by poets. I love good stand-up. And, by good stand-up, I mean people like Tom Lehrer or Woody Allen. Or Lenny Bruce. You go back to some of these old Lenny Bruce albums and, my God, the acting and the performance and the timing is magnificent. English guys? Alexie Sale, he's a fascinating performer, fascinating stand-up. Eddie Izzard, who has managed somehow to create an entire vocabulary that didn't exist before in terms of timing and beats. But much more important than any of that is my Dad. My Dad is a wonderful public speaker. As a kid, I used to watch him get up and talk and think, how does he do that? And Richard Curtis, who wrote *Black Adder* and *Four Weddings and a Funeral* and *Notting Hill.* I've been privileged occasionally to be around Richard when he has to get up in front of an audience, normally of major-league celebrities and things, and make a short speech. He says exactly the right thing, and it's funny and it's heart-warming and it's brilliant and it's from the heart. So Dick Curtis is definitely someone who I'd be influenced by as a speaker. But so much of it is just doing it long enough and finding your own voice. It's the same with writing. I know Jerry Garcia said it once, but I know many people have said it before him, which is "Style is the stuff you can't help doing." Style in some ways is the stuff that you do wrong. Because perfect technique would be completely without style. Stuff that lets everybody know that it's you playing is the falling away from perfect technique. So after you've written a few million words, the thing that lets anybody picking up a page read it and say, "Neil wrote that," is style, it's the stuff you can't help doing. You're not thinking, how can I write this like a Neil Gaiman sentence? You're writing a sentence. If you've been writing long enough and well enough, than it's going to be a Neil Gaiman sentence, because that's what they do. And I think it's the same for me up on stage in front of a large audience. You get the beat of an audience, you find out where they are, get a kind of sense of them, and then . . .

*You ride it?*

You ride it, and you talk to them, and you have fun. And you don't make fun of them. It's the only thing that I've always figured with an audience. As an audience, they're nervous enough already. They're terrified they've asked a stupid question. So even if somebody does ask a stupid question—which they don't very often—I'm never going to say, "Well, that was a stupid question." I'm much more likely to say, "Well, I think what you're trying to say is—" or "Okay, let me phrase that another way for you" or even "Fascinating question, let me answer it by saying that—" and get away from it after they've asked a stupid question with a yes-or-no answer, because you don't want them to feel uncomfortable.

*In addition to your creative work, I think posterity is going to remember you for what you've done for the Comic Book Legal Defense Fund. You've raised hundreds of thousands of dollars for that organization. I'm sure you've expressed your feelings toward this before, but—*

I feel that freedom of speech is an incredibly valuable thing, coming from England, which has no freedom of speech enshrined under law. It has Obscene Publications Acts, it has repressive customs laws, it has all sorts of weird things, laws against horror comics, laws against this and that. Coming out to a country where freedom of speech is actually enshrined in the constitution is incredibly important. And I felt like somebody coming to a country in which every citizen is, at birth, handed a large gold egg, and most of them find it an embarrassment, and lose it, or hide it, or think maybe things would be better if the gold egg were taken away from everybody and put somewhere where it's not going to offend anyone. It's just weird. And I just think the Comic Book Legal Defense Fund is *right*. It's this really good thing. Literature has won most of its battles. Comics is still fighting its battles. And I'm going to be out on the front line helping it fight the battles. The price of freedom is not cheap in this country. The price of freedom *may* be eternal vigilance, but the price of justice is several hundred thousand pounds per annum, so I'm getting out there and helping to raise it.

*Thank you very much, Neil.*

You're very welcome.

## Anita L. Burkam (review date November-December 2002)

SOURCE: Burkam, Anita L. Review of *Coraline,* by Neil Gaiman. *Horn Book Magazine* 78, no. 6 (November-December 2002): 755, 757.

[*In the following review, Burkam asserts that* Coraline *is an amusing story, but comments that it could be strengthened by more backstory and greater character development.*]

Out of sorts in her new home, Coraline finds a bricked-up door in the drawing room and, when her mother is out for the afternoon, discovers the bricks have gone and she can pass through to a very similar house with an "other mother" and an "other father." These two creepy specimens (with paper-white skin and black button eyes) want her to stay and be their little girl. Back in her own home, Coraline waits in vain for her parents to return, until at last she catches sight of a mirror image of them and determines she must head back into the alternate house to try to rescue them. What started out as a world set slightly askew turns nightmarish as Coraline joins the other mother in a game of hide-and-seek for her parents—winner take all. Images (white grub-like creatures in cobwebs; a toy box full of wind-up angels and tiny chatter-mouthed dinosaur skulls; the ubiquitous shiny black button eyes pictured in McKean's occasional dark and unsettling sketches as actual buttons) fly at the reader thick and fast, fully evoking the irrational yet unperturbing world of dreams, creating an avant-garde cinematic sweep of charged and often horrific flotsam from the subconscious. One wishes for a little more backstory to add depth and unity to the disparate images and a little more structure around the identity of the other mother (it turns out she resembles a kind of trap-door spider for souls, although exactly what she is or why she set up shop in Coraline's drawing room is left unstated). Still, the danger is convincingly dangerous, the heroine is convincingly brave, and the whirlwind denouement (helped along by a friendly cat and a *rather* clever ploy on the part of Coraline) will leave readers bemused but elated and slightly breathless.

## Charles De Lint (review date February 2003)

SOURCE: De Lint, Charles. Review of *Coraline,* by Neil Gaiman. *Fantasy & Science Fiction* 104, no. 2 (February 2003): 30-1.

[*In the following review, De Lint asserts that* Coraline *is Gaiman's best work of children's fiction yet, and comments that the story is enjoyable for adults as well as children.*]

Is there anything Gaiman doesn't do well?

*Coraline* isn't his first foray into children's fiction, but it's certainly his most successful. In fact, it's astonishingly good—an instant classic, if you'll excuse the hyperbole—and one that I can imagine both children and adults reading a hundred years from now with the same enjoyment they do Lewis Carroll's *Alice* books.

Carroll is actually a good touchstone, since *Coraline* reminds me of nothing so much as a macabre *Alice in Wonderland*. The title character doesn't go through a mirror or fall down a rabbit hole, but she does go through a door that normally opens on a brick wall to find herself in a twisted version of her own world. There she meets her other parents, the ones with buttons for eyes who want only the very best for Coraline, which includes making her one of their own.

Our plucky heroine escapes, only to find that her real parents have now been kidnapped and taken into that other world. Calling the police doesn't help—they only suggest she's having a nightmare and that she should go wake her mother and have her make a cup of hot chocolate. So it's up to Coraline to rescue not only her real parents, but also the spirits of the dead children that were taken before the "other mother" set her sights on Coraline.

The book is illustrated throughout by Dave McKean's pen and ink drawings that are both charming and strange. The prose is simple and lovely, the subject matter both dark and whimsical (sometimes whimsically dark, other times darkly whimsical—you get the idea). In accompanying material Gaiman writes that it's a story "that children experienced as an adventure, but which gave adults nightmares," and while I didn't get nightmares (I'm too much of a child, I suppose) I can easily see how both hold true. I do know that images from the book pop into my head at surprising times with an accompanying little shiver and thrill, and that I plan to reread it very soon. Now that I know the story, I want to savor the wonderful prose.

Collectors might be interested in tracking down a signed (by the author) limited edition that Harper-Collins has also produced. It features a color frontispiece by the book's illustrator as well as almost twenty pages of extra material that includes some more black and white art as well as commentaries by Gaiman himself. At around twenty-five dollars, it's a good price for a collectible book.

Or you can buy the peanutpress e-book version, which also includes the additional material, at around eleven dollars.

## Jeff Zaleski (essay date 28 July 2003)

SOURCE: Zaleski, Jeff. "Comics! Books! Films!: The Arts and Ambitions of Neil Gaiman." *Publishers Weekly* 250, no. 30 (28 July 2003): 46-57.

[*In the following essay, Zaleski provides an overview of Gaiman's writing projects in the media of comics, books, and film. Zaleski includes interview material with Gaiman, his agent, and his publishers.*]

COMICS

*LOS ANGELES: CHA CHA CHA!*

It's a warm L.A. night and Cha Cha Cha! is jumping. The staff of DC Comics and their supporters are crowded into the trendy restaurant on this first night of

BEA [Book Expo America] 2003. Everyone is talking, laughing, sometimes shouting. *PW* has to lean forward to hear what Karen Berger is saying. The executive editor of DC's Vertigo imprint has just placed pages from Neil Gaiman's *The Sandman: Endless Nights* on our table.

Berger tells us how Gaiman collaborated with an international "dream team" of artists for his return to the comics series that made his reputation, seven years after he quit comics to concentrate on books and screenplays. We flick through the pages. There are gorgeously colored drawings of two armies clashing, and of a man—or is it a woman?—of great beauty, with yellow eyes. Elsewhere a young woman, her face white and her hair black, peers out at us as if she knows us. The pages are bold, seductive, kinetic.

DC has big hopes for this September hardcover release—bestseller hopes. There's recently been a "dramatic growth" in the bookstore market for graphic novels, Berger says; reason enough, we think, for BEA organizers to have granted comics their own pavilion and a day of seminars. Yet "dramatic" is relative; in 2002, while the graphic novel market reached an estimated $100 million, a 33% hike from 2001, graphic novels accounted for fewer than 1% of the books sold in America. Graphic novels remain the wayward child of the publishing world, as apt to be found in comics retail stores, which aren't tracked on bestseller lists, as in bookstores, as understood and appreciated by most in book publishing as a nose-ringed teen is by her parents.

Guests migrate from table to table as others arrive. Music thrums over us from the bar area, adding to the din. Plates of spicy salad and jerked chicken clatter onto our table, nearly splashing the *Sandman* pages. A man walks up to us and speaks with fervor about the importance of comics to the world. Perhaps comics, he exclaims, are creating a mythology every bit as important as those created by the Greeks and Romans thousands of years ago.

Gaiman's *Sandman* series is considered by some to offer a new mythology. Published in 75 monthly 24-page issues by DC from December 1988 to March 1996, plus one special double issue, and now collected into 10 graphic novels, the series rocked the comics world with its literate, visionary tales of the godlike siblings known as the Endless. Gaiman's stories about Dream, aka the Sandman, Lord of the Dreaming, about his pale, black-haired sister Death, and about Delirium, Desire, Destruction, Despair and Destiny crowned comics bestseller lists for years, drawing an unprecedented number of female readers, and won awards galore. With its vast scale, encompassing eons from the birth of time to today, with its gallery of unforgettable characters, from gods to serial killers to Shakespeare and Marlowe, with its marvelous art and wit, ferocity, compassion and astonishing hipness, it spun comics in a more sophisticated direction and earned the indelible loyalty of fans, many of whom took it as a guide to life, the figure of the Sandman, tall, thin and brooding, helping to spawn the Goth movement along the way.

To comics folk, Gaiman's return to *Sandman* is a second coming. How will it play in the mainstream book market? The last graphic novel to scale national lists, Art Spiegelman's *Maus,* did so more than 10 years ago, but the excitement at BEA about graphic novels and *Endless Nights* reflects a medium climbing to the edge of commercial and critical embrace. Perhaps all that comics need is that one book, that one author, to pull them over the edge. Will *Endless Nights* be the tipping point?

We've heard that Gaiman might show for dinner, but he doesn't. The next day we spot him at the fair. He could be an older brother to the woman we saw in *Endless Nights,* in his black T-shirt, jeans and leather jacket, dark hair shagging over his pale face. A gawky guy clutching a mess of comics and books is standing close to Gaiman, handing him item after item. Gaiman signs each one quietly, patiently.

## Manhattan: DC Comics

The seventh-floor elevators at DC Comics open to a panoramic view of Metropolis, a huge mural of the city centered by the rising bulk of the *Daily Planet* building. The mural extends to a waiting area of four boxy chairs in red, yellow and blue. They're Superman's colors, and they're repeated in the nearby life-size statue of the Man of Steel, his arms thrust high in flight. Three phone booths stand along a wall, as does a pedestal displaying a chunk of mysterious green rock.

As Peggy Burns, DC's publicity manager, leads us to the office of Paul Levitz, we spot the DC president and publisher seated in a conference room; at another chair sits a life-size statue of Clark Kent. Levitz's office is a showcase of comic books, graphic novels and superhero figurines; near his desk hangs a embroidered portrait of Batman. Levitz joins us within moments. He's trim with glasses and wears a suit. Noticing the can and glass of Diet Coke we've placed on his desk, he slips a coaster beneath each and responds to our first question.

"Will *Endless Nights* be a tipping point?" Levitz raps twice on the desk. "The product itself is the first step in whether or not you can make this the tipping point. We're putting out a product that is literally world class." He considers his words. "In many ways," he suggests, "the American comic industry has been evolving, like a child saying, 'When I grow up I wanna be . . .'"

Comics have been growing up for more than a century. The first comic strip, *The Yellow Kid,* appeared in the 1890s. Forty years later came the first comic book, the familiar serial tabloid sold mostly in comic book stores, with *Funnies on Parade.* Detective Comics, or DC, was formed in 1937. A year later DC introduced the first superhero, Superman, in *Action Comics* #1, joined by Batman in 1939 and, in the '50s and '60s, by the wonders created by Stan Lee and Jack Kirby at Marvel. The industry's growth has been seriously arrested twice, first by the adoption in 1954 of the infamous Comics Code, which imposed censorship and stifled creativity, then by the collapse of the collectors' bubble market in the early '90s, which sent sales plummeting. Yet comics continued to mature. Underground work like R. Crumb's *Zap Comix* swarmed to prominence in the 1960s, and 1978 saw the birth of the graphic novel with Will Eisner's *A Contract with God,* followed by revelatory works like Alan Moore's *Watchmen,* Frank Miller's *Dark Knight* (Batman) series and Gaiman's *Sandman.*

"At last," continues Levitz, "you reach that point in maturity when you begin saying, 'I want to create something that will matter beyond me.' And that's when you have something that's worthy of being the tipping point." Levitz raps on the desk again. "Neil," he adds, "is one of a very short list of creative people who altered the limits of what the field can do. *Endless Nights* will be viewed as a benchmark."

Burns offers a tour of the DC offices. In the library, cliffs of steel cabinets secure vast archives. We roll one drawer open to extract a copy of *Action Comics* #1. In mint condition this comic can fetch up to $200,000 on the collectors' market, but someone has dismembered DC's vault copy, separating and laminating each page. On another floor, we visit the offices of the perpetually rambunctious *MAD Magazine.* Front and center stands a bronze bust of Alfred E. Neuman as combat soldier; original artwork for classic *MAD* covers lines the walls. Another elevator ride brings us to a virtual Gotham, backdropped by a mural of Batman's fabled city and embellished with a projected Bat Signal, a small-scale Batmobile and George Clooney's Batman costume. Steel containers and siding, looking cold and rusty, hulk in corners, while around them DC staffers, mostly young, bustle at their tasks.

## The Minneapolis Area: Neil Gaiman

Neil Gaiman writes far from Gotham's debris. Today, the sky is heavy with thunderheads, darkening the surrounding fields to emerald, as Lorraine Garland drives us up to a large brick Victorian house. Within this countryside where cows outnumber people and farms abound, Gaiman lives with his wife, Mary, his youngest daughter, Maddy, and Garland, the Gaimans' general assistant.

The author and his wife greet us in an immaculate kitchen. Gaiman is dressed in black again and hasn't shaved. He looks rested, and fit enough despite a slight paunch. He asks after our flight, and suggests a cup of tea as a restorative, then takes us outside, where he shows us his small garden and frets about a row of drooping pea plants. He's been away on a European tour, he explains, and hasn't been able "to pass on his complete knowledge" about pea-growing to Garland. He seems genuinely apologetic about the peas.

Gaiman was born in [Portchester], England, in 1960, his father a businessman and his mother a pharmacist. After graduating from the Whiting School in 1977, he skipped higher education in favor of a writing career, initially as a journalist. He married Mary McGrath in 1985 and, in 1992, moved to America with her and his two older children. He settled in this area, he says, mostly for the privacy, and to keep fans away; he prefers that we not mention the exact location of his home. The land is a refuge of trees and fresh air, and clearly Gaiman loves it; he happily shows us his blueberry bushes and, down a path, a gazebo where he used to write. But 10 years in America, plus the reach of the Internet, have rendered him a man without a country.

"When I go back to England," he explains in the English accent he retains, "I am no longer regarded as English. But here I'm not regarded as American. From 1992 to 1997 I worked very hard at living in America. I watched a lot of late night TV. Now the world is redefined. My paper of choice is the *Guardian,* which I read online, and my TV is as likely to come from Australia as from the US. So I don't think of myself as anything anymore. It's not a bad thing for a writer not to feel at home. Writers—we're much more comfortable at parties standing in the corner watching everybody else having a good time than we are mingling."

We go back inside, dodging a Super-Soaker wielded by Maddy, and pass through rooms graced with fine furniture. A glorious painting in red by illustrator Yoshitaka Amano brightens a Japanese-themed living room, and Gaiman points with pride to an ink drawing by Harry Clarke, an Irish artist in the Beardsley manner whom he collects. We go down to the basement, into an archive room crammed with comics and books preserved in plastic bins. Gaiman checks on the several humidifiers in one corner, plugging one in and pouring dirty water from a can labeled "Humidifier in a Can" into a hole in the floor. The next room is his library, centerpieced by a leatherbound 9th edition of the *Encyclopedia Britannica.* The walls are dense with books, awards and plaques tucked into every cranny, including one congratulating Gaiman as the Most Collectible Author of 2002. But it's now getting late, so Gaiman drives us in his cluttered Toyota Camry back to our hotel. We will meet tomorrow for our formal interview.

BOOKS

*MANHATTAN: WRITER'S HOUSE*

In 1872, a descendant of John Jacob Astor built a mansion on a leafy Manhattan side street to serve as his counting and money house. The building's walls of marble, plaster and dark wood, its slate tile floors and its stained glass windows made it a fitting home for the man's fortune, as did the walk-in safe in the building's basement. Today the mansion hosts one of publishing's most veteran dealmakers, literary agent Al Zuckerman, and the firm he founded in 1974 and still heads, Writers House.

Gaiman's agent, Merrilee Heifetz, works here. Dressed in a black pants suit that sets off her red hair, she greets *PW* in her office, where bookshelves (built by Zuckerman's son, Heifetz says) support editions by Gaiman and her other clients, including Laurell K. Hamilton, Bruce Sterling and Octavia Butler. Joining us for a minute, Zuckerman, smooth and cordial in an expensive suit, informs us that the building is in the manner of Aesthetic Movement, then takes his leave.

Heifetz explains that she first encountered Gaiman in 1988, when, as the American rep for a publishing house owned by the Who's Pete Townshend, she sold a book by "this young guy named Neil Gaiman, about Douglas Adams, for far more money than anyone thought it would." She looks steadily at us over glasses perched on her nose. "And of course half of that money belonged to this young journalist who barely had two pennies to rub together." Gaiman soon signed with Heifetz, proclaiming, she recalls, that "I write comic books, and I'm going to write novels someday."

Heifetz repped mostly Gaiman's comics until, in 1990, he kept his promise, producing *Good Omens,* a humorous tale of Armageddon co-authored with Terry Pratchett—the first major step into the shape-shifting that would mark his career. Six years later he took another step, delivering to the BBC six half-hour teleplays for *Neverwhere,* about a young man's adventures in a fantastic underground London. Intending to novelize *Neverwhere* himself, Gaiman told Heifetz that "I want a really big book deal with this. A million-dollar book deal, and I want a really good film agent. We're going to have to go to L.A. and meet people."

"We came away with Jon Levin of CAA," says Heifetz. "I made the book deal first. It was with Morrow/Avon. They bought *Neverwhere* and a short story collection [*Smoke and Mirrors*] and another novel [*Stardust*]. It was for nearly a million." Spending that much on an author who'd yet to crack bestseller lists was a shot in the dark, but one that paid off with strong sales on *Neverwhere* and, in 2000, a major national bestseller in

*American Gods.* That epic about a struggle between ancient European gods and younger, brasher American deities outsold Gaiman's previous books by nearly two to one.

"What made the difference was his Web site," Heifetz says. "Six months before *American Gods* was to come out, he started the site, and he started his blogger. And people started to visit. By the time *American Gods* came out, they went out and bought, and the book hit the lists." There are dozens of sites devoted to *Sandman* and Gaiman, but none like Gaiman's own (www.neilgaiman.com). It's a slick, immensely entertaining information and promotion machine, featuring a message board with more than 3,000 registered members and 200,000 posts, but most impressively Gaiman's blogger, where he converses at length with fans nearly every day about anything, but most often about his work. The site reportedly draws hundreds of thousands of regular visitors.

Gaiman followed *American Gods* with another shift, his first children's chapter book, *Coraline,* about a girl trapped in a parallel home with her "other parents," who have buttons for eyes. "He had been writing it for years," Heifetz says. "The advance was not huge. But the royalties have been, and now it's won awards [two ALA citations; a Stoker from the Horror Writers Association]. And it's broken Neil out to a new audience." An audience, we point out, he's expanding further this summer with *The Wolves in the Walls,* a whimsical HarperChildren's tale of wolves invading a home that looks a lot like Gaiman's, featuring a girl who looks just like his daughter Maddy. English artist Dave McKean contributed the rich, jazzy illustrations to *Wolves.* McKean collaborates with Gaiman on nearly all of Gaiman's illustrated books, and he created all the *Sandman* covers, including the one for *Endless Nights.*

Gaiman works at a furious pace to produce all this product—and to promote it. He's known for extensive tours jammed with overflow signings. "He just doesn't stop," says Heifetz. "He went to Brazil, and he got this huge turnout. Who knew? And they want him to come back. I said, 'Neil, you cannot go to Brazil again, it's going to take two weeks of your life.' And he said, 'Yes, but I could be the #1 bestselling author in Brazil.'" Heifetz suggests that Gaiman's primary goal is neither fortune nor fame, however, but the freedom to create what he wants when he wants.

THE MINNEAPOLIS AREA: NEIL GAIMAN

Gaiman picks us up 45 minutes early this morning, explaining that he's lost his broadband so he couldn't watch "digital dailies" of the fantasy film *Mirror Mask,* a Jim Henson Pictures production that he wrote and that Dave McKean is now directing in England. We drive for 20 minutes, through a small town and forest, until we reach a wood-framed motel situated above a gleaming lake. Gaiman rents the end unit, and it is here, in what he calls his "cabin," that he writes in splendid isolation, with two rules: no reading and no Web surfing. The one-bedroom unit can get hot, so he turns on a fan that will drone noisily throughout our talk.

"I know that I'm an oddity," Gaiman tells us with a characteristically complex mix of humor, frankness and self-awareness. "I seem to be fairly good at moving from medium to medium. What I really am is a storyteller. And what I'm fighting for is just to be allowed to do what I want to do next. It isn't the idea that I'm the 'bestselling author that no one's ever heard of' [a title given to Gaiman by *Forbes* magazine] that rankles. What rankles is that I'm sitting here with a readership and an audience in numbers that most people never dream of, and that every time I do a tour with a new publicity organization, they do not understand this."

Gaiman draws from more discrete readerships than probably any other bestselling writer, because he works successfully in so many media—serial comics, graphic novels, adult novels, children's chapter books and picture books, plays and teleplays and, now, films. It's difficult, he suggests, for professionals in any one field to grasp his success in the others. At the core of his readership are the *Sandman* fans, as loyal to Gaiman as Potter fans are to Rowling. He recalls that in 1997, when his and Dave McKean's illustrated children's book, *The Day I Swapped My Dad for Two Goldfish,* came out, the book "did over 20,000 straight off in hardcover in the comic stores to the Neil Gaiman fans. So there's a built-in readership." Gaiman cultivates his fan base, not only via his Web site but through the extensive in-person appearances, sometimes building a groundswell of interest far in advance of publication. "I've been doing *Wolves in the Walls* at readings ever since I wrote it, so from about late '98, early '99. I'm filling 1,000-seater bowls and now each of those 1,000 people is waiting for the book to come out."

"Why do so many people show up at your signings?" we ask. Like few other authors, Dean Koontz and Clive Barker among them, Gaiman will sign for hours, until the last fan is satisfied.

"I think they want to say 'thank you.' Sometimes they don't even have a book. Sometimes they bring you presents, sometimes they burst into tears. One girl fainted. I think you've given them something and you took them somewhere they couldn't have gone on their own."

Gaiman's work, his ambitions and his will to achieve them are creating greater public awareness of him, and his personal look speeds the process. Like Clancy in his quasi-uniforms and King in his country-cracker duds, Gaiman conjures up an easy-to-grasp image, of a handsome youngish man, sometimes unshaven, clad in all black and, for many years, in shades. "The shades were fun," Gaiman says, laughing. "The shades mostly came from trying to give people something to cartoon.

"But I'm kind of nervous about the upcoming three months," he adds. "Because for the last eight, nine years I've been every bit as famous as I would like to be, famous enough to get my phone calls returned. Which is probably saying stuff that I shouldn't be saying, but I really do like existing under the radar. It's a really cool and comfortable place to be."

We notice a sheaf of comics pages on a sofa. They are in black-and-white, the panels depicting men and women in old English dress—and there's an angel locked in a dungeon. We ask Gaiman what it is.

"It's something I'm doing for Marvel."

## Comics

### Manhattan: Marvel Enterprises

Joe Quesada, editor-in-chief of Marvel Enterprises, is rushing around his office. "There's been an asbestos explosion!" he shouts as he bends to pick up stuff off the floor. Quesada continues to straighten among his piles of comics and books and toys until we sit in the low chair opposite his desk. He then takes the much higher chair behind it and indicates that we should begin.

A celebrated comics writer/artist who took over Marvel editorial in 2000, Quesada has been credited with saving the comics giant from financial and artistic disaster. "Marvel needed to build some bridges with the creative community," he admits. "There were several key creators over the course of 10 or 15 years that we didn't do the right thing by, so consequently as a company we looked around and wondered why our books weren't that good. Neil was one of the first bridges that I wanted to build."

Quesada, stocky and solidly built, exudes a vigor that goes with his open-necked black knit shirt and gold chain. "*1602* was an instant green light," he says. "We were raring to go, and I was incredibly honored that Neil was going to do his next big comics project here at Marvel." The publication in August of the first issue of *1602,* illustrated by Andy Kubert, an eight-part series set in Elizabethan England and concerning mutants, a powerful object and an ancestral version of the Marvel universe, marks Gaiman's return to serial comics.

"Why were you 'incredibly honored'"?

"Neil is one of the top five writers in the history of our industry. He brings a certain amount of cachet. And he *always* brings his A game." Quesada's heavy watch clacks against his desk as he makes his point.

*1602* initially will appear only in comics stores. But Quesada expects the series to be collected into bookstores by July or August of next year. Marvel's drive for bookstore attention began three years ago, he tells us. "We perceive bookstores as the next feeder system for our industry. Every Wednesday is new comic day at the comic shops. So every Wednesday the true and faithful are there waiting for the boxes to be opened. Most human beings don't shop for *anything* that way. But there are people who go to the bookstore, and they love the product." And looking beyond comics, Marvel has just made its first foray into prose books, with the YA novel *Mary Jane,* about Spider-Man's girlfriend.

When we conclude, Quesada shows us out to a lobby stoppered on one end by huge double doors aflame with images of Marvel's superheroes. An impossibly muscled Hulk rages at the center.

### The Minneapolis Area: Neil Gaiman

It's interesting to see these black-and-white pages of *1602,* to observe a graphic novel in gestation. Like film, comics are a collaborative medium. The most important contributor is often the writer, who dreams the story and provides a script that includes not only storyline, commentary and dialogue but also art direction. "Foreground—the phone. In the background we can see Rick, heading for the phone, and Felix, picking up his bag, and preparing to leave," runs the script description for page 2, panel 4 of the *Sandman* episode **"Calliope."** An artist will then draw the story (Gaiman has worked with dozens); a letterer will add the words (Gaiman's longtime letterer is Todd Klein); an inker will go over the drawing in ink, and a colorer will transform black-and-white into a rainbow.

Gaiman likes to collaborate and is intent, he says, on playing to the strengths of his colleagues; that's why he refuses to write a comics script until he knows who will draw it. He's also intensely loyal, as evidenced by the duration of his collaborations—not only with Dave McKean and Todd Klein but with Merrilee Heifetz, DC Comics and Harper-Collins. He has a reputation within publishing as a good man. Certainly his work for the Comic Book Legal Defense Fund bears this out.

Back at the cabin, Gaiman sits by the front window. He's only a shadow against the intense sunlight that floods the room from behind him. There's fire in his voice as he talks about the Legal Defense Fund, citing cases it has fought, beginning with the State of California's attempt to reclassify comics from "literature" to "signed paintings," their aim, Gaiman says, "being that if it was signed painting they could collect sales tax on it." Other cases he relates involve obscenity arrests. For years, Gaiman participated in grueling tours to support the fund. He feels so passionately about its work, he says, because "the First Amendment is something that I think is really, really cool. I'm from England. There is no First Amendment there, no guaranteed freedom of speech."

## FILMS

### LOS ANGELES: CAA

Gaiman's film agent is Jon Levin, who speaks with us by phone from his offices at Creative Artists Agency. To date, Gaiman's best-known work in film is his English-language adaptation of the acclaimed Japanese animated movie **Princess Mononoke,** and the only Gaiman film project currently in production is **Mirror Mask.** But the author's screen future looks bright. "We're very active on a couple of books of his," Levin says. "One is **Stardust.** And he has **American Gods,** which sundry filmmakers are interested in, like George Clooney and Steven Soderbergh's Section Eight Films. He has a project in development at Pandemonium, which has a deal at Disney, for **Coraline.** He has a project that is in development at Warner Brothers, called **Books of Magic.**"

"What is Gaiman's appeal to the film world?" we ask. Levin pauses. "His unique vision. Neil is able to synthesize ancient mythology with the current zeitgeist. His characters, no matter how fantastical the world, are essentially human. And I will tell you that on top of all things, he is an amazing human being, and his work stems from his essence as a human being."

### THE MINNEAPOLIS AREA: NEIL GAIMAN

"In 1995, '96," Gaiman recalls at the cabin, "when I first started getting seriously wooed by Hollywood, I went out with Merrilee and interviewed agents. We got the full William Morris gang bang, all of the different agencies came out to see us. It was very obvious that very few of them got who I was or what I did. And everybody seemed to be out to make a real quick buck on me. Nobody was long term, which is why I wound up with Jon. He got who I was and what I did."

Gaiman's film dreams are huge but he knows how Hollywood works. He mentions an article in last year's *Variety* about how "I was the person who had sold the most properties and scripts in Hollywood and had not actually had anything made." But, he adds, "I think the odds are very good that the next one that I've written will actually happen, which is *The Fermata* [Nicholson Baker's erotic novel about a man who can stop time], for Robert Zemeckis. After I finished **American Gods,** I

re-read the novel and thought, 'Okay, it is completely un-filmable but I could do this. . . .' We plan to start shooting in the beginning of the year." Gaiman also expects to spend up to eight months of next year directing his first film, his own adaptation of his **Sandman** spin-off graphic novel **Death: The High Cost of Living,** for Pandemonium/Warner Brothers.

The string of recent $100-million grosses for movies based on Marvel properties have doubled Marvel's stock price, and DC intends to follow suit, with *Catwoman* filming this fall with Halle Berry, and other DC properties in development or pre-production. So what of **Sandman**? "It's in limbo," Gaiman says. "The book is much too weird and complicated to be a nice 100-minute movie. Or even three Hollywood movies à la *Lord of the Rings*." Numerous screenwriters have chipped their teeth chewing on **Sandman,** which ran to nearly 2,000 pages in comics form. "The worst of the scripts was the last one I read," Gaiman recalls. "The Sandman was completely powerless, had been kept under New York for a long time by giant electromagnets, and when they were turned off he was free but he had no superpowers of any kind, and his identical brother had taken over the Dreaming, and . . . as I'm reading this I'm going, 'I don't know who this is being written for.'"

## BOOKS

### MANHATTAN: HARPERCOLLINS

Jane Friedman and Cathy Hemming look summer-relaxed yet dressed for business, Friedman in pearls and a pale lime linen suit, Hemming in a black skirt and gray jacket. We can see the sun beating on the terrace adjoining Friedman's office, but the air inside is cool, the light subdued. Gaiman has no new book coming out from Harper adult trade this fall but the house is pushing him, issuing **Neverwhere** and **American Gods** in trade paperback. "Why are you making this additional investment in Neil Gaiman?" we ask the Harper CEO.

"We think he is a great talent," Friedman answers. "And there are people who have not yet discovered him. Once people read Neil they want to read all of Neil, and we should have the books in the right format."

"He's been successful as a children's author," adds Hemming, president and publisher of the house's general books group. "He has been very successful as a graphic novelist, and his audios are very successful. He's developing all these constituencies in all these different formats."

We suggest that by publishing books pitched at varied ages, Gaiman, who is 42, and HarperCollins are training younger readers to enjoy him from the go and to continue reading him as they grow up.

"How wonderful," Friedman says. "How wonderful! Which is interesting because this is exactly what we used to talk with Michael Crichton about, as his career was building. How do you get the ones who are 14 to become the lifelong fans? It worked with Crichton. There are the fans of *Coraline,* and there are the parents who are fans of *Coraline,* so we are building a generation that will follow suit."

Does Harper have any plans to move into graphic novels in a big way? "I doubt that we'll have a HarperCollins graphic books imprint," says Friedman. "Of course, if the right illustrated novel comes to us, we would publish it. We're open to anything, but we want to play to our strengths. We're better off sticking to the business we know."

Gaiman is currently contracted to HarperCollins adult trade for two unpublished novels and a collection of short stories. He has published books with the house since the mid-'90s, weathering a shock when his longtime editor Jennifer Hersey left (Jennifer Brehl now edits him). Friedman expects him to remain. "I think it's a great relationship. There's so much behind him and yet so much in front of him. We're married. We're in the Neil Gaiman business forever. Forever."

To get an insight into Gaiman's work for children, we call Susan Katz, president and publisher of the house's children's division, whose enthusiasm for Gaiman erupts into a shouted "Yay!" time and again. "He's one of the handful of successful adult writers who knows how to talk to children effectively without talking down to them," Katz suggests. She mentions that Gaiman "has another children's book in the pipeline. It has a lot to do with graveyards [which also figure in Gaiman's entry in the third volume of the *Little Lit* series, edited by Art Spiegelman, a graphic novel for kids due out from Harper's Joanna Cotler Books in August]." And Katz expects Gaiman's forthcoming tour for *Wolves* to excel, because "when Neil tours, all of his fan base turns out. Yay!"

The *Sandman* mythos has generated a cottage industry in related product. The primary publisher of *Sandman* sidelines is Chronicle. According to executive editor Sarah Malarkey, current offerings include a Sandman wall calendar and collectible postcards, plus two journals. This fall, Chronicle will publish *Sandman: King of Dreams,* an illustrated study of the series by Alisa Kwitney. Then there is *The Sandman: The Book of Dreams,* from Harper-Collins, with stories about the Endless from genre stars including Clive Barker, Gene Wolfe and Tad Williams. DC has issued a collection of Dave McKean's *Sandman* covers, as well as Hy Bender's *The Sandman Companion.* And an array of *Sandman* toys. And smaller presses, too, are hitching to Gaiman's star. Wildside Press has just published

Stephen Rauch's scholarly study of the Sandman mythos, *Neil Gaiman's "The Sandman" and Joseph Campbell: In Search of the Modern Myth,* and the British publisher Titan is releasing in America a newly revised edition of **Don't Panic.**

*THE MINNEAPOLIS AREA: NEIL GAIMAN*

For lunch we drive to a cozy spot that features an array of fantastic pies. We each select sour-cream-and-raisin, topped by a cloud of meringue.

"Why do you write fantasy?" we ask.

"You can do so many things with fantasy. At a rock-bottom level, you can concretize a metaphor. Part of it is that, if you're a writer, you can play God. This is my world, you are welcome to come, but I get to call the shots, and I won't be embarrassed to pull in anything I need or want."

Calling the shots means deciding not only what to write but how to write it, and in *American Gods* Gaiman tried something new. "There's a style of writing," he says, forking some meringue, "that I had always admired, which I think of—although there couldn't be two writers further apart—as a Stephen King/Elmore Leonard thing, where what the writer is trying to do is to become invisible. What I tended to do before was the very English thing of saying, 'Lovely to see you, I am your host, please sit down, I'm going to make you comfortable, I'll bring you a drink, would you like a story?' The American voice is almost pretending there's nobody writing the story." Gaiman's gambit worked: *American Gods* is the only fiction ever to have won all four major speculative fiction awards, including a Hugo, Nebula, Stoker and World Fantasy.

Gaiman informs us that his next novel will be *Anansi Boys,* set in the world of *American Gods* but this time with a comedic spin. He considers writing humor a particular challenge, pointing out that "humor and horror and pornography are incredibly similar—you know immediately whether you've got them right or not because they should provoke physiological changes in the person reading."

COMICS

*MANHATTAN: DC COMICS*

Karen Berger, slim and blonde and casually dressed, greets us warmly. She has worked with Gaiman for 15 years, ever since the young author, a lifelong comics fan who was trained to write a comics script by Alan Moore, approached her with his plan to revitalize—and totally transform—a defunct DC superhero known as the Sandman, who caught criminals by knocking them out with sleeping gas. For the past 10 years she has edited Vertigo, DC's prestigious graphic novels line, which publishes all of Gaiman's DC work. "I think it was Vertigo's 10th anniversary that got Neil to commit to a big book for us," she tells us. "And this was what I was able to get out of Neil. It sounds desperate my saying it that way, but the guy's getting a hell of a lot more money as a book author than he is here. I'm thrilled to get whatever he'll write for us."

What Gaiman has written for DC is a comics masterpiece, a book that, in its seven tales, one devoted to each of the Endless, each illustrated by a different artist, demonstrates the enormous range of the comics medium both in content and style. The seven artists bring visuals as disparate as the sharply delineated, reader-friendly work of P. Craig Russell, who drew the **"Death"** story, and the deliriously jagged paintings of Barron Storey for **"Fifteen Portraits of Despair."** Berger comments, "Each story is like a novella, rich in narrative and character and texture. And that's even without the art. It's such a great deal, too, $25 to get 160 pages of amazing story and art."

A great deal, but will the public buy? "I think the tide is just starting to turn," says Berger. "We're moving up to crest but we obviously haven't crested yet. We've lined up a ton of publicity, including *ET, USA Today,* bookstores. The buyers recognize this book, so we're getting a lot of support."

"You'll want to convince folk who never bought a graphic novel to buy one."

"If it's going to happen with anyone, it's going to happen with Neil and *Sandman.*"

*THE MINNEAPOLIS AREA: NEIL GAIMAN*

After lunch, we return to the cabin to wrap things up. We ask Gaiman about his thinking process in the creation of *Endless Nights.*

"I'm often asked, 'Where do ideas come from?' The best that I can point to is that ideas come from two or more things coming together. You combine them and suddenly it's, 'Oh, nobody's ever done that before. That will be really fun.' In comics, very often for me it's somebody asking, "How would you like to do something for artist X?'

"Manara [Milo Manara, the artist for the Desire story in *Endless Nights,* about a young woman who finds love briefly only to see her lover slain, and who then takes revenge] is a lovely example. I had this great odd idea of a way to write the story. And if it works, by the time I get to the end page, where she's turning around and she's talking directly to us over a span of 50 years and essentially dying in the last panel, it's going to be

absolutely beautiful. I pulled that off only because Manara gave me that last page, where she ages from 20 to 70 and is somehow recognizable. This is a comics thing because you're seeing her age on the page, while the images remain static in a way that wouldn't have worked in a film. In a film she'd be talking to us and you'd have to do a 60-years dissolve. As a prose story you might well have wanted to end it earlier. Here there are six inexorable panels that do something in comics that I couldn't have done in any other medium."

The sun moves low over the lake and we return to the house. There we admire a World Fantasy Award, shaped as a craggy bust of H. P. Lovecraft, and one of Gaiman's Stokers, a casting of Poe's House of Usher, with a little door that opens at the front. Gaiman says that he doesn't want *Coraline*'s Stoker mentioned on the paperback edition of the novel, as "it would frighten too many parents."

Driving us back to our hotel, Gaiman muses. "Do you know what the coolest thing about *Endless Nights* is? It's seven short stories that are, respectively, a very realistic short story about a contemporary soldier that is melded with a weird sort of Casanova fantasy. A really cool historical thing based on a fragment of an anecdote about a Scottish clan related by George Fraser. A high fantasy set at the beginning of the universe with an animated sun. An out-there, para-literary, post-modern sequence. . . . Not one of those stories is even in the same genre as any of the other stories.

"I did it right, I did the thing that people remember and love. I did this thing that now, what, 10 million people have read, 20 million people have read, you know?"

Later that night we're channel surfing when we come across a show on the History Channel about comics. There's Stan Lee, and *Batman* writer Frank Miller, and there's Gaiman, unshaven and in black, caught while on tour, his face worn from lack of sleep, speaking with passion about the medium he loves, a medium that has found its lead title, and perhaps even its tipping point, in his latest work.

**John Giuffo (review date 17 September 2003)**

SOURCE: Giuffo, John. "Re-Enter *Sandman*." *Village Voice* 48, no. 38 (17 September 2003): 48.

[*In the following review, Giuffo offers high praise for Gaiman's* Sandman: Endless Nights.]

Neil Gaiman's improbable recipe for delicious literary success: Take one young British journalist disillusioned with the comics he loved as a teen, introduce an issue of Alan Moore's early-'80s boundary-expanding *Swamp Thing,* stir in a formerly cornball but reclaimed Golden Age DC Comics character called Sandman, season liberally with history, myth, and biblical allegory, stir in generous helpings of word of mouth, and simmer for eight years. Let congeal, then cut into 11 volumes. When cool, add a healthy dollop of gripping fantastic prose, a dash of TV fame (preferably of the BBC miniseries variety), and swaddle in black. Garnish with more *Sandman* for texture, Serves millions.

One glance at the giddy crowd during a Gaiman reading held last month at the Wall Street Borders and it's obvious just how popular he is. While he read from *The Wolves in the Walls,* his latest book for children, it's safe to say that most in attendance were drawn by their love of Gaiman's brooding, lanky personification of dreams, the Sandman. After a seven-year break from writing the fantastical-historical-mythical stories that made him famous, Gaiman has returned to his best-loved characters with *The Sandman: Endless Nights,* a dizzyingly lush grouping of seven tales, each focused on a different sibling in the family known as the Endless. The intervening years have been busy ones for the prolific Gaiman—three children's books, three novels, two collections, and a smattering of TV and movie projects—but it's still *The Sandman* that inspires the most fervent dedication.

Lisa Feuer is one such devotee: a thin, pale goth mom—that's right, a goth mom—who brought her 13-month-old son, Sasha, to the signing. "He actually came to Neil's last signing when he was 10 days old," beams Feuer, an a&r rep for darkwave label Projekt Records.

When I tell Gaiman at a breakfast interview the following day that I don't want to pigeonhole him, but that I plan to quote her for this piece, he chuckles and says, "Of course you will." The 43-year-old Gaiman has a well-earned reputation for being generous to his readers, usually staying at readings for hours until every last fan gets a signature. "But for every goth mom, you have a skinny art chick or a tall science fiction fan or a grandma," he says. "The thing that fascinates me is this incredibly weird, wonderful cross section."

Credit his ever diversifying body of work; from the Douglas Adams-y comic novel *Good Omens* (co-written with Terry Pratchett) to his *New York Times* bestseller, *American Gods,* to his growing collection of children's books. In addition to attracting an increasingly eclectic readership, Gaiman's forays into prose fiction have had the effect of getting his comics work—and, indeed, the comics medium—taken more seriously by mainstream media bent on infantilizing the form.

That's not to say that Gaiman set out to create a seminal, genre-busting work of modern mythmaking. "When I was writing *Sandman,* if I had an agenda, the agenda was purely and simply the idea of, 'Can I write a comic that will get somebody like me to go down to a comics shop once a month and spend money to find out what happens next?'" he says, "I was my audience."

Luckily, that audience has grown: The *Sandman* series has sold over 7 million copies to date, in 19 countries and 13 languages. DC Comics is betting that *Endless Nights* will be a huge hit, and Gaiman expects that it will be the first graphic novel since Art Spiegelman's 1992 Pulitzer-winning *Maus* to reach the *Times* best-seller list.

One look at the book proves that such hopes aren't unfounded. With illustrations by an impressive group of international artists, including Barron Storey, Bill Sienkiewicz, and Miguelanxo Prado, *Endless Nights* both delivers on the high expectations of longtime readers and surprises with its millennium-spanning variety. Each of the seven short stories focuses on one member of the Endless family—Death, Desire, Dream (the Sandman), Despair, Delirium, Destruction, and Destiny—and explores the histories and evolution of these anthropomorphized manifestations of human constants. Whereas Gaiman's *Sandman* series, which ran from 1988 to 1996, often used the title character to explore mythology and history through the prism of Dream, and of dreams, this latest installment uses contemporary allusion and mythological allegory to explore the roles played by the seven Endless siblings in human—and cosmic—events. They aren't gods, Gaiman takes pains to explain, though they are godlike, and their existence doesn't depend on belief in them (a theme Gaiman visited in *American Gods,* to a different, though familiar, end).

One of the most impressive stories in *Endless Nights* is the second, **"What I've Tasted of Desire."** Set in a medieval Nordic village, it tells the tale of a beautiful townswoman who wants nothing more than to capture the heart of the tribe's comely, virile prince. She finds his philandering infuriating, however, and she seeks out the assistance of the hermaphroditic Desire in her efforts to snag her man. Her mastery of desire (though, finally, not of Desire) proves to be, for all of its thirst-quenching satisfaction, but one early, oft remembered episode in her otherwise unremarkable life. Gaiman had Italian eroticist Milo Manara's work in mind when he wrote the tale, and the final product is a seamless melding of the author's mytho-historical storytelling skill and of Manara's *Heavy Metal*-style spank-mag tendencies. It's an amazing instance of an author bringing out an artist's best, and, without revealing too much, the last page is a prime example of something that's only possible in comics. "That's my fuck-off page," explains Gaiman. "If you're telling me that comics are a lesser medium, you can fuck off because you can't do this in any other medium."

Even without the novels, the children's books, the BBC miniseries (*Neverwhere*), and the movies-in-development (his *Sandman* onetime spin-off *Death: The High Cost of Living* is slated to start production next year), Gaiman still would have had a profound impact on comics, opening the form up to new styles, subjects, and possibilities.

"I remember once ranting [about the state of the comics industry] to Dave Sim, who did *Cerebus,* and he said, 'So what are you doing about it?'" Gaiman says, "And I thought about it for a minute, and I said, Well, I'm writing good comics. And I'm really pleased I did, because now I can look at those 10 volumes of *Sandman* and go, Look, this was something that meant something."

## Charles De Lint (review date December 2003)

SOURCE: De Lint, Charles. Review of *The Wolves in the Walls,* by Neil Gaiman and Dave McKean. *Fantasy & Science Fiction* 105, no. 6 (December 2003): 26-7.

[*In the following review, De Lint describes* The Wolves in the Walls *as "a splendid foray into the dark and strange mind of Gaiman."*]

I'd been looking forward to this book [*The Wolves in the Walls*] ever since I first heard Gaiman talk about it on a panel at the 2002 World Fantasy Convention. Gaiman, it turns out, is one of those rare writers who can make a work-in-progress sound really fascinating. Usually, listening to that sort of thing makes for more tedium than I care to experience (don't tell me about the book, write it and let me read it on my own!), but Gaiman's brief description of a plucky young girl who realizes that wolves live inside the walls of her parents' house, and who then goes on to drive the family out so that they have to live at the bottom of the garden, promised to deliver a welcome helping of dark whimsy.

I was disappointed, however, when a galley arrived in my P.O. box and I realized that *The Wolves in the Walls* wasn't so much like *Coraline* (a short novel with illustrations) as *The Day I Swapped My Dad for Two Goldfish* (a children's picture book). But the disappointment only lasted as long as it took me to get to the third page where Lucy first hears noises in the walls.

What follows is another splendid foray into the dark and strange mind of Gaiman, who, if nothing else, never delivers a story that takes you where you think it will. The prose here is very simple. There's no age given—probably because the publisher knows that adults will pick up a Gaiman book for themselves as readily as they buy one for their children—but I'd guess it's in

the neighborhood of five and up. You might want to vet the story and pictures for possible nightmare inducing, though kids are far more resilient than we adults think they are.

McKean's art won't necessarily be to everyone's taste—it's a bit confrontational, rather than typical picture book pretty—but I love the look of it, and I'm sure children will, too.

## Stephen Rauch (essay date 2003)

SOURCE: Rauch, Stephen. "'Dream a Little Dream of Me . . .': The Relationship of Dreams and Myth in Campbell, Jung, and Gaiman's *Sandman,*" and "The Role of the Artist and the Art of Storytelling in *The Sandman.*" In *Neil Gaiman's "The Sandman" and Joseph Campbell: In Search of the Modern Myth,* pp. 22-37; 117-37. Holicong, Penn.: Wildside Press, 2003.

[*In the following two essays, Rauch discusses the relationship between dream and myth in Gaiman's* Sandman *series, drawing on the theories of Carl Jung and Joseph Campbell to demonstrate the ways in which the stories function as a modern myth. The second essay focuses specifically on the role of stories and storytelling in the* Sandman *stories.*]

"'DREAM A LITTLE DREAM OF ME . . .': THE RELATIONSHIP OF DREAMS AND MYTH IN CAMPBELL, JUNG, AND GAIMAN'S *SANDMAN,*"

"A dream is a personal experience of that deep, dark ground that is the support of our conscious lives, and a myth is the society's dream. The myth is the public dream and the dream is the private myth."

—Joseph Campbell

"Dreams are weird and stupid and they scare me."

—Rose Walker

To associate myths and dreams with one another is hardly a new enterprise. Religious traditions going back thousands of years have viewed dreams as a source of knowledge and intuition, and have connected this information with the central narratives of their traditions. If myth is to be seen as a living phenomenon that connects to all aspects of people's lives, then dreams cannot be ignored—after all, we spend a third of our lives in the realm of dreams. Modern psychologists tell us that dreams are essential to mental and physical health, but they are only telling us what we knew all along. Still, in modern times, the connection between myths and dreams has come even more into the fore. In the early twentieth century, doctors began to notice that the dreams and visions of their patients bore a striking resemblance to the motifs and narratives of various religious traditions, traditions with which the patients often had no familiarity. With the advent of Carl Jung's theory of the collective unconscious, a new era of relationship between myth and dream was ushered in. The claim was that not only do myths and dreams share material and patterns, they come from the same place: the human psyche. This theory was developed even further by later scholars, such as Joseph Campbell, who drew analogies between the dreams of an individual, and the myths of a people.

Campbell's theory brings us to the matter at hand: what is the relationship between myth and dream in *The Sandman*? Certainly, this is at least a good place to start, as the series is a myth that in many places is about dreams and how they affect the lives of dreamers. Of course, the connection is even stronger than that. The central character in *Sandman* is Morpheus, the Lord of Dreams. He presides over the Dreaming, the collective realm where dreams do not merely reflect reality; they *are* reality. Simply put, he lives in dreams, and as a constituent of consciousness, he *is* the psychological function of dreaming. Beyond Dream (the character), the structure of *Sandman* reflects the kinship between myths and dreams. The Dreaming is inhabited by characters taken from myth, most notably Eve, Cain, and Abel. The Dreaming itself, I would argue, is a dramatization of Jung's "collective unconscious," making concrete what he perceived in metaphor. Finally, according to both Gaiman and Campbell, the gods themselves come from dreams, and are born and nurtured in dreams (of course, there are also other characters in the Dreaming besides gods). And in *The Sandman,* dreams are respected as their own form of reality. While some theories reductively pigeonhole dreams as reflections of neuroses, in Gaiman's universe, dreams are real, and this fact points to another theme in Gaiman's work, respect for inner realities. It is never "just" a dream. Rather, it is a dream, but dreams have a supreme importance. What better place, then, to start with a series about how myths are made, born, and die, than with an examination of the role of dreams. Thus, we take a ride into dreams. Pay no attention to the man in black.

One of the key principles of the relationship between myths and dreams is that they are somehow connected. Campbell says that "indeed, between the worlds of myth and dream there are many instructive analogies. When we leave the field of our waking lives . . . we descend into a timeless realm of the unconscious" (*Transformations* 206). He continues, that in dreams, "the logic, the heroes, and the deeds of myth survive into modern times" (*Hero with a Thousand Faces,* 4). Gaiman takes this idea to the next level, and in doing so makes a pronouncement about the nature of the gods themselves: that gods are in fact magnified dreams. With a psychological interpretation of myths, such as

that used by Campbell and Jung, saying "the gods" does not refer to some outer reality, but to an inner one. Campbell says "the archetypes of mythology (God, angels, incarnations, and so forth) . . . are of the mind" (*Masks* 583). He also refers to the transformative power of religion as leading "not into outer space but into inward space, to the place from which all being comes, into the consciousness that is the source of all things, the kingdom of heaven within" (*Power* 56). In a similar vein, the gods become metaphors of inner "potentialities;" thus, myth, at its heart, is about people, and their inner worlds. Campbell asks, "What is a god? A god is a personification of a motivating power or a value system that functions in human life and the universe— the powers of your own body and of nature. The myths are metaphorical of spiritual potentiality in the human being, and the same powers that animate our life animate the life of the world" (*Power* 22). Thus, myths are metaphorical of a deeper truth. Elsewhere, Campbell states that "gods are all metaphors of this ultimate mystery, the mystery of your own being" (*Transformations* 155). Beyond the fact that the gods are metaphors lies a second point, that gods are only as valid in that they reflect some aspect of our being. We care about gods not because they control fire or water or lightning, but because they are a part of us. Campbell also says that "all the gods are within: within you— within the world" (*Masks* 650). Put another way, "the source of the gods is in your own heart" (*Hero's Journey* 128). Thus, ultimately, myths are about *us.* And the realization of this fact is an important step for more than one character in *Sandman.* Of course, although dreams and myth are related, there are important differences between them, as we will see.

With this shift, from gods as physical beings to gods as metaphors of aspects of ourselves, the relationship of myth to dream comes into focus. Just as gods can function as symbols, so can elements from our dreams. The next step, then, is to identify the gods with dreams. Campbell says that "all the gods, all the heavens, all the worlds, are within us. They are magnified dreams, and dreams are manifestations in image form of the energies of the body in conflict with each other. That is what myth is. Myth is a manifestation in symbolic images, in metaphorical images, of the energies of the organs in conflict with each other" (*Power* 39). Then, he states that "the myth is the public dream and the dream is the private myth" (40). Elsewhere, he says "Dream is the personalized myth, myth the depersonalized dream; both myth and dream are symbolic in the same general way of the dynamics of the psyche" (Campbell, *Hero with a Thousand Faces,* 19). At this point, if we are to accept Campbell's psychological reading of myth, the relationship between myth and dream seems well-established.

In the *Power of Myth* videos, Campbell also says that "myths and dreams come from the same place" (Tape 1). Of course, exactly what that "place" is may be a matter of debate. For Campbell (as for Jung) it was the unconscious, or at least the psyche. For Gaiman, it is the Dreaming. From Campbell's discussion, the most important concept in relation to *The Sandman* is that of gods as magnified dreams. At first glance, however, such a reading might seem as reductive as those against which Campbell rails. After all, if the gods are all metaphors, then they do not *really* exist. However, with *The Sandman,* we are dealing with a myth, a work of art, in which such beings can exist without our having to worry about whether or not they exist in the real world. In fact, one of the lessons of *Sandman* is that inner, imaginary worlds are just as real and valid as the solid, "real" world, and that each one of us has not just one inner world, but many.

Returning to Campbell, then, the flip-side of the gods' status as metaphors and magnified dreams, (the other side of the coin, if you will) is what happens after the gods have left the realm of dreams. In Gaiman's work, this stage is eloquently described by Ishtar, once Astarte, a goddess, now working in a seedy strip club, just before she goes off to her death: "I know how gods begin, Roger. We start as dreams. Then we walk out of dreams into the land. We are worshipped and loved, and take power to ourselves. And then one day there's no one left to worship us. And in the end, each little god and goddess takes its last journey back into dreams . . . And what comes after, not even *we* know" (*Sandman* 45:20). This quotation is filled with implications. First, of course, is the association of gods with dreams. Gods and goddesses start their journey in dreams. From one dreamer, they can spread to others, until an entire people believes in them. And one day, after being nurtured in dreams, they step out into the world, becoming gods in their own right. The immediate implication of this journey is to confirm Campbell's notion of gods as magnified dreams. However, Gaiman's treatment of the subject also runs much deeper. One implication of this is that gods, often said to be immortal, are in fact very mortal. They depend on people's worship for their very lives. *Sandman* is full of stories of gods who have been forced to deal with the loss of worship. For some, their time has passed, while for others, the modern "demythologization" has taken its toll. And without worship, they will die. The character Death, at one point, tells us that this process takes a while, but it is bound to happen, as "Mythologies take longer to die than people believe. They linger on in a kind of dream country" (*Sandman* 20:21). This "dream country" is the province of the Sandman. And while religious traditions are filled with accounts of the gods "needing" the sacrifices that people make to them, nowhere else is the gods' dependence identified with belief to the degree that it is in *Sandman*. And this need for belief works in both directions. Just as gods need us, so do we have a need to believe in them.

As Destruction tells us, there is no such thing as a one-sided coin. And the flip-side to the gods' needing people for worship is that we need them just as much. Frank McConnell, in his preface to the *Sandman: Book of Dreams,* asks the question, "How do gods die? And when they do, what happens to them *then?* You might as well ask, how do gods get born? All three questions are, really, the same question. And they all have a common assumption: *that humankind can no more live without gods than you can kill yourself by holding your breath*" (2, emphasis mine). Just as gods need us, so do we need them. Since the time of the Enlightenment, people have moved further and further into secularization. If we take Freud as the high-water mark of demythization and post-Enlightenment positivism, then his *Future of an Illusion* epitomizes the already existing argument that religious belief is, in fact, an illusion, and an illusion that mankind can and will (even must) learn to live without. However, we now stand almost a century later, and whether the loss of religious belief has truly helped us is a dubious claim indeed. In other words, we have killed the gods, and are only now beginning to wonder whether doing so was a good idea. For many, the loss of religion has meant the loss of meaning and purpose in life.

Like others, Gaiman understands this situation, what has been called "the spiritual problem of modern humans." Destruction's formulation of this problem led him to abandon his realm (albeit for slightly different reasons—see part 4). Still, the point here is not simply that the increasing march toward rationality has taken a toll in our spiritual lives. It is that people who think they are living in a world without God (or gods) are really just fooling themselves. If the old gods are lost, we will simply invent new ones. The central point here is the importance of *belief*. It is belief that is central to keeping gods alive, and it is belief that is equally important for people. McConnell continues his discussion, that "We need gods . . . not so much to worship or sacrifice to, but because they satisfy our need—distinctive from that of all the other animals—to imagine a meaning, a sense to our lives, to satisfy our hunger to believe that the muck and chaos of daily existence does, after all *tend* somewhere" (Preface 2). This kind of belief is born of a need for meaning, and it powers the "gods as magnified dreams" dynamic. And this sense of meaning is what makes life worth living.

The second major point in the relationship between myths and dreams lies in the psychological background of both. This background, quite literally, is Carl Jung's idea of the "collective unconscious," which shows a strong kinship with Gaiman's "Dreaming." It is from the collective unconscious that both myths and dreams spring. According to Jung, this layer of the unconscious is "not individual but universal," and "more or less the same in all individuals" (Jung, *Archetypes* 3-4). Jung agrees with Campbell, that gods and heroes "[dwell] nowhere except in the soul of man," and that "the psyche contains all the images that have ever given rise to myths" (*Archetypes* 6-7). It is this part of the psyche that is the source of the images and stories that so captivate us. According to Jung, the collective unconscious is inherited biologically, "[owing its] existence exclusively to heredity" (42). And although the collective unconscious is the source for myths as well, it is dreams that are the "main source" of knowledge about it—being unconscious, dreams are "pure products of nature not falsified by any conscious purpose" (Jung, *Archetypes* 48). Thus, this layer of the psyche is passed down through the generations biologically, and is the result of the same process of evolution that produced our other forms of instinctive behavior.

The second major point about the collective unconscious, after its residency in the psyche, is that it is the same in all people. Jung says that "from the unconscious there emanate determining influences which, independently of tradition, guarantee in every single individual a similarity and even a sameness of experience, and also of the way it is represented imaginatively. One of the main proofs of this is the almost universal parallelism between mythological motifs, which, on account of their quality as primordial images, I have called *archetypes*" (*Archetypes* 58). Under this scheme, the archetypes are the inner psychic images that we form instinctively, and which are the precursors of the religious and mythological images we create. Although I am not qualified to address the veracity of this claim, it might well be that, as other theorists do, Jung overestimated the similarities between mythic traditions and ignored their differences, as some critics have claimed. Still, it is important to note that Jung is not saying that all mythologies are the same. Archetypes are not the images of myth themselves; "it is not, therefore, a question of inherited *ideas,* but of inherited *possibilities* of ideas" (Jung, *Archetypes* 66).

Elsewhere, Jung calls the archetypes "primordial," at least as old as the human species. He also says that "they are the 'human quality' of the human being, and the specifically human form his activities take" (*Archetypes* 78), thus forming one of the things that define us. He claims "the true history of the mind is not preserved in learned volumes but in the living mental organism of everyone" (*Psychology and Religion* 41). It is difficult to overestimate the importance of these phenomena; Jung says, "I am of the opinion that the psyche is the most tremendous fact of human life" (*Archetypes* 116). He also says that "psyche is existent, even existence itself" (*Psychology and Religion* 12). Elsewhere, Jung lays out the psyche as consisting of

both the conscious mind and "an indefinitely large hinterland of unconscious psyche" (*Psychology and Religion* 47). Finally, Campbell has commented on Jung's ideas, as he was influenced by them was well; "The psyche is the inward experience of the human body, which is essentially the same in all human beings . . . Out of this common ground have come what Jung has called the archetypes, which are the common idea of myths" (Campbell, *Power* 51). Here, we have an etiological explanation for Campbell's statement that dreams and myths come from the same place; that place is the collective unconscious. And although dreams and myths have important differences, they are inextricably linked.

In another work, *Modern Man in Search of a Soul,* Jung discusses the collective unconscious further. In particular, the production of dreams is important, as "dreams may give expression to ineluctable truths, to philosophical pronouncements, illusions, wild fantasies, memories, [etc] . . . One thing we ought never to forget: almost half of our lives is passed in a more or less unconscious state" (*Modern Man* 11). In arguing for the importance of the unconscious, he says "When we see that at least a half of man's life is passed in this realm, that consciousness has its roots there, and that the unconscious operates in and out of waking existence, it would seem incumbent upon medical psychology to sharpen its perceptions by a systematic study of dreams. No one doubts the importance of conscious experience; why then should we question the importance of unconscious happenings?" (15). Later, he tells us that "the collective unconscious, moreover, seems not to be a person, but something like an unceasing stream or perhaps an ocean of images and figures which drift into consciousness in our dreams . . ." (*Modern Man* 186). And connected with dreams, always, is myth, and while this connection was made more forcefully by later theorists like Campbell, Jung still makes the connection, as "myth for Jung *is* the naked expression of the unconscious" (Segal, *Jung on Mythology* 25-6). At one point, Campbell quotes Jung as saying "the typical motifs in dreams . . . permit a comparison with the motifs of mythology" (*Masks* 644). Jung also says that "man has, everywhere and always, spontaneously developed religious forms of expression, and that the human psyche from time immemorial has been shot through with religious ideas. Whoever cannot see this aspect of the human psyche is blind" (*Modern Man* 122). Commenting on this idea, Anne Ulanov says that "operating in us, independent of our will, [the religious instinct] is a capacity for and urge toward conscious relationship to transpersonal deity" (18). The idea of the psyche as being naturally religious also opens a dialogue between Jung and scholars of religion.

While some depth psychologists have tried to explain religion away as a relic of a past age, and to envision myth as a "quaint" but outmoded system of belief, Jung saw religious experience as an integral part of psychic life, and began to study religion in order to more fully understand the psyche. In *Psychology and Religion,* he calls religion "one of the earliest and most universal activities of the human mind" (1). In particular, Jung focuses on what Rudolf Otto calls the "numinosum," which Jung defines as "a dynamic existence or affect, not caused by an arbitrary act of will" (4). In light of this, he defines religion as "the term that designates the attitude peculiar to a consciousness which has been altered by the experience of the numinosum" (Psychology 6). Anne Ulanov comments on Jung's interest in religion, that he "valued the numinous above all, and he conceived of health as finding life's meaning" (Ulanov 1). Ulanov also sees the need to "humanize archetypal symbols into livable forms in our ordinary lives" (2). As we will see, one of the ways of looking at *Sandman* is as a story of the humanization of myth. Again speaking of Jung's impact on religion, Ulanov says that he "works to reconnect religion to its archaic instinctive roots, from which the symbols of theology and ritual spring. When we reach and link ourselves to the primordial religious experience deep within us . . . Religion ceases to be merely an intellectual activity or a systematic exploration of abstract principles of being. *Instead, it reaches into our hearts, our souls, our bowels*" (23, emphasis mine). It is exactly this immediacy of experience that is missing in many people's lives today. Thus, while he wrote in the field of psychology, Jung was intensely interested in religious experience. It is perhaps his greatest expression of humanity's religious impulse that Jung says "one could almost say that if all the world's traditions were cut off at a single blow, the whole of mythology and the whole history of religion would start over again with the next generation" (Jung on Mythology 211). Under this scheme, it is indeed appropriate to speak of a religious *instinct.* Asking these kinds of religious questions is as much a part of what it means to be human as anything else.

Having established the relevance of Jung and his theory of the collective unconscious to religion, we can look at these ideas' relevance to *The Sandman.* First and most apparent is Gaiman's formulation of "the Dreaming," Morpheus's realm. Essentially, the Dreaming is a place that contains everything that has ever been dreamed or that has been produced in dreams. As Campbell says about dreams, "it is the realm we enter in sleep. We carry it within ourselves forever . . . All the life-potentialities that we never managed to bring to adult realization, those other portions of oneself, are there; for such golden seeds do not die" (*Hero with a Thousand Faces* 17). Everything is there, and more than once Dream moves between people's dreams, taking items as he needs them, or moving through them to where he needs to go (*Sandman* 1:31 and 5:18,

respectively). It is in dreams that Dream's power is paramount, and he has the power to influence them, even as they happen to people.

Another example of the collective unconscious in *Sandman* is Lucien's library. The library, maintained by Lucien, one of Dream's most conscientious helpers, is unusual indeed, as "somewhere in here is every story that has ever been dreamed," including stories that were only finished or written in dreams (*Sandman* 22:2). Elsewhere, Lucien says "the library of Dream is the largest library there never was" (*Vertigo Jam* 2). It contains "every book that's ever been dreamed. Every book that's ever been imagined. Every book that's ever been lost" (*Sandman* 57:12). One major divergence between Jung's theory and the Dreaming might be that dreams are (for Jung) to a large extent unstructured, while the Dreaming is somewhat ordered (at least the parts inhabited by Dream). There are other areas of the Dreaming, however: lands and skerries that operate largely without Dream's control (one example being the land in *A Game of You*). Still, this difference could be attributed to a small scope of vision. At best, in our dreams, we only manage to experience aspects of Dream, and of the Dreaming. But if we were able to see both in a more systematic manner (as we do when we read *Sandman*), then perhaps our vision would look more like Gaiman's vision. Still, it seems that at least a rough approximation can be made that "the Dreaming" is essentially the same as Jung's collective unconscious, or at least an artist's interpretation of it. The rest comes rather quickly. If we know that there are certain images and motifs that are embedded in our consciousness, then what would happen if they existed with some systematicity or purpose? It might look like the Dreaming.

Another point of dialogue between Jung's theory and *The Sandman* is the presence of archetypes in the Dreaming. If the archetypes are the way in which the collective unconscious expresses itself, and the Dreaming is the collective unconscious, then one would expect to find the archetypes in the Dreaming. And, in fact, many archetypes do "live" in the Dreaming. Cain and Abel, the first pair of brothers, live next to each other as the keepers of the houses of mysteries and secrets, respectively. And in typical archetypal form, the pair act out the primordial fratricidal killing over and over again (*Sandman* 2:15). After being killed by Cain, Abel revives, picks himself up, and continues with his duties (*Sandman* 2:22). Moreover, the archetypes of brothers in conflict and fratricide, represented by Cain and Abel, are revealed to go back even farther than the Jewish and Christian Biblical story we know today. In **"A Parliament of Rooks,"** Abel reveals that when they came to inhabit the Dreaming, they lived in another world, and did not look even remotely human (*Sandman* 40:21). This and other passages have led to a mini-controversy among Gaiman's readers. Some have supposed that Gaiman privileges Jewish and Christian mythologies over other systems. Gaiman, however, denies this. The figures these readers point to—Eve, Cain, and Abel among them—are, for Gaiman, part of a pattern much older than the Bible. Eve, who lives in a cave on the borders of nightmare, is there less as the Biblical Eve than as the archetypal mother, and as an expression of the archetypal female, as when the Furies (or the Kindly Ones) visit the Dreaming, they do not attack Eve because "she is an aspect of ourselves" (*Sandman* 65:14). This is not to say that the characters do not borrow aspects of the Biblical accounts; one of the joys of reading *Sandman* is to watch Gaiman interweaving different mythologies. Essentially, all the myths are true, in one form or another, in that they coexist in the world of *Sandman.* Other "archetypal" but less famous characters include the Corinthian (nightmare par excellence), Brute and Glob (force and cunning), Fiddler's Green (who is somewhere between a person and a place) and Mervyn Pumkinhead, the comic relief of the Dreaming. And of course, many other gods and archetypal figures may not live in the Dreaming, but visit there, as in the case of *A Season of Mists,* or Odin in *The Kindly Ones.*

After familiarizing ourselves with Jung's ideas concerning the psyche, Campbell's formulations make more sense. Just as the psyche contains a hidden level behind the conscious mind, so Campbell interprets myth as establishing an invisible plane of support for our lives in the world, as "I would say that is the basic theme of all mythology—that there is an invisible plane supporting the visible one" (*Power* 71). Also, he says that "there are dimensions of your being and a potential for realization and consciousness that are not included in your concept of yourself. Your life is much deeper and broader than you conceive it to be here" (*Power* 58). Similarly, in *Sandman,* at the end of *The Doll's House,* Rose Walker writes that "If my dream was true, then everything we know, everything we think we know is a lie. It means the world's about as solid and as reliable as a layer of scum on the top of a well of black water that goes down forever, and there are things in the depths that I don't even want to think about. It means more than that. It means we're just dolls. We don't have a clue what's really going down, we just kid ourselves that we're in control of our lives" (*Sandman* 16:17-8). What Rose is grappling with is the idea that the world has hidden depths, very similar to Campbell's "invisible plane of support." Still, Rose also comes face to face with the fact that pure, unadulterated religious experience can be scary as hell. She finds it in herself to regain hope and move on with her life. Campbell also speaks of mythology as going "down and down and down" (*Power* 39). The theme of hidden depths runs throughout the series.

And at the same time Rose uses the metaphor of the Doll's House to describe the influence of unseen archetypal forces, Dream makes a similar claim about the gods, or even the Endless themselves, being influenced by men and women. As he tells Desire, "We the Endless are the servants of the living—we are not their masters. We exist because they know, deep in their hearts, that we exist. When the last living thing has left the universe, then our task will be done. And we do not manipulate them. If anything, they manipulate us. We are their toys. Their dolls, if you will" (*Sandman* 16:22). Here, we have, perfectly balanced against Rose's claims of powerlessness in the face of the gods, a contrasting assessment from Dream, that the gods and even the Endless exist because people *know* they exist. Thus, not only the world, but individual people too have hidden depths to them. Here, we connect with the earlier formulation of the gods' owing their existence to belief on the part of the people who worship them. Without the belief of humans, the gods wither and die. And again, we have the mutual dependence between deities and people, a dependence that is mediated by inner worlds. The concept of inner worlds also surfaces at the end of *A Game of You,* as the positive, inner side to Rose's lament. Barbie says at Wanda's grave, "Everybody has a secret world inside of them. I mean everybody. All of the people in the whole world—no matter how dull and boring they are on the outside. Inside them they've all got unimaginable, magnificent, wonderful, stupid, amazing worlds . . . Not just one world. Hundreds of them. Thousands, maybe" (*Sandman* 37:19). This means that no matter how people appear, they all have unexplored, hidden depths inside them . . . secret worlds.

Finally, just as myth and dream are linked, and just as we have seen "the power of myth" (from Campbell), so in *Sandman* we see the power of dreams. One example of this is the **"Dream of a Thousand Cats."** In it, we are told the tale that cats were once the dominant species on earth, but that one day the humans rose up, as a leader said, "Dream! Dreams shape the world. Dreams create the world anew, every night" (*Sandman* 18:17). The humans began to dream of a world in which *they* were the dominant species, and when enough of them (say, 1000) did so, they changed the world. However, they did more than change the world as it was. Dream (as a cat) tells a cat leader that "they dreamed the world so it always was the way it is now . . . There never was a world of high cat-ladies and cat-lords. They changed the universe from the beginning of all things, until the end of time" (*Sandman* 18:19). The issue ends with the cat urging her fellow cats to join together and dream of the world in which they were the lords of it. And although one cat doubts whether you could get a thousand cats to do anything together, the fact remains: dreams have the power to change and shape the world. In theory, there is no telling how many times this has happened, as each time it occurs, the world is changed so that it always was the way it is now. This shows the tremendous power of dreams, as they can recreate the entire world. Here, we see an example of Gaiman's statement that the business of fantasy is to make metaphors concrete. In this case, dreams literally change the world. Further, from this principle, we can accept any number of alternate worlds and histories, places in which things happened differently. Such a system is hinted at in **"The Golden Boy,"** as different Americas are mentioned according to who was elected president, but the possibilities for dreams to change the world are endless. Put another way, the world we know is but one of many, or even infinite worlds.

Also, there is the episode in which Dream goes to Hell in search of his stolen helmet. After he regains it, Lucifer threatens not to let him leave, and asks what power dreams have in Hell. Dream responds "ask yourselves, all of you . . . What power would Hell have if those here imprisoned were not able to dream of Heaven?" (*Sandman* 4:22). The demons are unable to meet his challenge, and he leaves unscathed. Thus, even in Hell, dreams have power, and as in **"A Dream of a Thousand Cats,"** they can change worlds.

Finally, one last qualification must be made concerning the relationship between myths and dreams. Although many useful parallels can be drawn between the two, there are key differences between the two classes of phenomena. Campbell says that "we must note that myths are not exactly comparable to dream. Their figures originate from the same sources—the unconscious wells of fantasy . . . but [myths] are not the spontaneous products of sleep. On the contrary, their patterns are consciously controlled" (*Hero with a Thousand Faces* 256). Likewise, Jung says that "strictly speaking, a myth is a historical document. It is told, it is recorded, but it is not itself a dream. It is the product of an unconscious process in a particular social group, at a particular time, at a particular place" (*Jung on Mythology* 107). While myths are consciously shaped and created, dreams are the raw product of the unconscious mind. Analogous to the split between dream and myth, Gaiman speaks about the difference between "dream-logic" and "story-logic," as the contents of a dream often do not translate to making a good story. With dreams, "for you it was interesting and fascinating; but it's not a story. And dreams very, very rarely contain stories; but they will contain images" that you can pull up from the depths (Sound & Spirit interview). Thus, crafting stories (or myths) is a very different process than dreaming. It is easy to overlook in one's enthusiasm that dreams and myth are not identical; however, similarities do exist, and both are rich worlds into which we can delve.

At this point, the kinship between dreams and myths should be apparent. Both spring from the biologically-ingrained collective unconscious, and "live" in what Jung called the "vast hinterland of the psyche." In addition, gods can be seen as magnified dreams, as has been pointed out by both Campbell and Gaiman, revealing a two-way process, in which people need to believe in *something* to bring meaning to their lives, and gods need people to believe in them in order to survive. On both sides, belief is the key step. The Dreaming can be seen as an approximation of the collective unconscious, and it not only contains many archetypal figures, but also reveals a hidden plane of existence behind the visible one. We spend a third of our lives in Morpheus's realm, and dreams, whether true dreams or waking dreams, have the power to change the world.

Given the relationship between myths and dreams, it makes sense that a modern myth, one that recognizes the "inner" religious life, should be concerned with dreams. By setting so much of *The Sandman* in dreams, Gaiman is able to weave his own myth with characters from the full body of world mythology. Jung says that the modern gods "are as powerful and as awe-inspiring as ever, in spite of their new disguise—the so-called psychical functions" (*Psychology* 102). Of course, the formulation of "new" gods coincides exactly with the Endless, who are manifestations of consciousness. What Gaiman adds, though, is that the Endless are so much more than gods; they provide the background and the secret cause by which the gods exist. Gaiman then crafts a new mythology around the existing mythologies. And, as with the older myths, dreams are key in shaping these mythic narratives. We will return later to what exactly is meant by "myth." In terms of an overall study, Gaiman's use of the Endless and incorporation of many mythologies constitutes what Campbell calls the cosmological function of myth. And the important lesson to take from this discussion is that the myths (and dreams) are *real*.

. . . . .

### "THE ROLE OF THE ARTIST AND THE ART OF STORYTELLING IN *THE SANDMAN*."

"Myth must be kept alive. The people who can keep it alive are artists of one kind or another. The function of the artist is the mythologization of the environment and the world."

—Joseph Campbell

"I learned that we have the right, or the obligation, to tell the old stories in our own ways, because they are our stories, and they must be told."

—Neil Gaiman

We have been exploring what is old and new about the modern myth, and have seen the delicate balancing act that is creating such a work. However, this duality of new and old also exists for a final important theme in *The Sandman*: the art of storytelling. Of course, the act of telling stories is as old as the human race, but there is something new about the way that the modern storyteller is placed in the role of mythmaker. And if myths are gone, then what we have to replace them is stories. David Miller, in his discussion of the form of the next spiritual movement, remarked that the new theology would be a theology of stories and narrative (75), and this seems to be as good a guess as any. We have already examined various aspects of myth, and although we have alluded to it a few times, there remains one final step: for what are myths, if not stories? Myths are important stories, even central to our lives, or just, as I would suggest, the *big* stories. Still, if we are to believe the critics of modernity, then those of us who can claim to live with a story, to feel it in your bones (or as Delirium would say, in your socks), are the lucky few. You may remember from childhood a state somewhat similar to this, of being gripped by tales of fantastic and far-away worlds, or the inspired lunacy of a beloved children's writer. In this age of instant publishing, it seems that anyone can be an author, but only a few can truly be called "storytellers." For what is mythmaking, if not storytelling? Campbell, who seems to have foreseen so much of Gaiman's work, was far from the first to note that the storytellers are the mythmakers of today, when he said that mythology is "the homeland of the muses," the motivating force behind literature and art (*Power* 55). And if the storytellers are "the new mythmakers," this arrangement is hardly new—good storytellers have always been held in high reverence. Put another way, the death of wonder, or of meaning, which people have referred to is in many ways a death of storytelling. Of course, nothing as central to human existence as storytelling could ever truly die, but we do have to ask the question: when was the last time a story held you in full aesthetic arrest, unable to think about anything else but to marvel at its composition and fluidity of movement, as it unfurled itself across the room?

The point of all this, of course, it that Gaiman is just such a storyteller. It has always been a truism of the writing world that writers love to write about nothing more than the process of writing. So it seems fitting that a master storyteller would have lots to say about the art of storytelling. And *Sandman* is filled with all facets of storytelling: people telling stories, writing stories, listening to stories, *living* stories. Frank McConnell, speaking of the story about stories (in his introduction to *The Kindly Ones*) says "this is the kind of writing literary critics like to call 'postmodern:' letting the reader know you're conscious of what you're doing at the very time you do it. And a writer like Gaiman is smart enough to realize that kind of performance is about as 'modern' as the Divine Comedy. The great storytellers have always wanted to tell us as much about the business of storytelling as about the stories themselves" (4). And as we will see, *Sandman* also

takes us into the mind of storytellers, both mundane (the doomed waitress Bettie in **"24 Hours"**), fanciful (the tricksterish faery Cluracan), and masterful (the Bard himself), for a "behind the scenes" look at the creative process. In a sense, *Sandman* is what might be called a "metanarrative," a story about stories. In addition, *Sandman* emerges as a hybrid text, with oral and written elements, in a blending of myth and folklore. More than that, Dream is, simply put, the reason we tell stories. Both oral and written storytelling are explored, and it seems that oral storytellers are somewhat privileged, at least in places. Still, both media are vital to the process of mythmaking. However, first we will examine the role of the artist in fashioning the modern myth. And just as we have an instinct for religion, so do we have one for storytelling. Stories are also capable of evoking Campbell's first (mystical) and fourth (psychological) functions of myth.

The strongest statements about the artist as mythmaker come, fittingly (because of his artistic temperament) from Campbell. In *The Power of Myth,* he writes "Myth must be kept alive. The people who can keep it alive are artists of one kind or another. The function of the artist is the mythologization of the environment and the world" (85). Later, Bill Moyers asks Campbell who are to be the shamans of today, and Campbell answers "It is the function of the artist to do this. The artist is the one who communicates myth for today. But he has to be an artist who understands mythology and humanity and isn't simply a sociologist with a program for you" (*Power* 99). It should be apparent by now that Gaiman has a firm grasp of the world's mythological traditions. And an understanding of human nature is critical to any artist's success. But Campbell's words hold another implication; if the artist is the one who creates the new mythology, then he or she holds a vital importance to the mind and soul of a society. In a sense, for those with the talent to do so, being an artist is *the highest good one can achieve.* Campbell speaks of mythology as "the secret opening through which the inexhaustible energies of the cosmos pour into human cultural manifestation" (*Hero with a Thousand Faces* 3). It is the role of the artist, then, to take this experience and translate it into a form that people can comprehend. In this sense, the artist and certain kinds of mystics have something in common: both experience something available to only a few and bring it back to the people as something they can understand.

It might also go without saying, but Campbell also lists myth as being behind the work of artists, even if they are not consciously seeking to create the new myth. He says that "mythology teaches you what's behind literature and the arts, it teaches you about your own life" (*Power* 11). He also states that "I think of mythology as the homeland of the muses, the inspirers of art, the inspirers of poetry. To see life as a poem and yourself participating in a poem is what myth does for you" (*Power* 55). Campbell also lays out the connection of the artist to mythology as: "it's to see the experience and archetypology of a *living* moment. What the artist must render is a living moment somehow, a living moment actually in action or an inward experience" (*Hero's Journey* 184). One might take issue with Campbell's admittedly quite elastic definition of mythology, but the spirit of his remarks is important. One of the qualifications of a myth, then, is for a narrative to grip you, so that you see it as a part of your life, or see your life as a part of it. Campbell said that "When the story is in your mind, then you see its relevance to something happening in your own life. It gives you perspective on what's happening to you" (*Power* 4). Later, we will address some of the criticisms of Campbell, but for now it is enough to note that, at heart, he was more artist than academic. He had a reverence for the creative life that I have not found an equal to anywhere else. Elsewhere, he writes: "[the] personal creative act is related to the realm of myth, the realm of the muses, because myth is the homeland of the inspiration of the arts. The muses are the children of the goddess of memory, which is not the memory from up there, from the head; it is the memory of down here, from the heart" (*Mythic* 151).

So far we have encountered many descriptions of being gripped by a story; to this we would add "Proper art is static. It holds you in ecstatic arrest . . . Because the rhythm before you is the rhythm of nature. It is the rhythm of *your* nature . . . And why is it that you are held in aesthetic arrest? It is because the nature you are looking at is *your* nature. There is an accord between you and the object, and that is why you say, 'Aha!'" (Campbell, *Mythic* 154). Elsewhere, Campbell says, "that *Aha!* That you get when you see an artwork that really hits you is 'I am that.' I am the radiance and energy that is talking to me through this painting" (*Hero's Journey* 38). What we have seen, then, are various ways to describe a narrative's resonance with the reader (or listener). It may require a leap of faith to accept, but what is being argued for the magic of storytelling, and the transformative power of mythic narratives. As Bender says, "transforming lives is what stories are for" (178).

Like Campbell, Jung also recognizes the role of the artist in shaping myth. And he presents a corollary to Campbell, that the arts, mythology included, come from the psyche. He says that "the human psyche is the womb of all the sciences and arts" (*Modern Man* 152). Nancy Mellon adds that "a treasure-trove of imaginative powers lives within us all" (1). Jung also makes a distinction between psychological and visionary art. While psychological art involves the realm of human life, with the visionary, "the experience that furnishes the material for artistic expression is no longer familiar. It is a strange something that derives its existence from the hinterland of man's mind—that suggests the abyss of time separating us from pre-human ages, or evokes a super-human world of contrasting light and darkness. It is a primordial experience . . . It is a vision of other worlds" (Modern Man 156-7). For Jung, the "primordial experience" is essential, as "we must admit that the vision represents a deeper and more impressive experience than human passion . . . we cannot doubt that the vision is a genuine, primordial experience" (162). He also writes that "It is therefore to be expected of the poet that he will resort to mythology in order to give his experience its most fitting expression" (164). As strange and unusual as this sort of art may be, "it is not wholly unfamiliar. Man has known of it from time immemorial—here, there, and everywhere" (163). This kind of implicit knowledge and memory, then, is built into our very psyches.

Among psychologists, the term for such an art is "fantasy," which is also one of the genres into which **Sandman** is placed. Of course, as a genre, "fantasy" has garnered its share of critical disdain. However, to call it fantasy is not necessarily to deprecate it, as Jung tells us, "Truth to tell, I have a very high opinion of fantasy . . . When all is said and done, we are never proof against fantasy . . . All the works of man have their origin in creative fantasy. What right have we then to deprecate imagination? In the ordinary course of things, fantasy does not easily go astray; it is too deep for that, and too closely bound up with the tap-root of human and animal instinct" (*Modern Man* 66). He closes his statement by saying "As Schiller says, man is completely human only when he is playing" (66). Among psychologists, especially David Winnicott, playing, far from being a waste of time, is vital to establishing a person's relationships with others and the world. To identify fantasy with children, as many critics do, is really a backhanded slight (as being "childish" has become in our society a criticism) that reveals a deeper truth. For it is with children that we identify the feeling of wide-eyed wonder and mystery, the same kind of wonder that comprises Campbell's first function of mythology. Perhaps this is what Jesus meant when he said that in order to enter the kingdom of heaven, we must be like children (Matthew 18:3). Finally, as a caution, it is important to note that for Jung, the "primordial experience" is unconscious and inexpressible to the conscious mind, while for Campbell, the process of fashioning myth is a conscious act. And while I lean towards the latter view, Jung is helpful in recognizing a level deeper than consciousness at which a narrative can grip a person. And if the old mythic forms are gone, then the modern situation is that our storytellers must find a way to replace them. Put another way, we can only create myths if we dare to tell stories.

Having thus established the role of the artist in fashioning myth, and as our greatest hope for creating a distinctively modern myth, and having seen how a story can grip a person *below* the consciousness, we are ready to examine the role of stories and storytelling in *The Sandman*, with which the series is filled. And although Dream is the "Prince of Stories" (*Sandman* 2:3), and himself the reason we tell stories in the first place, it is often when the focus shifts away from Dream that the theme of storytelling moves to the forefront. At this point, Dream becomes a facilitator for the stories; we have already examined the relationship between myth and dreams, so it should seem fitting that the King of Dreams is also the Prince of Stories.

We have already alluded to the idea of claiming a story of one's own, and interpreting one's own life through that story. This is what it means to *live* a myth. In theology, there is a movement called "narrative theology" that proposes we do just this. Speaking of narrative theology, George Stroup says that "every philosophical anthropology . . . must come to terms with the narrative structure of human identity" (87). Using the example of Christian narratives, he says that "to understand Christian narrative properly is to be able to interpret one's personal identity by means of biblical texts" (96). Next, he adds that "it is no accident that when they are asked to identify themselves most people recite a narrative or story" (Stroup 111). Furthermore, it soon becomes apparent that there is more to every person than meets the eye (111), a theme picked up on in Barbie's "secret worlds" speech. The more artistic side of these ideas is the fact that "if we experience the reality of each part of the story as an aspect of ourselves, no matter how grand or dilapidated, or fantastical it may be, it will be an enlivening experience" (Mellon 2). For us, the impact of these ideas is that stories and storytelling, of both the secular and sacred kind, are vital to our collective and individual identities. This is why I am spending so much time discussing the art of storytelling. Again and again, we see the importance of *living* a story.

While *The Sandman* contains examples of both oral and written stories, perhaps it would be advantageous to begin with written tales, since they are the closest to what Gaiman is doing, and since, after all, we live in a culture of the book. The key writers to appear in the series are Richard Madoc in **"Calliope"** (issue 17), the waitress Bettie from **"24 Hours"** (issue 6), the playwright in **"Fear of Falling,"** . . . and an aspiring poet and playwright named William Shakespeare.

The story of the writer in **"Fear of Falling"** is perhaps the simplest of the accounts of storytellers. One reason for this is that it did not occur in a regular issue of *Sandman,* but in a publication of shorter stories by many of the artists on Gaiman's Vertigo label. Still, Gaiman saw fit to include it in one of the short story collections. It involves a playwright named Todd Faber, who is in the middle of directing a play he wrote. He is afraid, either of failure or of success, or of both, so he decides to abandon the production and run away. That night, he has a dream in which he is climbing up a cliff, and when he reaches the top, he encounters Dream, who questions him. Todd answers "It's all getting to be too much for me. I feel I'm out of my depth. I'm scared. I'm scared I'm going to do something stupid" (*Fables & Reflections* 7). Dream answers, "And if you do something stupid, what then?" Todd says that he is afraid of falling, to which Dream replies, "It is sometimes a mistake to climb; it is always a mistake never even to make the attempt . . . If you do not climb you will not fall. This is true. But is it that bad to fail, that hard to fall? Sometimes you wake, and sometimes, yes, you die. But there is a third alternative" (7-8). At this point, Todd falls, and we do not find out what happens until the next morning, when he returns to the rehearsal, and says, "Sometimes you wake up. Sometimes the fall kills you. And sometimes, when you fall, you fly" (11). This story is the least complicated, and the most straightforwardly romantic, of the author narratives. It is addressed to anyone trying to find the courage to create, to take that great risk of putting oneself on the line and coming up with something no one has ever produced before. The falling, of course, is symbolic of a great many fears of failure. Everyone falls at one time or another, but sometimes, the result of the fall is that you learn how to fly. As Dream says, it may sometimes be a mistake to climb, but it is always a mistake not to try at all. If we are to continue to have myths in our world, then we must have men and women who are brave enough to risk failure and create them. Also, the story underscores the point that dreams, like myths, can be filled with wisdom and guidance.

The other narratives of writers involve, in one way or another, cautions about the dangers of writing. The second story (and the first chronologically) is of the waitress Bettie in **"24 Hours."** The narrator tells us that "On her days off, after she's tidied the house, Bette Munroe writes stories. She writes them in longhand on yellow legal pads. Sometimes she writes about her ex-husband Bernard, and about her son, Bernard Jr., who went off to college and never came back to her. She makes these stories end happily. Most of her stories, however, are about her customers" (*Sandman* 6:1). Although the stories might not be much as far as the craft goes, they add meaning to Bette's life, as "They look at her and they just see a waitress; they don't know she's nursing a secret. A secret that keeps her aching calf-muscles and her coffee-scalded fingers and her weariness from dragging her down . . . It's her secret. She's never shown anyone her stories" (6:1-2). Her dreams become all the more poignant as we begin to see through them. She dreams of sending her stories to a famous writer, who would publish them, of becoming famous, even being interviewed by Johnny Carson:

"But you're a writer,' Johnny Carson will say to her, 'How do you know what it's like to be a waitress?' She'll smile. She won't tell him. It'll be her secret" (6:2). She does not seem to realize that almost all writers start out working day jobs; however, the important thing for her is the dream. We have already seen how dreams can change the world, but for Bette, it is enough that her dream keep the monotony of working in a greasy spoon at bay. Gaiman also uses Bette to show the contrast between people's appearances, or the way we *want* to see them, and the harsh realities of life. In her stories, everyone gets a happy ending, as "All Bette's stories have happy endings. That's because she knows where to stop. She's realized the real problem with stories—if you keep them going long enough, they always end in death" (6:4). Besides almost tipping Gaiman's hand for what he has planned for the whole series, with the death of Dream, it shows her blind optimism, and what happens when you refuse to see reality.

"24 Hours" is also one of the truly horrific tales in *Sandman*; everyone ends up dead, either by his or her own hand or each other's, because of the machinations of John Dee and Dream's stolen ruby. Over the rest of the story, we find out the customers' stories. There is Judy, who just has a fight with her girlfriend, Donna (who later appears as Foxglove). Bette feels "sorry" for them, and in her stories marries them off to "fine young men" (6:3). She describes the Fletchers as "like lovebirds," but he dreams of having sex with a prostitute in his car and then beating her up, while she dreams of putting his head on a platter ("no more infidelities"). Marsh confesses that he "as good as killed" his wife by giving her, an alcoholic, a crate of vodka and going out of town for a week (6:18). Moreover, we learn that Bette's son ended up in prison after getting into prostitution. The whole story is shocking in its visceral nature, so it is somewhat difficult to know what to make of it all. But one thing is that Bette does not see the truth, and in her quest for happy endings, ignores reality. She is surely not a mythmaker, then; however, she does have the dream of being a writer, and for someone with her station in life, it is enough, until supernatural forces intervene. As an episode in the greater myth, "24 Hours" is also about the problem of evil, and the failure of moral and ethical systems to address it. For this slaughter has no meaning, no higher explanation of why God would allow such a thing to happen. It is as senseless as it is sudden, and there is no one to stop the madman with the ruby. Although Bette is flawed as a writer, she does not deserve what happens to her (neither do most of the rest of them), but such is often the way with cautionary tales, in which the protagonists come to a gruesome fate they did not deserve. After all, their story is also a plot device, in showing the twisted mind of John Dee when he takes hold of Dream's stolen ruby. A bad guy always needs victims.

Only slightly better off than Bette is Richard Madoc, the main character in **"Calliope."** The author of a successful first novel, he is nine months overdue on his second, and has been unable to write anything. As a result, he makes a deal with Erasmus Fry, an aging author, for his special "property:" the Muse Calliope who he had imprisoned years ago while in Greece. His treatment of her is horrific, as "His first action was to rape her, nervously, on the musty old camp bed. She's not even human, he told himself. She's thousands of years old. But her flesh was warm, and her breath was sweet, and she choked back tears like a child whenever he hurt her. It occurred to him momentarily that the old man might have cheated him: given him a real girl. That he, Rick Madoc, might possibly have done something wrong, even criminal" (*Sandman* 17:8). The irony compounds as the tale continues, as Madoc becomes wildly successful. He keeps Calliope until Dream shows up and gives him an excess of ideas that overwhelm him (reminiscent of the "ironic punishment" division of the Greek Hades), until he lets her go. The tale might also work as a way for Gaiman to assuage his conscience as a writer, as it may seem that all authors are "raping the muse," figuratively if not literally. Thus, it may have been a Gaiman-style autobiography. At a party, Madoc is praised for transcending the bounds of genre fiction—enough to be nominated for a mainstream literary award. Gaiman won the World Fantasy Award for the **"Midsummer Night's Dream"** story—making it the first and only time a comic has won a mainstream award. In the same panel, a female fan praises him for the strong women in his work, to which he responds "Actually, I do tend to regard myself as a feminist writer" (17:12). I do not know if Gaiman has made any such claim himself, but his work has been praised by many as containing strong female characters. The tale ends when Madoc lets Calliope go, and he says "it's gone. I've got no idea any more. No idea at all" (17:24). Even if Madoc is not some kind of twisted alter-ego of the writer, it reveals what some people will do to avoid or get rid of writer's block. On theme here, that we have seen elsewhere, is that people are capable of committing terrible wrongs, and that we should try to reduce people's suffering whenever we can. With Madoc, the problem is not that he is a monster, but that he is very human; as he does something terrible, he is a reminder of the evil that exists around and especially within us.

From **"24 Hours"** and **"Calliope,"** one might think that the outlook for writers is rather bleak. Either they blind themselves to reality and use their dreams to stave off the boredom of a meaningless life, or they will resort to terrible measures in order to ensure that the ideas keep coming. Compared to them, then, the outlook for William Shakespeare is positively rosy. Still, even though Shakespeare makes his deal to become the greatest storyteller of his age (and some would say of any age), in the end, he comes to half-regret his choice. Will's story begins when he and Marlowe are eating in the same inn where Dream meets Hob for their once-a-century drink. At this point, Shakespeare is a hack, who Marlowe encourages to give up writing, and who wants more than anything to become a great writer. He tells Marlowe that "I would give anything to have your gifts. Or more than anything to give men dreams, that would live on long after I am dead. I'd bargain, like your Faustus, for that boon" (*Sandman* 13:12). Dream overhears the conversation and asks Will, "Would you write great plays? Create new dreams to spur the minds of men?" (13:13). They go off and talk, and although we do not see their exchange, we know that Dream unlocks the doors in Will's mind, to allow him to become a vehicle of the great stories. Will, in exchange, promises to write two plays for Morpheus, celebrating dreams, which turn out to be *A Midsummer Night's Dream* and *The Tempest.*

The story of **"Midsummer"** is told in issue 19, as Shakespeare's players perform in front of an audience of faery folk, including Titania and Auberon (the queen and king of Faerie). By this time, we can see the seeds of discontent, even in the face of Will's greatness. His son, Hamnet, traveling with him for the Summer, says "He's very distant . . . Anything that happens he just makes stories out of it. I'm less real to him than any of the characters in his plays" (*Sandman* 19:13). He says that his sister Judith jokes that if he died, Will would just write a play about it . . . "Hamnet." (Of course, just this happens.) Hamnet ends the exchange by saying "All that matters to him . . . All that matters is the stories" (19:13). Even Dream begins to wonder if he did the right thing, as he is beginning to ponder his role and influence in people's lives. He tells Titania, "I wonder, Titania. I wonder if I have done right. And I wonder why I wonder. Will is a willing vehicle for the great stories. Through him they will live for an age of man; and his words will echo down through time. But he did not understand the price. Mortals never do. They only see the prize, their heart's desire, their dream . . . But the price of getting what you want, is getting what you once wanted" (19:19). This statement seems pessimistic, that even if you get what you want, you won't be happy because you won't be the same person who wanted it. But, fundamentally, it amounts to another affirmation of change, the radical change that can go on inside each one of us, that we must accept as part of our lives.

Shakespeare's story continues in the final *Sandman* (issue 75), which takes place as he is writing his second play for Dream, *The Tempest,* which also happened to be the last play he wrote alone. This time, an older Shakespeare is actively questioning the deal he made with Dream. He talks to a priest, asking how to redeem the magician Prospero, but of course he is also asking about himself. When he meets Dream, he asks him what his life would have been like, had he not made their deal, but then he shrinks away when Dream starts to tell him (*Sandman* 75:179). He says, "I wonder . . . I wonder if it was all worth it. Whatever happened to me in life, happened to me as a writer of plays. I'd fall in love, or fall in lust. And at the height of my passion, I would think, 'So this is how it feels,' and I would tie it up with pretty words. I watched my life as if it were happening to someone else. My son died. And I was hurt; but I watched my hurt, and even relished it, a little, for now I could write a real death, a true loss" (75:180). Again, here it seems that Gaiman is trying to tell the reader about the mind of the writer, and the terrible price it exacts on those who follow the craft. My brother, who is much more of a writer than I will ever be, tells me that the feeling of watching your own life with detachment, as a way of gathering material, is quite true. Dream reveals to Will that even if he did open the door in the playwright's mind, it was Will who still did the writing, and all the work. Will then asks Dream why he chose *The Tempest,* and Dream (in one of the series' most heartbreaking moments) tells him that he "wanted a play about graceful ends . . . about a King who drowns his books, and breaks his staff, and leaves his kingdom. About a magician who becomes a man. About a man who turns his back on magic" (75:181). When asks why, Dream continues, "Because I will never leave my island," and later, "I am not a man. And I do not change. I asked you earlier if you saw yourself reflected in your tale. I do not. I may not. I am prince of stories, Will; but I have no story of my own. Nor shall I ever" (75:182). The tale (Gaiman's, that is) also tells about the terrible price of writing by examining the life of one of the great storytellers of any age. Frank McConnell writes that the choice of Shakespeare is especially fitting, as "in [the Renaissance], our myths began to be humanized; beginning, say, with Shakespeare, we began to realize that the gods had not invented us, but that we were in the process of inventing our gods" ("Epic Comics"). Thus, Shakespeare makes an ideal study for Gaiman's purposes, to say nothing of the artistic nerve necessary to take on the Bard, with which fortunately for us, Gaiman is quite blessed. Incidentally, it is worth noting that Gaiman chose Shakespeare's story as the final issue of the series. Thus, the last we see of Dream is (the old Dream) lamenting his lack of story (which is, of course, pure irony: we are reading his story). From this, I believe we can infer that for Gaiman, the storytelling material is an essential part of the series as a whole.

Overall, the depictions of writers depict the terrible price the craft exacts: from them, and from those close to them. How are we to reconcile this with the idea of the storyteller as mythmaker? The answer, I believe, lies in the instances of oral storytelling that appear in *Sandman.* In a sense, there is something pure about oral narratives, and about people who view storytelling as an *art,* as opposed to writers, who view it as a *profession.* And while myths can be oral, more often the oral narratives are folklore, *the stories people tell each other.* There are even more examples of told stories in *Sandman* than written ones: the travelers in *World's End,* the grandfather in "Tales in the Sand," Gilbert in *The Doll's House,* and the storytellers of "Convergence" (issues 38-40). The best example of this is in *World's End,* in which travelers from different worlds are trapped by a storm (a reality storm) in an inn and pass the time by telling tales. The frame of the story, of course, goes back to Chaucer's *Canterbury Tales.* On this choice of models, Gaiman remarks, "I liked the idea of using one of the oldest storytelling devices in the English language. If you're going to steal, you might as well do so from a great source, and *Canterbury Tales* definitely qualifies" (Bender 176).

The storytellers come from a variety of worlds and races: there are Brant and Charlene, whose car crashes on the way to Chicago, the centaur Chiron, the blue-skinned apprentice mortician Petrefax, the English sailor girl-passing-for-boy Jim, and the wily faerie Cluracan. Chaucer's story used characters from all different walks of life; Gaiman does him one better by bringing together characters *literally* from different worlds. And as seems to be the instinct, when we find ourselves among strangers for an extended period of time, we tell stories. Another notable feature of *World's End* is the nesting of stories within stories. In "Cerements," we have Petrefax telling his stories of life as an apprentice in the great Necropolis Litharge. He tells of attending a burial in which the participants all told stories. One of these tellers tells a story about meeting a traveler (Destruction) who was passing through the city. And the stranger tells his listener the story of the first Necropolis, and how its charter was revoked when its inhabitants became hardened and no longer loved their duties and recognized the importance of the funeral rites. And, at the end of the collection, we find that the whole thing has been a story, of Brant Tucker, our narrator, talking to a bartender. So we have a story, within a story, within a story . . . within another story. The frame story is a common story device, but to the best of my knowledge no one else has matched this depth of recursion.

Either way, the recursion certainly boggles the mind. Another thing to notice about *World's End* is the economy with which Gaiman works with elements of the larger tale. In "Cerements," we learn that one of the Endless has died in the past (the first Despair), and we see the room that holds the materials and the ritual to accompany the death of one of the Endless. Of course, this foreshadows Dream's demise, and the envoy Eblis O'Shaunnesey's (named by Delirium, if you can tell) seeking out the proper materials. Another foreshadowing event takes place in the last issue of the collec-

tion, as we see the funeral train going across the sky. We have already discussed this scene at some length; suffice it to say that it makes it clear that mourning is going to be a theme for a while. Overall, the storytelling, both in scope, levels, and humanity (as these are some of the finest examples of stories told for stories' sake), is (not to use a word too much) magical. It transforms the experience of everyone listening, and, just as Bender says, changes lives. After hearing all the stories, Brant's image of the world is shaken, Charlene decides to stay at the inn, and Petrefax decides to seek adventure outside the Necropolis. It is also worth noting that in most of these stories, Dream shows up rarely, if at all. It is as if Gaiman decided to put off the main plot for a while and focus for a while on storytelling, which is another thing that *The Sandman* is about.

In keeping with the theme, there are other accounts of oral storytelling in *Sandman,* and they all seem to focus on bringing people of different worlds together. The one that rises to mythic quality comes in "Tales in the Sand," the prelude to *The Doll's House.* Here, we see a telling of the foundation myth of an African people, which is also a rite of passage. One of Eliade's criteria for sacred myths is that they are told only at certain times. This story is heard only once in a man's life, when he is initiated, and told only once, when he goes to initiate a relative of his. The story, which tells of Dream's disastrous affair with Nada (minus the condemning her to Hell part), also contains many elements of folklore and myth. In a sense, then, *The Sandman* is a hybrid text. The people are held to be the first people on earth, as "the first people were of our tribe. That is our secret, and we never tell outsiders, for they would kill us if they knew. But it is the truth" (*Sandman* 9:5). Campbell and others have noticed that just about every group has some myth in which they were "the first people." Gaiman's attention to detail is key here; the tale also features animals in important roles and other folkloristic devices. It is the little weaverbird that finds the fruit that will allow Nada to find Dream. However, the trip carrying the burning berry burns it, causing its color to change from white to brown. Also, a prohibition is set against killing the weaverbird, because of its service. All these are standard folkloristic elements. Finally, there is mention made of another version of the tale, in the stories that the women tell, "in their private language that the men-children are not taught, and that the old men are too wise to learn" (9:24). Here and in a few other places, a distinction is made between male and female stories, and it would make an interesting project to examine the gendering of stories as a greater theme in *Sandman.* (Gaiman has made some interesting comments about the "genders" of his stories as well.)

Also, with Nada's tale, we see an intact culture, with a living mythology. The uncle telling the story to his nephew shows that his people's religion and rites of passage sustain them in the way that, according to the critics of modernity, modern religion no longer does. If nothing else, this story serves as a reminder that, no matter how much we enjoy stories today, there was a time when people believed in stories completely, and it sustained them. The challenge for the modern myth, then, is to sustain us as traditional myths once did.

Finally, there are other instances of storytelling in *Sandman,* with the underlying theme, that stories bring people together. First, there is the mini-story-arc titled **"Convergence"** (issues 38-40), which features stories being told between generations and across worlds. In **"The Hunt,"** a grandfather (who is secretly also a werewolf) tells his somewhat unwilling granddaughter about his adventures as a young man. On the theme of Gaiman's self-consciousness, at one point the granddaughter says "It all sounds suspiciously post-modern to me, Grandpa. Are you sure this is really a story from the old country?" (*Sandman* 38:11). In **"Soft Places,"** a young Marco Polo meets a friend of his from later in life, and Gilbert, who is trying to get away from Dream and his new love (Thessaly). This story also introduces the idea that there are "soft places," where the fabric of space and time and reality grows thin and people can encounter others from other worlds and times. In **"A Parliament of Rooks"** (issue 40), Eve and Cain and Abel set about entertaining a pre-transfiguration Daniel. Eve tells the story of the three wives of Adam, Abel the story of how he and Cain came to live in the Dreaming (with the cutest Li'l Endless you ever saw). Cain, for his part, sets out a mystery about the behavior of rooks (a type of bird in the same family of ravens). Their plural is called a parliament, because of a strange behavior. They gather in a field in a circle, with one bird in the middle. That bird then begins to chatter for a time, until the group of birds either flies away or pecks the one in the middle to death. At the end of the issue, Abel tells Matthew and Daniel that the rook in the middle is really telling a story, and that the other birds either approve of the story (and fly away), or disapprove (and peck it to death). Thus, if we are to believe Gaiman, even animals have an instinct for storytelling. Again, as with much myth or folklore, a narrative occurs as a conversation between two or more people, including gods or archetypes. There are other instances of storytelling in the series, Gilbert telling Rose the original "Little Red Riding Hood" story, or the cat in **"Dream of a Thousand Cats"** telling her story, or the interlude of the old women telling Rose the story in the nursing home, but the point is clear: storytelling is the act that brings us all together, and is a part of why we have myths in the first place.

The amount and space and attention Gaiman devotes to storytelling is clear: what remains is to establish *why* he does so. And here, I can offer some suggestions why. In terms of the modern myth, we have already seen from

Miller that the new theology would be a theology of stories. And *Sandman* is, in many ways, a story about stories. There are too many instances of story-telling, both oral and written, for us to ignore them. Of course, for metanarratives (stories about stories) we can go all the way back to *The Odyssey*. And the reason the great storytellers have always told us about the business of telling stories (besides a sense of their own importance) is their tremendous importance for the vitality of a culture. What we can get from Jung is that we might even be able to say that we have an *instinct* for story-telling. Nancy Mellon puts it that "there is a natural sto-rytelling urge and ability in all human beings" (172). And if myths are really about the human condition, then one important aspect of myth should focus on *why* we tell myths in the first place. It seems to me that myths are an attempt to come to terms with the world we find around us. In our limited understanding, we create. Of course, we know more about the world than we did 3000 years ago, but in the things that really matter: our minds, our souls, our spirits, we still have much to learn. The point here is that *Sandman* is not only a story about stories: Dream, as the prefect of Dreaming and tales, is the reason we tell stories . . . and create myths. As Dream tells Titania of Faerie at one point, "Tales and dreams are the shadow-truths that will endure when mere facts are dust and ashes, and forgot" (*Sandman* 19:21).

Finally, there is another example of the creative life we have yet to mention: Destruction. Since he abandoned his realm, he has traveled far and wide, but eventually came to rest on a small island. There, he engages actively in creative pursuits: he paints, composes poems, cooks, and sculpts. It is not that he is a master crafts-man; in fact, if we are to believe Barnabas, he is uniformly terrible at these tasks. But the important thing is that he finds happiness and meaning in the creative life as an artist, albeit a mediocre one.

Yet, if we pay attention to *Sandman,* then another important feature of myths is that they are, at bottom, stories. Here, we come to an important step in the definition of myth. How are myths different from stories? How are they related? In traditional societies, they seem intimately connected, as stories about people also involved divine beings, and stories about divine beings also involved people. In modern society, however, he have had a clearer line of demarcation. We have myths (which we call "religion") of our own culture on one level, then stories (which we call "literature") and other people's myths on another level. Folklore, if given a place, would lie somewhere between myths and stories. Finally, there is a firm line between literature—high culture, and low culture, which includes "comic books." What *Sandman* should make clear is that the line between high and low culture is a false distinction. Here, in comics, we have a story that has all the meaning, all the grace, and all the subtlety, if not more, of "high-culture" literature. And if this distinction is false, then maybe the line between stories and myths is too. We have already seen "postmodern" writers taking on elements of the mythic in literature, and of course, literature is filled with mythic elements. Perhaps, then, what we are left with are *stories*. Myths, after all, have always been stories—what I have called the BIG stories, which ask the big questions of life. Who are we? Why are we here? Who made the world? Why do we die? And so on. Is it not possible that the difference between myths and stories is simply one of quality? That myths are simply well-told stories?

Of course, this criteria opens up the question of what makes a story well-told. Part of it is the emotional appeal, which we will discuss soon. The story must be good enough to become beloved, to reach the point where people order their lives according to it. And here, the criteria seems to be a depth of humanity that we find by feeling rather than reason. For emotional involvement with the characters is the beginning of living your life through a story. The key action here is to read (or hear) a story and see yourself reflected in it. In time, such a story can even provide identity, as myth once did for people. Part of the criteria should be subtlety, something that can be read and reread, and can reveal something new each time. Depending on the book, I have read through *Sandman* 6 or 7 times, and I have found something new in the stories every time. Finally, there is something hard to define, but I will call "command of the devices of storytelling." Simply put, Gaiman is a master storyteller: he knows how stories work, how people read them, how to lead a reader, and how to make the story curve at the last minute for maximum effect. Finally, a good story, if it is to rise to the level of myth, should fulfill Campbell's four functions of myth. First, *Sandman* is full of wonder, both overt and subtle. Second, it tells us about the structure of the macrocosm, what the universe is like and who rules it. Third, it provides a sociology, telling us how to be good, or *human,* to each other. Finally, fourth, it tells us how to move through the stages of our lives, from birth to the various rites of passage of puberty, marriage, and old age, and finally, death (the BIG change). The point here is that stories and storytelling bring people together. It is for all these reasons that *Sandman* is a good story. And more important, why it is a myth.

The art of storytelling is, of course, older than anyone can remember. However, it also contains the paradox of the modern myth of being both old and new. Whoever created the original myths, their torch has been passed to the storytellers of today, secular as well as religious. Just like the high-culture/low-culture divide has been broken down, so has that which formerly separated stories from myths proper. We previously spent some time lamenting the loss of meaning and religion in the modern world. And while it is certainly true that the old traditions no longer sustain many of us, we must also not be swept away by pessimism; rather, we must look at what has emerged to take their place. The purpose of the discussion of the role of the art of storytelling in *The Sandman* has been to emphasize that storytelling is not dead. And just as the mythmakers helped sustain the life of their communities in ancient times, so do the storytellers of today. If one is willing to look, there are many storytellers who incorporate the mythic into their works (Charles de Lint, Garth Ennis, Joss Whedon, to name a few). Furthermore, it is not just on their shoulders that we place the weighty task of creating meaning; the "collective unconscious" and the example of Destruction tell us that we all have it in us to be creative beings. The old ways are gone, just like Dream's Ruby was destroyed by John Dee. And like Dream, we cannot go back to the way it once was. However, the positive side of this is that all the energies we put into them have been freed for our use. So it is that in the modern world, we make our own meanings. *And we're doing fine.*

*Bibliography*

PRIMARY SOURCES:

Gaiman, Neil. *Death: The High Cost of Living.* New York: DC Comics, 1994.

———. *Death: The Time of Your Life.* New York: DC Comics, 1997.

———. "Murder Mysteries." *Angels and Visitations.* Minneapolis: DreamHaven Books, 1993, 139-166.

———. *The Sandman: Brief Lives.* New York: DC Comics, 1994

———. *The Sandman: The Doll's House.* New York: DC Comics, 1990.

———. *The Sandman: Dream Country.* New York: DC Comics, 1990.

———. *The Sandman: Fables and Reflections.* New York: DC Comics, 1993.

———. *The Sandman: A Game of You.* New York: DC Comics, 1993.

———. *The Sandman: The Kindly Ones.* New York: DC Comics, 1996.

———. *The Sandman: Preludes and Nocturnes.* New York: DC Comics, 1988.

———. *The Sandman: A Season of Mists.* New York: DC Comics, 1992.

———. *The Sandman: The Wake.* New York: DC Comics, 1997.

————. *The Sandman: World's End.* New York: DC Comics, 1994.

SECONDARY SOURCES:

Amos, Tori. "Introduction." *Death: The High Cost of Living.* New York: DC Comics, 1994, 5-7.

Arendt, Hannah. *Eichmann in Jerusalem: A Report on the Banality of Evil.* London: Russell Square, 1963.

Becker, Ernest. *The Denial of Death.* New York: Free Press Paperbacks, 1973.

Bender, Hy. *The Sandman Companion.* New York: DC Comics, 1999.

Campbell, Joseph. "Editor's Introduction." *The Portable Jung.* Ed. Joseph Campbell. New York: Penguin Books, 1971, vii-xxxii.

————. *The Hero with a Thousand Faces.* New York: MJF Books, 1949.

————. *The Hero's Journey: Joseph Campbell on his Life and Work.* Ed. Phil Cousineau. San Francisco: Harper & Row, 1990.

————. *The Masks of God, Vol. 4: Creative Mythology.* New York: Penguin Books, 1968.

————. *The Mythic Dimension.* Ed. Antony Van Couvering. San Francisco: HarperCollins, 1967.

————. *Myths to Live By.* New York: Penguin Group, 1972.

————. *The Power of Myth* with Bill Moyers. New York: Doubleday, 1988.

Caputi, Jane. "On Psychic Activism: Feminist Mythmaking." *The Feminist Companion to Mythology.* Ed. Caroline Larrington. London: Pandora, 1992, 425-440.

Dundes, Alan. *Essays in Folkloristics.* Meerut: Folklore Institute, 1978.

Eliade, Mircea. *The Sacred and the Profane: The Nature of Religion.* Trans. by Willard Trask. San Diego: Harcourt Brace & Co., 1957.

Gilmore, Mikal. "Introduction." *The Sandman: The Wake.* New York: DC Comics, 1997, 9-12.

Guiley, Rosemary Ellen. "Witchcraft as Goddess Worship." *The Feminist Companion to Mythology.* Ed. Caroline Larrington. London: Pandora, 1992, 411-424.

Hollis, James. *Tracking the Gods: The Place of Myth in Modern Life.* Toronto: Inner City Books, 1995.

Jaffe, Lawrence. *Celebrating Soul: Preparing for the New Religion.* Toronto: Inner City Books, 1999.

Johnson, Robert. *The Fisher King & The Handless Maiden.* San Francisco: HarperCollins Publishers, 1993.

Jung, Carl. *The Archetypes and the Collective Unconscious.* New York: Bollingen Foundation, 1959.

————. *Encountering Jung on Mythology.* Ed. Robert Segal. Princeton: Princeton UP, 1998.

————. *Modern Man in Search of a Soul.* San Diego: Harcourt Brace & Co., 1933.

————. *Psychology and Religion.* New Haven: Yale UP, 1938.

Kushner, Ellen. "Neil Gaiman Interview." From National Public Radio's "Sound & Spirit" Program, episode entitled "Dreams," originally aired July 14, 1997.

Larrington, Carolyne. "Introduction." *The Feminist Companion to Mythology.* Ed. Caroline Larrington. London: Pandora, 1992, ix-xiii.

Leeming, David Adams. *Mythology: The Voyage of the Hero.* New York: Oxford UP, 1998.

Malinowski, Bronislaw. *Malinowski and the Work of Myth.* Ed. Ivan Stranski. Princeton: Princeton UP, 1992.

McConnell, Frank. "Epic Comics." *Commonweal.* October 20, 1995, v.122, p. 21-22.

————. "Introduction." *The Sandman: The Kindly Ones.* New York: DC Comics, 1996, 6-11.

————. "Preface." *The Sandman: Book of Dreams.* Ed. Neil Gaiman & Ed Kramer. New York: HarperPrism, 1996. 2-6.

Melgrim, Stanley. *Obedience to Authority.* New York: Harper Perennial, 1974.

Mellon, Nancy. *The Art of Storytelling.* Boston: Element Books Unlimited, 1992.

Miller, David. *The New Polytheism: Rebirth of the Gods and Goddesses.* New York: Harper & Row, 1974.

Morrow, Greg, and Goldfarb, David. "The *Sandman* Annotations." Taken from the web at: http://rtt.colorado.edu/~jnmiller/Sandman.html

Niebuhr, Reinhold. *The Nature and Destiny of Man.* Volume 1: *Human Nature.* New York: Charles Scribner's Sons, 1941.

————. *The Nature and Destiny of Man.* Volume 2: *Human Destiny.* New York: Charles Scribner's Sons, 1943.

Olson, Robert. *An Introduction to Existentialism.* New York: Dover Publications, Inc., 1962.

Ovid. *Metamorphoses.* Trans by A. D. Melville. Oxford: Oxford UP, 1986.

Personal communications with *Sandman* fans.

Real, Terrence. *I Don't Want to Talk About it: Overcoming the Secret Legacy of Male Depression.* New York: Scribner, 1997.

Ricoeur, Paul. *Figuring the Sacred: Religion, Narrative, and Imagination.* Ed. Mark Wallace. Minneapolis: Fortress Press, 1995.

———. *The Symbolism of Evil.* New York: Harper & Row, 1967.

Segal, Robert. *Joseph Campbell: An Introduction.* New York: Garland Publishing, Inc, 1987.

Smith, Huston. *Why Religion Matters: the Fate of the Human Spirit in an Age of Disbelief.* San Francisco: HarperCollins Publishers, 2001.

Straub, Peter. "Afterword: On Mortality and Change." *The Sandman: Brief Lives.* New York: DC Comics, 1994.

Strenski, Ivan. *Malinowski and the Work of Myth.* Ed. Ivan Stranski. Princeton: Princeton UP, 1992.

Stroup, George. *The Promise of Narrative Theology.* Atlanta: John Knox Press, 1981.

Tillich, Paul. *The Courage to Be.* New Haven: Yale University Press, 1952.

Ulanov, Ann. *Religion and the Spiritual in Carl Jung.* New York: Paulist Press, 1999.

Wilson, Terry. "The Big Sleep: Popular 'Sandman' Comic Reaches the End of the Line." *The Chicago Tribune,* November 27, 1995, section C, page 1.

## Charles De Lint (review date February 2004)

SOURCE: De Lint, Charles. Review of *The Sandman: Endless Nights,* by Neil Gaiman. *Fantasy & Science Fiction* 106, no. 2 (February 2004): 31-2.

[*In the following review of* Sandman: Endless Nights, *De Lint praises Gaiman as an accomplished storyteller of dark, whimsical tales.*]

Has it really been seven years since Gaiman finished off his lengthy **Sandman** saga? Though I suppose, once you start counting up the projects in between—which include fascinating books such as **Neverwhere, American Gods,** and **Coraline**—you start to wonder where he found the time to write the seven stories collected here.

Because they aren't light, throwaway stories.

A quick recap for the uninitiated: years ago, Gaiman scripted an ongoing series for DC Comics about seven siblings he called the Endless (all the issues of which have been collected in trade paperback format and are currently in print). They're not gods, but they're most certainly not human either, though they do occasionally fall prey to human foibles. What they are is the physical representation of the names by which they're known: Dream, Death, Desire, Delirium, Despair, Destruction, and Destiny.

For this return to their world, Gaiman has written a story for each of the siblings, each illustrated by a different artist. The talent Gaiman has gathered to help him tell these stories is staggering: you need only flip through the pages to be seduced by their artistic vision. Some tell a story in the traditional panel-following-panel method, others explore different approaches to illustrated narrative. Their only similarity is that they are giants in terms of their talent.

But unlike some comic books where the art overshadows the story (much like contemporary film where too often the FX does the same), Gaiman reminds us once again of just how accomplished he is in this field. Each of the Endless get their fair share of time on stage—even if often the story ebbs and flows around their presence—but longtime fans will probably appreciate **"The Heart of a Star"** the most. This is where Gaiman has the audacity to strip away all the mysteries of his long-running series and give us the truth behind its mythology. Though curiously, in doing so, he has only increased the power of those same mysteries.

Anyone who has dismissed comic books over the past couple of decades would do well to have a look at this new collection to see just how fascinating a medium it has become. For the rest of us, sit back and enjoy this visit to the dark—though sometimes whimsical—twisting tales brought to us by Gaiman and his collaborators.

## Bruce Allen (essay date 2004)

SOURCE: Allen, Bruce. "The Dreaming of Neil Gaiman." In *Contemporary Literary Criticism,* 195. Farmington Hills, Mich.: Thomson Gale, 2004.

[*In the following essay, Allen provides a comprehensive overview of Gaiman's career as a graphic novelist.*]

### THE DREAMING OF NEIL GAIMAN

In a feat of literary legerdemain and metamorphosis that many of his characters and creations might envy, an unassuming Englishman who began his career as a freelance writer edging into the comic book industry has become one of (his adopted country) America's best-loved storytellers.

From a path-breaking graphic novel series through television and film scripts, continuing distinguished work in the comics field, charmingly offbeat children's stories, and—by virtually universal agreement—the finest adult fantasy fiction currently being written, Neil Gaiman has risen steadily to the summit of his profession.

A frequent honored guest at comic book and fantasy conventions (where he's known for his endless patience with autograph-seeking fans), Gaiman also remains prominently in the public eye via a state-of-the-art website (www.neilgaiman.com) that enables him to "chat" with countless adoring readers. He has socialized with celebrities like rock star Tori Amos (with whom Gaiman has in fact toured), and has collected such prestigious admirers as Norman Mailer—who has memorably proclaimed Gaiman's multi-volume graphic novel *The Sandman* "a comic strip for intellectuals," adding "and I say it's about time."

Gaiman has received numerous accolades, ranging from his designation as Most Collectible Author of 1992 to several Will Eisner Comic Industry Awards (including the only one yet given to a single issue of a comic book), and the unprecedented sweep accomplished by his 2001 fantasy novel *American Gods,* which won all four of its genre's most coveted prizes: the Hugo, Nebula, Stoker, and World Fantasy Awards.

His books have been translated into many languages, and the illustrated fiction on which he has collaborated with several of the finest contemporary graphic artists is generally credited with having crucially boosted the current boom in adult comics, thanks previously to works like Alan Moore's popular *Swamp Thing* (an influence graciously acknowledged by Gaiman) and Art Spiegelman's innovative Holocaust tale *Maus.*

Recent Gaiman projects include an English-language adaptation of the beloved Japanese animated film *Princess Mononoke,* an agreeably scary children's story *The Wolves in the Walls,* that has grown-ups sneaking into bookstore children's sections to browse it greedily (I have been one such retrograde adult), and a 2003 continuation of *The Sandman,* presenting seven lavishly illustrated new stories.

Two of Gaiman's stories, **"Snow, Glass, Apples"** and **"Murder Mysteries"** have been adapted for radio performance and are available on audiocassette. His illustrated fantasy tale *1602* has recently been published by Marvel Comics. And this year will bring a feature film scripted by Gaiman, **Mirror Mask,** produced by Jim Henson Studios and directed by its author's longtime illustrator Dave McKean.

And the beat goes on. Shock radio personality Howard Stern's claim to the title "King of All Media" notwithstanding, there's constantly increasing evidence that Gaiman's seemingly tireless creative energy and versatility, and his high visibility, have placed him somewhere very near the epicenter of contemporary popular culture.

Neil Gaiman was born in 1960 in Portchester, England. Though his family is Jewish, Neil was raised in a manner that seems to have been neither Orthodox nor orthodox, by supportive parents who were themselves accomplished professionals (his father a businessman, his mother a pharmacist).

In interviews, Gaiman routinely refers to himself as "the kid with a book," perpetually stealing moments to indulge his quickly discovered love of fantasy, adventure, and supernatural fiction. His mother strongly encouraged this passion for reading, which came to encompass not only landmark works like J. R. R. Tolkien's *Lord of the Rings* and Mervyn Peake's *Gormenghast* and their many imitations, but also the work of genre writers less commonly detected by literary-critical radar—such as thriller writer Edgar Wallace, the polymathic G. K. Chesterton, Hope Mirrlees, Lord Dunsany, and the American fantasist whom Gaiman names his favorite such author, Virginia novelist James Branch Cabell.

The ambition to emulate his favorites and become a writer himself was thus implanted early in young Neil, and after graduating from public school, he decided against committing to higher formal education and began working as a freelance journalist. Commissions for miscellaneous articles and interviews, successfully carried out throughout the early 1980s, led him to place work in such top-of-the-line publications as *Time Out,* the Sunday *London Times, The Observer,* and *Punch.* A "quickie" book about rock music group Duran Duran followed, as did a collection of amusing hyperbolic excerpts from science fiction novels and movies, **Ghastly beyond Belief** (1985), which Gaiman co-edited with novelist Kim Newman.

His name becoming known, and his interests settling into their distinctive groove, Gaiman made contacts with influential people in the comic book industry, and began producing original scripts. Early works in this form included **Violent Cases** (1987), **Outrageous: Tales of the Old Testament** (1987), **Black Orchid** (1988-89), **Signal to Noise** (1989-90), **Miracleman: The Golden Age** (1992), **Death: The High Cost of Living** (1993), and **The Tragical Comedy or Comical Tragedy of Mr. Punch** (1994).

Meanwhile, Gaiman had married (in 1985), edited a decidedly unconventional poetry anthology (pace Wordsworth) **Now We Are Sick** (1987), authored the informal critical study **The Official Hitchhiker's Guide to the Galaxy Companion** (1988), and—in 1992—

moved with his wife and two young children to the U.S., settling in Minnesota (a third child, his daughter Maddy, has since been born, in America).

During the 1990s, Gaiman spearheaded Comic Relief, a movement that developed into the Comic Legal Defense Fund, offering support to comics artists and writers who have been victims of censorship. He has remained an active participant in its activities, despite a workload that has increased exponentially as Gaiman has kept branching out into new venues and forms of expression.

In 1990 he collaborated with the wildly popular British fantasist Terry Pratchett (author of the mega-bestselling *Discworld* Novels) on **Good Omens,** a comic novel about the end of the world as observed and experienced by miscellaneous divinities, demons, and humans, replete with satanic nuns, fallen angels, a deity who has gotten really tired of humanity, and a riptide of millennial gags undoubtedly inspired by the aforementioned *Hitchhiker's Guide to the Galaxy,* the late Douglas Adams's 1979 cult favorite.

**Good Omens** is a very funny (if more than slightly overstuffed, and minimally self-indulgent) romp, whose quality may best be suggested by this tribute from Gaiman's peer (and fellow American emigrant), horror novelist Clive Barker: "The apocalypse has never been funnier."

In 1996, Gaiman wrote an original script for BBC Television: a tale of fantastic adventure set in a mythical "London Below" the real city, which story would soon be reshaped into his first adult novel written alone. A year later, he conquered yet another field with his first fiction for young adults, **The Day I Swapped My Dad for Two Goldfish.** This agreeably whimsical story became a bestseller, and was chosen one of the Best Children's Books of 1997 and cited as Recommended Reading by *Scholastic Magazine.*

But by this time, Gaiman's name had already become widely known via the medium that was his first love and to which he would continue to return.

The first installment of **The Sandman,** a comic book that appropriated and altered a character from a 1970s comic (created by Joe Simon and Jack Kirby) appeared in 1988. Its eponymous protagonist, formerly an avenging superhero who used "sleeping gas" to subdue criminals, was reimagined by Gaiman into a reclusive nonhuman reminiscent of the legendary figures of the Wandering Jew and Flying Dutchman.

Sandman, also known as Dream (and Morpheus, Lord of Dreams, among other cognomens and titles), is one of seven immortal siblings, all personifications of elemental entities that inhabit and shape human consciousness. His counterparts-and a strangely dysfunctional, perpetually conflicted "family" they are indeed—are Destiny, Desire, Delirium, Despair, Destruction, and Death.

The Sandman, who presides over a realm known as The Dreaming and who in effect orchestrates the dreams—and hence the imaginations—of all living beings, is, as envisioned by graphic artist Dave McKean (who drew all the individual issues' cover images), a brooding Byronic presence whose dark good looks and preference for black clothing have struck multiple responsive chords in readers. For one thing, this "Dream" rather resembles the striking-looking Neil Gaiman himself. For another, his likeness is credited with being one of the major inspirations for the Goth Movement of the 1990s.

Dream is a somewhat morose character, detached from any real communion or empathy with his peers or with humans (no matter how much he interacts with others). And the thrust of the entire **Sandman** series is the arduous process through which he comes to terms with his mission, his fallibility, and his future.

The original **Sandman** (for there have been successors) consists of seventy-five monthly issues (plus a 1991 "extra" installment, **The Sandman Special**), which ran from 1988 to 1996 and are collected in ten more-or-less sequential paperback anthologies. Gaiman had been granted considerable freedom to develop the concept of **The Sandman** in whatever way struck his imagination. The hugely exfoliating storyline he created immediately attracted some of the fantasy genre's most renowned graphic artists, and soon drew critical praise (expressed in "Introductions" written for the paperback volumes) from such genre luminaries as Stephen King, Peter Straub, Harlan Ellison, and Samuel R. Delany.

**Sandman** was likewise a huge commercial success, and still sells more than a million copies annually. It won multiple Eisner Awards for both text and artwork, and has since been optioned by Warner Brothers for a major motion picture (because, as Gaiman has slyly commented, "nothing is ever soon to be a minor motion picture").

Each of the ten paperback **Sandman** volumes groups individual issues thematically rather than in consistent chronological order. In **Preludes and Nocturnes** (issues # 1-8), a moribund British antiquarian, Roderick Burgess, while attempting to capture Death (and thus live forever), instead seizes Death's brother Dream, who is imprisoned for seventy-two years and stripped of his otherworldly powers by the theft of his magical "tools": a pouch, helmet, and ruby. Dream's absence from his usual duties produces a worldwide epidemic of sleeping sickness (rendered in stunning visual images).

When Dream finally escapes, the quest to recover his tools takes him to Hell itself, thence the home of John Dee, the son of Burgess's mistress Ethel Cripps, and a fugitive from the Arkham Asylum for the Criminally Insane (in a grimly humorous nod to the creator of fictional Arkham, Massachusetts: H. P. Lovecraft).

These lively melodramatics are followed by Dream's encounter (in **"The Sound of Her Wings"**) with his sister Death, a forthright street punk who basically tells her sibling to stop feeling sorry for himself and tend to his business as lord of The Dreaming.

Subsequent issues alternate between concentrating on Dream's progress (or lack of it) in shouldering his burdens and separate stories both intimately and only tangentially related to it. In *The Doll's House* (issues #9-16), for example, the escape of several rebellious Dreams from the Sandman's realm lead him to fear that his world is falling apart—and introduces the characters of self-sacrificing Rose Walker; British author G. K. Chesterton; 14th-century commoner Hob Gadling, who bargains successfully with Dream and is rewarded with immortality; and the sinister Corinthian, who appears to be Dream's murderous alter ego.

This volume's stories include a faux African folktale (**"Tales in the Sand"**) that describes Dream's love affair with black queen Nada, and a mordantly amusing account of a serial killers' convention.

*Dream Country* (issues # 17-20), which incidentally reveals the gradual erosion of Dream's abstracted indifference to the world around him, ranges farther afield, to depict the Muse Calliope captured and sexually exploited by a blocked writer, a gorgeously detailed alternate reality in which felines hold dominion over humans (**"A Dream of a Thousand Cats"**), and—in one of the series's most gratifying high points—a marvelous fantastical retelling of Shakespeare's matchless comedy "A Midsummer Night's Dream."

In Gaiman's inspired version, a summary of the play's action is surrounded and enriched by the story of its first production (and the involvement therein of its author's twin children Hamnet and Judith) and an explanation of how it came to be written: out of a Faustian pact with Dream, whereby the struggling playwright came into his full artistic maturity.

It was **"A Midsummer Night's Dream"** (issue # 19) that received the World Fantasy Award as its year's Best Short Story—the only comic book issue ever to be so honored. *Season of Mists* (issues # 21-28) depicts the consequences of Lucifer's decision to abandon Hell (which perhaps echoes God's annoyance with His creation in *Good Omens*) and give the key to its gates to Dream, who is thereupon importuned by numerous beings eager to seize control of the infernal regions. Deities from various theologies and mythologies keep popping up (thus prefiguring Gaiman's later novel *American Gods*), as do the troublemaking demon Azazel and the Norse god of mischief Loki (who is in many ways Dream's exact temperamental opposite).

This entertaining volume, whose resonant title is derived from Keats's great "Ode to Autumn," is notable also for its very interesting characterization of a sensitive and ethically complex Lucifer, and as a further development of growing rifts among the increasingly distracted Dream and his squabbling Endless siblings.

In *A Game of You* (issues # 32-37), a previously encountered character named Barbie (and obviously inspired by the popular doll of the 1950s) becomes a princess reigning over a "dreamworld" imperiled by The Cuckoo, a destroyer bent on holding sway over a world purged of living beings. Dream is essentially an offstage presence in this somewhat surprising sequence, which contains teasing echoes of *The Wizard of Oz* (with Barbie as Dorothy, and her valiant dog Martin Tenbones as Toto), and strongly suggests the dangers of living within one's imagination—perhaps another warning signal to the Sandman.

*Fables and Reflections,* a ragbag volume that contains issues # 29-31, 38-40, 50, the aforementioned *Sandman Special,* and a new story entitled **"Fear of Falling,"** offers several crucial stories. These include Emperor Augustus Caesar's disclosure of the real reasons why Rome fell; the adventures of the (historical) self-proclaimed "Emperor of America," late 19th-century San Francisco eccentric Joshua Norton (who was befriended by a much amused Mark Twain); and envisionings of Baghdad then and now, ranging from the fabulous caliphate of Haroun Al-Raschid (immortalized in *The Arabian Nights*) to its contemporary wartime state.

And, in a return to Dream's own preoccupations, **"The Song of Orpheus"** retells the familiar myth, adding the complication that Dream—who is revealed to be Orpheus's father—declines to restore the latter's beloved Eurydice to life.

*Brief Lives* (issues # 41-49), whose title denotes its emphases, involves Dream—at his sister Delirium's request—in a search for his missing brother Destruction, who has grown weary of humanity's misappropriation of his gift, and become estranged from The Endless. This almost unrelentingly grim sequence (relieved intermittently by such charming spectacles as that of Babylonian goddess Ishtar moonlighting as an exotic dancer) focuses further on Dream's embattled condition, when he is obliged—like the biblical patriarch Abraham—to take the life of his own son. Fewer specifics should be revealed about the succeeding volumes.

*World's End* (issues # 51-56) indeed anticipates the promise of its title, as travelers stranded during a "reality storm" exchange stories, in the manner made famous by Boccaccio and Chaucer. The choicest tales are a flavorful sea story (**"Hob's Leviathan"**) reminiscent of Stevenson and Melville, and an ingenious Horatio Alger-like story of a teenager (**"The Golden Boy"**) who miraculously becomes President of the United States.

*The Kindly Ones* (issues # 57-69) brings The Dreaming under siege, by the classical Furies to whom its title alludes, and by the malicious mischief-making of Loki and Puck. The Sandman's "sin" is a careless remark, made much earlier in the series, that initiated a chain of devastating consequences, taking the form of wrongs that can only be righted—as gathering events make clear—by a purifying sacrificial act.

Volume ten *The Wake* (issues # 70-75) is very much a tying up of loose ends, in which a haunting Chinese tale memorably dramatizes the complex relationships of fathers to sons, Dream converses once more with the undying Hob Gadling, and the full truth of Will Shakespeare's bargain is revealed, with the second and last of his plays devoted to dreams and their consequences: "The Tempest." Suffice it to say that *The Wake* literally is a wake, that celebrates as it mourns the nature of Dream (and dreaming), his gift to the world over which he broods with such sorrowful contemplation, and his destiny.

More than two thousand pages long, crammed with arresting and strangely beautiful images, featuring both an absorbing central narrative and a bountiful array of old and new stories, *The Sandman* revolutionized the graphic novel form, in effect creating an entirely new readership for comic books, and spreading Neil Gaiman's name throughout the land. And it was only the beginning.

Gaiman returned to the *Sandman* conception in 1999 with *The Dream Hunters,* a gorgeously illustrated short novel about a fox who befriends, then comes to love a gentle monk—and travels to the land of dreams in order to save her beloved from a malevolent landowner. Like the earlier *Sandman* episode **"A Dream of a Thousand Cats,"** it's a wonderful modern version of the traditional beast fable: "an old Japanese fable," Gaiman has since said of this limpid work, "[that] I completely made up."

A new *Sandman* collection, *Endless Nights,* appeared in 2003. It contains seven stories, each related to or featuring one of The Endless. One of its best is **"Death and Venice,"** in which a pleasure-loving nobleman's plot to cheat time (and thus death as well) is juxtaposed with an introverted soldier's lifelong emotional momentum toward the nameless woman he met in his youth:

Death herself. Another is a dark and intriguing miscellany entitled **"Fifteen Portraits of Despair"** (which includes two ironically apposite observations: "It is a writer, with nothing left that he knows how to say" and "It is an artist, and fingers that will never catch the vision"). Even better is **"On the Peninsula,"** an ingeniously unsettling tale of archaeologists who explore a presumably post-nuclear future.

Gaiman's expertly "caught" vision has extended itself still further, in *The Sandman: Book of Dreams* (1996), a collection of stories written and illustrated by admirers of the original series; and in *The Sandman Presents: The Furies* (2003), written by Mike Carey and illustrated by John Bolton, which is a sequel to the series' penultimate volume, *The Kindly Ones.*

Additional to this evidence that Dream will not really die are Gaiman's several affirmative responses whenever he's asked by interviewers whether he will return again to this material. *Endless Nights* is, in all likelihood, not the end of this story.

Meanwhile, this protean author's mastery of adult fiction was evidenced by *Smoke and Mirrors: Short Fictions and Illusions* (1998), an expanded version of Gaiman's 1993 gathering of shorter work, *Angels and Visitations.*

This is a richly varied collection of thirty short stories and narrative poems, many of which transform classic figures from well-known myths, legends, and folktales into their darker (and, in some cases, funnier equivalents). **"Nicholas Was,"** for example, introduces a disturbingly unconventional Santa Claus. **"Don't Ask Jack"** (which may have been inspired by Walter de la Mare's great story "The Riddle") features an evil Jack-in-the-box. And the poem **"Bay Wolf"** updates the grim Anglo-Saxon epic Beowulf by shifting it into the giggly suntanned world of television's cluelessly inane *Baywatch.*

Gaiman rewrites the story of *Snow White* from the viewpoint of the jealous Queen (**"Snow, Glass, Apples"**), retells a folktale of magical revenge (**"The Daughter of Owls"**) in the style of seventeenth-century British antiquarian John Aubrey, and appropriates H. P. Lovecraft's dank haunted New England landscape of Innsmouth in **"Only the End of the World Again"** and **"Shoggoth's Old Peculiar"** (in the latter story, an American student traveling through England learns through unfortunate chance meetings that "there were things that lurked beneath gray raincoats that man was not meant to know").

These "messages from Looking-Glass Land and pictures in shifting clouds" (so identified in Gaiman's **"Introduction"** to them) pay other homages—to fantasy writer

Michael Moorcock and his contemporaries in a ruminative memoir of Gaiman's early reading (**"One Life, Furnished in Early Moorcock"**) and to those masters of narrative concision John Collier and Ray Bradbury in **"We Can Get Them for You Wholesale,"** the story of a jealous lover who patronizes an assassination service and discovers the pleasures of megalomania and mass murder. There are also more strictly contemporary stories, including **"Looking for the Girl,"** set in "the London club scene in the early seventies," and **"Tastings,"** which portrays a female succubus, or lamia, in a hair-raisingly graphic manner.

But these pale in comparison with the collection's finest story **"Chivalry"** (which Gaiman has singled out as a favorite piece for public readings). Told in the most restrained plain style imaginable, this is a perfect little fantasy, whose widowed protagonist Mrs. Whitaker happens one day to purchase the Holy Grail in a second-hand shop. Having brought it home, she is visited by the Arthurian knight Galahad, who has long sought it. Mrs. Whitaker's "temptation" by the handsome adventurer, and the sensible decision she makes, are quite movingly conveyed, in a tale that effortlessly blends the world of her own dowdy routine with the realm of chivalric romance. It's a great story, not nearly well enough known: the centerpiece of a remarkable collection that proved Neil Gaiman's continuing success with every task and challenge he had set himself.

In 1998 Gaiman published the novel **Neverwhere,** an expansion of the script written earlier for television performance. It's the story of Richard Mayhew, a young man from a provincial town who moves to London, makes his fortune (in a manner of speaking), and acquires a beauteous fiancée named Jessica.

Richard's life changes abruptly when he encounters a witch-like old woman who solemnly announces that he will soon undergo a remarkable experience that "starts with doors." Sure enough, Richard meets a frail, comely girl who calls herself Door, and aids her in her flight from a pair of grotesque assassins for hire, Mr. Croup and Mr. Vandemar (whose communal demeanor may be indicated by the way they answer their telephone, thus: "Croup and Vandemar, . . . Eyes gouged, noses twisted, tongues pierced, chins cleft, throats slit"). These distinctly uncharming partners were, Door surmises, undoubtedly implicated in the murder of her family, which she and Richard thereupon set out to solve.

Richard follows Door to "London Below," a city beneath the "real" London ("where the people who fall through the cracks go"). Here he wanders through a tumultuous Floating Market, meeting various angelic and demonic persons and personifications, and proving his mettle by doing battle with the fearsome Great Beast of London. The novel ends with Richard restored to the life for which he is best suited, and the two Londons continue to exist in a richly suggestively symbolic mutual relationship.

*Neverwhere* is Gaiman's best novel so far. Its likable hero (whose surname evokes the historical Henry Mayhew, author of the classic nineteenth-century sociological study London Labour and the London Poor) is a vivid contemporary equivalent of the archetypal innocent youth who grows by fits and starts into his herohood; Croup and Vandemar make a splendid psychopathic vaudeville time (they resemble nothing so much as a bloodthirsty Laurel and Hardy); and the eerily detailed landscape of London below is etched with bravura nightmarish precision: it's a setting that might have been invented by a Kafka-influenced Dickens.

Its successor *Stardust* (1999) is made of somewhat gentler stuff, though the spell it casts is scarcely less seductive. This beguiling adult fairy tale begins in rural England in the 1830s, in the town of Wall, named thus for the "high grey rock wall" between it and an otherworldly "meadow" in which not-quite-human figures are frequently glimpsed. The inhabitants of this meadow ("Faerie") are quite willing to mingle occasionally with mortals. And, on one such occasion, during Wall's annual April fair, young Dunstan Thorn falls in love with a maiden from the meadow and conceives a child with her.

The latter, who grows up in Wall, becomes Tristran Thorn. And, like his father Dunstan before him, young Tristran becomes enamored of a bewitching girl, Victoria Forester—who, in a playful moment, agrees to accept Tristran's love if he retrieves for her the streaking star they had together observed falling to earth; or, more precisely, beyond the rock wall, within the boundaries of Faerie.

The bulk of the novel recounts Tristran's amazing adventures, as he learns he is not the star's only pursuer. The murderous sons of the villainous Lord of Stormhold (accompanied by the dead brothers whom they the living have murdered) are his chief rivals, but they're only part of a phantasmagoric parade that includes assorted trolls and spell-mumbling hags, a farm boy transformed into a goat, and a wood nymph turned into a tree, among others. Tristran finds the star (which turns out to be, rather than an astral body, a person—and not a particularly agreeable one), but not before exploits aboard a passing "sky ship," his own metamorphosis (into a dormouse), and a bittersweet return to Wall, upon which he learns—as did Richard Mayhew in *Neverwhere*—that his destiny is neither as commonplace nor as earthbound as he had been brought up to believe.

The protagonists of *Neverwhere* and *Stardust,* heroes though they may be, are fairly simply drawn characters compared with "Shadow" Moon, the central figure of Gaiman's multiple-prizewinning next novel *American Gods* (2001).

A bit of hint as to who Shadow really is is dropped when we learn that he is thirty-two, has served three years of a prison term for "aggravated assault and battery," and has just been freed, after learning that his wife Laura has died in an automobile accident. Shadow travels by plane to Indiana for Laura's funeral, and the story's real complications begin.

En route, Shadow meets a loquacious "businessman" of uncertain identity ("Call me Wednesday," he affably declares), and impulsively accepts an equally undefined job as the latter's chauffeur and "handyman."

Shadow's subsequent waking and dreaming moments are populated by bizarre otherworldly figures. A human with the head of a buffalo offers him sonorous cryptic advice. Laura's ghost visits him, taking unusual corporeal form.

At this point the narrative begins expanding to include several interpolated stories. An 18th-century Irish girl, Essie Tregowan, is "transported" to America. Salim, a Middle Eastern immigrant, becomes the lover of a mischievous spirit (an ifrit) working as a Manhattan cabdriver. Boy and girl twins sold by their wicked uncle are brought to America on a slave ship: the boy grows up to participate in a bloody slave rebellion; the girl becomes a healer, and the forerunner of "voudon" queen Marie Laveau.

Meanwhile, Shadow and Wednesday travel throughout middle America, establishing a kind of base in Lakeside, Wisconsin, making preparations for a "meeting" Wednesday is arranging. The schemes related to it are described by one suspicious colleague as follows: "he wants a last stand. He wants to go out in a blaze of glory."

Shadow is repeatedly warned that a storm is approaching. Reality seems to be losing its bearings: as Shadow watches television in a motel room, Rob Petrie physically abuses his Laura; and Lucy Ricardo speaks from the screen directly to Shadow.

Even more sinister omens pile onto one another. In Chicago, a ruffian named Czernobog wins a game of checkers, and reserves the right to beat Shadow's brains out on an unspecified later occasion. Wednesday has some strange business with mortician Mr. Ibis and his associate Mr. Jacquel. A murderous old man named Hinzelmann poses yet another threat to the increasingly bewildered Shadow.

The reader gradually understands that the "old gods" worshipped around the world have followed the emigrants who believe in them to America—where they are confronted by the "new gods" of consumerism and mass communication (Media, for example—who is at one point mistaken for the classical antiheroine "who killed her children")—and that Wednesday (who is the Norse god Wotan, not all that carefully disguised) has, with Shadow's aid, summoned them to a climactic, perhaps apocalyptic gathering.

Shadow's function in this götterdämmerung is made clear by the novel's climactic events. When the slain Wednesday is buried (beneath an ancient "world tree"), Shadow keeps the required vigil over his grave, tied to the tree, denied food and water, until Mr. Ibis conducts him on a subsequent journey that involves a flight by "thunderbird" (and no, Virginia, it's not an automobile), the payment of what he owes to the patient Czernobog, a Dantean task accomplished on a "frozen lake," and a terrific surprise contained in an ironic concluding "Postscript."

*American Gods* is, arguably, a bit too playful and hectic for its own good. But much of the very considerable pleasure this rich novel offers consists in recognizing the theological and mythological sources of its boldly drawn characters. Most readers who are attuned to Gaiman's encyclopedic imagination will note that the ibis and the jackal are key figures in Egyptian myth, that Shadow's light-fingered former cellmate "Low Key" Lyesmith has his own divine counterpart—perhaps even that the blowsy good-time gal "Easter" somewhat resembles pagan goddess of spring Eostre, the spry little black man Mr. Nancy has many of the qualities of the West African trickster-creator Anansi, and that the buffalo-headed sage of Shadow's dreams has many antecedents in Native American folklore.

The novel's key incidents and incidental details are similarly freighted with symbolic suggestiveness. Shadow's hobby of "coin manipulation," at which he's particularly adept, marks him as one potentially capable of magic. His "combat" with Czernobog closely echoes the medieval tale of Arthurian knight Sir Gawain's fateful encounter with the mysteriously powerful Green Knight. His ordeal on that frozen lake emphatically implies a journey to the infernal regions and back. And when Wednesday rises from the dead to inform Shadow that "there's power in the sacrifice of a son," we understand that America's gods, native and newly arrived, are not the only ones involved in the drama of Shadow's passage from sin and error to purification through suffering.

This big novel received numerous mainstream reviews (unusual for a book by an author associated with the fantasy genre) and effectively confirmed Gaiman's reputation as a "serious" writer. When he followed it with *Coraline* (2002), a scary young adult novel about a preadolescent girl who discovers an alternate reality within her family's house, even more rapturous reviews greeted the book. *Coraline* (a story that adult readers should not overlook) won the Hugo, Bram Stoker, and British Science Fiction Association Awards, and is already spoken of as a contemporary classic.

Gaiman's seemingly indefatigable energies have produced, within the last four years, several more graphic novels: a shivery tale of lycanthropy (*Only the End of the World Again* [an illustrated version of Gaiman's short story] 2000); a chilling love story based on commedia dell' arte characters and motifs (*Harlequin Valentine,* 2001); a weird tale of a sinister "rock legend" (*The Last Temptation,* 2001); and the story behind the story of the angel Lucifer's fall from heaven (*Murder Mysteries,* 2003), expanded from a story that had appeared in *Smoke and Mirrors.*

The aforementioned feature film *Mirror Mask* will be along later this year. Other Gaiman works optioned for film include *Death: The High Cost of Living, Neverwhere,* and *Stardust.* Gaiman websites advise that a sequel to *American Gods* is in the works.

In a 1999 interview with the internet journal *Writers Write,* Gaiman said "As far as I'm concerned, the entire reason for becoming a writer is not having to get up in the morning." Perhaps. But when a storyteller so generous and gifted dreams to such stunning effect, one wants only to say: Sleep well. Dream well. Then get up, as late as you please, and write down for us all that you have dreamed.

## Kent Worcester (essay date 2004)

SOURCE: Worcester, Kent. "The Graphic Novels of Neil Gaiman." In *Contemporary Literary Criticism,* 195. Farmington Hills, Mich.: Thomson Gale, 2004.

[*In the following essay, Worcester examines the works, life, and career of Neil Gaiman.*]

### INTRODUCTION

Neil Gaiman (b. 1960) is an imaginative, prolific and highly popular contemporary author whose impact has been felt in a variety of media and genres. He is the author of several fantasy novels (*Neverwhere, Stardust, Good Omens* (with Terry Pratchett), and *American Gods*), and numerous short stories (some of which are collected in *Smoke and Mirrors*), as well as stories for younger readers (*Coraline, The Day I Swapped My Dad for Two Goldfish,* and *The Wolves in the Walls*). While Gaiman has written for film, television, stage, magazines, and newspapers, he is probably best known for his work in comic books. In recent years Gaiman has received the Hugo, the Nebula, the Harvey, the Eis-

ner, the World Fantasy Award, the Bram Stoker Award, and other honors in the fields of fantasy, science fiction, children's fiction, literary fiction, and comics. Gaiman's website (www.neilgaiman.com) receives thousands of hits per day and offers links to comprehensive bibliographies as well as interviews, essays, message boards, and a web journal.

Gaiman was born in Portchester, England, where his father owned a vitamin company. He was educated at Ardingly College Junior School and the Whitgift School. In the early 1980s he worked as a freelance journalist in London, contributing articles, reviews and interviews on popular culture topics. While he was a fan of Marvel and DC comics as a child, he stopped reading comic books in his teen years and only reluctantly looked at them again as an adult. In an interview with Hy Bender, Gaiman described "waiting for a train at Victoria Station" in 1984, when he "noticed a newsstand with piles of comics, and *Swamp Thing* 25, "The Sleep of Reason," caught my eye. I was dead set against buying it, but I read it just standing there and flipping. As I did so, I started thinking, 'This is really good. But it can't be, because comics are no good" (Bender 15). The following year he became friends with both Alan Moore (b. 1953), the British comics writer who had already achieved critical acclaim for his work on *Swamp Thing,* and Dave McKean (b. 1963), an innovative young artist. Alan Moore's burgeoning success helped convinced Gaiman that a career as a comics writer was not only possible, but worthwhile, while his numerous conversations with Dave McKean helped him to lay out an ambitious agenda for comics. As Gaiman later recalled, he and McKean "had very definite ideas about the kind of comics we wanted to see, the kind of comics we liked. They were heady times. We were both intoxicated by the potential of the medium, by the then-strange idea that comics weren't exclusively for kids anymore (if they ever had been): that the possibilities were endless" (*Violent Cases* 3).

The comics industry in the mid-to-late 1980s was undergoing a period of change and transformation. Independent companies were being set up to take advantage of the specialist comics shops opening in Britain, the United States, and elsewhere. Politically minded figures such as Moore, Frank Miller, Paul Chadwick, and Art Spiegelman were part of a creative turn that emphasized the contribution that multilayered scripts and unconventional artwork could make to a supposedly lowbrow medium. DC Comics, then as now part of Time Warner, one of the world's largest entertainment corporations, performed an important catalytic function by signing and promoting UK writers who brought a distinctive sensibility to a U.S. dominated industry. These writers included not only Alan Moore and Neil Gaiman, but Grant Morrison, Peter Milligan, Warren Ellis, Garth Ennis, and a handful of others.

Meanwhile, a growing number of comics creators experimented with longer, self-contained stories for adult readers—a format that became known as the graphic novel.

Gaiman played a starring role in this period of creative ferment and he remains one of the biggest names in the field. His friendship with Dave McKean led to a series of high-profile collaborations, beginning with the remarkable *Violent Cases* as well as the "prestige format," three-part series, *Black Orchid.* While the former drew readers via word of mouth, the latter was enthusiastically received in the comics subculture and helped mark the arrival of a "British wave" in comics. With the success of *Black Orchid,* DC invited Gaiman to develop a new monthly series, which led to the launch of *The Sandman* at the end of 1988. *The Sandman* featured Gaiman's densely plotted, emotionally resonant scripts, McKean's fanciful cover art, and interior artwork by a procession of talented illustrators. It was possibly the most critically acclaimed English-language comic series of the 1990s. Gaiman further consolidated his reputation with *Signal to Noise* (1992) and *Mr. Punch* (1994) both with McKean, as well as his scripts for *Miracleman* (1990-1994) and various side projects, including *Sandman* spin-offs *Death: The High Cost of Living* (1994) and *Death: The Time of Your Life* (1997). While Gaiman brought the monthly series to a close in 1996, he returned to "the Dreaming" with his illustrated story collaboration with Yoshitaka Amano, *The Sandman: The Dream Hunters* (1999), and in *The Sandman: Endless Nights* (2003).

This essay focuses on the longer and more ambitious comics that Neil Gaiman has undertaken over the past two decades. These projects can be divided into two main groups: first, the experimental, boundary-expanding projects with McKean, and second, *The Sandman* and related graphic novels. The essay refers only in passing to his other comics writings and does not address his prose fiction. In the concluding section the essay takes stock of Gaiman's influence on contemporary comics and his contribution to the revival of fantasy in mainstream comics. The conclusion also considers whether and to what extent Gaiman and McKean were able to implement the sweeping artistic and cultural agenda they laid out for the comics medium in the mid-1980s.

## COLLABORATIONS WITH DAVE MCKEAN

Comics often involve a group undertaking that brings together writers and illustrators and sometimes inkers, letterers, and colorists. While there are many individuals who write and draw their own comics, comics published by the larger companies (such as DC) tend to be produced by creative teams whose rosters change from time to time. In the case of the seventy-five issues of *The Sandman,* Neil Gaiman worked alongside no fewer than 50 artists, letterers, and colorists, along with 3 editors and assistant editors, and one cover artist, over a span of eight years. This turnover in personnel can be explained in part by the pressures of monthly publication, but Gaiman also wanted to deploy different artists for distinct storytelling purposes.

The graphic novels *Violent Cases, Signal to Noise,* and *Mr. Punch* were produced under very different conditions from *The Sandman.* Each is a self-contained, coauthored package designed to appeal to culturally literate readers who would normally never pay attention to comics or genre-based fiction more generally. As McKean wrote in the dedication to *Violent Cases,* "For my teacher, Malcolm Hatton. You see? This is what I mean by comics." In each case, their purpose was to explore the medium's largely unrealized potential, to combine words and pictures in ways that took full advantage of the form—panels, word balloons, and sequential storytelling—without invoking the familiar conventions and tropes of mainstream comics. The stories themselves diverge from the norm as much as the artwork. Rather than telling heroic adventure stories, these books are concerned with intrinsically grown up themes, such as memory's imperfections and the solace that meaningful work can provide in the face of death.

Gaiman and McKean's distinctive visual-verbal agenda is also promulgated in their only slightly more cheerful books for younger readers, each of which recapitulate aspects of the graphic novel, but under a different publishing rubric. The term "children's book" would be misapplied to these stories, especially *Coraline,* given their edgy content. "Graphic novel" might be more accurate, even if they do not consistently use a panel-by-panel illustrated narrative structure as such. But, in contrast to *Violent Cases, Signal to Noise,* and *Mr. Punch, Coraline, The Wolves in the Walls,* and *The Day I Swapped my Dad for Two Goldfish* are mainly sold in bookstores and are not retailed or consumed as comics.

*Violent Cases* is the earliest of the Gaiman-McKean collaborations and yet it holds up quite nicely. It tells a quasi-autobiographical story about a four-year old boy in provincial southern England who meets (or at least recalls meeting) Al Capone's osteopath. Almost everything about the book departs from the traditional comic book—from the cover, which features a disturbingly indistinct, puffy-cheeked older man in a gray suit, to the inside pages, which veer from collages and oversize panels to dense overlays of penciled sketches and exploding borders. The story itself rests on precarious foundations—the memories of a child, for whom violin cases are "violent cases" and "the giants always looked like my father." "The actual subject matter of *Violent Cases,*" Gaiman explained, "is a subject matter that fascinates and obsesses me: violence, cruelty, madness, and what it's like to be a kid in an adult world, and how horrible parties are, and all that stuff" (Thompson 71).

The book opens with a disturbing childhood incident in which Gaiman's shoulder was sprained or dislocated by his father. "I wouldn't want to gloss over the true facts," Gaiman explains, as he addresses the reader via multiple panels. "Without true facts, where are we?" The action centers around three successive conversations with the osteopath, whose appearance changes over the course of the book, as the narrator tries to form a clear image from his unreliable memory. The porous nature of mental images is something that the book captures quite effectively. As Gaiman later said, "I think we pulled off something you couldn't do anywhere other than in comics, where the osteopath suddenly looks younger, and for the rest of the book he looks that way. You couldn't do that in prose, because by that time the reader would have built up a mental picture of what he looks like. In film or TV people would be distracted by looking at the make-up job required, or the fact that a different actor was suddenly playing the part" (Lawley and Whitaker 47). This sense of makeshift recollections is further suggested by McKean's fragmented pages, which combine odd details with abstracted depictions of imperfectly remembered episodes.

The four-year old Gaiman chats with the talkative osteopath for the last time at "Louisa Singer's fifth birthday party at the Queen's Hotel." Sipping a cola at the Hotel bar he hears about the time when Al Capone tied up and then clubbed some of his closest associates to death. In Gaiman's mind Louisa Singer's party and Al Capone's orgy of violence merge, so that in one panel, Capone's men are screaming, and in another, "four children run around three chairs . . . and a little girl—Louisa Singer herself, the birthday girl—stomps away from the others, her lower lip trembling." This leads to a genuinely unnerving page in which a thick spray of black ink, symbolizing blood, splashes over the men's tortured faces. "Nobody was sick, which kind of surprised me," Gaiman intones at the bottom of the page, in a borderless image that features party favors and a handgun. "I thought of the other children. Their heads bloody caved-in lumps. I felt fine about it. I felt happy." Despite the seething hostility that this passage reveals—a rage that has its roots, presumably, in the behavior of his parents, and particularly his argumentative father, who has a taste for bickering and empty threats—the young Gaiman merely says "thank you for having me" to Louisa's mother at the end of the party. While Neil Gaiman has a reputation for being one of the nicest people in comics, *Violent Cases* suggests that his knack for writing tragic and occasionally morbid stories has at least partly autobiographical origins.

*Signal to Noise* similarly juxtaposes two apparently unrelated themes—the impending death of a well-known film director, and the end-of-the-world anxieties that ordinary Europeans felt on the eve of the last millennium—just as *Violent Cases* contrasts and then conflates kid's parties with the mafia. Here too the ending unites the two themes, with the now spectral film director joining the crowds on a hillside at the end of 999 AD. This volume is more optimistic than *Violent Cases,* insofar as the director hopefully peers upward in the final panels, and the reader learns that the script he's been working on has found an audience. "The world is always ending, for someone," muses the director. But in this case art can outlive the artist, whereas in *Violent Cases* all that's left are memories. Art carries the signal that distinguishes meaning from the "noise" of meaninglessness. In this book at least, Gaiman seems to suggest that the dying are threatened by noise rather than peace.

In mainstream comics one of Gaiman's best-known characters is Death, the older sister of Dream (aka the Sandman), who wears a stylish black costume and is everyone's best friend. The faintly menacing aspect of her character is occasionally acknowledged, but her high spirits and *savoir-faire* suggest that the universal experience she embodies is a thrilling mystery rather than a source of dread. In *Signal to Noise,* death is not stylish. "My chest began to hurt, and I told myself I should not have walked," the unnamed director says to himself as a dull orange colored glow hovers above his outstretched hand. The fact that the main character is aging, balding, and thickening around the waist—decaying, in other words—is another form of "noise" that comics have not always been willing to contend with. *The Sandman* has its deeply tragic elements, but it is mostly about people who look and act as if they are under 35 (even if some are elemental beings that predate homo sapiens). By way of contrast, the concept of youthful glamour is almost entirely absent from the core Gaiman-McKean collaborations, even if their coauthored pages are often stunning in their artistic virtuosity.

With *Signal to Noise* Gaiman and McKean introduced new approaches to their assigned roles. Gaiman's prose is more epigrammatic this time around, with whole pages devoted to terse and sometimes elusive phrases: "I had a lie," states the narrator on one page; "stop looking at me!" says the director in another, as he shouts at the photos in his study. In one particularly unconventional two-page spread, rows and rows of photocopied, blue-tinted eyes stare out at the reader while the text reads "And I saw as it was a sea of glass mingled with fire." McKean's trademark blurry sketches turn up on some pages, but there are a greater variety of visual styles on hand, from full-page paintings and photographic collages, to computerized mindscapes and disturbing paintings of each of the four riders of the apocalypse. Many of these pages achieve a sense of paintings-that-talk that is generally absent from the action-oriented, plot-derived graphics that accompany most comic book stories.

While *Violent Cases* and *Signal to Noise* appeared under small press imprints, *Mr. Punch* was published by DC's Vertigo line of mature reader comics. Even by Vertigo standards *Mr. Punch* is an unusual project, one that was presumably facilitated by Gaiman's growing fame as the guiding spirit behind *The Sandman.* Once again, the emphasis is on each page as a thing in itself rather than incessant narrative stimulation. In many pages McKean places dark gray borders between panels, which lends these passages the feel of a family portrait album. The panels themselves are mostly brown, sepia, and gray, with occasional discordant splash of green, purple or blue, depending on the storyline. It's an unusually bleak look for a major comics publisher. The story itself—which returns to Gaiman's childhood, when he is introduced to the time-honored secrets of Punch and Judy, by way of his grandfather's dilapidated seaside amusement arcade—is no lighter in tone than artwork. The story culminates, after all, in a miserable scene in which the arcade's pregnant "mermaid" is whacked in the stomach and face with a two-by-four by a shadowy figure (quite possibly a family member). *Mr. Punch* revisits such familiar Gaimanesque riffs as memory, uncertainty, incipient violence, and family mysteries, but it also introduces an ambivalent romance with archaic forms of English folk culture, a theme that also surfaces in *The Sandman.* While there may be less emphasis on formal experimentation in this book, there is never any danger that McKean's pages could be mistaken for anyone else's in comics.

Both the adult-oriented graphic novels described here and the illustrated books for younger readers referred to earlier are the products of an unusually long-lived creative partnership. Gaiman and McKean's careers have operated on slightly different tracks, however. In a 1993 interview, Gaiman said "Me and Dave, we're like Venn diagrams: There are places of intersection, but then we have completely different tastes and sensibilities going off on each side. I miss him appallingly, terribly. We only used to see each other once every couple of months, but we probably talked on the phone practically every night for years" (Thompson 68). While they continue to share a passion for taking comics in new directions, Gaiman exhibits a far greater fondness for genre. "I tend to like genres: I like to play with them and take them apart and put them back together," Gaiman said in the same interview. "But Dave, I think, feels that genres are essentially slightly silly things" (Thompson 68). Even his covers for *The Sandman,* while popular with many regular comic fans, looked quite unlike anything else on the racks. While McKean's dense, melancholy, and painterly covers invoked

a sense of mystery and sometimes horror, they did so without playing on horror comic conventions. Nor did they connect with the rest of the "DC universe" (DCU) in any obvious way.

*Black Orchid* is the only long form Gaiman-McKean collaboration that takes place within a mainstream comics environment. Lex Luthor, Swamp Thing, Poison Ivy, and other hardy DC perennials play supporting roles in a story that reintroduces readers to a pair of gentle, bioengineered flower creatures who share the power of flight. Gaiman seems especially attuned to the ecological underpinnings of the story, with its lyrical contrast between Luthor's looming office tower and the lush green forests of the Amazon. The story's final resolution is a little easy, perhaps, but some of the pages are stunning, with their mix of Gaiman's snappy dialogue and McKean's vivid greens and purples. In an interview with *Comics Forum,* Gaiman confessed that "*Orchid* has a lot of flaws. We were having to do our learning in public. We'd figured out our manifesto of how to do comics, and we were trying to apply it" (Lawley and Whitaker 59). McKean's characteristically bold page compositions looked cramped in a standard format comic book, and some of the plotting seemed forced. Two years later, Gaiman penned a four-part story called *The Books of Magic,* also for DC, which introduced a significant new character, the young magician Timothy Hunter, into the DCU. This book represented an enjoyable but similarly strained compromise between Gaiman's literary sensibility and the existing DC mythos and ethos. Gaiman's other DC universe stories are collected in *Green Lantern/Superman: Legend of the Green Flame* and *Neil Gaiman's Midnight Days.*

### THE SANDMAN AND RELATED PROJECTS

With *The Sandman,* Neil Gaiman was granted a license to construct an entire world (or, more accurately, entire worlds) of fairies, monsters, demons, humans, and ancient godlike creatures at the fringes of the DCU. He also retained a greater degree of control over his domain than creators had previously negotiated from the major companies, including the power to bring his own series to an end. "*Sandman* is a fantasy," Gaiman once said in an interview. "It wanders around and smudges the border of genre from time to time and is often historical; it will go off and very occasionally be horror. But mostly it's fantasy, that's what it is. It's a story about things that do not exist" (Groth 76). While some of the series' minor characters were already part of the DC universe, they were mostly obscure figures from non-superhero titles of the 1960s and 1970s who had been languishing in comic book limbo before Gaiman dusted them off and placed them within *The Sandman.* The key cast members are the seven Endless: Destiny, Death, Dream (i.e., the Sandman), Destruction, Desire, Despair, and Delirium, formerly known as Delight. With the partial exception of Destiny, they are all Gaiman's inventions. Each represent intrinsic aspects of the human condition, and as such they are older and more powerful than humanity's gods. It is suggested that the Endless will outlive humanity and that Death will outlive the universe itself. They regard themselves as members of a single family, but like all families they argue and bicker and quarrel.

In the course of the story we learn that Destruction has given up his role (he now dedicates himself to such pursuits as painting, writing and music), a dereliction of duty that unnerves some of his siblings, especially his brother Dream. We also find out that Desire has a penchant for stirring up trouble, which indirectly sets into motion the concluding story arc, in which Dream more or less allows himself to be snuffed out by "the kindly ones," the famous weird sisters of European mythology. The kindly ones take some pleasure in taking down one of the Endless, but another Dream soon takes his place. *The Sandman* closes with the first Dream's wake, in which various characters, human and non-human, come to terms with Dream's passing.

By making Dream, who is sometimes referred to as Morpheus, the main protagonist, Gaiman is able to write about stories themselves, the ways in which dreams, nightmares, and narratives exert a powerful hold on the contemporary imagination, even as modernity seeks to diminish myth in favor of science, logic, and instrumental reason. Myths, Gaiman insists, retain the power to tell us about ourselves. But according to Gaiman we don't always want to obtain that kind of knowledge. As a character named Rose Walker tells herself at the end of *The Doll's House* story arc, "the world's about as solid and reliable as a layer of scum on the top of a well of black water which goes down forever, and there are things in the depths that I don't even want to think about." Or as Gaiman said in one interview, "One of the things I wanted specifically to look at was, what does the twentieth century do with, to and about myth . . . myths and legends still have power; they get buried and forgotten, but they're like land-mines" (Lawley and Whitaker 51).

The first issue of *The Sandman* introduces Roderick Burgess, an eccentric English magus along the lines of Aleister Crowley, who attempts to kidnap Death via a pagan ceremony. While Death eludes them, Burgess and his followers manage to capture Dream, and for a period of seventy years, 1916 to 1986, Dream remains locked away—trapped and stripped of his powers—in the basement of an English manor house. The dreams of the twentieth century were as troubled as they were, it turns out, because the Sandman went missing. When Morpheus finally escapes his captors, his first thoughts are of revenge, and recovering the possessions that had been taken from him. Vengeance, for the king of dreams, is relatively easy to arrange; retrieving his belongings, and throne, proves a little more difficult.

Most difficult of all is the fact that his involuntary leave of absence leads him to reopen uncomfortable questions about his past, and his unbending personality structure, which generates unfamiliar feelings of remorse and misgiving. He especially regrets his decision to banish his one-time human lover, Nada, to Hell (on the grounds that she spurned him), and even more importantly, he feels guilty about the tragic disregard he has previously shown his son Orpheus. These feelings, and Morpheus's struggle to come to terms with their ramifications, motivate much of the series' meta-story, although there are numerous points where Gaiman slows things down and presents stories in which the Sandman plays a minor role or in which we see the Sandman in earlier incarnations, prior to his traumatic imprisonment.

"*Sandman* is incredibly traditional," (Lawley and Whitaker 55) Gaiman once admitted. Rather than trying to incite political action, or moral outrage, the comic spins a series of fine yarns, the kind that deserve a deep chair and a warm fire. In *The Sandman* Gaiman borrows freely from ancient fables, myths, and legends, and somehow fashions them into an appropriately oversized postmodern mythology for modern-day readers, complete with a sprawling setting and an eccentric cast of characters that lends itself to endless adventures in myth-making, where the reader's imagination becomes as important as the recorded stories themselves. At the same time, every story ever told is part of the Dreaming, the other-worldly realm ruled by Morpheus, and therefore every story is part of *The Sandman,* at least in theory—which allows Gaiman to incorporate everything from Elizabethan drama (William Shakespeare is featured in two stories and writes both *A Midsummer's Night Dream* and *The Tempest* at Morpheus' behest), to the countless books that have been dreamed rather than written down, which can only be found in Morpheus' library. The reason that Dream has to die, perhaps, is because new myths and stories are needed; but Dream can never die, at least not as long as there are dreamers.

As this suggests, the dream world, for Neil Gaiman, is a vital source of collective myths and stories rather than an expression of the subjugated forces of the id, as Sigmund Freud famously argued. Dreams, Gaiman suggests, are a kind of "shadow-truth" that haunt and inspire entire societies, rather than highly individualized experiences. Interestingly, Freud's name is never invoked in a self-consciously literary comics series that explores the relationship between stories, consciousness, and dreams. Arguably, *The Sandman* is more about what Freud referred to as the super-ego than the id, and it is at least debatable that the comic blurs any distinction between storytelling and dreaming, thus ignoring or downplaying the psychological dimensions of dreaming.

The shape of *The Sandman*'s larger story only gradually came into focus for readers, who were teased with hints of Dream's growing self-doubt throughout the course of the series. Two smaller-scale stories that proved especially popular with readers were **"Ramadan,"** illustrated by P. Craig Russell, and **"A Dream of a Thousand Cats,"** illustrated by Kelley Jones and Malcolm Jones III, in which alley cats dream of a world in which "no cats are killed by human caprice." Both stories confirm Gaiman's talent for crafting emotionally engaging characters, even or especially non-human ones, and they also exemplify the Dreaming's extraordinary flexibility as a storytelling device. Furthermore, they offer stories in which dreamers are represented as heroic figures, and important leaders, rather than easy marks. Gaiman's comics work is free of the cynical impulse that characterizes many contemporary comics, both alternative and mainstream.

Many readers were reportedly less enthusiastic about *A Game of You,* the fifth volume in *The Sandman* reprint series, which Gaiman has nevertheless described as a personal favorite. On one level this volume takes up the story of one of Dream's many responsibilities, which involves keeping an eye on "distant islets in the shoals of dream." One particular islet, where much of the drama unfolds, is a fantasyland for emotionally neglected girls, complete with princesses, evildoers, and talking stuffed animals. The fate of this remote skerry is determined in the course of the story. On another level the volume concerns a circle of eccentric New Yorkers, bohemian residents of the lower East Side, who make their way to the islet by way of lunar magic to assist their friend Barbie, who lives in their building. Each of these Manhattanites is struggling with issues of identity—from Barbie herself, who cannot say with any confidence where she belongs, to their neighbor George, who is not who or what he appears to be, to Barbie's good friend Wanda, a vivacious pre-op transsexual. The reader also meets the memorable witch Thessaly, who was "born in the day of greatest darkness, in the year the bear totem was shattered" and who certainly knows her way around a corpse.

Witchcraft occupies a pivotal position in this story, as it does in several *Sandman* issues, and as is true in the case of the Dreaming the reader finds that magic is not without its perils, and terrors. But the most powerful parts of the story have to do with good old punk rock New York, its rhythms and personalities, rather than fantasy or the supernatural. Some readers may have been turned off by the book's uncompromising sexual politics, its unconventional mishmash of imaginary worlds and street scenes, and its unapologetic gore (what happens in the bathtub is not for the faint of heart). But it nevertheless showcases Gaiman's talent for placing fully realized, three-dimensional characters in unworldly and some might say ungodly situations and letting them discover for themselves how dangerous things are "out there" and how little they (and we) know.

The artwork in *The Sandman* is usually excellent, although it is also tremendously varied. It ranges from Marc Hempel's argumentative, staccato lines to P. Craig Russell's lovingly detailed renderings; from Jill Thompson's engagingly busy pages to Mike Allred's colorful hippie vibe. Some of the earlier stories are firmly rooted in horror, and these feature murky pages by Mike Dringenberg and Malcolm Jones III, who specialize in dark corridors and ghastly visages. In some of the historical episodes, such as those having to do with medieval or early modern England, the artwork is far more refined and delicate. The English artist Bryan Talbot proved a splendidly muscular choice for handling ancient Rome in **"August,"** in which Emperor Augustus spends a day disguised as a beggar in the marketplace. Gaiman specifically asked each illustrator he worked with what kinds of things they liked to draw, and then tried to accommodate their requests in his stories. Judging from "August," Talbot may have specifically expressed an interest in drawing pock marked faces amid the sculptural splendors the ancient world.

In 1993 DC launched a new imprint, Vertigo, which was designed to take advantage of the renewed interest in more intellectually ambitious comics that the British wave, Neil Gaiman very much included, helped generated. In part this move reflected DC's unabashed interest in building on the success of *The Sandman* itself, and in the intervening years Vertigo has issued a stream of monthly series, one-off titles, and mini-series based in and on the Dreaming. While DC has agreed not to publish any stories about the Endless, unless written by Gaiman himself, this has left ample room for stories about Faerie, dreams, Timothy Hunter, and Merv Pumpkinhead (the dream world's wise-cracking handyman). DC also spared no expense in packaging and promoting Gaiman's recent *Sandman*-related titles, *The Sandman: The Dream Hunters,* and *The Sandman: Endless Nights.* While Vertigo should not be considered synonymous with Gaiman-derived fantasy, a substantial share of the company's output over the past decade has been directly based on worlds and characters that Gaiman introduced in his best known title.

Many observers rate *The Sandman* in particular, and Neil Gaiman's comics and graphic novels in general, as milestones in the development of literary-minded comics. Gaiman's work is beginning to attract attention from scholars and researchers in literature and media studies. (Rauch 2003; Sanders 1997; see also www.holycow/dreaming/academia) At least one cultural historian, however, has argued that Gaiman's writings lack the political bite of other UK comics writers, such as Alan Moore and Grant Morrison. "The quality of Gaiman's writing, his inventiveness, his wit, his sensitivity," Newsinger concedes, "all combined to produce a contemporary romantic hero, Morpheus, Lord of Dreams, the protagonist of a series of classic Gothic tales. There is, however, another reason for *The Sandman*'s cult status and critical acclaim. The comic was conservative with a small 'c', resolutely middle class in its appeal. It posed no challenges, cast down no icons, trashed no temples, violated no taboos. Instead it provided a conservative exploration of the 'human condition', of our existential predicament, abstracted from any social or political context. This is certainly not to dispute the quality of Gaiman's writing or the pleasures to be got from it, but rather to point to a dimension of his achievement that is not generally recognized: *The Sandman* is horror for the middle classes" (Newsinger 81).

Gaiman would probably accept the charge of showing scant interest in explicitly political topics. As he once conceded in a long interview with Gary Groth: "Would I describe myself as a rebel? No!" (Groth 85) Feminists might point to the substantial number of strong female characters who feature in Gaiman's stories (up to and including Eve, of Adam and Eve fame, who lives on the edge of the Dreaming), and environmentalists might reasonably view Gaiman as one of their own, given his obvious appreciation for animals and nature. But Newsinger is onto something when he contrasts Gaiman, who is at root an entertainer, albeit an unusually inventive one, to the more agitational minded members of his pop-literary generation. At the same time, there are plenty of hints that Gaiman holds to a social democratic sensibility that does not exactly command the center stage in U.S. politics. As Gaiman recently told a web-blogger: "Of course, when stood next to the choice of American political parties ("So, would you like Right Wing, or Supersized Right Wing with Extra Fries?") my English fuzzy middle-of-the-roadness probably translates easily as bomb-throwing Trotskyist, but when I get to chat to proper lefties like Ken McLeod or China Mieville I feel myself retreating rapidly back into the woffly *Guardian*-reading why-can't-people-just-be-nice-to-each-otherhood of the politically out of his depth" (See nielsenhayden.com/electrolite/archives/002700.html).

CONCLUSION

Many fine writers and artists have contributed to the vitalization of the comics medium in recent years. Even without Gaiman's persuasive voice it seems likely that

greater numbers of comics would have been marketed to older readers with a taste for something other than pulp formulas and percussive, four color fisticuffs. Vertigo, or something very much like it, probably would have occurred to the decision makers at DC, even without the example of *The Sandman* to work from. And it is difficult to see how the so-called alternative wing of the comics industry, exemplified by the prize-winning output of Fantagraphics, and Drawn and Quarterly, would be affected one way or the other by Gaiman's hypothetical absence, except insofar as *The Sandman* helped push readers to try out other, non-super hero titles that emphasize good writing and visuals rather than splash pages and witless score-settling. *The Sandman,* in other words, may have fostered a taste for good comics that worked and continues to work to the benefit of the independents, even if they mainly traffic in autobiography, comedy, politics, and deadpan irony rather than genre based entertainment.

In part, Neil Gaiman's special contribution lies in his deft rehabilitation of the fantasy genre. While there are not nearly as many fantasy titles on the market as superhero stories, the genre nevertheless received an enormous push by *The Sandman* and its various spin-offs. After all, fantasy offers a distinct set of problems and scenarios for artists and writers to grapple with, and it almost certainly holds greater appeal for many older readers, and female readers, than superheroes. To the extent that more women are now reading comics it is in large measure due to Gaiman's constructive influence. Ongoing efforts to rethink and transform comics presumably depend on appealing to new cohorts of readers with new kinds of stories. *The Sandman,* more than any other comic book of the 1990s, helped realize this goal.

The Gaiman-McKean collaborations, as reflected in *Violent Cases, Signal to Noise,* and *Mr. Punch,* also constitute a major strand in Gaiman's comic book legacy. It is in these volumes, as much or more so than in *The Sandman,* that Gaiman realized the lofty ambitions that he and Dave McKean articulated when they first set out to turn the world of comics upside down. The fact that Gaiman walks with ease between two worlds—on the one hand, the world of serial, genre based fiction, and on the other, the world of edgy, experimental art—is an indication of his category-defying achievements. Gaiman and McKean have both accomplished more than they had any right to expect.

*Bibliography*

COLLABORATIONS WITH DAVE MCKEAN

Neil Gaiman and Dave McKean. *Black Orchid,* books 1-3. New York: DC, 1988-1989.

————. *Coraline.* New York: HarperCollins, 2002.

———. *The Day I Swapped My Dad for Two Goldfish.* Clarkston, GA: White Wolf Publishing, 1997.

———. *Mr. Punch. [The Tragical Comedy or Comical Tragedy of Mr. Punch: A Romance]* New York: DC/Vertigo, 1994.

———. *Signal to Noise.* Milwaukee, OR: Dark Horse, 1992.

———. *The Wolves in the Walls.* HarperCollins, 2003.

THE SANDMAN LIBRARY AND RELATED TITLES

The ten *Sandman* volumes:

I. *Preludes and Nocturnes*

II. *The Doll's House*

III. *Dream Country*

IV. *Season of Mists*

V. *A Game of You*

VI. *Fables & Reflections*

VII. *Brief Lives*

VIII. *World's End*

IX. *The Kindly Ones*

X. *The Wake*

Neil Gaiman. *The Sandman: Preludes and Nocturnes.* New York: DC Comics, 1991. Collecting *The Sandman,* issues 1-8. Art by Sam Keith, Mike Dringenberg, and Malcolm Jones III.

———. *The Sandman: The Doll's House.* New York: DC Comics, 1990. Collecting *The Sandman,* issues 8-16. Art by Mike Dringenberg and Malcolm Jones III.

———. *The Sandman: Dream Country.* New York: DC Comics, 1991. Collecting *The Sandman,* issues 17-20. Art by Kelley Jones, Charles Vess, Colleen Doran, and Malcolm Jones III.

———. *The Sandman: Season of Mists.* New York: DC Comics, 1992. Collecting *The Sandman,* issues 21-28. Art by Kelley Jones, Mike Dringenberg, Malcolm Jones III, Matt Wagner, Dick Giordano, George Pratt, and P. Craig Russell.

———. *The Sandman: A Game of You.* New York: DC Comics, 1993. Collecting *The Sandman,* issues 32-37. Art by Shawn McManus, Colleen Doran, Bryan Talbot, George Pratt, Stan Woch, and Dick Giordano.

———. *The Sandman: Brief Lives.* New York: DC Comics, 1993. Collecting *The Sandman,* issues 41-49. Art by Jill Thompson and Vince Locke.

———. *The Sandman: Fables and Recollections.* New York DC Comics, 1993. Collecting *The Sandman,* issues 29-31, 38-40, 50, *Sandman Special* 1, and *Vertigo*

*Preview.* Art by Bryan Talbot, Stan Woch, P. Craig Russell, Shawn McManus, John Watkiss, Jill Thompson, Duncan Eagleson, and Kent Williams.

———. *The Sandman: World's End.* New York: DC Comics, 1994. Collecting *The Sandman,* issues 51-56. Art by Michael Allred, Gary Amaro, Mark Buckingham, Dick Giordano, Tony Harris, Steve Leialoha, Vince Locke, Shea Anton Pensa, Alec Stevens, Bryan Talbot, John Watkiss, and Michael Zulli.

———. *The Sandman: The Kindly Ones.* New York: DC Comics, 1996. Collecting *The Sandman,* 57-69. Art by Marc Hempel, Richard Case, D'Israeli, Teddy Kristiansen, Glyn Dillon, Charles Vess, Dean Ormston, and Kevin Nowlan.

———. *The Sandman: The Wake.* New York: DC Comics, 1997. Collecting *The Sandman,* issues 70-75. Art by Michael Zulli, Jon J. Muth and Charles Vess.

———. *Death: The High Cost of Living.* New York: DC/Vertigo, 1994. Art by Chris Bachalo, Mark Buckingham, and Dave McKean.

———. *Death: The Time of Your Life.* DC/Vertigo, 1997. Art by Chris Bachalo, Mark Buckingham, and Mark Pennington.

———. *The Sandman: The Dream Hunters.* New York: DC/Vertigo, 1999. Art by Yoshitaka Amano.

———. *The Sandman: Endless Nights.* New York: DC/Vertigo, 2003. Art by Glenn Fabry, Milo Manara, Miguelanxo Prado, Frank Quitely, P. Craig Russell, Bill Sienkiewicz, and Barron Storey.

OTHER WORKS BY NEIL GAIMAN

Neil Gaiman. *American Gods.* New York: William Morrow, 2001.

———. *The Books of Magic,* parts 1-4. New York: DC Comics, 1990-1991. Art by John Bolton, Scott Hampton, Charles Vess, and Paul Johnson.

———. *Green Lantern/Superman: Legend of the Green Flame.* New York: DC, 2000. Art by Michael D. Allred and Terry Austin, Mark Buckingham, John Totleben, Matt Wagner, Eric Shanower and Arthur Adams, Jim Aparo, Kevin Nowlan, and Jason Little.

———. *Harlequin Valentine.* Milwaukee, OR: Dark Horse, 2001. Art by John Bolton.

———. *Neil Gaiman's Midnight Days.* New York: DC/Vertigo, 1999. Art by Richard Piers Rayner, Dave McKean, Mike Hoffman, Mike Mignola, Steve Bissette, Kim DeMulder, and John Totleben.

———. *Neverwhere.* New York: Avon Books, 1998.

———. *Smoke and Mirrors: Short Fictions and Illusions.* New York: Perennial, 2001.

———. *Stardust.* New York: Perennial, 2001.

Neil Gaiman and Terry Pratchett. *Good Omens.* New York: Ace Books, 1996.

Neil Gaiman and P. Craig Russell. *Murder Mysteries.* Milwaukee, OR: Dark Horse, 2002.

SECONDARY WORKS

Bender, Hy. *The Sandman Companion.* New York: DC/Vertigo, 1999.

Groth, Gary. "Interview with Neil Gaiman." *The Comics Journal* 169 (July 1994): 54-108.

Lawley, Guy and Steve Whitaker. "Interview with Neil Gaiman, Part One." *Comics Forum* 1:1 (spring 1992): 24-46.

———. "Interview with Neil Gaiman, Part Two." *Comics Forum* 1:2 (summer 1992): 46-59.

Newsinger, John. *The Dredd Phenomenon: Comics and Contemporary Society.* Bristol: Libertarian Education, 1999.

Rauch, Stephen. *Neil Gaiman's "The Sandman" and Joseph Campbell: In Search of the Modern Myth.* Holicong, PA: Wildside Press, 2003.

Sanders, Joe. "Of Parents and Children and Dreams in Neil Gaiman's *Mr. Punch* and *The Sandman.*" *Foundation: The International Review of Science Fiction* 71 (autumn 1997).

Thompson, Kim. "Interview with Neil Gaiman." *The Comics Journal* 155 (January 1993): 64-83.

---

# FURTHER READING

## Criticism

Bender, Hy. *The Sandman Companion.* New York: DC Comics, 1999, 273 p.

Provides an overview of Gaiman's work on the *Sandman* series, including plot summaries, interviews with Gaiman, and anecdotes about the stories.

Gaiman, Neil, and George Khoury. "Gaijin Mononoke: An Interview with Neil Gaiman." *Creative Screenwriting* 6, no. 6 (November-December 1999): 63-5.

Provides discussion with Gaiman regarding his English language dialogue adaptation for the Japanese animated film *Miyazaki Hayao* (*Princess Mononoke*).

Goldweber, David E. "Mr. Punch, Dangerous Savior." *International Journal of Comic Art* 1, no. 1 (spring-summer 1999): 157-70.

Presents analysis and discussion of plot, style, and themes within Gaiman's *The Tragical Comedy or Comical Tragedy of Mr. Punch.*

McCarty, Michael, ed. "Good Omens: An Interview with Neil Gaiman." In *Giants of the Genre,* pp. 46-52. Holicong, Pa.: Wildside Press, 2003.

Brief interview with Gaiman focusing on his novel *Good Omens,* his children's work *Coraline,* his feelings about writer Douglas Adams, and an interview postscript describing a reading and book signing in 2001.

Sanders, Joe. "Of Parents and Children and Dreams in Neil Gaiman's *Mr. Punch* and *The Sandman.*" *Foundation: The International Review of Science Fiction* 71 (autumn 1997): 18-32.

Focuses on parent-child relationships as portrayed in various stories within *The Sandman* and *The Tragical Comedy or Comical Tragedy of Mr. Punch.*

# Shena Mackay
## 1944-

Scottish novelist, short-story and novella writer, and editor.

The following entry presents an overview of Mackay's career through 2003.

## INTRODUCTION

Mackay is recognized as a talented novelist and short fiction writer. Her work focuses on eccentric and complex individuals struggling with poverty, alienation, and despair. Critics praise her fiction for its dark and absurdist humor and its adroit use of detail.

## BIOGRAPHICAL INFORMATION

Mackay was born in Edinburgh, Scotland, in 1944. When she was a young child, her family settled in Shoreham, Kent, England. Later the family moved to southeast London, where she grew up in an urbane, literary environment. Unhappy in school, she left when she was sixteen years old. Mackay was already interested in writing, and won a poetry prize right after she left school. She worked in an antique shop owned by the parents of art critic David Sylvester and managed by playwright Frank Marcus. Through her friendship with these two men, Mackay was introduced to the London art world of the 1960s; she became acquainted with such renowned artists as Lucian Freud, Francis Bacon, Henry Moore, and David Hockney. Many critics have noted the painterly qualities of Mackay's fiction. In 1964 a collection of two of her novellas, *Dust Falls on Eugene Schlumburger and Toddler on the Run,* was published. She was an immediate sensation in London literary and social circles. After her marriage in 1964, she published less frequently. In fact, after the publication of her novel *An Advent Calendar* in 1971, she did not publish another book until 1983. She did continue to write short stories during that period. In 1980 she became a friend to novelist Brigid Brophy, who helped her find a publisher for her book, *A Bowl of Cherries* (1984). Her 1995 novel, *The Orchard on Fire,* was on the shortlist for the prestigious Booker Prize. Mackay lives in south London, and remains a well-established literary figure in England.

## MAJOR WORKS

In Mackay's first novel, *Music Upstairs* (1965), she explores the bohemian life of 1960s London through the emotional and sexual relationship between a young English girl from the suburbs and her two landlords, Pam and Lenny. *The Advent Calendar* touches on such controversial topics as cannibalism, pedophilia, adultery, and animal cruelty. In *A Bowl of Cherries,* Mackay explores the issue of redemption through the relationship of twin brothers: Rex, a successful novelist, and Stanley, his poor and friendless brother. When it is revealed that Rex's literary success is a fraud—his popular novel was actually written by Stanley—a wealth of family secrets is exposed. Considered one of her best works, *Redhill Rococo* (1986) is an amusing story of the love affair between the ex-con Luke and the prostitute Pearl Slattery. Mackay's next novel, *Dunedin* (1992), chronicles the hard-luck lives of the Mackenzie family from 1902 New Zealand to 1989 London. *The Orchard on Fire* focuses on the intense friendship between two English girls, April and Ruby. Both are being abused; Ruby is physically beaten by her father and April is being molested by an elderly man in the neighborhood. The novel ends with an embittered April, now much older, reflecting on the importance of her friendship with Ruby. Mackay's 1998 novel, *The Artist's Widow,* is set within the contemporary art scene in London. Her latest novel, *Heligoland* (2000), follows the lives of several aging artists living in a communal, utopian community. Critics praise the sharp and complex cast of characters in the book. In addition to her novels, Mackay has received favorable critical attention for her short stories. Collections such as *Babies in Rhinestones and Other Stories* (1983) and *The World's Smallest Unicorn: Stories* (1999) highlight what critics consider Mackay's satirical view of modern culture as well as her poignant and insightful perspective on human relationships.

## CRITICAL RECEPTION

Mackay has been widely praised for her lovely prose style and her intelligent and evocative fiction. In particular, reviewers applaud her effective use of satire, dark humor, eroticism, and dialogue. Her powers of description are considered well developed, and many commentators have discussed the accurate and shrewd use of detail in her novels, novellas, and short stories. Critics contend that she creates compassionate and vivid portrayals of people living in desolation, isolation, and desperation. However, some reviewers have accused Mackay of failing to create likable characters, particularly male ones, and denigrate the bleak circumstances and plaintive tone of her work. Her combination of absurdist humor, pathos, and compassion has led some commentators to compare her work with that of Charles Dickens. Mackay is regarded as a distinctive and gifted voice in contemporary English literature.

## PRINCIPAL WORKS

*Dust Falls on Eugene Schlumburger and Toddler on the Run* (novellas) 1964
*Music Upstairs* (novel) 1965
*Old Crow* (novel) 1967
*An Advent Calendar* (novel) 1971
*Babies in Rhinestones and Other Stories* (short stories) 1983
*A Bowl of Cherries* (novel) 1984
*Redhill Rococo* (novel) 1986
*Dreams of Dead Women's Handbags* (short stories) 1987
*Dunedin* (novel) 1992
*The Laughing Academy* (short stories) 1993
*Collected Short Stories* (short stories) 1994
*The Orchard on Fire* (novel) 1995
*The Artist's Widow* (novel) 1998
*The World's Smallest Unicorn: Stories* (short stories) 1999
*Heligoland* (novel) 2000

## CRITICISM

### Clive Jordan (review date 2 July 1971)

SOURCE: Jordan, Clive. "Dislocations." *New Statesman and Society* 82 (2 July 1971): 24.

[*In the following excerpt, Jordan provides a favorable review of* An Advent Calendar.]

*An Advent Calendar* provides a slight but raffishly entertaining excursion to the rundown territory Shena Mackay has staked out as her own. Here again, observed rather less cruelly than before, is the quagmire of a ghastly urban sub-culture. 'Marguerite lay in bed thinking of the long road of days that led to a goat's dripping beard in East Finchley.' However improbable, the logic of the road of days is remorseless. Here it brings an impoverished young family to spend the pre-Christmas period with a decrepit uncle, the goat's

owner. The resultant complexities include the wife's affair with the goat's vet, and the seduction of a dreadful 15-year-old schoolgirl by a middle-aged poet. I particularly admire the way Shena Mackay makes it appear that both people and things have been formed from the same messy organic substance. The 'wild white drowned hair of the spaghetti' is not too fanciful when we already know that the meat sauce contains a human finger.

### Hugh Barnes (review date 6 February 1986)

SOURCE: Barnes, Hugh. "Scenes from British Life." *London Review of Books* 8, no. 2 (6 February 1986): 7.

[*In the following excerpt, Barnes offers a mixed review of* Redhill Rococo.]

*Redhill Rococo* experiments in a little-known genre: the 'Condition of Surrey' novel. The main feature of the style is the barrage of acronyms and initials facing the reader: DHSS, YTS, HMP, C of E, WPC, SDP; even UCCA plays a part and among vegetarians $B_{12}$ gets an honourable mention. At PTA meetings mothers abbreviate each other blithely, into Mrs H-J or Mrs S; and trendy Christians daub their surroundings—a Ricky Nelson poster comes in for special punishment, a macabre touch—with the graffito 'GOD RULES OK.' You get from the novel what you don't expect: Pearl Slattery (Mrs S) strikes a radical blow against the State. Towards the end she turns up for work at Snashfold's Sweet Factory to find locked gates and sleeping machinery. It is suggested that the plant has shut down due to the recession: a nail-file in the butterscotch and a plaster in the Jelly Teddies can't have helped. Anxious about the upkeep of her family, about her son's unpunctuality on his Youth Training Scheme and about her daughter who has eloped with the Bible-punchers, Pearl opts to go out in a blaze of glory—or rather a shop steward takes that option for her. Her arrest for criminal damage to Snashfold's property equips her neighbours with an unfamiliar item of conversation—martyrdom to class struggle.

Mackay excels at a comedy of self-abasement, intermittently deprecating and cruel. But unhappily she has a propensity for overkill. Bad jokes sneak in and the insubstantial narrative indicates weakness. Pearl's lodger attempts to seduce her but in vain, despite a liberal sprinkling of love-potion (purchased from Redhill's obeah man) in her Horlicks. The Slattery children gesture at rebellion or disappoint, and a climax that involves Pearl escaping in a Range Rover seems relatively pointless. At other times Mackay shows herself to be susceptible to patches of purple prose concerning liberation. In this context such an idea, although she milks it for a laugh or two, appears whimsical and out of place.

## Anne Duchêne (review date 14 February 1986)

SOURCE: Duchêne, Anne. "The Distant Sound of Breaking Glass." *Times Literary Supplement* (14 February 1986): 163.

[*In the following review, Duchêne commends the combination of humor and sadness she finds in* Redhill Rococo.]

In Shena Mackay's new novel [*Redhill Rococo*], the fuddled vicar, finding himself at a wedding reception, toasts "the horse and groom"; the local librarian gives the over-seventies double fines for returning books late, as they should know better; the local paper reports "CO-OP RAIDED: NOTHING TAKEN"; a cookery book is called "Take aLeek". . . . It all sounds rather like a script for *The Two Ronnies*; and yet, like all Shena Mackay's novels, it is also painfully sad.

For twenty years now (dust-jacket photographs suggest she began publishing around the age of fifteen), Mackay has written with exuberant glee and compassionate horror about people living in suburban sorriness and desolation, gasping for what Forster called "a breathing-hole for the human spirit"; and she has always held both the exuberance and the compassion suspended in her writing, not allowing them to settle into any new composition that might commit her either to a purely, surrealistically funny novel, or to a distressingly sad and serious one. This formula does not make for a seamless novel, and confines her to a minor genre; but it furnishes a great deal to be enjoyed and admired along the way.

*Redhill Rococo* is set in her favourite stamping-ground, suburbia's Surrey outposts. Redhill is presented as "in essence a carpark, or a series of carparks strung together with links of smouldering rubble and ragwort, buddleia and willowherb" (the time is late summer), and many of the short sections into which the short chapters are divided stamp out its properties pretty harshly: "Saturday night in Redhill; from Busby's the distant sound of breaking glass, a short scream, a police siren. . . . Sunday morning: a pale pinkish-yellow plasmatic smell of half-cooked meat hung over the back gardens. In the Slatterys' kitchen their Sunday lunch, five tubs of pot noodles, steamed gently . . .". Demolition and polystyrene prevail.

Just down the road, but in another socio-economic world, is genteel Reigate (where the author herself lives), with bijou cottages, kempt gardens, and "bedizened ladies discreetly buying gin" at Cullens, or putting on rubber gloves to fold their rotary dryers into plastic covers. The two worlds are to meet, because children attend the same schools. Chiefly, we see the Redhill mother, Pearl, a brave slattern and defeated romantic, who works in a local sweet-factory. As a girl, daughter of a level-crossing keeper whose wife defected, she attended Tonbridge Girls' Grammar School, where poverty constrained her to wear wellingtons throughout the school year and all its activities. Now, she wishes life could be "more like *The Bells of St Mary's,* where Bing Crosby tucked Barry Fitzgerald up in bed, crooning an Irish lullaby". The Samaritans hung up on her when she confessed to eating fried bread while they talked; the local library's information officer, when she telephoned to ask the Meaning of Life, promised to call back, but never did.

Pearl's present husband, Jack Slattery, is in prison. She does not visit, but sends one postcard. They aren't actually married, but she and their children carry his name—Sean, a punk with a heavy line in irony, Cherry, taking A-levels, and Tiffany, a pre-pubertal drum-majorette. Sometimes she is visited by the child of her first marriage, a brown young man called Elvis, his black wife, a nurse, called Precious, and their two small black daughters. Now and then, with dignified repugnance, Pearl sleeps, for financial reasons, with the local publican, whose tongue is "like a slug in her ear".

The Reigate mother, Helen Headley-Jones, drives a Range Rover, distributes Meals on Wheels, wears a *Guardian* jogging-suit, and makes pastry on a marble slab; also "toilet rolls in the shape of crinoline ladies in delicate shades of green and mauve and yellow foam rubber" for SDP sales. "Helen tried hard to be good." The lack of satisfaction this achieves bewilders her, and also her husband, who recommends she find herself a new dog. (Jeremy's birthday dinner—Helen has given him "personalized golf-tees"—with their daughters in an Indian restaurant is a beautifully modulated Reigate set-piece.)

Into the Slattery household, as a lodger, stumbles Luke, aged seventeen, after Borstal. A nice boy, he over-reacted to the "ante-chamber of Death" in the local sub-post-office where pensions were being loquaciously claimed, and feigned a hold-up with a toy pistol off the shelves: one of his many jokes that miscarry. He doesn't want to return to his home in nearby Purley because his mother ("hadn't she been nice to him once?") now lives in the bath, sleeping at night on piles of towels, and his father, the Rev Ichabod Ribbons, has taken to the cooking sherry after being evicted from his church by the evangelical curate and the "waves of ecumenical laughter" engendered during services. ("There was a lot of kissing after Communion, and what the Vicar found hardest to bear was that they all looked so damned happy.")

Various things happen. Luke falls in thoroughly unrequited love with Pearl. The sweet-factory closes. The curate falls in love with Cherry. None of this matters much Plot, as usual with this author, is pretty perfunctory: detail is all, and the seeping desolation it communicates, along with the cheerfulness. Most of the characters are imprisoned in a kind of atomic isolation, only now and then bumping into one another. They breach this isolation, fitfully; Pearl and Cherry, for instance, have an "old easy love", almost forgotten under the detritus of life, and at the end Pearl and Helen draw together in their common perplexity. The author turns a gentle eye on them; and her very gentlest on youth, the only straggly seedling of hope which she allows. Luke is as yet undefeated, and still believes his own wit and charm are irresistible; Cherry still hopes to go to university.

One cannot feel much hope, though, that their goodness will not be soiled and wasted, with time, like that of their elders. This is a very black comedy, in which the hearts of gold glint like mica. The brightness it does give off, and which suffuses it as one reads, comes from the author's endearing inability to resist a joke or to refrain from going too far, so that her frightening view topples over into preposterousness—Pearl's wellies, Helen's toilet-roll covers, Luke's mother in the bath. One might doubtless take Mackay to task for writing a book in which the impurities rise so exuberantly to the surface. But, if England has to sink giggling into the sea, she contributes a great deal to the cruel comedy of decomposition.

## Adam Mars-Jones (review date 21 August 1987)

SOURCE: Mars-Jones, Adam. "Running through the Recipes." *Times Literary Supplement* (21 August 1987): 897.

[*In the following review, Mars-Jones offers a mixed assessment of the stories in* Dreams of Dead Women's Handbags, *asserting that Mackay's "faults are intermittent, her virtues—her eye, her inventiveness—constant."*]

Moving as it does from the sombre to the absurdly trivial without becoming unambiguously comic, the splendid title of Shena Mackay's new collection [*Dreams of Dead Women's Handbags*] well represents the tonal range of the book. Sometimes she invokes the simplicities of melodrama or pathos, sometimes she transforms them at the last moment into some more sophisticated compound.

The title story is unusual in falling off from the eerie confidence of its opening: "It was a black evening bag sequined with salt. . . . This image, the wreckage of a dream beached on the morning, would not float away; as empty as an open shell, the black bivalve emitted a silent howl of despair; clouds passed through its mir-

ror." In the story, the dreamer—a writer of mystery novels—imagines the dream to be a fiction-germ stirring, and waits for it to root itself in a plot or a cast of characters. Mackay's parallel attempt to derive a story from the dream produces some fine passages of surrealistic unease, as the mystery writer encounters minor madness and coincidence on her way by train to a reading of her work, but lapses into an almost wilful baldness when the dream turns out to be a memory of the writer's innocent killing of her parents as a child—not the sort of thing that even the most professionally productive unconscious could mistake for the first glimmerings of Detective Inspector Hartshorn's next case.

The short story is in many ways an unforgiving form, which calls like any tricky recipe for careful regulation of temperature and timing. But a story can also be a salvageable souffle, whose sagging texture can be restored by a gust of invention even on the way to the table. An example is the story **"Violets and Strawberries in the Snow",** an account of an alcoholic ex-writer spending Christmas in a mental hospital, which is almost pure cliché throughout. The writer is visited by his three daughters, who put a brave face on things until one of them inadvertently sums up the situation with the words, "Satsumas are horrible this year." After their visit the writer sits down to write a story with that title: "It would not be very good, he knew, but at least it would come from that pulpy, sodden satsuma that was all that remained of his heart." This is Mackay at her most over-explicit, her least respectful of the balance that is struck in any story between the said and the unsaid.

But the story is saved by her manipulation of her own more oblique title phrase, first when the daughters enter: "they came in, smelling of fresh air and rain, with unseasonal daffodils and chocolates, like children, he thought, in a fairytale, sent by their cruel stepmother up the mountainside to find violets and strawberries in the snow". There is a piercing poignancy in the way the character sees his children's visit more easily in terms of the fulfilment of a bizarre quest than as a natural expression of feelings.

Then, after they have left, the phrase recurs with its terms reversed, as the character sees in memory "his children smiling and waving at the door, their resolute backs as they walked to the car concealing their wounds under their coats, forgiving and brave, and carrying his own weak and dissolute genes in their young and beautiful bodies. Violets and strawberries in the snow."

Most of these stories are brief, little more than ten pages. **"All the Pubs in Soho"** is by some way the longest and the most substantial. It tells the story of summer 1965 as it affects eight-year-old Joe, bullied and ignored at home, who finds something like friendship with Arthur and Guido, a couple who move into a cottage in the village. There is nothing about a child's point of view likely to defeat a writer of Shena Mackay's quality, but she seems reluctant in general to commit herself—either to fully inhabiting a character's point of view or to maintaining a fixed distance from it—in a way that hampers this particular story. The first paragraph, for instance, describes with an adult's aesthetic scrupulousness (flowers resembling "blue and copper velvety kitten's faces freaked with black") Joe's misinterpretation of the words "those bloody pansies", which refer in fact to Arthur and Guido. Since Joe's age has yet to be revealed, the effect is curiously irrelevant and confusing.

There is more to be revealed about Joe than age. Joe is actually Josephine, but refers to herself—and is referred to by the narrative voice—as a boy. Arthur and Guido guess this secret before the reader is likely to do so. Joe's resentment of her gender and the limitations it imposes is focused on her academic future, since the school her parents have chosen for her has a uniform which will prevent her from equivocating. She will be fatally a tomboy in a skirt.

The story builds to a climax as the school term approaches, and as Arthur and Guido's stay in the village comes to an abrupt end. But along the way Shena Mackay produces some of her few clumsy sentences:

> The child from a house where a veneer of anxiety lay on every surface like dust, where at any moment a bark might rip up comics and scatter toys, where a fist thumping the table might make cups leap in fear vomiting their contents on to the tablecloth, just as Joe had once been sick when his father caught the side of his head with his knuckles and where Mummy's forehead wrinkled like the skin on cocoa and her chin puckered in fear and placation, expected every domestic disclosure between two adults to degenerate into a battle in which by being co-opted to one side, he was considered the enemy by the other, and so always ended as the loser whoever else was in power when a truce was called.

Even this disastrously rambling sentence is not a ruin but a ramshackle, uninhabitable mansion that could easily be subdivided into a number of splendid flats. Shena Mackay's faults are intermittent, her virtues—her eye, her inventiveness—constant. They give a reliable pleasure.

**Sara Maitland (review date 28 August 1987)**

SOURCE: Maitland, Sara. "Pain Killer." *New Statesman* 114, no. 2944 (28 August 1987): 21-2.

[*In the following review, Maitland derides the plaintive tone and psychological density of the stories in* Dreams of Dead Women's Handbags.]

Shena Mackay has an uncomfortably accurate and shrewd eye for the details of bourgeois life, and an appropriately shrewd and elegant style to tell us what she has seen. This is a combination that suits the satirist well and in *Redhill Rococo,* her last novel, she showed how well she could handle satire: hilarity without loss of compassion is a rare and lovely thing.

But it works less well in this collection of stories—because here Mackay is not, I think, trying to be funny, though too many sentences do stretch longingly towards a snappy, witty conclusion. Real pain and madness lurk within almost all these stories: the pain and madness of loneliness, isolation and failure. And there is something almost plaintive in the tone—as though the stories themselves, or at least the characters in them, know and fear that they may be laughed at and feel they don't deserve it. Are we expected to laugh at poor Miss Agnew, doomed, by the death of her woman lover, to live out her life despised, along with an odd group of other social exiles, on an upper story of a seaside hotel in **'Where the Carpet Ends'**? Or at the agony of a writer's loss of faith in her own talent in **'The Thirty First of October'**? Or at the fierce intensity and pyromanic despair of poor little Joe, misunderstood child, who finds herself a frail friendship with two artistic homosexuals in **'All the Pubs in Soho'** (my favourite of this collection)?

Mackay compounds her problems of tone by taking a very firm hand and insisting, too much, on a rigorous social realism. Many of the stories—the title one, for example, or **'The Most Beautiful Dress in the World'**, in which the conflict between maternal love and creative self-fulfilment leads to the disintegration of the protagonist—end up by 'explaining' too much. As in the gothic novels of the early 19th century, everything has to have a clear and literal explanation; dream and imagination are clearly separated from the 'real world' and their own reality is thus denied, along with the imaginative capacity of the reader. I actually do not need to know whether the mayhem committed by the mother in **'The Most Beautiful Dress'** *really* happened, and I certainly do not want to have my experience of her panic distanced by the unnecessary and clumsy intrusion of the police force.

Since, for most of Mackay's characters, imaginary life is central, crucial to their experience, it is almost mean of her to drag them continually back into social realism. Even in the most supernatural of the stories, such as **'Perpetual Spinach'**, where the insensitivity of some gentrifying yuppies towards their aged neighbours is appropriately punished, the ending is laboured lest the reader miss the point. The characters, the readers and the potency of the imagination itself: all deserve more respect.

So, despite the accuracy and the delicious prose, this collection left me uneasy: not only in the way that it is obviously meant to (have I looked hard enough at the lives of 'ordinary people'? am I aware of the lurking depths, the strange kinks, the tangled pasts of these superficially dull folk?) but also in a more literary sense.

Can the structure of the traditional short story (which is what these predominantly are) with its lavish piling on of the social detail, with its deft ending which both explains and skews what has gone before, actually carry the emotional weight, the imaginative, psychological density that it is being asked to here? And the answer, here at least, is 'not quite'.

**Patricia Craig (review date 17 September 1987)**

SOURCE: Craig, Patricia. "Getting On." *London Review of Books* 9, no. 16 (17 September 1987): 18.

[*In the following excerpt, Craig offers a mixed review of the stories included in* Dreams of Dead Women's Handbags.]

The women characters of Shena Mackay [in *Dreams of Dead Women's Handbags*] are apt to get into an overwrought state: domestic annoyances and shortcomings conspire to agitate them until they lash out with the nearest weapon to hand—in one instance, a vegetable marrow. The unsatisfactoriness of life is something they all know well and resent. One spends her days in an out-of-season hotel full of society's rejects; another regrets her dwindled celebrity as a writer, and acts in a way to cause retrospective embarrassment to herself at a literary party. The heroine of the title story, also a writer (of detective fiction), has a difficult time on a train, where her overnight bag keeps getting mixed up with the bag of a woman in a synthetic fur coat who orders her gin and tonic by the double. We learn a little about the writer's past, and the accident that befell her parents on a clifftop. Did she cause it, or was the whole thing a dream? In any case, there remains the theatrical image of a handbag falling after its owner down the side of a cliff. 'The black bivalve emitted a silent howl of despair.' Shena Mackay needs to tone down her trimmings. At one point, we find a pier striding on shivery legs into a sea of gun-metal silk edged with flounces of creamy lace. Nevertheless, *Dead Women's Handbags* contains some gems, including two stories about children, **'Cardboard City'** and **'All the Pubs in Soho'**. In the first, two stepdaughters of a despised stepfather, 12 and 14, wangle a day in London on their own; in **'Soho'**, a girl who would rather be a boy attaches herself to an ostracised twosome (a pair of bloody pansies, say the locals) in a Kentish village. **'Perpetual Spinach'** has a workers' row of houses, an up-and-coming couple, and their edgy relations with two of the workers next door; when the latter are killed in a road accident, there's a comic implication that the couple's cats have taken over their role. Shena Mackay is a sharp and often funny observer of the deficiencies in ordinary lives.

**Angela Huth (review date 4 July 1992)**

SOURCE: Huth, Angela. "Accents Yet Unknown." *Spectator* 269, no. 8556 (4 July 1992): 30-1.

[*In the following review, Huth lauds Mackay's eye for detail in* Dunedin, *but faults the unevenness of the novel.*]

It is a puzzling fact in the literary world that while some writers' names lodge in the public mind from the start, others, for all their eligibility, remain for years—sometimes for ever—'vaguely heard of' rather than a public name.

One of those upon whom the unfairness of fashion has rendered this disservice is Shena Mackay, first published 28 years ago. Her last collection of stories, **Dreams of Dead Women's Handbags**, received particular critical acclaim. But, singular writer though she is, Mackay does not yet share the popularity of O'Brien, Brookner or Bainbridge, and it's hard to know why.

**Dunedin** is her seventh novel. The story begins in 1909, in New Zealand. Presbyterian minister Jack Mackenzie, with his wife and family, arrive from Scotland to start a new life. In Jack's case, this does not mean giving up old ways. He was 'at his nicest when being botanical'. When it came to women, he continued in his customary churlish ways.

Mackay's evocation of small community life in New Zealand almost a century ago is masterful. Here we find Miss Kettle, spinster of the parish, whose days 'spread out around her like the repeated pattern of a dingy patchwork,' and who harbours a secret passion for the minister. He in turn lusts after Myrtille, 'the dark skinned launderess,' who keeps the head of her great-grandfather on a shelf. Beneath the domestic exteriors, misery and deceit rumble menacingly in all quarters.

It is not just that Mackay has that cliché, a woman's eye for detail (which she has), but that her delight in detail is infectious. No moment is too small to burnish; no texture is too humble to bring to life. She makes the most ordinary things sparkle, describes with extraordinary vibrance objects and moments that are familiar to us all.

Many years later, Kitty would come across this book in a drawer lined with brittle paper of bleached and breaking roses exuding a distillation of summers locked in wood, and would weep at the schoolgirlish hand in which the sheets, pillowcases, towels . . . were listed so importantly and painstakingly in ink which had rusted to the colour of old thin blood.

Mackay also has a piquant sense of humour. Louisa, the parrot-shooting minister's wife,

> . . . started to hum: flocks of parrots might well explode in shuttlecocks of brilliant bloody green feathers if that would take her husband away from Dunedin for a day or two. He could make the feathers into a headdress for all she cared, and perform a grotesque stamping war dance and protrude his tongue . . . a feathered spear impaling his chest. 'May God forgive me, I didn't mean it,' Louisa muttered as she realised she had just committed murder in her heart.

In the general charge of her exuberance, Mackay is prepared to take risks.

> Lilian had a singing voice that reminded Madge of rowan jelly when you held the jar up to the light.

Had the words of this sentence been one millimetre out, it could have been material for Pseuds Corner. As it is, you know exactly what she means.

Unfortunately, on p. 52, New Zealand ends, but for a few pages of epilogue. We are then whirled forward 80 years to London, and the bleak lives of the Mackenzie grandchildren. The misfortune for the reader is not that Mackay's writing in any way declines, but the antipodean episode is so bewitching that it is hard not to feel some reluctance to being transported to the more familiar shores of grotty London. If anyone can bring humour and sparkle to delapidated houses, the agony in the mind of a baby-snatcher and the horrifying fate of a homeless young New Zealander, Mackay it is. We are in turn sympathetic, intrigued, shocked, entertained—but oh the yearning for the world she magically conjured in the first part. Would she had mixed her proportions of time and place differently. But perhaps she was unaware of how good her beginning is, and had no notion of what an ache for more she would cause in her reader.

As it is, her depiction of different kinds of misery in different generations of the same family manages not to be depressing. There is a kind of persistence of spirit among her characters, which is not a bad substitute for hope.

## Chris Savage King (review date 10 July 1992)

SOURCE: King, Chris Savage. "Urban Jungle." *New Statesman and Society* 5, no. 210 (10 July 1992): 34.

[*In the following review, King draws comparisons between* Dunedin *and the work of Charles Dickens.*]

When the dust has settled on the millennium and readers want to find out how people lived in our age, they will discover all they need to know in the work of Shena Mackay. In *Dunedin,* the Mackenzies, a Scottish Presbyterian family who landed in New Zealand in 1909, are tracked down to their dispersed scions in the chaotic mess of 1980s South London. The suspended, ominous drift of middle-class Edwardian life is harshly contrasted with the more precarious present: a world of dishevelled corner shops, cackling street life, battered parks and end-of-the-line public services. General pathology is stoked until it explodes in random and irrevocable acts.

Olive, a shopkeeper with a heart full to bursting, snatches a black baby in an indifferent tube crowd. Her brother William, a headmaster, retires early when one of his pupils, Pragna Patel, is murdered by an ambling psychotic on a school trip. Meanwhile, Jay—the product of an illicit liaison between the Reverend Mackenzie and a Maori woman—arrives in London and lands at Crystal Palace, to end up in a private enterprise prison.

Despite being politically on the side of the angels, Shena Mackay's aim is as comic as it is bleak. In highly distinctive dialogue, she captures genteel convolutions disguising viciousness, and a masquerade of wisdom in jargon and cliché. Her characters, both irascible and resigned, have a natural antagonism and suspicion towards one another. This is relieved by sheer exhaustion as much as by goodwill.

Yet she carries an easy empathy with a range of defeated underdogs and gritty survivors, and a redemptive sensuous attention to the natural or debased objects that surround them. In her hands, dead cars shielded by blossoms, a discarded crisp wrapper in a front garden, Jay's fantasies of non-existent matey employers, and a Clapham restaurant meal shared by two middle-aged people about to fall in love, have a vividness and immediacy that elevate local incidents and the unexceptional people who experience them to an intense expressiveness and beauty. Her perspective on the usually unrecorded delights in the rush and snarl of the city make it seem at times as if she is forging a unique urban pastoral.

Enjoyable, shaggy-dog plotting and a sprawling cast make *Dunedin* as rumbustious and socially engaged as Dickens. With him she shares hot splashes of satire and an eye for idiosyncrasy, but is probably more faithful to her source material.

The realist school to which she notionally belongs is shallow in its most trumpeted offerings. Semi-public figures who write about semi-public figures deliver all the insight of a lengthy press release. Mackay's talent is more similar to friendlier forms: the songs of Ray Davies and Morrissey, the plays of Alan Bennett and Joe Orton, and Victoria Wood's sketches.

Like them, she writes about the extraordinariness of ordinary lives: the stuff that launched the novel in the 18th century, when it became the guiding light of secular humanism and displaced a dried-out aristocratic taste for metaphysics and archetypes. Ever since, hard men have been getting in on the act, and have stuffed novels with all manner of importance-seeking material. The literary "artist" of our age, assuming obsolete Romantic rights, produces works almost wholly vacated of active, contemporary life. This, in turn, has produced an understandable and blameless public who don't read "literary" novels.

Shena Mackay puts these efforts in the shade. She reveals the intellectual ambition of the boy, and female wannabe-boy, novelists for what it is: self-absorption, empty technique and, worst of all, imaginative deficiency. Still, never mind: the British novel thrives! Read Shena Mackay—the best writer we've got.

### Lorna Sage (review date 10 July 1992)

SOURCE: Sage, Lorna. "A Light Touch with the Horrors." *Times Literary Supplement* (10 July 1992): 21.

[*In the following review, Sage describes* Dunedin *as "exuberant, cruel, depressed and hilarious by turns—a manic-depressive book, all ups and downs."*]

The street-theatre of "community care" and the brand-new towering monuments to recession have inspired some interesting London novels, from Michael Moorcock's carnivalesque *Mother London* to Penelope Lively's brittle, see-through *City of the Mind*—but none has quite the high-spirited style of *Dunedin.* Shena Mackay writes about South East London with such penetrating familiarity and ingenuity that it becomes the focus for a whole world of dreams and disasters and guilty histories. And it is done with a special lightness of touch that lets you levitate out of the horrors, without in the least obscuring them. Here, for instance, is bad-tempered, menopausal and witty Olive Mackenzie, simply getting from A to B, sometime in 1989.

> She drove past buildings faded like old music-hall queens, raddled, with dust in the folds of their skirts and broken fans, past people hitting their children while waiting for buses that would never come. Rain hit the windscreen, and at once it, and the road, were full of what they used to call dancing dollies; silver spirals pirouetting on glass and tarmac.

This kind of openly artful—but none the less easy-going—writing, which doesn't feel embarrassed about similes, and pounces on any chance association that promises pleasure, marks out Mackay as a traditionalist. She reminds one just enough of Dickens, and (at different time) of Iris Murdoch and Angus Wilson, to call up a rich receding background of fictions of society, leading up to her own.

Indeed, a severed head broods symbolically over the action—a Maori shrunken head in a biscuit tin under the floorboards of a derelict mansion called "Dunedin", both house-name and head commemorating a shaming and abortive colonial excursion by the Mackenzie family, when grandfather Jack, the preacher, took them all the way to New Zealand, only to be sent back for blotting his copybook with the part-Maori laundress, Myrtille. The novel's first and last sections are set back in that brief antipodean idyll, and act as a sunlit and ironical frame for the lives of the present generation. Jack Mackenzie's grandchildren, official and unofficial.

Once upon a time, the British went out into the world with outrageous colonizing confidence; now, the wide world washes up here, like flotsam and jetsam: we're back "home". The Mackenzies, as it were, anticipated this receding, homecoming tide of ex-empire by being chucked back in, eighty years ago. Divorced Olive and her brother William—an ex-headmaster disgraced when one of his pupils was killed on a school trip—look set to be "the last rotting fruit on their branch of the family tree".

But, true to the tradition she's working in, which generates elaborate and endlessly proliferating plots. Mackay produces one surprise after another; a baby out of a hat here, a lost young life there. . . . Decay is after all a form of life, and what look like the last days of London from one horrific angle are the first days of new sorts of life from another. Not that things "balance out", at all. Under cover of curiosity and humour, she is a relentless moralist, and juxtaposes moments of euphoria with black hopelessness and violence, just to make the point that there is no common denominator—no way of sharing out either happiness or suffering. Dickens, defending the melodrama of *Oliver Twist* against supposed-realists, said that actually city life *was* like streaky bacon, and Mackay, I am sure, would agree. Her characters are at once ordinarily plausible and on the margins of nightmare, and she demonstrates brilliantly how little divides daily looniness from the kind of thing you read about in the newspapers (both Olive and William get into the papers in the course of the story). Then again, there are the things too terrible to be in the papers, yet.

Perhaps the most obvious sign of the novel's slyness and ambition is its excursion into dystopian "fantasy", in the form of a secret concentration camp for vagrants, run by the Department of the Environment. Can we be sure? you're meant to ask yourself. Also, this strand of subplot is a reminder that for all its connections with past novels. *Dunedin* is not at all comforting. Instead, it is exuberant, cruel, depressed and hilarious by turns—a manic-depressive book, all ups and downs.

There is space in this formula for a lot of supposedly "minor characters", including a couple of very nasty pen-portraits of the kind of writer Shena Mackay *isn't*; Terry Turner and Derek Mothersole, who vie with each other in trendiness, coolly pornographic when it suits, "caring" when that's in vogue, but never able to lose themselves in London, as this book can. It's a small but sufficiently savage authorial gesture on behalf of openness, which should not be mistaken for ease or cosiness. You need, in fact, to be on the edge of hysteria to cope with what she calls—in a nice portmanteau pun— these last days of "empirical follies".

### Susannah Clapp (review date 5 November 1992)

SOURCE: Clapp, Susannah. "Bully Off." *London Review of Books* 21, no. 5 (5 November 1992): 28-9.

[*In the following favorable review of* Dunedin, *Clapp elucidates the defining characteristics of Mackay's fiction.*]

Shena Mackay has written the first anti-speciesist novel. *Dunedin* does not feature animals in any large anthropomorphic or allegorical capacity, and there is hardly a pet in sight. But what happens at the edges of Mackay's novels, what is taken for granted, has always been vital in establishing their distinctive flavour and their point. *Dunedin* is about London, poverty and pinched lives, but the background imagery is consistently, though often quietly animal. This imagery helps to make *Dunedin* as original as any of Mackay's earlier books. It was one of the few things not praised in the unexpected eulogy bestowed upon Mackay by the pit-bull of the literary pages Julie Burchill when, in *Elle* magazine, she dismissed other contemporary women authors as 'a mannered, marginal bunch of second bananas', and went on to proclaim Mackay as 'the best writer in the world today'.

Plot has never been a central attraction in Mackay's fiction: she introduces topics, strands of subject-matter and characters, and lets them unravel, sometimes intertwine, often fade away and frequently get dumped. There is as much meander as development—appropriately, for she writes about dreamers and ditherers. She is a writer of moments, of sharp touches, who has found as many fervent advocates for her short stories as for her novels.

*Dunedin* is more conventional in subject-matter and structure than most of her books. The novel's opening is strikingly—for Mackay, weirdly—traditional, seem-

ing to promise a historical costume drama, in which a Scots minister and his family, arriving at the New Zealand port of Dunedin in 1909, find a mixing of traditions: there is shortbread and pursed lips and the tawse; there are also preserved human heads. Mackay makes less than she could of the distinctive cultural blend of the place: New Zealand émigrés report that the gold-rush town of Dunedin (founded by Scottish Presbyterians in the 1840s) was almost entirely determined by the idea of re-creating Edinburgh. It sports a George Street, a Hanover Street and an Albany Street, as well as a Castle Street (without the castle) and a Princes Street (with no prince); even in the 1960s, the statue of Robert Burns in the middle of the main street was surrounded by Highland dancers every Friday night. The Scottishness of Mackay's Dunedin is more a matter of moral style than of civic life, and her New Zealand a place of lush temptations and hazards—of bubbling geysers, sweet-briared verandas and black thighs. It is a place where a family's lives are narrowed by an oppressive father—while the father's own fantasy and fancy wander. It is also a place where the family's maid-servants, though preyed upon by their master, are in the end allowed their free range of fun:

> 'I keep seeing his terrible face, staring at us. Like God and Adam and Eve.'
>
> Madge came over to Lilian's bed. 'Is it wrong? Does it feel wrong when I take you in my arms?'

Mackay's books have often been, as here, quite casually bisexual. In 1965 *Music Upstairs* provided an account of a young woman's drift through London—half-drunk, mostly miserable, half-tranced—to which the heroine's love affairs with her landlady and landlord are retailed with a wonderfully off-hand assurance. Mackay was 18 when she wrote *Music Upstairs*—a book whose title suggests the in-the-wings and off-the-wall nature of the heroine's life, and which gains from its suggestion of the Thirties use of 'musical' for homosexual. She was a prodigy who, a year before, had produced another account of two wastrels or escapers. *Dust Falls on Eugene Schlumburger* stars an ancient-seeming 30-year-old man and a schoolgirl only a year or so younger than the author who created her, who run off together (her headmistress informs the girl that her Uncle Eugene has just phoned the school with a request that she go to her mother's sickbed), crash a stolen car and become severally imprisoned and a secretary.

Some pages early on in *Eugene Schlumburger* set the tone of the novella and are a gauge of Mackay's particular mix of talents. It is assembly-time at the heroine's school: 'schoolgirls in collars and ties singing of sailors in the hard electric glare of the depth of winter'; the heroine is listening to prayers for the county councils and thinking of an encounter behind the Portsmouth Odeon. And it is snowing:

Abigail thought: snow is filling the hockey nets and glittering on the yellow mud, freezing the drive and filling the hedges. Mounting in desolation on the windowsills, wailing at the pane, drifting under doors. Soon it will cover the desks and the algebra books, fill the crucible and the belljar and thoroughly obliterate the blackboard. Blue glaciers will form in the inkwells. Perhaps Benthall's car will skid on the drive and hurtle in frozen flames through the hollyhedge. Supposing they all broke their legs on the hockey pitch. 'Bully off!' and they charged, and their legs broke like hockeysticks, their faces like netballs sank into the snow.

If you don't like this, or the way a lyrical passage is then slapped up against a piece of satire—'In addition to this bestiality,' complains the headmistress about a recent misdemeanour, 'not one of these girls was wearing her beret'—you won't like any of Mackay's work. Her preoccupations and style haven't changed much in the course of a thirty-year writing career. She still makes a lot of jokes. Her protagonists are still semi-detached from society. She still takes off in fantastic flights of visual imagery.

*Dunedin* profits from these characteristics, though it is not her best novel. It is bigger than her previous books—there are more pages, more characters, more countries, more overt themes—and its bigness exposes a tendency to inconsequentiality which can seem a triumph of coolness but can seem merely careless. The New Zealand scenes which begin and end the novel are barely tethered to the central London chapters. One of the characters who could integrate the different parts of the novel—a young vagrant from New Zealand who is related to more people in London than he suspects—is sketchily presented. A series of scenes involving him describes a dystopia in which dissident members of the population are rounded up, imprisoned, patrolled by thugs and beaten up: both the baddies (E-type-owning adulterers who get their opponents bumped off) and the goodies (kind-eyed intuitives with sweet-smelling babies) are spectral.

These unsatisfactory parts stick out: they read as if they have been implanted to make *Dunedin* an evidently ambitious book. But they don't damage the fabric of the novel. Mackay's real ambitiousness has little to do with making overt moral or political statements. It has everything to do with seeing and expressing things in a completely individual way. Apparently effortlessly. Throughout her work painterly touches pop up. She looks at the closed eyes of a baby and sees that they are 'like the seams along broad beans'. She gives a picture of a marriage that is worthy of Francis Bacon: 'As the sound of a plane ebbed in the darkness a rumbling came from Nigel's side of the bed and Jean's stomach gave a timid answering bleat. She could have felt sorry for those two stomachs had they lain side by side in white bloody trays in a butcher's window.' And she has a quick car:

'Sometimes I feel I can't go on, Doctor . . .'

'Go on, Mrs Roe.'

There is nothing precious about her effects. Novelists have recently been excoriated for escapism, for not addressing themselves to bad news. Mackay has always written about recognisably bleak contemporary circumstances. Women novelists, on the other hand, are always being accused of concentrating too narrowly on what's going on around them: of being too polite, too middle-class (this seems to matter more in the case of women), too domestic. Mackay, who is no chronicler of china or linen or stable families, writes to a large extent about women who are called sluts or slags, centring her fiction on desolates or drifters, on characters who are more often glimpsed as part of a backdrop of urban disintegration. The protagonists of *Dunedin* are less obviously imperilled than earlier Mackay characters: they own houses and have—or have had—respectable jobs. Nevertheless, one middle aged woman turns into a baby-snatcher; her brother is an ex-headmaster who has never recovered from a tragedy on a school outing; her ex-lover is a spectacular drunk. Mackay is most pointedly satirical when dealing with this last character, a writer, and his creative-writing-class exploits. His way of dealing with unfavourable reviews of his work is to ring up the reviewer in the middle of the night and do heavy breathing ('There were ways of handling these things if you were a pro'); when an author kills herself shortly after a sneering review by him: '"Probably done old Enid the biggest favour of her career," Terry muttered as he cracked open a can of Red Stripe. "She'll be a Virago Modern Classic before you can say 'knife'."' Mackay became a Virago Modern Classic several years ago.

Mackay's books are scattered with topical and period references—to Jimmy Saville's T and T Club, to Double Biological Ariel, to *Home and Away*. They are savvy but never studiously realistic: there is always something strange and elusive going on. In *Dunedin* it is the animals. They are everywhere, and they are an indicator of the author's temperament: dark, funny and attracted to the bizarre. This is the book of, among other things, a vegetarian: meals and garb have a particular aspect—people munch 'bits of dead animals in buns' and wear sandals 'hacked from the hide of an animal recently dead'; routine icons of dismemberment—a pub sign showing 'a hare about to be torn apart by a pack of hounds'—are seen as savagely intrusive. The edges of scenes are busy with the normally undetected movements of small creatures: snails are squelched, toads are threatened, fish bump around in tiny tanks, lobsters claw their way out of boiling cauldrons. Every now and then the scenes shift slightly in composition and the beasts come to the fore in ways characteristic of Mackay's writing. This can be calmly humorous: 'Ashley smiled, knowing that her friends laughed at her close relationship with the cats: recently she had been stung into telling Rosemary that her children were substitute cats.' Or violent and paradoxical: Smithfield porters, 'the bloodstained conscience of London', protest in gory aprons against hospital cuts. Or grim and extraordinary: a man beats on the door of his prison, 'howling his dog's name'. The focus on everyday life is altered not incredibly but irrevocably: it is as if one looked at the Cabinet and found that all bar two of its members were women. The result is a world which is recognisable, peculiar and amusing. And full of unsuspected animation. Thank Pan.

## Trev Broughton (review date 30 July 1993)

SOURCE: Broughton, Trev. "Affirmation of Life." *Times Literary Supplement* (30 July 1993): 21.

[*In the following favorable review, Broughton identifies the unifying theme of the stories in* The Laughing Academy *to be "the limits of responsibility and compassion."*]

Here are nine perfectly crafted stories from a master of her medium. Shena Mackay's most striking characters are an unlikely, unprepossessing bunch—dry old sticks and wallflowers, the weedy and the seedy—but she somehow confers on them vivid beauty and coherence. The most benighted old codger, the frumpiest drudge, acquire a curious but unmistakable dignity and stature. In **"Cloud-Cuckoo-Land"**, Roy Rowley's borrowed spectacles reveal, with sudden, harrowing clarity, the shoals of salmonella in the kitchen, the pills and bobbles on his wife's jumper, and, between the cuff of the tracksuit bottoms and his brogues, the nightmare of his own ankles:

> Roy could not believe the knobs and nodules below the fringe of black-grey foliage, the wormcasts and bits of dead elastic. . . . "These aren't my feet," he said. "Some old man has made off with Roy Rowley's feet while he wasn't looking and dumped these on me."

More devastating still, the glasses expose to him his own pretensions as a do-gooder, as a "baggy-trousered philanthropist". For a few hours, he sees the signs of ugliness and decay in the community he has been trying to salvage; sees himself as a symptom rather than a solution. "He stood, what else could he do, a well-intentioned bloke in an anorak; a drone."

Taking the classic short-fiction formula of a few "red letter" minutes or hours in a single life, moments of heightened awareness and urgent deliberation, Mackay draws us swiftly inside her characters through their unique relationship to language. For Mackay, this relationship is not just about thoughts: it is joyful flesh, aching bone, erratic pulse, stubborn immune system. Mackay insists that the rhythms and contours of experience are defined as decisively by this relationship—by old jokes and corny lyrics, by the bad puns and daft sayings of childhood—as by the rigidities of conscious thought. Moreover, she brings to the musings and chunterings of her characters a comic range which extends from Fay Weldon to Leonard Rossiter. There is overblown Monica who plays the harmonica, and Violet Greene who likes her own name ("pre-Raphaelite purple and viridian . . . the hectic hues of Arthur Hughes").

Even the most incidental, monosyllabic characters have their own idiom, as individual as a fingerprint. In **"A Pair of Spoons"**, Bonnie and Vivien are lesbian Lovejoys, savvy rural antique dealers conning the locals out of their Clarice Cliff crockery. The man from the CID catches the couple celebrating their latest heist with a glass of champagne and a smoochy dance. "Good evening, ladies", he announces. "Filth."

Unlike the soggy inverts of D. H. Lawrence's "The Fox", of which Mackay's story is a sly revision, this pair manage to outwit both the male intruder and their own mutual jealousies and fears: "the Friendly Old-Established Firm, back in business". Mackay is not always so upbeat. In **"Shinty"**, Margaret and Suzy attend a book-launch to confirm to themselves that Veronica Sharples, the primary-school sadist of their childhood memories, has flowered into a best-selling, politically correct . . . primary-school sadist. Their satisfaction dwindles, however, as the evening progresses and they piece together their own complicity in "Ronnie's" regime.

If there is a connecting thread in these stories, it is this probing of the limits of responsibility and compassion. It is a question for the 1990s: what would happen if, strained to breaking-point by the Welfare recession, our emotional infrastructure gave way? What would happen if our resources of caring, of *minding,* came to an end? If the voice at the end of the telephone counselling service for phoneline addicts (Roy Rowley's Helpline Helpline) told us to "try a bit of aversion therapy—piss off!"? Mackay's vignettes allow us a glimpse of all these possibilities. But even at their grimmest—and there is betrayal, disappointment and horror in *The Laughing Academy*—the stories gasp out an affirmation of life. When a character wonders "whether we should love one another if we were made of glass, with all the workings visible, like transparent factories", the answer is a brisk, non-negotiable, "We should have to."

## Judy Cooke (review date 30 July 1993)

SOURCE: Cooke, Judy. "City Lights." *New Statesman and Society* (30 July 1993): 39.

[*In the following positive review of* The Laughing Academy, *Cooke underscores Mackay's widespread appeal as a fiction writer.*]

You have to laugh at life's absurdities. It's better than being taught how to cope in the Laughing Academy, aka the Funny Farm, remembered fearfully by one of the most vulnerable characters in these stories [of *The Laughing Academy*] as "a sort of stale amyl-nitratey whiff, a sniff of sad, sour institutional air or a thick meaty odour."

Shena Mackay's keen ear for dialogue is complemented by the precision of her descriptive writing. She can evoke a mood or point up a meaning with one or two carefully chosen images—dead foliage clinging to a thorn bush, or plane trees in autumn standing like "dappled benign giraffes". The humour in this hugely entertaining new book is often hilarious, over-the-top surreal; the prose style stays close to home, interweaving snatches of conversation, pop lyrics, jargon, advertising slogans, puns and scraps of poetry.

In one of the shorter pieces, **"Glass",** a woman has to decide whether or not to leave her lover. She scrutinises every object she finds on her walk from "the little squares of opaque glass" in the pavement to the powder compact in the shop window, "a lid of butterflies' wings". It is a lonely moment of choice but not an isolated one. Her decision is made in a renewed understanding of her own temperament, informed by everything that she has seen. Mackay's romanticism, like Allen Ginsberg's, suggests that the diversity of city life, all its perplexing phenomena, can be a comforting blanket keeping us warm.

She has a great talent for comedy in the English tradition: one of the strengths of contemporary fiction overlooked by those critics who like to diagnose its decline. I recommend they read **"Cloud-Cuckoo-Land",** a study of blinkered do-gooding that bears comparison with Dickens' attack on Mrs Jellyby. The Rowleys are a family possessed. Ron works for Helpline Helpline, "established to counsel people addicted to ringing, or setting up, Helplines". His wife is the charity worker from hell. His daughter escapes for a time by becoming a Jehovah's Witness. In the spirit of N F Simpson, the Glums, and the best of Alan Bennett, the writing builds to a crescendo of appalled observation.

Even funnier is the group portrait of the politically correct sisterhood, gathered to worship Ronnie Sharples at a women-only reading in the Charing Cross Road. Jean and Margaret, schoolfellows of the erstwhile Veronica, can pack a pretty mean punch themselves. But Ronnie's entrance, flanked by twin Tonton Macoutes and attended by her latest partner, Mog ("rumour had it that she had been bought as a slave in Camden Market") subdues them temporarily. Ronnie is narcissitic, predatory, violent and richly deserving of her eventual humiliation. Could such a one exist in literary London?

Shena Mackay appeals to a wide readership, as was evident in the success of last year's novel, *Dunedin.* The broad range of her material probably has something to do with this, together with the sheer hedonistic fun of what she has to say. My favourite story, **"A Pair of Spoons",** is the cleverest, sexiest piece of writing I've read since Angela Carter's *The Bloody Chamber.* Indeed, there is a fairytale element in Bonnie and Vivien's adventure: the Friendly Old-Established Firm of dealers, whose relationship is threatened by an Aladdin's cave known only to one of them. Love triumphs, as does Beauty. Don't miss this story of the Wolf, the Fox and the Filth.

## Penny Smith (essay date 1995)

SOURCE: Smith, Penny. "Hell Innit: The Millennium in Alasdair Gray's *Lanark,* Martin Amis's *London Fields,* and Shena Mackay's *Dunedin.*" *Essays and Studies* 48 (1995): 115-28.

[*In the following essay, Smith comments on the influences of World War II in Mackay's* Dunedin, *Martin Amis's* London Fields, *and Alasdair Gray's* Lanark.]

While it can be argued that mere *fin de siecle* inevitably courts disillusionment, the recognition that there is to be no brave new world just around the corner, it is useful to keep in mind that 'for most of human history the idea of the millennium itself has been essentially hopeful' (O'Toole, 29). After Apocalypse comes judgement, and thereafter the thousand-year rule by Christ and a panoply of saints. As we approach the third millennium, however, any belief in resurrection has increasingly become the province of suicidal cults: for the rest of us the dancing on the Berlin Wall is over and we watch in growing alarm as the spectres of civil war, genocide, and nuclear vandalism slouch across the landscape of a disintegrating Europe. According to the historian Eric Hobsbawm:

> the European 20th century has already ended with the collapse of the last great utopia of communism and the return of the map of Europe to a shape similar to that before the first world war.

> (cited O'Toole, 29)

If, then, the millennium has already encroached into the European consciousness by a couple of decades might it not be that the state of mind that we have come to describe as postmodern is actually better understood as being 'postmillennial'? (A possibility that postmodernism, with its underlying sense of ending and crisis, has long been hinting at anyway.) And might it not also be possible that the end of the twentieth century can be pushed back even further than Hobsbawm suggests? As far, say, as the mid twentieth century? For in the three texts to be discussed here, *Lanark* (1981), *London Fields* (1989), and **Dunedin** (1992), there is a sense that as we approach the year 2000 we find ourselves looking not forward but back, to the catastrophe that has cast its shadow across the second half of the twentieth century, the Second World War.

I

If the period since the war has witnessed the occasional preemptive obituary of history, the death of the novel has been hailed with even greater regularity. What call for the novel when narrative has leapt from the printed page to the computer screen? In the last decade of the twentieth century the once-upon-a-time reader is transformed into either a hero/player, negotiating/narrating a path through levels of increasing difficulty, or a writer/programmer disappearing into the variable choice that is the hypertext, where it is guaranteed that no readings can ever possibly be the same. Whereas narrative as was, on the page, on the stage, on the cinema and television screen, did (despite readings translated through gender, race, class, age, sexuality) have a certain, albeit fragile, stability, we are now faced with the possibility of endless instability, of no shared readings being possible, or desirable.

Postmodernism supposes the predominance of the electronic media, but it is also apparent that narrative is demonstrating a determination to survive in a resurgence of oral tradition and in the novel's own ability to incorporate, and even to thrive on, instability. Readers can no longer be entirely sure of just where they are, or when the next leap—in genre, difficulty, *faith*—will be necessary. Alasdair Gray's *Lanark*—'possibly the first Scottish metafiction' (Imhoff, 75)—is a prime example of this.

The fragmented text that is *Lanark* reflects, however, not only contemporary pressures on narrative but, more specifically, the fragmented consciousness of the protagonist(s), Thaw/Lanark, and the state of late capitalist society. We begin with what appears to be a realist text, as a man of about twenty-four sits on the balcony of a bohemian cafe in what might be any decade, in any city, of the twentieth century. Realism, however, quickly lurches into science fantasy: the man sits staring out into the darkness not in hope of enlightenment, but in the hope of catching a glimpse of sunlight. The city he finds himself in is Unthank (a fact not discovered till the next stage of his journey, this piece of information being kept secret by the civic authorities for 'security reasons', 31). Unthank is a thankless place, where it is always dark, it is impossible to keep track of time's passing, and people are afflicted with attacks of 'dragonhide' (from which Lanark suffers), 'twittering rigor', 'softs' or 'mouths'. Comparing his symptoms with those of Gay, a woman patron of the cafe, Lanark is appalled when she unclenches her palm to reveal a mouth, through which Sludden, the leader of one of the cafe's cliques speaks to him. Gay is Sludden's mouthpiece, in every sense, and Lanark suddenly realizes where he is: '. . . this is hell!' (45).

Up till now he hasn't been sure. He's arrived in the city on a train, nameless and with no memory (something he's made sure of by throwing away the papers and diary he discovers in his knapsack). All he is sure of is that he craves sunlight, that he couldn't be an artist—when Sludden suggests this occupation he says he has nothing to tell people (6)—and that he has arrived in a place where people randomly disappear when the lights (the electric variety) go out. Some individuals refuse to disappear quietly: her last lodger, Lanark's landlady informs him, 'left a hell of a mess . . . And his screams!' (13). But when Lanark's turn comes he goes voluntarily. A giant mouth (or vagina) opens in the ground at his feet announcing 'I am the way out' (47), and Lanark leaps in. Only to find himself reborn in an even stranger place, the institute.

For the reader the institute links the worlds of *Lanark* with our own: Lanark is tended by a doctor who informs him that this is an establishment which has 'been isolated since the outbreak of the second world war' (53), and his supply of reading material includes *Our Wullie's Annual for 1938* and *No Orchids for Miss Blandish*. What we have, then, is a parallel universe, a fracturing of the world as we know it that occurred during the war. This connection with our own here and now is subsequently made clear in the story Lanark hears from the oracle in the Prologue and Books One and Two (the novel begins with Book Three). The connecting passage between the parallel worlds is death: Lanark, Duncan Thaw in his previous life, commits suicide and so finds himself as the nameless man on the train, shunting into an alternative existence.

Or does he? Douglas Gifford argues that the only consistent way to read Gray's novel is as hallucination resulting from mental breakdown (Gifford, 111). But while such a reading is certainly consistent with the realist characterization of Duncan Thaw, the text as a whole strains against such consistency. *Lanark,* with its disrupted chronology and structure, self-reflective notes, allegorically-laden illustrations (see Lee), extravagant layout and typography, not only demands but also deserves an exuberant suspension of disbelief. Duncan Thaw is reborn as Lanark. Lanark *does* find himself in the institute, where he falls in love with Rima, with whom he travels through time and space. To read Lanark's adventures as hallucination confines Hell to that small area within Duncan Thaw's tormented psyche, whereas the whole point of the novel is that Hell is vast and we are in it. Unthank is Glasgow is the industrial, post-war world.

The institute, still running after having been set up during the war, represents a fragmenting of space and time, and Thaw's childhood world is fragmented in much the same way, and for the same reason. Book One begins with Chapter Twelve: 'The War Begins'. It's 1939 and Thaw's working-class family is evacuated from Glasgow. Thaw's view of the war is the view from boyhood: he can play at German spies on the beach and confidently announce to the local minister that he doesn't believe in Hell. To which Dr McPhedron prophetically replies: 'When you have more knowledge of life you will mibby find Hell more believable' (143). Young Thaw doesn't know it but Hell starts here and at a later date he will be able to point out its exact landmarks to his father:

> 'Look at Belsen!' cried Thaw. 'And Nagasaki, and the Russians in Hungary and Yanks in South America and French in Algeria and the British bombing Egypt without declaring war on her! Half the folk on this planet die of malnutrition before they're thirty, we'll be twice as many before the century ends, and the only governments with the skill and power to make a decent home of the world are plundering their neighbours and planning to atom bomb each other. We cooperate in millions when it comes to killing, but when it comes to generous, beautiful actions we work in tens and hundreds.'
>
> (295)

Social and industrial decline follow the war. Thaw's father can only find work as a labourer and his friends leave school for jobs which are boring, and dangerous: '. . . this business of being a *man* keeps you happy for mibby a week, then on your second Monday it hits you' (215). One half of the planet's population dies of malnutrition while the other half thrives: 'Men are pies that bake and eat themselves' (188). A metaphor that, in the institute, becomes fact; Lanark discovers that the patients who aren't cured are used as fuel and food, despite many sections of the institute being owned by decent people 'who don't know they are cannibals and wouldn't believe it if you told them' (102).

*Lanark* is a study of the way power, particularly political power, works, and how it is fuelled by greed, hate, separation, and the inability to love. When, in the Epilogue, Lanark encounters his maker, the author/conjurer Nastler, he is told that: 'The Thaw narrative shows a man dying because he is bad at loving. It is enclosed by your narrative which shows civilization collapsing for the same reason' (484). Thaw, the schoolboy who doesn't believe in Hell, goes on to become Thaw the adolescent, wracked with asthma and eczema and the awareness that 'Hell was the one truth and pain the one fact that nullified all others' (160). Thaw the art student struggles against class, poverty, and an inflexible education system; but his most important failures are his own. He is a man who, like the society around him, is bad at loving. A man who, in his final breakdown, believes he has—and in fact might have—killed Marjory, the woman he loves but who doesn't love him back.

Duncan Thaw throws himself into the sea in 1956; toward the close of the century Lanark is an old man who has ventured into alternative worlds, and across time zones, in an unsuccessful attempt to save Unthank from destruction. Lanark's, however, is a different failure from Thaw's because, although inept and easily manipulated, he is capable of love. 'I never wanted anything', he tells Nastler, 'but some sunlight, some love, some very ordinary happiness' (484). He saves the life of Rima (once Marjory) in the institute, and is willing to risk his own life to save their son, Alexander. Love does triumph. And Alexander's existence confounds Lanark's creator:

> The conjuror stared and said, 'You have no son.'
>
> 'I have a son called Alexander who was born in the Cathedral.'
>
> (498)

*Lanark's* final chapter is simply entitled 'End'. Nastler warns his character that 'my whole imagination has a carefully reined-back catastrophic tendency' (498) and when Lanark demands to know what will happen to his son, his creator simply replies: 'I can't change my overall plan now. Why should I be kinder than my century? The millions of children who've been vilely murdered this century . . .' (498-99).

Time has run out. In Unthank people pay for what they need now by pledging their futures (437), and there is no future left: 'let us thrill the readers with a description of you ending *in company*. Let the ending be worldwide, for such a calamity is likely nowadays' (496). There is a promise of a catastrophe of biblical proportions, although at the last the immediate threat abates, leaving Lanark aware of his own approaching death but relatively at peace with himself: 'a slightly worried, ordinary old man but glad to see the light in the sky' (560). Around him, however, a war continues to rage and there is little doubt that Unthank will finally succumb, swallowed by the creature which is otherwise manifested in the power structures known as as the institute, the council, the foundation (409).

## II

Where Alasdair Gray is a better writer than he sometimes seems, Martin Amis sometimes seems to be better a writer than he actually is. The most common criticism of Amis's work is that the parts are better than the whole, a contagious style ultimately failing to make up for lack of content. At the same time, there is no doubt that *London Fields* is both an indicator of the *zeitgeist,* as well as an influence, and no discussion of the millennium in contemporary British fiction can afford to leave it off the list.

Amis's text shares *Lanark*'s sense of there not being much time left: 'Oh, Christ, no, the hell of time. . . . Time *takes* from you, with both hands. Things just disappear into it' (239). As the Note to *London Fields* explains, an alternative title could have been *Millennium.* However as 'M.A.' (the text is a prolonged tease and we're never sure whether we're in the hands of Martin Amis, real author, or Mark Asprey, fictional creation) explains: '*everything* is called *Millennium* just now'. So *London Fields* it is: 'This book is called *London Fields. London Fields . . .*' [p. vii].

Although the year is supposed to be 1999, 1989 is how it reads, with the bubble of the Eighties about to burst and recession immediately around the corner. London is at crisis point—although it is difficult to identify what form the crisis will actually take. Certainly the weather is behaving very oddly, there are cyclonic winds (killing 'nineteen people, and thirty-three million trees' (43). The animals are dying (97), and rumour has it that there is to be massive flooding, cosmic rays, and the Second Coming (118). The natural world is on fastforward, rushing toward catastrophe with the political situation racing to keep up. There's danger of 'A flare-up. A flashpoint somewhere' (105). The international situation is mysteriously linked to the ill-health of Faith, the First Lady (207), and the 'new buzz word' is '*Cathartic war*' (417). The sun is daily sinking lower as the earth tilts on its axis in anticipation of a full eclipse on November 5, at which point, so the rumours go, two nuclear bombs will explode, 'one over the Palace of Culture in Warsaw, one over Marble Arch' (394).

It's the end of the century and the planet is braced for impact (197) because while previous millenniums didn't really mean the end of the world ('Nobody had the hardware', 369), this time things are different. But when November 5 does come around, there isn't a bang but a whimper. The comet doesn't hit, the bombs don't explode, the sun returns to its normal position. A woman, however, is murdered and we are back with what we were promised on the novel's first page: 'This is' the story of a murder.'

*London Fields* is a murder story, popular fiction dressed up as high art, a text that functions as much as a textbook (designed for the undergraduate seminar requiring neat examples of the metafictional and postmodern) as a novel. Where in *Lanark* there are 'two' novels, one an experiment in realism, the other science fiction, *London Fields* is also multi-layered, the commentary of the narrator, Samson Young, sandwiching the fiction he is writing. The commentary, of course, tells us that this fiction is 'real' ('This is a true story but I can't believe it's really happening,' 1): a woman— Nicola Six, 'the murderee'—dumps her diaries in a London rubbish bin (26) and an author finds a ready-made story. At the same time Nicola Six finds her murderer. Or, rather, potential murderer for while, in Lawrentian terms, a murderee is always a murderee, 'The murderer was not yet a murderer' (18). A murderer has to be made, and so Samson Young describes how Nicola goes to work on Keith Talent who, although 'a very bad guy', working class, petty crook, wife-beater, rapist, is not yet 'the very worst ever' (4). It is up to Nicola to turn him into that, and in order to transform Keith into what is required she plays him off against Guy Clinch—upper class, nice guy, handsome, rich (27).

Nicola Six (a blend of sex and an Apocalyptic 666) has from an early age always known 'what was going to happen next' (15), and in the case of her own murder is playing both prophet and author. Why she wants to die is another matter: 'It's what she's always wanted' (1). Nicola Six is a heart, and ball, breaker: 'She pauperized gigilos, she spayed studs, she hospitalized heartbreakers' (21). For Guy, Nicola plays the virgin, teasing him into a state whereby he loses dignity, sanity, family. For Keith she's the whore. Nicola is all things to all men: 'I'm worried', Samson Young tells her, 'they're going to say you're a male fantasy figure.' To which the reply is 'I *am* a male fantasy figure. I've been one for fifteen years. It really takes it out of a girl' (260).

If this is the writer (the real writer, Martin Amis) attempting to cover himself the attempt is less than a success. Geoff Dyer confides that 'youngish male writers' find themselves struggling against the influence of the Amis style ('. . . the guy has got it. I mean, really') and 'accusing each other of imitating him' (Dyer, 8). Some women critics, however, appear to find Amis less difficult to resist (Ellison, 21) and it is easy to see how the depiction of Nicola Six invites accusations of misogyny, even though Amis's apparent intention is for his female character to be read as a symbol of her age rather than a sign of her gender. Nicola is self-destructive, compelled not just to cancel love but to murder it (21), a perversion of emotion which, according to this text, is reflected in a predeliction for sodomy: 'It was the only thing about herself that she couldn't understand and wouldn't forgive' (67). But while Nicola can't quite comprehend her own desires she is aware that 'Literature *did* go on about sodomy, and increasingly' (67). Joyce, Lawrence, Beckett, Updike,

Mailer, Roth, Naipaul (68), compiling her list of (male) writers she is tempted to see sodomy as a 'twentieth-century theme', and Nicola 'would be perfectly prepared to represent her century' (67-8). Sodomy, for Nicola, is about negation—'*That's what I am,* she used to whisper to herself after sex. *A black hole. Nothing can escape from me.*' (67)—and that too is the motto of the suicidal last century of the second millennium.

The twentieth century has 'come along and after several try-outs and test-drives it put together an astonishing new offer: death for everybody . . .' (297). At the end, however, death calls only for Nicola, who barely whimpers. This doesn't mean that the big bang won't happen, but is more a recognition that it has happened already. We've already seen the big one, and are living in its aftermath. The big one was the Second World War and what it unleashed, the possibility of nuclear holocaust. Just as Nicola has known since childhood what was going to happen next she's been accompanied by an invisible companion: '. . . Enola Gay. Enola wasn't real. Enola came from inside the head of Nicola Six' (16). As part of her effort to humiliate Guy, Nicola extracts large amounts of money from him on the pretext of trying to save Enola Gay and her little boy, stranded in south-east Asia as a result of the Cambodian war. But just as Enola Gay isn't really a refugee in Thailand or Burma, she isn't a fantasy either:

> 'Enola Gay' was the plane that flew the mission to Hiroshima. The pilot named the aircraft after his mother. He was once her little boy. But Little Boy was the name of the atom bomb. It killed 50,000 people in 120 seconds.
>
> (445)

Nicola has been able to con Guy because, like the vast majority, he hasn't known one of the most important facts in his sad century's history. Similarly, Keith has to be told that the bikini Nicola dons is named after the Bikini Atoll:

> 'What American men did there—one of the greatest crimes in human history. If you got the world's most talented shits and cruelty experts together, they couldn't come up with anything worse than Bikini. And how do we commemorate the crime, Keith?' She indicated the two small pieces of her two-piece. 'Certain women go about wearing this trash. It's very twentieth-century, don't you think?'
>
> 'Yeah. Diabolical.'
>
> (127)

So diabolical in fact that it's as if the Second World War never really ended: '. . . it seemed possible to argue that Hitler was still running the century. Hitler, the great bereaver' (395). History ended mid-century and what we are caught in in *London Fields* is the hell of the perpetual present.

Nicola Six, the murderee, walks in the shadow of Enola Gay, and so too does her murderer. When Nicola appears in the Black Cross pub Samson Young leaps to the conclusion that she's recognized her murderer in Keith. But this is one of those whodunnits in which the unwitting narrator turns out to be the 'who'. 'She leaned forward. "You," she said, with intense recognition. "Always you . . ."' (465). Nicola had known him from the start (466). And Young should have known too because he and Nicola are linked by the fact that they're both as good as dead already (260). However where Nicola, representative of a self-destructive century, wills her own death, Young has had his willed on him as a legacy of the work his father did, in London Fields, on High Explosives Research (120, 161).

Samson Young is 'pre-nuked and dead-already' (323). So when Guy is about to kill Nicola, Young can make a deal with him and take his place because he has nothing to lose. 'After the first blow she gave a moan of visceral assent' (467) and the narrator is left to take a suicide pill. A murder and a suicide and everything goes back to normal. Which is the problem with *London Fields* because, ultimately, any political message there is about the destructive temperament of the century, the madness of things nuclear, is lost as the skies clear and the novel, like other of Amis's novels, concludes by valorizing class and gender (Doan, 79). The woman gets what she's asking for and her death is, ultimately, engineered by Guy who beats up the already-humiliated Keith and reasserts himself as the dominant, upper-class male. The post-war, postmodern, postmillennial world gets back to normal.

### III

Hannah Arendt's explorations of the dynamics of holocaust have demonstrated the banality of evil, and this is the premise behind Shena Mackay's powerful, and alarming novel, ***Dunedin.*** Mackay's text begins as a realist novel set in 1909, effortlessly jumps forward into a dark comedy about middle-class, suburban life in south London, 1989, then skews sideways into a surreal, alternative world which serves as a nightmarish vision of the future.

In the early years of the new century the minister Jack Mackenzie and his family, fresh from Scotland, sail into Dunedin harbour, New Zealand, and find: 'the New World glittering at the end of the beams which streamed from the fingers of God as a sign that all would be well' (3). In this last century of the second millennium, however, God's influence is decidedly weak. Jack Mackenzie, hypocrite and sensualist, disregards the needs of his flock, tyrannises over his family, and is more interested in science than religion. Nothing is well at all.

Where cause and effect are tenuous in both *Lanark* and *London Fields,* the equation is carefully worked out in

***Dunedin.*** Thus Sandy, Jack Mackenzie's son, will become overtly what his father is covertly, a professional con-man. The minister brings bad luck on his son, and on his son's children, the Mackenzie family representing in miniature the repercussions of imperialism and colonialism on future generations. When they leave Dunedin they take bad luck with them back to the Old World in the form of a preserved head which Jack steals—as a scientific curiosity—from his Maori lover, Myrtille. But the head is '*tapu* . . . sacred or magic (27): in 1811 a sailor stole a similar one and six years later was killed, along with some of his shipmates, by the natives he'd robbed. In revenge the Maori city of Otago was set alight and destroyed (10-11). Jack Mackenzie knows the story, but doesn't heed its lesson.

Eighty years later the English, once with a mighty empire to exploit, can only exploit each other. South London in 1989 is, like the rest of Europe, a frightening and dangerous place where it is no longer safe to let children play in the park alone (60). A fact recognized only too well by William Mackenzie, Jack Mackenzie's grandson, whose career as a headmaster comes to an end when one of his students is murdered on a school trip. William blames himself:

> almost every moment of the day and night, waking screaming in a sodden, strangling tangle of sheets. The horror of the child's going.
>
> (61)

It is for their lost children that William and his sister, Olive, grieve. Olive finds a solution in the simple expedient of child-napping. The pretty black baby in his mother's arms on the tube is irresistible and when Olive gets him back home she announces that he is named Theodore: the next morning her brother leaves this 'Gift of God' (81) outside a local hospital.

Olive sees the baby as a desirable object; less desirable is the scruffy boy she meets in the Horniman Museum. Nineteen-year-old Jay Pascal, newly arrived from New Zealand, is beaten and robbed on his arrival in London (280), and is appalled by the 'vastness, noise and dirt' of the city (66). Should she ask him, Jay—who might not be a gift from God but is certainly one of God's holy fools—would be only too happy to go and live in Olive's house. But all Olive offers is a lift, and even when he asks to be dropped off at 'Dunedin', once the Mackenzie family home but now a derelict squat, she fails to ask why this young New Zealander has come to stay at this particular address. If she did ask she would discover that Jay, brought up in an orphanage in New Zealand, has made his way 'home': Jack Mackenzie not only stole the sacred head from Myrtille, but left her pregnant, and Jay is his great-grandson.

Jay soon joins the ranks of the 'ruined people' (70). This is the wasteland of the Eighties, the Thatcher years: the hospitals and asylums are in the process of being demolished and the patients have been left to make their own way in 'what they had been taught to call the community' (73). The disaffected, deranged, and dispossessed, sleep in doorways, beg at tube stations—and it is at this point that Mackay's vision of the future begins to shape itself along the lines of what is, after all, not a remote past. Because before long:

> There were those who had decided that something must be done about them. Private enterprise was engaged to trawl the streets in the dead hours before dawn. . . . Rumours of disappearances circulated in crypts and park benches and in derelict houses but nobody walked into a police station to register a vagrant as a missing person.
>
> (73-4)

The reality of late-Eighties England, the increase in begging and homelessness, the well-publicized moves to 'clean up' areas like the Strand and the cardboard city clustered around the South Bank, reverberates with the reality of late-Thirties Nazi Germany. The millennium is on the doorstep and its shape is that of the Holocaust, the 'T4' euthenasia programme and the removal of 'asocials' to concentration, and death, camps.

Late one night Jay is bundled into a windowless van 'marked Department of the Environment' (187) and finds himself at St Anne's, a vast Victorian house which has quietly been removed from the Ordnance Survey maps and isn't listed in the telephone book: 'it was as if it did not exist' (185). And the people who have been brought here, 'herded into the reek of misery and rot', might as well not exist any longer either:

> They were being addressed by a man in a quasi-uniform of navy blue: '. . . and just in case there should be any barrack-room lawyers among you, with any fancy ideas about Human Rights, I should point out that you lot have renounced any claim you might once have had to humanity. You are no longer human beings. You are the scum of the earth. Your subsciptions to Amnesty International have been cancelled. If you have any friends, which I very much doubt, they won't find you here. Oh yes, one more thing, there is no way out, so don't even think about it.'
>
> (188)

This is the discourse of power and brutality, legitimized as 'the Vagrancy Act' (318), and in the face of this Jay's appeal for justice on behalf of himself and his fellow prisoners is not only futile but dangerous: 'Why am I being kept prisoner here? And it's not just me, all of us, we haven't committed any crimes and if we had we're entitled to a hearing, not just to be locked up and beaten . . .' (318). A sign above a row of bins reads 'Refuse To Be Incinerated', which is how the institution's staff regard the inmates. Jay reads the same sign and determines to survive: 'I will refuse . . . I am still myself. I won't let them destroy me. I will get out of here' (236).

The reader is tantalized with the hope that Jay might escape the incinerators. Father Jeremy, a vicar who in these last days of the century cherishes a touching faith in God, also harbours the suspicion that something is dreadfully wrong at St Anne's: 'I know that God wants me to find out what it is' (193). He eventually hears the truth from the director's secretary:

> As Cheryl spoke of vans disgorging broken people into the courtyard, of black-windowed private ambulances, the secret laboratories, locked rooms where naked men and women rocked silently in filth, the faint far-off cries of children, it was as though a troop of demons streamed from those rosebud lips.
>
> (315)

Jeremy, blessed with a loving wife, a baby son, and the ability sometimes to read others' thoughts, seems to be just the person to blow Dr Barrables' establishment sky-high. This is the conclusion that Barrables comes to himself, with the result that Olive later reads about: 'a curate and his family, wife and child, who had been killed in a freak accident, when their Volkswagen Beetle had run off a seemingly empty country road in broad daylight and somersaulted down a chalky bank (326). 'Hell on Earth', Olive reads in her paper, 'Greek Island of the Insane Exposed. Why it couldn't happen here . . .' (325). But Hell is here already, experienced by 'a monkey with . . . tubes and electrodes coming out of his scalped head' (193), 'galvanised animal concentration camps set in stinking yards' (265). It is only a short step from here to the conclusion that if people like Jay are 'no longer human beings' (188) then genocide is, *humane*. Like with animals . . . the kindest thing . . .' (241).

Olive, wrapped in her cloak of self-centred, middle-class *angst,* can read the newspaper article about the dead curate and his family without reading it: '"They'll be all right," she thought dully, turning the page' (326). Passing a boy huddled outside a pub she does briefly remember Jay and 'if goodwill had any power against evil a spark flared for a second in the darkness' (329). But in the gathering gloom that is the end of the second millennium, evil has won out and for Olive the only answer left is a return to the God that her grandfather turned his back on at the beginning of the century: '"Well," she thought. "Seeing as no one else bloody well wants me, I'd better see if God will take me back"' (330). In this black comedy this might either be a reference to suicide, or to the Evangelicals who have just passed by.

The suggestion of suicide links Olive to Thaw/Lanark, and Samson Young. However a stronger link among **Dunedin,** *Lanark,* and *London Fields,* is the fear we feel not so much for ourselves but for our children, and our anxiety that they should be kept safe. In **Dunedin** successive generations fail their children and in the last

years of the century there is no assurance that anyone can keep a child safe. However the one sliver of hope that the novel does offer is the fact that Olive's brother, William, has found a lover and conceived a child.

As Nastler reminds Lanark, this is a century in which millions of children have been vilely murdered. Lanark, a child of the Second World War, is desperate to know what will happen to his son Alexander in the war which is to engulf Unthank. And Alexander, in turn, is quick to assure Lanark that his own daughter is 'in a safer place than this, thank goodness' (556). Meanwhile, in *London Fields,* Nicola Six is finally murdered for the sake of a child. Samson Young loves Keith's baby daughter, Kim. Kim, however, is being abused by her mother, Kath, who is abused by Keith. The deal Young strikes with Guy means that Kath and Kim will be looked after financially, and Kim will be safe in the future.

With the Second World War history entered hell's gates, and never came out again. Apocalypse but with no Second Coming, no heavenly jurisdiction. But while history might have ended some fifty years ago it is still possible to hope that it can move forward once again through future generations. Thus, as the sun sets on the battleground that was the twentieth century time becomes even more urgent, for it is now: 'time to do this, time to look for our children and see how many we can find' (*London Fields,* 469).

### Works Cited

Amis, Martin, 1990 (1989). *London Fields,* Penguin.

Doan, Laura L., 1990. '"Sexy Greedy *Is* the Late Eighties": Power Systems in Amis's *Money* and Churchill's *Serious Money,*' *Minnesota Review* 34-5, Spring-Fall, 69-80.

Dyer, Geoff, 1993. 'Mad about the boy,' *The Guardian,* 2 Nov., 8.

Ellison, Jane, 1989. 'Battlefields,' *The Guardian,* 12 Oct., 21.

Gifford, Douglas, 1987. 'Private Confession and Public Satire in the Fiction of Alasdair Gray,' *Chapman* 10.i and ii, Summer, 101-16.

Gray, Alasdair, 1991 (1981). *Lanark,* Picador.

Imhoff, Rudiger, 1990. 'Chinese Box: Flann O'Brien in the Metafiction of Alasdair Gray, John Fowles, and Robert Coover,' *Eire-Ireland* 25.i, Spring, 64-79.

Lee, Alison, 1990. 'Un-mastering masterful images,' in *Realism and Power: Postmodern British Fiction,* Routledge, 99-127.

Mackay, Shena, 1992. *Dunedin,* Penguin.

O'Toole, Fintan, 1995. 'The Dredd of 2000 AD,' *The Guardian,* 7 Jan., 29.

## Katy Emck (review date 14 June 1996)

SOURCE: Emck, Katy. "Down Rabbit Lane." *Times Literary Supplement* (14 June 1996): 22.

[*In the following review, Emck deems* The Orchard on Fire *as "a bittersweet, gentle novel, not given to grandstanding or preaching, but shot through with humour and compassion."*]

Shena MacKay's new novel [*The Orchard on Fire*] opens in an elegiac mood. April, a middle-aged teacher, a divorcee, sits brooding in her low-rental London garden on one of those ruefully lovely summer evenings when every cranny of decayed wall erupts with dust-covered plant-life. Her reflection is broken by her neighbour, the jauntily-named Jaz, the author "of several unpublished manuscripts of the depilatory school", who refers to April's attempt to stem the floodtide of weeds as "a spot of ethnic cleansing". But for all her urban cynicism, Jaz is really Janette from Northumbria, "a damp fungus grown from a spore blown on to London plaster", while April is "a brittler accretion, but as rootless". The pair are as diasporic as the pheasant berry, which "seeds itself everywhere, leaving dead canes where it cannot stand the competition, that rattle and creak".

The mood of creeping disaffection is premonitory. It prepares us for April's return to the Kent village where she grew up in a teashop called the Copper Kettle. English teashops are as immemorial as English weeds. They suggest a 1950s never-never land of discreet curtains, cosily steamed-up windows and scones with "lashings of jam". Middle-aged April is still April the eight-year-old: "it was the time that coloured everything for me, that set my weakness for the gaudy and ephemeral. . . ." April loves fairy lights, hanging spider plants, electric candles. And Shena MacKay picks up on details which are so *right* that April's memories of childhood seem to be one's own. For instance there is Veronica, the schoolgirl who smells of Marmite and—obviously, since she can't shake off the smell of food—lacks spirit.

The village of Stonebridge, for all its staid appearance, is a theatre of English eccentrics. There are the local female artists, greenery-yallery types, theatrical but kind. There is April's grandfather, whose pet project is to build the Crystal Palace using matchsticks, silver cigarette paper, pipe cleaners and bits of sponge dipped in green ink (for the trees). There are April's parents, London publicans turned country-teashop owners and Communists. Less cosily, Stonebridge sports a young man who hangs around in lonely places cadging kisses from girls by jamming them up against walls with his bike. It is also inhabited by Mr Greenidge, ageing but dapper in a panama hat, the wolf in the woods where April plays.

The child's sense of melodrama, her love for secret refuges and morbid, sensational fictions—*Deathcap Cottage* is one—is threaded into a fearful tale that is not imagined but real. On arriving in Stonebridge, April makes friends with the fiery-headed Ruby. They share a taste for adventure, a passion for illicit hide-outs and stories about murder and code-breaking. Slowly April comes to see that Ruby is being beaten by her publican father and neglected by her harridan of a mother. However, neither Ruby nor April's parents are aware of the pact that has sprung up between April and Mr Greenidge. The Edenic orchard and thrilling train carriage where the children play are refuges from the adult world in more senses than one. Lovers Lane is no longer a childish joke, and the dark intruder they imagine beyond the confines of their camp is all too real.

But April never tells. And the easy good humour of her family life continues for the most part undisturbed, along with the quiet hum of village existence. *The Orchard on Fire* is an elegy for a lost time as much as a deconstruction of its cosy virtues. The portrait of the passionate, anarchic friendship of April and her red-headed friend, Ruby, makes the novel a celebration of childhood as well as a mourning for the loss of innocence. Their friendship is made in the immediate, absolute, instinctive way that only children can imagine. It forms the heart of the novel, along with April's enduring love for "ANTIQUES BYGONES KITCHENALIA. . . . Utensils with scorched handles of yellow banded in green, rusted bun tins that print fancy leaves on the bottom of your fairy cakes . . . a Chad Valley swan and a big tin Triang tortoise". Yet April reacts ironically when she finds that the Copper Kettle is selling off its "kitchenalia" to nostalgia tourists, wryly observing that "they are trying to buy their way into the past they think we had, they want to be snug and safe down Rabbit Lane".

*The Orchard on Fire* is written more in sorrowful affection than in anger. It is a bitter-sweet, gentle novel, not given to grandstanding or preaching, but shot through with humour and compassion. Shena MacKay is effortlessly amusing but never plays for laughs. Her writing brilliantly captures the spirit of place, where every present sensation has ghostly overtones that make experience all the more sad and lovely.

## Carol Birch (review date 21 June 1996)

SOURCE: Birch, Carol. "Remembered Ills." *New Statesman* 125, no. 4288 (21 June 1996): 45-6.

[*In the following review, Birch offers a mixed review of* The Orchard on Fire.]

At the heart of *The Orchard on Fire* is an intense best-friendship between two little girls in a fictional Kent village in 1953. Kingfishers flash on the river, the meadows are lush with wild flowers and the bloom is on the plums in the forgotten orchard where they have their den in an abandoned railway carriage. Theirs is a symbiotic relationship, cemented by pacts, codes and secret understandings.

Over this rural idyll hangs the awful guillotine shadow of child abuse, threatening to break the friendship and ensuring their ultimate separation. For Ruby the abuse is brutal and physical and comes from her own parents. For April, the narrator, it's more subtle. She falls prey to white-haired Mr Greenidge, the "charming man" who walks his ailing wife's dachshund through the village and lures April into a world equally private but infinitely more damaging, of stolen old man's kisses and pathetic trysts.

There is an assurance to Shena Mackay's prose that is up and running from the first line. Her descriptions and evocations of place and atmosphere are very fine indeed. "We forced open the door," says April, speaking of that first breathless entry into the secret railway carriage, "and stood in the smell of trapped time." One almost hears the scuttling of spiders outraged at the intrusion, senses the light filtered through "earthy, rain-streaked, bird-squirted, berry-smeared windows."

Less successful are the depictions of minor characters. April and Ruby inhabit a world of stereotypes whose delineation is so shallow that at times you feel you have wandered into the pages of a children's book. Villains practically twirl their moustaches. Artists are dippy and fey, professors absent-minded, Cockney grannies the salt of the earth. The local communist family is so saintly it glows with Waltonesque warmth.

April herself is convincingly rounded. She has picked up on the inconsistent moral reasonings of the adults around her and struggles to make sense of them. Capital and corporal punishment are, for example, condemned but "Lex [Ruby's father] ought to be put up against a wall and shot." The clear consensus is that some people are very nasty indeed and deserve a good kicking. Smug in her disdain for the failings of others, April is less than kind to a would-be friend whose main sin seems to be that "she smelled of Marmite and had warts on her hands."

April and Ruby, despite their abuse, are cocky, confident children, surprisingly well-balanced; at least it would seem so if the story were not planted, by way of an introduction and epilogue, firmly in the here and now.

Ruby we do not see as an adult but April, recalling the past at fiftysomething, has clearly suffered. The child has become "a hard-faced woman with a mascara'd tissue crumpled in her lap applying lipstick in the cruel sunshine." The book's triumph is in capturing the sense of grief for a friendship untimely ripped apart almost half a century ago and the evocation of the magical intensity with which childhood cloaks landscape—the sadness and treachery of those "blue remembered hills".

### Anita Brookner (review date 29 June 1996)

SOURCE: Brookner, Anita. "A Memory of Yesterday's Pleasures." *Spectator* 276, no. 8763 (29 June 1996): 35-6.

[*In the following positive review of* The Orchard on Fire, *Brookner contends that "in her misleadingly straightforward novel the author has set out a rite of passage which will leave few readers unaffected."*]

It can be no accident that on reading the first few pages of this haunting novel [*The Orchard on Fire*] one is enveloped by a feeling of nostalgia, not for Provence, not for Tuscany, but for hot sun in a London garden, and a July evening spent with a book under a dusty tree. Shena Mackay is the celebrant of unfashionable suburbs, Streatham and Sydenham, Norwood and Herne Hill: her richly subversive *Dunedin,* in which her disconcerting talent was given its head, took place within these confines. The nostalgia, in the present case, expands to take in Kent, equally unfashionable, and the village of Stonebridge, where her protagonist, April Harlency, grows up after her parents, gallant losers in the licensed trade, take over the Copper Kettle Tea Room.

And that is it, the story of an almost happy childhood, into which the occasional disturbed adult intrudes, posing problems for April and her friend Ruby Richards, daughter of the landlord of The Rising Sun. April and Ruby are heroines, with the peculiar loyalty and truthfulness of inseparables, free to play in the fields, to wheel about on their bicycles, to make a hideout in a disused railway carriage. Their minds and characters are complementary, until their complicity is arbitrarily broken up. Left to themselves they are invulnerable, but of course they are not left to themselves.

It is 1953; television sets are rare and the wireless reigns supreme. 'Let's have a bit of entertainment', says April's mother, and they tune in to Family Favourites. Into this almost prelapsarian setting a dissonant note is sounded by Ruby's brutal father, and even more so by the jovial and priapic Mr Greenidge. In both cases their wives are compliant, knowing and accepting. This might almost be an exemplary story for children, warning them of the dangers of the adult world. The date is important: in 1953 politeness inhibited children from denouncing aberrant behaviour. Today there would be help lines, social workers, counselling. The crux of the story is the incorruptibility of the children, although they are not proof against fear. One might say that even so they are too ignorant to be truly frightened. How could they be? Their reading matter consists of *Little Women* and *Anne of Green Gables*; they have neither witnessed nor imagined a primal scene. April remains mystified by Mr Greenidge's friendship, although she grows increasingly uncomfortable as he requests a meeting by the telephone box. It was only his dog which attracted her, but even a dog can be an instrument of seduction.

The friendship between April and Ruby is beautifully done, and here a further nostalgia is brought into play, this time for a life before knowingness, calculation, bargaining. The afterword is therefore all the more shocking. An adult April goes back to Stonebridge to recapture, or to try to recapture—the attempt is doomed—something of those early years. She is hard-faced, lonely, a teacher of English. She has learned how to dissemble, how never to give a straight answer. She has been brought to this condition by the process of ageing and the loss of a friend. This is the final nostalgia, then, for the friends of one's youth, whose memory is all the more poignant when they are no longer there to comfort one for the mistakes made in later life.

Shena Mackay has brought off something quite rare, a completely unpretentious story written with the benefit of hindsight. She embraces no modish theories, alludes to no wider themes, is sparing with historical and local colour. The writing is functional, but natural and easy, so easy that one accedes immediately to the girls' private language and concerns. It would be equally easy to dismiss *The Orchard on Fire* as an agreeable diversion in an era of heavyweight literary exercises. This would be a mistake. The subtlety with which it traces misplaced causes and effects is calculated. Love and friendship are at stake, although apparently explored only in two children who inevitably lose their innocence. That is the tragedy, of course, the tragedy which befalls most children. In her misleadingly straightforward novel the author has set out a rite of passage which will leave few readers unaffected.

**Michele Field (review date 2 December 1996)**

SOURCE: Field, Michele. "Shena Mackay: The Menace of the Domestic." *Publishers Weekly* 243, no. 49 (2 December 1996): 36-8.

[*In the following positive review of* The Orchard on Fire, *Field praises Mackay's sense of the macabre and provides an overview of her literary career.*]

The annals of contemporary fiction are full of authors of highly praised but little-known books. Few have produced a body of work that is as fresh and evocative

as the 11 volumes that Shena Mackay has written since 1964. Her latest, *The Orchard on Fire,* a Booker Prize nominee, recently published Stateside by Moyer-Bell, displays her sharp eye for the macabre and humorous domestic dramas of the English middle class.

Mackay (pronounced to rhyme with "reply") is the most mysterious of the six authors to be shortlisted for this year's Booker. This is partly because she attends fewer literary parties than she is invited to: she lives in an outer-London neighborhood that is beyond the reach of the tube. But it is not only her seclusion that has maintained her mystery—she also doesn't belong to a literary clique that might spread gossip about her.

In person, Mackay, 52, is a striking figure, whose beautiful white pageboy haircut and quiet voice lend her an air of invulnerability; it somehow takes 10 minutes to absorb the fact that she is also nervous. Mackay answers *PW*'s questions as if she were in a doctor's office and is careful to be accurate. She refuses to hedge, freely telling her American audience more about herself than most British readers know from the few interviews she's given in recent years.

The narrator of *The Orchard on Fire* is a young girl with whom an elderly married man has fallen in love, and who is beset by feelings of bewilderment and entrapment as his pursuit turns into psychological molestation. The novel subtly shows how life goes on with girlish things despite the bad scripts of adult lives. All of Mackay's books are about the charged emotional lives of very ordinary middle-class nailbiters.

Mackay was born in Edinburgh, the second of three sisters. Her parents were intellectuals who had met in college, but none of the girls pursued higher education. The burned plastic smell of families melting apart surrounds Mackay's life story and the stories in her books. "My mother was a schoolteacher, but she got rheumatoid arthritis when she was in her 30s and got progressively worse," says Mackay. "It was a fairly tempestuous marriage and I left home at 16, around the time they split up. They had ambitions for their daughters initially, but the ambitions petered out.

"My mother died about four years ago, and I see my dad quite regularly now. I never lost touch with him entirely [as the rest of the family did]. But I don't consciously put my family into my books, and the family in *The Orchard on Fire* is not my family; it is more Louisa May Alcott, an invented ideal family that is not mine. There is some of my childhood in *The Orchard,* but it is more a feeling than specific incidents."

Unlike the protagonist of *The Orchard on Fire,* Mackay grew up in an urbane, literary environment. Her parents knew various Scottish writers who were living in

London and had a circle of painter friends. "The bohemian lifestyle did seem interesting," Mackay laughs. "It was what I wanted to do."

## A Precocious Start

At age 16, Mackay won her first literary competition (with a poem she wrote at 14) and through that met other writers. Throughout her life, she has been close to art critic David Sylvester (who recently curated the Francis Bacon show at the Pompidou Center in Paris). "I did meet lots of painters—the old Colony Room crowd like Francis Bacon and Lucian Freud," she says.

When Mackay left school at 16, she worked in an antique shop in Chancery Lane owned by David Sylvester's sister Jackie, who in turn was married to Frank Marcus (who wrote *The Killing of Sister George*). "Frank Marcus was manager of the silver shop and I was 17 when I showed him something I'd written, and he showed it to his agent, who showed it to a publisher. It was **Dust Falls on Eugene Schlumberger** and it was far too short, but they said if I would write something else they would publish it. So I wrote **Toddler on the Run.**"

Mackay had just turned 20 when both works were published in one volume by Andre Deutsch. She found her first agent immediately in Peter JansonSmith. Shortly thereafter, when another member of the firm, Deborah Rogers, left to form her own agency (now Rogers, Coleridge & White Ltd), Mackay moved with her. "II think I am her oldest living client," she muses.

Mackay married a former school friend, a petro-chemist named Robin Brown (whom she divorced in the 1980s), moved out of London and wrote three more books while raising three daughters—two by Brown, one by Sylvester. Then from 1971 to 1983, nothing was heard of her.

Pressed to explain why she left the literary fast lane after such a promising start, it becomes clear that the pressures of raising three daughters, often singlehand-edly, played a significant role. "It was not so much deliberate as it just happened. I didn't give up, but I did write a novel which has never been published—which now looks like a rough draft of *A Bowl of Cherries,* which was published in 1984. Indeed my publisher, Jonathan Cape, rejected *A Bowl of Cherries,* too, but I was friends at that time with the writer Brigid Brophy and she showed it to Iris Murdoch, who helped see that it was published by a firm called Harvester." She pauses, and adds with a smile: "I think Harvester just does CD-ROMs now."

Apart from small jobs in libraries and shops, Mackay has always written. Her first novel to be published in the States was her third in Britain, *Old Crow* (McGraw-Hill, 1967). Later that year, Simon & Schuster brought out **Toddler on the Run** as its own volume. "Then nothing in the States at all," she says. "'Too English,' I was told.

"But a few years ago, I heard from Moyer-Bell." It was critic and novelist Francis Wyndham, whose Whitbread Award-winning novel, *The Other Garden,* is also published by the small, Rhode-Island-based press, who first introduced co-publisher Jennifer Moyer to Mackay's work. Moyer-Bell has since released a collection of Mackay's stories called **Dreams of Dead Women's Handbags** (1994), two novels in 1992, **Dunedin** and *A Bowl of Cherries,* and an anthology of short stories about sisters that Mackay edited called *Such Devoted Sisters* (1994).

## Harold Pinter in the Kitchen

Mackay's signature is recognizable from book to book: a sense of menace below the check-pattern of middle-class life; a subliminal eroticism charging everything ("but no blow-by-blow sex scenes," Mackay points out); and a very sharp definition of time and place, of brand names and domestic manners—altogether, as if Harold Pinter were taking you through the contents of his kitchen cupboards.

Why does nothing in her discussion of these books suggest that most of them end in death? "Well, there is a death per page in the first two novellas, and I think I have fewer deaths now," she laughs. "Still, one or two."

"*Old Crow,* like **The Orchard on Fire,** is set in Kent," Mackay says when asked what in her life has given rise to the peculiar mix of hilarity, surrealism and gloom that animate the commonplace world of her books. "I lived in Kent from the age of eight to 15—though it is a very fictionalized version of a village called Shore-ham, where William Blake and Samuel Palmer once lived. I don't actually have roots—though I feel Scottish and I go back there—but I do feel very strongly about Kent.

"You can read my biography," she says, in the two books that followed **Old Crow, Music Upstairs** (1965) and **An Advent Calendar** (1971), both of which concern a young married couple. "Both, I think, have a mixture of humor and sadness and ends on a note of muted optimism. 'Black humor' is what the reviewers said, and of course there is that, but it is a very easy label. A lot of my humor is punning as well, and slapstick."

**Redhill Roccoco** (1986) was written around the time of her divorce, when she and the girls moved to a suburb of "happy-clappy" Christians, as she calls them. "I used to like going to church, but I hate this kind of enthusi-asm, so I don't go to church now. I like an evensong, the pews three-quarters empty, a few candles." She is being ironic but truthful. Her eldest daughter, Sarah, and her husband are members of a Christian organization that has sent them to Pakistan to work with Afghan refugees. Mackay hopes to visit them in March.

*Dunedin* stands out among Mackay's work because it abandons the suburbs of modern London that she has made her own for New Zealand at the beginning of the century ("a New Zealand of my imagination, since I hadn't been there"). It is the only occasion when she has not written about a remembered past. "The book was about empire and the damage colonialists can do. And the contemporary scenes are set among vagrants on the streets of London. I was drawing an analogy between a Scottish family who went out to New Zealand and how it all went wrong for them; and how everything has gone wrong in London."

When she wrote *The Orchard on Fire,* Mackay returned to the same tone as her earlier books, but for the first time she wrote in the first person. "And I wrote it in a completely narrative-linear way: I mean I just sat down and wrote it after putting it off and putting it off. I know I put writing off because once you enter it, you know you will be in a very intense state and won't want to be interrupted. So if you have other commitments in life, it is very easy not to start."

Mackay is slowly making inroads with American readers. Both *Dreams of Dead Women's Handbags* and *A Bowl of Cherries,* a novel about two unhappily married authors of detective fiction, received glowing reviews in the *New York Times Book Review.* At press time, she has just concluded her first American book tour, which culminated at the Illinois Humanities Council Literary Festival in Chicago, where 250 fans turned out to hear her read from her four books published here.

She has previously made just two trips to New York, both private holidays for less than a week. "I actually hate book tours but I pretend to like them when I want to go somewhere like Chicago, which I have only seen in the movies. I remind myself that there is no such thing as a free lunch," she says wryly.

Today, Mackay is as prolific as ever. Moyer-Bell's edition of *Dreams* is a compilation of three short story collections previously issued in England and she is building up to the publication of still another story collection. Mackay has continued to write short stories although her longer fiction is in demand. The novels are more lucrative, but the money question does not hound her. "Let's say money has always been problematic, up and down, and often more down than up."

Mackay lives in a one-bedroom flat and when she has people to stay "well, it would be lovely to have them stay comfortably. My second daughter, Rebecca, is mar-

ried and has a little boy, Harry, who is 18 months, and she is expecting another baby in December. Grandchildren are the most wonderful thing, and I want to be able to afford a house somewhere for them and me." Cecily Brown, 27, Mackay's third daughter (the daughter of David Sylvester), is a painter living in New York who illustrated the jacket of the British edition of *The Orchard on Fire.*

British critics have compared Mackay to authors ranging from Dickens to Ronald Firbank and Muriel Spark, but she seems far too vivid to be a clone of somebody else. An unconventionally glamorous woman, doting grandmother and a writer who sees the world with witty intelligence and heartbreaking clarity, she deserves her own place in the literary pantheon.

## Denise Chong (review date 28 January 1997)

SOURCE: Chong, Denise. "In the Playground of Good and Evil." *Washington Post Book World* (28 January 1997): D10.

[*In the following positive review, Chong views* The Orchard on Fire *as a charming and evocative novel.*]

You can have a near out-of-body experience with Shena Mackay's latest novel, *The Orchard on Fire.* In its opening pages the narrator, April Harlency, remembers her childhood: "I was never a particularly balletic or acrobatic child, but sometimes when I was happy I could see another self slip from my body and run leaping and doing cartwheels, somersaulting through the air beside me. I almost glimpse her now, running along an undulating hedge and telegraph poles' tightropes." Few readers can help but see their other self slip from between the pages. By the time they catch their breath at this compact novel's end, they will both welcome and regret the inevitable journey back to adulthood.

Deservedly, *The Orchard on Fire* was short-listed for last year's Booker Prize. For American readers, it can be an introduction to Mackay, a Scottish-born writer living in London and previously published but little-known in the United States. Mackay's publisher says it "aims to change that" with this novel, yet it makes a couple of irritating mistakes about the story on the inside jacket. No matter, as reading *The Orchard on Fire* (and Mackay) for the first time, I fell under its spell and found myself wanting other titles by her on the bedside table. To my delight, Shena Mackay, first published at age 20 in 1964, has amassed a body of work that includes not only novels but stories.

*The Orchard on Fire* begins with an adult's reminiscences, when April, living alone and her parents both dead, takes a day trip from London to the village of

Stonebridge. At the end she makes a haunting discovery about what has become of her best childhood friend, redheaded Ruby Richards. In between is a richly wrought story of an intense friendship that takes place almost a half-century earlier between two girls, both 8 years old.

April's and Ruby's lives come together when April's parents move from London to Stonebridge to try to make a go of the Copper Kettle Tea-room, in the same village where Ruby's parents run the local pub, the Rising Sun. Where April's parents radiate a cozy warmth, complete with a baby sister or brother for April on the way, Ruby's are ill-tempered, hateful and destructive. Although the girls create a secure world in a secret hideaway in a forgotten orchard, whenever they go back to the world of adults, the novel is gripped with nervous tension. Lurking from page to page is the white-haired Mr. Greenidge, in a Panama hat and with a dachshund on a leash, who conspires to find himself alone with April. He is unwittingly aided by her parents, who insist that she accept his invitations to Sunday tea with him and his childless, ailing wife. Also in April's cast of evil is Ruby's father, as she makes a connection between his unprovoked rages and her friend's passing references to being "locked in the cellar."

Such harm and cruelty would today be labeled sexual abuse and domestic violence, which in the novel's 1950s setting didn't exist as neighborly suspicion, much less criminal offenses. Between April and Ruby, there are no answers and fewer questions about the infallibility of the adults around them. Mackay delivers her verdict on the irrevocable damage done without a hint of raw preaching but rather by telling the story from a child's point of view and by exquisitely preserving in the girls' friendship a corner of that world that is unassailable by adults.

For all the bleakness of stolen innocence, there is no drabness in *The Orchard on Fire.* Mackay populates the novel with an array of colorful characters who make the village complete, including teacher, constable, butcher and cheeseman, as well as the occasional outside visitors, such as weekend arty guests and twin professors. The sense of place is rendered sensuously and lovingly: When April's parents first see the Copper Kettle, its windows are sealed with "gravy-colored paint" and the living accommodation is decorated in "tones of meat and two veg"; they redo it in hanging spider plants, fairy lights and lace curtains.

If the author's words charm us, the pace of the story makes us charge compulsively through them. Still, the effect of the book, infused with compassion and the bemusement and unintentional humor of children, Engers. *The Orchard on Fire* is a wondrous novel that will birth emotions anew, age them with experience and tinge them with an aching melancholy.

## Jan Clausen (review date July 1997)

SOURCE: Clausen, Jan. "Passionate Friendship." *Women's Review of Books* 14, nos. 10-11 (July 1997): 35.

[*In the following review, Clausen surveys the strengths and weaknesses of* The Orchard on Fire.]

When eight-year-old April Harlency, "born into the licensed trade," arrives in Stonebridge, Kent, the first person she meets is red-haired Ruby Richards, busy setting toilet paper afire in the ladies' room of her parents' pub. As the Harlencies settle in to run the Copper Kettle Tearoom, the two girls form a passionate, nearly seamless friendship. Though plagued by a gendered terror of public spaces ("None of the village girls would have dreamed of walking down Station Hill at night . . . because everybody knew there was a man with a sack and a knife waiting to jump out on you"), they push the envelope. Ruby takes the lead; she knows that terror begins at home.

Their glorious alliance can't alleviate the solitude in which each girl faces her own powerlessness. Neither April nor her loving but preoccupied parents can do much about Ruby's troubles (a father who belts her, a mother who justifies it). And April can't tell Ruby of her own panic at the behavior of Mr. Greenidge, the dapper gentleman with the dachshund and the dying wife, who lures her to tea and plies her with hideous kisses.

Its jacket slathered with predictable references to "coming of age" and loss of "innocence," this fierce and gentle novel [*The Orchard on Fire*] in fact depicts the world of little girls—and the reputedly "safe" era of the early 1950s—as always already tainted, disillusioned, compromised. Ruby believes her parents hated her from birth. The beauty of rural Kent looks like this: "You might catch the flash of a kingfisher or the scuttle of a crayfish into a glinting tin can on the river bed." When first embraced by Mr. Greenidge, April already knows not only that it's "wrong because Mr. Greenidge was married to Mrs. Greenidge," but that she mustn't be rude to him. Later we watch her wield unwanted power and understand her adult question: "Had I been the destroying angel in a cotton frock and wellingtons?"

The social scene is understated gothic, numbering among the dramatis personae cracked old Mrs. Chacksfield, said to have slept for weeks with her husband's corpse; two unattractive middle-aged teachers, Miss Fay and Major Morton, spied in a moment of disoriented lust; a visiting professor, wildly inebriated, who drops—literally—dead at the prospect of having to lecture on art history to a bunch of "bacchantes with sketchbooks." Mackay nicely captures the weird moral autonomy of certain childhoods, the sense of being utterly on one's own with problems too grave to entrust to adult solutions.

CONTEMPORARY LITERARY CRITICISM, Vol. 195

Stonebridge is poor and narrow, but possesses an integrity to which Mackay pays homage via immaculately observed physical detail and inspired rendering of a child's garden of language. (April pictures the Iron Curtain as "rusting corrugated iron hung with white convolvulus"; she puzzles over the "dicky ticker" to which Mr. Greenidge attributes his wife's invalidism.) It's a world of rank odors ("piss and biscuits," strong drink), suffused with cruelty and patchy splendor. Splendid indeed is the abandoned orchard, a "dark-green and purple-blue paradise" where the girls establish the "camp of our dreams."

The story of how those fragile dreams are wrecked seems to me the least successful portion of the novel. Ruby and April are lost to one another, while the hovering Mr. Greenidge is dispatched with a melodramatic flourish that feels rushed, as though Mackay had belatedly perceived a need for plot. Compounding the problem, flashback machinery creaks annoyingly, and the adult April evinces little of her remembered child self's tough grace. A self-pitying divorcee, she's capable of greeting a misdelivered pizza with the thought: "It's not for me. I ordered the dust and ashes special, with extra acrimony."

Why didn't grownup April search for Ruby, her most important friend ever? The offhand explanation that she'd "thought we had all the time in the world to find each other" doesn't satisfy when the loss of this friendship is asked to bear so much symbolic weight. *The Orchard on Fire* ends on a note reminiscent of the lament for lost friendship in Toni Morrison's *Sula,* but in the latter novel it's Morrison's demonstration of how the bitter logic of womanhood dooms the friends that gives Nel's elegiac "We was girls together" its tragic force. If Mackay neglects to show us where the magic went, she triumphs in conveying how it felt while it lasted.

**Richard Eder (review date 26 October 1997)**

SOURCE: Eder, Richard. "Chop Shop." *Los Angeles Times Book Review* (26 October 1997): 2.

[*In the following review, Eder commends the absurdist humor and social satire he finds in* An Advent Calendar.]

John is buying chopped meat in his rundown North London neighborhood when Mick, the butcher's assistant, lands his cleaver on his own finger. In an uproar of blood, towels and hysteria, the finger somehow falls into the meat grinder.

An hour or so later, John's semi-invalid Uncle Cecil comes to the table with an anticipatory grunt of "lovely grub" and guzzles up the meat sauce despite the odd

bits of bone and gristle. Soon the butcher is at the door demanding the return of the finger. The dog ate it, John lies, stricken. Rather than remark on the manifest absence of a dog, the butcher inveighs furiously at the idea of anyone feeding good meat to a pet.

With this beginning, a reader will expect *An Advent Calendar* to be a work of absurdist humor and perhaps—bearing in mind Shena Mackay's British (Scottish) nationality and the purposeful use of such humor by writers like Joe Orton and Brendan Behan—of social satire as well.

There is social commentary in *Calendar,* but it is something more desolate than satire. The humor is mainly dark, but there is nothing absurdist about the struggling and penniless young family of John, his wife Marguerite and their two children, the decrepit but sweet Uncle Cecil and one or two friends and neighbors.

Absurdity is in the world they try to manage. They themselves are frail and only shakily competent, but their integral humanity is unquestionable even if it has holes in it, like their breakfast toast (the mold spots having been cut out beforehand). They bear a resemblance to Mr. and Mrs. Antrobus in Thornton Wilder's *The Skin of Our Teeth,* who try to hold out through our planet's upheavals from the ice age to the present. Mackay's characters lack Wilder's soft-edged whimsicality. Their ice is real, though it dazzles unexpectedly and even harbors, like igloo blocks, a sporadic warmth.

The upheaval that Mackay depicts is specifically the changed ethos of Thatcherite and post-Thatcherite Britain, though it could apply to a more generally troubling contemporary world. In the dismal gray London neighborhood, the social fabric has frayed.

A slaughterhouse and a garbage dump stand near Uncle Cecil's once pleasant, now decayed house. Electric wires dangle from the walls, the dust is an inch thick and the kitchen is so greasy that when Marguerite lights a burner, the whole stove flames up. The plant nursery Cecil used to run is abandoned, its signboard lying "in a black slime of petals, among slug-trailed panes where long worms and roots writhed through fiber pots."

Two decades of free-enterprise retreat from the concepts and practices of a welfare state have created more than economic hardship in the neighborhood. The social connective tissue has withered; there is a bleak emptiness between one character and the next. Even those bound by love and family find the links straining.

John, a college dropout, desperately wants to support his family but is too absorbed in his private musings and too disconnected from the world around him for steady work. On his first job for a house-cleaning company, he attaches the vacuum hose backward. When it spews out dirt, he berates the outraged client for keeping a filthy house and, in passing, for her prissy clothes.

Marguerite resumes an old affair with Aaron, a veterinarian, after he turns up to examine Uncle Cecil's sick goat. She loves John and her children; she also loves Aaron, and Aaron loves her. The world around her is too unstructured to help her with a choice. All three are good and endearing people. They try hard, but just as society's center has collapsed—a sense of the public as well as the private good—their own centers won't hold.

There is little action in the book; instead, there is lethargic, random activity, like fish swimming in a murky aquarium. While John and Mary struggle to work, keep house, confront and retreat from each other, their neighbors intersect with various degrees of incompetent good will or sheer malevolence.

Particularly malevolent—he is evil, defined in the theological sense as the absence of good—is Eric Turle, a self-indulgent middle-aged poet. He seduces Joy, a passionate teenage misfit. Besotted with poetry—and eventually destined to work in the slaughterhouse—she hides for hours in the school lavatory reading the "Golden Treasury" anthology and ignoring the insistent paging of the public address system.

In his wife's absences, Eric wins Joy by reading poems and plying her with Camembert. When they manage to spend a night together, she scribbles a love poem, awkward but quite lovely, in the notebook he keeps beside the bed in the event of inspiration. (There has been no such event for years; the pages are blank.) When his outraged wife discovers it, he claims that he has written the poem for her; they both turn on Joy, a heroine though ill-fated.

Another incompetent innocent is Elizabeth, a teacher who tries to befriend Joy and do other bits of good, all of which turn out badly. She impulsively invites a drunken street-cleaner for Christmas dinner, then practices cutting her hand for an excuse to put him off. She harbors an insatiably needy and vindictive school friend, who tries to hang herself from the shower rail and, failing, proposes going out for a drink.

Neither good nor evil is concerted. Just as society has disconnected from the individual, the individuals have disconnected from each other, despite their yearnings, and eventually from themselves. Even the most appealing of them lack the dimension of hope: that is, a sense of the future implicit in their present. One dimension less does not result in flatness but in a poignant evanescence.

Mackay suggests evanescence quite wonderfully with a prose that alights, vanishes, pops up elsewhere, interrupts itself and turns up again with unexpected finds. It can be disconcerting; no sooner do we delight in a person or passage than it breaks off. It is as if the author is keeping a distance from authorship; as if what she provides is something found by chance, undependably and possibly illegally.

## Jonathan Yardley (review date 29 October 1997)

SOURCE: Yardley, Jonathan. "Bleak, Blue-Collar and British." *Washington Post Book World* (29 October 1997): D2.

[*In the following review, Yardley regards* An Advent Calendar *as a proletariat novel.*]

No doubt about it, this is a very strange novel. Written by a British novelist who has published numerous other books, it ventures into territory not often occupied by the novel, which is in essence a middle-class institution. *An Advent Calendar* by contrast is working-class fiction: not proletarian, guided by political and/or ideological purposes, but descriptive and empathetic, a look inside a world that is familiar to few regular readers of conventional fiction.

Shena Mackay sets the tone immediately. John, a young married man in difficult economic circumstances, stops by the butcher's for a bit of meat to share with his uncle, Cecil, with whom he and his small, unhappy family are temporarily lodging. He buys ground meat, which at home he tosses into spaghetti sauce. "Piece of gristle," he remarks to Cecil, and pushes the offending morsel to the side of his plate. "I'll have it," Cecil says and gobbles up the last of the grub.

Gristle, indeed. That hard piece of meat was a human finger, sliced from Mick, the butcher, as he wielded his cleaver. When John comprehends what has happened, he feels compelled to atone for Mick's loss but can only shout at him: "Do you want to know what happened to your finger? It got minced up by accident and my uncle and I ate it. That's right! I've eaten part of you!"

We are not, to put it mildly, in the world of haute cuisine. This is blue-collar England, a place where anonymous people struggle through bleak lives that offer little prospect of advancement and not much more of happiness. Marguerite, John's wife, feels weighed down by gloom as she "put on John's corduroy trousers, another sweater and socks, got into bed and lay too cold to move between the ancient sheets, thinking that she must lie there for at least thirty-one nights, because it was December 1st, and saw each day open like a dark door in an Advent Calendar."

She has ample reason to feel blue. Not merely does her family have almost no money—John is reduced to swabbing for a cleaning service—but she must share close quarters with the eccentric Cecil, and she is utterly out of sorts with her husband. "He is completely indifferent to me," she thinks as, a few feet away, he thinks. "How strange that that exotic bird should choose to perch for the duration of its one life on the chair opposite mine. Why does it stay, why not simply fly away?"

This in a fashion is what Marguerite ends up doing. She becomes involved with another man, one of some means who is happy to reward her with gifts of cash in exchange for the favors she extends. Yet rather than estrange her from her husband and children, this extramarital adventure gives her the freedom to buy Christmas gifts and bring something like pleasure into the household. Happiness may not be easy to come by, Mackay reminds us, but it is often nearer to our grasp than we are able to realize.

A similar lesson is learned in somewhat different ways by others who cross the family's path. Elizabeth, John's sister, had her own dread; she "couldn't remember how long she had known that she was going to be murdered, but could remember as a child lying stricken in a bath of congealing water, afraid to emerge lest her family had been silently slaughtered with an axe and the killer awaited her." Yet rather than succumb and withdraw, she tries to befriend a student in the school where she teaches. Joy—never has a child been more cruelly misnamed—is a sad droopy creature, by her own account "the odd one out," teased at school and neglected at home; "her heart was so conditioned by dread that it lurched, on holidays and weekdays alike."

Elizabeth helps Joy find work babysitting for a friend, but what lies in wait is the friend's husband, a mediocre poet who promptly seduces Joy. What the two commit is "an unspeakable crime," yet for the joyless Joy it arouses a feeling that might almost be called love, a connection with another human being, however illicit and abusive, that brings her alive for a few moments.

Happiness, Mackay seems to be saying, is where one must find it and does not often arrive in the form desired. This is true, and *An Advent Calendar* has the ring of truth. Mackay keeps her distance from her characters, but she never condescends to them. What humanity they achieve may seem parched to those who are more fortunate, but it is humanity all the same and must be recognized and honored as such. This Mackay does in a book that catches the reader by surprise: Terse and economical, *Advent Calendar* has far more to it than one first apprehends.

## Nicola Shulman (review date 10 July 1998)

SOURCE: Shulman, Nicola. "Working the Party." *Times Literary Supplement* (10 July 1998): 23.

[*In the following review, Shulman compares* The Artist's Widow *to the work of Charles Dickens and praises Mackay as a highly talented novelist.*]

It is traditional for novelists to write about painters, and with good reason. Paint makes manifest the invisible concerns of the writer; and the task of describing the painter at his work does not overload the burden of authorial research. So when Shena Mackay opens her new novel [*The Artist's Widow*]—about a painter—with an opening, it seems almost a nod of recognition to this arrangement of long standing.

The opening in question is a private view of works by John Crane, a painter whose credentials—British, Academic, representational, painterly, given to forming artistic communities in English seaside towns—ensure him a place at the furthest conceivable remove from the centre of fashion. It is an opening that, we are told on the dust jacket, "will change [the characters'] lives for ever", an odd assertion in view of the fact that there is nobody there whose life is changed by it at all. Certainly not the painter Lyris Crane; her life was changed for ever when the death of her husband, John, turned her into the Artist's Widow of the title. For her, this party is the occasion when all the humiliations of her new position are borne irresistibly home to her.

Mackay is capable of compressing whole predicaments and their histories into a phrase. At this party, she works the room with such skill that, in just a few pages, we, like Lyris, can see it all. Here is Lyris asking Louis, the gallery owner (who has inherited the dealership of John Crane, along with the gallery, from his mother), if he could "go and be nice" to a couple who know no one and whose portraits are on the wall:

> "John was very fond of them. Before you ask them what they do, Tony has a washing machine repair business and Anne's a dinner lady at our local school."
>
> Louis made a derisively submissive little bow and left her.

In this gesture, Mackay has managed to communicate not only the precise and relative standing, in the scale of Louis's opinion, of Anne and Tony, of John Crane and of Lyris, but the full force of that compound insult as it strikes Lyris. One hopes there are readers for novels in which people's lives are not changed for every, only realized in sentences sprung like that.

Also at the party is young Nathan Pursey, the great-nephew of John Crane. Nathan is a conceptual artist of the kind that feeds the vacuum of their talent with atrocities and narcissism. He works in rotten meat and sweetie wrappers and cyberspace, but his preferred medium is publicity, or would be if he could attract any. Plainly he is everything Lyris is not; and just as his brief peckings at the surfaces of ideas echo his faithlessness as a friend and lover, so Lyris's endless fascination with paint evokes her lifelong love of a single man. But Mackay is too economical to leave Nathan as a simple foil. He is also son and heir to the great comic characters of this book, the Purley Purseys.

I am well aware that any dodgy family appearing to comic effect in a London novel will, like a leech, draw out the words "Charles Dickens". However, the righteous venality of the Purley Purseys and the author's most evident relish in creating them make the comparison unavoidable. Mackay is nowhere wittier than in her treatment of Nathan's family and their business (they are purveyors, mainly to gangland, of artistic floral tributes) which reflects so hilariously on Nathan's own line of work. A glorious scene with the Purseys at dinner in an Italian restaurant shows Mackay as a superb comic writer ("'I wonder if I can make room for a knickerbocker glory, Pat?', Sonia said, bringing her into the conversation"), but able also to reveal, through the comedy, exactly how the family favour has been distributed, and with what crushing results.

As a novelist, Shena Mackay is highly talented: she can do dialogue, description, characterization, drama, humour, pathos; moreover, she achieves her effects without adverting to them, as though she expects the reader to take a point lightly made. Indeed, what makes *The Artist's Widow* an unmistakable work of maturity is that it employs the author's every accomplishment while displaying none. For example, she puts her gift for idiom at the service of the book's central theme of loneliness.

Everyone here is lonely: Candy, an MP's abandoned mistress; Clovis the bookseller, damned by an act of gross cowardice; Jacki, Nathan's conciliatory girlfriend who wants to be liked and is not. But the loneliness of Lyris is the most acute; so much so that she is, crucially, vulnerable to the limited charms of Nathan. Mackay never alludes to it, but—making us first aware that here is a woman habituated, over fifty years of marriage, to being perfectly understood—she then beautifully demonstrates it in conversations where nobody can read Lyris's idiom and, with the typical condescension of the young, think she is perhaps misusing theirs. Only an expert mimic could bring this off.

There is one important lapse of judgment here. The events of this novel occur over the latter part of last summer. At length a horrible suspicion arises that we are all hastening towards a tunnel on the banks of the Seine; and so it proves. Doubtless Mackay could not foresee how the repeated batterings of the past ten months would make us dead to this subject, which now numbs everything that touches it. All the same, it's sad when a good book comes to a bad end.

**Gabriele Annan (review date 16 July 1998)**

SOURCE: Annan, Gabriele. "Lyris, Clovis, Nat and Candy." *London Review of Books* (16 July 1998): 19.

[*In the following review, Annan surveys the broad range of characters in* The Artist's Widow.]

Shena Mackay's latest novel [*The Artist's Widow*] invites you to observe the Zeitgeist of 1997 addling the brains and hearts of quite a large number of Londoners. They seem an incongruous lot, but with her usual ingenuity she manages to portion out the action among them and to make them connect (not necessarily in the Forsterian sense). They tend to come in pairs locked in ideological conflict, which doesn't have to be verbal: it can be expressed in their behaviour, their domestic arrangements, their clothes. Altogether it is a Dickensian assemblage, vivid, lively, quirky and woven into a network that stretches from Dulwich to Maida Vale, and from Tufnell Park to the art galleries in Mayfair. Every bit of the novel is either topographical or topical, or both: like Hoxton, the new cool place for artists to have their studios.

Mackay has an uncommon ability to focus on environmental details and find evocative metaphors for them. Her prose, though, tends to go what her characters would call 'OTT', switching from relentless parody of the latest jargon to passages of the purplest prose. 'The cotoneaster, gemmate with red berries, had spread in a peacock's tail over the grass' is perhaps an unfair example, because when she notices the shrub behaving like that, the heroine, Lyris Crane, is thinking about Edith Sitwell's unhappy childhood. Lyris is very recently widowed and herself an artist. On another occasion she hears a suspicious noise in the hall, and 'her slippery heart hurt as it leapt. As a dark shape bulked into the studio doorway she seized a large bottle of turpentine and flung it.' She is a plucky old girl; and anyway the bulky thing is not exactly a burglar; only her ghastly great-nephew Nat, who manages to make off with her purse at the end of a chatty visit. His parents own a flower stall and have got rich by illegal means, so minor crime comes naturally to Nat. He is a conceptual artist and has just set up a group in Hoxton, but failed to make it into the Royal Academy's *Sensation* show.

Because of this rebuff, he is toying with the idea of moving on from brutalist imitations of Damien Hirst to art on the Net. Great-Aunt Lyris, on the other hand, pushing eighty and brought up a vegetarian Fabian, is a traditionalist painter. Her work sounds post-Bonnardian, and she regards art as a combination of public service and hymn to beauty. 'My role,' she lectures Nat, 'is to record such things'—rose-hips seen against a green-painted wall—'not only for their intrinsic beauty and for myself, but on behalf of people whose hearts are touched in precisely the same way'; and she quotes a little chunk of Walter de la Mare to reinforce her point. Lyris combines literacy, stoicism and personal austerity with charity and humour, and spreads inter-racial and inter-class tolerance. Her best friend is a school dinner lady married to a washing-machine repairman. The trouble is that it is difficult to emphasise the admirable nature of Lyris's attitude without making her sound patronising.

The rest of the cast is divided into goodies, baddies and what you might call lost girls. Some (not all) of the baddies are converted in the course of the novel, while the lost girls are found, or rather led to find themselves. One is Candy, a pretty, warm-hearted, middle-aged woman who sits alone at a café table in Maida Vale, while her bunch of little dogs wind their leads round the chair legs. Her lover of more than twenty years has left her. He lost his seat as a Conservative MP in the last election and has decided to spend more time with his wife in the country. However, by the end of the book it looks as though she will settle down with a nice divorced bookseller called Clovis who has a shop nearby.

The other lost girl is Jacki: 'Jackee', as she calls herself at the start of the novel when she wears her hair in dreadlocks and wants to be taken for a Caribbean half-caste instead of the middle-class white girl with affectionate parents that she is. Her black lover jilts her just the same, and so does Nat, the next man she shacks up with. So she falls into a depression from which Lyris rescues her by taking her in and getting her to help redecorate her house and lose weight by eating less comfort food. A happy ending seems in sight for her, too: on the last page, crass Nat is seen moving towards his great-aunt's house, a reformed character bearing the purse he stole from her at the beginning of the story. Perhaps he, too, will now paint flower pieces in vivid colours; and set up home with Jacki.

*The Artist's Widow* is indefatigably up to date. It has everything: conceptual art and Conservatives with lost seats and abandoned mistresses, paedophilia, snuff movies, public relations women in suits, TV interviewers, suburban developments with integral garages and names like Joekin's Mead and Biggs's Coppice, Ofsted, air pollution (with special reference to nannies driving their charges to private schools while primary school children breathe in their petrol fumes), education cutbacks, young offenders committing suicide in prison,

baseball caps and cloned sheep. The deaths of Diana and Dodi provide the grand finale.

They coincide with the 50th-birthday party of Clovis's ex-wife Isobel, who lives in the country with their teenage daughter Miranda. Clovis and Candy have been asked, and they give a lift to Lyris. All the other guests have been disinvited because of the collision in the Paris underpass, but these three haven't even heard the news. They find Miranda in tears and Isobel too: 'How can you stand there and congratulate me?' she sobs. 'Wishing me a happy birthday, how could you both? Have you no feelings at all?' Candy, too, bursts into tears, and 'Clovis envied her her ability to express the emotions he felt but could not have articulated.' Isobel, however, goes too far: 'I'm so pleased that Clovis has you, Candy,' she says. 'We must all take great care of each other.' She is thinking of joining a Contemplative Order as soon as Miranda is settled. Or even establishing 'my own Order. A sort of unofficially recognised community, a band of folk dedicated to living simply, dressing perhaps in some unobtrusive uniform, going about the world helping in little ways, righting wrongs by stealth'. This is too much for Lyris: 'Everybody seems so determined to do good lately,' she whispers to Clovis. 'Do you think it would be a refreshing change to meet someone avowed to doing something really *bad*?' Still, even she returns home 'drained' with 'her eyelids . . . sore from weeping'. She has, presumably, achieved exactly the right measure of grief and compassion. You could see her as the Lady Troubridge of the emotions.

All the same, she has something in common with Olive, the embittered middle-class, middle-aged spinster baby-snatcher in Mackay's 1992 novel *Dunedin*. *Dunedin* covers the same territory socially and geographically—a brilliantly envisaged London stretching from one end to the other of the Central, Northern and District Lines. Olive, like Lyris, is appalled by the conditions and behaviour of the age she lives in. The difference is that she looks at them with disgust, whereas Lyris does so with a mixture of pity, irony and truly righteous indignation. Both books are as moralistic as *Little Lord Fauntleroy*; tracts, in fact, but ironic tracts. The irony is sometimes heavy, but mostly enjoyable and funny. 'Wise and funny' is how the blurb describes the novel—a publisher's cliché to put one on one's guard. Still, it deserves to be on the syllabus for students of social anthropology.

### Natasha Fairweather (review date 19 July 1998)

SOURCE: Fairweather, Natasha. "It May Look Like a Sack of Cement to You. To Me, It's a Dead Sheep." *Observer* (19 July 1998): 14.

[*In the following review, Fairweather considers* The Artist's Widow *to be a disappointing novel.*]

At some juncture in her lengthy career as a writer, Shena Mackay must have encountered the publisher's publicist from hell. For in her new novel, *The Artist's Widow,* Mackay sketches a vicious cameo portrait of Nancy Carmody, the glossy, publicist daughter of a Conservative MP who lost his seat in the 1997 election. More interested in her funeral clothes than the reasons behind the suicide of one of her authors, Nancy is described as a slippery eel while her philandering father is likened to a weevil.

Writing with what reads like personal bitterness, Mackay describes the branch of publishing to which Nancy belongs: 'All those people with their fat salaries [who] have no conception of life at the other end of their industries. They take more holidays than hairdressers. They should remember who pays for their fine clothes. They pick people up when it suits them, make them jump through hoops and then toss them aside.'

Perhaps Mackay was put off the publicity game during the hoopla which accompanied the nomination of her previous novel, *The Orchard on Fire,* for the Booker Prize of 1996. Although she did not win, the novel—an intimate, touching and memorably funny evocation of a rural Fifties childhood—was widely praised for the authenticity of its voice and the brilliance of its polish. Readers coming to *The Artist's Widow* looking for more of the same lustre will be disappointed. In spite of Mackay's technical adroitness, this novel is much less alluring.

Written in the less intimate third person, *The Artist's Widow* draws a disparate group of Londoners into a plot which revolves slowly and uneventfully around an artist's widow called Lyris Crane who is also an artist in her own right. In her eighties, and rattling, increasingly breathlessly, around a large house in Dulwich, Lyris is potential prey to many of the parasites of the artistic world. Louis, an oleaginous Mayfair art dealer, knows how to humiliate Lyris in a hundred tiny, patronising ways. The exotic and coke-sniffing Zoe Rifaat wants to depict Lyris not as an individual, but as a type, by featuring her in a film she is making for Channel 4 about unjustly neglected women in artistic partnerships. And Nathan Pursey, her great nephew by marriage, who is pursuing a high-profile but financially unrewarding career as a conceptual artist, has designs on her money, her art collection and her house.

Through the absurd and despicable figure of Nathan, Mackay is able to parody the contemporary art scene where traditional craftsmanship and a true desire to communicate through the medium are overshadowed by the flashy installations and half-baked concepts of many of the artists who feature, for example, in Charles Saatchi's private collection. Nathan, who submitted a photocopy of his bottom in his degree show at the

Chelsea Arts College and still came away with a degree, was catapulted briefly to celebrity when he discovered a sack of old cement in the backyard which looked like a felled sheep. 'Dead Sheep' went on to lead a contemporary art exhibition.

.But when we encounter Nathan in the novel, he is on a downhill trajectory. Sophie, the most talented painter in his artistic collective (and the only woman), has decided to strike out alone. And he is reduced to masturbating on his childhood bed as he vacillates about whether his sister's old doll's house is simply a child's plaything or an ironic statement about contemporary life.

Although Mackay begins to develop some ideas about the relationship between the quality of an artist's work and the integrity of their personal character, the novel's biggest problem is that Mackay appears to have nothing to say. Lyris, questioning Nathan about his cultural milieu, insists that she needs to know about the Zeitgeist since: 'Everything is remixed and recycled nowadays and I want to be able to take the references in some multi-media project.' But as Mackay peppers her text with the full monty of contemporary cultural references—from Di and Dodi's high-impact death, to the Spice Girls (admittedly before the departure of Geri), and boy bands in general—it feels as though she is less concerned about capturing the spirit of the times and more about using style to disguise a critical lack of substance.

Perhaps Mackay was hurried into print by a publisher keen to capitalise on the previous Booker nomination. But it is a shame that *The Artist's Widow* falls short of her writing at its best, for there are moments in this novel when the reader is reminded of how good she can be. There is the dazzlingly original comic portrait (a welcome break in a novel short on laughs) of Jacki Wigram, the wigga (white nigga) who once passed herself off as a dread-locked half-caste, but has now had to acknowledge the full disaster of her Caucasian origins.

Although the novel focuses on the visual senses, it is the passages of acute olfactory observation, when a character's body odour is broken down to the last stale glass of wine and day-old dip in a bowl of hummus, which are most striking. And the ungrammatical description of Lyris's fear when Nathan enters her house stealthily, as uninvited as a mugger, will strike terror in the hearts of anyone who has ever spent a vulnerable night alone regretting the teenage years of horror-film apprenticeship: 'Her heart thrashing about like a hooked fish: newsprint and television horror coursing through her brain while she sat paralysed, anticipating pain and even death: her body sprawled on the floor in a disorder of clothes.'

## Sylvia Brownrigg (review date 5 March 1999)

SOURCE: Brownrigg, Sylvia. "The Objects of Life." *Times Literary Supplement* (5 March 1999): 22.

[*In the following review, Brownrigg views Mackay as a talented short story writer and touches on the key thematic concerns of the stories in* The World's Smallest Unicorn.]

A common, self-deprecating wisdom holds that the English (with the acknowledged exception of V. S. Pritchett) are not much good at short stories; that the nation has produced no master of the form with the calibre of Chekhov or Raymond Carver. A. S. Byatt went some way to correcting this gloomy picture in her rich anthology compiled for Oxford last year. There, she put forward a convincing argument that English writers have worked against the taut, "well-crafted" model of the short story. The best English stories, Byatt claimed, "pack together comedy and tragedy, farce and delicacy, elegance and the grotesque".

This is an apt description of the work of Shena Mackay, who may be claimed for the Scots but who in her themes and settings is predominantly English, and increasingly metropolitan. (Born in Edinburgh, Mackay was brought up and educated in Kent.) Since the early 1980s, Mackay has produced several acclaimed collections of stories, pursuing the form with the same cool care and strange intensity she has brought to novels like *Dunedin* (1992) or *The Orchard on Fire* (1996). Her stories are dark, compelling excursions, and they cut with an edge that is distinctive to Mackay: an edge of humour and hostility that startles and unnerves, even as it amuses.

Some writers use the story collection strategically, to build a world: one reads through a volume of Raymond Carver or Alice Munro with an urgency based on the compulsion to understand a complete fictional environment. Mackay operates quite differently. There is unity neither in this collection as a whole, nor in each individual story. Mackay darts and dashes, sampling stark realism and gaudy fantasy; her narratives start and stop, and start again. She moves from Sheldon's Silver and Antiques in early 1960s Chancery Lane to a Home for Retired Clowns in Kent; from a lost expat returning from Hong Kong, to a hopeful publisher seeking romantic and literary salvation in Goa. Mackay's short fiction has been likened to a junk-shop window, and it is a fitting image; busy with objects, jewellery, clothes and an encyclopaedic range of plants, her stories are cluttered with material—with, to borrow Byatt's phrase on Sylvia Townsend Warner, the "thinginess of things". Scotland appears briefly in a couple of stories—generally as a place people leave—but most are set in London. Within the capital itself, Mackay travels widely, taking in tree-sheltered terrace houses and a luxurious Sloane Square home; visiting club bores in the West End and well-off parents who reside in "one of those parts of London that thinks itself a village". Mackay has a grim lyricism when conveying urban bleakness, and the south London in several stories is alive with a wonderful damp gloom. One of the collection's best stories, **"The Index of Embarrassment"**, has a gay nephew visiting his misanthropic uncle, whose great labour is compiling the index of the title, a comprehensive catalogue of song lyrics and clips, jokes and clichés. Uncle Bob experiences a malicious satisfaction at a neighbour's suicide in this bleary suburb, and his nephew tries to protect the grieving mother from Bob, whose "sharp nose would sniff out the loneliness masked by her rather shrill perfume".

Mackay is frequently drawn to encounters between old and young. At her most sympathetic, she gently teases those on both sides of the generational divide, vividly chronicling the expat uncle's bewildered appreciation of his teenage nieces, a mother's jealousy of her son's Goth girlfriend, and, most movingly, the cross-generational encounter in **"Trouser Ladies"**, in which an ageing journalist, Beatrice, dines with the daughter of her dead best friend. (The younger lesbian has intuited Beatrice's lifelong passion for her own late mother, and that unspoken empathy warms their meal.) At Mackay's brittlest, the old become pathetic and the young merely predatory. In **"The Day of the Gecko"**, Allie, a publisher, takes her PA, Tasha, along to Goa on her wistful search for a vanished author, but she is wary of too-attractive Tasha: "to Allie, her face was like a cat's, who rubs against your legs while knowing there is a dead bird behind the sofa".

A similar envy and suspicion undermine the relationship between the successful, lonely author, Andrea, and ambitious Lily, whom Andrea takes on as a protégée-cum-cleaner, after Lily's story fails to win a literary competition for which Andrea was a judge. Mackay has had to bear the burden of being a Whitbread and now a Booker judge, and so the comically weary tone she allows here is understandable, but it makes the conflict between the two women rather schematic. (Mackay gets considerable pleasure throughout the volume in penning imagined titles to bad literary productions, whether it's Andrea's remaindered Virago classic *Mistletoe in a Dirty Glass* or a gritty television play called *Pigs and Spigots*.) As in her last novel, *The Artist's Widow* (1998), Mackay occasionally chooses soft targets for her cultural satire. The smug couple in **"Barbarians"** run a Benetton-like children's clothing business, for whose catalogues they blithely encourage the children of their Asian workers to model. Here, Mackay's broad brush paints the loathsome father not just as a philanderer but also as an arch-capitalist who argues with his daughter about the minimum wage, and accuses his ailing son of looking "like some homeless layabout in a shop doorway begging for change".

The book is scattered with examples of the lovely, precise prose for which Mackay is celebrated, as when two young boys wait in "the raw noon of a motherless, shapeless Saturday". But there are moments when Mackay's eye fails her, producing a baffling description such as "the dark bobbles of the plane tree in the square where she lived were draggling like trimmings of frowsty curtains in a sky of mushroom soup". Mackay shows subtle compassion when her imagination turns to troubled or less privileged characters, as is common in her earlier stories, but can also write with a detachment that keeps her tone quite cold. She shows an ease and confidence with this form. There may not be anything in this volume to match the smooth menace of *Dreams of Dead Women's Handbags* (1987), but there are elegance and delicacy, farce and tragedy, and colours and textures to awaken any alert reader's senses.

### Francis King (review date 27 March 1999)

SOURCE: King, Francis. "Laughter and Tears." *Spectator* 282, no. 8903 (27 March 1999): 36.

[*In the following mixed review, King notes the humor and poignancy of the tales collected in* The World's Smallest Unicorn.]

As one of the most gifted contenders in the literary Olympic games, Shena Mackay has always struck me as being a sparkish, spunky sprinter rather than a patient, persistent long-distance runner. Her novels may at first seem slight, sometimes even insubstantial; but their specific gravity is so high that long after one has read them they still leave a dense residue in one's mind. Even her shortest short stories can, like those of Jane Gardam, be usually relied on to tell one far more about the turbulent passions and twisted motives of her characters than many a jumbo of a novel by a writer less concise and adroit.

In this latest collection [*The World's Smallest Unicorn*], many of these characters belong to the world either of entertainment or of books. But in those worlds their positions are nearly always humble, even humiliating. In **'Crossing the Border',** one of the funniest and most poignant of the stories (Mackay's stories are usually both those things), a feisty young woman pays a visit to the Grimaldi Home for Retired Clowns, where her great-uncle, his undistinguished career long over, has been incarcerated. Sadly, she arrives too late, death having already visited him before her. His sole bequest to her is a pair of clown's shoes.

In another story, full of alert observation, **'The Last Sand Dance',** Zinnia, married to a once successful television writer whom no one now wishes to employ,

is an actress with an 'unreconstructedly West End glamour about her', who has not appeared on a stage north of Wimbledon for many years. The jangling relationship between her and her husband is beautifully adumbrated, with a mixture of tenderness and mockery. Of another character Mackay writes that he 'fantasised about being a pop star until an audition for *New Faces* smashed his dreams'. In her fiction, people's dreams, particularly if they are of fame, all too often get smashed.

In one of the two dud stories in the book, **'Death by Art Deco'**—its satire of the literary world too crude and unforgiving, its dénouement too mechanical—the theme is the relationship, at first affectionate and mutually supportive but eventually doomed to disillusion and destruction, between an established woman author (her last novel is a remaindered Virago Classic, *Mistletoe in a Dirty Glass*), whose life and work are both entering a decline, and a young would-be one, full of ardour and hope. In the far better **'The Day of the Gecko'** the aging editorial director of a publishing house and her sexually adventurous young assistant travel to Goa in vain search of a vanished author. The accelerating friction between the two women is skillfully realised, as is the exotic setting; and there is the added bonus of the presence in the Da Silva Guest House, where the women are lodging, of two old troupers, Jonty and Jilly, who have achieved fame as irascible husband and long-suffering wife in a dozen indistinguishable sitcoms.

Children, wise beyond their years and therefore even more cynical than their parents, also figure prominently. In the splendid title story, a pair of twin girls cruelly exacerbate the sense of defeat and shame of a man who returns, his job with a Hong Kong firm called The Pink Panda Stationery Company abruptly terminated, to sponge off his brother and the sister-in-law whom, many years before, he nonchalantly seduced.

Even the less successful of the stories remain a joy to read because of the way in which the style now buffets one into attention and now caresses one into delight. 'Trainers like two dead pigeons on the carpet'; 'her roots growing out until her hair looked like burnt toast spread with margarine'; 'an umbrella like an injured fruitbat': such similes at first make one think 'How ludicrous!' and then, immediately afterwards, 'How absolutely right!'

Mackay writes of one of her characters that she 'saw eternity in a plastic flower'. It is her own special gift to see eternity in what to other, less perceptive, less humorous and less compassionate writers might merely seem to be rubbishy ephemera. Hers is a talent to cherish.

## Ian Hamilton (essay date 10 July 1999)

SOURCE: Hamilton, Ian. "Bohemian Rhapsodist." *Guardian* (10 July 1999): 6.

[*In the following essay, Hamilton traces Mackay's life and literary development.*]

Shena Mackay has never been one for trendy self-promotion. Like Lyris, the neglected painter in her most recent novel, *The Artist's Widow,* Mackay would—on balance—rather be overlooked than vulgarly exposed. "A publicist's nightmare" is how her own publicists have now and then described her, and Mackay takes a certain pride in their exasperation.

Even today, with 10 highly-praised books in print (two, *The Artist's Widow,* and *Dunedin,* are out in Vintage paperback this month), and with a paean from Julie Burchill to amplify her blurbs (Burchill recently called her "the best writer in the world today"), Mackay cannot quite bring herself to bustle on the circuits.

As she told me recently: "I do think the whole climate for writers these days is so vulgar. It's all so money-led. I hate going into book shops and seeing, you know, the Top Ten Bestsellers, a sort of self-fulfilling prophecy. I just find the whole thing so vulgar: the books pages, and the way writers are portrayed—snippets in diaries about so-and-so's advance. It all just creates a climate of anxiety for the majority of writers and gets them into the feeling that it's all a competition".

A publicist's nightmare, to be sure, and yet Mackay, when she first started out, seemed quite the opposite. When I first heard of her, in the early 60s, she was being touted as the youngest and prettiest girl-novelist in town. She was featured in style sections of the tabloids, along with figures like Marianne Faithful, and seemed to be heading for a starring role in the about-to-happen youthquake. She had written her first novel when she was 16, we were told, and by 20 had clocked up quite a few foam-flecked reviews: "Macabre, zany, scoffingly droll, sadly beautiful, wildly funny, glitteringly stylish—and quite brilliant . . . She stands on her own—an original and a very hot property". And that was just the Daily Mail.

As for the prettiness—this too was the stuff of dazed hyperbole. A poet friend of mine, who can't be named, remembers meeting Mackay at a mid-60s literary festival: "A vision of blonde, schoolgirl loveliness", he says, "but sexy and flirtatious too. You should have seen those corduroyed belletrists swoon whenever she timidly sashayed into the hotel bar. They all wanted to, well, protect her, advise her, and so on—and in spite of the deadpan wit with which she kept them all at bay,

she did somehow seem to need protecting. Let's just say that she was the kind of novelist who didn't really need to write another novel."

Mackay did write other novels, though, and in many of them the lustful male is skewered with brutal finesse. Her early novels in particular are full of bristly predators, and we are spared none of the repulsive details: the starings and the gropings, the bad breath, the drunken bullshit, the love-talk that turns nasty when our heroine sees through it, and so on.

I asked Mackay the other day if she had ever invented an admirable male character. The question seemed to take her by surprise, and in the end she came up with Stanley in *A Bowl of Cherries*: a wan and ineffectual bedsit loser. "And what's so terrific about Stanley?" "Well, he's nice to children", she replied.

Shena Mackay (nee Mackey) was born in Edinburgh in 1944, on D-Day. Her father was in the army; her mother was training to be a teacher. They had met as students at St Andrews University. He was the son of a headmaster; she the daughter of a Presbyterian minister, and according to Mackay the marriage was a "genuine love-match". After the war, the family moved to England, at first to Hampstead (where, for a time, they lived next door to the Saatchis; little Charles, says Mackay, would now and then come crawling through their hedge) and later, via various London locations, to the village of Shoreham in Kent.

Benjamin Mackey, Shena's father, had problems "settling down" after the war, not least because he seems to have been the victim of a somewhat volatile Scottish temper. He took a succession of short-term jobs, ranging from coal-miner to ship's purser. There were frequent parental absences: not all of these unwelcome to Shena and her two sisters. Nor, maybe, to their mother.

Mrs Mackey was steadfast, intrepid and self-sacrificing. During the family's eight years in Shoreham, the years of Shena's growing up, it was the mother who kept everything together. Although of an arty disposition, counting as friends many poets and painters of the day, she was also a rigorously conscientious coper. According to Valerie Foster, a childhood friend, the Mackey girls were always "stylishly turned out", although the family was invariably short of cash.

Certainly it was from her mother that Mackay picked up several habits and interests that would stay with her later on: her vegetarianism, her interest in modern painting, her passion for wild flowers. "My mother made us learn the names of all the flowers in Kent", she says, and there is no book of hers, I think, that does not contain at least one flourish of botanical expertise.

Mackay's mother also encouraged her to read. "Shena was always, always reading", says her sister Frances, and Foster remembers her friend poring over Sherlock Holmes and Billy Bunter.

Mackay herself recalls her mother scolding her, along the lines of "A big girl of eight and you haven't read *Crime and Punishment!*" But the scolding is remembered with intense affection: "I adored my mother", Mackay says today, "I got all sorts of values from her. She was a trouper, if you like, and lots of fun. But she had very high standards. We were brought up with quite liberal values but with a Presbyterian moral codes as well".

Mrs Mackey made sure that her daughters attended the village church and that they went to Sunday school. Mackay sang in the church choir, and although Foster recalls a few moments of Sunday irreverence, Mackay always remembered the words of all the hymns, and has worked quite a few of them into her books.

These childhood years left a deep imprint, to be sure, and Foster remembers them as an "enchanted" time. Mackay, she recalls, was always the mischievous tomboy, forever embarking on escapades and getting into scrapes. "She was always more daring than I was. She liked danger and even then she had a macabre sense of humour." At Tonbridge Grammar School, the two girls were co-conspirators—mocking the teachers, playing truant and so on—but Mackay (brilliant at English, bad at maths) always came out top of the detentions league. And she had begun writing poems and short stories: dark, horrid stuff, apparently, with lots of gratuitously sudden deaths (which also feature fairly often in her adult work). Even in these early, schoolgirl years, Valerie Foster was in no doubt that her naughty little friend would one day be "a very well-known writer".

Mackay's Shoreham childhood features repeatedly in her grown-up writings and is still looked back on with a sense of loss. In some ways, all of her novels and short stories, whatever their actual settings, can seem like attempts to reclaim the sharply circumscribed intensities of village life. She is celebrated now as "the tenth muse of suburbia", "the supreme lyricist of daily grot", but her beady-eyed dissections of the London suburb always seem guided by what one might call a villager's sensibility.

She is always on the lookout for oddballs and eccentrics, for tiny gaffes and small-scale self-delusions, and even when she is at her most caustically satirical there is usually an elegiac undertone. She has a wonderfully good ear for bus-stop dialogue ("for reasons best known to themselves"; "it's the children I feel sorry for") and she always wants to know what's going on behind the counter at the corner shop.

Unglamorous community endeavours—flower shows, amateur dramatics, church socials, and the like—always bring out the mordant best in her writing. She has on the whole been happier with close-ups than long-shots. At the same time, the village schoolgirl was, from early on, enticed by the idea of the metropolis. She had observed her mother's arty visitors and friends—the poet W S Graham and the painter Glyn Collins seem to have been regulars—and she nurtured adolescent fantasies of the artistic London life.

In 1960, she edged a step closer to metropolitan Bohemia. Her parents moved to Blackheath in south east London, and the children were switched from Tonbridge Grammar to Kidbrooke comprehensive, which Mackay hated from the start.

Kidbrooke does seem to have transformed her from a mischievous rural tomboy into a trainee urban-disaffiliate. She began to put on beatnik airs, failed most of her O levels, listened to Radio Luxemburg and got herself an art-student boyfriend, with whom she enjoyed exciting weekend trysts in Soho. On school-days, she and a friend would sometimes bunk off to the big city, encountering predators everywhere.

By this stage, she was reading *Catcher in the Rye* and *On the Road,* classic truant texts, and there were few pop songs that she hadn't learned by heart. Mackay spent one restless year at Kidbrooke before announcing, at 16, that she wanted to leave school. She won a £25 prize in a *Daily Mirror* poetry competition—"Windscattered little bones of birds / Lie on this fallow field"—and began to see herself as thoroughly committed to the writing life.

She applied for jobs in London and eventually landed a quite good one which, as things transpired, would change her life. "Girl Wanted for Antiques Shop. Easy Hours. Good Wages." The antique shop was in London's Chancery Lane and it was one of a pair owned by the parents of the art critic David Sylvester. One of the two shops sold antiques (jewellery, porcelain, etc) and the other specialised in silver. Mackay's job was in the silver shop, which was managed by the soon-to-be famous playwright Frank Marcus (his hit play, *The Killing of Sister George,* is not at all, says Mackay, based on her).

Marcus, now dead, was married to the Sylvesters' daughter, Jackie. In no time at all, it appears, Mackay had the Sylvester household at her feet. Marcus helped her to get moving as a writer, by introducing her to publishers and agents, and David Sylvester began to escort her to art galleries and Soho drinking clubs. Mackay became a Colony Room regular (even the notoriously misanthropic Muriel, the Colony's grande dame, seem to have quite liked her), and with a shuddering heart found herself getting introduced to legendary art-world figures like Lucian Freud, Frank Auerbach and Francis Bacon: "Francis could be vicious but he never was to me".

And nor was anybody else, so it would seem. Before long there was scarcely a big-name painter in England with whom Mackay was not on friendly terms: "David took me to galleries, openings, parties, painters' houses and studios and introduced me to the greatest British and American artists of the day, and to the Australians Sidney Nolan and Brett Whiteley. We visited Henry Moore at Much Hadham and had tea and whisky in bone china cups with David Hockney in Powis Square. I had the great privilege of meeting Giacometti not long before he died. He was gracious and kind, his noble lined face weary beneath his grizzled hair."

All this was a far cry from Blackheath, where her parents' marriage had gone into terminal decline. Worse still, Mackay's mother had become seriously ill, with rheumatoid arthritis. With both parents out of action, so to speak, the anxious Mackay (who might otherwise have been pressed to sign up at some university or college) was free to immerse herself in the Marcus/Sylvester world of publishers and painters. She took a flat-share in Earls Court and for a period drank deeply at the well of urban dereliction.

In Earls Court in the early 1960s she has said low life ran parallel to, and sometimes encroached on, backpackers' paradise; corruption coexisted with the conventions. And this, for Mackay was the perfect mix: Bohemia meets Presbyteria. Her Earls Court experience coincided with the publication of her first work of fiction—two novellas, published in one volume by Andre Deutsch in 1964—and she soon had enough money (just about) to enable her to give up her full-time job at the antique shop.

*Music Upstairs* (1965) her second book, was a witty and candidly bisexual romp around the sleaze-spots of Earls Court, and *Old Crow,* two years later, was a murky and staccato rendering of rustic angst: surreal lyricism combined with a high body-count is how she now describes. it. In these early books Mackay's gift for the killing simile and the surprising, spot-on image was splendidly in evidence. The plotting was half-hearted and oblique and some of the characters were caricatures, but line by line the writing had a studied and altogether individual brilliance.

Quite clearly, hers was an authentic talent. At the age of 22, she was a presence to be reckoned with. "People often remark," she says "that it must have been exciting to be published so young, and it was, but it was also terrifying. I was both blase and shy, and I was entering an entirely new world, with holes in my shoes, and, as often as not, a dog in tow."

In the early 1960s she recalls, all books by young persons were treated in the papers as dispatches from frontline Swinging London. She was regularly interrogated on matters youthful by magazines and TV shows. Her opinion, she says was sought on everything from the Beatles to reasons why a pretty girl should waste her time on writing novels. And she was certainly not getting rich. In spite of a small subsidy from Andre Deutsch, she still had to look for part time jobs: "I was a model for classes taught by gruff, white-bearded Chelsea artists, and a shop assistant for a morning at Chic of Hampstead—I fled at lunchtime because I could not fold cashmere sweaters—and I worked at a greetings card warehouse where we had the perfect line-up for a sitcom along the lines of *Are You Being Served?*"

In 1964, Mackay got married, to a boyfriend she had left behind in Blackheath. Robin Brown was an engineering student and not in the least literary, indeed, those kind of people, made him nervous. "But I married him for love, and we had many happy times together."

Three daughters followed, and one further novel, *The Advent Calendar,* published in 1971. Then came what critics have described as Mackay's doldrum years, from 1971 until 1983, the year of her next publication. Doldrum they may have been for admirers of her work, but for the author herself these were the years of young motherhood and marriage, and pretty busy years at that. "Maybe I was exhausted," she suggests, "I didn't have much time. I was running a big house. My mother was unwell. We took in lodgers. And there were three children to bring up."

As a mother, Mackay is extolled by her friends as wonderfully conscientious. "She always made sure they had their name tags sewed on," was just one of many accolades. In 1972 she and Robin moved the family from East Finchley to Brockham, a village in Surrey where Mackay perhaps hoped to give her daughters a taste of her own enchanted childhood, and thence to Reigate, scene of several of her subsequent suburban tales.

During the 1970s, though, her marriage began to falter. David Sylvester had reappeared (indeed, he is the father of her youngest daughter, Cecily Brown, now a highly thought of artist who recently sold a painting to the Tate Gallery). Why didn't she go off with Sylvester? "When it came to the point neither of us could do it. I couldn't do it to my children and he couldn't do it to his. We would probably have driven each other mad very quickly."

During the so-called "doldrum years" Mackay continued writing—several of her most incisive and merciless short stories belong to this period—but found it hard to get to grips with anything large-scale. One novel, *The*

*Firefly Motel,* was completed, then abandoned, although some of it was salvaged for *A Bowl of Cherries,* her next full length work, which was submitted to Jonathan Cape, with whom she had a contract.

Cape turned it down. Approaching her forties, Mackay found herself without a publisher, a dispiriting situation, considering her early triumphs, and all the more galling, maybe, because with this new book she had made a conscious effort to move beyond the disjointed lyricism of her first three novels. She wanted, she says, more narrative straightforwardness, more explanation.

It was around this time that she met Brigid Brophy, then a highly prominent figure on the literary scene. Over the ensuing years, Brophy would become one of Mackay's closest friends. In 1982, her help was crucial. She read *A Bowl of Cherries* in manuscript, liked it a lot (she had already admiringly reviewed some of Mackay's early work) and passed it on to Iris Murdoch who in turn recommended it to a small publisher, the Harvester Press.

Harvester published the book in 1984, to excellent reviews. Shena Mackay's barren years—"barren, indeed" she says—were over. In 1984, she turned 40, her children were getting ready to leave home, she was finally divorced (in 1982), and she was enjoying a second wave of recognition. Her life had become simpler in some ways but, as she points out, it was not quite a bowl of cherries. She had to support herself with part-time work at Reigate Library, her mother was still seriously ill and needed much attention (she would die in 1993) and Brigid Brophy was also in poor health (she died in 1995), and there were other turbulences too, some of them to do with drink.

On this topic, Mackay is undeniably reluctant to hold forth, but she does admit to having suffered from a "genetic predisposition to use drink as an anaesthetic against anxiety and depression. To deny it would be to deny the wonderful people who have helped me . . . I wouldn't be the artist I am if I didn't know about the dark side of life and the dark night of the soul."

Nowadays, Mackay doesn't touch a drop, but it has not been easy. It obviously pains Shena Mackay to talk about such matters, just as it pains her to be quizzed about her sometimes close relationships with other women. She loathes the word "bisexual" and visibly winces when the subject is touched on. "If you love someone", she says, "it doesn't matter what sex they are. I go along with Keats in being certain of nothing but the holiness of the heart's affections and the truth of the imagination." And it would be a vulgar inquisitor, indeed, who could insist on pressing for more details.

For a shy person, Diet Coke is not a great loosener of tongues. For her, though, the correct place for eloquence is on the page, and over the last decade she has been

eloquent indeed. Since 1984, there have been four novels and three volumes of short stories. There has also been some progress in the marketplace, her 1996 novel: *The Orchard on Fire,* was short-listed for the Booker Prize and paperback sales are heading for six figures.

Mackay despises book-hype but on the other hand she has no wish to be marked down as merely "quirky" or "stylishly off-beat". Her mother used to warn her, in jest: "Please don't end up like Jean Rhys"—by which she meant "neglected and admired". Perhaps Mackay's fictions are still more likely to be valued for their brilliant detail than for their narrative excitements. When I asked a few of her admirers to nominate the features of her writing that they most admired, nearly all of them remembered similes, plane trees in the sunshine looking like giraffes, the flames of a gas fire like lupins, a collapsed umbrella like an injured fruitbat, and so on. Or they mentioned her sly, semi-private jokes.

For myself, I always chuckle when I recall one of her characters attempting to quote Yeats: "The falcon cannot bear the falconer", he says. "That's not a misprint, is it?" I once asked her: "What do you think?" she replied. (The "bear" in case you don't know, should be "hear").

It is not common for compulsively "visual" writers to be good at telling stories; they are always dawdling so that they can take a closer look. But with recent novels like *Dunedin* and *The Orchard on Fire,* Mackay does seem to have been trying for a new structural surefootedness. And she is nicer to her characters these days, although, it must be said, she's still not very nice to them. As one of her admirers pointed out to me the other day: "Mackay simply does not know that she is being cruel to people in her books. She says that she means them to be sympathetic". And this does seem to be the case. When I put it to Mackay that the pervert Greenidge in *The Orchard on Fire* is a triumph in sheer loathsomeness, she looked seriously troubled. Apparently we are meant to feel sorry for this child-seducing wretch.

But then feeling sorry for people—and feeling sorry for flowers, animals, insects and sometimes the whole planet—seems to be ingrained in Mackay's nature. "I can't see a distressed pigeon in the street without wanting to look after it", she says. "And if I come across a snail on a pavement, I have to move it to a safer place, where it won't be trodden on." Does all this make her better than the rest of us? "Oh no, not at all. I wish I didn't feel like this. It's sometimes a real nuisance, an affliction."

A new Mackay novel will be finished by the end of the year, she tells me, but that's all she wants to tell. Her life now is industrious and calm. She has a circle of devoted and protective friends, not all of them literary, and she has what she calls "a huge extended family", including two grandchildren, on whom she evidently dotes. She sits on committees (she is a Booker Prize judge this year), supports environmental causes, is indignant about Nato and her favourite politician is Tony Benn.

"You can say that I live quietly in south London with my cats," she says. But what about the old days? Has the Bohemian been altogether vanquished by the Presbyterian? She smiles what I take to be an enigmatic smile. "There's a wonderful play by Rodney Ackland", she says. "It's called *The Pink Room* [later renamed *Absolute Hell*] and it's set in a club rather like the old Colony Room. The production I saw a few years ago ended with Judi Dench, who played the club owner, alone on the stage. The club is closing down. It has to, for some reason. And Judi Dench's last despairing cry is: 'Where are the pink lights? For God's sake let's have the pink lights on!' There's still part of me that wants the pink lights, the vie en rose, the artifice, the tawdry glamour. Outside is the cruel daylight and all that. But most of me doesn't want that. Most of me wants to live in the country, really."

### Barbara Croft (review date May 2001)

SOURCE: Croft, Barbara. "Tangled Tales." *Women's Review of Books* 18, no. 8 (May 2001): 21-2.

[*In the following review, Croft contends that the stories in* The World's Smallest Unicorn *are "unique, bittersweet stories, full of fun but far from light reading."*]

The stories of Scottish author Shena Mackay [in *The World's Smallest Unicorn*] are a lot more cheerful, but she too has an eye for the bizarre: an old folks home for retired clowns, a world traveler who ingests historic monuments, an eccentric old man's catalogue of life's embarrassments, an aging theatrical couple who act out the subtle jealousies of the film *A Star Is Born*.

Mackay, who has written a number of novels, including *The Orchard on Fire* and, more recently, *The Artist's Widow*, draws deliciously eccentric characters—Uncle Bob in **"The Index of Embarrassment,"** for example, who believes "that soap and water destroy the skin's essential oils," and Tusker Laidlaw, the official Bore of the Wilderness Club. Several are involved in writing: an aspiring young novelist, a journalist in disguise on a secret assignment, a young woman setting out to write the biography of her famous uncle, an editor eager to reprint the works of an aging, reclusive author. Their efforts to communicate, however, never quite succeed, and the stories are full of misunderstandings and misap-

plied blame. Characters say the wrong thing, twist the truth; they lie. They lash out at one another, hurling insults they don't really mean. An incident fraught with significance for one person is hardly remembered by another. Some are haunted by words that have never been spoken.

Ghosts drift through these stories, old grievances, unfulfilled longings. Teddy, for example, a melancholy expatriate who has returned from Hong Kong to an unwelcoming family and a London he hardly recognizes, feels like a *gweilo* (Chinese for ghost) and longs to see "the world's smallest unicorn"—a bit of magic advertised in a circus poster. Beatrice in **"Trouser Ladies"** broods for years over an ill-conceived visit to the family of an old friend, the secret love of her life.

Mackay doesn't indulge her characters' sorrows. Instead she embeds their tragedies in a wild and witty web of slang, puns, jokes, song cues and brand names. References to pop culture abound, and the stories sizzle with fast-paced flip dialogue. Like the fiction of the aspiring writer in **"Death by Art Deco,"** Mackay's densely textured stories are "gaudily painted, glittering and flamboyant."

The sense of melancholy in **"Trouser Ladies"** and **"The World's Smallest Unicorn"** is balanced by other stories that are freewheeling comedies. These seem to race forward, freely shifting point of view and offering delightful glimpses of the characters' backgrounds in passing, often with just a convoluted, one-sentence sketch: "Janet Richards, who worked as a home help, blamed Lily's father, a telephone engineer who had fantasized about being a pop star until an audition for *New Faces* smashed his dreams, for not having backed her up in her bid to persuade Lily to go to college." The pace never slows in these stories. It's just one damn thing after another: "My father was a second violinist. He was run over by a taxi while nipping out for an interval drink, and it was a struggle for my mother to provide for us. We were always keeping up appearances."

But, despite the incredible complications Mackay piles up for her characters, the collection is light on story. In **"A Silver Summer,"** a young shop girl, Tessa, meets the boy of her dreams, only to lose him when another boy, who has been making unwanted advances, tells him lies about her character. Tessa vows revenge. End of story. In **"Death by Art Deco,"** a young would-be writer becomes the personal assistant to a famous woman novelist. The junior writer worships her boss and mentor, but manages, through a complicated psychological tangle, to get on her bad side. Eventually, she's fired.

There's little sense of movement. The characters don't change. What makes this book a delightful read is not the narrative line, but the writing itself. Mackay's prose sparkles with precise and beautifully worded observations, often mingling the poetic and the mundane. Here, for example, she pinpoints a precise shade of turquoise: "True turquoise, not peacock blue or eau-de-nil or aquamarine or the debased hues of lacy bedjackets and babies' cardigans and velour leisure-suits that call themselves turquoise, but the vibrant stone of scarab and torque and misshapen ancient beads and Islamic glaze." Always, the description mirrors the character, as for example when she shows us an elegant older woman's worn embroidered silk kimono, "faded from peacock to azure and worn to patches of gossamer grids and loose hammocks of threads slung between blossoms and birds."

Ultimately, though, it is character that anchors fiction, and Mackay's people are wonderfully human. They delight and frequently move us, but we never pity even the most tragic of them because, however sad their circumstances, they have a wry sort of wisdom. These are unique, bittersweet stories, full of fun but far from light reading.

## Philip Hensher (review date 22 February 2003)

SOURCE: Hensher, Philip. "Radiance in Suburbia." *Spectator* 291, no. 9107 (22 February 2003): 35-6.

[*In the following review, Hensher assesses Mackay's literary accomplishment and asserts that* Heligoland *"has a deceptive simplicity which conceals great art, and it manages to convey a big emotional journey in a relatively brief span."*]

Shena Mackay has had a difficult and unconventional career, and it has taken a long time for most readers to register what a powerful and original novelist she is. Several things have counted, unfairly, against her: her subjects are not just domestic, but often suburban, which she presents with a disconcerting rapture. She does not write long books, nor polemical ones; it is hard to say what any given novel by her is 'about', although various fiercely held convictions may, from time to time, be discerned. They are primarily about human beings living their lives, rendered with increasing mastery and a hard-won truth; and there is nothing harder in the world to defend than that. In her prime, she reminds me sometimes of a very different novelist, Elizabeth Taylor; both have a rare gift of making their characters interesting whether their acts and situations are objectively so or not. She can make you watch a girl walking up a country road with nothing much at the end of it; and that takes some skill.

Perhaps the greatest difficulty for the conventionally minded critic is that her career has followed an unusual path. She was a child prodigy among novelists, and her very early novels, written in her teens, such as *Music Upstairs* and *Toddler on the Run*—my favourite of all her titles—are flip, brilliant miniatures out of the school of Brigid Brophy. They are wonderfully funny and effortless, but tiny and short-breathed; and then she fell suddenly silent. When she started to publish again, some years later, her style had broadened and deepened, and become much less easy to classify. The glorious, glamorous *Redhill Rococo* and *A Bowl of Cherries* were like nothing else being written at the time; their mood must have been hard to catch, and they were often either misread as satires or dismissed by metropolitan readers as naive books about suburban people.

She has been patient, and taught us how to read her books, and slowly we have caught up with her. What were always beautiful books have become steadily more expert, and now she is generally acknowledged as a unique voice of exceptional confidence and range. She has always been greatly loved by her readership; with the increasing accomplishment of her recent novels, *The Orchard on Fire, The Artist's Widow* and, especially, *Heligoland,* there can be no excuse for not taking her seriously.

Her books give the impression of great generosity. Certainly, she is a writer who finds ecstatic delight in mundane things, and there are loving descriptions of bright plastic hair-clips, cheap sweets and gaudy, suburban flower-beds. There is no irony in any of this; she is capable of loving them as Iris Murdoch could love a rock. She believes fervently that the world is full of beauty, and the aesthetic pleasures of the uneducated taste are as profoundly experienced as those of the learned. Indeed, her novels, and, particularly, many of her short stories come from a belief that the life of, say, a girl growing up in the suburbs is richer in wonder and beauty than the lives of sophisticated aesthetes. A simple person will respond ecstatically to ordinary objects, to birds, flowers, angel fish in a pet shop, even a neon sign; a sophisticated one will save his delight for museums, and his life has less beauty in it.

Her world is full of objects, lovingly assembled in massive, exact lists; she loves gardens—*The Orchard on Fire,* her most rapturous book, is full of precise renderings of plants and flowers—but they melt, very often, into similarly ecstatic accounts of broken toys or cheap jewellery. Many of her boldest effects come simply from an observation of colour; the moment at the end of the first chapter of *The Artist's Widow* when Lyris, returning from an exhausting and depressing party, sits down in her painter's chair and 'squeezes out a bead of aquamarine'. Her ability to see spiritual beauty everywhere is almost Japanese; in particular, her excellent short stories often start from physical facts, such as a tank of tropical fish, and then construct lives around them. In *A Bowl of Cherries,* the lavish evocation of a ratty old novelty shop produces a rhapsody:

Heaps of glittering excelsior, red, green, gold, blue, silver foil trumpets, feathered squeakers, paper fans, black eye-masks and animal faces, a skull, peashooters, magic daggers, tricks, jokes, little silk chinese drums, paper accordions, flutes, indoor fireworks, joss sticks, balloons, spangles, sparklers, sequins; gimcrack gewgaws, evanescent glitter.

Here, there is no overt judgment until the very end of the list, and then the word 'gimcrack' is austerely set apart from the rapture with a semi-colon, as if it is quite a different voice from her own. Her interests are very appealing; I adore the girls' schools episodes in so many of her books, from *Dust Falls on Eugene Schlumberger* onwards; they are much like the first chapter of Iris Murdoch's *The Flight from the Enchanter,* a vein Murdoch ought to have pursued. She has, too, the precision of an Opie in her recall of playground chants, and a jolly schoolgirl taste for the really silly joke which is always irresistible—the sign at the beginning of *Redhill Rococo* which reads 'Redhill Exhausts and Tyres', or the character in *The Artist's Widow* who observes that a girl called Paige 'sounds like something from a book'. Her novels are full of happy, relieved journeys towards home, with a tart and unindulgent nostalgia, and exist in a densely evoked physical world.

They seem, in recollection, like infinitely generous books; it is surprising to see that, in reality, she makes uncompromising judgments. Again like Murdoch, she likes and closely observes animals; butchers and people affecting to dislike cats are given a rough ride. (She once gave me a very hard time when I was rude about a cat in a novel; I'm not sure I've ever been entirely forgiven.) That's probably just a foible, but a more interesting judgment is a recurrent one on artistic dabblers. Nathan in *The Artist's Widow* or Jaz in *The Orchard on Fire* come off particularly badly.

Perhaps this is because Mackay herself is a writer who takes her art very seriously, and who sets herself challenges with each book. As a result, she has grown steadily in authority. *A Bowl of Cherries* is a deliberate attempt to write more expansively than the clipped, witty style of *Music Upstairs*; the characters talk, not always quite successfully, as if they have been let off the leash, rather than in a sequence of *bons mots.* *Dunedin,* the most varied of her books, is an attempt at a more complicated structure than before; dazzling as it is, the experiment doesn't quite come off. But a novelist who never risks anything is not a novelist worth reading, and the experience of *Dunedin* went into the intricately patterned, but immensely satisfying *The Orchard on Fire,* one of the best novels of the 1990s. It is the book of hers where everything seems to come together effortlessly.

*Heligoland* has a deceptive simplicity which conceals great art, and it manages to convey a big emotional journey in a relatively brief span. It is set in an idealistic urban community, a 1930s experiment in communal liv-ing which is still staggering on decades later. In the Nautilus building, a motley collection of aging architects, poets, artists rub along somehow, their grand friends and sorry hangers-on popping in from time to time.

The description of the atmosphere of such a place, the crabby utopianism struggling on in the middle of a philistine and cynical world, is a delight, and the novel is full of brilliant, sharp character sketches—the cast of *The Artist's Widow* reappears here, seen from a slightly colder angle. Both dreamily speculative and physically precise, the book has a tone and flavour uniquely Mackay's own. At the core of the novel is a profoundly moving study of loneliness, in the central figure of Rowena Snow. She is one of Mackay's uprooted and uncertain heroines; her life has followed no clear path, and at each stage she seems baffled by her own circumstances. From a terrible progressive boarding school, working as a home-help, to her strange and not quite established place at the Nautilus, half cleaner, half patient muse, she has had consistent bad luck and consistent isolation.

It is an extremely sad story, utterly plausible in the gruesome details—the 'advanced' school is appallingly enjoyable—but it ends in consolation and optimism, as Rowena starts to see that she might, after all, be able to enjoy a birthday party she never had and thought she never wanted. By then, we are mildly surprised to discover how much we want her to be happy, and in the end she almost is. 'Rowena doesn't know how to have birthday parties, but suddenly it all seems to be going quite well.' In Mackay's world, that counts as an epiphany, and if there is a constant conviction in her books that most people worry that they don't know 'how to do it', nevertheless, despite everything, in the end things seem to 'go quite well'. It is a modest sounding triumph, but in the event a deeply moving one, and, like the best of her books, this one concludes in the atmosphere of a long-anticipated quiet homecoming.

**Peter Bradshaw (review date 1 March 2003)**

SOURCE: Bradshaw, Peter. "Muddling Through." *Guardian* (1 March 2003): 26.

[*In the following review, Bradshaw lauds as gorgeous the prose of* Heligoland.]

Shena Mackay's elegant, elusive new book [*Heligoland*] sketches out the circumstances of marginal and defeated lives in what are almost short stories, loosely threaded like beads on a string. Her theme is elderly or middle-aged people living fretfully in genteel obscurity, but doing so in such a way that they seem like bright, observant but powerless children. This is drawn so playfully and so compassionately—and with such consistently beautiful writing—that the experience is mysteriously comic and sweet.

The venue is the Nautilus, an eccentric house designed in the 1930s which resembles a seashell and whose rooms look like a shell's chambers. Set amid heavy gravel in which an anchor and chain have been whimsically placed, it seems as if the house should be on a seashore, but it is in fact in the London suburbs. This was established as the location of a Bloomsbury-ish bohemian community of yore, with lavish bar, magnificent library and a printing press long since fallen into disuse.

It now houses just two of its elderly pioneers. Francis Campion is a querulous minor poet, worrying away at slights and glancing condescensions in various biographies and literary histories; Celeste Zylberstein is of Jewish and central European extraction, the widow of Arkady, another man of letters. New tenant Gus Crabb, an antiques dealer of faintly roguish mien who has moved into the Nautilus having just been left by his wife and children, is quite without these literary credentials. And the heroine is Rowena Snow, who applies for the post of housekeeper at the Nautilus: an Asian woman brought up as an orphan in an ecstatically remembered arcadia of remote Scotland, then unhappily sent south to an experimental boarding school called Chestnuts before drifting into ill-paid work in the caring professions.

This is a world of people who listen to Radio 4 last thing at night: who drift off to sleep to "Sailing By" and then, as often as not, get jerked sharply awake by "Lillibulero" at two in the morning as the station makes way for the World Service. The Heligoland of the title is an island off the German coast that used to be mentioned in the incantation of the shipping forecast but is now omitted, and which Rowena's childish self—a self that bleeds into her adult persona—fantasises as a promised land of happiness.

That Radio 4 trope is part of the book's intense and exotic Englishness, and its delicate, pre-modern feel. This is a book in which drum and bass can be heard thudding from young people's cars, but these novelties do not impinge greatly on a world in which people unselfconsciously refer to "the wireless". Celeste's Jewish mannerisms and Yiddish phrases are effortlessly subsumed into the Anglo-Saxon mix, and it is difficult to remember that Rowena is of a different ethnic group from everyone else. Apart from one possibly racially motivated incident, in which a crowd of yobs throw an egg at her from a car, it does not register as a very important factor. Like the black African character in

*The Archers* whose colour was never remarked upon, Rowena does not seem alienated from the rest of the cast, or at least no more than they all are from each other.

The driving force at the centre of this book is not really the narrative, because the impetus that that provides is pretty low: nothing very much happens, and the story is always turning left, right and backwards into diverting sidestreets and culs-de-sac. (Bafflingly, one very important event, the husband of an old friend falling in love with Rowena, gets only a brief mention.) It is Mackay's gorgeous prose that does the work, along with the seductive, sad and hilarious vignettes that she conjures up, sequences and setpieces that are often themselves in a subordinate position to the flashbacks appended to the main narrative.

The writing is superb, and of that unassuming, unworked-up kind that comes only from an author whose gentle mastery of language is quite beyond showy displays of technique. There are too many felicities to cite here, but the description of the snowy scene at the book's beginning is wonderfully achieved, while there are laugh-out-loud descriptions of Mrs Diggins, the cantankerous cook at Rowena's old school, who has a face like a "cruel spoon", and a preposterous boho couple who hope to persuade Francis to get their execrable dramatic monologues performed on the radio.

*Heligoland* can be a bemusing book in some ways: we see glimpses of lives, fragments and shards, rather than amply delineated, rounded existences. But the peripheral nature of all this is precisely the point: these are vulnerable people in the evening of lives of which they have no clear view, living in a muddle, and muddling through. It is this partial victory on which Mackay bestows her gentle, lenient and generous imagination.

---

# FURTHER READING

## Criticism

Allardice, Lisa. "Nautilus, Not Nice." *Observer* (2 March 2003): 17.
> Provides a negative assessment of *Heligoland*, maintaining that the novel might work better as a short story.

**Additional information on Mackay's life and career is contained in the following sources published by Thomson Gale: *Contemporary Authors*, Vol. 104; *Contemporary Authors New Revision Series*, Vol. 88; *Dictionary of Literary Biography*, Vol. 231; and *Literature Resource Center*.**

# Susan Sontag
## 1933 -

American essayist, novelist, short-story writer, critic, playwright, screenplay writer, and film director.

The following entry provides an overview of Sontag's career through 2004. For further information on her life and works, see *CLC*, Volumes 1, 2, 10, 13, 31, and 105.

## INTRODUCTION

Sontag is widely noted as one of the most influential and controversial contemporary American essayists and social commentators. Considered a popular icon for her role in the development of modern culture and intellectual thought, Sontag addresses issues of interpretation and has exposed Americans to the works of modern European intellectuals. Through her essays on illness, she has discredited many of the misinformed opinions and negative associations attached to such diseases as cancer and AIDS, and she has argued for a new understanding of disease based on clinical evidence and free from social stigma. In her fiction Sontag frequently experiments with form and style and uses narrative to underscore the universality of human emotion and actions, to illustrate the fine line between reality and fiction, and to ponder the bounds of free will.

## BIOGRAPHICAL INFORMATION

Sontag was born on January 16, 1933, in New York City, but spent her youth in Tucson and Los Angeles. She was a gifted student and skipped several years in school, graduating from high school at age fifteen. She then entered the University of California, Berkeley, and transferred after one year to the University of Chicago, where she earned a bachelor's degree in philosophy in 1951. While attending the University of Chicago, Sontag met Philip Rieff, a social psychologist. The couple married in 1950 and had a son, David, but divorced nine years later. Sontag pursued graduate studies at Harvard from 1951 to 1957, earning master's degrees in English (1954) and philosophy (1955). She later continued her graduate studies at St. Anne's College, Oxford, and at the Sorbonne, Paris. Sontag was a regular contributor to the *Partisan Review, Harper's Weekly,* the *Nation,* and the *New York Review of Books* while holding teaching positions at institutions including the University of Connecticut, City College of the City University of New York, Sarah Lawrence College, and Rutgers University. Sontag soon retired from her academic career and began writing full-time; her first

novel, *The Benefactor,* was published in 1963 and her first collection of essays, *Against Interpretation and Other Essays,* appeared in 1966. In the early 1970s Sontag was diagnosed with breast cancer and her experiences with disease as well as others' reaction to it served as the basis for her *Illness as a Metaphor* (1978), which in turn led to the writing of *AIDS and Its Metaphors* (1989). In the early 1990s, Sontag made numerous trips to war-torn Yugoslavia for humanitarian purposes. While there, she also directed a production of Samuel Beckett's *Waiting for Godot.* Sontag has received numerous fellowships and awards, including a National Book Award nomination in 1966 for *Against Interpretation and Other Essays,* a National Book Critics Circle prize in 1978 for *On Photography* (1977), and the National Book Award in 2000 for the novel *In America* (2000).

## MAJOR WORKS

Sontag addresses social, artistic, and political issues, as well as contemporary complacency in her essays. In her first collection, *Against Interpretation and Other Essays,* Sontag eschewed standard critical methods that rely on analysis of content and various levels of meaning, asserting instead that the function of criticism is to show "how it is what it is, even that it is what it is, rather than show what it means." Included in this collection is the famous essay "Notes on 'Camp'," in which Sontag defends "camp" as a serious art form. *Styles of Radical Will* (1969) contains the essay "The Pornographic Imagination," in which Sontag argues that pornography is a valid literary genre. *Illness as Metaphor* and *AIDS and Its Metaphors* both deal with the way in which western society interprets and creates cultural myths about diseases. In *Illness as Metaphor,* Sontag examines the stigma associated with cancer and cancer patients and attempts to defuse the negative power that words have in dealing with such an illness. She takes this approach one step further in *AIDS and Its Metaphors* exposing misconceptions and confusion about AIDS and AIDS patients. *Under the Sign of Saturn* (1980) is a volume of essays that explore theories in literary criticism. Sontag further delves into the arts and the artist in *Where the Stress Falls* (2001); this volume also includes the essay titled "Waiting for Godot in Sarajevo," which focuses on her time in Sarajevo during the war in Yugoslavia. Sontag studies photographs and images and their effects on viewers in *On Photography* and *Regarding the Pain of Others* (2003) and comments on humanity's reaction to and morbid fascination with photos and images of the pain of others. Sontag emphasizes the dangerous desensitizing of Westerners who are bombarded by such images on television, in magazines, and films. Sontag has also written several works of fiction, including a play, *Alice in Bed* (1993), about Alice James, sister to Henry and William James; the novels *The Benefactor* and *Death Kit* (1967); and a collection of short stories titled *I, etcetera* (1978). Most notable among her fiction are *The Volcano Lover* (1992) and *In America* (2000). *The Volcano Lover* is an unusual account of Emma Hamilton and Horatio Nelson's love affair as told from the point of view of Hamilton's husband, Sir William Hamilton. This novel provides a sweeping look at Italian society between 1764 and 1780, with which the author contrasts contemporary culture and highlights the timeless repetition of human folly and foibles. *In America* is also a historical novel, and concerns a Polish actress and immigrant and her quest for fame, fortune, and the American dream.

## CRITICAL RECEPTION

Sontag's work has generated much reaction from reviewers and ordinary readers alike. Many of her views have run contrary to majority political and intellectual thought and Sontag has actually reversed some of her earlier opinions. Her studies of American culture have earned her both favorable and negative criticism, as well as observations that her own work proves her points in ironic, presumably unintentional ways. For example, some commentators have asserted that her essays censuring American culture of the 1960s and early 1970s are actually themselves a product of the era's discourse. While some reviewers have praised her novel interpretation of modern culture and her championing of contemporary European writers and intellectuals, others contend that Sontag's arguments are not supported adequately and that she often diverges from her central themes. Sontag's groundbreaking works on the power of words to create associations for certain physical ailments are universally well received. Although some note that Sontag's use of epigrams and clichés is at times tedious, most critics approve of her descriptive narrative style and her depiction of historical trends and settings, praising her experiments with language and literary form.

---

# PRINCIPAL WORKS

*The Benefactor* (novel) 1963
*Against Interpretation and Other Essays* (essays) 1966
*Death Kit* (novel) 1967
*Duet for Cannibals* [and director] (screenplay) 1969
*Styles of Radical Will* (essays) 1969
*Trip to Hanoi* (essay) 1969
*Brother Carl: A Filmscript* [and director] (screenplay) 1971
*Promised Lands* [and director] (screenplay) 1974
*On Photography* (nonfiction) 1977
*I, etcetera* (short stories) 1978
*Illness as Metaphor* (nonfiction) 1978
*Under the Sign of Saturn* (essays) 1980
*A Susan Sontag Reader* (essay collection) 1982
*Unguided Tour* [and director] (screenplay) 1983
"The Way We Live Now" [republished as a novella in 1991] (short story) 1986
*AIDS and Its Metaphors* (nonfiction) 1989
*The Volcano Lover: A Romance* (novel) 1992
*Alice in Bed: A Play in Eight Scenes* (drama) 1993
*In America: A Novel* (novel) 2000
*Where the Stress Falls* (essays) 2001
*Regarding the Pain of Others* (nonfiction) 2003

---

# CRITICISM

## John Simon (review date 15 December 1980)

SOURCE: Simon, John. "From Sensibility toward Sense." *New Leader* 63, no. 23 (15 December 1980): 22-4.

[*In the following review, Simon judges that many of the phrases in Sontag's collection* Under the Sign of Saturn *are nonsensical and overly verbose, creating confusion for the reader.*]

According to an adage that often performs also as an analogy, if we watched ourselves walking, we could not walk at all. In the process of speculating about just how we propel ourselves forward by putting one foot in front of the other, we would end up paralyzed or falling on our faces. Whether or not this is the truth about ambulation, it unfortunately is not true of criticism: Entire schools of contemporary criticism watch themselves—anxiously, self-importantly, gloatingly—perform in essays that, far from freezing, flow unremittingly on. If anyone becomes numb, it is the reader, unlucky fellow, who finds himself in the position of an innocent traveler pressed into archaeological spade work without being given the necessary equipment or training. Structuralist and semiological criticism, and their various offshoots, have not only buried the texts they belabor under impermeable rubble, they are also hell-bent on burying us.

Susan Sontag is not uninfluenced by the prevailing French or French-derived criticism, witness the tribute to Roland Barthes in her new collection, *Under the Sign of Saturn.* Although she is basically a comprehensible, generally even lucid, critic, she has a tendency to sprinkle complication into her writing, as for instance in the opening section of her essay on Antonin Artaud, the longest and most interesting in the book. One is reminded of the story about Mallarmé dawdling at a café table over a funerary poem for Verlaine and explaining his holding up the obsequies with: "I am just adding a little obscurity." Aside from the short mortuary tribute to Barthes, a similar one to Paul Goodman—the latter really a lament over his snubbing her, as well as a portrait of herself as an isolated artist in a Paris garret—and the piece on Artaud that served as the introduction to his *Selected Writings,* Sontag's book includes essays on Walter Benjamin (himself no mean shedder of obscurity), on Elias Canetti, on Hans-Jürgen Syberberg's seven-hour film about Hitler, and on **"Fascinating Fascism,"** which deals with both Leni Riefenstahl and a coffee-table book of photographs called *SS Regalia.*

What is the sign of Saturn, and why are these writers and filmmakers under it? Miss Sontag quotes Walter Benjamin, the complicated German philosopher-critic who alone can compete with the French master obfuscators in current popularity among the literary élite: "I came into the world under the sign of Saturn—the star of the slowest revolution, the planet of detours and delays. . . ." The umbrella of Saturn does not really cover every one of the other artists discussed, but they are all, in one sense or another, extreme cases—*cas limites,* as the French would say: artists who are at the limits of the possible or the permissable. Sontag refers to them admiringly as "the great, daring mapmakers of consciousness *in extremis.*

Actually, some do not enjoy her full favor: she is against Leni Riefenstahl, Hitler's favorite filmmaker, at least ideologically. It is characteristic of Miss Sontag's new critical stance that moral considerations matter. Thus she shows us Riefenstahl's career as a triptych: the early mountaineering films where Leni was both star and director, and physical effort triumphed; the Nazi period's panegyrics to bodily beauty, strength and achievement—*Triumph of the Will* and *Olympia*; and the more recent book of photographs about a handsome but vanishing African tribe, *The Last of the Nuba.* In her *Sturm und Drang* phase, Miss Sontag would have hailed Riefenstahl's esthetic achievements and disregarded the political and moral aspects; now, at last, she gives us a carefully researched and documented moral-political case against Riefenstahl and her alleged reformation, though Sontag rightly concedes a certain philosophy to the Nazis and admires the unquestionable cinematic values of the Nazi filmmaker's two great documentaries.

Here Sontag reintroduces the concept of "camp" that she championed without ever fully admitting it, essentially to renounce it, albeit not without some reservations and regrets. She speaks of "formalist appreciations" backed up by "the sensibility of camp, which is unfettered by the scruples of high seriousness: and the modern sensibility relies on continuing trade-offs between the formalist approach and camp taste." This is an irresponsible statement: Neither in her celebrated **"Notes on 'Camp'"** (1964) nor in **"Fascinating Fascism"** (1974) does Sontag show how "high seriousness" or "the formalist approach" trades off with camp taste; indeed, not even the meaning of "modern sensibility" is made entirely clear.

But, then, Sontag has a trying habit of issuing wonderfully challenging statements throughout this collection (and elsewhere) without elaborating and elucidating them. She will tell us, "I admire Norman Mailer as a writer, but I don't really believe in his voice," a voice that she finds "too baroque, somehow fabricated." Since her statement occurs in the tribute to Paul Goodman, whose voice, apparently, "is the real thing," we must, perhaps, settle for this foreshortened explanation of what is wrong with Mailer; yet, whatever the context, we must be told how someone with an inauthentic voice can still be admired as a writer.

Similarly, we learn next that although Goodman "was not often graceful as a writer, his writing and his mind were touched with grace." This means one of three things. Either grace as a writer can coexist with gracelessness in the writing, or being touched with grace is in some mysterious way different from having it, or Miss Sontag tosses off hasty, high-sounding paradoxes without thinking through what, if anything, they mean.

The last hypothesis gains credibility when considered in conjunction with other assertions in the book. We are told that the major works of Baudelaire and Lautréamont "are equally dependent . . . upon the idea of the author as a tormented self raping its own unique subjectivity." Quite aside from the clumsiness of that image, the extremely disciplined verse and controlled audacity of *Les Fleurs du mal* are in no way comparable to the torrential flow of poetic prose and surreal vision of *Les Chants de Maldoror*; as for the artist's driving himself to the limit and beyond, this applies equally to a good many 19th-and 20th-century poets. But what really confuses the issue is Miss Sontag's wording: What is this "idea of the author"? Is it in the author's or in the reading public's mind? Is it a legitimate concept or a self-deluding notion? Or is it merely verbiage?

Again, when Sontag casually asserts that "Walt Disney's *Fantasia,* Busby Berkeley's *The Gang's All Here,* and Kubrick's *2001* . . . strikingly exemplify certain formal structures and themes of fascist art," we cannot accept her parenthetic aside without any further discussion; at the very least we want to know *which* structures and themes. And if it is true, it requires an examination of what that says about contemporary American society. In fact, if Sontag could prove her glibly dropped point, an essay on *it* would be much more interesting than the virtually self-evident demonstration of Riefenstahl's fascism.

But to return to camp. Sontag tries to exonerate it, first, on the basis of "continuing trade-offs" between it and high seriousness—which conjures up the image of a close collaboration between Matthew Arnold and Ronald Firbank; soon, contradictorily, she attempts a defense on the grounds of something quite ephemeral: fashion. "Art that seemed eminently worth defending 10 years ago [i.e., in '64 as against '74], as a minority or adversary taste, no longer seems defensible today, because the ethical and cultural issues it raises have become serious, even dangerous, in a way they were not then." This is, to put it mildly, bizarre.

To begin with, can something that ceases to be defensible as art in a mere decade still be considered art at all? Whatever outlives its artistic usefulness in 10 short years is precisely a fleeting fashion and the exemplar of nonart. Second, is critical evaluation meant to be a kind of politics of contrariness? That would automatically foster the enshrinement of what the majority resents or ignores—the very procedure that, for a while, raised camp to the level of art.

The giveaway follows apace: "The hard truth is that what may be acceptable in élite culture may not be acceptable in mass culture, that tastes which pose only innocuous ethical issues as the property of a minority become corrupting when they become more established.

Taste is context, and the context has changed." Yet how did camp become a majority taste? It achieved its eminence precisely because the brilliant, young, glamorous Susan Sontag published **"Notes on 'Camp'"**—to be sure, in *Partisan Review,* not exactly the stomping grounds of hoi polloi, but where are the temples of the unco-optable nowadays? Soon enough the media latched on to that essay and its topic, and especially to its eloquent, charming, highly saleable author. Nothing succeeds better than highbrow endorsement of lowbrow tastes: Who would not, at no extra cost, prefer to be a *justified* sinner? Miss Sontag's "hard truth" strikes me as very soft indeed.

Next, by what right, human or divine, is what is good for the élite taboo for the masses? This kind of intellectual *droit du seigneur* may well be the epitome of fascist criticism. If, as responsible critics, we preconize, say, Proust, Mallarmé, Joyce, and Beckett, it is not because we want to keep them to ourselves; it is, on the contrary, in the hope, often forlorn, that we may bring more people to the pleasure and insight to be gathered from them. If, on the other hand, our taste is deleterious and culpable—or foolish and irresponsible—we have no business promulgating it either in *Partisan Review* or in *Time* magazine. Taste is precisely *not* context, but that which transcends context; everything else is addiction, fashionable or unfashionable, and, even if pleasing for the moment, headed for the waste basket. But, of course, this is presuming that taste refers to esthetics and not to erotics, and that we do not, as Miss Sontag did in another famous 1964 essay, **"Against Interpretation,"** celebrate and demand a mere "erotics of art."

Miss Sontag no longer militantly espouses this outlook, but she continues to hover in its vicinity. Scattered throughout **Under the Sign of Saturn** are such bits of questionable praise as that for Artaud's "aesthetics of thought . . . theology of culture . . . phenomenology of suffering." Now, I can see how one might worship culture, though I am not sure how this applies to a craving for Artaud; I can likewise see how a phenomenology of suffering might make for a riveting case history for psychiatrists and even some lay readers. But "aesthetics of thought"—surely this is just the "erotics of art" turned inside out and being sneaked, in sheep's clothing, through the back door.

And touting Artaud, that "hero of self-exacerbation," as "the greatest prose poet in the French language since the Rimbaud of *Illuminations* and *A Season in Hell,*" rashly ignores the Mallarmé of *Divagations* and does scant justice to Valéry, Claudel, Gide, and Jules Renard, among others. Of course, if your criterion is self-exacerbation—"the greatest *quantity* of suffering in the history of literature"—your candidate may be the greatest prose poet *before* Rimbaud as well, although even then one might wonder about what kinds of scales, or calipers are needed for the quantitative assessment of suffering. Or does one judge simply by the loudness of the screams?

Yet how silly of me to raise such questions in these post-R. D. Laing and post-Michel Foucault days. Obviously, Miss Sontag is influenced by both these "minority or adversary" thinkers, as witness her condemnation of Jacques Rivière's moving attempts to bring Artaud back to relative sanity (a lost cause, if ever there was one), followed by her Foucaultian definition of sanity as what makes sense to a particular culture, a particular society; whereas "what is called insane denotes that which in the determination of a particular society must not be thought." Aside from the fact that this statement overlooks the not insignificant distinction in most societies between thought and action, it implies that to a shallow society profundity will appear insane, i.e., madness is context, and the context changes. Yet even if there is something arbitrary about most prevailing definitions of madness, there is nothing specious about regarding acts of violence against others as dangerous, illicit and mad.

But do not consider the foregoing strictures a complete rejection of Miss Sontag's book. Whenever she takes the trouble to be a historian, as in her pointing out the ahistoricity of Riefenstahl's view of the Nuba, or a theological historian, as when she traces Artaud's indebtedness to Gnosticism, she performs with noteworthy acumen and ability. So, too, when she analyzes the quiddity of a work and its background, as with Syberberg's *Hitler, a Film from Germany,* a seven-hour endurance test she had the stamina (or eccentricity) to see five or six times, to discuss at length with its author, and (apparently) to read up on in great detail. Although my own regard for this film is qualified, I have nothing but respect for a critic who goes to such lengths to understand and interpret (yes, interpret; no "against interpretation" here!) a difficult work.

Regrettably, in the case of this film, too, Miss Sontag indulges in what strikes me as an exaggeration. Just as she asserted that "the course of all recent serious theater in Western Europe and the Americas can be said to divide into two periods—before Artaud and after Artaud" (which, assuming that it is meant as more than a chronological division, sounds like a whopping overstatement), she now tells us that *Hitler* is "probably the most ambitious Symbolist work of this century," a masterpiece having "in the era of cinema's unprecedented mediocrity . . . something of the character of a posthumous event." It is "like an unwanted baby in the era of zero population growth." The trouble with *Hitler,* as I see it, is precisely that it is the equivalent of too many babies in any era, an act of overpopulation on screen—and of decimation in the auditorium.

That, however, is one of the hallmarks of Miss Sontag's criticism; a boundless enthusiasm for certain favorites that ignores or minimizes their shortcomings. In Elias Canetti she loves "his staunchless capacity for admiration and enthusiasm, and his civilized contempt for complaining." This may be splendid in a novelist and essayist; in a critic, complaining is often necessary where it hurts most, and enthusiasm frequently in need of a little staunching. Thank goodness, Miss Sontag no longer comes out in enthusiastic defense of such stuff as Jack Smith's *Flaming Creatures,* yet not even Canetti, whose work I do not know, should (in my opinion) be praised unqualifiedly for his tribute to "a brown bundle emitting a single sound (*e-e-e-e-e*) which is brought every day to a square in Marrakesh." Canetti's "I was proud of the bundle because it was alive" strikes me not as a moving tribute, but as endorsement of a horrible misery for the sake of displaying one's enlightened affirmation of life.

Susan Sontag can write well: "One is always in arrears to oneself" is exquisite and compelling; "Surrealism's great gift . . . was to make melancholy cheerful," though debatable, is equally stimulating and exquisite. There is much to be said, too, for this maxim: "One cannot use the life to interpret the work. But one can use the work to interpret the life." Other boldly hurled maxims boomerang. I find it hard to accept, in a context of her high praise for Walter Benjamin, that "his major essays seem to end just in time, before they self-destruct."

Rash and unhelpful, again, is the assertion that, though one can be inspired, scorched and changed by Artaud, "there is no way of applying him." Can any poet-seer be applied? Sontag's argument is not helped by careless use of words: How can Artaud be "profoundly indigestible"? On some deeper level than that of the stomach? And I should be happier if Miss Sontag stopped hinting, especially about the dead, and instead of referring to Barthes as "consciously interested in the perverse" and as "a man of his sexual tastes," allowed her observations to come out of the closet.

She might also, profitably, stop reaching for grand but nebulous criteria. To praise, as she does, identification "with something beyond achievement" is very much like arguing "against interpretation." A critic as capable of subtle and illuminating interpretations as Susan Sontag should come down all the way from the cloudy heights of metacriticism.

### Walter Goodman (review date 13 December 1982)

SOURCE: Goodman, Walter. "Fair Game." *New Leader* 65, no. 23 (13 December 1982): 9-10.

[*In the following review of* A Susan Sontag Reader, *Goodman studies the vehemence and political leanings of Sontag's essays throughout her career. Goodman as-*

*serts that Sontag is becoming less radical and extremist as she matures, detecting a more moderate stance in her views and writings.*]

### UNDER THE SIGN OF SONTAG

Her position has been certified everywhere from *Vogue* to *Rolling Stone*. Readers of *People* magazine know her as "America's *prima intellectual assoluta*," and she also holds the ambiguous title of "the Natalie Wood of the U.S. avant garde." Yet the crowning of Susan Sontag as this country's exemplary intellectual remains a puzzlement. As *A Susan Sontag Reader,* her new collection of "the work I'm proudest of," confirms, she is more akin to a species of European intelligentsia than to any homegrown strain, and has no great affection for American society.

Sontag became the talk of the literati in the mid-'60s, with several now-famous essays that were as striking for their combative tone as for their substance. In **"Against Interpretation"** and **"On Style,"** she took on critics who, in her view, were so intent on "explaining" what a work of art "meant" that they missed the essence of the work itself. She condemned the seekers after interpretation as "reactionary, impertinent, cowardly, stifling." Her attention-grabbing **"Notes on 'Camp',"** written around the same time, was all about a way of seeing the world that exaggerated style to the point of parody and laughed away content.

For conservative critics like Hilton Kramer, who devoted considerable space to his distaste for Sontag in the premier issue of his magazine, *The New Criterion,* Sontag was guilty of promoting a doctrine that would "release high culture from its obligations to be entirely serious." Her essay's catchiest line, "Camp is a woman walking around in a dress made of three million feathers," was an uncharacteristic flash of humor from a writer whose prose is not usually much fun. The Sontag camp has had to grapple with sentences like this one from her essay, **"The Aesthetics of Silence":** "Toward such an ideal plenitude to which the audience can add nothing, analogous to the aesthetic relation to nature, a great deal of contemporary art aspires—through various strategies of blandness, of reduction, of deindividuation, of alogicality."

Would these early essays have brought fame to a homely middle-aged man? An invidious question—but Sontag grants that her gender has contributed to her celebrity. America likes its intellectual glamour girls. If she lacked the wit of Mary McCarthy or the weight of Hannah Arendt, it cannot have hurt to be a good-looking woman in her early 30s, as well as a highly intelligent, formidably read, fiercely assertive one.

During the '70s, Sontag made a mark as the foremost publicist for European bearers of the Modernist sensibility, whose writings even devotees of cultural criticism and philosophy may find hard going. These "master obscurantists," as John Simon calls them, include Walter Benjamin, the melancholic German-Jewish essayist who was driven to suicide in 1940; the anguished Antonin Artaud, who tried to transmogrify delirium into drama; the misogynistic Nobel Prize-winner Elias Canetti, author of "Crowds and Power"; and the influential French man of letters Roland Barthes, propounder of "semiotics" or the study of signs, who was killed in a traffic accident in 1980.

Sontag is powerfully drawn to outsiders, writers removed from bourgeois society and most of its works. Among the few Americans to engage her enthusiasm are Paul Goodman, unrecognized for most of his writing life, who found attention in the 1960s when raging against America was all the rage, and Norman O. Brown, who won an audience for his assaults on the West's sexual hangups during the same giddy period. The spirit that draws Sontag to such alien minds also impels her, as David Bromwich put it, to champion a kind of art that "stands outside the mainstream of culture and sometimes at the very periphery of human experience." *Extremity,* in art and criticism, is a key to the enthusiasm of this self-described "besotted esthete" and "obsessed moralist."

### IMAGE OF AMERICA

It is difficult not to detect a certain trendiness in Sontag's political as well as her esthetic tastes. Her vision of America in the '60s was drenched in New Leftism. In 1966, she contributed to *Partisan Review* a response to a set of questions on **"What's Happening in America"** that condemned every aspect of the country except its alienated "kids," who were extolled for "the way they dance, dress, wear their hair, riot, make love," and for their homage to Oriental thought and ritual and their interest in drugs. For the rest, America was "a violent, ugly, unhappy country, passionately racist," run by "genuine yahoos." She called the white race "the cancer of history."

Her treatments of Cuba, China and North Vietnam were notably kinder, in the fashion on the Left of the time. In the Third World, she discovered "moral beauty." Even Sontag's fans do not claim much for her assays into political philosophy. The fuss over her recent Town Hall attack on Communism, which Leon Wieseltier dismissed in *Partisan Review* as "the political apology of an unpolitical person," owed less to its novelty than to the fact that it was delivered to an audience that would rather not have heard it.

The omission of the 1966 anti-American diatribe from her new collection may be evidence of a softening of Sontag's attitude toward her country as her hopes for the evolution of Communist regimes toward more openness has faded. As she put it in an interview, "I wrote, **'What's Happening in America'** at a time of great anguish over Vietnam. I still think this is a crazy, violent, dangerous, horrifying country and that there are other, better possibilities for a prosperous democratic capitalist society than we have here. But between our empire and the Communist empire, I prefer ours."

Despite or because of her role as adversary of American culture and society, Sontag has gotten her share of praise, grants and awards from the Establishment. Her most popular book, **On Photography,** won a National Book Critics Circle Award in 1978. These ruminations exhibited her mind at its most venturesome, as it speculated upon the blurring in this age of photography of the line between images and things, between copies and the original.

Even here, however, she could not resist a dig at capitalism so tendentious that it distracted one from the main picture, like the antics of a crackpot in a gallery. She wrote: "A capitalist society requires a culture based on images. It needs to furnish vast amounts of entertainment in order to stimulate buying and anesthetize the injuries of class, race and sex. And it needs to gather unlimited amounts of information, the better to exploit natural resources, increase productivity, keep order, make war, give jobs to bureaucrats." Sontag has always had a sharper eye for the image than for the reality. Numerous magazines have used images of her, sometimes in dramatic poses, the better to stimulate sales of boots perhaps. She has confessed that she finds it "hard to resist the invitation to manifest oneself. . . ."

As for pictures that move, the filmmakers whom she admires and has borrowed from in her own tries at movie-making are mainly European moderns like Jean-Luc Godard, Robert Bresson and Hans-Jurgen Syberberg, whose *Hitler, a Film from Germany* she hailed, typically, for "the extremity of its achievement." She has soured on Leni Riefenstahl, Hitler's favorite filmmaker. The ***Susan Sontag Reader*** contains a vigorous assault on Riefenstahl, written in 1974, that is startling when set against Sontag's previous, thoroughly admiring approach to her work. In 1965, Sontag wrote that the content of *Triumph of the Will and Olympia* had "come to play a purely formal role," owing to Riefenstahl's genius; a triumph of the Style. But by 1974, Sontag was exceedingly harsh with those who would blink away the filmmaker's connection with Nazism. The aggressive tone of both these contradictory pieces supports the observation of Denis Donoghue that Sontag's mind is "powerful but not subtle."

### REALITY OF CANCER

A few years ago, after her recovery from cancer, Sontag vowed to devote more time to fiction, but finds herself now completing a long essay on the travels of intel-

lectuals to Communist countries; it promises to display yet another change of her heart and mind. Her fiction so far has received mixed notices—kinder probably, and more of them certainly, than would have been garnered by a lesser name.

None of her stories, which abjure conventional plot and characterization, carries the passion of her 1978 polemic, **Illness as Metaphor.** Moved by her personal experience, she inveighed against the literary penchant for using disease, particularly cancer, as a metaphor for all manner of evil, thereby making the victim to a degree responsible for his sufferings, and diverting attention from the cruel reality of the illness. "I just wanted to say that cancer is real and ought to be diagnosed and treated." (She now regrets having called the white race a cancer.) It is an indication of Sontag's bookish approach to life that even in this deeply personal work there is no mention of her own mastectomy. Her emotions are channelled into an attack on words and their power to do damage.

Benjamin DeMott, who has noted a "thinness of experience, lack of conversance with common life" in Sontag's work, suggests that **Illness as Metaphor** can be read as a questioning of the "murky Modernist blackishness . . . the dogmas about the human condition that [have] shaped the work of the artists she has most admired and imitated." DeMott catches flickerings here of a "genuine affection for middle ways" and advances the possibility that Sontag may have arrived at a belated recognition that "modesty and moderation deserve respect as civilizing values."

Do the essay on illness, the public split with her former political allies, the turnabout on Riefenstahl represent a shift in the Sontag sensibility, a movement from the extreme toward the middle, some reconciliation with the country that she seems to have written off on the day that she began to write? The question is open. After nearly two decades of "manifesting oneself," Sontag remains the beneficiary of a society that enjoys conferring celebrity on its most disdainful critics.

### Geoff Dyer (review date 17 March 1989)

SOURCE: Dyer, Geoff. "The Way We Live Now." *New Statesman* 2, no. 41 (17 March 1989): 34-5.

[*In the following review, Dyer judges Sontag as a master of the essay form, praising her work* AIDS and Its Metaphors *as well as the earlier essay* Illness as Metaphor.]

Twelve years ago, when Susan Sontag became a cancer patient, she felt compelled to write a book about the disease, not a confessional account of the struggle against illness—"a narrative, it seemed to me, would be less useful than an idea"—but a broader genealogy and history of the metaphors associated with disease. Like a vaccine for which the world had been waiting, *Illness as Metaphor* achieved the immediate status of a classic, one of those books which seem always to have been around.

Disease, she argues in that book, should be seen as just that, otherwise the sick have to suffer not only physically but also from the weight of associations that a given sickness brings in its wake. At any time there tends to be one disease whose associations become so ideologically loaded as to make it seem a threat to society's economic or political health. In the era of early capitalist accumulation TB was seen as typifying the dangers of squandering, over-consumption—over-budgeting the body's resources. In the era of advanced capitalism, which requires speculation, credit and expenditure, cancer serves to express the dangers of repressing spontaneity, holding back and hoarding.

And now there is AIDS. With characteristic assurance Sontag notes [in *AIDS and Its Metaphors*] the way that this new disease has lent itself to military metaphors of invasion, how it quickly assumed the status of a plague against which the nation arms itself with a rhetoric of vague authoritarianism.

After two decades of steadily increasing sexual freedom—"sexual inflation"—we now find ourselves in the midst of a sexual depression. Even before AIDS a counter-current of moderation—diets, looking after yourself—was already challenging the sixties ideal of wild self-realisation; but with AIDS that self-restraining impulse had become an urgent imperative. So it has been in the arts, with a return to landscape and figure in painting, with jazz showing a retreat from free improvisation to the tighter structures of bebop. Neo-classicism, in a word.

So far so predictable, but Sontag extends her inquiry to consider the way that AIDS has taken its place among other possible catastrophes that are *in the process of threatening* the earth (the ozone layer, nuclear war). From there the argument *soars* as she wonders how "even an apocalypse can be made to seem part of the ordinary horizon of expectation"—but I want to stop there, just as we are getting to the best part.

It's a convention of fiction reviewing that you don't give the story away and this slim, beautifully produced book offers many of the pleasures of fiction (pleasures almost absent, incidentally, from Sontag's own laboriously modernist novels) as the pattern of ideas, clues and evidence emerges. It is in no way to diminish the content of *AIDS and Its Metaphors*—or Sontag's stature as a thinker—to emphasise how in her hands the essay becomes the most sensuous of literary forms. Sentences unfold with unruffled calm, bearing an imperceptibly increasing weight of meaning without ever becoming cumbersome. There is none of the back-wrenching strain of John Berger—though she has his urgency—none of the clause-twisting formulations of Raymond Williams—though her arguments have his force—no sense of sweating under the weight of accumulated erudition that we find in George Steiner—though she ranges as widely.

*AIDS and Its Metaphors* ranks alongside the best essays of any of these three: it is an important book about "the way we live now"—to lift the title of her own story about AIDS published in the *New Yorker*—and it is also the work of a stylist who, like Barthes, has mastered all the most difficult forms of writing: the colon, parentheses, italics, the semi-colon, ellipses . . .

## Sara Maitland (review date 25 March 1989)

SOURCE: Maitland, Sara. "Practising Safe Language." *Spectator* 262, no. 8385 (25 March 1989): 29.

[*In the following review, Maitland agrees with Sontag's assessment in* AIDS and Its Metaphors *that society views certain diseases as more than physical ailments, but also as social issues centering on the contraction of the disease.*]

Compared to heart attacks, cancer, even road deaths, few people have died of Aids. Yet we have rushed to attach *meaning* to the condition more than to any other. (We have proliferated so much *meaning,* indeed, that we have, by and large, lost any *sense:* 'God's punishment on homosexuals' suggests a very bizarre view of God's justice, given that one of the lowest possible risk groups is women homosexuals.) As usual when human communities struggle to create meaning, we have also created a language, a set of metaphors, to use about Aids, which are meant to be descriptive, explanatory, but in fact—as usual—end up being prescriptive, formative and continually read back into the subject that they are supposed to elucidate.

In this essay [*AIDS and Its Metaphors*] (a postscript to her book *Illness as Metaphor,* which she wrote ten years ago and which anyone seriously interested in this subject ought to read), Susan Sontag attempts to decode some of these metaphors, exposing them to scientific knowledge and linguistic understanding. She is the right person for the job: Sontag continually struggles to find meaning in the texts and language of society. No postmodernist severance for her; the words we use are words about actual things and they shape our understanding, our ways of seeing and dealing with those things. Language, metaphor, image, sense, do matter; they actually have effect outside the text.

Of course, this insistence on meaning ironically undercuts her commitment to 'the effort to detach [Aids] from these meanings, these metaphors' (p. 94)—and by extension all illness—from metaphorical language, because one language must necessarily be replaced by another, as she herself admits: 'Much in the way of individual experience and social policy depends on the struggle for rhetorical ownership of the illness: how it is possessed, assimilated in argument and cliché.' We need counter-metaphors not no metaphors as she seems to imply. (For example, she praises the 'wholesome dedramatisation' of leprosy in its new name—Hansen's Disease—without acknowledging that to name a disease after the scientist who discovered its causal virus is to enter into a metaphor about individual ownership and the power of scientists.)

But these methodological quibbles apart, Sontag has done an interesting job, particularly in exposing the militaristic metaphors too often employed and linking them with the xenophobia that is common to all infectious diseases, but particularly powerful within the Aids discourse. These wily foreigners invade the body, lurk hidden in the fabric of the microcosm—even as they do in society. While Europe plots the journey of Aids from Africa via Haiti and the USA, Africa—far more seriously affected—traces the germ warfare of a malicious CIA (America). Such an attack 'justifies' all-out war, waged by the medical profession and by the larger society, on the disease: internment of suspected or even potential 'enemy sympathisers' (read: people who have the disease, the anti-bodies to the disease, life styles which might encourage the spread of the disease, and even those known to consort with such) becomes an option. But a virus cannot actually *be* 'crafty', 'single-minded', 'naked'; it cannot 'lurk', 'attack' or 'mobilise'. It certainly cannot be 'evil', wicked or treacherous; nor can it select 'victims' because of its God-given moral sensibilities about human sexual options.

Of course it can't, we say, but continue to use language structures which blame or victimise or degrade the sufferers of any disease which has to carry the weight of panicked, fear-full meanings that society lays upon it. Aids, with its sexual—and other deviant—transmission, its slow invisible development, its difficulty of treatment, its painful death, its physically disfiguring symptoms—is, Sontag makes clear, a perfect vehicle for social obsession; indeed it has managed even to 'banalise' cancer, the previous, but much less amenable, candidate for this rôle.

Aids is a social construct, Sontag argues, which should be deconstructed through language, sense and science. This is the importance of Sontag's essay: it returns the subject of Aids to us all; gives a focus which could be set against both the patronage, or stigmatisation, of the sufferer and the dangerous liberal tendency of laying

claim to the sufferings of others. We may not 'get' Aids, but we have all got the metaphors of Aids as loose in our brain cells as the virus is in the blood cells.

## Leon S. Roudiez (review date autumn 1989)

SOURCE: Roudiez, Leon S. Review of *AIDS and Its Metaphors,* by Susan Sontag. *World Literature Today* 63, no. 4 (autumn 1989): 685.

[*In the following review, Roudiez contends that* AIDS and Its Metaphors *is not as cohesive as* Illness as Metaphor, *but contends that the new essay effectively clarifies confusing facts and misconceptions regarding AIDS.*]

In *Illness as Metaphor* (1977) Susan Sontag had contrasted tuberculosis, the disease that the nineteenth century found "interesting" and even "romantic," with the "great epidemic diseases of the past, which strike each person as a member of an afflicted community." In the seventies it was indeed assumed that such major epidemics were a curse of the past; and then AIDS burst upon us—or rather, it spread to the West and spawned a primal fear expressed by means of ugly metaphors.

These metaphors are viewed by [in *AIDS and Its Metaphors*] Sontag as having been produced by the cultural atmosphere of the eighties. There was, for instance, a reaction against the sexually permissive attitude that prevailed in the sixties; there was also the hyper-Christian, somewhat xenophobic stance affirmed during the early years of the Reagan administration and, in Europe, an increasing resistance to Third World immigrants; later, ecological concerns over the depletion of the ozone layer, dwindling rain forests, and atomic accidents encouraged a doomsday rhetoric. As a result, a complex cluster of metaphors has developed in which none is able to dominate discourse. Whereas cancer, which was at the center of *Illness as Metaphor,* was seen as "domestic subversion," in the case of AIDS it is an outside agent that affects the system, giving birth to a "language of political paranoia" in which the vocabulary of science fiction reinforces military metaphors. However, AIDS, in the West, so far has not affected the entire population. Because at first it struck mostly homosexual men, these could be stigmatized as sinners, and metaphors of divine punishment were resurrected. Since the "source" of the disease has been identified as Africa, racist metaphors have inevitably surfaced.

A curious development is that, as the scope of the epidemic became obvious and no cure was in sight, the doomsday metaphors acted as a catalytic agent; nevertheless, "With the inflation of apocalyptic rhetoric has come the increasing unreality of the apocalypse." There have been so many dire predictions in various domains that we have become inured, mainly because we are still alive and doing well. Who are "we," however, if not the privileged, cultured, well-to-do elite of the West? And what does our attitude portend concerning the future of humanity?

The disease, like the times we live in, is fearsome and unsettling. Sontag's book, as it deals with the variegated metaphors people use in talking about AIDS, inevitably lacks the focus that made *Illness as Metaphor* so effective. This is hardly her fault, nor can I in a brief review adequately deal with the tight complexity of her account. It is, however, to her considerable credit that *AIDS and Its Metaphors* reveals the mental confusion—to say the least—that afflicts our society, as the meaning of John Donne's words, the scope of which he himself could not have fully grasped, is finally understood—"No man is an Iland, intire of itself; every man is a peece of the Continent, a part of the maine."

## Sohnya Sayres (essay date autumn 1989)

SOURCE: Sayres, Sohnya. "Susan Sontag and the Practice of Modernism." *American Literary History* 1, no. 3 (autumn 1989): 593-611.

[*In the following essay, Sayres examines both Sontag's fiction and her essays, focusing on her epigrammatic style, her multilayered studies into contradictions and negations, and modernist theories.*]

Most of Sontag's fictional characters are neither heroes nor antiheroes as we have come to understand these figures. They lack the appeal of having mirrored our condition, satirically or otherwise. They live too separately; they are too much governed by dreams. In a sense, her fiction itself displays what the characters suffer from—excessive control: enigmas tend to reverberate interiorly. Dilemmas and glimpses of the other, nonself-referential world are replaced too often by closed possibilities and imposed wisdoms. Into these hermetically sealed lives come these intrusions, these truncated, pithy, antithetical statements seemingly in the mouths of her characters yet distinctly like Sontag in her other aspects. They are one of her most recognizable devices.

In her essays, she includes so many of these kinds of statements that the logic of her arguments jigsaws. One comes to understand that sharpness and objection matter more than development and substantiation. She cannot be much of a theorist then, some complain. Her interest in the individual work is too slight. Her statements have a melodramatic cast, her thoughts are

merely compiled in that moralizing, French epigrammatic way. Then too, occasionally, in the midst of her "reason-dictates" tone, she tosses hand grenades.

How striking is the difference between her voice in her first volume of essays and Trilling's graceful, methodological circumventions of virtually the same years—in *Beyond Culture* (1965). What Sontag has to say is held in tension, the terms of her questions are more directed, as if she were prompted by a determination to enter the arena, during that lull in the critical controversies, readier to fight. She writes as if she is taking up a gauntlet, however gingerly it had been laid down before her.

That was a time when criticism was smothering modernism in its welcome, a welcome so reasonable that Trilling could write in "The Fate of Pleasure" (1963): "The energy, the consciousness, and the wit of modern literature derive from its violence against the specious good. We instinctively resent questions which suggest that there is fault to be found with the one saving force in our moral situation—that extruded 'high' segment of our general culture which, with its exigent, violently subversive spirituality, has the power of arming us against, and setting us apart from, all in the general culture that we hate and fear" (*BC* [*Beyond Culture*] 70).

Obscured in Trilling's impenetrable "we" lies a challenge: "whether the perverse and morbid idealism of modern literature is not to be thought of as being precisely political, whether it does not express a demand which in its own way is rational and positive and which may be taken into account by a rational and positive politics" (73). What Trilling means by this is a general permission, given in other times to heroes, saints, martyrs, and in these times to artists, to lead exemplary subversive lives or to create exemplary subversive works.

Sontag recently told an interviewer that she remembers being moved by Trilling's essay. While that remark is an off-handed hint only to the origins of her own search for a method, her essays are full of queries into the exemplariness of this age's spiritual project, full of discussions with herself about what this politics might be like. She is spying into tenets of modernism as if it were a practice, as if it could be put to the test of a politics. What's more, Sontag had just published a novel in which she examines that inheritance of the "perverse and morbid" in literature, especially as it might have been reinterpreted by the younger writers in France in the 1950s from the generation that had preceded them. When Trilling makes his call for "a novelist we do not yet have but must surely have one day, who will take into serious and comic account the actualities of the spiritual life of our time" (71), she had just finished being that kind of novelist. In response to Trilling's thought that the "life of competition for spiritual status is not without its own peculiar sordidness and absurdity," she could have pointed to the whole character of her protagonist and episode after episode in his story.

Sontag had acceded to a time in America's critical life when the residues of Left puritanism were blowing away, when the hard work to drum out the 1930s broad realist aesthetic (of sentiment, type, and brotherhood of victims and the folk) was finished. What was still being done were efforts to accommodate that "extruded 'high'" art into American ideals. That became Sontag's stepping-off place, almost certain as she was from the beginning that this was an aesthetic that forbade accommodation. Trilling, on his side, could end his essay with the reassurances that "before we conclude that the tendencies in our literature which we have remarked on are nothing but perverse and morbid, let us recall that although Freud did indeed say that 'the aim of all life is death,' the course of his argument leads him to the statement that 'the organism wishes to die only in its own fashion,' only through the complex fullness of its appropriate life" (76).

For Sontag, the impact of those lines might have come too close to the other forms of pious fellow-traveling to which Americans are all too prone. What was this complex fullness of a life in such extreme negation? Sontag would write with a sure and quick defense for artworks that shared next to nothing with this imperious aesthetic, such as Jack Smith's *Flaming Creatures* or Camp, grateful, as she says, for the release they offered. But that question kept returning to her, sending her to Europe to become a critic of all manner of Europe's coming to grips with its recent past. She would skirt the revivals of Left Hegelianism, Left Freudianism, Left Nietzscheanism, Left existentialism and Left structuralism, listening and thinking about them, but not captured. What captures her is the attempt to "name the contours of the sensibility" Trilling felt came after pleasure as a motive in art and life.

The following is a discussion of the terms of her discourse. I have emphasized features that filtered out over time and give some thoughts to their individual troubles. This is not offered as an anatomy of a system—Sontag has avoided systems—rather as spotlights on certain repeated elements that lead her through her questions, while revealing her instincts, and that begin to have a dialogue one with the other. These form part of her practice, for want of a better word, as a writer and critic.

## 1. EPIGRAMMATICAL MODE

Sontag's writing is epigrammatical, though this is no special observation about her unless one keeps in mind that the epigram, unlike its close cousins the aphorism and the apothegm, includes a sense of inversion. The contradictory inspires a writer given to writing in epigrams, as a mode of thought in itself. The epigram rests on its turn of thought away from sense, as in C. L. Kline's "the sacred duty of lawlessness." The epigram may be sage and witty but it rarely assumes the burden, in good faith, of addressing the principle of the thing it observes—that is the aphorism's function. Mouthed often, epigrams instead profess, as one character in Sontag's fiction explains, a "line of gnomic crap."

The epigrammatical mode can be recognized, overall, by the penchant of the writer to make these quizzical statements as little or as large as his or her subject warrants (the set piece for the whole plot, perhaps) and then confound them. The point of the statement seems to be its pointedness, the encapsulation of what is experienced as a paradox—the interminable way in which meanings turn in on themselves, values reverse, and the only worthy gestures are the disruptive ones. The modern epigrammatist writes wisdoms, but not for the sake of enlightenment. They are instead intended as didacticisms of the perverse—truths that hold true because of their power to evoke the negation of what seems. Or truths neatly conceived yet so bland they blow away under the force of the contrary evidence of the story. Combine the hyperreflexivity of modern writing with the later focus on the independence of writing, reading, and interpretation, and the effect is to move the writer towards a voiceless speech that comes from nowhere. In Sontag's fiction, for example, even though the fate of her characters tends to belie what they offer as rationalizations, their voices carry their neutralized assertions out of the story in all headiness. That is, Sontag's characters are often shown to be quite mistaken about what they think they are doing, yet their formulations, suddenly in heaps, are not really to be disregarded. The vacuity of their experience is already presumed. They have explored nether values and the diminution of things, and in that realm their observations hold.

Yet Sontag aches for simpler truths, for aphoristic writing, perhaps the homiletic. Proverbs and folk sayings, everyone's favorite mottoes lie strewn about on placards in the charnel house of the last pages of *Death Kit*. The dead there have marched to their graves carrying their little judgments. The next reader finds these doomed, happier assurances in splinters.

As for irony—the epigrammatist works inside the strictures of an elaborated awareness of forms; to that extent she or he participates in the spirit of modernist gamesmanship. But the game takes on an edge when the language approaches the discursive wisdom of the epigram. Because the epigram is about reality and its negation, it may be the joke of jokes. Few writers find it a whimsical matter.

As for suffering—the epigram bears the writer away from suffering, being abstract and not dependent on things of the senses. In fact, a text composed of epigrams is tighter than one in which the eye passes over detail. One feels the precision with which the writer's intelligence (Sontag's most revered quality) confers on the world as a triumph for the speaker, against some lesser successes such as the connoisseur enjoys. "Intelligence" finds these other modes a little lugubrious, a little obsequious, a little rhetorical.

This mode attracts the philosophical writer strongly given to thoughts about the Enlightenment's demise, who, nonetheless, takes no delight in the irrational, rather discounts metaphorical vehicles, and distrusts nothing as much as the springs of feeling. The thrilling possibilities of living in media-vision, a melee of fired perceptions, which so excites some recent writers, barely touches the epigrammatist. Sometimes, she may feel left out of the party, and tries to get into the swing of things, high on analytical wit. But she dances in weighted shoes.

## 2. On Silences

I have emphasized the efficacy of the mode of writing in epigrams, when of course epigrams give pleasure. They let the space around them grow rich, like the grass around tombstones, on what is buried. To the very extent they are pointed, precise, they outline the silence of what they do not speak. The pleasure is in the poise won. All around the silences reverberate anew. This is the kind of pleasure that entices the writer who sits reflecting before a commitment or a journey. Afterward the experience may want telling for its own sake. So she stops in unfinished propositions, readying herself against surprises, content to explore some of the contradictions before meeting them. She means to undermine the fallible, or to pay homage to mortality before disappearing beneath.

This mode fits Sontag's purpose well, for example, in her short story **"Project for a Trip to China."** We are invited to sit with Sontag as she considers what it means to her to go to China after so many years thinking about it as the place of her father's death and of herself as a political figure. She works downward just as she tells about how, when she was ten years old (her father had died a few years before):

> . . . I dug a hole in the back yard. I stopped when it got to be six feet by six feet by six feet. "What are you trying to do?" said the maid. "Dig all the way to China?"

> No. I just wanted a place to sit in. . . . The ivory and quartz elephants had been auctioned.

> —my refuge

> —my cell

> —my study

> —my grave.

(***I, e*** [***I, etcetera***] 8)

In this story Sontag creates that epigrammatical feel—that uncertainty structured into the assertions—by the interlocking of thought and objects rather than by letting the statement brush up against its foil. What she evokes is a latticework of spaces in which she can place the accounts of what she will see. In this spareness, we do find an Orient of the heart, a porcelain beauty, a world dignified by silences. She prefers not to write about what is consecrated by history. In this hesitation, we recognize a tribute to enormity.

The end story in ***I, etcetera,* "Unguided Tour"** (made into a film by Sontag), pulls her themes of repetitions, pain, language, and literature along on another journey. The woman speaker confesses to her weariness with travel, to the predictability of thought and feeling. She knows before she begins, "all the possibilities of travel," "all the words I am going to utter again." Wherever she travels, "it's to say goodbye." Yet she continues to wander insatiably; some wound compels her. And only the wound is sufficient to give "lyricism" to the going which words would otherwise make redundant.

Silence restrains that self, protects it from contact, from being measured by life. This aspect of the "aesthetics of silence" goes unexamined in Sontag's longish study. There is hardly any mention of a personal or historical correlative to the artist's use of silence, as if it were so ubiquitous a choice in the twentieth century, the century itself has borne it.

What Sontag intends for us to understand, though I always suspect she is thinking of the European epoch after the war, is that sensibility which had been nurtured by Gide, Artaud, Genet—composite figures in her fiction—and which came up in the silences of Blanchot or Duras. They walked about as emotional skeletons, these postwar survivors. If they chose life it was from some incomprehensible, innate desire, of the kind Frau Anders displays in Sontag's ***The Benefactor.***

After the war the cruelty in themselves damned them to equations: "I am like them," writes Duras in *The Lover.* "Collaborators, the Fernandezes were. And I, two years after the war, I was a member of the French Communist Party. The parallel is complete and absolute. The two things are the same, the same pity, the same call for help, the same lack of judgment, the same superstition if you like, that consists in believing in a political solution to a personal problem." Survivors by accident, they link themselves to survivors by cowardice and betrayal, and conclude: "It's in the silence that the war is still here." Toward the cool, distant silences, or above the feverish ones, their language strikes poses. It is that kind of voice which plagues Sontag, so close in tone and purpose to Blanchot's narrator in *Death Sentence* (1948): "The unfortunate thing is that after having waited for so many years, during which silence, immobility, and patience carried to the point of inertia did not for one single day stop deceiving me, I had to open my eyes all at once and allow myself to be tempted by a splendid thought, which I am trying in vain to bring to its knees. Perhaps these precautions will not be precautions" (30).

Lately Sontag is more prone to wandering in the halls of old cathedrals via their paintings, musing on the melancholy of the body as it is transformed by paint and camera. Even so, her language strains for the epigrammatical effect embedded in the silences of those experiences.

### 3. Spirit of Negation

One cannot be a modern epigrammatist without the spirit of negation running through one's head. The "no" advanced the project of the Enlightenment in its strike at authority; the "no" sends one's defiance out against destiny. The "no" outlines the self from all that would incorporate it. The "no" is the movable force of the dialectic, and as such it thus affirms what it negates. Negation's spirit is vigorous, astute, independent. It does not, however, lighten one's way. It sees the world in terms of powerful, weighty oppositions. In the sway of that spirit one is apt to give oneself moral dignity, so strong is the sense that what one is battling against is the necessary enemy.

In 1967, Sontag writes in **"The Aesthetics of Silence"** that the modern artist is "committed to the idea that the power of art is located in its power to negate." From the comfort of that widely held assumption, Sontag can enter the silence that beckons her with a brisk, objective mind. Silence can then exist "as a *decision*—in the exemplary suicide of the artist"; and it can also exist "as a *punishment*—self-punishment, in the exemplary madness of artists" (*AI* [*Against Interpretation*] 9). She continues to feel along the walls for the limits of the artistic uses of silence, "boundary notions," not to be understood without the dialectic.

The dialectic calls up the "leading terms of a particular spiritual and cultural rhetoric" (*AI* 11). From the earliest part of this century, the dialectic of negation of contemporary values upheld the widest promise of experiencing a whole set of new relations. In art, negation was that tenet of modernism which called upon creation at the moment of destruction of older artistic forms. In the realm of the spirit, for the sake of the autonomy of the spirit, negation was to be exercised in all spheres. In Sontag's carefully retired language of

"that particular rhetoric," one can hear that she senses, faintly concurs in the idea, that by the middle of the century that credo was slipping away.

Curiously, when one considers how she was identified with 1960s radicalism, her phrase was deaf to or cynical about the reenlistment of the ethos of negation in the political upswing of those times. The Frankfurt School had taught that negative dialectics had the power to break through those dementing forces of modern life—its monolithic structures, its paradoxical tolerances, the loony ways it fed consumerism and anesthetized with media. Perhaps Sontag sensed that despite its apocalyptic moods, the age's allegiance to negation was thin. There were too many benefits in living in a very rich, compulsively expansive society. Or as Sontag puts it: "in the post-political, electronically connected cosmopolis in which all serious modern artists have taken out premature citizenship . . ." (*AI* 34). The age's feeling for negation, at least as evidenced in its art, was growing more attenuated and mannered. In her words, the aesthetics of negation was living off of myths.

"In my opinion," she writes, "the myths of silence and emptiness are about as nourishing and viable as might be devised in an 'unwholesome' time—which is, of necessity, a time in which 'unwholesome' psychic states furnish the energies for most superior work in the arts. Yet one can't deny the pathos of these myths" (*AI* 11).

### 4. Pathos of Heroes

That "pathos" cues Sontag's readers that an iconic evaluation is going on. Her moderns possess pathos, as some gift they have for endurance. Pathos keeps futility at bay, when it fixes on that subject with all of its attention. Then the two emotions lock in a kind of tug-of-war. This is the struggle of tragic heroes, and it is tragedy that brightens the star of pathos in the pantheon of sentiments. In any other sense of the word, we tend to be less sure of its virtues.

Sontag has spoken of the pathos of children, by which she invokes our more commonplace appreciation of their fragility and their neediness. A touch of these qualities can be felt in that intimate and bonded way of hers of addressing the hauteur of the modernist aesthetic. But only a touch—the hopefulness of the childhood of an aesthetic. Mostly, it is her modern's steadfastness in suffering that raises them to heroic stature. She admires the inexorability of their ideals, which drive them step by step to self-dissolve, or should they be heroes of the mind, their inexorable pursuit of self-confrontation. They have claims to some of tragedy's merits, if only in their pathos. She would be the first to acknowledge that they would not themselves believe that they are worthy of tragedy's impulses or even believe in its forms.

This pathos is the opposite of the quality of voice and approach to ideas the young Sontag liked to make, that is, those epigrammatical incursions. To steal a phrase from Sontag's essay on Sartre, where she describes his solution "to his disgust," the epigrammatical mode is "impertinent" (*AI* 98). Only later, into the 1970s, does the other side of her yearn toward the fullness of pathos.

By then, she has had more time to wrestle with several sides of herself and more time to test the climate in which her respectful, ambivalent looking back at the ethos of modernism is being received. Our sympathy with the pathos of heroes includes the luxury of afterthought. Their stories tend to be conclusive. The pathos we carry away becomes a lovely haze in which we recall the world of their struggles, a far slighter thing than if we thought we were subject to the same purposes. Sontag, having directed her critical energies to the new temperament, had to sense what double or triple ironic release survived in her italicized references to the "heroic age" of modernism and the "pathos" of its myths. Or rather, her statements are an attempt at a release, because to her all serious art, such as the impassioned minimalism of that period, called forth and relied upon these modernist "unwholesome" tenets.

## 5. ETHICS

There is much at stake in these clashes of formal temperaments, that is, between what might be called the classical or "heroic" modernism and its later variety, the literature and arts of the '40s and '50s (and, arguably, modernism's rollover into the postmodernism of the late 1960s and on). Two kinds of nourishments of consciousness are at stake, and thus, for Sontag, two kinds of ethical groundings.

As Maire Jaanus Kurrik formulates the matter, classical (modern) novels *negate,* modernist (or, in my terms, late modernist) novels *delete.* Admittedly, this is an oversimplification, a conceit. However, by taking a sight along this single line of inquiry, how negation metamorphoses, Kurrik can say things like this: later modernist novels make us uncomfortable not for what the books attack, but for what they override. The old humanist complaints against modernism—that modernism is nihilistic, tradition-destroying, the lamentable outcome of the excesses of Romantic mystification—can be countered with the argument that modernists say no to the power of God, destiny, authority, because the power of these things is mighty. The newer novelists are far less ambivalent; seemingly they can give up, erase, elide in a dispersed totality. The feel of deletion as it acts, then, is one of lessening, while the feel of negation is making something serious, complex, noble, and ignoble.

One of the problems with deletion, as Kurrik writes, is that while "it may bypass the corruption of our yesses and noes" (236), "its own violence displaces the violence of negation" (232). It is left with a state of "nolition"—an inability to wish or want anything. Negativity turns to negativism, and from there a person descends to a deracinated, dematerialized, "gutted," and "drained" state.

Sontag's characters in her fiction play these scenarios out, literally perform these operations on themselves. Hippolyte sets out to "delete" himself; Diddy to die while his stomach is being pumped. Their stories are exercises in the farcical underside of pathos of modernism's myths. They are meant to be "despised": that is, they are meant to be analyzed with wonder and indignation, sympathy and revulsion, in a paradigmatically ambivalent fashion. They are antithetical portraits of a sensibility towards which Sontag has tried to establish a position that neither judges nor interprets.

But Sontag is motivated by a larger set of values. The ethics of negation can lift the spirit to the mountaintop of mystical oneness; here the ethical secularist in Sontag is wary. The ethos of nolition of the new novel, on the other hand, cannot be abided with either, not directly, not by a moralist. It challenges Sontag to investigate Nietzsche's thought that art is a "complex kind of willing" set alongside this world, a way of nourishing through its graces our capacity for willing. We are fed by the artist's autonomous spirit; we are provoked to will. But if that spirit claims no autonomy, if it likens the world to a rush of reception—then the challenge moves to the reader, to that artist inside the critic. It forces her to save the seriousness of the modernist project by herself working through it, until she has "exhausted it," silenced it imaginatively, or in that cryptic word of hers, "disburdened" herself of it. In Sontag's practice, modernism's turn towards deletion begins to dress itself in the vestments of an allegorical struggle.

## 6. THE AUTHENTIC MORAL SPIRIT

If all this battling with the paradoxes of deletion only mires one more deeply in the paradoxical, it has to be thus. Paradox is a way of construing how it is to live in a time dominated by metacritical concerns, a time, as Sontag describes, that patronizes itself infinitely. One has to learn to live with that sense of being watched too closely, at every level too aware of historical indebtedness, structural imperatives or deceptive motives about one's own behavior and ideas. Looking back on the modernist flight from bad faith (the failed, incomplete project of negation) into nothingness, one realizes that the moment of pure freedom and creativity—the "present" of modernism—can never be achieved. One is hopelessly bound by the self thinking about the self striving for authentic life. One longs to be disburdened.

The authentic moral spirit, however, does not compromise with the world, and disburdenment can seem a compromise. So a kind of deal is struck: specifically, in the modernist scheme, one achieves authenticity by negating the authorities and conventions generating from one's own work. The self that is then transcended is not suspected of being the originator of sin, error, pollution, or arrogance (the mystic's demons); rather it is seen as an agent imposing false constraints. This self is both imperious and alienated from its own liberation. It can be won back to itself only by a downward slide to the very edge of existence.

Trilling finds in this ideal something he dislikes. He writes in *Sincerity and Authenticity* (1970)—his way of retreating from that call for a positive politics of 1963—that it is indicative of our times that our intellectuals advocate the overcoming of alienation by completing it.[1] What bothers Trilling, what he distrusts in all that negating business of the rule of authenticity, is that the advocacy of completing alienation "involves no actual credence." To which argument, Sontag, in effect, replies: no actual credence, to be sure, for no artist or intellectual can completely silence his or her own speech, adopt madness over sanity, destroy the creation upon which he or she experiences being an artist or intellectual without ceasing to be one. Short of that final, actual negation—utter silence, complete madness, successful suicide—there is that promise of acting out, and thereby learning from, the paradoxes of one's own positions.

Perhaps another explanation for the modernist phenomenon Trilling dislikes so much—the advocacy of overcoming alienation by completing it—is that advocacy playacts the brave stance of negation while fulfilling a more primitive desire: self-consistency. In a state of total alienation a person finds a certainty of his or her own making. The insane person wills chaos and thereby escapes the disorientation of the sane person who merely suffers it. So does the artist of the aesthetic of silence. The sad realization comes upon the modernist, though (perhaps then covering them with the honor of pathos), that in the self-made world of the alienated there can be a sense of being justified, but there is no justice; of being truthful to oneself, but of sharing no truth. There can only be an affirmation of a negative state in which we find others who are lost.

In Sontag's fiction and in a strain of her criticism—on Artaud, Cioran, Benjamin, for example—there is an advocacy (sharply curtailed, argued with) for the allegorized world in which the artist pursues the negative state in order to know self-completion. And she is quick to point out that that state is morbid, like death, if not a death itself. What surprises her is her own indelible "fascination with morbidity." Her frequent references to the need to "disburden" the self, to call modern thinking "disembowelment"—seemingly she regrets these capitulations to the reigning ideal. The political side of Sontag, the side that cares for moral action, repudiates

both this apocalyptic sense of negation and its encroachment on well-being. She is always buttressing the citadels of modernism to keep them from leaking into the present, spilling out their creeds into our lives.

## 7. POLITICS

History, though, has to offer at least a vision of that future where solitude is overcome and action is meaningful in order for it to sustain hope. Mailer thought he saw such a vision in the sea of demonstrators marching to the Pentagon. In the 1960s there was a near devotional enthusiasm for pageantry, as if making a scene could reinforce the dream that progressive forces were alive. Sontag's politics had little interest in such events; she was more interested in having vision reflect on the categorical struggles within herself. Perhaps this is the one reason why *Trip to Hanoi* appeared to some as a romance. North Vietnam in the midst of its war with America provided a place to witness the instance of the opposite, a place making an "ethical fairytale." It offered her the chance to compare the spirit of positive action against the passivity of Western intellectualism, with that particular Western concern for individual style. In North Vietnam Sontag thought she found a unity of commitment, a simplicity of purposes and values. To her it was a place of unashamed moralism and nonironical values. It was a place, moreover, where there was no avant-garde. She believed North Vietnam challenged the premise she had helped establish—that the power of art was located in its power to negate; North Vietnam refuted her prescription for intelligence. There, excessive self-consciousness did not even have an audience.

That she writes of her impression of the North Vietnamese with nothing less than the full presence of her complicating, modernist consciousness should not arouse the reader's cynicism. Sontag never intends to complete the transformation of herself into her negated self, since that transformation is an allegory. It suggests only that the self has to look to defeat its own material, intellectual, historical recalcitrance. Sontag's work is an exploration of the desire to negate, of the will to do it, not of the extent. The extent always troubles her.

What she would rather have us contemplate are the styles of this radical willing. She addresses these various styles in her first two collections of essays. By the time she writes of photography in the mid-1970s, she has come around again to adopt the position of some of the Left-humanist critics before her. The modernist era had accomplished what she fears is a terrifying distortion of perception. Modernism, while negating itself as art, turned the world into art. It aestheticized life. Modernism had made antiform, disaster, horror as much subject for aesthetic pleasure as beauty; it forced pleasurable regard beyond all boundaries until it became a wholly inadequate response. Experience and imagination could both be treated as spectacle. All that was needed was a certain, very minimal, integrity of elements.

Readiness, style, demonstration, action: these were the critical terms for the 1960s; Sontag's title **Styles of Radical Will** captures the essence of that preparedness, that nourishing of contemplation that provokes the will. Still, consciously or not, the paradox of modernist action is already built into the phrase: having a style of radical will stands for the ultimate expression of the aestheticization of life, just as it stands for a complete response to the conditions of alienation.

One can live with contradictions as long as a greater cause by which one justifies oneself remains irrefutable. It is only later, under the sense that something has gone wrong, that paradoxical intentions are examined for what they are. After the radical culture faded in influence, it was not difficult to point out that its impact was weakened by its emphasis on modes or styles of being. Sontag was caught up in the same kinds of corrections, not repudiations, as were many others. In fact, Sontag soon distrusted the politics of style (see her essay on Cuba, 1969) shortly after and perhaps even while she was writing about it. The arguments for such a politics come too close to paralleling arguments for modernist art. In practice, this politics took too much from the ideals of freedom, and had too much the sense of individual volition, or rather, it dematerialized its sense of opposition, was too trusting of and too dependent on notions of the will.

But it has to be said, that in reading Sontag's **Trip to Hanoi** and the later **"Project for a Trip to China,"** one realizes that Sontag cannot give up the essential esteem she has for both trips as trips and both places as opposites to her sensibilities. Rather than her attitude being romantic, or pastoral, or Orientalist, her attitude reflects that tendency in her towards abstraction, a certain mechanical sense of negation, the very one that has been her target all along. She may "despise" her protagonists; she may be exasperated with the trajectory of modernist thinking—she spotted and roundly criticized this problem as early as her 1963 essay on Lévi-Strauss. She knows its power, nonetheless.

### 8. MELANCHOLIC ALLEGORIST

In **Under the Sign of Saturn,** which is her sign as well as Walter Benjamin's (and by implication that of the others in this volume), melancholics seek to be contented with the ironies of mortality. But it seems that life is always outpacing them. Nervously, melancholics have a determination to sequester loss. They descend the path to the contemplation of death and vileness and there, at that base, they find they are thinking in allegories. Faithlessly, they have been given a vehicle of redemption. Benjamin writes:

Ultimately in the death signs of the baroque the direction of allegorical reflection is reversed; on the second part of its wide arc it returns, to redeem. . . . And this is the essence of the melancholy immersion: that its ultimate objects, in which it believes it can most fully secure for itself that which is vile, turn into allegories, and that these allegories fill out and deny the void in which they are represented, just as, ultimately, the intention does not faithfully rest in the contemplation of bones, but faithlessly leaps forward to the ideal of redemption.

(232-33)

Part of what Benjamin means by redemption is that which is gathered up into the idea, into a process which has its own essences but which at the same time bespeaks the totality. "That is its Platonic 'redemption'" (46). The melancholic here, in the German baroque drama, awaits a transfiguration that would bring him or her back into the eddies of becoming an authentic idea, presumably a tragic hero, or perhaps even a lesser being who is about to experience the satisfaction of self-discovery. Otherwise, the melancholic's "wisdom is subject to the nether world," as a contemplator of dead things.

How strange that Sontag and others should take up as part of the idea of consciousness of our times this obscure art form, the German *Trauerspiel,* the emblem-ridden, allegorically coded ceremony of sorrow which the seventeenth century fetishized as melancholic contemplation. Perhaps some of that presumed affinity comes from the desire to write like Benjamin; another cause is that which Benjamin himself characterizes as the "fatal, pathological suggestibility" that is "characteristic of our age" (53). "Like expressionism," he continues, "the baroque is not so much an age of genuine artistic achievement as an age possessed of an unremitting artistic will. . . . To this should be added the desire for a vigorous style of language, which would make it seem equal to the violence of world-events" (54-55).

It is an art of epigones, given to exaggeration, the "spectacle of spiritual contradiction" and the antithetical; its common practice is to "pile up fragments ceaselessly, without any strict idea of a goal, and, in the unrelenting expectation of a miracle, to take the repetition of a stereotype for the process of intensification" (178). The melancholic hero of the allegories adopts the world in ruins as his or her natural place, a place beyond beauty and without revelation, where the "events of history shrivel up and become absorbed in the setting" (179).

"To be exploited as muted cultural commentary does not exhaust the eloquence of ruins. As an allegory of personal as well as historical loss which cannot be repaired, they are an old figure in the aesthetic of melancholy," Sontag writes in 1986 in her introduction to *Veruschka: Transfigurations.* "What characterizes the aesthetic of melancholy is that there is no witness, only a single, unmoving protagonist—one who does not witness desolation but *is* desolation—and whose complete identification with the desolate scene precludes feeling (its exemplary forms: tears), whose gaze is unresponsive, withdrawn" (12). In Sontag's rendering of the sensibility of our age, she begins to tire of finding "the politics of the perverse and the morbid" that Trilling had called for with a half-raised flag. Instead, she is beckoned by the melancholic allegorist. To her, late modernism passes into the shadows, becomes a shade of contemplation of the infernal; to her, the allegorical dimension of thinking sanctions the emptying out of colossal events and turns them into plays of the disembodied that await their and our "faithless leaps." The principle, as she says in her essay on Cioran, is that one save oneself.

In the baroque world of the seventeenth century, emblems, mottoes, and allegorical narrative were used unmistakably to promote obeisance to the court, church, or some other ideal of incorporated glory. If allegory has returned as a favored explanation of our art and sensibility, it augurs this one felicity: allegory is inaccessible to ironic deflation. The nearly dogmatic commitment to self-traducing—to Sontag, modernism's gnostic complaint—in allegory is relieved of its ironic trivializing. Something is believed in allegory, something stands behind and supports the whole apparatus. There is no meaning immanent in the ruins. But the alienation that exposed rituals—our more common modern experience—turns to the pathos of admiring what is lost. What could that be now but the energy and confidence of heroic modernism, now sheltered by its monumentality in a landscape of horrors?

On those topics she likes, Sontag writes very slowly. In that pace comes the melancholic attachment which sets out to devolve its reasons for empathy. From these dead objects and fallen virtues she discovers and forges a dramaturgy of relinquishment. Inside the writer of the "new" is the writer searching to name the contours of the modern sensibility in the already just past.

In Sontag's first twenty-five years of writing, she is never far from this strange allegory of disburdenment. Her fiction is a tale told from these ending processes; in her essays she puts herself to the task: she exacts from herself the charge of exhausting the Westernizing, metacritical, self-patronizing consciousness that "digests" and "cannibalizes" itself in order to recover a longed for, lighter state. In describing Sontag's choice, I have tried to take her advice and consider "that it is what it is." That the allegory of disburdenment has crystallized in her work, with its special, inner constitution and outward predilections, has given her work a

center and personality. It has become her way of "soliciting self-knowledge" as Cary Nelson has phrased it, a way of doing criticism as a "zone of permission, a special site on which self-extinction can be desired and verbally pursued" (726).

## CODA

I have to remark upon how highly selective these eight points are. I have dug grooves into Sontag's work in order to make tributaries flow into a river. I protest myself. This is a violation. Sontag deserves a wider, livelier appreciation. *Against Interpretation* and **"The Aesthetics of Silence"** are much quoted and taught. Principles from her **"The Pornographic Imagination"** are drawn upon virtually whenever the subject is discussed. *Trip to Hanoi* has been under continuous review since its publication in 1968, and *On Photography* (1977) has enjoyed a few attempts at "application" of its theories. *Illness as Metaphor* (1978), simply, has helped people, and *AIDS and Its Metaphors* (1989) most likely will too when the scientific evidence is more certain and the political climate less explosive around issues of responsibility. Its long view is grating on AIDS workers, while its sympathies seem a little late. Older essays such as **"Notes on 'Camp'"** and **"Fascinating Fascism"** gave permission to a whole new class of intellectuals to look more deeply into popular culture. What she accomplished in keeping alive a debate, on Riefenstahl or Syberberg, not surprisingly, is still fought over. Equally, she set standards and made a lasting contribution to the culture of the United States in introducing European thinkers. It has been said, not so generously, that that has been her chief role. She is less well remembered for how she set out to correct our understanding of Lukács, Lévi-Strauss, Weil, Sartre, Camus, Barthes, Artaud, or for the way she emphasized the moral nature of the form—in disaster films, piety in the secular age, the novel, metatheater. This is a period where she is being more closely watched for her political fumbles, in her place under the spotlights as that kind (the older type) of intellectual who makes statements, takes on polemics, goes to enemy lands, and fights for artistic freedom.

Why then have I here stuck to the trying themes of negation and disburdenment in the face of all these separate, explicit, fulminating, and controversial accomplishments? Answer: to advance the case Sontag herself likes to put forth about her work. She is to herself a complete artist, welding her essays and fiction and films into one aesthetic. She told an interviewer in May 1988, while in Lisbon at an international conference of writers, that she does not "write about things, period. Everything that I write is fiction even when I write an essay. When I write an essay it is a type of fiction." She starts, in the morning at her desk, with language, "and then I go on an adventure for the next sentence. I try to follow ideas of seriousness and good use in language" (Rattner A-31). She wishes to present herself thus, as a formalist and an artist. This essay takes her at her word, for the sake of what she is after.

### Note

1. Trilling also quietly responds to Sontag's *Against Interpretation* in the essay "The Heroic, The Beautiful, the Authentic." She is mentioned in the text, and pointedly, in a footnote in which Trilling shows that his essay "The Fate of Pleasure" came first (171). By implication Sontag is linked to the likes of Sarraute's "relentlessly censorious tone [which] suggests the moral intensity we now direct upon the questions of authenticity" (101). She, like Gide, Lawrence, and Sartre himself has added to the "gabble"—those conventions, maxims, etc., of "anyone who undertakes to satisfy our modern demand for reminders of our fallen state and for reasons why we are to be ashamed of our lives" (105).

### Works Cited

Benjamin, Walter. *The Origin of German Tragic Drama.* Trans. John Osborne. London: New Left Books, 1977.

Blanchot, Maurice. *Death Sentence.* Trans. Lydia Davis. Barrytown, NY: Station Hill Press, 1978.

Kurrik, Maire Jaanus. *Literature and Negation.* New York: Columbia UP, 1979.

Nelson, Cary. "Soliciting Self-Knowledge: The Rhetoric of Susan Sontag's Criticism." *Critical Inquiry* 7 (Summer 1980): 726.

Rattner, Jair. "Sontag diz que há uma superpopulação de escritores." *Fohla De S. Paulo* 28 May 1988: A-31.

Sontag, Susan. *Against Interpretation.* New York: Farrar, 1966.

——. *AIDS and Its Metaphors.* New York: Farrar, 1989.

——. *The Benefactor.* New York: Farrar, 1963.

——. *Death Kit.* New York: Farrar, 1967.

——. *I, etcetera.* New York: Farrar, 1978.

——. *Illness as Metaphor.* New York: Farrar, 1978.

——. Introduction. *Veruschka: Transfigurations.* By Vera Lehndorff and Holger Trulzsch. New York: Little, 1986. 6-12.

——. *On Photography.* New York: Farrar, 1977.

——. *Styles of Radical Will.* New York: Farrar, 1969.

——. *Trip to Hanoi.* New York: Farrar, 1968.

——. *Under the Sign of Saturn.* New York: Farrar, 1980.

Trilling, Lionel. "The Authentic Unconscious." *Sincerity and Authenticity.* Cambridge: Harvard UP, 1971.

——. "The Fate of Pleasure." *Beyond Culture.* New York: Harcourt, 1965.

——. "The Heroic, the Beautiful, the Authentic." *Sincerity and Authenticity.*

## Harriet Gilbert (essay date 29 March 1991)

SOURCE: Gilbert, Harriet. "Education of the Heart." *New Statesman and Society* 4, no. 144 (29 March 1991): 23-4.

[*In the following essay, Gilbert discusses Sontag's writings on cancer and AIDS, using interview quotes to illustrate the author's opinions and confusion surrounding the social implications involved with these diseases.*]

Like Woody Allen in *Zelig,* Susan Sontag appears to have been there, boots planted centre-stage, at every cultural high spot of the last quarter-century: the "youth movement" of the 1960s; opposition to the Vietnam war; feminism; anti-censorship . . . Aptly enough, she even popped up in *Zelig* itself.

This week, she has been in London raising money for Aids, an event centred on the re-publication of her *New Yorker* story **"The Way We Live Now"**—about a network of friends, of whom one is in hospital with Aids—in book form, with lithograph illustrations by Howard Hodgkin, the Turner Prize-winning British artist. In a gap between readings, fund-raising dinners and interviews, I met Susan Sontag in her Soho hotel and asked her how this "campaigning" persona clashed with her other existence, as one of our era's most complex and subtle analysts.

Her answer was swift: she has never *been* a campaigner. "The amount that I do is vastly exaggerated. I mean, what's the last political statement I made? I organised the American writers' response to the *fatwa* against Salman Rushdie. Since then I haven't opened my *mouth.*"

The last should not be taken literally. Sontag speaks fluently and likes to speak. Both language and ideas give her so much palpable pleasure that you feel that, were strangers to accost her in the street, she would want to answer whatever they asked. This explains why she may under-estimate the number of platforms on which she has stood; but it also explains why people exaggerate her presence in the public arena. Not only is she mesmerising, with great intellectual and physical grace; but her mixture of thoughtfulness, mercury awareness and non-stop internal argument continues to echo long after the voice has stopped.

Writing, however, is what she does. "I really try to convey what I think in a way that has pockets, you know; that does acknowledge the complexity. That's why I don't generally like to do television. When I'm talking, I can't remember all the different sides of it. But then, when I write . . . it's a kind of layering process. You know, I lay down one layer and then I lay down another layer and then that sort of modifies the first thing, and then I get something that seems not too simple and seems eloquent and seems powerful and *that's* the argument that I want to make: one that one might want to re-read; not one that one would want to summarise and say, 'Oh, I know what she thinks about this, she's against it, she's for it.'"

The problem is that Sontag bestrides a crossroads where art, academe, politics and street-life converge. She is therefore particularly vulnerable to having her feet run over. In her youth, fellow academics accused her of debasing critical writing by using its rigour to examine popular culture. Now she is charged that *AIDS and Its Metaphors,* the non-fiction book she wrote after **"The Way We Live Now",** could reduce the pressure for action on Aids by its calm assurance that a cure *will* be found, and its undermining of the metaphors by which the syndrome is made into something more portentous than an illness.

"Oh, that's absurd," said Sontag. "What else could it be but an illness? Even if it were some of the things that people act as if it were, if it were a state of mind, if it were a symptom of social disorder or moral degeneracy, would that make it *more* imperative to do something about it? Oh, you know, it's so . . . I often have the feeling that people don't really read what you write. I mean, there's all sorts of arguments in the book to try to understand why people *need* to use these metaphors."

**"The Way We Live Now"** was also written, in part, to help in understanding: what Sontag describes as "an education of the heart". It does this by weaving a lattice of voices expressing the pain, fear, compassion and euphoria (Sontag refuses to ignore this last) that greet the arrival of probable death within a close-knit community. The comfort that it offers is an artist's: not the comfort of meaning but of *shape*. This does not, however, make either it or its need less emotionally real.

The story's catalyst was the news that Sontag's friend Robert Mapplethorpe, the photographer, was in hospital. She wrote it fast, and talks about it now as a "kind of premonition", Mapplethorpe being the first of 30 close friends in whose death from Aids she has since been involved. However, as with the non-fiction book that she wrote about her cancer, *Illness as Metaphor,* the personal experience at once rippled out to form a larger, more general statement, thus feeding into the criticism that Sontag is distanced, uncommitted.

In a study of Sontag published last year, Sohnya Sayres points particularly to a passage in *AIDS and Its Metaphors* where Sontag writes that fear of Aids has enforced "a much more moderate exercise of appetite". Sayres reads this as approval, a sign of Sontag's ever-increasing "conservatism". The truth is less straightforward.

"I start *absolutely* by assuming that what is desirable is a pluralistic society, a society that does not impede a number of ways of being and feeling, and that includes different kinds of sexual relations. So, in that sense, I couldn't possibly be censorious about sexual experimentation. But, on the other hand—there's always another hand—I've lived long enough to see become publicly acceptable extremely cynical and callous ideas about personal relations, about sexuality."

As illustration, Sontag cited such films as *The Silence of the Lambs* and David Lynch's *Wild at Heart,* the second of which she has been appalled to hear described as a "charming comedy". "I wear turtle-neck sweaters when I go to the movies, so that I can pull the thing over my head, and I turn around and everyone's sitting there, not even blinking; so I mean, there is a kind of mutation of feeling and a rise in the tolerance for brutality." The crucial point, however, is this: when I asked her whether this "tolerance" was growing in real as well as in representational life, she looked for a moment surprised that there might be a difference. Similarly, when I asked her whether she felt moral conflict about raising funds, some part of which could be paying for experiments on chimpanzees, she sounded sincerely perplexed. "I don't know what to say. I'm horrified by cruelty to animals and all the examples of unnecessary use of animals in laboratories, and I don't know what the practical consequences of disapproving of it so much . . . I don't know whether one should want *not* to use animals, if it could mean finding proper treatment earlier. I just don't know . . . I don't know how to think about it."

"Practical consequences" ought, perhaps, to be marginally better considered. But then, as she said, Sontag is not a campaigner. She is a public figure whom we still desperately need: someone for whom imagining, thinking, saying and feeling are indivisible. If some of us know more clearly where we "stand" on, for example, vivisection, we should also know the ambivalence that we trampled in order to get there. As much as political positions, or more so, contradictions need a guardian.

### Elin Elgaard (review date autumn 1993)

SOURCE: Elgaard, Elin. Review of *The Volcano Lover,* by Susan Sontag. *World Literature Today* 67, no. 4 (autumn 1993): 825-26.

[*In the following review, Elgaard finds flaws in the narrative style in* The Volcano Lover, *yet compliments Son-*

*tag's characterizations, and especially the development of the protagonist, Emma.*]

Set in revolution-threatened, late-eighteenth-century Naples and subtitled "A Romance," **The Volcano Lover** casts a net of passions: a British envoy's for Vesuvius, his first wife Catherine's for him, his own for second wife Emma, and finally hers, *requited,* for Admiral Nelson. Crisscrossing the net run other loves: the collecting envoy's for art; the starving mob's (as is the king's hunting lust) for butchery; that of the queen's confidant, Scarpia, for power. The storyteller (of *ancient* origin, now termed "postmodern") freely manipulates and interrupts action—even letters!—in comments witty, scathing, and wistful, tightening the net till there is scarcely room for the reader. Deliberate tense shifts—often in midsentence—may serve artistically, like filmic *stills* (the momentous moment), but also irritate as mere mannerism.

Forestalling character delusions ("Catherine may have thought, wrongly, that she had escaped male egoism") or coloring reader reception ("What we agree with leaves us inactive, but contradiction makes us productive—a wisdom and a brand of felicity unavailable to the Collector which he would never miss") may be *mock*-Victorian, but any such intention is vitiated by *tah*some impact. Led by the nose, and mostly within earshot of Vesuvius—variously androgyne, monster, principle of disaster, projection of ourselves (even willed identification)—we soonest see the connection between humanity's lust for destruction (*spectacle* at all cost) and appropriation: both are "appetitive." A wholly negative cuneiform is the *cuccagna,* an obscene, live mountain of terrified animals built to entertain and feed the poor on feast days; and equally Swiftian is the inverted(?) volcano of the King's protracted bowel movements.

Preachily explicit on the societally oppressed, as in many a feminist dictum, the novel yet triumphs in its portrayal of Emma. Related to mythical Galatea (and Balzac's *Sarrasine* story), she is statue come alive, endearing and empowering herself through sheer vitality. Fat and faded, she meets her one-armed, one-eyed hero, and in a marvelous "funhouse" full of Bacchanalian statuary, they kiss. With their separate imperfections they attain perfect passion: "She never imagined that a man could feel as she did—that he wanted to be taken by her as much as she by him. We are all, in that *best* sense, little volcanoes, even Jack the monkey, whom the Collector mistakenly saw as "comocker" (versus embracer) of life and who died for lack of affection—to be resurrected "sitting on my breast" in the envoy's death delirium, a reminder of failure.

Since obsession is here defined as the opposite of ecstasy, even the martyred intellectual Eleanora, who comes to judge *all* posthumously, must, in her desire to be "pure flame," be seen as having failed; the sybil Efrosina, whom the Collector sought *and* feared as the erotic connection to life, remains (with Emma) closer to the pulse.

## Tess Lewis (review date spring 1994)

SOURCE: Lewis, Tess. "Wild Fancies." *Belles Lettres* 9, no. 3 (spring 1994): 25-6.

[*In the following review, Lewis provides a negative assessment of* Alice in Bed, *contending that the character's words and actions are inaccurate, implausible, and laden with banalities and trite cliches.*]

"How wild can be the fancies of the unimaginative female!" the bedridden Alice James wrote in her diary in 1891. Unfortunately, wild, self-indulgent fancy rather than quickening imagination is the guiding spirit of **Alice in Bed,** Susan Sontag's play based on Henry and William James's invalid sister. Intended as a play "about women, about women's anguish and women's consciousness" and about the imagination, **Alice in Bed** is in fact little more than a procession of emblematic figures uttering portentous, clipped sentences at one another. Rather than bring the historical and fictional figures to life on stage, Sontag exploits them for all the sociocultural atmosphere they are worth, leaving the intellectual heavy lifting to the spectator. Alice, for example, informs Emily Dickinson, "I think your interest in death is more interesting than mine." That may well be, but how, and why, and what difference does it make? Such pronouncements as the fictional Dickinson's "Death is the lining. The lines." hardly clear things up.

Sontag's emblematic use of historical and literary figures was far more successful in her recent novel **The Volcano Lover,** in which the main characters—Sir William Hamilton; his wife, Emma; and Lord Nelson—are not referred to by name, but as the Cavaliere, the Cavaliere's wife, and the hero. Goethe; William Beckford, the notorious collector, amateur architect, and author of *Vathek*—the scandalous tale of a sadistic sultan; and the Baron Scarpia from *Tosca* also make their appearances. But whereas **The Volcano Lover**'s elaborate settings and dramatic action bring most of the characters convincingly to life, **Alice in Bed**'s intellectual scaffolding remains woefully bare.

**Alice in Bed** opens in 1890 with a 40-ish Alice in bed under several thin mattresses bickering with her nurse about whether she can, will, or even wants to get up. She eventually does, smokes opium, delivers a monologue, and gets back into bed. Throughout the play, the mattresses—social pressures, family expectations, etc.—are piled upon her or taken away by a man and a woman in sailor outfits. In the central scene, inspired by a fusion of Alice James with the heroine of Lewis Carroll's *Alice in Wonderland,* Alice is joined for a mad tea party by Margaret Fuller; Emily Dickinson; Alice's mother; Kundry from Wagner's *Parsifal,* who wishes to sleep away her adulterous guilt; and Myrtha, the Queen of the Wilis—a group of women in Adolphe Adam's ballet *Giselle* who died before their wedding days and returned to torment unfaithful lovers. Utterly devoid of humor, this scene reduces such eloquent, passionate women as Fuller and Dickinson to mouthing superficial banalities. For example, Sontag has Dickinson say, "I trust that my flowers have the good grace to be seared by our shouts," and Margaret Fuller, "Women despair differently. I've observed that. We can be very stoical."

Henry James makes an appearance, quoting from Alice's diary and from his own writings about her. In another scene a younger Alice asks her father's permission to commit suicide, a request the senior Henry James did in fact grant his then 30-year old daughter. However, that he should then remove his wooden leg and beat it with a hammer is dramatically, not to mention historically, implausible.

A touch of *nostalgie de la boue* enters in the form of a gentle, bumbling young thief with "a Cockney or Irish accent." Assured that Alice was ill and would not wake up, he agrees, despite his inexperience, to break into her room only to find a suddenly energetic Alice who drinks his gin, points out the choice pieces he should steal, and reveals her dark visions.

Intended as proof of Alice's victorious imagination as well as the imaginative climax of the play, Scene 6 consists of a monologue delivered by a shrunken Alice in an oversized bed. She describes her mental flight to Rome but fails to draw the reader in. Her constant repetition of the qualifier "in my mind" not only ensures that the imagined scene remains Alice's alone, but also prevents us from believing that she herself is wholly caught up in her imaginative displacement. Alice has, it seems here, constructed an insurmountable barrier between her self and her imagination. Moreover, if this monologue reflects Sontag's view of the limitations and advantages of the mental defense mechanisms of 19th-century women, why does she not illustrate her view at greater length and with greater subtlety? We are offered no insight into the suffering and invalidism prevalent among intelligent women in the 19th century, into the pressures suffered by such women as James, Fuller, and Dickinson, or into their very different reactions to these pressures.

The best thing about the book is the afterword, lumbering though it is. In this "Note on the Play" Sontag explains what she has tried to accomplish. In fact, she explains her intentions so thoroughly that there is no real need for the play at all. Sontag ends her afterword with the rallying cry: "But the victories of the imagination are not enough." Yes, and how dismal are its failures.

Henry James, himself a surprisingly unsuccessful playwright, wrote that "the dramatist only wants more liberties than he can really take." Sontag has clearly taken far too many here.

### Susan Sontag and Edward Hirsch (interview date July 1994)

SOURCE: Sontag, Susan, and Edward Hirsch. "Susan Sontag: The Art of Fiction CXLIII." *Paris Review* 37, no. 137 (winter 1995): 176-208.

[*In the following interview, conducted in July, 1994, Sontag reveals the authors who have inspired and influenced her literary career, comments on the craft of writing, and elaborates on the different approaches she takes between writing essays and writing fiction.*]

Susan Sontag was interviewed in her Manhattan apartment on three blisteringly hot days in July, 1994. She had been traveling back and forth to Sarajevo—she has now been there nine times—and it was gracious of her to set aside time for the interview. Sontag is a prodigious talker—candid, informal, learned, ardent—and each day at a wooden kitchen table held forth for seven and eight-hour stretches. The kitchen is a mixed-use room, but the fax machine and the photocopier were silent; the telephone seldom rang. The conversation ranged over a vast array of subjects—later the texts would be scoured and revised—but always returned to the pleasures and distinctions of literature. Sontag is interested in all things concerning writing—from the mechanism of the process to the high nature of the calling. She has many missions, but foremost among them is the vocation of the writer.

Sontag was born in 1933 in New York City, grew up in Arizona and later, Southern California. She graduated from high school at fifteen, attended Berkeley for a year, graduated from the University of Chicago (1951) and received two M.A.s from Harvard: one in English (1954), one in philosophy (1955). In 1950, she married Philip Rieff, with whom she had a son, the writer David Rieff; the marriage lasted nine years. Since 1957, when she spent a year in France, Sontag has often lived abroad, though New York City has generally served as her base. In the early sixties she taught philosophy and the history of religion at various universities, but since then has eschewed academic life. She has won many awards and fellowships, including the National Book Critics Circle Award for *On Photography,* and a five-year MacArthur Fellowship.

Sontag has published fifteen books, including the novels *The Benefactor* (1963), *Death Kit* (1967) and *The Volcano Lover* (1992), a collection of short stories, *I, etcetera* (1978) and three collections of essays: *Against Interpretation* (1966), *Styles of Radical Will* (1969) and *Under the Sign of Saturn* (1980). *On Photography,* a collection of related essays, was published in 1977. *A Susan Sontag Reader* appeared in 1982. *Illness as Metaphor* (1978) and its companion volume, *AIDS and Its Metaphors* (1989), anatomize the putative uses of metaphors for tuberculosis, cancer and AIDS in our culture. Her latest work is a play employing elements from the life of Alice James entitled *Alice in Bed* (1993). Sontag has also written and directed four films— *Duet for Cannibals* (1969), *Brother Carl* (1971), *Promised Lands* (1974) and *Unguided Tour* (1983)—and edited and introduced writings by Antonin Artaud (1976), Roland Barthes (1981) and, most recently, Danilo Kiš (1995), as well as written prefaces to books by Robert Walser (1982), Marina Tsvetaeva (1983), Machado de Assis (1990) and Juan Rulfo (1995), among others.

Sontag lives in a sparsely furnished five-room apartment on the top floor of a building in Chelsea on the west side of Manhattan. Books—as many as fifteen thousand—and papers are everywhere. A lifetime could be spent browsing through the books on art and architecture, theater and dance, philosophy and psychiatry, the history of medicine and the history of religion, photography and opera and so on. The various European literatures—French, German, Italian, Spanish, Russian, etc., as well as hundreds of books of Japanese literature and books on Japan—are arranged by language in a loosely chronological way. So is American literature as well as English literature, which runs from *Beowulf* to, say, James Fenton. Sontag is an inveterate clipper, and the books are filled with scraps of paper ("each book is marked and filleted," she says), the bookcases festooned with notes scrawled with the names of additional things to read.

Sontag usually writes by hand on a low marble table in the living room. Small theme notebooks are filled with notes for her novel-in-progress, *In America.* An old book on Chopin sits atop a history of table manners. The room is lit by a lovely Fortuny lamp, or a replica of one. Piranesi prints decorate the wall (architectural prints are one of her passions).

Everything in Sontag's apartment testifies to the range of her interests, but it is the work itself, like her conversation, that demonstrates the passionate nature of her commitments. She is eager to follow a subject wherever it leads, as far as it will go—and beyond. What she has said about Roland Barthes is true about her as well: "It was not a question of knowledge . . . but of alertness, a fastidious transcription of what could

be thought about something, once it swam into the stream of attention."

[*Hirsch*]: *When did you begin writing?*

[Sontag]: I'm not sure. But I know I was self-publishing when I was about nine: I started a four-page monthly newspaper, which I hectographed (a very primitive method of duplication) in about twenty copies and sold for five cents to the neighbors. The paper, which I kept going for several years, was filled with imitations of things I was reading. There were stories, poems and two plays that I remember, one inspired by Čapek's *R.U.R.*, the other by Edna St. Vincent Millay's *Aria de Capo.* And accounts of battles—Midway, Stalingrad and so on; remember, this was 1942, 1943, 1944— dutifully condensed from articles in real newspapers.

*We've had to postpone this interview several times because of your frequent trips to Sarajevo which, you've told me, have been one of the most compelling experiences of your life. I was thinking how war recurs in your work and life.*

It does. I made two trips to North Vietnam under American bombardment, the first of which I recounted in **"Trip to Hanoi,"** and when the Yom Kippur War started in 1973 I went to Israel to shoot a film, *Promised Lands,* on the front lines. Bosnia is actually my third war.

*There's the denunciation of military metaphors in* **Illness as Metaphor.** *And the narrative climax of* **The Volcano Lover,** *a horrifying evocation of the viciousness of war. And when I asked you to contribute to a book I was editing,* Transforming Vision: Writers on Art, *the work you chose to write about was Goya's* The Disasters of War.

I suppose it could seem odd to travel to a war, and not just in one's imagination—even if I do come from a family of travelers. My father, who was a fur trader in northern China, died there during the Japanese invasion: I was five. I remember hearing about "world war" in September 1939, entering elementary school, where my best friend in the class was a Spanish Civil War refugee. I remember panicking on December 7, 1941. And one of the first pieces of language I ever pondered over was "for the duration"—as in "there's no butter for the duration." I recall savoring the oddity, and the optimism, of that phrase.

*In* **"Writing Itself,"** *on Roland Barthes, you express surprise that Barthes, whose father was killed in one of the battles of the First World War (Barthes was an infant) and who, as a young man himself, lived through the Second World War—the Occupation—never once mentions the word* war *in any of his writings. But your work seems haunted by war.*

I could answer that a writer is someone who pays attention to the world.

*You once wrote of* **Promised Lands***: "My subject is war, and anything about any war that does not show the appalling concreteness of destruction and death is a dangerous lie."*

That prescriptive voice rather makes me cringe. But . . . yes.

*Are you writing about the siege of Sarajevo?*

No. I mean, not yet, and probably not for a long time. And almost certainly not in the form of an essay or report. David Rieff, who is my son, and who started going to Sarajevo before I did, has published such an essay-report, a book called *Slaughterhouse*—and one book in the family on the Bosnian genocide is enough. So I'm not spending time in Sarajevo to write about it. For the moment it's enough for me just to be there as much as I can: to witness, to lament, to offer a model of non-complicity, to pitch in. The duties of a human being, one who believes in right action, not of a writer.

*Did you always want to be a writer?*

I read the biography of Madame Curie by her daughter Eve Curie when I was about six, so at first I thought I was going to be a chemist. Then for a long time, most of my childhood, I wanted to be a physician. But literature swamped me. What I really wanted was every kind of life, and the writer's life seemed the most inclusive.

*Did you have any role models as a writer?*

Of course I thought I was Jo in *Little Women*. But I didn't want to write what Jo wrote. Then in *Martin Eden* I found a writer-protagonist with whose writing I could identify, so then I wanted to be Martin Eden—minus, of course, the dreary fate Jack London gives him. I saw myself as, I guess I was, a heroic autodidact. I looked forward to the struggle of the writing life. I thought of being a writer as a heroic vocation.

*Any other models?*

Later, when I was thirteen, I read the journals of André Gide, which described a life of great privilege and relentless avidity.

*Do you remember when you started reading?*

When I was three, I'm told. Anyway, I remember reading real books—biographies, travel books—when I was about six. And then free fall into Poe and Shakespeare

and Dickens and the Brontës and Victor Hugo and Schopenhauer and Pater, and so on. I got through my childhood in a delirium of literary exaltations.

*You must have been very different from other children.*

Was I? I was good at dissembling, too. I didn't think that much about myself, I was so glad to be on to something better. But I so wanted to be elsewhere. And reading produced its blissful, confirming alienations. Because of reading—and music—my daily experience was of living in a world of people who didn't give a hoot about the intensities to which I had pledged myself. I felt as if I were from another planet—a fantasy borrowed from the innocent comic books of that era, to which I was also addicted. And of course I didn't really have much sense of how I was seen by others. Actually, I never thought people were thinking of me at all. I do remember—I was about four—a scene in a park, hearing my Irish nanny saying to another giant in a starched white uniform, "Susan is very high-strung," and thinking, "That's an interesting word. Is it true?"

*Tell me something about your education.*

All in public schools, quite a number of them, each one more lowering than the one before. But I was lucky to have started school before the era of the child psychologists. Since I could read and write I was immediately put into the third grade, and later I was skipped another semester, so I was graduated from high school—North Hollywood High School—when I was still fifteen. After that, I had a splendid education at Berkeley, then in the so-called Hutchins College of the University of Chicago, and then as a graduate student in philosophy at Harvard and Oxford. I was a student for most of the 1950s and I never had a teacher from whom I didn't learn. But at Chicago, the most important of my universities, there were not just teachers I admired but three to whose influence I gratefully submitted: Kenneth Burke, Richard McKeon and Leo Strauss.

*What was Burke like as a teacher?*

Completely inside his own enthralling way of unpacking a text. He spent almost a year with the class reading Conrad's *Victory* word by word, image by image. It was from Burke that I learned how to read. I still read the way he taught me. He took some interest in me. I had already read some of his books before he was my teacher in Humanities III; remember, he wasn't well-known then and he'd never met an undergraduate who had read him while still in high school. He gave me a copy of his novel, *Towards a Better Life,* and told me stories about sharing an apartment in Greenwich Village in the 1920s with Hart Crane and Djuna Barnes—you can imagine what that did to me. He was the first person I met who had written books that I owned. (I except an audience I was roped into with Thomas Mann when I was fourteen years old, which I recounted in a story called **"Pilgrimage."**) Writers were as remote to me as movie stars.

*You had your B.A. from the University of Chicago at eighteen. Did you know by then you would become a writer?*

Yes, but I still went to graduate school. It never occurred to me that I could support myself as a writer. I was a grateful, militant student. I thought I would be happy teaching, and I was. Of course, I had been careful to prepare myself to teach not literature, but philosophy and the history of religion.

*But you taught only through your twenties, and have refused countless invitations to return to university teaching. Is this because you came to feel that being an academic and being a creative writer are incompatible?*

Yes. Worse than incompatible. I've seen academic life destroy the best writers of my generation.

*Do you mind being called an intellectual?*

Well, one never likes to be called anything. And the word makes more sense to me as an adjective than as a noun, though, even so, I suppose there will always be a presumption of graceless oddity—especially if one is a woman. Which makes me even more committed to my polemics against the ruling anti-intellectual cliches: heart versus head, feeling versus intellect, and so forth.

*Do you think of yourself as a feminist?*

That's one of the few labels I'm content with. But even so . . . is it a noun? I doubt it.

*What women writers have been important to you?*

Many. Sei Shōnagon, Austen, George Eliot, Dickinson, Woolf, Tsvetayeva, Akhmatova, Elizabeth Bishop, Elizabeth Hardwick . . . the list is much longer than that. Because women are, culturally speaking, a minority, with my minority consciousness I always rejoice in the achievement of women. With my writer's consciousness, I rejoice in any writer I can admire, women writers no more or less than men.

*Whatever the models of a literary vocation that inspired you as a child, I have the impression that your adult idea of a literary vocation is more European than American.*

I'm not so sure. I think it's my own private brand. But what is true is that, living in the second half of the twentieth century, I could indulge my Europhile tastes without actually expatriating myself, while still spend-ing a lot of my adult life in Europe. That's been my way of being an American. As Gertrude Stein remarked, "What good are roots if you can't take them with you?" One might say that's very Jewish, but it's also very American.

*Your third novel,* **The Volcano Lover,** *seems to me a very American book, even though the story it tells takes place in eighteenth-century Europe.*

It is. Nobody but an American would have written **The Volcano Lover.**

*And* **The Volcano Lover***'s subtitle: "A Romance." That's a reference to Hawthorne, right?*

Exactly. I was thinking of what Hawthorne says in the preface to *The House of Seven Gables*: "When a writer calls his work a romance, it need hardly be observed that he wishes to claim a certain latitude, both as to its fashion and material, which he would not have felt himself entitled to assume had he been writing a novel." My imagination is very marked by nineteenth-century American literature—first by Poe, whom I read at a precocious age and whose mixture of speculativeness, fantasy and gloominess enthralled me. Poe's stories still inhabit my head. Then by Hawthorne and Melville. I love Melville's obsessiveness. *Clarel, Moby-Dick.* And *Pierre*—another novel about the terrible thwarting of a heroic solitary writer.

*Your first book was a novel,* **The Benefactor.** *Since then you've written essays, travel narratives, stories, plays, as well as two more novels. Have you ever started something in one form and then changed it to another?*

No. From the beginning I always know what something is going to be: every impulse to write is born of an idea of form, for me. To begin I have to have the shape, the architecture. I can't say it better than Nabokov did: "The pattern of the thing precedes the thing."

*How fluent are you as a writer?*

I wrote **The Benefactor** quickly, almost effortlessly, on weekends and during two summers (I was teaching in the Department of Religion at Columbia College); I thought I was telling a pleasurably sinister story that illustrated the fortune of certain heretical religious ideas that go by the name of Gnosticism. The early essays came easily, too. But writing is an activity that in my experience doesn't get easier with practice. On the contrary.

*How does something get started for you?*

It starts with sentences, with phrases, and then I know something is being transmitted. Often it's an opening line. But sometimes I hear the closing line, instead.

*How do you actually write?*

I write with a felt-tip pen, or sometimes a pencil, on yellow or white legal pads, that fetish of American writers. I like the slowness of writing by hand. Then I type it up and scrawl all over that. And keep on retyping it, each time making corrections both by hand and directly on the typewriter, until I don't see how to make it any better. Up to five years ago, that was it. Since then there is a computer in my life. After the second or third draft it goes into the computer, so I don't retype the whole manuscript anymore, but continue to revise by hand on a succession of hard-copy drafts from the computer.

*Is there anything that helps you get started writing?*

Reading—which is rarely related to what I'm writing, or hoping to write. I read a lot of art history, architectural history, musicology, academic books on many subjects. And poetry. Getting started is partly stalling, stalling by way of reading and of listening to music, which energizes me and also makes me restless. Feeling guilty about *not* writing.

*Do you write every day?*

No. I write in spurts. I write when I have to because the pressure builds up and I feel enough confidence that something has matured in my head and I can write it down. But once something is really under way, I don't want to do anything else. I don't go out, much of the time I forget to eat, I sleep very little. It's a very undisciplined way of working and makes me not very prolific. But I'm too interested in many other things.

*Yeats said famously that one must choose between the life and the work. Do you think that is true?*

As you know, he actually said that one must choose between perfection of the life and perfection of the work. Well, writing *is* a life—a very peculiar one. Of course, if by life you mean life with other people, Yeats's dictum is true. Writing requires huge amounts of solitude. What I've done to soften the harshness of that choice is that I don't write all the time. I like to go out—which includes traveling; I can't write when I travel. I like to talk. I like to listen. I like to look and to watch. Maybe I have an Attention Surplus Disorder. The easiest thing in the world for me is to pay attention.

*Do you revise as you go along or do you wait until you have an entire draft and then revise the whole thing?*

I revise as I go along. And that's quite a pleasurable task. I don't get impatient and I'm willing to go over and over something until it works. It's beginnings that

are hard. I always begin with a great sense of dread and trepidation. Nietzsche says that the decision to start writing is like leaping into a cold lake. Only when I'm about a third of the way can I tell if it's good enough. Then I have my cards, and I can play my hand.

*Is there a difference between writing fiction and writing essays?*

Writing essays has always been laborious. They go through many drafts, and the end result may bear little relation to the first draft: often I completely change my mind in the course of writing an essay. Fiction comes much easier, in the sense that the first draft contains the essentials—tone, lexicon, velocity, passions—of what I eventually end up with.

*Do you regret anything you've written?*

Nothing in its entirety except two theater chronicles I did in the mid-1960s for *Partisan Review,* and unfortunately included in the first collection of essays, *Against Interpretation*—I'm not suited for that kind of pugnacious, impressionistic task. Obviously, I don't agree with everything in the early essays. I've changed, and I know more. And the cultural context which inspired them has altogether changed. But there would be no point in modifying them now. I think I would like to take a blue pencil to the first two novels, though.

**The Benefactor,** *which you wrote in your late twenties, is narrated in the voice of a Frenchman in his sixties. Did you find it easy to impersonate someone so different from yourself?*

Easier than writing about myself. But writing is impersonation. Even when I write about events in my own life, as I did in **"Pilgrimage"** and **"Project for a Trip to China,"** it's not really me. But I admit that, with *The Benefactor,* the difference was as broad as I could make it. I wasn't celibate, I wasn't a recluse, I wasn't a man, I wasn't elderly, I wasn't French.

*But the novel seems very influenced by French literature.*

Is it? It seems many people think that it was influenced by the *nouveau roman.* But I don't agree. There were ironic allusions to two French books, hardly contemporary ones: Descartes' *Meditations* and Voltaire's *Candide.* But those weren't influences. If there was an influence on *The Benefactor,* though one I wasn't at all conscious of at the time, it was Kenneth Burke's *Towards a Better Life.* I reread Burke's novel recently, after many decades (I may never have reread it since he gave me a copy when I was sixteen), and discovered in its programmatic preface what seems like a model for *The Benefactor.* The novel as sequence of arias and fictive moralizing. The coquetry of a protagonist—Burke dared to call his the novel's hero—so ingeniously self-absorbed that no reader could be tempted to identify with him.

*Your second novel,* **Death Kit,** *is quite different from* **The Benefactor.**

**Death Kit** invites identification with its miserable protagonist. I was in the lamenting mood—it's written in the shadow of the Vietnam War. It's a book of grief, veils and all.

*Hardly a new emotion in your work. Wasn't your first published story entitled* **"Man with a Pain"**?

Juvenilia. You won't find it in *I, etcetera.*

*How did you come to write those theater chronicles for* Partisan Review?

Well you have to understand that the literary world then was defined by so-called small magazines—hard to imagine because it's so different now. My sense of literary vocation had been shaped by reading literary magazines—*Kenyon Review, Sewanee Review, The Hudson Review, Partisan Review*—at the end of the 1940s, while still in high school in Southern California. By the time I came to New York in 1960, those magazines still existed. But it was already the end of an era. Of course, I couldn't have known that. My highest ambition had been and still was to publish in one of these magazines, where five thousand people would read me. That seemed to me very heaven.

Soon after I moved to New York, I saw William Phillips at a party and got up my nerve to go over and ask him, "How does one get to write for *Partisan Review*?" He answered, "You come down to the magazine and I give you a book to review on spec." I was there the next day. And he gave me a novel. Not one I was interested in, but I wrote something decent, and the review was printed. And so the door was opened. But then there was some inappropriate fantasy, which I tried to squelch, that I was going to be "the new Mary McCarthy"—as Phillips made plain to me by asking me to do a theater chronicle. "You know, Mary used to do it," he said. I told him I didn't want to write theater reviews. He insisted. And so, much against my better judgment (I certainly had no desire to be the new Mary McCarthy, a writer who'd never mattered to me), I did turn out two of them. I reviewed plays by Arthur Miller and James Baldwin and Edward Albee and said they were bad and tried to be witty and hated myself for doing it. After the second round I told Phillips I couldn't go on.

*But you did go on and write those famous essays, some of which were published in* Partisan Review?

Yes, but those subjects were all of my own choosing. I've hardly ever written anything on commission. I am not at all interested in writing about work I don't admire. And even among what I've admired, by and large I've written only about things I felt were neglected or relatively unknown. I am not a critic, which is something else than an essayist; I thought of my essays as cultural work. They were written out of a sense of what *needed* to be written.

I was assuming that a principal task of art was to strengthen the adversarial consciousness. And that led me to reach for relatively eccentric work. I took for granted that the liberal consensus about culture—I was and am a great admirer of Lionel Trilling—would stay in place, that the traditional canon of great books could not be threatened by work that was more transgressive or playful. But taste has become so debauched in the thirty years I've been writing that now simply to defend the idea of seriousness has become an adversarial act. Just to be serious or to care about things in an ardent, disinterested way is becoming incomprehensible to most people. Perhaps only those who were born in the 1930s—and maybe a few stragglers—are going to understand what it means to talk about art as opposed to art projects. Or artists as opposed to celebrities. As you see, I'm chock-full of indignation about the barbarism and relentless vacuity of this culture. How tedious always to be indignant.

*Is it old-fashioned to think that the purpose of literature is to educate us about life?*

Well, it does educate us about life. I wouldn't be the person I am, I wouldn't understand what I understand, were it not for certain books. I'm thinking of the great question of nineteenth-century Russian literature: how should one live? A novel worth reading is an education of the heart. It enlarges your sense of human possibility, of what human nature is, of what happens in the world. It's a creator of inwardness.

*Do writing an essay and writing a piece of fiction come from different parts of yourself?*

Yes. The essay is a constrained form. Fiction is freedom. Freedom to tell stories and freedom to be discursive, too. But essayistic discursiveness, in the context of fiction, has an entirely different meaning. It is always voiced.

*It seems as if you have pretty much stopped writing essays.*

I have. And most of the essays I've succumbed to writing in the past fifteen years are requiems or tributes. The essays on Canetti, Barthes and Benjamin are about elements in their work and sensibility that I feel close to: Canetti's cult of admiration and hatred of cruelty, Barthes's version of the aesthete's sensibility, Benjamin's poetics of melancholy. I was very aware that there's much to be said about them which I didn't say.

*Yes, I can see that those essays are disguised self-portraits. But weren't you doing much the same thing in early essays, including some of those in* **Against Interpretation***?*

I suppose it can't be helped that it all hangs together. Still, something else was going on in the essays that went into the last collection, **Under the Sign of Saturn.** I was having a kind of slow-motion, asymptomatic nervous breakdown writing essays. I was so full of feeling and ideas and fantasies that I was still trying to cram into the essay mode. In other words, I'd come to the end of what the essay form could do for me. Maybe the essays on Benjamin, Canetti and Barthes were self-portraits, but they were also really fictions. My volcano lover, the Cavaliere, is the fully realized fictional form of what I'd been trying to say, in an impacted way, in the essay-portraits of Canetti and Benjamin.

*Writing fiction, is your experience one of inventing or figuring out a plot?*

Oddly enough, the plot is what seems to come all of a piece—like a gift. It's very mysterious. Something I hear or see or read conjures up a whole story in all its concreteness: scenes, characters, landscapes, catastrophes. With **Death Kit,** it was hearing someone utter the childhood nickname of a mutual friend named Richard—just the hearing of the name: Diddy. With **The Volcano Lover,** it was browsing in a print shop near the British Museum and coming across some images of volcanic landscapes that turned out to be from Sir William Hamilton's *Campi Phlegraei.* For the new novel, it was reading something in Kafka's diaries, a favorite book, so I must have already read this paragraph, which may be an account of a dream, more than once. Reading it this time the story of a whole novel, like a movie I'd seen, leaped into my head.

*The whole story?*

Yes, the whole story. The plot. But what the story can carry or accumulate—*that* I discover in the writing. If **The Volcano Lover** starts in a flea market and ends with Eleonora's beyond-the-grave monologue, it isn't as if I knew before I started writing all the implications of that journey, which goes from an ironic, down-market vignette of a collector on the prowl to Eleonora's moral wide-shot view of the whole story that the reader has experienced. Ending with Eleonora, and her denunciation of the protagonists, is as far as you can get from the point of view with which the novel starts.

*At the beginning of your legendary essay "Notes on 'Camp'," which appeared in 1964, you wrote that your attitude was one of "deep sympathy modified by revul-*

sion." *This seems a typical attitude of yours: both yes and no to camp. Both yes and no to photography. Both yes and no to narrative . . .*

It isn't that I like it and I don't like it: that's too simple. Or, if you will, it isn't "both yes and no." It's "this but also that." I'd love to settle in on a strong feeling or reaction. But, having seen whatever I see, my mind keeps on going and I see something else. It's that I quickly see the limitations of whatever I say or whatever judgment I make about anything. There's a wonderful remark of Henry James: "Nothing is my last word on anything." There's always more to be said, more to be felt.

*I think most people might imagine that you bring some theoretical agenda to fiction—if not as a writer of novels, at least as a reader of them.*

But I don't. I need to care about and be touched by what I read. I can't care about a book that has nothing to contribute to the wisdom project. And I'm a sucker for a fancy prose style. To put it less giddily, my model for prose is poet's prose: many of the writers I most admire were poets when young or could have been poets. Nothing theoretical in all that. In fact, my taste is irrepressibly catholic. I shouldn't care to be prevented from doting on Dreiser's *Jennie Gerhardt* and Didion's *Democracy,* Glenway Wescott's *The Pilgrim Hawk* and Donald Barthelme's *The Dead Father.*

*You're mentioning a number of contemporaries you admire. Would you also say you've been influenced by them?*

Whenever I avow to being influenced, I'm never sure I'm telling the truth. But here goes. I think I learned a lot about punctuation and speed from Donald Barthelme, about adjectives and sentence rhythms from Elizabeth Hardwick. I don't know if I learned from Nabokov and Thomas Bernhard, but their incomparable books help me keep my standards for myself as severe as they ought to be. And Godard—Godard has been a major nourishment to my sensibility and therefore, inevitably, to my writing. And I've certainly learned something as a writer from the way Schnabel plays Beethoven, Glenn Gould plays Bach, and Mitsuko Uchida plays Mozart.

*Do you read the reviews of your work?*

No. Not even those I'm told are entirely favorable. All reviews upset me. But friends give me a certain thumbs-up, thumbs-down sense of what they are.

*After* **Death Kit** *you didn't write much for a few years.*

I'd been very active in the anti-war movement since 1964, when it couldn't yet be called a movement. And that took up more and more time. I got depressed. I waited. I read. I lived in Europe. I fell in love. My admirations evolved. I made some movies. I had a crisis of confidence of how to write because I've always thought that a book should be something necessary, and that each book by me should be better than the one before. Punishing standards, but I'm quite loyal to them.

*How did you come to write* **On Photography***?*

I was having lunch with Barbara Epstein of *The New York Review of Books* in early 1972 and going on about the Diane Arbus show at the Museum of Modern Art, which I'd just seen, and she said, "Why don't you write a piece about the show?" I thought that maybe I could. And then when I began writing it I thought that it should start with a few paragraphs about photography in general and then move to Arbus. And soon there was a lot more than a few paragraphs, and I couldn't extricate myself. The essays multiplied—I felt often like the hapless sorcerer's apprentice—and they got harder and harder to write, I mean, to get right. But I'm stubborn—I was on the third essay before I managed to place some paragraphs about Arbus and the show—and, feeling I'd committed myself, wouldn't give up. It took five years to write the six essays that make up *On Photography.*

*But you told me that you wrote your next book,* **Illness as Metaphor,** *very fast.*

Well, it's shorter. One long essay, the non-fiction equivalent of a novella. And being ill—while writing it I was a cancer patient with a gloomy prognosis—was certainly very focusing. It gave me energy to think I was writing a book that would be helpful to other cancer patients and those close to them.

*All along you'd been writing stories . . .*

Revving up for a novel.

*Soon after finishing* **The Volcano Lover** *you started another novel. Does that mean that you're more drawn to longer, rather than shorter, forms of fiction?*

Yes. There are a few of my stories which I like a lot—from *I, etcetera,* "Debriefing" and "Unguided Tour," and "The Way We Live Now," which I wrote in 1987. But I feel more drawn to polyphonic narratives, which need to be long—or longish.

*How much time did it take you to write* **The Volcano Lover***?*

From the first sentence of the first draft to the galleys, two and a half years. For me that's fast.

*Where were you?*

I started *The Volcano Lover* in September 1989 in Berlin, where I had gone to hang out thinking that I was going to a place that was both very isolated and the Berkeley of Central Europe. Although only two months after I arrived Berlin had started to become a very different place, it still retained its main advantages for me: I wasn't in my apartment in New York, with all my books, and I wasn't in the place that I was writing about either. That sort of double distancing works very well for me.

About half of *The Volcano Lover* was written between late 1989 and the end of 1990 in Berlin. The second half was written in my apartment in New York, except for two chapters that I wrote in a hotel room in Milan (a two-week escapade) and another chapter which I wrote in the Mayflower Hotel in New York. That was the Cavaliere's deathbed interior monologue, which I thought I had to write in one go, in complete isolation, and knew—I don't know how I knew—that I could do in three days. So I left my apartment and checked into the hotel with my typewriter and legal-sized pads and felt-tip pens, and ordered up BLTs until I was done.

*Did you write the novel in sequence?*

Yes. I write chapter by chapter and I don't go on to the next chapter until the one I'm working on is in final form. That was frustrating at first because from the beginning I knew much of what I wanted the characters to say in the final monologues, but I feared that if I wrote them early on I wouldn't be able to go back to the middle. I was also afraid that maybe by the time I got to it I would have forgotten some of the ideas or no longer be connected to those feelings. The first chapter, which is about fourteen typewritten pages, took me four months to write. The last five chapters, some one hundred typewritten pages, took me two weeks.

*How much of the book did you have in mind before you started?*

I had the title; I can't write something unless I already know its title. I had the dedication; I knew I would dedicate it to my son. I had the *Così fan tutte* epigraph. And of course I had the story in some sense, and the span of the book. And what was most helpful, I had a very strong idea of a structure. I took it from a piece of music, Hindemith's *The Four Temperaments*—a work I know very well, since it's the music of one of Balanchine's most sublime ballets, which I've seen countless times. The Hindemith starts with a triple prologue, three very short pieces. Then come four movements: melancholic, sanguinic, phlegmatic, choleric. In that order. I knew I was going to have a triple prologue and then four sections or parts corresponding to the four temperaments—though I saw no reason to belabor the idea by actually labeling Parts I to IV "melancholic," "sanguinic," etc. I knew all of that, plus the novel's last sentence: "Damn them all." Of course, I didn't know who was going to utter it. In a sense, the whole work of writing the novel consisted of making something that would justify that sentence.

*That sounds like a lot to know before beginning.*

Yes, but for all that I knew about it, I still didn't understand all that it could be. I started off thinking that **The Volcano Lover** was the story of the volcano lover, Sir William Hamilton, the man I call the Cavaliere; that the book would stay centered on him. And I was going to develop the character of the self-effacing first Lady Hamilton, Catherine, at the expense of the story of his second wife, which everyone knows. I knew her story and the relation with Nelson had to figure in the novel, but I intended to keep it in the background. The triple prologue and Part I, with its many variations on the theme of melancholy (or depression, as we call it)—the melancholy of the collector, the ecstatic sublimation of that melancholy—all that went as planned. Part I never leaves the Cavaliere. But then, when I started my Part II—which was to have variations on the theme of blood, from the sanguinic Emma, this person bursting with energy and vitality, to the literal blood of the Neapolitan revolution—Emma kidnapped the book. And that permitted the novel to open out (the chapters got longer and longer) into a furor of storytelling and of reflections about justice, war and cruelty. That was the end of the main narrative, told in the third person. The rest of the novel was to be in the first person. A very short Part III: the Cavaliere—delirious, "phlegmatic"—enacts, in words, his dying. That went exactly as I'd imagined it, but then I was back in the Cavaliere-centered world of Part I. There were more surprises for me when I came to write the monologues of Part IV, "choleric": women, angry women, speaking from beyond the grave.

*Why beyond the grave?*

A supplementary fiction, making it more plausible that they are speaking with such insistent, heartfelt, heartbreaking truthfulness. My equivalent of the unmediated, acutely rueful directness of an operatic aria. And how could I resist the challenge of ending each monologue with the character describing her own death?

*Were they always going to be all women?*

Yes, definitely. I always knew the book would end with women's voices, the voices of some of the women characters in the book, who would finally have their say.

*And give the woman's point of view.*

Well, you're assuming that there is a woman's, or female, point of view. I don't. Your question reminds me that, whatever their numbers, women are always

regarded, are culturally constructed, as a minority. It's to minorities that we impute having a unitary point of view. Lord what do women want? etc. Had I ended the novel with the voices of four men, no one would suppose I was giving the male point of view; the differences among the four voices would be too striking. These women are as different from each other as any of four men characters in the novel I might have chosen. Each retells the story (or part of it) already known to the reader from her own point of view. Each has a truth to tell.

*Do they have anything in common?*

Of course. They all know, in different ways, that the world is run by men. So, with respect to the great public events that have touched their lives, they have the insight of the disenfranchised to contribute. But they don't speak only about public events.

*Did you know who the women would be?*

I knew pretty soon that the first three beyond-the-grave monologues would be by Catherine, Emma's mother and Emma. But I was already in the middle of writing Part II, Chapter 6 and boning up on the Neapolitan Revolution of 1799, before I found the speaker of the fourth and last monologue: Eleonora de Fonseca Pimentel, who makes a brief appearance toward the end of that chapter, the narrative climax of the novel. And, finding her, I finally understood the unwrapped gift of that last line, which I'd heard in my head before I'd even started writing—that hers would be the voice that had the right to utter it. The events, public and private, of her life, as well as her atrocious death, follow the historical record, but her principles—her ethical ardor—are the novelist's invention. While I'd felt sympathy for the characters in **The Benefactor** and **Death Kit,** what I feel for the characters in **The Volcano Lover** is love (I had to borrow a stage villain, Scarpia, to have one character in **The Volcano Lover** I didn't love). But I can live with their becoming small at the end. I mean, it *is* the end of the novel. I was thinking in cinematic terms as I did throughout Part II, Chapter 6. Remember how so many French films of the early 1960s ended with the camera in long shot starting to pull back, and the character moving further and further into the rear of the pictured space, becoming smaller and smaller as the credits start to roll. Seen in the ethical wide shot that Eleonora de Fonseca Pimentel provides, Nelson and the Cavaliere and Emma should be judged as harshly as she judges them. Although they do end badly in one way or another, they are extremely privileged, they're still winners—except for poor Emma, and even she has quite a ride for a while. The last word should be given to someone who speaks for victims.

*There are so many voices—stories and sub-stories.*

Until the late 1980s most of what I did in fiction was going on inside a single consciousness, whether it was actually in the first person like **The Benefactor** or nominally in the third person like **Death Kit.** Until **The Volcano Lover,** I wasn't able to give myself permission to tell a story, a real story, as opposed to the adventures of somebody's consciousness. The key was this structure that I borrowed from the Hindemith composition. I'd had the idea for a long time that my third novel was going to have the title *The Anatomy of Melancholy.* But I was resisting it—I don't mean fiction, but *that* novel, whose story hadn't yet been given to me. But it's obvious to me now that I didn't really want to write it. I mean a book written under the aegis of that title, which is just another way of saying "under the sign of Saturn." Most of my work had projected only one of the old temperaments: melancholy. I didn't want to write just about melancholy. The musical structure, with its arbitrary order, freed me. Now I could do all four.

With **The Volcano Lover** the door opened and I have a wider entry. That's the great struggle, for more access and more expressiveness, isn't it? You don't—I'm adapting a phrase of Philip Larkin—write the novels you really want to write. But I think I'm coming closer.

*It seems as if some of your essayistic impulses are also part of the novel's form.*

I suppose it's true that if you strung together all the passages about collecting in **The Volcano Lover** you'd have a discontinuous, aphoristic essay that might well stand on its own. Still, the degree of essayistic speculation in **The Volcano Lover** seems restrained if compared with a central tradition of the European novel. Think of Balzac and Tolstoy and Proust, who go on for pages and pages that could really be excerpted as essays. Or *The Magic Mountain,* perhaps the thinkiest great novel of all. But speculation, rumination, direct address to the reader are entirely indigenous to the novel form. The novel is a big boat. It's not so much that I was able to salvage the banished essayist in myself. It's that the essayist in me was only part of the novelist I've finally given myself permission to be.

*Did you have to do a lot of research?*

You mean reading? Yes, some. The me who is a self-defrocked academic found that part of writing a novel set in the past very pleasurable.

*Why set a novel in the past?*

To escape the inhibitions connected with my sense of the contemporary, my sense of how degraded and debased the way we live and feel and think is now. The past is bigger than the present. Of course, the present is

always there, too. The narrating voice of **The Volcano Lover** is very much of the late twentieth century, driven by late twentieth-century concerns. It was never my idea to write a "you are there" historical novel, even while it was a matter of honor to make the historical substance of the novel as dense and accurate as I could. It felt even more spacious that way. But having decided to give myself one more romp in the past—with **In America,** the novel I'm writing now—I'm not sure it will work out the same way this time.

*When is it set?*

From the mid-1870s almost to the end of the nineteenth century. And, like **The Volcano Lover,** it's based on a real story, that of a celebrated Polish actress and her entourage who left Poland and went to Southern California to create a utopian community. The attitudes of my principal characters are wonderfully exotic to me—Victorian, if you will. But the America they arrive in is not so exotic, though I'd thought that to set a book in late nineteenth-century America would feel almost as remote as late eighteenth-century Naples and London. It's not. There is an astonishing continuity of cultural attitudes in our country. I never cease to be surprised that the America Tocqueville observed in the early 1830s is, in most respects, recognizably the America of the end of the twentieth century—even though the demographic and ethnographic composition of the country has totally changed. It's as if you had changed both the blade and handle of a knife and it is still the same knife.

*Your play,* **Alice in Bed,** *is also about a late nineteenth-century sensibility.*

Yes—Alice James plus the nineteenth century's most famous Alice, Lewis Carroll's. I was directing a production of Pirandello's *As You Desire Me* in Italy, and one day Adriana Asti, who played the lead, said to me—dare I say it?—playfully: "Please write a play for me. And remember, I have to be on stage all the time." And then Alice James, thwarted writer and professional invalid, fell into my head, and I made up the play on the spot and told it to Adriana. But I didn't write it for another ten years.

*Are you going to write more plays? You've always been very involved with theater.*

Yes. I hear voices. That's why I like to write plays. And I've lived in the world of theater artists for much of my life. When I was very young, acting was the only way I knew how to insert myself into what happens on a stage: starting at ten, I was taken on for some kiddie roles in Broadway plays put on by a community theater (this was in Tucson); I was active in student theater—Sophocles, Shakespeare—at the University of Chicago;

and in my early twenties did a bit of summer stock. Then I stopped. I'd much rather direct plays (though not my own). And make films (I hope to make better ones than the four I wrote and directed in Sweden, Israel and Italy in the 1970s and early 1980s). And direct operas, which I haven't done yet. I'm very drawn to opera—the art form that most regularly and predictibly produces ecstasy (at least in this opera lover). Opera is one of the inspirations of *The Volcano Lover*: stories from operas and operatic emotions.

*Does literature produce ecstasy?*

Sure, but less reliably than music and dance: literature has more on its mind. One must be strict with books. I want to read only what I'll want to reread—the definition of a book worth reading once.

*Do you ever go back and reread your work?*

Except to check translations, no. Definitely no. I'm not curious. I'm not attached to the work I've already done. Also, perhaps I don't want to see how it's all the same. Maybe I'm always reluctant to reread anything I wrote more than ten years ago because it would destroy my illusion of endless new beginnings. That's the most American part of me: I feel that it's always a new start.

*But your work is so diverse.*

Well it's supposed to be diverse, though of course there is a unity of temperament, of preoccupation—certain predicaments, certain emotions that recur: ardor and melancholy. And an obsessive concern with human cruelty, whether cruelty in personal relations or the cruelty of war.

*Do you think your best work is still to come?*

I hope so. Or . . . yes.

*Do you think much about the audience for your books?*

Don't dare. Don't want to. But, anyway, I don't write because there's an audience. I write because there is literature.

## Stacy Olster (essay date spring 1995)

SOURCE: Olster, Stacy. "Remakes, Outtakes, and Updates in Susan Sontag's *The Volcano Lover.*" *Modern Fiction Studies* 41, no. 1 (spring 1995): 117-39.

[*In the following essay, Olster analyzes the imagery and the romantic form of* The Volcano Lover, *examining the novel within the context of postmodern theories and focusing on Sontag's use of language to depict the continuity of human experiences and actions through the ages.*]

> Our friend Sir William is well. He has lately got a piece of modernity from England which I am afraid will fatigue and exhaust him more than all the Volcanos and antiquities in the Kingdom of Naples.
>
> —James Byres to the Bishop of Killala, 14 June 1786[1]

The "piece of modernity" in question was Emma Hart, formerly Emily Hart, formerly Emy Lyon, recently arrived in Naples after having been dispatched from London by her erstwhile protector Charles Greville in an attempt to exchange the financial burdens of supporting her for the financial rewards that might accrue from a lucrative marriage. The marriage Greville anticipated for himself did not take place; the one he never contemplated did, though, as Emma became the wife of his uncle William Hamilton on September 6, 1791. In so doing, she, whom nephew had dangled before uncle as "a modern piece of virtu,"[2] one more beautiful item to add to Hamilton's antiquarian collections, became more than just a companion whose status had been sanctioned legally and whose name could be prefaced with the title "Lady." She became the heroine of a romance, peculiarly modern perhaps in that her virtue did not hinge on her virginity (which was long lost), but certainly romantic in that the wedding between low-born servant girl and plenipotentiary of British royalty both confirmed the prospects presented in *Pamela*'s fiction and anticipated those socially unequal liaisons, such as that between William Randolph Hearst and Marion Davies, that later would occur in fact. (And that was before Nelson ever entered the picture.)

That Byres, an art dealer, should refer to Emma as a "piece of modernity" in particular is most appropriate when considering Susan Sontag's re-telling of her story in *The Volcano Lover,* for Sontag—from whose vocabulary the word "postmodernism" is noticeably absent—professes that "most everything we think of as natural is historical and has roots—specifically in the late-eighteenth and early-nineteenth centuries, the so called Romantic revolutionary period" (Cott 49), the very period during which the marriage between Emma and Hamilton and her subsequent affair with Horatio Nelson took place. But that Byres's fears should focus on the possible exhaustion that Hamilton's piece of modernity might exact upon a significantly older benefactor unintentionally raises questions about literary exhaustion—a distinctly postmodern concern—with respect to any contemporary re-telling of the story of the Hamiltons and Lord Nelson as a romance, to cite the subtitle that Sontag appends to her historical novel.

Such distinctly postmodern concerns about literary exhaustion, moreover, are not the only ones that link Sontag to a cultural phenomenon she never identifies by name. Admittedly, different postmodernisms exist for different postmodernist commentators (the, by now, *de rigueur* caveat by which the work of each is prefaced);

that being the case, many of Sontag's remarks neverthe-less conform to almost every defining element upon which commentators agree as basic assumptions. Her evolutionary conception of aesthetic forms, in which "exhausted" forms are periodically "replaced by new forms which are at the same time anti-forms" (*Against Interpretation* 180), actually predates John Barth's 1967 and 1980 pronouncements on exhaustion and replenish-ment respectively. Her rejection of grand narratives, whether exemplified in the myth imposed by Lévi-Strauss upon all cultures over all times or the single scenario by which the North Vietnamese understand their entire history (*Against Interpretation* 79; *Radical Will* [*Styles of Radical Will*] 219), is no different from Lyotard's repudiation of totalizing systems. Her view of images that displace the reality of their referents, as il-lustrated by photography's "hyping up the real" (*On Photography* 169), virtually duplicates Baudrillard's simulacra (not to mention his wording). And if her trac-ing the production of those images within advanced industrial societies does not duplicate Fredric Jameson's wording in quite the same manner (he would prefer multinational), her proposing that "freedom to consume a plurality of images and goods is equated with freedom itself" (*On Photography* 178-179) as the ideological upshot of a proliferation of images corresponds completely with his diagnosis.[3]

Why then the confusion among literary critics, who designate Sontag as, alternately, late modernist and early postmodernist?[4] Part, no doubt, is attributable to Son-tag's refusal to strait-jacket her conception of the modern—the word she typically employs when delineat-ing the qualities listed above—to a single chronological period. In contrast to a theorist like Jameson, who derives postmodernism's historical situation from its multinationalism being the cultural dominant of "our own period" (36), Sontag conceives different cultures experiencing the historical conditions that promote particular kinds of art at different chronological times. Yet far more categoric confusion, I would argue, results from that admiration of the artist/auteur's will and insistence on the work of art's autonomy that signal, particularly in Sontag's early writings, the lingering perspective of the aesthete who adamantly rejects all notions of "putting art to use" and whose anti-interpretive refusal to "dig 'behind' the text, to find a sub-text" presumes that texts are best experienced as ends in themselves rather than as ideologically con-structed (*Against Interpretation* 21, 6).

The importance of a later work like *The Volcano Lover* thus derives, in large part, from the way it directly ad-dresses Sontag's straddling of the modernist/postmodernist divide. Framed with respect to cinematic techniques, yet always aware of the moral element inherent in choosing different forms of representational media, Sontag's recycling the story of the Hamilton-Nelson triangle as a historical novel yields a perfect example of the kind of self-reflexive postmodern novel that Linda Hutcheon has dubbed historiographic metafiction (14). At the same time, Sontag's dubbing that same historical novel a romance recycles a narra-tive form whose representation of an idealized world in which "all the arts and adornments of language are used to embellish the narrative," to quote Robert Scholes and Robert Kellogg (14), "signifies a fiction composed by an individual author for esthetic ends" (248)—a narra-tive, in other words, perfectly suited to the modernist in Sontag who began her career advancing the priority of form over content.

As Gillian Beer has pointed out, however, the romance is not quite as "esthetic" a production as Scholes and Kellogg presume. While the idealized world presented in romance "is never fully equivalent to our own," it nevertheless "must remind us of it if we are to understand it at all" (3)—and for the very didactic purposes of instruction. (After all, once Nelson enters the picture, Emma Hamilton's story shifts from a chronicle of upward mobility to a testament to the folly of flouting social conventions.) As a result, in choosing a form with such an implicit utilitarian component, Sontag provides not just a postmodern parody of an earlier admonitory tale, she provides a postmodern parody of her own early aesthetic pronouncements.

PREVIEWS

"The Romance is an heroic fable, which treats of fabulous persons and things.—The Novel is a picture of real life and manners, and of the times in which it is written," wrote Clara Reeve in *The Progress of Romance* (1785). Continuing with this line of thought, she went on to distinguish between the two literary forms on the basis of the approximation of verisimilitude each provided:

> The Romance in lofty and elevated language, describes what never happened nor is likely to happen.—The Novel gives a familiar relation of such things, as pass every day before our eyes, such as may happen to our friend, or to ourselves; and the perfection of it, is to represent every scene, in so easy and natural a manner, and to make them appear so probable, as to deceive us into a persuasion (at least while we are reading) that all is real, until we are affected by the joys or distresses, of the persons in the story, as if they were our own.
>
> (111)

As Reeve also admitted, such neat distinctions did not apply quite so well in an age of "modern Romances" that "were written with more regularity, and brought nearer to probability," having "tak[en] for their founda-tion some obscure parts of true history, and building fictitious stories upon them," to the extent that "truth and fiction were so blended together, that a common reader could not distinguish them" (64-65). Reeve was not alone in her concern. Distinguishing between those recent works of fiction he termed "comed[ies] of romance" and those earlier works of Knight-Errantry he called "heroic romance[s]," Samuel Johnson warned of the imprudent messages that the modern incarnations could send to their readers:

> In the romances formerly written, every transaction and sentiment was so remote from all that passes among men, that the reader was in very little danger of making any applications to himself; the virtues and crimes were equally beyond his sphere of activity. . . . But when an adventurer is levelled with the rest of the world, and acts in such scenes of the universal drama, as may be the lot of any other man; young spectators fix their eyes upon him with closer attention, and hope by observing his behaviour and success to regulate their own practices, when they shall be engaged in the like part.
>
> (67, 69)

The solution was not to dispense with romance, however, but to employ romance for purposes of moral education, for "under proper restrictions and regulations they will afford much useful instruction, as well as rational and elegant amusement" (Reeve xvi). Thus, Johnson advised careful selection of material, based on his belief that an awareness of the excellence of art imitating nature should be tempered by an awareness of which parts of nature were most worthy of being imitated (70). Yet far from such strictures being an imposition upon romance, they in many ways just made more explicit the duties that were always implicit in a genre that, for all the temporal or social distance separating its stories from their audiences, was allusive from the very beginning. As Gillian Beer notes, "[t]he romance tends to use and re-use well-known stories whose familiarity reassures" in such a way that "remote sources are domesticated and brought close to present experience primarily because they are peopled with figures whose emotions and relationships are directly registered and described with profuse sensuous detail" (2), with results of which Doctor Johnson would most certainly have approved: "Because romance shows us the ideal it is implicitly instructive as well as escapist" (9).

Particularly illustrative of this instructive component of romance is the most familiar precursor of Sontag's own re-telling of the Hamilton-Nelson triangle, Alexander Korda's *That Hamilton Woman* (1941, released in England as *Lady Hamilton*), which, for all its director's emphasizing amorous passion as defining his principal characters' desires while filming ("Vincikém," he reputedly admonished his set designer brother upon viewing the lavish library constructed for Lord Hamilton's home in Naples, "it's a love story. I can't shoot it in a bloody library. Make me a bedroom!" [Korda 150; Walker

152]), was intended from its inception as a piece of propaganda to mobilize support for Britain during World War II. (As Korda informed his screenwriters, "Propaganda needs sugar coating" [Edwards 127].) Suggested as a subject in 1940 by Winston Churchill, who was interested in a vehicle that would promote Britain's historic role as a scourge of tyrants (Hitler here equated with Bonaparte); funded by Korda himself, who had been secretly serving as a courier for transatlantic messages and whose New York City offices were already supplying cover to MI-5 agents gathering intelligence on both German activities in the United States and isolationist sentiments among makers of American foreign policy; and starring Vivien Leigh and Laurence Olivier, who were interested in quick cash to stabilize their finances in order to evacuate their respective children from Britain for the remainder of the war, the movie repeatedly sacrifices the passion of romantic love in order to send the message that "England expects that every man will do his duty," as the sails raised prior to the Battle of Trafalgar signal.

And not only men, as it turns out. "Well, we both have our duty, haven't we?" says Alan Mowbray's doddering William Hamilton to his wife, when asking her to convince Nelson of her imminent move to Cairo so that he will return to London as ordered by the Admiralty. "I feel it my duty to tell you of these things," says Nelson to the Admiralty officers, when imploring them to convince the prime minister not to ratify any peace plan with Napoleon. So clearly, in fact, did the film send its message about the need for continued vigilance against the threat of "men who for the sake of their insane ambition want to destroy what other people build," so loudly did it proclaim the centuries-old role of Britain (a "tiny little bit," as Emma says, when first shown its position on the globe) in maintaining a Commonwealth "in which every little spot has its purpose and value to the balanced line of life" against "madmen" who "want to get hold of the whole world" and "dictate their will to others," that it became Exhibit A in a case brought against Korda by the Senate Foreign Relations Committee. The Committee had accused him of operating an espionage and propaganda center for Britain in the United States—a charge Korda only escaped by virtue of the fact that his scheduled appearance before the committee on December 12, 1941 was preempted by the Japanese bombing of Pearl Harbor five days earlier (Holden 166).[5]

This is not the movie scenario viewers remember, of course, no more than they remember the film's peculiar abstemiousness that qualifies, if not condemns, the very lushness its romantic surroundings are meant to herald: a Nelson who renounces the Neapolitan fete held in his honor as a "tragic carnival" of "paper caps and toy balloons," an Emma who replaces banana curls and oversized white hats with sensible dark clothes and embroidery hoops. That viewers remember a love story is due to the fact that the real romance involved in the film's production occurred off-screen, between two actors (who had just completed a run of *Romeo and Juliet*—another real romance—just prior to the start of filming), each married to another person, who in having "loved before their time," to quote *Life* magazine (20 May 1940), had entered the pantheon of "great American lovers—the Duke and Duchess of Windsor, John Barrymore and Elaine Barrie, and John Smith and Pocahontas" (Vickers 128). It did not matter that the two actors in question had obtained their respective divorces and married in secret before production began, for it was the image of two adulterous actors playing two adulterous historical figures that lent the movie the aura of romance that is now remembered.

According to Sontag, such a sentimental residue is, in part, a function of film's being the artistic medium "most heavily burdened with memory," so much so that "practically all films older than four or five years are saturated with pathos" (**Radical Will** 113, 114). In even greater part, it testifies to the substitution of image for actuality that Sontag, citing the 1843 preface to the second edition of Feuerbach's *The Essence of Christianity,* sees as forming "a widely agreed-on diagnosis" of a society's modernity (**On Photography** 153). Just how relativistic that diagnosis is to different societies and different times, however, is suggested by the particularly heavy burden of cinematic imagery with which Sontag has to contend in **The Volcano Lover,** for Korda's version was not the only movie made of the Hamilton-Nelson affair. Preceding and succeeding it were so many celluloid versions of Lady Hamilton's story produced in so many countries as to make Emma an international commodity: Malvina Longfellow in *Nelson* and *The Romance of Lady Hamilton* (Great Britain, 1918 and 1919), Liane Haid in *The Affairs of Lady Hamilton* (Germany, 1921), Gertrude McCoy in *Nelson* (Great Britain, 1926), Corinne Griffith in *The Divine Lady* (USA, 1929), Michele Mercier in *Lady Hamilton* (West Germany, Italy, France, USA, 1969), and Glenda Jackson in *Bequest to the Nation* (Great Britain, 1973) (Pickard 91-92). Representing the romance of Lady Hamilton and Lord Nelson in a contemporary novel thus means representing an image of an image of an image ad infinitum, the cumulative burdens of which Sontag portrays in the deliberately hyperbolic rhetoric she chooses to delineate the most clichéd (and hence parodied) feature of her narrative, the volcano itself: "a monstrous living body, both male and female," "an abyss," "[a] constant menace," "[t]he slumbering giant that wakes," "[t]he lumbering giant who turns his attentions to *you*" (5-6).

This is not to suggest that Sontag reduces her historical personages to celluloid phantasms and their ménage to mirage. "The question is never whether the events of the past actually took place," Linda Hutcheon remarks in an important qualification:

> The past did exist—independently of our capacity to know it. Historiographic metafiction accepts this philosophically realist view of the past and then proceeds to confront it with an anti-realist one that suggests that, however true that independence may be, nevertheless the past exists *for us—now*—only as traces on and in the present. The absent past can only be inferred from circumstantial evidence.
>
> (73)

And the evidence in question, as Sontag's inclusion of letters and other written documents attests, is specifically textual. Therefore, while Sontag's deconstructed rendering of a bloated and boozy Emma may result in a more accurate Emma, in that it corresponds more closely to the Emma described by those of her time as "a dull creature" (Goethe 316) and "terribly fat" (Vigée Lebrun 68), it does not (and cannot) arrive at a truthful Emma because the evidence upon which she bases her own portrait is itself compromised.

In the case of Emma in particular, more than human bias contributes to that compromised quality of her representations. "Few ever see what is not already inside their heads," Sontag writes in her novel (56), and Emma was very much in the heads of late eighteenth- and early nineteenth-century Europe. ("She is becoming a local marvel with an international reputation, like the volcano" [137].) Having been painted or drawn by George Romney, Sir Joshua Reynolds, Benjamin West, John Raphael Smith, Gavin Hamilton, Frederick Rehberg, Louise-Elisabeth Vigée-Lebrun, Dominique Vivant De Non, Constantina Coltellini, Henry Fuseli, Thomas Lawrence, Jean Baptiste Monnoyer, Wilhelm Tischbein, Angelica Kauffmann, and James Masquerier; and having in those pictures incarnated such varied figures from history, myth, and literature as Joan of Arc, Magdalen, St. Cecilia, Nature, Circe, Medea, Agrippina, Thetis, Calypso, Hebe, Sibyl, Ariadne, innumerable Bacchanates, Shakespeare's Miranda and Constance, Goethe's Iphigenia, and William Hayley's *The Triumph of Temper* heroine Serena, Emma *as visual image* was very much in the heads of Europeans at that time, and often *prior to her arrival* on the Continent. "Hers was the beauty he had adored on canvas, as a statue, on the side of a vase," muses Hamilton, referred to throughout the novel as the Cavaliere, who has himself contributed to the advance of Emma's image by commissioning a portrait of her from Reynolds: "Nothing had ever seemed to him as beautiful as certain objects and images—the reflection, no, the memorial, of a beauty that never really existed, or existed no longer. Now he realized the images were not only the record of beauty but its harbinger, its forerunner" (130). Thus, Sontag amends Feuerbach's conception of a modern age's *preference* for "the image to the thing, the copy to the original" and presents her own version of Baudrillard's précéssion of simulacra that precedes even Baudrillard's conceptualization:[6] because notions of reality change as certainly as notions of image, the "true modern primitivism," in her view, "is not to regard the image as a real thing," but to define what is real to the degree that it conforms to the visual image that precedes it" (*On Photography* 153, 161). To put it another way, when the time comes for Emma to sit as portrait *subject* instead of portrait *model,* as occurs with Romney's painting her as *The Ambassadress* in 1791, there is no Emma left to paint, for, as Romney's Sitters's Diaries show, even the image of Emma married to the Ambassador to the Kingdom of the Two Sicilies precedes her actual marriage to him, the nuptials in question taking place on the third day after her sittings begin (177; Great Britain Arts Council 45).

When Sontag then writes that Emma "does not know who she is anymore, but she knows herself to be ascending" (134), she describes not just the indeterminate subject of postmodern writing, as the apparent ease of the actual Emma's changes of name might indicate (heightened in Sontag's book by the character's remaining without any name until the last page), but the overdetermined subject. Even her transformation is depicted with respect to an old familiar story—"Pygmalion in reverse" (144). Any "ascension" Emma undergoes is simply a function of having replaced less reputable artistic transposers, like London sex therapist Doctor Graham, in whose tableaux vivants she models at fifteen, with more reputable ones, like society portrait painter George Romney, for whom she begins posing two years later (146). Perhaps more to the point, any "ascension" Emma undergoes proves to be short-lived in the extreme, as renderings of the actual historical figure confirm, for at the same time that her body begins to expand, her images start to shrink—from early canvases of her in classical dress (95" × 80-1/2" for Romney's Thetis, 53" × 62" for Vigée-Lebrun's Bacchante, 51" × 38" for Hamilton's Sibyl), to later likenesses of Emma as herself both anatomized (Joseph Nellekens's 22-15/16"-high marble bust, Thomas Laurence's 7-7/8" × 6" penciled head) and miniaturized (Henry Bone's 3-1/2" × 3" ivory). Indeed, so many representations of her begin to appear (a 1-3/8" enamel brooch in Naples's De Ciccio Collection), or are alleged to appear (the figure of Hope on the Duke of Clarence's porcelain dinner service), and in so many different mediums (a 3-1/4" × 2-1/2" tortoise-shell snuff box with miniature ivory inset) that all sense of her uniqueness vanishes.[7] No longer an artifact of high culture, but available to all through mass merchandising, she becomes easily disposable, as in fact happens when she dies in Calais, penniless and indolent.

### FREEZE-FRAMES

The paradigm in Sontag's book for the transformation that Emma undergoes is the transformation of Hamilton's Portland Vase into Etruria Ware at the hands of Josiah Wedgwood, an emblematizing that Sontag highlights through an anthropomorphic rendering of the vase with respect to features of human anatomy. The process delineated is the one sketched by Walter Benjamin concerning the fate of a work of art in an age of mechanical reproduction, and the lesson taught applies as much to the romantic form in which Sontag works as it does to the image of the romantic figure at its center:[8]

> Some twenty replicas of the midnight-blue glass vase were made in smooth black stoneware—the industrial potter and professed lover of simplified forms was to consider it his masterpiece. Wedgwood did not even attempt to match the color or patina of the original and, by simplifying, vitiated its aristocratic contours. The vase's handles lean inward instead of following the curve of the body, the shoulders are more rounded, the neck is shortened. Perhaps the Cavaliere found the slightly dumpy rendering acceptable, having long ago overcome any patrician resistance to this new, mercantile way of spreading the influence of his collections. But he would surely have been startled by the progeny of the vase that the Wedgwood firm began turning out by the tens of thousands in the next century. Olive-green, yellow, pale pink, lilac, lavender-blue, grey, black, and brown Portland vases; Portland vases in many sizes, including small, medium, and large. Everyone could have, should have a Portland vase— and however desired: that was the company's plan. It grew, it shrank, it could be any color. The vase became a notion, a tribute to itself.
>
> Who can really love the Portland Vase now?
>
> (137-138)

According to Donald Barthelme, who portrayed the per-capita production of trash as increasing over the years, the question was moot; with production approaching the one hundred percent mark, disposal of trash was impossible and appreciation inevitable (97). Sontag concurs, if for slightly different reasons. Inheriting an aesthetic artifact that so epitomizes all those overstylized "derelict, inane, *démodé* objects of modern civilization" enables Sontag to treat it as an artifact of Camp, to be dismembered as part of her long-standing Surrealist program of "cultural disburdenment" and then reassembled with the aim of "destroying conventional meanings, and creating new meanings or countermeanings through radical juxtaposition" (*Against Interpretation* 271, 269; *Radical Will* 167). Far from hampering Sontag in her task, the vulgarization that the history of the vase typifies is an absolute prerequisite for such recycling as depends on objects that cannot be considered "high art or [in] good taste"—indeed, "the more despised the material or the more banal the sentiments expressed, the better" (*Against Interpretation* 271).

Complementing the description of the Portland Vase's descent into Wedgwood's crass commodification, therefore, is a second description that traces its later re-valuation in the British Museum after it is "decreated" at the hands of a young man in 1845 and subsequently repaired (345). "Can something shattered, then expertly repaired, be the same, the same as it was?" Sontag asks of the restoration that yields a "new vase, neither replica nor original" (347). Again, the answer that she provides applies as much to the romance narrative that she herself is recycling as it does to the piece of first-century B.C. Roman cameo glass that she describes in it:

> A perfect job of reconstruction, for the time. Until time wears it out. Transparent glue yellows and bulges, making seamless joints visible. The jeopardous decision to attempt a better reconstruction of the vase was made in 1989. First, it had to be restored to its shattered condition. A team of experts immersed the vase in a desiccating solvent to soften the old adhesive, peeled off the one hundred and eighty-nine fragments one by one, washed each in a solution of warm water and non-ionic soap, and reassembled them with a new adhesive, which hardens naturally, and resin, which can be cured with ultraviolet light in thirty seconds. . . . The result is optimal. The vase will last forever, now.
>
> (347)

Not quite. Sontag ends the passage by qualifying the longevity of the reconstructed artifact—"Well, at least another hundred years"—thereby signaling the limited shelf life that any single rendering can hope to have within an ongoing process of aesthetic fluctuation.

Towards the end of reassembling her own version of the Hamilton-Nelson affair, Sontag sets the story of romantic passion commemorated by antecedents against a story of revolutionary passion that in most earlier accounts serves as mere backdrop.[9] Prefigured by the fall of the Bastille, portrayed with respect to those same volcanic eruptions that previously signified amorous desire (Vesuvius's worst eruption since 1631 coinciding here with the Terror in France reaching its climax in 1794 [185]), and embodied in those Jacobin intellectuals and aristocrats who turn Naples into a Parthenopean Republic on January 29, 1799 (celebrated by Vesuvius on the evening of its proclamation [277]), the depiction of political passion in Sontag's book rescues from oblivion those omitted from earlier artistic renderings. In contrast to Emma Hamilton's superfluity of images, these are the people of whom no popular images remain.

Such an absence does not result from lack of desire, however, for Sontag's historically marginalized revolutionaries are as interested in their imagerial renderings as those monarchists at the other end of the political spectrum. And by the time that Sontag introduces the Revolution of 1799 into her book, it is not just the confidante-to-the-Queen-of-Naples Emma who is concerned with the way she will appear to posterity. Nelson, who, as performing self, has envisioned his image "in history paintings, as a portrait bust, as a statue on a pedestal, or even atop a high column in a public square" from the beginning (193), resorts to cosmetic enhancement when the likenesses he has imagined start being crafted upon his return to England (330). True, the martyred revolutionaries contemplate transformation into images at a particular time (prior to their executions) and under particular circumstances (struck by the need to embolden themselves before they die) that the monarchists never have to consider. But in seeking images of themselves that will not just remember them to future generations (much like Julius and Ethel Rosenberg in Robert Coover's *The Public Burning*[10]) but specifically set an example for future generations, they embark upon a program of instruction that is no different from that pursued by those who seek imagerial transposition for different ideological and social purposes.

Nowhere is this common proclivity of romantic passions better illustrated than in Sontag's juxtaposition of Emma Hamilton, privileged for being at center stage of the book's romantic drama, against Eleonora de Fonseca Pimentel, privileged for providing the voice that concludes her historical novel. It is not just a question of Emma's desire for amorous passion to make her "pure sensation" (263) mirroring Fonseca Pimentel's yearning for political passion to turn her into "pure flame" (417). Even more, it is a question of the vehicles through which both women express their differing forms of passion having instruction as their primary ends. "The instruction of the people and their conversion to republican ideas—propaganda—was the only one of the revolution's tasks on which everyone could agree" (280), Sontag writes, and in the newspaper articles that Fonseca Pimentel herself writes, she proposes forms of art that can contribute to that purpose: "puppet shows with more edifying escapades for their Punchinellos," "operas with allegorical subjects such as those being staged in France" (280). Yet when Emma, draped in tunics and shawls, performs her Attitudes before invited company, the poses she assumes in succession are intended to provide edifying illustrations to her guests, precisely the kind of edifying illustrations, in fact, that the romance writer seeks to evoke through recourse to ancient prototypes. Specifically, Emma is to "[i]llustrate the passion" of figures from antiquity (both male and female) because "[w]hat people made of antiquity then was a model for the present, a set of ideal examples," with the past providing "familiar names (the gods, the great sufferers, the heroes and heroines) representing familiar virtues (constancy, nobility, courage, grace)" (146, 148). So successful an instructress does Emma become, eventually, that when she poses as successive figures from an earlier age,

> [s]he was not just impersonating Cleopatra now, she was Cleopatra, ensnaring Antony; a Dido whose charms detain Aeneas; an Armida who has bewitched Rinaldo— the familiar stories from ancient history and epic everyone knew, in which a man destined for glory makes a brief stop in the course of his great mission,

succumbs to the charms of an irresistible woman, and stays. And stays. And stays.

(235-236)

That Emma misses the whole point of the poses she incarnates results from the fact that the images with which she seeks to instruct are static, each governed by the selection of a single moment, "the right moment, the moment that presents meaning, that sums up the essence of a character, a story, an emotion," the combination of which leaves Emma not with a continuous narrative, but with a set of snapshots, "a living slide show of the iconic moments of ancient myth and literature" (146). And because the significant moment privileged by neoclassical aesthetics is one that "showed suffering with decorum, dignity in the midst of horror," it "evoked the worst without showing us the worst" (295). Therefore, when those revolutionaries about to mount the scaffold seek to "show an example" through "the didactic art of the significant moment," these "future citizens of the world of history painting" choose an image of themselves that represents stoicism in the face of death, based on the assumption that "[a]n image, even of the most lamentable events, should also give hope. Even the most horrifying stories can be told in a way that does not make us despair" (295).

Unfortunately, in choosing an image that omits the full extent of the horror they undergo, they leave the future citizens of the world who view their (imagined) portraits unable to reconstruct the story that would provide the greatest amount of edification. Moreover, in assuming that image-makers control image apprehension, they neglect the role of what Victor Burgin has called the seeing subject and that subject's "preconstituted field of discourse" with which images interact to produce a story (69, 65). When all those who live by the image in Sontag's novel (which is to say everybody) thus try to reconstruct a historical narrative, they invariably get the story wrong. Nelson, whose dreams even take the form of disconnected pictures, casts the story of Emma and Hamilton as a sentimental morality play: "the fallen woman, taken under the Cavaliere's protection, who had become an irreproachable wife" (196, 195). Queen Maria Carolina of Naples tells the story of a tragic diva (Sontag's recycling of *Tosca*), and "the whole story came out, backward" (325). Emma relates to dinner guests the tale of a band of murderers who occupy the Cavaliere's courtyard a few weeks after her arrival, not realizing that the events she describes have occurred a quarter of a century earlier and not even to her (170-172).

What Emma's complete bypassing of all sense of temporal relations reveals, finally, is the ahistorical component of the static image, typified for Sontag in the photographic image that atomizes experience into "a series of unrelated, freestanding particles" and turns "history, past and present, [into] a set of anecdotes and *faits divers*" (*On Photography* 23). Psychologically useful, such a separation of actions and consequences can "suppress, or at least reduce, moral and sensory queasiness" (*On Photography* 40): the Cavaliere, who wants "nothing to disturb the beautiful images he preserved of Naples," is spared the hangings, shootings, and beheadings of revolutionaries that occur in his fair city, for Naples remains "like a picture," always "seen from the same point of view" to those who view it from aboard Nelson's ship (284, 294). As a vehicle for transmitting any edifying knowledge of history, however, the static image proves extremely limited. As Sontag again illustrates with respect to the photograph, the static image may goad conscience but never result in any "ethical or political knowledge," and, as a result, "[t]he knowledge gained through still photographs will always be some kind of sentimentalism, whether cynical or humanist. It will be a knowledge at bargain prices" (*On Photography* 24).

The question, then, concerns what vehicle will transmit the experience of the past most efficaciously—pictures or words, images or narratives. As mediating texts, neither, of course, can presume to transmit that experience accurately. Nonetheless, in Sontag's view, the two encourage very different responses, complicity or responsibility, from their audiences: "While images invite the spectator to identify with what is seen, the presence of words makes the spectator into a critic" (*Radical Will* 185). The two, moreover, encourage very different temporal and spatial responses in particular. "In contrast to the amorous relation, which is based on how something looks, understanding is based on how it functions," she writes. "And functioning takes place in time, and must be explained in time. Only that which narrates can make us understand" (*On Photography* 23). Writing *of* a period in English history when only ten thousand people read newspapers and *during* a period of history in which increased literacy is matched by increased media imagery, Sontag has no choice but to maintain "the right velocity of narration" (328, 349), as she describes it, in order for her work to facilitate greater understanding. For that she must move from the image of abbreviated temporality to the narrative of conscious temporal relations.

### Coming Attractions

Ironically, the narrative of temporal relations that Sontag composes as a romance novel takes its cue from the insufficiency of words to describe fully what needs to be communicated, particularly when the subject at hand evokes the most extreme form of sensory response. "How can the Cavaliere communicate to an auditor *how* disgusting the King is," she questions, only to conclude that he cannot: "An odor. A taste. A touch. Impossible to describe" (44). How can the Cavaliere communicate how beautiful the cameos, vases, and paintings that decorate his treasure-congested study are? "Their forms, he wrote, were simple, beautiful, and varied beyond description" (73). So frequently do such moments of inadequacy occur, in fact, that *"Impossible to Describe"* turns into a heading for a list (129).

Faced with this representational insufficiency of language, the Cavaliere opts for narratives that sanitize history. "He only relates," Sontag writes of his experiences with Naples's flatulent young king, "and in the relating, the sheer odiousness of it dwindles into a tale, nothing to get wrought up over" (44). Hamilton may ease the burden of his conscience by reminding himself that the king is "just one item" that beggars description, but Sontag's Naples, a "kingdom of the immoderate, of excess, of overflow" (44), is a place with more than one source of odious behavior that beggars description in words—this, after all, is a city where people rip apart live animals tied to the base of a mountain of food built for all court celebrations. "And where everyone is shocked is a place where everyone tells stories" (38). Safe stories, like those of the Cavaliere; stories designed to minimize, not dramatize, shock and spectacle.

Sontag, who has long advocated an art of "shock therapy" to awaken those in the West from the "massive sensory anesthesia" that she sees plaguing them since the time of the Industrial Revolution (*Against Interpretation* 302), takes the opposite approach. If the narrative of linear temporal relations cannot convey the extent of her subject's shock adequately, she fractures the seamless narrative of strict chronology to suggest the shock of her subject analogously, with Hamilton's Vesuvius juxtaposed against Las Vegas's fifty-four-foot-high fiberglass replica (327); Pompeii and Herculaneum against Hiroshima and Nagasaki (113); William Beckford's Fonthill Abbey against Ludwig II's "Disneyesque" Neuschwanstein (344); and gallows against gas chambers (217). With language from one period yoked to phenomena of another, winds of southern Europe promote "a collective PMS that comes on seasonally" (86), and a naval commander who disobeys orders becomes a hero "who has in effect gone AWOL" (319).

The method informing the whole is cinematic, reflecting Sontag's belief that "the distinctive cinematic unit is not the image but the principle of connection between the images" (*Radical Will* 108), and the specific governing principle of connection is montage. Emma's emotionally charged character raises questions about women's power in patriarchal societies, and with a "flash-forward" Sontag relates the tale of Tosca (309), the story she later has Queen Maria Carolina relate in summary form backwards (325). The Cavaliere normally observes Naples from behind windows and terraces, and with a "reverse shot" Sontag shows how he later

views it while at sea aboard the *Foudroyant* during the 1799 Revolution (298).

"You'll lose track of the time," the novel's narrator warns in Sontag's opening *mise-en-scène* in a Manhattan flea market, spring of 1992, prior to the jump-cut that leaves her in a London picture auction, autumn of 1772 (3). In a very real way one does, of course, for what these fragmentations of linear time and space do— techniques comparable to the "rhetoric of disorientation" that Sontag admires in the films of Jean-Luc Godard (*Radical Will* 165)—is make past, present, and future equally present, as suggested in the oxymoronic phrase that introduces the story of Tosca as an illustration of woman's powerlessness that "a flash-forward may serve to recall" (309). As a result, the narrative perspective of the novel grants its readers the same kind of "dual citizenship in the past and in the future" that the Neapolitan fortune teller Hamilton consults is granted by her oracular vision (58). "The future exists in the present, she said. The future, as she described it, seemed to be the present gone awry" (58). The coming attractions, in short, are already here.

As Efrosina also warns the Cavaliere, "[t]he future is a hole. . . . When you fall in it, you cannot be sure how far you will go" (55). And what one falls into within Sontag's comparativist history are Derridean "[m]oments of slippage, when anything seems possible and not everything makes sense" (120), the most compelling of which concern that concept of cultural hybridity defined by Homi Bhabha and Edward Said. Naples, the wealthiest, most populous city on the Italian peninsula, and, "after Paris, the second largest city on the European continent" (20), becomes "Ireland (or Greece, or Turkey, or Poland)," another "refractory colony, or a country on Europe's margin," to be disciplined and dealt with accordingly (298). Palermo is shown to be to Naples what Saigon is to Hanoi, and what Rio is to São Paulo, and what Calcutta is to Delhi—a southern culture in which people who are "never on time" (but who do possess "a wonderful sense of rhythm") just "charm, charm, charm"—only what Palermo is to Naples is also what Naples is to Rome (225-226). Perhaps most unsettling, the 1799 Neapolitan "fairy-tale revolution" doomed to defeat from the very beginning is also presented as the republic that seeks, in Sontag's deliberately loaded phrasing, "to win the hearts and minds of the people" in the five short (renamed) months of its existence (278, 281).

More than anything else, these moments of slippage call into question all notions of historical progress. The King of Naples decrees that animals tied to the mountain of food are to be slaughtered first and then hung in quarters on a fence. "As you see," he tells the Cavaliere, "there is progress even here, in this city" (44), a statement whose meaning its own ironic tone immediately cancels. In contrast, then, to a novel like *Ragtime,* which undermines complacent notions about America "then" being better than "now" in order to show historical continuities and patterns between the early and late periods of the twentieth century, *The Volcano Lover* offers contiguities and parallels between circumstances that prevail in those late capitalist countries that Sontag terms modern. Viewed in this context, turn-of-the-century (eighteenth to nineteenth) Naples in Sontag's Romantic self-fashioning (to parody Stephen Greenblatt) is no better *or* worse than turn-of-the-century (twentieth to twenty-first) America—a statement as unsatisfying to liberals who harbor hopes for the future as it is to conservatives who venerate the inheritance of the past.

Writing about the seventeen-million-dollar villa built by J. Paul Getty to house his antiquities and paintings, an architectural structure whose garish appearance seemed at odds with the Renaissance and Baroque art contained within it, Joan Didion saw a similar lesson being taught: that "the past was perhaps different from the way we like to perceive it," that "[t]he old world was once discomfitingly new, or even nouveau," finally, that "not much changes," indeed, "that we were never any better than we are and will never be any better than we were"—a lesson she considered "a profoundly unpopular political statement" (76). As Didion also noted, the Getty was modeled upon a villa buried in 79 A.D. by mud from Vesuvius, unearthed in part by digging around Herculaneum that took place during the eighteenth century (75). Writing about the eighteenth century directly, Sontag offers the massiveness of Vesuvius itself, "instructive as well as thrilling" (6), both "[e]ntertainment and apocalypse" (129), whose unpredictable yet imminent eruptions signal the sense of historical irresolution to which the lesson of her book is ultimately devoted: the "permanent modern scenario" she sketched earlier in which "apocalypse looms . . . and it doesn't occur. And it still looms" (*AIDS* [*AIDS and Its Metaphors*] 175). At the time she first depicted that scenario, she, fittingly, framed it as cinematic narrative, "a long-running serial." Equally fitting was the name she gave to the soap opera that comprised her view of the process of history: not "Apocalypse Now," but "Apocalypse From Now On" (*AIDS* 176)—a variation on another old scenario admittedly, but, then again, what artifact in Sontag's aesthetic flea market isn't?

### Notes

1. James Byres, Historical Manuscripts Collection, London, 24: Rutland MSS, vol. 3, 311; qtd. in Fraser, *Emma, Lady Hamilton* 80. I am indebted to Catherine Belling for bringing this biography, as well as the pamphlet accompanying the 1972 *Lady Hamilton in Relation to the Art of Her Time* exhibition, to my attention.

2. Charles Greville, letter to William Hamilton, 10 Mar. 1785, qtd. in Fraser 55.

3. See Barth, "The Literature of Exhaustion" 29-34, and "The Literature of Replenishment" 65-71; Lyotard, *The Postmodern Condition: A Report on Knowledge* 37-41; Baudrillard, *Simulacra and Simulation* 1-42; and Jameson, *Postmodernism, or, The Cultural Logic of Late Capitalism* 1-54.

4. For an extended discussion of Sontag's sensibilities as reflecting the paradoxes of late modernist aesthetics, see Sayres 10-12. For representative citations of Sontag as an early postmodernist, see Brooker 10-11, 17; Maltby 17; and Hutcheon 10. For consideration of Sontag's theorizing as compared with that of more recent French post-structuralists, see Kennedy 30-31.

5. Even Nelson's return to Naples to evacuate the Hamiltons and the royal family—problematic in that it was in direct defiance of Lord Keith's order to take his fleet to the Mediterranean—is presented in Korda's film as an act of duty, justified by Nelson with the phrase, "I will not see those I love and those I owe loyalty to left alone." So big a fan of the finished film was Winston Churchill that he had a copy shown to those accompanying him on the *Prince of Wales* for the Atlantic Charter meeting with Franklin Delano Roosevelt in August of 1941. He also had a private print of his own kept at Chartwell that he used for private screenings (Vickers 132).

6. Baudrillard's "La précéssion de simulacres" appeared in *Traverses* 11 (1978): 3-37. Sontag's emendation of Feuerbach first appeared in the *New York Review of Books,* 23 June 1977: 25-27, as part of her essay on "Photography Unlimited" prior to its inclusion in *On Photography.*

7. For a listing of the dimensions of these renderings of Emma Hamilton, see *Lady Hamilton in Relation to the Art of Her Time,* a pamphlet accompanying the 18 July—16 October 1972 exhibition of the same name, organized by the Arts Council of Great Britain and the Greater London Council at the Iveagh Bequest, Kenwood.

8. For Sontag's reading of Walter Benjamin as exhibiting a paradigmatically Surrealist temperament, see the title essay in *Under the Sign of Saturn* 109-134.

9. For an earlier example of Sontag's portrayal of political revolution as an expression of passion, see her 1969 piece, "Some Thoughts on the Right Way (for us) to Love the Cuban Revolution" 6, 10, 14, 16, 18-19.

10. Coover's sympathetic portrayal of this desire in *The Public Burning* is, in large part, a response to those much more critical charges lodged against Julius and Ethel Rosenberg while incarcerated. See Fiedler 25-45, and Warshow 69-81.

### Works Cited

Barth, John. "The Literature of Exhaustion." *Atlantic Monthly* Aug. 1967: 29-34.

———. "The Literature of Replenishment." *Atlantic Monthly* Jan. 1980: 65-71.

Barthelme, Donald. *Snow White.* 1967. New York: Atheneum, 1980.

Baudrillard, Jean. "La précéssion de simulacres." *Traverses* 10 (1978): 3-37.

———. *Simulacra and Simulation.* 1981. Trans. Sheila Faria Glaser. Ann Arbor: U of Michigan P, 1994.

Beer, Gillian. *The Romance.* London: Methuen, 1970.

Brooker, Peter. "Introduction: Reconstructions." *Modernism/Postmodernism.* London: Longman, 1992. 1-33.

Burgin, Victor. *The End of Art Theory: Criticism and Postmodernity.* Atlantic Highlands: Humanities Press International, 1986.

Coover, Robert. *The Public Burning.* 1977. New York: Bantam, 1978.

Cott, Jonathan. "The *Rolling Stone* Interview: Susan Sontag." *Rolling Stone* 4 Oct. 1979: 46-53.

Didion, Joan. "The Getty." 1977. *The White Album.* 1979. New York: Pocket, 1980. 74-78.

Doctorow, E. L. *Ragtime.* New York: Random, 1975.

Edwards, Anne. *Vivien Leigh: A Biography.* New York: Simon and Schuster, 1977.

Fiedler, Leslie A. "Afterthoughts on the Rosenbergs." 1952. *An End To Innocence: Essays On Politics and Culture.* 2nd ed. 1955. New York: Stein and Day, 1972. 25-45.

Fraser, Flora. *Emma, Lady Hamilton.* New York: Knopf, 1987.

Goethe, J. W. *Italian Journey: [1786-1788].* Trans. W. H. Auden and Elizabeth Mayer. 1962. New York: Penguin, 1970.

Great Britain. Arts Council of Great Britain and Greater London. Council at Iveagh Bequest, Kenwood. *Lady Hamilton in Relation to the Art of Her Time.* Shenval, 1972.

Holden, Anthony. *Laurence Olivier.* New York: Atheneum-Macmillan, 1988.

Hutcheon, Linda. *The Politics of Postmodernism.* London: Routledge, 1989.

Jameson, Fredric. *Postmodernism, or, The Cultural Logic of Late Capitalism.* Durham: Duke UP, 1991.

Johnson, Samuel. *Rasselas, Poems, and Selected Prose.* Ed. Bertrand H. Bronson. 1958. San Francisco: Rinehart, 1971.

Kennedy, Liam. "Precious Archaeology: Susan Sontag and the Criticism of Culture." *Journal of American Studies* 24 (1990): 23-39.

Korda, Michael. *Charmed Lives: A Family Romance.* New York: Random, 1979.

Lyotard, Jean-François. *The Postmodern Condition: A Report on Knowledge.* 1979. Trans. Geoff Bennington and Brian Massumi. Minneapolis: U of Minnesota P, 1984.

Maltby, Paul. *Dissident Postmodernists: Barthelme, Coover, Pynchon.* Philadelphia: U of Pennsylvania P, 1991.

Pickard, Roy. *Who Played Who in the Movies: An A-Z.* New York: Schocken, 1981.

Reeve, Clara. *The Progress of Romance and the History of Charoba, Queen of Egypt.* 1785. New York: Facsimile Text Society, 1930.

Sayres, Sohnya. *Susan Sontag: The Elegiac Modernist.* New York: Routledge, 1990.

Scholes, Robert, and Robert Kellogg. *The Nature of Narrative.* 1966. New York: Oxford UP, 1976.

Sontag, Susan. *Against Interpretation.* 1966. New York: Anchor, 1990.

———. *Illness as Metaphor and AIDS and Its Metaphors.* 1978, 1989. New York: Anchor, 1990.

———. *On Photography.* 1977. New York: Anchor, 1990.

———. "Photography Unlimited." *New York Review of Books* 23 June 1977: 25-32.

———. "Some Thoughts on the Right Way (for us) to Love the Cuban Revolution." *Ramparts* April 1969: 6, 10, 14, 16, 18-19.

———. *Styles of Radical Will.* 1969. New York: Anchor, 1991.

———. *Under the Sign of Saturn.* 1980. New York: Anchor, 1991.

———. *The Volcano Lover: A Romance.* New York: Farrar, 1992.

*That Hamilton Woman.* Dir. and prod. Alexander Korda. Written by Walter Reisch and R. C. Sherriff. United Artists, 1941.

Vickers, Hugo. *Vivien Leigh.* Boston: Little, Brown, 1988.

Vigée Lebrun, Madame Louise-Elisabeth. *Memoirs of Madame Vigée Lebrun.* Trans. Lionel Strachey. New York: Doubleday, 1903.

Walker, Alexander. *Vivien: The Life of Vivien Leigh.* New York: Weidenfeld and Nicholson, 1987.

Warshow, Robert. "The 'Idealism' of Julius and Ethel Rosenberg." 1953. *The Immediate Experience: Movies, Comics, Theatre and Other Aspects of Popular Culture.* New York: Doubleday, 1962.

## Roger Kimball (essay date February 1998)

SOURCE: Kimball, Roger. "Reflections on a Cultural Revolution-VI: The New Sensibility." *New Criterion* 16, no. 6 (February 1998): 5-11.

[*In the following essay, Kimball explores the inconsistencies he has found in several of Sontag's essays. Kimball argues against many of Sontag's conclusions, noting that she frequently contradicts herself in her own essays.*]

> Everyone who feels bored cries out for change. With this demand I am in complete sympathy, but it is necessary to act in accordance with some settled principle. . . . *Nil admirari* [nothing is to be marveled at] is . . . the real philosophy. No moment must be permitted so great a significance that it cannot be forgotten when convenient; each moment ought, however, to have so much significance that it can be recollected at will. . . . From the beginning one should keep the enjoyment under control, never spreading every sail to the wind in any resolve; one ought to devote oneself to pleasure with a certain suspicion, a certain wariness, if one desires to give the lie to the proverb which says that no one can eat his cake and have it too.
>
> —Søren Kierkegaard, *Either/Or*

> Like all great aesthetes, Barthes was an expert at having it both ways.
>
> —Susan Sontag, **"On Roland Barthes"**

In an earlier installment of these reflections, we noted that America's cultural revolution, despite the insurrectionary rhetoric that accompanied it, differed in important ways from political revolutions as traditionally understood. To be sure, the endless demonstrations, sit-ins, rallies, petitions, marches, and "non-negotiable demands" that were such a prominent feature of the 1960s and 1970s had myriad political ramifications. Everything that has come under the Orwellian rubric of "affirmative action" is a case in point. Nevertheless, the result of the counterculture's political activism was not to overthrow a government but to transform morals—using "morals" broadly, as Matthew Arnold did in his famous essay on Wordsworth, to encompass "whatever bears upon the question, 'how to live.'"

There are other distinctions to be observed. For if America's cultural revolution must be distinguished on one side from genuine political revolution, so it must be distinguished on another side from a genuine intellectual or artistic revolution. Of course, talk about "innovation," "creativity," and a new "avant-garde" was deafening in the 1960s and 1970s. But looking back on that period—and looking around now at its sordid aftermath—one is left mostly with the embarrassing sensation of hyperactive sterility. What was all the sound and fury about? What did that putative unleashing of "creativity" create? It is as if an entire generation had somehow conspired to infantilize itself, substituting overblown intellectual impersonation for serious cultural endeavor. When one compares it to the last truly important era of artistic and cultural innovation—the era of high modernism, which culminated in the 1920s—one is struck above all by the extent to which the "radical" artistic and intellectual gestures of the counterculture were unwitting repetitions or jejune parodies of ideas that had seemed old before World War II.

Partly, no doubt, what we saw in the Sixties was a venerable case of history repeating itself as farce. But if its combination of vacuousness, self-infatuation, and political grandstanding seems mostly preposterous now, that should not lead us to underestimate its destructive effects. America's cultural revolution was not itself an intellectual or artistic revolution; but it nevertheless has had immense consequences for artistic and intellectual life. It is not simply that there has been a disastrous lowering of standards. There has also been a wholesale attack on the very idea of standards: a process of blurring or (more accurately) inversion that has made critical discrimination seem like an antiquarian pursuit. What we have witnessed is a corruption of taste that is at the same time the triumph of a certain species of aestheticizing decadence.

No one has more lovingly delineated, or more perfectly epitomized, the mandarin ambiguities of this situation than Susan Sontag, the critic, novelist, playwright, filmmaker, theatrical director, professional aesthete, and political radical. Sontag burst upon the New York intellectual scene in the mid Sixties with a handful of remarkable essays: **"Notes on 'Camp'"** (1964) and **"On Style"** (1965) in *Partisan Review*; **"Against Interpretation"** (1964) in *Evergreen Review*; **"One Culture and the New Sensibility"** (1965), an abridged version of which first appeared in *Mademoiselle*; and several essays and reviews in the newly launched *New York Review of Books*. (Sontag contributed a short review of Simone Weil's essays for the *Review*'s inaugural issue in 1963.) Almost overnight, it seemed, these essays electrified intellectual debate and catapulted their author to celebrity.

Not that Sontag's efforts were unanimously praised. Far from it. The critic John Simon, to take just one example, wondered in a sharp letter to *Partisan Review* whether Sontag's **"Notes on 'Camp'"** was itself "only a piece of 'camp.'" No, the important thing was the *attentiveness* of the response. Pro or con, Sontag's essays galvanized debate: indeed, they contributed mightily to changing the very climate of intellectual debate. Her demand, at the end of **"Against Interpretation,"** that "in place of a hermeneutics we need an erotics of art"; her praise of camp, the "whole point" of which "is to dethrone the serious"; her encomium to the "new sensibility" of the Sixties, whose acolytes, she observed, "have broken, whether they know it or not, with the Matthew Arnold notion of culture, finding it historically and humanly obsolescent": in these and other such pronouncements Sontag offered not arguments but a mood, a tone, an atmosphere.

Never mind that a lot of it was mere verbiage: it was nevertheless *irresistible* verbiage. It somehow didn't matter, for example, that the whole notion of "an erotics of art" was arrant nonsense. Everyone likes sex, and talking about "erotics" seems so much sexier than talking about "sex"; and of course everyone likes art: how was it that no one had thought of putting them together in this clever way before? Who would bother with something so boring as mere "interpretation"—which, Sontag had suggested, was these days "reactionary, impertinent, cowardly, stifling," "the revenge of the intellect upon art"—when he could have (or pretend to have) an erotics instead?

It was a remarkable performance, all the more so as Sontag was then barely thirty years old. In truth, there had always been something precocious—not to say hasty—about her. Born in New York City in 1933, she had been brought up mostly in Arizona and California (her father died in 1938; Sontag is her stepfather's name). She began skipping grades when she was six. Graduating from high school when she was barely sixteen, Sontag went first to the University of California at Berkeley and then, in the fall of 1949, to the University of Chicago. In December of 1950, when she was seventeen, she met the critic Philip Rieff (author of *The Triumph of the Therapeutic* [1966], among other works), then a twenty-eight-year-old instructor, who was giving a course that Sontag audited. As she was leaving after the first class, Sontag recalled, "He was standing at the door and he grabbed my arm and asked my name. I apologized and told him I had only come to audit. 'No, what's your name?' he persisted. 'Will you have lunch with me.'" Married ten days later, they found themselves with a son—who would grow up to be the left-wing writer David Rieff—in 1952 and a divorce in 1958. Meanwhile Sontag, having picked up a bachelor's degree at Chicago after three years, had also spent time studying at Harvard—where she took a master's degree in philosophy—and at Oxford and the Sorbonne. Armed with a battery of French names few people knew about here, she returned to New York in 1959, worked briefly at *Commentary* and elsewhere before taking up, in 1960, a teaching position at Columbia in (*mirabile dictu*) the department of religion.

But all this was prolegomenon. Looking back on it now, it seems obvious that throughout those years Sontag was constructing, burnishing, perfecting—what to call it? A style, partly; a tone, assuredly; but in the end, perhaps, it might be best described as an *altitude.* By

the time she began publishing in highbrow journals like *Partisan Review,* Sontag had made herself the mistress of a new brand of cultural hauteur. It was ferociously intellectual without necessarily being intelligent; it deployed, but did not rely upon, arguments. Its invariable direction was *de haut en bas.* "Formal" and "formalist" are among Sontag's favorite words. In her early essays, she never tires of telling us that works of art must be judged for their formal properties, not their "content." If we judge Sontag's own essays in "formal" terms, they may appear as models of chic daring; but judged in terms of content, they are little more than a repository of intellectual clichés—witness the insistence, as if it were something original, on judging art for its formal excellence and not its "message," one of the hoariest of modern half-truths. "The satisfactions of *Paradise Lost,*" she writes in **"On Style,"** do not lie in its views on God and man, but in the superior kinds of energy, vitality, expressiveness which are incarnated in the poem." What she doesn't say is that the energy, vitality, and expressiveness of Milton's poem are unintelligible apart from the truths it aspires to articulate. If this were not the case, *Paradise Lost* might just as well be about baked beans as about "justify[ing] the ways of God to man."

It goes without saying that what we are dealing with here is only partly a matter of *intellectual* style. Sontag was creating a *Gesamtkunstwerk,* and it had sartorial as well as cerebral leitmotifs. We get a hint of this in the introduction to **Conversations with Susan Sontag,** a collection of interviews published in 1995. The editor of that volume quotes a description of an author's photograph depicting Sontag "in black trousers, black polo-neck and wearing cowboy boots. She is stretched out on a window-sill with a pile of books and papers under her arm. The seriousness is lightened by the faint flicker of pleasure: this is an image which pleases the author. At home, with books, wearing black." It is not said whether this was before or after the publication of *Texas Boots,* David Rieff's celebration of cowboy boots. In any event, it is clear that a less physically attractive woman could never have aspired to be Susan Sontag.

It is hardly surprising that one of Sontag's indisputable contributions has been to the art of pretension—or perhaps it should be called "intellectual impersonation." It is not every day, for example, that a writer, asked when his interest in "the moral" began, will reply as did Sontag that

> I believe that it began when I was three years old. In other aspects, I am not very clear about when I was young, which is a source of strength and a problem at the same time. I remember that I would think much on the things that I think about now before I was ten years old.

It is almost enough to make one join Sontag in her campaign against interpretation.

In one early essay, Sontag described the bombastic dramatic events known as "happenings" as "an art of radical juxtaposition." The same can be said of her essays, singly and taken in comparison with one another. What she produces are not essays, really, but verbal collages. *Against Interpretation* (1966), her first collection, contains pieces on Sartre *and* science fiction novels, the literary criticism of the Marxist Georg Lukács *and* a paean to Jack Smith's *Flaming Creatures,* a cult film in which, as Sontag cheerfully puts it, "a couple of women and a much larger number of men, most of them clad in flamboyant thrift-shop women's clothes, frolic about, pose and posture, dance with one another, and enact various scenes of voluptuousness, sexual frenzy, romance, and vampirism," including scenes of masturbation, gang rape, and oral sex. Sontag castigates the "indifference or hostility" of "the mature intellectual and artistic community" to this "small but valuable work" in the tradition of "the cinema of shock." She praises the "extraordinary charge and beauty of [Smith's] images" and—a signature Sontag touch—the film's "exhilarating freedom from moralism." Sontag is very big on that "exhilarating freedom from moralism." Acknowledging that "by ordinary standards"—but not, of course, by hers—*Flaming Creatures* is composed of themes that are "perverse, decadent," she insists that really the film "is about joy and innocence," not least because it is "both too full of pathos and too ingenuous to be prurient."

This sort of thing was catnip to the intellectual establishment of the mid 1960s. Not that any of it was new, exactly. *Nostalgie de la boue* has long been a defining disease of bourgeois intellectuals, and has been effectively peddled by many before the advent of S. Sontag. But few if any writers commanded Sontag's air of perfect knowingness, which managed to combine commendation, indifference, and disdain with breathtaking virtuosity.

In his review of *Under the Sign of Saturn,* a collection of Sontag's essays published in 1980, John Simon noted that "nothing succeeds better than highbrow endorsement of lowbrow tastes." Sontag's great trick was not merely to endorse lowbrow tastes, but to create the illusion that for the truly sophisticated all intellectual, artistic, and moral distinctions of merit were otiose, dispensable, *de trop.* This is one reason that she championed the camp sensibility. "Camp," she observed, "is the consistently aesthetic experience of the world. It incarnates a victory of 'style' over 'content,' 'aesthetics' over 'morality,' of irony over tragedy." Camp, she went on to say, "is a solvent of morality," concluding with one of her famous paradoxes: "The ultimate Camp statement: it's good *because* it's awful." (She immediately adds: "of course, one can't always say that. Only under certain conditions"—thus letting you know that not just anyone is allowed to indulge in contradiction and win praise for it.)

One of Sontag's characteristic productions was **"The Pornographic Imagination"** (1967), which appears in *Styles of Radical Will* (1969), her second collection. In essence, it is a defense of pornography, not, of course, as something merely salacious—that would grant too much recognition of its "content"—but for its "formal" resources as a means of transcendence. It is hardly news that sexual ecstasy has often poached on religious rhetoric and vice versa; nor is it news that pornography often employs religious metaphors. That is part of its perversity. But Sontag decides to take pornography seriously as a solution to the spiritual desolations of modern secular culture. Writing about Pauline Réage's pornographic *Story of O,* she solemnly tells us that

> O is an adept; whatever the cost in pain and fear, she is grateful for the opportunity to be initiated into a mystery. That mystery is the loss of self. O learns, she suffers, she changes. Step by step she becomes more what she is, a process identical with the emptying out of herself. In the vision of the world presented by *The Story of O,* the highest good is the transcendence of personality.

Which is about as accurate as saying that the Marquis de Sade's books are essentially about exercise.

One of Sontag's great gifts has been her ability to enlist her politics in the service of her aestheticism. For her, it is the work of a moment to move from admiring pornography—or at least "the pornographic imagination"—to castigating

> the traumatic failure of capitalist society to provide authentic outlets for the perennial human flair for high-temperature visionary obsession, to satisfy the appetite for exalted self-transcending modes of concentration and seriousness. The need of human beings to transcend "the person" is no less profound than the need to be a person, an individual.

**"The Pornographic Imagination,"** like most of Sontag's essays, is full of powerful phrases, seductive insights, and extraordinary balderdash. Sontag dilates on pornography's "peculiar access to some truth." What she doesn't say is that *The Story of O* (for example) presents not an instance of mystical fulfillment but a graphic depiction of human degradation. Only someone who had allowed "form" to triumph over "content" could have ignored this. In a way, **"The Pornographic Imagination"** is itself the perfect camp gesture: for if camp aims to "dethrone the serious" it is also, as Sontag points out, "deadly serious" about the demotic and the trivial. Sontag is a master at both ploys. Having immersed herself in the rhetoric of traditional humanistic learning, she is expert at using it against itself. This of course is a large part of what has made her writing so successful among would-be "avant-garde" intellectuals: playing with the empty forms of traditional moral and aesthetic thought, she is able to appear simultaneously unsettling and edifying, daringly "beyond good and evil" and yet passionately *engagé*.

**"The Pornographic Imagination"** also exhibits the seductive Sontag hauteur in full flower. After telling us that pornography can be an exciting version of personal transcendence, she immediately remarks that "not everyone is in the same condition as knowers or potential knowers. Perhaps most people don't need 'a wider scale of experience.' It may be that, without subtle and extensive psychic preparation, any widening of experience and consciousness is destructive for most people." Not for you and me, Dear Reader: we are among the elect. We deserve that "wider scale of experience"; but as for the rest, as for "most people," well. . . .

It doesn't always work. As a writer, Sontag is essentially a coiner of epigrams. At their best they are witty, well phrased, provocative. A few are even true: "Nietzsche was a histrionic thinker but not a lover of the histrionic." But Sontag's striving for effect (unlike Nietzsche, she *is* a lover of the histrionic) often leads her into muddle. In **"One Culture and the New Sensibility,"** for example, she enthusiastically reasons that "if art is understood as a form of discipline of the feelings and a programming of sensations, then the feeling (or sensation) given off by a Rauschenberg painting might be like that of a song by the Supremes." But of course the idea that art is a "programming of the sensations" (a phrase, alas, of which Sontag is particularly fond) is wrong, incoherent, or both, as is the idea that feelings or sensations might be "given off" by any song or painting, even one by Rauschenberg (odors, yes; sensations, no). As often happens, her passion for synesthesia and effacing boundaries leads her into nonsense.

Charity dictates that we pass lightly over Sontag's fiction and drama. Most of it reminds one of Woody Allen's parody of Kafka. "Should I marry K.? Only if she tells me the other letters of her name"—that sort of thing. Here's a sample from *I, etcetera* (a book whose title might be reused for Sontag's collected works): "Dearest M. I cannot telephone. I am six years old. My grief falls like snowflakes on the warm soil of your indifference. You are inhaling your own pain." Readers looking for the comic side of Sontag's *oeuvre* will want to dip into her fiction: *The Benefactor* (1963) and *Death Kit* (1967) are particularly fine, provided they are read as parodies of intellectual solemnity. In *Either/Or,* Kierkegaard advised the aspiring aesthete to look for "a

very different kind of enjoyment from that which the author has been so kind as to plan for you." It is advice that is particularly relevant when approaching Sontag's "creative writing."

If one wanted to sum up Sontag's allure in a single phrase, it would be difficult to do better than Tom Wolfe's "radical chic." In her manner, her opinions, her politics, Sontag has always been a walking inventory of radical chic attitudes. Writing about Camus's notebooks in 1963, she naturally patronizes him as having been "acclaimed beyond his purely literary merits," assuring us that, unlike Sartre (but like George Orwell), he was not "a thinker of importance." In 1963, Jean-Paul Sartre was still an Approved Radical Figure, whose Communist sympathies and virulent anti-Americanism made him beloved of American intellectuals. Camus, who had had the temerity to criticize Communism, was distinctly not-ARF and had to be taken down a peg or two.

And then there were Sontag's own political activities. Cuba and North Vietnam in 1968, China in 1973, Sarajevo in 1993 (where she went to direct a production of *Waiting for Godot*—surely the consummate radical chic gesture of all time). Few people have managed to combine naïve idealization of foreign tyranny with violent hatred of their own country to such deplorable effect. Consider her essay "Some Thoughts on the Right Way (for us) to Love the Cuban Revolution," which appeared in *Ramparts* magazine in April 1969. She begins with some ritualistic denunciations of American culture as "inorganic, dead, coercive, authoritarian." "America is a cancerous society with a runaway rate of productivity that inundates the country with increasingly unnecessary commodities, services, gadgets, images, information." One of the few spots of light, Sontag tells us, is Eldridge Cleaver's *Soul on Ice,* which teaches that "America's psychic survival entails her transformation through a political revolution." (It also teaches that, for blacks, rape can be a noble "insurrectionary act," a "defying and trampling on the white man's laws," but Sontag doesn't bother with that detail.)

According to her, "the power structure derives its credibility, its legitimacy, its energies from the dehumanization of the individuals who operate it. The people staffing IBM and General Motors, and the Pentagon, and United Fruit are the living dead." Since the counterculture is not strong enough to overthrow IBM, the Pentagon, etc., it must opt for subversion. "Rock, grass, better orgasms, freaky clothes, grooving on nature— really grooving on anything—unfits, maladapts a person for the American way of life." And here is where the Cubans come in: they come by this "new sensibility" naturally, possessing as they do a "southern spontaneity which we feel our own too white, death-ridden culture denies us. . . . The Cubans know a lot about spontaneity, gaiety, sensuality and freaking out. They are not linear, desiccated creatures of print culture."

Indeed not: supine, desiccated creatures of a Communist tyranny would be more like it, though patronizing honky talk about "southern spontaneity" doubtless made things seem much better when this was written. In the great contest for writing the most fatuous line of political drivel, Sontag is always a contender. This essay contains at least two gems: after ten years, she writes, "the Cuban revolution is astonishingly free of repression and bureaucratization," and, even better perhaps, is this passing remark delivered in parentheses: "No Cuban writer has been or is in jail, or is failing to get his work published." Readers wishing to make a reality check should consult Paul Hollander's classic study *Political Pilgrims: Western Intellectuals in Search of the Good Society* (fourth edition, 1998), which cites Sontag's claim and then lists, in two or three pages, some of the many writers and artists who have been jailed, tortured, or executed by Castro's spontaneous gaiety.

Sontag concocted a similar fairy tale when she went to Vietnam in 1968 courtesy of the North Vietnamese government. Her long essay **"Trip to Hanoi"** (1968) is another classic in the literature of political mendacity. Connoisseurs of the genre will especially savor Sontag's observation that the real problem for the North Vietnamese is that they "aren't good enough haters." Their fondness for Americans, she explains, keeps getting in the way of the war effort. "They genuinely care about the welfare of the hundreds of captured American pilots and give them bigger rations than the Vietnamese population gets, 'because they're bigger than we are,' as a Vietnamese army officer told me." Sontag acknowledges that her account tended somewhat to idealize North Vietnam; but that was only because it was a country that "in many respects, *deserves* to be idealized."

Unlike any country in Western Europe, and above all unlike the United States. In **"What's Happening in America** (1966),"** Sontag tells readers that what America "deserves" is to have its wealth "taken away" by the Third World. In one particularly notorious passage, she writes that "the truth is that Mozart, Pascal, Boolean algebra, Shakespeare, parliamentary government, baroque churches, Newton, the emancipation of women, Kant, Marx, and Balanchine ballets don't redeem what this particular civilization has wrought upon the world. The white race *is* the cancer of human history." After a bout with cancer in the 1970s, Sontag emended that last observation because on reflection she had come to realize that it was unfair—to cancer.

What can one say? Sontag excoriates the American economy for its "runaway rate of productivity." But she has had no scruples about enjoying the fruits of that productivity: a Rockefeller Foundation grant in 1964, a Merrill Foundation grant in 1965, a Guggenheim Foundation Fellowship in 1966, etc., etc., culminating in 1990 with a MacArthur Foundation "genius" award.

But it is not simply in such mundane terms that Sontag wants to have it both ways. Inveterate aestheticism entails intractable intellectual and moral frivolity. Sontag went on to blast the Castro regime for its brutal treatment of certain approved writers, but her condemnation meant little more than her initial enthusiasm. It was, as she might put it, merely "formal": the content didn't count. It was the same with her famous announcement at a left-wing symposium in 1982 that "Communism *is* fascism." How piquant that Susan Sontag should utter this elementary truth! In her essay **"On Style,"** Sontag had assured her readers that Leni Riefenstahl's Nazi films "transcend the categories of propaganda or even reportage": the content of the films—i.e., their endorsement of Nazi ideology—has come "to play a purely formal role." Ten years later, in an essay called **"Fascinating Fascism"** (1974) she says the opposite: that the "very conception" of *Triumph of the Will* "negates the possibility of the filmmaker's having an aesthetic conception independent of propaganda." Taxed by an interviewer with the contradiction, Sontag replies that "both statements illustrate the richness of the form-content distinction, as long as one is careful always to use it against itself." "Rich" is indeed the *mot juste*. In her book *On Photography* (1977), Sontag says that photography transforms people into "tourists of reality." It is a neat phrase: vivid, arresting, overstated. But as she has shown over and over, Sontag herself is just such a tourist. One day she embraces camp, the next day she warns about the "perils of over-generalizing the aesthetic view of life." As Hilton Kramer observed, "it is not that Sontag was ever prepared to abandon her stand on aestheticism and all its implications. It was only that she did not want it to cost her anything." Sontag once noted that "the relation between boredom and Camp taste cannot be overestimated." One suspects that boredom underlies a good deal of her unhappy radicalism. Discontented with "the Matthew Arnold notion of culture," she abandoned the question of "how to live" and became instead a prophet of the new sensibility of aesthetic nihilism.

**Michael Silverblatt (review date 27 February 2000)**

SOURCE: Silverblatt, Michael. "For You O Democracy." *Los Angeles Times Book Review* (27 February 2000): 1-2.

[*In the following review, Silverblatt comments on the disillusionment and Americanization of the characters in Sontag's novel* In America.]

## I

Susan Sontag's new novel is a brilliant and profound investigation into the fate of thought and culture in America. Like Sontag's previous novel, *The Volcano Lover, In America* masquerades as historical fiction, flaunting the stuff of drama and romance. It is something restless, hybrid, disturbing, original.

At its center is a true story. As Sontag tells us in a prefatory statement, she was inspired by "the emigration to America in 1876 of Helena Modrzejewska, Poland's most celebrated actress, accompanied by her husband Count Karol Chlapowski, her fifteen-year-old son Rudolf, the young journalist and future author of *Quo Vadis* Henryk Sienkiewicz, and a few friends; their brief sojourn in Anaheim, California; and Modrzejewska's subsequent triumphant career on the American stage under the name of Helena Modjeska." Sontag goes on to explain that most of the characters in the novel "are invented, and those who are not depart in radical ways from their real-life models."

In fact, *In America* is a picaresque fable, a historical tragicomedy. The story revolves around a Polish actress, Maryna Zalezowska. More than an actress, she is a national symbol for the triply besieged and conquered Poland, a symbol of patriotism, of seriousness, of achievement on a grand scale in the arts. She is dissatisfied, restless; her brother has died; rival actresses are producing travesties of her work. She decides to surrender, give up the stage and move to California, where she will toil with her comrades on a commune in Anaheim founded on the utopian principles of Charles Fourier. There they discover they have neither the radical ideals nor the practical abilities to maintain a communal farm. They go into debt and disperse. Maryna Zalezowska returns to the stage renamed Marina Zaleska. She tours America, performing in English, and in the process of winning national and even international recognition, she betrays her loves and her artistic beliefs. The book is a melancholic comedy about the defeat of every kind of integrity. In America, Maryna goes from being what Sontag calls "an orphaned talent" to being what Maryna herself calls "a monster," She becomes a cultured freak, an emotionally overwrought publicity whore: a very American type.

But here are the book's genius and originality. We see Maryna through carefully selected lenses: her own moody self-adoring monologues and arias, the diaries of Bogdan, her patient husband (who, like the husbands of other divas, uses his marriage as a blind for his mostly resisted attraction to boys) and the letters and effusions of Ryszard, her young and besotted would-be lover. Add to these a Polish citizenry mourning the loss of its revered national symbol and a claque of young actors and older impresarios whose well-being depends on keeping brilliant Maryna's self-absorption well-flattered and under control. No one in this book has the freedom to tell Maryna who she is, what she is becoming or what is actually happening to her.

To put it more precisely: Only two characters can break through Maryna's lacquered self-deception. One is Susan Sontag, who has an opening monologue and narrates sections of the book. She is "outside" the tale and cannot speak directly to Maryna. The other is Edwin Booth, the great tragedian, brother of John Wilkes Booth, who makes his appearance in the final monologue. He confronts Maryna with terrifying directness, and she asks him to stop—and the novel ends.

In their monologues, Sontag and Booth are pitiless, anti-sentimental, truth-telling. They stand at a remove from the deceit and vulgarity growing at the heart of the novel, embodied by Maryna's passion for lying and display, her willingness to flatter, conciliate and compromise. Willing to sacrifice everything, even her art, for success, Maryna thinks that she is learning how to live in America, that she is learning the lessons of the dawning of America's celebrity culture.

Sontag's monologue, "Chapter Zero," which begins with a description of a dream in which she enters, like Alice into the Looking Glass, the world of this novel, stands outside the novel, presenting in small compass the themes, the dislocations, the recreations of the novel in full. Read it carefully, for this chapter, a single 25-page paragraph, shows what prose can achieve in our time. It is a model of the modern split sensibility achieving what integration it can with the past. Not the broken fragments of a modernist text but rather the unfalling and beautiful glide of a long take, it is a prose style that sees consciousness as continuous with what it observes. Sontag has achieved this style over time, from such short fictions as "Description (of a Description)" and "The Letter Scene," an exploration of the effect, but not the content, of the classical operatic letter aria. Inspired by a passage from one of Kafka's blue octavo diary notebooks and by the eerie first-person obsessional novels of Thomas Bernhard, Sontag has arrived in her new novel at a supple, dream-waltz prose that can look at the world and look at itself looking. Here is a sentence in the form of a cascade; there, one, that opens like a fan. The result is elegant and vertiginous.

The image for best apprehending the book is one Sontag herself has suggested (in a recent interview in *Bookforum*): "a Scheherazade Rubik's cube." It is only after you have reconfigured the surfaces, bringing the various facets of the novel together onto the correct planes, that you see that the major characters suffer four distinct American fates.

Ryszard, who rejects America, begins his life again and again, marrying and remarrying, waiting for a jump-start. Bogdan disappears into America, into a peculiar

American anonymity: He is freed to follow his sexual yearnings but rejects his freedom, choosing to remain the stage husband, Maryna's consoler and keeper. Booth, the novel's darkest figure, flickers memorably in its final chapter—morose, alcoholic, broken but uncompromised, an American tragedy. Maryna, poor Maryna, deserts her art and her loves and remains untouchable, martyred by her bottomless will and talent for self-reinvention. Maryna succeeds, but she becomes inured to a life without satisfaction. She ends up lonely, humbled, ludicrous.

Along the way, we encounter a regular circus bill of attractions and thrilling sideshows: the theater world of besieged Poland; transatlantic voyages; child prostitutes on shipboard and a chance encounter with a writer in a Manhattan bordello; romance in the California desert moonlight; homosexual yearnings; transcontinental train rides; the Centennial Exhibition in Philadelphia; a love triangle; an attempted suicide; silver mines; opening nights; productions of "Camille," "As You Like It," "Romeo and Juliet," "A Doll's House"; the saloon of Minnie, the girl of the Golden West; the hard-bitten story of an itinerant lady photographer's romance with light; a cameo appearance by Henry James; tale telling and debates about narrative. In other words, enough incident, psychology, local color and fascinating detail to stock a flotilla of popular novels, a couple of *Ragtimes* and a brace of theatrical memoirs.

But though Sontag masters the amusing clockwork trains and trick miniature effects of historical travelogue, she is after something more than showmanship: Showmanship, P.T. Barnum-style, is in fact what American culture uses to conceal what occurs backstage, the vast arena where classically trained actresses are turned into divas, where plays become spectacles and where ideas become entertainment.

It is here that Sontag lets us see Maryna without the filters and lenses of adoring friends, lovers and countrymen. Sontag pours everything she knows about being an artist, an actress, an activist, a diva into this character, Maryna is a flood of uncertainties, resolutions, anguishes resolved by will, manipulations, Intensities. She intrigues; she flirts. She accepts the protection of the wife of an occupying Russian official when her production of "Hamlet" is endangered, hardly the action of a Polish patriot. She is indomitable but easy to flatter. She is often inflexibly wrong but passionately convincing. She ages before our eyes and loses her beauty, but she will still play Juliet. She will go on shopping sprees, and she will tour week after week, spending only a day in an American nowhere before moving on to the next engagement. Sontag gives us a convincing portrait of an artist who is losing her way, and it would be a pity if all the structural brilliance that surrounds her were to distract readers from her imperious, self-dramatizing and fallible character.

## II

What do the Poles learn in America? They learn the usefulness of a happy ending. Here's how:

Anaheim is visited by the traveling Stappenbeck Circus from Los Angeles. And the commune is visited by an obese Polish kleptomaniac from San Francisco. Each visit brings a transgression: A lynch mob forms after the circus; the fatso steals Maryna's jewels (and much more). One cannot trust visitors; even one's own countrymen are treacherous.

This truth is too painful and impolite; it necessitates that most American of alterations: the happy ending, kissing cousin of the American success story. Writing about the circus, Ryszard, the young Polish novelist, decides to alter reality. He lets the escaped lovers elude the lynch mob and sends them to hidden bliss in a romantic cave. And Maryna refuses to mourn her stolen jewels: There must be a lesson and a moral. "One should be ready to part with anything," she says. Loss and violence give rise to the instinct for transcendence, the American happy ending.

And if success requires a happy ending, then beginnings must be altered as well; the means must justify the end. Everything must be renamed: the names of plays, of people, of towns. Why? To fool the censor, to entice the public, to make things more exotic—and less foreign—to facilitate the myth of the new beginning." Immigrant children like Piotr, Maryna's son, want to become Peter to be more like other American children.

Even the strongman of the Stappenbeck Circus, the child of a Cahuilla squaw, changes his name. "His real name U-wa-ka died with his mother; in the village and the foothills he was known as Big Neck." In the circus he gets a circus name, Zambo, the American Hercules. How different is this from the fate of Maryna Zalezowska, who becomes Marina Zalenska, "Countess Zalenska of the Russian Imperial Theater, Warsaw"? She, too, has been given "a circus name," Unfortunate inconveniences, which she is willing to overlook: that the Russians were the Poles' oppressors, that Marina is the Russian spelling of Maryna and that Maryna is not, and has never been, a countess (the title belongs to her husband).

It is not long before this search for "the enhancing falsehood"—the happy ending—affects the artistic impulses as well. On tour, after abandoning Anaheim in debt, Marina Zalenska will ultimately take on something ambitious, a production of Ibsen's *A Doll's House*. But as vultures devour a corpse, American concerns descend en masse. The title must be changed: What if people should think it is a play for children? The character's name must be changed: Nora might be an American name and no American woman would behave so perfidiously as to abandon husband and children. Why not call her Thora? It sounds more Scandinavian and, just to be safe, give it a happy ending: "Nora—no, Thora!—will think of leaving. But won't. Will forgive her husband. Should it go well here, we can restore the real ending when we bring it to New York." Ibsen's "Thora," with Marina Zalenska in the title role, has its only performance in Louisville, Ky. "Reviewers irate, even with the happy ending. Just as I feared. Offense to Christian morals and the American family."

Marina retitles "Romeo and Juliet"; she tours in something called "Juliet"; after all, isn't she the main attraction? She thereafter becomes a specialist in tearjerking dramas like "East Lynne" and "Frou-Frou"; her job is to provoke tears and command attention. "In Poland, you were allowed some practice of the arts of self-indulgence, but you were expected to be sincere and also to have high ideals—people respected you for that. In America, you were expected to exhibit the confusions of inner vehemence, to express opinions no one need take seriously, and have eccentric foibles and extravagant needs, which exhibited the force of your will, your appetitiveness, the spread of your self-regard—all excellent things."

### III

Why, at this hour of the world, a historical novel built out of letters, diaries, compacted facts? Is this a conservative, traditional novel? If one defines modernism as the set of energies inscribed in the work of Picasso, Stravinsky, Joyce, Pound, Eliot—a belief that the world can be seen only in fragments and that these fragments cannot be reassembled, that the world is in ruins—then Sontag owes much more to Proust, to the belief that the past can be recaptured and that this recaptured past includes eruptions, dissolution and breakage.

In this way, Sontag's earlier historical novel. *The Volcano Lover,* and her new one, *In America,* attempt to reroute the novel away from further fragmentation. Sontag's stance is one of abject mourning for the tragedies of the past and for what these tragedies have done to our culture and our ideas about art. By means of this acceptance, she has found a way to connect the modern novel to the great monuments of the past, the works of Stendhal, Tolstoy, George Eliot. She embarks upon a journey of construction—the novel is composed as a succession of microstructures—and arrives at a new use of tradition, one that seemed unavailable to the postmodernist sensibility. She is giving us, in fiction, the history of the loss that led to irony and fragmentation, the death of so much that could formerly be called culture, and she bravely attempts a journey beyond that loss.

Sontag has managed to structure a paradox—call it hopeful inconsolability or optimistic pessimism—a belief that the destruction of our ideals and our long-lost innocence can still be narrated, that there is still a story to be told about us and about how we came to be the way we are or to see, as the title of one of her past stories has it (borrowing from Anthony Trollope), the seeds of the past in **"The Way We Live Now."**

### James Wood (review date 27 March 2000)

SOURCE: Wood, James. "The Palpable Past-Intimate." *New Republic* 222, no. 13 (27 March 2000): 29-33.

[*In the following review, Wood contends that in contemporary society the historical novel has become an overworked and tedious genre, but that* In America *is an exception, characterizing the book as nicely balanced with insight, theatricality, and riveting narration.*]

Is it still possible to write the historical novel? There would seem to be powerful arguments, and powerful modern instances, against it. First, it is the least innocent of forms in an all-too-knowing age; one might say, paradoxically, that at this late stage it represents the novel at its most complacently alienated from itself. This has primarily to do with the pace of historical change in the last century. It is true that *War and Peace* is an historical novel, but rather as *The Prelude* is an historical poem. Tolstoy felt confident about reaching back sixty or so years from his age to the Napoleonic wars, because he was so sure that nothing essential had changed that he could proceed to write what was, in effect, a contemporary novel.

But there is now a large gulf between, say, the beginning of this century and the beginning of the last, and into this breach may run our quivering self-consciousness. For nowadays we know how acute our historical separateness is, and it is this knowledge that is so dangerous to the unthinking freedom of fiction. It is this knowledge that lends a certain desperate quality to the detail that writers of historical fiction choose to mention. Of course, they do not really choose their detail; it chooses them. If a writer is painting London or New York in 1900, we must be told about coachmen and dandies with canes, or 1900 will not have been evoked. And the characters in historical fiction—especially the minor characters—are not free either, for they are continually being forced to say things like, "Have you seen *The Tramp* yet?", just so that we know that it is 1915. Such characters can end up sounding like the paradoxical mathematician described by Plato, who, when counting numbers that he must already know, "sets out to learn from himself anew something he must already be familiar with."

This is one reason why the historical novel may nowadays be merely science-fiction facing backwards, with the same crudities of detail. Without the ability to move freely, detail is converted from the accidental into the determined, and the book may become stagy, and essentially unliterary. It may also become essentially unhistorical, for if a great deal of time is being wasted on the confirmation of the past, then history is being confirmed in its crudest particulars, rather than challenged or even explored. All these large alienations drive the historical novel away from what Henry James, in the letter to Sarah Orne Jewett in which he condemned the historical novel, called "the palpable present-intimate."

Alessandro Manzoni, who wrote the historical novel *The Betrothed* in 1827, argued against the historical novel, surprisingly enough, in his essay *On The Historical Novel.* Always a great believer in the science of historical inquiry, Manzoni felt that the historical novel could not succeed because it mixed the literary (what he called "the verisimilar") with actual, historical fact (what he called "positive truth"). He argued that this blending of history and invention mangled both modes of writing, and robbed the historical novel of any purity of purpose: "the historical novel is a work in which the necessary turns out to be impossible . . . it does not have a logical purpose of its own."

And yet Manzoni wrote a great historical novel. He reconciled what he saw as the lumpy disjunction of the historical and the invented by combining standard novelistic (or invented) narration with historically aware essayism—by refusing to leave alone his own fictional detail, but often pointing readers towards its actual historical status. In other words, he was self-conscious about his self-consciousness. This was a liberty for Manzoni, but it may be the only possible way to write historical fiction now. It is the method that Susan Sontag adopts in her historical novel *In America,* and alongside other techniques and contexts, it more than saves her novel from the confident awkwardness of the genre.

Sontag's novel tells the story of a group of educated and adventurous Poles, led by a great actress already famous in her homeland, who leave Poland for America in the 1870s, and settle briefly in a rural commune in Anaheim, California. It is loosely based on the true story of the Polish actress Helena Modrzejewska, who emigrated to America in 1876, along with her husband and son, and with the young writer Henryk Sienkiewicz. In America, after a short time in California, Helena reinvented herself as an American actress, with the name Helena Modjeska.

Immediately Sontag inserts herself into the foreground of the novel, as she did in her last historical fiction, *The Volcano Lover.* The book's first chapter, which is fanci-ful but oddly moving, gathers the characters in a hotel dining-room in a town in Poland, and Sontag—so the conceit goes—wanders unnoticed around the room, deciding what her characters will do and what names they should have, and generally, as she finely puts it, "scattering seeds of prediction." The chapter is an introductory confession; indeed, it is startlingly confessional. Referring to her early marriage to a well-known scholar, Sontag writes that at the age of seventeen she read *Middlemarch* and cried, because she realized that she was Dorothea Brooke and that she had married Casaubon. She tells us that she has perhaps been drawn to write about Poland because all four of her grandparents came from that country; and before we can resist the sentimentality of this thought, she undermines it herself by admitting that she had tried to describe a hotel room in Sarajevo at the same historical moment, and failed.

So we are reading an historical fiction, and we are to be reminded periodically of this throughout the book. This kind of self-reflexiveness can come to seem in weaker books like a repetitive and doomed attempt at self-cleansing—like someone washing her hands again and again—but after the first chapter it is only delicately pressed on. (We hear no more from Sontag, as such.) Yet it is intellectually important, for it suspends the characters in a fluid of modernity (or post-modernity), and releases them from the category of historical idiocy. We know that they know they are being watched by a contemporary writer; but inside this careful panopticon they live and breathe fully as free fictional characters.

In fact, the heroine of the novel, the actress Maryna Załeżowska, is used to being watched, and used to watching herself. Histrionic, imperious, willful, and demanding, she spends her life in a crowd of mirrors; her loving entourage, which includes her loyal husband Bogdan and her ardent admirer and subsequent lover Ryszard (he is based on Sienkiewicz), reflect her glory back to her. Maryna is a powerful creation, alive, not exactly likeable but fizzy with her own essence. She has more than a hint in her of Irina Arkadin, Chekhov's impossible actress in *The Seagull.*

Sontag shrewdly uses the stageyness of the world, this actress's world—we travel with Maryna on her triumphant American tour—further to complicate the certainties of the historical novel. For the book is suffused with a certain plush, melodramatic stageyness of its own, half-parody and half-innocence; it is always proposing *performance.* Its world is being watched, but it is also watching itself, and watching us, too. And this is done in a manner that seems both self-conscious and genuinely unconscious on Sontag's part. One is reminded of her unfashionable belief in the theater, which is similarly innocent and now necessarily also a self-consciousness. The result is that the inevitable artificiality of historical detail is coated in a certain buoyant irony, which breaks into true creative gaiety.

In general, it is striking how little historical detail seems to clog the surface of this novel; it has been smoothed into underground discretion. The book is not a disquisition on the America of the 1870s. That is not to say that Sontag does not occasionally bully her data into historical confession. There is a somewhat crude moment, for instance, when Ryszard is buttonholed by a man who seems to want to talk about someone he calls "Tockveel," and "Tockveel's" visit to America fifty years before. It is one of those encounters that happens only in novels. And later in the book the reader becomes restless when Sontag writes that the Poles were nostalgic for Polish music: "they had longed for the sound of Polish composers, a song by Kurpiński, a waltz by Ogiński . . ." The Poles, being Polish, would not have had to name these familiar composers to themselves (shades of Plato's mathematician); and since the names mean little to us non-Poles, it is simply a matter of homework being presented for reward by the author.

At such moments, the joists of the enterprise of the historical novel are exposed. This leads to a further suspicion of the form as currently practiced, which is that historical fiction may get a borrowed gravity from its subject, a gravity for which fiction set in its own time must more dirtily labor. Hasn't Sontag avoided some of the messy chanciness of fiction by choosing to write about educated Poles in the 1870s? A certain language and grammar of manners—a set of conventions that are themselves derived from nineteenth-century fiction—is already in place, not to mention the furniture and the couture of the period (lorgnettes, hats, silks, and so on). These things come already solemnized by literature, whereas the novelist who wants to write about modern Brooklyn or modern Knightsbridge must strive for his or her own solemnity.

To be fair, Sontag uses the story of this emigration precisely to throw a nineteenth-century (or "European") gravity into the unclaimed space of an America that does not recognize these conventions. And Sontag is very subtle in the way she approaches historical detail, properly treating it as fictive detail. The description of the Atlantic crossing made by Ryszard and a friend is extremely good. It includes a painful scene in which Ryszard, seeking journalistic information, wanders below decks into steerage, where he encounters an Irishman who is pimping for his six captive "nieces." Ryszard is cajoled into having lukewarm sex with one of the girls, who is barely fifteen, but he cannot do it, and only pretends to go through the motions behind a dirty curtain, so that the "uncle" will not beat his "niece" afterwards for rejecting the gentleman visitor.

Once in America, Maryna takes her little son Piotr to the Centennial Exposition in Philadelphia. There she marvels at the new American inventions, and writes to an old friend in Poland of what she has seen. But Sontag does not overplay her hand here. Maryna is especially taken with a typewriter, which she describes as "a porcupine-like machine for stamping inked letters on blank paper." And she is enthusiastic about the telephone, which she imagines will one day be in every household. But since she cannot imagine the television, she thinks that the telephone will be a kind of television, and expresses educated caution: "And what a boon to humanity that will be, when, by means of this device, anyone can have an Italian opera, a play of Shakespeare, a debate in the Congress, a sermon by their favorite preacher laid on like gas in one's own house . . . Still, I worry about the consequences of this invention, human laziness being what it is, for nothing can replace the experience of entering a temple of dramatic art . . ." This is just the right pressure of self-conscious irony; we enjoy the fatalism of our televisual retrospect, and subtly correct Maryna's fatalism in our minds. Delicacy is all, here; for anything heavier would fail.

Eventually, after several weeks on the east coast, the group find their separate ways to California, and it is California that prompts some of Sontag's finest writing. Sontag grew up in California, and this novel may be seen as almost invisibly watermarked by her own nostalgia for that early landscape. "Even now . . . it thrills me to write CALIFORNIA," writes Maryna to her old friend, and one feels this to be Sontag's sentiment, also. A kind of ecstasy takes over her prose when she writes of the California desert, and she is both lyrical and precise:

> Hardly anything is near anything here: those slouching braided sentinels, the yucca trees, and bouquets of drooping spears, the agaves, and the squat clusters of prickly pears, all so widely spaced, so unresembling— and nothing had to do with anything else . . . The purity of the vista, its uncompromising bleakness, seemed first like a menace, then an excitement, then a numbing, then a different arousal. Their real initiation into the seductive nihilism of the desert had begun. The soundless, odorless, monochrome landscape, so drastically untenanted, had the same effect on everyone: an intoxicating impression of aloneness . . .

At first, the quixotic European attempt at frontier farming seems to prosper. Maryna, though famous in Europe, is a mere immigrant in California, and involved, like the rest of her family and friends, with the graft of subsistence. She loves it, and loves America, if complicatedly, feeling that "the sudden drop in the volume of meanings in the new life worked on her like a thinning out of oxygen." But schism soon threatens, as if in a secular mimicry of religious fracture: two of their number are lured away to a rival commune, and another couple returns to Poland after the unhappy wife tries to kill herself. Those left are not especially good farmers; in a nice detail, Sontag writes that none of the women were very good at milking, for "they felt they were torturing the cows."

Meanwhile Maryna, Bogdan, and Ryszard, who constitute the novel's controlling trio, are becoming restless. Bogdan, a faithful husband but a repressed homosexual, is attracted by novel American flesh, and confides secret desires to his tense diary. Ryszard, who is in love with Maryna, veers between elation and depression. On the one hand, "even if my life ended now, he said to himself, I would still think, My God, what a journey I have made." On the other hand, he feels that farming ill becomes his heroine, and that to extract the most from America one must stay on the move, as the hunter does.

Eventually Maryna decides to return to the stage—in America. Thus begins the last third of the book, an intensely imagined, superbly Dreiserian account of Maryna's lavish American victory. What may surprise some readers of Sontag's criticism is how easily she subjugates her intelligence, and yields to the fairy-tale textures of this episode. An initially skeptical theater manager, Angus Barton of the California Theatre in San Francisco, is won over, and soon Maryna—now retitled Marina Zalenska, because a Russian name sounds more impressive to the American public than a Polish one—is playing various melodramatic hits of the day, such as *Adrienne Lecouvreur* and *East Lynne* (which she disdainfully calls *Beast Lynne*).

As her fame grows, Maryna is given a private train to travel in, and crosses America. Some of Sontag's detail may have been taken from the historical record; but most of it must have been invented, and it has the high zest of invention on it like a sheen. In Jacksonville, a man presents her with two lime-green baby alligators, and her manager immediately converts the place of donation to New Orleans, because it sounds more glamorous. In Fort Wayne, an obese man wearing a yellow wig gives her a dog. He has already "pressed on her a bronze statuette of Hiawatha, the collected speeches of Ulysses S. Grant, and a music box, set on a nearby table and repeatedly wound up to unwind 'Carnival in Venice.'" In a curiously affecting scene, one admirer writes her a poem after her performance; and the last couplet, "Keep Polish memories in your heart alone, / America now claims you for her own," makes her weep. Soaps and scents named after her are being sold. Her only rival is Sarah Bernhardt.

The novel ends where, in a sense, it began, with Maryna occupying the only home she knows, the only one she is unnostalgic about: the theater. The book shuttles between homelessnesses. Being Polish, these men and women were already nostalgic for their country even while living in it. Maryna suspects that they are now suffering not only from nostalgia, but also from "a new illness, the inability to become attached to anything." In a way, the novel combines old nostalgia and new homelessness; these are the epochs that it moves between, for one might say that these characters are nostalgic for what they cannot be attached to anyway. And this means that they are out of place in America, too, because the America that Sontag portrays is a country of brutal, adhesive immigration. Yet these educated, upper-class, artistic Poles are emigrants rather than immigrants, and thus somehow both lost and found in America. And so Ryszard and Maryna exist most fully in their respective arts, the novel and the theater, and America becomes both a novel and a theater—for them, and, designedly, for the reader of this book.

For Sontag's other area of intellectual exploration is that of theatrical illusion. Here she braves didacticism, even un-originality. After all, there is not much new to say about masks and the diabolical flexibility of the actor. Yet Sontag novelistically grounds her discussion in the concrete, and in the arrogantly anxious bosom of her heroine. Maryna is an intensely nineteenth-century creation, after all. Though she has played Schiller and Shakespeare, her most popular roles are watery melodramas, in which the very air of the theater is dropleted with the audience's cheap tears, and at the end of which the adulterous heroine must make sacrificial expiration.

Maryna is expert at these dying falls, practically a mortician of the melodramatic. As such, she is a luridly expressive actress, accustomed to the raucous support of her adoring Polish audiences. She is torn between a cold professionalism, in which, in the classic theatrical way, she is simply a soul for hire, ready to inhabit any emotion; and a Romantic authenticity, in which she exhaustingly undergoes the same emotions that she plays on stage. She argues, early in the novel, that acting ought to be about "*not* feeling," and longs to be more restrained in her playing. Yet her heart vibrates with the language of Shakespeare, and it is clear that, in an equally classic theatrical manner, she has become her roles.

The novel wisely does not seek to adjudicate between these rival approaches, but lets them lie complicatedly in the same woman. Is the theater, then, an art of easy falsity, or is it a difficult, self-expressive form, worthy of taking its place with the other mimetic arts, such as writing and painting? I take Sontag to be nudging us to such a question, and perhaps finally to be suggesting that of course the theater is both falsity and authenticity, for mimesis is never innocent.

Certainly, Maryna does not attempt to reconcile these attitudes, and we are grateful for it. In a striking scene, Sontag dramatizes what might have been presented essayistically: the inevitable corruption of mimesis. Maryna, surrounded by her American actors, begins to speak, lyrically and expressively, some words of Polish. They are perhaps a hymn or a recitation, perhaps a poem. She finishes, and her colleagues express their delight. Then Maryna tells them that she has simply been reciting the Polish alphabet. She has been acting meaningless letters, and has almost brought her audience to tears.

This, presumably, is what Horace meant when he asked, rhetorically, "do good poems come by nature, or by art?" The same question might be asked of good novels, such as this one. One suspects that Sontag wants us to ask such a question, wants us to use the dilemma of theater's mimesis as a way of reflecting on the dilemma of the historical novel's relation to reality. For her book is both Romantically expressive and artfully sly; it is unconscious and self-conscious in equal measure. If this is the only possible way to write historical fiction in a postmodern time, then Sontag has magnificently managed to make it look like freedom rather than determination. It is certainly an achievement; but surely fiction has more primary duties than the recovery (even the enraptured recovery) of the past, and I wish that Sontag would release herself into the wide and even more unsettled straits of the palpable present-intimate.

## Carl Rollyson (review date April 2000)

SOURCE: Rollyson, Carl. "The Will & the Way." *New Criterion* 18, no. 8 (April 2000): 80-2.

[*In the following review, Rollyson judges Sontag's* In America *as a trite, underdeveloped historical novel.*]

*In America* begins with an epigraph from Langston Hughes: "America will be!" It is a fitting start to the story of a group of Poles who travel to Anaheim, California in 1876 to establish a utopian community. Their leader is Maryna Zaleska, Poland's greatest actress, who has forsaken her career in order to establish a farming commune. She is aware of the likelihood of failure, but the romance of starting anew, the challenge of succeeding where communities such as Brook Farm failed, is too enticing not to pursue. She takes with her a devoted husband, Bogdan; a young son, Piotr; and a young writer, Ryszard, who aspires to win her love.

In a note on the copyright page, Sontag explains that her novel was inspired by the career of Helena Modrzejewska, Poland's renowned actress, who did indeed emigrate to America in 1876 and settle in Anaheim with her husband Count Karol Chapowski; Rudolf, their fifteen-year-old son; Henryk Sienkiewicz, the future Nobel-Prize-winning writer; and a group of friends. Sontag insists on the word "inspired," since she does not follow the historical record too closely. She has allowed herself, she emphasizes, the freedom to invent.

Thus the journey to the new world and the making of a new community are yoked to Sontag's effort to create a new story out of the material of history. I insist on the word "effort" because in the novel's preface, "Zero," Sontag explores her personal relationship to her characters. She fancies herself a Nathaniel Hawthorne in the Custom House telling his readers how he acquired the scarlet letter.

Sontag once said to Pete Hamill that she would not be able to write a detective novel unless she could first invent the writer writing the story. "Zero" tells us who the writer of *In America* is. Sontag rehearses a good deal from the interviews she has given over the past thirty years: she grew up in Arizona and California wanting to be, like Marie Curie, a great scientist and humanitarian; her grandparents came from Poland; at eighteen she read *Middlemarch* and "burst into tears because I realized not only that *I* was Dorothea but that, a few months earlier, I had married Mr. Casaubon" (i.e., Philip Rieff). She has been to Sarajevo (the novel is dedicated to "my friends in Sarajevo"), and thinks of the Poles she overhears talking in a room (she has been magically transported to the past) as precursors of her beloved Bosnians—like the Poles, suffering occupation and partition.

The Sontag narrator of "Zero" appears only once in the novel—and then very briefly. What, then, is the point of "Zero"? It portends some grand link between past and present, author and material that the novel itself never delivers. "Zero" is important only because it is written in Susan Sontag's own voice, and Susan Sontag must be noticed as the writer. In her interviews (conveniently collected in *Conversations with Susan Sontag*), she is at pains to explain that she became a writer not to express herself, but to contribute to the body of great literature. To be recognized as a writer means more to her than what she writes. Style predominates over content—to apply the terms of her famous essay, **"Against Interpretation,"** to herself.

Therein lies the problem. Sontag has never come to ground. She dreams of herself as a writer just as she dreams of an America that will be. The America that is has rarely appealed to her, and has usually merited her disapproval. In her essays, she has dismissed most of American fiction, and her comments on American history are about as superficial and ill-informed as those of any writer who has achieved her prominence.

It is very American to think of oneself as being in a constant state of becoming. But to soar one needs a firm launchpad, and Sontag has never been able to see herself or her native land in terms concrete enough to create palpable fiction. In the essay form, her abstract longing for becoming has a certain flair and speaks to a yearning that readers, especially in the 1960s and 1970s, find appealing. The very idea of a "new sensibility"—as she called it in her first book of essays, *Against Interpretation* (1966)—had a rousing sound to it. Having been there before, however, and with no startling new Sontag work to exemplify the new sensibility, "Zero" lands with a thud.

Reviews of Sontag's fiction often speak of a willed enterprise. She takes her cue from the Romanian philosopher E. M. Cioran, who advocates a spiritual strenuousness that requires us to "sever our roots" and become "metaphysically foreigners." Her essay on Cioran perfectly captures her own *willed* existence. In it, she embraces a thinker who counsels extrication from the world and from domestic commitments in order to experience life as "a series of situations" that leaves the consciousness free to explore its own labyrinth. What Sontag loves most about Cioran is his elevation of the "*will* and its capacity to transform the world."

Not surprisingly, then, **In America** evokes the "power of the will." While acknowledging her utopian tendencies and her doubts that she will prevail in America, Maryna declares, "I must and I will!" She is reminiscent of the earlier Sontag who weighed the risks of idealizing North Vietnam but then insisted the country deserved to be idealized! Maryna writes to a Polish friend that with a "strong enough will one can surmount any obstacle." America, Maryna concludes, is a "whole country of people who believe in the will."

**In America** fails because so much of it is declaiming without dramatizing. Even Sontag's fabled talent for epigram eludes her here: "passion is a beautiful thing, and so is understanding, the coming to understand something, which is a passion, which is a journey, too." Banal expressions make the novel a bore.

Only rarely does a character or a scene catch fire, as with Angus Barton, the theater impresario, who auditions Maryna when she decides to forsake her utopia for a career on the American stage. Henry James enters the narrative for a few pages, and Sontag does a nice parody of his style. But her effort to close the novel, as she did *The Volcano Lover,* with a dramatic monologue is inept, even though the speaker is Edwin Booth. We are invited to measure his anguished, if successful, career against Maryna's faith in the American promise of a new life, but the effort falls flat.

The biggest disappointment is Maryna herself. Sontag mentions in "Zero" how taken she is with divas. She even describes a scene she witnessed between Maria Callas and Rudolf Bing that occurred just as Sontag herself was beginning to establish a reputation in New York. But we learn little from Maryna or from the other characters about what it means to be a diva. Divahood, seemingly, would once have made an ideal subject for a Sontag essay, but she no longer seems willing to exercise the discipline demanded by the genre.

Sontag told a Polish interviewer in Warsaw last year that she had always wanted to write a novel about an actress. Sontag emphasized that she knew a lot about acting, having been in productions Mike Nichols staged at the University of Chicago. But her Maryna, rather like Sontag herself, takes refuge in the aesthetics of silence. Maryna does chatter on about her hopes for America, her attitude toward her husband, son, and lover, and about all manner of subjects—except the one that would engage readers. What does it feel like to be a diva? Her silence abut this matter, like Sontag's, seems almost perverse.

Although Sontag says she felt free to invent in her new novel, much of **In America** reads like a diligently researched report, replete with quaint passages about what America was like in nineteenth-century New York and the Western United States. Popular novelists like Caleb Carr have done a much better job with similar material, and it is hard to see why Sontag bothered. Without a driving plot, the historical background only makes a static novel more static.

In *The Scarlet Letter,* the introductory Custom House section succeeds because Hawthorne takes on the burden of the past, establishing his link to the seventeenth century even as he would like, in some ways, to shed its influence. The past was unquestionably an ineluctable part of the novelist and his novel. History was palpable, and it suffused both his style and content. Sontag writes like an exile who believes she can through sheer force of will conjure up the past. The reader soon tires of the novelist as eavesdropper, one who never commits herself to her characters, who in fact seems to feel superior to her creations, since, after all, they are only products of her will.

## Diana Postlewaite (review date June 2000)

SOURCE: Postlewaite, Diana. "Scene Stealer." *Women's Review of Books* 17, no. 9 (June 2000): 5-6.

[*In the following review, Postlewaite maintains that* In America *is not only a superbly written historical novel, but that Sontag's characterization of protagonist Maryna provides insight into Sontag's mind and personality.*]

In 1992, critics were surprised and readers delighted when Susan Sontag, formidable essayist of the au courant, published **The Volcano Lover,** a romantic historical fiction set in late eighteenth-century Naples. And now she's done it again: a nineteenth-century tale based on the true story of Polish actress Helena Modrzejewska, who emigrated to a farming commune in Anaheim, California, in 1876 and subsequently became a darling of the American stage.

Sontagians have made much of this writer's later-life new beginnings, her protean self-reinvention (qualities she shares with the heroine of her latest fiction). But Susan Sontag's avant-garde postmodernism and her old-guard historicism, her fierce intellectualism and her equally fiery romanticism, were there all along, inverted images of one another—photograph and negative, to use a metaphor from an art form which continues to fascinate her.

If Sontag was a prophet, she's always been a historian, too. Re-read today, her famous 1964 essay **"On 'Camp'"** from *Against Interpretation* offers an uncanny prevision of the retro-crazed, sensibility-in-cheek way we live now. Sontag got famous writing about **"The Way We Live Now"** (her short story by that title was recently chosen for *The Best American Short Stories of the Century*); but it's worth noting she borrowed that title from a classic novel by Anthony Trollope. Even as she denominated "the canon of Camp," from Cuban pop singers to old Flash Gordon comics, she was reminding us of the "pantheon of high culture: truth, beauty, and seriousness." George Eliot's *Middlemarch* made it onto Sontag's "high culture" list back in 1964, and it pops up again in Chapter Zero of *In America,* wherein our narrator (manifestly Susan Sontag herself) engages in some "alert eavesdropping" on her heroine-to be: "If I thought of Maryna as a character in a novel, I would have liked her to have something of Dorothea Brooke (I remember when I first read *Middlemarch.* I had just turned eighteen, and a third of the way through the book burst into tears because I realized not only that I was Dorothea, but that, a few months earlier, I had married Mr. Casaubon)." No doubt we are to read this as a reference to Sontag's youthful marriage to academician Phillip Rieff.

Poor old Henry James (glimpsed at a dinner-party walk-on in *In America* as a "fattish, wordy, manifestly brilliant man") was relegated to the corridors of Camp back in 1964 for his "quality of excruciation." Nonetheless, James' eyewitness description of George Eliot came to mind as I read *In America*: "Her manner is extremely good though rather too intense and her speech, in the way of accent and syntax peculiarly agreeable. Altogether, she has a larger circumference than any woman I have ever seen."[1] He could be describing Susan Sontag.

In America, fourteen Polish emigrés pose for a group photograph by Mrs. Eliza Withington, Photographic Artist extraordinaire ("Secure the shadow 'ere the substance fade," her card reads). At their center, poised on the brink of the modern age and "the far edge of . . . the American sublime," stands the charismatic actress Maryna Zalezowska, who has left behind stardom at Warsaw's Imperial Theater to join a utopian commune at the western border of the national experi-

ment. "Picture-taking transported everyone into the future," Sontag writes of her little band of European adventurers, "when their more youthful selves would be only a memory. The photograph was evidence . . . that they were really here, pursuing their valiant new life; to themselves, one day, it would be a relic of that life at its hard, rude beginning or, should their venture not succeed . . . of what they had attempted."

Photographs and historical novels, literary snapshots of the past, have something in common. "To take a photograph," Sontag wrote in 1977 in *On Photography,* "is to participate in . . . mutability. Precisely by slicing out this moment and freezing it, all photographs testify to time's relentless melt." But a photograph is also a treasured "relic," a testimony to the human spirit, that which those who came before us valiantly attempted.

Shortly after Mrs. Withington freezes that moment, the commune disbands: some return to Poland, others seek their fortunes in America. "Time's relentless melt" haunts the pages of *In America.* Our heroine, fashioning yet another "new self," returns triumphantly to the stage, touring the western states under a new name, "Marina Zaleska." That's the novel's fairy-tale plot in a nutshell: idealistic agrarian isolata reinvents herself as imperial, media-darling diva.

But "with this story you feel you can tell many stories," the narrator of Chapter Zero tells her readers. This wonder-full, unapologetically overreaching and unabashedly exuberant novel tells us stories about (among other things): the idea of "America"; the actor's art; the Old World versus the New; the earnest sensibilities of the nineteenth century and the self-conscious sensibilities of intellectuals in every century; the birth of the modern; self-transformation; history, memory and mutability; and—above all—the splendid prerogatives of diva-dom.

"Authority, idiosyncrasy, velvetiness—these are what make a star. And an unforgettable voice." Not since George Eliot's Princess Halm-Eberstein, the Jewish birth-mother of Daniel Deronda, has there been a more fascinating, egomaniacal nineteenth-century fictional actress than Maryna Zalezowska. "This woman's nature was one in which all feeling . . . immediately became a matter of conscious representation: experience immediately passed into drama, and she acted her own emotions," Eliot wrote of her histrionic heroine—words which perfectly describe Maryna. But in 1876, George Eliot was profoundly (or at least publicly) ambivalent about a woman who placed her art above motherhood and religion: "I am not a monster, but I have not felt exactly what other women feel—or say they feel, for being thought unlike others," the Princess tells her long-lost son—just before revealing her fatal illness.

No such guilt or retributive health problems for Sontag's Polish stage-princess, "vibrant," "fluent" and "agile"—whose story also happens to begin in 1876, the same year as Deronda's. "I need ordeals, challenges, mystery. I need to feel *not* at home. That's what makes me strong," Maryna freely confesses. Maryna has a young son, Piotr, with no father in sight, but motherhood doesn't cramp her style. She also has the three men in her life every woman needs: a (rich) husband, a (romantic) lover and a (wise) friend. Wealthy husband Bogdan, estranged from his aristocratic Polish family, is latently homosexual, openly adoring of Maryna's every flamboyant move and calmly accepting of lovers and absences ("Bogdan brought support; Bogdan brought harmony"). Ryszard, novelist and Don Juan, follows Maryna to America and gets his reward ("quick bruising kisses") after the star takes eleven curtain calls on her triumphant American opening night ("I can give you my heart, Ryszard. But I can't give you my life"). To complete the triumvirate, there's Henryk, an urbane doctor straight out of a Chekhov play, who remains in Poland to give Maryna an outlet for epistolary musings.

This isn't the first time Susan Sontag has placed a divine diva center stage in a historical novel. Emma Hamilton, heroine of *The Volcano Lover,* notoriously unfaithful wife of the British Ambassador to Naples and paramour of British naval hero Horatio Nelson, was famous in her day for her striking "living statues" of famous historical/mythological figures. "Once she was in possession of the subject, came the challenging part—finding the . . . moment that represents meaning, that sums up the essence of a character, a story, an emotion. It was the same hard choice painters [and novelists, too, I would add] were supposed to make." Like Maryna, Emma isn't just an artist, she's a star. Although Emma's life ends in poverty and decrepitude, she comes back from her grave at the end of *The Volcano Lover* to address us directly: "there was some magic about me. . . . I had [something] that was more inclusive [than talent, intelligence, and beauty], that compelled attention, like a ring of light."

Sontag has said repeatedly that she'll never write her memoirs. They'd be a bestseller, of course: from being buddies with Mike Nichols at the University of Chicago in the 1950s to dodging bombs in Sarajevo in the 1990s, Sontag has, like her fictional heroines, toured widely. But to read *In America* is to know more than you could ever have hoped to learn about Susan Sontag: to tour not her life, but her brain. "We're always talking about ourselves when we talk of anything else," Maryna tells her husband.

The cover of *In America* presents a vintage photograph of an elaborately-coiffured nineteenth-century woman— her back, startlingly, to the camera. In what direction is this faceless woman gazing: backwards, or forwards? "Like many writers," Sontag writes of her novel's novelist, "Ryszard did not really believe in the present,

but only in the past and in the future." Like the photograph, the novel is, paradoxically, a memento mori that lives on. "Every limit is a beginning as well as an ending," writes George Eliot in *Middlemarch*'s "Finale." And the final line of *In America*? "We have a long tour ahead of us."

### Notes

1. Henry James, letter to his father, 10 May 1869; quoted in Gordon Haight, *George Eliot* (Oxford University Press, 1968), p. 417.

## Sven Birkerts (review date October 2000)

SOURCE: Birkerts, Sven. "Fiction in Review." *Yale Review* 88, no. 4 (October 2000): 158-62.

[*In the following review, Birkerts contends that* In America *lacks dramatic tension and character plausibility.*]

"In place of a hermeneutics," wrote Susan Sontag in 1964 at the conclusion of her essay **"Against Interpretation,"** "we need an erotics of art." It may have been the first arresting formulation in what has become a venerable career of pronouncements and instigatory postures, not to mention achieved works of prose in diverse genres. Through it all—and because of it all— Sontag has made herself into one of our very few brandname intellectuals. She is striking, memorable, the bearer of the standard of high seriousness in a culture that has essentially capitulated to the easy lifting of the ironic mode or the ready clasp of pure entertainment.

This early pronouncement serves us as an immediate point of departure, not least because of the utterly grating contradiction between message and manner. It is as intellectualized a plea for getting past the intellectualizing reflex as one could imagine. And somewhere in its lumbering insistence I catch a hint of what has irritated and frustrated me about Sontag's most recent novel, *In America.*

Although it is true that Sontag's plea for an erotics of art was directed not at the novelist—or artist—but at the critic, the fact is that Sontag has for many years now been trying to refashion herself from critic-intellectual into something more like artist-creator, a private battle (or evolution) that in many ways wants to enact the displacement of the hermeneutic by the erotic. But as the apothegm cannot unbend itself—get funky or erotic—neither in the largest sense can its author. *In America,* though it shows us how much can be achieved by the energized and purposeful will, also shows us exactly the limits of a fiction filtered through intellect that nevertheless refuses to become a fiction of ideas.

First erotics, then hermeneutics. *In America,* as anyone who has perused any of the myriad reviews knows, is a novel loosely premised on the real-life story of Polish stage actress Helena Modrzejewska, who, with her husband, son, and writer-friend Henryk Sienkiewicz, moved to America in the 1870s to remake her life. Sontag's protagonist, Maryna Zalezowska, is the very prototype of the successful, temperamental performer. Think of Bette Davis as Margo Channing in *All About Eve.* Maryna, too, is proud, willful, forever angling her face in the available light, and maturely practiced in the arts of frontal and oblique emotional assault. She lives for her nightly bath of adoration, an occupational narcissism that thrusts the rest of her life—her stolid husband, Bogdan, and the impetuous if somewhat self-regarding writer-friend, Ryszard—into the shadowy areas at stage left and right.

But Maryna dreams of change, of rebirth, of something outside the pale of her by-now familiar success, and when she quits the national stage to sail to America, it is to settle—with believable improbability—in a commune in Anaheim, California. There are some socialist political ideals percolating in the background, but Sontag is plainly not interested in exploring these for themselves.

The immersion in rural self-sufficiency proves short-lived for Maryna. An actress of her caliber—and artistic will—cannot live long away from the footlights. Sontag has her thinking thus in her phase of reconsidering: "Happiness depended on not being trapped in your individual existence, a container with your name on it. You have to forget yourself, your container. You have to attach yourself to what takes you outside yourself, what stretches the world." The counterpointing irony, of course, is that Maryna finds her roles—standard romantic leads—a perfect home for her inchoate longings and her grandiosity.

Before long, then, Maryna has hooked up with an enterprising impresario, has brushed up her roles, and is on her way to an American acting career as Marina Zalenska. She will achieve a triumph commensurate with the scale and appetites of her adopted land. Bogdan recedes, psychologically and literally, into the distance (he stays behind to tend his land), Ryszard breaks into the foreground briefly as an ardent lover—is taken up, dropped—and Maryna's son, well, he might as well not even exist.

Sontag ends the novel with Maryna in full career, spending an evening with the great American thespian—and grandiloquent drunk—Edwin Booth, who tries to articulate his feelings, his torments, but has become so grown together with his vocation that he cannot pry apart the suffering man and the posturing, self-dramatizing player. Maryna's final words in the book are: "Stop, Edwin."

Given how much *In America* turns on the themes of dramatic impersonation and self-invention, there is surprisingly little drama or tension in the work itself. Indeed, so smoothly does Sontag render Maryna living her life in her historical moment, and with such studied-up rightness does she set out her mise-en-scène, the half-tamed American West, the rude whistlestop towns where Maryna travels to reprise her roles, that there is precious little for the reader to engage with—no nap or burr. What's more, the complexity of Maryna herself is so opaque, so finished, so closed off to any speculative entry, that the reader must watch her move as upon a stage of her own devising. The whole thing is so artfully done, so combed into place. And in the absence of any sustained emotional conflict—there are only local weather patterns, situational storms (Maryna and Bogdan, Maryna and Ryszard)—we meet with nothing that can destroy, or even rupture, the closed circle of her self-regard. We are neither moved nor provoked by anything that happens, really. What Maryna said to Booth, we want to say, more stridently, to our heroine. Stop. Stop being so cunningly and coquettishly yourself all the time, with such wan regrets and ineffectual countermanding impulses. Bend, break, change, grow, do something besides strutting the boards and drinking the mead of inevitable applause. Young America slides by beautifully outside the windows of your personal railroad car, but it is not enough to hold us.

Because Sontag is such a reflective and self-conscious artist, the problem with *In America* runs deeper than a mere failure to dramatize her material. There is a flaw in the very conception, one that takes us back, I believe, to the author's willed determination to transform herself from intellectual to creator. Simply, she has tried but has not been able to go far enough; she has not killed off the gnawing worm, the consciousness that is so fatal—not to the novel necessarily, but to the kind of novel that Sontag seems to have aspired to write.

The opening chapter—"Zero"—is, in this sense, a giveaway. Here Sontag ventures the risky postmodern move of inserting herself into the period and place, enacting, in effect, how it is that a novelist's imagination comes to possess its subject. "Irresolute, no, shivering, I'd crashed a party in the private dining room of a hotel." So she begins. Moving through the room, ghost from the future come back to haunt the past, she studies the people, searching for her characters. Then she spots the woman she wants:

> No longer in her first youth, as people then said of an attractive woman past thirty, of medium height, straight-spined, with a pile of ash-blond hair into which she nervously tucked a few escaping strands, she was not exceptionally beautiful. But she became more compelling the longer I watched her. She could be, she must be, the woman they were discussing. When she moved about the room, she was always surrounded;

when she spoke she was always listened to. It seemed to me I'd caught her name, it was either Helena or Maryna—and supposing it would help me to decipher the story if I could identify the couple or the trio, what better start than to give them names. I decided to think of her as Maryna.

The gambit is intriguing, and sustained with subtle care for pages. Sontag gives body, motion, and growing particularity to what are finally figments of imagination. And how concisely she dramatizes the opportunistic motions of inspiration. But in thus intruding herself, she also begins to undermine the whole ensuing enterprise. For with this bit of sketching, these revealed flights of the modeling fancy—which compel us and draw us in—she effectively fills the gap we require in order to suspend our readerly disbelief. At a stroke, Sontag breaches the conventions of the stage, which the novel is otherwise so keen to memorialize, spilling the action into the aisles and compromising the illusionism by suggesting real-life personalities behind the assumed roles.

Don't get me wrong. I'm not suggesting that this breach of artifice—itself, as suggested, a postmodern artifice—cannot or ought not be attempted. Milan Kundera, for one, makes similar gestures all the time to brilliant effect. But Kundera does so in the service of the novel of ideas, a cause he has argued for persuasively in *The Art of the Novel* and elsewhere. Sontag, by contrast, in her project of self-remaking, not only has turned away from the procedures of critical intellect but seems bent on *not* writing a novel of ideas. She has almost perversely deprived herself of the resource of her powerful idea-making faculty, which, freed to the task, might have compensated for what feels to the reader like a considerable dramatic shortfall. If we can't get a real erotics (and true drama is erotic), we could be won over by something a bit more hermeneutic. As it is we're in a neither-nor situation.

## Michael Wood (review date summer 2001)

SOURCE: Wood, Michael. "Susan Sontag and the American Will." *Raritan* 21, no. 1 (summer 2001): 141-47.

[*In the following review, Wood analyzes the depiction of self-determination in* In America, *noting that many of Sontag's theories on society, American culture, and human will are apparent in the novel.*]

For Roland Barthes photographs were announcements of mortality, "imperious signs" of future death. The characters in Susan Sontag's new novel feel the same but at the moment of being photographed, not when they contemplate the result. And what dies for them is

not a self but a project, a hope. In the very act of photography, one character writes—we are in California in 1876—there is "a kind of foreboding. Or regret—as if we were taking the first step toward accepting the eventual failure of our colony, by making sure that we would have in our possession an image of what we are now." A few pages earlier another character thinks of a photograph as both "evidence" and "a relic"; proof for the future that the present will have existed. Why would they need proof? Why wouldn't memory and their senses be enough? One answer is that these characters are "in America," as the title of the novel says, in a place so prone to hope that time and reality seem to be effects of the will rather than material measurements or resistances. The photograph doesn't create this mythology or the concurrent anxiety about it, but it does crystallize the perception, display its secret kinship with defeat and melancholy.

*In America* is a historical novel which is also a subtle and complex meditation on America as the land of the will. More precisely, as a land where the will is not so much a presence or a force as the object of a collective act of faith, "a whole country of people who believe in the will," as the central character suggests. The same character, a page or so later, recognizes "the old American tune, which conflates willing strenuously and taking for granted." The singer of the tune in this case is Henry James, imagining he is more English than he is, taking himself for English because that is what he wants to be. "Henry James was very American after all," our heroine concludes. "He'd contrived to have at his disposal a vast allotment of willing."

Who is this expert on the American will? She is a Polish actress, and it's important to remember that this novel is mainly peopled by Europeans, and that virtually all of its many fine reflections on the idea of America come from them. It's also important to remember that the expert on the Polish actress and on the European view of America is an American novelist, Sontag herself, fully present in this text as an imagining and reimagining mind. America is not a fantasy or an illusion in such a framework, but it is doubly dreamed as well as geographically real. It's a European idea, as its name suggests; but not only a European idea. There are Americans who have forgotten Europe, and there are Americans who never knew it. And there are Americans, Sontag's intricate fiction suggests, who need to keep starting out again from Europe in order to arrive in their own history and their own present time.

The novel begins "Irresolute, no, shivering, I'd crashed a party in the private dining room of a hotel." The party is taking place in Warsaw in 1876, but the gate-crasher already knows about Maria Callas and 1960s New York and the "besieged Sarajevo" of our day. She doesn't understand Polish ("I was in a country I'd visited only once, thirteen years ago"), but she picks up scraps of meaning from the conversations she hears, and she tells us something about herself. "For it should be mentioned, why not here, that all four of my grandparents were born in this country (hence, born in a country that had ceased to exist some eighty years earlier), indeed, born around the very year to which I'd traveled in my mind in order to co-inhabit this room with its old-timey conversations, though the couple that engendered me were quite unlike these people, being poor unworldly villagers with occupations like peddler, innkeeper, woodcutter, Talmud student." The narrator also tells us that she has "tried conjuring up a hotel dining room from the same era in Sarajevo, and failed," and more intimately that she first read *Middlemarch* at the age of eighteen and cried "because I realized not only that *I* was Dorothea but that, a few months earlier, I had married Mr. Casaubon."

Our narrator clearly much resembles our novelist, but we should pause over the careful descriptions of her activities. She travels in her mind, she tries to conjure up. "These people" are not her people, they are Polish aristocrats and artists and intellectuals, and there is a difference between a mental journey to a remembered place and the same journey to an imagined place, and still another difference between either of those trips and a journey to a place which is both actual and imagined, both documentable and dreamed. I hear the voice of Salman Rushdie reminding us (in *Midnight's Children*) that "reality can have a metaphorical content," and Sontag's narrator comments shrewdly and elegiacally on the same topic:

> The past is the biggest country of all, and there's a reason one gives in to the desire to set stories in the past: almost everything good seems to be located in the past, perhaps that's an illusion, but I feel nostalgic for every era before I was born; and one is freer of modern inhibitions, perhaps because one bears no responsibility for the past, sometimes I feel simply ashamed of the time in which I live. And this past will also be the present, because it was I in the private dining room of the hotel, scattering seeds of prediction. I did not belong there, I was an alien presence . . . but even what I misunderstood would be a kind of truth, if only about the time in which I live.

The compelling truth here seems to be the felt shame of the present. The innocence of the past is perhaps not entirely an invention but it is inseparable now from the fallen time it precedes and rebukes. What speaks in a nostalgia "for every era before I was born" is not the historical imagination but a lyrical scorn for the writer's own day.

But the historical imagination is at work here too. The well-known historical events of the period are alluded to very discreetly. There is an American financial panic "of three years ago"; there is the "ignominious defeat" of General Custer "early this summer." And there is the less recent assassination of President Lincoln "by a deranged actor, as you'll recall." The deranged actor is the younger brother of a more famous actor, Edwin Booth, who is given a long soliloquy (a conversation in the form of a brilliant monologue) at the close of the novel, which rests in all its major details on further historical events which are not exactly unknown. The Polish actress Helena Modrzejewska, her name later shortened to Modjeska, emigrated to America in the late nineteenth century, founded a utopian colony in California, and became the age's most famous stage diva, rivaled only by Sarah Bernhardt. She was accompanied to America by her husband and her son and her friend and lover the writer Henryk Sienkiewicz, later to become known as the author of *Quo Vadis*. Sontag's novel is "inspired by" these travels and these figures, she says, "no less and no more." The historical Modjeska becomes the fictional Maryna Zalezowska, shortened to Zalenska; her husband, the count, is Bogdan; her son is Piotr; Sienkiewicz is Ryszard. We even watch the writer handing out these names—"yes, I know it could have been Helena, but I'd decided that it would be, or must be, Maryna," "I ruled that he could not be a Karol, that I had misheard his name, and gave myself permission to rechristen him Bogdan." The point, I take it, is not only to express the liberty of fiction to rework and complement history, but to remind us of fiction's haunting by history, the substantive, continuing existence of what is there to be reworked.

*In America* takes us from Zalenska's Warsaw to her rural retreat in the Tatra mountains; follows the outriders of her community across the Atlantic as they explore possibilities for settlement in America, and decide on Anaheim in California; traces Maryna's own travels from Hoboken through the Panama Canal; describes the start-up and ongoing life and abrupt failure of the community; and chronicles in rich detail Maryna's return to the stage, including a visit to Poland and a tour in England, complete with conversation with Henry James. The last sentences of the book record Edwin Booth's hatred of improvisation, and strike the same complicated note about history and reality and their alternatives. "An actor can't just *make it up*," Booth says to Maryna. "Shall we promise each other, here and now, always to tell first when we're going to do something new? We have a long tour ahead of us." They may be actors and have a long tour ahead of them, but they are also versions of the historical novelist. They will do something new, but they won't just make it up.

Maryna didn't want to feel like a child, even as a child, and certainly not when she was an adult. "It was partly so as not to feel like a child, ever, that she had become an actress." To be a child, in this perspective, is to be vulnerable, prey to parents and memory and your old submissive habits. An actress, in the same perspective, is something like an American as the novel thinks of this brave creature, an instance of perpetual self-invention. And to become an American actress, having been a Polish one, is to carry the sense of an always renewable world to extreme lengths. To be an American, Ryszard thinks at the beginning of his voyage, is "to be free to think yourself something you're not (not yet), something better than what you are." Bogdan writes in his journal: "In Poland I thought that I was what I had to be. America means one can strive with fate."

This is very traditional, and familiar, and a long way from the bitterly negative America Sontag evokes in *Styles of Radical Will* and elsewhere. But the ideology has its cracks. Would the equation of actress and America mean that America never felt like a child, however much its inhabitants might boast of their innocence and claim to think like children? Even America, Ryszard thinks, "has its America." If Poles dream of New York, New Yorkers dream of California. The deferral of the dream evokes Langston Hughes, and sure enough, there he is, in the epigraph to the whole novel: "America will be!" That sounds positive enough, but gets a little gloomy if the future is always somewhere else, and gloomier still if the "will" in that sentence expresses effort or even desperation as well as tomorrow's tense. "America is supposed to repair the European scale of injury," Bogdan writes, "or simply make one forget what one wanted, to substitute other desires." The supposed repair seems a little remote, and just forgetting what one wanted isn't the most dynamic form of the American dream. "In America," Bogdan writes again, thinking now of the faltering utopian community, "everything is supposed to be possible. And everything *is* possible here, abetted by the American inventiveness and the American talent for desecration. America lived up to its part of the bargain. The fault, the failure, is ours." What happens is different from what's possible, in America or anywhere else, and the very idea of possibility can become a reproach, a source of shame about the actual.

"Every marriage," Maryna thinks, "every community is a failed utopia. Utopia is not a kind of place but a kind of time, those all too brief moments when one would not wish to be anywhere else." This is not just European pessimism, or a Polish taste for martyrdom, which are amply celebrated and mocked within the novel. It is an evocation of America as neither repair for injury nor substitution of desire nor sheer bland possibility but as something that can be constantly sought but scarcely ever found. Early in the novel Maryna believes firmly in "the power of the will," in what she calls the "utopian" idea "that everything we wish can be obtained," and she achieves a considerable amount of success in this vein. But she realizes that charm and

persistence and charisma are not the same as wishing, and begins to think that will is "just another name for desire." In other words, there are two very different kinds of will to be invoked. One is the planning, originating desire, the one that seeks and finds means for its fulfillment. This is what gets Europeans to America, and gets anyone, Europeans or Americans, to achieve anything at all. Then there is the other, lonelier, powerless evocation of the will, which represents lingering desire without any hope or means of fulfillment, since all we have is the willing itself, supposed to be capable of magically turning thought into action, of unilaterally taking the place of all the now broken instruments of desire.

When Americans conflate "willing strenuously with taking for granted," they are using the second kind of willing to disguise the absence or failure of the first. And when they are said to "believe in the will," both senses of the word are in play. Americans believe in wanting things and getting things, Sontag is suggesting, but they are not sure how much they have to do beyond the wanting. Ryszard is described as "one of those extremely intelligent people who become writers because they cannot imagine a better use of their watchfulness," and the narrator says something very similar about herself and her notion "that steadfastness and caring more than the others about what was important would take me wherever I wanted to go." "I thought if I listened and watched and ruminated, taking as much time as I needed, I could understand the people in this room, that theirs would be a story that would speak to me."

Watchers see all kinds of sights, of course, but in this novel they register two things above all. First, America is a place infiltrated with ideas which keep threatening to take it out of place, and out of time, although it can't finally escape history's clutches. Second, the will is a fiction which moves many facts around, which can't be ignored and can't be believed in. The watcher finds these insights in the large country of the past, but the territory is easier to enter than to bring up to date. "I don't consider devotion to the past a form of snobbery," one of the characters says in a story in Sontag's *I, etcetera.* "Just one of the more disastrous forms of unrequited love." *In America* displays the same unrequited love, but converts it into utopia, the place we can't go beyond and don't wish to leave. The vision is alluring, and Sontag is suggesting we need both to understand its appeal and to shake it off. It is not a style of radical will but rather the reverse: a longing for a historical time when wishing was an option, and for the fantasy time when wishing was enough.

**Scott McLemee (review date 16 September 2001)**

SOURCE: McLemee, Scott. "Notes from the Pedestal." *Washington Post Book World* (16 September 2001): 9.

[*In the following review, McLemee expresses his disappointment with the essays in* Where the Stress Falls, *finding Sontag's approach egotistical and clichéd, and asserting the writing lacks the biting observations of her earlier writings.*]

Anyone who admires the work of Susan Sontag can only greet the publication of a new volume of her essays with mixed emotions, a blend of hope and worry. Her last collection appeared in 1980. That same year, she told an interviewer in Poland that there were no really great writers in America but that the country did have "ten extremely good prose writers, of which," she helpfully noted, "I am one." During this same period she began announcing that she would henceforth spend less time writing criticism, in order to concentrate on fiction—a promise she has, unfortunately, kept.

In other words, **Where the Stress Falls** was written during a period of Sontag's waning commitment to the work for which she has a real gift. Over the past 20 years, I have worn out a few copies of **Against Interpretation** (1966) and subsequent collections. The authority of that voice, the sensuousness of mind that it evoked, the intellectual restlessness and energy, the knack for the adamantine aphorism—these made for essays in an almost classical vein. In her best writing on literature, film and ideas, Sontag captures the intrinsic drama of moral and aesthetic questions.

But in Sontag's fiction, by contrast, mere will does the work of the imagination. At its worst, the effect is that of an unintentional parody of Borges, lacking the wit or grace of the original. With **The Volcano Lover** (1992), she overcame the narrative anemia of her previous novels through a transfusion of full-blooded historical drama. But this was temporary. Last year, **In America** recycled her bestselling formula (adulterous romance among sophisticated emigres in an exotic setting) while also revealing a formidable gift for the platitude. The book was sprinkled with dozens of passages in which her wandering band of Polish intellectuals ponder the American way of life as a ceaseless abolition of history, responsibility, complexity, etc. The line between profundity and triteness has seldom been drawn more finely.

**Where the Stress Falls** reprints more than 40 essays written while Sontag has been trying to reconfigure herself as novelist—or rather, perhaps, as Nobelist. (With her regular invocation of "the idea of literary greatness" and the frequent suggestion that she is among the last defenders of "seriousness," she sounds as if she has her eyes on the prize.) The volume includes one of her very best essays, **"Writing Itself: On Roland Barthes"** (1982), plus a half-dozen or so other pieces that bear up to more than one reading. As her own remarks over the years have indicated, rereading is indeed the test. A durable literary work cannot be exhausted the first time through; returning to it is a curious process of defamiliarization, of renegotiating an understanding with something you have already experienced.

A few of Sontag's essays from the past two decades can induce that experience. Most don't. Several essays written as prefaces to collections of photographs read like indifferent paraphrases of the densely textured argument of her book **On Photography** (1978). The items on dance and opera are pleasantly effusive, but not much else. Her comments on Robert Walser and Danilo Kis sent me scrambling to the library when she first published them years ago; they leave you wishing she would write critical essays on their work, instead of brief introductions.

A short item titled **"DQ"** is not, alas, about a visit to the Dairy Queen. Rather, it offers five paragraphs about *Don Quixote* that are both unexceptional and remarkably uninteresting: She writes that "Cervantes's book is the very image of that glorious *mise-en-abime* which is literature, and of that fragile delirium that is authorship, its manic expressiveness." The staleness of that thought has scarcely been forgotten when (two pages later, in an essay on Borges) she denies that reading is escapism: "Books are much more. They are a way of being fully human." A bold thought, to be sure—though nothing can quite compare to this one, in an essay on Adam Zagajewski: "From a great Polish writer we expect Slavic intensities."

What gives? The early Sontag was ruthless about cultural clichés. Her favorite term of scorn was "philistine," and her essays embodied, as she says about Barthes, "an ideology of taste which makes of the familiar something vulgar and facile." Her manner now is virtually indistinguishable from that of George Steiner in his lugubrious moments as Last Intellectual, striking that solemn pose as embodiment of high seriousness—perched atop the Nintendo ruins of Western Civilization. Of course, this attitude can itself be something "familiar . . . vulgar and facile"—not to mention self-aggrandizing.

Eagerness to mount one's portable pedestal is a definite liability to a writer. For one thing, you can see only so much from that great height. Instead of writing and speaking to her fellow American citizens on behalf of military action against Serbian aggression in Bosnia, Sontag gave another well-rehearsed performance of her contempt for the people who would actually do the fighting. (She has never been shy about expressing her belief that the butt-ugly aesthetics of our mass society is no better than its inhabitants deserve.) Nor has her writing on the arts exactly benefited from her proclamation that she is ultimately responsible to "the republic of letters"—the self-selected cosmopolitan elite of self-regulating excellence. Her essays were better in the early '60s, when she was hanging around with the methamphetaminized drag queens and Eurotrash sponges at Andy Warhol's studio.

The habit of high disdain has its own rewards, of course. But the long-term effect, to judge by *Where the Stress Falls,* is ultimately impoverishing. At several points, Sontag evokes the idea that a great artist's goal is "wisdom." That belief is honorable. But what about the belief that one is among the great? It seems the better part of wisdom to keep such thoughts to oneself.

## Deborah L. Nelson (review date October 2001)

SOURCE: Nelson, Deborah L. "Public Intellectual." *Women's Review of Books* 19, no. 1 (October 2001): 4-6.

[*In the following review, Nelson examines the changing tones amongst the essays collected in* Where the Stress Falls.]

You showed that it was not necessary to be unhappy," Susan Sontag writes in **"A Letter to Borges,"** "even while one is clear-eyed and undeluded about how terrible everything is." Sontag's new collection of essays, *Where the Stress Falls,* drawn from her work of the past twenty years championing artists, art forms and causes, salvages tremendous comfort from acute disappointment. Her idiosyncratic moral aestheticism, which provokes the Left and the Right in this country, sets the terms for the collection, providing the grounds of her esteem for artists in a wide variety of media and her disillusionment with her fellow intellectuals. For the "barely closeted moralist," as she describes the younger self that wrote *Against Interpretation* (and she has long since come out of this closet), it is a given that "there is no possibility of true culture without altruism."

*Where the Stress Falls* is not a typical Sontag essay collection. First, it contains none of the extended sieges on an idea or form that make up *Against Interpretation, Styles of Radical Will, On Photography, Illness as Metaphor* and *Under the Sign of Saturn.* Instead, it offers forty essays parceled out under three headings—"Reading," "Seeing" and "There and Here"—in just under 350 pages. These pieces are mostly brief, many as short as three pages, most under ten, and only two of

roughly 25 pages: **"Writing Itself: On Roland Barthes"** and **"Waiting for Godot in Sarajevo."** These two are among the most satisfying essays in the volume because Sontag has room to explore, detour and elaborate. Second, the vast majority of these essays—prefaces, introductions and program notes—originally addressed not a general audience but one made up of enthusiasts: those who attended a performance of Bunraku (Japanese puppetry) or a Wagner opera, or who bought a catalogue of painter Howard Hodgkin, a translation of a novel by W. G. Sebald, or a collection celebrating one hundred years of Italian photography.

It is the mark of Sontag's immense authority as a generalist that there is virtually no stylistic difference between an introduction to a new translation of *Pedro Páramo* and an exploration of the appeal of the grotto in *House and Garden.* All the same, the obligations of preface-or program-writing require Sontag to restrain the sweep and ambition that marked her most famous work in order to turn attention toward, not compete with, the artists she so fervently admires.

Attention is the coin of Sontag's realm and, sadly for the feminist reader, she rarely chooses to bestow it on women. Only three women artists receive consideration: Russian poet Marina Tsvetaeva, cultural critic and novelist Elizabeth Hardwick (to whom she dedicates the volume) and dancer/choreographer Lucinda Childs, the subject of **"Lexicon for *Available Light.*"** One wishes this were not so, not only because when she chooses to, Sontag writes thoughtfully about the stubborn asymmetries of gender. The author of the best essay on the position of women never anthologized, **"The Third World of Women"** from *Partisan Review* in 1973, Sontag has been extremely astute about feminist concerns. (That essay could have been written yesterday, it anticipates, so many of the later fractures within feminism.) But while never simple-minded about questions of gender, Sontag is no longer at the vanguard, as we can see in the smart but by no means groundbreaking introduction to *Women,* Annie Liebovitz's extraordinary collection of photographs. She seems to have as little interest in recent feminist thinking as contemporary feminists have had in her. That is, to my mind, regrettable for both.

Perhaps the fact that Sontag feels the injuries of her position as a woman is the reason she rarely elects to write about it. She seems to admire most in Elizabeth Hardwick her refusal to dwell on wounds to the self: "Not a breath of complaint (and there is much to complain of) . . ." One's own pain is simply never a tasteful or ethical subject of contemplation, taste being a form of ethics for Sontag. Women are not the only ones praised for this reticence. She respects poet Joseph Brodsky's ability to bear "[i]ntractable grief . . . with great indignation, great sobriety" as much as Hardwick's "[c[auterizing the torment of personal relations with hot lexical choices, jumpy punctuation, mercurial sentence rhythms." Indeed, disciplined self-transcendence in form is a value extolled in everything from writing to dance (Childs, Lincoln Kirstein and Mikhail Baryshnikov) to painting (Hodgkin).

Gender simply isn't where the stress falls. But to speculate on why this might be violates the terms of reading that she lays out in **"Singleness,"** one of the essays in which she describes her relationship to her own writing. She warns strenuously against making assumptions about her person from either what she has chosen to write or what she hasn't: "I write what I can: that is, what's given to me and what seems worth writing, by me. I care passionately about many things that don't get into my fiction and essays . . . My books aren't me—all of me. And in some ways, I am less than them." While Sontag is more willing to insert herself into some of these essays than one might expect, the entire collection is laced with caveats about autobiography, its capacity to conceal as well as reveal, and her dismay at the indefatigable self-exposure of so much contemporary writing. Autobiography *can* be a "wisdom project" but only when, like Adam Zagajewski's *Another Beauty,* it "purges [one] of vanity" or, like Roland Barthes' late work, it is "artfully anti-confessional."

So where does the stress fall? What is it that absorbs her attention and draws forth her most passionate moral commitments and aesthetic appreciation? In the third of the volume's three sections, "There and Here," we see a point of moral crisis that unifies the collection as a whole. This section includes essays Sontag wrote about her experiences in Sarajevo in the early 1990s; they deliver both a moving account of the Sarajevans' plight and a stinging rebuke to the European and American intellectual community.

> If the intellectuals of the 1930s and 1960s often showed themselves too gullible, too prone to appeals to idealism to take in what was really happening in certain beleaguered, newly radicalized societies that they may or may not have visited (briefly), the morosely depoliticized intellectuals of today with their cynicism always at the ready, their addiction to entertainment, their reluctance to inconvenience themselves for any cause, their devotion to personal safety, seem at least equally deplorable.
>
> (p. 328)

Beyond personal failure, she censures a more general collapse of international solidarity and attenuation of political engagement; this is a time, she concludes, when "[o]nly domestic political commitments seem plausible." The provincialism and timidity excoriated in "There and Here" provide stark contrast to the heroism extolled in the essays of "Reading" and "Seeing." The moral compass that US intellectuals have so tragically lost she finds in writers like Yugoslavia's Danilo Kiš, "who spoke up against nationalism and fomented-from-the-top ethnic hatreds" but "could not save Europe's honor, Europe's better idea," and Poland's Witold Gombrowicz, who in "strengthening his disaffection from nationalist pieties and self-congratulation" became "a consummate citizen of world literature."

Sontag indirectly explains the diminished expectations of *Where the Stress Falls* in **"Thirty Years Later . . . ,"** her introduction to a new edition of *Against Interpretation,* reprinted here. "The world in which these essays were written no longer exists," she concludes, but "How one wishes some of its boldness, its optimism, its disdain for commerce had survived." Suffusing this collection is her awareness that neither aesthetic value nor moral commitment claims serious reflection in advanced capitalist cultures, which have witnessed a "vertiginous shift of moral attitudes" whose "hallmark is the discrediting of all idealisms, of altruism itself; of high standards of all kinds, cultural as well as moral." The narrower address of *Where the Stress Falls* and its more limited ambition predict that it will not engender the controversy or the esteem of Sontag's earlier work. But as **"Thirty Years Later . . ."** suggests, perhaps it is not so much Sontag who has changed, but the world around her.

Such a powerful sense of disaffection from the present moment might induce a deep nostalgia for the better times of thirty years ago. Thankfully, with one possible exception (**"A Century of Cinema,"** which yearns for the cinephilia of that era) Sontag does not indulge. The pervasive sorrow of the essays is tempered by her boundless capacity for admiration and pleasure in literature, dance, painting, photography, opera and film. *Where the Stress Falls* oscillates between melancholy and delight, outrage and a cautious optimism. Collecting these exercises in advanced appreciation, she seems not to have abandoned the hopefulness that supplied the energy of her early work, her then unwavering belief in the value of serious reflection. That hopefulness is muted, but not extinguished: "There is desolation and, as well, so many fortifying pleasures supplied by the genius of others."

## Carl Rollyson (essay date 2001)

SOURCE: Rollyson, Carl. "The Benefactor." In *Reading Susan Sontag: A Critical Introduction to Her Work,* pp. 44-54. Chicago, Ill.: Ivan R. Dee, 2001.

*[In the following essay, Rollyson explores the similarities between Hippolyte, the main character in* The Benefactor, *and John Neal, the protagonist in Kenneth Burke's* Towards a Better Life.*]*

## The Benefactor

*Synopsis*

In certain respects, "Dreams of Hippolyte" is a more satisfying title for Sontag's first novel [*The Benefactor*]. For it is a book of dreams, a reverie reminiscent of Poe. In the first chapter, Hippolyte, the narrator, declares in French, "I Dream Therefore I Am." He takes a retrospective tone, contrasting the difference between "those days" and "now." He has written an article that excites comment in the literary world and gains him an invitation to the salon of Frau Anders. In retrospect, it is difficult not to see in Hippolyte the emerging figure of Susan Sontag, about to attain fame for an essay, **"Notes on 'Camp,'"** even as she enters the literary circle centered on *Partisan Review*. But in the novel autobiography becomes allegory, and New York City is displaced by a foreign capital similar to Paris but not named as such. True to her aesthetic, Sontag does not wish to make her novel a report on reality but rather a counterweight to it.

In the second chapter, Hippolyte relates his dream of two rooms that imprison him. He is ordered about by a sadist in a black wool bathing suit. The sadist limps and carries a flute. Hippolyte tells his dream to Jean-Jacques, a writer, homosexual prostitute, and former boxer, who tells him to live his dream and go beyond it. But to Hippolyte, the dream is an end in itself, or rather, it is a prelude to more dreams. In other words, rather than attempting to connect his dreams (imagination) to the outer world, he prefers to invert Jean-Jacques's advice—Hippolyte moves away from the world and further into his dreams.

In Chapters Three and Four, sexually charged versions of the "two rooms dream" lead Hippolyte to begin a new project: the seduction of Frau Anders. More dreams with pornographic and religious connotations prompt Hippolyte to discuss them with Father Trissotin, who considers whether they are inspired by the devil. Like Sontag, the essayist who resists critiquing art in moral terms, Hippolyte steadfastly refuses to reduce his dreams to psychological or moral terms. Rather, he desires to expand the experience of his dreams by seducing Frau Anders. The sex in his dreams is just that—sex—which Sontag later calls (in **"The Pornographic Imagination"**) a form of pure pleasure that should be immune to moralistic debates and assessments. Just as literature should be appreciated in its own terms, so Hippolyte's dreams are not to be reduced to an interpretation of their contents. Hippolyte insists that his dreams are a dialogue with himself. He declares he wants to "rid my dreams of me"—implying, apparently, a desire to dissolve himself into his creation, just as Sontag would later argue in her essays that the work is the writer, that no writer is separable from the work.

To expunge himself, then, is to attain a "silence," a kind of state of perfect equilibrium, apart from words, that Sontag will later name, in an important essay, **"The Aesthetics of Silence."**

Debating his quest for silence with Jean-Jacques in Chapter Five, Hippolyte announces that he hopes to fashion dreams like silent movies. Although Jean-Jacques has been a kind of model for Hippolyte, the men split on the subject of silence, since Jean-Jacques is very much a man of the world and a believer in theatricality and role playing. He is a participant, Hippolyte is an observer. Hippolyte treasures the sheer sensuousness of images in silent film; Jean-Jacques is a man of the word.

In Chapters Six and Seven, the logic of Hippolyte's dreams drives him to kidnap Frau Anders, to drug her, to share his dreams with her, and then to sell her to an Arab barman in an Arab city. Returning to the capital in Chapter Seven, he has dreams of an old man who becomes his patron, who makes him dig a hole and throw a cat in it. Like other similar dreams, Hippolyte abases himself to an authority who degrades him. Although he awakes cursing the "captivity of his dreams," a conversation with Professor Bulgaraux convinces him that the dreams are a form of psychic cleansing. Rather than feeling ashamed or humiliated, he appears liberated—evidently because he has divested himself of his worldly personality and submitted himself to the power of his dreams.

To submit to the dream is to relinquish the craving for interpretation, Hippolyte implies in Chapter Eight. He recounts his last role as an actor. Playing the part of a father confessor to a child-murderer, Hippolyte argues with the director who wants to explain the psychology of the criminal. Hippolyte objects to the director's belief that the criminal is passionate. Just the opposite is true, Hippolyte argues: the murderer is supremely indifferent to his crime. Psychology is only a form of exoneration, Hippolyte implies.

When Frau Anders's daughter, Lucrezia, receives a ransom note, Hippolyte agrees to pay the sum for Frau Anders's return. He discusses with Lucrezia, his lover, his theory that dreams are perpetually present—unlike real events which vanish after they occur and are, in a sense, revocable.

In Chapter Nine, Herr Anders, anticipating his wife's return, seeks Hippolyte's help in obtaining a divorce, since he wishes to remarry. Hippolyte's friend, Monique, delivers a letter from Frau Anders, who then appears. She has been maimed by the Arab and demands that Hippolyte tell her what to do. Hippolyte dreams of a piano lesson in which he crawls into a piano played by a Mother Superior in the garden of an ice palace.

Inside the piano he meets "a young man with a tiny mustache" and advises him to crawl into a hole in the floor while students attack the piano. Hippolyte then shoots the Mother Superior and everyone in the room. Then he is pulled out of a tree by the man in the black bathing suit. Noticing that the Mother Superior resembles Frau Anders, Hippolyte sets fire to her apartment.

Suspecting that he has murdered Frau Anders, Hippolyte visits Monique in Chapter Ten. She is jealous about his relationship with Frau Anders. He tells her that he is guilty of "real murder." With Jean-Jacques he explores the concept of individualism, which can be creative or destructive. Hippolyte then leaves the capital to visit his sick father, with whom he discusses marriage and murder. When he returns to the capital, Monique has married, and Frau Anders tells him: "My dear, you're no better as a murderer than as a white-slaver." When he inherits his father's estate, Hippolyte decides to surprise Frau Anders by refurbishing a town house for her, thus becoming her benefactor.

In Chapter Eleven, Hippolyte takes Frau Anders on a tour of the house and is relieved and delighted to see that she accepts his gift. When he obeys her command to make love to her, he discovers, as in a dream, that in his "erotic fury" he has healed her. The "dream of the mirror" follows in Chapter Twelve. Hippolyte is standing in a ballroom trying to remember a name. When he strips naked and encounters a footman, he announces that he is a "potential amputee" and rips off his own left leg. He then struggles into an operating theatre where he is among volunteers waiting to have their eyes put out with knitting needles. He proposes to donate his body and worldly goods to the man in the black bathing suit if his leg and his sight are restored to him. When he is told to run, he finds himself in the street watching his own house burn. Rescuing his journal, a book of ancient history, and a tray with cups, he confronts his father. What will Hippolyte call his wife? his father asks. This long sequence of dreams involving dismemberment, destruction, and reunification, and the fact that Hippolyte seems to be waking up to see his dream in the mirror, suggests that perhaps the world of waking and dreaming are coming together. He goes back to his country home, marries an officer's daughter, and returns to the capital.

In Chapter Thirteen, Hippolyte seems content with his happy wife, even though Jean-Jacques suggests that Hippolyte expresses his guilt by being a benefactor to Frau Anders. Hippolyte tells his wife the story of a nearly blind princess who marries a talking bear that decides not to talk. They live happily ever after, perhaps because she cannot see whom she has married. Hippolyte's wife makes friends with a Jewess who is being pursued by the authorities. The Jewess turns out to be Frau Anders. Meanwhile Hippolyte thinks about how self-love so perfectly contains the lover.

Hippolyte discovers in Chapter Fourteen that his wife is dying of leukemia. He attends her and they play with tarot cards. Jean-Jacques appears, masquerading as an officer who dies in a fight with Hippolyte, who then delivers (with the assistance of a delivery boy) an unconscious Jean-Jacques to his flat. Hippolyte's wife dies after three days in a coma. Professor Bulgaraux performs a private service, delivering a sermon entitled "On the Death of a Virgin Soul." Like the criminal, the virgin discovers innocence in the act of defiance, Bulgaraux declares. A tense Hippolyte feels the need of another dream.

Although increasingly estranged from Jean-Jacques, Hippolyte renews their friendship in Chapter Fifteen after learning that Jean-Jacques has been accused of collaboration (the novel is vaguely set during the years of the Spanish Civil War and World War II). The two men argue, with Jean-Jacques accusing Hippolyte of being a "character without a story." Hippolyte dreams again, and this time he is dismembered several times by three acrobats. He then retires to his town house to live with Frau Anders.

In Chapter Sixteen, Hippolyte reaches the end of his story and suddenly doubts its veracity. What has he been dreaming? What has been "real"? Have the two rooms of his dreams been an expression of his two modes of existence? Apparently evicted from his house, Hippolyte considers that perhaps he has been confined to a mental institution. Has his story been only the outline of a novel he finds in his notebooks? How can he separate his waking from his dreaming?

### SONTAG READING SONTAG

**The Benefactor,** as Sontag admitted in 1974 to interviewer Joe David Bellamy, contains "systematically obscure elements . . . because I want to leave several possible readings open." On the one hand, the novel is the "dreams of Hippolyte," and like all dreams his contain unresolvable elements and events that cannot be reduced to a definitive interpretation. Sontag seems to have set out to construct a novel that defies or is "against interpretation." Even Hippolyte cannot say for sure what his dreams mean and how much he has dreamed. As Sontag told Jonathan Cott in 1979, Hippolyte is a "kind of Candide who, instead of looking for the best of all possible worlds, searches for some clear state of consciousness, for a way in which he could be properly disburdened." The idea that he can jettison reality, Sontag suggests, is ludicrous, and she means for some of his apparently solemn statements to be taken comically and ironically. He cannot abolish the waking world any more than he can stifle his dreams. The novel's ending, then, is ironic. By attempting to live entirely in his dreams, Hippolyte has no basis for comparison; he cannot know how much he has been dreaming because he has not kept careful track of his waking moments. His problem is not psychological; it is ontological. Like a Poe narrator, his problem is not that he is insane; it is that he has lost a standard or objective by which to measure himself. This is perhaps why Sontag told Edward Hirsch in 1995 that she "thought I was telling a pleasurably sinister story that illustrated the fortune of certain heretical religious ideas that go by the name of Gnosticism." She seems to have in mind the notion that Hippolyte's Gnostic search for esoteric or privileged knowledge is ironic because in his desire to be unique he destroys any way of grounding his uniqueness.

Sontag also told Hirsch that in retrospect she realized that the model for her first novel was Kenneth Burke's *Towards a Better Life.* He had given her a copy of the novel when she was at the University of Chicago. Years later he would say that she was his best student, and not surprisingly he wrote to her later to tell her how much he enjoyed *The Benefactor.* Burke, more renowned for his literary criticism than his fiction, had published a work, Sontag explained to Hirsch, full of "arias and fictive moralizing. The coquetry of a protagonist—Burke dared to call the novel's hero [John Neal]—so ingeniously self-absorbed that no reader could be tempted to identify with him." Similarly, Sontag had picked a narrator who was a Frenchman in his sixties to forestall any identification between herself and Hippolyte. (Burke's novel and its relationship to *The Benefactor* is discussed in the next section.)

Sontag resisted any autobiographical reading of *The Benefactor,* insisting to James Toback in 1968 that "I'm *nothing* like Hippolyte: at least I certainly *hope* I'm not. He fascinates me, but I dislike him intensely. He's purposeless and wasteful and evil."

CRITICAL COMMENTARY

Reviews of *The Benefactor* were respectful but mixed. In the *New York Times Book Review,* Daniel Stern commented, "It has been said of the French that they develop an idea and then assume it is the world. Hippolyte has decided that *he* is the world, and has proceeded to explore it." He compared Sontag's work to the *nouveau roman.* In *Against Interpretation,* she would secure her status as the foremost interpreter of the French new novel, selecting the work of Nathalie Sarraute and Alain Robbe-Grillet for her admiration. What her novel had in common with her French colleagues was a style that "concentrates . . . on itself," noted reviewer John Wain in the *New Republic.* She repudiated the American tradition of psychological realism. James Frakes in the *New York Herald Tribune* was

perhaps the novel's greatest advocate, calling it "a very special book, written with care, polish, daring, and certainty. Very sure. Very tough." Yet he took note of *The Benefactor*'s "frustrating precise design." Though it reminded him of Kafka, to other readers Sontag's absolute exclusion of psychological insight squeezed life out of the novel. What she gained in purity of form, she lost in chapters that became monotonous. In the *New York Review of Books,* Robert Adams appreciated Sontag's original depiction of a "mind lost in its own intricate dialectic." He thought of *Candide* but complained that Sontag did not have Voltaire's wit or gift for comedy.

Later critics, drawing on Sontag's essays, perceived that Hippolyte resembled her culture heroes such as E. M. Cioran (an alienated Romanian exile who lived and wrote in Paris) and Antonin Artaud (a great writer about the modern theatre's need to explore extreme states of mind, who himself went mad). Sohnya Sayres pointed to Sontag's comment that these writers' "uninhibited display of egotism devolves into the heroic quest for the cancellation of the self." Although Sontag told interviewer James Toback that she was nothing like Hippolyte and that she found him wasteful and evil, Sayres suspected that Sontag was "hiding from a complex set of feelings." She was ambivalent about the aesthetic view of the world—the one in which Hippolyte's dreams have first claim on him—because it seems to lead to a solipsism that negates the idea of the individual's ethical obligation to others. Ultimately Hippolyte's devotion to his own vision results in his self-disintegration. Yet the Sontag of the early essays she was soon to include in *Against Interpretation* extols precisely those artists who favor the beauty of form over the urgency of the message, the content. *The Benefactor* seems to subvert as much as it supports Sontag's essays. Sontag's first novel has buried in it the seeds of doubt about her aesthetic position that would begin to surface in interviews she gave to coincide with the publication of her most recent novel, *In America.*

No critic spotted the resemblance between Kenneth Burke's *Towards a Better Life* and *The Benefactor.* Burke's protagonist, John Neal, laments, rejoices, beseeches, admonishes, moralizes, and rages against the world, the status quo. He is a Hippolyte, a narcissist concerned with perfecting himself. As critic Merle Brown points out, Neal's language is "pure artifice"; that is, it does not arise out of character development or plot. Instead, he is his arias as much as Hippolyte is his dreams. Both Neal and Hippolyte are fashioning narratives that represent themselves, not the world. In his preface to *Towards a Better Life,* Burke favors the essayistic over the narrative, admitting that in the books "I had especially admired, I had found many desirable qualities which threatened them as novels." This is, no doubt, why he taught Joseph Conrad's novel *Victory* during one of Sontag's semesters with him. In Conrad's narrator, Marlow, Burke seized on the intruding figure—the writer who reminds the reader that stories are artifice.

Burke argues in his preface that the verisimilitude of the nineteenth-century novel that has come to dominate fiction is but a blip in the history of literature, which has traditionally prized form over lifelike content. Here he is foreshadowing Sontag's soon-to-be-published essays fulminating against content, psychologizing, and so-called realism in literature. Her key term will be "artifice" as she argues for an art that is enclosed in its own language—as Neal and Hippolyte are enveloped in theirs. Rejecting the value of pure story, Burke concludes that his hero's bewilderment "charts a process, and in the charting of this process there is 'understanding.'" Of what? Apparently of how the self construes an identity through words—or, in Hippolyte's case, through dreams.

Sontag seems to acknowledge Burke in Hippolyte's assertion: "I am interested in my dreams as acts, and as models for action and motives for action." That key phrase, "motives for action," alludes to Burke titles such as *A Grammar of Motives* and *A Rhetoric of Motives,* both of which reveal a sensibility interested in why people or characters in literature act as they do, but which also treats the idea of motives dispassionately—as separate from the notion of a unique personality that must be understood in biographical terms. In his novel, as in his criticism, Burke is simply not taken with the project of analyzing—really psychoanalyzing—the self. Like Sontag's Hippolyte, he explores the range of action open to the individual, which Hippolyte says constitutes his freedom. Otherwise, to inspect his dreams in order to understand himself would be "considering my dreams from the point of view of bondage." To Sontag, as to Burke, the idea that one is bound to a psychological matrix established in childhood is deeply offensive; it is a provocation to the *sui generis.*

The denouement of Burke's novel reads like a stencil for *The Benefactor,* for as critic Merle Brown concludes, "Toward the end . . . Neal talks to others who are only projections of himself and who reply to him in his own voice. He has lost all sense of an outer world." Hippolyte, who has been, he thinks, moving toward a better life, suddenly discovers journals and a novel-like narrative similar to the one he has been relating that call into question whether his present account is fiction or fact, a history of what has actually happened to him or simply a delusion. Friends treat him as though he has been in a mental institution. And Hippolyte concedes there are six years of his life about which he is doubtful—his memory wavers. The consequences of choosing himself—as Hippolyte puts it—include not merely narcissism but solipsism.

This impasse of the self-involved is precisely what modern novels have tended toward, Sontag observes in **"Demons and Dreams,"** her review of an Isaac Singer novel. Why not, then, as in Burke, make that solipsism not just denouement of the novel but its subject? Why not suggest that Hippolyte's desire to become his dreams is the equivalent of the modern novel's desire to free itself from the world, from mimesis, and to become what Poe said a poem is: "a poem and nothing more—this poem written solely for the poem's sake."

What can be attractive as well as off-putting about this kind of self-contained fiction is that it is so *ouvre.* Critic Malcolm Cowley admired the virtuosity of Burke's style, its finished quality, but that very *rondeur* also robs the novel of vitality. Burke tried in *Towards a Better Life* to return to more "formalized modes of writing," to what he called the "structural" sentence, the "Johnsonese" manner as opposed to the modern, informal, conversational style. Sontag affects a Johnsonese grandeur in her passive constructions, which she tries to offset by quaint, teasing chapter headings reminiscent of eighteenth-century novels. But, like Burke, she turns away from what he calls the "impromptu toward the studied." At best such fiction has the alternation of excitement and depression that characterized, in Poe's view, the poetic principle. So much of Poe seems to take place in a dream—or rather, the nightmare that Sontag evokes in her Singer review. Poe's stories, like Hippolyte's dreams, have a redundancy that is both compelling and alienating. Poe wisely measured out his aesthetic in small doses; to string his short story structure into a novel is enervating. If Hippolyte is going mad at the end of the novel—as many critics have supposed—just as Neal appears headed for insanity, both Burke and Sontag confound their readers by insisting on narrators who write, as Merle Brown puts it, in the "same well-rounded, periodic sentences." Brown is applying this judgment only to Burke, but it holds for his pupil as well; she, like him, remains a "verbalizer and analyst."

Although Sontag would publish another novel, *Death Kit,* closely related to *The Benefactor*'s exploration of a disintegrating self, she was already writing herself into a dead end. It would take her twenty-five years to reverse her theories of fiction and to recoup her confidence as a writer of fiction. Roger Straus, an astute observer of her developing talent, suggested that her next book be a collection of essays. He recognized that Sontag's nonfiction was bold and provocative. Compared to the attentive but not exactly enthusiastic reviews of her first novel, the reception of *Against Interpretation,* Straus seemed to foresee, would be intense and wide ranging, so that the name of Susan Sontag would become a cynosure for controversy.

*Works Cited in the Text*

*Note:* For the biographical details of this study I draw on *Susan Sontag: The Making of an Icon*. Where I have used traditional print (hard-copy) sources, I have cited page numbers. For articles retrieved from websites, I have supplied the website address.

Adams, Robert M. "Nacht und Tag." *New York Review of Books,* October 17, 1963, 19.

Bellamy, Joe David. "Susan Sontag." *The New Fiction: Interviews with Innovative American Writers.* Urbana: University of Illinois Press, 1974. Reprinted in Poague, 35-48.

Brown, Merle E. *Kenneth Burke.* Minneapolis: University of Minnesota Press, 1969.

Burke, Kenneth. *Towards a Better Life: Being a Series of Epistles, or Declamations.* New York: Harcourt, Brace, 1932.

Cott, Jonathan. "Susan Sontag: The *Rolling Stone* Interview." *Rolling Stone,* October 4, 1979, 46-53. Reprinted in Poague, 106-136.

Frakes, James R. "Where Dreaming Is Believing." *New York Herald Tribune Book Week,* September 22, 1963, 10.

Hirsch, Edward. "The Art of Fiction: Susan Sontag." *Paris Review* 137 (Winter 1995): 175-208.

Sayres, Sohnya. *Susan Sontag: Elegiac Modernist.* New York: Routledge, 1990.

Stern, Daniel. "Life Becomes a Dream." *New York Times Book Review,* September 8, 1963, 5.

Toback, James. "Whatever You'd Like Susan Sontag to Think, She Doesn't." *Esquire,* July 1968, 59-61, 114.

Wain, John. "Song of Myself." *New Republic,* September 21, 1963, 26-27, 30.

**Carl Rollyson (essay date 2001)**

SOURCE: Rollyson, Carl. "*AIDS.*" In *Reading Susan Sontag: A Critical Introduction to Her Work,* pp. 143-55. Chicago, Ill.: Ivan R. Dee, 2001.

[*In the following essay, Rollyson examines Sontag's short story "The Way We Live Now" and her book-length essay* AIDS and Its Metaphors, *comparing and contrasting the two, their respective critical appraisals, and includes some commentary on each by Sontag herself.*]

Stirred by the deaths of friends who had succumbed to a new, terrifying, and bewildering disease, Susan Sontag responded by writing two very different treatments of how AIDS attacked the health of individuals and society. Her story **"The Way We Live Now"** (1986) and book-length essay *AIDS and Its Metaphors* (1989) epitomize the way she has tried to bridge the gap between the dramatic and expository modes of her imagination. The story became an instant classic, reprinted at the beginning of *The Best American Short Stories, 1987,* dramatized in performances across the country, and widely discussed in books and articles surveying the literary treatments of AIDS. Why the story much more than her essay has won critical acclaim will be explored in the critical commentary section of this chapter.

"THE WAY WE LIVE NOW"

*SYNOPSIS*

The word "AIDS" is never used in the story, which is, like so much of Sontag's fiction, generic and allegorical, a moving away from the specifics of culture to the platonic universals or first principles she has pursued so persistently. What makes **"The Way We Live Now"** compelling, however, is her grounding in the human voice, in the twenty-six narrators (one for each letter of the alphabet) who comprise the society that reacts to the AIDS phenomenon. The story's title is taken from Anthony Trollope's monumental novel, a classic study of mid-Victorian society, especially of its social manners and political life.

The plight of Max, who has AIDS, is told entirely through the voices of his friends. They observe his first reactions to his illness—denying that he has it and delaying a trip to the doctor for the blood test that will establish his condition definitively. Each friend has a different reaction to Max's dilemma. Some sympathize with his state of denial; others worry that he is not seeking medical attention early enough. Aileen thinks of herself. Is she at risk? She doubts it, but her friend Frank reminds her that this is an unprecedented illness; no one can be sure he or she is not vulnerable. Stephen hopes that Max realizes he has options; he should not consider himself helpless at the onset of the disease.

The next stage is Max's hospitalization. Ursula says that Max has received the AIDS diagnosis almost as a relief after his months of anxiety. Friends wonder how to treat him. They decide to indulge him with the things he likes—chocolate, for example. They visit him frequently, and his mood seems to lighten.

But does Max really want to see so many people? Are they doing the right thing by visiting him so frequently? Aileen asks. Sure they are, Ursula answers, who is certain Max values the company and is not judging people's motives. Friends such as Stephen question Max's doctor, trying to assess the gravity of this stage of Max's illness. The doctor is willing to treat him with experimental drugs, but she disconcerts Stephen by saying the chocolate might bolster Max's spirit and do as much good as anything else. Stephen, who has followed all the recent efforts to treat the disease, is dismayed by this old-fashioned advice.

Kate shudders when she realizes that Max's friends have started talking about him in the past tense, as if he has already died. Several friends suspect their visits have begun to pall on him. Other friends argue that he has come to expect their daily presence. There is a brief respite from anxiety as Max's friends welcome him home and observe him put on weight. Xavier thinks they should stop worrying about how their visits affect Max; they are getting as much out of trying to help him as he is. They realize that they are dreading the possibility that they might also get the disease, that it is just a matter of time before they or their friends succumb to it. Betsy says "everybody is worried about everybody now . . . that seems to be the way we live, the way we live now."

Max's friends think about how he has managed his life. He practiced unsafe sex, saying it was so important to him that he would risk getting the disease. But Betsy thinks he must feel foolish now—like someone who kept on smoking cigarettes until he contracted a fatal disease. When it happens to you, Betsy believes, you no longer feel fatalistic; you feel instead that you have been reckless with your life. Lewis angrily rejects her thinking, pointing out that AIDS infected people long before they took any precautions. Max might have been more prudent and still have caught AIDS. Unlike cigarettes, all that is needed is one exposure to the disease.

Friends report the various phases of Max's reaction to the disease. He is afraid to sleep because it is too much like dying. Some days he feels so good that he thinks he can beat it. Other days he looks upon the disease as giving him a remarkable experience. He likes all the attention he is getting. It gives him a sort of distinction and a following. Some friends find his temperament softened and sweetened; others reject this attitudinizing about Max as sentimental. Each friend clings stubbornly to a vision of Max, the story ending with Stephen's insistent statement that "He's still alive."

As the narrators speculate about what Max is going through, it is as though they are suffering from the disease themselves, trying to keep him alive in their thoughts and wishes. How they react to his disease depends very much on the kind of people they are. They argue with each other and sometimes support each other, desperately seeking ways to cope with the imminence of death. Max's approaching fate forces them to confront their own mortality, though they rarely acknowledge that they are indeed thinking of themselves as much as they are of him.

Death has many faces, many manifestations, Sontag seems to be implying. For some, it is to be evaded. Some of Max's friends visit him rarely—one supposing that they have never been close friends anyway. Other friends—such as Stephen—almost seem to want to take over the fight against death, quizzing the doctors, boning up on the latest medical research, and conducting a kind of campaign against any capitulation to the disease. Very few friends are fatalistic; almost all of them hope for a medical breakthrough that will rescue Max.

They live in fear. One friend finds out that his seventy-five-year-old mother has contracted AIDS through a blood transfusion she received five years ago. No one is immune to the disease; even if everyone does not get it, someone close to them probably will. It is the extraordinary vulnerability of these people that makes them argue with or reassure each other, to question what is the best behavior. Everyone encounters an ethical dilemma about how to lead his or her life and how to respond to those who are afflicted with the disease.

The blending and clash of voices reveals a society in argument with itself, testing ways of responding to AIDS, advancing, then rejecting, certain attitudes. Voices overlap each other, as they do in real conversation:

> He seemed optimistic, Kate thought, his appetite was good, and what he said, Orson reported, was that he agreed when Stephen advised him that the main thing was to keep in shape, he was a fighter, right, he wouldn't be who he was if he weren't, and was he ready for the big fight, Stephen asked rhetorically (as Max told it to Donny), and he said you bet. . . .

A complex layering of speeches within speeches, and of social and psychological observation, are emphasized by long sentences that continually switch speakers, so that a community of friends and points of view get expressed sentence by sentence. The story is like compressing the one hundred chapters of Trollope's novel into one hundred sentences.

It is the rhythm of these voices, of the ups and downs in their moods, of the phases people go through in responding to the disease, that is one of the most impressive accomplishments of Sontag's techniques. She presents the tragedy of one man, yet from the first to the last sentence the story is also a society's tragedy as well. It is the society that is ill. The speakers retain their individuality, yet they also become a chorus—almost like one in a Greek tragedy. They do not speak the same thoughts at once, but the syntax of the sentences make them seem bound to one another—as enclosed by their community of feeling as are the clauses in Sontag's sentences enclosed by commas. The speaker's thought at the beginning of a sentence is carried on, refuted, modified, or added to by speakers in later parts of the sentence. The sentence as a grammatical unit links speakers to each other. Whatever their attitudes toward the disease, they cannot escape the thought of it. Thinking of it is, as one of them says, the way they live now.

### Sontag Reading Sontag

Sontag told interviewer Kenny Fries that she wrote her story after receiving a phone call from a friend who told her he had AIDS. Later that night, crying and unable to sleep, she took a bath and the story began to take shape: "It was given to me, ready to be born. I got out of the bathtub and starting writing standing up," she told Fries. "I wrote the story very quickly, in two days, drawing on experiences of my own cancer and a friend's stroke. Radical experiences are similar." The urgency of creation and the frankness of fiction appealed to her: "Fiction is closer to my private life, more immediate, direct, less constrained—more reckless. Essays involve more effort in layering and condensation, more revisions." Fries noted that Sontag was "very proud" of her story.

In a radio interview, Sontag called the story a "stunt" but also one of her best pieces of writing, because it captured both the "velocity" and the "static quality" of enduring a mortal illness. She thought the story explored the human issues of illness more deeply than an essay could, for the former reveals deep emotions and feelings whereas the latter has a tendency to encourage "superficial" moral judgments.

### Critical Commentary

Novelist David Leavitt thought the story therapeutic, making him feel "less alone in my dread, and therefore brave enough to read more." The story "transcended horror and grief, and . . . was therefore redemptive, if not of AIDS itself, then at least of the processes by which people cope with it. . . . It offered a possibility of catharsis, and at that point catharsis was something we all badly needed." Leavitt is referring to a time when contracting AIDS seemed an immediate death sentence, when artists such as Robert Mapplethorpe, suspecting they had AIDS, refused to be tested for the disease. Sontag saw that the stigma attached to AIDS made patients feel isolated and fearful, much as cancer had earlier made society shun the ill and the ill shun society. (Mapplethorpe was finally diagnosed with AIDS in the fall of 1986, about two months before Sontag published her story.)

But as Sontag would say about *AIDS and Its Metaphors,* **"The Way We Live Now"** is not just about AIDS, it is about extreme changes in society. Like the overarching theme of Trollope's great novel, Sontag's story is about "a loss of community and ethical value," to quote Elaine Showalter. Joseph Cady calls **"The Way We Live Now"** a "counterimmersive" story, one of several that do not involve readers directly with scenes of suffering and physical descriptions of AIDS but rather avoid specific mention of the disease, concentrating instead on the stages of denial among the ill and society at large. Such counterimmersive stories he calls "deferential," since they protect readers from "too jarring a confrontation with the subject through a variety of distancing devices." In **"The Way We Live Now,"** the relay race of narrators provides the distancing, which is perhaps why Sylvie Drake called a dramatization of the story "bloodless." Cady finds it troubling that the disease is not named in counterimmersive stories, thereby playing to society's sense of delicacy and phobia about the illness: "Sontag offers no forceful alternative to the characters' perspective in her text, and denying readers could still finish the story with their defenses largely intact."

On the other hand, critic Emmanuel S. Nelson argues that in Sontag's story "there is no reassuring voice the reader can comfortably connect with; her insistence that AIDS puts all of us at risk disrupts the complacency of those readers who consider themselves quite safe from the epidemic." True, the story does not name the disease, but Nelson notes this sentence: "And it was encouraging he was willing to say the name of the disease, pronounce it often and easily, as if it were just another word, like a boy or gallery . . . because . . . to utter the name is a sign of health."

Annie Dawid, who taught the story to students born after 1972, reports they found its fast pace and multiple narrators confusing and upsetting. It was hard to root for Max because they never got to know him. Of all the AIDS stories Dawid taught, **"The Way We Live Now"** was the "harshest . . . the least gentle by way of assuring the readers that they can all return to their lives, business as usual."

To some extent, these differences in critical opinion mirror Sontag's own swaying arguments about the import of literature, about art as form and art as content, art that makes a statement and art that is all style and refuses to be pinned to a point. There is a kind of decorum observed in the story, a "none dare speak its name" resonance, a reticence about "coming out" that certain gay and lesbian critics in the late 1980s and early 1990s would scorn. For them, the story's reluctance to be more specific drains it of potential power. For the proponents of reticence (see Rochelle Gurstein's provocative *The Repeal of Reticence*), on the contrary, **"The Way We Live Now"** is powerful precisely because it is not explicit; it does not strip the person with AIDS of his most intimate moments; it does not provide the gory details; it is not, in short, pornographic in its handling of the disease. **"The Way We Live Now"** might almost be taken as an illustration of Gurstein's brief for a reticence our society no longer respects, a reticence that once preserved the "inherent fragility of intimate life, the tone of public conversation, standards of taste and morality, and reverence owed to mysteries."

### *AIDS AND ITS METAPHORS*

*SYNOPSIS*

Sontag begins by examining the compulsion to use metaphor, by which she means Aristotle's definition: "giving the thing a name that belongs to something else." Metaphors are inescapable, Sontag concedes, but that does not mean that some of them should not be "retired" or that, in some instances, it is not correct to be "against interpretation." For inevitably metaphors distort as much as they describe phenomena. Based on her own experience with cancer, Sontag doubts that military metaphors do anything more than victimize the sufferer—and it does not matter whether the victim of the "war" against disease is regarded as innocent or guilty. Either way the ill feel attacked, invaded, and vulnerable.

AIDS shares with earlier illnesses this overwrought use of metaphor. To contract AIDS is tantamount to receiving a death sentence. AIDS stigmatizes individuals. Like cancer, the reputation of the disease isolates the patient. During her own cancer treatment Sontag saw how patients became disgusted with themselves. The metaphorical atmosphere around such diseases simply increases suffering and is unnecessary, Sontag asserts. By stringently abstaining from the use of metaphors, her aim is to deprive illness of its accreted meanings. Illness, in other words, has been interpreted too much. Sontag feels her approach has been vindicated in the new attitude evinced by doctors, who now treat illnesses such as cancer more frankly and without the secrecy or mystery that once surrounded sickness.

As a sexually transmitted disease, AIDS has been subject to the vehement use of metaphors. It is an invasive virus that must be combated. It is an alien that victims harbor in their bodies, and it is a contaminant—in other words, a spreading evil. In the first phase of awareness of the disease, AIDS patients were thought of as guilty parties punished for their sexual deviancy—especially since the first cases were discovered in homosexuals. Unlike such diseases as tuberculosis or cancer, however, AIDS speaks to a more primitive sense of disease, for the AIDS sufferer is thought to be morally blameworthy. In other words, his illness is not merely a function of his psychology; rather the disease is a condemnation of character. Thus AIDS is a throwback to medieval notions of a plague—in this case a "gay plague."

Conservatives find in AIDS a convenient metaphor for the ravages of a permissive society, in which permitting all abominations leads to certain death. AIDS is a calamity that society has brought upon itself, according to this line of reasoning. AIDS and permissiveness become, through the agency of metaphor, one and the same thing: contagious. Sontag rejects this argument, pointing out that AIDS, which has only recently been identified, cannot be regarded as always leading to death. (In the decade since her book was published, this aspect of her argument has been vindicated.)

Concentrating on AIDS as an inevitable death warrant obscures the fact that early deaths from the disease were at least in part the result of ignorance and ineffective therapies. It is the disease that has to treated without the emotional overlay of metaphors—especially since so much about the etiology of the disease has yet to be studied.

Yet Sontag acknowledges that AIDS must also be viewed in terms of a society that has become more sexually permissive and ever more consumer oriented. "How could sexuality *not* come to be, for some, a consumer option: an exercise of liberty, of increased mobility, of the pushing back of limits." This broad change in cultural mores is "hardly an invention of the male homosexual subculture," she points out. And the response to AIDS has been to adopt "programs of self-management and self-discipline (diet, exercise). Watch your appetites. Take care of yourself. Don't let yourself go"—these are the watchwords, Sontag suggests. These calls to "stricter limits in the conduct of personal life" earn her approval—as do a return to the conventions of society that help to regulate individual behavior.

Sontag understands but wants to resist the sense of apocalypse associated with diseases like AIDS. The world is not coming to an end, but each new campaign or "war" on disease makes it seem as though it is. "Apocalypse is now a long-running serial: not 'Apocalypse Now' but 'Apocalypse from Now On,'" she quips. Such constant evocations of catastrophe are, in the end, exhausting and counterproductive. The worst outcome, she concludes, is to treat AIDS or any other disease as a "total" anything. She argues that illness should be regarded as "ordinary" and treatable.

*SONTAG READING SONTAG*

To Kenny Fries, Sontag characterized her book as a "literary performance. It is an essay, a literary form with a tradition and speculative purpose." Her reiteration of the obvious was in response to a barrage of reviews that took issue with both her facts and her arguments. She was not trying to take a position on AIDS in the way an activist might but rather exploring the mindset about AIDS and other diseases. "My ideas of AIDS alone, stripped of the associations, are the same as any civilized, compassionate, liberal's." In a similar vein, she pointed out to Margaria Fichtner: "This book . . . isn't really about AIDS. It's what AIDS makes you think about. It's about things that AIDS reveals or points to."

Sontag also acknowledged that her rational view of disease and her resistance to psychologizing it with metaphors was a position she arrived at only during the sixth draft of her book. Until then, she too had succumbed to calling AIDS a plague. Her book was an effort to reject both "hysteria and facile pessimism."

## CRITICAL COMMENTARY

*AIDS and Its Metaphors* appeared in a cultural climate far different from the one that acclaimed *Illness as Metaphor.* Charles Perrow, in the *Chicago Tribune,* spoke for many reviewers when he regretted that Sontag's emphasis on metaphors obscured practical matters—what could be done immediately in terms of education, social conditions, and politics to combat the disease. Simone Watney, in the *Guardian Weekly,* chastised her for writing in a vacuum; she failed to take account of the mounting literature on AIDS. Jan Grover, in the *Women's Review of Books,* criticized Sontag for her apparent ignorance that AIDS was being psychologized in the gay community. Similarly Gregory Kolovakos, in the *Nation,* rejected her praise of monogamy as "shallow revisionism." Her insensitivity to the mood and mores of the gay community was an underlying theme of many responses to the book.

There were many positive responses to Sontag's approach as well, including Patricia W. Dideriksen and John A. Bartlett in the *New England Journal of Medicine* who called the book "noble." Deborah Stone, in the *Journal of Health Politics, Policy and Law,* found the book "brilliant," and Francine Prose, in *Savvy Woman,* admired Sontag's compassion and intensity. While Randy Shilts, one of the country's foremost authorities on AIDS, was severely critical of Sontag, he admired the way she integrated AIDS into her discussion of other diseases. Perhaps the highest compliment paid to *AIDS and Its Metaphors* came from Anatole Broyard in the *New York Times Book Review* who asserted that Sontag's book was to "illness what William Empson's *Seven Types of Ambiguity* is to literature"—that is, she had written a classic text certain to become part of the canon of modern literature.

Surely one of the reasons Sontag's book sparked critical animosity was because of its rather lofty tone. She deliberately divorced herself from the crisis atmosphere that surrounded her subject. Whereas she saw herself as advocating a quieter but just as determined an attitude toward treating the disease as those who were militantly

calling for a national campaign or war against AIDS, her critics saw an aloof and even conservative figure apparently out of touch with people's feelings and needs.

Unlike cancer, which for all its threatening associations had become (in part thanks to Sontag) more like an ordinary disease afflicting people, AIDS was put into a special category because it still seemed in 1989 like a plague that modern medicine had not learned how to control, let alone eradicate. Sontag's reflective temper collided with the very hysteria she was attempting to alleviate. Instead of being received as therapeutic, the book was rejected as abrasive.

Sontag herself realized that another kind of book was wanted from her. But it was a book she was not prepared to write, a book that did not appeal to her sensibility, a book that would have looked too much like the other books written about AIDS. Sontag's own notion of herself as a writer destined her to write a book that many readers could not accept. As she pointed out to Kenny Fries, "I have the kind of mind that, whenever I think of something, it makes me think of something else. With this book I do what I do best. This book has more to do with Emerson than with Randy Shilts." Like Emerson, Sontag was using AIDS as another instance of how people use metaphor and how they think about illness. To those readers exercised more about the devastating spread of AIDS and more concerned with the disease itself than with its cultural or historical context, Sontag's approach seemed almost callous. She had not focused specifically enough on the anguish of the dying and on their caretakers. And she seemed to show almost no sympathy at all for gays—the first major community to be affected by the disease.

Perhaps the only way Sontag might have remained true to her sensibility and at the same time satisfied her critics would have been to reveal more of the process by which she came to reject the emotional metaphors used to describe and treat the disease. For example, what happened to her on that sixth draft when she rejected the plague metaphor? Throughout her career, Sontag has tended to use the interview form as a substitute for autobiography, evidently equating autobiography with a more informal, inexact mode of expression that conflicts with the formal elements of her essays—the decorum and rationality she has cultivated as a nonfiction writer. That sense of propriety has contributed significantly to her authority as an essayist, but it has also put off many readers who cannot connect a human voice with the ideas she explores in her essays.

## *Works Cited in the Text*

*Note.* For the biographical details of this study I draw on *Susan Sontag: The Making of an Icon.* Where I have used traditional print (hard-copy) sources, I have cited page numbers. For articles retrieved from websites, I have supplied the website address.

Broyard, Anatole. "Good Books About Being Sick." *New York Times Book Review,* April 1, 1990, 1, 28-29.

Cady, Joseph. "Immersive and Counterimmersive Writing About AIDS: The Archives of Paul Monette's *Love Alone,*" in *Writing AIDS: Gay Literature, Language, and Analysis,* ed. Timothy F. Murphy and Suzanne Poirier (New York: Columbia University Press, 1993), 244-264.

Dawid, Annie. "The Way We Teach Now: Three Approaches to AIDS Literature," in *AIDS: The Literary Response,* ed. Emmanuel S. Nelson. New York: Twayne, 1992.

Dideriksen, Patricia W., and John A. Bartlett. [Review of *AIDS and Its Metaphors.*] *New England Journal of Medicine,* February 8, 1990, 415.

Drake, Sylvie. "Bearing the Pain of AIDS in 'The Way We Live Now.'" *Los Angeles Times,* February 24, 1989, Section 6, p. 8.

Fichtner, Margaria. "Susan Sontag's Train of Thought Rolls into Town." *Miami Herald,* February 19, 1989, 1G.

Fries, Kenny. "*AIDS and Its Metaphors*: A Conversation with Susan Sontag." *Coming Up* (March 1989): 49-50. Reprinted in Poague, 255-260.

Grover, Jan. "AIDS: Metaphors and Real Life." *Christianity and Crisis,* September 11, 1989, 268-270.

Gurstein, Rochelle. *The Repeal of Reticence: A History of American Cultural and Legal Struggles Over Free Speech, Obscenity, Sexual Liberation, and Modern Art.* New York: Hill and Wang, 1996.

Kolovakos, Gregory. "AIDS Words." *The Nation,* May 1, 1989, 598-602.

Leavitt, David. "The Way I Live Now." *New York Times Magazine,* July 9, 1989, 28-32, 80, 82-83. Reprinted in Ann Charters, ed., *The Story and Its Writer: An Introduction to Short Fiction* (Boston: St. Martin's Press, 1991).

Nelson, Emmanuel, S., ed. *AIDS: The Literary Response.* New York: Twayne, 1992.

Perrow, Charles. "Healing Words." *Tribune Books (Chicago Tribune),* January 22, 1989, 6.

Prose, Francine. "Words That Wound." *Savvy Woman,* January 1989, 100-101.

Showalter, Elaine. *Sexual Anarchy: Gender and Culture at the Fin de Siecle.* New York: Viking, 1990.

Stone, Deborah. [Review of *AIDS and Its Metaphors.*] *Journal of Health Politics, Policy and Law* 14 (1989): 850-852.

Watney, Simon. "Sense and Less Than Sense About AIDS." *Guardian Weekly,* March 26, 1989, 28.

## Frances Spalding (review date 21 January 2002)

SOURCE: Spalding, Frances. "Writer in a Critical Condition." *New Statesman* 131, no. 4571 (21 January 2002): 49-50.

[*In the following review, Spalding finds that Sontag's essays in* Where the Stress Falls *appear pessimistic concerning the state of current arts and society, and deems that Sontag is at her best when indignantly taking an unpopular stance on issues.*]

Susan Sontag is America's most successful woman of letters, but she is also, right now, in a curious position, unable to please either the right or the left. Ten days after 11 September, the *New Yorker* carried an article by her in which she fired off at the "sanctimonious, reality-concealing rhetoric spouted by American officials and media commentators in recent days". To her, it seemed "unworthy of a mature democracy". There followed howls of rage. Although much of what she said echoed opinions being voiced in British newspapers, she was labelled an intellectual crank and a detractor from American solidarity.

Meanwhile, her relations with left-wing academics continue to deteriorate. Writing as she does for the common reader and from an untheoretical position, she is regarded as a magisterial exponent of a literary mode that is amateur and outmoded. She, in turn, has scant respect for today's academy, which she lambasts in this new book [*Where the Stress Falls*] for using ideas "devoid of common sense or respect for the practice of writing". Her recent transformation into a successful novelist (*The Volcano Lover* has been translated into 20 languages) may have aggravated the situation. Academics, always so conscious of positioning, are suspicious of anyone with Sontag's range, and tend also to prefer the safety of tenure to the dangers and discomforts of Sarajevo under siege.

However, few would deny the influence that her first collection of essays, *Against Interpretation* (1966), had on radical thinking about modern culture, or, in what followed, how stimulating she could be, on Aids and illness, the pornographic imagination, drugs, authors and literary theorists, photography, dance, film and theatre; even when the reader disagreed with her arguments or conclusions. Her insights also made her influential among those involved with the creative and performing arts. As she herself once said of her chosen art form, an essay can be as much an event, a transforming event, as a novel or a poem. But this new collection, written over the past 20 years, strikes a somewhat doleful note. At times, it seems that what is on offer is less a transforming experience than a jeremiad.

Nevertheless, many will find this book hard to resist. It is wrapped seductively in a painting by Howard Hodgkin (who is the subject of one of these essays), and it offers a fresh opportunity to enter Sontag's mind and share her curiosity, enthusiasms and pleasures. The now familiar manner, which Elizabeth Hardwick once described as the "liberality of her floating, restless expositions", at first disguises the tenacity of Sontag's thought. Because, although she finds much to praise, the underlying burden of these essays is a protest at the degradation of culture in the capitalist world of today.

Evidence of this can be found both on screen and in books. In the essay **"A Century of Cinema"**, Sontag, who once said her life could be divided into two—before and after her discovery of Jean-Luc Godard—recounts the love affair with films which made her an incorrigible cinephile. But whereas cinema once seemed to her quintessentially modern, accessible, poetic, mysterious, erotic and moral, it is now a decadent art form, engaged in an "ignominious, irreversible decline". Literature fares no better. Alongside the "implacable devolution" of literary ambition, she notes "the concurrent ascendancy of the tepid, the glib and the senselessly cruel as normative fictional subjects". The question asked by the Polish writer Adam Zagajewski at a Danish university in 1998—"Is literary greatness still possible?"—must have reverberated in her mind, for it became the opening sentence of her lead article on W G Sebald in the *Times Literary Supplement,* which is reprinted here. It is also one of the main themes of this book.

Her recurrent emphasis on "greatness" and "seriousness" is out of step with contemporary issues, and will irritate cultural relativists. It also casts Sontag in the role of cultural priestess. All of this will invite dispraise, inevitably. She insists, however, that critics cannot ally her with George Steiner and other professional mourners of the death of high art; the breadth of her interests supports this claim. Her thought chimes best with present-day concerns in her constant brooding on the significance of memory. "All writing is a species of remembering," she argues, in her essay on Sebald, whom she admires for the "passionate bleakness" of his voice, his lament and mental restlessness. She continues: "The recovery of memory, of course, is an ethical obligation: the obligation to persist in the effort to apprehend the truth." Elsewhere, her understanding of the role of memory in Hodgkin's art makes her his most percipient commentator. She is also the first to link his paintings and his passion for collecting and travelling with the artist's gratitude for that which is not himself, "the world that resists and survives the ego and its discontents".

What saves her in places from a higher form of grumbling is her radicalism and eloquence. Take, for instance, her description of "the tide of indecipherable signatures of mutinous adolescents which has washed over and bitten into the façades of monuments and the surfaces of public vehicles in the city where I live—graffiti as an assertion of disrespect, but most of all simply an assertion: the powerless saying, I'm here, too". Elsewhere, she detects a political conservatism behind the new cultural populism.

At times, it feels necessary to resist her recurrent sense of mourning and loss. It informs **"The Idea of Europe (One More Elegy)"**, which builds on how Europhilia has been a significant ingredient in her work since the 1960s. What gave an interesting slant to her appreciation of European culture was the American consciousness she brought to it. But her Europe cannot be elided with the economic issues and challenges that have surrounded the adoption of the euro, nor with Euro-festivals, Euro-exhibitions. Euro-journalism and Euro-television, all of which Sontag dismisses as kitsch, mere parodies of art and literature. Europe, for her, is a collection of standards—a legacy derived from the "diversity, seriousness, fastidiousness, density" of its culture. This, she claims, provides her with a reference point, a mental ground from which to explore the world.

Sontag does not ignore the ways in which this ideal has at times been hideously perverted, used to promote an idea of Europe that augments power and suppresses or erases cultural differences. There is nevertheless a lack of balance in her threnody for a shrinking Europe, a Europe of "high art and ethical seriousness, of the values of privacy and inwardness and an unamplified, non-machine-made discourse". She cites the films of Krzysztof Zanussi, the prose of Thomas Bernhard, the poetry of Seamus Heaney and the music of Arvo Pärt. "That Europe still exists," she concludes, "will continue to exist for some time. But it will occupy less territory. And increasing numbers of its citizens and adherents will understand themselves as émigrés, exiles and foreigners."

Is this conclusion the product of "seriousness"? Or the outcome of a romantic idealism that has petrified into received opinion? It left me wanting to protest the ingenuity of rap, the versatility of much present-day animation, the notion of pilgrimage in relation to football matches, and the gains assimilated from the American language. ("Why look how sappy it is, full of juice isn't it, real live growing stuff," as Stevie Smith wrote in the 1940s.) But Sontag is always a step ahead of her readers and, with a sudden twist at the end of her essay on the idea of a fading Europe, consoles us with a story about Gertrude Stein. When asked if, after 40 years residing in France, she was worried about losing her American roots, Stein replied: "But what good are roots if you can't take them with you?"

Ultimately, so Sontag concludes her essay on American fiction, "it's where the stress falls". With this new collection, neither the stress nor the place where it falls will find universal favour. But the tug and flow of Sontag's ideas is irresistible, and nowhere more so than in the essay that follows her account of war-torn Sarajevo, where she directed a performance of *Waiting for Godot.* Titled "**'There' and 'Here'"**, it reveals her at her angriest and best, her activism to the fore as she indicts intellectuals for making so little response to the Bosnian war.

## Maggie McDonald (review date 1 March 2003)

SOURCE: McDonald, Maggie. "Show Me." *New Scientist* 177, no. 2384 (1 March 2003): 49.

[*In the following review, McDonald comments on Sontag's study* Regarding the Pain of Others, *noting the various potential effects that photographs can produce in modern viewers constantly inundated with images from news sources, advertising, and entertainment.*]

"When Capa's falling soldier appeared in *Life* opposite a Vitalis ad, there was a huge, unbridgeable difference in look between the two kinds of photographs, 'editorial' and 'advertising'. Now there is not," says Susan Sontag in *Regarding the Pain of Others.*

Sontag is examining the way in which we see images, how the lack of context in art, reportage and advertising impoverish our understanding of the world. This smearing of boundaries between those categories means that we cannot be certain about the authenticity of the photograph itself. For an advertisement, a scene is staged. Until the widespread use of the SLR camera in the Vietnam War, says Sontag, we could not be certain that war scenes—including that of Capa's falling soldier—were not staged or restaged for the photographer. The length of time it then took to capture an image made it more likely that this was done than not.

But photographs are sometimes the only way we can understand what happens in a war. Sontag mentions the British air force bombing in Iraq during the 1920s. Photographs of a destroyed village, Kushan-Al-Ajaza, are part of the evidence a young squadron leader offers to show that in under an hour a few planes can practically wipe out a place, killing a third of its inhabitants.

But we are less likely to see that kind of evidence these days. Censorship too plays a part: Sontag describes the careful editing of access by photographers to war theatres, from the Crimea to the Falklands, and points out we are increasingly denied that access.

What can be seen is often disturbing, and Sontag explores the fascination that the shocking has. Sometimes the distancing of atrocity is a palliative for viewers: from the people dying from starvation in Ethiopia to a wounded Taliban soldier begging for his life, these pictures are from a Western point of view exotic, even colonised, thus safer to see.

Why are we fascinated by the shocking anyway? Sontag's passionate exploration of what it is we see and how the destruction of context impoverishes our world view is compelling. She offers uncomfortable answers. To pursue this further, try Nigel Spivey's brilliant cultural history, *Enduring Creation,* in which he explores the representation of pain in Western art. He examines our response to, for example, a tortured crucifixion, asking why and if we can find pain beautiful. The viscera of a Benetton advertisement and pictures of mass graves in Kosovo both catch our eyes. Understanding why and how is vital.

## Tzvetan Todorov (essay date 21-28 April 2003)

SOURCE: Todorov, Tzvetan. "Exposures." *New Republic* 228, nos. 4605-06 (21-28 April 2003): 28-31.

[*In the following essay, Todorov analyzes human preoccupation with suffering, and categorizes* Regarding the Pain of Others *as a valuable study in this phenomenon.*]

One of the great platitudes of our epoch is that images, in particular photographic or filmed images, transmit messages that are much clearer and stronger than words, which disguise the truth more than they reveal it. But in truth nothing could be less certain: a photograph can stun us, but taken out of context it may not convey any significant meaning. You see a mutilated corpse, you are moved and overcome by shock or pity; but you do not yet know who this corpse is, nor why this person has been killed, nor by whom; nor whether this is a case that warrants an appeal to vengeance, or on the contrary an appeal for peace, or whether it is only an incitement to meditate on the fragility of human existence. Sentences have a subject and a predicate, a part that delimits what is being discussed and another part that says something about it. But images are subjects without predicates: they evoke the world intensely, but they do not tell us, of themselves, what we should think about it.

Susan Sontag's small and rather digressive book [*Regarding the Pain of Others*] suggests this idea, among many others; but in a way the book resembles its subject, the photographic image, in that it contains more evocations than judgments. Sontag summons facts, and summarizes the different interpretations to which they lend themselves, but she does not hasten to formulate arguments. Often her analyses end with a question for which we must ourselves find the answer; or indeed by refuting all the possible answers that come to mind.

The essay's structure is not scholarly. Its principal theme is articulated by its title: why do we take pleasure in seeing the suffering of others? And, supposing that we do, does this not entail certain political and moral perplexities? Around this vast subject Sontag hangs observations and musings on a variety of themes. One sometimes has the impression of a long fireside conversation from which we have only the contributions of one participant. Sontag knows her subject well, and she expresses herself elegantly. She is at ease in the history of photography and in the history of painting, in the analysis of history and in the analysis of the media, and she never slides into pedantry. Nor does she seek to force her ideas upon us, but rather to make us reflect, with some melancholy, upon a range of troublesome topics.

Even if it does not directly pertain to the book's central subject, for example, there is the fact, well known by twentieth-century historians, that military action was long considered perfectly legitimate as long as its victims were colonized populations, far away and exotic. When they took place in Europe, however, such actions risked being seen as war crimes. Thus General Franco commanded the extermination of "enemies" in Morocco in the 1920s without provoking a single raised eyebrow; but transposed to his native country in the 1930s, these same methods aroused widespread indignation. Arthur Harris, a young commander in the Royal Air Force, could boast in 1924 of the systematic destruction that he wreaked upon the "rebel" villages of Iraq, when "within forty-five minutes a full-sized village can be practically wiped out and a third of its inhabitants killed by four or five machines which offer them no real target." He could do the same again when, on February 13, 1945, he ordered the incineration of "more than a hundred thousand civilians, three-fourths of them women," during the RAF firebombing of Dresden. But sixty years later many people question the legitimacy of this latter massacre. We continue to discriminate between "us" and "them" in the infinitely less murderous domain that is the circulation of photographic images: "we" appear in images as individuals, if not with proper names; "they" illustrate always and only a situation, an attitude, an emotion.

Then, too, there are the multiple uses that we make of memory—a human capacity that is much more ambiguous than the new cultural popularity of commemoration would have us believe. For one thing, the constant reminders of the past keep wounds open, and thereby lead to violence. "Too much remembering (of ancient grievances: Serbs, Irish) embitters," Sontag remarks. "To make peace is to forget." Moreover, memory usually serves simply as a reinforcement of the self—a pardonable but not particularly laudable activity. One likes to recall one's past as a hero or a victim, rather than the situations in which one's group played a less

glorious role. In this regard Sontag writes that "to have a museum chronicling the great crime that was African slavery in the United States of America would be to acknowledge that the evil was here. Americans prefer to picture the evil that was *there,* and from which the United States is exempt."

The simple evocation of a painful past awakens emotion, but this of itself is an insufficient response: it is always better to analyze and to think. The compassion felt in the face of disaster must not become a substitute for the need for action. And a lucid analysis, in its turn, demands that we discard our egocentric preconceptions. Sontag recounts, in this regard, a very telling anecdote about the inhabitants of Sarajevo, who protested against an exhibition that mixed the images of their sufferings with those of similar atrocities committed in Somalia: "It's intolerable to have one's own sufferings twinned with anybody else's." Intolerable, yes; but it is also indispensable to anyone who wishes to think, rather than simply to be outraged.

Finally, too—though the list of possible subjects is far from being exhausted—there is the singular status of images, and in particular of photographic images. Wherein does their specificity lie? Is it that, unlike words, but also unlike painted pictures, they present us with an authentic piece of reality and lead us, by this shortcut, directly to the truth? Clearly not. It is hardly necessary to mention the many cases in which photographs have been retouched, or, more numerous still, in which the photographed objects have been arranged to create a better effect. (This was the case with some of the most celebrated war photographs by Roger Fenton and Matthew Brady, by Robert Capa and Yevgeny Khaldei.) What is decisive is the choice to photograph *this* and not *that.* "It is always the image that someone chose," Sontag observes; "to photograph is to frame, and to frame is to exclude." For this reason, photography is as subjective as drawing or narrative—even if it has a less determined meaning than the latter. The specificity of the photographic image lies elsewhere: not in the greatest fidelity to the exterior world, but in the physical continuity between the object represented and the subject taking the picture. That is why we experience a certain discomfort when the scene photographed is particularly violent: looking at images of lynchings and executions, one wonders whether the photographer, rather than seeking a better angle for his photograph, ought not to have thrown himself upon the torturers in an effort to disarm them.

Sontag's main theme is hardly new. Since time immemorial we have been aware of the fascination provoked by the misery of others. She cites a famous passage from Plato's *Republic,* to which one might add Lucretius: "Tis sweet, when the sea is high and winds are driving, / To watch from shore another's anguished striving." Or Montaigne: "In the midst of compassion we feel within us I know not what bittersweet pricking of malicious pleasure in seeing others suffer." Or La Rochefoucauld: "We all have strength enough to endure the troubles of others." Or Burke, or Hazlitt, or Balzac. Or the French writer and philosopher Georges Bataille, who admitted that he gazed at least once a day at an especially atrocious photograph from China in which one sees a man skinned alive. But why? What is gained from the contemplation of such sadistic images? Why does a great proportion of Western painting represent the Massacre of the Innocents, and the flaying of Marsyas, and the agony of Laocoön—when it is not depicting the slow and agonizing death of a man named Jesus?

It is not enough to say that suffering sells better than happiness; this only begs the question. The moralists of the past provided a first reply to the question, which one could summarize thus: watching the suffering of others brings us a certain pleasure because we recognize at the same time that we ourselves are exempt from this distress. No man is an island; whether we wish it or not, we are constantly comparing ourselves to others, and to see them unhappy throws into relief our own happiness, just as the sight of their triumphs can plunge us into melancholy. Why do they enjoy such good fortune, and we do not?

But this explanation seems limited when one tries to comprehend the spell that has been cast upon the faithful, for centuries, by the bloodied body of the crucified messiah. And the same is true, in its way, of Bataille's tortured Chinese prisoner. The answer here would be, rather, that the image of Christ's suffering has this effect because it embodies, for believing Christians, an essential aspect of the human condition. Christ sacrificed himself to save mankind; owing to his sacrifice, salvation is possible. He suffered greatly, to be sure, but he thereby fulfilled the divine plan, and we owe him gratitude. In a similar but secular way, when we look— without pleasure, perhaps, but with an undeniable fascination—at the bodies of lynched African Americans, or at Japanese carbonized by atomic explosions, or at Vietnamese transformed into purulent sores by napalm, we, too, discover an essential truth—about human nature or, more modestly, about human politics. Such images remind us of the evil of which we and those like us are capable, and so they are very welcome, in all their disturbing ugliness, because they shake us out of our complacence about ourselves. We generally prefer to anesthetize ourselves with notions that are more flattering to us, to see ourselves as rational beings toiling ceaselessly for the universal good.

It is a good thing, therefore, that these horrific images exist. "It seems a good in itself," Sontag suggests, "to acknowledge, to have enlarged, one's sense of how much suffering caused by human wickedness there is in the world we share with others." But many other questions are born of this answer. Doesn't the multiplicity— and therefore the familiarity—of these images destroy the disabused feeling about the world that they are charged with eliciting? By seeing so many massacres, do we not become numbed to the blood? Sontag does not think so. Anyway, there is a practical consideration: it is hard to imagine a way of supervising all the world's televisions so that they do not exceed some daily quota of brutality. Another facet of the same problem concerns the blurring of fiction and reality, of virtual images and real wars: having seen so many disaster films, so many acted murders, will we still be able to be moved by a catastrophe in our own town? Sontag thinks this danger is exaggerated, that most people are morally and cognitively sound enough to see the difference between entertainment and reality. "To speak of reality becoming a spectacle is a breathtaking provincialism," she properly asserts. "It universalizes the viewing habits of a small, educated population living in the rich part of the world. . . . It assumes that everyone is a spectator. It suggests, perversely, unseriously, that there is no real suffering in the world. . . . There are hundreds of millions of television watchers who are far from inured to what they see on television. They do not have the luxury of patronizing reality."

Images of distress and suffering are threatened also from another side: they risk being beautiful. We experience a certain malaise when we come away with this perversely pleasing impression. It is a reproach frequently leveled at Sebastião Salgado, and in particular at his series *Migrations*. The offense here is aestheticism: to avoid making a moral judgment by making an aesthetic one, to limit one's reaction to "it's beautiful" or "it's not beautiful," even in the face of revolting events to which one expects the reaction "this is evil." Nero fiddled while Rome burned, and Ukrainian scientists stood on a balcony to admire the fireworks produced by the explosion of the central reactor at Chernobyl.

There are several sides to this problem. One is linked to the presence of the photographer: he must not give us the impression that he could have prevented the disaster but refrained from doing so in order to come away with a fine photograph or to experience an intense sensation. What can shock in some of Salgado's images is not their beauty but their generality—all the exoduses of the earth are confused and run together, severed from their concrete political contexts—and the anonymity of his photographic subjects, stripped of their individuality and transformed into symbols of distress. "It is significant," Sontag notes, "that the powerless are not named in the captions."

Moreover, the discomfort evoked by certain images of catastrophe—the ones that we say are "too beautiful to be true"—proceeds from an aesthetic judgment rather than an ethical one. They lack internal coherence. If their purpose is to make us more sensitive to disaster, then the very beauty of the image becomes a distraction and a discomfort. And if they are designed to make us admire beauty, why focus only upon the children in rags, or upon the emaciated man? What we call the truth of an image—which is not reducible to the fact that the object photographed exists somewhere in the world—is at the same time its beauty; and if the truth and the beauty are separated, both suffer.

That we choose to look at the suffering of others should not make us feel guilty, but neither should it be a source of pride. For the word is as necessary as the image: the latter strikes the imagination (which is always too weak), the former helps us to understand. Moreover, representation, even with the best will in the world, cannot replace experience. No filmed bombardment can reproduce the effect of actual falling bombs, of the bodies of loved ones dug from the ruins. This is doubtless one of the reasons why wars, the most abundantly represented events in the history of mankind, still continue. We never seem to know them well enough.

## Alexander Nehamas (review date September 2003)

SOURCE: Nehamas, Alexander. "The Other Eye of the Beholder." *American Prospect* 14, no. 8 (September 2003): 62-3.

[*In the following review, Nehamas praises Sontag's opinions in* Regarding the Pain of Others, *contending that she makes honest assertions about the effects that pictures depicting brutality and suffering can have on the public.*]

"Ever since cameras were invented in 1839, photography has kept company with death": Thirty years after the first of the essays eventually collected in *On Photography,* which was published in 1977, Susan Sontag is still troubled by the aesthetic, moral and political ambiguities of the medium. *Regarding the Pain of Others* is her erudite, subtle and provocative—though also tentative and sometimes inconclusive—meditation on the tensions inherent in photographs of war, death and devastation. Such pictures seem to multiply with every passing day. Does that make their horrors more palpable or less? Many are technically proficient; some are even beautiful. Does beauty celebrate violence and ferocity or does it simply entice a larger audience to confront them? They seem to establish a bond between viewer and victim. Does compassion incite us to fight injustice or does it permit us to feel innocent of it and impotent against it?

Photography is not the only visual medium to go hand in hand with death. Death has been the constant companion of all visual representation since its very beginnings. In the oldest historic work of art, a bronze palette from 3150 B.C., Menes, king of Upper Egypt, is about to crush an enemy's head with his mace and add the body to the mound of corpses lying at his feet. Unlike the painter's hand or the sculptor's arm, however, the camera is a machine. It registers physical traces of things. A photograph seems to be more than just a representation because, somehow, the representation allows us to look through it and see its subject directly, as if it were literally before our eyes. A photograph is "a record of the real."

That is one reason pictures of pain and suffering are so unsettling: A photograph of starving mothers and their children in Biafra makes us feel, willy-nilly, that we are standing before them, at best unable and at worst unwilling to intervene. That is not to say that all pictures of horror have similar effects; ambiguity is inescapable. An image of dead civilians in the Middle East may draw me to the victims on humanitarian grounds or confirm your abhorrence of war, though to Israelis or Palestinians it may simply be proof of the other side's brutality. Sontag shows that context is critical to determining whom a photograph will outrage and whom it will delight. The same pictures of dead children, with different captions, served to denounce both Serb and Croat atrocities in the early 1990s. Still, photographs that appall present their own special problems.

Why, for example, is it so difficult to tear oneself away from them? In 1968, Gen. Nguyen Ngoc Loan executed a Vietcong suspect on a Saigon street. In a terrifying photograph—much more disturbing than the tape of the whole sequence—Eddie Adams captured the moment of the shooting. Contorted by pain, fear and the sheer force of the bullet that has just struck him, the prisoner's face also expresses a kind of sad resignation. It is the face of a man who knows that he has already died. Whenever I see it again (and I have seen it many times already), I find myself gazing at it intently, with a curiosity that is almost morbid. Although I am, to be sure, horrified, I also suspect that, as I study the man's face for a hint of what that moment feels like, part of me is glad that it is he who is dead and not I. (Plato showed that speaking of oneself as a collection of fragments is inevitable here.)

What does it say about me that I may find pleasure in another's death? And what does it say about us that I am not alone? Sontag, too, is disturbed by the photograph. "As for the viewer, this viewer," she confesses in the hesitating manner characteristic of this book, "even many years after the picture was taken . . . well, one can gaze at these faces for a long time and not come to the end of the mystery, and the indecency, of such co-spectatorship." Averting our gaze is not the solution, she writes, as, "The gruesome invites us to be either spectators or cowards, unable to look."

Photographs of contemporary atrocities, at least, may provoke effective action. The purpose of looking at photographs of the past—such as the lynching souvenirs in James Allen's collection *Without Sanctuary,* published in 2000—is much more disputable. Old or new, however, no picture can speak for itself; neither the photographer's intention nor its visual content determines its meaning, purpose or effect. Adams' photograph (to his dismay) galvanized the anti-war movement, but only because the movement was already in place, ready to circulate its own interpretation. But where opponents of the war saw callous indifference in Gen. Loan's impassive profile, supporters of U.S. policy could discern stoic devotion to duty.

Despite being mute, pictures can still be manipulative. Some of the most famous war photographs, for example, turn out to have been staged. The Light Brigade never rode into the plain that Roger Fenton, the first war photographer, chose to depict in "The Valley of the Shadow of Death" (1855) and over which he carefully arranged the cannonballs that litter the landscape. Alexander Gardner's "The Home of a Rebel Sharpshooter, Gettysburg" (1863) is of an imaginary scene, created specially for the occasion. Some suspect that even Robert Capa's "Falling Soldier" (1936)—the model of "spontaneous" photography—may have been posed for the camera. Sontag doesn't find that surprising; what strikes her as odd is that "we are surprised to learn that they were staged, and always disappointed."

Actually, when photographs of contemporary events, which we might still affect, are at issue, we are more likely to be angry than disappointed—a staged picture is a kind of false advertising. It is when we discover that older photographs were staged that we are disappointed, especially if they are well known. Perhaps, then, we might begin to find an explanation in the relationship between photography and memory. Images, often provided in the first instance by photographs, are essential to memory. For example, the war in Bosnia is inseparable in my mind from an image of a Serb militiaman about to kick a Muslim woman lying on the ground—inseparable, that is, from Ron Haviv's 1992 photograph. If it turned out that Bosnian propaganda had staged the scene, I would be very angry (these are still recent events), but I would also have to ask: Would my feelings today be the same had the picture, and the turmoil it caused me, not been a factor in my life? My stand on the new Balkan wars? My political views? How can we help being disappointed with ourselves when we are made to see how easily we might have been somebody else?

Turning from viewer to victim, Sontag criticizes Sebastião Salgado's photographs—not, like most others, for being beautiful but for always leaving the powerless they represent nameless and so reducing them to their generic features, just as under the single heading "Migration" Salgado groups together different kinds of misery produced by different causes in different countries. His vast and abstract scale makes suffering seem almost natural and certainly too uniform and widespread to be affected by any specific political action. "All politics," however, "like all of history, is concrete." That's why, I think, Serajevans, as Sontag reports, would yell at photographers as the bombs fell around them, "Are you waiting for a shell to go off so you can photograph some corpses?" *Some corpses.* In anticipation, it seems as if it doesn't matter whose as long as there is something to shoot; naming, if it comes at all, can only come later and is no consolation to the victim.

Sontag now rightly rejects the view, central to *On Photography,* that as images of violence and devastation proliferate, their horrors turn into mere spectacle and their viewers become inured to them. Her reasons are not clear, but she is convinced that exposure to these images does not dull their impact. They serve as reminders that "this is what human beings are capable of doing—may volunteer to do, enthusiastically, self-righteously. Don't forget." But Sontag, I think, is overlooking the fact that this is something pictures can do only if someone of her intelligence and sensibility lends them her voice. In the book's closing sections, the ambiguities of photography recede further and further into the background as looking is gradually transformed into "elective attention," "thinking" and, finally, "the function of the mind itself." At that point its guilty pleasures have also disappeared. Sontag writes, "There's nothing wrong with standing back and thinking, . . . 'Nobody can think and hit someone at the same time.'"

Perhaps. But nobody can hurt and think at the same time, either. The only pain we can ever regard is necessarily the pain of others—most often remote and exotic others but sometimes also those whose only difference from us is in the pain they feel. In the distance that separates observer and observed there is always room for the thought, "At least it is not happening *to me,*" and, with it, for photography's questionable pleasures. To those who have felt them, these pleasures intimate that we can never be sure whose role we would play if we were to find ourselves in a world of real violence. Or, as Sontag writes about the ordinary people posing for snapshots with the charred bodies of their lynched victims in *Without Sanctuary*: "Maybe they *were* barbarians. Maybe *this* is what most barbarians look like. (They look like everybody else.)"

Although *Regarding the Pain of Others* is brimming with questions, its answers are few and seldom more definite than this tentative statement, which is typical of the book as a whole and fitting to its equivocal subject. That has irritated some of the book's reviewers; to me it is one of its strengths. Looking at photographs of human horrors is, in many ways, inescapably ambiguous, and to pretend otherwise is either arrogant or complacent. Readers of Susan Sontag's record of honest perplexity will be a little more self-conscious as they read the morning newspaper or watch the evening news—not a mean feat if we agree with her, as we should, that all politics is concrete.

### Arthur M. Kleinman (review date fall 2003)

SOURCE: Kleinman, Arthur M. Review of *Regarding the Pain of Others,* by Susan Sontag. *Literature and Medicine* 22, no. 4 (fall 2003): 257-61.

[*In the following review, Kleinman praises* Regarding the Pain of Others *for not only displaying human fascination with images of death and pain, but for urging readers to view such images with sympathy and compassion.*]

Susan Sontag has been, since the 1970s, one of the leading public literary figures in the United States. In addition to six novels, two film scripts, and a play, she has written eight books of essays. Two of the latter are widely cited meditations on medically relevant topics. ***Illness as Metaphor*** and ***AIDS and Its Metaphors,*** books that are taught to medical students in courses in the medical humanities and social sciences, illustrate the power of meaning to shape experiences of pain and suffering, often in ways that create problems for patients and practitioners.

Sontag also wrote one of the earliest and most penetrating and influential interpretations of photography in modern society, ***On Photography.*** In the early 1990s, during the horrific civil war in Bosnia, Sontag traveled to Sarajevo, from where she penned powerful pieces on the brutal effects of the fighting and the social forces that fueled its explosions of inhuman political violence, pieces that also burned with passionate criticism of the seeming incapacity of Europe, the United States, and international agencies to intervene effectively to stop the bloodshed, psychological trauma, and societal destruction.

All of these themes come together in a powerful and disturbing way in her brilliant new book, ***Regarding the Pain of Others.*** Sontag focuses on photographs of pain and suffering that are caused by "hellish events," especially war (p. 26). Photographs, she avers, unite opposites: objectivity and a special point of view. Sontag insists "to photograph is to frame, to frame is to exclude . . . it has always been possible for a photograph to misrepresent" (p. 46). Yet, in commonsense realism, "A photograph is supposed not to evoke but to show. That is why photographs, unlike handmade images, can count as evidence" (p. 47).

Sontag reminds us of Ernst Friedrich's *Krieg dem Krieg!* (*War Against War!*), a book of photographs from the First World War that was deemed unpublishable by German censors while the war was being fought because of the horror the photos portray, including close-ups of soldiers with difficult-to-look-at gaping facial wounds. The purpose of this picture book was to shock readers with graphic evidence of the immense destructiveness of the Great War, a war in which 1.7 million Germans died. Here photography not only acknowledges social suffering but also offers a protest. That this protesting image and the many others used by antiwar activists offered no serious resistance to the gathering storm of fascism and Nazism that only a generation later would create a second world war, with at least fifty million deaths, reminds us soberingly of the limits of images to prevent the very real dangers in human experience. To be sure, Sontag also reminds us that images of horror and gore can feed a prurient voyeurism that many of us are capable of experiencing.

Sontag joins earlier critics of the famous war photographer Robert Capa's iconic photograph of the Spanish Civil War depicting a Republican soldier at the very instant he is killed by enemy fire. Other evidence suggests that this universally recognized photo was almost certainly staged and may have recorded a training exercise. Many of the most memorable pictures from the Second World War were indeed staged, including that quintessential picture of American military bravery that conjures patriotic sentiments each Veteran's Day, the photo of American servicemen raising the Stars and Stripes over Iwo Jima in the winter of 1945. Live television broadcasts, such as those by "embedded" reporters in the Iraq War, may prevent staging; still, the ability to frame and interpret make point of view as crucial to photography now as in the past, as anyone comparing images from Iraq on American and Arab television can attest.

One widely cited picture of human suffering that Sontag does not discuss, but that makes many of her points, is a picture that won the South African photojournalist, Kevin Carter, a Pulitzer Prize.[1] It frames an isolated toddler bent over in a stubble field in southern Sudan during a famine. Near the dying child is a large black vulture poised, it seems, to move in for the kill. The message is stark and terrible: look at what a basket case Africa is. Africans can't even protect their own children from natural disaster. Leading international nongovernmental organizations featured the picture in their campaigns for funds to relieve the dire plight of famine victims. Almost everything the picture depicts is seriously misleading. It took Carter days of tramping through the brush to find a child separated from its family. The so-called natural disaster is in fact a political strategy in Sudan's decades-long civil war by which the government, dominated by northern Muslims, seeks to subdue the Christian Nilotic tribes of the south. The evil symbolized by the menacing vulture is actually situated in the political offices and military barracks in Khartoum. Although Leonardo da Vinci ordered artists who depict war to be "pitiless" and to appall, critics of Kevin Carter (who, shortly after receiving his prize, committed suicide) wanted to know how he could take such a picture while the vulture acutely threatened the child. How long did he wait before he intervened? Was he inhuman and unethical? Sontag's powerful essay includes at least one troubling ethical issue in every chapter.

> It used to be thought, when the candid images were not common, that showing something that needed to be seen, bringing a painful reality closer, was bound to goad viewers to feel more. In a world in which photography is brilliantly at the service of consumerist manipulations, no effect of a photograph of a doleful scene can be taken for granted. As a consequence, morally alert photographers and ideologues of photography have become increasingly concerned with the issues of exploitation of sentiment (pity, compassion, indignation) in war photography and of rote ways of provoking feeling.
>
> (Pp. 79-80)

Pictures, actually home photos, taken by whites watching the lynching of black men in the American South "tell us about human wickedness. About inhumanity" (p. 91). Sontag is attracted to the notion that "there exists an innate tropism toward the gruesome" (p. 97). Pain and suffering can be represented to beautify, to uglify, to steel the observer, to numb her, to "acknowledge the incorrigible," to haunt, and to transform (p. 98). Just as pain transforms the sufferer, pictures of pain can transform the observer, making a bystander into a witness, a member of a lonely crowd into a social activist, a nonengaged observer into a healer.

In the essay's closing pages, and to her great credit, Sontag turns from "regarding the pain of others," with its primary emphasis on representation and interpretation, to the reality of the suffering itself, the experience of injury and loss. Without explicitly saying so, Sontag is criticizing writers who so readily forget that images of pain are not only images, who may even seek to weaken the authority of the real world. Trauma and dying are lived. Danger is at the very core of the experience of most men and women. Sontag has been in the thick of battle; she knows what violence is about. She knows that to be there demands practical action:

> To speak of reality becoming a spectacle is a breathtaking provincialism. It universalizes the viewing habits of

a small, educated population living in the rich part of the world, where news has been converted into entertainment. . . . It assumes that everyone is a spectator. It suggests, perversely, unseriously, that there is no real suffering in the world. But it is absurd to identify the world with those zones in the well-off countries where people have the dubious privilege of being spectators, or of declining to be spectators, of other people's pain, just as it is absurd to generalize about the ability to respond to the sufferings of others on the basis of the mind-set of those consumers of news who know nothing at first hand about war and massive injustice and terror. There are hundreds of millions of television watchers who are far from inured to what they see on television. They do not have the luxury of patronizing reality.
>
> (P. 110)

So much has been made of the moral duty to remember trauma through pictures that Sontag's admonition to forget, to allow pictures to lapse into amnesia in order to stop the cycles of killing, comes as a shock, as does her argument that there is no difference between watching suffering at a distance and up close. One wants to argue back, and that is a virtue of the great clarity of her writing and the compelling logic it conveys—a forceful position moves the reader to want to argue back.

Interpreting an art photo of dead Russian soldiers in Afghanistan, intended by its creator to haunt the everyday, Sontag concludes,

> What would they have to say to us? "We"—this "we" is everyone who has never experienced anything like what they went through—don't understand. We don't get it. We truly can't imagine what it was like. We can't imagine how dreadful, how terrifying war is, and how normal it becomes. Can't understand, can't imagine. That's what every soldier, and every journalist and aid worker and independent observer who has put in time under fire, and had the luck to elude the death that struck down others nearby, stubbornly feels. And they are right.
>
> (Pp. 125-6)

And this is also the issue for physicians involved in responses to war and other forms of political violence: Can we project to policy makers the actual horrors of war, so that the terrible burden of our experiences can bring the reality of social suffering to weigh on those who are responsible for waging war, to move them to prevent it?

*Note*

1. Arthur Kleinman and Joan Kleinman, "The Appeal of Experience; The Dismay of Images: Cultural Appropriations of Suffering in Our Times," *Daedalus* 125, no. 1 (Winter 1996): 1-23.

## Paul Lester (review date winter 2004)

SOURCE: Lester, Paul. Review of *Regarding the Pain of Others,* by Susan Sontag. *Journalism & Mass Communication Educator* 58, no. 4 (winter 2004): 392-94.

[*In the following review, Lester compares and contrasts* Regarding the Pain of Others *with Brian Goldfarb's* Visual Pedagogy: Media Cultures in and beyond the Classroom.]

> All images that display the violation of an attractive body are, to a certain degree, pornographic.
>
> —Susan Sontag in ***Regarding the Pain of Others,*** p. 95

> I do not mean to downplay the radical potential of programs that engage students in the visual, the popular, or the technical means of media production.
>
> —Brian Goldfarb in *Visual Pedagogy,* p. 7

An interesting and valued feature for this journal would be for AEJMC members to periodically report what books they read for pleasure—ones chosen for no other purpose than to learn about topics unrelated to career paths, and yet, if the authors do it right, ways of incorporating their teaching into ours can be found. I tend to choose nonfiction books to read for fun with one-word main titles: *Beauty, Crying, Dust, Salt,* and *Stiff,* for example. Recently, I have made two exceptions: ***Regarding the Pain of Others*** and *Visual Pedagogy.* Guess which one I was asked to review for this journal?

I must confess at the onset that *pedagogy,* the word, is one of those "fingernails on the blackboard" haughty terms like *hegemony* and *paradigm* that I usually avoid when selecting books and articles to read or conference presentations to attend. (Perhaps part of the problem I have with the word is I am never sure if it is peda-GAAgee or pedaGOgee. My wife and writing collaborator says the former, but I prefer the sound of the latter. But I digress.)

As soon as I saw the recent Sontag collection of essays on the shelf of a bookstore at a mall. I snatched it up and devoured the articles in one afternoon, pausing only to underline phrases and write comments here and there. Back in 1977 when Sontag's first collection, ***On Photography,*** was published, I was a green, 24-year-old photojournalist living in the French Quarter. Her book taught me, among other things, that I could be intellectually challenged while working as a professional. ***On Photography*** was one of the most influential works about the nature of images, image making, and our responses to the artifact and the artist. Just as its predecessor, ***Regarding the Pain of Others*** should be more than simply regarded. It is a vital addition to the ever-expanding literature of visual culture that all of us—word and picture people alike—should read (although in truth, how many are reading this review?). In this age of MTV music videos, "Headline News" crowded screens, and even university professors trying to jazz up their lectures for their bored undergraduates, there is a good chance that our media-driven culture dulls and dilutes the message somewhere between the pupil and the hippocampus.

And nowhere are there better examples than with images from war. Think of the pictures of those killed and those grieving over their profound loss—regardless of sides—during the on-going Iraqi conflict and judge whether you were truly moved by such grotesque agony.

Quite simply, visual messages, as necessary as they are to fully tell important stories of the day, cause us to be weary—weary of the war on terrorism, weary of another dead soldier, and weary of Laci Peterson.

Part of the weariness many feel is not connected to 9/11, wars, or real crime subjects closer to home. It is an outgrowth of a trend in photo-journalism that has long-established and honored roots. Photojournalists at conventions receive standing ovations, Pulitzer Prizes, and community and professional accolades for photographing others during their worst moments. Through reading magazines and newspapers, watching television and motion pictures, and using the World Wide Web, we can find all manner of agony: desperate and inexperienced miners in South America, kids doing tricks to buy crack, a beautiful young woman forever altered by a fiery crash caused by a drunk driver, or close-up shots of those shot during battles. These depictions of grief neatly framed and sometimes explained with words is a form of commercialized voyeurism rendering the viewer impotent and useless, and are as objectifying as any pornographic image. That is the message of Sontag's essays. Unfortunately, we may never learn the proper response to her challenge.

But as educators—excuse me—as enlightened pedagogues—we are challenged, it must be said, by two factors in our teaching: our students must be made aware of the pornography of grief that causes us to disregard the pain of others *and* they must be given the tools—intellectually as well as technically—to affect change. Otherwise, we have not only failed them, but we have failed all.

Knowing this challenge, we are left with always the disquieting question of what to do about it. Despite my initial hesitancy because of its title, *Visual Pedagogy* offers a possible way out of this cycle of cynical criminality.

Goldfarb teaches media production at the University of California, San Diego. His educational experiences within traditional and alternative classroom settings combined with his position as Curator of Education at the New Museum of Contemporary Art in New York City make him a unique force in the field of teaching students how to engage their audiences with their stories using innovative technologies or traditional methods with innovative ideas.

Imagine a journalism in which readers and viewers become as engaged with the plight of others as our students do during a semester-long project. In two parts, Goldfarb describes how that feat might be possible. The four chapters of part one look at innovative technology and ideas within traditional classroom settings: the advent of television instruction from Washington, D.C., to American Samoa, empowering students as video producers, learning from lessons from sex education, and implementing peer instruction in which students teach students through a variety of technological methods. The final three chapters take us outside the box of the classroom: using the philosophy and history of the museum space as an educational tool, studying African filmmakers and films in which the African viewer "functions finally as the crucial figure of pedagogical authority" (p. 189), and seeing how local television and community politics collide and interact in São Paulo, Brazil.

Engagement is the link between Sontag's concern and Goldfarb's solution. Journalism should engage a reader, viewer, user, and/or consumer with the facts and people involved in a story. Too often, however, it does not. Mass communication and journalism instructors should take the initiative and meet with instructors from other disciplines that in the past have been separated by traditional modes of thinking. Instructors and students from theatre, art, music, computer science, and philoso-phy should work together to produce trans-media collaborations. Grant applications should be completed to obtain funds for equipment, instructor time, conferences, and new media centers. Engagement can lead to connections among users, the people who are a part of the story, and the producers of the story. But that's not all. Engagement also can lead to what has been described by philosopher Albert Borgmann as "the good life."

---

# FURTHER READING

## Criticism

Bedient, Calvin. "Passion and War: Reading Sontag, Viola, Forche and Others." *Salmagundi,* nos. 141-142 (winter 2004): 243-62.
>   Provides discussion of visual and textual representations of war, focusing on several works including Sontag's *Regarding the Pain of Others.*

Sontag, Susan, and Caroline Brothers. "Educating the Heart." *Meanjin* 63, no. 1 (March 2004): 73-86.
>   Sontag describes her experiences in war torn Yugoslavia, elaborates on her views of wars past and present, and discusses her works and how they relate to her social and political views.

Sorensen, Sue. "Susan Sontag and the Violent Image." *Afterimage* 31, no. 6 (May-June 2004): 16-17.
>   Presents a critical analysis of the essays in *Regarding the Pain of Others.*

---

**Additional coverage of Sontag's life and career is contained in the following sources published by Thomson Gale:** *American Writers Supplement,* **Vol. 3;** *Contemporary Authors,* **Vols. 17-20R;** *Contemporary Authors New Revision Series,* **Vols. 25, 51, 74, 97;** *Contemporary Literary Criticism,* **Vols. 1, 2, 10, 13, 31, 105;** *Contemporary Novelists,* **Ed. 7;** *Contemporary Popular Writers; Dictionary of Literary Biography,* **Vols. 2, 67;** *DISCovering Authors Modules, Popular Fiction and Genre Authors; DISCovering Authors 3.0; Encyclopedia of World Literature in the 20th Century,* **Ed. 3;** *Literature Resource Center; Major 20th-Century Writers,* **Eds. 1, 2;** *Modern American Women Writers; Reference Guide to American Literature,* **Ed. 4;** *Short Stories for Students,* **Vol. 10; and** *Twentieth-Century Romance and Historical Writers.*

# How to Use This Index

### The main references

---
**Calvino, Italo**
   1923-1985 ....... CLC **5, 8, 11, 22, 33, 39,**
                               **73; SSC 3, 48**
---

**list all author entries in the following Gale Literary Criticism series:**

*AAL* = *Asian American Literature*
*BG* = *The Beat Generation: A Gale Critical Companion*
*BLC* = *Black Literature Criticism*
*BLCS* = *Black Literature Criticism Supplement*
*CLC* = *Contemporary Literary Criticism*
*CLR* = *Children's Literature Review*
*CMLC* = *Classical and Medieval Literature Criticism*
*DC* = *Drama Criticism*
*HLC* = *Hispanic Literature Criticism*
*HLCS* = *Hispanic Literature Criticism Supplement*
*HR* = *Harlem Renaissance: A Gale Critical Companion*
*LC* = *Literature Criticism from 1400 to 1800*
*NCLC* = *Nineteenth-Century Literature Criticism*
*NNAL* = *Native North American Literature*
*PC* = *Poetry Criticism*
*SSC* = *Short Story Criticism*
*TCLC* = *Twentieth-Century Literary Criticism*
*WLC* = *World Literature Criticism, 1500 to the Present*
*WLCS* = *World Literature Criticism Supplement*

### The cross-references

---
See also CA 85-88, 116; CANR 23, 61;
DAM NOV; DLB 196; EW 13; MTCW 1, 2;
RGSF 2; RGWL 2; SFW 4; SSFS 12
---

**list all author entries in the following Gale biographical and literary sources:**

*AAYA* = *Authors & Artists for Young Adults*
*AFAW* = *African American Writers*
*AFW* = *African Writers*
*AITN* = *Authors in the News*
*AMW* = *American Writers*
*AMWR* = *American Writers Retrospective Supplement*
*AMWS* = *American Writers Supplement*
*ANW* = *American Nature Writers*
*AW* = *Ancient Writers*
*BEST* = *Bestsellers*
*BPFB* = *Beacham's Encyclopedia of Popular Fiction: Biography and Resources*
*BRW* = *British Writers*
*BRWS* = *British Writers Supplement*
*BW* = *Black Writers*
*BYA* = *Beacham's Guide to Literature for Young Adults*
*CA* = *Contemporary Authors*
*CAAS* = *Contemporary Authors Autobiography Series*
*CABS* = *Contemporary Authors Bibliographical Series*
*CAD* = *Contemporary American Dramatists*
*CANR* = *Contemporary Authors New Revision Series*
*CAP* = *Contemporary Authors Permanent Series*
*CBD* = *Contemporary British Dramatists*
*CCA* = *Contemporary Canadian Authors*
*CD* = *Contemporary Dramatists*
*CDALB* = *Concise Dictionary of American Literary Biography*
*CDALBS* = *Concise Dictionary of American Literary Biography Supplement*
*CDBLB* = *Concise Dictionary of British Literary Biography*

*CMW* = *St. James Guide to Crime & Mystery Writers*
*CN* = *Contemporary Novelists*
*CP* = *Contemporary Poets*
*CPW* = *Contemporary Popular Writers*
*CSW* = *Contemporary Southern Writers*
*CWD* = *Contemporary Women Dramatists*
*CWP* = *Contemporary Women Poets*
*CWRI* = *St. James Guide to Children's Writers*
*CWW* = *Contemporary World Writers*
*DA* = *DISCovering Authors*
*DA3* = *DISCovering Authors 3.0*
*DAB* = *DISCovering Authors: British Edition*
*DAC* = *DISCovering Authors: Canadian Edition*
*DAM* = *DISCovering Authors: Modules*
   *DRAM:* *Dramatists Module;* *MST:* *Most-studied Authors Module;*
   *MULT:* *Multicultural Authors Module;* *NOV:* *Novelists Module;*
   *POET:* *Poets Module;* *POP:* *Popular Fiction and Genre Authors Module*
*DFS* = *Drama for Students*
*DLB* = *Dictionary of Literary Biography*
*DLBD* = *Dictionary of Literary Biography Documentary Series*
*DLBY* = *Dictionary of Literary Biography Yearbook*
*DNFS* = *Literature of Developing Nations for Students*
*EFS* = *Epics for Students*
*EXPN* = *Exploring Novels*
*EXPP* = *Exploring Poetry*
*EXPS* = *Exploring Short Stories*
*EW* = *European Writers*
*FANT* = *St. James Guide to Fantasy Writers*
*FW* = *Feminist Writers*
*GFL* = *Guide to French Literature,* Beginnings to 1789, 1798 to the Present
*GLL* = *Gay and Lesbian Literature*
*HGG* = *St. James Guide to Horror, Ghost & Gothic Writers*
*HW* = *Hispanic Writers*
*IDFW* = *International Dictionary of Films and Filmmakers: Writers and Production Artists*
*IDTP* = *International Dictionary of Theatre: Playwrights*
*LAIT* = *Literature and Its Times*
*LAW* = *Latin American Writers*
*JRDA* = *Junior DISCovering Authors*
*MAICYA* = *Major Authors and Illustrators for Children and Young Adults*
*MAICYAS* = *Major Authors and Illustrators for Children and Young Adults Supplement*
*MAWW* = *Modern American Women Writers*
*MJW* = *Modern Japanese Writers*
*MTCW* = *Major 20th-Century Writers*
*NCFS* = *Nonfiction Classics for Students*
*NFS* = *Novels for Students*
*PAB* = *Poets: American and British*
*PFS* = *Poetry for Students*
*RGAL* = *Reference Guide to American Literature*
*RGEL* = *Reference Guide to English Literature*
*RGSF* = *Reference Guide to Short Fiction*
*RGWL* = *Reference Guide to World Literature*
*RHW* = *Twentieth-Century Romance and Historical Writers*
*SAAS* = *Something about the Author Autobiography Series*
*SATA* = *Something about the Author*
*SFW* = *St. James Guide to Science Fiction Writers*
*SSFS* = *Short Stories for Students*
*TCWW* = *Twentieth-Century Western Writers*
*WLIT* = *World Literature and Its Times*
*WP* = *World Poets*
*YABC* = *Yesterday's Authors of Books for Children*
*YAW* = *St. James Guide to Young Adult Writers*

# Literary Criticism Series
# Cumulative Author Index

**20/1631**
See Upward, Allen

**A/C Cross**
See Lawrence, T(homas) E(dward)

**Abasiyanik, Sait Faik** 1906-1954
See Sait Faik
See also CA 123

**Abbey, Edward** 1927-1989 .......... **CLC 36, 59**
See also AMWS 13; ANW; CA 45-48; 128;
CANR 2, 41, 131; DA3; DLB 256, 275;
LATS 1:2; MTCW 2; TCWW 2

**Abbott, Edwin A.** 1838-1926 ........ **TCLC 139**
See also DLB 178

**Abbott, Lee K(ittredge)** 1947- .......... **CLC 48**
See also CA 124; CANR 51, 101; DLB 130

**Abe, Kobo** 1924-1993 ...... **CLC 8, 22, 53, 81;
SSC 61; TCLC 131**
See also CA 65-68; 140; CANR 24, 60;
DAM NOV; DFS 14; DLB 182; EWL 3;
MJW; MTCW 1, 2; RGWL 3; SFW 4

**Abe Kobo**
See Abe, Kobo

**Abelard, Peter** c. 1079-c. 1142 ...... **CMLC 11**
See also DLB 115, 208

**Abell, Kjeld** 1901-1961 ...................... **CLC 15**
See also CA 191; 111; DLB 214; EWL 3

**Abercrombie, Lascelles**
1881-1938 .............................. **TCLC 141**
See also CA 112; DLB 19; RGEL 2

**Abish, Walter** 1931- ........... **CLC 22; SSC 44**
See also CA 101; CANR 37, 114; CN 7;
DLB 130, 227

**Abrahams, Peter (Henry)** 1919- ......... **CLC 4**
See also AFW; BW 1; CA 57-60; CANR
26, 125; CDWLB 3; CN 7; DLB 117, 225;
EWL 3; MTCW 1, 2; RGEL 2; WLIT 2

**Abrams, M(eyer) H(oward)** 1912- ... **CLC 24**
See also CA 57-60; CANR 13, 33; DLB 67

**Abse, Dannie** 1923- ......... **CLC 7, 29; PC 41**
See also CA 53-56; CAAS 1; CANR 4, 46,
74, 124; CBD; CP 7; DAB; DAM POET;
DLB 27, 245; MTCW 1

**Abutsu** 1222(?)-1283 ...................... **CMLC 46**
See Abutsu-ni

**Abutsu-ni**
See Abutsu
See also DLB 203

**Achebe, (Albert) Chinua(lumogu)**
1930- ...... **BLC 1; CLC 1, 3, 5, 7, 11, 26,
51, 75, 127, 152; WLC**
See also AAYA 15; AFW; BPFB 1; BRWC
2; BW 2, 3; CA 1-4R; CANR 6, 26, 47,
124; CDWLB 3; CLR 20; CN 7; CP 7;
CWRI 5; DA; DA3; DAB; DAC; DAM
MST, MULT, NOV; DLB 117; DNFS 1;
EWL 3; EXPN; EXPS; LAIT 2; LATS
1:2; MAICYA 1, 2; MTCW 1, 2; NFS 2;
RGEL 2; RGSF 2; SATA 38, 40; SATA-
Brief 38; SSFS 3, 13; TWA; WLIT 2;
WWE 1

**Acker, Kathy** 1948-1997 ............ **CLC 45, 111**
See also AMWS 12; CA 117; 122; 162;
CANR 55; CN 7

**Ackroyd, Peter** 1949- .......... **CLC 34, 52, 140**
See also BRWS 6; CA 123; 127; CANR 51,
74, 99, 132; CN 7; DLB 155, 231; HGG;
INT CA-127; MTCW 1; RHW; SATA
153; SUFW 2

**Acorn, Milton** 1923-1986 ................... **CLC 15**
See also CA 103; CCA 1; DAC; DLB 53;
INT CA-103

**Adamov, Arthur** 1908-1970 .......... **CLC 4, 25**
See also CA 17-18; 25-28R; CAP 2; DAM
DRAM; EWL 3; GFL 1789 to the Present;
MTCW 1; RGWL 2, 3

**Adams, Alice (Boyd)** 1926-1999 .. **CLC 6, 13,
46; SSC 24**
See also CA 81-84; 179; CANR 26, 53, 75,
88; CN 7; CSW; DLB 234; DLBY 1986;
INT CANR-26; MTCW 1, 2; SSFS 14

**Adams, Andy** 1859-1935 ................. **TCLC 56**
See also TCWW 2; YABC 1

**Adams, (Henry) Brooks**
1848-1927 .............................. **TCLC 80**
See also CA 123; 193; DLB 47

**Adams, Douglas (Noel)** 1952-2001 .. **CLC 27,
60**
See also AAYA 4, 33; BEST 89:3; BYA 14;
CA 106; 197; CANR 34, 64, 124; CPW;
DA3; DAM POP; DLB 261; DLBY 1983;
JRDA; MTCW 1; NFS 7; SATA 116;
SATA-Obit 128; SFW 4

**Adams, Francis** 1862-1893 ............. **NCLC 33**

**Adams, Henry (Brooks)**
1838-1918 ........................... **TCLC 4, 52**
See also AMW; CA 104; 133; CANR 77;
DA; DAB; DAC; DAM MST; DLB 12,
47, 189, 284; EWL 3; MTCW 1; NCFS 1;
RGAL 4; TUS

**Adams, John** 1735-1826 ............... **NCLC 106**
See also DLB 31, 183

**Adams, Richard (George)** 1920- ... **CLC 4, 5,
18**
See also AAYA 16; AITN 1, 2; BPFB 1;
BYA 5; CA 49-52; CANR 3, 35, 128;
CLR 20; CN 7; DAM NOV; DLB 261;
FANT; JRDA; LAIT 5; MAICYA 1, 2;
MTCW 1, 2; NFS 11; SATA 7, 69; YAW

**Adamson, Joy(-Friederike Victoria)**
1910-1980 ................................ **CLC 17**
See also CA 69-72; 93-96; CANR 22;
MTCW 1; SATA 11; SATA-Obit 22

**Adcock, Fleur** 1934- ........................ **CLC 41**
See also CA 25-28R, 182; CAAE 182;
CAAS 23; CANR 11, 34, 69, 101; CP 7;
CWP; DLB 40; FW; WWE 1

**Addams, Charles (Samuel)**
1912-1988 ................................ **CLC 30**
See also CA 61-64; 126; CANR 12, 79

**Addams, (Laura) Jane** 1860-1935 . **TCLC 76**
See also AMWS 1; CA 194; DLB 303; FW

**Addison, Joseph** 1672-1719 .................. **LC 18**
See also BRW 3; CDBLB 1660-1789; DLB
101; RGEL 2; WLIT 3

**Adler, Alfred (F.)** 1870-1937 .......... **TCLC 61**
See also CA 119; 159

**Adler, C(arole) S(chwerdtfeger)**
1932- ........................................ **CLC 35**
See also AAYA 4, 41; CA 89-92; CANR
19, 40, 101; CLR 78; JRDA; MAICYA 1,
2; SAAS 15; SATA 26, 63, 102, 126;
YAW

**Adler, Renata** 1938- ...................... **CLC 8, 31**
See also CA 49-52; CANR 95; CN 7;
MTCW 1

**Adorno, Theodor W(iesengrund)**
1903-1969 .............................. **TCLC 111**
See also CA 89-92; 25-28R; CANR 89;
DLB 242; EWL 3

**Ady, Endre** 1877-1919 .................... **TCLC 11**
See also CA 107; CDWLB 4; DLB 215;
EW 9; EWL 3

**A.E.** ................................................. **TCLC 3, 10**
See Russell, George William
See also DLB 19

**Aelfric** c. 955-c. 1010 .................... **CMLC 46**
See also DLB 146

**Aeschines** c. 390B.C.-c. 320B.C. .... **CMLC 47**
See also DLB 176

**Aeschylus** 525(?)B.C.-456(?)B.C. .. **CMLC 11,
51; DC 8; WLCS**
See also AW 1; CDWLB 1; DA; DAB;
DAC; DAM DRAM, MST; DFS 5, 10;
DLB 176; LMFS 1; RGWL 2, 3; TWA

**Aesop** 620(?)B.C.-560(?)B.C. ......... **CMLC 24**
See also CLR 14; MAICYA 1, 2; SATA 64

**Affable Hawk**
See MacCarthy, Sir (Charles Otto) Desmond

**Africa, Ben**
See Bosman, Herman Charles

**Afton, Effie**
See Harper, Frances Ellen Watkins

**Agapida, Fray Antonio**
See Irving, Washington

**Agee, James (Rufus)** 1909-1955 ...... **TCLC 1,
19**
See also AAYA 44; AITN 1; AMW; CA 108;
148; CANR 131; CDALB 1941-1968;
DAM NOV; DLB 2, 26, 152; DLBY
1989; EWL 3; LAIT 3; LATS 1:2; MTCW
1; RGAL 4; TUS

**Aghill, Gordon**
See Silverberg, Robert

**Agnon, S(hmuel) Y(osef Halevi)**
1888-1970 .......... **CLC 4, 8, 14; SSC 30; TCLC 151**
See also CA 17-18; 25-28R; CANR 60, 102; CAP 2; EWL 3; MTCW 1, 2; RGSF 2; RGWL 2, 3

**Agrippa von Nettesheim, Henry Cornelius**
1486-1535 ..................................... **LC 27**

**Aguilera Malta, Demetrio**
1909-1981 ................................... **HLCS 1**
See also CA 111; 124; CANR 87; DAM MULT, NOV; DLB 145; EWL 3; HW 1; RGWL 3

**Agustini, Delmira** 1886-1914 ........... **HLCS 1**
See also CA 166; DLB 290; HW 1, 2; LAW

**Aherne, Owen**
See Cassill, R(onald) V(erlin)

**Ai** 1947- ..................................... **CLC 4, 14, 69**
See also CA 85-88; CAAS 13; CANR 70; DLB 120; PFS 16

**Aickman, Robert (Fordyce)**
1914-1981 ................................. **CLC 57**
See also CA 5-8R; CANR 3, 72, 100; DLB 261; HGG; SUFW 1, 2

**Aidoo, (Christina) Ama Ata**
1942- ............................. **BLCS; CLC 177**
See also AFW; BW 1; CA 101; CANR 62; CD 5; CDWLB 3; CN 7; CWD; CWP; DLB 117; DNFS 1, 2; EWL 3; FW; WLIT 2

**Aiken, Conrad (Potter)** 1889-1973 .... **CLC 1, 3, 5, 10, 52; PC 26; SSC 9**
See also AMW; CA 5-8R; 45-48; CANR 4, 60; CDALB 1929-1941; DAM NOV, POET; DLB 9, 45, 102; EWL 3; EXPS; HGG; MTCW 1, 2; RGAL 4; RGSF 2; SATA 3, 30; SSFS 8; TUS

**Aiken, Joan (Delano)** 1924-2004 ...... **CLC 35**
See also AAYA 1, 25; CA 9-12R, 182; 223; CAAE 182; CANR 4, 23, 34, 64, 121; CLR 1, 19, 90; DLB 161; FANT; HGG; JRDA; MAICYA 1, 2; MTCW 1; RHW; SAAS 1; SATA 2, 30, 73; SATA-Essay 109; SATA-Obit 152; SUFW 2; WYA; YAW

**Ainsworth, William Harrison**
1805-1882 ................................. **NCLC 13**
See also DLB 21; HGG; RGEL 2; SATA 24; SUFW 1

**Aitmatov, Chingiz (Torekulovich)**
1928- ..................................... **CLC 71**
See Aytmatov, Chingiz
See also CA 103; CANR 38; CWW 2; DLB 302; MTCW 1; RGSF 2; SATA 56

**Akers, Floyd**
See Baum, L(yman) Frank

**Akhmadulina, Bella Akhatovna**
1937- ........................... **CLC 53; PC 43**
See also CA 65-68; CWP; CWW 2; DAM POET; EWL 3

**Akhmatova, Anna** 1888-1966 ..... **CLC 11, 25, 64, 126; PC 2, 55**
See also CA 19-20; 25-28R; CANR 35; CAP 1; DA3; DAM POET; DLB 295; EW 10; EWL 3; MTCW 1, 2; PFS 18; RGWL 2, 3

**Aksakov, Sergei Timofeyvich**
1791-1859 ................................... **NCLC 2**
See also DLB 198

**Aksenov, Vasilii (Pavlovich)**
See Aksyonov, Vassily (Pavlovich)
See also CWW 2

**Aksenov, Vassily**
See Aksyonov, Vassily (Pavlovich)

**Akst, Daniel** 1956- ........................... **CLC 109**
See also CA 161; CANR 110

**Aksyonov, Vassily (Pavlovich)**
1932- ............................... **CLC 22, 37, 101**
See Aksenov, Vasilii (Pavlovich)
See also CA 53-56; CANR 12, 48, 77; DLB 302; EWL 3

**Akutagawa Ryunosuke** 1892-1927 ... **SSC 44; TCLC 16**
See also CA 117; 154; DLB 180; EWL 3; MJW; RGSF 2; RGWL 2, 3

**Alabaster, William** 1568-1640 ............. **LC 90**
See also DLB 132; RGEL 2

**Alain** 1868-1951 ............................. **TCLC 41**
See also CA 163; EWL 3; GFL 1789 to the Present

**Alain de Lille** c. 1116-c. 1203 ....... **CMLC 53**
See also DLB 208

**Alain-Fournier** ................................. **TCLC 6**
See Fournier, Henri-Alban
See also DLB 65; EWL 3; GFL 1789 to the Present; RGWL 2, 3

**Al-Amin, Jamil Abdullah** 1943- ......... **BLC 1**
See also BW 1, 3; CA 112; 125; CANR 82; DAM MULT

**Alanus de Insluis**
See Alain de Lille

**Alarcon, Pedro Antonio de**
1833-1891 ................... **NCLC 1; SSC 64**

**Alas (y Urena), Leopoldo (Enrique Garcia)**
1852-1901 ................................. **TCLC 29**
See also CA 113; 131; HW 1; RGSF 2

**Albee, Edward (Franklin) (III)**
1928- .. **CLC 1, 2, 3, 5, 9, 11, 13, 25, 53, 86, 113; DC 11; WLC**
See also AAYA 51; AITN 1; AMW; CA 5-8R; CABS 3; CAD; CANR 8, 54, 74, 124; CD 5; CDALB 1941-1968; DA; DA3; DAB; DAC; DAM DRAM, MST; DFS 2, 3, 8, 10, 13, 14; DLB 7, 266; EWL 3; INT CANR-8; LAIT 4; LMFS 2; MTCW 1, 2; RGAL 4; TUS

**Alberti (Merello), Rafael**
See Alberti, Rafael
See also CWW 2

**Alberti, Rafael** 1902-1999 ................... **CLC 7**
See Alberti (Merello), Rafael
See also CA 85-88; 185; CANR 81; DLB 108; EWL 3; HW 2; RGWL 2, 3

**Albert the Great** 1193(?)-1280 ...... **CMLC 16**
See also DLB 115

**Alcaeus** c. 620B.C.- ......................... **CMLC 65**
See also DLB 176

**Alcala-Galiano, Juan Valera y**
See Valera y Alcala-Galiano, Juan

**Alcayaga, Lucila Godoy**
See Godoy Alcayaga, Lucila

**Alcott, Amos Bronson** 1799-1888 .... **NCLC 1**
See also DLB 1, 223

**Alcott, Louisa May** 1832-1888 . **NCLC 6, 58, 83; SSC 27; WLC**
See also AAYA 20; AMWS 1; BPFB 1; BYA 2; CDALB 1865-1917; CLR 1, 38; DA; DA3; DAB; DAC; DAM MST, NOV; DLB 1, 42, 79, 223, 239, 242; DLBD 14; FW; JRDA; LAIT 2; MAICYA 1, 2; NFS 12; RGAL 4; SATA 100; TUS; WCH; WYA; YABC 1; YAW

**Alcuin** c. 730-804 ........................... **CMLC 69**
See also DLB 148

**Aldanov, M. A.**
See Aldanov, Mark (Alexandrovich)

**Aldanov, Mark (Alexandrovich)**
1886(?)-1957 ........................... **TCLC 23**
See also CA 118; 181

**Aldington, Richard** 1892-1962 .......... **CLC 49**
See also CA 85-88; CANR 45; DLB 20, 36, 100, 149; LMFS 2; RGEL 2

**Aldiss, Brian W(ilson)** 1925- . **CLC 5, 14, 40; SSC 36**
See also AAYA 42; CA 5-8R, 190; CAAE 190; CAAS 2; CANR 5, 28, 64, 121; CN 7; DAM NOV; DLB 14, 261, 271; MTCW 1, 2; SATA 34; SFW 4

**Aldrich, Bess Streeter**
1881-1954 ................................. **TCLC 125**
See also CLR 70

**Alegria, Claribel**
See Alegria, Claribel
See also CWW 2; DLB 145, 283

**Alegria, Claribel** 1924- .... **CLC 75; HLCS 1; PC 26**
See Alegria, Claribel
See also CA 131; CAAS 15; CANR 66, 94; DAM MULT; EWL 3; HW 1; MTCW 1; PFS 21

**Alegria, Fernando** 1918- ................. **CLC 57**
See also CA 9-12R; CANR 5, 32, 72; EWL 3; HW 1, 2

**Aleichem, Sholom** ....... **SSC 33; TCLC 1, 35**
See Rabinovitch, Sholem
See also TWA

**Aleixandre, Vicente** 1898-1984 ....... **HLCS 1; TCLC 113**
See also CANR 81; DLB 108; EWL 3; HW 2; RGWL 2, 3

**Aleman, Mateo** 1547-1615(?) .............. **LC 81**

**Alencon, Marguerite d'**
See de Navarre, Marguerite

**Alepoudelis, Odysseus**
See Elytis, Odysseus
See also CWW 2

**Aleshkovsky, Joseph** 1929-
See Aleshkovsky, Yuz
See also CA 121; 128

**Aleshkovsky, Yuz** ............................. **CLC 44**
See Aleshkovsky, Joseph

**Alexander, Lloyd (Chudley)** 1924- ... **CLC 35**
See also AAYA 1, 27; BPFB 1; BYA 5, 6, 7, 9, 10, 11; CA 1-4R; CANR 1, 24, 38, 55, 113; CLR 1, 5, 48; CWRI 5; DLB 52; FANT; JRDA; MAICYA 1, 2; MAICYAS 1; MTCW 1; SAAS 19; SATA 3, 49, 81, 129, 135; SUFW; TUS; WYA; YAW

**Alexander, Meena** 1951- ................. **CLC 121**
See also CA 115; CANR 38, 70; CP 7; CWP; FW

**Alexander, Samuel** 1859-1938 ........ **TCLC 77**

**Alexie, Sherman (Joseph, Jr.)**
1966- ........ **CLC 96, 154; NNAL; PC 53**
See also AAYA 28; BYA 15; CA 138; CANR 65, 95, 133; DA3; DAM MULT; DLB 175, 206, 278; LATS 1:2; MTCW 1; NFS 17; SSFS 18

**al-Farabi** 870(?)-950 ...................... **CMLC 58**
See also DLB 115

**Alfau, Felipe** 1902-1999 .................... **CLC 66**
See also CA 137

**Alfieri, Vittorio** 1749-1803 ........... **NCLC 101**
See also EW 4; RGWL 2, 3

**Alfred, Jean Gaston**
See Ponge, Francis

**Alger, Horatio, Jr.** 1832-1899 .... **NCLC 8, 83**
See also CLR 87; DLB 42; LAIT 2; RGAL 4; SATA 16; TUS

**Al-Ghazali, Muhammad ibn Muhammad**
1058-1111 ............................... **CMLC 50**
See also DLB 115

**Algren, Nelson** 1909-1981 ..... **CLC 4, 10, 33; SSC 33**
See also AMWS 9; BPFB 1; CA 13-16R; 103; CANR 20, 61; CDALB 1941-1968; DLB 9; DLBY 1981, 1982, 2000; EWL 3; MTCW 1, 2; RGAL 4; RGSF 2

**al-Hariri, al-Qasim ibn 'Ali Abu Muhammad al-Basri**
1054-1122 ................................. **CMLC 63**
See also RGWL 3

**Ali, Ahmed** 1908-1998 ...................... **CLC 69**
See also CA 25-28R; CANR 15, 34; EWL 3

**Ali, Tariq** 1943- ................................ **CLC 173**
See also CA 25-28R; CANR 10, 99

**Alighieri, Dante**
See Dante

**Allan, John B.**
See Westlake, Donald E(dwin)

**Allan, Sidney**
See Hartmann, Sadakichi

**Allan, Sydney**
See Hartmann, Sadakichi

**Allard, Janet** ........................................ **CLC 59**

**Allen, Edward** 1948- ........................... **CLC 59**

**Allen, Fred** 1894-1956 ...................... **TCLC 87**

**Allen, Paula Gunn** 1939- ..... **CLC 84; NNAL**
See also AMWS 4; CA 112; 143; CANR 63, 130; CWP; DA3; DAM MULT; DLB 175; FW; MTCW 1; RGAL 4

**Allen, Roland**
See Ayckbourn, Alan

**Allen, Sarah A.**
See Hopkins, Pauline Elizabeth

**Allen, Sidney H.**
See Hartmann, Sadakichi

**Allen, Woody** 1935- ............. **CLC 16, 52, 195**
See also AAYA 10, 51; CA 33-36R; CANR 27, 38, 63, 128; DAM POP; DLB 44; MTCW 1

**Allende, Isabel** 1942- ... **CLC 39, 57, 97, 170; HLC 1; SSC 65; WLCS**
See also AAYA 18; CA 125; 130; CANR 51, 74, 129; CDWLB 3; CLR 99; CWW 2; DA3; DAM MULT, NOV; DLB 145; DNFS 1; EWL 3; FW; HW 1, 2; INT CA-130; LAIT 5; LAWS 1; LMFS 2; MTCW 1, 2; NCFS 1; NFS 6, 18; RGSF 2; RGWL 3; SSFS 11, 16; WLIT 1

**Alleyn, Ellen**
See Rossetti, Christina (Georgina)

**Alleyne, Carla D.** .............................. **CLC 65**

**Allingham, Margery (Louise)**
1904-1966 ........................................ **CLC 19**
See also CA 5-8R; 25-28R; CANR 4, 58; CMW 4; DLB 77; MSW; MTCW 1, 2

**Allingham, William** 1824-1889 ...... **NCLC 25**
See also DLB 35; RGEL 2

**Allison, Dorothy E.** 1949- .......... **CLC 78, 153**
See also AAYA 53; CA 140; CANR 66, 107; CSW; DA3; FW; MTCW 1; NFS 11; RGAL 4

**Alloula, Malek** .................................. **CLC 65**

**Allston, Washington** 1779-1843 ....... **NCLC 2**
See also DLB 1, 235

**Almedingen, E. M.** ........................... **CLC 12**
See Almedingen, Martha Edith von
See also SATA 3

**Almedingen, Martha Edith von** 1898-1971
See Almedingen, E. M.
See also CA 1-4R; CANR 1

**Almodovar, Pedro** 1949(?)- ........... **CLC 114; HLCS 1**
See also CA 133; CANR 72; HW 2

**Almqvist, Carl Jonas Love**
1793-1866 ........................................ **NCLC 42**

**al-Mutanabbi, Ahmad ibn al-Husayn Abu al-Tayyib al-Jufi al-Kindi**
915-965 .................................... **CMLC 66**
See also RGWL 3

**Alonso, Damaso** 1898-1990 .............. **CLC 14**
See also CA 110; 131; 130; CANR 72; DLB 108; EWL 3; HW 1, 2

**Alov**
See Gogol, Nikolai (Vasilyevich)

**al'Sadaawi, Nawal**
See El Saadawi, Nawal
See also FW

**Al Siddik**
See Rolfe, Frederick (William Serafino Austin Lewis Mary)
See also GLL 1; RGEL 2

**Alta** 1942- ............................................ **CLC 19**
See also CA 57-60

**Alter, Robert B(ernard)** 1935- .......... **CLC 34**
See also CA 49-52; CANR 1, 47, 100

**Alther, Lisa** 1944- ........................... **CLC 7, 41**
See also BPFB 1; CA 65-68; CAAS 30; CANR 12, 30, 51; CN 7; CSW; GLL 2; MTCW 1

**Althusser, L.**
See Althusser, Louis

**Althusser, Louis** 1918-1990 ............. **CLC 106**
See also CA 131; 132; CANR 102; DLB 242

**Altman, Robert** 1925- ................. **CLC 16, 116**
See also CA 73-76; CANR 43

**Alurista** .............................................. **HLCS 1**
See Urista (Heredia), Alberto (Baltazar)
See also DLB 82; LLW 1

**Alvarez, A(lfred)** 1929- .................. **CLC 5, 13**
See also CA 1-4R; CANR 3, 33, 63, 101; CN 7; CP 7; DLB 14, 40

**Alvarez, Alejandro Rodriguez** 1903-1965
See Casona, Alejandro
See also CA 131; 93-96; HW 1

**Alvarez, Julia** 1950- .......... **CLC 93; HLCS 1**
See also AAYA 25; AMWS 7; CA 147; CANR 69, 101, 133; DA3; DLB 282; LATS 1:2; LLW 1; MTCW 1; NFS 5, 9; SATA 129; WLIT 1

**Alvaro, Corrado** 1896-1956 ............ **TCLC 60**
See also CA 163; DLB 264; EWL 3

**Amado, Jorge** 1912-2001 ... **CLC 13, 40, 106; HLC 1**
See also CA 77-80; 201; CANR 35, 74; CWW 2; DAM MULT, NOV; DLB 113; EWL 3; HW 2; LAW; LAWS 1; MTCW 1, 2; RGWL 2, 3; TWA; WLIT 1

**Ambler, Eric** 1909-1998 ............. **CLC 4, 6, 9**
See also BRWS 4; CA 9-12R; 171; CANR 7, 38, 74; CMW 4; CN 7; DLB 77; MSW; MTCW 1, 2; TEA

**Ambrose, Stephen E(dward)**
1936-2002 ................................ **CLC 145**
See also AAYA 44; CA 1-4R; 209; CANR 3, 43, 57, 83, 105; NCFS 2; SATA 40, 138

**Amichai, Yehuda** 1924-2000 .. **CLC 9, 22, 57, 116; PC 38**
See also CA 85-88; 189; CANR 46, 60, 99, 132; CWW 2; EWL 3; MTCW 1

**Amichai, Yehudah**
See Amichai, Yehuda

**Amiel, Henri Frederic** 1821-1881 .... **NCLC 4**
See also DLB 217

**Amis, Kingsley (William)**
1922-1995 ...... **CLC 1, 2, 3, 5, 8, 13, 40, 44, 129**
See also AITN 2; BPFB 1; BRWS 2; CA 9-12R; 150; CANR 8, 28, 54; CDBLB 1945-1960; CN 7; CP 7; DA; DA3; DAB; DAC; DAM MST, NOV; DLB 15, 27, 100, 139; DLBY 1996; EWL 3; HGG; INT CANR-8; MTCW 1, 2; RGEL 2; RGSF 2; SFW 4

**Amis, Martin (Louis)** 1949- .... **CLC 4, 9, 38, 62, 101**
See also BEST 90:3; BRWS 4; CA 65-68; CANR 8, 27, 54, 73, 95, 132; CN 7; DA3; DLB 14, 194; EWL 3; INT CANR-27; MTCW 1

**Ammianus Marcellinus** c. 330-c. 395 ............................................ **CMLC 60**
See also AW 2; DLB 211

**Ammons, A(rchie) R(andolph)**
1926-2001 ...... **CLC 2, 3, 5, 8, 9, 25, 57, 108; PC 16**
See also AITN 1; AMWS 7; CA 9-12R; 193; CANR 6, 36, 51, 73, 107; CP 7; CSW; DAM POET; DLB 5, 165; EWL 3; MTCW 1, 2; PFS 19; RGAL 4

**Amo, Tauraatua i**
See Adams, Henry (Brooks)

**Amory, Thomas** 1691(?)-1788 .............. **LC 48**
See also DLB 39

**Anand, Mulk Raj** 1905- .............. **CLC 23, 93**
See also CA 65-68; CANR 32, 64; CN 7; DAM NOV; EWL 3; MTCW 1, 2; RGSF 2

**Anatol**
See Schnitzler, Arthur

**Anaximander** c. 611B.C.-c. 546B.C. ...................................... **CMLC 22**

**Anaya, Rudolfo A(lfonso)** 1937- ...... **CLC 23, 148; HLC 1**
See also AAYA 20; BYA 13; CA 45-48; CAAS 4; CANR 1, 32, 51, 124; CN 7; DAM MULT, NOV; DLB 82, 206, 278; HW 1; LAIT 4; LLW 1; MTCW 1, 2; NFS 12; RGAL 4; RGSF 2; WLIT 1

**Andersen, Hans Christian**
1805-1875 ....... **NCLC 7, 79; SSC 6, 56; WLC**
See also AAYA 57; CLR 6; DA; DA3; DAB; DAC; DAM MST, POP; EW 6; MAICYA 1, 2; RGSF 2; RGWL 2, 3; SATA 100; TWA; WCH; YABC 1

**Anderson, C. Farley**
See Mencken, H(enry) L(ouis); Nathan, George Jean

**Anderson, Jessica (Margaret) Queale**
1916- .......................................... **CLC 37**
See also CA 9-12R; CANR 4, 62; CN 7

**Anderson, Jon (Victor)** 1940- ........... **CLC 9**
See also CA 25-28R; CANR 20; DAM POET

**Anderson, Lindsay (Gordon)**
1923-1994 ........................................ **CLC 20**
See also CA 125; 128; 146; CANR 77

**Anderson, Maxwell** 1888-1959 ........ **TCLC 2, 144**
See also CA 105; 152; DAM DRAM; DFS 16, 20; DLB 7, 228; MTCW 2; RGAL 4

**Anderson, Poul (William)**
1926-2001 ........................................ **CLC 15**
See also AAYA 5, 34; BPFB 1; BYA 6, 8, 9; CA 1-4R; 181; 199; CAAE 181; CAAS 2; CANR 2, 15, 34, 64, 110; CLR 58; DLB 8; FANT; INT CANR-15; MTCW 1, 2; SATA 90; SATA-Brief 39; SATA-Essay 106; SCFW 2; SFW 4; SUFW 1, 2

**Anderson, Robert (Woodruff)**
1917- .......................................... **CLC 23**
See also AITN 1; CA 21-24R; CANR 32; DAM DRAM; DLB 7; LAIT 5

**Anderson, Roberta Joan**
See Mitchell, Joni

**Anderson, Sherwood** 1876-1941 .. **SSC 1, 46; TCLC 1, 10, 24, 123; WLC**
See also AAYA 30; AMW; AMWC 2; BPFB 1; CA 104; 121; CANR 61; CDALB 1917-1929; DA; DA3; DAB; DAC; DAM MST, NOV; DLB 4, 9, 86; DLBD 1; EWL 3; EXPS; GLL 2; MTCW 1, 2; NFS 4; RGAL 4; RGSF 2; SSFS 4, 10, 11; TUS

**Andier, Pierre**
See Desnos, Robert

**Andouard**
See Giraudoux, Jean(-Hippolyte)

**Andrade, Carlos Drummond de** ..... **CLC 18**
See Drummond de Andrade, Carlos
See also EWL 3; RGWL 2, 3

**Andrade, Mario de** ........................ **TCLC 43**
See de Andrade, Mario
See also EWL 3; LAW; RGWL 2, 3; WLIT
1

**Andreae, Johann V(alentin)**
1586-1654 ...................................... **LC 32**
See also DLB 164

**Andreas Capellanus** fl. c. 1185- .... **CMLC 45**
See also DLB 208

**Andreas-Salome, Lou** 1861-1937 ... **TCLC 56**
See also CA 178; DLB 66

**Andreev, Leonid**
See Andreyev, Leonid (Nikolaevich)
See also DLB 295; EWL 3

**Andress, Lesley**
See Sanders, Lawrence

**Andrewes, Lancelot** 1555-1626 ............. **LC 5**
See also DLB 151, 172

**Andrews, Cicily Fairfield**
See West, Rebecca

**Andrews, Elton V.**
See Pohl, Frederik

**Andreyev, Leonid (Nikolaevich)**
1871-1919 .................................... **TCLC 3**
See Andreev, Leonid
See also CA 104; 185

**Andric, Ivo** 1892-1975 ......... **CLC 8; SSC 36;**
**TCLC 135**
See also CA 81-84; 57-60; CANR 43, 60;
CDWLB 4; DLB 147; EW 11; EWL 3;
MTCW 1; RGSF 2; RGWL 2, 3

**Androvar**
See Prado (Calvo), Pedro

**Angelique, Pierre**
See Bataille, Georges

**Angell, Roger** 1920- ......................... **CLC 26**
See also CA 57-60; CANR 13, 44, 70; DLB
171, 185

**Angelou, Maya** 1928- ... **BLC 1; CLC 12, 35,**
**64, 77, 155; PC 32; WLCS**
See also AAYA 7, 20; AMWS 4; BPFB 1;
BW 2, 3; BYA 2; CA 65-68; CANR 19,
42, 65, 111, 133; CDALBS; CLR 53; CP
7; CPW; CSW; CWP; DA; DA3; DAB;
DAC; DAM MST, MULT, POET, POP;
DLB 38; EWL 3; EXPN; EXPP; LAIT 4;
MAICYA 2; MAICYAS 1; MAWW;
MTCW 1, 2; NCFS 2; NFS 2; PFS 2, 3;
RGAL 4; SATA 49, 136; WYA; YAW

**Angouleme, Marguerite d'**
See de Navarre, Marguerite

**Anna Comnena** 1083-1153 ............ **CMLC 25**

**Annensky, Innokentii Fedorovich**
See Annensky, Innokenty (Fyodorovich)
See also DLB 295

**Annensky, Innokenty (Fyodorovich)**
1856-1909 ................................. **TCLC 14**
See also CA 110; 155; EWL 3

**Annunzio, Gabriele d'**
See D'Annunzio, Gabriele

**Anodos**
See Coleridge, Mary E(lizabeth)

**Anon, Charles Robert**
See Pessoa, Fernando (Antonio Nogueira)

**Anouilh, Jean (Marie Lucien Pierre)**
1910-1987 . **CLC 1, 3, 8, 13, 40, 50; DC**
**8, 21**
See also CA 17-20R; 123; CANR 32; DAM
DRAM; DFS 9, 10, 19; EW 13; EWL 3;
GFL 1789 to the Present; MTCW 1, 2;
RGWL 2, 3; TWA

**Anselm of Canterbury**
1033(?)-1109 ........................... **CMLC 67**
See also DLB 115

**Anthony, Florence**
See Ai

**Anthony, John**
See Ciardi, John (Anthony)

**Anthony, Peter**
See Shaffer, Anthony (Joshua); Shaffer,
Peter (Levin)

**Anthony, Piers** 1934- ....................... **CLC 35**
See also AAYA 11, 48; BYA 7; CA 200;
CAAE 200; CANR 28, 56, 73, 102, 133;
CPW; DAM POP; DLB 8; FANT; MAI-
CYA 2; MAICYAS 1; MTCW 1, 2; SAAS
22; SATA 84, 129; SATA-Essay 129; SFW
4; SUFW 1, 2; YAW

**Anthony, Susan B(rownell)**
1820-1906 ................................. **TCLC 84**
See also CA 211; FW

**Antiphon** c. 480B.C.-c. 411B.C. .... **CMLC 55**

**Antoine, Marc**
See Proust, (Valentin-Louis-George-Eugene)
Marcel

**Antoninus, Brother**
See Everson, William (Oliver)

**Antonioni, Michelangelo** 1912- ........ **CLC 20,**
**144**
See also CA 73-76; CANR 45, 77

**Antschel, Paul** 1920-1970
See Celan, Paul
See also CA 85-88; CANR 33, 61; MTCW
1; PFS 21

**Anwar, Chairil** 1922-1949 ............. **TCLC 22**
See Chairil Anwar
See also CA 121; 219; RGWL 3

**Anzaldua, Gloria (Evanjelina)**
1942-2004 ................................. **HLCS 1**
See also CA 175; 227; CSW; CWP; DLB
122; FW; LLW 1; RGAL 4

**Apess, William** 1798-1839(?) ........ **NCLC 73;**
**NNAL**
See also DAM MULT; DLB 175, 243

**Apollinaire, Guillaume** 1880-1918 ....... **PC 7;**
**TCLC 3, 8, 51**
See Kostrowitzki, Wilhelm Apollinaris de
See also CA 152; DAM POET; DLB 258;
EW 9; EWL 3; GFL 1789 to the Present;
MTCW 1; RGWL 2, 3; TWA; WP

**Apollonius of Rhodes**
See Apollonius Rhodius
See also AW 1; RGWL 2, 3

**Apollonius Rhodius** c. 300B.C.-c.
220B.C. ..................................... **CMLC 28**
See Apollonius of Rhodes
See also DLB 176

**Appelfeld, Aharon** 1932- ... **CLC 23, 47; SSC**
**42**
See also CA 112; 133; CANR 86; CWW 2;
DLB 299; EWL 3; RGSF 2

**Apple, Max (Isaac)** 1941- .... **CLC 9, 33; SSC**
**50**
See also CA 81-84; CANR 19, 54; DLB
130

**Appleman, Philip (Dean)** 1926- ....... **CLC 51**
See also CA 13-16R; CAAS 18; CANR 6,
29, 56

**Appleton, Lawrence**
See Lovecraft, H(oward) P(hillips)

**Apteryx**
See Eliot, T(homas) S(tearns)

**Apuleius, (Lucius Madaurensis)**
125(?)-175(?) ........................... **CMLC 1**
See also AW 2; CDWLB 1; DLB 211;
RGWL 2, 3; SUFW

**Aquin, Hubert** 1929-1977 ................. **CLC 15**
See also CA 105; DLB 53; EWL 3

**Aquinas, Thomas** 1224(?)-1274 ..... **CMLC 33**
See also DLB 115; EW 1; TWA

**Aragon, Louis** 1897-1982 ............. **CLC 3, 22;**
**TCLC 123**
See also CA 69-72; 108; CANR 28, 71;
DAM NOV, POET; DLB 72, 258; EW 11;

EWL 3; GFL 1789 to the Present; GLL 2;
LMFS 2; MTCW 1, 2; RGWL 2, 3

**Arany, Janos** 1817-1882 ................. **NCLC 34**

**Aranyos, Kakay** 1847-1910
See Mikszath, Kalman

**Aratus of Soli** c. 315B.C.-c.
240B.C. .................................... **CMLC 64**
See also DLB 176

**Arbuthnot, John** 1667-1735 .................. **LC 1**
See also DLB 101

**Archer, Herbert Winslow**
See Mencken, H(enry) L(ouis)

**Archer, Jeffrey (Howard)** 1940- ....... **CLC 28**
See also AAYA 16; BEST 89:3; BPFB 1;
CA 77-80; CANR 22, 52, 95; CPW; DA3;
DAM POP; INT CANR-22

**Archer, Jules** 1915- ......................... **CLC 12**
See also CA 9-12R; CANR 6, 69; SAAS 5;
SATA 4, 85

**Archer, Lee**
See Ellison, Harlan (Jay)

**Archilochus** c. 7th cent. B.C.- ........ **CMLC 44**
See also DLB 176

**Arden, John** 1930- ................... **CLC 6, 13, 15**
See also BRWS 2; CA 13-16R; CAAS 4;
CANR 31, 65, 67, 124; CBD; CD 5;
DAM DRAM; DFS 9; DLB 13, 245;
EWL 3; MTCW 1

**Arenas, Reinaldo** 1943-1990 .. **CLC 41; HLC**
**1**
See also CA 124; 128; 133; CANR 73, 106;
DAM MULT; DLB 145; EWL 3; GLL 2;
HW 1; LAW; LAWS 1; MTCW 1; RGSF
2; RGWL 3; WLIT 1

**Arendt, Hannah** 1906-1975 ........ **CLC 66, 98**
See also CA 17-20R; 61-64; CANR 26, 60;
DLB 242; MTCW 1, 2

**Aretino, Pietro** 1492-1556 ................... **LC 12**
See also RGWL 2, 3

**Arghezi, Tudor** ................................. **CLC 80**
See Theodorescu, Ion N.
See also CA 167; CDWLB 4; DLB 220;
EWL 3

**Arguedas, Jose Maria** 1911-1969 .... **CLC 10,**
**18; HLCS 1; TCLC 147**
See also CA 89-92; CANR 73; DLB 113;
EWL 3; HW 1; LAW; RGWL 2, 3; WLIT
1

**Argueta, Manlio** 1936- ...................... **CLC 31**
See also CA 131; CANR 73; CWW 2; DLB
145; EWL 3; HW 1; RGWL 3

**Arias, Ron(ald Francis)** 1941- ........... **HLC 1**
See also CA 131; CANR 81; DAM MULT;
DLB 82; HW 1, 2; MTCW 2

**Ariosto, Ludovico** 1474-1533 ... **LC 6, 87; PC**
**42**
See also EW 2; RGWL 2, 3

**Aristides**
See Epstein, Joseph

**Aristophanes** 450B.C.-385B.C. ....... **CMLC 4,**
**51; DC 2; WLCS**
See also AW 1; CDWLB 1; DA; DA3;
DAB; DAC; DAM DRAM, MST; DFS
10; DLB 176; LMFS 1; RGWL 2, 3; TWA

**Aristotle** 384B.C.-322B.C. ........... **CMLC 31;**
**WLCS**
See also AW 1; CDWLB 1; DA; DA3;
DAB; DAC; DAM MST; DLB 176;
RGWL 2, 3; TWA

**Arlt, Roberto (Godofredo Christophersen)**
1900-1942 .................. **HLC 1; TCLC 29**
See also CA 123; 131; CANR 67; DAM
MULT; DLB 305; EWL 3; HW 1, 2; LAW

**Armah, Ayi Kwei** 1939- . **BLC 1; CLC 5, 33,**
**136**
See also AFW; BW 1; CA 61-64; CANR
21, 64; CDWLB 3; CN 7; DAM MULT,
POET; DLB 117; EWL 3; MTCW 1;
WLIT 2

Armatrading, Joan 1950- .................. **CLC 17**
See also CA 114; 186
Armitage, Frank
See Carpenter, John (Howard)
Armstrong, Jeannette (C.) 1948- ....... **NNAL**
See also CA 149; CCA 1; CN 7; DAC;
SATA 102
Arnette, Robert
See Silverberg, Robert
Arnim, Achim von (Ludwig Joachim von
Arnim) 1781-1831 ..... **NCLC 5; SSC 29**
See also DLB 90
Arnim, Bettina von 1785-1859 ...... **NCLC 38,
123**
See also DLB 90; RGWL 2, 3
Arnold, Matthew 1822-1888 ..... **NCLC 6, 29,
89, 126; PC 5; WLC**
See also BRW 5; CDBLB 1832-1890; DA;
DAB; DAC; DAM MST, POET; DLB 32,
57; EXPP; PAB; PFS 2; TEA; WP
Arnold, Thomas 1795-1842 ............ **NCLC 18**
See also DLB 55
Arnow, Harriette (Louisa) Simpson
1908-1986 .......................... **CLC 2, 7, 18**
See also BPFB 1; CA 9-12R; 118; CANR
14; DLB 6; FW; MTCW 1, 2; RHW;
SATA 42; SATA-Obit 47
Arouet, Francois-Marie
See Voltaire
Arp, Hans
See Arp, Jean
Arp, Jean 1887-1966 ....... **CLC 5; TCLC 115**
See also CA 81-84; 25-28R; CANR 42, 77;
EW 10
Arrabal
See Arrabal, Fernando
Arrabal, Fernando 1932- ... **CLC 2, 9, 18, 58**
See Arrabal (Teran), Fernando
See also CA 9-12R; CANR 15; EWL 3;
LMFS 2
Arrabal (Teran), Fernando 1932-
See Arrabal, Fernando
See also CWW 2
Arreola, Juan Jose 1918-2001 ....... **CLC 147;
HLC 1; SSC 38**
See also CA 113; 131; 200; CANR 81;
CWW 2; DAM MULT; DLB 113; DNFS
2; EWL 3; HW 1, 2; LAW; RGSF 2
Arrian c. 89(?)-c. 155(?) ............... **CMLC 43**
See also DLB 176
Arrick, Fran ............................ **CLC 30**
See Gaberman, Judie Angell
See also BYA 6
Arrley, Richmond
See Delany, Samuel R(ay), Jr.
Artaud, Antonin (Marie Joseph)
1896-1948 ............... **DC 14; TCLC 3, 36**
See also CA 104; 149; DA3; DAM DRAM;
DLB 258; EW 11; EWL 3; GFL 1789 to
the Present; MTCW 1; RGWL 2, 3
Arthur, Ruth M(abel) 1905-1979 ..... **CLC 12**
See also CA 9-12R; 85-88; CANR 4; CWRI
5; SATA 7, 26
Artsybashev, Mikhail (Petrovich)
1878-1927 ................................. **TCLC 31**
See also CA 170; DLB 295
Arundel, Honor (Morfydd)
1919-1973 .................................. **CLC 17**
See also CA 21-22; 41-44R; CAP 2; CLR
35; CWRI 5; SATA 4; SATA-Obit 24
Arzner, Dorothy 1900-1979 ............... **CLC 98**
Asch, Sholem 1880-1957 .................... **TCLC 3**
See also CA 105; EWL 3; GLL 2
Ascham, Roger 1516(?)-1568 ............. **LC 101**
See also DLB 236
Ash, Shalom
See Asch, Sholem

Ashbery, John (Lawrence) 1927- .. **CLC 2, 3,
4, 6, 9, 13, 15, 25, 41, 77, 125; PC 26**
See Berry, Jonas
See also AMWS 3; CA 5-8R; CANR 9, 37,
66, 102, 132; CP 7; DA3; DAM POET;
DLB 5, 165; DLBY 1981; EWL 3; INT
CANR-9; MTCW 1, 2; PAB; PFS 11;
RGAL 4; WP
Ashdown, Clifford
See Freeman, R(ichard) Austin
Ashe, Gordon
See Creasey, John
Ashton-Warner, Sylvia (Constance)
1908-1984 .................................. **CLC 19**
See also CA 69-72; 112; CANR 29; MTCW
1, 2
Asimov, Isaac 1920-1992 ..... **CLC 1, 3, 9, 19,
26, 76, 92**
See also AAYA 13; BEST 90:2; BPFB 1;
BYA 4, 6, 7, 9; CA 1-4R; 137; CANR 2,
19, 36, 60, 125; CLR 12, 79; CMW 4;
CPW; DA3; DAM POP; DLB 8; DLBY
1992; INT CANR-19; JRDA; LAIT 5;
LMFS 2; MAICYA 1, 2; MTCW 1, 2;
RGAL 4; SATA 1, 26, 74; SCFW 2; SFW
4; SSFS 17; TUS; YAW
Askew, Anne 1521(?)-1546 .................. **LC 81**
See also DLB 136
Assis, Joaquim Maria Machado de
See Machado de Assis, Joaquim Maria
Astell, Mary 1666-1731 ........................ **LC 68**
See also DLB 252; FW
Astley, Thea (Beatrice May) 1925- .. **CLC 41**
See also CA 65-68; CANR 11, 43, 78; CN
7; DLB 289; EWL 3
Astley, William 1855-1911
See Warung, Price
Aston, James
See White, T(erence) H(anbury)
Asturias, Miguel Angel 1899-1974 .... **CLC 3,
8, 13; HLC 1**
See also CA 25-28; 49-52; CANR 32; CAP
2; CDWLB 3; DA3; DAM MULT, NOV;
DLB 113, 290; EWL 3; HW 1; LAW;
LMFS 2; MTCW 1, 2; RGWL 2, 3; WLIT
1
Atares, Carlos Saura
See Saura (Atares), Carlos
Athanasius c. 295-c. 373 ................. **CMLC 48**
Atheling, William
See Pound, Ezra (Weston Loomis)
Atheling, William, Jr.
See Blish, James (Benjamin)
Atherton, Gertrude (Franklin Horn)
1857-1948 .................................. **TCLC 2**
See also CA 104; 155; DLB 9, 78, 186;
HGG; RGAL 4; SUFW 1; TCWW 2
Atherton, Lucius
See Masters, Edgar Lee
Atkins, Jack
See Harris, Mark
Atkinson, Kate 1951- .......................... **CLC 99**
See also CA 166; CANR 101; DLB 267
Attaway, William (Alexander)
1911-1986 .................... **BLC 1; CLC 92**
See also BW 2, 3; CA 143; CANR 82;
DAM MULT; DLB 76
Atticus
See Fleming, Ian (Lancaster); Wilson,
(Thomas) Woodrow
Atwood, Margaret (Eleanor) 1939- ... **CLC 2,
3, 4, 8, 13, 15, 25, 44, 84, 135; PC 8;
SSC 2, 46; WLC**
See also AAYA 12, 47; AMWS 13; BEST
89:2; BPFB 1; CA 49-52; CANR 3, 24,
33, 59, 95, 133; CN 7; CP 7; CPW; CWP;
DA; DA3; DAB; DAC; DAM MST, NOV,
POET; DLB 53, 251; EWL 3; EXPN; FW;
INT CANR-24; LAIT 5; MTCW 1, 2;

NFS 4, 12, 13, 14, 19; PFS 7; RGSF 2;
SATA 50; SSFS 3, 13; TWA; WWE 1;
YAW
Aubigny, Pierre d'
See Mencken, H(enry) L(ouis)
Aubin, Penelope 1685-1731(?) ............... **LC 9**
See also DLB 39
Auchincloss, Louis (Stanton) 1917- .. **CLC 4,
6, 9, 18, 45; SSC 22**
See also AMWS 4; CA 1-4R; CANR 6, 29,
55, 87, 130; CN 7; DAM NOV; DLB 2,
244; DLBY 1980; EWL 3; INT CANR-
29; MTCW 1; RGAL 4
Auden, W(ystan) H(ugh) 1907-1973 . **CLC 1,
2, 3, 4, 6, 9, 11, 14, 43, 123; PC 1;
WLC**
See also AAYA 18; AMWS 2; BRW 7;
BRWR 1; CA 9-12R; 45-48; CANR 5, 61,
105; CDBLB 1914-1945; DA; DA3;
DAB; DAC; DAM DRAM, MST, POET;
DLB 10, 20; EWL 3; EXPP; MTCW 1, 2;
PAB; PFS 1, 3, 4, 10; TUS; WP
Audiberti, Jacques 1899-1965 ........... **CLC 38**
See also CA 25-28R; DAM DRAM; EWL 3
Audubon, John James 1785-1851 . **NCLC 47**
See also ANW; DLB 248
Auel, Jean M(arie) 1936- .......... **CLC 31, 107**
See also AAYA 7, 51; BEST 90:4; BPFB 1;
CA 103; CANR 21, 64, 115; CPW; DA3;
DAM POP; INT CANR-21; NFS 11;
RHW; SATA 91
Auerbach, Erich 1892-1957 ............ **TCLC 43**
See also CA 118; 155; EWL 3
Augier, Emile 1820-1889 ................. **NCLC 31**
See also DLB 192; GFL 1789 to the Present
August, John
See De Voto, Bernard (Augustine)
Augustine, St. 354-430 ....... **CMLC 6; WLCS**
See also DA; DA3; DAB; DAC; DAM
MST; DLB 115; EW 1; RGWL 2, 3
Aunt Belinda
See Braddon, Mary Elizabeth
Aunt Weedy
See Alcott, Louisa May
Aurelius
See Bourne, Randolph S(illiman)
Aurelius, Marcus 121-180 ............. **CMLC 45**
See Marcus Aurelius
See also RGWL 2, 3
Aurobindo, Sri
See Ghose, Aurabinda
Aurobindo Ghose
See Ghose, Aurabinda
Austen, Jane 1775-1817 ...... **NCLC 1, 13, 19,
33, 51, 81, 95, 119; WLC**
See also AAYA 19; BRW 4; BRWC 1;
BRWR 2; BYA 3; CDBLB 1789-1832;
DA; DA3; DAB; DAC; DAM MST, NOV;
DLB 116; EXPN; LAIT 2; LATS 1:1;
LMFS 1; NFS 1, 14, 18, 20; TEA; WLIT
3; WYAS 1
Auster, Paul 1947- ..................... **CLC 47, 131**
See also AMWS 12; CA 69-72; CANR 23,
52, 75, 129; CMW 4; CN 7; DA3; DLB
227; MTCW 1; SUFW 2
Austin, Frank
See Faust, Frederick (Schiller)
See also TCWW 2
Austin, Mary (Hunter) 1868-1934 . **TCLC 25**
See Stairs, Gordon
See also ANW; CA 109; 178; DLB 9, 78,
206, 221, 275; FW; TCWW 2
Averroes 1126-1198 ........................ **CMLC 7**
See also DLB 115
Avicenna 980-1037 .......................... **CMLC 16**
See also DLB 115
Avison, Margaret 1918- ........... **CLC 2, 4, 97**
See also CA 17-20R; CP 7; DAC; DAM
POET; DLB 53; MTCW 1

**Axton, David**
See Koontz, Dean R(ay)

**Ayckbourn, Alan** 1939- ...... **CLC 5, 8, 18, 33, 74; DC 13**
See also BRWS 5; CA 21-24R; CANR 31, 59, 118; CBD; CD 5; DAB; DAM DRAM; DFS 7; DLB 13, 245; EWL 3; MTCW 1, 2

**Aydy, Catherine**
See Tennant, Emma (Christina)

**Ayme, Marcel (Andre)** 1902-1967 ... **CLC 11; SSC 41**
See also CA 89-92; CANR 67; CLR 25; DLB 72; EW 12; EWL 3; GFL 1789 to the Present; RGSF 2; RGWL 2, 3; SATA 91

**Ayrton, Michael** 1921-1975 ................ **CLC 7**
See also CA 5-8R; 61-64; CANR 9, 21

**Aytmatov, Chingiz**
See Aitmatov, Chingiz (Torekulovich)
See also EWL 3

**Azorin** ................................................ **CLC 11**
See Martinez Ruiz, Jose
See also EW 9; EWL 3

**Azuela, Mariano** 1873-1952 .. **HLC 1; TCLC 3, 145**
See also CA 104; 131; CANR 81; DAM MULT; EWL 3; HW 1, 2; LAW; MTCW 1, 2

**Ba, Mariama** 1929-1981 ....................... **BLCS**
See also AFW; BW 2; CA 141; CANR 87; DNFS 2; WLIT 2

**Baastad, Babbis Friis**
See Friis-Baastad, Babbis Ellinor

**Bab**
See Gilbert, W(illiam) S(chwenck)

**Babbis, Eleanor**
See Friis-Baastad, Babbis Ellinor

**Babel, Isaac**
See Babel, Isaak (Emmanuilovich)
See also EW 11; SSFS 10

**Babel, Isaak (Emmanuilovich)**
1894-1941(?) ......... **SSC 16; TCLC 2, 13**
See Babel, Isaac
See also CA 104; 155; CANR 113; DLB 272; EWL 3; MTCW 1; RGSF 2; RGWL 2, 3; TWA

**Babits, Mihaly** 1883-1941 ............... **TCLC 14**
See also CA 114; CDWLB 4; DLB 215; EWL 3

**Babur** 1483-1530 .................................. **LC 18**

**Babylas** 1898-1962
See Ghelderode, Michel de

**Baca, Jimmy Santiago** 1952- . **HLC 1; PC 41**
See also CA 131; CANR 81, 90; CP 7; DAM MULT; DLB 122; HW 1, 2; LLW 1

**Baca, Jose Santiago**
See Baca, Jimmy Santiago

**Bacchelli, Riccardo** 1891-1985 .......... **CLC 19**
See also CA 29-32R; 117; DLB 264; EWL 3

**Bach, Richard (David)** 1936- ............ **CLC 14**
See also AITN 1; BEST 89:2; BPFB 1; BYA 5; CA 9-12R; CANR 18, 93; CPW; DAM NOV, POP; FANT; MTCW 1; SATA 13

**Bache, Benjamin Franklin**
1769-1798 ....................................... **LC 74**
See also DLB 43

**Bachelard, Gaston** 1884-1962 ...... **TCLC 128**
See also CA 97-100; 89-92; DLB 296; GFL 1789 to the Present

**Bachman, Richard**
See King, Stephen (Edwin)

**Bachmann, Ingeborg** 1926-1973 ....... **CLC 69**
See also CA 93-96; 45-48; CANR 69; DLB 85; EWL 3; RGWL 2, 3

**Bacon, Francis** 1561-1626 .............. **LC 18, 32**
See also BRW 1; CDBLB Before 1660; DLB 151, 236, 252; RGEL 2; TEA

**Bacon, Roger** 1214(?)-1294 ........... **CMLC 14**
See also DLB 115

**Bacovia, George** 1881-1957 ............ **TCLC 24**
See Vasiliu, Gheorghe
See also CDWLB 4; DLB 220; EWL 3

**Badanes, Jerome** 1937-1995 .............. **CLC 59**

**Bagehot, Walter** 1826-1877 ............ **NCLC 10**
See also DLB 55

**Bagnold, Enid** 1889-1981 .................. **CLC 25**
See also BYA 2; CA 5-8R; 103; CANR 5, 40; CBD; CWD; CWRI 5; DAM DRAM; DLB 13, 160, 191, 245; FW; MAICYA 1, 2; RGEL 2; SATA 1, 25

**Bagritsky, Eduard** .......................... **TCLC 60**
See Dzyubin, Eduard Georgievich

**Bagrjana, Elisaveta**
See Belcheva, Elisaveta Lyubomirova

**Bagryana, Elisaveta** ........................ **CLC 10**
See Belcheva, Elisaveta Lyubomirova
See also CA 178; CDWLB 4; DLB 147; EWL 3

**Bailey, Paul** 1937- .............................. **CLC 45**
See also CA 21-24R; CANR 16, 62, 124; CN 7; DLB 14, 271; GLL 2

**Baillie, Joanna** 1762-1851 ............... **NCLC 71**
See also DLB 93; RGEL 2

**Bainbridge, Beryl (Margaret)** 1934- . **CLC 4, 5, 8, 10, 14, 18, 22, 62, 130**
See also BRWS 6; CA 21-24R; CANR 24, 55, 75, 88, 128; CN 7; DAM NOV; DLB 14, 231; EWL 3; MTCW 1, 2

**Baker, Carlos (Heard)**
1909-1987 .............................. **TCLC 119**
See also CA 5-8R; 122; CANR 3, 63; DLB 103

**Baker, Elliott** 1922- ............................. **CLC 8**
See also CA 45-48; CANR 2, 63; CN 7

**Baker, Jean H.** ............................. **TCLC 3, 10**
See Russell, George William

**Baker, Nicholson** 1957- ............. **CLC 61, 165**
See also AMWS 13; CA 135; CANR 63, 120; CN 7; CPW; DA3; DAM POP; DLB 227

**Baker, Ray Stannard** 1870-1946 .... **TCLC 47**
See also CA 118

**Baker, Russell (Wayne)** 1925- ........... **CLC 31**
See also BEST 89:4; CA 57-60; CANR 11, 41, 59; MTCW 1, 2

**Bakhtin, M.**
See Bakhtin, Mikhail Mikhailovich

**Bakhtin, M. M.**
See Bakhtin, Mikhail Mikhailovich

**Bakhtin, Mikhail**
See Bakhtin, Mikhail Mikhailovich

**Bakhtin, Mikhail Mikhailovich**
1895-1975 .................................. **CLC 83**
See also CA 128; 113; DLB 242; EWL 3

**Bakshi, Ralph** 1938(?)- ...................... **CLC 26**
See also CA 112; 138; IDFW 3

**Bakunin, Mikhail (Alexandrovich)**
1814-1876 ......................... **NCLC 25, 58**
See also DLB 277

**Baldwin, James (Arthur)** 1924-1987 . **BLC 1; CLC 1, 2, 3, 4, 5, 8, 13, 15, 17, 42, 50, 67, 90, 127; DC 1; SSC 10, 33; WLC**
See also AAYA 4, 34; AFAW 1, 2; AMWR 2; AMWS 1; BPFB 1; BW 1; CA 1-4R; 124; CABS 1; CAD; CANR 3, 24; CDALB 1941-1968; CPW; DA; DA3; DAB; DAC; DAM MST, MULT, NOV, POP; DFS 11, 15; DLB 2, 7, 33, 249, 278; DLBY 1987; EWL 3; EXPS; LAIT 5; MTCW 1, 2; NCFS 4; NFS 4; RGAL 4; RGSF 2; SATA 9; SATA-Obit 54; SSFS 2, 18; TUS

**Bale, John** 1495-1563 ......................... **LC 62**
See also DLB 132; RGEL 2; TEA

**Ball, Hugo** 1886-1927 ................... **TCLC 104**

**Ballard, J(ames) G(raham)** 1930- . **CLC 3, 6, 14, 36, 137; SSC 1, 53**
See also AAYA 3, 52; BRWS 5; CA 5-8R; CANR 15, 39, 65, 107, 133; CN 7; DA3; DAM NOV, POP; DLB 14, 207, 261; EWL 3; HGG; MTCW 1, 2; NFS 8; RGEL 2; RGSF 2; SATA 93; SFW 4

**Balmont, Konstantin (Dmitriyevich)**
1867-1943 ................................. **TCLC 11**
See also CA 109; 155; DLB 295; EWL 3

**Baltausis, Vincas** 1847-1910
See Mikszath, Kalman

**Balzac, Honore de** 1799-1850 ... **NCLC 5, 35, 53; SSC 5, 59; WLC**
See also DA; DA3; DAB; DAC; DAM MST, NOV; DLB 119; EW 5; GFL 1789 to the Present; LMFS 1; RGSF 2; RGWL 2, 3; SSFS 10; SUFW; TWA

**Bambara, Toni Cade** 1939-1995 ........ **BLC 1; CLC 19, 88; SSC 35; TCLC 116; WLCS**
See also AAYA 5, 49; AFAW 2; AMWS 11; BW 2, 3; BYA 12, 14; CA 29-32R; 150; CANR 24, 49, 81; CDALBS; DA; DA3; DAC; DAM MST, MULT; DLB 38, 218; EXPS; MTCW 1, 2; RGAL 4; RGSF 2; SATA 112; SSFS 4, 7, 12

**Bamdad, A.**
See Shamlu, Ahmad

**Bamdad, Alef**
See Shamlu, Ahmad

**Banat, D. R.**
See Bradbury, Ray (Douglas)

**Bancroft, Laura**
See Baum, L(yman) Frank

**Banim, John** 1798-1842 .................. **NCLC 13**
See also DLB 116, 158, 159; RGEL 2

**Banim, Michael** 1796-1874 ............. **NCLC 13**
See also DLB 158, 159

**Banjo, The**
See Paterson, A(ndrew) B(arton)

**Banks, Iain**
See Banks, Iain M(enzies)

**Banks, Iain M(enzies)** 1954- ............ **CLC 34**
See also CA 123; 128; CANR 61, 106; DLB 194, 261; EWL 3; HGG; INT CA-128; SFW 4

**Banks, Lynne Reid** .......................... **CLC 23**
See Reid Banks, Lynne
See also AAYA 6; BYA 7; CLR 86

**Banks, Russell (Earl)** 1940- ....... **CLC 37, 72, 187; SSC 42**
See also AAYA 45; AMWS 5; CA 65-68; CAAS 15; CANR 19, 52, 73, 118; CN 7; DLB 130, 278; EWL 3; NFS 13

**Banville, John** 1945- .................. **CLC 46, 118**
See also CA 117; 128; CANR 104; CN 7; DLB 14, 271; INT CA-128

**Banville, Theodore (Faullain) de**
1832-1891 .................................. **NCLC 9**
See also DLB 217; GFL 1789 to the Present

**Baraka, Amiri** 1934- .... **BLC 1; CLC 1, 2, 3, 5, 10, 14, 33, 115; DC 6; PC 4; WLCS**
See Jones, LeRoi
See also AFAW 1, 2; AMWS 2; BW 2, 3; CA 21-24R; CABS 3; CAD; CANR 27, 38, 61, 133; CD 5; CDALB 1941-1968; CP 7; CPW; DA; DA3; DAC; DAM MST, MULT, POET, POP; DFS 3, 11, 16; DLB 5, 7, 16, 38; DLBD 8; EWL 3; MTCW 1, 2; PFS 9; RGAL 4; TUS; WP

**Baratynsky, Evgenii Abramovich**
1800-1844 ............................... **NCLC 103**
See also DLB 205

**Barbauld, Anna Laetitia**
1743-1825 ............................... **NCLC 50**
See also DLB 107, 109, 142, 158; RGEL 2

**Barbellion, W. N. P.** ........................ **TCLC 24**
　See Cummings, Bruce F(rederick)
**Barber, Benjamin R.** 1939- ............. **CLC 141**
　See also CA 29-32R; CANR 12, 32, 64, 119
**Barbera, Jack (Vincent)** 1945- ......... **CLC 44**
　See also CA 110; CANR 45
**Barbey d'Aurevilly, Jules-Amedee**
　1808-1889 .................... **NCLC 1; SSC 17**
　See also DLB 119; GFL 1789 to the Present
**Barbour, John** c. 1316-1395 .......... **CMLC 33**
　See also DLB 146
**Barbusse, Henri** 1873-1935 ............... **TCLC 5**
　See also CA 105; 154; DLB 65; EWL 3;
　RGWL 2, 3
**Barclay, Bill**
　See Moorcock, Michael (John)
**Barclay, William Ewert**
　See Moorcock, Michael (John)
**Barea, Arturo** 1897-1957 ................ **TCLC 14**
　See also CA 111; 201
**Barfoot, Joan** 1946- ........................... **CLC 18**
　See also CA 105
**Barham, Richard Harris**
　1788-1845 ................................. **NCLC 77**
　See also DLB 159
**Baring, Maurice** 1874-1945 ............... **TCLC 8**
　See also CA 105; 168; DLB 34; HGG
**Baring-Gould, Sabine** 1834-1924 ... **TCLC 88**
　See also DLB 156, 190
**Barker, Clive** 1952- ............. **CLC 52; SSC 53**
　See also AAYA 10, 54; BEST 90:3; BPFB
　1; CA 121; 129; CANR 71, 111, 133;
　CPW; DA3; DAM POP; DLB 261; HGG;
　INT CA-129; MTCW 1, 2; SUFW 2
**Barker, George Granville**
　1913-1991 ............................... **CLC 8, 48**
　See also CA 9-12R; 135; CANR 7, 38;
　DAM POET; DLB 20; EWL 3; MTCW 1
**Barker, Harley Granville**
　See Granville-Barker, Harley
　See also DLB 10
**Barker, Howard** 1946- ....................... **CLC 37**
　See also CA 102; CBD; CD 5; DLB 13,
　233
**Barker, Jane** 1652-1732 ................. **LC 42, 82**
　See also DLB 39, 131
**Barker, Pat(ricia)** 1943- ...... **CLC 32, 94, 146**
　See also BRWS 4; CA 117; 122; CANR 50,
　101; CN 7; DLB 271; INT CA-122
**Barlach, Ernst (Heinrich)**
　1870-1938 ................................. **TCLC 84**
　See also CA 178; DLB 56, 118; EWL 3
**Barlow, Joel** 1754-1812 .................. **NCLC 23**
　See also AMWS 2; DLB 37; RGAL 4
**Barnard, Mary (Ethel)** 1909- .......... **CLC 48**
　See also CA 21-22; CAP 2
**Barnes, Djuna** 1892-1982 .... **CLC 3, 4, 8, 11,
　29, 127; SSC 3**
　See Steptoe, Lydia
　See also AMWS 3; CA 9-12R; 107; CAD;
　CANR 16, 55; CWD; DLB 4, 9, 45; EWL
　3; GLL 1; MTCW 1, 2; RGAL 4; TUS
**Barnes, Jim** 1933- ............................... **NNAL**
　See also CA 108; 175; CAAE 175; CAAS
　28; DLB 175
**Barnes, Julian (Patrick)** 1946- . **CLC 42, 141**
　See also BRWS 4; CA 102; CANR 19, 54,
　115; CN 7; DAB; DLB 194; DLBY 1993;
　EWL 3; MTCW 1
**Barnes, Peter** 1931-2004 ............... **CLC 5, 56**
　See also CA 65-68; CAAS 12; CANR 33,
　34, 64, 113; CBD; CD 5; DFS 6; DLB
　13, 233; MTCW 1
**Barnes, William** 1801-1886 ........... **NCLC 75**
　See also DLB 32
**Baroja (y Nessi), Pio** 1872-1956 ........ **HLC 1;
　TCLC 8**
　See also CA 104; EW 9

**Baron, David**
　See Pinter, Harold
**Baron Corvo**
　See Rolfe, Frederick (William Serafino
　Austin Lewis Mary)
**Barondess, Sue K(aufman)**
　1926-1977 .................................... **CLC 8**
　See Kaufman, Sue
　See also CA 1-4R; 69-72; CANR 1
**Baron de Teive**
　See Pessoa, Fernando (Antonio Nogueira)
**Baroness Von S.**
　See Zangwill, Israel
**Barres, (Auguste-)Maurice**
　1862-1923 ................................. **TCLC 47**
　See also CA 164; DLB 123; GFL 1789 to
　the Present
**Barreto, Afonso Henrique de Lima**
　See Lima Barreto, Afonso Henrique de
**Barrett, Andrea** 1954- ...................... **CLC 150**
　See also CA 156; CANR 92
**Barrett, Michele** .............................. **CLC 65**
**Barrett, (Roger) Syd** 1946- .............. **CLC 35**
**Barrett, William (Christopher)**
　1913-1992 ................................... **CLC 27**
　See also CA 13-16R; 139; CANR 11, 67;
　INT CANR-11
**Barrie, J(ames) M(atthew)**
　1860-1937 .................................... **TCLC 2**
　See also BRWS 3; BYA 4, 5; CA 104; 136;
　CANR 77; CDBLB 1890-1914; CLR 16;
　CWRI 5; DA3; DAB; DAM DRAM; DFS
　7; DLB 10, 141, 156; EWL 3; FANT;
　MAICYA 1, 2; MTCW 1; SATA 100;
　SUFW; WCH; WLIT 4; YABC 1
**Barrington, Michael**
　See Moorcock, Michael (John)
**Barrol, Grady**
　See Bograd, Larry
**Barry, Mike**
　See Malzberg, Barry N(athaniel)
**Barry, Philip** 1896-1949 .................. **TCLC 11**
　See also CA 109; 199; DFS 9; DLB 7, 228;
　RGAL 4
**Bart, Andre Schwarz**
　See Schwarz-Bart, Andre
**Barth, John (Simmons)** 1930- ... **CLC 1, 2, 3,
　5, 7, 9, 10, 14, 27, 51, 89; SSC 10**
　See also AITN 1, 2; AMW; BPFB 1; CA
　1-4R; CABS 1; CANR 5, 23, 49, 64, 113;
　CN 7; DAM NOV; DLB 2, 227; EWL 3;
　FANT; MTCW 1; RGAL 4; RGSF 2;
　RHW; SSFS 6; TUS
**Barthelme, Donald** 1931-1989 ... **CLC 1, 2, 3,
　5, 6, 8, 13, 23, 46, 59, 115; SSC 2, 55**
　See also AMWS 4; BPFB 1; CA 21-24R;
　129; CANR 20, 58; DA3; DAM NOV;
　DLB 2, 234; DLBY 1980, 1989; EWL 3;
　FANT; LMFS 2; MTCW 1, 2; RGAL 4;
　RGSF 2; SATA 7; SATA-Obit 62; SSFS
　17
**Barthelme, Frederick** 1943- ...... **CLC 36, 117**
　See also AMWS 11; CA 114; 122; CANR
　77; CN 7; CSW; DLB 244; DLBY 1985;
　EWL 3; INT CA-122
**Barthes, Roland (Gerard)**
　1915-1980 ...... **CLC 24, 83; TCLC 135**
　See also CA 130; 97-100; CANR 66; DLB
　296; EW 13; EWL 3; GFL 1789 to the
　Present; MTCW 1, 2; TWA
**Bartram, William** 1739-1823 ....... **NCLC 145**
　See also ANW; DLB 37
**Barzun, Jacques (Martin)** 1907- ..... **CLC 51,
　145**
　See also CA 61-64; CANR 22, 95
**Bashevis, Isaac**
　See Singer, Isaac Bashevis

**Bashkirtseff, Marie** 1859-1884 ....... **NCLC 27**
**Basho, Matsuo**
　See Matsuo Basho
　See also PFS 18; RGWL 2, 3; WP
**Basil of Caesaria** c. 330-379 .......... **CMLC 35**
**Basket, Raney**
　See Edgerton, Clyde (Carlyle)
**Bass, Kingsley B., Jr.**
　See Bullins, Ed
**Bass, Rick** 1958- ......... **CLC 79, 143; SSC 60**
　See also ANW; CA 126; CANR 53, 93;
　CSW; DLB 212, 275
**Bassani, Giorgio** 1916-2000 ................ **CLC 9**
　See also CA 65-68; 190; CANR 33; CWW
　2; DLB 128, 177, 299; EWL 3; MTCW 1;
　RGWL 2, 3
**Bastian, Ann** ...................................... **CLC 70**
**Bastos, Augusto (Antonio) Roa**
　See Roa Bastos, Augusto (Antonio)
**Bataille, Georges** 1897-1962 ........... **CLC 29;
　TCLC 155**
　See also CA 101; 89-92; EWL 3
**Bates, H(erbert) E(rnest)**
　1905-1974 ..................... **CLC 46; SSC 10**
　See also CA 93-96; 45-48; CANR 34; DA3;
　DAB; DAM POP; DLB 162, 191; EWL
　3; EXPS; MTCW 1, 2; RGSF 2; SSFS 7
**Bauchart**
　See Camus, Albert
**Baudelaire, Charles** 1821-1867 . **NCLC 6, 29,
　55; PC 1; SSC 18; WLC**
　See also DA; DA3; DAB; DAC; DAM
　MST, POET; DLB 217; EW 7; GFL 1789
　to the Present; LMFS 2; PFS 21; RGWL
　2, 3; TWA
**Baudouin, Marcel**
　See Peguy, Charles (Pierre)
**Baudouin, Pierre**
　See Peguy, Charles (Pierre)
**Baudrillard, Jean** 1929- ..................... **CLC 60**
　See also DLB 296
**Baum, L(yman) Frank** 1856-1919 .. **TCLC 7,
　132**
　See also AAYA 46; BYA 16; CA 108; 133;
　CLR 15; CWRI 5; DLB 22; FANT; JRDA;
　MAICYA 1, 2; MTCW 1, 2; NFS 13;
　RGAL 4; SATA 18, 100; WCH
**Baum, Louis F.**
　See Baum, L(yman) Frank
**Baumbach, Jonathan** 1933- .......... **CLC 6, 23**
　See also CA 13-16R; CAAS 5; CANR 12,
　66; CN 7; DLBY 1980; INT CANR-12;
　MTCW 1
**Bausch, Richard (Carl)** 1945- ........... **CLC 51**
　See also AMWS 7; CA 101; CAAS 14;
　CANR 43, 61, 87; CSW; DLB 130
**Baxter, Charles (Morley)** 1947- . **CLC 45, 78**
　See also CA 57-60; CANR 40, 64, 104, 133;
　CPW; DAM POP; DLB 130; MTCW 2
**Baxter, George Owen**
　See Faust, Frederick (Schiller)
**Baxter, James K(eir)** 1926-1972 ....... **CLC 14**
　See also CA 77-80; EWL 3
**Baxter, John**
　See Hunt, E(verette) Howard, (Jr.)
**Bayer, Sylvia**
　See Glassco, John
**Baynton, Barbara** 1857-1929 ......... **TCLC 57**
　See also DLB 230; RGSF 2
**Beagle, Peter S(oyer)** 1939- ....... **CLC 7, 104**
　See also AAYA 47; BPFB 1; BYA 9, 10,
　16; CA 9-12R; CANR 4, 51, 73, 110;
　DA3; DLBY 1980; FANT; INT CANR-4;
　MTCW 1; SATA 60, 130; SUFW 1, 2;
　YAW
**Bean, Normal**
　See Burroughs, Edgar Rice

**Beard, Charles A(ustin)**
1874-1948 ................................. **TCLC 15**
See also CA 115; 189; DLB 17; SATA 18

**Beardsley, Aubrey** 1872-1898 .......... **NCLC 6**

**Beattie, Ann** 1947- ..... **CLC 8, 13, 18, 40, 63, 146; SSC 11**
See also AMWS 5; BEST 90:2; BPFB 1; CA 81-84; CANR 53, 73, 128; CN 7; CPW; DA3; DAM NOV, POP; DLB 218, 278; DLBY 1982; EWL 3; MTCW 1, 2; RGAL 4; RGSF 2; SSFS 9; TUS

**Beattie, James** 1735-1803 ............... **NCLC 25**
See also DLB 109

**Beauchamp, Kathleen Mansfield** 1888-1923
See Mansfield, Katherine
See also CA 104; 134; DA; DA3; DAC; DAM MST; MTCW 2; TEA

**Beaumarchais, Pierre-Augustin Caron de**
1732-1799 .......................... **DC 4; LC 61**
See also DAM DRAM; DFS 14, 16; EW 4; GFL Beginnings to 1789; RGWL 2, 3

**Beaumont, Francis** 1584(?)-1616 .. **DC 6; LC 33**
See also BRW 2; CDBLB Before 1660; DLB 58; TEA

**Beauvoir, Simone (Lucie Ernestine Marie Bertrand) de** 1908-1986 .... **CLC 1, 2, 4, 8, 14, 31, 44, 50, 71, 124; SSC 35; WLC**
See also BPFB 1; CA 9-12R; 118; CANR 28, 61; DA; DA3; DAB; DAC; DAM MST, NOV; DLB 72; DLBY 1986; EW 12; EWL 3; FW; GFL 1789 to the Present; LMFS 2; MTCW 1, 2; RGSF 2; RGWL 2, 3; TWA

**Becker, Carl (Lotus)** 1873-1945 ..... **TCLC 63**
See also CA 157; DLB 17

**Becker, Jurek** 1937-1997 ............... **CLC 7, 19**
See also CA 85-88; 157; CANR 60, 117; CWW 2; DLB 75, 299; EWL 3

**Becker, Walter** 1950- ......................... **CLC 26**

**Beckett, Samuel (Barclay)**
1906-1989 .. **CLC 1, 2, 3, 4, 6, 9, 10, 11, 14, 18, 29, 57, 59, 83; DC 22; SSC 16, 74; TCLC 145; WLC**
See also BRWC 2; BRWR 1; BRWS 1; CA 5-8R; 130; CANR 33, 61; CBD; CDBLB 1945-1960; DA; DA3; DAB; DAC; DAM DRAM, MST, NOV; DFS 2, 7, 18; DLB 13, 15, 233; DLBY 1990; EWL 3; GFL 1789 to the Present; LATS 1:2; LMFS 2; MTCW 1, 2; RGSF 2; RGWL 2, 3; SSFS 15; TEA; WLIT 4

**Beckford, William** 1760-1844 ........ **NCLC 16**
See also BRW 3; DLB 39, 213; HGG; LMFS 1; SUFW

**Beckham, Barry (Earl)** 1944- ............ **BLC 1**
See also BW 1; CA 29-32R; CANR 26, 62; CN 7; DAM MULT; DLB 33

**Beckman, Gunnel** 1910- ..................... **CLC 26**
See also CA 33-36R; CANR 15, 114; CLR 25; MAICYA 1, 2; SAAS 9; SATA 6

**Becque, Henri** 1837-1899 .... **DC 21; NCLC 3**
See also DLB 192; GFL 1789 to the Present

**Becquer, Gustavo Adolfo**
1836-1870 ............. **HLCS 1; NCLC 106**
See also DAM MULT

**Beddoes, Thomas Lovell** 1803-1849 .. **DC 15; NCLC 3**
See also DLB 96

**Bede** c. 673-735 ............................. **CMLC 20**
See also DLB 146; TEA

**Bedford, Denton R.** 1907-(?) ............. **NNAL**

**Bedford, Donald F.**
See Fearing, Kenneth (Flexner)

**Beecher, Catharine Esther**
1800-1878 ............................... **NCLC 30**
See also DLB 1, 243

**Beecher, John** 1904-1980 .................... **CLC 6**
See also AITN 1; CA 5-8R; 105; CANR 8

**Beer, Johann** 1655-1700 ........................ **LC 5**
See also DLB 168

**Beer, Patricia** 1924- ........................... **CLC 58**
See also CA 61-64; 183; CANR 13, 46; CP 7; CWP; DLB 40; FW

**Beerbohm, Max**
See Beerbohm, (Henry) Max(imilian)

**Beerbohm, (Henry) Max(imilian)**
1872-1956 ........................... **TCLC 1, 24**
See also BRWS 2; CA 104; 154; CANR 79; DLB 34, 100; FANT

**Beer-Hofmann, Richard**
1866-1945 ............................... **TCLC 60**
See also CA 160; DLB 81

**Beg, Shemus**
See Stephens, James

**Begiebing, Robert J(ohn)** 1946- ....... **CLC 70**
See also CA 122; CANR 40, 88

**Begley, Louis** 1933- ......................... **CLC 197**
See also CA 140; CANR 98; DLB 299

**Behan, Brendan (Francis)**
1923-1964 ........... **CLC 1, 8, 11, 15, 79**
See also BRWS 2; CA 73-76; CANR 33, 121; CBD; CDBLB 1945-1960; DAM DRAM; DFS 7; DLB 13, 233; EWL 3; MTCW 1, 2

**Behn, Aphra** 1640(?)-1689 .. **DC 4; LC 1, 30, 42; PC 13; WLC**
See also BRWS 3; DA; DA3; DAB; DAC; DAM DRAM, MST, NOV, POET; DFS 16; DLB 39, 80, 131; FW; TEA; WLIT 3

**Behrman, S(amuel) N(athaniel)**
1893-1973 ............................... **CLC 40**
See also CA 13-16; 45-48; CAD; CAP 1; DLB 7, 44; IDFW 3; RGAL 4

**Belasco, David** 1853-1931 .................... **TCLC 3**
See also CA 104; 168; DLB 7; RGAL 4

**Belcheva, Elisaveta Lyubomirova**
1893-1991 ............................... **CLC 10**
See Bagryana, Elisaveta

**Beldone, Phil "Cheech"**
See Ellison, Harlan (Jay)

**Beleno**
See Azuela, Mariano

**Belinski, Vissarion Grigoryevich**
1811-1848 ................................. **NCLC 5**
See also DLB 198

**Belitt, Ben** 1911- ............................. **CLC 22**
See also CA 13-16R; CAAS 4; CANR 7, 77; CP 7; DLB 5

**Bell, Gertrude (Margaret Lowthian)**
1868-1926 ............................... **TCLC 67**
See also CA 167; CANR 110; DLB 174

**Bell, J. Freeman**
See Zangwill, Israel

**Bell, James Madison** 1826-1902 ........ **BLC 1; TCLC 43**
See also BW 1; CA 122; 124; DAM MULT; DLB 50

**Bell, Madison Smartt** 1957- ...... **CLC 41, 102**
See also AMWS 10; BPFB 1; CA 111, 183; CAAE 183; CANR 28, 54, 73; CN 7; CSW; DLB 218, 278; MTCW 1

**Bell, Marvin (Hartley)** 1937- ........ **CLC 8, 31**
See also CA 21-24R; CAAS 14; CANR 59, 102; CP 7; DAM POET; DLB 5; MTCW 1

**Bell, W. L. D.**
See Mencken, H(enry) L(ouis)

**Bellamy, Atwood C.**
See Mencken, H(enry) L(ouis)

**Bellamy, Edward** 1850-1898 ..... **NCLC 4, 86, 147**
See also DLB 12; NFS 15; RGAL 4; SFW 4

**Belli, Gioconda** 1949- ........................ **HLCS 1**
See also CA 152; CWW 2; DLB 290; EWL 3; RGWL 3

**Bellin, Edward J.**
See Kuttner, Henry

**Bello, Andres** 1781-1865 ............... **NCLC 131**
See also LAW

**Belloc, (Joseph) Hilaire (Pierre Sebastien Rene Swanton)** 1870-1953 ......... **PC 24; TCLC 7, 18**
See also CA 106; 152; CWRI 5; DAM POET; DLB 19, 100, 141, 174; EWL 3; MTCW 1; SATA 112; WCH; YABC 1

**Belloc, Joseph Peter Rene Hilaire**
See Belloc, (Joseph) Hilaire (Pierre Sebastien Rene Swanton)

**Belloc, Joseph Pierre Hilaire**
See Belloc, (Joseph) Hilaire (Pierre Sebastien Rene Swanton)

**Belloc, M. A.**
See Lowndes, Marie Adelaide (Belloc)

**Belloc-Lowndes, Mrs.**
See Lowndes, Marie Adelaide (Belloc)

**Bellow, Saul** 1915- . **CLC 1, 2, 3, 6, 8, 10, 13, 15, 25, 33, 34, 63, 79, 190; SSC 14; WLC**
See also AITN 2; AMW; AMWC 2; AMWR 2; BEST 89:3; BPFB 1; CA 5-8R; CABS 1; CANR 29, 53, 95, 132; CDALB 1941-1968; CN 7; DA; DA3; DAB; DAC; DAM MST, NOV, POP; DLB 2, 28, 299; DLBD 3; DLBY 1982; EWL 3; MTCW 1, 2; NFS 4, 14; RGAL 4; RGSF 2; SSFS 12; TUS

**Belser, Reimond Karel Maria de** 1929-
See Ruyslinck, Ward
See also CA 152

**Bely, Andrey** ......................... **PC 11; TCLC 7**
See Bugayev, Boris Nikolayevich
See also DLB 295; EW 9; EWL 3; MTCW 1

**Belyi, Andrei**
See Bugayev, Boris Nikolayevich
See also RGWL 2, 3

**Bembo, Pietro** 1470-1547 ..................... **LC 79**
See also RGWL 2, 3

**Benary, Margot**
See Benary-Isbert, Margot

**Benary-Isbert, Margot** 1889-1979 .... **CLC 12**
See also CA 5-8R; 89-92; CANR 4, 72; CLR 12; MAICYA 1, 2; SATA 2; SATA-Obit 21

**Benavente (y Martinez), Jacinto**
1866-1954 .................. **HLCS 1; TCLC 3**
See also CA 106; 131; CANR 81; DAM DRAM, MULT; EWL 3; GLL 2; HW 1, 2; MTCW 1, 2

**Benchley, Peter (Bradford)** 1940- .. **CLC 4, 8**
See also AAYA 14; AITN 2; BPFB 1; CA 17-20R; CANR 12, 35, 66, 115; CPW; DAM NOV, POP; HGG; MTCW 1, 2; SATA 3, 89

**Benchley, Robert (Charles)**
1889-1945 ........................... **TCLC 1, 55**
See also CA 105; 153; DLB 11; RGAL 4

**Benda, Julien** 1867-1956 ................. **TCLC 60**
See also CA 120; 154; GFL 1789 to the Present

**Benedict, Ruth (Fulton)**
1887-1948 ............................... **TCLC 60**
See also CA 158; DLB 246

**Benedikt, Michael** 1935- .............. **CLC 4, 14**
See also CA 13-16R; CANR 7; CP 7; DLB 5

**Benet, Juan** 1927-1993 ..................... **CLC 28**
See also CA 143; EWL 3

**Benet, Stephen Vincent** 1898-1943 ... SSC 10;
TCLC 7
　　See also AMWS 11; CA 104; 152; DA3;
　　DAM POET; DLB 4, 48, 102, 249, 284;
　　DLBY 1997; EWL 3; HGG; MTCW 1;
　　RGAL 4; RGSF 2; SUFW; WP; YABC 1
**Benet, William Rose** 1886-1950 ..... TCLC 28
　　See also CA 118; 152; DAM POET; DLB
　　45; RGAL 4
**Benford, Gregory (Albert)** 1941- ..... CLC 52
　　See also BPFB 1; CA 69-72, 175; CAAE
　　175; CAAS 27; CANR 12, 24, 49, 95;
　　CSW; DLBY 1982; SCFW 2; SFW 4
**Bengtsson, Frans (Gunnar)**
　　1894-1954 ................................. TCLC 48
　　See also CA 170; EWL 3
**Benjamin, David**
　　See Slavitt, David R(ytman)
**Benjamin, Lois**
　　See Gould, Lois
**Benjamin, Walter** 1892-1940 .......... TCLC 39
　　See also CA 164; DLB 242; EW 11; EWL
　　3
**Ben Jelloun, Tahar** 1944-
　　See Jelloun, Tahar ben
　　See also CA 135; CWW 2; EWL 3; RGWL
　　3; WLIT 2
**Benn, Gottfried** 1886-1956 .. PC 35; TCLC 3
　　See also CA 106; 153; DLB 56; EWL 3;
　　RGWL 2, 3
**Bennett, Alan** 1934- ..................... CLC 45, 77
　　See also BRWS 8; CA 103; CANR 35, 55,
　　106; CBD; CD 5; DAB; DAM MST;
　　MTCW 1, 2
**Bennett, (Enoch) Arnold**
　　1867-1931 ............................ TCLC 5, 20
　　See also BRW 6; CA 106; 155; CDBLB
　　1890-1914; DLB 10, 34, 98, 135; EWL 3;
　　MTCW 2
**Bennett, Elizabeth**
　　See Mitchell, Margaret (Munnerlyn)
**Bennett, George Harold** 1930-
　　See Bennett, Hal
　　See also BW 1; CA 97-100; CANR 87
**Bennett, Gwendolyn B.** 1902-1981 ....... HR 2
　　See also BW 1; CA 125; DLB 51; WP
**Bennett, Hal** ......................................... CLC 5
　　See Bennett, George Harold
　　See also DLB 33
**Bennett, Jay** 1912- ............................. CLC 35
　　See also AAYA 10; CA 69-72; CANR 11,
　　42, 79; JRDA; SAAS 4; SATA 41, 87;
　　SATA-Brief 27; WYA; YAW
**Bennett, Louise (Simone)** 1919- ........ BLC 1;
CLC 28
　　See also BW 2, 3; CA 151; CDWLB 3; CP
　　7; DAM MULT; DLB 117; EWL 3
**Benson, A. C.** 1862-1925 ............... TCLC 123
　　See also DLB 98
**Benson, E(dward) F(rederic)**
　　1867-1940 ............................... TCLC 27
　　See also CA 114; 157; DLB 135, 153;
　　HGG; SUFW 1
**Benson, Jackson J.** 1930- ................. CLC 34
　　See also CA 25-28R; DLB 111
**Benson, Sally** 1900-1972 .................... CLC 17
　　See also CA 19-20; 37-40R; CAP 1; SATA
　　1, 35; SATA-Obit 27
**Benson, Stella** 1892-1933 ............... TCLC 17
　　See also CA 117; 154, 155; DLB 36, 162;
　　FANT; TEA
**Bentham, Jeremy** 1748-1832 .......... NCLC 38
　　See also DLB 107, 158, 252
**Bentley, E(dmund) C(lerihew)**
　　1875-1956 ............................... TCLC 12
　　See also CA 108; DLB 70; MSW
**Bentley, Eric (Russell)** 1916- ............ CLC 24
　　See also CA 5-8R; CAD; CANR 6, 67;
　　CBD; CD 5; INT CANR-6

**ben Uzair, Salem**
　　See Horne, Richard Henry Hengist
**Beranger, Pierre Jean de**
　　1780-1857 ................................ NCLC 34
**Berdyaev, Nicolas**
　　See Berdyaev, Nikolai (Aleksandrovich)
**Berdyaev, Nikolai (Aleksandrovich)**
　　1874-1948 ................................ TCLC 67
　　See also CA 120; 157
**Berdyayev, Nikolai (Aleksandrovich)**
　　See Berdyaev, Nikolai (Aleksandrovich)
**Berendt, John (Lawrence)** 1939- ...... CLC 86
　　See also CA 146; CANR 75, 93; DA3;
　　MTCW 1
**Beresford, J(ohn) D(avys)**
　　1873-1947 ................................ TCLC 81
　　See also CA 112; 155; DLB 162, 178, 197;
　　SFW 4; SUFW 1
**Bergelson, David (Rafailovich)**
　　1884-1952 ................................ TCLC 81
　　See Bergelson, Dovid
　　See also CA 220
**Bergelson, Dovid**
　　See Bergelson, David (Rafailovich)
　　See also EWL 3
**Berger, Colonel**
　　See Malraux, (Georges-)Andre
**Berger, John (Peter)** 1926- ........... CLC 2, 19
　　See also BRWS 4; CA 81-84; CANR 51,
　　78, 117; CN 7; DLB 14, 207
**Berger, Melvin H.** 1927- ................... CLC 12
　　See also CA 5-8R; CANR 4; CLR 32;
　　SAAS 2; SATA 5, 88; SATA-Essay 124
**Berger, Thomas (Louis)** 1924- .. CLC 3, 5, 8,
11, 18, 38
　　See also BPFB 1; CA 1-4R; CANR 5, 28,
　　51, 128; CN 7; DAM NOV; DLB 2;
　　DLBY 1980; EWL 3; FANT; INT CANR-
　　28; MTCW 1, 2; RHW; TCWW 2
**Bergman, (Ernst) Ingmar** 1918- ...... CLC 16,
72
　　See also CA 81-84; CANR 33, 70; CWW
　　2; DLB 257; MTCW 2
**Bergson, Henri(-Louis)** 1859-1941 . TCLC 32
　　See also CA 164; EW 8; EWL 3; GFL 1789
　　to the Present
**Bergstein, Eleanor** 1938- .................... CLC 4
　　See also CA 53-56; CANR 5
**Berkeley, George** 1685-1753 ............... LC 65
　　See also DLB 31, 101, 252
**Berkoff, Steven** 1937- ........................ CLC 56
　　See also CA 104; CANR 72; CBD; CD 5
**Berlin, Isaiah** 1909-1997 .............. TCLC 105
　　See also CA 85-88; 162
**Bermant, Chaim (Icyk)** 1929-1998 ... CLC 40
　　See also CA 57-60; CANR 6, 31, 57, 105;
　　CN 7
**Bern, Victoria**
　　See Fisher, M(ary) F(rances) K(ennedy)
**Bernanos, (Paul Louis) Georges**
　　1888-1948 .................................. TCLC 3
　　See also CA 104; 130; CANR 94; DLB 72;
　　EWL 3; GFL 1789 to the Present; RGWL
　　2, 3
**Bernard, April** 1956- ........................ CLC 59
　　See also CA 131
**Bernard of Clairvaux** 1090-1153 .. CMLC 71
　　See also DLB 208
**Berne, Victoria**
　　See Fisher, M(ary) F(rances) K(ennedy)
**Bernhard, Thomas** 1931-1989 ..... CLC 3, 32,
61; DC 14
　　See also CA 85-88; 127; CANR 32, 57; CD-
　　WLB 2; DLB 85, 124; EWL 3; MTCW 1;
　　RGWL 2, 3
**Bernhardt, Sarah (Henriette Rosine)**
　　1844-1923 ................................ TCLC 75
　　See also CA 157

**Bernstein, Charles** 1950- ................ CLC 142,
　　See also CA 129; CAAS 24; CANR 90; CP
　　7; DLB 169
**Bernstein, Ingrid**
　　See Kirsch, Sarah
**Berriault, Gina** 1926-1999 ....... CLC 54, 109;
SSC 30
　　See also CA 116; 129; 185; CANR 66; DLB
　　130; SSFS 7,11
**Berrigan, Daniel** 1921- ....................... CLC 4
　　See also CA 33-36R, 187; CAAE 187;
　　CAAS 1; CANR 11, 43, 78; CP 7; DLB 5
**Berrigan, Edmund Joseph Michael, Jr.**
　　1934-1983
　　See Berrigan, Ted
　　See also CA 61-64; 110; CANR 14, 102
**Berrigan, Ted** ................................... CLC 37
　　See Berrigan, Edmund Joseph Michael, Jr.
　　See also DLB 5, 169; WP
**Berry, Charles Edward Anderson** 1931-
　　See Berry, Chuck
　　See also CA 115
**Berry, Chuck** .................................... CLC 17
　　See Berry, Charles Edward Anderson
**Berry, Jonas**
　　See Ashbery, John (Lawrence)
　　See also GLL 1
**Berry, Wendell (Erdman)** 1934- ... CLC 4, 6,
8, 27, 46; PC 28
　　See also AITN 1; AMWS 10; ANW; CA
　　73-76; CANR 50, 73, 101, 132; CP 7;
　　CSW; DAM POET; DLB 5, 6, 234, 275;
　　MTCW 1
**Berryman, John** 1914-1972 ... CLC 1, 2, 3, 4,
6, 8, 10, 13, 25, 62
　　See also AMW; CA 13-16; 33-36R; CABS
　　2; CANR 35; CAP 1; CDALB 1941-1968;
　　DAM POET; DLB 48; EWL 3; MTCW 1,
　　2; PAB; RGAL 4; WP
**Bertolucci, Bernardo** 1940- ...... CLC 16, 157
　　See also CA 106; CANR 125
**Berton, Pierre (Francis Demarigny)**
　　1920- ..................................... CLC 104
　　See also CA 1-4R; CANR 2, 56; CPW;
　　DLB 68; SATA 99
**Bertrand, Aloysius** 1807-1841 ........ NCLC 31
　　See Bertrand, Louis oAloysiusc
**Bertrand, Louis oAloysiusc**
　　See Bertrand, Aloysius
　　See also DLB 217
**Bertran de Born** c. 1140-1215 ........ CMLC 5
**Besant, Annie (Wood)** 1847-1933 ..... TCLC 9
　　See also CA 105; 185
**Bessie, Alvah** 1904-1985 ................... CLC 23
　　See also CA 5-8R; 116; CANR 2, 80; DLB
　　26
**Bestuzhev, Aleksandr Aleksandrovich**
　　1797-1837 .............................. NCLC 131
　　See also DLB 198
**Bethlen, T. D.**
　　See Silverberg, Robert
**Beti, Mongo** ........................... BLC 1; CLC 27
　　See Biyidi, Alexandre
　　See also AFW; CANR 79; DAM MULT;
　　EWL 3; WLIT 2
**Betjeman, John** 1906-1984 ...... CLC 2, 6, 10,
34, 43
　　See also BRW 7; CA 9-12R; 112; CANR
　　33, 56; CDBLB 1945-1960; DA3; DAB;
　　DAM MST, POET; DLB 20; DLBY 1984;
　　EWL 3; MTCW 1, 2
**Bettelheim, Bruno** 1903-1990 .......... CLC 79;
TCLC 143
　　See also CA 81-84; 131; CANR 23, 61;
　　DA3; MTCW 1, 2
**Betti, Ugo** 1892-1953 ........................ TCLC 5
　　See also CA 104; 155; EWL 3; RGWL 2, 3

**Betts, Doris (Waugh)** 1932- ..... **CLC 3, 6, 28; SSC 45**
See also CA 13-16R; CANR 9, 66, 77; CN 7; CSW; DLB 218; DLBY 1982; INT CANR-9; RGAL 4

**Bevan, Alistair**
See Roberts, Keith (John Kingston)

**Bey, Pilaff**
See Douglas, (George) Norman

**Bialik, Chaim Nachman** 1873-1934 ................................. **TCLC 25**
See also CA 170; EWL 3

**Bickerstaff, Isaac**
See Swift, Jonathan

**Bidart, Frank** 1939- ........................... **CLC 33**
See also CA 140; CANR 106; CP 7

**Bienek, Horst** 1930- ................... **CLC 7, 11**
See also CA 73-76; DLB 75

**Bierce, Ambrose (Gwinett)** 1842-1914(?) ..... **SSC 9, 72; TCLC 1, 7, 44; WLC**
See also AAYA 55; AMW; BYA 11; CA 104; 139; CANR 78; CDALB 1865-1917; DA; DA3; DAC; DAM MST; DLB 11, 12, 23, 71, 74, 186; EWL 3; EXPS; HGG; LAIT 2; RGAL 4; RGSF 2; SSFS 9; SUFW 1

**Biggers, Earl Derr** 1884-1933 ........ **TCLC 65**
See also CA 108; 153; DLB 306

**Billiken, Bud**
See Motley, Willard (Francis)

**Billings, Josh**
See Shaw, Henry Wheeler

**Billington, (Lady) Rachel (Mary)** 1942- ....................................... **CLC 43**
See also AITN 2; CA 33-36R; CANR 44; CN 7

**Binchy, Maeve** 1940- ...................... **CLC 153**
See also BEST 90:1; BPFB 1; CA 127; 134; CANR 50, 96; CN 7; CPW; DA3; DAM POP; INT CA-134; MTCW 1; RHW

**Binyon, T(imothy) J(ohn)** 1936- ....... **CLC 34**
See also CA 111; CANR 28

**Bion** 335B.C.-245B.C. ..................... **CMLC 39**

**Bioy Casares, Adolfo** 1914-1999 ... **CLC 4, 8, 13, 88; HLC 1; SSC 17**
See Casares, Adolfo Bioy; Miranda, Javier; Sacastru, Martin
See also CA 29-32R; 177; CANR 19, 43, 66; CWW 2; DAM MULT; DLB 113; EWL 3; HW 1, 2; LAW; MTCW 1, 2

**Birch, Allison** ................................... **CLC 65**

**Bird, Cordwainer**
See Ellison, Harlan (Jay)

**Bird, Robert Montgomery** 1806-1854 ................................. **NCLC 1**
See also DLB 202; RGAL 4

**Birkerts, Sven** 1951- ...................... **CLC 116**
See also CA 128; 133, 176; CAAE 176; CAAS 29; INT CA-133

**Birney, (Alfred) Earle** 1904-1995 .. **CLC 1, 4, 6, 11; PC 52**
See also CA 1-4R; CANR 5, 20; CP 7; DAC; DAM MST, POET; DLB 88; MTCW 1; PFS 8; RGEL 2

**Biruni, al** 973-1048(?) .................... **CMLC 28**

**Bishop, Elizabeth** 1911-1979 ..... **CLC 1, 4, 9, 13, 15, 32; PC 3, 34; TCLC 121**
See also AMWR 1; AMWS 1; CA 5-8R; 89-92; CABS 2; CANR 26, 61, 108; CDALB 1968-1988; DA; DA3; DAC; DAM MST, POET; DLB 5, 169; EWL 3; GLL 2; MAWW; MTCW 1, 2; PAB; PFS 6, 12; RGAL 4; SATA-Obit 24; TUS; WP

**Bishop, John** 1935- ........................... **CLC 10**
See also CA 105

**Bishop, John Peale** 1892-1944 ..... **TCLC 103**
See also CA 107; 155; DLB 4, 9, 45; RGAL 4

**Bissett, Bill** 1939- .................. **CLC 18; PC 14**
See also CA 69-72; CAAS 19; CANR 15; CCA 1; CP 7; DLB 53; MTCW 1

**Bissoondath, Neil (Devindra)** 1955- ......................................... **CLC 120**
See also CA 136; CANR 123; CN 7; DAC

**Bitov, Andrei (Georgievich)** 1937- ... **CLC 57**
See also CA 142; DLB 302

**Biyidi, Alexandre** 1932-
See Beti, Mongo
See also BW 1, 3; CA 114; 124; CANR 81; DA3; MTCW 1, 2

**Bjarme, Brynjolf**
See Ibsen, Henrik (Johan)

**Bjoernson, Bjoernstjerne (Martinius)** 1832-1910 ........................... **TCLC 7, 37**
See also CA 104

**Black, Robert**
See Holdstock, Robert P.

**Blackburn, Paul** 1926-1971 .......... **CLC 9, 43**
See also BG 2; CA 81-84; 33-36R; CANR 34; DLB 16; DLBY 1981

**Black Elk** 1863-1950 ......... **NNAL; TCLC 33**
See also CA 144; DAM MULT; MTCW 1; WP

**Black Hawk** 1767-1838 ....................... **NNAL**

**Black Hobart**
See Sanders, (James) Ed(ward)

**Blacklin, Malcolm**
See Chambers, Aidan

**Blackmore, R(ichard) D(oddridge)** 1825-1900 ................................. **TCLC 27**
See also CA 120; DLB 18; RGEL 2

**Blackmur, R(ichard) P(almer)** 1904-1965 ............................. **CLC 2, 24**
See also AMWS 2; CA 11-12; 25-28R; CANR 71; CAP 1; DLB 63; EWL 3

**Black Tarantula**
See Acker, Kathy

**Blackwood, Algernon (Henry)** 1869-1951 ................................. **TCLC 5**
See also CA 105; 150; DLB 153, 156, 178; HGG; SUFW 1

**Blackwood, Caroline** 1931-1996 .... **CLC 6, 9, 100**
See also BRWS 9; CA 85-88; 151; CANR 32, 61, 65; CN 7; DLB 14, 207; HGG; MTCW 1

**Blade, Alexander**
See Hamilton, Edmond; Silverberg, Robert

**Blaga, Lucian** 1895-1961 ................... **CLC 75**
See also CA 157; DLB 220; EWL 3

**Blair, Eric (Arthur)** 1903-1950 .... **TCLC 123**
See Orwell, George
See also CA 104; 132; DA; DA3; DAB; DAC; DAM MST, NOV; MTCW 1, 2; SATA 29

**Blair, Hugh** 1718-1800 .................... **NCLC 75**

**Blais, Marie-Claire** 1939- .... **CLC 2, 4, 6, 13, 22**
See also CA 21-24R; CAAS 4; CANR 38, 75, 93; CWW 2; DAC; DAM MST; DLB 53; EWL 3; FW; MTCW 1, 2; TWA

**Blaise, Clark** 1940- ........................... **CLC 29**
See also AITN 2; CA 53-56; CAAS 3; CANR 5, 66, 106; CN 7; DLB 53; RGSF 2

**Blake, Fairley**
See De Voto, Bernard (Augustine)

**Blake, Nicholas**
See Day Lewis, C(ecil)
See also DLB 77; MSW

**Blake, Sterling**
See Benford, Gregory (Albert)

**Blake, William** 1757-1827 . **NCLC 13, 37, 57, 127; PC 12; WLC**
See also AAYA 47; BRW 3; BRWR 1; CD-BLB 1789-1832; CLR 52; DA; DA3; DAB; DAC; DAM MST, POET; DLB 93, 163; EXPP; LATS 1:1; LMFS 1; MAI-CYA 1, 2; PAB; PFS 2, 12; SATA 30; TEA; WCH; WLIT 3; WP

**Blanchot, Maurice** 1907-2003 ......... **CLC 135**
See also CA 117; 144; 213; DLB 72, 296; EWL 3

**Blasco Ibanez, Vicente** 1867-1928 . **TCLC 12**
See also BPFB 1; CA 110; 131; CANR 81; DA3; DAM NOV; EW 8; EWL 3; HW 1, 2; MTCW 1

**Blatty, William Peter** 1928- ................. **CLC 2**
See also CA 5-8R; CANR 9, 124; DAM POP; HGG

**Bleeck, Oliver**
See Thomas, Ross (Elmore)

**Blessing, Lee** 1949- ........................... **CLC 54**
See also CAD; CD 5

**Blight, Rose**
See Greer, Germaine

**Blish, James (Benjamin)** 1921-1975 . **CLC 14**
See also BPFB 1; CA 1-4R; 57-60; CANR 3; DLB 8; MTCW 1; SATA 66; SCFW 2; SFW 4

**Bliss, Frederick**
See Card, Orson Scott

**Bliss, Reginald**
See Wells, H(erbert) G(eorge)

**Blixen, Karen (Christentze Dinesen)** 1885-1962
See Dinesen, Isak
See also CA 25-28; CANR 22, 50; CAP 2; DA3; DLB 214; LMFS 1; MTCW 1, 2; SATA 44; SSFS 20

**Bloch, Robert (Albert)** 1917-1994 .... **CLC 33**
See also AAYA 29; CA 5-8R; 179; 146; CAAE 179; CAAS 20; CANR 5, 78; DA3; DLB 44; HGG; INT CANR-5; MTCW 1; SATA 12; SATA-Obit 82; SFW 4; SUFW 1, 2

**Blok, Alexander (Alexandrovich)** 1880-1921 .................... **PC 21; TCLC 5**
See also CA 104; 183; DLB 295; EW 9; EWL 3; LMFS 2; RGWL 2, 3

**Blom, Jan**
See Breytenbach, Breyten

**Bloom, Harold** 1930- ................. **CLC 24, 103**
See also CA 13-16R; CANR 39, 75, 92, 133; DLB 67; EWL 3; MTCW 1; RGAL 4

**Bloomfield, Aurelius**
See Bourne, Randolph S(illiman)

**Bloomfield, Robert** 1766-1823 ..... **NCLC 145**
See also DLB 93

**Blount, Roy (Alton), Jr.** 1941- .......... **CLC 38**
See also CA 53-56; CANR 10, 28, 61, 125; CSW; INT CANR-28; MTCW 1, 2

**Blowsnake, Sam** 1875-(?) ................... **NNAL**

**Bloy, Leon** 1846-1917 ..................... **TCLC 22**
See also CA 121; 183; DLB 123; GFL 1789 to the Present

**Blue Cloud, Peter (Aroniawenrate)** 1933- ............................................. **NNAL**
See also CA 117; CANR 40; DAM MULT

**Bluggage, Oranthy**
See Alcott, Louisa May

**Blume, Judy (Sussman)** 1938- .... **CLC 12, 30**
See also AAYA 3, 26; BYA 1, 8, 12; CA 29-32R; CANR 13, 37, 66, 124; CLR 2, 15, 69; CPW; DA3; DAM NOV, POP; DLB 52; JRDA; MAICYA 1, 2; MAICYAS 1; MTCW 1, 2; SATA 2, 31, 79, 142; WYA; YAW

**Blunden, Edmund (Charles)** 1896-1974 ............................. **CLC 2, 56**
See also BRW 6; CA 17-18; 45-48; CANR 54; CAP 2; DLB 20, 100, 155; MTCW 1; PAB

**Bly, Robert (Elwood)** 1926- ....... **CLC 1, 2, 5, 10, 15, 38, 128; PC 39**
See also AMWS 4; CA 5-8R; CANR 41, 73, 125; CP 7; DA3; DAM POET; DLB 5; EWL 3; MTCW 1, 2; PFS 6, 17; RGAL 4

**Boas, Franz** 1858-1942 .................... **TCLC 56**
See also CA 115; 181

**Bobette**
See Simenon, Georges (Jacques Christian)

**Boccaccio, Giovanni** 1313-1375 ... **CMLC 13, 57; SSC 10**
See also EW 2; RGSF 2; RGWL 2, 3; TWA

**Bochco, Steven** 1943- ........................ **CLC 35**
See also AAYA 11; CA 124; 138

**Bode, Sigmund**
See O'Doherty, Brian

**Bodel, Jean** 1167(?)-1210 ............... **CMLC 28**

**Bodenheim, Maxwell** 1892-1954 .... **TCLC 44**
See also CA 110; 187; DLB 9, 45; RGAL 4

**Bodenheimer, Maxwell**
See Bodenheim, Maxwell

**Bodker, Cecil** 1927-
See Bodker, Cecil

**Bodker, Cecil** 1927- ........................ **CLC 21**
See also CA 73-76; CANR 13, 44, 111; CLR 23; MAICYA 1, 2; SATA 14, 133

**Boell, Heinrich (Theodor)** 1917-1985 ..... **CLC 2, 3, 6, 9, 11, 15, 27, 32, 72; SSC 23; WLC**
See Boll, Heinrich
See also CA 21-24R; 116; CANR 24; DA; DA3; DAB; DAC; DAM MST, NOV; DLB 69; DLBY 1985; MTCW 1, 2; SSFS 20; TWA

**Boerne, Alfred**
See Doeblin, Alfred

**Boethius** c. 480-c. 524 .................... **CMLC 15**
See also DLB 115; RGWL 2, 3

**Boff, Leonardo (Genezio Darci)** 1938- ............................. **CLC 70; HLC 1**
See also CA 150; DAM MULT; HW 2

**Bogan, Louise** 1897-1970 ....... **CLC 4, 39, 46, 93; PC 12**
See also AMWS 3; CA 73-76; 25-28R; CANR 33, 82; DAM POET; DLB 45, 169; EWL 3; MAWW; MTCW 1, 2; PFS 21; RGAL 4

**Bogarde, Dirk**
See Van Den Bogarde, Derek Jules Gaspard Ulric Niven
See also DLB 14

**Bogosian, Eric** 1953- .................. **CLC 45, 141**
See also CA 138; CAD; CANR 102; CD 5

**Bograd, Larry** 1953- ........................ **CLC 35**
See also CA 93-96; CANR 57; SAAS 21; SATA 33, 89; WYA

**Boiardo, Matteo Maria** 1441-1494 ........ **LC 6**

**Boileau-Despreaux, Nicolas** 1636-1711 . **LC 3**
See also DLB 268; EW 3; GFL Beginnings to 1789; RGWL 2, 3

**Boissard, Maurice**
See Leautaud, Paul

**Bojer, Johan** 1872-1959 .................. **TCLC 64**
See also CA 189; EWL 3

**Bok, Edward W(illiam)** 1863-1930 ............................. **TCLC 101**
See also CA 217; DLB 91; DLBD 16

**Boker, George Henry** 1823-1890 . **NCLC 125**
See also RGAL 4

**Boland, Eavan (Aisling)** 1944- .. **CLC 40, 67, 113; PC 58**
See also BRWS 5; CA 143, 207; CAAE 207; CANR 61; CP 7; CWP; DAM POET; DLB 40; FW; MTCW 2; PFS 12

**Boll, Heinrich**
See Boell, Heinrich (Theodor)
See also BPFB 1; CDWLB 2; EW 13; EWL 3; RGSF 2; RGWL 2, 3

**Bolt, Lee**
See Faust, Frederick (Schiller)

**Bolt, Robert (Oxton)** 1924-1995 ....... **CLC 14**
See also CA 17-20R; 147; CANR 35, 67; CBD; DAM DRAM; DFS 2; DLB 13, 233; EWL 3; LAIT 1; MTCW 1

**Bombal, Maria Luisa** 1910-1980 .... **HLCS 1; SSC 37**
See also CA 127; CANR 72; EWL 3; HW 1; LAW; RGSF 2

**Bombet, Louis-Alexandre-Cesar**
See Stendhal

**Bomkauf**
See Kaufman, Bob (Garnell)

**Bonaventura** ................................. **NCLC 35**
See also DLB 90

**Bond, Edward** 1934- .......... **CLC 4, 6, 13, 23**
See also AAYA 50; BRWS 1; CA 25-28R; CANR 38, 67, 106; CBD; CD 5; DAM DRAM; DFS 3, 8; DLB 13; EWL 3; MTCW 1

**Bonham, Frank** 1914-1989 ................ **CLC 12**
See also AAYA 1; BYA 1, 3; CA 9-12R; CANR 4, 36; JRDA; MAICYA 1, 2; SAAS 3; SATA 1, 49; SATA-Obit 62; TCWW 2; YAW

**Bonnefoy, Yves** 1923- . **CLC 9, 15, 58; PC 58**
See also CA 85-88; CANR 33, 75, 97; CWW 2; DAM MST, POET; DLB 258; EWL 3; GFL 1789 to the Present; MTCW 1, 2

**Bonner, Marita** ................................. **HR 2**
See Occomy, Marita (Odette) Bonner

**Bonnin, Gertrude** 1876-1938 .............. **NNAL**
See Zitkala-Sa
See also CA 150; DAM MULT

**Bontemps, Arna(ud Wendell)** 1902-1973 ..... **BLC 1; CLC 1, 18; HR 2**
See also BW 1; CA 1-4R; 41-44R; CANR 4, 35; CLR 6; CWRI 5; DA3; DAM MULT, NOV, POET; DLB 48, 51; JRDA; MAICYA 1, 2; MTCW 1, 2; SATA 2, 44; SATA-Obit 24; WCH; WP

**Boot, William**
See Stoppard, Tom

**Booth, Martin** 1944-2004 .................. **CLC 13**
See also CA 93-96; 188; 223; CAAE 188; CAAS 2; CANR 92

**Booth, Philip** 1925- ........................ **CLC 23**
See also CA 5-8R; CANR 5, 88; CP 7; DLBY 1982

**Booth, Wayne C(layson)** 1921- ......... **CLC 24**
See also CA 1-4R; CAAS 5; CANR 3, 43, 117; DLB 67

**Borchert, Wolfgang** 1921-1947 ........ **TCLC 5**
See also CA 104; 188; DLB 69, 124; EWL 3

**Borel, Petrus** 1809-1859 ................. **NCLC 41**
See also DLB 119; GFL 1789 to the Present

**Borges, Jorge Luis** 1899-1986 ... **CLC 1, 2, 3, 4, 6, 8, 9, 10, 13, 19, 44, 48, 83; HLC 1; PC 22, 32; SSC 4, 41; TCLC 109; WLC**
See also AAYA 26; BPFB 1; CA 21-24R; CANR 19, 33, 75, 105, 133; CDWLB 3; DA; DA3; DAB; DAC; DAM MST, MULT; DLB 113, 283; DLBY 1986; DNFS 1, 2; EWL 3; HW 1, 2; LAW; LMFS 2; MSW; MTCW 1, 2; RGSF 2; RGWL 2, 3; SFW 4; SSFS 17; TWA; WLIT 1

**Borowski, Tadeusz** 1922-1951 .......... **SSC 48; TCLC 9**
See also CA 106; 154; CDWLB 4; DLB 215; EWL 3; RGSF 2; RGWL 3; SSFS 13

**Borrow, George (Henry)** 1803-1881 .................................. **NCLC 9**
See also DLB 21, 55, 166

**Bosch (Gavino), Juan** 1909-2001 ..... **HLCS 1**
See also CA 151; 204; DAM MST, MULT; DLB 145; HW 1, 2

**Bosman, Herman Charles** 1905-1951 ................................ **TCLC 49**
See Malan, Herman
See also CA 160; DLB 225; RGSF 2

**Bosschere, Jean de** 1878(?)-1953 ... **TCLC 19**
See also CA 115; 186

**Boswell, James** 1740-1795 ... **LC 4, 50; WLC**
See also BRW 3; CDBLB 1660-1789; DA; DAB; DAC; DAM MST; DLB 104, 142; TEA; WLIT 3

**Bottomley, Gordon** 1874-1948 ..... **TCLC 107**
See also CA 120; 192; DLB 10

**Bottoms, David** 1949- ........................ **CLC 53**
See also CA 105; CANR 22; CSW; DLB 120; DLBY 1983

**Boucicault, Dion** 1820-1890 ........... **NCLC 41**

**Boucolon, Maryse**
See Conde, Maryse

**Bourget, Paul (Charles Joseph)** 1852-1935 ................................. **TCLC 12**
See also CA 107; 196; DLB 123; GFL 1789 to the Present

**Bourjaily, Vance (Nye)** 1922- ........ **CLC 8, 62**
See also CA 1-4R; CAAS 1; CANR 2, 72; CN 7; DLB 2, 143

**Bourne, Randolph S(illiman)** 1886-1918 ................................. **TCLC 16**
See also AMW; CA 117; 155; DLB 63

**Bova, Ben(jamin William)** 1932- ...... **CLC 45**
See also AAYA 16; CA 5-8R; CAAS 18; CANR 11, 56, 94, 111; CLR 3, 96; DLBY 1981; INT CANR-11; MAICYA 1, 2; MTCW 1; SATA 6, 68, 133; SFW 4

**Bowen, Elizabeth (Dorothea Cole)** 1899-1973 ... **CLC 1, 3, 6, 11, 15, 22, 118; SSC 3, 28, 66; TCLC 148**
See also BRWS 2; CA 17-18; 41-44R; CANR 35, 105; CAP 2; CDBLB 1945-1960; DA3; DAM NOV; DLB 15, 162; EWL 3; EXPS; FW; HGG; MTCW 1, 2; NFS 13; RGSF 2; SSFS 5; SUFW 1; TEA; WLIT 4

**Bowering, George** 1935- ............. **CLC 15, 47**
See also CA 21-24R; CAAS 16; CANR 10; CP 7; DLB 53

**Bowering, Marilyn R(uthe)** 1949- ... **CLC 32**
See also CA 101; CANR 49; CP 7; CWP

**Bowers, Edgar** 1924-2000 .................. **CLC 9**
See also CA 5-8R; 188; CANR 24; CP 7; CSW; DLB 5

**Bowers, Mrs. J. Milton** 1842-1914
See Bierce, Ambrose (Gwinett)

**Bowie, David** .................................... **CLC 17**
See Jones, David Robert

**Bowles, Jane (Sydney)** 1917-1973 ..... **CLC 3, 68**
See Bowles, Jane Auer
See also CA 19-20; 41-44R; CAP 2

**Bowles, Jane Auer**
See Bowles, Jane (Sydney)
See also EWL 3

**Bowles, Paul (Frederick)** 1910-1999 . **CLC 1, 2, 19, 53; SSC 3**
See also AMWS 4; CA 1-4R; 186; CAAS 1; CANR 1, 19, 50, 75; CN 7; DA3; DLB 5, 6, 218; EWL 3; MTCW 1, 2; RGAL 4; SSFS 17

**Bowles, William Lisle** 1762-1850 . **NCLC 103**
See also DLB 93

**Box, Edgar**
See Vidal, (Eugene Luther) Gore
See also GLL 1

**Boyd, James** 1888-1944 ................ **TCLC 115**
See also CA 186; DLB 9; DLBD 16; RGAL 4; RHW

**Boyd, Nancy**
See Millay, Edna St. Vincent
See also GLL 1

**Boyd, Thomas (Alexander)**
1898-1935 ................................ **TCLC 111**
See also CA 111; 183; DLB 9; DLBD 16

**Boyd, William** 1952- ............. **CLC 28, 53, 70**
See also CA 114; 120; CANR 51, 71, 131;
CN 7; DLB 231

**Boyesen, Hjalmar Hjorth**
1848-1895 ................................ **NCLC 135**
See also DLB 12, 71; DLBD 13; RGAL 4

**Boyle, Kay** 1902-1992 ........ **CLC 1, 5, 19, 58,
121; SSC 5**
See also CA 13-16R; 140; CAAS 1; CANR
29, 61, 110; DLB 4, 9, 48, 86; DLBY
1993; EWL 3; MTCW 1, 2; RGAL 4;
RGSF 2; SSFS 10, 13, 14

**Boyle, Mark**
See Kienzle, William X(avier)

**Boyle, Patrick** 1905-1982 ................... **CLC 19**
See also CA 127

**Boyle, T. C.**
See Boyle, T(homas) Coraghessan
See also AMWS 8

**Boyle, T(homas) Coraghessan**
1948- ............... **CLC 36, 55, 90; SSC 16**
See Boyle, T. C.
See also AAYA 47; BEST 90:4; BPFB 1;
CA 120; CANR 44, 76, 89, 132; CN 7;
CPW; DA3; DAM POP; DLB 218, 278;
DLBY 1986; EWL 3; MTCW 2; SSFS 13,
19

**Boz**
See Dickens, Charles (John Huffam)

**Brackenridge, Hugh Henry**
1748-1816 ................................ **NCLC 7**
See also DLB 11, 37; RGAL 4

**Bradbury, Edward P.**
See Moorcock, Michael (John)
See also MTCW 2

**Bradbury, Malcolm (Stanley)**
1932-2000 ............................. **CLC 32, 61**
See also CA 1-4R; CANR 1, 33, 91, 98;
CN 7; DA3; DAM NOV; DLB 14, 207;
EWL 3; MTCW 1, 2

**Bradbury, Ray (Douglas)** 1920- .... **CLC 1, 3,
10, 15, 42, 98; SSC 29, 53; WLC**
See also AAYA 15; AITN 1, 2; AMWS 4;
BPFB 1; BYA 4, 5, 11; CA 1-4R; CANR
2, 30, 75, 125; CDALB 1968-1988; CN
7; CPW; DA; DA3; DAB; DAC; DAM
MST, NOV, POP; DLB 2, 8; EXPN;
EXPS; HGG; LAIT 3, 5; LATS 1:2;
LMFS 2; MTCW 1, 2; NFS 1; RGAL 4;
RGSF 2; SATA 11, 64, 123; SCFW 2;
SFW 4; SSFS 1, 20; SUFW 1, 2; TUS;
YAW

**Braddon, Mary Elizabeth**
1837-1915 ................................ **TCLC 111**
See also BRWS 8; CA 108; 179; CMW 4;
DLB 18, 70, 156; HGG

**Bradfield, Scott (Michael)** 1955- ....... **SSC 65**
See also CA 147; CANR 90; HGG; SUFW
2

**Bradford, Gamaliel** 1863-1932 ....... **TCLC 36**
See also CA 160; DLB 17

**Bradford, William** 1590-1657 ............. **LC 64**
See also DLB 24, 30; RGAL 4

**Bradley, David (Henry), Jr.** 1950- .... **BLC 1;
CLC 23, 118**
See also BW 1, 3; CA 104; CANR 26, 81;
CN 7; DAM MULT; DLB 33

**Bradley, John Ed(mund, Jr.)** 1958- . **CLC 55**
See also CA 139; CANR 99; CN 7; CSW

**Bradley, Marion Zimmer**
1930-1999 ................................ **CLC 30**
See Chapman, Lee; Dexter, John; Gardner,
Miriam; Ives, Morgan; Rivers, Elfrida
See also AAYA 40; BPFB 1; CA 57-60; 185;
CAAS 10; CANR 7, 31, 51, 75, 107;
CPW; DA3; DAM POP; DLB 8; FANT;
FW; MTCW 1, 2; SATA 90, 139; SATA-
Obit 116; SFW 4; SUFW 2; YAW

**Bradshaw, John** 1933- ..................... **CLC 70**
See also CA 138; CANR 61

**Bradstreet, Anne** 1612(?)-1672 ...... **LC 4, 30;
PC 10**
See also AMWS 1; CDALB 1640-1865;
DA; DA3; DAC; DAM MST, POET; DLB
24; EXPP; FW; PFS 6; RGAL 4; TUS;
WP

**Brady, Joan** 1939- ............................ **CLC 86**
See also CA 141

**Bragg, Melvyn** 1939- ....................... **CLC 10**
See also BEST 89:3; CA 57-60; CANR 10,
48, 89; CN 7; DLB 14, 271; RHW

**Brahe, Tycho** 1546-1601 ..................... **LC 45**
See also DLB 300

**Braine, John (Gerard)** 1922-1986 . **CLC 1, 3,
41**
See also CA 1-4R; 120; CANR 1, 33; CD-
BLB 1945-1960; DLB 15; DLBY 1986;
EWL 3; MTCW 1

**Braithwaite, William Stanley (Beaumont)**
1878-1962 ............ **BLC 1; HR 2; PC 52**
See also BW 1; CA 125; DAM MULT; DLB
50, 54

**Bramah, Ernest** 1868-1942 ............. **TCLC 72**
See also CA 156; CMW 4; DLB 70; FANT

**Brammer, William** 1930(?)-1978 ...... **CLC 31**
See also CA 77-80

**Brancati, Vitaliano** 1907-1954 ........ **TCLC 12**
See also CA 109; DLB 264; EWL 3

**Brancato, Robin F(idler)** 1936- ........ **CLC 35**
See also AAYA 9; BYA 6; CA 69-72; CANR
11, 45; CLR 32; JRDA; MAICYA 1;
MAICYAS 1; SAAS 9; SATA 97; WYA;
YAW

**Brand, Dionne** 1953- ....................... **CLC 192**
See also BW 2; CA 143; CWP

**Brand, Max**
See Faust, Frederick (Schiller)
See also BPFB 1; TCWW 2

**Brand, Millen** 1906-1980 .................... **CLC 7**
See also CA 21-24R; 97-100; CANR 72

**Branden, Barbara** ........................... **CLC 44**
See also CA 148

**Brandes, Georg (Morris Cohen)**
1842-1927 ................................ **TCLC 10**
See also CA 105; 189; DLB 300

**Brandys, Kazimierz** 1916-2000 ......... **CLC 62**
See also EWL 3

**Branley, Franklyn M(ansfield)**
1915-2002 ................................ **CLC 21**
See also CA 33-36R; 207; CANR 14, 39;
CLR 13; MAICYA 1, 2; SAAS 16; SATA
4, 68, 136

**Brant, Beth (E.)** 1941- ....................... **NNAL**
See also CA 144; FW

**Brathwaite, Edward Kamau**
1930- ................ **BLCS; CLC 11; PC 56**
See also BW 2, 3; CA 25-28R; CANR 11,
26, 47, 107; CDWLB 3; CP 7; DAM
POET; DLB 125; EWL 3

**Brathwaite, Kamau**
See Brathwaite, Edward Kamau

**Brautigan, Richard (Gary)**
1935-1984 .... **CLC 1, 3, 5, 9, 12, 34, 42;
TCLC 133**
See also BPFB 1; CA 53-56; 113; CANR
34; DA3; DAM NOV; DLB 2, 5, 206;
DLBY 1980, 1984; FANT; MTCW 1;
RGAL 4; SATA 56

**Brave Bird, Mary** ............................... **NNAL**
See Crow Dog, Mary (Ellen)

**Braverman, Kate** 1950- ..................... **CLC 67**
See also CA 89-92

**Brecht, (Eugen) Bertolt (Friedrich)**
1898-1956 ..... **DC 3; TCLC 1, 6, 13, 35;
WLC**
See also CA 104; 133; CANR 62; CDWLB
2; DA; DA3; DAB; DAC; DAM DRAM,
MST; DFS 4, 5, 9; DLB 56, 124; EW 11;
EWL 3; IDTP; MTCW 1, 2; RGWL 2, 3;
TWA

**Brecht, Eugen Berthold Friedrich**
See Brecht, (Eugen) Bertolt (Friedrich)

**Bremer, Fredrika** 1801-1865 .......... **NCLC 11**
See also DLB 254

**Brennan, Christopher John**
1870-1932 ................................ **TCLC 17**
See also CA 117; 188; DLB 230; EWL 3

**Brennan, Maeve** 1917-1993 ... **CLC 5; TCLC
124**
See also CA 81-84; CANR 72, 100

**Brent, Linda**
See Jacobs, Harriet A(nn)

**Brentano, Clemens (Maria)**
1778-1842 ................................ **NCLC 1**
See also DLB 90; RGWL 2, 3

**Brent of Bin Bin**
See Franklin, (Stella Maria Sarah) Miles
(Lampe)

**Brenton, Howard** 1942- ..................... **CLC 31**
See also CA 69-72; CANR 33, 67; CBD;
CD 5; DLB 13; MTCW 1

**Breslin, James** 1930-
See Breslin, Jimmy
See also CA 73-76; CANR 31, 75; DAM
NOV; MTCW 1, 2

**Breslin, Jimmy** ............................... **CLC 4, 43**
See Breslin, James
See also AITN 1; DLB 185; MTCW 2

**Bresson, Robert** 1901(?)-1999 ........... **CLC 16**
See also CA 110; 187; CANR 49

**Breton, Andre** 1896-1966 .. **CLC 2, 9, 15, 54;
PC 15**
See also CA 19-20; 25-28R; CANR 40, 60;
CAP 2; DLB 65, 258; EW 11; EWL 3;
GFL 1789 to the Present; LMFS 2;
MTCW 1, 2; RGWL 2, 3; TWA; WP

**Breytenbach, Breyten** 1939(?)- .. **CLC 23, 37,
126**
See also CA 113; 129; CANR 61, 122;
CWW 2; DAM POET; DLB 225; EWL 3

**Bridgers, Sue Ellen** 1942- ................. **CLC 26**
See also AAYA 8, 49; BYA 7, 8; CA 65-68;
CANR 11, 36; CLR 18; DLB 52; JRDA;
MAICYA 1, 2; SAAS 1; SATA 22, 90;
SATA-Essay 109; WYA; YAW

**Bridges, Robert (Seymour)**
1844-1930 ..................... **PC 28; TCLC 1**
See also BRW 6; CA 104; 152; CDBLB
1890-1914; DAM POET; DLB 19, 98

**Bridie, James** ................................... **TCLC 3**
See Mavor, Osborne Henry
See also DLB 10; EWL 3

**Brin, David** 1950- ............................. **CLC 34**
See also AAYA 21; CA 102; CANR 24, 70,
125, 127; INT CANR-24; SATA 65;
SCFW 2; SFW 4

**Brink, Andre (Philippus)** 1935- . **CLC 18, 36,
106**
See also AFW; BRWS 6; CA 104; CANR
39, 62, 109, 133; CN 7; DLB 225; EWL
3; INT CA-103; LATS 1:2; MTCW 1, 2;
WLIT 2

**Brinsmead, H. F(ay)**
See Brinsmead, H(esba) F(ay)

**Brinsmead, H. F.**
See Brinsmead, H(esba) F(ay)

**Brinsmead, H(esba) F(ay)** 1922- ...... **CLC 21**
See also CA 21-24R; CANR 10; CLR 47;
CWRI 5; MAICYA 1, 2; SAAS 5; SATA
18, 78

**Brittain, Vera (Mary)** 1893(?)-1970 . **CLC 23**
See also CA 13-16; 25-28R; CANR 58;
CAP 1; DLB 191; FW; MTCW 1, 2

**Broch, Hermann** 1886-1951 ........... **TCLC 20**
See also CA 117; 211; CDWLB 2; DLB 85,
124; EW 10; EWL 3; RGWL 2, 3

**Brock, Rose**
See Hansen, Joseph
See also GLL 1

**Brod, Max** 1884-1968 .................... **TCLC 115**
See also CA 5-8R; 25-28R; CANR 7; DLB
81; EWL 3

**Brodkey, Harold (Roy)** 1930-1996 .. **CLC 56;
TCLC 123**
See also CA 111; 151; CANR 71; CN 7;
DLB 130

**Brodsky, Iosif Alexandrovich** 1940-1996
See Brodsky, Joseph
See also AITN 1; CA 41-44R; 151; CANR
37, 106; DA3; DAM POET; MTCW 1, 2;
RGWL 2, 3

**Brodsky, Joseph** . **CLC 4, 6, 13, 36, 100; PC
9**
See Brodsky, Iosif Alexandrovich
See also AMWS 8; CWW 2; DLB 285;
EWL 3; MTCW 1

**Brodsky, Michael (Mark)** 1948- ....... **CLC 19**
See also CA 102; CANR 18, 41, 58; DLB
244

**Brodzki, Bella ed.** ............................ **CLC 65**

**Brome, Richard** 1590(?)-1652 ............. **LC 61**
See also DLB 58

**Bromell, Henry** 1947- ........................ **CLC 5**
See also CA 53-56; CANR 9, 115, 116

**Bromfield, Louis (Brucker)**
1896-1956 ................................. **TCLC 11**
See also CA 107; 155; DLB 4, 9, 86; RGAL
4; RHW

**Broner, E(sther) M(asserman)**
1930- ..................................... **CLC 19**
See also CA 17-20R; CANR 8, 25, 72; CN
7; DLB 28

**Bronk, William (M.)** 1918-1999 ........ **CLC 10**
See also CA 89-92; 177; CANR 23; CP 7;
DLB 165

**Bronstein, Lev Davidovich**
See Trotsky, Leon

**Bronte, Anne** 1820-1849 ..... **NCLC 4, 71, 102**
See also BRW 5; BRWR 1; DA3; DLB 21,
199; TEA

**Bronte, (Patrick) Branwell**
1817-1848 ............................... **NCLC 109**

**Bronte, Charlotte** 1816-1855 ...... **NCLC 3, 8,
33, 58, 105; WLC**
See also AAYA 17; BRW 5; BRWC 2;
BRWR 1; BYA 2; CDBLB 1832-1890;
DA; DA3; DAB; DAC; DAM MST, NOV;
DLB 21, 159, 199; EXPN; LAIT 2; NFS
4; TEA; WLIT 4

**Bronte, Emily (Jane)** 1818-1848 ... **NCLC 16,
35; PC 8; WLC**
See also AAYA 17; BPFB 1; BRW 5;
BRWC 1; BRWR 1; BYA 3; CDBLB
1832-1890; DA; DA3; DAB; DAC; DAM
MST, NOV, POET; DLB 21, 32, 199;
EXPN; LAIT 1; TEA; WLIT 3

**Brontes**
See Bronte, Anne; Bronte, Charlotte; Bronte,
Emily (Jane)

**Brooke, Frances** 1724-1789 ............. **LC 6, 48**
See also DLB 39, 99

**Brooke, Henry** 1703(?)-1783 .................. **LC 1**
See also DLB 39

**Brooke, Rupert (Chawner)**
1887-1915 ..... **PC 24; TCLC 2, 7; WLC**
See also BRWS 3; CA 104; 132; CANR 61;
CDBLB 1914-1945; DA; DAB; DAC;
DAM MST, POET; DLB 19, 216; EXPP;
GLL 2; MTCW 1, 2; PFS 7; TEA

**Brooke-Haven, P.**
See Wodehouse, P(elham) G(renville)

**Brooke-Rose, Christine** 1926(?)- ..... **CLC 40,
184**
See also BRWS 4; CA 13-16R; CANR 58,
118; CN 7; DLB 14, 231; EWL 3; SFW 4

**Brookner, Anita** 1928- .. **CLC 32, 34, 51, 136**
See also BRWS 4; CA 114; 120; CANR 37,
56, 87, 130; CN 7; CPW; DA3; DAB;
DAM POP; DLB 194; DLBY 1987; EWL
3; MTCW 1, 2; TEA

**Brooks, Cleanth** 1906-1994 . **CLC 24, 86, 110**
See also CA 17-20R; 145; CANR 33, 35;
CSW; DLB 63; DLBY 1994; EWL 3; INT
CANR-35; MTCW 1, 2

**Brooks, George**
See Baum, L(yman) Frank

**Brooks, Gwendolyn (Elizabeth)**
1917-2000 ... **BLC 1; CLC 1, 2, 4, 5, 15,
49, 125; PC 7; WLC**
See also AAYA 20; AFAW 1, 2; AITN 1;
AMWS 3; BW 2, 3; CA 1-4R; 190; CANR
1, 27, 52, 75, 132; CDALB 1941-1968;
CLR 27; CP 7; CWP; DA; DA3; DAC;
DAM MST, MULT, POET; DLB 5, 76,
165; EWL 3; EXPP; MAWW; MTCW 1,
2; PFS 1, 2, 4, 6; RGAL 4; SATA 6;
SATA-Obit 123; TUS; WP

**Brooks, Mel** ................................... **CLC 12**
See Kaminsky, Melvin
See also AAYA 13, 48; DLB 26

**Brooks, Peter (Preston)** 1938- ........... **CLC 34**
See also CA 45-48; CANR 1, 107

**Brooks, Van Wyck** 1886-1963 .......... **CLC 29**
See also AMW; CA 1-4R; CANR 6; DLB
45, 63, 103; TUS

**Brophy, Brigid (Antonia)**
1929-1995 ................. **CLC 6, 11, 29, 105**
See also CA 5-8R; 149; CAAS 4; CANR
25, 53; CBD; CN 7; CWD; DA3; DLB
14, 271; EWL 3; MTCW 1, 2

**Brosman, Catharine Savage** 1934- ..... **CLC 9**
See also CA 61-64; CANR 21, 46

**Brossard, Nicole** 1943- ............ **CLC 115, 169**
See also CA 122; CAAS 16; CCA 1; CWP;
CWW 2; DLB 53; EWL 3; FW; GLL 2;
RGWL 3

**Brother Antoninus**
See Everson, William (Oliver)

**The Brothers Quay**
See Quay, Stephen; Quay, Timothy

**Broughton, T(homas) Alan** 1936- ..... **CLC 19**
See also CA 45-48; CANR 2, 23, 48, 111

**Broumas, Olga** 1949- ................... **CLC 10, 73**
See also CA 85-88; CANR 20, 69, 110; CP
7; CWP; GLL 2

**Broun, Heywood** 1888-1939 ......... **TCLC 104**
See also DLB 29, 171

**Brown, Alan** 1950- ............................ **CLC 99**
See also CA 156

**Brown, Charles Brockden**
1771-1810 .................. **NCLC 22, 74, 122**
See also AMWS 1; CDALB 1640-1865;
DLB 37, 59, 73; FW; HGG; LMFS 1;
RGAL 4; TUS

**Brown, Christy** 1932-1981 ................ **CLC 63**
See also BYA 13; CA 105; 104; CANR 72;
DLB 14

**Brown, Claude** 1937-2002 ... **BLC 1; CLC 30**
See also AAYA 7; BW 1, 3; CA 73-76; 205;
CANR 81; DAM MULT

**Brown, Dee (Alexander)**
1908-2002 ............................ **CLC 18, 47**
See also AAYA 30; CA 13-16R; 212; CAAS
6; CANR 11, 45, 60; CPW; CSW; DA3;
DAM POP; DLBY 1980; LAIT 2; MTCW
1, 2; NCFS 5; SATA 5, 110; SATA-Obit
141; TCWW 2

**Brown, George**
See Wertmueller, Lina

**Brown, George Douglas**
1869-1902 ................................. **TCLC 28**
See Douglas, George
See also CA 162

**Brown, George Mackay** 1921-1996 ... **CLC 5,
48, 100**
See also BRWS 6; CA 21-24R; 151; CAAS
6; CANR 12, 37, 67; CN 7; CP 7; DLB
14, 27, 139, 271; MTCW 1; RGSF 2;
SATA 35

**Brown, (William) Larry** 1951- ......... **CLC 73**
See also CA 130; 134; CANR 117; CSW;
DLB 234; INT CA-134

**Brown, Moses**
See Barrett, William (Christopher)

**Brown, Rita Mae** 1944- ........ **CLC 18, 43, 79**
See also BPFB 1; CA 45-48; CANR 2, 11,
35, 62, 95; CN 7; CPW; CSW; DA3;
DAM NOV, POP; FW; INT CANR-11;
MTCW 1, 2; NFS 9; RGAL 4; TUS

**Brown, Roderick (Langmere) Haig-**
See Haig-Brown, Roderick (Langmere)

**Brown, Rosellen** 1939- ............... **CLC 32, 170**
See also CA 77-80; CAAS 10; CANR 14,
44, 98; CN 7

**Brown, Sterling Allen** 1901-1989 ...... **BLC 1;
CLC 1, 23, 59; HR 2; PC 55**
See also AFAW 1, 2; BW 1, 3; CA 85-88;
127; CANR 26; DA3; DAM MULT,
POET; DLB 48, 51, 63; MTCW 1, 2;
RGAL 4; WP

**Brown, Will**
See Ainsworth, William Harrison

**Brown, William Hill** 1765-1793 ........... **LC 93**
See also DLB 37

**Brown, William Wells** 1815-1884 ...... **BLC 1;
DC 1; NCLC 2, 89**
See also DAM MULT; DLB 3, 50, 183,
248; RGAL 4

**Browne, (Clyde) Jackson** 1948(?)- ... **CLC 21**
See also CA 120

**Browning, Elizabeth Barrett**
1806-1861 ... **NCLC 1, 16, 61, 66; PC 6;
WLC**
See also BRW 4; CDBLB 1832-1890; DA;
DA3; DAB; DAC; DAM MST, POET;
DLB 32, 199; EXPP; PAB; PFS 2, 16;
TEA; WLIT 4; WP

**Browning, Robert** 1812-1889 . **NCLC 19, 79;
PC 2; WLCS**
See also BRW 4; BRWC 2; BRWR 2; CD-
BLB 1832-1890; CLR 97; DA; DA3;
DAB; DAC; DAM MST, POET; DLB 32,
163; EXPP; LATS 1:1; PAB; PFS 1, 15;
RGEL 2; TEA; WLIT 4; WP; YABC 1

**Browning, Tod** 1882-1962 ................. **CLC 16**
See also CA 141; 117

**Brownmiller, Susan** 1935- .............. **CLC 159**
See also CA 103; CANR 35, 75; DAM
NOV; FW; MTCW 1, 2

**Brownson, Orestes Augustus**
1803-1876 ............................... **NCLC 50**
See also DLB 1, 59, 73, 243

**Bruccoli, Matthew J(oseph)** 1931- ... **CLC 34**
See also CA 9-12R; CANR 7, 87; DLB 103

**Bruce, Lenny** ..................................... **CLC 21**
See Schneider, Leonard Alfred

**Bruchac, Joseph III** 1942- .................. **NNAL**
See also AAYA 19; CA 33-36R; CANR 13,
47, 75, 94; CLR 46; CWRI 5; DAM

MULT; JRDA; MAICYA 2; MAICYAS 1;
MTCW 1; SATA 42, 89, 131

**Bruin, John**
See Brutus, Dennis

**Brulard, Henri**
See Stendhal

**Brulls, Christian**
See Simenon, Georges (Jacques Christian)

**Brunner, John (Kilian Houston)**
1934-1995 ............................. **CLC 8, 10**
See also CA 1-4R; 149; CAAS 8; CANR 2,
37; CPW; DAM POP; DLB 261; MTCW
1, 2; SCFW 2; SFW 4

**Bruno, Giordano** 1548-1600 ................ **LC 27**
See also RGWL 2, 3

**Brutus, Dennis** 1924- ... **BLC 1; CLC 43; PC
24**
See also AFW; BW 2, 3; CA 49-52; CAAS
14; CANR 2, 27, 42, 81; CDWLB 3; CP
7; DAM MULT, POET; DLB 117, 225;
EWL 3

**Bryan, C(ourtlandt) D(ixon) B(arnes)**
1936- ................................................... **CLC 29**
See also CA 73-76; CANR 13, 68; DLB
185; INT CANR-13

**Bryan, Michael**
See Moore, Brian
See also CCA 1

**Bryan, William Jennings**
1860-1925 ................................. **TCLC 99**
See also DLB 303

**Bryant, William Cullen** 1794-1878 . **NCLC 6,
46; PC 20**
See also AMWS 1; CDALB 1640-1865;
DA; DAB; DAC; DAM MST, POET;
DLB 3, 43, 59, 189, 250; EXPP; PAB;
RGAL 4; TUS

**Bryusov, Valery Yakovlevich**
1873-1924 ................................. **TCLC 10**
See also CA 107; 155; EWL 3; SFW 4

**Buchan, John** 1875-1940 ................ **TCLC 41**
See also CA 108; CMW 4; DAB;
DAM POP; DLB 34, 70, 156; HGG;
MSW; MTCW 1; RGEL 2; RHW; YABC
2

**Buchanan, George** 1506-1582 ................ **LC 4**
See also DLB 132

**Buchanan, Robert** 1841-1901 ....... **TCLC 107**
See also CA 179; DLB 18, 35

**Buchheim, Lothar-Guenther** 1918- .... **CLC 6**
See also CA 85-88

**Buchner, (Karl) Georg**
1813-1837 ........................ **NCLC 26, 146**
See also CDWLB 2; DLB 133; EW 6;
RGSF 2; RGWL 2, 3; TWA

**Buchwald, Art(hur)** 1925- ................. **CLC 33**
See also AITN 1; CA 5-8R; CANR 21, 67,
107; MTCW 1, 2; SATA 10

**Buck, Pearl S(ydenstricker)**
1892-1973 ................ **CLC 7, 11, 18, 127**
See also AAYA 42; AITN 1; AMWS 2;
BPFB 1; CA 1-4R; 41-44R; CANR 1, 34;
CDALBS; DA; DA3; DAB; DAC; DAM
MST, NOV; DLB 9, 102; EWL 3; LAIT
3; MTCW 1, 2; RGAL 4; RHW; SATA 1,
25; TUS

**Buckler, Ernest** 1908-1984 ................ **CLC 13**
See also CA 11-12; 114; CAP 1; CCA 1;
DAC; DAM MST; DLB 68; SATA 47

**Buckley, Christopher (Taylor)**
1952- ................................................... **CLC 165**
See also CA 139; CANR 119

**Buckley, Vincent (Thomas)**
1925-1988 ................................. **CLC 57**
See also CA 101; DLB 289

**Buckley, William F(rank), Jr.** 1925- . **CLC 7,
18, 37**
See also AITN 1; BPFB 1; CA 1-4R; CANR
1, 24, 53, 93, 133; CMW 4; CPW; DA3;

DAM POP; DLB 137; DLBY 1980; INT
CANR-24; MTCW 1, 2; TUS

**Buechner, (Carl) Frederick** 1926- . **CLC 2, 4,
6, 9**
See also AMWS 12; BPFB 1; CA 13-16R;
CANR 11, 39, 64, 114; CN 7; DAM NOV;
DLBY 1980; INT CANR-11; MTCW 1, 2

**Buell, John (Edward)** 1927- .............. **CLC 10**
See also CA 1-4R; CANR 71; DLB 53

**Buero Vallejo, Antonio** 1916-2000 ... **CLC 15,
46, 139; DC 18**
See also CA 106; 189; CANR 24, 49, 75;
CWW 2; DFS 11; EWL 3; HW 1; MTCW
1, 2

**Bufalino, Gesualdo** 1920-1996 .......... **CLC 74**
See also CWW 2; DLB 196

**Bugaev, Boris Nikolayevich**
1880-1934 ...................... **PC 11; TCLC 7**
See Bely, Andrey; Belyi, Andrei
See also CA 104; 165; MTCW 1

**Bukowski, Charles** 1920-1994 ... **CLC 2, 5, 9,
41, 82, 108; PC 18; SSC 45**
See also CA 17-20R; 144; CANR 40, 62,
105; CPW; DA3; DAM NOV, POET;
DLB 5, 130, 169; EWL 3; MTCW 1, 2

**Bulgakov, Mikhail (Afanas'evich)**
1891-1940 ............. **SSC 18; TCLC 2, 16**
See also BPFB 1; CA 105; 152; DAM
DRAM, NOV; DLB 272; EWL 3; NFS 8;
RGSF 2; RGWL 2, 3; SFW 4; TWA

**Bulgya, Alexander Alexandrovich**
1901-1956 ................................. **TCLC 53**
See Fadeev, Aleksandr Aleksandrovich;
Fadeev, Alexandr Alexandrovich; Fadeyev,
Alexander
See also CA 117; 181

**Bullins, Ed** 1935- ... **BLC 1; CLC 1, 5, 7; DC
6**
See also BW 2, 3; CA 49-52; CAAS 16;
CAD; CANR 24, 46, 73; CD 5; DAM
DRAM, MULT; DLB 7, 38, 249; EWL 3;
MTCW 1, 2; RGAL 4

**Bulosan, Carlos** 1911-1956 .................... **AAL**
See also CA 216; RGAL 4

**Bulwer-Lytton, Edward (George Earle
Lytton)** 1803-1873 .............. **NCLC 1, 45**
See also DLB 21; RGEL 2; SFW 4; SUFW
1; TEA

**Bunin, Ivan Alexeyevich** 1870-1953 ... **SSC 5;
TCLC 6**
See also CA 104; EWL 3; RGSF 2; RGWL
2, 3; TWA

**Bunting, Basil** 1900-1985 ...... **CLC 10, 39, 47**
See also BRWS 7; CA 53-56; 115; CANR
7; DAM POET; DLB 20; EWL 3; RGEL
2

**Bunuel, Luis** 1900-1983 ... **CLC 16, 80; HLC
1**
See also CA 101; 110; CANR 32, 77; DAM
MULT; HW 1

**Bunyan, John** 1628-1688 ..... **LC 4, 69; WLC**
See also BRW 2; BYA 5; CDBLB 1660-
1789; DA; DAB; DAC; DAM MST; DLB
39; RGEL 2; TEA; WCH; WLIT 3

**Buravsky, Alexandr** ......................... **CLC 59**

**Burckhardt, Jacob (Christoph)**
1818-1897 ................................. **NCLC 49**
See also EW 6

**Burford, Eleanor**
See Hibbert, Eleanor Alice Burford

**Burgess, Anthony** . **CLC 1, 2, 4, 5, 8, 10, 13,
15, 22, 40, 62, 81, 94**
See Wilson, John (Anthony) Burgess
See also AAYA 25; AITN 1; BRWS 1; CD-
BLB 1960 to Present; DAB; DLB 14, 194,
261; DLBY 1998; EWL 3; MTCW 1;
RGEL 2; RHW; SFW 4; YAW

**Burke, Edmund** 1729(?)-1797 ........ **LC 7, 36;
WLC**
See also BRW 3; DA; DA3; DAB; DAC;
DAM MST; DLB 104, 252; RGEL 2;
TEA

**Burke, Kenneth (Duva)** 1897-1993 ... **CLC 2,
24**
See also AMW; CA 5-8R; 143; CANR 39,
74; DLB 45, 63; EWL 3; MTCW 1, 2;
RGAL 4

**Burke, Leda**
See Garnett, David

**Burke, Ralph**
See Silverberg, Robert

**Burke, Thomas** 1886-1945 .............. **TCLC 63**
See also CA 113; 155; CMW 4; DLB 197

**Burney, Fanny** 1752-1840 ....... **NCLC 12, 54,
107**
See also BRWS 3; DLB 39; NFS 16; RGEL
2; TEA

**Burney, Frances**
See Burney, Fanny

**Burns, Robert** 1759-1796 ... **LC 3, 29, 40; PC
6; WLC**
See also AAYA 51; BRW 3; CDBLB 1789-
1832; DA; DA3; DAB; DAC; DAM MST,
POET; DLB 109; EXPP; PAB; RGEL 2;
TEA; WP

**Burns, Tex**
See L'Amour, Louis (Dearborn)
See also TCWW 2

**Burnshaw, Stanley** 1906- ........ **CLC 3, 13, 44**
See also CA 9-12R; CP 7; DLB 48; DLBY
1997

**Burr, Anne** 1937- .................................. **CLC 6**
See also CA 25-28R

**Burroughs, Edgar Rice** 1875-1950 . **TCLC 2,
32**
See also AAYA 11; BPFB 1; BYA 4, 9; CA
104; 132; CANR 131; DA3; DAM NOV;
DLB 8; FANT; MTCW 1, 2; RGAL 4;
SATA 41; SCFW 2; SFW 4; TUS; YAW

**Burroughs, William S(eward)**
1914-1997 .. **CLC 1, 2, 5, 15, 22, 42, 75,
109; TCLC 121; WLC**
See Lee, William; Lee, Willy
See also AITN 2; AMWS 3; BG 2; BPFB
1; CA 9-12R; 160; CANR 20, 52, 104;
CN 7; CPW; DA; DA3; DAB; DAC;
DAM MST, NOV, POP; DLB 2, 8, 16,
152, 237; DLBY 1981, 1997; EWL 3;
HGG; LMFS 2; MTCW 1, 2; RGAL 4;
SFW 4

**Burton, Sir Richard F(rancis)**
1821-1890 ................................. **NCLC 42**
See also DLB 55, 166, 184

**Burton, Robert** 1577-1640 .................... **LC 74**
See also DLB 151; RGEL 2

**Buruma, Ian** 1951- ........................... **CLC 163**
See also CA 128; CANR 65

**Busch, Frederick** 1941- ... **CLC 7, 10, 18, 47,
166**
See also CA 33-36R; CAAS 1; CANR 45,
73, 92; CN 7; DLB 6, 218

**Bush, Barney (Furman)** 1946- ........... **NNAL**
See also CA 145

**Bush, Ronald** 1946- ........................... **CLC 34**
See also CA 136

**Bustos, F(rancisco)**
See Borges, Jorge Luis

**Bustos Domecq, H(onorio)**
See Bioy Casares, Adolfo; Borges, Jorge
Luis

**Butler, Octavia E(stelle)** 1947- .. **BLCS; CLC
38, 121**
See also AAYA 18, 48; AFAW 2; AMWS
13; BPFB 1; BW 2, 3; CA 73-76; CANR
12, 24, 38, 73; CLR 65; CPW; DA3;
DAM MULT, POP; DLB 33; LATS 1:2;

MTCW 1, 2; NFS 8; SATA 84; SCFW 2;
SFW 4; SSFS 6; YAW

**Butler, Robert Olen, (Jr.)** 1945- ...... **CLC 81,
162**
   See also AMWS 12; BPFB 1; CA 112;
   CANR 66; CSW; DAM POP; DLB 173;
   INT CA-112; MTCW 1; SSFS 11

**Butler, Samuel** 1612-1680 ............. **LC 16, 43**
   See also DLB 101, 126; RGEL 2

**Butler, Samuel** 1835-1902 ......... **TCLC 1, 33;
WLC**
   See also BRWS 2; CA 143; CDBLB 1890-
   1914; DA; DA3; DAB; DAC; DAM MST,
   NOV; DLB 18, 57, 174; RGEL 2; SFW 4;
   TEA

**Butler, Walter C.**
   See Faust, Frederick (Schiller)

**Butor, Michel (Marie Francois)**
   1926- ............... **CLC 1, 3, 8, 11, 15, 161**
   See also CA 9-12R; CANR 33, 66; CWW
   2; DLB 83; EW 13; EWL 3; GFL 1789 to
   the Present; MTCW 1, 2

**Butts, Mary** 1890(?)-1937 ............... **TCLC 77**
   See also CA 148; DLB 240

**Buxton, Ralph**
   See Silverstein, Alvin; Silverstein, Virginia
   B(arbara Opshelor)

**Buzo, Alex**
   See Buzo, Alexander (John)
   See also DLB 289

**Buzo, Alexander (John)** 1944- .......... **CLC 61**
   See also CA 97-100; CANR 17, 39, 69; CD
   5

**Buzzati, Dino** 1906-1972 .................... **CLC 36**
   See also CA 160; 33-36R; DLB 177; RGWL
   2, 3; SFW 4

**Byars, Betsy (Cromer)** 1928- ........... **CLC 35**
   See also AAYA 19; BYA 3; CA 33-36R,
   183; CAAE 183; CANR 18, 36, 57, 102;
   CLR 1, 16, 72; DLB 52; INT CANR-18;
   JRDA; MAICYA 1, 2; MAICYAS 1;
   MTCW 1; SAAS 1; SATA 4, 46, 80;
   SATA-Essay 108; WYA; YAW

**Byatt, A(ntonia) S(usan Drabble)**
   1936- .............................. **CLC 19, 65, 136**
   See also BPFB 1; BRWC 2; BRWS 4; CA
   13-16R; CANR 13, 33, 50, 75, 96, 133;
   DA3; DAM NOV, POP; DLB 14, 194;
   EWL 3; MTCW 1, 2; RGSF 2; RHW;
   TEA

**Byrne, David** 1952- ............................ **CLC 26**
   See also CA 127

**Byrne, John Keyes** 1926-
   See Leonard, Hugh
   See also CA 102; CANR 78; INT CA-102

**Byron, George Gordon (Noel)**
   1788-1824 ..... **DC 24; NCLC 2, 12, 109;
PC 16; WLC**
   See also BRW 4; BRWC 2; CDBLB 1789-
   1832; DA; DA3; DAB; DAC; DAM MST,
   POET; DLB 96, 110; EXPP; LMFS 1;
   PAB; PFS 1, 14; RGEL 2; TEA; WLIT 3;
   WP

**Byron, Robert** 1905-1941 ............... **TCLC 67**
   See also CA 160; DLB 195

**C. 3. 3.**
   See Wilde, Oscar (Fingal O'Flahertie Wills)

**Caballero, Fernan** 1796-1877 ......... **NCLC 10**

**Cabell, Branch**
   See Cabell, James Branch

**Cabell, James Branch** 1879-1958 .... **TCLC 6**
   See also CA 105; 152; DLB 9, 78; FANT;
   MTCW 1; RGAL 4; SUFW 1

**Cabeza de Vaca, Alvar Nunez**
   1490-1557(?) ................................. **LC 61**

**Cable, George Washington**
   1844-1925 .................... **SSC 4; TCLC 4**
   See also CA 104; 155; DLB 12, 74; DLBD
   13; RGAL 4; TUS

**Cabral de Melo Neto, Joao**
   1920-1999 .................................. **CLC 76**
   See Melo Neto, Joao Cabral de
   See also CA 151; DAM MULT; LAW;
   LAWS 1

**Cabrera Infante, G(uillermo)** 1929- . **CLC 5,
25, 45, 120; HLC 1; SSC 39**
   See also CA 85-88; CANR 29, 65, 110; CD-
   WLB 3; CWW 2; DA3; DAM MULT;
   DLB 113; EWL 3; HW 1, 2; LAW; LAWS
   1; MTCW 1, 2; RGSF 2; WLIT 1

**Cade, Toni**
   See Bambara, Toni Cade

**Cadmus and Harmonia**
   See Buchan, John

**Caedmon** fl. 658-680 ........................ **CMLC 7**
   See also DLB 146

**Caeiro, Alberto**
   See Pessoa, Fernando (Antonio Nogueira)

**Caesar, Julius** ................................. **CMLC 47**
   See Julius Caesar
   See also AW 1; RGWL 2, 3

**Cage, John (Milton, Jr.)**
   1912-1992 ......................... **CLC 41; PC 58**
   See also CA 13-16R; 169; CANR 9, 78;
   DLB 193; INT CANR-9

**Cahan, Abraham** 1860-1951 ........... **TCLC 71**
   See also CA 108; 154; DLB 9, 25, 28;
   RGAL 4

**Cain, G.**
   See Cabrera Infante, G(uillermo)

**Cain, Guillermo**
   See Cabrera Infante, G(uillermo)

**Cain, James M(allahan)** 1892-1977 .. **CLC 3,
11, 28**
   See also AITN 1; BPFB 1; CA 17-20R; 73-
   76; CANR 8, 34, 61; CMW 4; DLB 226;
   EWL 3; MSW; MTCW 1; RGAL 4

**Caine, Hall** 1853-1931 .................... **TCLC 97**
   See also RHW

**Caine, Mark**
   See Raphael, Frederic (Michael)

**Calasso, Roberto** 1941- .................... **CLC 81**
   See also CA 143; CANR 89

**Calderon de la Barca, Pedro**
   1600-1681 .......... **DC 3; HLCS 1; LC 23**
   See also EW 2; RGWL 2, 3; TWA

**Caldwell, Erskine (Preston)**
   1903-1987 .... **CLC 1, 8, 14, 50, 60; SSC
19; TCLC 117**
   See also AITN 1; AMW; BPFB 1; CA 1-4R;
   121; CAAS 1; CANR 2, 33; DA3; DAM
   NOV; DLB 9, 86; EWL 3; MTCW 1, 2;
   RGAL 4; RGSF 2; TUS

**Caldwell, (Janet Miriam) Taylor (Holland)**
   1900-1985 ......................... **CLC 2, 28, 39**
   See also BPFB 1; CA 5-8R; 116; CANR 5;
   DA3; DAM NOV, POP; DLBD 17; RHW

**Calhoun, John Caldwell**
   1782-1850 ................................. **NCLC 15**
   See also DLB 3, 248

**Calisher, Hortense** 1911- ..... **CLC 2, 4, 8, 38,
134; SSC 15**
   See also CA 1-4R; CANR 1, 22, 117; CN
   7; DA3; DAM NOV; DLB 2, 218; INT
   CANR-22; MTCW 1, 2; RGAL 4; RGSF
   2

**Callaghan, Morley Edward**
   1903-1990 ..... **CLC 3, 14, 41, 65; TCLC
145**
   See also CA 9-12R; 132; CANR 33, 73;
   DAC; DAM MST; DLB 68; EWL 3;
   MTCW 1, 2; RGEL 2; RGSF 2; SSFS 19

**Callimachus** c. 305B.C.-c.
   240B.C. ................................. **CMLC 18**
   See also AW 1; DLB 176; RGWL 2, 3

**Calvin, Jean**
   See Calvin, John
   See also GFL Beginnings to 1789

**Calvin, John** 1509-1564 ........................ **LC 37**
   See Calvin, Jean

**Calvino, Italo** 1923-1985 .... **CLC 5, 8, 11, 22,
33, 39, 73; SSC 3, 48**
   See also CA 85-88; 116; CANR
   23, 61, 132; DAM NOV; DLB 196; EW
   13; EWL 3; MTCW 1, 2; RGSF 2; RGWL
   2, 3; SFW 4; SSFS 12

**Camara Laye**
   See Laye, Camara
   See also EWL 3

**Camden, William** 1551-1623 ................ **LC 77**
   See also DLB 172

**Cameron, Carey** 1952- ....................... **CLC 59**
   See also CA 135

**Cameron, Peter** 1959- ........................ **CLC 44**
   See also AMWS 12; CA 125; CANR 50,
   117; DLB 234; GLL 2

**Camoens, Luis Vaz de** 1524(?)-1580
   See Camoes, Luis de
   See also EW 2

**Camoes, Luis de** 1524(?)-1580 . **HLCS 1; LC
62; PC 31**
   See Camoens, Luis Vaz de
   See also DLB 287; RGWL 2, 3

**Campana, Dino** 1885-1932 ............. **TCLC 20**
   See also CA 117; DLB 114; EWL 3

**Campanella, Tommaso** 1568-1639 ....... **LC 32**
   See also RGWL 2, 3

**Campbell, John W(ood, Jr.)**
   1910-1971 ................................. **CLC 32**
   See also CA 21-22; 29-32R; CANR 34;
   CAP 2; DLB 8; MTCW 1; SCFW; SFW 4

**Campbell, Joseph** 1904-1987 ........... **CLC 69;
TCLC 140**
   See also AAYA 3; BEST 89:2; CA 1-4R;
   124; CANR 3, 28, 61, 107; DA3; MTCW
   1, 2

**Campbell, Maria** 1940- ....... **CLC 85; NNAL**
   See also CA 102; CANR 54; CCA 1; DAC

**Campbell, (John) Ramsey** 1946- ..... **CLC 42;
SSC 19**
   See also AAYA 51; CA 57-60; CANR 7,
   102; DLB 261; HGG; INT CANR-7;
   SUFW 1, 2

**Campbell, (Ignatius) Roy (Dunnachie)**
   1901-1957 .................................. **TCLC 5**
   See also AFW; CA 104; 155; DLB 20, 225;
   EWL 3; MTCW 2; RGEL 2

**Campbell, Thomas** 1777-1844 ....... **NCLC 19**
   See also DLB 93, 144; RGEL 2

**Campbell, Wilfred** ............................. **TCLC 9**
   See Campbell, William

**Campbell, William** 1858(?)-1918
   See Campbell, Wilfred
   See also CA 106; DLB 92

**Campion, Jane** 1954- ......................... **CLC 95**
   See also AAYA 33; CA 138; CANR 87

**Campion, Thomas** 1567-1620 ............. **LC 78**
   See also CDBLB Before 1660; DAM POET;
   DLB 58, 172; RGEL 2

**Camus, Albert** 1913-1960 ...... **CLC 1, 2, 4, 9,
11, 14, 32, 63, 69, 124; DC 2; SSC 9,
76; WLC**
   See also AAYA 36; AFW; BPFB 1; CA 89-
   92; CANR 131; DA; DA3; DAB; DAC;
   DAM DRAM, MST, NOV; DLB 72; EW
   13; EWL 3; EXPN; EXPS; GFL 1789 to
   the Present; LATS 1:2; LMFS 2; MTCW
   1, 2; NFS 6, 16; RGSF 2; RGWL 2, 3;
   SSFS 4; TWA

**Canby, Vincent** 1924-2000 ................. **CLC 13**
   See also CA 81-84; 191

**Cancale**
   See Desnos, Robert

Author Index

**Canetti, Elias** 1905-1994 .. **CLC 3, 14, 25, 75, 86; TCLC 157**
See also CA 21-24R; 146; CANR 23, 61, 79; CDWLB 2; CWW 2; DA3; DLB 85, 124; EW 12; EWL 3; MTCW 1, 2; RGWL 2, 3; TWA

**Canfield, Dorothea F.**
See Fisher, Dorothy (Frances) Canfield

**Canfield, Dorothea Frances**
See Fisher, Dorothy (Frances) Canfield

**Canfield, Dorothy**
See Fisher, Dorothy (Frances) Canfield

**Canin, Ethan** 1960- ............ **CLC 55; SSC 70**
See also CA 131; 135

**Cankar, Ivan** 1876-1918 ................ **TCLC 105**
See also CDWLB 4; DLB 147; EWL 3

**Cannon, Curt**
See Hunter, Evan

**Cao, Lan** 1961- .................................. **CLC 109**
See also CA 165

**Cape, Judith**
See Page, P(atricia) K(athleen)
See also CCA 1

**Capek, Karel** 1890-1938 ........ **DC 1; SSC 36; TCLC 6, 37; WLC**
See also CA 104; 140; CDWLB 4; DA; DA3; DAB; DAC; DAM DRAM, MST, NOV; DFS 7, 11; DLB 215; EW 10; EWL 3; MTCW 1; RGSF 2; RGWL 2, 3; SCFW 2; SFW 4

**Capote, Truman** 1924-1984 . **CLC 1, 3, 8, 13, 19, 34, 38, 58; SSC 2, 47; WLC**
See also AMWS 3; BPFB 1; CA 5-8R; 113; CANR 18, 62; CDALB 1941-1968; CPW; DA; DA3; DAB; DAC; DAM MST, NOV, POP; DLB 2, 185, 227; DLBY 1980, 1984; EXPS; GLL 1; LAIT 3; MTCW 1, 2; NCFS 2; RGAL 4; RGSF 2; SATA 91; SSFS 2; TUS

**Capra, Frank** 1897-1991 .................. **CLC 16**
See also AAYA 52; CA 61-64; 135

**Caputo, Philip** 1941- ........................... **CLC 32**
See also CA 73-76; CANR 40; YAW

**Caragiale, Ion Luca** 1852-1912 ...... **TCLC 76**
See also CA 157

**Card, Orson Scott** 1951- ....... **CLC 44, 47, 50**
See also AAYA 11, 42; BPFB 1; BYA 5, 8; CA 102; CANR 27, 47, 73, 102, 106, 133; CPW; DA3; DAM POP; FANT; INT CANR-27; MTCW 1, 2; NFS 5; SATA 83, 127; SCFW 2; SFW 4; SUFW 2; YAW

**Cardenal, Ernesto** 1925- ......... **CLC 31, 161; HLC 1; PC 22**
See also CA 49-52; CANR 2, 32, 66; CWW 2; DAM MULT, POET; DLB 290; EWL 3; HW 1, 2; LAWS 1; MTCW 1, 2; RGWL 2, 3

**Cardinal, Marie** 1929-2001 ............ **CLC 189**
See also CA 177; CWW 2; DLB 83; FW

**Cardozo, Benjamin N(athan)** 1870-1938 ................................. **TCLC 65**
See also CA 117; 164

**Carducci, Giosue (Alessandro Giuseppe)** 1835-1907 .................. **PC 46; TCLC 32**
See also CA 163; EW 7; RGWL 2, 3

**Carew, Thomas** 1595(?)-1640 . **LC 13; PC 29**
See also BRW 2; DLB 126; PAB; RGEL 2

**Carey, Ernestine Gilbreth** 1908- ...... **CLC 17**
See also CA 5-8R; CANR 71; SATA 2

**Carey, Peter** 1943- ........ **CLC 40, 55, 96, 183**
See also CA 123; 127; CANR 53, 76, 117; CN 7; DLB 289; EWL 3; INT CA-127; MTCW 1, 2; RGSF 2; SATA 94

**Carleton, William** 1794-1869 .......... **NCLC 3**
See also DLB 159; RGEL 2; RGSF 2

**Carlisle, Henry (Coffin)** 1926- ......... **CLC 33**
See also CA 13-16R; CANR 15, 85

**Carlsen, Chris**
See Holdstock, Robert P.

**Carlson, Ron(ald F.)** 1947- ............... **CLC 54**
See also CA 105, 189; CAAE 189; CANR 27; DLB 244

**Carlyle, Thomas** 1795-1881 ..... **NCLC 22, 70**
See also BRW 4; CDBLB 1789-1832; DA; DAB; DAC; DAM MST; DLB 55, 144, 254; RGEL 2; TEA

**Carman, (William) Bliss** 1861-1929 ... **PC 34; TCLC 7**
See also CA 104; 152; DAC; DLB 92; RGEL 2

**Carnegie, Dale** 1888-1955 ............... **TCLC 53**
See also CA 218

**Carossa, Hans** 1878-1956 ............... **TCLC 48**
See also CA 170; DLB 66; EWL 3

**Carpenter, Don(ald Richard)** 1931-1995 ................................. **CLC 41**
See also CA 45-48; 149; CANR 1, 71

**Carpenter, Edward** 1844-1929 ....... **TCLC 88**
See also CA 163; GLL 1

**Carpenter, John (Howard)** 1948- ... **CLC 161**
See also AAYA 2; CA 134; SATA 58

**Carpenter, Johnny**
See Carpenter, John (Howard)

**Carpentier (y Valmont), Alejo** 1904-1980 . **CLC 8, 11, 38, 110; HLC 1; SSC 35**
See also CA 65-68; 97-100; CANR 11, 70; CDWLB 3; DAM MULT; DLB 113; EWL 3; HW 1, 2; LAW; LMFS 2; RGSF 2; RGWL 2, 3; WLIT 1

**Carr, Caleb** 1955- ............................. **CLC 86**
See also CA 147; CANR 73; DA3

**Carr, Emily** 1871-1945 .................... **TCLC 32**
See also CA 159; DLB 68; FW; GLL 2

**Carr, John Dickson** 1906-1977 .......... **CLC 3**
See Fairbairn, Roger
See also CA 49-52; 69-72; CANR 3, 33, 60; CMW 4; DLB 306; MSW; MTCW 1, 2

**Carr, Philippa**
See Hibbert, Eleanor Alice Burford

**Carr, Virginia Spencer** 1929- ........... **CLC 34**
See also CA 61-64; DLB 111

**Carrere, Emmanuel** 1957- ................ **CLC 89**
See also CA 200

**Carrier, Roch** 1937- ..................... **CLC 13, 78**
See also CA 130; CANR 61; CCA 1; DAC; DAM MST; DLB 53; SATA 105

**Carroll, James Dennis**
See Carroll, Jim

**Carroll, James P.** 1943(?)- ................. **CLC 38**
See also CA 81-84; CANR 73; MTCW 1

**Carroll, Jim** 1951- ..................... **CLC 35, 143**
See Carroll, James Dennis
See also AAYA 17; CA 45-48; CANR 42, 115; NCFS 5

**Carroll, Lewis** ..... **NCLC 2, 53, 139; PC 18; WLC**
See Dodgson, Charles L(utwidge)
See also AAYA 39; BRW 5; BYA 5, 13; CD-BLB 1832-1890; CLR 2, 18; DLB 18, 163, 178; DLBY 1998; EXPN; EXPP; FANT; JRDA; LAIT 1; NFS 7; PFS 11; RGEL 2; SUFW 1; TEA; WCH

**Carroll, Paul Vincent** 1900-1968 ...... **CLC 10**
See also CA 9-12R; 25-28R; DLB 10; EWL 3; RGEL 2

**Carruth, Hayden** 1921- ..... **CLC 4, 7, 10, 18, 84; PC 10**
See also CA 9-12R; CANR 4, 38, 59, 110; CP 7; DLB 5, 165; INT CANR-4; MTCW 1, 2; SATA 47

**Carson, Anne** 1950- ........................ **CLC 185**
See also AMWS 12; CA 203; DLB 193; PFS 18

**Carson, Rachel**
See Carson, Rachel Louise
See also AAYA 49; DLB 275

**Carson, Rachel Louise** 1907-1964 .... **CLC 71**
See Carson, Rachel
See also AMWS 9; ANW; CA 77-80; CANR 35; DA3; DAM POP; FW; LAIT 4; MTCW 1, 2; NCFS 1; SATA 23

**Carter, Angela (Olive)** 1940-1992 ...... **CLC 5, 41, 76; SSC 13; TCLC 139**
See also BRWS 3; CA 53-56; 136; CANR 12, 36, 61, 106; DA3; DLB 14, 207, 261; EXPS; FANT; FW; MTCW 1, 2; RGSF 2; SATA 66; SATA-Obit 70; SFW 4; SSFS 4, 12; SUFW 2; WLIT 4

**Carter, Nick**
See Smith, Martin Cruz

**Carver, Raymond** 1938-1988 ..... **CLC 22, 36, 53, 55, 126; PC 54; SSC 8, 51**
See also AAYA 44; AMWS 3; BPFB 1; CA 33-36R; 126; CANR 17, 34, 61, 103; CPW; DA3; DAM NOV; DLB 130; DLBY 1984, 1988; EWL 3; MTCW 1, 2; PFS 17; RGAL 4; RGSF 2; SSFS 3, 6, 12, 13; TCWW 2; TUS

**Cary, Elizabeth, Lady Falkland** 1585-1639 .................................. **LC 30**

**Cary, (Arthur) Joyce (Lunel)** 1888-1957 ........................... **TCLC 1, 29**
See also BRW 7; CA 104; 164; CDBLB 1914-1945; DLB 15, 100; EWL 3; MTCW 2; RGEL 2; TEA

**Casal, Julian del** 1863-1893 ......... **NCLC 131**
See also DLB 283; LAW

**Casanova de Seingalt, Giovanni Jacopo** 1725-1798 ..................................... **LC 13**

**Casares, Adolfo Bioy**
See Bioy Casares, Adolfo
See also RGSF 2

**Casas, Bartolome de las** 1474-1566
See Las Casas, Bartolome de
See also WLIT 1

**Casely-Hayford, J(oseph) E(phraim)** 1866-1903 ................... **BLC 1; TCLC 24**
See also BW 2; CA 123; 152; DAM MULT

**Casey, John (Dudley)** 1939- ............. **CLC 59**
See also BEST 90:2; CA 69-72; CANR 23, 100

**Casey, Michael** 1947- ......................... **CLC 2**
See also CA 65-68; CANR 109; DLB 5

**Casey, Patrick**
See Thurman, Wallace (Henry)

**Casey, Warren (Peter)** 1935-1988 .... **CLC 12**
See also CA 101; 127; INT CA-101

**Casona, Alejandro** ........................... **CLC 49**
See Alvarez, Alejandro Rodriguez
See also EWL 3

**Cassavetes, John** 1929-1989 ............. **CLC 20**
See also CA 85-88; 127; CANR 82

**Cassian, Nina** 1924- ........................... **PC 17**
See also CWP; CWW 2

**Cassill, R(onald) V(erlin)** 1919-2002 ............................. **CLC 4, 23**
See also CA 9-12R; 208; CAAS 1; CANR 7, 45; CN 7; DLB 6, 218; DLBY 2002

**Cassidorus, Flavius Magnus** c. 490(?)-c. 583(?) ...................................... **CMLC 43**

**Cassirer, Ernst** 1874-1945 .............. **TCLC 61**
See also CA 157

**Cassity, (Allen) Turner** 1929- ....... **CLC 6, 42**
See also CA 17-20R; 223; CAAE 223; CAAS 8; CANR 11; CSW; DLB 105

**Castaneda, Carlos (Cesar Aranha)** 1931(?)-1998 ..................... **CLC 12, 119**
See also CA 25-28R; CANR 32, 66, 105; DNFS 1; HW 1; MTCW 1

**Castedo, Elena** 1937- ........................ **CLC 65**
See also CA 132

**Castedo-Ellerman, Elena**
See Castedo, Elena

**Castellanos, Rosario** 1925-1974 ....... **CLC 66; HLC 1; SSC 39, 68**
See also CA 131; 53-56; CANR 58; CD-WLB 3; DAM MULT; DLB 113, 290; EWL 3; FW; HW 1; LAW; MTCW 1; RGSF 2; RGWL 2, 3

**Castelvetro, Lodovico** 1505-1571 ........ **LC 12**

**Castiglione, Baldassare** 1478-1529 ...... **LC 12**
See Castiglione, Baldesar
See also LMFS 1; RGWL 2, 3

**Castiglione, Baldesar**
See Castiglione, Baldassare
See also EW 2

**Castillo, Ana (Hernandez Del)**
1953- ......................................... **CLC 151**
See also AAYA 42; CA 131; CANR 51, 86, 128; CWP; DLB 122, 227; DNFS 2; FW; HW 1; LLW 1; PFS 21

**Castle, Robert**
See Hamilton, Edmond

**Castro (Ruz), Fidel** 1926(?)- .............. **HLC 1**
See also CA 110; 129; CANR 81; DAM MULT; HW 2

**Castro, Guillen de** 1569-1631 ............. **LC 19**

**Castro, Rosalia de** 1837-1885 ... **NCLC 3, 78; PC 41**
See also DAM MULT

**Cather, Willa (Sibert)** 1873-1947 . **SSC 2, 50; TCLC 1, 11, 31, 99, 132, 152; WLC**
See also AAYA 24; AMW; AMWC 1; AMWR 1; BPFB 1; CA 104; 128; CDALB 1865-1917; CLR 98; DA; DA3; DAB; DAC; DAM MST, NOV; DLB 9, 54, 78, 256; DLBD 1; EWL 3; EXPN; EXPS; LAIT 3; LATS 1:1; MAWW; MTCW 1, 2; NFS 2, 19; RGAL 4; RGSF 2; RHW; SATA 30; SSFS 2, 7, 16; TCWW 2; TUS

**Catherine II**
See Catherine the Great
See also DLB 150

**Catherine the Great** 1729-1796 .......... **LC 69**
See Catherine II

**Cato, Marcus Porcius**
234B.C.-149B.C. ...................... **CMLC 21**
See Cato the Elder

**Cato, Marcus Porcius, the Elder**
See Cato, Marcus Porcius

**Cato the Elder**
See Cato, Marcus Porcius
See also DLB 211

**Catton, (Charles) Bruce** 1899-1978 . **CLC 35**
See also AITN 1; CA 5-8R; 81-84; CANR 7, 74; DLB 17; SATA 2; SATA-Obit 24

**Catullus** c. 84B.C.-54B.C. .............. **CMLC 18**
See also AW 2; CDWLB 1; DLB 211; RGWL 2, 3

**Cauldwell, Frank**
See King, Francis (Henry)

**Caunitz, William J.** 1933-1996 ......... **CLC 34**
See also BEST 89:3; CA 125; 130; 152; CANR 73; INT CA-130

**Causley, Charles (Stanley)**
1917-2003 ................................... **CLC 7**
See also CA 9-12R; 223; CANR 5, 35, 94; CLR 30; CWRI 5; DLB 27; MTCW 1; SATA 3, 66; SATA-Obit 149

**Caute, (John) David** 1936- ............... **CLC 29**
See also CA 1-4R; CAAS 4; CANR 1, 33, 64, 120; CBD; CD 5; CN 7; DAM NOV; DLB 14, 231

**Cavafy, C(onstantine) P(eter)** .......... **PC 36; TCLC 2, 7**
See Kavafis, Konstantinos Petrou
See also CA 148; DA3; DAM POET; EW 8; EWL 3; MTCW 1; PFS 19; RGWL 2, 3; WP

**Cavalcanti, Guido** c. 1250-c.
1300 ........................................ **CMLC 54**

**Cavallo, Evelyn**
See Spark, Muriel (Sarah)

**Cavanna, Betty** .............................. **CLC 12**
See Harrison, Elizabeth (Allen) Cavanna
See also JRDA; MAICYA 1; SAAS 4; SATA 1, 30

**Cavendish, Margaret Lucas**
1623-1673 ................................. **LC 30**
See also DLB 131, 252, 281; RGEL 2

**Caxton, William** 1421(?)-1491(?) ......... **LC 17**
See also DLB 170

**Cayer, D. M.**
See Duffy, Maureen

**Cayrol, Jean** 1911- ........................... **CLC 11**
See also CA 89-92; DLB 83; EWL 3

**Cela (y Trulock), Camilo Jose**
See Cela, Camilo Jose
See also CWW 2

**Cela, Camilo Jose** 1916-2002 ....... **CLC 4, 13, 59, 122; HLC 1; SSC 71**
See Cela (y Trulock), Camilo Jose
See also BEST 90:2; CA 21-24R; 206; CAAS 10; CANR 21, 32, 76; DAM MULT; DLBY 1989; EW 13; EWL 3; HW 1; MTCW 1, 2; RGSF 2; RGWL 2, 3

**Celan, Paul** .......... **CLC 10, 19, 53, 82; PC 10**
See Antschel, Paul
See also CDWLB 2; DLB 69; EWL 3; RGWL 2, 3

**Celine, Louis-Ferdinand** .. **CLC 1, 3, 4, 7, 9, 15, 47, 124**
See Destouches, Louis-Ferdinand
See also DLB 72; EW 11; EWL 3; GFL 1789 to the Present; RGWL 2, 3

**Cellini, Benvenuto** 1500-1571 ............... **LC 7**

**Cendrars, Blaise** ....................... **CLC 18, 106**
See Sauser-Hall, Frederic
See also DLB 258; EWL 3; GFL 1789 to the Present; RGWL 2, 3; WP

**Centlivre, Susanna** 1669(?)-1723 ......... **LC 65**
See also DLB 84; RGEL 2

**Cernuda (y Bidon), Luis** 1902-1963 . **CLC 54**
See also CA 131; 89-92; DAM POET; DLB 134; EWL 3; GLL 1; HW 1; RGWL 2, 3

**Cervantes, Lorna Dee** 1954- ..... **HLCS 1; PC 35**
See also CA 131; CANR 80; CWP; DLB 82; EXPP; HW 1; LLW 1

**Cervantes (Saavedra), Miguel de**
1547-1616 .... **HLCS; LC 6, 23, 93; SSC 12; WLC**
See also AAYA 56; BYA 1, 14; DA; DAB; DAC; DAM MST, NOV; EW 2; LAIT 1; LATS 1:1; LMFS 1; NFS 8; RGSF 2; RGWL 2, 3; TWA

**Cesaire, Aime (Fernand)** 1913- ......... **BLC 1; CLC 19, 32, 112; DC 22; PC 25**
See also BW 2, 3; CA 65-68; CANR 24, 43, 81; CWW 2; DA3; DAM MULT, POET; EWL 3; GFL 1789 to the Present; MTCW 1, 2; WP

**Chabon, Michael** 1963- ... **CLC 55, 149; SSC 59**
See also AAYA 45; AMWS 11; CA 139; CANR 57, 96, 127; DLB 278; SATA 145

**Chabrol, Claude** 1930- ..................... **CLC 16**
See also CA 110

**Chairil Anwar**
See Anwar, Chairil
See also EWL 3

**Challans, Mary** 1905-1983
See Renault, Mary
See also CA 81-84; 111; CANR 74; DA3; MTCW 2; SATA 23; SATA-Obit 36; TEA

**Challis, George**
See Faust, Frederick (Schiller)
See also TCWW 2

**Chambers, Aidan** 1934- ..................... **CLC 35**
See also AAYA 27; CA 25-28R; CANR 12, 31, 58, 116; JRDA; MAICYA 1, 2; SAAS 12; SATA 1, 69, 108; WYA; YAW

**Chambers, James** 1948-
See Cliff, Jimmy
See also CA 124

**Chambers, Jessie**
See Lawrence, D(avid) H(erbert Richards)
See also GLL 1

**Chambers, Robert W(illiam)**
1865-1933 ................................. **TCLC 41**
See also CA 165; DLB 202; HGG; SATA 107; SUFW 1

**Chambers, (David) Whittaker**
1901-1961 ................................. **TCLC 129**
See also CA 89-92; DLB 303

**Chamisso, Adelbert von**
1781-1838 ................................. **NCLC 82**
See also DLB 90; RGWL 2, 3; SUFW 1

**Chance, James T.**
See Carpenter, John (Howard)

**Chance, John T.**
See Carpenter, John (Howard)

**Chandler, Raymond (Thornton)**
1888-1959 ............... **SSC 23; TCLC 1, 7**
See also AAYA 25; AMWC 2; AMWS 4; BPFB 1; CA 104; 129; CANR 60, 107; CDALB 1929-1941; CMW 4; DA3; DLB 226, 253; DLBD 6; EWL 3; MSW; MTCW 1, 2; NFS 17; RGAL 4; TUS

**Chang, Diana** 1934- ............................ **AAL**
See also CWP; EXPP

**Chang, Eileen** 1921-1995 ......... **AAL; SSC 28**
See Chang Ai-Ling; Zhang Ailing
See also CA 166

**Chang, Jung** 1952- ........................... **CLC 71**
See also CA 142

**Chang Ai-Ling**
See Chang, Eileen
See also EWL 3

**Channing, William Ellery**
1780-1842 ................................. **NCLC 17**
See also DLB 1, 59, 235; RGAL 4

**Chao, Patricia** 1955- ........................ **CLC 119**
See also CA 163

**Chaplin, Charles Spencer**
1889-1977 ................................. **CLC 16**
See Chaplin, Charlie
See also CA 81-84; 73-76

**Chaplin, Charlie**
See Chaplin, Charles Spencer
See also DLB 44

**Chapman, George** 1559(?)-1634 . **DC 19; LC 22**
See also BRW 1; DAM DRAM; DLB 62, 121; LMFS 1; RGEL 2

**Chapman, Graham** 1941-1989 ......... **CLC 21**
See Monty Python
See also CA 116; 129; CANR 35, 95

**Chapman, John Jay** 1862-1933 ....... **TCLC 7**
See also CA 104; 191

**Chapman, Lee**
See Bradley, Marion Zimmer
See also GLL 1

**Chapman, Walker**
See Silverberg, Robert

**Chappell, Fred (Davis)** 1936- .... **CLC 40, 78, 162**
See also CA 5-8R, 198; CAAE 198; CAAS 4; CANR 8, 33, 67, 110; CN 7; CP 7; CSW; DLB 6, 105; HGG

**Char, Rene(-Emile)** 1907-1988 .... **CLC 9, 11, 14, 55; PC 56**
See also CA 13-16R; 124; CANR 32; DAM POET; DLB 258; EWL 3; GFL 1789 to the Present; MTCW 1, 2; RGWL 2, 3

**Charby, Jay**
See Ellison, Harlan (Jay)

**Chardin, Pierre Teilhard de**
See Teilhard de Chardin, (Marie Joseph) Pierre

**Chariton** fl. 1st cent. (?)- ............... **CMLC 49**

**Charlemagne** 742-814 .................... **CMLC 37**

**Charles I** 1600-1649 ............................. **LC 13**

**Charriere, Isabelle de** 1740-1805 .. **NCLC 66**

**Chartier, Alain** c. 1392-1430 ................ **LC 94**
See also DLB 208

**Chartier, Emile-Auguste**
See Alain

**Charyn, Jerome** 1937- ............... **CLC 5, 8, 18**
See also CA 5-8R; CAAS 1; CANR 7, 61, 101; CMW 4; CN 7; DLBY 1983; MTCW 1

**Chase, Adam**
See Marlowe, Stephen

**Chase, Mary (Coyle)** 1907-1981 ........... **DC 1**
See also CA 77-80; 105; CAD; CWD; DFS 11; DLB 228; SATA 17; SATA-Obit 29

**Chase, Mary Ellen** 1887-1973 ........... **CLC 2; TCLC 124**
See also CA 13-16; 41-44R; CAP 1; SATA 10

**Chase, Nicholas**
See Hyde, Anthony
See also CCA 1

**Chateaubriand, Francois Rene de** 1768-1848 ......................... **NCLC 3, 134**
See also DLB 119; EW 5; GFL 1789 to the Present; RGWL 2, 3; TWA

**Chatterje, Sarat Chandra** 1876-1936(?)
See Chatterji, Saratchandra
See also CA 109

**Chatterji, Bankim Chandra** 1838-1894 ................................. **NCLC 19**

**Chatterji, Saratchandra** ................ **TCLC 13**
See Chatterje, Sarat Chandra
See also CA 186; EWL 3

**Chatterton, Thomas** 1752-1770 ....... **LC 3, 54**
See also DAM POET; DLB 109; RGEL 2

**Chatwin, (Charles) Bruce** 1940-1989 ...................... **CLC 28, 57, 59**
See also AAYA 4; BEST 90:1; BRWS 4; CA 85-88; 127; CPW; DAM POP; DLB 194, 204; EWL 3

**Chaucer, Daniel**
See Ford, Ford Madox
See also RHW

**Chaucer, Geoffrey** 1340(?)-1400 .. **LC 17, 56; PC 19, 58; WLCS**
See also BRW 1; BRWC 1; BRWR 2; CD-BLB Before 1660; DA; DA3; DAB; DAC; DAM MST, POET; DLB 146; LAIT 1; PAB; PFS 14; RGEL 2; TEA; WLIT 3; WP

**Chavez, Denise (Elia)** 1948- .............. **HLC 1**
See also CA 131; CANR 56, 81; DAM MULT; DLB 122; FW; HW 1, 2; LLW 1; MTCW 2

**Chaviaras, Strates** 1935-
See Haviaras, Stratis
See also CA 105

**Chayefsky, Paddy** ......................... **CLC 23**
See Chayefsky, Sidney
See also CAD; DLB 7, 44; DLBY 1981; RGAL 4

**Chayefsky, Sidney** 1923-1981
See Chayefsky, Paddy
See also CA 9-12R; 104; CANR 18; DAM DRAM

**Chedid, Andree** 1920- ......................... **CLC 47**
See also CA 145; CANR 95; EWL 3

**Cheever, John** 1912-1982 ..... **CLC 3, 7, 8, 11, 15, 25, 64; SSC 1, 38, 57; WLC**
See also AMWS 1; BPFB 1; CA 5-8R; 106; CABS 1; CANR 5, 27, 76; CDALB 1941-1968; CPW; DA; DA3; DAB; DAC; DAM MST, NOV, POP; DLB 2, 102, 227;

DLBY 1980, 1982; EWL 3; EXPS; INT CANR-5; MTCW 1, 2; RGAL 4; RGSF 2; SSFS 2, 14; TUS

**Cheever, Susan** 1943- .................. **CLC 18, 48**
See also CA 103; CANR 27, 51, 92; DLBY 1982; INT CANR-27

**Chekhonte, Antosha**
See Chekhov, Anton (Pavlovich)

**Chekhov, Anton (Pavlovich)** 1860-1904 ...... **DC 9; SSC 2, 28, 41, 51; TCLC 3, 10, 31, 55, 96; WLC**
See also BYA 14; CA 104; 124; DA; DA3; DAB; DAC; DAM DRAM, MST; DFS 1, 5, 10, 12; DLB 277; EW 7; EWL 3; EXPS; LAIT 3; LATS 1:1; RGSF 2; RGWL 2, 3; SATA 90; SSFS 5, 13, 14; TWA

**Cheney, Lynne V.** 1941- ..................... **CLC 70**
See also CA 89-92; CANR 58, 117; SATA 152

**Chernyshevsky, Nikolai Gavrilovich**
See Chernyshevsky, Nikolay Gavrilovich
See also DLB 238

**Chernyshevsky, Nikolay Gavrilovich** 1828-1889 ................................ **NCLC 1**
See Chernyshevsky, Nikolai Gavrilovich

**Cherry, Carolyn Janice** 1942-
See Cherryh, C. J.
See also CA 65-68; CANR 10

**Cherryh, C. J.** ................................... **CLC 35**
See Cherry, Carolyn Janice
See also AAYA 24; BPFB 1; DLBY 1980; FANT; SATA 93; SCFW 2; SFW 4; YAW

**Chesnutt, Charles W(addell)** 1858-1932 .... **BLC 1; SSC 7, 54; TCLC 5, 39**
See also AFAW 1, 2; BW 1, 3; CA 106; 125; CANR 76; DAM MULT; DLB 12, 50, 78; EWL 3; MTCW 1, 2; RGAL 4; RGSF 2; SSFS 11

**Chester, Alfred** 1929(?)-1971 ............. **CLC 49**
See also CA 196; 33-36R; DLB 130

**Chesterton, G(ilbert) K(eith)** 1874-1936 . **PC 28; SSC 1, 46; TCLC 1, 6, 64**
See also AAYA 57; BRW 6; CA 104; 132; CANR 73, 131; CDBLB 1914-1945; CMW 4; DAM NOV, POET; DLB 10, 19, 34, 70, 98, 149, 178; EWL 3; FANT; MSW; MTCW 1, 2; RGEL 2; RGSF 2; SATA 27; SUFW 1

**Chiang, Pin-chin** 1904-1986
See Ding Ling
See also CA 118

**Chief Joseph** 1840-1904 ..................... **NNAL**
See also CA 152; DA3; DAM MULT

**Chief Seattle** 1786(?)-1866 .................. **NNAL**
See also DA3; DAM MULT

**Ch'ien, Chung-shu** 1910-1998 .......... **CLC 22**
See Qian Zhongshu
See also CA 130; CANR 73; MTCW 1, 2

**Chikamatsu Monzaemon** 1653-1724 ... **LC 66**
See also RGWL 2, 3

**Child, L. Maria**
See Child, Lydia Maria

**Child, Lydia Maria** 1802-1880 .. **NCLC 6, 73**
See also DLB 1, 74, 243; RGAL 4; SATA 67

**Child, Mrs.**
See Child, Lydia Maria

**Child, Philip** 1898-1978 ............... **CLC 19, 68**
See also CA 13-14; CAP 1; DLB 68; RHW; SATA 47

**Childers, (Robert) Erskine** 1870-1922 ................................. **TCLC 65**
See also CA 113; 153; DLB 70

**Childress, Alice** 1920-1994 . **BLC 1; CLC 12, 15, 86, 96; DC 4; TCLC 116**
See also AAYA 8; BW 2, 3; BYA 2; CA 45-48; 146; CAD; CANR 3, 27, 50, 74; CLR 14; CWD; DA3; DAM DRAM, MULT, NOV; DFS 2, 8, 14; DLB 7, 38, 249; JRDA; LAIT 5; MAICYA 1, 2; MAIC-YAS 1; MTCW 1, 2; RGAL 4; SATA 7, 48, 81; TUS; WYA; YAW

**Chin, Frank (Chew, Jr.)** 1940- ..... **CLC 135; DC 7**
See also CA 33-36R; CANR 71; CD 5; DAM MULT; DLB 206; LAIT 5; RGAL 4

**Chin, Marilyn (Mei Ling)** 1955- ......... **PC 40**
See also CA 129; CANR 70, 113; CWP

**Chislett, (Margaret) Anne** 1943- ...... **CLC 34**
See also CA 151

**Chitty, Thomas Willes** 1926- ............. **CLC 11**
See Hinde, Thomas
See also CA 5-8R; CN 7

**Chivers, Thomas Holley** 1809-1858 ................................. **NCLC 49**
See also DLB 3, 248; RGAL 4

**Choi, Susan** 1969- ............................. **CLC 119**
See also CA 223

**Chomette, Rene Lucien** 1898-1981
See Clair, Rene
See also CA 103

**Chomsky, (Avram) Noam** 1928- ..... **CLC 132**
See also CA 17-20R; CANR 28, 62, 110, 132; DA3; DLB 246; MTCW 1, 2

**Chona, Maria** 1845(?)-1936 ............... **NNAL**
See also CA 144

**Chopin, Kate** ........... **SSC 8, 68; TCLC 127; WLCS**
See Chopin, Katherine
See also AAYA 33; AMWR 2; AMWS 1; BYA 11, 15; CDALB 1865-1917; DA; DAB; DLB 12, 78; EXPN; EXPS; FW; LAIT 3; MAWW; NFS 3; RGAL 4; RGSF 2; SSFS 17; TUS

**Chopin, Katherine** 1851-1904
See Chopin, Kate
See also CA 104; 122; DA3; DAC; DAM MST, NOV

**Chretien de Troyes** c. 12th cent. - . **CMLC 10**
See also DLB 208; EW 1; RGWL 2, 3; TWA

**Christie**
See Ichikawa, Kon

**Christie, Agatha (Mary Clarissa)** 1890-1976 .. **CLC 1, 6, 8, 12, 39, 48, 110**
See also AAYA 9; AITN 1, 2; BPFB 1; BRWS 2; CA 17-20R; 61-64; CANR 10, 37, 108; CBD; CDBLB 1914-1945; CMW 4; CPW; CWD; DA3; DAB; DAC; DAM NOV; DFS 2; DLB 13, 77, 245; MSW; MTCW 1, 2; NFS 8; RGEL 2; RHW; SATA 36; TEA; YAW

**Christie, Philippa** ............................. **CLC 21**
See Pearce, Philippa
See also BYA 5; CANR 109; CLR 9; DLB 161; MAICYA 1; SATA 1, 67, 129

**Christine de Pizan** 1365(?)-1431(?) ....... **LC 9**
See also DLB 208; RGWL 2, 3

**Chuang Tzu** c. 369B.C.-c. 286B.C. ..................................... **CMLC 57**

**Chubb, Elmer**
See Masters, Edgar Lee

**Chulkov, Mikhail Dmitrievich** 1743-1792 ....................................... **LC 2**
See also DLB 150

**Churchill, Caryl** 1938- ....... **CLC 31, 55, 157; DC 5**
See Churchill, Chick
See also BRWS 4; CA 102; CANR 22, 46, 108; CBD; CWD; DFS 12, 16; DLB 13; EWL 3; FW; MTCW 1; RGEL 2

**Churchill, Charles** 1731-1764 ............... **LC 3**
See also DLB 109; RGEL 2
**Churchill, Chick** 1938-
See Churchill, Caryl
See also CD 5
**Churchill, Sir Winston (Leonard Spencer)**
1874-1965 ............................. **TCLC 113**
See also BRW 6; CA 97-100; CDBLB
1890-1914; DA3; DLB 100; DLBD 16;
LAIT 4; MTCW 1, 2
**Chute, Carolyn** 1947- ......................... **CLC 39**
See also CA 123
**Ciardi, John (Anthony)** 1916-1986 . **CLC 10,
40, 44, 129**
See also CA 5-8R; 118; CAAS 2; CANR 5,
33; CLR 19; CWRI 5; DAM POET; DLB
5; DLBY 1986; INT CANR-5; MAICYA
1, 2; MTCW 1, 2; RGAL 4; SAAS 26;
SATA 1, 65; SATA-Obit 46
**Cibber, Colley** 1671-1757 ..................... **LC 66**
See also DLB 84; RGEL 2
**Cicero, Marcus Tullius**
106B.C.-43B.C. ......................... **CMLC 3**
See also AW 1; CDWLB 1; DLB 211;
RGWL 2, 3
**Cimino, Michael** 1943- ...................... **CLC 16**
See also CA 105
**Cioran, E(mil) M.** 1911-1995 ............ **CLC 64**
See also CA 25-28R; 149; CANR 91; DLB
220; EWL 3
**Cisneros, Sandra** 1954- .... **CLC 69, 118, 193;
HLC 1; PC 52; SSC 32, 72**
See also AAYA 9, 53; AMWS 7; CA 131;
CANR 64, 118; CWP; DA3; DAM MULT;
DLB 122, 152; EWL 3; EXPN; FW; HW
1, 2; LAIT 5; LATS 1:2; LLW 1; MAI-
CYA 2; MTCW 2; NFS 2; PFS 19; RGAL
4; RGSF 2; SSFS 3, 13; WLIT 1; YAW
**Cixous, Helene** 1937- ......................... **CLC 92**
See also CA 126; CANR 55, 123; CWW 2;
DLB 83, 242; EWL 3; FW; GLL 2;
MTCW 1, 2; TWA
**Clair, Rene** ............................................... **CLC 20**
See Chomette, Rene Lucien
**Clampitt, Amy** 1920-1994 .... **CLC 32; PC 19**
See also AMWS 9; CA 110; 146; CANR
29, 79; DLB 105
**Clancy, Thomas L., Jr.** 1947-
See Clancy, Tom
See also CA 125; 131; CANR 62, 105;
DA3; INT CA-131; MTCW 1, 2
**Clancy, Tom** ............................... **CLC 45, 112**
See Clancy, Thomas L., Jr.
See also AAYA 9, 51; BEST 89:1, 90:1;
BPFB 1; BYA 10, 11; CANR 132; CMW
4; CPW; DAM NOV, POP; DLB 227
**Clare, John** 1793-1864 .. **NCLC 9, 86; PC 23**
See also DAB; DAM POET; DLB 55, 96;
RGEL 2
**Clarin**
See Alas (y Urena), Leopoldo (Enrique
Garcia)
**Clark, Al C.**
See Goines, Donald
**Clark, (Robert) Brian** 1932- ............. **CLC 29**
See also CA 41-44R; CANR 67; CBD; CD
5
**Clark, Curt**
See Westlake, Donald E(dwin)
**Clark, Eleanor** 1913-1996 ............. **CLC 5, 19**
See also CA 9-12R; 151; CANR 41; CN 7;
DLB 6
**Clark, J. P.**
See Clark Bekederemo, J(ohnson) P(epper)
See also CDWLB 3; DLB 117
**Clark, John Pepper**
See Clark Bekederemo, J(ohnson) P(epper)
See also AFW; CD 5; CP 7; RGEL 2

**Clark, Kenneth (Mackenzie)**
1903-1983 ............................. **TCLC 147**
See also CA 93-96; 109; CANR 36; MTCW
1, 2
**Clark, M. R.**
See Clark, Mavis Thorpe
**Clark, Mavis Thorpe** 1909-1999 ...... **CLC 12**
See also CA 57-60; CANR 8, 37, 107; CLR
30; CWRI 5; MAICYA 1, 2; SAAS 5;
SATA 8, 74
**Clark, Walter Van Tilburg**
1909-1971 ............................... **CLC 28**
See also CA 9-12R; 33-36R; CANR 63,
113; DLB 9, 206; LAIT 2; RGAL 4;
SATA 8
**Clark Bekederemo, J(ohnson) P(epper)**
1935- ................. **BLC 1; CLC 38; DC 5**
See Clark, J. P.; Clark, John Pepper
See also BW 1; CA 65-68; CANR 16, 72;
DAM DRAM, MULT; DFS 13; EWL 3;
MTCW 1
**Clarke, Arthur C(harles)** 1917- .... **CLC 1, 4,
13, 18, 35, 136; SSC 3**
See also AAYA 4, 33; BPFB 1; BYA 13;
CA 1-4R; CANR 2, 28, 55, 74, 130; CN
7; CPW; DA3; DAM POP; DLB 261;
JRDA; LAIT 5; MAICYA 1, 2; MTCW 1,
2; SATA 13, 70, 115; SCFW; SFW 4;
SSFS 4, 18; YAW
**Clarke, Austin** 1896-1974 ............... **CLC 6, 9**
See also CA 29-32; 49-52; CAP 2; DAM
POET; DLB 10, 20; EWL 3; RGEL 2
**Clarke, Austin C(hesterfield)** 1934- .. **BLC 1;
CLC 8, 53; SSC 45**
See also BW 1; CA 25-28R; CAAS 16;
CANR 14, 32, 68; CN 7; DAC; DAM
MULT; DLB 53, 125; DNFS 2; RGSF 2
**Clarke, Gillian** 1937- ......................... **CLC 61**
See also CA 106; CP 7; CWP; DLB 40
**Clarke, Marcus (Andrew Hislop)**
1846-1881 ............................... **NCLC 19**
See also DLB 230; RGEL 2; RGSF 2
**Clarke, Shirley** 1925-1997 ................. **CLC 16**
See also CA 189
**Clash, The**
See Headon, (Nicky) Topper; Jones, Mick;
Simonon, Paul; Strummer, Joe
**Claudel, Paul (Louis Charles Marie)**
1868-1955 ............................. **TCLC 2, 10**
See also CA 104; 165; DLB 192, 258; EW
8; EWL 3; GFL 1789 to the Present;
RGWL 2, 3; TWA
**Claudian** 370(?)-404(?) ................... **CMLC 46**
See also RGWL 2, 3
**Claudius, Matthias** 1740-1815 ....... **NCLC 75**
See also DLB 97
**Clavell, James (duMaresq)**
1925-1994 ......................... **CLC 6, 25, 87**
See also BPFB 1; CA 25-28R; 146; CANR
26, 48; CPW; DA3; DAM NOV, POP;
MTCW 1, 2; NFS 10; RHW
**Clayman, Gregory** ........................... **CLC 65**
**Cleaver, (Leroy) Eldridge**
1935-1998 ............. **BLC 1; CLC 30, 119**
See also BW 1, 3; CA 21-24R; 167; CANR
16, 75; DA3; DAM MULT; MTCW 2;
YAW
**Cleese, John (Marwood)** 1939- ......... **CLC 21**
See Monty Python
See also CA 112; 116; CANR 35; MTCW 1
**Cleishbotham, Jebediah**
See Scott, Sir Walter
**Cleland, John** 1710-1789 ................. **LC 2, 48**
See also DLB 39; RGEL 2
**Clemens, Samuel Langhorne** 1835-1910
See Twain, Mark
See also CA 104; 135; CDALB 1865-1917;
DA; DA3; DAB; DAC; DAM MST, NOV;
DLB 12, 23, 64, 74, 186, 189; JRDA;

LMFS 1; MAICYA 1, 2; NCFS 4; NFS
20; SATA 100; SSFS 16; YABC 2
**Clement of Alexandria**
150(?)-215(?) ......................... **CMLC 41**
**Cleophil**
See Congreve, William
**Clerihew, E.**
See Bentley, E(dmund) C(lerihew)
**Clerk, N. W.**
See Lewis, C(live) S(taples)
**Cleveland, John** 1613-1658 ............... **LC 106**
See also DLB 126; RGEL 2
**Cliff, Jimmy** ....................................... **CLC 21**
See Chambers, James
See also CA 193
**Cliff, Michelle** 1946- .......... **BLCS; CLC 120**
See also BW 2; CA 116; CANR 39, 72; CD-
WLB 3; DLB 157; FW; GLL 2
**Clifford, Lady Anne** 1590-1676 ........... **LC 76**
See also DLB 151
**Clifton, (Thelma) Lucille** 1936- ......... **BLC 1;
CLC 19, 66, 162; PC 17**
See also AFAW 2; BW 2, 3; CA 49-52;
CANR 2, 24, 42, 76, 97; CLR 5; CP 7;
CSW; CWP; CWRI 5; DA3; DAM MULT,
POET; DLB 5, 41; EXPP; MAICYA 1, 2;
MTCW 1, 2; PFS 1, 14; SATA 20, 69,
128; WP
**Clinton, Dirk**
See Silverberg, Robert
**Clough, Arthur Hugh** 1819-1861 ... **NCLC 27**
See also BRW 5; DLB 32; RGEL 2
**Clutha, Janet Paterson Frame** 1924-2004
See Frame, Janet
See also CA 1-4R; 224; CANR 2, 36, 76;
MTCW 1, 2; SATA 119
**Clyne, Terence**
See Blatty, William Peter
**Cobalt, Martin**
See Mayne, William (James Carter)
**Cobb, Irvin S(hrewsbury)**
1876-1944 ............................. **TCLC 77**
See also CA 175; DLB 11, 25, 86
**Cobbett, William** 1763-1835 .......... **NCLC 49**
See also DLB 43, 107, 158; RGEL 2
**Coburn, D(onald) L(ee)** 1938- .......... **CLC 10**
See also CA 89-92
**Cocteau, Jean (Maurice Eugene Clement)**
1889-1963 ...... **CLC 1, 8, 15, 16, 43; DC
17; TCLC 119; WLC**
See also CA 25-28; CANR 40; CAP 2; DA;
DA3; DAB; DAC; DAM DRAM, MST,
NOV; DLB 65, 258; EW 10; EWL 3; GFL
1789 to the Present; MTCW 1, 2; RGWL
2, 3; TWA
**Codrescu, Andrei** 1946- ............. **CLC 46, 121**
See also CA 33-36R; CAAS 19; CANR 13,
34, 53, 76, 125; DA3; DAM POET;
MTCW 2
**Coe, Max**
See Bourne, Randolph S(illiman)
**Coe, Tucker**
See Westlake, Donald E(dwin)
**Coen, Ethan** 1958- ........................... **CLC 108**
See also AAYA 54; CA 126; CANR 85
**Coen, Joel** 1955- ............................... **CLC 108**
See also AAYA 54; CA 126; CANR 119
**The Coen Brothers**
See Coen, Ethan; Coen, Joel
**Coetzee, J(ohn) M(axwell)** 1940- ..... **CLC 23,
33, 66, 117, 161, 162**
See also AAYA 37; AFW; BRWS 6; CA 77-
80; CANR 41, 54, 74, 114, 133; CN 7;
DA3; DAM NOV; DLB 225; EWL 3;
LMFS 2; MTCW 1, 2; WLIT 2; WWE 1
**Coffey, Brian**
See Koontz, Dean R(ay)

**Coffin, Robert P(eter) Tristram**
1892-1955 .................................. **TCLC 95**
See also CA 123; 169; DLB 45
**Cohan, George M(ichael)**
1878-1942 .............................. **TCLC 60**
See also CA 157; DLB 249; RGAL 4
**Cohen, Arthur A(llen)** 1928-1986 ...... **CLC 7,**
**31**
See also CA 1-4R; 120; CANR 1, 17, 42;
DLB 28
**Cohen, Leonard (Norman)** 1934- ...... **CLC 3,**
**38**
See also CA 21-24R; CANR 14, 69; CN 7;
CP 7; DAC; DAM MST; DLB 53; EWL
3; MTCW 1
**Cohen, Matt(hew)** 1942-1999 ........... **CLC 19**
See also CA 61-64; 187; CAAS 18; CANR
40; CN 7; DAC; DLB 53
**Cohen-Solal, Annie** 19(?)- ................. **CLC 50**
**Colegate, Isabel** 1931- ...................... **CLC 36**
See also CA 17-20R; CANR 8, 22, 74; CN
7; DLB 14, 231; INT CANR-22; MTCW
1
**Coleman, Emmett**
See Reed, Ishmael
**Coleridge, Hartley** 1796-1849 ........ **NCLC 90**
See also DLB 96
**Coleridge, M. E.**
See Coleridge, Mary E(lizabeth)
**Coleridge, Mary E(lizabeth)**
1861-1907 .............................. **TCLC 73**
See also CA 116; 166; DLB 19, 98
**Coleridge, Samuel Taylor**
1772-1834 ...... **NCLC 9, 54, 99, 111; PC**
**11, 39; WLC**
See also BRW 4; BRWR 2; BYA 4; CD-
BLB 1789-1832; DA; DA3; DAB; DAC;
DAM MST, POET; DLB 93, 107; EXPP;
LATS 1:1; LMFS 1; PAB; PFS 4, 5;
RGEL 2; TEA; WLIT 3; WP
**Coleridge, Sara** 1802-1852 ............. **NCLC 31**
See also DLB 199
**Coles, Don** 1928- ............................... **CLC 46**
See also CA 115; CANR 38; CP 7
**Coles, Robert (Martin)** 1929- ......... **CLC 108**
See also CA 45-48; CANR 3, 32, 66, 70;
INT CANR-32; SATA 23
**Colette, (Sidonie-Gabrielle)**
1873-1954 ......... **SSC 10; TCLC 1, 5, 16**
See Willy, Colette
See also CA 104; 131; DA3; DAM NOV;
DLB 65; EW 9; EWL 3; GFL 1789 to the
Present; MTCW 1, 2; RGWL 2, 3; TWA
**Collett, (Jacobine) Camilla (Wergeland)**
1813-1895 .................................. **NCLC 22**
**Collier, Christopher** 1930- ................. **CLC 30**
See also AAYA 13; BYA 2; CA 33-36R;
CANR 13, 33, 102; JRDA; MAICYA 1,
2; SATA 16, 70; WYA; YAW 1
**Collier, James Lincoln** 1928- ........... **CLC 30**
See also AAYA 13; BYA 2; CA 9-12R;
CANR 4, 33, 60, 102; CLR 3; DAM POP;
JRDA; MAICYA 1, 2; SAAS 21; SATA 8,
70; WYA; YAW 1
**Collier, Jeremy** 1650-1726 ..................... **LC 6**
**Collier, John** 1901-1980 . **SSC 19; TCLC 127**
See also CA 65-68; 97-100; CANR 10;
DLB 77, 255; FANT; SUFW 1
**Collier, Mary** 1690-1762 ...................... **LC 86**
See also DLB 95
**Collingwood, R(obin) G(eorge)**
1889(?)-1943 ........................... **TCLC 67**
See also CA 117; 155; DLB 262
**Collins, Hunt**
See Hunter, Evan
**Collins, Linda** 1931- .......................... **CLC 44**
See also CA 125

**Collins, Tom**
See Furphy, Joseph
See also RGEL 2
**Collins, (William) Wilkie**
1824-1889 ...................... **NCLC 1, 18, 93**
See also BRWS 6; CDBLB 1832-1890;
CMW 4; DLB 18, 70, 159; MSW; RGEL
2; RGSF 2; SUFW 1; WLIT 4
**Collins, William** 1721-1759 .............. **LC 4, 40**
See also BRW 3; DAM POET; DLB 109;
RGEL 2
**Collodi, Carlo** ................................. **NCLC 54**
See Lorenzini, Carlo
See also CLR 5; WCH
**Colman, George**
See Glassco, John
**Colman, George, the Elder**
1732-1794 ..................................... **LC 98**
See also RGEL 2
**Colonna, Vittoria** 1492-1547 ............... **LC 71**
See also RGWL 2, 3
**Colt, Winchester Remington**
See Hubbard, L(afayette) Ron(ald)
**Colter, Cyrus J.** 1910-2002 ............... **CLC 58**
See also BW 1; CA 65-68; 205; CANR 10,
66; CN 7; DLB 33
**Colton, James**
See Hansen, Joseph
See also GLL 1
**Colum, Padraic** 1881-1972 ................ **CLC 28**
See also BYA 4; CA 73-76; 33-36R; CANR
35; CLR 36; CWRI 5; DLB 19; MAICYA
1, 2; MTCW 1; RGEL 2; SATA 15; WCH
**Colvin, James**
See Moorcock, Michael (John)
**Colwin, Laurie (E.)** 1944-1992 .... **CLC 5, 13,**
**23, 84**
See also CA 89-92; 139; CANR 20, 46;
DLB 218; DLBY 1980; MTCW 1
**Comfort, Alex(ander)** 1920-2000 ........ **CLC 7**
See also CA 1-4R; 190; CANR 1, 45; CP 7;
DAM POP; MTCW 1
**Comfort, Montgomery**
See Campbell, (John) Ramsey
**Compton-Burnett, I(vy)**
1892(?)-1969 .......... **CLC 1, 3, 10, 15, 34**
See also BRW 7; CA 1-4R; 25-28R; CANR
4; DAM NOV; DLB 36; EWL 3; MTCW
1; RGEL 2
**Comstock, Anthony** 1844-1915 ...... **TCLC 13**
See also CA 110; 169
**Comte, Auguste** 1798-1857 ............. **NCLC 54**
**Conan Doyle, Arthur**
See Doyle, Sir Arthur Conan
See also BPFB 1; BYA 4, 5, 11
**Conde (Abellan), Carmen**
1901-1996 .................................. **HLCS 1**
See also CA 177; CWW 2; DLB 108; EWL
3; HW 2
**Conde, Maryse** 1937- ....... **BLCS; CLC 52, 92**
See also BW 2, 3; CA 110, 190; CAAE 190;
CANR 30, 53, 76; CWW 2; DAM MULT;
EWL 3; MTCW 1
**Condillac, Etienne Bonnot de**
1714-1780 ................................... **LC 26**
**Condon, Richard (Thomas)**
1915-1996 ........ **CLC 4, 6, 8, 10, 45, 100**
See also BEST 90:3; BPFB 1; CA 1-4R;
151; CAAS 1; CANR 2, 23; CMW 4; CN
7; DAM NOV; INT CANR-23; MTCW 1,
2
**Condorcet** 1743-1794 ......................... **LC 104**
See also GFL Beginnings to 1789
**Confucius** 551B.C.-479B.C. .... **CMLC 19, 65;**
**WLCS**
See also DA; DA3; DAB; DAC; DAM
MST

**Congreve, William** 1670-1729 ... **DC 2; LC 5,**
**21; WLC**
See also BRW 2; CDBLB 1660-1789; DA;
DAB; DAC; DAM DRAM, MST, POET;
DFS 15; DLB 39, 84; RGEL 2; WLIT 3
**Conley, Robert J(ackson)** 1940- ......... **NNAL**
See also CA 41-44R; CANR 15, 34, 45, 96;
DAM MULT
**Connell, Evan S(helby), Jr.** 1924- . **CLC 4, 6,**
**45**
See also AAYA 7; CA 1-4R; CAAS 2;
CANR 2, 39, 76, 97; CN 7; DAM NOV;
DLB 2; DLBY 1981; MTCW 1, 2
**Connelly, Marc(us Cook)** 1890-1980 . **CLC 7**
See also CA 85-88; 102; CANR 30; DFS
12; DLB 7; DLBY 1980; RGAL 4; SATA-
Obit 25
**Connor, Ralph** ................................... **TCLC 31**
See Gordon, Charles William
See also DLB 92; TCWW 2
**Conrad, Joseph** 1857-1924 ..... **SSC 9, 67, 69,**
**71; TCLC 1, 6, 13, 25, 43, 57; WLC**
See also AAYA 26; BPFB 1; BRW 6;
BRWC 1; BRWR 2; BYA 2; CA 104; 131;
CANR 60; CDBLB 1890-1914; DA; DA3;
DAB; DAC; DAM MST, NOV; DLB 10,
34, 98, 156; EWL 3; EXPN; EXPS; LAIT
2; LATS 1:1; LMFS 1; MTCW 1, 2; NFS
2, 16; RGEL 2; RGSF 2; SATA 27; SSFS
1, 12; TEA; WLIT 4
**Conrad, Robert Arnold**
See Hart, Moss
**Conroy, (Donald) Pat(rick)** 1945- ... **CLC 30,**
**74**
See also AAYA 8, 52; AITN 1; BPFB 1;
CA 85-88; CANR 24, 53, 129; CPW;
CSW; DA3; DAM NOV, POP; DLB 6;
LAIT 5; MTCW 1, 2
**Constant (de Rebecque), (Henri) Benjamin**
1767-1830 ................................... **NCLC 6**
See also DLB 119; EW 4; GFL 1789 to the
Present
**Conway, Jill K(er)** 1934- ................. **CLC 152**
See also CA 130; CANR 94
**Conybeare, Charles Augustus**
See Eliot, T(homas) S(tearns)
**Cook, Michael** 1933-1994 ................. **CLC 58**
See also CA 93-96; CANR 68; DLB 53
**Cook, Robin** 1940- ............................ **CLC 14**
See also AAYA 32; BEST 90:2; BPFB 1;
CA 108; 111; CANR 41, 90, 109; CPW;
DA3; DAM POP; HGG; INT CA-111
**Cook, Roy**
See Silverberg, Robert
**Cooke, Elizabeth** 1948- ..................... **CLC 55**
See also CA 129
**Cooke, John Esten** 1830-1886 .......... **NCLC 5**
See also DLB 3, 248; RGAL 4
**Cooke, John Estes**
See Baum, L(yman) Frank
**Cooke, M. E.**
See Creasey, John
**Cooke, Margaret**
See Creasey, John
**Cooke, Rose Terry** 1827-1892 ...... **NCLC 110**
See also DLB 12, 74
**Cook-Lynn, Elizabeth** 1930- ........... **CLC 93;**
**NNAL**
See also CA 133; DAM MULT; DLB 175
**Cooney, Ray** ....................................... **CLC 62**
See also CBD
**Cooper, Anthony Ashley** 1671-1713 .. **LC 107**
See also DLB 101
**Cooper, Douglas** 1960- ....................... **CLC 86**
**Cooper, Henry St. John**
See Creasey, John
**Cooper, J(oan) California** (?)- .......... **CLC 56**
See also AAYA 12; BW 1; CA 125; CANR
55; DAM MULT; DLB 212

**Cooper, James Fenimore**
1789-1851 ...................... **NCLC 1, 27, 54**
See also AAYA 22; AMW; BPFB 1;
CDALB 1640-1865; DA3; DLB 3, 183,
250, 254; LAIT 1; NFS 9; RGAL 4; SATA
19; TUS; WCH

**Cooper, Susan Fenimore**
1813-1894 ............................... **NCLC 129**
See also ANW; DLB 239, 254

**Coover, Robert (Lowell)** 1932- ...... **CLC 3, 7, 15, 32, 46, 87, 161; SSC 15**
See also AMWS 5; BPFB 1; CA 45-48;
CANR 3, 37, 58, 115; CN 7; DAM NOV;
DLB 2, 227; DLBY 1981; EWL 3;
MTCW 1, 2; RGAL 4; RGSF 2

**Copeland, Stewart (Armstrong)**
1952- .......................................... **CLC 26**

**Copernicus, Nicolaus** 1473-1543 ......... **LC 45**

**Coppard, A(lfred) E(dgar)**
1878-1957 ...................... **SSC 21; TCLC 5**
See also BRWS 8; CA 114; 167; DLB 162;
EWL 3; HGG; RGEL 2; RGSF 2; SUFW
1; YABC 1

**Coppee, Francois** 1842-1908 .......... **TCLC 25**
See also CA 170; DLB 217

**Coppola, Francis Ford** 1939- ... **CLC 16, 126**
See also AAYA 39; CA 77-80; CANR 40,
78; DLB 44

**Copway, George** 1818-1869 ................. **NNAL**
See also DAM MULT; DLB 175, 183

**Corbiere, Tristan** 1845-1875 .......... **NCLC 43**
See also DLB 217; GFL 1789 to the Present

**Corcoran, Barbara (Asenath)**
1911- .......................................... **CLC 17**
See also AAYA 14; CA 21-24R, 191; CAAE
191; CAAS 2; CANR 11, 28, 48; CLR
50; DLB 52; JRDA; MAICYA 2; MAIC-
YAS 1; RHW; SAAS 20; SATA 3, 77;
SATA-Essay 125

**Cordelier, Maurice**
See Giraudoux, Jean(-Hippolyte)

**Corelli, Marie** ...................... **TCLC 51**
See Mackay, Mary
See also DLB 34, 156; RGEL 2; SUFW 1

**Corinna** c. 225B.C.-c. 305B.C. ...... **CMLC 72**

**Corman, Cid** ...................... **CLC 9**
See Corman, Sidney
See also CAAS 2; DLB 5, 193

**Corman, Sidney** 1924-2004
See Corman, Cid
See also CA 85-88; 225; CANR 44; CP 7;
DAM POET

**Cormier, Robert (Edmund)**
1925-2000 ............................... **CLC 12, 30**
See also AAYA 3, 19; BYA 1, 2, 6, 8, 9;
CA 1-4R; CANR 5, 23, 76, 93; CDALB
1968-1988; CLR 12, 55; DA; DAB; DAC;
DAM MST, NOV; DLB 52; EXPN; INT
CANR-23; JRDA; LAIT 5; MAICYA 1,
2; MTCW 1, 2; NFS 2, 18; SATA 10, 45,
83; SATA-Obit 122; WYA; YAW

**Corn, Alfred (DeWitt III)** 1943- ....... **CLC 33**
See also CA 179; CAAE 179; CAAS 25;
CANR 44; CP 7; CSW; DLB 120, 282;
DLBY 1980

**Corneille, Pierre** 1606-1684 ... **DC 21; LC 28**
See also DAB; DAM MST; DLB 268; EW
3; GFL Beginnings to 1789; RGWL 2, 3;
TWA

**Cornwell, David (John Moore)**
1931- .......................................... **CLC 9, 15**
See le Carre, John
See also CA 5-8R; CANR 13, 33, 59, 107,
132; DA3; DAM POP; MTCW 1, 2

**Cornwell, Patricia (Daniels)** 1956- . **CLC 155**
See also AAYA 16, 56; BPFB 1; CA 134;
CANR 53, 131; CMW 4; CPW; CSW;
DAM POP; DLB 306; MSW; MTCW 1

**Corso, (Nunzio) Gregory** 1930-2001 . **CLC 1, 11; PC 33**
See also AMWS 12; BG 2; CA 5-8R; 193;
CANR 41, 76, 132; CP 7; DA3; DLB 5,
16, 237; LMFS 2; MTCW 1, 2; WP

**Cortazar, Julio** 1914-1984 ... **CLC 2, 3, 5, 10, 13, 15, 33, 34, 92; HLC 1; SSC 7, 76**
See also BPFB 1; CA 21-24R; CANR 12,
32, 81; CDWLB 3; DA3; DAM MULT,
NOV; DLB 113; EWL 3; EXPS; HW 1,
2; LAW; MTCW 1, 2; RGSF 2; RGWL 2,
3; SSFS 3, 20; TWA; WLIT 1

**Cortes, Hernan** 1485-1547 ................... **LC 31**

**Corvinus, Jakob**
See Raabe, Wilhelm (Karl)

**Corwin, Cecil**
See Kornbluth, C(yril) M.

**Cosic, Dobrica** 1921- ........................... **CLC 14**
See also CA 122; 138; CDWLB 4; CWW
2; DLB 181; EWL 3

**Costain, Thomas B(ertram)**
1885-1965 ............................... **CLC 30**
See also BYA 3; CA 5-8R; 25-28R; DLB 9;
RHW

**Costantini, Humberto** 1924(?)-1987 . **CLC 49**
See also CA 131; 122; EWL 3; HW 1

**Costello, Elvis** 1954- ........................... **CLC 21**
See also CA 204

**Costenoble, Philostene**
See Ghelderode, Michel de

**Cotes, Cecil V.**
See Duncan, Sara Jeannette

**Cotter, Joseph Seamon Sr.**
1861-1949 ................... **BLC 1; TCLC 28**
See also BW 1; CA 124; DAM MULT; DLB
50

**Couch, Arthur Thomas Quiller**
See Quiller-Couch, Sir Arthur (Thomas)

**Coulton, James**
See Hansen, Joseph

**Couperus, Louis (Marie Anne)**
1863-1923 ............................... **TCLC 15**
See also CA 115; EWL 3; RGWL 2, 3

**Coupland, Douglas** 1961- .......... **CLC 85, 133**
See also AAYA 34; CA 142; CANR 57, 90,
130; CCA 1; CPW; DAC; DAM POP

**Court, Wesli**
See Turco, Lewis (Putnam)

**Courtenay, Bryce** 1933- ..................... **CLC 59**
See also CA 138; CPW

**Courtney, Robert**
See Ellison, Harlan (Jay)

**Cousteau, Jacques-Yves** 1910-1997 .. **CLC 30**
See also CA 65-68; 159; CANR 15, 67;
MTCW 1; SATA 38, 98

**Coventry, Francis** 1725-1754 ............... **LC 46**

**Coverdale, Miles** c. 1487-1569 ............. **LC 77**
See also DLB 167

**Cowan, Peter (Walkinshaw)**
1914-2002 .................................. **SSC 28**
See also CA 21-24R; CANR 9, 25, 50, 83;
CN 7; DLB 260; RGSF 2

**Coward, Noel (Peirce)** 1899-1973 . **CLC 1, 9, 29, 51**
See also AITN 1; BRWS 2; CA 17-18; 41-
44R; CANR 35, 132; CAP 2; CDBLB
1914-1945; DA3; DAM DRAM; DFS 3,
6; DLB 10, 245; EWL 3; IDFW 3, 4;
MTCW 1, 2; RGEL 2; TEA

**Cowley, Abraham** 1618-1667 ............... **LC 43**
See also BRW 2; DLB 131, 151; PAB;
RGEL 2

**Cowley, Malcolm** 1898-1989 ............. **CLC 39**
See also AMWS 2; CA 5-8R; 128; CANR
3, 55; DLB 4, 48; DLBY 1981, 1989;
EWL 3; MTCW 1, 2

**Cowper, William** 1731-1800 ..... **NCLC 8, 94; PC 40**
See also BRW 3; DA3; DAM POET; DLB
104, 109; RGEL 2

**Cox, William Trevor** 1928-
See Trevor, William
See also CA 9-12R; CANR 4, 37, 55, 76,
102; DAM NOV; INT CANR-37; MTCW
1, 2; TEA

**Coyne, P. J.**
See Masters, Hilary

**Cozzens, James Gould** 1903-1978 . **CLC 1, 4, 11, 92**
See also AMW; BPFB 1; CA 9-12R; 81-84;
CANR 19; CDALB 1941-1968; DLB 9,
294; DLBD 2; DLBY 1984, 1997; EWL
3; MTCW 1, 2; RGAL 4

**Crabbe, George** 1754-1832 .... **NCLC 26, 121**
See also BRW 3; DLB 93; RGEL 2

**Crace, Jim** 1946- ............... **CLC 157; SSC 61**
See also CA 128; 135; CANR 55, 70, 123;
CN 7; DLB 231; INT CA-135

**Craddock, Charles Egbert**
See Murfree, Mary Noailles

**Craig, A. A.**
See Anderson, Poul (William)

**Craik, Mrs.**
See Craik, Dinah Maria (Mulock)
See also RGEL 2

**Craik, Dinah Maria (Mulock)**
1826-1887 .................................. **NCLC 38**
See Craik, Mrs.; Mulock, Dinah Maria
See also DLB 35, 163; MAICYA 1, 2;
SATA 34

**Cram, Ralph Adams** 1863-1942 ..... **TCLC 45**
See also CA 160

**Cranch, Christopher Pearse**
1813-1892 ............................... **NCLC 115**
See also DLB 1, 42, 243

**Crane, (Harold) Hart** 1899-1932 ......... **PC 3; TCLC 2, 5, 80; WLC**
See also AMW; AMWR 2; CA 104; 127;
CDALB 1917-1929; DA; DA3; DAB;
DAC; DAM MST, POET; DLB 4, 48;
EWL 3; MTCW 1, 2; RGAL 4; TUS

**Crane, R(onald) S(almon)**
1886-1967 .................................. **CLC 27**
See also CA 85-88; DLB 63

**Crane, Stephen (Townley)**
1871-1900 ...... **SSC 7, 56, 70; TCLC 11, 17, 32; WLC**
See also AAYA 21; AMW; AMWC 1; BPFB
1; BYA 3; CA 109; 140; CANR 84;
CDALB 1865-1917; DA; DA3; DAB;
DAC; DAM MST, NOV, POET; DLB 12,
54, 78; EXPN; EXPS; LAIT 2; LMFS 2;
NFS 4, 20; PFS 9; RGAL 4; RGSF 2;
SSFS 4; TUS; WYA; YABC 2

**Cranmer, Thomas** 1489-1556 ............... **LC 95**
See also DLB 132, 213

**Cranshaw, Stanley**
See Fisher, Dorothy (Frances) Canfield

**Crase, Douglas** 1944- .......................... **CLC 58**
See also CA 106

**Crashaw, Richard** 1612(?)-1649 .......... **LC 24**
See also BRW 2; DLB 126; PAB; RGEL 2

**Cratinus** c. 519B.C.-c. 422B.C. ..... **CMLC 54**
See also LMFS 1

**Craven, Margaret** 1901-1980 ........... **CLC 17**
See also BYA 2; CA 103; CCA 1; DAC;
LAIT 5

**Crawford, F(rancis) Marion**
1854-1909 .................................. **TCLC 10**
See also CA 107; 168; DLB 71; HGG;
RGAL 4; SUFW 1

**Crawford, Isabella Valancy**
1850-1887 ....................... **NCLC 12, 127**
See also DLB 92; RGEL 2

**Crayon, Geoffrey**
See Irving, Washington
**Creasey, John** 1908-1973 ................... **CLC 11**
See Marric, J. J.
See also CA 5-8R; 41-44R; CANR 8, 59;
CMW 4; DLB 77; MTCW 1
**Crebillon, Claude Prosper Jolyot de (fils)**
1707-1777 ................................. **LC 1, 28**
See also GFL Beginnings to 1789
**Credo**
See Creasey, John
**Credo, Alvaro J. de**
See Prado (Calvo), Pedro
**Creeley, Robert (White)** 1926- .. **CLC 1, 2, 4,
8, 11, 15, 36, 78**
See also AMWS 4; CA 1-4R; CAAS 10;
CANR 23, 43, 89; CP 7; DA3; DAM
POET; DLB 5, 16, 169; DLBD 17; EWL
3; MTCW 1, 2; PFS 21; RGAL 4; WP
**Crevecoeur, Hector St. John de**
See Crevecoeur, Michel Guillaume Jean de
See also ANW
**Crevecoeur, Michel Guillaume Jean de**
1735-1813 ............................... **NCLC 105**
See Crevecoeur, Hector St. John de
See also AMWS 1; DLB 37
**Crevel, Rene** 1900-1935 ................ **TCLC 112**
See also GLL 2
**Crews, Harry (Eugene)** 1935- ..... **CLC 6, 23,
49**
See also AITN 1; AMWS 11; BPFB 1; CA
25-28R; CANR 20, 57; CN 7; CSW; DA3;
DLB 6, 143, 185; MTCW 1, 2; RGAL 4
**Crichton, (John) Michael** 1942- .... **CLC 2, 6,
54, 90**
See also AAYA 10, 49; AITN 2; BPFB 1;
CA 25-28R; CANR 13, 40, 54, 76, 127;
CMW 4; CN 7; CPW; DA3; DAM NOV,
POP; DLB 292; DLBY 1981; INT CANR-
13; JRDA; MTCW 1, 2; SATA 9, 88;
SFW 4; YAW
**Crispin, Edmund** ............................. **CLC 22**
See Montgomery, (Robert) Bruce
See also DLB 87; MSW
**Cristofer, Michael** 1945(?)- ............... **CLC 28**
See also CA 110; 152; CAD; CD 5; DAM
DRAM; DFS 15; DLB 7
**Criton**
See Alain
**Croce, Benedetto** 1866-1952 ........... **TCLC 37**
See also CA 120; 155; EW 8; EWL 3
**Crockett, David** 1786-1836 .............. **NCLC 8**
See also DLB 3, 11, 183, 248
**Crockett, Davy**
See Crockett, David
**Crofts, Freeman Wills** 1879-1957 .. **TCLC 55**
See also CA 115; 195; CMW 4; DLB 77;
MSW
**Croker, John Wilson** 1780-1857 .... **NCLC 10**
See also DLB 110
**Crommelynck, Fernand** 1885-1970 .. **CLC 75**
See also CA 189; 89-92; EWL 3
**Cromwell, Oliver** 1599-1658 ................ **LC 43**
**Cronenberg, David** 1943- ................ **CLC 143**
See also CA 138; CCA 1
**Cronin, A(rchibald) J(oseph)**
1896-1981 ................................... **CLC 32**
See also BPFB 1; CA 1-4R; 102; CANR 5;
DLB 191; SATA 47; SATA-Obit 25
**Cross, Amanda**
See Heilbrun, Carolyn G(old)
See also BPFB 1; CMW; CPW; DLB 306;
MSW
**Crothers, Rachel** 1878-1958 ........... **TCLC 19**
See also CA 113; 194; CAD; CWD; DLB
7, 266; RGAL 4
**Croves, Hal**
See Traven, B.

**Crow Dog, Mary (Ellen)** (?)- ............ **CLC 93**
See Brave Bird, Mary
See also CA 154
**Crowfield, Christopher**
See Stowe, Harriet (Elizabeth) Beecher
**Crowley, Aleister** ............................. **TCLC 7**
See Crowley, Edward Alexander
See also GLL 1
**Crowley, Edward Alexander** 1875-1947
See Crowley, Aleister
See also CA 104; HGG
**Crowley, John** 1942- ........................ **CLC 57**
See also AAYA 57; BPFB 1; CA 61-64;
CANR 43, 98; DLBY 1982; FANT; SATA
65, 140; SFW 4; SUFW 2
**Crowne, John** 1641-1712 ................... **LC 104**
See also DLB 80; RGEL 2
**Crud**
See Crumb, R(obert)
**Crumarums**
See Crumb, R(obert)
**Crumb, R(obert)** 1943- ..................... **CLC 17**
See also CA 106; CANR 107
**Crumbum**
See Crumb, R(obert)
**Crumski**
See Crumb, R(obert)
**Crum the Bum**
See Crumb, R(obert)
**Crunk**
See Crumb, R(obert)
**Crustt**
See Crumb, R(obert)
**Crutchfield, Les**
See Trumbo, Dalton
**Cruz, Victor Hernandez** 1949- ... **HLC 1; PC
37**
See also BW 2; CA 65-68; CAAS 17;
CANR 14, 32, 74, 132; CP 7; DAM
MULT, POET; DLB 41; DNFS 1; EXPP;
HW 1, 2; LLW 1; MTCW 1; PFS 16; WP
**Cryer, Gretchen (Kiger)** 1935- ......... **CLC 21**
See also CA 114; 123
**Csath, Geza** 1887-1919 .................. **TCLC 13**
See also CA 111
**Cudlip, David R(ockwell)** 1933- ....... **CLC 34**
See also CA 177
**Cullen, Countee** 1903-1946 .... **BLC 1; HR 2;
PC 20; TCLC 4, 37; WLCS**
See also AFAW 2; AMWS 4; BW 1; CA
108; 124; CDALB 1917-1929; DA; DA3;
DAC; DAM MST, MULT, POET; DLB 4,
48, 51; EWL 3; EXPP; LMFS 2; MTCW
1, 2; PFS 3; RGAL 4; SATA 18; WP
**Culleton, Beatrice** 1949- ..................... **NNAL**
See also CA 120; CANR 83; DAC
**Cum, R.**
See Crumb, R(obert)
**Cummings, Bruce F(rederick)** 1889-1919
See Barbellion, W. N. P.
See also CA 123
**Cummings, E(dward) E(stlin)**
1894-1962 .. **CLC 1, 3, 8, 12, 15, 68; PC
5; TCLC 137; WLC**
See also AAYA 41; AMW; CA 73-76;
CANR 31; CDALB 1929-1941; DA;
DA3; DAB; DAC; DAM MST, POET;
DLB 4, 48; EWL 3; EXPP; MTCW 1, 2;
PAB; PFS 1, 3, 12, 13, 19; RGAL 4; TUS;
WP
**Cummins, Maria Susanna**
1827-1866 ............................... **NCLC 139**
See also DLB 42; YABC 1
**Cunha, Euclides (Rodrigues Pimenta) da**
1866-1909 ................................. **TCLC 24**
See also CA 123; 219; LAW; WLIT 1
**Cunningham, E. V.**
See Fast, Howard (Melvin)

**Cunningham, J(ames) V(incent)**
1911-1985 ............................ **CLC 3, 31**
See also CA 1-4R; 115; CANR 1, 72; DLB
5
**Cunningham, Julia (Woolfolk)**
1916- ...................................... **CLC 12**
See also CA 9-12R; CANR 4, 19, 36; CWRI
5; JRDA; MAICYA 1, 2; SAAS 2; SATA
1, 26, 132
**Cunningham, Michael** 1952- ............ **CLC 34**
See also CA 136; CANR 96; DLB 292;
GLL 2
**Cunninghame Graham, R. B.**
See Cunninghame Graham, Robert
(Gallnigad) Bontine
**Cunninghame Graham, Robert (Gallnigad)
Bontine** 1852-1936 .................. **TCLC 19**
See Graham, R(obert) B(ontine) Cunning-
hame
See also CA 119; 184
**Curnow, (Thomas) Allen (Monro)**
1911-2001 ..................................... **PC 48**
See also CA 69-72; 202; CANR 48, 99; CP
7; EWL 3; RGEL 2
**Currie, Ellen** 19(?)- ........................... **CLC 44**
**Curtin, Philip**
See Lowndes, Marie Adelaide (Belloc)
**Curtin, Phillip**
See Lowndes, Marie Adelaide (Belloc)
**Curtis, Price**
See Ellison, Harlan (Jay)
**Cusanus, Nicolaus** 1401-1464 ............. **LC 80**
See Nicholas of Cusa
**Cutrate, Joe**
See Spiegelman, Art
**Cynewulf** c. 770- ............................. **CMLC 23**
See also DLB 146; RGEL 2
**Cyrano de Bergerac, Savinien de**
1619-1655 ..................................... **LC 65**
See also DLB 268; GFL Beginnings to
1789; RGWL 2, 3
**Cyril of Alexandria** c. 375-c. 430 . **CMLC 59**
**Czaczkes, Shmuel Yosef Halevi**
See Agnon, S(hmuel) Y(osef Halevi)
**Dabrowska, Maria (Szumska)**
1889-1965 ................................... **CLC 15**
See also CA 106; CDWLB 4; DLB 215;
EWL 3
**Dabydeen, David** 1955- ..................... **CLC 34**
See also BW 1; CA 125; CANR 56, 92; CN
7; CP 7
**Dacey, Philip** 1939- ........................... **CLC 51**
See also CA 37-40R; CAAS 17; CANR 14,
32, 64; CP 7; DLB 105
**Dafydd ap Gwilym** c. 1320-c. 1380 ..... **PC 56**
**Dagerman, Stig (Halvard)**
1923-1954 ................................... **TCLC 17**
See also CA 117; 155; DLB 259; EWL 3
**D'Aguiar, Fred** 1960- ....................... **CLC 145**
See also CA 148; CANR 83, 101; CP 7;
DLB 157; EWL 3
**Dahl, Roald** 1916-1990 ....... **CLC 1, 6, 18, 79**
See also AAYA 15; BPFB 1; BRWS 4; BYA
5; CA 1-4R; 133; CANR 6, 32, 37, 62;
CLR 1, 7, 41; CPW; DA3; DAB; DAC;
DAM MST, NOV, POP; DLB 139, 255;
HGG; JRDA; MAICYA 1, 2; MTCW 1,
2; RGSF 2; SATA 1, 26, 73; SATA-Obit
65; SSFS 4; TEA; YAW
**Dahlberg, Edward** 1900-1977 .. **CLC 1, 7, 14**
See also CA 9-12R; 69-72; CANR 31, 62;
DLB 48; MTCW 1; RGAL 4
**Daitch, Susan** 1954- ......................... **CLC 103**
See also CA 161
**Dale, Colin** ....................................... **TCLC 18**
See Lawrence, T(homas) E(dward)
**Dale, George E.**
See Asimov, Isaac

**Dalton, Roque** 1935-1975(?) ..... **HLCS 1; PC 36**
See also CA 176; DLB 283; HW 2

**Daly, Elizabeth** 1878-1967 ................ **CLC 52**
See also CA 23-24; 25-28R; CANR 60; CAP 2; CMW 4

**Daly, Mary** 1928- ........................... **CLC 173**
See also CA 25-28R; CANR 30, 62; FW; GLL 1; MTCW 1

**Daly, Maureen** 1921- ......................... **CLC 17**
See also AAYA 5, 58; BYA 6; CANR 37, 83, 108; CLR 96; JRDA; MAICYA 1, 2; SAAS 1; SATA 2, 129; WYA; YAW

**Damas, Leon-Gontran** 1912-1978 .... **CLC 84**
See also BW 1; CA 125; 73-76; EWL 3

**Dana, Richard Henry Sr.**
1787-1879 .................................... **NCLC 53**

**Daniel, Samuel** 1562(?)-1619 .............. **LC 24**
See also DLB 62; RGEL 2

**Daniels, Brett**
See Adler, Renata

**Dannay, Frederic** 1905-1982 ............. **CLC 11**
See Queen, Ellery
See also CA 1-4R; 107; CANR 1, 39; CMW 4; DAM POP; DLB 137; MTCW 1

**D'Annunzio, Gabriele** 1863-1938 ... **TCLC 6, 40**
See also CA 104; 155; EW 8; EWL 3; RGWL 2, 3; TWA

**Danois, N. le**
See Gourmont, Remy(-Marie-Charles) de

**Dante** 1265-1321 .... **CMLC 3, 18, 39, 70; PC 21; WLCS**
See also DA; DA3; DAB; DAC; DAM MST, POET; EFS 1; EW 1; LAIT 1; RGWL 2, 3; TWA; WP

**d'Antibes, Germain**
See Simenon, Georges (Jacques Christian)

**Danticat, Edwidge** 1969- ........... **CLC 94, 139**
See also AAYA 29; CA 152; 192; CAAE 192; CANR 73, 129; DNFS 1; EXPS; LATS 1:2; MTCW 1; SSFS 1; YAW

**Danvers, Dennis** 1947- ...................... **CLC 70**

**Danziger, Paula** 1944-2004 ............... **CLC 21**
See also AAYA 4, 36; BYA 6, 7, 14; CA 112; 115; CANR 37, 132; CLR 20; JRDA; MAICYA 1, 2; SATA 36, 63, 102, 149; SATA-Brief 30; WYA; YAW

**Da Ponte, Lorenzo** 1749-1838 ........ **NCLC 50**

**Dario, Ruben** 1867-1916 ....... **HLC 1; PC 15; TCLC 4**
See also CA 131; CANR 81; DAM MULT; DLB 290; EWL 3; HW 1, 2; LAW; MTCW 1, 2; RGWL 2, 3

**Darley, George** 1795-1846 ................ **NCLC 2**
See also DLB 96; RGEL 2

**Darrow, Clarence (Seward)**
1857-1938 .................................... **TCLC 81**
See also CA 164; DLB 303

**Darwin, Charles** 1809-1882 ........... **NCLC 57**
See also BRWS 7; DLB 57, 166; LATS 1:1; RGEL 2; TEA; WLIT 4

**Darwin, Erasmus** 1731-1802 ........ **NCLC 106**
See also DLB 93; RGEL 2

**Daryush, Elizabeth** 1887-1977 ...... **CLC 6, 19**
See also CA 49-52; CANR 3, 81; DLB 20

**Das, Kamala** 1934- ............. **CLC 191; PC 43**
See also CA 101; CANR 27, 59; CP 7; CWP; FW

**Dasgupta, Surendranath**
1887-1952 .................................... **TCLC 81**
See also CA 157

**Dashwood, Edmee Elizabeth Monica de la Pasture** 1890-1943
See Delafield, E. M.
See also CA 119; 154

**da Silva, Antonio Jose**
1705-1739 .............................. **NCLC 114**

**Daudet, (Louis Marie) Alphonse**
1840-1897 .................................. **NCLC 1**
See also DLB 123; GFL 1789 to the Present; RGSF 2

**d'Aulnoy, Marie-Catherine** c.
1650-1705 .................................. **LC 100**

**Daumal, Rene** 1908-1944 ............... **TCLC 14**
See also CA 114; EWL 3

**Davenant, William** 1606-1668 ............. **LC 13**
See also DLB 58, 126; RGEL 2

**Davenport, Guy (Mattison, Jr.)**
1927- ................. **CLC 6, 14, 38; SSC 16**
See also CA 33-36R; CANR 23, 73; CN 7; CSW; DLB 130

**David, Robert**
See Nezval, Vitezslav

**Davidson, Avram (James)** 1923-1993
See Queen, Ellery
See also CA 101; 171; CANR 26; DLB 8; FANT; SFW 4; SUFW 1, 2

**Davidson, Donald (Grady)**
1893-1968 .................... **CLC 2, 13, 19**
See also CA 5-8R; 25-28R; CANR 4, 84; DLB 45

**Davidson, Hugh**
See Hamilton, Edmond

**Davidson, John** 1857-1909 ............. **TCLC 24**
See also CA 118; 217; DLB 19; RGEL 2

**Davidson, Sara** 1943- ........................ **CLC 9**
See also CA 81-84; CANR 44, 68; DLB 185

**Davie, Donald (Alfred)** 1922-1995 .... **CLC 5, 8, 10, 31; PC 29**
See also BRWS 6; CA 1-4R; 149; CAAS 3; CANR 1, 44; CP 7; DLB 27; MTCW 1; RGEL 2

**Davie, Elspeth** 1919-1995 .................. **SSC 52**
See also CA 120; 126; 150; DLB 139

**Davies, Ray(mond Douglas)** 1944- ... **CLC 21**
See also CA 116; 146; CANR 92

**Davies, Rhys** 1901-1978 .................... **CLC 23**
See also CA 9-12R; 81-84; CANR 4; DLB 139, 191

**Davies, (William) Robertson**
1913-1995 ....... **CLC 2, 7, 13, 25, 42, 75, 91; WLC**
See Marchbanks, Samuel
See also BEST 89:2; BPFB 1; CA 33-36R; 150; CANR 17, 42, 103; CN 7; CPW; DA; DA3; DAB; DAC; DAM MST, NOV, POP; DLB 68; EWL 3; HGG; INT CANR-17; MTCW 1, 2; RGEL 2; TWA

**Davies, Sir John** 1569-1626 ................. **LC 85**
See also DLB 172

**Davies, Walter C.**
See Kornbluth, C(yril) M.

**Davies, William Henry** 1871-1940 ... **TCLC 5**
See also CA 104; 179; DLB 19, 174; EWL 3; RGEL 2

**Da Vinci, Leonardo** 1452-1519 ..... **LC 12, 57, 60**
See also AAYA 40

**Davis, Angela (Yvonne)** 1944- .......... **CLC 77**
See also BW 2, 3; CA 57-60; CANR 10, 81; CSW; DA3; DAM MULT; FW

**Davis, B. Lynch**
See Bioy Casares, Adolfo; Borges, Jorge Luis

**Davis, Frank Marshall** 1905-1987 ...... **BLC 1**
See also BW 2, 3; CA 125; 123; CANR 42, 80; DAM MULT; DLB 51

**Davis, Gordon**
See Hunt, E(verette) Howard, (Jr.)

**Davis, H(arold) L(enoir)** 1896-1960 . **CLC 49**
See also ANW; CA 178; 89-92; DLB 9, 206; SATA 114

**Davis, Rebecca (Blaine) Harding**
1831-1910 ................... **SSC 38; TCLC 6**
See also CA 104; 179; DLB 74, 239; FW; NFS 14; RGAL 4; TUS

**Davis, Richard Harding**
1864-1916 ................................ **TCLC 24**
See also CA 114; 179; DLB 12, 23, 78, 79, 189; DLBD 13; RGAL 4

**Davison, Frank Dalby** 1893-1970 ..... **CLC 15**
See also CA 217; 116; DLB 260

**Davison, Lawrence H.**
See Lawrence, D(avid) H(erbert Richards)

**Davison, Peter (Hubert)** 1928- ......... **CLC 28**
See also CA 9-12R; CAAS 4; CANR 3, 43, 84; CP 7; DLB 5

**Davys, Mary** 1674-1732 ................... **LC 1, 46**
See also DLB 39

**Dawson, (Guy) Fielding (Lewis)**
1930-2002 ...................................... **CLC 6**
See also CA 85-88; 202; CANR 108; DLB 130; DLBY 2002

**Dawson, Peter**
See Faust, Frederick (Schiller)
See also TCWW 2, 2

**Day, Clarence (Shepard, Jr.)**
1874-1935 .................................. **TCLC 25**
See also CA 108; 199; DLB 11

**Day, John** 1574(?)-1640(?) .................. **LC 70**
See also DLB 62; 170; RGEL 2

**Day, Thomas** 1748-1789 ....................... **LC 1**
See also DLB 39; YABC 1

**Day Lewis, C(ecil)** 1904-1972 . **CLC 1, 6, 10; PC 11**
See Blake, Nicholas
See also BRWS 3; CA 13-16; 33-36R; CANR 34; CAP 1; CWRI 5; DAM POET; DLB 15, 20; EWL 3; MTCW 1, 2; RGEL 2

**Dazai Osamu** .................. **SSC 41; TCLC 11**
See Tsushima, Shuji
See also CA 164; DLB 182; EWL 3; MJW; RGSF 2; RGWL 2, 3; TWA

**de Andrade, Carlos Drummond**
See Drummond de Andrade, Carlos

**de Andrade, Mario** 1892-1945
See Andrade, Mario de
See also CA 178; HW 2

**Deane, Norman**
See Creasey, John

**Deane, Seamus (Francis)** 1940- ...... **CLC 122**
See also CA 118; CANR 42

**de Beauvoir, Simone (Lucie Ernestine Marie Bertrand)**
See Beauvoir, Simone (Lucie Ernestine Marie Bertrand) de

**de Beer, P.**
See Bosman, Herman Charles

**de Brissac, Malcolm**
See Dickinson, Peter (Malcolm)

**de Campos, Alvaro**
See Pessoa, Fernando (Antonio Nogueira)

**de Chardin, Pierre Teilhard**
See Teilhard de Chardin, (Marie Joseph) Pierre

**Dee, John** 1527-1608 ............................ **LC 20**
See also DLB 136, 213

**Deer, Sandra** 1940- .......................... **CLC 45**
See also CA 186

**De Ferrari, Gabriella** 1941- ............. **CLC 65**
See also CA 146

**de Filippo, Eduardo** 1900-1984 ... **TCLC 127**
See also CA 132; 114; EWL 3; MTCW 1; RGWL 2, 3

**Defoe, Daniel** 1660(?)-1731 .... **LC 1, 42, 108; WLC**
See also AAYA 27; BRW 3; BRWR 1; BYA 4; CDBLB 1660-1789; CLR 61; DA; DA3; DAB; DAC; DAM MST, NOV; DLB 39, 95, 101; JRDA; LAIT 1; LMFS

1; MAICYA 1, 2; NFS 9, 13; RGEL 2;
SATA 22; TEA; WCH; WLIT 3

**de Gourmont, Remy(-Marie-Charles)**
See Gourmont, Remy(-Marie-Charles) de

**de Gournay, Marie le Jars**
1566-1645 ..................................... **LC 98**
See also FW

**de Hartog, Jan** 1914-2002 ................ **CLC 19**
See also CA 1-4R; 210; CANR 1; DFS 12

**de Hostos, E. M.**
See Hostos (y Bonilla), Eugenio Maria de

**de Hostos, Eugenio M.**
See Hostos (y Bonilla), Eugenio Maria de

**Deighton, Len** .................... **CLC 4, 7, 22, 46**
See Deighton, Leonard Cyril
See also AAYA 6; BEST 89:2; BPFB 1; CD-
BLB 1960 to Present; CMW 4; CN 7;
CPW; DLB 87

**Deighton, Leonard Cyril** 1929-
See Deighton, Len
See also AAYA 57; CA 9-12R; CANR 19,
33, 68; DA3; DAM NOV, POP; MTCW
1, 2

**Dekker, Thomas** 1572(?)-1632 ..... **DC 12; LC
22**
See also CDBLB Before 1660; DAM
DRAM; DLB 62, 172; LMFS 1; RGEL 2

**de Laclos, Pierre Ambroise Franois**
See Laclos, Pierre Ambroise Francois

**Delacroix, (Ferdinand-Victor-)Eugene**
1798-1863 ............................... **NCLC 133**
See also EW 5

**Delafield, E. M.** .............................. **TCLC 61**
See Dashwood, Edmee Elizabeth Monica
de la Pasture
See also DLB 34; RHW

**de la Mare, Walter (John)**
1873-1956 . **SSC 14; TCLC 4, 53; WLC**
See also CA 163; CDBLB 1914-1945; CLR
23; CWRI 5; DA3; DAB; DAC; DAM
MST, POET; DLB 19, 153, 162, 255, 284;
EWL 3; EXPP; HGG; MAICYA 1, 2;
MTCW 1; RGEL 2; RGSF 2; SATA 16;
SUFW 1; TEA; WCH

**de Lamartine, Alphonse (Marie Louis Prat)**
See Lamartine, Alphonse (Marie Louis Prat)
de

**Delaney, Franey**
See O'Hara, John (Henry)

**Delaney, Shelagh** 1939- ..................... **CLC 29**
See also CA 17-20R; CANR 30, 67; CBD;
CD 5; CDBLB 1960 to Present; CWD;
DAM DRAM; DFS 7; DLB 13; MTCW 1

**Delany, Martin Robison**
1812-1885 ................................. **NCLC 93**
See also DLB 50; RGAL 4

**Delany, Mary (Granville Pendarves)**
1700-1788 ................................... **LC 12**

**Delany, Samuel R(ay), Jr.** 1942- ........ **BLC 1;
CLC 8, 14, 38, 141**
See also AAYA 24; AFAW 2; BPFB 1; BW
2, 3; CA 81-84; CANR 27, 43, 115, 116;
CN 7; DAM MULT; DLB 8, 33; FANT;
MTCW 1, 2; RGAL 4; SATA 92; SCFW;
SFW 4; SUFW 2

**De la Ramee, Marie Louise (Ouida)**
1839-1908
See Ouida
See also CA 204; SATA 20

**de la Roche, Mazo** 1879-1961 .......... **CLC 14**
See also CA 85-88; CANR 30; DLB 68;
RGEL 2; RHW; SATA 64

**De La Salle, Innocent**
See Hartmann, Sadakichi

**de Laureamont, Comte**
See Lautreamont

**Delbanco, Nicholas (Franklin)**
1942- ............................. **CLC 6, 13, 167**
See also CA 17-20R, 189; CAAE 189;
CAAS 2; CANR 29, 55, 116; DLB 6, 234

**del Castillo, Michel** 1933- ................. **CLC 38**
See also CA 109; CANR 77

**Deledda, Grazia (Cosima)**
1875(?)-1936 ........................... **TCLC 23**
See also CA 123; 205; DLB 264; EWL 3;
RGWL 2, 3

**Deleuze, Gilles** 1925-1995 ............. **TCLC 116**
See also DLB 296

**Delgado, Abelardo (Lalo) B(arrientos)**
1930-2004 .................................... **HLC 1**
See also CA 131; CAAS 15; CANR 90;
DAM MST, MULT; DLB 82; HW 1, 2

**Delibes, Miguel** ........................... **CLC 8, 18**
See Delibes Setien, Miguel
See also EWL 3

**Delibes Setien, Miguel** 1920-
See Delibes, Miguel
See also CA 45-48; CANR 1, 32; CWW 2;
HW 1; MTCW 1

**DeLillo, Don** 1936- ..... **CLC 8, 10, 13, 27, 39,
54, 76, 143**
See also AMWC 2; AMWS 6; BEST 89:1;
BPFB 1; CA 81-84; CANR 21, 76, 92,
133; CN 7; CPW; DA3; DAM NOV, POP;
DLB 6, 173; EWL 3; MTCW 1, 2; RGAL
4; TUS

**de Lisser, H. G.**
See De Lisser, H(erbert) G(eorge)
See also DLB 117

**De Lisser, H(erbert) G(eorge)**
1878-1944 ................................. **TCLC 12**
See de Lisser, H. G.
See also BW 2; CA 109; 152

**Deloire, Pierre**
See Peguy, Charles (Pierre)

**Deloney, Thomas** 1543(?)-1600 ........... **LC 41**
See also DLB 167; RGEL 2

**Deloria, Ella (Cara)** 1889-1971(?) ..... **NNAL**
See also CA 152; DAM MULT; DLB 175

**Deloria, Vine (Victor), Jr.** 1933- ...... **CLC 21,
122; NNAL**
See also CA 53-56; CANR 5, 20, 48, 98;
DAM MULT; DLB 175; MTCW 1; SATA
21

**del Valle-Inclan, Ramon (Maria)**
See Valle-Inclan, Ramon (Maria) del

**Del Vecchio, John M(ichael)** 1947- .. **CLC 29**
See also CA 110; DLBD 9

**de Man, Paul (Adolph Michel)**
1919-1983 .................................. **CLC 55**
See also CA 128; 111; CANR 61; DLB 67;
MTCW 1, 2

**DeMarinis, Rick** 1934- ...................... **CLC 54**
See also CA 57-60, 184; CAAE 184; CAAS
24; CANR 9, 25, 50; DLB 218

**de Maupassant, (Henri Rene Albert) Guy**
See Maupassant, (Henri Rene Albert) Guy
de

**Dembry, R. Emmet**
See Murfree, Mary Noailles

**Demby, William** 1922- ........... **BLC 1; CLC 53**
See also BW 1, 3; CA 81-84; CANR 81;
DAM MULT; DLB 33

**de Menton, Francisco**
See Chin, Frank (Chew, Jr.)

**Demetrius of Phalerum** c.
307B.C.- ................................... **CMLC 34**

**Demijohn, Thom**
See Disch, Thomas M(ichael)

**De Mille, James** 1833-1880 ......... **NCLC 123**
See also DLB 99, 251

**Deming, Richard** 1915-1983
See Queen, Ellery
See also CA 9-12R; CANR 3, 94; SATA 24

**Democritus** c. 460B.C.-c. 370B.C. . **CMLC 47**

**de Montaigne, Michel (Eyquem)**
See Montaigne, Michel (Eyquem) de

**de Montherlant, Henry (Milon)**
See Montherlant, Henry (Milon) de

**Demosthenes** 384B.C.-322B.C. ...... **CMLC 13**
See also AW 1; DLB 176; RGWL 2, 3

**de Musset, (Louis Charles) Alfred**
See Musset, (Louis Charles) Alfred de

**de Natale, Francine**
See Malzberg, Barry N(athaniel)

**de Navarre, Marguerite** 1492-1549 ..... **LC 61**
See Marguerite d'Angouleme; Marguerite
de Navarre

**Denby, Edwin (Orr)** 1903-1983 ........ **CLC 48**
See also CA 138; 110

**de Nerval, Gerard**
See Nerval, Gerard de

**Denham, John** 1615-1669 ..................... **LC 73**
See also DLB 58, 126; RGEL 2

**Denis, Julio**
See Cortazar, Julio

**Denmark, Harrison**
See Zelazny, Roger (Joseph)

**Dennis, John** 1658-1734 ...................... **LC 11**
See also DLB 101; RGEL 2

**Dennis, Nigel (Forbes)** 1912-1989 ...... **CLC 8**
See also CA 25-28R; 129; DLB 13, 15, 233;
EWL 3; MTCW 1

**Dent, Lester** 1904-1959 .................. **TCLC 72**
See also CA 112; 161; CMW 4; DLB 306;
SFW 4

**De Palma, Brian (Russell)** 1940- ...... **CLC 20**
See also CA 109

**De Quincey, Thomas** 1785-1859 ..... **NCLC 4,
87**
See also BRW 4; CDBLB 1789-1832; DLB
110, 144; RGEL 2

**Deren, Eleanora** 1908(?)-1961
See Deren, Maya
See also CA 192; 111

**Deren, Maya** ............................. **CLC 16, 102**
See Deren, Eleanora

**Derleth, August (William)**
1909-1971 ................................. **CLC 31**
See also BPFB 1; BYA 9, 10; CA 1-4R; 29-
32R; CANR 4; CMW 4; DLB 9; DLBD
17; HGG; SATA 5; SUFW 1

**Der Nister** 1884-1950 ..................... **TCLC 56**
See Nister, Der

**de Routisie, Albert**
See Aragon, Louis

**Derrida, Jacques** 1930- .............. **CLC 24, 87**
See also CA 124; 127; CANR 76, 98, 133;
DLB 242; EWL 3; LMFS 2; MTCW 1;
TWA

**Derry Down Derry**
See Lear, Edward

**Dersonnes, Jacques**
See Simenon, Georges (Jacques Christian)

**Desai, Anita** 1937- ......... **CLC 19, 37, 97, 175**
See also BRWS 5; CA 81-84; CANR 33,
53, 95, 133; CN 7; CWRI 5; DA3; DAB;
DAM NOV; DLB 271; DNFS 2; EWL 3;
FW; MTCW 1, 2; SATA 63, 126

**Desai, Kiran** 1971- ........................... **CLC 119**
See also BYA 16; CA 171; CANR 127

**de Saint-Luc, Jean**
See Glassco, John

**de Saint Roman, Arnaud**
See Aragon, Louis

**Desbordes-Valmore, Marceline**
1786-1859 ................................. **NCLC 97**
See also DLB 217

**Descartes, Rene** 1596-1650 ........... **LC 20, 35**
See also DLB 268; EW 3; GFL Beginnings
to 1789

**Deschamps, Eustache** 1340(?)-1404 .. **LC 103**
   See also DLB 208
**De Sica, Vittorio** 1901(?)-1974 ......... **CLC 20**
   See also CA 117
**Desnos, Robert** 1900-1945 ............. **TCLC 22**
   See also CA 121; 151; CANR 107; DLB
      258; EWL 3; LMFS 2
**Destouches, Louis-Ferdinand**
   1894-1961 ............................... **CLC 9, 15**
   See Celine, Louis-Ferdinand
   See also CA 85-88; CANR 28; MTCW 1
**de Tolignac, Gaston**
   See Griffith, D(avid Lewelyn) W(ark)
**Deutsch, Babette** 1895-1982 ............. **CLC 18**
   See also BYA 3; CA 1-4R; 108; CANR 4,
      79; DLB 45; SATA 1; SATA-Obit 33
**Devenant, William** 1606-1649 ............. **LC 13**
**Devkota, Laxmiprasad** 1909-1959 . **TCLC 23**
   See also CA 123
**De Voto, Bernard (Augustine)**
   1897-1955 ................................. **TCLC 29**
   See also CA 113; 160; DLB 9, 256
**De Vries, Peter** 1910-1993 ..... **CLC 1, 2, 3, 7,**
   **10, 28, 46**
   See also CA 17-20R; 142; CANR 41; DAM
      NOV; DLB 6; DLBY 1982; MTCW 1, 2
**Dewey, John** 1859-1952 .................. **TCLC 95**
   See also CA 114; 170; DLB 246, 270;
      RGAL 4
**Dexter, John**
   See Bradley, Marion Zimmer
   See also GLL 1
**Dexter, Martin**
   See Faust, Frederick (Schiller)
   See also TCWW 2
**Dexter, Pete** 1943- ......................... **CLC 34, 55**
   See also BEST 89:2; CA 127; 131; CANR
      129; CPW; DAM POP; INT CA-131;
      MTCW 1
**Diamano, Silmang**
   See Senghor, Leopold Sedar
**Diamond, Neil** 1941- .......................... **CLC 30**
   See also CA 108
**Diaz del Castillo, Bernal**
   1496-1584 ..................... **HLCS 1; LC 31**
   See also LAW
**di Bassetto, Corno**
   See Shaw, George Bernard
**Dick, Philip K(indred)** 1928-1982 ... **CLC 10,**
   **30, 72; SSC 57**
   See also AAYA 24; BPFB 1; BYA 11; CA
      49-52; 106; CANR 2, 16, 132; CPW;
      DA3; DAM NOV, POP; DLB 8; MTCW
      1, 2; NFS 5; SCFW; SFW 4
**Dickens, Charles (John Huffam)**
   1812-1870 ... **NCLC 3, 8, 18, 26, 37, 50,**
   **86, 105, 113; SSC 17, 49; WLC**
   See also AAYA 23; BRW 5; BRWC 1, 2;
      BYA 1, 2, 3, 13, 14; CDBLB 1832-1890;
      CLR 95; CMW 4; DA; DA3; DAB; DAC;
      DAM MST, NOV; DLB 21, 55, 70, 159,
      166; EXPN; HGG; JRDA; LAIT 1, 2;
      LATS 1:1; LMFS 1; MAICYA 1, 2; NFS
      4, 5, 10, 14, 20; RGEL 2; RGSF 2; SATA
      15; SUFW 1; TEA; WCH; WLIT 4; WYA
**Dickey, James (Lafayette)**
   1923-1997 .... **CLC 1, 2, 4, 7, 10, 15, 47,**
   **109; PC 40; TCLC 151**
   See also AAYA 50; AITN 1, 2; AMWS 4;
      BPFB 1; CA 9-12R; 156; CABS 2; CANR
      10, 48, 61, 105; CDALB 1968-1988; CP
      7; CPW; CSW; DA3; DAM NOV, POET,
      POP; DLB 5, 193; DLBD 7; DLBY 1982,
      1993, 1996, 1997, 1998; EWL 3; INT
      CANR-10; MTCW 1, 2; NFS 9; PFS 6,
      11; RGAL 4; TUS
**Dickey, William** 1928-1994 .......... **CLC 3, 28**
   See also CA 9-12R; 145; CANR 24, 79;
      DLB 5

**Dickinson, Charles** 1951- ................. **CLC 49**
   See also CA 128
**Dickinson, Emily (Elizabeth)**
   1830-1886 ... **NCLC 21, 77; PC 1; WLC**
   See also AAYA 22; AMW; AMWR 1;
      CDALB 1865-1917; DA; DA3; DAB;
      DAC; DAM MST, POET; DLB 1, 243;
      EXPP; MAWW; PAB; PFS 1, 2, 3, 4, 5,
      6, 8, 10, 11, 13, 16; RGAL 4; SATA 29;
      TUS; WP; WYA
**Dickinson, Mrs. Herbert Ward**
   See Phelps, Elizabeth Stuart
**Dickinson, Peter (Malcolm)** 1927- .. **CLC 12,**
   **35**
   See also AAYA 9, 49; BYA 5; CA 41-44R;
      CANR 31, 58, 88; CLR 29; CMW 4; DLB
      87, 161, 276; JRDA; MAICYA 1, 2;
      SATA 5, 62, 95, 150; SFW 4; WYA; YAW
**Dickson, Carr**
   See Carr, John Dickson
**Dickson, Carter**
   See Carr, John Dickson
**Diderot, Denis** 1713-1784 ..................... **LC 26**
   See also EW 4; GFL Beginnings to 1789;
      LMFS 1; RGWL 2, 3
**Didion, Joan** 1934- . **CLC 1, 3, 8, 14, 32, 129**
   See also AITN 1; AMWS 4; CA 5-8R;
      CANR 14, 52, 76, 125; CDALB 1968-
      1988; CN 7; DA3; DAM NOV; DLB 2,
      173, 185; DLBY 1981, 1986; EWL 3;
      MAWW; MTCW 1, 2; NFS 3; RGAL 4;
      TCWW 2; TUS
**Dietrich, Robert**
   See Hunt, E(verette) Howard, (Jr.)
**Difusa, Pati**
   See Almodovar, Pedro
**Dillard, Annie** 1945- .............. **CLC 9, 60, 115**
   See also AAYA 6, 43; AMWS 6; ANW; CA
      49-52; CANR 3, 43, 62, 90, 125; DA3;
      DAM NOV; DLB 275, 278; DLBY 1980;
      LAIT 4, 5; MTCW 1, 2; NCFS 1; RGAL
      4; SATA 10, 140; TUS
**Dillard, R(ichard) H(enry) W(ilde)**
   1937- ............................................ **CLC 5**
   See also CA 21-24R; CAAS 7; CANR 10;
      CP 7; CSW; DLB 5, 244
**Dillon, Eilis** 1920-1994 ...................... **CLC 17**
   See also CA 9-12R, 182; 147; CAAE 182;
      CAAS 3; CANR 4, 38, 78; CLR 26; MAI-
      CYA 1, 2; MAICYAS 1; SATA 2, 74;
      SATA-Essay 105; SATA-Obit 83; YAW
**Dimont, Penelope**
   See Mortimer, Penelope (Ruth)
**Dinesen, Isak** ..... **CLC 10, 29, 95; SSC 7, 75**
   See Blixen, Karen (Christentze Dinesen)
   See also EW 10; EWL 3; EXPS; FW; HGG;
      LAIT 3; MTCW 1; NCFS 2; NFS 9;
      RGSF 2; RGWL 2, 3; SSFS 3, 6, 13;
      WLIT 2
**Ding Ling** ......................................... **CLC 68**
   See Chiang, Pin-chin
   See also RGWL 3
**Diphusa, Patty**
   See Almodovar, Pedro
**Disch, Thomas M(ichael)** 1940- ... **CLC 7, 36**
   See Disch, Tom
   See also AAYA 17; BPFB 1; CA 21-24R;
      CAAS 4; CANR 17, 36, 54, 89; CLR 18;
      CP 7; DA3; DLB 8; HGG; MAICYA 1, 2;
      MTCW 1, 2; SAAS 15; SATA 92; SCFW;
      SFW 4; SUFW 2
**Disch, Tom**
   See Disch, Thomas M(ichael)
   See also DLB 282
**d'Isly, Georges**
   See Simenon, Georges (Jacques Christian)
**Disraeli, Benjamin** 1804-1881 ... **NCLC 2, 39,**
   **79**
   See also BRW 4; DLB 21, 55; RGEL 2

**Ditcum, Steve**
   See Crumb, R(obert)
**Dixon, Paige**
   See Corcoran, Barbara (Asenath)
**Dixon, Stephen** 1936- ......... **CLC 52; SSC 16**
   See also AMWS 12; CA 89-92; CANR 17,
      40, 54, 91; CN 7; DLB 130
**Djebar, Assia** 1936- .......................... **CLC 182**
   See also CA 188; EWL 3; RGWL 3; WLIT
      2
**Doak, Annie**
   See Dillard, Annie
**Dobell, Sydney Thompson**
   1824-1874 ................................. **NCLC 43**
   See also DLB 32; RGEL 2
**Doblin, Alfred** ....................... **TCLC 13**
   See Doeblin, Alfred
   See also CDWLB 2; EWL 3; RGWL 2, 3
**Dobroliubov, Nikolai Aleksandrovich**
   See Dobrolyubov, Nikolai Alexandrovich
   See also DLB 277
**Dobrolyubov, Nikolai Alexandrovich**
   1836-1861 ................................... **NCLC 5**
   See Dobroliubov, Nikolai Aleksandrovich
**Dobson, Austin** 1840-1921 ............. **TCLC 79**
   See also DLB 35, 144
**Dobyns, Stephen** 1941- ..................... **CLC 37**
   See also AMWS 13; CA 45-48; CANR 2,
      18, 99; CMW 4; CP 7
**Doctorow, E(dgar) L(aurence)**
   1931- ....... **CLC 6, 11, 15, 18, 37, 44, 65,**
   **113**
   See also AAYA 22; AITN 2; AMWS 4;
      BEST 89:3; BPFB 1; CA 45-48; CANR
      2, 33, 51, 76, 97, 133; CDALB 1968-
      1988; CN 7; CPW; DA3; DAM NOV,
      POP; DLB 2, 28, 173; DLBY 1980; EWL
      3; LAIT 3; MTCW 1, 2; NFS 6; RGAL 4;
      RHW; TUS
**Dodgson, Charles L(utwidge)** 1832-1898
   See Carroll, Lewis
   See also CLR 2; DA; DA3; DAB; DAC;
      DAM MST, NOV, POET; MAICYA 1, 2;
      SATA 100; YABC 2
**Dodsley, Robert** 1703-1764 ................. **LC 97**
   See also DLB 95; RGEL 2
**Dodson, Owen (Vincent)** 1914-1983 .. **BLC 1;**
   **CLC 79**
   See also BW 1; CA 65-68; 110; CANR 24;
      DAM MULT; DLB 76
**Doeblin, Alfred** 1878-1957 .............. **TCLC 13**
   See Doblin, Alfred
   See also CA 110; 141; DLB 66
**Doerr, Harriet** 1910-2002 .................. **CLC 34**
   See also CA 117; 122; 213; CANR 47; INT
      CA-122; LATS 1:2
**Domecq, H(onorio Bustos)**
   See Bioy Casares, Adolfo
**Domecq, H(onorio) Bustos**
   See Bioy Casares, Adolfo; Borges, Jorge
      Luis
**Domini, Rey**
   See Lorde, Audre (Geraldine)
   See also GLL 1
**Dominique**
   See Proust, (Valentin-Louis-George-Eugene)
      Marcel
**Don, A**
   See Stephen, Sir Leslie
**Donaldson, Stephen R(eeder)**
   1947- ................................... **CLC 46, 138**
   See also AAYA 36; BPFB 1; CA 89-92;
      CANR 13, 55, 99; CPW; DAM POP;
      FANT; INT CANR-13; SATA 121; SFW
      4; SUFW 1, 2
**Donleavy, J(ames) P(atrick)** 1926- .... **CLC 1,**
   **4, 6, 10, 45**
   See also AITN 2; BPFB 1; CA 9-12R;
      CANR 24, 49, 62, 80, 124; CBD; CD 5;

CN 7; DLB 6, 173; INT CANR-24; MTCW 1, 2; RGAL 4

**Donnadieu, Marguerite**
See Duras, Marguerite

**Donne, John** 1572-1631 ... **LC 10, 24, 91; PC 1, 43; WLC**
See also BRW 1; BRWC 1; BRWR 2; CD-BLB Before 1660; DA; DAB; DAC; DAM MST, POET; DLB 121, 151; EXPP; PAB; PFS 2, 11; RGAL 3; TEA; WLIT 3; WP

**Donnell, David** 1939(?)- ..................... **CLC 34**
See also CA 197

**Donoghue, P. S.**
See Hunt, E(verette) Howard, (Jr.)

**Donoso (Yanez), Jose** 1924-1996 ... **CLC 4, 8, 11, 32, 99; HLC 1; SSC 34; TCLC 133**
See also CA 81-84; 155; CANR 32, 73; CD-WLB 3; CWW 2; DAM MULT; DLB 113; EWL 3; HW 1, 2; LAW; LAWS 1; MTCW 1, 2; RGSF 2; WLIT 1

**Donovan, John** 1928-1992 ................. **CLC 35**
See also AAYA 20; CA 97-100; 137; CLR 3; MAICYA 1, 2; SATA 72; SATA-Brief 29; YAW

**Don Roberto**
See Cunninghame Graham, Robert (Gallnigad) Bontine

**Doolittle, Hilda** 1886-1961 . **CLC 3, 8, 14, 31, 34, 73; PC 5; WLC**
See H. D.
See also AMWS 1; CA 97-100; CANR 35, 131; DA; DAC; DAM MST, POET; DLB 4, 45; EWL 3; FW; GLL 1; LMFS 2; MAWW; MTCW 1, 2; PFS 6; RGAL 4

**Doppo, Kunikida** ........................... **TCLC 99**
See Kunikida Doppo

**Dorfman, Ariel** 1942- ......... **CLC 48, 77, 189; HLC 1**
See also CA 124; 130; CANR 67, 70; CWW 2; DAM MULT; DFS 4; EWL 3; HW 1, 2; INT CA-130; WLIT 1

**Dorn, Edward (Merton)**
1929-1999 ............................ **CLC 10, 18**
See also CA 93-96; 187; CANR 42, 79; CP 7; DLB 5; INT CA-93-96; WP

**Dor-Ner, Zvi** ...................................... **CLC 70**

**Dorris, Michael (Anthony)**
1945-1997 ......................... **CLC 109; NNAL**
See also AAYA 20; BEST 90:1; BYA 12; CA 102; 157; CANR 19, 46, 75; CLR 58; DA3; DAM MULT, NOV; DLB 175; LAIT 5; MTCW 2; NFS 3; RGAL 4; SATA 75; SATA-Obit 94; TCWW 2; YAW

**Dorris, Michael A.**
See Dorris, Michael (Anthony)

**Dorsan, Luc**
See Simenon, Georges (Jacques Christian)

**Dorsange, Jean**
See Simenon, Georges (Jacques Christian)

**Dorset**
See Sackville, Thomas

**Dos Passos, John (Roderigo)**
1896-1970 ... **CLC 1, 4, 8, 11, 15, 25, 34, 82; WLC**
See also AMW; BPFB 1; CA 1-4R; 29-32R; CANR 3; CDALB 1929-1941; DA; DA3; DAB; DAC; DAM MST, NOV; DLB 4, 9, 274; DLBD 1, 15; DLBY 1996; EWL 3; MTCW 1, 2; NFS 14; RGAL 4; TUS

**Dossage, Jean**
See Simenon, Georges (Jacques Christian)

**Dostoevsky, Fedor Mikhailovich**
1821-1881 .. **NCLC 2, 7, 21, 33, 43, 119; SSC 2, 33, 44; WLC**
See Dostoevsky, Fyodor
See also AAYA 40; DA; DA3; DAB; DAC; DAM MST, NOV; EW 7; EXPN; NFS 3, 8; RGSF 2; RGWL 2, 3; SSFS 8; TWA

**Dostoevsky, Fyodor**
See Dostoevsky, Fedor Mikhailovich
See also DLB 238; LATS 1:1; LMFS 1, 2

**Doty, M. R.**
See Doty, Mark (Alan)

**Doty, Mark**
See Doty, Mark (Alan)

**Doty, Mark (Alan)** 1953(?)- .... **CLC 176; PC 53**
See also AMWS 11; CA 161, 183; CAAE 183; CANR 110

**Doty, Mark A.**
See Doty, Mark (Alan)

**Doughty, Charles M(ontagu)**
1843-1926 ............................... **TCLC 27**
See also CA 115; 178; DLB 19, 57, 174

**Douglas, Ellen** ................................. **CLC 73**
See Haxton, Josephine Ayres; Williamson, Ellen Douglas
See also CN 7; CSW; DLB 292

**Douglas, Gavin** 1475(?)-1522 ............... **LC 20**
See also DLB 132; RGEL 2

**Douglas, George**
See Brown, George Douglas
See also RGEL 2

**Douglas, Keith (Castellain)**
1920-1944 ................................. **TCLC 40**
See also BRW 7; CA 160; DLB 27; EWL 3; PAB; RGEL 2

**Douglas, Leonard**
See Bradbury, Ray (Douglas)

**Douglas, Michael**
See Crichton, (John) Michael

**Douglas, (George) Norman**
1868-1952 ................................. **TCLC 68**
See also BRW 6; CA 119; 157; DLB 34, 195; RGEL 2

**Douglas, William**
See Brown, George Douglas

**Douglass, Frederick** 1817(?)-1895 ..... **BLC 1; NCLC 7, 55, 141; WLC**
See also AAYA 48; AFAW 1, 2; AMWC 1; AMWS 3; CDALB 1640-1865; DA; DA3; DAC; DAM MST, MULT; DLB 1, 43, 50, 79, 243; FW; LAIT 2; NCFS 2; RGAL 4; SATA 29

**Dourado, (Waldomiro Freitas) Autran**
1926- ..................................... **CLC 23, 60**
See also CA 25-28R; 179; CANR 34, 81; DLB 145; HW 2

**Dourado, Waldomiro Autran**
See Dourado, (Waldomiro Freitas) Autran
See also CA 179

**Dove, Rita (Frances)** 1952- . **BLCS; CLC 50, 81; PC 6**
See also AAYA 46; AMWS 4; BW 2; CA 109; CAAS 19; CANR 27, 42, 68, 76, 97, 132; CDALBS; CP 7; CSW; CWP; DA3; DAM MULT, POET; DLB 120; EWL 3; EXPP; MTCW 1; PFS 1, 15; RGAL 4

**Doveglion**
See Villa, Jose Garcia

**Dowell, Coleman** 1925-1985 .............. **CLC 60**
See also CA 25-28R; 117; CANR 10; DLB 130; GLL 2

**Dowson, Ernest (Christopher)**
1867-1900 ................................. **TCLC 4**
See also CA 105; 150; DLB 19, 135; RGEL 2

**Doyle, A. Conan**
See Doyle, Sir Arthur Conan

**Doyle, Sir Arthur Conan**
1859-1930 ....... **SSC 12; TCLC 7; WLC**
See Conan Doyle, Arthur
See also AAYA 14; BRWS 2; CA 104; 122; CANR 131; CDBLB 1890-1914; CMW 4; DA; DA3; DAB; DAC; DAM MST, NOV; DLB 18, 70, 156, 178; EXPS; HGG; LAIT 2; MSW; MTCW 1, 2; RGEL 2; RGSF 2; RHW; SATA 24; SCFW 4; SFW 4; SSFS 2; TEA; WCH; WLIT 4; WYA; YAW

**Doyle, Conan**
See Doyle, Sir Arthur Conan

**Doyle, John**
See Graves, Robert (von Ranke)

**Doyle, Roddy** 1958(?)- ............... **CLC 81, 178**
See also AAYA 14; BRWS 5; CA 143; CANR 73, 128; CN 7; DA3; DLB 194

**Doyle, Sir A. Conan**
See Doyle, Sir Arthur Conan

**Dr. A**
See Asimov, Isaac; Silverstein, Alvin; Silverstein, Virginia B(arbara Opshelor)

**Drabble, Margaret** 1939- ...... **CLC 2, 3, 5, 8, 10, 22, 53, 129**
See also BRWS 4; CA 13-16R; CANR 18, 35, 63, 112, 131; CDBLB 1960 to Present; CN 7; CPW; DA3; DAB; DAC; DAM MST, NOV, POP; DLB 14, 155, 231; EWL 3; FW; MTCW 1, 2; RGEL 2; SATA 48; TEA

**Drakulic, Slavenka** 1949- ................ **CLC 173**
See also CA 144; CANR 92

**Drakulic-Ilic, Slavenka**
See Drakulic, Slavenka

**Drapier, M. B.**
See Swift, Jonathan

**Drayham, James**
See Mencken, H(enry) L(ouis)

**Drayton, Michael** 1563-1631 .................. **LC 8**
See also DAM POET; DLB 121; RGEL 2

**Dreadstone, Carl**
See Campbell, (John) Ramsey

**Dreiser, Theodore (Herman Albert)**
1871-1945 .... **SSC 30; TCLC 10, 18, 35, 83; WLC**
See also AMW; AMWC 2; AMWR 2; BYA 15, 16; CA 106; 132; CDALB 1865-1917; DA; DA3; DAC; DAM MST, NOV; DLB 9, 12, 102, 137; DLBD 1; EWL 3; LAIT 2; LMFS 2; MTCW 1, 2; NFS 8, 17; RGAL 4; TUS

**Drexler, Rosalyn** 1926- ................... **CLC 2, 6**
See also CA 81-84; CAD; CANR 68, 124; CD 5; CWD

**Dreyer, Carl Theodor** 1889-1968 ...... **CLC 16**
See also CA 116

**Drieu la Rochelle, Pierre(-Eugene)**
1893-1945 ................................. **TCLC 21**
See also CA 117; DLB 72; EWL 3; GFL 1789 to the Present

**Drinkwater, John** 1882-1937 .......... **TCLC 57**
See also CA 109; 149; DLB 10, 19, 149; RGEL 2

**Drop Shot**
See Cable, George Washington

**Droste-Hulshoff, Annette Freiin von**
1797-1848 .......................... **NCLC 3, 133**
See also CDWLB 2; DLB 133; RGSF 2; RGWL 2, 3

**Drummond, Walter**
See Silverberg, Robert

**Drummond, William Henry**
1854-1907 ................................. **TCLC 25**
See also CA 160; DLB 92

**Drummond de Andrade, Carlos**
1902-1987 .............. **CLC 18; TCLC 139**
See Andrade, Carlos Drummond de
See also CA 132; 123; LAW

**Drummond of Hawthornden, William**
1585-1649 ................................. **LC 83**
See also DLB 121, 213; RGEL 2

**Drury, Allen (Stuart)** 1918-1998 ....... **CLC 37**
See also CA 57-60; 170; CANR 18, 52; CN 7; INT CANR-18

**Dryden, John** 1631-1700 ..... **DC 3; LC 3, 21; PC 25; WLC**
    See also BRW 2; CDBLB 1660-1789; DA; DAB; DAC; DAM DRAM, MST, POET; DLB 80, 101, 131; EXPP; IDTP; LMFS 1; RGEL 2; TEA; WLIT 3

**du Bellay, Joachim** 1524-1560 ............. **LC 92**
    See also GFL Beginnings to 1789; RGWL 2, 3

**Duberman, Martin (Bauml)** 1930- ..... **CLC 8**
    See also CA 1-4R; CAD; CANR 2, 63; CD 5

**Dubie, Norman (Evans)** 1945- .......... **CLC 36**
    See also CA 69-72; CANR 12, 115; CP 7; DLB 120; PFS 12

**Du Bois, W(illiam) E(dward) B(urghardt)** 1868-1963 ..... **BLC 1; CLC 1, 2, 13, 64, 96; HR 2; WLC**
    See also AAYA 40; AFAW 1, 2; AMWC 1; AMWS 2; BW 1, 3; CA 85-88; CANR 34, 82, 132; CDALB 1865-1917; DA; DA3; DAC; DAM MST, MULT, NOV; DLB 47, 50, 91, 246, 284; EWL 3; EXPP; LAIT 2; LMFS 2; MTCW 1, 2; NCFS 1; PFS 13; RGAL 4; SATA 42

**Dubus, Andre** 1936-1999 ..... **CLC 13, 36, 97; SSC 15**
    See also AMWS 7; CA 21-24R; 177; CANR 17; CN 7; CSW; DLB 130; INT CANR-17; RGAL 4; SSFS 10

**Duca Minimo**
    See D'Annunzio, Gabriele

**Ducharme, Rejean** 1941- ................... **CLC 74**
    See also CA 165; DLB 60

**du Chatelet, Emilie** 1706-1749 ............ **LC 96**

**Duchen, Claire** ..................................... **CLC 65**

**Duclos, Charles Pinot-** 1704-1772 ........ **LC 1**
    See also GFL Beginnings to 1789

**Dudek, Louis** 1918-2001 ............. **CLC 11, 19**
    See also CA 45-48; 215; CAAS 14; CANR 1; CP 7; DLB 88

**Duerrenmatt, Friedrich** 1921-1990 ... **CLC 1, 4, 8, 11, 15, 43, 102**
    See Durrenmatt, Friedrich
    See also CA 17-20R; CANR 33; CMW 4; DAM DRAM; DLB 69, 124; MTCW 1, 2

**Duffy, Bruce** 1953(?)- ......................... **CLC 50**
    See also CA 172

**Duffy, Maureen** 1933- ........................ **CLC 37**
    See also CA 25-28R; CANR 33, 68; CBD; CN 7; CP 7; CWD; CWP; DFS 15; DLB 14; FW; MTCW 1

**Du Fu**
    See Tu Fu
    See also RGWL 2, 3

**Dugan, Alan** 1923-2003 ................... **CLC 2, 6**
    See also CA 81-84; 220; CANR 119; CP 7; DLB 5; PFS 10

**du Gard, Roger Martin**
    See Martin du Gard, Roger

**Duhamel, Georges** 1884-1966 ............. **CLC 8**
    See also CA 81-84; 25-28R; CANR 35; DLB 65; EWL 3; GFL 1789 to the Present; MTCW 1

**Dujardin, Edouard (Emile Louis)** 1861-1949 ................................. **TCLC 13**
    See also CA 109; DLB 123

**Duke, Raoul**
    See Thompson, Hunter S(tockton)

**Dulles, John Foster** 1888-1959 ....... **TCLC 72**
    See also CA 115; 149

**Dumas, Alexandre (pere)** 1802-1870 ............. **NCLC 11, 71; WLC**
    See also AAYA 22; BYA 3; DA; DA3; DAB; DAC; DAM MST, NOV; DLB 119, 192; EW 6; GFL 1789 to the Present; LAIT 1, 2; NFS 14, 19; RGWL 2, 3; SATA 18; TWA; WCH

**Dumas, Alexandre (fils)** 1824-1895 ...... **DC 1; NCLC 9**
    See also DLB 192; GFL 1789 to the Present; RGWL 2, 3

**Dumas, Claudine**
    See Malzberg, Barry N(athaniel)

**Dumas, Henry L.** 1934-1968 ......... **CLC 6, 62**
    See also BW 1; CA 85-88; DLB 41; RGAL 4

**du Maurier, Daphne** 1907-1989 .. **CLC 6, 11, 59; SSC 18**
    See also AAYA 37; BPFB 1; BRWS 3; CA 5-8R; 128; CANR 6, 55; CMW 4; CPW; DA3; DAB; DAC; DAM MST, POP; DLB 191; HGG; LAIT 3; MSW; MTCW 1, 2; NFS 12; RGEL 2; RGSF 2; RHW; SATA 27; SATA-Obit 60; SSFS 14, 16; TEA

**Du Maurier, George** 1834-1896 ..... **NCLC 86**
    See also DLB 153, 178; RGEL 2

**Dunbar, Paul Laurence** 1872-1906 ... **BLC 1; PC 5; SSC 8; TCLC 2, 12; WLC**
    See also AFAW 1, 2; AMWS 2; BW 1, 3; CA 104; 124; CANR 79; CDALB 1865-1917; DA; DA3; DAC; DAM MST, MULT, POET; DLB 50, 54, 78; EXPP; RGAL 4; SATA 34

**Dunbar, William** 1460(?)-1520(?) ........ **LC 20**
    See also BRWS 8; DLB 132, 146; RGEL 2

**Dunbar-Nelson, Alice** ........................... **HR 2**
    See Nelson, Alice Ruth Moore Dunbar

**Duncan, Dora Angela**
    See Duncan, Isadora

**Duncan, Isadora** 1877(?)-1927 ....... **TCLC 68**
    See also CA 118; 149

**Duncan, Lois** 1934- ........................... **CLC 26**
    See also AAYA 4, 34; BYA 6, 8; CA 1-4R; CANR 2, 23, 36, 111; CLR 29; JRDA; MAICYA 1, 2; MAICYAS 1; SAAS 2; SATA 1, 36, 75, 133, 141; SATA-Essay 141; WYA; YAW

**Duncan, Robert (Edward)** 1919-1988 .... **CLC 1, 2, 4, 7, 15, 41, 55; PC 2**
    See also BG 2; CA 9-12R; 124; CANR 28, 62; DAM POET; DLB 5, 16, 193; EWL 3; MTCW 1, 2; PFS 13; RGAL 4; WP

**Duncan, Sara Jeannette** 1861-1922 ................................ **TCLC 60**
    See also CA 157; DLB 92

**Dunlap, William** 1766-1839 .............. **NCLC 2**
    See also DLB 30, 37, 59; RGAL 4

**Dunn, Douglas (Eaglesham)** 1942- .... **CLC 6, 40**
    See also CA 45-48; CANR 2, 33, 126; CP 7; DLB 40; MTCW 1

**Dunn, Katherine (Karen)** 1945- ....... **CLC 71**
    See also CA 33-36R; CANR 72; HGG; MTCW 1

**Dunn, Stephen (Elliott)** 1939- .......... **CLC 36**
    See also AMWS 11; CA 33-36R; CANR 12, 48, 53, 105; CP 7; DLB 105; PFS 21

**Dunne, Finley Peter** 1867-1936 ...... **TCLC 28**
    See also CA 108; 178; DLB 11, 23; RGAL 4

**Dunne, John Gregory** 1932-2003 ..... **CLC 28**
    See also CA 25-28R; 222; CANR 14, 50; CN 7; DLBY 1980

**Dunsany, Lord** ........................... **TCLC 2, 59**
    See Dunsany, Edward John Moreton Drax Plunkett
    See also DLB 77, 153, 156, 255; FANT; IDTP; RGEL 2; SFW 4; SUFW 1

**Dunsany, Edward John Moreton Drax Plunkett** 1878-1957
    See Dunsany, Lord
    See also CA 104; 148; DLB 10; MTCW 1

**Duns Scotus, John** 1266(?)-1308 ... **CMLC 59**
    See also DLB 115

**du Perry, Jean**
    See Simenon, Georges (Jacques Christian)

**Durang, Christopher (Ferdinand)** 1949- ................................... **CLC 27, 38**
    See also CA 105; CAD; CANR 50, 76, 130; CD 5; MTCW 1

**Duras, Marguerite** 1914-1996 . **CLC 3, 6, 11, 20, 34, 40, 68, 100; SSC 40**
    See also BPFB 1; CA 25-28R; 151; CANR 50; CWW 2; DLB 83; EWL 3; GFL 1789 to the Present; IDFW 4; MTCW 1, 2; RGWL 2, 3; TWA

**Durban, (Rosa) Pam** 1947- ............... **CLC 39**
    See also CA 123; CANR 98; CSW

**Durcan, Paul** 1944- ...................... **CLC 43, 70**
    See also CA 134; CANR 123; CP 7; DAM POET; EWL 3

**Durfey, Thomas** 1653-1723 ................. **LC 94**
    See also DLB 80; RGEL 2

**Durkheim, Emile** 1858-1917 .......... **TCLC 55**

**Durrell, Lawrence (George)** 1912-1990 ..... **CLC 1, 4, 6, 8, 13, 27, 41**
    See also BPFB 1; BRWS 1; CA 9-12R; 132; CANR 40, 77; CDBLB 1945-1960; DAM NOV; DLB 15, 27, 204; DLBY 1990; EWL 3; MTCW 1, 2; RGEL 2; SFW 4; TEA

**Durrenmatt, Friedrich**
    See Duerrenmatt, Friedrich
    See also CDWLB 2; EW 13; EWL 3; RGWL 2, 3

**Dutt, Michael Madhusudan** 1824-1873 ................................ **NCLC 118**

**Dutt, Toru** 1856-1877 ...................... **NCLC 29**
    See also DLB 240

**Dwight, Timothy** 1752-1817 .......... **NCLC 13**
    See also DLB 37; RGAL 4

**Dworkin, Andrea** 1946- ............. **CLC 43, 123**
    See also CA 77-80; CAAS 21; CANR 16, 39, 76, 96; FW; GLL 1; INT CANR-16; MTCW 1, 2

**Dwyer, Deanna**
    See Koontz, Dean R(ay)

**Dwyer, K. R.**
    See Koontz, Dean R(ay)

**Dybek, Stuart** 1942- .......... **CLC 114; SSC 55**
    See also CA 97-100; CANR 39; DLB 130

**Dye, Richard**
    See De Voto, Bernard (Augustine)

**Dyer, Geoff** 1958- ............................ **CLC 149**
    See also CA 125; CANR 88

**Dyer, George** 1755-1841 ............... **NCLC 129**
    See also DLB 93

**Dylan, Bob** 1941- .... **CLC 3, 4, 6, 12, 77; PC 37**
    See also CA 41-44R; CANR 108; CP 7; DLB 16

**Dyson, John** 1943- ............................ **CLC 70**
    See also CA 144

**Dzyubin, Eduard Georgievich** 1895-1934
    See Bagritsky, Eduard
    See also CA 170

**E. V. L.**
    See Lucas, E(dward) V(errall)

**Eagleton, Terence (Francis)** 1943- .. **CLC 63, 132**
    See also CA 57-60; CANR 7, 23, 68, 115; DLB 242; LMFS 2; MTCW 1, 2

**Eagleton, Terry**
    See Eagleton, Terence (Francis)

**Early, Jack**
    See Scoppettone, Sandra
    See also GLL 1

**East, Michael**
    See West, Morris L(anglo)

**Eastaway, Edward**
    See Thomas, (Philip) Edward

**Eastlake, William (Derry)**
1917-1997 ..................... **CLC 8**
See also CA 5-8R; 158; CAAS 1; CANR 5, 63; CN 7; DLB 6, 206; INT CANR-5; TCWW 2

**Eastman, Charles A(lexander)**
1858-1939 ........... **NNAL; TCLC 55**
See also CA 179; CANR 91; DAM MULT; DLB 175; YABC 1

**Eaton, Edith Maude** 1865-1914 ........... **AAL**
See Far, Sui Sin
See also CA 154; DLB 221; FW

**Eaton, (Lillie) Winnifred** 1875-1954 .... **AAL**
See also CA 217; DLB 221; RGAL 4

**Eberhart, Richard (Ghormley)**
1904- ..................... **CLC 3, 11, 19, 56**
See also AMW; CA 1-4R; CANR 2, 125; CDALB 1941-1968; CP 7; DAM POET; DLB 48; MTCW 1; RGAL 4

**Eberstadt, Fernanda** 1960- .............. **CLC 39**
See also CA 136; CANR 69, 128

**Echegaray (y Eizaguirre), Jose (Maria Waldo)** 1832-1916 .... **HLCS 1; TCLC 4**
See also CA 104; CANR 32; EWL 3; HW 1; MTCW 1

**Echeverria, (Jose) Esteban (Antonino)**
1805-1851 ................... **NCLC 18**
See also LAW

**Echo**
See Proust, (Valentin-Louis-George-Eugene) Marcel

**Eckert, Allan W.** 1931- ..................... **CLC 17**
See also AAYA 18; BYA 2; CA 13-16R; CANR 14, 45; INT CANR-14; MAICYA 2; MAICYAS 1; SAAS 21; SATA 29, 91; SATA-Brief 27

**Eckhart, Meister** 1260(?)-1327(?) ... **CMLC 9**
See also DLB 115; LMFS 1

**Eckmar, F. R.**
See de Hartog, Jan

**Eco, Umberto** 1932- ........... **CLC 28, 60, 142**
See also BEST 90:1; BPFB 1; CA 77-80; CANR 12, 33, 55, 110, 131; CPW; CWW 2; DA3; DAM NOV, POP; DLB 196, 242; EWL 3; MSW; MTCW 1, 2; RGWL 3

**Eddison, E(ric) R(ucker)**
1882-1945 ..................... **TCLC 15**
See also CA 109; 156; DLB 255; FANT; SFW 4; SUFW 1

**Eddy, Mary (Ann Morse) Baker**
1821-1910 ............................. **TCLC 71**
See also CA 113; 174

**Edel, (Joseph) Leon** 1907-1997 .. **CLC 29, 34**
See also CA 1-4R; 161; CANR 1, 22, 112; DLB 103; INT CANR-22

**Eden, Emily** 1797-1869 ................... **NCLC 10**

**Edgar, David** 1948- ........................... **CLC 42**
See also CA 57-60; CANR 12, 61, 112; CBD; CD 5; DAM DRAM; DFS 15; DLB 13, 233; MTCW 1

**Edgerton, Clyde (Carlyle)** 1944- ...... **CLC 39**
See also AAYA 17; CA 118; 134; CANR 64, 125; CSW; DLB 278; INT CA-134; YAW

**Edgeworth, Maria** 1768-1849 .... **NCLC 1, 51**
See also BRWS 3; DLB 116, 159, 163; FW; RGEL 2; SATA 21; TEA; WLIT 3

**Edmonds, Paul**
See Kuttner, Henry

**Edmonds, Walter D(umaux)**
1903-1998 ............................. **CLC 35**
See also BYA 2; CA 5-8R; CANR 2; CWRI 5; DLB 9; LAIT 1; MAICYA 1, 2; RHW; SAAS 4; SATA 1, 27; SATA-Obit 99

**Edmondson, Wallace**
See Ellison, Harlan (Jay)

**Edson, Margaret** 1961- ...................... **DC 24**
See also CA 190; DFS 13; DLB 266

**Edson, Russell** 1935- ......................... **CLC 13**
See also CA 33-36R; CANR 115; DLB 244; WP

**Edwards, Bronwen Elizabeth**
See Rose, Wendy

**Edwards, G(erald) B(asil)**
1899-1976 ............................. **CLC 25**
See also CA 201; 110

**Edwards, Gus** 1939- ......................... **CLC 43**
See also CA 108; INT CA-108

**Edwards, Jonathan** 1703-1758 ........ **LC 7, 54**
See also AMW; DA; DAC; DAM MST; DLB 24, 270; RGAL 4; TUS

**Edwards, Sarah Pierpont** 1710-1758 .. **LC 87**
See also DLB 200

**Efron, Marina Ivanovna Tsvetaeva**
See Tsvetaeva (Efron), Marina (Ivanovna)

**Egeria** fl. 4th cent. - ......................... **CMLC 70**

**Egoyan, Atom** 1960- ......................... **CLC 151**
See also CA 157

**Ehle, John (Marsden, Jr.)** 1925- ..... **CLC 27**
See also CA 9-12R; CSW

**Ehrenbourg, Ilya (Grigorevich)**
See Ehrenburg, Ilya (Grigoryevich)

**Ehrenburg, Ilya (Grigoryevich)**
1891-1967 ..................... **CLC 18, 34, 62**
See Erenburg, Il'ia Grigor'evich
See also CA 102; 25-28R; EWL 3

**Ehrenburg, Ilyo (Grigoryevich)**
See Ehrenburg, Ilya (Grigoryevich)

**Ehrenreich, Barbara** 1941- ............. **CLC 110**
See also BEST 90:4; CA 73-76; CANR 16, 37, 62, 117; DLB 246; FW; MTCW 1, 2

**Eich, Gunter**
See Eich, Gunter
See also RGWL 2, 3

**Eich, Gunter** 1907-1972 ..................... **CLC 15**
See Eich, Gunter
See also CA 111; 93-96; DLB 69, 124; EWL 3

**Eichendorff, Joseph** 1788-1857 ........ **NCLC 8**
See also DLB 90; RGWL 2, 3

**Eigner, Larry** ..................................... **CLC 9**
See Eigner, Laurence (Joel)
See also CAAS 23; DLB 5; WP

**Eigner, Laurence (Joel)** 1927-1996
See Eigner, Larry
See also CA 9-12R; 151; CANR 6, 84; CP 7; DLB 193

**Eilhart von Oberge** c. 1140-c. 1195 ............................. **CMLC 67**
See also DLB 148

**Einhard** c. 770-840 ......................... **CMLC 50**
See also DLB 148

**Einstein, Albert** 1879-1955 ............. **TCLC 65**
See also CA 121; 133; MTCW 1, 2

**Eiseley, Loren**
See Eiseley, Loren Corey
See also DLB 275

**Eiseley, Loren Corey** 1907-1977 ......... **CLC 7**
See Eiseley, Loren
See also AAYA 5; ANW; CA 1-4R; 73-76; CANR 6; DLBD 17

**Eisenstadt, Jill** 1963- ......................... **CLC 50**
See also CA 140

**Eisenstein, Sergei (Mikhailovich)**
1898-1948 ............................. **TCLC 57**
See also CA 114; 149

**Eisner, Simon**
See Kornbluth, C(yril) M.

**Ekeloef, (Bengt) Gunnar**
1907-1968 ..................... **CLC 27; PC 23**
See Ekelof, (Bengt) Gunnar
See also CA 123; 25-28R; DAM POET

**Ekelof, (Bengt) Gunnar** 1907-1968
See Ekeloef, (Bengt) Gunnar
See also DLB 259; EW 12; EWL 3

**Ekelund, Vilhelm** 1880-1949 .......... **TCLC 75**
See also CA 189; EWL 3

**Ekwensi, C. O. D.**
See Ekwensi, Cyprian (Odiatu Duaka)

**Ekwensi, Cyprian (Odiatu Duaka)**
1921- ............................. **BLC 1; CLC 4**
See also AFW; BW 2, 3; CA 29-32R; CANR 18, 42, 74, 125; CDWLB 3; CN 7; CWRI 5; DAM MULT; DLB 117; EWL 3; MTCW 1, 2; RGEL 2; SATA 66; WLIT 2

**Elaine** ............................................. **TCLC 18**
See Leverson, Ada Esther

**El Crummo**
See Crumb, R(obert)

**Elder, Lonne III** 1931-1996 ..... **BLC 1; DC 8**
See also BW 1, 3; CA 81-84; 152; CAD; CANR 25; DAM MULT; DLB 7, 38, 44

**Eleanor of Aquitaine** 1122-1204 ... **CMLC 39**

**Elia**
See Lamb, Charles

**Eliade, Mircea** 1907-1986 ................. **CLC 19**
See also CA 65-68; 119; CANR 30, 62; CD-WLB 4; DLB 220; EWL 3; MTCW 1; RGWL 3; SFW 4

**Eliot, A. D.**
See Jewett, (Theodora) Sarah Orne

**Eliot, Alice**
See Jewett, (Theodora) Sarah Orne

**Eliot, Dan**
See Silverberg, Robert

**Eliot, George** 1819-1880 ...... **NCLC 4, 13, 23, 41, 49, 89, 118; PC 20; SSC 72; WLC**
See Evans, Mary Ann
See also BRW 5; BRWC 1, 2; BRWR 2; CDBLB 1832-1890; CN 7; CPW; DA; DA3; DAB; DAC; DAM MST, NOV; DLB 21, 35, 55; LATS 1:1; LMFS 1; NFS 17; RGEL 2; RGSF 2; SSFS 8; TEA; WLIT 3

**Eliot, John** 1604-1690 ........................... **LC 5**
See also DLB 24

**Eliot, T(homas) S(tearns)**
1888-1965 ...... **CLC 1, 2, 3, 6, 9, 10, 13, 15, 24, 34, 41, 55, 57, 113; PC 5, 31; WLC**
See also AAYA 28; AMW; AMWC 1; AMWR 1; BRW 7; BRWR 2; CA 5-8R; 25-28R; CANR 41; CDALB 1929-1941; DA; DA3; DAB; DAC; DAM DRAM, MST, POET; DFS 4, 13; DLB 7, 10, 45, 63, 245; DLBY 1988; EWL 3; EXPP; LAIT 3; LATS 1:1; LMFS 2; MTCW 1, 2; NCFS 5; PAB; PFS 1, 7, 20; RGAL 4; RGEL 2; TUS; WLIT 4; WP

**Elizabeth** 1866-1941 ....................... **TCLC 41**

**Elkin, Stanley L(awrence)**
1930-1995 .. **CLC 4, 6, 9, 14, 27, 51, 91; SSC 12**
See also AMWS 6; BPFB 1; CA 9-12R; 148; CANR 8, 46; CN 7; CPW; DAM NOV, POP; DLB 2, 28, 218, 278; DLBY 1980; EWL 3; INT CANR-8; MTCW 1, 2; RGAL 4

**Elledge, Scott** ................................... **CLC 34**

**Elliott, Don**
See Silverberg, Robert

**Elliott, George P(aul)** 1918-1980 ........ **CLC 2**
See also CA 1-4R; 97-100; CANR 2; DLB 244

**Elliott, Janice** 1931-1995 ................... **CLC 47**
See also CA 13-16R; CANR 8, 29, 84; CN 7; DLB 14; SATA 119

**Elliott, Sumner Locke** 1917-1991 ..... **CLC 38**
See also CA 5-8R; 134; CANR 2, 21; DLB 289

**Elliott, William**
See Bradbury, Ray (Douglas)

**Ellis, A. E.** ............................................. **CLC 7**

**Ellis, Alice Thomas** ........................... **CLC 40**
See Haycraft, Anna (Margaret)
See also DLB 194; MTCW 1

**Ellis, Bret Easton** 1964- ...... **CLC 39, 71, 117**
See also AAYA 2, 43; CA 118; 123; CANR 51, 74, 126; CN 7; CPW; DA3; DAM POP; DLB 292; HGG; INT CA-123; MTCW 1; NFS 11

**Ellis, (Henry) Havelock**
1859-1939 ................................. **TCLC 14**
See also CA 109; 169; DLB 190

**Ellis, Landon**
See Ellison, Harlan (Jay)

**Ellis, Trey** 1962- ................................. **CLC 55**
See also CA 146; CANR 92

**Ellison, Harlan (Jay)** 1934- ... **CLC 1, 13, 42, 139; SSC 14**
See also AAYA 29; BPFB 1; BYA 14; CA 5-8R; CANR 5, 46, 115; CPW; DAM POP; DLB 8; HGG; INT CANR-5; MTCW 1, 2; SCFW 2; SFW 4; SSFS 13, 14, 15; SUFW 1, 2

**Ellison, Ralph (Waldo)** 1914-1994 .... **BLC 1; CLC 1, 3, 11, 54, 86, 114; SSC 26; WLC**
See also AAYA 19; AFAW 1, 2; AMWC 2; AMWR 2; AMWS 2; BPFB 1; BW 1, 3; BYA 2; CA 9-12R; 145; CANR 24, 53; CDALB 1941-1968; CSW; DA; DA3; DAB; DAC; DAM MST, MULT, NOV; DLB 2, 76, 227; DLBY 1994; EWL 3; EXPN; EXPS; LAIT 4; MTCW 1, 2; NCFS 3; NFS 2; RGAL 4; RGSF 2; SSFS 1, 11; YAW

**Ellmann, Lucy (Elizabeth)** 1956- ..... **CLC 61**
See also CA 128

**Ellmann, Richard (David)**
1918-1987 ................................. **CLC 50**
See also BEST 89:2; CA 1-4R; 122; CANR 2, 28, 61; DLB 103; DLBY 1987; MTCW 1, 2

**Elman, Richard (Martin)**
1934-1997 ................................. **CLC 19**
See also CA 17-20R; 163; CAAS 3; CANR 47

**Elron**
See Hubbard, L(afayette) Ron(ald)

**El Saadawi, Nawal** 1931- ................ **CLC 196**
See also al'Sa'adawi, Nawal; Sa'adawi, al-Nawal; Saadawi, Nawal El; Sa'dawi, Nawal al-
See also CA 118; CAAS 11; CANR 44, 92

**Eluard, Paul** .................. **PC 38; TCLC 7, 41**
See Grindel, Eugene
See also EWL 3; GFL 1789 to the Present; RGWL 2, 3

**Elyot, Thomas** 1490(?)-1546 ................. **LC 11**
See also DLB 136; RGEL 2

**Elytis, Odysseus** 1911-1996 ........ **CLC 15, 49, 100; PC 21**
See Alepoudelis, Odysseus
See also CA 102; 151; CANR 94; CWW 2; DAM POET; EW 13; EWL 3; MTCW 1, 2; RGWL 2, 3

**Emecheta, (Florence Onye) Buchi**
1944- .............. **BLC 2; CLC 14, 48, 128**
See also AFW; BW 2, 3; CA 81-84; CANR 27, 81, 126; CDWLB 3; CN 7; CWRI 5; DA3; DAM MULT; DLB 117; EWL 3; FW; MTCW 1, 2; NFS 12, 14; SATA 66; WLIT 2

**Emerson, Mary Moody**
1774-1863 ................................. **NCLC 66**

**Emerson, Ralph Waldo** 1803-1882 . **NCLC 1, 38, 98; PC 18; WLC**
See also AMW; ANW; CDALB 1640-1865; DA; DA3; DAB; DAC; DAM MST, POET; DLB 1, 59, 73, 183, 223, 270;

EXPP; LAIT 2; LMFS 1; NCFS 3; PFS 4, 17; RGAL 4; TUS; WP

**Eminescu, Mihail** 1850-1889 .. **NCLC 33, 131**

**Empedocles** 5th cent. B.C.- ........... **CMLC 50**
See also DLB 176

**Empson, William** 1906-1984 ... **CLC 3, 8, 19, 33, 34**
See also BRWS 2; CA 17-20R; 112; CANR 31, 61; DLB 20; EWL 3; MTCW 1, 2; RGEL 2

**Enchi, Fumiko (Ueda)** 1905-1986 ..... **CLC 31**
See Enchi Fumiko
See also CA 129; 121; FW; MJW

**Enchi Fumiko**
See Enchi, Fumiko (Ueda)
See also DLB 182; EWL 3

**Ende, Michael (Andreas Helmuth)**
1929-1995 ................................. **CLC 31**
See also BYA 5; CA 118; 124; 149; CANR 36, 110; CLR 14; DLB 75; MAICYA 1, 2; MAICYAS 1; SATA 61, 130; SATA-Brief 42; SATA-Obit 86

**Endo, Shusaku** 1923-1996 ..... **CLC 7, 14, 19, 54, 99; SSC 48; TCLC 152**
See Endo Shusaku
See also CA 29-32R; 153; CANR 21, 54, 131; DA3; DAM NOV; MTCW 1, 2; RGSF 2; RGWL 2, 3

**Endo Shusaku**
See Endo, Shusaku
See also CWW 2; DLB 182; EWL 3

**Engel, Marian** 1933-1985 .... **CLC 36; TCLC 137**
See also CA 25-28R; CANR 12; DLB 53; FW; INT CANR-12

**Engelhardt, Frederick**
See Hubbard, L(afayette) Ron(ald)

**Engels, Friedrich** 1820-1895 .. **NCLC 85, 114**
See also DLB 129; LATS 1:1

**Enright, D(ennis) J(oseph)**
1920-2002 ........................... **CLC 4, 8, 31**
See also CA 1-4R; 211; CANR 1, 42, 83; CP 7; DLB 27; EWL 3; SATA 25; SATA-Obit 140

**Enzensberger, Hans Magnus**
1929- ............................. **CLC 43; PC 28**
See also CA 116; 119; CANR 103; CWW 2; EWL 3

**Ephron, Nora** 1941- ..................... **CLC 17, 31**
See also AAYA 35; AITN 2; CA 65-68; CANR 12, 39, 83

**Epicurus** 341B.C.-270B.C. ............. **CMLC 21**
See also DLB 176

**Epsilon**
See Betjeman, John

**Epstein, Daniel Mark** 1948- ............... **CLC 7**
See also CA 49-52; CANR 2, 53, 90

**Epstein, Jacob** 1956- .......................... **CLC 19**
See also CA 114

**Epstein, Jean** 1897-1953 ................. **TCLC 92**

**Epstein, Joseph** 1937- ....................... **CLC 39**
See also CA 112; 119; CANR 50, 65, 117

**Epstein, Leslie** 1938- ........................ **CLC 27**
See also AMWS 12; CA 73-76, 215; CAAE 215; CAAS 12; CANR 23, 69; DLB 299

**Equiano, Olaudah** 1745(?)-1797 . **BLC 2; LC 16**
See also AFAW 1, 2; CDWLB 3; DAM MULT; DLB 37, 50; WLIT 2

**Erasmus, Desiderius** 1469(?)-1536 ..... **LC 16, 93**
See also DLB 136; EW 2; LMFS 1; RGWL 2, 3; TWA

**Erdman, Paul E(mil)** 1932- ............... **CLC 25**
See also AITN 1; CA 61-64; CANR 13, 43, 84

**Erdrich, Louise** 1954- ........ **CLC 39, 54, 120, 176; NNAL; PC 52**
See also AAYA 10, 47; AMWS 4; BEST 89:1; BPFB 1; CA 114; CANR 41, 62, 118; CDALBS; CN 7; CP 7; CPW; CWP; DA3; DAM MULT, NOV, POP; DLB 152, 175, 206; EWL 3; EXPP; LAIT 5; LATS 1:2; MTCW 1; NFS 5; PFS 14; RGAL 4; SATA 94, 141; SSFS 14; TCWW 2

**Erenburg, Ilya (Grigoryevich)**
See Ehrenburg, Ilya (Grigoryevich)

**Erickson, Stephen Michael** 1950-
See Erickson, Steve
See also CA 129; SFW 4

**Erickson, Steve** ................................. **CLC 64**
See Erickson, Stephen Michael
See also CANR 60, 68; SUFW 2

**Erickson, Walter**
See Fast, Howard (Melvin)

**Ericson, Walter**
See Fast, Howard (Melvin)

**Eriksson, Buntel**
See Bergman, (Ernst) Ingmar

**Eriugena, John Scottus** c.
810-877 ................................... **CMLC 65**
See also DLB 115

**Ernaux, Annie** 1940- ................. **CLC 88, 184**
See also CA 147; CANR 93; NCFS 3, 5

**Erskine, John** 1879-1951 ................ **TCLC 84**
See also CA 112; 159; DLB 9, 102; FANT

**Eschenbach, Wolfram von**
See Wolfram von Eschenbach
See also RGWL 3

**Eseki, Bruno**
See Mphahlele, Ezekiel

**Esenin, Sergei (Alexandrovich)**
1895-1925 ................................. **TCLC 4**
See Yesenin, Sergey
See also CA 104; RGWL 2, 3

**Eshleman, Clayton** 1935- ................... **CLC 7**
See also CA 33-36R, 212; CAAE 212; CAAS 6; CANR 93; CP 7; DLB 5

**Espriella, Don Manuel Alvarez**
See Southey, Robert

**Espriu, Salvador** 1913-1985 ............... **CLC 9**
See also CA 154; 115; DLB 134; EWL 3

**Espronceda, Jose de** 1808-1842 ..... **NCLC 39**

**Esquivel, Laura** 1951(?)- ... **CLC 141; HLCS 1**
See also AAYA 29; CA 143; CANR 68, 113; DA3; DNFS 2; LAIT 3; LMFS 2; MTCW 1; NFS 5; WLIT 1

**Esse, James**
See Stephens, James

**Esterbrook, Tom**
See Hubbard, L(afayette) Ron(ald)

**Estleman, Loren D.** 1952- ................. **CLC 48**
See also AAYA 27; CA 85-88; CANR 27, 74; CMW 4; CPW; DA3; DAM NOV, POP; DLB 226; INT CANR-27; MTCW 1, 2

**Etherege, Sir George** 1636-1692 . **DC 23; LC 78**
See also BRW 2; DAM DRAM; DLB 80; PAB; RGEL 2

**Euclid** 306B.C.-283B.C. .................. **CMLC 25**

**Eugenides, Jeffrey** 1960(?)- ............... **CLC 81**
See also AAYA 51; CA 144; CANR 120

**Euripides** c. 484B.C.-406B.C. ....... **CMLC 23, 51; DC 4; WLCS**
See also AW 1; CDWLB 1; DA; DA3; DAB; DAC; DAM DRAM, MST; DFS 1, 4, 6; DLB 176; LAIT 1; LMFS 1; RGWL 2, 3

**Evan, Evin**
See Faust, Frederick (Schiller)

**Evans, Caradoc** 1878-1945 ... **SSC 43; TCLC 85**
See also DLB 162

**Evans, Evan**
See Faust, Frederick (Schiller)
See also TCWW 2
**Evans, Marian**
See Eliot, George
**Evans, Mary Ann**
See Eliot, George
See also NFS 20
**Evarts, Esther**
See Benson, Sally
**Everett, Percival**
See Everett, Percival L.
See also CSW
**Everett, Percival L.** 1956- ................. **CLC 57**
See Everett, Percival
See also BW 2; CA 129; CANR 94
**Everson, R(onald) G(ilmour)**
1903-1992 ................................ **CLC 27**
See also CA 17-20R; DLB 88
**Everson, William (Oliver)**
1912-1994 .......................... **CLC 1, 5, 14**
See also BG 2; CA 9-12R; 145; CANR 20;
DLB 5, 16, 212; MTCW 1
**Evtushenko, Evgenii Aleksandrovich**
See Yevtushenko, Yevgeny (Alexandrovich)
See also CWW 2; RGWL 2, 3
**Ewart, Gavin (Buchanan)**
1916-1995 ........................... **CLC 13, 46**
See also BRWS 7; CA 89-92; 150; CANR
17, 46; CP 7; DLB 40; MTCW 1
**Ewers, Hanns Heinz** 1871-1943 ..... **TCLC 12**
See also CA 109; 149
**Ewing, Frederick R.**
See Sturgeon, Theodore (Hamilton)
**Exley, Frederick (Earl)** 1929-1992 .... **CLC 6, 11**
See also AITN 2; BPFB 1; CA 81-84; 138;
CANR 117; DLB 143; DLBY 1981
**Eynhardt, Guillermo**
See Quiroga, Horacio (Sylvestre)
**Ezekiel, Nissim (Moses)** 1924-2004 .. **CLC 61**
See also CA 61-64; 223; CP 7; EWL 3
**Ezekiel, Tish O'Dowd** 1943- ............. **CLC 34**
See also CA 129
**Fadeev, Aleksandr Aleksandrovich**
See Bulgya, Alexander Alexandrovich
See also DLB 272
**Fadeev, Alexandr Alexandrovich**
See Bulgya, Alexander Alexandrovich
See also EWL 3
**Fadeyev, A.**
See Bulgya, Alexander Alexandrovich
**Fadeyev, Alexander** ...................... **TCLC 53**
See Bulgya, Alexander Alexandrovich
**Fagen, Donald** 1948- .......................... **CLC 26**
**Fainzilberg, Ilya Arnoldovich** 1897-1937
See Ilf, Ilya
See also CA 120; 165
**Fair, Ronald L.** 1932- ...................... **CLC 18**
See also BW 1; CA 69-72; CANR 25; DLB
33
**Fairbairn, Roger**
See Carr, John Dickson
**Fairbairns, Zoe (Ann)** 1948- ............. **CLC 32**
See also CA 103; CANR 21, 85; CN 7
**Fairfield, Flora**
See Alcott, Louisa May
**Fairman, Paul W.** 1916-1977
See Queen, Ellery
See also CA 114; SFW 4
**Falco, Gian**
See Papini, Giovanni
**Falconer, James**
See Kirkup, James
**Falconer, Kenneth**
See Kornbluth, C(yril) M.
**Falkland, Samuel**
See Heijermans, Herman

**Fallaci, Oriana** 1930- ................. **CLC 11, 110**
See also CA 77-80; CANR 15, 58; FW;
MTCW 1
**Faludi, Susan** 1959- ...................... **CLC 140**
See also CA 138; CANR 126; FW; MTCW
1; NCFS 3
**Faludy, George** 1913- ........................ **CLC 42**
See also CA 21-24R
**Faludy, Gyoergy**
See Faludy, George
**Fanon, Frantz** 1925-1961 .... **BLC 2; CLC 74**
See also BW 1; CA 116; 89-92; DAM
MULT; DLB 296; LMFS 2; WLIT 2
**Fanshawe, Ann** 1625-1680 ............... **LC 11**
**Fante, John (Thomas)** 1911-1983 .... **CLC 60; SSC 65**
See also AMWS 11; CA 69-72; 109; CANR
23, 104; DLB 130; DLBY 1983
**Far, Sui Sin** ................................... **SSC 62**
See Eaton, Edith Maude
See also SSFS 4
**Farah, Nuruddin** 1945- ...... **BLC 2; CLC 53, 137**
See also AFW; BW 2, 3; CA 106; CANR
81; CDWLB 3; CN 7; DAM MULT; DLB
125; EWL 3; WLIT 2
**Fargue, Leon-Paul** 1876(?)-1947 .... **TCLC 11**
See also CA 109; CANR 107; DLB 258;
EWL 3
**Farigoule, Louis**
See Romains, Jules
**Farina, Richard** 1936(?)-1966 ............ **CLC 9**
See also CA 81-84; 25-28R
**Farley, Walter (Lorimer)**
1915-1989 ................................ **CLC 17**
See also AAYA 58; BYA 14; CA 17-20R;
CANR 8, 29, 84; DLB 22; JRDA; MAI-
CYA 1, 2; SATA 2, 43, 132; YAW
**Farmer, Philip Jose** 1918- ............. **CLC 1, 19**
See also AAYA 28; BPFB 1; CA 1-4R;
CANR 4, 35, 111; DLB 8; MTCW 1;
SATA 93; SCFW 2; SFW 4
**Farquhar, George** 1677-1707 ............... **LC 21**
See also BRW 2; DAM DRAM; DLB 84;
RGEL 2
**Farrell, J(ames) G(ordon)**
1935-1979 ................................. **CLC 6**
See also CA 73-76; 89-92; CANR 36; DLB
14, 271; MTCW 1; RGEL 2; RHW; WLIT
4
**Farrell, James T(homas)** 1904-1979 . **CLC 1, 4, 8, 11, 66; SSC 28**
See also AMW; BPFB 1; CA 5-8R; 89-92;
CANR 9, 61; DLB 4, 9, 86; DLBD 2;
EWL 3; MTCW 1, 2; RGAL 4
**Farrell, Warren (Thomas)** 1943- ...... **CLC 70**
See also CA 146; CANR 120
**Farren, Richard J.**
See Betjeman, John
**Farren, Richard M.**
See Betjeman, John
**Fassbinder, Rainer Werner**
1946-1982 ................................ **CLC 20**
See also CA 93-96; 106; CANR 31
**Fast, Howard (Melvin)** 1914-2003 .. **CLC 23, 131**
See also AAYA 16; BPFB 1; CA 1-4R, 181;
214; CAAE 181; CAAS 18; CANR 1, 33,
54, 75, 98; CMW 4; CN 7; CPW; DAM
NOV; DLB 9; INT CANR-33; LATS 1:1;
MTCW 1; RHW; SATA 7; SATA-Essay
107; TCWW 2; YAW
**Faulcon, Robert**
See Holdstock, Robert P.
**Faulkner, William (Cuthbert)**
1897-1962 ....... **CLC 1, 3, 6, 8, 9, 11, 14, 18, 28, 52, 68; SSC 1, 35, 42; TCLC 141; WLC**
See also AAYA 7; AMW; AMWR 1; BPFB
1; BYA 5, 15; CA 81-84; CANR 33;

CDALB 1929-1941; DA; DA3; DAB;
DAC; DAM MST, NOV; DLB 9, 11, 44,
102; DLBD 2; DLBY 1986, 1997; EWL
3; EXPN; EXPS; LAIT 2; LATS 1:1;
LMFS 2; MTCW 1, 2; NFS 4, 8, 13;
RGAL 4; RGSF 2; SSFS 2, 5, 6, 12; TUS
**Fauset, Jessie Redmon**
1882(?)-1961 .. **BLC 2; CLC 19, 54; HR 2**
See also AFAW 2; BW 1; CA 109; CANR
83; DAM MULT; DLB 51; FW; LMFS 2;
MAWW
**Faust, Frederick (Schiller)**
1892-1944(?) ............................ **TCLC 49**
See Austin, Frank; Brand, Max; Challis,
George; Dawson, Peter; Dexter, Martin;
Evans, Evan; Frederick, John; Frost, Fred-
erick; Manning, David; Silver, Nicholas
See also CA 108; 152; DAM POP; DLB
256; TUS
**Faust, Irvin** 1924- ............................... **CLC 8**
See also CA 33-36R; CANR 28, 67; CN 7;
DLB 2, 28, 218, 278; DLBY 1980
**Faustino, Domingo** 1811-1888 ...... **NCLC 123**
**Fawkes, Guy**
See Benchley, Robert (Charles)
**Fearing, Kenneth (Flexner)**
1902-1961 ................................ **CLC 51**
See also CA 93-96; CANR 59; CMW 4;
DLB 9; RGAL 4
**Fecamps, Elise**
See Creasey, John
**Federman, Raymond** 1928- .......... **CLC 6, 47**
See also CA 17-20R, 208; CAAE 208;
CAAS 8; CANR 10, 43, 83, 108; CN 7;
DLBY 1980
**Federspiel, J(uerg) F.** 1931- ............. **CLC 42**
See also CA 146
**Feiffer, Jules (Ralph)** 1929- ...... **CLC 2, 8, 64**
See also AAYA 3; CA 17-20R; CAD; CANR
30, 59, 129; CD 5; DAM DRAM; DLB 7,
44; INT CANR-30; MTCW 1; SATA 8,
61, 111
**Feige, Hermann Albert Otto Maximilian**
See Traven, B.
**Feinberg, David B.** 1956-1994 .......... **CLC 59**
See also CA 135; 147
**Feinstein, Elaine** 1930- ..................... **CLC 36**
See also CA 69-72; CAAS 1; CANR 31,
68, 121; CN 7; CP 7; CWP; DLB 14, 40;
MTCW 1
**Feke, Gilbert David** ......................... **CLC 65**
**Feldman, Irving (Mordecai)** 1928- ..... **CLC 7**
See also CA 1-4R; CANR 1; CP 7; DLB
169
**Felix-Tchicaya, Gerald**
See Tchicaya, Gerald Felix
**Fellini, Federico** 1920-1993 ......... **CLC 16, 85**
See also CA 65-68; 143; CANR 33
**Felltham, Owen** 1602(?)-1668 ............. **LC 92**
See also DLB 126, 151
**Felsen, Henry Gregor** 1916-1995 ..... **CLC 17**
See also CA 1-4R; 180; CANR 1; SAAS 2;
SATA 1
**Felski, Rita** ...................................... **CLC 65**
**Fenno, Jack**
See Calisher, Hortense
**Fenollosa, Ernest (Francisco)**
1853-1908 ................................ **TCLC 91**
**Fenton, James Martin** 1949- ............. **CLC 32**
See also CA 102; CANR 108; CP 7; DLB
40; PFS 11
**Ferber, Edna** 1887-1968 ............. **CLC 18, 93**
See also AITN 1; CA 5-8R; 25-28R; CANR
68, 105; DLB 9, 28, 86, 266; MTCW 1,
2; RGAL 4; RHW; SATA 7; TCWW 2
**Ferdowsi, Abu'l Qasem** 940-1020 . **CMLC 43**
See also RGWL 2, 3

**Ferguson, Helen**
  See Kavan, Anna
**Ferguson, Niall** 1964- ...................... **CLC 134**
  See also CA 190
**Ferguson, Samuel** 1810-1886 ......... **NCLC 33**
  See also DLB 32; RGEL 2
**Fergusson, Robert** 1750-1774 .............. **LC 29**
  See also DLB 109; RGEL 2
**Ferling, Lawrence**
  See Ferlinghetti, Lawrence (Monsanto)
**Ferlinghetti, Lawrence (Monsanto)**
  1919(?)- .... **CLC 2, 6, 10, 27, 111; PC 1**
  See also CA 5-8R; CANR 3, 41, 73, 125;
  CDALB 1941-1968; CP 7; DA3; DAM
  POET; DLB 5, 16; MTCW 1, 2; RGAL 4;
  WP
**Fern, Fanny**
  See Parton, Sara Payson Willis
**Fernandez, Vicente Garcia Huidobro**
  See Huidobro Fernandez, Vicente Garcia
**Fernandez-Armesto, Felipe** ............ **CLC 70**
**Fernandez de Lizardi, Jose Joaquin**
  See Lizardi, Jose Joaquin Fernandez de
**Ferre, Rosario** 1938- ...... **CLC 139; HLCS 1;**
  **SSC 36**
  See also CA 131; CANR 55, 81; CWW 2;
  DLB 145; EWL 3; HW 1, 2; LAWS 1;
  MTCW 1; WLIT 1
**Ferrer, Gabriel (Francisco Victor) Miro**
  See Miro (Ferrer), Gabriel (Francisco
  Victor)
**Ferrier, Susan (Edmonstone)**
  1782-1854 .................................. **NCLC 8**
  See also DLB 116; RGEL 2
**Ferrigno, Robert** 1948(?)- ................ **CLC 65**
  See also CA 140; CANR 125
**Ferron, Jacques** 1921-1985 .............. **CLC 94**
  See also CA 117; 129; CCA 1; DAC; DLB
  60; EWL 3
**Feuchtwanger, Lion** 1884-1958 ........ **TCLC 3**
  See also CA 104; 187; DLB 66; EWL 3
**Feuerbach, Ludwig** 1804-1872 ..... **NCLC 139**
  See also DLB 133
**Feuillet, Octave** 1821-1890 ............. **NCLC 45**
  See also DLB 192
**Feydeau, Georges (Leon Jules Marie)**
  1862-1921 ................................ **TCLC 22**
  See also CA 113; 152; CANR 84; DAM
  DRAM; DLB 192; EWL 3; GFL 1789 to
  the Present; RGWL 2, 3
**Fichte, Johann Gottlieb**
  1762-1814 ................................ **NCLC 62**
  See also DLB 90
**Ficino, Marsilio** 1433-1499 ................ **LC 12**
  See also LMFS 1
**Fiedeler, Hans**
  See Doeblin, Alfred
**Fiedler, Leslie A(aron)** 1917-2003 ..... **CLC 4,**
  **13, 24**
  See also AMWS 13; CA 9-12R; 212; CANR
  7, 63; CN 7; DLB 28, 67; EWL 3; MTCW
  1, 2; RGAL 4; TUS
**Field, Andrew** 1938- .......................... **CLC 44**
  See also CA 97-100; CANR 25
**Field, Eugene** 1850-1895 ................... **NCLC 3**
  See also DLB 23, 42, 140; DLBD 13; MAI-
  CYA 1, 2; RGAL 4; SATA 16
**Field, Gans T.**
  See Wellman, Manly Wade
**Field, Michael** 1915-1971 ............... **TCLC 43**
  See also CA 29-32R
**Field, Peter**
  See Hobson, Laura Z(ametkin)
  See also TCWW 2
**Fielding, Helen** 1958- ...................... **CLC 146**
  See also CA 172; CANR 127; DLB 231

**Fielding, Henry** 1707-1754 ....... **LC 1, 46, 85;**
  **WLC**
  See also BRW 3; BRWR 1; CDBLB 1660-
  1789; DA; DA3; DAB; DAC; DAM
  DRAM, MST, NOV; DLB 39, 84, 101;
  NFS 18; RGEL 2; TEA; WLIT 3
**Fielding, Sarah** 1710-1768 ............... **LC 1, 44**
  See also DLB 39; RGEL 2; TEA
**Fields, W. C.** 1880-1946 .................. **TCLC 80**
  See also DLB 44
**Fierstein, Harvey (Forbes)** 1954- ..... **CLC 33**
  See also CA 123; 129; CAD; CD 5; CPW;
  DA3; DAM DRAM, POP; DFS 6; DLB
  266; GLL
**Figes, Eva** 1932- ................................ **CLC 31**
  See also CA 53-56; CANR 4, 44, 83; CN 7;
  DLB 14, 271; FW
**Filippo, Eduardo de**
  See de Filippo, Eduardo
**Finch, Anne** 1661-1720 .............. **LC 3; PC 21**
  See also BRWS 9; DLB 95
**Finch, Robert (Duer Claydon)**
  1900-1995 .................................. **CLC 18**
  See also CA 57-60; CANR 9, 24, 49; CP 7;
  DLB 88
**Findley, Timothy (Irving Frederick)**
  1930-2002 ........................... **CLC 27, 102**
  See also CA 25-28R; 206; CANR 12, 42,
  69, 109; CCA 1; CN 7; DAC; DAM MST;
  DLB 53; FANT; RHW
**Fink, William**
  See Mencken, H(enry) L(ouis)
**Firbank, Louis** 1942-
  See Reed, Lou
  See also CA 117
**Firbank, (Arthur Annesley) Ronald**
  1886-1926 .................................. **TCLC 1**
  See also BRWS 2; CA 104; 177; DLB 36;
  EWL 3; RGEL 2
**Fish, Stanley**
  See Fish, Stanley Eugene
**Fish, Stanley E.**
  See Fish, Stanley Eugene
**Fish, Stanley Eugene** 1938- ............. **CLC 142**
  See also CA 112; 132; CANR 90; DLB 67
**Fisher, Dorothy (Frances) Canfield**
  1879-1958 ................................ **TCLC 87**
  See also CA 114; 136; CANR 80; CLR 71,;
  CWRI 5; DLB 9, 102, 284; MAICYA 1,
  2; YABC 1
**Fisher, M(ary) F(rances) K(ennedy)**
  1908-1992 ........................... **CLC 76, 87**
  See also CA 77-80; 138; CANR 44; MTCW
  1
**Fisher, Roy** 1930- ............................. **CLC 25**
  See also CA 81-84; CAAS 10; CANR 16;
  CP 7; DLB 40
**Fisher, Rudolph** 1897-1934 .... **BLC 2; HR 2;**
  **SSC 25; TCLC 11**
  See also BW 1, 3; CA 107; 124; CANR 80;
  DAM MULT; DLB 51, 102
**Fisher, Vardis (Alvero)** 1895-1968 .... **CLC 7;**
  **TCLC 140**
  See also CA 5-8R; 25-28R; CANR 68; DLB
  9, 206; RGAL 4; TCWW 2
**Fiske, Tarleton**
  See Bloch, Robert (Albert)
**Fitch, Clarke**
  See Sinclair, Upton (Beall)
**Fitch, John IV**
  See Cormier, Robert (Edmund)
**Fitzgerald, Captain Hugh**
  See Baum, L(yman) Frank
**FitzGerald, Edward** 1809-1883 ....... **NCLC 9**
  See also BRW 4; DLB 32; RGEL 2

**Fitzgerald, F(rancis) Scott (Key)**
  1896-1940 ... **SSC 6, 31, 75; TCLC 1, 6,**
  **14, 28, 55, 157; WLC**
  See also AAYA 24; AITN 1; AMW; AMWC
  2; AMWR 1; BPFB 1; CA 110; 123;
  CDALB 1917-1929; DA; DA3; DAB;
  DAC; DAM MST, NOV; DLB 4, 9, 86,
  219, 273; DLBD 1, 15, 16; DLBY 1981,
  1996; EWL 3; EXPN; EXPS; LAIT 3;
  MTCW 1, 2; NFS 2, 19, 20; RGAL 4;
  RGSF 2; SSFS 4, 15; TUS
**Fitzgerald, Penelope** 1916-2000 . **CLC 19, 51,**
  **61, 143**
  See also BRWS 5; CA 85-88; 190; CAAS
  10; CANR 56, 86, 131; CN 7; DLB 14,
  194; EWL 3; MTCW 2
**Fitzgerald, Robert (Stuart)**
  1910-1985 .................................. **CLC 39**
  See also CA 1-4R; 114; CANR 1; DLBY
  1980
**FitzGerald, Robert D(avid)**
  1902-1987 .................................. **CLC 19**
  See also CA 17-20R; DLB 260; RGEL 2
**Fitzgerald, Zelda (Sayre)**
  1900-1948 ................................ **TCLC 52**
  See also AMWS 9; CA 117; 126; DLBY
  1984
**Flanagan, Thomas (James Bonner)**
  1923-2002 ........................... **CLC 25, 52**
  See also CA 108; 206; CANR 55; CN 7;
  DLBY 1980; INT CA-108; MTCW 1;
  RHW
**Flaubert, Gustave** 1821-1880 .... **NCLC 2, 10,**
  **19, 62, 66, 135; SSC 11, 60; WLC**
  See also DA; DA3; DAB; DAC; DAM
  MST, NOV; DLB 119, 301; EW 7; EXPS;
  GFL 1789 to the Present; LAIT 2; LMFS
  1; NFS 14; RGSF 2; RGWL 2, 3; SSFS
  6; TWA
**Flavius Josephus**
  See Josephus, Flavius
**Flecker, Herman Elroy**
  See Flecker, (Herman) James Elroy
**Flecker, (Herman) James Elroy**
  1884-1915 ................................ **TCLC 43**
  See also CA 109; 150; DLB 10, 19; RGEL
  2
**Fleming, Ian (Lancaster)** 1908-1964 . **CLC 3,**
  **30**
  See also AAYA 26; BPFB 1; CA 5-8R;
  CANR 59; CDBLB 1945-1960; CMW 4;
  CPW; DA3; DAM POP; DLB 87, 201;
  MSW; MTCW 1, 2; RGEL 2; SATA 9;
  TEA; YAW
**Fleming, Thomas (James)** 1927- ...... **CLC 37**
  See also CA 5-8R; CANR 10, 102; INT
  CANR-10; SATA 8
**Fletcher, John** 1579-1625 .......... **DC 6; LC 33**
  See also BRW 2; CDBLB Before 1660;
  DLB 58; RGEL 2; TEA
**Fletcher, John Gould** 1886-1950 .... **TCLC 35**
  See also CA 107; 167; DLB 4, 45; LMFS
  2; RGAL 4
**Fleur, Paul**
  See Pohl, Frederik
**Flieg, Helmut**
  See Heym, Stefan
**Flooglebuckle, Al**
  See Spiegelman, Art
**Flora, Fletcher** 1914-1969
  See Queen, Ellery
  See also CA 1-4R; CANR 3, 85
**Flying Officer X**
  See Bates, H(erbert) E(rnest)
**Fo, Dario** 1926- ........... **CLC 32, 109; DC 10**
  See also CA 116; 128; CANR 68, 114;
  CWW 2; DA3; DAM DRAM; DLBY
  1997; EWL 3; MTCW 1, 2
**Fogarty, Jonathan Titulescu Esq.**
  See Farrell, James T(homas)

**Follett, Ken(neth Martin)** 1949- ....... **CLC 18**
See also AAYA 6, 50; BEST 89:4; BPFB 1;
CA 81-84; CANR 13, 33, 54, 102; CMW
4; CPW; DA3; DAM NOV, POP; DLB
87; DLBY 1981; INT CANR-33; MTCW
1

**Fontane, Theodor** 1819-1898 ......... **NCLC 26**
See also CDWLB 2; DLB 129; EW 6;
RGWL 2, 3; TWA

**Fontenot, Chester** ............................ **CLC 65**

**Fonvizin, Denis Ivanovich**
1744(?)-1792 ................................... **LC 81**
See also DLB 150; RGWL 2, 3

**Foote, Horton** 1916- .................... **CLC 51, 91**
See also CA 73-76; CAD; CANR 34, 51,
110; CD 5; CSW; DA3; DAM DRAM;
DFS 20; DLB 26, 266; EWL 3; INT
CANR-34

**Foote, Mary Hallock** 1847-1938 .. **TCLC 108**
See also DLB 186, 188, 202, 221

**Foote, Samuel** 1721-1777 ................... **LC 106**
See also DLB 89; RGEL 2

**Foote, Shelby** 1916- ........................... **CLC 75**
See also AAYA 40; CA 5-8R; CANR 3, 45,
74, 131; CN 7; CPW; CSW; DA3; DAM
NOV, POP; DLB 2, 17; MTCW 2; RHW

**Forbes, Cosmo**
See Lewton, Val

**Forbes, Esther** 1891-1967 ................. **CLC 12**
See also AAYA 17; BYA 2; CA 13-14; 25-
28R; CAP 1; CLR 27; DLB 22; JRDA;
MAICYA 1, 2; RHW; SATA 2, 100; YAW

**Forche, Carolyn (Louise)** 1950- ....... **CLC 25,
83, 86; PC 10**
See also CA 109; 117; CANR 50, 74; CP 7;
CWP; DA3; DAM POET; DLB 5, 193;
INT CA-117; MTCW 1; PFS 18; RGAL 4

**Ford, Elbur**
See Hibbert, Eleanor Alice Burford

**Ford, Ford Madox** 1873-1939 ... **TCLC 1, 15,
39, 57**
See Chaucer, Daniel
See also BRW 6; CA 104; 132; CANR 74;
CDBLB 1914-1945; DA3; DAM NOV;
DLB 34, 98, 162; EWL 3; MTCW 1, 2;
RGEL 2; TEA

**Ford, Henry** 1863-1947 ................... **TCLC 73**
See also CA 115; 148

**Ford, Jack**
See Ford, John

**Ford, John** 1586-1639 ............... **DC 8; LC 68**
See also BRW 2; CDBLB Before 1660;
DA3; DAM DRAM; DFS 7; DLB 58;
IDTP; RGEL 2

**Ford, John** 1895-1973 ......................... **CLC 16**
See also CA 187; 45-48

**Ford, Richard** 1944- ..................... **CLC 46, 99**
See also AMWS 5; CA 69-72; CANR 11,
47, 86, 128; CN 7; CSW; DLB 227; EWL
3; MTCW 1; RGAL 4; RGSF 2

**Ford, Webster**
See Masters, Edgar Lee

**Foreman, Richard** 1937- ................... **CLC 50**
See also CA 65-68; CAD; CANR 32, 63;
CD 5

**Forester, C(ecil) S(cott)** 1899-1966 . **CLC 35;
TCLC 152**
See also CA 73-76; 25-28R; CANR 83;
DLB 191; RGEL 2; RHW; SATA 13

**Forez**
See Mauriac, Francois (Charles)

**Forman, James**
See Forman, James D(ouglas)

**Forman, James D(ouglas)** 1932- ....... **CLC 21**
See also AAYA 17; CA 9-12R; CANR 4,
19, 42; JRDA; MAICYA 1, 2; SATA 8,
70; YAW

**Forman, Milos** 1932- ....................... **CLC 164**
See also CA 109

**Fornes, Maria Irene** 1930- ......... **CLC 39, 61,
187; DC 10; HLCS 1**
See also CA 25-28R; CAD; CANR 28, 81;
CD 5; CWD; DLB 7; HW 1, 2; INT
CANR-28; LLW 1; MTCW 1; RGAL 4

**Forrest, Leon (Richard)**
1937-1997 ........................... **BLCS; CLC 4**
See also AFAW 2; BW 2; CA 89-92; 162;
CAAS 7; CANR 25, 52, 87; CN 7; DLB
33

**Forster, E(dward) M(organ)**
1879-1970 .... **CLC 1, 2, 3, 4, 9, 10, 13,
15, 22, 45, 77; SSC 27; TCLC 125;
WLC**
See also AAYA 2, 37; BRW 6; BRWR 2;
BYA 12; CA 13-14; 25-28R; CANR 45;
CAP 1; CDBLB 1914-1945; DA; DA3;
DAB; DAC; DAM MST, NOV; DLB 34,
98, 162, 178, 195; DLBD 10; EWL 3;
EXPN; LAIT 3; LMFS 1; MTCW 1, 2;
NCFS 1; NFS 3, 10, 11; RGEL 2; RGSF
2; SATA 57; SUFW 1; TEA; WLIT 4

**Forster, John** 1812-1876 ................. **NCLC 11**
See also DLB 144, 184

**Forster, Margaret** 1938- .................. **CLC 149**
See also CA 133; CANR 62, 115; CN 7;
DLB 155, 271

**Forsyth, Frederick** 1938- .......... **CLC 2, 5, 36**
See also BEST 89:4; CA 85-88; CANR 38,
62, 115; CMW 4; CN 7; CPW; DAM
NOV, POP; DLB 87; MTCW 1, 2

**Forten, Charlotte L.** 1837-1914 ......... **BLC 2;
TCLC 16**
See Grimke, Charlotte L(ottie) Forten
See also DLB 50, 239

**Fortinbras**
See Grieg, (Johan) Nordahl (Brun)

**Foscolo, Ugo** 1778-1827 ............. **NCLC 8, 97**
See also EW 5

**Fosse, Bob** ............................................ **CLC 20**
See Fosse, Robert Louis

**Fosse, Robert Louis** 1927-1987
See Fosse, Bob
See also CA 110; 123

**Foster, Hannah Webster**
1758-1840 ................................. **NCLC 99**
See also DLB 37, 200; RGAL 4

**Foster, Stephen Collins**
1826-1864 ................................. **NCLC 26**
See also RGAL 4

**Foucault, Michel** 1926-1984 . **CLC 31, 34, 69**
See also CA 105; 113; CANR 34; DLB 242;
EW 13; EWL 3; GFL 1789 to the Present;
GLL 1; LMFS 2; MTCW 1, 2; TWA

**Fouque, Friedrich (Heinrich Karl) de la
Motte** 1777-1843 ....................... **NCLC 2**
See also DLB 90; RGWL 2, 3; SUFW 1

**Fourier, Charles** 1772-1837 ............ **NCLC 51**

**Fournier, Henri-Alban** 1886-1914
See Alain-Fournier
See also CA 104; 179

**Fournier, Pierre** 1916- ....................... **CLC 11**
See Gascar, Pierre
See also CA 89-92; CANR 16, 40

**Fowles, John (Robert)** 1926- . **CLC 1, 2, 3, 4,
6, 9, 10, 15, 33, 87; SSC 33**
See also BPFB 1; BRWS 1; CA 5-8R;
CANR 25, 71, 103; CDBLB 1960 to
Present; CN 7; DA3; DAB; DAC; DAM
MST; DLB 14, 139, 207; EWL 3; HGG;
MTCW 1, 2; RGEL 2; RHW; SATA 22;
TEA; WLIT 4

**Fox, Paula** 1923- ..................... **CLC 2, 8, 121**
See also AAYA 3, 37; BYA 3, 8; CA 73-76;
CANR 20, 36, 62, 105; CLR 1, 44, 96;
DLB 52; JRDA; MAICYA 1, 2; MTCW
1; NFS 12; SATA 17, 60, 120; WYA;
YAW

**Fox, William Price (Jr.)** 1926- ......... **CLC 22**
See also CA 17-20R; CAAS 19; CANR 11;
CSW; DLB 2; DLBY 1981

**Foxe, John** 1517(?)-1587 ...................... **LC 14**
See also DLB 132

**Frame, Janet** .. **CLC 2, 3, 6, 22, 66, 96; SSC
29**
See Clutha, Janet Paterson Frame
See also CN 7; CWP; EWL 3; RGEL 2;
RGSF 2; TWA

**France, Anatole** ............................... **TCLC 9**
See Thibault, Jacques Anatole Francois
See also DLB 123; EWL 3; GFL 1789 to
the Present; MTCW 1; RGWL 2, 3;
SUFW 1

**Francis, Claude** ............................... **CLC 50**
See also CA 192

**Francis, Dick** 1920- ......... **CLC 2, 22, 42, 102**
See also AAYA 5, 21; BEST 89:3; BPFB 1;
CA 5-8R; CANR 9, 42, 68, 100; CDBLB
1960 to Present; CMW 4; CN 7; DA3;
DAM POP; DLB 87; INT CANR-9;
MSW; MTCW 1, 2

**Francis, Robert (Churchill)**
1901-1987 ...................... **CLC 15; PC 34**
See also AMWS 9; CA 1-4R; 123; CANR
1; EXPP; PFS 12

**Francis, Lord Jeffrey**
See Jeffrey, Francis
See also DLB 107

**Frank, Anne(lies Marie)**
1929-1945 ..................... **TCLC 17; WLC**
See also AAYA 12; BYA 1; CA 113; 133;
CANR 68; CLR 101; DA; DA3; DAB;
DAC; DAM MST; LAIT 4; MAICYA 2;
MAICYAS 1; MTCW 1, 2; NCFS 2;
SATA 87; SATA-Brief 42; WYA; YAW

**Frank, Bruno** 1887-1945 ................. **TCLC 81**
See also CA 189; DLB 118; EWL 3

**Frank, Elizabeth** 1945- ..................... **CLC 39**
See also CA 121; 126; CANR 78; INT CA-
126

**Frankl, Viktor E(mil)** 1905-1997 ...... **CLC 93**
See also CA 65-68; 161

**Franklin, Benjamin**
See Hasek, Jaroslav (Matej Frantisek)

**Franklin, Benjamin** 1706-1790 .......... **LC 25;
WLCS**
See also AMW; CDALB 1640-1865; DA;
DA3; DAB; DAC; DAM MST; DLB 24,
43, 73, 183; LAIT 1; RGAL 4; TUS

**Franklin, (Stella Maria Sarah) Miles
(Lampe)** 1879-1954 ................... **TCLC 7**
See also CA 104; 164; DLB 230; FW;
MTCW 2; RGEL 2; TWA

**Fraser, Antonia (Pakenham)** 1932- . **CLC 32,
107**
See also AAYA 57; CA 85-88; CANR 44,
65, 119; CMW; DLB 276; MTCW 1, 2;
SATA-Brief 32

**Fraser, George MacDonald** 1925- ...... **CLC 7**
See also AAYA 48; CA 45-48, 180; CAAE
180; CANR 2, 48, 74; MTCW 1; RHW

**Fraser, Sylvia** 1935- ........................... **CLC 64**
See also CA 45-48; CANR 1, 16, 60; CCA
1

**Frayn, Michael** 1933- . **CLC 3, 7, 31, 47, 176**
See also BRWC 2; BRWS 7; CA 5-8R;
CANR 30, 69, 114, 133; CBD; CD 5; CN
7; DAM DRAM, NOV; DLB 13, 14, 194,
245; FANT; MTCW 1, 2; SFW 4

**Fraze, Candida (Merrill)** 1945- ........ **CLC 50**
See also CA 126

**Frazer, Andrew**
See Marlowe, Stephen

**Frazer, J(ames) G(eorge)**
1854-1941 ................................ **TCLC 32**
See also BRWS 3; CA 118; NCFS 5

**Frazer, Robert Caine**
See Creasey, John
**Frazer, Sir James George**
See Frazer, J(ames) G(eorge)
**Frazier, Charles** 1950- ...................... **CLC 109**
See also AAYA 34; CA 161; CANR 126;
CSW; DLB 292
**Frazier, Ian** 1951- ........................... **CLC 46**
See also CA 130; CANR 54, 93
**Frederic, Harold** 1856-1898 .......... **NCLC 10**
See also AMW; DLB 12, 23; DLBD 13;
RGAL 4
**Frederick, John**
See Faust, Frederick (Schiller)
See also TCWW 2
**Frederick the Great** 1712-1786 .......... **LC 14**
**Fredro, Aleksander** 1793-1876 ........ **NCLC 8**
**Freeling, Nicolas** 1927-2003 ............. **CLC 38**
See also CA 49-52; 218; CAAS 12; CANR
1, 17, 50, 84; CMW 4; CN 7; DLB 87
**Freeman, Douglas Southall**
1886-1953 ................................ **TCLC 11**
See also CA 109; 195; DLB 17; DLBD 17
**Freeman, Judith** 1946- ..................... **CLC 55**
See also CA 148; CANR 120; DLB 256
**Freeman, Mary E(leanor) Wilkins**
1852-1930 ............ **SSC 1, 47; TCLC 9**
See also CA 106; 177; DLB 12, 78, 221;
EXPS; FW; HGG; MAWW; RGAL 4;
RGSF 2; SSFS 4, 8; SUFW 1; TUS
**Freeman, R(ichard) Austin**
1862-1943 ................................ **TCLC 21**
See also CA 113; CANR 84; CMW 4; DLB
70
**French, Albert** 1943- .......................... **CLC 86**
See also BW 3; CA 167
**French, Antonia**
See Kureishi, Hanif
**French, Marilyn** 1929- .. **CLC 10, 18, 60, 177**
See also BPFB 1; CA 69-72; CANR 3, 31;
CN 7; CPW; DAM DRAM, NOV, POP;
FW; INT CANR-31; MTCW 1, 2
**French, Paul**
See Asimov, Isaac
**Freneau, Philip Morin** 1752-1832 .. **NCLC 1,**
**111**
See also AMWS 2; DLB 37, 43; RGAL 4
**Freud, Sigmund** 1856-1939 ............. **TCLC 52**
See also CA 115; 133; CANR 69; DLB 296;
EW 8; EWL 3; LATS 1:1; MTCW 1, 2;
NCFS 3; TWA
**Freytag, Gustav** 1816-1895 .......... **NCLC 109**
See also DLB 129
**Friedan, Betty (Naomi)** 1921- ........... **CLC 74**
See also CA 65-68; CANR 18, 45, 74; DLB
246; FW; MTCW 1, 2; NCFS 5
**Friedlander, Saul** 1932- ..................... **CLC 90**
See also CA 117; 130; CANR 72
**Friedman, B(ernard) H(arper)**
1926- ........................................ **CLC 7**
See also CA 1-4R; CANR 3, 48
**Friedman, Bruce Jay** 1930- ...... **CLC 3, 5, 56**
See also CA 9-12R; CAD; CANR 25, 52,
101; CD 5; CN 7; DLB 2, 28, 244; INT
CANR-25; SSFS 18
**Friel, Brian** 1929- .... **CLC 5, 42, 59, 115; DC**
**8; SSC 76**
See also BRWS 5; CA 21-24R; CANR 33,
69, 131; CBD; CD 5; DFS 11; DLB 13;
EWL 3; MTCW 1; RGEL 2; TEA
**Friis-Baastad, Babbis Ellinor**
1921-1970 ................................. **CLC 12**
See also CA 17-20R; 134; SATA 7
**Frisch, Max (Rudolf)** 1911-1991 ... **CLC 3, 9,**
**14, 18, 32, 44; TCLC 121**
See also CA 85-88; 134; CANR 32, 74; CD-
WLB 2; DAM DRAM, NOV; DLB 69,
124; EW 13; EWL 3; MTCW 1, 2; RGWL
2, 3

**Fromentin, Eugene (Samuel Auguste)**
1820-1876 ........................ **NCLC 10, 125**
See also DLB 123; GFL 1789 to the Present
**Frost, Frederick**
See Faust, Frederick (Schiller)
See also TCWW 2
**Frost, Robert (Lee)** 1874-1963 .. **CLC 1, 3, 4,**
**9, 10, 13, 15, 26, 34, 44; PC 1, 39;**
**WLC**
See also AAYA 21; AMW; AMWR 1; CA
89-92; CANR 33; CDALB 1917-1929;
CLR 67; DA; DA3; DAB; DAC; DAM
MST, POET; DLB 54, 284; DLBD 7;
EWL 3; EXPP; MTCW 1, 2; PAB; PFS 1,
2, 3, 4, 5, 6, 7, 10, 13; RGAL 4; SATA
14; TUS; WP; WYA
**Froude, James Anthony**
1818-1894 ................................. **NCLC 43**
See also DLB 18, 57, 144
**Froy, Herald**
See Waterhouse, Keith (Spencer)
**Fry, Christopher** 1907- ........... **CLC 2, 10, 14**
See also BRWS 3; CA 17-20R; CAAS 23;
CANR 9, 30, 74, 132; CBD; CD 5; CP 7;
DAM DRAM; DLB 13; EWL 3; MTCW
1, 2; RGEL 2; SATA 66; TEA
**Frye, (Herman) Northrop**
1912-1991 ............................ **CLC 24, 70**
See also CA 5-8R; 133; CANR 8, 37; DLB
67, 68, 246; EWL 3; MTCW 1, 2; RGAL
4; TWA
**Fuchs, Daniel** 1909-1993 .............. **CLC 8, 22**
See also CA 81-84; 142; CAAS 5; CANR
40; DLB 9, 26, 28; DLBY 1993
**Fuchs, Daniel** 1934- .......................... **CLC 34**
See also CA 37-40R; CANR 14, 48
**Fuentes, Carlos** 1928- .. **CLC 3, 8, 10, 13, 22,**
**41, 60, 113; HLC 1; SSC 24; WLC**
See also AAYA 4, 45; AITN 2; BPFB 1;
CA 69-72; CANR 10, 32, 68, 104; CD-
WLB 3; CWW 2; DA; DA3; DAB; DAC;
DAM MST, MULT, NOV; DLB 113;
DNFS 2; EWL 3; HW 1, 2; LAIT 3; LATS
1:2; LAW; LAWS 1; LMFS 2; MTCW 1,
2; NFS 8; RGSF 2; RGWL 2, 3; TWA;
WLIT 1
**Fuentes, Gregorio Lopez y**
See Lopez y Fuentes, Gregorio
**Fuertes, Gloria** 1918-1998 ................... **PC 27**
See also CA 178, 180; DLB 108; HW 2;
SATA 115
**Fugard, (Harold) Athol** 1932- . **CLC 5, 9, 14,**
**25, 40, 80; DC 3**
See also AAYA 17; AFW; CA 85-88; CANR
32, 54, 118; CD 5; DAM DRAM; DFS 3,
6, 10; DLB 225; DNFS 1, 2; EWL 3;
LATS 1:2; MTCW 1; RGEL 2; WLIT 2
**Fugard, Sheila** 1932- ......................... **CLC 48**
See also CA 125
**Fukuyama, Francis** 1952- .............. **CLC 131**
See also CA 140; CANR 72, 125
**Fuller, Charles (H.), (Jr.)** 1939- ......... **BLC 2;**
**CLC 25; DC 1**
See also BW 2; CA 108; 112; CAD; CANR
87; CD 5; DAM DRAM, MULT; DFS 8;
DLB 38, 266; EWL 3; INT CA-112;
MTCW 1
**Fuller, Henry Blake** 1857-1929 .... **TCLC 103**
See also CA 108; 177; DLB 12; RGAL 4
**Fuller, John (Leopold)** 1937- ........... **CLC 62**
See also CA 21-24R; CANR 9, 44; CP 7;
DLB 40
**Fuller, Margaret**
See Ossoli, Sarah Margaret (Fuller)
See also AMWS 2; DLB 183, 223, 239
**Fuller, Roy (Broadbent)** 1912-1991 ... **CLC 4,**
**28**
See also BRWS 7; CA 5-8R; 135; CAAS
10; CANR 53, 83; CWRI 5; DLB 15, 20;
EWL 3; RGEL 2; SATA 87

**Fuller, Sarah Margaret**
See Ossoli, Sarah Margaret (Fuller)
**Fuller, Sarah Margaret**
See Ossoli, Sarah Margaret (Fuller)
See also DLB 1, 59, 73
**Fulton, Alice** 1952- ........................... **CLC 52**
See also CA 116; CANR 57, 88; CP 7;
CWP; DLB 193
**Furphy, Joseph** 1843-1912 .............. **TCLC 25**
See Collins, Tom
See also CA 163; DLB 230; EWL 3; RGEL
2
**Fuson, Robert H(enderson)** 1927- .... **CLC 70**
See also CA 89-92; CANR 103
**Fussell, Paul** 1924- ........................... **CLC 74**
See also BEST 90:1; CA 17-20R; CANR 8,
21, 35, 69; INT CANR-21; MTCW 1, 2
**Futabatei, Shimei** 1864-1909 .......... **TCLC 44**
See Futabatei Shimei
See also CA 162; MJW
**Futabatei Shimei**
See Futabatei, Shimei
See also DLB 180; EWL 3
**Futrelle, Jacques** 1875-1912 ........... **TCLC 19**
See also CA 113; 155; CMW 4
**Gaboriau, Emile** 1835-1873 ........... **NCLC 14**
See also CMW 4; MSW
**Gadda, Carlo Emilio** 1893-1973 ...... **CLC 11;**
**TCLC 144**
See also CA 89-92; DLB 177; EWL 3
**Gaddis, William** 1922-1998 ... **CLC 1, 3, 6, 8,**
**10, 19, 43, 86**
See also AMWS 4; BPFB 1; CA 17-20R;
172; CANR 21, 48; CN 7; DLB 2, 278;
EWL 3; MTCW 1, 2; RGAL 4
**Gaelique, Moruen le**
See Jacob, (Cyprien-)Max
**Gage, Walter**
See Inge, William (Motter)
**Gaiman, Neil (Richard)** 1960- ........ **CLC 195**
See also AAYA 19, 42; CA 133; CANR 81,
129; DLB 261; HGG; SATA 85, 146;
SFW 4; SUFW 2
**Gaines, Ernest J(ames)** 1933- .. **BLC 2; CLC**
**3, 11, 18, 86, 181; SSC 68**
See also AAYA 18; AFAW 1, 2; AITN 1;
BPFB 2; BW 2, 3; BYA 6; CA 9-12R;
CANR 6, 24, 42, 75, 126; CDALB 1968-
1988; CLR 62; CN 7; CSW; DA3; DAM
MULT; DLB 2, 33, 152; DLBY 1980;
EWL 3; EXPN; LAIT 5; LATS 1:2;
MTCW 1, 2; NFS 5, 7, 16; RGAL 4;
RGSF 2; RHW; SATA 86; SSFS 5; YAW
**Gaitskill, Mary (Lawrence)** 1954- .... **CLC 69**
See also CA 128; CANR 61; DLB 244
**Gaius Suetonius Tranquillus** c. 70-c. 130
See Suetonius
**Galdos, Benito Perez**
See Perez Galdos, Benito
See also EW 7
**Gale, Zona** 1874-1938 ...................... **TCLC 7**
See also CA 105; 153; CANR 84; DAM
DRAM; DFS 17; DLB 9, 78, 228; RGAL
4
**Galeano, Eduardo (Hughes)** 1940- . **CLC 72;**
**HLCS 1**
See also CA 29-32R; CANR 13, 32, 100;
HW 1
**Galiano, Juan Valera y Alcala**
See Valera y Alcala-Galiano, Juan
**Galilei, Galileo** 1564-1642 .................... **LC 45**
**Gallagher, Tess** 1943- ....... **CLC 18, 63; PC 9**
See also CA 106; CP 7; CWP; DAM POET;
DLB 120, 212, 244; PFS 16

**Gallant, Mavis** 1922- ..... **CLC 7, 18, 38, 172;**
    **SSC 5**
    See also CA 69-72; CANR 29, 69, 117;
    CCA 1; CN 7; DAC; DAM MST; DLB
    53; EWL 3; MTCW 1, 2; RGEL 2; RGSF
    2
**Gallant, Roy A(rthur)** 1924- ............. **CLC 17**
    See also CA 5-8R; CANR 4, 29, 54, 117;
    CLR 30; MAICYA 1, 2; SATA 4, 68, 110
**Gallico, Paul (William)** 1897-1976 ..... **CLC 2**
    See also AITN 1; CA 5-8R; 69-72; CANR
    23; DLB 9, 171; FANT; MAICYA 1, 2;
    SATA 13
**Gallo, Max Louis** 1932- ..................... **CLC 95**
    See also CA 85-88
**Gallois, Lucien**
    See Desnos, Robert
**Gallup, Ralph**
    See Whitemore, Hugh (John)
**Galsworthy, John** 1867-1933 ............ **SSC 22;**
    **TCLC 1, 45; WLC**
    See also BRW 6; CA 104; 141; CANR 75;
    CDBLB 1890-1914; DA; DA3; DAB;
    DAC; DAM DRAM, MST, NOV; DLB
    10, 34, 98, 162; DLBD 16; EWL 3;
    MTCW 1; RGEL 2; SSFS 3; TEA
**Galt, John** 1779-1839 ................ **NCLC 1, 110**
    See also DLB 99, 116, 159; RGEL 2; RGSF
    2
**Galvin, James** 1951- ............................ **CLC 38**
    See also CA 108; CANR 26
**Gamboa, Federico** 1864-1939 ......... **TCLC 36**
    See also CA 167; HW 2; LAW
**Gandhi, M. K.**
    See Gandhi, Mohandas Karamchand
**Gandhi, Mahatma**
    See Gandhi, Mohandas Karamchand
**Gandhi, Mohandas Karamchand**
    1869-1948 ................................. **TCLC 59**
    See also CA 121; 132; DA3; DAM MULT;
    MTCW 1, 2
**Gann, Ernest Kellogg** 1910-1991 ..... **CLC 23**
    See also AITN 1; BPFB 2; CA 1-4R; 136;
    CANR 1, 83; RHW
**Gao Xingjian** 1940- .......................... **CLC 167**
    See Xingjian, Gao
**Garber, Eric** 1943(?)-
    See Holleran, Andrew
    See also CANR 89
**Garcia, Cristina** 1958- ...................... **CLC 76**
    See also AMWS 11; CA 141; CANR 73,
    130; DLB 292; DNFS 1; EWL 3; HW 2;
    LLW 1
**Garcia Lorca, Federico** 1898-1936 ...... **DC 2;**
    **HLC 2; PC 3; TCLC 1, 7, 49; WLC**
    See Lorca, Federico Garcia
    See also AAYA 46; CA 104; 131; CANR
    81; DA; DA3; DAB; DAC; DAM DRAM,
    MST, MULT, POET; DFS 4, 10; DLB
    108; EWL 3; HW 1, 2; LATS 1:2; MTCW
    1, 2; TWA
**Garcia Marquez, Gabriel (Jose)**
    1928- .... **CLC 2, 3, 8, 10, 15, 27, 47, 55,**
    **68, 170; HLC 1; SSC 8; WLC**
    See also AAYA 3, 33; BEST 89:1, 90:4;
    BPFB 2; BYA 12, 16; CA 33-36R; CANR
    10, 28, 50, 75, 82, 128; CDWLB 3; CPW;
    CWW 2; DA; DA3; DAB; DAC; DAM
    MST, MULT, NOV, POP; DLB 113;
    DNFS 1, 2; EWL 3; EXPN; EXPS; HW
    1, 2; LAIT 2; LATS 1:2; LAW; LAWS 1;
    LMFS 2; MTCW 1, 2; NCFS 3; NFS 1,
    5, 10; RGSF 2; RGWL 2, 3; SSFS 1, 6,
    16; TWA; WLIT 1
**Garcilaso de la Vega, El Inca**
    1503-1536 ................................... **HLCS 1**
    See also LAW
**Gard, Janice**
    See Latham, Jean Lee

**Gard, Roger Martin du**
    See Martin du Gard, Roger
**Gardam, Jane (Mary)** 1928- ............. **CLC 43**
    See also CA 49-52; CANR 2, 18, 33, 54,
    106; CLR 12; DLB 14, 161, 231; MAI-
    CYA 1, 2; MTCW 1; SAAS 9; SATA 39,
    76, 130; SATA-Brief 28; YAW
**Gardner, Herb(ert George)**
    1934-2003 ................................... **CLC 44**
    See also CA 149; 220; CAD; CANR 119;
    CD 5; DFS 18, 20
**Gardner, John (Champlin), Jr.**
    1933-1982 ...... **CLC 2, 3, 5, 7, 8, 10, 18,**
    **28, 34; SSC 7**
    See also AAYA 45; AITN 1; AMWS 6;
    BPFB 2; CA 65-68; 107; CANR 33, 73;
    CDALBS; CPW; DA3; DAM NOV, POP;
    DLB 2; DLBY 1982; EWL 3; FANT;
    LATS 1:2; MTCW 1; NFS 3; RGAL 4;
    RGSF 2; SATA 40; SATA-Obit 31; SSFS
    8
**Gardner, John (Edmund)** 1926- ....... **CLC 30**
    See also CA 103; CANR 15, 69, 127; CMW
    4; CPW; DAM POP; MTCW 1
**Gardner, Miriam**
    See Bradley, Marion Zimmer
    See also GLL 1
**Gardner, Noel**
    See Kuttner, Henry
**Gardons, S. S.**
    See Snodgrass, W(illiam) D(e Witt)
**Garfield, Leon** 1921-1996 .................. **CLC 12**
    See also AAYA 8; BYA 1, 3; CA 17-20R;
    152; CANR 38, 41, 78; CLR 21; DLB
    161; JRDA; MAICYA 1, 2; MAICYAS 1;
    SATA 1, 32, 76; SATA-Obit 90; TEA;
    WYA; YAW
**Garland, (Hannibal) Hamlin**
    1860-1940 .................. **SSC 18; TCLC 3**
    See also CA 104; DLB 12, 71, 78, 186;
    RGAL 4; RGSF 2; TCWW 2
**Garneau, (Hector de) Saint-Denys**
    1912-1943 ................................... **TCLC 13**
    See also CA 111; DLB 88
**Garner, Alan** 1934- ............................ **CLC 17**
    See also AAYA 18; BYA 3, 5; CA 73-76,
    178; CAAE 178; CANR 15, 64; CLR 20;
    CPW; DAB; DAM POP; DLB 161, 261;
    FANT; MAICYA 1, 2; MTCW 1, 2; SATA
    18, 69; SATA-Essay 108; SUFW 1, 2;
    YAW
**Garner, Hugh** 1913-1979 ................... **CLC 13**
    See Warwick, Jarvis
    See also CA 69-72; CANR 31; CCA 1; DLB
    68
**Garnett, David** 1892-1981 ................... **CLC 3**
    See also CA 5-8R; 103; CANR 17, 79; DLB
    34; FANT; MTCW 2; RGEL 2; SFW 4;
    SUFW 1
**Garos, Stephanie**
    See Katz, Steve
**Garrett, George (Palmer)** 1929- .. **CLC 3, 11,**
    **51; SSC 30**
    See also AMWS 7; BPFB 2; CA 1-4R, 202;
    CAAE 202; CAAS 5; CANR 1, 42, 67,
    109; CN 7; CP 7; CSW; DLB 2, 5, 130,
    152; DLBY 1983
**Garrick, David** 1717-1779 ................... **LC 15**
    See also DAM DRAM; DLB 84, 213;
    RGEL 2
**Garrigue, Jean** 1914-1972 .............. **CLC 2, 8**
    See also CA 5-8R; 37-40R; CANR 20
**Garrison, Frederick**
    See Sinclair, Upton (Beall)
**Garro, Elena** 1920(?)-1998 .. **HLCS 1; TCLC**
    **153**
    See also CA 131; 169; CWW 2; DLB 145;
    EWL 3; HW 1; LAWS 1; WLIT 1
**Garth, Will**
    See Hamilton, Edmond; Kuttner, Henry

**Garvey, Marcus (Moziah, Jr.)**
    1887-1940 ....... **BLC 2; HR 2; TCLC 41**
    See also BW 1; CA 120; 124; CANR 79;
    DAM MULT
**Gary, Romain** ................................... **CLC 25**
    See Kacew, Romain
    See also DLB 83, 299
**Gascar, Pierre** ................................... **CLC 11**
    See Fournier, Pierre
    See also EWL 3
**Gascoigne, George** 1539-1577 ........... **LC 108**
    See also DLB 136; RGEL 2
**Gascoyne, David (Emery)**
    1916-2001 ................................... **CLC 45**
    See also CA 65-68; 200; CANR 10, 28, 54;
    CP 7; DLB 20; MTCW 1; RGEL 2
**Gaskell, Elizabeth Cleghorn**
    1810-1865 .... **NCLC 5, 70, 97, 137; SSC**
    **25**
    See also BRW 5; CDBLB 1832-1890; DAB;
    DAM MST; DLB 21, 144, 159; RGEL 2;
    RGSF 2; TEA
**Gass, William H(oward)** 1924- . **CLC 1, 2, 8,**
    **11, 15, 39, 132; SSC 12**
    See also AMWS 6; CA 17-20R; CANR 30,
    71, 100; CN 7; DLB 2, 227; EWL 3;
    MTCW 1, 2; RGAL 4
**Gassendi, Pierre** 1592-1655 ................. **LC 54**
    See also GFL Beginnings to 1789
**Gasset, Jose Ortega y**
    See Ortega y Gasset, Jose
**Gates, Henry Louis, Jr.** 1950- ... **BLCS; CLC**
    **65**
    See also BW 2, 3; CA 109; CANR 25, 53,
    75, 125; CSW; DA3; DAM MULT; DLB
    67; EWL 3; MTCW 1; RGAL 4
**Gautier, Theophile** 1811-1872 .. **NCLC 1, 59;**
    **PC 18; SSC 20**
    See also DAM POET; DLB 119; EW 6;
    GFL 1789 to the Present; RGWL 2, 3;
    SUFW; TWA
**Gawsworth, John**
    See Bates, H(erbert) E(rnest)
**Gay, John** 1685-1732 ........................... **LC 49**
    See also BRW 3; DAM DRAM; DLB 84,
    95; RGEL 2; WLIT 3
**Gay, Oliver**
    See Gogarty, Oliver St. John
**Gay, Peter (Jack)** 1923- ................... **CLC 158**
    See also CA 13-16R; CANR 18, 41, 77;
    INT CANR-18
**Gaye, Marvin (Pentz, Jr.)**
    1939-1984 ................................... **CLC 26**
    See also CA 195; 112
**Gebler, Carlo (Ernest)** 1954- ........... **CLC 39**
    See also CA 119; 133; CANR 96; DLB 271
**Gee, Maggie (Mary)** 1948- ............... **CLC 57**
    See also CA 130; CANR 125; CN 7; DLB
    207
**Gee, Maurice (Gough)** 1931- ........... **CLC 29**
    See also AAYA 42; CA 97-100; CANR 67,
    123; CLR 56; CN 7; CWRI 5; EWL 3;
    MAICYA 2; RGSF 2; SATA 46, 101
**Geiogamah, Hanay** 1945- .................. **NNAL**
    See also CA 153; DAM MULT; DLB 175
**Gelbart, Larry (Simon)** 1928- .... **CLC 21, 61**
    See Gelbart, Larry
    See also CA 73-76; CANR 45, 94
**Gelbart, Larry** 1928-
    See Gelbart, Larry (Simon)
    See also CAD; CD 5
**Gelber, Jack** 1932-2003 ...... **CLC 1, 6, 14, 79**
    See also CA 1-4R; 216; CAD; CANR 2;
    DLB 7, 228
**Gellhorn, Martha (Ellis)**
    1908-1998 ............................. **CLC 14, 60**
    See also CA 77-80; 164; CANR 44; CN 7;
    DLBY 1982, 1998

**Genet, Jean** 1910-1986 .. **CLC 1, 2, 5, 10, 14, 44, 46; TCLC 128**
See also CA 13-16R; CANR 18; DA3; DAM DRAM; DFS 10; DLB 72; DLBY 1986; EW 13; EWL 3; GFL 1789 to the Present; GLL 1; LMFS 2; MTCW 1, 2; RGWL 2, 3; TWA

**Gent, Peter** 1942- ................................ **CLC 29**
See also AITN 1; CA 89-92; DLBY 1982

**Gentile, Giovanni** 1875-1944 .......... **TCLC 96**
See also CA 119

**Gentlewoman in New England, A**
See Bradstreet, Anne

**Gentlewoman in Those Parts, A**
See Bradstreet, Anne

**Geoffrey of Monmouth** c. 1100-1155 ................................ **CMLC 44**
See also DLB 146; TEA

**George, Jean**
See George, Jean Craighead

**George, Jean Craighead** 1919- .......... **CLC 35**
See also AAYA 8; BYA 2, 4; CA 5-8R; CANR 25; CLR 1; 80; DLB 52; JRDA; MAICYA 1, 2; SATA 2, 68, 124; WYA; YAW

**George, Stefan (Anton)** 1868-1933 . **TCLC 2, 14**
See also CA 104; 193; EW 8; EWL 3

**Georges, Georges Martin**
See Simenon, Georges (Jacques Christian)

**Gerald of Wales** c. 1146-c. 1223 ... **CMLC 60**

**Gerhardi, William Alexander**
See Gerhardie, William Alexander

**Gerhardie, William Alexander** 1895-1977 ...................................... **CLC 5**
See also CA 25-28R; 73-76; CANR 18; DLB 36; RGEL 2

**Gerson, Jean** 1363-1429 ...................... **LC 77**
See also DLB 208

**Gersonides** 1288-1344 ................... **CMLC 49**
See also DLB 115

**Gerstler, Amy** 1956- ............................ **CLC 70**
See also CA 146; CANR 99

**Gertler, T.** ............................................ **CLC 34**
See also CA 116; 121

**Gertsen, Aleksandr Ivanovich**
See Herzen, Aleksandr Ivanovich

**Ghalib** ........................................ **NCLC 39, 78**
See Ghalib, Asadullah Khan

**Ghalib, Asadullah Khan** 1797-1869
See Ghalib
See also DAM POET; RGWL 2, 3

**Ghelderode, Michel de** 1898-1962 ..... **CLC 6, 11; DC 15**
See also CA 85-88; CANR 40, 77; DAM DRAM; EW 11; EWL 3; TWA

**Ghiselin, Brewster** 1903-2001 .......... **CLC 23**
See also CA 13-16R; CAAS 10; CANR 13; CP 7

**Ghose, Aurabinda** 1872-1950 ......... **TCLC 63**
See Ghose, Aurobindo
See also CA 163

**Ghose, Aurobindo**
See Ghose, Aurabinda
See also EWL 3

**Ghose, Zulfikar** 1935- ........................ **CLC 42**
See also CA 65-68; CANR 67; CN 7; CP 7; EWL 3

**Ghosh, Amitav** 1956- ................. **CLC 44, 153**
See also CA 147; CANR 80; CN 7; WWE 1

**Giacosa, Giuseppe** 1847-1906 .......... **TCLC 7**
See also CA 104

**Gibb, Lee**
See Waterhouse, Keith (Spencer)

**Gibbon, Edward** 1737-1794 ................ **LC 97**
See also BRW 3; DLB 104; RGEL 2

**Gibbon, Lewis Grassic** .................... **TCLC 4**
See Mitchell, James Leslie
See also RGEL 2

**Gibbons, Kaye** 1960- ........... **CLC 50, 88, 145**
See also AAYA 34; AMWS 10; CA 151; CANR 75, 127; CSW; DA3; DAM POP; DLB 292; MTCW 1; NFS 3; RGAL 4; SATA 117

**Gibran, Kahlil** 1883-1931 . **PC 9; TCLC 1, 9**
See also CA 104; 150; DA3; DAM POET, POP; EWL 3; MTCW 2

**Gibran, Khalil**
See Gibran, Kahlil

**Gibson, William** 1914- ...................... **CLC 23**
See also CA 9-12R; CAD 2; CANR 9, 42, 75, 125; CD 5; DA; DAB; DAC; DAM DRAM, MST; DFS 2; DLB 7; LAIT 2; MTCW 2; SATA 66; YAW

**Gibson, William (Ford)** 1948- ... **CLC 39, 63, 186, 192; SSC 52**
See also AAYA 12, 59; BPFB 2; CA 126; 133; CANR 52, 90, 106; CN 7; CPW; DA3; DAM POP; DLB 251; MTCW 2; SCFW 2; SFW 4

**Gide, Andre (Paul Guillaume)** 1869-1951 ..... **SSC 13; TCLC 5, 12, 36; WLC**
See also CA 104; 124; DA; DA3; DAB; DAC; DAM MST, NOV; DLB 65; EW 8; EWL 3; GFL 1789 to the Present; MTCW 1, 2; RGSF 2; RGWL 2, 3; TWA

**Gifford, Barry (Colby)** 1946- ............ **CLC 34**
See also CA 65-68; CANR 9, 30, 40, 90

**Gilbert, Frank**
See De Voto, Bernard (Augustine)

**Gilbert, W(illiam) S(chwenck)** 1836-1911 .................................. **TCLC 3**
See also CA 104; 173; DAM DRAM, POET; RGEL 2; SATA 36

**Gilbreth, Frank B(unker), Jr.** 1911-2001 ................................ **CLC 17**
See also CA 9-12R; SATA 2

**Gilchrist, Ellen (Louise)** 1935- .. **CLC 34, 48, 143; SSC 14, 63**
See also BPFB 2; CA 113; 116; CANR 41, 61, 104; CN 7; CPW; CSW; DAM POP; DLB 130; EWL 3; EXPS; MTCW 1, 2; RGAL 4; RGSF 2; SSFS 9

**Giles, Molly** 1942- ............................. **CLC 39**
See also CA 126; CANR 98

**Gill, Eric** 1882-1940 ........................ **TCLC 85**
See Gill, (Arthur) Eric (Rowton Peter Joseph)

**Gill, (Arthur) Eric (Rowton Peter Joseph)** 1882-1940
See Gill, Eric
See also CA 120; DLB 98

**Gill, Patrick**
See Creasey, John

**Gillette, Douglas** ................................ **CLC 70**

**Gilliam, Terry (Vance)** 1940- .... **CLC 21, 141**
See Monty Python
See also AAYA 19, 59; CA 108; 113; CANR 35; INT CA-113

**Gillian, Jerry**
See Gilliam, Terry (Vance)

**Gilliatt, Penelope (Ann Douglass)** 1932-1993 ................. **CLC 2, 10, 13, 53**
See also AITN 2; CA 13-16R; 141; CANR 49; DLB 14

**Gilman, Charlotte (Anna) Perkins (Stetson)** 1860-1935 ...... **SSC 13, 62; TCLC 9, 37, 117**
See also AMWS 11; BYA 11; CA 106; 150; DLB 221; EXPS; FW; HGG; LAIT 2; MAWW; MTCW 1; RGAL 4; RGSF 2; SFW 4; SSFS 1, 18

**Gilmour, David** 1946- ........................ **CLC 35**

**Gilpin, William** 1724-1804 ............. **NCLC 30**

**Gilray, J. D.**
See Mencken, H(enry) L(ouis)

**Gilroy, Frank D(aniel)** 1925- ............. **CLC 2**
See also CA 81-84; CAD; CANR 32, 64, 86; CD 5; DFS 17; DLB 7

**Gilstrap, John** 1957(?)- ...................... **CLC 99**
See also CA 160; CANR 101

**Ginsberg, Allen** 1926-1997 .... **CLC 1, 2, 3, 4, 6, 13, 36, 69, 109; PC 4, 47; TCLC 120; WLC**
See also AAYA 33; AITN 1; AMWC 1; AMWS 2; BG 2; CA 1-4R; 157; CANR 2, 41, 63, 95; CDALB 1941-1968; CP 7; DA; DA3; DAB; DAC; DAM MST, POET; DLB 5, 16, 169, 237; EWL 3; GLL 1; LMFS 2; MTCW 1, 2; PAB; PFS 5; RGAL 4; TUS; WP

**Ginzburg, Eugenia** ........................... **CLC 59**
See Ginzburg, Evgeniia

**Ginzburg, Evgeniia** 1904-1977
See Ginzburg, Eugenia
See also DLB 302

**Ginzburg, Natalia** 1916-1991 ....... **CLC 5, 11, 54, 70; SSC 65; TCLC 156**
See also CA 85-88; 135; CANR 33; DFS 14; DLB 177; EW 13; EWL 3; MTCW 1, 2; RGWL 2, 3

**Giono, Jean** 1895-1970 .... **CLC 4, 11; TCLC 124**
See also CA 45-48; 29-32R; CANR 2, 35; DLB 72; EWL 3; GFL 1789 to the Present; MTCW 1; RGWL 2, 3

**Giovanni, Nikki** 1943- ...... **BLC 2; CLC 2, 4, 19, 64, 117; PC 19; WLCS**
See also AAYA 22; AITN 1; BW 2, 3; CA 29-32R; CAAS 6; CANR 18, 41, 60, 91, 130; CDALBS; CLR 6, 73; CP 7; CSW; CWP; CWRI 5; DA; DA3; DAB; DAC; DAM MST, MULT, POET; DLB 5, 41; EWL 3; EXPP; INT CANR-18; MAICYA 1, 2; MTCW 1, 2; PFS 17; RGAL 4; SATA 24, 107; TUS; YAW

**Giovene, Andrea** 1904-1998 ............... **CLC 7**
See also CA 85-88

**Gippius, Zinaida (Nikolaevna)** 1869-1945
See Hippius, Zinaida (Nikolaevna)
See also CA 106; 212

**Giraudoux, Jean(-Hippolyte)** 1882-1944 ............................... **TCLC 2, 7**
See also CA 104; 196; DAM DRAM; DLB 65; EW 9; EWL 3; GFL 1789 to the Present; RGWL 2, 3; TWA

**Gironella, Jose Maria (Pous)** 1917-2003 ................................... **CLC 11**
See also CA 101; 212; EWL 3; RGWL 2, 3

**Gissing, George (Robert)** 1857-1903 ....... **SSC 37; TCLC 3, 24, 47**
See also BRW 5; CA 105; 167; DLB 18, 135, 184; RGEL 2; TEA

**Giurlani, Aldo**
See Palazzeschi, Aldo

**Gladkov, Fedor Vasil'evich**
See Gladkov, Fyodor (Vasilyevich)
See also DLB 272

**Gladkov, Fyodor (Vasilyevich)** 1883-1958 ................................. **TCLC 27**
See Gladkov, Fedor Vasil'evich
See also CA 170; EWL 3

**Glancy, Diane** 1941- ........................... **NNAL**
See also CA 136; 225; CAAE 225; CAAS 24; CANR 87; DLB 175

**Glanville, Brian (Lester)** 1931- .......... **CLC 6**
See also CA 5-8R; CAAS 9; CANR 3, 70; CN 7; DLB 15, 139; SATA 42

**Glasgow, Ellen (Anderson Gholson)**
1873-1945 .............. **SSC 34; TCLC 2, 7**
See also AMW; CA 104; 164; DLB 9, 12;
MAWW; MTCW 2; RGAL 4; RHW;
SSFS 9; TUS

**Glaspell, Susan** 1882(?)-1948 ..... **DC 10; SSC 41; TCLC 55**
See also AMWS 3; CA 110; 154; DFS 8,
18; DLB 7, 9, 78, 228; MAWW; RGAL
4; SSFS 3; TCWW 2; TUS; YABC 2

**Glassco, John** 1909-1981 .................... **CLC 9**
See also CA 13-16R; 102; CANR 15; DLB
68

**Glasscock, Amnesia**
See Steinbeck, John (Ernst)

**Glasser, Ronald J.** 1940(?)- ............. **CLC 37**
See also CA 209

**Glassman, Joyce**
See Johnson, Joyce

**Gleick, James (W.)** 1954- ............... **CLC 147**
See also CA 131; 137; CANR 97; INT CA-
137

**Glendinning, Victoria** 1937- ............. **CLC 50**
See also CA 120; 127; CANR 59, 89; DLB
155

**Glissant, Edouard (Mathieu)**
1928- ................................... **CLC 10, 68**
See also CA 153; CANR 111; CWW 2;
DAM MULT; EWL 3; RGWL 3

**Gloag, Julian** 1930- ........................... **CLC 40**
See also AITN 1; CA 65-68; CANR 10, 70;
CN 7

**Glowacki, Aleksander**
See Prus, Boleslaw

**Gluck, Louise (Elisabeth)** 1943- .. **CLC 7, 22, 44, 81, 160; PC 16**
See also AMWS 5; CA 33-36R; CANR 40,
69, 108, 133; CP 7; CWP; DA3; DAM
POET; DLB 5; MTCW 2; PFS 5, 15;
RGAL 4

**Glyn, Elinor** 1864-1943 .................... **TCLC 72**
See also DLB 153; RHW

**Gobineau, Joseph-Arthur**
1816-1882 ................................. **NCLC 17**
See also DLB 123; GFL 1789 to the Present

**Godard, Jean-Luc** 1930- ................... **CLC 20**
See also CA 93-96

**Godden, (Margaret) Rumer**
1907-1998 ................................. **CLC 53**
See also AAYA 6; BPFB 2; BYA 2, 5; CA
5-8R; 172; CANR 4, 27, 36, 55, 80; CLR
20; CN 7; CWRI 5; DLB 161; MAICYA
1, 2; RHW; SAAS 12; SATA 3, 36; SATA-
Obit 109; TEA

**Godoy Alcayaga, Lucila** 1899-1957 .. **HLC 2; PC 32; TCLC 2**
See Mistral, Gabriela
See also BW 2; CA 104; 131; CANR 81;
DAM MULT; DNFS; HW 1, 2; MTCW 1,
2

**Godwin, Gail (Kathleen)** 1937- ..... **CLC 5, 8, 22, 31, 69, 125**
See also BPFB 2; CA 29-32R; CANR 15,
43, 69, 132; CN 7; CPW; CSW; DA3;
DAM POP; DLB 6, 234; INT CANR-15;
MTCW 1, 2

**Godwin, William** 1756-1836 .. **NCLC 14, 130**
See also CDBLB 1789-1832; CMW 4; DLB
39, 104, 142, 158, 163, 262; HGG; RGEL
2

**Goebbels, Josef**
See Goebbels, (Paul) Joseph

**Goebbels, (Paul) Joseph**
1897-1945 ................................. **TCLC 68**
See also CA 115; 148

**Goebbels, Joseph Paul**
See Goebbels, (Paul) Joseph

**Goethe, Johann Wolfgang von**
1749-1832 ....... **DC 20; NCLC 4, 22, 34, 90; PC 5; SSC 38; WLC**
See also CDWLB 2; DA; DA3; DAB;
DAC; DAM DRAM, MST, POET; DLB
94; EW 5; LATS 1; LMFS 1:1; RGWL 2,
3; TWA

**Gogarty, Oliver St. John**
1878-1957 ................................. **TCLC 15**
See also CA 109; 150; DLB 15, 19; RGEL
2

**Gogol, Nikolai (Vasilyevich)**
1809-1852 ......... **DC 1; NCLC 5, 15, 31; SSC 4, 29, 52; WLC**
See also DA; DAB; DAC; DAM DRAM,
MST; DFS 12; DLB 198; EW 6; EXPS;
RGSF 2; RGWL 2, 3; SSFS 7; TWA

**Goines, Donald** 1937(?)-1974 ... **BLC 2; CLC 80**
See also AITN 1; BW 1, 3; CA 124; 114;
CANR 82; CMW 4; DA3; DAM MULT,
POP; DLB 33

**Gold, Herbert** 1924- ... **CLC 4, 7, 14, 42, 152**
See also CA 9-12R; CANR 17, 45, 125; CN
7; DLB 2; DLBY 1981

**Goldbarth, Albert** 1948- ................. **CLC 5, 38**
See also AMWS 12; CA 53-56; CANR 6,
40; CP 7; DLB 120

**Goldberg, Anatol** 1910-1982 ............. **CLC 34**
See also CA 131; 117

**Goldemberg, Isaac** 1945- ................... **CLC 52**
See also CA 69-72; CAAS 12; CANR 11,
32; EWL 3; HW 1; WLIT 1

**Golding, Arthur** 1536-1606 ............... **LC 101**
See also DLB 136

**Golding, William (Gerald)**
1911-1993 ..... **CLC 1, 2, 3, 8, 10, 17, 27, 58, 81; WLC**
See also AAYA 5, 44; BPFB 2; BRWR 1;
BRWS 1; BYA 2; CA 5-8R; 141; CANR
13, 33, 54; CDBLB 1945-1960; CLR 94;
DA; DA3; DAB; DAC; DAM MST, NOV;
DLB 15, 100, 255; EWL 3; EXPN; HGG;
LAIT 4; MTCW 1, 2; NFS 2; RGEL 2;
RHW; SFW 4; TEA; WLIT 4; YAW

**Goldman, Emma** 1869-1940 ........... **TCLC 13**
See also CA 110; 150; DLB 221; FW;
RGAL 4; TUS

**Goldman, Francisco** 1954- ................ **CLC 76**
See also CA 162

**Goldman, William (W.)** 1931- ...... **CLC 1, 48**
See also BPFB 2; CA 9-12R; CANR 29,
69, 106; CN 7; DLB 44; FANT; IDFW 3,
4

**Goldmann, Lucien** 1913-1970 ........... **CLC 24**
See also CA 25-28; CAP 2

**Goldoni, Carlo** 1707-1793 .................... **LC 4**
See also DAM DRAM; EW 4; RGWL 2, 3

**Goldsberry, Steven** 1949- .................. **CLC 34**
See also CA 131

**Goldsmith, Oliver** 1730-1774 ... **DC 8; LC 2, 48; WLC**
See also BRW 3; CDBLB 1660-1789; DA;
DAB; DAC; DAM DRAM, MST, NOV,
POET; DFS 1; DLB 39, 89, 104, 109, 142;
IDTP; RGEL 2; SATA 26; TEA; WLIT 3

**Goldsmith, Peter**
See Priestley, J(ohn) B(oynton)

**Gombrowicz, Witold** 1904-1969 .... **CLC 4, 7, 11, 49**
See also CA 19-20; 25-28R; CANR 105;
CAP 2; CDWLB 4; DAM DRAM; DLB
215; EW 12; EWL 3; RGWL 2, 3; TWA

**Gomez de Avellaneda, Gertrudis**
1814-1873 .............................. **NCLC 111**
See also LAW

**Gomez de la Serna, Ramon**
1888-1963 ................................... **CLC 9**
See also CA 153; 116; CANR 79; EWL 3;
HW 1, 2

**Goncharov, Ivan Alexandrovich**
1812-1891 ............................. **NCLC 1, 63**
See also DLB 238; EW 6; RGWL 2, 3

**Goncourt, Edmond (Louis Antoine Huot) de**
1822-1896 .................................. **NCLC 7**
See also DLB 123; EW 7; GFL 1789 to the
Present; RGWL 2, 3

**Goncourt, Jules (Alfred Huot) de**
1830-1870 .................................. **NCLC 7**
See also DLB 123; EW 7; GFL 1789 to the
Present; RGWL 2, 3

**Gongora (y Argote), Luis de**
1561-1627 .................................... **LC 72**
See also RGWL 2, 3

**Gontier, Fernande** 19(?)- ................... **CLC 50**

**Gonzalez Martinez, Enrique**
See Gonzalez Martinez, Enrique
See also DLB 290

**Gonzalez Martinez, Enrique**
1871-1952 ................................. **TCLC 72**
See Gonzalez Martinez, Enrique
See also CA 166; CANR 81; EWL 3; HW
1, 2

**Goodison, Lorna** 1947- ....................... **PC 36**
See also CA 142; CANR 88; CP 7; CWP;
DLB 157; EWL 3

**Goodman, Paul** 1911-1972 ..... **CLC 1, 2, 4, 7**
See also CA 19-20; 37-40R; CAD; CANR
34; CAP 2; DLB 130, 246; MTCW 1;
RGAL 4

**GoodWeather, Harley**
See King, Thomas

**Googe, Barnabe** 1540-1594 ................. **LC 94**
See also DLB 132; RGEL 2

**Gordimer, Nadine** 1923- ..... **CLC 3, 5, 7, 10, 18, 33, 51, 70, 123, 160, 161; SSC 17; WLCS**
See also AAYA 39; AFW; BRWS 2; CA
5-8R; CANR 3, 28, 56, 88, 131; CN 7;
DA; DA3; DAB; DAC; DAM MST, NOV;
DLB 225; EWL 3; EXPS; INT CANR-28;
LATS 1:2; MTCW 1, 2; NFS 4; RGEL 2;
RGSF 2; SSFS 2, 14, 19; TWA; WLIT 2;
YAW

**Gordon, Adam Lindsay**
1833-1870 ................................. **NCLC 21**
See also DLB 230

**Gordon, Caroline** 1895-1981 . **CLC 6, 13, 29, 83; SSC 15**
See also AMW; CA 11-12; 103; CANR 36;
CAP 1; DLB 4, 9, 102; DLBD 17; DLBY
1981; EWL 3; MTCW 1, 2; RGAL 4;
RGSF 2

**Gordon, Charles William** 1860-1937
See Connor, Ralph
See also CA 109

**Gordon, Mary (Catherine)** 1949- .... **CLC 13, 22, 128; SSC 59**
See also AMWS 4; BPFB 2; CA 102;
CANR 44, 92; CN 7; DLB 6; DLBY
1981; FW; INT CA-102; MTCW 1

**Gordon, N. J.**
See Bosman, Herman Charles

**Gordon, Sol** 1923- ........................... **CLC 26**
See also CA 53-56; CANR 4; SATA 11

**Gordone, Charles** 1925-1995 .. **CLC 1, 4; DC 8**
See also BW 1, 3; CA 93-96; 180; 150;
CAAE 180; CAD; CANR 55; DAM
DRAM; DLB 7; INT CA-93-96; MTCW
1

**Gore, Catherine** 1800-1861 ........... **NCLC 65**
See also DLB 116; RGEL 2

**Gorenko, Anna Andreevna**
See Akhmatova, Anna

**Gorky, Maxim** ....... **SSC 28; TCLC 8; WLC**
See Peshkov, Alexei Maximovich
See also DAB; DFS 9; DLB 295; EW 8;
EWL 3; MTCW 2; TWA

**Goryan, Sirak**
See Saroyan, William
**Gosse, Edmund (William)**
1849-1928 ................................ **TCLC 28**
See also CA 117; DLB 57, 144, 184; RGEL 2
**Gotlieb, Phyllis (Fay Bloom)** 1926- .. **CLC 18**
See also CA 13-16R; CANR 7; DLB 88, 251; SFW 4
**Gottesman, S. D.**
See Kornbluth, C(yril) M.; Pohl, Frederik
**Gottfried von Strassburg** fl. c.
1170-1215 ................................ **CMLC 10**
See also CDWLB 2; DLB 138; EW 1; RGWL 2, 3
**Gotthelf, Jeremias** 1797-1854 ....... **NCLC 117**
See also DLB 133; RGWL 2, 3
**Gottschalk, Laura Riding**
See Jackson, Laura (Riding)
**Gould, Lois** 1932(?)-2002 .............. **CLC 4, 10**
See also CA 77-80; 208; CANR 29; MTCW 1
**Gould, Stephen Jay** 1941-2002 ....... **CLC 163**
See also AAYA 26; BEST 90:2; CA 77-80; 205; CANR 10, 27, 56, 75, 125; CPW; INT CANR-27; MTCW 1, 2
**Gourmont, Remy(-Marie-Charles) de**
1858-1915 ................................ **TCLC 17**
See also CA 109; 150; GFL 1789 to the Present; MTCW 2
**Gournay, Marie le Jars de**
See de Gournay, Marie le Jars
**Govier, Katherine** 1948- .................... **CLC 51**
See also CA 101; CANR 18, 40, 128; CCA 1
**Gower, John** c. 1330-1408 ....... **LC 76; PC 59**
See also BRW 1; DLB 146; RGEL 2
**Goyen, (Charles) William**
1915-1983 .................... **CLC 5, 8, 14, 40**
See also AITN 2; CA 5-8R; 110; CANR 6, 71; DLB 2, 218; DLBY 1983; EWL 3; INT CANR-6
**Goytisolo, Juan** 1931- .... **CLC 5, 10, 23, 133; HLC 1**
See also CA 85-88; CANR 32, 61, 131; CWW 2; DAM MULT; EWL 3; GLL 2; HW 1, 2; MTCW 1, 2
**Gozzano, Guido** 1883-1916 .................. **PC 10**
See also CA 154; DLB 114; EWL 3
**Gozzi, (Conte) Carlo** 1720-1806 .... **NCLC 23**
**Grabbe, Christian Dietrich**
1801-1836 ................................ **NCLC 2**
See also DLB 133; RGWL 2, 3
**Grace, Patricia Frances** 1937- .......... **CLC 56**
See also CA 176; CANR 118; CN 7; EWL 3; RGSF 2
**Gracian y Morales, Baltasar**
1601-1658 ................................ **LC 15**
**Gracq, Julien** .............................. **CLC 11, 48**
See Poirier, Louis
See also CWW 2; DLB 83; GFL 1789 to the Present
**Grade, Chaim** 1910-1982 .................. **CLC 10**
See also CA 93-96; 107; EWL 3
**Graduate of Oxford, A**
See Ruskin, John
**Grafton, Garth**
See Duncan, Sara Jeannette
**Grafton, Sue** 1940- .......................... **CLC 163**
See also AAYA 11, 49; BEST 90:3; CA 108; CANR 31, 55, 111; CMW 4; CPW; CSW; DA3; DAM POP; DLB 226; FW; MSW
**Graham, John**
See Phillips, David Graham
**Graham, Jorie** 1951- .... **CLC 48, 118; PC 59**
See also CA 111; CANR 63, 118; CP 7; CWP; DLB 120; EWL 3; PFS 10, 17

**Graham, R(obert) B(ontine) Cunninghame**
See Cunninghame Graham, Robert (Gallnigad) Bontine
See also DLB 98, 135, 174; RGEL 2; RGSF 2
**Graham, Robert**
See Haldeman, Joe (William)
**Graham, Tom**
See Lewis, (Harry) Sinclair
**Graham, W(illiam) S(idney)**
1918-1986 ................................ **CLC 29**
See also BRWS 7; CA 73-76; 118; DLB 20; RGEL 2
**Graham, Winston (Mawdsley)**
1910-2003 ................................ **CLC 23**
See also CA 49-52; 218; CANR 2, 22, 45, 66; CMW 4; CN 7; DLB 77; RHW
**Grahame, Kenneth** 1859-1932 ...... **TCLC 64, 136**
See also BYA 5; CA 108; 136; CANR 80; CLR 5; CWRI 5; DA3; DAB; DLB 34, 141, 178; FANT; MAICYA 1, 2; MTCW 2; NFS 20; RGEL 2; SATA 100; TEA; WCH; YABC 1
**Granger, Darius John**
See Marlowe, Stephen
**Granin, Daniil** 1918- ........................ **CLC 59**
See also DLB 302
**Granovsky, Timofei Nikolaevich**
1813-1855 ................................ **NCLC 75**
See also DLB 198
**Grant, Skeeter**
See Spiegelman, Art
**Granville-Barker, Harley**
1877-1946 ................................ **TCLC 2**
See Barker, Harley Granville
See also CA 104; 204; DAM DRAM; RGEL 2
**Granzotto, Gianni**
See Granzotto, Giovanni Battista
**Granzotto, Giovanni Battista**
1914-1985 ................................ **CLC 70**
See also CA 166
**Grass, Guenter (Wilhelm)** 1927- ... **CLC 1, 2, 4, 6, 11, 15, 22, 32, 49, 88; WLC**
See Grass, Gunter (Wilhelm)
See also BPFB 2; CA 13-16R; CANR 20, 75, 93, 133; CDWLB 2; DA; DA3; DAB; DAC; DAM MST, NOV; DLB 75, 124; EW 13; EWL 3; MTCW 1, 2; RGWL 2, 3; TWA
**Grass, Gunter (Wilhelm)**
See Grass, Guenter (Wilhelm)
See also CWW 2
**Gratton, Thomas**
See Hulme, T(homas) E(rnest)
**Grau, Shirley Ann** 1929- ....... **CLC 4, 9, 146; SSC 15**
See also CA 89-92; CANR 22, 69; CN 7; CSW; DLB 2, 218; INT CA-89-92; CANR-22; MTCW 1
**Gravel, Fern**
See Hall, James Norman
**Graver, Elizabeth** 1964- .................... **CLC 70**
See also CA 135; CANR 71, 129
**Graves, Richard Perceval**
1895-1985 ................................ **CLC 44**
See also CA 65-68; CANR 9, 26, 51
**Graves, Robert (von Ranke)**
1895-1985 .. **CLC 1, 2, 6, 11, 39, 44, 45; PC 6**
See also BPFB 2; BRW 7; BYA 4; CA 5-8R; 117; CANR 5, 36; CDBLB 1914-1945; DA3; DAB; DAC; DAM MST, POET; DLB 20, 100, 191; DLBD 18; DLBY 1985; EWL 3; LATS 1:1; MTCW 1, 2; NCFS 2; RGEL 2; RHW; SATA 45; TEA
**Graves, Valerie**
See Bradley, Marion Zimmer

**Gray, Alasdair (James)** 1934- .......... **CLC 41**
See also BRWS 9; CA 126; CANR 47, 69, 106; CN 7; DLB 194, 261; HGG; INT CA-126; MTCW 1, 2; RGSF 2; SUFW 2
**Gray, Amlin** 1946- ............................ **CLC 29**
See also CA 138
**Gray, Francine du Plessix** 1930- ..... **CLC 22, 153**
See also BEST 90:3; CA 61-64; CAAS 2; CANR 11, 33, 75, 81; DAM NOV; INT CANR-11; MTCW 1, 2
**Gray, John (Henry)** 1866-1934 ...... **TCLC 19**
See also CA 119; 162; RGEL 2
**Gray, Simon (James Holliday)**
1936- ................................ **CLC 9, 14, 36**
See also AITN 1; CA 21-24R; CAAS 3; CANR 32, 69; CD 5; DLB 13; EWL 3; MTCW 1; RGEL 2
**Gray, Spalding** 1941-2004 ........ **CLC 49, 112; DC 7**
See also CA 128; 225; CAD; CANR 74; CD 5; CPW; DAM POP; MTCW 2
**Gray, Thomas** 1716-1771 .... **LC 4, 40; PC 2; WLC**
See also BRW 3; CDBLB 1660-1789; DA; DA3; DAB; DAC; DAM MST; DLB 109; EXPP; PAB; PFS 9; RGEL 2; TEA; WP
**Grayson, David**
See Baker, Ray Stannard
**Grayson, Richard (A.)** 1951- ............ **CLC 38**
See also CA 85-88; 210; CAAE 210; CANR 14, 31, 57; DLB 234
**Greeley, Andrew M(oran)** 1928- ...... **CLC 28**
See also BPFB 2; CA 5-8R; CAAS 7; CANR 7, 43, 69, 104; CMW 4; CPW; DA3; DAM POP; MTCW 1, 2
**Green, Anna Katharine**
1846-1935 ................................ **TCLC 63**
See also CA 112; 159; CMW 4; DLB 202, 221; MSW
**Green, Brian**
See Card, Orson Scott
**Green, Hannah**
See Greenberg, Joanne (Goldenberg)
**Green, Hannah** 1927(?)-1996 .............. **CLC 3**
See also CA 73-76; CANR 59, 93; NFS 10
**Green, Henry** ........................ **CLC 2, 13, 97**
See Yorke, Henry Vincent
See also BRWS 2; CA 175; DLB 15; EWL 3; RGEL 2
**Green, Julian (Hartridge)** 1900-1998
See Green, Julien
See also CA 21-24R; 169; CANR 33, 87; CWW 2; DLB 4, 72; MTCW 1
**Green, Julien** ........................ **CLC 3, 11, 77**
See Green, Julian (Hartridge)
See also EWL 3; GFL 1789 to the Present; MTCW 2
**Green, Paul (Eliot)** 1894-1981 .......... **CLC 25**
See also AITN 1; CA 5-8R; 103; CANR 3; DAM DRAM; DLB 7, 9, 249; DLBY 1981; RGAL 4
**Greenaway, Peter** 1942- ................. **CLC 159**
See also CA 127
**Greenberg, Ivan** 1908-1973
See Rahv, Philip
See also CA 85-88
**Greenberg, Joanne (Goldenberg)**
1932- ................................ **CLC 7, 30**
See also AAYA 12; CA 5-8R; CANR 14, 32, 69; CN 7; SATA 25; YAW
**Greenberg, Richard** 1959(?)- ............ **CLC 57**
See also CA 138; CAD; CD 5
**Greenblatt, Stephen J(ay)** 1943- ...... **CLC 70**
See also CA 49-52; CANR 115

**Greene, Bette** 1934- ............................ **CLC 30**
See also AAYA 7; BYA 3; CA 53-56; CANR 4; CLR 2; CWRI 5; JRDA; LAIT 4; MAI-CYA 1, 2; NFS 10; SAAS 16; SATA 8, 102; WYA; YAW

**Greene, Gael** ............................................ **CLC 8**
See also CA 13-16R; CANR 10

**Greene, Graham (Henry)**
1904-1991 .... **CLC 1, 3, 6, 9, 14, 18, 27, 37, 70, 72, 125; SSC 29; WLC**
See also AITN 2; BPFB 2; BRWR 2; BRWS 1; BYA 3; CA 13-16R; 133; CANR 35, 61, 131; CBD; CDBLB 1945-1960; CMW 4; DA; DA3; DAB; DAC; DAM MST, NOV; DLB 13, 15, 77, 100, 162, 201, 204; DLBY 1991; EWL 3; MSW; MTCW 1, 2; NFS 16; RGEL 2; SATA 20; SSFS 14; TEA; WLIT 4

**Greene, Robert** 1558-1592 ................... **LC 41**
See also BRWS 8; DLB 62, 167; IDTP; RGEL 2; TEA

**Greer, Germaine** 1939- ...................... **CLC 131**
See also AITN 1; CA 81-84; CANR 33, 70, 115, 133; FW; MTCW 1, 2

**Greer, Richard**
See Silverberg, Robert

**Gregor, Arthur** 1923- ........................... **CLC 9**
See also CA 25-28R; CAAS 10; CANR 11; CP 7; SATA 36

**Gregor, Lee**
See Pohl, Frederik

**Gregory, Lady Isabella Augusta (Persse)**
1852-1932 ...................................... **TCLC 1**
See also BRW 6; CA 104; 184; DLB 10; IDTP; RGEL 2

**Gregory, J. Dennis**
See Williams, John A(lfred)

**Grekova, I.** .............................................. **CLC 59**
See Ventsel, Elena Sergeevna
See also CWW 2

**Grendon, Stephen**
See Derleth, August (William)

**Grenville, Kate** 1950- ........................... **CLC 61**
See also CA 118; CANR 53, 93

**Grenville, Pelham**
See Wodehouse, P(elham) G(renville)

**Greve, Felix Paul (Berthold Friedrich)**
1879-1948
See Grove, Frederick Philip
See also CA 104; 141, 175; CANR 79; DAC; DAM MST

**Greville, Fulke** 1554-1628 ................... **LC 79**
See also DLB 62, 172; RGEL 2

**Grey, Lady Jane** 1537-1554 ................ **LC 93**
See also DLB 132

**Grey, Zane** 1872-1939 ...................... **TCLC 6**
See also BPFB 2; CA 104; 132; DA3; DAM POP; DLB 9, 212; MTCW 1, 2; RGAL 4; TCWW 2; TUS

**Griboedov, Aleksandr Sergeevich**
1795(?)-1829 ......................... **NCLC 129**
See also DLB 205; RGWL 2, 3

**Grieg, (Johan) Nordahl (Brun)**
1902-1943 ...................................... **TCLC 10**
See also CA 107; 189; EWL 3

**Grieve, C(hristopher) M(urray)**
1892-1978 ............................... **CLC 11, 19**
See MacDiarmid, Hugh; Pteleon
See also CA 5-8R; 85-88; CANR 33, 107; DAM POET; MTCW 1; RGEL 2

**Griffin, Gerald** 1803-1840 ................ **NCLC 7**
See also DLB 159; RGEL 2

**Griffin, John Howard** 1920-1980 ..... **CLC 68**
See also AITN 1; CA 1-4R; 101; CANR 2

**Griffin, Peter** 1942- ........................... **CLC 39**
See also CA 136

**Griffith, D(avid Lewelyn) W(ark)**
1875(?)-1948 ......................... **TCLC 68**
See also CA 119; 150; CANR 80

**Griffith, Lawrence**
See Griffith, D(avid Lewelyn) W(ark)

**Griffiths, Trevor** 1935- ................ **CLC 13, 52**
See also CA 97-100; CANR 45; CBD; CD 5; DLB 13, 245

**Griggs, Sutton (Elbert)**
1872-1930 ...................................... **TCLC 77**
See also CA 123; 186; DLB 50

**Grigson, Geoffrey (Edward Harvey)**
1905-1985 ............................... **CLC 7, 39**
See also CA 25-28R; 118; CANR 20, 33; DLB 27; MTCW 1, 2

**Grile, Dod**
See Bierce, Ambrose (Gwinett)

**Grillparzer, Franz** 1791-1872 ............ **DC 14; NCLC 1, 102; SSC 37**
See also CDWLB 2; DLB 133; EW 5; RGWL 2, 3; TWA

**Grimble, Reverend Charles James**
See Eliot, T(homas) S(tearns)

**Grimke, Angelina (Emily) Weld**
1880-1958 ...................................... **HR 2**
See Weld, Angelina (Emily) Grimke
See also BW 1; CA 124; DAM POET; DLB 50, 54

**Grimke, Charlotte L(ottie) Forten**
1837(?)-1914
See Forten, Charlotte L.
See also BW 1; CA 117; 124; DAM MULT, POET

**Grimm, Jacob Ludwig Karl**
1785-1863 ............. **NCLC 3, 77; SSC 36**
See also DLB 90; MAICYA 1, 2; RGSF 2; RGWL 2, 3; SATA 22; WCH

**Grimm, Wilhelm Karl** 1786-1859 .. **NCLC 3, 77; SSC 36**
See also CDWLB 2; DLB 90; MAICYA 1, 2; RGSF 2; RGWL 2, 3; SATA 22; WCH

**Grimmelshausen, Hans Jakob Christoffel von**
See Grimmelshausen, Johann Jakob Christoffel von
See also RGWL 2, 3

**Grimmelshausen, Johann Jakob Christoffel von** 1621-1676 ................................. **LC 6**
See Grimmelshausen, Hans Jakob Christoffel von
See also CDWLB 2; DLB 168

**Grindel, Eugene** 1895-1952
See Eluard, Paul
See also CA 104; 193; LMFS 2

**Grisham, John** 1955- ........................... **CLC 84**
See also AAYA 14, 47; BPFB 2; CA 138; CANR 47, 69, 114, 133; CMW 4; CN 7; CPW; CSW; DA3; DAM POP; MSW; MTCW 2

**Grosseteste, Robert** 1175(?)-1253 . **CMLC 62**
See also DLB 115

**Grossman, David** 1954- ...................... **CLC 67**
See also CA 138; CANR 114; CWW 2; DLB 299; EWL 3

**Grossman, Vasilii Semenovich**
See Grossman, Vasily (Semenovich)
See also DLB 272

**Grossman, Vasily (Semenovich)**
1905-1964 ...................................... **CLC 41**
See Grossman, Vasilii Semenovich
See also CA 124; 130; MTCW 1

**Grove, Frederick Philip** ................. **TCLC 4**
See Greve, Felix Paul (Berthold Friedrich)
See also DLB 92; RGEL 2

**Grubb**
See Crumb, R(obert)

**Grumbach, Doris (Isaac)** 1918- . **CLC 13, 22, 64**
See also CA 5-8R; CAAS 2; CANR 9, 42, 70, 127; CN 7; INT CANR-9; MTCW 2

**Grundtvig, Nicolai Frederik Severin**
1783-1872 ...................................... **NCLC 1**
See also DLB 300

**Grunge**
See Crumb, R(obert)

**Grunwald, Lisa** 1959- ........................ **CLC 44**
See also CA 120

**Gryphius, Andreas** 1616-1664 ............. **LC 89**
See also CDWLB 2; DLB 164; RGWL 2, 3

**Guare, John** 1938- .... **CLC 8, 14, 29, 67; DC 20**
See also CA 73-76; CAD; CANR 21, 69, 118; CD 5; DAM DRAM; DFS 8, 13; DLB 7, 249; EWL 3; MTCW 1, 2; RGAL 4

**Guarini, Battista** 1537-1612 ............... **LC 102**

**Gubar, Susan (David)** 1944- .......... **CLC 145**
See also CA 108; CANR 45, 70; FW; MTCW 1; RGAL 4

**Gudjonsson, Halldor Kiljan** 1902-1998
See Halldor Laxness
See also CA 103; 164

**Guenter, Erich**
See Eich, Gunter

**Guest, Barbara** 1920- ........... **CLC 34; PC 55**
See also BG 2; CA 25-28R; CANR 11, 44, 84; CP 7; CWP; DLB 5, 193

**Guest, Edgar A(lbert)** 1881-1959 ... **TCLC 95**
See also CA 112; 168

**Guest, Judith (Ann)** 1936- ........... **CLC 8, 30**
See also AAYA 7; CA 77-80; CANR 15, 75; DA3; DAM NOV, POP; EXPN; INT CANR-15; LAIT 5; MTCW 1, 2; NFS 1

**Guevara, Che** ........................ **CLC 87; HLC 1**
See Guevara (Serna), Ernesto

**Guevara (Serna), Ernesto**
1928-1967 ...................... **CLC 87; HLC 1**
See Guevara, Che
See also CA 127; 111; CANR 56; DAM MULT; HW 1

**Guicciardini, Francesco** 1483-1540 ..... **LC 49**

**Guild, Nicholas M.** 1944- .................. **CLC 33**
See also CA 93-96

**Guillemin, Jacques**
See Sartre, Jean-Paul

**Guillen, Jorge** 1893-1984 . **CLC 11; HLCS 1; PC 35**
See also CA 89-92; 112; DAM MULT, POET; DLB 108; EWL 3; HW 1; RGWL 2, 3

**Guillen, Nicolas (Cristobal)**
1902-1989 .... **BLC 2; CLC 48, 79; HLC 1; PC 23**
See also BW 2; CA 116; 125; 129; CANR 84; DAM MST, MULT, POET; DLB 283; EWL 3; HW 1; LAW; RGWL 2, 3; WP

**Guillen y Alvarez, Jorge**
See Guillen, Jorge

**Guillevic, (Eugene)** 1907-1997 .......... **CLC 33**
See also CA 93-96; CWW 2

**Guillois**
See Desnos, Robert

**Guillois, Valentin**
See Desnos, Robert

**Guimaraes Rosa, Joao** 1908-1967 .... **HLCS 2**
See Rosa, Joao Guimaraes
See also CA 175; LAW; RGSF 2; RGWL 2, 3

**Guiney, Louise Imogen**
1861-1920 ...................................... **TCLC 41**
See also CA 160; DLB 54; RGAL 4

**Guinizelli, Guido** c. 1230-1276 ...... **CMLC 49**

**Guiraldes, Ricardo (Guillermo)**
1886-1927 ...................................... **TCLC 39**
See also CA 131; EWL 3; HW 1; LAW; MTCW 1

**Gumilev, Nikolai (Stepanovich)**
 1886-1921 ................................. **TCLC 60**
 See Gumilyov, Nikolay Stepanovich
 See also CA 165; DLB 295
**Gumilyov, Nikolay Stepanovich**
 See Gumilev, Nikolai (Stepanovich)
 See also EWL 3
**Gump, P. Q.**
 See Card, Orson Scott
**Gunesekera, Romesh** 1954- ............... **CLC 91**
 See also CA 159; CN 7; DLB 267
**Gunn, Bill** ................................... **CLC 5**
 See Gunn, William Harrison
 See also DLB 38
**Gunn, Thom(son William)**
 1929-2004 . **CLC 3, 6, 18, 32, 81; PC 26**
 See also BRWS 4; CA 17-20R; 227; CANR
 9, 33, 116; CDBLB 1960 to Present; CP
 7; DAM POET; DLB 27; INT CANR-33;
 MTCW 1; PFS 9; RGEL 2
**Gunn, William Harrison** 1934(?)-1989
 See Gunn, Bill
 See also AITN 1; BW 1, 3; CA 13-16R;
 128; CANR 12, 25, 76
**Gunn Allen, Paula**
 See Allen, Paula Gunn
**Gunnars, Kristjana** 1948- ................. **CLC 69**
 See also CA 113; CCA 1; CP 7; CWP; DLB
 60
**Gunter, Erich**
 See Eich, Gunter
**Gurdjieff, G(eorgei) I(vanovich)**
 1877(?)-1949 ............................ **TCLC 71**
 See also CA 157
**Gurganus, Allan** 1947- ...................... **CLC 70**
 See also BEST 90:1; CA 135; CANR 114;
 CN 7; CPW; CSW; DAM POP; GLL 1
**Gurney, A. R.**
 See Gurney, A(lbert) R(amsdell), Jr.
 See also DLB 266
**Gurney, A(lbert) R(amsdell), Jr.**
 1930- ..................... **CLC 32, 50, 54**
 See Gurney, A. R.
 See also AMWS 5; CA 77-80; CAD; CANR
 32, 64, 121; CD 5; DAM DRAM; EWL 3
**Gurney, Ivor (Bertie)** 1890-1937 ... **TCLC 33**
 See also BRW 6; CA 167; DLBY 2002;
 PAB; RGEL 2
**Gurney, Peter**
 See Gurney, A(lbert) R(amsdell), Jr.
**Guro, Elena (Genrikhovna)**
 1877-1913 ................................. **TCLC 56**
 See also DLB 295
**Gustafson, James M(oody)** 1925- ... **CLC 100**
 See also CA 25-28R; CANR 37
**Gustafson, Ralph (Barker)**
 1909-1995 ................................. **CLC 36**
 See also CA 21-24R; CANR 8, 45, 84; CP
 7; DLB 88; RGEL 2
**Gut, Gom**
 See Simenon, Georges (Jacques Christian)
**Guterson, David** 1956- ...................... **CLC 91**
 See also CA 132; CANR 73, 126; DLB 292;
 MTCW 2; NFS 13
**Guthrie, A(lfred) B(ertram), Jr.**
 1901-1991 ................................. **CLC 23**
 See also CA 57-60; 134; CANR 24; DLB 6,
 212; SATA 62; SATA-Obit 67
**Guthrie, Isobel**
 See Grieve, C(hristopher) M(urray)
**Guthrie, Woodrow Wilson** 1912-1967
 See Guthrie, Woody
 See also CA 113; 93-96
**Guthrie, Woody** ................................. **CLC 35**
 See Guthrie, Woodrow Wilson
 See also DLB 303; LAIT 3
**Gutierrez Najera, Manuel**
 1859-1895 .............. **HLCS 2; NCLC 133**
 See also DLB 290; LAW

**Guy, Rosa (Cuthbert)** 1925- ............. **CLC 26**
 See also AAYA 4, 37; BW 2; CA 17-20R;
 CANR 14, 34, 83; CLR 13; DLB 33;
 DNFS 1; JRDA; MAICYA 1, 2; SATA 14,
 62, 122; YAW
**Gwendolyn**
 See Bennett, (Enoch) Arnold
**H. D.** ........... **CLC 3, 8, 14, 31, 34, 73; PC 5**
 See Doolittle, Hilda
**H. de V.**
 See Buchan, John
**Haavikko, Paavo Juhani** 1931- .. **CLC 18, 34**
 See also CA 106; CWW 2; EWL 3
**Habbema, Koos**
 See Heijermans, Herman
**Habermas, Juergen** 1929- ............... **CLC 104**
 See also CA 109; CANR 85; DLB 242
**Habermas, Jurgen**
 See Habermas, Juergen
**Hacker, Marilyn** 1942- ...... **CLC 5, 9, 23, 72,**
 **91; PC 47**
 See also CA 77-80; CANR 68, 129; CP 7;
 CWP; DAM POET; DLB 120, 282; FW;
 GLL 2; PFS 19
**Hadewijch of Antwerp** fl. 1250- ... **CMLC 61**
 See also RGWL 3
**Hadrian** 76-138 ............................. **CMLC 52**
**Haeckel, Ernst Heinrich (Philipp August)**
 1834-1919 ................................. **TCLC 83**
 See also CA 157
**Hafiz** c. 1326-1389(?) ..................... **CMLC 34**
 See also RGWL 2, 3
**Hagedorn, Jessica T(arahata)**
 1949- ........................................ **CLC 185**
 See also CA 139; CANR 69; CWP; RGAL
 4
**Haggard, H(enry) Rider**
 1856-1925 ................................. **TCLC 11**
 See also BRWS 3; BYA 4, 5; CA 108; 148;
 CANR 112; DLB 70, 156, 174, 178;
 FANT; LMFS 1; MTCW 2; RGEL 2;
 RHW; SATA 16; SCFW; SFW 4; SUFW
 1; WLIT 4
**Hagiosy, L.**
 See Larbaud, Valery (Nicolas)
**Hagiwara, Sakutaro** 1886-1942 .......... **PC 18;**
 **TCLC 60**
 See Hagiwara Sakutaro
 See also CA 154; RGWL 3
**Hagiwara Sakutaro**
 See Hagiwara, Sakutaro
 See also EWL 3
**Haig, Fenil**
 See Ford, Ford Madox
**Haig-Brown, Roderick (Langmere)**
 1908-1976 ................................. **CLC 21**
 See also CA 5-8R; 69-72; CANR 4, 38, 83;
 CLR 31; CWRI 5; DLB 88; MAICYA 1,
 2; SATA 12
**Haight, Rip**
 See Carpenter, John (Howard)
**Hailey, Arthur** 1920- ........................... **CLC 5**
 See also AITN 2; BEST 90:3; BPFB 2; CA
 1-4R; CANR 2, 36, 75; CCA 1; CN 7;
 CPW; DAM NOV, POP; DLB 88; DLBY
 1982; MTCW 1, 2
**Hailey, Elizabeth Forsythe** 1938- ..... **CLC 40**
 See also CA 93-96, 188; CAAE 188; CAAS
 1; CANR 15, 48; INT CANR-15
**Haines, John (Meade)** 1924- ............. **CLC 58**
 See also AMWS 12; CA 17-20R; CANR
 13, 34; CSW; DLB 5, 212
**Hakluyt, Richard** 1552-1616 ................ **LC 31**
 See also DLB 136; RGEL 2
**Haldeman, Joe (William)** 1943- ....... **CLC 61**
 See Graham, Robert
 See also AAYA 38; CA 53-56, 179; CAAE
 179; CAAS 25; CANR 6, 70, 72, 130;
 DLB 8; INT CANR-6; SCFW 2; SFW 4

**Hale, Janet Campbell** 1947- ............... **NNAL**
 See also CA 49-52; CANR 45, 75; DAM
 MULT; DLB 175; MTCW 2
**Hale, Sarah Josepha (Buell)**
 1788-1879 ................................. **NCLC 75**
 See also DLB 1, 42, 73, 243
**Halevy, Elie** 1870-1937 ................. **TCLC 104**
**Haley, Alex(ander Murray Palmer)**
 1921-1992 ......... **BLC 2; CLC 8, 12, 76;**
 **TCLC 147**
 See also AAYA 26; BPFB 2; BW 2, 3; CA
 77-80; 136; CANR 61; CDALBS; CPW;
 CSW; DA; DA3; DAB; DAC; DAM MST,
 MULT, POP; DLB 38; LAIT 5; MTCW
 1, 2; NFS 9
**Haliburton, Thomas Chandler**
 1796-1865 ................................. **NCLC 15**
 See also DLB 11, 99; RGEL 2; RGSF 2
**Hall, Donald (Andrew, Jr.)** 1928- ...... **CLC 1,**
 **13, 37, 59, 151**
 See also CA 5-8R; CAAS 7; CANR 2, 44,
 64, 106, 133; CP 7; DAM POET; DLB 5;
 MTCW 1; RGAL 4; SATA 23, 97
**Hall, Frederic Sauser**
 See Sauser-Hall, Frederic
**Hall, James**
 See Kuttner, Henry
**Hall, James Norman** 1887-1951 ..... **TCLC 23**
 See also CA 123; 173; LAIT 1; RHW 1;
 SATA 21
**Hall, Joseph** 1574-1656 ........................ **LC 91**
 See also DLB 121, 151; RGEL 2
**Hall, (Marguerite) Radclyffe**
 1880-1943 ................................. **TCLC 12**
 See also BRWS 6; CA 110; 150; CANR 83;
 DLB 191; MTCW 2; RGEL 2; RHW
**Hall, Rodney** 1935- ........................... **CLC 51**
 See also CA 109; CANR 69; CN 7; CP 7;
 DLB 289
**Hallam, Arthur Henry**
 1811-1833 ............................... **NCLC 110**
 See also DLB 32
**Halldor Laxness** ............................... **CLC 25**
 See Gudjonsson, Halldor Kiljan
 See also DLB 293; EW 12; EWL 3; RGWL
 2, 3
**Halleck, Fitz-Greene** 1790-1867 .... **NCLC 47**
 See also DLB 3, 250; RGAL 4
**Halliday, Michael**
 See Creasey, John
**Halpern, Daniel** 1945- ...................... **CLC 14**
 See also CA 33-36R; CANR 93; CP 7
**Hamburger, Michael (Peter Leopold)**
 1924- ................................... **CLC 5, 14**
 See also CA 5-8R, 196; CAAE 196; CAAS
 4; CANR 2, 47; CP 7; DLB 27
**Hamill, Pete** 1935- ............................ **CLC 10**
 See also CA 25-28R; CANR 18, 71, 127
**Hamilton, Alexander**
 1755(?)-1804 ............................. **NCLC 49**
 See also DLB 37
**Hamilton, Clive**
 See Lewis, C(live) S(taples)
**Hamilton, Edmond** 1904-1977 ........... **CLC 1**
 See also CA 1-4R; CANR 3, 84; DLB 8;
 SATA 118; SFW 4
**Hamilton, Eugene (Jacob) Lee**
 See Lee-Hamilton, Eugene (Jacob)
**Hamilton, Franklin**
 See Silverberg, Robert
**Hamilton, Gail**
 See Corcoran, Barbara (Asenath)
**Hamilton, (Robert) Ian** 1938-2001 . **CLC 191**
 See also CA 106; 203; CANR 41, 67; CP 7;
 DLB 40, 155
**Hamilton, Jane** 1957- ...................... **CLC 179**
 See also CA 147; CANR 85, 128
**Hamilton, Mollie**
 See Kaye, M(ary) M(argaret)

**Hamilton, (Anthony Walter) Patrick**
1904-1962 ............................... **CLC 51**
See also CA 176; 113; DLB 10, 191

**Hamilton, Virginia (Esther)**
1936-2002 ............................. **CLC 26**
See also AAYA 2, 21; BW 2, 3; BYA 1, 2,
8; CA 25-28R; 206; CANR 20, 37, 73,
126; CLR 1, 11, 40; DAM MULT; DLB
33, 52; DLBY 01; INT CANR-20; JRDA;
LAIT 5; MAICYA 1, 2; MAICYAS 1;
MTCW 1, 2; SATA 4, 56, 79, 123; SATA-
Obit 132; WYA; YAW

**Hammett, (Samuel) Dashiell**
1894-1961 .... **CLC 3, 5, 10, 19, 47; SSC
17**
See also AAYA 59; AITN 1; AMWS 4;
BPFB 2; CA 81-84; CANR 42; CDALB
1929-1941; CMW 4; DA3; DLB 226, 280;
DLBD 6; DLBY 1996; EWL 3; LAIT 3;
MSW; MTCW 1, 2; RGAL 4; RGSF 2;
TUS

**Hammon, Jupiter** 1720(?)-1800(?) .... **BLC 2;
NCLC 5; PC 16**
See also DAM MULT, POET; DLB 31, 50

**Hammond, Keith**
See Kuttner, Henry

**Hamner, Earl (Henry), Jr.** 1923- ...... **CLC 12**
See also AITN 2; CA 73-76; DLB 6

**Hampton, Christopher (James)**
1946- ......................................... **CLC 4**
See also CA 25-28R; CD 5; DLB 13;
MTCW 1

**Hamsun, Knut** ............ **TCLC 2, 14, 49, 151**
See Pedersen, Knut
See also DLB 297; EW 8; EWL 3; RGWL
2, 3

**Handke, Peter** 1942- .... **CLC 5, 8, 10, 15, 38,
134; DC 17**
See also CA 77-80; CANR 33, 75, 104, 133;
CWW 2; DAM DRAM, NOV; DLB 85,
124; EWL 3; MTCW 1, 2; TWA

**Handy, W(illiam) C(hristopher)**
1873-1958 ............................... **TCLC 97**
See also BW 3; CA 121; 167

**Hanley, James** 1901-1985 ..... **CLC 3, 5, 8, 13**
See also CA 73-76; 117; CANR 36; CBD;
DLB 191; EWL 3; MTCW 1; RGEL 2

**Hannah, Barry** 1942- ............ **CLC 23, 38, 90**
See also BPFB 2; CA 108; 110; CANR 43,
68, 113; CN 7; CSW; DLB 6, 234; INT
CA-110; MTCW 1; RGSF 2

**Hannon, Ezra**
See Hunter, Evan

**Hansberry, Lorraine (Vivian)**
1930-1965 ... **BLC 2; CLC 17, 62; DC 2**
See also AAYA 25; AFAW 1, 2; AMWS 4;
BW 1, 3; CA 109; 25-28R; CABS 3;
CAD; CANR 58; CDALB 1941-1968;
CWD; DA; DA3; DAB; DAC; DAM
DRAM, MST, MULT; DFS 2; DLB 7, 38;
EWL 3; FW; LAIT 4; MTCW 1, 2; RGAL
4; TUS

**Hansen, Joseph** 1923- ....................... **CLC 38**
See Brock, Rose; Colton, James
See also BPFB 2; CA 29-32R; CAAS 17;
CANR 16, 44, 66, 125; CMW 4; DLB
226; GLL 1; INT CANR-16

**Hansen, Martin A(lfred)**
1909-1955 ............................... **TCLC 32**
See also CA 167; DLB 214; EWL 3

**Hansen and Philipson eds.** ............... **CLC 65**

**Hanson, Kenneth O(stlin)** 1922- ....... **CLC 13**
See also CA 53-56; CANR 7

**Hardwick, Elizabeth (Bruce)** 1916- . **CLC 13**
See also AMWS 3; CA 5-8R; CANR 3, 32,
70, 100; CN 7; CSW; DA3; DAM NOV;
DLB 6; MAWW; MTCW 1, 2

**Hardy, Thomas** 1840-1928 ....... **PC 8; SSC 2,
60; TCLC 4, 10, 18, 32, 48, 53, 72, 143,
153; WLC**
See also BRW 6; BRWC 1, 2; BRWR 1;
CA 104; 123; CDBLB 1890-1914; DA;
DA3; DAB; DAC; DAM MST, NOV,
POET; DLB 18, 19, 135, 284; EWL 3;
EXPN; EXPP; LAIT 2; MTCW 1, 2; NFS
3, 11, 15, 19; PFS 3, 4, 18; RGEL 2;
RGSF 2; TEA; WLIT 4

**Hare, David** 1947- ............... **CLC 29, 58, 136**
See also BRWS 4; CA 97-100; CANR 39,
91; CBD; CD 5; DFS 4, 7, 16; DLB 13;
MTCW 1; TEA

**Harewood, John**
See Van Druten, John (William)

**Harford, Henry**
See Hudson, W(illiam) H(enry)

**Hargrave, Leonie**
See Disch, Thomas M(ichael)

**Hariri, Al- al-Qasim ibn 'Ali Abu
Muhammad al-Basri**
See al-Hariri, al-Qasim ibn 'Ali Abu Mu-
hammad al-Basri

**Harjo, Joy** 1951- ..... **CLC 83; NNAL; PC 27**
See also AMWS 12; CA 114; CANR 35,
67, 91, 129; CP 7; CWP; DAM MULT;
DLB 120, 175; EWL 3; MTCW 2; PFS
15; RGAL 4

**Harlan, Louis R(udolph)** 1922- ........ **CLC 34**
See also CA 21-24R; CANR 25, 55, 80

**Harling, Robert** 1951(?)- .................. **CLC 53**
See also CA 147

**Harmon, William (Ruth)** 1938- ........ **CLC 38**
See also CA 33-36R; CANR 14, 32, 35;
SATA 65

**Harper, F. E. W.**
See Harper, Frances Ellen Watkins

**Harper, Frances E. W.**
See Harper, Frances Ellen Watkins

**Harper, Frances E. Watkins**
See Harper, Frances Ellen Watkins

**Harper, Frances Ellen**
See Harper, Frances Ellen Watkins

**Harper, Frances Ellen Watkins**
1825-1911 ... **BLC 2; PC 21; TCLC 14**
See also AFAW 1, 2; BW 1, 3; CA 111; 125;
CANR 79; DAM MULT, POET; DLB 50,
221; MAWW; RGAL 4

**Harper, Michael S(teven)** 1938- ... **CLC 7, 22**
See also AFAW 2; BW 1; CA 33-36R, 224;
CAAE 224; CANR 24, 108; CP 7; DLB
41; RGAL 4

**Harper, Mrs. F. E. W.**
See Harper, Frances Ellen Watkins

**Harpur, Charles** 1813-1868 .......... **NCLC 114**
See also DLB 230; RGEL 2

**Harris, Christie**
See Harris, Christie (Lucy) Irwin

**Harris, Christie (Lucy) Irwin**
1907-2002 ................................... **CLC 12**
See also CA 5-8R; CANR 6, 83; CLR 47;
DLB 88; JRDA; MAICYA 1, 2; SAAS 10;
SATA 6, 74; SATA-Essay 116

**Harris, Frank** 1856-1931 ............... **TCLC 24**
See also CA 109; 150; CANR 80; DLB 156,
197; RGEL 2

**Harris, George Washington**
1814-1869 ................................. **NCLC 23**
See also DLB 3, 11, 248; RGAL 4

**Harris, Joel Chandler** 1848-1908 ..... **SSC 19;
TCLC 2**
See also CA 104; 137; CANR 80; CLR 49;
DLB 11, 23, 42, 78, 91; LAIT 2; MAI-
CYA 1, 2; RGSF 2; SATA 100; WCH;
YABC 1

**Harris, John (Wyndham Parkes Lucas)
Beynon** 1903-1969
See Wyndham, John
See also CA 102; 89-92; CANR 84; SATA
118; SFW 4

**Harris, MacDonald** ........................... **CLC 9**
See Heiney, Donald (William)

**Harris, Mark** 1922- ........................... **CLC 19**
See also CA 5-8R; CAAS 3; CANR 2, 55,
83; CN 7; DLB 2; DLBY 1980

**Harris, Norman** ............................... **CLC 65**

**Harris, (Theodore) Wilson** 1921- .... **CLC 25,
159**
See also BRWS 5; BW 2, 3; CA 65-68;
CAAS 16; CANR 11, 27, 69, 114; CD-
WLB 3; CN 7; CP 7; DLB 117; EWL 3;
MTCW 1; RGEL 2

**Harrison, Barbara Grizzuti**
1934-2002 ............................... **CLC 144**
See also CA 77-80; 205; CANR 15, 48; INT
CANR-15

**Harrison, Elizabeth (Allen) Cavanna**
1909-2001
See Cavanna, Betty
See also CA 9-12R; 200; CANR 6, 27, 85,
104, 121; MAICYA 2; SATA 142; YAW

**Harrison, Harry (Max)** 1925- ........... **CLC 42**
See also CA 1-4R; CANR 5, 21, 84; DLB
8; SATA 4; SCFW 2; SFW 4

**Harrison, James (Thomas)** 1937- ...... **CLC 6,
14, 33, 66, 143; SSC 19**
See Harrison, Jim
See also CA 13-16R; CANR 8, 51, 79; CN
7; CP 7; DLBY 1982; INT CANR-8

**Harrison, Jim**
See Harrison, James (Thomas)
See also AMWS 8; RGAL 4; TCWW 2;
TUS

**Harrison, Kathryn** 1961- .......... **CLC 70, 151**
See also CA 144; CANR 68, 122

**Harrison, Tony** 1937- ............... **CLC 43, 129**
See also BRWS 5; CA 65-68; CANR 44,
98; CBD; CD 5; CP 7; DLB 40, 245;
MTCW 1; RGEL 2

**Harriss, Will(ard Irvin)** 1922- .......... **CLC 34**
See also CA 111

**Hart, Ellis**
See Ellison, Harlan (Jay)

**Hart, Josephine** 1942(?)- .................. **CLC 70**
See also CA 138; CANR 70; CPW; DAM
POP

**Hart, Moss** 1904-1961 ....................... **CLC 66**
See also CA 109; 89-92; CANR 84; DAM
DRAM; DFS 1; DLB 7, 266; RGAL 4

**Harte, (Francis) Bret(t)**
1836(?)-1902 ... **SSC 8, 59; TCLC 1, 25;
WLC**
See also AMWS 2; CA 104; 140; CANR
80; CDALB 1865-1917; DA; DA3; DAC;
DAM MST; DLB 12, 64, 74, 79, 186;
EXPS; LAIT 2; RGAL 4; RGSF 2; SATA
26; SSFS 3; TUS

**Hartley, L(eslie) P(oles)** 1895-1972 ... **CLC 2,
22**
See also BRWS 7; CA 45-48; 37-40R;
CANR 33; DLB 15, 139; EWL 3; HGG;
MTCW 1, 2; RGEL 2; RGSF 2; SUFW 1

**Hartman, Geoffrey H.** 1929- ............. **CLC 27**
See also CA 117; 125; CANR 79; DLB 67

**Hartmann, Sadakichi** 1869-1944 ... **TCLC 73**
See also CA 157; DLB 54

**Hartmann von Aue** c. 1170-c.
1210 ....................................... **CMLC 15**
See also CDWLB 2; DLB 138; RGWL 2, 3

**Hartog, Jan de**
See de Hartog, Jan

**Haruf, Kent** 1943- ............................. **CLC 34**
See also AAYA 44; CA 149; CANR 91, 131

**Harvey, Caroline**
See Trollope, Joanna
**Harvey, Gabriel** 1550(?)-1631 ............. **LC 88**
See also DLB 167, 213, 281
**Harwood, Ronald** 1934- .................... **CLC 32**
See also CA 1-4R; CANR 4, 55; CBD; CD
5; DAM DRAM, MST; DLB 13
**Hasegawa Tatsunosuke**
See Futabatei, Shimei
**Hasek, Jaroslav (Matej Frantisek)**
1883-1923 ................... **SSC 69; TCLC 4**
See also CA 104; 129; CDWLB 4; DLB
215; EW 9; EWL 3; MTCW 1, 2; RGSF
2; RGWL 2, 3
**Hass, Robert** 1941- ... **CLC 18, 39, 99; PC 16**
See also AMWS 6; CA 111; CANR 30, 50,
71; CP 7; DLB 105, 206; EWL 3; RGAL
4; SATA 94
**Hastings, Hudson**
See Kuttner, Henry
**Hastings, Selina** ................................ **CLC 44**
**Hathorne, John** 1641-1717 .................. **LC 38**
**Hatteras, Amelia**
See Mencken, H(enry) L(ouis)
**Hatteras, Owen** ................................ **TCLC 18**
See Mencken, H(enry) L(ouis); Nathan,
George Jean
**Hauptmann, Gerhart (Johann Robert)**
1862-1946 ................... **SSC 37; TCLC 4**
See also CA 104; 153; CDWLB 2; DAM
DRAM; DLB 66, 118; EW 8; EWL 3;
RGSF 2; RGWL 2, 3; TWA
**Havel, Vaclav** 1936- ..... **CLC 25, 58, 65, 123;
DC 6**
See also CA 104; CANR 36, 63, 124; CD-
WLB 4; CWW 2; DA3; DAM DRAM;
DFS 10; DLB 232; EWL 3; LMFS 2;
MTCW 1, 2; RGWL 3
**Haviaras, Stratis** ............................. **CLC 33**
See Chaviaras, Strates
**Hawes, Stephen** 1475(?)-1529(?) .......... **LC 17**
See also DLB 132; RGEL 2
**Hawkes, John (Clendennin Burne, Jr.)**
1925-1998 .. **CLC 1, 2, 3, 4, 7, 9, 14, 15,
27, 49**
See also BPFB 2; CA 1-4R; 167; CANR 2,
47, 64; CN 7; DLB 2, 7, 227; DLBY
1980, 1998; EWL 3; MTCW 1, 2; RGAL
4
**Hawking, S. W.**
See Hawking, Stephen W(illiam)
**Hawking, Stephen W(illiam)** 1942- . **CLC 63,
105**
See also AAYA 13; BEST 89:1; CA 126;
129; CANR 48, 115; CPW; DA3; MTCW
2
**Hawkins, Anthony Hope**
See Hope, Anthony
**Hawthorne, Julian** 1846-1934 ........ **TCLC 25**
See also CA 165; HGG
**Hawthorne, Nathaniel** 1804-1864 ... **NCLC 2,
10, 17, 23, 39, 79, 95; SSC 3, 29, 39;
WLC**
See also AAYA 18; AMW; AMWC 1;
AMWR 1; BPFB 2; BYA 3; CDALB
1640-1865; DA; DA3; DAB; DAC; DAM
MST, NOV; DLB 1, 74, 183, 223, 269;
EXPN; EXPS; HGG; LAIT 1; NFS 1, 20;
RGAL 4; RGSF 2; SSFS 1, 7, 11, 15;
SUFW 1; TUS; WCH; YABC 2
**Haxton, Josephine Ayres** 1921-
See Douglas, Ellen
See also CA 115; CANR 41, 83
**Hayaseca y Eizaguirre, Jorge**
See Echegaray (y Eizaguirre), Jose (Maria
Waldo)
**Hayashi, Fumiko** 1904-1951 .......... **TCLC 27**
See Hayashi Fumiko
See also CA 161

**Hayashi Fumiko**
See Hayashi, Fumiko
See also DLB 180; EWL 3
**Haycraft, Anna (Margaret)** 1932-
See Ellis, Alice Thomas
See also CA 122; CANR 85, 90; MTCW 2
**Hayden, Robert E(arl)** 1913-1980 ..... **BLC 2;
CLC 5, 9, 14, 37; PC 6**
See also AFAW 1, 2; AMWS 2; BW 1, 3;
CA 69-72; 97-100; CABS 2; CANR 24,
75, 82; CDALB 1941-1968; DA; DAC;
DAM MST, MULT, POET; DLB 5, 76;
EWL 3; EXPP; MTCW 1, 2; PFS 1;
RGAL 4; SATA 19; SATA-Obit 26; WP
**Haydon, Benjamin Robert**
1786-1846 ............................... **NCLC 146**
See also DLB 110
**Hayek, F(riedrich) A(ugust von)**
1899-1992 ............................. **TCLC 109**
See also CA 93-96; 137; CANR 20; MTCW
1, 2
**Hayford, J(oseph) E(phraim) Casely**
See Casely-Hayford, J(oseph) E(phraim)
**Hayman, Ronald** 1932- ..................... **CLC 44**
See also CA 25-28R; CANR 18, 50, 88; CD
5; DLB 155
**Hayne, Paul Hamilton** 1830-1886 . **NCLC 94**
See also DLB 3, 64, 79, 248; RGAL 4
**Hays, Mary** 1760-1843 ................. **NCLC 114**
See also DLB 142, 158; RGEL 2
**Haywood, Eliza (Fowler)**
1693(?)-1756 ........................... **LC 1, 44**
See also DLB 39; RGEL 2
**Hazlitt, William** 1778-1830 ...... **NCLC 29, 82**
See also BRW 4; DLB 110, 158; RGEL 2;
TEA
**Hazzard, Shirley** 1931- .................... **CLC 18**
See also CA 9-12R; CANR 4, 70, 127; CN
7; DLB 289; DLBY 1982; MTCW 1
**Head, Bessie** 1937-1986 ...... **BLC 2; CLC 25,
67; SSC 52**
See also AFW; BW 2, 3; CA 29-32R; 119;
CANR 25, 82; CDWLB 3; DA3; DAM
MULT; DLB 117, 225; EWL 3; EXPS;
FW; MTCW 1, 2; RGSF 2; SSFS 5, 13;
WLIT 2; WWE 1
**Headon, (Nicky) Topper** 1956(?)- ..... **CLC 30**
**Heaney, Seamus (Justin)** 1939- ..... **CLC 5, 7,
14, 25, 37, 74, 91, 171; PC 18; WLCS**
See also BRWR 1; BRWS 2; CA 85-88;
CANR 25, 48, 75, 91, 128; CDBLB 1960
to Present; CP 7; DA3; DAB; DAM
POET; DLB 40; DLBY 1995; EWL 3;
EXPP; MTCW 1, 2; PAB; PFS 2, 5, 8,
17; RGEL 2; TEA; WLIT 4
**Hearn, (Patricio) Lafcadio (Tessima Carlos)**
1850-1904 ................................. **TCLC 9**
See also CA 105; 166; DLB 12, 78, 189;
HGG; RGAL 4
**Hearne, Samuel** 1745-1792 ................. **LC 95**
See also DLB 99
**Hearne, Vicki** 1946-2001 ................... **CLC 56**
See also CA 139; 201
**Hearon, Shelby** 1931- ....................... **CLC 63**
See also AITN 2; AMWS 8; CA 25-28R;
CANR 18, 48, 103; CSW
**Heat-Moon, William Least** ............. **CLC 29**
See Trogdon, William (Lewis)
See also AAYA 9
**Hebbel, Friedrich** 1813-1863 . **DC 21; NCLC
43**
See also CDWLB 2; DAM DRAM; DLB
129; EW 6; RGWL 2, 3
**Hebert, Anne** 1916-2000 ....... **CLC 4, 13, 29**
See also CA 85-88; 187; CANR 69, 126;
CCA 1; CWP; CWW 2; DA3; DAC;
DAM MST, POET; DLB 68; EWL 3; GFL
1789 to the Present; MTCW 1, 2; PFS 20

**Hecht, Anthony (Evan)** 1923- ...... **CLC 8, 13,
19**
See also AMWS 10; CA 9-12R; CANR 6,
108; CP 7; DAM POET; DLB 5, 169;
EWL 3; PFS 6; WP
**Hecht, Ben** 1894-1964 ...... **CLC 8; TCLC 101**
See also CA 85-88; DFS 9; DLB 7, 9, 25,
26, 28, 86; FANT; IDFW 3, 4; RGAL 4
**Hedayat, Sadeq** 1903-1951 ............. **TCLC 21**
See also CA 120; EWL 3; RGSF 2
**Hegel, Georg Wilhelm Friedrich**
1770-1831 ............................... **NCLC 46**
See also DLB 90; TWA
**Heidegger, Martin** 1889-1976 .......... **CLC 24**
See also CA 81-84; 65-68; CANR 34; DLB
296; MTCW 1, 2
**Heidenstam, (Carl Gustaf) Verner von**
1859-1940 ............................... **TCLC 5**
See also CA 104
**Heidi Louise**
See Erdrich, Louise
**Heifner, Jack** 1946- ........................... **CLC 11**
See also CA 105; CANR 47
**Heijermans, Herman** 1864-1924 .... **TCLC 24**
See also CA 123; EWL 3
**Heilbrun, Carolyn G(old)**
1926-2003 .......................... **CLC 25, 173**
See Cross, Amanda
See also CA 45-48; 220; CANR 1, 28, 58,
94; FW
**Hein, Christoph** 1944- ..................... **CLC 154**
See also CA 158; CANR 108; CDWLB 2;
CWW 2; DLB 124
**Heine, Heinrich** 1797-1856 ....... **NCLC 4, 54,
147; PC 25**
See also CDWLB 2; DLB 90; EW 5; RGWL
2, 3; TWA
**Heinemann, Larry (Curtiss)** 1944- .. **CLC 50**
See also CA 110; CAAS 21; CANR 31, 81;
DLBD 9; INT CANR-31
**Heiney, Donald (William)** 1921-1993
See Harris, MacDonald
See also CA 1-4R; 142; CANR 3, 58; FANT
**Heinlein, Robert A(nson)** 1907-1988 . **CLC 1,
3, 8, 14, 26, 55; SSC 55**
See also AAYA 17; BPFB 2; BYA 4, 13;
CA 1-4R; 125; CANR 1, 20, 53; CLR 75;
CPW; DA3; DAM POP; DLB 8; EXPS;
JRDA; LAIT 5; LMFS 2; MAICYA 1, 2;
MTCW 1, 2; RGAL 4; SATA 9, 69;
SATA-Obit 56; SCFW 1; SFW 4; SSFS 7;
YAW
**Helforth, John**
See Doolittle, Hilda
**Heliodorus** fl. 3rd cent. - ................ **CMLC 52**
**Hellenhofferu, Vojtech Kapristian z**
See Hasek, Jaroslav (Matej Frantisek)
**Heller, Joseph** 1923-1999 . **CLC 1, 3, 5, 8, 11,
36, 63; TCLC 131, 151; WLC**
See also AAYA 24; AITN 1; AMWS 4;
BPFB 2; BYA 1; CA 5-8R; 187; CABS 1;
CANR 8, 42, 66, 126; CN 7; CPW; DA;
DA3; DAB; DAC; DAM MST, NOV,
POP; DLB 2, 28, 227; DLBY 1980, 2002;
EWL 3; EXPN; INT CANR-8; LAIT 4;
MTCW 1, 2; NFS 1; RGAL 4; TUS; YAW
**Hellman, Lillian (Florence)**
1906-1984 .. **CLC 2, 4, 8, 14, 18, 34, 44,
52; DC 1; TCLC 119**
See also AAYA 47; AITN 1, 2; AMWS 1;
CA 13-16R; 112; CAD; CANR 33; CWD;
DA3; DAM DRAM; DFS 1, 3, 14; DLB
7, 228; DLBY 1984; EWL 3; FW; LAIT
3; MAWW; MTCW 1, 2; RGAL 4; TUS
**Helprin, Mark** 1947- ......... **CLC 7, 10, 22, 32**
See also CA 81-84; CANR 47, 64, 124;
CDALBS; CPW; DA3; DAM NOV, POP;
DLBY 1985; FANT; MTCW 1, 2; SUFW
2

**Helvetius, Claude-Adrien** 1715-1771 .. **LC 26**

**Helyar, Jane Penelope Josephine** 1933-
See Poole, Josephine
See also CA 21-24R; CANR 10, 26; CWRI 5; SATA 82, 138; SATA-Essay 138

**Hemans, Felicia** 1793-1835 ...... **NCLC 29, 71**
See also DLB 96; RGEL 2

**Hemingway, Ernest (Miller)**
1899-1961 .... **CLC 1, 3, 6, 8, 10, 13, 19, 30, 34, 39, 41, 44, 50, 61, 80; SSC 1, 25, 36, 40, 63; TCLC 115; WLC**
See also AAYA 19; AMW; AMWC 1; AMWR 1; BPFB 2; BYA 2, 3, 13, 15; CA 77-80; CANR 34; CDALB 1917-1929; DA; DA3; DAB; DAC; DAM MST, NOV; DLB 4, 9, 102, 210; DLBD 1, 15, 16; DLBY 1981, 1987, 1996, 1998; EWL 3; EXPN; EXPS; LAIT 3, 4; LATS 1:1; MTCW 1, 2; NFS 1, 5, 6, 14; RGAL 4; RGSF 2; SSFS 17; TUS; WYA

**Hempel, Amy** 1951- ........................... **CLC 39**
See also CA 118; 137; CANR 70; DA3; DLB 218; EXPS; MTCW 2; SSFS 2

**Henderson, F. C.**
See Mencken, H(enry) L(ouis)

**Henderson, Sylvia**
See Ashton-Warner, Sylvia (Constance)

**Henderson, Zenna (Chlarson)**
1917-1983 ...................................... **SSC 29**
See also CA 1-4R; 133; CANR 1, 84; DLB 8; SATA 5; SFW 4

**Henkin, Joshua** ............................... **CLC 119**
See also CA 161

**Henley, Beth** .................. **CLC 23; DC 6, 14**
See Henley, Elizabeth Becker
See also CABS 3; CAD; CD 5; CSW; CWD; DFS 2; DLBY 1986; FW

**Henley, Elizabeth Becker** 1952-
See Henley, Beth
See also CA 107; CANR 32, 73; DA3; DAM DRAM, MST; MTCW 1, 2

**Henley, William Ernest** 1849-1903 .. **TCLC 8**
See also CA 105; DLB 19; RGEL 2

**Hennissart, Martha** 1929-
See Lathen, Emma
See also CA 85-88; CANR 64

**Henry VIII** 1491-1547 ......................... **LC 10**
See also DLB 132

**Henry, O.** ..... **SSC 5, 49; TCLC 1, 19; WLC**
See Porter, William Sydney
See also AAYA 41; AMWS 2; EXPS; RGAL 4; RGSF 2; SSFS 2, 18

**Henry, Patrick** 1736-1799 .................... **LC 25**
See also LAIT 1

**Henryson, Robert** 1430(?)-1506(?) ...... **LC 20**
See also BRWS 7; DLB 146; RGEL 2

**Henschke, Alfred**
See Klabund

**Henson, Lance** 1944- ........................... **NNAL**
See also CA 146; DLB 175

**Hentoff, Nat(han Irving)** 1925- ......... **CLC 26**
See also AAYA 4, 42; BYA 6; CA 1-4R; CAAS 6; CANR 5, 25, 77, 114; CLR 1, 52; INT CANR-25; JRDA; MAICYA 1, 2; SATA 42, 69, 133; SATA-Brief 27; WYA; YAW

**Heppenstall, (John) Rayner**
1911-1981 ...................................... **CLC 10**
See also CA 1-4R; 103; CANR 29; EWL 3

**Heraclitus** c. 540B.C.-c. 450B.C. ... **CMLC 22**
See also DLB 176

**Herbert, Frank (Patrick)**
1920-1986 .......... **CLC 12, 23, 35, 44, 85**
See also AAYA 21; BPFB 2; BYA 4, 14; CA 53-56; 118; CANR 5, 43; CDALBS; CPW; DAM POP; DLB 8; INT CANR-5; LAIT 5; MTCW 1, 2; NFS 17; SATA 9, 37; SATA-Obit 47; SCFW 2; SFW 4; YAW

**Herbert, George** 1593-1633 ...... **LC 24; PC 4**
See also BRW 2; BRWR 2; CDBLB Before 1660; DAB; DAM POET; DLB 126; EXPP; RGEL 2; TEA; WP

**Herbert, Zbigniew** 1924-1998 ..... **CLC 9, 43; PC 50**
See also CA 89-92; 169; CANR 36, 74; CD-WLB 4; CWW 2; DAM POET; DLB 232; EWL 3; MTCW 1

**Herbst, Josephine (Frey)**
1897-1969 ...................................... **CLC 34**
See also CA 5-8R; 25-28R; DLB 9

**Herder, Johann Gottfried von**
1744-1803 ...................................... **NCLC 8**
See also DLB 97; EW 4; TWA

**Heredia, Jose Maria** 1803-1839 ....... **HLCS 2**
See also LAW

**Hergesheimer, Joseph** 1880-1954 ... **TCLC 11**
See also CA 109; 194; DLB 102, 9; RGAL 4

**Herlihy, James Leo** 1927-1993 .......... **CLC 6**
See also CA 1-4R; 143; CAD; CANR 2

**Herman, William**
See Bierce, Ambrose (Gwinett)

**Hermogenes** fl. c. 175- ................... **CMLC 6**

**Hernandez, Jose** 1834-1886 ........... **NCLC 17**
See also LAW; RGWL 2, 3; WLIT 1

**Herodotus** c. 484B.C.-c. 420B.C. ... **CMLC 17**
See also AW 1; CDWLB 1; DLB 176; RGWL 2, 3; TWA

**Herrick, Robert** 1591-1674 ....... **LC 13; PC 9**
See also BRW 2; BRWC 2; DA; DAB; DAC; DAM MST, POP; DLB 126; EXPP; PFS 13; RGAL 4; RGEL 2; TEA; WP

**Herring, Guilles**
See Somerville, Edith Oenone

**Herriot, James** 1916-1995 ................ **CLC 12**
See Wight, James Alfred
See also AAYA 1, 54; BPFB 2; CA 148; CANR 40; CLR 80; CPW; DAM POP; LAIT 3; MAICYA 2; MAICYAS 1; MTCW 2; SATA 86, 135; TEA; YAW

**Herris, Violet**
See Hunt, Violet

**Herrmann, Dorothy** 1941- ................ **CLC 44**
See also CA 107

**Herrmann, Taffy**
See Herrmann, Dorothy

**Hersey, John (Richard)** 1914-1993 .... **CLC 1, 2, 7, 9, 40, 81, 97**
See also AAYA 29; BPFB 2; CA 17-20R; 140; CANR 33; CDALBS; CPW; DAM POP; DLB 6, 185, 278, 299; MTCW 1, 2; SATA 25; SATA-Obit 76; TUS

**Herzen, Aleksandr Ivanovich**
1812-1870 ........................... **NCLC 10, 61**
See Herzen, Alexander

**Herzen, Alexander**
See Herzen, Aleksandr Ivanovich
See also DLB 277

**Herzl, Theodor** 1860-1904 .............. **TCLC 36**
See also CA 168

**Herzog, Werner** 1942- ....................... **CLC 16**
See also CA 89-92

**Hesiod** c. 8th cent. B.C.- ................... **CMLC 5**
See also AW 1; DLB 176; RGWL 2, 3

**Hesse, Hermann** 1877-1962 ... **CLC 1, 2, 3, 6, 11, 17, 25, 69; SSC 9, 49; TCLC 148; WLC**
See also AAYA 43; BPFB 2; CA 17-18; CAP 2; CDWLB 2; DA; DA3; DAB; DAC; DAM MST, NOV; DLB 66; EW 9; EWL 3; EXPN; LAIT 1; MTCW 1, 2; NFS 6, 15; RGWL 2, 3; SATA 50; TWA

**Hewes, Cady**
See De Voto, Bernard (Augustine)

**Heyen, William** 1940- .................. **CLC 13, 18**
See also CA 33-36R; 220; CAAE 220; CAAS 9; CANR 98; CP 7; DLB 5

**Heyerdahl, Thor** 1914-2002 .............. **CLC 26**
See also CA 5-8R; 207; CANR 5, 22, 66, 73; LAIT 4; MTCW 1, 2; SATA 2, 52

**Heym, Georg (Theodor Franz Arthur)**
1887-1912 ...................................... **TCLC 9**
See also CA 106; 181

**Heym, Stefan** 1913-2001 ................... **CLC 41**
See also CA 9-12R; 203; CANR 4; CWW 2; DLB 69; EWL 3

**Heyse, Paul (Johann Ludwig von)**
1830-1914 ...................................... **TCLC 8**
See also CA 104; 209; DLB 129

**Heyward, (Edwin) DuBose**
1885-1940 ...................... **HR 2; TCLC 59**
See also CA 108; 157; DLB 7, 9, 45, 249; SATA 21

**Heywood, John** 1497(?)-1580(?) .......... **LC 65**
See also DLB 136; RGEL 2

**Hibbert, Eleanor Alice Burford**
1906-1993 ...................................... **CLC 7**
See Holt, Victoria
See also BEST 90:4; CA 17-20R; 140; CANR 9, 28, 59; CMW 4; CPW; DAM POP; MTCW 2; RHW; SATA 2; SATA-Obit 74

**Hichens, Robert (Smythe)**
1864-1950 ...................................... **TCLC 64**
See also CA 162; DLB 153; HGG; RHW; SUFW

**Higgins, Aidan** 1927- ........................ **SSC 68**
See also CA 9-12R; CANR 70, 115; CN 7; DLB 14

**Higgins, George V(incent)**
1939-1999 .................... **CLC 4, 7, 10, 18**
See also BPFB 2; CA 77-80; 186; CAAS 5; CANR 17, 51, 89, 96; CMW 4; CN 7; DLB 2; DLBY 1981, 1998; INT CANR-17; MSW; MTCW 1

**Higginson, Thomas Wentworth**
1823-1911 .................................... **TCLC 36**
See also CA 162; DLB 1, 64, 243

**Higgonet, Margaret** ed. .................... **CLC 65**

**Highet, Helen**
See MacInnes, Helen (Clark)

**Highsmith, (Mary) Patricia**
1921-1995 ............ **CLC 2, 4, 14, 42, 102**
See Morgan, Claire
See also AAYA 48; BRWS 5; CA 1-4R; 147; CANR 1, 20, 48, 62, 108; CMW 4; CPW; DA3; DAM NOV, POP; DLB 306; MSW; MTCW 1, 2

**Highwater, Jamake (Mamake)**
1942(?)-2001 ................................. **CLC 12**
See also AAYA 7; BPFB 2; BYA 4; CA 65-68; 199; CAAS 7; CANR 10, 34, 84; CLR 17; CWRI 5; DLB 52; DLBY 1985; JRDA; MAICYA 1, 2; SATA 32, 69; SATA-Brief 30

**Highway, Tomson** 1951- ...... **CLC 92; NNAL**
See also CA 151; CANR 75; CCA 1; CD 5; DAC; DAM MULT; DFS 2; MTCW 2

**Hijuelos, Oscar** 1951- .......... **CLC 65; HLC 1**
See also AAYA 25; AMWS 8; BEST 90:1; CA 123; CANR 50, 75, 125; CPW; DA3; DAM MULT, POP; DLB 145; HW 1, 2; LLW 1; MTCW 2; NFS 17; RGAL 4; WLIT 1

**Hikmet, Nazim** 1902(?)-1963 ............ **CLC 40**
See also CA 141; 93-96; EWL 3

**Hildegard von Bingen** 1098-1179 . **CMLC 20**
See also DLB 148

**Hildesheimer, Wolfgang** 1916-1991 .. **CLC 49**
See also CA 101; 135; DLB 69, 124; EWL 3

**Hill, Geoffrey (William)** 1932- ...... **CLC 5, 8, 18, 45**
See also BRWS 5; CA 81-84; CANR 21, 89; CDBLB 1960 to Present; CP 7; DAM POET; DLB 40; EWL 3; MTCW 1; RGEL 2

**Hill, George Roy** 1921-2002 ............ **CLC 26**
  See also CA 110; 122; 213
**Hill, John**
  See Koontz, Dean R(ay)
**Hill, Susan (Elizabeth)** 1942- ...... **CLC 4, 113**
  See also CA 33-36R; CANR 29, 69, 129;
  CN 7; DAB; DAM MST, NOV; DLB 14,
  139; HGG; MTCW 1; RHW
**Hillard, Asa G. III** ........................... **CLC 70**
**Hillerman, Tony** 1925- ............. **CLC 62, 170**
  See also AAYA 40; BEST 89:1; BPFB 2;
  CA 29-32R; CANR 21, 42, 65, 97; CMW
  4; CPW; DA3; DAM POP; DLB 206, 306;
  MSW; RGAL 4; SATA 6; TCWW 2; YAW
**Hillesum, Etty** 1914-1943 .............. **TCLC 49**
  See also CA 137
**Hilliard, Noel (Harvey)** 1929-1996 ... **CLC 15**
  See also CA 9-12R; CANR 7, 69; CN 7
**Hillis, Rick** 1956- ................................ **CLC 66**
  See also CA 134
**Hilton, James** 1900-1954 ............... **TCLC 21**
  See also CA 108; 169; DLB 34, 77; FANT;
  SATA 34
**Hilton, Walter** (?)-1396 .................. **CMLC 58**
  See also DLB 146; RGEL 2
**Himes, Chester (Bomar)** 1909-1984 .. **BLC 2;**
  **CLC 2, 4, 7, 18, 58, 108; TCLC 139**
  See also AFAW 2; BPFB 2; BW 2; CA 25-
  28R; 114; CANR 22, 89; CMW 4; DAM
  MULT; DLB 2, 76, 143, 226; EWL 3;
  MSW; MTCW 1, 2; RGAL 4
**Hinde, Thomas** ............................. **CLC 6, 11**
  See Chitty, Thomas Willes
  See also EWL 3
**Hine, (William) Daryl** 1936- ............. **CLC 15**
  See also CA 1-4R; CAAS 15; CANR 1, 20;
  CP 7; DLB 60
**Hinkson, Katharine Tynan**
  See Tynan, Katharine
**Hinojosa(-Smith), Rolando (R.)**
  1929- ................................................ **HLC 1**
  See Hinojosa-Smith, Rolando
  See also CA 131; CAAS 16; CANR 62;
  DAM MULT; DLB 82; HW 1, 2; LLW 1;
  MTCW 2; RGAL 4
**Hinton, S(usan) E(loise)** 1950- .. **CLC 30, 111**
  See also AAYA 2, 33; BPFB 2; BYA 2, 3;
  CA 81-84; CANR 32, 62, 92, 133;
  CDALBS; CLR 3, 23; CPW; DA; DA3;
  DAB; DAC; DAM MST, NOV; JRDA;
  LAIT 5; MAICYA 1, 2; MTCW 1, 2; NFS
  5, 9, 15, 16; SATA 19, 58, 115; WYA;
  YAW
**Hippius, Zinaida (Nikolaevna)** ....... **TCLC 9**
  See Gippius, Zinaida (Nikolaevna)
  See also DLB 295; EWL 3
**Hiraoka, Kimitake** 1925-1970
  See Mishima, Yukio
  See also CA 97-100; 29-32R; DA3; DAM
  DRAM; GLL 1; MTCW 1, 2
**Hirsch, E(ric) D(onald), Jr.** 1928- .... **CLC 79**
  See also CA 25-28R; CANR 27, 51; DLB
  67; INT CANR-27; MTCW 1
**Hirsch, Edward** 1950- ................. **CLC 31, 50**
  See also CA 104; CANR 20, 42, 102; CP 7;
  DLB 120
**Hitchcock, Alfred (Joseph)**
  1899-1980 ...................................... **CLC 16**
  See also AAYA 22; CA 159; 97-100; SATA
  27; SATA-Obit 24
**Hitchens, Christopher (Eric)**
  1949- .............................................. **CLC 157**
  See also CA 152; CANR 89
**Hitler, Adolf** 1889-1945 .................. **TCLC 53**
  See also CA 117; 147
**Hoagland, Edward** 1932- ................. **CLC 28**
  See also ANW; CA 1-4R; CANR 2, 31, 57,
  107; CN 7; DLB 6; SATA 51; TCWW 2

**Hoban, Russell (Conwell)** 1925- ... **CLC 7, 25**
  See also BPFB 2; CA 5-8R; CANR 23, 37,
  66, 114; CLR 3, 69; CN 7; CWRI 5; DAM
  NOV; DLB 52; FANT; MAICYA 1, 2;
  MTCW 1, 2; SATA 1, 40, 78, 136; SFW
  4; SUFW 2
**Hobbes, Thomas** 1588-1679 ................ **LC 36**
  See also DLB 151, 252, 281; RGEL 2
**Hobbs, Perry**
  See Blackmur, R(ichard) P(almer)
**Hobson, Laura Z(ametkin)**
  1900-1986 ............................... **CLC 7, 25**
  See Field, Peter
  See also BPFB 2; CA 17-20R; 118; CANR
  55; DLB 28; SATA 52
**Hoccleve, Thomas** c. 1368-c. 1437 ...... **LC 75**
  See also DLB 146; RGEL 2
**Hoch, Edward D(entinger)** 1930-
  See Queen, Ellery
  See also CA 29-32R; CANR 11, 27, 51, 97;
  CMW 4; DLB 306; SFW 4
**Hochhuth, Rolf** 1931- ........... **CLC 4, 11, 18**
  See also CA 5-8R; CANR 33, 75; CWW 2;
  DAM DRAM; DLB 124; EWL 3; MTCW
  1, 2
**Hochman, Sandra** 1936- .................. **CLC 3, 8**
  See also CA 5-8R; DLB 5
**Hochwaelder, Fritz** 1911-1986 .......... **CLC 36**
  See Hochwalder, Fritz
  See also CA 29-32R; 120; CANR 42; DAM
  DRAM; MTCW 1; RGWL 3
**Hochwalder, Fritz**
  See Hochwaelder, Fritz
  See also EWL 3; RGWL 2
**Hocking, Mary (Eunice)** 1921- ......... **CLC 13**
  See also CA 101; CANR 18, 40
**Hodgins, Jack** 1938- ........................... **CLC 23**
  See also CA 93-96; CN 7; DLB 60
**Hodgson, William Hope**
  1877(?)-1918 ............................. **TCLC 13**
  See also CA 111; 164; CMW 4; DLB 70,
  153, 156, 178; HGG; MTCW 2; SFW 4;
  SUFW 1
**Hoeg, Peter** 1957- ...................... **CLC 95, 156**
  See also CA 151; CANR 75; CMW 4; DA3;
  DLB 214; EWL 3; MTCW 2; NFS 17;
  RGWL 3; SSFS 18
**Hoffman, Alice** 1952- ........................ **CLC 51**
  See also AAYA 37; AMWS 10; CA 77-80;
  CANR 34, 66, 100; CN 7; CPW; DAM
  NOV; DLB 292; MTCW 1, 2
**Hoffman, Daniel (Gerard)** 1923- . **CLC 6, 13,**
  **23**
  See also CA 1-4R; CANR 4; CP 7; DLB 5
**Hoffman, Eva** 1945- .......................... **CLC 182**
  See also CA 132
**Hoffman, Stanley** 1944- ...................... **CLC 5**
  See also CA 77-80
**Hoffman, William** 1925- .................. **CLC 141**
  See also CA 21-24R; CANR 9, 103; CSW;
  DLB 234
**Hoffman, William M(oses)** 1939- ..... **CLC 40**
  See Hoffman, William M.
  See also CA 57-60; CANR 11, 71
**Hoffmann, E(rnst) T(heodor) A(madeus)**
  1776-1822 .................. **NCLC 2; SSC 13**
  See also CDWLB 2; DLB 90; EW 5; RGSF
  2; RGWL 2, 3; SATA 27; SUFW 1; WCH
**Hofmann, Gert** 1931- ......................... **CLC 54**
  See also CA 128; EWL 3
**Hofmannsthal, Hugo von** 1874-1929 ... **DC 4;**
  **TCLC 11**
  See also CA 106; 153; CDWLB 2; DAM
  DRAM; DFS 17; DLB 81, 118; EW 9;
  EWL 3; RGWL 2, 3

**Hogan, Linda** 1947- ..... **CLC 73; NNAL; PC**
  **35**
  See also AMWS 4; ANW; BYA 12; CA 120,
  226; CAAE 226; CANR 45, 73, 129;
  CWP; DAM MULT; DLB 175; SATA
  132; TCWW 2
**Hogarth, Charles**
  See Creasey, John
**Hogarth, Emmett**
  See Polonsky, Abraham (Lincoln)
**Hogg, James** 1770-1835 ........... **NCLC 4, 109**
  See also DLB 93, 116, 159; HGG; RGEL 2;
  SUFW 1
**Holbach, Paul Henri Thiry Baron**
  1723-1789 ...................................... **LC 14**
**Holberg, Ludvig** 1684-1754 .................. **LC 6**
  See also DLB 300; RGWL 2, 3
**Holcroft, Thomas** 1745-1809 ......... **NCLC 85**
  See also DLB 39, 89, 158; RGEL 2
**Holden, Ursula** 1921- ........................ **CLC 18**
  See also CA 101; CAAS 8; CANR 22
**Holderlin, (Johann Christian) Friedrich**
  1770-1843 ...................... **NCLC 16; PC 4**
  See also CDWLB 2; DLB 90; EW 5; RGWL
  2, 3
**Holdstock, Robert**
  See Holdstock, Robert P.
**Holdstock, Robert P.** 1948- ............... **CLC 39**
  See also CA 131; CANR 81; DLB 261;
  FANT; HGG; SFW 4; SUFW 2
**Holinshed, Raphael** fl. 1580- ............... **LC 69**
  See also DLB 167; RGEL 2
**Holland, Isabelle (Christian)**
  1920-2002 ...................................... **CLC 21**
  See also AAYA 11; CA 21-24R; 205; CAAE
  181; CANR 10, 25, 47; CLR 57; CWRI
  5; JRDA; LAIT 4; MAICYA 1, 2; SATA
  8, 70; SATA-Essay 103; SATA-Obit 132;
  WYA
**Holland, Marcus**
  See Caldwell, (Janet Miriam) Taylor
  (Holland)
**Hollander, John** 1929- .......... **CLC 2, 5, 8, 14**
  See also CA 1-4R; CANR 1, 52; CP 7; DLB
  5; SATA 13
**Hollander, Paul**
  See Silverberg, Robert
**Holleran, Andrew** 1943(?)- ................ **CLC 38**
  See Garber, Eric
  See also CA 144; GLL 1
**Holley, Marietta** 1836(?)-1926 ........ **TCLC 99**
  See also CA 118; DLB 11
**Hollinghurst, Alan** 1954- ............. **CLC 55, 91**
  See also CA 114; CN 7; DLB 207; GLL 1
**Hollis, Jim**
  See Summers, Hollis (Spurgeon, Jr.)
**Holly, Buddy** 1936-1959 .................. **TCLC 65**
  See also CA 213
**Holmes, Gordon**
  See Shiel, M(atthew) P(hipps)
**Holmes, John**
  See Souster, (Holmes) Raymond
**Holmes, John Clellon** 1926-1988 ...... **CLC 56**
  See also BG 2; CA 9-12R; 125; CANR 4;
  DLB 16, 237
**Holmes, Oliver Wendell, Jr.**
  1841-1935 ...................................... **TCLC 77**
  See also CA 114; 186
**Holmes, Oliver Wendell**
  1809-1894 .......................... **NCLC 14, 81**
  See also AMWS 1; CDALB 1640-1865;
  DLB 1, 189, 235; EXPP; RGAL 4; SATA
  34
**Holmes, Raymond**
  See Souster, (Holmes) Raymond
**Holt, Victoria**
  See Hibbert, Eleanor Alice Burford
  See also BPFB 2

**Holub, Miroslav** 1923-1998 ................. **CLC 4**
 See also CA 21-24R; 169; CANR 10; CD-
 WLB 4; CWW 2; DLB 232; EWL 3;
 RGWL 3

**Holz, Detlev**
 See Benjamin, Walter

**Homer** c. 8th cent. B.C.- .... **CMLC 1, 16, 61;**
 **PC 23; WLCS**
 See also AW 1; CDWLB 1; DA; DA3;
 DAB; DAC; DAM MST, POET; DLB
 176; EFS 1; LAIT 1; LMFS 1; RGWL 2,
 3; TWA; WP

**Hongo, Garrett Kaoru** 1951- ............... **PC 23**
 See also CA 133; CAAS 22; CP 7; DLB
 120; EWL 3; EXPP; RGAL 4

**Honig, Edwin** 1919- ........................... **CLC 33**
 See also CA 5-8R; CAAS 8; CANR 4, 45;
 CP 7; DLB 5

**Hood, Hugh (John Blagdon)** 1928- . **CLC 15,**
 **28; SSC 42**
 See also CA 49-52; CAAS 17; CANR 1,
 33, 87; CN 7; DLB 53; RGSF 2

**Hood, Thomas** 1799-1845 ............... **NCLC 16**
 See also BRW 4; DLB 96; RGEL 2

**Hooker, (Peter) Jeremy** 1941- .......... **CLC 43**
 See also CA 77-80; CANR 22; CP 7; DLB
 40

**Hooker, Richard** 1554-1600 ................ **LC 95**
 See also BRW 1; DLB 132; RGEL 2

**hooks, bell**
 See Watkins, Gloria Jean

**Hope, A(lec) D(erwent)** 1907-2000 .... **CLC 3,**
 **51; PC 56**
 See also BRWS 7; CA 21-24R; 188; CANR
 33, 74; DLB 289; EWL 3; MTCW 1, 2;
 PFS 8; RGEL 2

**Hope, Anthony** 1863-1933 .............. **TCLC 83**
 See also CA 157; DLB 153, 156; RGEL 2;
 RHW

**Hope, Brian**
 See Creasey, John

**Hope, Christopher (David Tully)**
 1944- ......................................... **CLC 52**
 See also AFW; CA 106; CANR 47, 101;
 CN 7; DLB 225; SATA 62

**Hopkins, Gerard Manley**
 1844-1889 ....... **NCLC 17; PC 15; WLC**
 See also BRW 5; BRWR 2; CDBLB 1890-
 1914; DA; DA3; DAB; DAC; DAM MST,
 POET; DLB 35, 57; EXPP; PAB; RGEL
 2; TEA; WP

**Hopkins, John (Richard)** 1931-1998 .. **CLC 4**
 See also CA 85-88; 169; CBD; CD 5

**Hopkins, Pauline Elizabeth**
 1859-1930 ................... **BLC 2; TCLC 28**
 See also AFAW 2; BW 2, 3; CA 141; CANR
 82; DAM MULT; DLB 50

**Hopkinson, Francis** 1737-1791 ........... **LC 25**
 See also DLB 31; RGAL 4

**Hopley-Woolrich, Cornell George** 1903-1968
 See Woolrich, Cornell
 See also CA 13-14; CANR 58; CAP 1;
 CMW 4; DLB 226; MTCW 2

**Horace** 65B.C.-8B.C. ......... **CMLC 39; PC 46**
 See also AW 2; CDWLB 1; DLB 211;
 RGWL 2, 3

**Horatio**
 See Proust, (Valentin-Louis-George-Eugene)
 Marcel

**Horgan, Paul (George Vincent**
 **O'Shaughnessy)** 1903-1995 .. **CLC 9, 53**
 See also BPFB 2; CA 13-16R; 147; CANR
 9, 35; DAM NOV; DLB 102, 212; DLBY
 1985; INT CANR-9; MTCW 1, 2; SATA
 13; SATA-Obit 84; TCWW 2

**Horkheimer, Max** 1895-1973 ........ **TCLC 132**
 See also CA 216; 41-44R; DLB 296

**Horn, Peter**
 See Kuttner, Henry

**Horne, Frank (Smith)** 1899-1974 ......... **HR 2**
 See also BW 1; CA 125; 53-56; DLB 51;
 WP

**Horne, Richard Henry Hengist**
 1802(?)-1884 ........................... **NCLC 127**
 See also DLB 32; SATA 29

**Hornem, Horace Esq.**
 See Byron, George Gordon (Noel)

**Horney, Karen (Clementine Theodore**
 **Danielsen)** 1885-1952 ............. **TCLC 71**
 See also CA 114; 165; DLB 246; FW

**Hornung, E(rnest) W(illiam)**
 1866-1921 ............................... **TCLC 59**
 See also CA 108; 160; CMW 4; DLB 70

**Horovitz, Israel (Arthur)** 1939- ........ **CLC 56**
 See also CA 33-36R; CAD; CANR 46, 59;
 CD 5; DAM DRAM; DLB 7

**Horton, George Moses**
 1797(?)-1883(?) ........................ **NCLC 87**
 See also DLB 50

**Horvath, odon von** 1901-1938
 See von Horvath, Odon
 See also EWL 3

**Horvath, Oedoen von** -1938
 See von Horvath, Odon

**Horwitz, Julius** 1920-1986 ................. **CLC 14**
 See also CA 9-12R; 119; CANR 12

**Hospital, Janette Turner** 1942- ........ **CLC 42,**
 **145**
 See also CA 108; CANR 48; CN 7; DLBY
 2002; RGSF 2

**Hostos, E. M. de**
 See Hostos (y Bonilla), Eugenio Maria de

**Hostos, Eugenio M. de**
 See Hostos (y Bonilla), Eugenio Maria de

**Hostos, Eugenio Maria**
 See Hostos (y Bonilla), Eugenio Maria de

**Hostos (y Bonilla), Eugenio Maria de**
 1839-1903 ............................... **TCLC 24**
 See also CA 123; 131; HW 1

**Houdini**
 See Lovecraft, H(oward) P(hillips)

**Houellebecq, Michel** 1958- .............. **CLC 179**
 See also CA 185

**Hougan, Carolyn** 1943- .................... **CLC 34**
 See also CA 139

**Household, Geoffrey (Edward West)**
 1900-1988 ................................. **CLC 11**
 See also CA 77-80; 126; CANR 58; CMW
 4; DLB 87; SATA 14; SATA-Obit 59

**Housman, A(lfred) E(dward)**
 1859-1936 ......... **PC 2, 43; TCLC 1, 10;**
 **WLCS**
 See also BRW 6; CA 104; 125; DA; DA3;
 DAB; DAC; DAM MST, POET; DLB 19,
 284; EWL 3; EXPP; MTCW 1, 2; PAB;
 PFS 4, 7; RGEL 2; TEA; WP

**Housman, Laurence** 1865-1959 ....... **TCLC 7**
 See also CA 106; 155; DLB 10; FANT;
 RGEL 2; SATA 25

**Houston, Jeanne (Toyo) Wakatsuki**
 1934- ................................................. **AAL**
 See also AAYA 49; CA 103; CAAS 16;
 CANR 29, 123; LAIT 4; SATA 78

**Howard, Elizabeth Jane** 1923- ..... **CLC 7, 29**
 See also CA 5-8R; CANR 8, 62; CN 7

**Howard, Maureen** 1930- ........ **CLC 5, 14, 46,**
 **151**
 See also CA 53-56; CANR 31, 75; CN 7;
 DLBY 1983; INT CANR-31; MTCW 1, 2

**Howard, Richard** 1929- .......... **CLC 7, 10, 47**
 See also AITN 1; CA 85-88; CANR 25, 80;
 CP 7; DLB 5; INT CANR-25

**Howard, Robert E(rvin)**
 1906-1936 ................................. **TCLC 8**
 See also BPFB 2; BYA 5; CA 105; 157;
 FANT; SUFW 1

**Howard, Warren F.**
 See Pohl, Frederik

**Howe, Fanny (Quincy)** 1940- ............ **CLC 47**
 See also CA 117; 187; CAAE 187; CAAS
 27; CANR 70, 116; CP 7; CWP; SATA-
 Brief 52

**Howe, Irving** 1920-1993 ................... **CLC 85**
 See also AMWS 6; CA 9-12R; 141; CANR
 21, 50; DLB 67; EWL 3; MTCW 1, 2

**Howe, Julia Ward** 1819-1910 ......... **TCLC 21**
 See also CA 117; 191; DLB 1, 189, 235;
 FW

**Howe, Susan** 1937- ....... **CLC 72, 152; PC 54**
 See also AMWS 4; CA 160; CP 7; CWP;
 DLB 120; FW; RGAL 4

**Howe, Tina** 1937- ............................. **CLC 48**
 See also CA 109; CAD; CANR 125; CD 5;
 CWD

**Howell, James** 1594(?)-1666 ................ **LC 13**
 See also DLB 151

**Howells, W. D.**
 See Howells, William Dean

**Howells, William D.**
 See Howells, William Dean

**Howells, William Dean** 1837-1920 ... **SSC 36;**
 **TCLC 7, 17, 41**
 See also AMW; CA 104; 134; CDALB
 1865-1917; DLB 12, 64, 74, 79, 189;
 LMFS 1; MTCW 2; RGAL 4; TUS

**Howes, Barbara** 1914-1996 .............. **CLC 15**
 See also CA 9-12R; 151; CAAS 3; CANR
 53; CP 7; SATA 5

**Hrabal, Bohumil** 1914-1997 ...... **CLC 13, 67;**
 **TCLC 155**
 See also CA 106; 156; CAAS 12; CANR
 57; CWW 2; DLB 232; EWL 3; RGSF 2

**Hrotsvit of Gandersheim** c. 935-c.
 1000 ...................................... **CMLC 29**
 See also DLB 148

**Hsi, Chu** 1130-1200 ....................... **CMLC 42**

**Hsun, Lu**
 See Lu Hsun

**Hubbard, L(afayette) Ron(ald)**
 1911-1986 ................................. **CLC 43**
 See also CA 77-80; 118; CANR 52; CPW;
 DA3; DAM POP; FANT; MTCW 2; SFW
 4

**Huch, Ricarda (Octavia)**
 1864-1947 ............................... **TCLC 13**
 See also CA 111; 189; DLB 66; EWL 3

**Huddle, David** 1942- ........................ **CLC 49**
 See also CA 57-60; CAAS 20; CANR 89;
 DLB 130

**Hudson, Jeffrey**
 See Crichton, (John) Michael

**Hudson, W(illiam) H(enry)**
 1841-1922 ............................... **TCLC 29**
 See also CA 115; 190; DLB 98, 153, 174;
 RGEL 2; SATA 35

**Hueffer, Ford Madox**
 See Ford, Ford Madox

**Hughart, Barry** 1934- ....................... **CLC 39**
 See also CA 137; FANT; SFW 4; SUFW 2

**Hughes, Colin**
 See Creasey, John

**Hughes, David (John)** 1930- ............. **CLC 48**
 See also CA 116; 129; CN 7; DLB 14

**Hughes, Edward James**
 See Hughes, Ted
 See also DA3; DAM MST, POET

**Hughes, (James Mercer) Langston**
 1902-1967 ...... **BLC 2; CLC 1, 5, 10, 15,**
 **35, 44, 108; DC 3; HR 2; PC 1, 53;**
 **SSC 6; WLC**
 See also AAYA 12; AFAW 1, 2; AMWR 1;
 AMWS 1; BW 1, 3; CA 1-4R; 25-28R;
 CANR 1, 34, 82; CDALB 1929-1941;
 CLR 17; DA; DA3; DAB; DAC; DAM
 DRAM, MST, MULT, POET; DFS 6, 18;
 DLB 4, 7, 48, 51, 86, 228; EWL 3; EXPP;
 EXPS; JRDA; LAIT 3; LMFS 2; MAI-

CYA 1, 2; MTCW 1, 2; PAB; PFS 1, 3, 6, 10, 15; RGAL 4; RGSF 2; SATA 4, 33; SSFS 4, 7; TUS; WCH; WP; YAW

**Hughes, Richard (Arthur Warren)**
1900-1976 .............................. **CLC 1, 11**
See also CA 5-8R; 65-68; CANR 4; DAM NOV; DLB 15, 161; EWL 3; MTCW 1; RGEL 2; SATA 8; SATA-Obit 25

**Hughes, Ted** 1930-1998 . **CLC 2, 4, 9, 14, 37, 119; PC 7**
See Hughes, Edward James
See also BRWC 2; BRWR 2; BRWS 1; CA 1-4R; 171; CANR 1, 33, 66, 108; CLR 3; CP 7; DAB; DAC; DLB 40, 161; EWL 3; EXPP; MAICYA 1, 2; MTCW 1, 2; PAB; PFS 4, 19; RGEL 2; SATA 49; SATA-Brief 27; SATA-Obit 107; TEA; YAW

**Hugo, Richard**
See Huch, Ricarda (Octavia)

**Hugo, Richard F(ranklin)**
1923-1982 ......................... **CLC 6, 18, 32**
See also AMWS 6; CA 49-52; 108; CANR 3; DAM POET; DLB 5, 206; EWL 3; PFS 17; RGAL 4

**Hugo, Victor (Marie)** 1802-1885 .... **NCLC 3, 10, 21; PC 17; WLC**
See also AAYA 28; DA; DA3; DAB; DAC; DAM DRAM, MST, NOV, POET; DLB 119, 192, 217; EFS 2; EW 6; EXPN; GFL 1789 to the Present; LAIT 1, 2; NFS 5, 20; RGWL 2, 3; SATA 47; TWA

**Huidobro, Vicente**
See Huidobro Fernandez, Vicente Garcia
See also DLB 283; EWL 3; LAW

**Huidobro Fernandez, Vicente Garcia**
1893-1948 ............................... **TCLC 31**
See Huidobro, Vicente
See also CA 131; HW 1

**Hulme, Keri** 1947- ..................... **CLC 39, 130**
See also CA 125; CANR 69; CN 7; CP 7; CWP; EWL 3; FW; INT CA-125

**Hulme, T(homas) E(rnest)**
1883-1917 ............................... **TCLC 21**
See also BRWS 6; CA 117; 203; DLB 19

**Humboldt, Wilhelm von**
1767-1835 ............................... **NCLC 134**
See also DLB 90

**Hume, David** 1711-1776 .................. **LC 7, 56**
See also BRWS 3; DLB 104, 252; LMFS 1; TEA

**Humphrey, William** 1924-1997 ......... **CLC 45**
See also AMWS 9; CA 77-80; 160; CANR 68; CN 7; CSW; DLB 6, 212, 234, 278; TCWW 2

**Humphreys, Emyr Owen** 1919- ........ **CLC 47**
See also CA 5-8R; CANR 3, 24; CN 7; DLB 15

**Humphreys, Josephine** 1945- ..... **CLC 34, 57**
See also CA 121; 127; CANR 97; CSW; DLB 292; INT CA-127

**Huneker, James Gibbons**
1860-1921 ............................... **TCLC 65**
See also CA 193; DLB 71; RGAL 4

**Hungerford, Hesba Fay**
See Brinsmead, H(esba) F(ay)

**Hungerford, Pixie**
See Brinsmead, H(esba) F(ay)

**Hunt, E(verette) Howard, (Jr.)**
1918- ...................................... **CLC 3**
See also AITN 1; CA 45-48; CANR 2, 47, 103; CMW 4

**Hunt, Francesca**
See Holland, Isabelle (Christian)

**Hunt, Howard**
See Hunt, E(verette) Howard, (Jr.)

**Hunt, Kyle**
See Creasey, John

**Hunt, (James Henry) Leigh**
1784-1859 ............................ **NCLC 1, 70**
See also DAM POET; DLB 96, 110, 144; RGEL 2; TEA

**Hunt, Marsha** 1946- ....................... **CLC 70**
See also BW 2, 3; CA 143; CANR 79

**Hunt, Violet** 1866(?)-1942 .............. **TCLC 53**
See also CA 184; DLB 162, 197

**Hunter, E. Waldo**
See Sturgeon, Theodore (Hamilton)

**Hunter, Evan** 1926- ..................... **CLC 11, 31**
See McBain, Ed
See also AAYA 39; BPFB 2; CA 5-8R; CANR 5, 38, 62, 97; CMW 4; CN 7; CPW; DAM POP; DLB 306; DLBY 1982; INT CANR-5; MSW; MTCW 1; SATA 25; SFW 4

**Hunter, Kristin** 1931-
See Lattany, Kristin (Elaine Eggleston) Hunter

**Hunter, Mary**
See Austin, Mary (Hunter)

**Hunter, Mollie** 1922- ..................... **CLC 21**
See McIlwraith, Maureen Mollie Hunter
See also AAYA 13; BYA 6; CANR 37, 78; CLR 25; DLB 161; JRDA; MAICYA 1, 2; SAAS 7; SATA 54, 106, 139; SATA-Essay 139; WYA; YAW

**Hunter, Robert** (?)-1734 ..................... **LC 7**

**Hurston, Zora Neale** 1891-1960 ........ **BLC 2; CLC 7, 30, 61; DC 12; HR 2; SSC 4; TCLC 121, 131; WLCS**
See also AAYA 15; AFAW 1, 2; AMWS 6; BW 1, 3; BYA 12; CA 85-88; CANR 61; CDALBS; DA; DA3; DAC; DAM MST, MULT, NOV; DFS 6; DLB 51, 86; EWL 3; EXPN; EXPS; FW; LAIT 3; LATS 1:1; LMFS 2; MAWW; MTCW 1, 2; NFS 3; RGAL 4; RGSF 2; SSFS 1, 6, 11, 19; TUS; YAW

**Husserl, E. G.**
See Husserl, Edmund (Gustav Albrecht)

**Husserl, Edmund (Gustav Albrecht)**
1859-1938 ............................... **TCLC 100**
See also CA 116; 133; DLB 296

**Huston, John (Marcellus)**
1906-1987 ............................... **CLC 20**
See also CA 73-76; 123; CANR 34; DLB 26

**Hustvedt, Siri** 1955- ......................... **CLC 76**
See also CA 137

**Hutten, Ulrich von** 1488-1523 ............. **LC 16**
See also DLB 179

**Huxley, Aldous (Leonard)**
1894-1963 ....... **CLC 1, 3, 4, 5, 8, 11, 18, 35, 79; SSC 39; WLC**
See also AAYA 11; BPFB 2; BRW 7; CA 85-88; CANR 44, 99; CDBLB 1914-1945; DA; DA3; DAB; DAC; DAM MST, NOV; DLB 36, 100, 162, 195, 255; EWL 3; EXPN; LAIT 5; LMFS 2; MTCW 1, 2; NFS 6; RGEL 2; SATA 63; SCFW 2; SFW 4; TEA; YAW

**Huxley, T(homas) H(enry)**
1825-1895 ............................... **NCLC 67**
See also DLB 57; TEA

**Huysmans, Joris-Karl** 1848-1907 ... **TCLC 7, 69**
See also CA 104; 165; DLB 123; EW 7; GFL 1789 to the Present; LMFS 2; RGWL 2, 3

**Hwang, David Henry** 1957- .... **CLC 55, 196; DC 4, 23**
See also CA 127; 132; CAD; CANR 76, 124; CD 5; DA3; DAM DRAM; DFS 11, 18; DLB 212, 228; INT CA-132; MTCW 2; RGAL 4

**Hyde, Anthony** 1946- ........................ **CLC 42**
See Chase, Nicholas
See also CA 136; CCA 1

**Hyde, Margaret O(ldroyd)** 1917- ..... **CLC 21**
See also CA 1-4R; CANR 1, 36; CLR 23; JRDA; MAICYA 1, 2; SAAS 8; SATA 1, 42, 76, 139

**Hynes, James** 1956(?)- ...................... **CLC 65**
See also CA 164; CANR 105

**Hypatia** c. 370-415 ......................... **CMLC 35**

**Ian, Janis** 1951- .............................. **CLC 21**
See also CA 105; 187

**Ibanez, Vicente Blasco**
See Blasco Ibanez, Vicente

**Ibarbourou, Juana de** 1895-1979 ..... **HLCS 2**
See also DLB 290; HW 1; LAW

**Ibarguengoitia, Jorge** 1928-1983 ..... **CLC 37; TCLC 148**
See also CA 124; 113; EWL 3; HW 1

**Ibn Battuta, Abu Abdalla**
1304-1368(?) ........................... **CMLC 57**
See also WLIT 2

**Ibn Hazm** 994-1064 ......................... **CMLC 64**

**Ibsen, Henrik (Johan)** 1828-1906 ........ **DC 2; TCLC 2, 8, 16, 37, 52; WLC**
See also AAYA 46; CA 104; 141; DA; DA3; DAB; DAC; DAM DRAM, MST; DFS 1, 6, 8, 10, 11, 15, 16; EW 7; LAIT 2; LATS 1:1; RGWL 2, 3

**Ibuse, Masuji** 1898-1993 .................. **CLC 22**
See Ibuse Masuji
See also CA 127; 141; MJW; RGWL 3

**Ibuse Masuji**
See Ibuse, Masuji
See also CWW 2; DLB 180; EWL 3

**Ichikawa, Kon** 1915- ......................... **CLC 20**
See also CA 121

**Ichiyo, Higuchi** 1872-1896 .............. **NCLC 49**
See also MJW

**Idle, Eric** 1943- ................................ **CLC 21**
See Monty Python
See also CA 116; CANR 35, 91

**Idris, Yusuf** 1927-1991 ...................... **SSC 74**
See also AFW; EWL 3; RGSF 2, 3; RGWL 3; WLIT 2

**Ignatow, David** 1914-1997 ....... **CLC 4, 7, 14, 40; PC 34**
See also CA 9-12R; 162; CAAS 3; CANR 31, 57, 96; CP 7; DLB 5; EWL 3

**Ignotus**
See Strachey, (Giles) Lytton

**Ihimaera, Witi (Tame)** 1944- ............ **CLC 46**
See also CA 77-80; CANR 130; CN 7; RGSF 2; SATA 148

**Ilf, Ilya** ............................................. **TCLC 21**
See Fainzilberg, Ilya Arnoldovich
See also EWL 3

**Illyes, Gyula** 1902-1983 ...................... **PC 16**
See also CA 114; 109; CDWLB 4; DLB 215; EWL 3; RGWL 2, 3

**Imalayen, Fatima-Zohra**
See Djebar, Assia

**Immermann, Karl (Lebrecht)**
1796-1840 ............................... **NCLC 4, 49**
See also DLB 133

**Ince, Thomas H.** 1882-1924 ............ **TCLC 89**
See also IDFW 3, 4

**Inchbald, Elizabeth** 1753-1821 ...... **NCLC 62**
See also DLB 39, 89; RGEL 2

**Inclan, Ramon (Maria) del Valle**
See Valle-Inclan, Ramon (Maria) del

**Infante, G(uillermo) Cabrera**
See Cabrera Infante, G(uillermo)

**Ingalls, Rachel (Holmes)** 1940- ......... **CLC 42**
See also CA 123; 127

**Ingamells, Reginald Charles**
See Ingamells, Rex

**Ingamells, Rex** 1913-1955 .............. **TCLC 35**
See also CA 167; DLB 260

**Inge, William (Motter)** 1913-1973 ..... **CLC 1, 8, 19**
See also CA 9-12R; CDALB 1941-1968; DA3; DAM DRAM; DFS 1, 3, 5, 8; DLB 7, 249; EWL 3; MTCW 1, 2; RGAL 4; TUS

**Ingelow, Jean** 1820-1897 ........ **NCLC 39, 107**
See also DLB 35, 163; FANT; SATA 33

**Ingram, Willis J.**
See Harris, Mark

**Innaurato, Albert (F.)** 1948(?)- ... **CLC 21, 60**
See also CA 115; 122; CAD; CANR 78; CD 5; INT CA-122

**Innes, Michael**
See Stewart, J(ohn) I(nnes) M(ackintosh)
See also DLB 276; MSW

**Innis, Harold Adams** 1894-1952 .... **TCLC 77**
See also CA 181; DLB 88

**Insluis, Alanus de**
See Alain de Lille

**Iola**
See Wells-Barnett, Ida B(ell)

**Ionesco, Eugene** 1912-1994 ... **CLC 1, 4, 6, 9, 11, 15, 41, 86; DC 12; WLC**
See also CA 9-12R; CANR 55, 132; CWW 2; DA; DA3; DAB; DAC; DAM DRAM, MST; DFS 4, 9; EW 13; EWL 3; GFL 1789 to the Present; LMFS 2; MTCW 1, 2; RGWL 2, 3; SATA 7; SATA-Obit 79; TWA

**Iqbal, Muhammad** 1877-1938 ........ **TCLC 28**
See also CA 215; EWL 3

**Ireland, Patrick**
See O'Doherty, Brian

**Irenaeus St.** 130- ............................. **CMLC 42**

**Irigaray, Luce** 1930- ...................... **CLC 164**
See also CA 154; CANR 121; FW

**Iron, Ralph**
See Schreiner, Olive (Emilie Albertina)

**Irving, John (Winslow)** 1942- ... **CLC 13, 23, 38, 112, 175**
See also AAYA 8; AMWS 6; BEST 89:3; BPFB 2; CA 25-28R; CANR 28, 73, 112, 133; CN 7; CPW; DA3; DAM NOV, POP; DLB 6, 278; DLBY 1982; EWL 3; MTCW 1, 2; NFS 12, 14; RGAL 4; TUS

**Irving, Washington** 1783-1859 . **NCLC 2, 19, 95; SSC 2, 37; WLC**
See also AAYA 56; AMW; CDALB 1640-1865; CLR 97; DA; DA3; DAB; DAC; DAM MST; DLB 3, 11, 30, 59, 73, 74, 183, 186, 250, 254; EXPS; LAIT 1; RGAL 4; RGSF 2; SSFS 1, 8, 16; SUFW 1; TUS; WCH; YABC 2

**Irwin, P. K.**
See Page, P(atricia) K(athleen)

**Isaacs, Jorge Ricardo** 1837-1895 ... **NCLC 70**
See also LAW

**Isaacs, Susan** 1943- ............................ **CLC 32**
See also BEST 89:1; BPFB 2; CA 89-92; CANR 20, 41, 65, 112; CPW; DA3; DAM POP; INT CANR-20; MTCW 1, 2

**Isherwood, Christopher (William Bradshaw)** 1904-1986 .... **CLC 1, 9, 11, 14, 44; SSC 56**
See also BRW 7; CA 13-16R; 117; CANR 35, 97, 133; DA3; DAM DRAM, NOV; DLB 15, 195; DLBY 1986; EWL 3; IDTP; MTCW 1, 2; RGAL 4; RGEL 2; TUS; WLIT 4

**Ishiguro, Kazuo** 1954- .. **CLC 27, 56, 59, 110**
See also AAYA 58; BEST 90:2; BPFB 2; BRWS 4; CA 120; CANR 49, 95, 133; CN 7; DA3; DAM NOV; DLB 194; EWL 3; MTCW 1, 2; NFS 13; WLIT 4; WWE 1

**Ishikawa, Hakuhin**
See Ishikawa, Takuboku

**Ishikawa, Takuboku** 1886(?)-1912 ..... **PC 10; TCLC 15**
See Ishikawa Takuboku
See also CA 113; 153; DAM POET

**Iskander, Fazil (Abdulovich)** 1929- .. **CLC 47**
See Iskander, Fazil' Abdulevich
See also CA 102; EWL 3

**Iskander, Fazil' Abdulevich**
See Iskander, Fazil (Abdulovich)
See also DLB 302

**Isler, Alan (David)** 1934- .................. **CLC 91**
See also CA 156; CANR 105

**Ivan IV** 1530-1584 ............................... **LC 17**

**Ivanov, Vyacheslav Ivanovich** 1866-1949 ............................ **TCLC 33**
See also CA 122; EWL 3

**Ivask, Ivar Vidrik** 1927-1992 ........... **CLC 14**
See also CA 37-40R; 139; CANR 24

**Ives, Morgan**
See Bradley, Marion Zimmer
See also GLL 1

**Izumi Shikibu** c. 973-c. 1034 ........ **CMLC 33**

**J. R. S.**
See Gogarty, Oliver St. John

**Jabran, Kahlil**
See Gibran, Kahlil

**Jabran, Khalil**
See Gibran, Kahlil

**Jackson, Daniel**
See Wingrove, David (John)

**Jackson, Helen Hunt** 1830-1885 .... **NCLC 90**
See also DLB 42, 47, 186, 189; RGAL 4

**Jackson, Jesse** 1908-1983 ................. **CLC 12**
See also BW 1; CA 25-28R; 109; CANR 27; CLR 28; CWRI 5; MAICYA 1, 2; SATA 2, 29; SATA-Obit 48

**Jackson, Laura (Riding)** 1901-1991 .... **PC 44**
See Riding, Laura
See also CA 65-68; 135; CANR 28, 89; DLB 48

**Jackson, Sam**
See Trumbo, Dalton

**Jackson, Sara**
See Wingrove, David (John)

**Jackson, Shirley** 1919-1965 . **CLC 11, 60, 87; SSC 9, 39; WLC**
See also AAYA 9; AMWS 9; BPFB 2; CA 1-4R; 25-28R; CANR 4, 52; CDALB 1941-1968; DA; DA3; DAC; DAM MST; DLB 6, 234; EXPS; HGG; LAIT 4; MTCW 2; RGAL 4; RGSF 2; SATA 2; SSFS 1; SUFW 1, 2

**Jacob, (Cyprien-)Max** 1876-1944 .... **TCLC 6**
See also CA 104; 193; DLB 258; EWL 3; GFL 1789 to the Present; GLL 2; RGWL 2, 3

**Jacobs, Harriet A(nn)** 1813(?)-1897 ............................ **NCLC 67**
See also AFAW 1, 2; DLB 239; FW; LAIT 2; RGAL 4

**Jacobs, Jim** 1942- ................................ **CLC 12**
See also CA 97-100; INT CA-97-100

**Jacobs, W(illiam) W(ymark)** 1863-1943 ................ **SSC 73; TCLC 22**
See also CA 121; 167; DLB 135; EXPS; HGG; RGEL 2; RGSF 2; SSFS 2; SUFW 1

**Jacobsen, Jens Peter** 1847-1885 .... **NCLC 34**

**Jacobsen, Josephine (Winder)** 1908-2003 ............................ **CLC 48, 102**
See also CA 33-36R; 218; CAAS 18; CANR 23, 48; CCA 1; CP 7; DLB 244

**Jacobson, Dan** 1929- ....................... **CLC 4, 14**
See also AFW; CA 1-4R; CANR 2, 25, 66; CN 7; DLB 14, 207, 225; EWL 3; MTCW 1; RGSF 2

**Jacqueline**
See Carpentier (y Valmont), Alejo

**Jacques de Vitry** c. 1160-1240 ...... **CMLC 63**
See also DLB 208

**Jagger, Mick** 1944- ............................. **CLC 17**

**Jahiz, al-** c. 780-c. 869 .................. **CMLC 25**

**Jakes, John (William)** 1932- ............ **CLC 29**
See also AAYA 32; BEST 89:4; BPFB 2; CA 57-60, 214; CAAE 214; CANR 10, 43, 66, 111; CPW; CSW; DA3; DAM NOV, POP; DLB 278; DLBY 1983; FANT; INT CANR-10; MTCW 1, 2; RHW; SATA 62; SFW 4; TCWW 2

**James I** 1394-1437 ............................... **LC 20**
See also RGEL 2

**James, Andrew**
See Kirkup, James

**James, C(yril) L(ionel) R(obert)** 1901-1989 ............... **BLCS; CLC 33**
See also BW 2; CA 117; 125; 128; CANR 62; DLB 125; MTCW 1

**James, Daniel (Lewis)** 1911-1988
See Santiago, Danny
See also CA 174; 125

**James, Dynely**
See Mayne, William (James Carter)

**James, Henry Sr.** 1811-1882 .......... **NCLC 53**

**James, Henry** 1843-1916 ........ **SSC 8, 32, 47; TCLC 2, 11, 24, 40, 47, 64; WLC**
See also AMW; AMWC 1; AMWR 1; BPFB 2; BRW 6; CA 104; 132; CDALB 1865-1917; DA; DA3; DAB; DAC; DAM MST, NOV; DLB 12, 71, 74, 189; DLBD 13; EWL 3; EXPS; HGG; LAIT 2; MTCW 1, 2; NFS 12, 16, 19; RGAL 4; RGEL 2; RGSF 2; SSFS 9; SUFW 1; TUS

**James, M. R.**
See James, Montague (Rhodes)
See also DLB 156, 201

**James, Montague (Rhodes)** 1862-1936 ................... **SSC 16; TCLC 6**
See James, M. R.
See also CA 104; 203; HGG; RGEL 2; RGSF 2; SUFW 1

**James, P. D.** ....................... **CLC 18, 46, 122**
See White, Phyllis Dorothy James
See also BEST 90:2; BPFB 2; BRWS 4; CDBLB 1960 to Present; DLB 87, 276; DLBD 17; MSW

**James, Philip**
See Moorcock, Michael (John)

**James, Samuel**
See Stephens, James

**James, Seumas**
See Stephens, James

**James, Stephen**
See Stephens, James

**James, William** 1842-1910 ....... **TCLC 15, 32**
See also AMW; CA 109; 193; DLB 270, 284; NCFS 5; RGAL 4

**Jameson, Anna** 1794-1860 ............. **NCLC 43**
See also DLB 99, 166

**Jameson, Fredric (R.)** 1934- .......... **CLC 142**
See also CA 196; DLB 67; LMFS 2

**Jami, Nur al-Din 'Abd al-Rahman** 1414-1492 ............................... **LC 9**

**Jammes, Francis** 1868-1938 .......... **TCLC 75**
See also CA 198; EWL 3; GFL 1789 to the Present

**Jandl, Ernst** 1925-2000 ..................... **CLC 34**
See also CA 200; EWL 3

**Janowitz, Tama** 1957- ................ **CLC 43, 145**
See also CA 106; CANR 52, 89, 129; CN 7; CPW; DAM POP; DLB 292

**Japrisot, Sebastien** 1931- ................... **CLC 90**
See Rossi, Jean-Baptiste
See also CMW 4; NFS 18

**Jarrell, Randall** 1914-1965 .... **CLC 1, 2, 6, 9, 13, 49; PC 41**
See also AMW; BYA 5; CA 5-8R; 25-28R; CABS 2; CANR 6, 34; CDALB 1941-

1968; CLR 6; CWRI 5; DAM POET; DLB 48, 52; EWL 3; EXPP; MAICYA 1, 2; MTCW 1, 2; PAB; PFS 2; RGAL 4; SATA 7

**Jarry, Alfred** 1873-1907 .... **SSC 20; TCLC 2, 14, 147**
See also CA 104; 153; DA3; DAM DRAM; DFS 8; DLB 192, 258; EW 9; EWL 3; GFL 1789 to the Present; RGWL 2, 3; TWA

**Jarvis, E. K.**
See Ellison, Harlan (Jay)

**Jawien, Andrzej**
See John Paul II, Pope

**Jaynes, Roderick**
See Coen, Ethan

**Jeake, Samuel, Jr.**
See Aiken, Conrad (Potter)

**Jean Paul** 1763-1825 ........................ **NCLC 7**

**Jefferies, (John) Richard**
1848-1887 ............................ **NCLC 47**
See also DLB 98, 141; RGEL 2; SATA 16; SFW 4

**Jeffers, (John) Robinson** 1887-1962 .. **CLC 2, 3, 11, 15, 54; PC 17; WLC**
See also AMWS 2; CA 85-88; CANR 35; CDALB 1917-1929; DA; DAC; DAM MST, POET; DLB 45, 212; EWL 3; MTCW 1, 2; PAB; PFS 3, 4; RGAL 4

**Jefferson, Janet**
See Mencken, H(enry) L(ouis)

**Jefferson, Thomas** 1743-1826 . **NCLC 11, 103**
See also AAYA 54; ANW; CDALB 1640-1865; DA3; DLB 31, 183; LAIT 1; RGAL 4

**Jeffrey, Francis** 1773-1850 .............. **NCLC 33**
See Francis, Lord Jeffrey

**Jelakowitch, Ivan**
See Heijermans, Herman

**Jelinek, Elfriede** 1946- ..................... **CLC 169**
See also CA 154; DLB 85; FW

**Jellicoe, (Patricia) Ann** 1927- .......... **CLC 27**
See also CA 85-88; CBD; CD 5; CWD; CWRI 5; DLB 13, 233; FW

**Jelloun, Tahar ben** 1944- ................. **CLC 180**
See Ben Jelloun, Tahar
See also CA 162; CANR 100

**Jemyma**
See Holley, Marietta

**Jen, Gish** .................................. **AAL; CLC 70**
See Jen, Lillian
See also AMWC 2

**Jen, Lillian** 1956(?)-
See Jen, Gish
See also CA 135; CANR 89, 130

**Jenkins, (John) Robin** 1912- ............. **CLC 52**
See also CA 1-4R; CANR 1; CN 7; DLB 14, 271

**Jennings, Elizabeth (Joan)**
1926-2001 ...................... **CLC 5, 14, 131**
See also BRWS 5; CA 61-64; 200; CAAS 5; CANR 8, 39, 66, 127; CP 7; CWP; DLB 27; EWL 3; MTCW 1; SATA 66

**Jennings, Waylon** 1937- ..................... **CLC 21**

**Jensen, Johannes V(ilhelm)**
1873-1950 ................................ **TCLC 41**
See also CA 170; DLB 214; EWL 3; RGWL 3

**Jensen, Laura (Linnea)** 1948- .......... **CLC 37**
See also CA 103

**Jerome, Saint** 345-420 ................... **CMLC 30**
See also RGWL 3

**Jerome, Jerome K(lapka)**
1859-1927 ................................ **TCLC 23**
See also CA 119; 177; DLB 10, 34, 135; RGEL 2

**Jerrold, Douglas William**
1803-1857 .................................. **NCLC 2**
See also DLB 158, 159; RGEL 2

**Jewett, (Theodora) Sarah Orne**
1849-1909 ......... **SSC 6, 44; TCLC 1, 22**
See also AMW; AMWC 2; AMWR 2; CA 108; 127; CANR 71; DLB 12, 74, 221; EXPS; FW; MAWW; NFS 15; RGAL 4; RGSF 2; SATA 15; SSFS 4

**Jewsbury, Geraldine (Endsor)**
1812-1880 ................................ **NCLC 22**
See also DLB 21

**Jhabvala, Ruth Prawer** 1927- . **CLC 4, 8, 29, 94, 138**
See also BRWS 5; CA 1-4R; CANR 2, 29, 51, 74, 91, 128; CN 7; DAB; DAM NOV; DLB 139, 194; EWL 3; IDFW 3, 4; INT CANR-29; MTCW 1, 2; RGSF 2; RGWL 2; RHW; TEA

**Jibran, Kahlil**
See Gibran, Kahlil

**Jibran, Khalil**
See Gibran, Kahlil

**Jiles, Paulette** 1943- ..................... **CLC 13, 58**
See also CA 101; CANR 70, 124; CWP

**Jimenez (Mantecon), Juan Ramon**
1881-1958 ......... **HLC 1; PC 7; TCLC 4**
See also CA 104; 131; CANR 74; DAM MULT, POET; DLB 134; EW 9; EWL 3; HW 1; MTCW 1, 2; RGWL 2, 3

**Jimenez, Ramon**
See Jimenez (Mantecon), Juan Ramon

**Jimenez Mantecon, Juan**
See Jimenez (Mantecon), Juan Ramon

**Jin, Ha** ............................................. **CLC 109**
See Jin, Xuefei
See also CA 152; DLB 244, 292; SSFS 17

**Jin, Xuefei** 1956-
See Jin, Ha
See also CANR 91, 130; SSFS 17

**Joel, Billy** ...................................... **CLC 26**
See Joel, William Martin

**Joel, William Martin** 1949-
See Joel, Billy
See also CA 108

**John, Saint** 10(?)-100 .............. **CMLC 27, 63**

**John of Salisbury** c. 1115-1180 ..... **CMLC 63**

**John of the Cross, St.** 1542-1591 ........ **LC 18**
See also RGWL 2, 3

**John Paul II, Pope** 1920- ............... **CLC 128**
See also CA 106; 133

**Johnson, B(ryan) S(tanley William)**
1933-1973 ............................. **CLC 6, 9**
See also CA 9-12R; 53-56; CANR 9; DLB 14, 40; EWL 3; RGEL 2

**Johnson, Benjamin F., of Boone**
See Riley, James Whitcomb

**Johnson, Charles (Richard)** 1948- .... **BLC 2; CLC 7, 51, 65, 163**
See also AFAW 2; AMWS 6; BW 2, 3; CA 116; CAAS 18; CANR 42, 66, 82, 129; CN 7; DAM MULT; DLB 33, 278; MTCW 2; RGAL 4; SSFS 16

**Johnson, Charles S(purgeon)**
1893-1956 ............................................. **HR 3**
See also BW 1, 3; CA 125; CANR 82; DLB 51, 91

**Johnson, Denis** 1949- . **CLC 52, 160; SSC 56**
See also CA 117; 121; CANR 71, 99; CN 7; DLB 120

**Johnson, Diane** 1934- .............. **CLC 5, 13, 48**
See also BPFB 2; CA 41-44R; CANR 17, 40, 62, 95; CN 7; DLBY 1980; INT CANR-17; MTCW 1

**Johnson, E. Pauline** 1861-1913 .......... **NNAL**
See also CA 150; DAC; DAM MULT; DLB 92, 175

**Johnson, Eyvind (Olof Verner)**
1900-1976 ............................................. **CLC 14**
See also CA 73-76; 69-72; CANR 34, 101; DLB 259; EW 12; EWL 3

**Johnson, Fenton** 1888-1958 ................ **BLC 2**
See also BW 1; 124; DAM MULT; DLB 45, 50

**Johnson, Georgia Douglas (Camp)**
1880-1966 ............................................. **HR 3**
See also BW 1; CA 125; DLB 51, 249; WP

**Johnson, Helene** 1907-1995 ................... **HR 3**
See also CA 181; DLB 51; WP

**Johnson, J. R.**
See James, C(yril) L(ionel) R(obert)

**Johnson, James Weldon** 1871-1938 .. **BLC 2; HR 3; PC 24; TCLC 3, 19**
See also AFAW 1, 2; BW 1, 3; CA 104; 125; CANR 82; CDALB 1917-1929; CLR 32; DA3; DAM MULT, POET; DLB 51; EWL 3; EXPP; LMFS 2; MTCW 1, 2; PFS 1; RGAL 4; SATA 31; TUS

**Johnson, Joyce** 1935- ........................ **CLC 58**
See also BG 3; CA 125; 129; CANR 102

**Johnson, Judith (Emlyn)** 1936- .... **CLC 7, 15**
See Sherwin, Judith Johnson
See also CA 25-28R; 153; CANR 34

**Johnson, Lionel (Pigot)**
1867-1902 ................................ **TCLC 19**
See also CA 117; 209; DLB 19; RGEL 2

**Johnson, Marguerite Annie**
See Angelou, Maya

**Johnson, Mel**
See Malzberg, Barry N(athaniel)

**Johnson, Pamela Hansford**
1912-1981 ............................. **CLC 1, 7, 27**
See also CA 1-4R; 104; CANR 2, 28; DLB 15; MTCW 1, 2; RGEL 2

**Johnson, Paul (Bede)** 1928- ............ **CLC 147**
See also BEST 89:4; CA 17-20R; CANR 34, 62, 100

**Johnson, Robert** ............................... **CLC 70**

**Johnson, Robert** 1911(?)-1938 ........ **TCLC 69**
See also BW 3; CA 174

**Johnson, Samuel** 1709-1784 ......... **LC 15, 52; WLC**
See also BRW 3; BRWR 1; CDBLB 1660-1789; DA; DAB; DAC; DAM MST; DLB 39, 95, 104, 142, 213; LMFS 1; RGEL 2; TEA

**Johnson, Uwe** 1934-1984 .. **CLC 5, 10, 15, 40**
See also CA 1-4R; 112; CANR 1, 39; CD-WLB 2; DLB 75; EWL 3; MTCW 1; RGWL 2, 3

**Johnston, Basil H.** 1929- ..................... **NNAL**
See also CA 69-72; CANR 11, 28, 66; DAC; DAM MULT; DLB 60

**Johnston, George (Benson)** 1913- .... **CLC 51**
See also CA 1-4R; CANR 5, 20; CP 7; DLB 88

**Johnston, Jennifer (Prudence)**
1930- ...................................... **CLC 7, 150**
See also CA 85-88; CANR 92; CN 7; DLB 14

**Joinville, Jean de** 1224(?)-1317 ..... **CMLC 38**

**Jolley, (Monica) Elizabeth** 1923- ..... **CLC 46; SSC 19**
See also CA 127; CAAS 13; CANR 59; CN 7; EWL 3; RGSF 2

**Jones, Arthur Llewellyn** 1863-1947
See Machen, Arthur
See also CA 104; 179; HGG

**Jones, D(ouglas) G(ordon)** 1929- ..... **CLC 10**
See also CA 29-32R; CANR 13, 90; CP 7; DLB 53

**Jones, David (Michael)** 1895-1974 .... **CLC 2, 4, 7, 13, 42**
See also BRW 6; BRWS 7; CA 9-12R; 53-56; CANR 28; CDBLB 1945-1960; DLB 20, 100; EWL 3; MTCW 1; PAB; RGEL 2

**Jones, David Robert** 1947-
See Bowie, David
See also CA 103; CANR 104

**Jones, Diana Wynne** 1934- ................ **CLC 26**
See also AAYA 12; BYA 6, 7, 9, 11, 13, 16;
CA 49-52; CANR 4, 26, 56, 120; CLR
23; DLB 161; FANT; JRDA; MAICYA 1,
2; SAAS 7; SATA 9, 70, 108; SFW 4;
SUFW 2; YAW

**Jones, Edward P.** 1950- ..................... **CLC 76**
See also BW 2, 3; CA 142; CANR 79; CSW

**Jones, Gayl** 1949- ...... **BLC 2; CLC 6, 9, 131**
See also AFAW 1, 2; BW 2, 3; CA 77-80;
CANR 27, 66, 122; CN 7; CSW; DA3;
DAM MULT; DLB 33, 278; MTCW 1, 2;
RGAL 4

**Jones, James** 1921-1977 ...... **CLC 1, 3, 10, 39**
See also AITN 1, 2; AMWS 11; BPFB 2;
CA 1-4R; 69-72; CANR 6; DLB 2, 143;
DLBD 17; DLBY 1998; EWL 3; MTCW
1; RGAL 4

**Jones, John J.**
See Lovecraft, H(oward) P(hillips)

**Jones, LeRoi** ............. **CLC 1, 2, 3, 5, 10, 14**
See Baraka, Amiri
See also MTCW 2

**Jones, Louis B.** 1953- ........................ **CLC 65**
See also CA 141; CANR 73

**Jones, Madison (Percy, Jr.)** 1925- ...... **CLC 4**
See also CA 13-16R; CAAS 11; CANR 7,
54, 83; CN 7; CSW; DLB 152

**Jones, Mervyn** 1922- .................... **CLC 10, 52**
See also CA 45-48; CAAS 5; CANR 1, 91;
CN 7; MTCW 1

**Jones, Mick** 1956(?)- ......................... **CLC 30**

**Jones, Nettie (Pearl)** 1941- ............... **CLC 34**
See also BW 2; CA 137; CAAS 20; CANR
88

**Jones, Peter** 1802-1856 ...................... **NNAL**

**Jones, Preston** 1936-1979 ................. **CLC 10**
See also CA 73-76; 89-92; DLB 7

**Jones, Robert F(rancis)** 1934-2003 .... **CLC 7**
See also CA 49-52; CANR 2, 61, 118

**Jones, Rod** 1953- ............................... **CLC 50**
See also CA 128

**Jones, Terence Graham Parry**
1942- ............................................ **CLC 21**
See Jones, Terry; Monty Python
See also CA 112; 116; CANR 35, 93; INT
CA-116; SATA 127

**Jones, Terry**
See Jones, Terence Graham Parry
See also SATA 67; SATA-Brief 51

**Jones, Thom (Douglas)** 1945(?)- ..... **CLC 81;
SSC 56**
See also CA 157; CANR 88; DLB 244

**Jong, Erica** 1942- ........... **CLC 4, 6, 8, 18, 83**
See also AITN 1; AMWS 5; BEST 90:2;
BPFB 2; CA 73-76; CANR 26, 52, 75,
132; CN 7; CP 7; CPW; DA3; DAM
NOV, POP; DLB 2, 5, 28, 152; FW; INT
CANR-26; MTCW 1, 2

**Jonson, Ben(jamin)** 1572(?)-1637 . **DC 4; LC
6, 33; PC 17; WLC**
See also BRW 1; BRWC 1; BRWR 1; CD-
BLB Before 1660; DA; DAB; DAC;
DAM DRAM, MST, POET; DFS 4, 10;
DLB 62, 121; LMFS 1; RGEL 2; TEA;
WLIT 3

**Jordan, June (Meyer)**
1936-2002 .. **BLCS; CLC 5, 11, 23, 114;
PC 38**
See also AAYA 2; AFAW 1, 2; BW 2, 3;
CA 33-36R; 206; CANR 25, 70, 114; CLR
10; CP 7; CWP; DAM MULT, POET;
DLB 38; GLL 2; LAIT 5; MAICYA 1, 2;
MTCW 1; SATA 4, 136; YAW

**Jordan, Neil (Patrick)** 1950- ........... **CLC 110**
See also CA 124; 130; CANR 54; CN 7;
GLL 2; INT CA-130

**Jordan, Pat(rick M.)** 1941- .............. **CLC 37**
See also CA 33-36R; CANR 121

**Jorgensen, Ivar**
See Ellison, Harlan (Jay)

**Jorgenson, Ivar**
See Silverberg, Robert

**Joseph, George Ghevarughese** ........ **CLC 70**

**Josephson, Mary**
See O'Doherty, Brian

**Josephus, Flavius** c. 37-100 ........... **CMLC 13**
See also AW 2; DLB 176

**Josiah Allen's Wife**
See Holley, Marietta

**Josipovici, Gabriel (David)** 1940- ...... **CLC 6,
43, 153**
See also CA 37-40R, 224; CAAE 224;
CAAS 8; CANR 47, 84; CN 7; DLB 14

**Joubert, Joseph** 1754-1824 ............... **NCLC 9**

**Jouve, Pierre Jean** 1887-1976 ........... **CLC 47**
See also CA 65-68; DLB 258; EWL 3

**Jovine, Francesco** 1902-1950 .......... **TCLC 79**
See also DLB 264; EWL 3

**Joyce, James (Augustine Aloysius)**
1882-1941 .... **DC 16; PC 22; SSC 3, 26,
44, 64; TCLC 3, 8, 16, 35, 52; WLC**
See also AAYA 42; BRW 7; BRWC 1;
BRWR 1; BYA 11, 13; CA 104; 126; CD-
BLB 1914-1945; DA; DA3; DAB; DAC;
DAM MST, NOV, POET; DLB 10, 19,
36, 162, 247; EWL 3; EXPN; EXPS;
LAIT 3; LMFS 1, 2; MTCW 1, 2; NFS 7;
RGSF 2; SSFS 1, 19; TEA; WLIT 4

**Jozsef, Attila** 1905-1937 .................. **TCLC 22**
See also CA 116; CDWLB 4; DLB 215;
EWL 3

**Juana Ines de la Cruz, Sor**
1651(?)-1695 ...... **HLCS 1; LC 5; PC 24**
See also DLB 305; FW; LAW; RGWL 2, 3;
WLIT 1

**Juana Inez de La Cruz, Sor**
See Juana Ines de la Cruz, Sor

**Judd, Cyril**
See Kornbluth, C(yril) M.; Pohl, Frederik

**Juenger, Ernst** 1895-1998 ............... **CLC 125**
See Junger, Ernst
See also CA 101; 167; CANR 21, 47, 106;
DLB 56

**Julian of Norwich** 1342(?)-1416(?) . **LC 6, 52**
See also DLB 146; LMFS 1

**Julius Caesar** 100B.C.-44B.C.
See Caesar, Julius
See also CDWLB 1; DLB 211

**Junger, Ernst**
See Juenger, Ernst
See also CDWLB 2; EWL 3; RGWL 2, 3

**Junger, Sebastian** 1962- .................. **CLC 109**
See also AAYA 28; CA 165; CANR 130

**Juniper, Alex**
See Hospital, Janette Turner

**Junius**
See Luxemburg, Rosa

**Just, Ward (Swift)** 1935- ............... **CLC 4, 27**
See also CA 25-28R; CANR 32, 87; CN 7;
INT CANR-32

**Justice, Donald (Rodney)**
1925-2004 ...................... **CLC 6, 19, 102**
See also AMWS 7; CA 5-8R; CANR 26,
54, 74, 121, 122; CP 7; CSW; DAM
POET; DLBY 1983; EWL 3; INT CANR-
26; MTCW 2; PFS 14

**Juvenal** c. 60-c. 130 ........................ **CMLC 8**
See also AW 2; CDWLB 1; DLB 211;
RGWL 2, 3

**Juvenis**
See Bourne, Randolph S(illiman)

**K., Alice**
See Knapp, Caroline

**Kabakov, Sasha** ............................... **CLC 59**

**Kabir** 1398(?)-1448(?) .......................... **PC 56**
See also RGWL 2, 3

**Kacew, Romain** 1914-1980
See Gary, Romain
See also CA 108; 102

**Kadare, Ismail** 1936- ................. **CLC 52, 190**
See also CA 161; EWL 3; RGWL 3

**Kadohata, Cynthia** 1956(?)- ..... **CLC 59, 122**
See also CA 140; CANR 124

**Kafka, Franz** 1883-1924 ... **SSC 5, 29, 35, 60;
TCLC 2, 6, 13, 29, 47, 53, 112; WLC**
See also AAYA 31; BPFB 2; CA 105; 126;
CDWLB 2; DA; DA3; DAB; DAC; DAM
MST, NOV; DLB 81; EW 9; EWL 3;
EXPS; LATS 1:1; LMFS 2; MTCW 1, 2;
NFS 7; RGSF 2; RGWL 2, 3; SFW 4;
SSFS 3, 7, 12; TWA

**Kahanovitsch, Pinkhes**
See Der Nister

**Kahn, Roger** 1927- ............................. **CLC 30**
See also CA 25-28R; CANR 44, 69; DLB
171; SATA 37

**Kain, Saul**
See Sassoon, Siegfried (Lorraine)

**Kaiser, Georg** 1878-1945 ................. **TCLC 9**
See also CA 106; 190; CDWLB 2; DLB
124; EWL 3; LMFS 2; RGWL 2, 3

**Kaledin, Sergei** ............................... **CLC 59**

**Kaletski, Alexander** 1946- ................. **CLC 39**
See also CA 118; 143

**Kalidasa** fl. c. 400-455 ........ **CMLC 9; PC 22**
See also RGWL 2, 3

**Kallman, Chester (Simon)**
1921-1975 .................................... **CLC 2**
See also CA 45-48; 53-56; CANR 3

**Kaminsky, Melvin** 1926-
See Brooks, Mel
See also CA 65-68; CANR 16

**Kaminsky, Stuart M(elvin)** 1934- ..... **CLC 59**
See also CA 73-76; CANR 29, 53, 89;
CMW 4

**Kamo no Chomei** 1153(?)-1216 .... **CMLC 66**
See also DLB 203

**Kamo no Nagaakira**
See Kamo no Chomei

**Kandinsky, Wassily** 1866-1944 ....... **TCLC 92**
See also CA 118; 155

**Kane, Francis**
See Robbins, Harold

**Kane, Henry** 1918-
See Queen, Ellery
See also CA 156; CMW 4

**Kane, Paul**
See Simon, Paul (Frederick)

**Kanin, Garson** 1912-1999 ................. **CLC 22**
See also AITN 1; CA 5-8R; 177; CAD;
CANR 7, 78; DLB 7; IDFW 3, 4

**Kaniuk, Yoram** 1930- ....................... **CLC 19**
See also CA 134; DLB 299

**Kant, Immanuel** 1724-1804 ..... **NCLC 27, 67**
See also DLB 94

**Kantor, MacKinlay** 1904-1977 ........... **CLC 7**
See also CA 61-64; 73-76; CANR 60, 63;
DLB 9, 102; MTCW 2; RHW; TCWW 2

**Kanze Motokiyo**
See Zeami

**Kaplan, David Michael** 1946- .......... **CLC 50**
See also CA 187

**Kaplan, James** 1951- ........................ **CLC 59**
See also CA 135; CANR 121

**Karadzic, Vuk Stefanovic**
1787-1864 ............................ **NCLC 115**
See also CDWLB 4; DLB 147

**Karageorge, Michael**
See Anderson, Poul (William)

**Karamzin, Nikolai Mikhailovich**
1766-1826 ................................ **NCLC 3**
See also DLB 150; RGSF 2

**Karapanou, Margarita** 1946- ........... **CLC 13**
See also CA 101

**Karinthy, Frigyes** 1887-1938 .......... **TCLC 47**
See also CA 170; DLB 215; EWL 3

**Karl, Frederick R(obert)**
1927-2004 ..................................... **CLC 34**
See also CA 5-8R; 226; CANR 3, 44

**Karr, Mary** 1955- ............................... **CLC 188**
See also AMWS 11; CA 151; CANR 100;
NCFS 5

**Kastel, Warren**
See Silverberg, Robert

**Kataev, Evgeny Petrovich** 1903-1942
See Petrov, Evgeny
See also CA 120

**Kataphusin**
See Ruskin, John

**Katz, Steve** 1935- ............................. **CLC 47**
See also CA 25-28R; CAAS 14, 64; CANR
12; CN 7; DLBY 1983

**Kauffman, Janet** 1945- ..................... **CLC 42**
See also CA 117; CANR 43, 84; DLB 218;
DLBY 1986

**Kaufman, Bob (Garnell)** 1925-1986 . **CLC 49**
See also BG 3; BW 1; CA 41-44R; 118;
CANR 22; DLB 16, 41

**Kaufman, George S.** 1889-1961 ...... **CLC 38;
DC 17**
See also CA 108; 93-96; DAM DRAM;
DFS 1, 10; DLB 7; INT CA-108; MTCW
2; RGAL 4; TUS

**Kaufman, Sue** ................................... **CLC 3, 8**
See Barondess, Sue K(aufman)

**Kavafis, Konstantinos Petrou** 1863-1933
See Cavafy, C(onstantine) P(eter)
See also CA 104

**Kavan, Anna** 1901-1968 .......... **CLC 5, 13, 82**
See also BRWS 7; CA 5-8R; CANR 6, 57;
DLB 255; MTCW 1; RGEL 2; SFW 4

**Kavanagh, Dan**
See Barnes, Julian (Patrick)

**Kavanagh, Julie** 1952- ..................... **CLC 119**
See also CA 163

**Kavanagh, Patrick (Joseph)**
1904-1967 ..................... **CLC 22; PC 33**
See also BRWS 7; CA 123; 25-28R; DLB
15, 20; EWL 3; MTCW 1; RGEL 2

**Kawabata, Yasunari** 1899-1972 ..... **CLC 2, 5,
9, 18, 107; SSC 17**
See Kawabata Yasunari
See also CA 93-96; 33-36R; CANR 88;
DAM MULT; MJW; MTCW 2; RGSF 2;
RGWL 2, 3

**Kawabata Yasunari**
See Kawabata, Yasunari
See also DLB 180; EWL 3

**Kaye, M(ary) M(argaret)**
1908-2004 ................................... **CLC 28**
See also CA 89-92; 223; CANR 24, 60, 102;
MTCW 1, 2; RHW; SATA 62; SATA-Obit
152

**Kaye, Mollie**
See Kaye, M(ary) M(argaret)

**Kaye-Smith, Sheila** 1887-1956 ....... **TCLC 20**
See also CA 118; 203; DLB 36

**Kaymor, Patrice Maguilene**
See Senghor, Leopold Sedar

**Kazakov, Iurii Pavlovich**
See Kazakov, Yuri Pavlovich
See also DLB 302

**Kazakov, Yuri Pavlovich** 1927-1982 . **SSC 43**
See Kazakov, Iurii Pavlovich; Kazakov,
Yury
See also CA 5-8R; CANR 36; MTCW 1;
RGSF 2

**Kazakov, Yury**
See Kazakov, Yuri Pavlovich
See also EWL 3

**Kazan, Elia** 1909-2003 ............ **CLC 6, 16, 63**
See also CA 21-24R; 220; CANR 32, 78

**Kazantzakis, Nikos** 1883(?)-1957 .... **TCLC 2,
5, 33**
See also BPFB 2; CA 105; 132; DA3; EW
9; EWL 3; MTCW 1, 2; RGWL 2, 3

**Kazin, Alfred** 1915-1998 ..... **CLC 34, 38, 119**
See also AMWS 8; CA 1-4R; CAAS 7;
CANR 1, 45, 79; DLB 67; EWL 3

**Keane, Mary Nesta (Skrine)** 1904-1996
See Keane, Molly
See also CA 108; 114; 151; CN 7; RHW

**Keane, Molly** ...................................... **CLC 31**
See Keane, Mary Nesta (Skrine)
See also INT CA-114

**Keates, Jonathan** 1946(?)- ................. **CLC 34**
See also CA 163; CANR 126

**Keaton, Buster** 1895-1966 ................. **CLC 20**
See also CA 194

**Keats, John** 1795-1821 ...... **NCLC 8, 73, 121;
PC 1; WLC**
See also AAYA 58; BRW 4; BRWR 1; CD-
BLB 1789-1832; DA; DA3; DAB; DAC;
DAM MST, POET; DLB 96, 110; EXPP;
LMFS 1; PAB; PFS 1, 2, 3, 9, 17; RGEL
2; TEA; WLIT 3; WP

**Keble, John** 1792-1866 .................... **NCLC 87**
See also DLB 32, 55; RGEL 2

**Keene, Donald** 1922- .......................... **CLC 34**
See also CA 1-4R; CANR 5, 119

**Keillor, Garrison** ....................... **CLC 40, 115**
See Keillor, Gary (Edward)
See also AAYA 2; BEST 89:3; BPFB 2;
DLBY 1987; EWL 3; SATA 58; TUS

**Keillor, Gary (Edward)** 1942-
See Keillor, Garrison
See also CA 111; 117; CANR 36, 59, 124;
CPW; DA3; DAM POP; MTCW 1, 2

**Keith, Carlos**
See Lewton, Val

**Keith, Michael**
See Hubbard, L(afayette) Ron(ald)

**Keller, Gottfried** 1819-1890 .... **NCLC 2; SSC
26**
See also CDWLB 2; DLB 129; EW; RGSF
2; RGWL 2, 3

**Keller, Nora Okja** 1965- .................. **CLC 109**
See also CA 187

**Kellerman, Jonathan** 1949- .............. **CLC 44**
See also AAYA 35; BEST 90:1; CA 106;
CANR 29, 51; CMW 4; CPW; DA3;
DAM POP; INT CANR-29

**Kelley, William Melvin** 1937- .......... **CLC 22**
See also BW 1; CA 77-80; CANR 27, 83;
CN 7; DLB 33; EWL 3

**Kellogg, Marjorie** 1922- ..................... **CLC 2**
See also CA 81-84

**Kellow, Kathleen**
See Hibbert, Eleanor Alice Burford

**Kelly, M(ilton) T(errence)** 1947- ...... **CLC 55**
See also CA 97-100; CAAS 22; CANR 19,
43, 84; CN 7

**Kelly, Robert** 1935- ........................... **SSC 50**
See also CA 17-20R; CAAS 19; CANR 47;
CP 7; DLB 5, 130, 165

**Kelman, James** 1946- .................... **CLC 58, 86**
See also BRWS 5; CA 148; CANR 85, 130;
CN 7; DLB 194; RGSF 2; WLIT 4

**Kemal, Yasar**
See Kemal, Yashar
See also CWW 2; EWL 3

**Kemal, Yashar** 1923(?)- ............... **CLC 14, 29**
See also CA 89-92; CANR 44

**Kemble, Fanny** 1809-1893 .............. **NCLC 18**
See also DLB 32

**Kemelman, Harry** 1908-1996 ............. **CLC 2**
See also AITN 1; BPFB 2; CA 9-12R; 155;
CANR 6, 71; CMW 4; DLB 28

**Kempe, Margery** 1373(?)-1440(?) ... **LC 6, 56**
See also DLB 146; RGEL 2

**Kempis, Thomas a** 1380-1471 .............. **LC 11**

**Kendall, Henry** 1839-1882 ............. **NCLC 12**
See also DLB 230

**Keneally, Thomas (Michael)** 1935- ... **CLC 5,
8, 10, 14, 19, 27, 43, 117**
See also BRWS 4; CA 85-88; CANR 10,
50, 74, 130; CN 7; CPW; DA3; DAM
NOV; DLB 289, 299; EWL 3; MTCW 1,
2; NFS 17; RGEL 2; RHW

**Kennedy, A(lison) L(ouise)** 1965- ... **CLC 188**
See also CA 168, 213; CAAE 213; CANR
108; CD 5; CN 7; DLB 271; RGSF 2

**Kennedy, Adrienne (Lita)** 1931- ........ **BLC 2;
CLC 66; DC 5**
See also AFAW 2; BW 2, 3; CA 103; CAAS
20; CABS 3; CANR 26, 53, 82; CD 5;
DAM MULT; DFS 9; DLB 38; FW

**Kennedy, John Pendleton**
1795-1870 ................................. **NCLC 2**
See also DLB 3, 248, 254; RGAL 4

**Kennedy, Joseph Charles** 1929-
See Kennedy, X. J.
See also CA 1-4R, 201; CAAE 201; CANR
4, 30, 40; CP 7; CWRI 5; MAICYA 2;
MAICYAS 1; SATA 14, 86, 130; SATA-
Essay 130

**Kennedy, William** 1928- ... **CLC 6, 28, 34, 53**
See also AAYA 1; AMWS 7; BPFB 2; CA
85-88; CANR 14, 31, 76; CN 7; DA3;
DAM NOV; DLB 143; DLBY 1985; EWL
3; INT CANR-31; MTCW 1, 2; SATA 57

**Kennedy, X. J.** ............................... **CLC 8, 42**
See Kennedy, Joseph Charles
See also CAAS 9; CLR 27; DLB 5; SAAS
22

**Kenny, Maurice (Francis)** 1929- ..... **CLC 87;
NNAL**
See also CA 144; CAAS 22; DAM MULT;
DLB 175

**Kent, Kelvin**
See Kuttner, Henry

**Kenton, Maxwell**
See Southern, Terry

**Kenyon, Jane** 1947-1995 ..................... **PC 57**
See also AMWS 7; CA 118; 148; CANR
44, 69; CP 7; CWP; DLB 120; PFS 9, 17;
RGAL 4

**Kenyon, Robert O.**
See Kuttner, Henry

**Kepler, Johannes** 1571-1630 ............... **LC 45**

**Ker, Jill**
See Conway, Jill K(er)

**Kerkow, H. C.**
See Lewton, Val

**Kerouac, Jack** 1922-1969 ...... **CLC 1, 2, 3, 5,
14, 29, 61; TCLC 117; WLC**
See Kerouac, Jean-Louis Lebris de
See also AAYA 25; AMWC 1; AMWS 3;
BG 3; BPFB 2; CDALB 1941-1968;
CPW; DLB 2, 16, 237; DLBD 3; DLBY
1995; EWL 3; GLL 1; LATS 1:2; LMFS
2; MTCW 2; NFS 8; RGAL 4; TUS; WP

**Kerouac, Jean-Louis Lebris de** 1922-1969
See Kerouac, Jack
See also AITN 1; CA 5-8R; 25-28R; CANR
26, 54, 95; DA; DA3; DAB; DAC; DAM
MST, NOV, POET, POP; MTCW 1, 2

**Kerr, (Bridget) Jean (Collins)**
1923(?)-2003 ............................... **CLC 22**
See also CA 5-8R; 212; CANR 7; INT
CANR-7

**Kerr, M. E.** .................................... **CLC 12, 35**
See Meaker, Marijane (Agnes)
See also AAYA 2, 23; BYA 1, 7, 8; CLR
29; SAAS 1; WYA

**Kerr, Robert** ..................................... **CLC 55**

**Kerrigan, (Thomas) Anthony** 1918- .. **CLC 4,
6**
See also CA 49-52; CAAS 11; CANR 4

**Kerry, Lois**
See Duncan, Lois

**Kesey, Ken (Elton)** 1935-2001 ... **CLC 1, 3, 6, 11, 46, 64, 184; WLC**
See also AAYA 25; BG 3; BPFB 2; CA 1-4R; 204; CANR 22, 38, 66, 124; CDALB 1968-1988; CN 7; CPW; DA; DA3; DAB; DAC; DAM MST, NOV, POP; DLB 2, 16, 206; EWL 3; EXPN; LAIT 4; MTCW 1, 2; NFS 2; RGAL 4; SATA 66; SATA-Obit 131; TUS; YAW

**Kesselring, Joseph (Otto)** 1902-1967 ......................... **CLC 45**
See also CA 150; DAM DRAM, MST; DFS 20

**Kessler, Jascha (Frederick)** 1929- ...... **CLC 4**
See also CA 17-20R; CANR 8, 48, 111

**Kettelkamp, Larry (Dale)** 1933- ...... **CLC 12**
See also CA 29-32R; CANR 16; SAAS 3; SATA 2

**Key, Ellen (Karolina Sofia)** 1849-1926 ............................... **TCLC 65**
See also DLB 259

**Keyber, Conny**
See Fielding, Henry

**Keyes, Daniel** 1927- ......................... **CLC 80**
See also AAYA 23; BYA 11; CA 17-20R, 181; CAAE 181; CANR 10, 26, 54, 74; DA; DA3; DAC; DAM MST, NOV; EXPN; LAIT 4; MTCW 2; NFS 2; SATA 37; SFW 4

**Keynes, John Maynard** 1883-1946 .......................... **TCLC 64**
See also CA 114; 162, 163; DLBD 10; MTCW 2

**Khanshendel, Chiron**
See Rose, Wendy

**Khayyam, Omar** 1048-1131 ... **CMLC 11; PC 8**
See Omar Khayyam
See also DA3; DAM POET

**Kherdian, David** 1931- ..................... **CLC 6, 9**
See also AAYA 42; CA 21-24R, 192; CAAE 192; CAAS 2; CANR 39, 78; CLR 24; JRDA; LAIT 3; MAICYA 1, 2; SATA 16, 74; SATA-Essay 125

**Khlebnikov, Velimir** ....................... **TCLC 20**
See Khlebnikov, Viktor Vladimirovich
See also DLB 295; EW 10; EWL 3; RGWL 2, 3

**Khlebnikov, Viktor Vladimirovich** 1885-1922
See Khlebnikov, Velimir
See also CA 117; 217

**Khodasevich, Vladislav (Felitsianovich)** 1886-1939 ............................. **TCLC 15**
See also CA 115; EWL 3

**Kielland, Alexander Lange** 1849-1906 ............................... **TCLC 5**
See also CA 104

**Kiely, Benedict** 1919- ... **CLC 23, 43; SSC 58**
See also CA 1-4R; CANR 2, 84; CN 7; DLB 15

**Kienzle, William X(avier)** 1928-2001 ............................. **CLC 25**
See also CA 93-96; 203; CAAS 1; CANR 9, 31, 59, 111; CMW 4; DA3; DAM POP; INT CANR-31; MSW; MTCW 1, 2

**Kierkegaard, Soren** 1813-1855 ..... **NCLC 34, 78, 125**
See also DLB 300; EW 6; LMFS 2; RGWL 3; TWA

**Kieslowski, Krzysztof** 1941-1996 .... **CLC 120**
See also CA 147; 151

**Killens, John Oliver** 1916-1987 ........ **CLC 10**
See also BW 2; CA 77-80; 123; CAAS 2; CANR 26; DLB 33; EWL 3

**Killigrew, Anne** 1660-1685 ............... **LC 4, 73**
See also DLB 131

**Killigrew, Thomas** 1612-1683 ............. **LC 57**
See also DLB 58; RGEL 2

**Kim**
See Simenon, Georges (Jacques Christian)

**Kincaid, Jamaica** 1949- ...... **BLC 2; CLC 43, 68, 137; SSC 72**
See also AAYA 13, 56; AFAW 2; AMWS 7; BRWS 7; BW 2, 3; CA 125; CANR 47, 59, 95, 133; CDALBS; CDWLB 3; CLR 63; CN 7; DA3; DAM MULT, NOV; DLB 157, 227; DNFS 1; EWL 3; EXPS; FW; LATS 1:2; LMFS 2; MTCW 2; NCFS 1; SSFS 5, 7; TUS; WWE 1; YAW

**King, Francis (Henry)** 1923- ....... **CLC 8, 53, 145**
See also CA 1-4R; CANR 1, 33, 86; CN 7; DAM NOV; DLB 15, 139; MTCW 1

**King, Kennedy**
See Brown, George Douglas

**King, Martin Luther, Jr.** 1929-1968 . **BLC 2; CLC 83; WLCS**
See also BW 2, 3; CA 25-28; CANR 27, 44; CAP 2; DA; DA3; DAB; DAC; DAM MST, MULT; LAIT 5; LATS 1:2; MTCW 1, 2; SATA 14

**King, Stephen (Edwin)** 1947- .... **CLC 12, 26, 37, 61, 113; SSC 17, 55**
See also AAYA 1, 17; AMWS 5; BEST 90:1; BPFB 2; CA 61-64; CANR 1, 30, 52, 76, 119; CPW; DA3; DAM NOV, POP; DLB 143; DLBY 1980; HGG; JRDA; LAIT 5; MTCW 1, 2; RGAL 4; SATA 9, 55; SUFW 1, 2; WYAS 1; YAW

**King, Steve**
See King, Stephen (Edwin)

**King, Thomas** 1943- .... **CLC 89, 171; NNAL**
See also CA 144; CANR 95; CCA 1; CN 7; DAC; DAM MULT; DLB 175; SATA 96

**Kingman, Lee** ..................................... **CLC 17**
See Natti, (Mary) Lee
See also CWRI 5; SAAS 3; SATA 1, 67

**Kingsley, Charles** 1819-1875 .......... **NCLC 35**
See also CLR 77; DLB 21, 32, 163, 178, 190; FANT; MAICYA 2; MAICYAS 1; RGEL 2; WCH; YABC 2

**Kingsley, Henry** 1830-1876 .......... **NCLC 107**
See also DLB 21, 230; RGEL 2

**Kingsley, Sidney** 1906-1995 .............. **CLC 44**
See also CA 85-88; 147; CAD; DFS 14, 19; DLB 7; RGAL 4

**Kingsolver, Barbara** 1955- . **CLC 55, 81, 130**
See also AAYA 15; AMWS 7; CA 129; 134; CANR 60, 96, 133; CDALBS; CPW; CSW; DA3; DAM POP; DLB 206; INT CA-134; LAIT 5; MTCW 2; NFS 5, 10, 12; RGAL 4

**Kingston, Maxine (Ting Ting) Hong** 1940- .......... **AAL; CLC 12, 19, 58, 121; WLCS**
See also AAYA 8, 55; AMWS 5; BPFB 2; CA 69-72; CANR 13, 38, 74, 87, 128; CDALBS; CN 7; DA3; DAM MULT, NOV; DLB 173, 212; DLBY 1980; EWL 3; FW; INT CANR-13; LAIT 5; MAWW; MTCW 1, 2; NFS 6; RGAL 4; SATA 53; SSFS 3

**Kinnell, Galway** 1927- ..... **CLC 1, 2, 3, 5, 13, 29, 129; PC 26**
See also AMWS 3; CA 9-12R; CANR 10, 34, 66, 116; CP 7; DLB 5; DLBY 1987; EWL 3; INT CANR-34; MTCW 1, 2; PAB; PFS 9; RGAL 4; WP

**Kinsella, Thomas** 1928- ........ **CLC 4, 19, 138**
See also BRWS 5; CA 17-20R; CANR 15, 122; CP 7; DLB 27; EWL 3; MTCW 1, 2; RGEL 2; TEA

**Kinsella, W(illiam) P(atrick)** 1935- . **CLC 27, 43, 166**
See also AAYA 7; BPFB 2; CA 97-100, 222; CAAE 222; CAAS 7; CANR 21, 35, 66, 75, 129; CN 7; CPW; DAC; DAM NOV, POP; FANT; INT CANR-21; LAIT 5; MTCW 1, 2; NFS 15; RGSF 2

**Kinsey, Alfred C(harles)** 1894-1956 ............................... **TCLC 91**
See also CA 115; 170; MTCW 2

**Kipling, (Joseph) Rudyard** 1865-1936 . **PC 3; SSC 5, 54; TCLC 8, 17; WLC**
See also AAYA 32; BRW 6; BRWC 1, 2; BYA 4; CA 105; 120; CANR 33; CDBLB 1890-1914; CLR 39, 65; CWRI 5; DA; DA3; DAB; DAC; DAM MST, POET; DLB 19, 34, 141, 156; EWL 3; EXPS; FANT; LAIT 3; LMFS 1; MAICYA 1, 2; MTCW 1, 2; RGEL 2; RGSF 2; SATA 100; SFW 4; SSFS 8; SUFW 1; TEA; WCH; WLIT 4; YABC 2

**Kirk, Russell (Amos)** 1918-1994 .. **TCLC 119**
See also AITN 1; CA 1-4R; 145; CAAS 9; CANR 1, 20, 60; HGG; INT CANR-20; MTCW 1, 2

**Kirkham, Dinah**
See Card, Orson Scott

**Kirkland, Caroline M.** 1801-1864 . **NCLC 85**
See also DLB 3, 73, 74, 250, 254; DLBD 13

**Kirkup, James** 1918- ......................... **CLC 1**
See also CA 1-4R; CAAS 4; CANR 2; CP 7; DLB 27; SATA 12

**Kirkwood, James** 1930(?)-1989 .......... **CLC 9**
See also AITN 2; CA 1-4R; 128; CANR 6, 40; GLL 2

**Kirsch, Sarah** 1935- ......................... **CLC 176**
See also CA 178; CWW 2; DLB 75; EWL 3

**Kirshner, Sidney**
See Kingsley, Sidney

**Kis, Danilo** 1935-1989 ...................... **CLC 57**
See also CA 109; 118; 129; CANR 61; CDWLB 4; DLB 181; EWL 3; MTCW 1; RGSF 2; RGWL 2, 3

**Kissinger, Henry A(lfred)** 1923- ..... **CLC 137**
See also CA 1-4R; CANR 2, 33, 66, 109; MTCW 1

**Kivi, Aleksis** 1834-1872 ................... **NCLC 30**

**Kizer, Carolyn (Ashley)** 1925- ... **CLC 15, 39, 80**
See also CA 65-68; CAAS 5; CANR 24, 70; CP 7; CWP; DAM POET; DLB 5, 169; EWL 3; MTCW 2; PFS 18

**Klabund** 1890-1928 ......................... **TCLC 44**
See also CA 162; DLB 66

**Klappert, Peter** 1942- ....................... **CLC 57**
See also CA 33-36R; CSW; DLB 5

**Klein, A(braham) M(oses)** 1909-1972 ............................... **CLC 19**
See also CA 101; 37-40R; DAB; DAC; DAM MST; DLB 68; EWL 3; RGEL 2

**Klein, Joe**
See Klein, Joseph

**Klein, Joseph** 1946- ......................... **CLC 154**
See also CA 85-88; CANR 55

**Klein, Norma** 1938-1989 ................... **CLC 30**
See also AAYA 2, 35; BPFB 2; BYA 6, 7, 8; CA 41-44R; 128; CANR 15, 37; CLR 2, 19; INT CANR-15; JRDA; MAICYA 1, 2; SAAS 1; SATA 7, 57; WYA; YAW

**Klein, T(heodore) E(ibon) D(onald)** 1947- ............................... **CLC 34**
See also CA 119; CANR 44, 75; HGG

**Kleist, Heinrich von** 1777-1811 ...... **NCLC 2, 37; SSC 22**
See also CDWLB 2; DAM DRAM; DLB 90; EW 5; RGSF 2; RGWL 2, 3

**Klima, Ivan** 1931- ...................... **CLC 56, 172**
See also CA 25-28R; CANR 17, 50, 91; CDWLB 4; CWW 2; DAM NOV; DLB 232; EWL 3; RGWL 3

**Klimentev, Andrei Platonovich**
See Klimentov, Andrei Platonovich
**Klimentov, Andrei Platonovich**
1899-1951 ................. **SSC 42; TCLC 14**
See Platonov, Andrei Platonovich; Platonov, Andrey Platonovich
See also CA 108
**Klinger, Friedrich Maximilian von**
1752-1831 ................................... **NCLC 1**
See also DLB 94
**Klingsor the Magician**
See Hartmann, Sadakichi
**Klopstock, Friedrich Gottlieb**
1724-1803 ......................... **NCLC 11**
See also DLB 97; EW 4; RGWL 2, 3
**Kluge, Alexander** 1932- ...................... **SSC 61**
See also CA 81-84; DLB 75
**Knapp, Caroline** 1959-2002 ............. **CLC 99**
See also CA 154; 207
**Knebel, Fletcher** 1911-1993 .............. **CLC 14**
See also AITN 1; CA 1-4R; 140; CAAS 3; CANR 1, 36; SATA 36; SATA-Obit 75
**Knickerbocker, Diedrich**
See Irving, Washington
**Knight, Etheridge** 1931-1991 ... **BLC 2; CLC 40; PC 14**
See also BW 1, 3; CA 21-24R; 133; CANR 23, 82; DAM POET; DLB 41; MTCW 2; RGAL 4
**Knight, Sarah Kemble** 1666-1727 ........ **LC 7**
See also DLB 24, 200
**Knister, Raymond** 1899-1932 ......... **TCLC 56**
See also CA 186; DLB 68; RGEL 2
**Knowles, John** 1926-2001 ... **CLC 1, 4, 10, 26**
See also AAYA 10; AMWS 12; BPFB 2; BYA 3; CA 17-20R; 203; CANR 40, 74, 76, 132; CDALB 1968-1988; CLR 98; CN 7; DA; DAC; DAM MST, NOV; DLB 6; EXPN; MTCW 1, 2; NFS 2; RGAL 4; SATA 8, 89; SATA-Obit 134; YAW
**Knox, Calvin M.**
See Silverberg, Robert
**Knox, John** c. 1505-1572 ...................... **LC 37**
See also DLB 132
**Knye, Cassandra**
See Disch, Thomas M(ichael)
**Koch, C(hristopher) J(ohn)** 1932- .... **CLC 42**
See also CA 127; CANR 84; CN 7; DLB 289
**Koch, Christopher**
See Koch, C(hristopher) J(ohn)
**Koch, Kenneth (Jay)** 1925-2002 .... **CLC 5, 8, 44**
See also CA 1-4R; 207; CAD; CANR 6, 36, 57, 97, 131; CD 5; CP 7; DAM POET; DLB 5; INT CANR-36; MTCW 2; PFS 20; SATA 65; WP
**Kochanowski, Jan** 1530-1584 .............. **LC 10**
See also RGWL 2, 3
**Kock, Charles Paul de** 1794-1871 . **NCLC 16**
**Koda Rohan**
See Koda Shigeyuki
**Koda Rohan**
See Koda Shigeyuki
See also DLB 180
**Koda Shigeyuki** 1867-1947 ............ **TCLC 22**
See Koda Rohan
See also CA 121; 183
**Koestler, Arthur** 1905-1983 ... **CLC 1, 3, 6, 8, 15, 33**
See also BRWS 1; CA 1-4R; 109; CANR 1, 33; CDBLB 1945-1960; DLBY 1983; EWL 3; MTCW 1, 2; NFS 19; RGEL 2
**Kogawa, Joy Nozomi** 1935- ...... **CLC 78, 129**
See also AAYA 47; CA 101; CANR 19, 62, 126; CN 7; CWP; DAC; DAM MST, MULT; FW; MTCW 2; NFS 3; SATA 99
**Kohout, Pavel** 1928- .......................... **CLC 13**
See also CA 45-48; CANR 3

**Koizumi, Yakumo**
See Hearn, (Patricio) Lafcadio (Tessima Carlos)
**Kolmar, Gertrud** 1894-1943 ........... **TCLC 40**
See also CA 167; EWL 3
**Komunyakaa, Yusef** 1947- .. **BLCS; CLC 86, 94; PC 51**
See also AFAW 2; AMWS 13; CA 147; CANR 83; CP 7; CSW; DLB 120; EWL 3; PFS 5, 20; RGAL 4
**Konrad, George**
See Konrad, Gyorgy
**Konrad, Gyorgy** 1933- ............ **CLC 4, 10, 73**
See also CA 85-88; CANR 97; CDWLB 4; CWW 2; DLB 232; EWL 3
**Konwicki, Tadeusz** 1926- ....... **CLC 8, 28, 54, 117**
See also CA 101; CAAS 9; CANR 39, 59; CWW 2; DLB 232; EWL 3; IDFW 3; MTCW 1
**Koontz, Dean R(ay)** 1945- ................ **CLC 78**
See also AAYA 9, 31; BEST 89:3, 90:2; CA 108; CANR 19, 36, 52, 95; CMW 4; CPW; DA3; DAM NOV, POP; DLB 292; HGG; MTCW 1; SATA 92; SFW 4; SUFW 2; YAW
**Kopernik, Mikolaj**
See Copernicus, Nicolaus
**Kopit, Arthur (Lee)** 1937- ...... **CLC 1, 18, 33**
See also AITN 1; CA 81-84; CABS 3; CD 5; DAM DRAM; DFS 7, 14; DLB 7; MTCW 1; RGAL 4
**Kopitar, Jernej (Bartholomaus)**
1780-1844 .............................. **NCLC 117**
**Kops, Bernard** 1926- .......................... **CLC 4**
See also CA 5-8R; CANR 84; CBD; CN 7; CP 7; DLB 13
**Kornbluth, C(yril) M.** 1923-1958 .... **TCLC 8**
See also CA 105; 160; DLB 8; SFW 4
**Korolenko, V. G.**
See Korolenko, Vladimir Galaktionovich
**Korolenko, Vladimir**
See Korolenko, Vladimir Galaktionovich
**Korolenko, Vladimir G.**
See Korolenko, Vladimir Galaktionovich
**Korolenko, Vladimir Galaktionovich**
1853-1921 .............................. **TCLC 22**
See also CA 121; DLB 277
**Korzybski, Alfred (Habdank Skarbek)**
1879-1950 .............................. **TCLC 61**
See also CA 123; 160
**Kosinski, Jerzy (Nikodem)**
1933-1991 .... **CLC 1, 2, 3, 6, 10, 15, 53, 70**
See also AMWS 7; BPFB 2; CA 17-20R; 134; CANR 9, 46; DA3; DAM NOV; DLB 2, 299; DLBY 1982; EWL 3; HGG; MTCW 1, 2; NFS 12; RGAL 4; TUS
**Kostelanetz, Richard (Cory)** 1940- .. **CLC 28**
See also CA 13-16R; CAAS 8; CANR 38, 77; CN 7; CP 7
**Kostrowitzki, Wilhelm Apollinaris de**
1880-1918
See Apollinaire, Guillaume
See also CA 104
**Kotlowitz, Robert** 1924- ...................... **CLC 4**
See also CA 33-36R; CANR 36
**Kotzebue, August (Friedrich Ferdinand) von**
1761-1819 .............................. **NCLC 25**
See also DLB 94
**Kotzwinkle, William** 1938- ..... **CLC 5, 14, 35**
See also BPFB 2; CA 45-48; CANR 3, 44, 84, 129; CLR 6; DLB 173; FANT; MAICYA 1, 2; SATA 24, 70, 146; SFW 4; SUFW 2; YAW
**Kowna, Stancy**
See Szymborska, Wislawa

**Kozol, Jonathan** 1936- ..................... **CLC 17**
See also AAYA 46; CA 61-64; CANR 16, 45, 96
**Kozoll, Michael** 1940(?)- ................... **CLC 35**
**Kramer, Kathryn** 19(?)- ................... **CLC 34**
**Kramer, Larry** 1935- ............ **CLC 42; DC 8**
See also CA 124; 126; CANR 60, 132; DAM POP; DLB 249; GLL 1
**Krasicki, Ignacy** 1735-1801 .............. **NCLC 8**
**Krasinski, Zygmunt** 1812-1859 ....... **NCLC 4**
See also RGWL 2, 3
**Kraus, Karl** 1874-1936 ...................... **TCLC 5**
See also CA 104; 216; DLB 118; EWL 3
**Kreve (Mickevicius), Vincas**
1882-1954 ................................ **TCLC 27**
See also CA 170; DLB 220; EWL 3
**Kristeva, Julia** 1941- ................. **CLC 77, 140**
See also CA 154; CANR 99; DLB 242; EWL 3; FW; LMFS 2
**Kristofferson, Kris** 1936- ................... **CLC 26**
See also CA 104
**Krizanc, John** 1956- .......................... **CLC 57**
See also CA 187
**Krleza, Miroslav** 1893-1981 ........ **CLC 8, 114**
See also CA 97-100; 105; CANR 50; CD-WLB 4; DLB 147; EW 11; RGWL 2, 3
**Kroetsch, Robert** 1927- .. **CLC 5, 23, 57, 132**
See also CA 17-20R; CANR 8, 38; CCA 1; CN 7; CP 7; DAC; DAM POET; DLB 53; MTCW 1
**Kroetz, Franz**
See Kroetz, Franz Xaver
**Kroetz, Franz Xaver** 1946- .............. **CLC 41**
See also CA 130; CWW 2; EWL 3
**Kroker, Arthur (W.)** 1945- ............... **CLC 77**
See also CA 161
**Kropotkin, Peter (Aleksieevich)**
1842-1921 .............................. **TCLC 36**
See Kropotkin, Petr Alekseevich
See also CA 119; 219
**Kropotkin, Petr Alekseevich**
See Kropotkin, Peter (Aleksieevich)
See also DLB 277
**Krotkov, Yuri** 1917-1981 ................... **CLC 19**
See also CA 102
**Krumb**
See Crumb, R(obert)
**Krumgold, Joseph (Quincy)**
1908-1980 ................................ **CLC 12**
See also BYA 1, 2; CA 9-12R; 101; CANR 7; MAICYA 1, 2; SATA 1, 48; SATA-Obit 23; YAW
**Krumwitz**
See Crumb, R(obert)
**Krutch, Joseph Wood** 1893-1970 ..... **CLC 24**
See also ANW; CA 1-4R; 25-28R; CANR 4; DLB 63, 206, 275
**Krutzch, Gus**
See Eliot, T(homas) S(tearns)
**Krylov, Ivan Andreevich**
1768(?)-1844 ............................ **NCLC 1**
See also DLB 150
**Kubin, Alfred (Leopold Isidor)**
1877-1959 ................................ **TCLC 23**
See also CA 112; 149; CANR 104; DLB 81
**Kubrick, Stanley** 1928-1999 ........... **CLC 16; TCLC 112**
See also AAYA 30; CA 81-84; 177; CANR 33; DLB 26
**Kumin, Maxine (Winokur)** 1925- ..... **CLC 5, 13, 28, 164; PC 15**
See also AITN 2; AMWS 4; ANW; CA 1-4R; CAAS 8; CANR 1, 21, 69, 115; CP 7; CWP; DA3; DAM POET; DLB 5; EWL 3; EXPP; MTCW 1, 2; PAB; PFS 18; SATA 12

**Kundera, Milan** 1929- . **CLC 4, 9, 19, 32, 68, 115, 135; SSC 24**
See also AAYA 2; BPFB 2; CA 85-88; CANR 19, 52, 74; CDWLB 4; CWW 2; DA3; DAM NOV; DLB 232; EW 13; EWL 3; MTCW 1, 2; NFS 18; RGSF 2; RGWL 3; SSFS 10

**Kunene, Mazisi (Raymond)** 1930- ... **CLC 85**
See also BW 1, 3; CA 125; CANR 81; CP 7; DLB 117

**Kung, Hans** ...................... **CLC 130**
See Kung, Hans

**Kung, Hans** 1928-
See Kung, Hans
See also CA 53-56; CANR 66; MTCW 1, 2

**Kunikida Doppo** 1869(?)-1908
See Doppo, Kunikida
See also DLB 180; EWL 3

**Kunitz, Stanley (Jasspon)** 1905- .. **CLC 6, 11, 14, 148; PC 19**
See also AMWS 3; CA 41-44R; CANR 26, 57, 98; CP 7; DA3; DLB 48; INT CANR-26; MTCW 1, 2; PFS 11; RGAL 4

**Kunze, Reiner** 1933- ...................... **CLC 10**
See also CA 93-96; CWW 2; DLB 75; EWL 3

**Kuprin, Aleksander Ivanovich**
1870-1938 ...................... **TCLC 5**
See Kuprin, Aleksandr Ivanovich; Kuprin, Alexandr Ivanovich
See also CA 104; 182

**Kuprin, Aleksandr Ivanovich**
See Kuprin, Aleksander Ivanovich
See also DLB 295

**Kuprin, Alexandr Ivanovich**
See Kuprin, Aleksander Ivanovich
See also EWL 3

**Kureishi, Hanif** 1954(?)- .......... **CLC 64, 135**
See also CA 139; CANR 113; CBD; CD 5; CN 7; DLB 194, 245; GLL 2; IDFW 4; WLIT 4; WWE 1

**Kurosawa, Akira** 1910-1998 ..... **CLC 16, 119**
See also AAYA 11; CA 101; 170; CANR 46; DAM MULT

**Kushner, Tony** 1956(?)- ........ **CLC 81; DC 10**
See also AMWS 9; CA 144; CAD; CANR 74, 130; CD 5; DA3; DAM DRAM; DFS 5; DLB 228; EWL 3; GLL 1; LAIT 5; MTCW 2; RGAL 4

**Kuttner, Henry** 1915-1958 .............. **TCLC 10**
See also CA 107; 157; DLB 8; FANT; SCFW 2; SFW 4

**Kutty, Madhavi**
See Das, Kamala

**Kuzma, Greg** 1944- ...................... **CLC 7**
See also CA 33-36R; CANR 70

**Kuzmin, Mikhail (Alekseevich)**
1872(?)-1936 ...................... **TCLC 40**
See also CA 170; DLB 295; EWL 3

**Kyd, Thomas** 1558-1594 .......... **DC 3; LC 22**
See also BRW 1; DAM DRAM; DLB 62; IDTP; LMFS 1; RGEL 2; TEA; WLIT 3

**Kyprianos, Iossif**
See Samarakis, Antonis

**L. S.**
See Stephen, Sir Leslie

**Laʒamon**
See Layamon
See also DLB 146

**Labrunie, Gerard**
See Nerval, Gerard de

**La Bruyere, Jean de** 1645-1696 .......... **LC 17**
See also DLB 268; EW 3; GFL Beginnings to 1789

**Lacan, Jacques (Marie Emile)**
1901-1981 ...................... **CLC 75**
See also CA 121; 104; DLB 296; EWL 3; TWA

**Laclos, Pierre Ambroise Francois**
1741-1803 ...................... **NCLC 4, 87**
See also EW 4; GFL Beginnings to 1789; RGWL 2, 3

**Lacolere, Francois**
See Aragon, Louis

**La Colere, Francois**
See Aragon, Louis

**La Deshabilleuse**
See Simenon, Georges (Jacques Christian)

**Lady Gregory**
See Gregory, Lady Isabella Augusta (Persse)

**Lady of Quality, A**
See Bagnold, Enid

**La Fayette, Marie-(Madelaine Pioche de la Vergne)** 1634-1693 .......... **LC 2**
See Lafayette, Marie-Madeleine
See also GFL Beginnings to 1789; RGWL 2, 3

**Lafayette, Marie-Madeleine**
See La Fayette, Marie-(Madelaine Pioche de la Vergne)
See also DLB 268

**Lafayette, Rene**
See Hubbard, L(afayette) Ron(ald)

**La Flesche, Francis** 1857(?)-1932 ...... **NNAL**
See also CA 144; CANR 83; DLB 175

**La Fontaine, Jean de** 1621-1695 ......... **LC 50**
See also DLB 268; EW 3; GFL Beginnings to 1789; MAICYA 1, 2; RGWL 2, 3; SATA 18

**Laforgue, Jules** 1860-1887 . **NCLC 5, 53; PC 14; SSC 20**
See also DLB 217; EW 7; GFL 1789 to the Present; RGWL 2, 3

**Lagerkvist, Paer (Fabian)**
1891-1974 ..... **CLC 7, 10, 13, 54; TCLC 144**
See Lagerkvist, Par
See also CA 85-88; 49-52; DA3; DAM DRAM, NOV; MTCW 1, 2; TWA

**Lagerkvist, Par** ...................... **SSC 12**
See Lagerkvist, Paer (Fabian)
See also DLB 259; EW 10; EWL 3; MTCW 2; RGSF 2; RGWL 2, 3

**Lagerloef, Selma (Ottiliana Lovisa)**
1858-1940 ...................... **TCLC 4, 36**
See Lagerlof, Selma (Ottiliana Lovisa)
See also CA 108; MTCW 2; SATA 15

**Lagerlof, Selma (Ottiliana Lovisa)**
See Lagerloef, Selma (Ottiliana Lovisa)
See also CLR 7; SATA 15

**La Guma, (Justin) Alex(ander)**
1925-1985 . **BLCS; CLC 19; TCLC 140**
See also AFW; BW 1, 3; CA 49-52; 118; CANR 25, 81; CDWLB 3; DAM NOV; DLB 117, 225; EWL 3; MTCW 1, 2; WLIT 2; WWE 1

**Laidlaw, A. K.**
See Grieve, C(hristopher) M(urray)

**Lainez, Manuel Mujica**
See Mujica Lainez, Manuel
See also HW 1

**Laing, R(onald) D(avid)** 1927-1989 . **CLC 95**
See also CA 107; 129; CANR 34; MTCW 1

**Laishley, Alex**
See Booth, Martin

**Lamartine, Alphonse (Marie Louis Prat) de**
1790-1869 ...................... **NCLC 11; PC 16**
See also DAM POET; DLB 217; GFL 1789 to the Present; RGWL 2, 3

**Lamb, Charles** 1775-1834 ..... **NCLC 10, 113; WLC**
See also BRW 4; CDBLB 1789-1832; DA; DAB; DAC; DAM MST; DLB 93, 107, 163; RGEL 2; SATA 17; TEA

**Lamb, Lady Caroline** 1785-1828 ... **NCLC 38**
See also DLB 116

**Lamb, Mary Ann** 1764-1847 ........ **NCLC 125**
See also DLB 163; SATA 17

**Lame Deer** 1903(?)-1976 ................... **NNAL**
See also CA 69-72

**Lamming, George (William)** 1927- ... **BLC 2; CLC 2, 4, 66, 144**
See also BW 2, 3; CA 85-88; CANR 26, 76; CDWLB 3; CN 7; DAM MULT; DLB 125; EWL 3; MTCW 1, 2; NFS 15; RGEL 2

**L'Amour, Louis (Dearborn)**
1908-1988 ...................... **CLC 25, 55**
See Burns, Tex; Mayo, Jim
See also AAYA 16; AITN 2; BEST 89:2; BPFB 2; CA 1-4R; 125; CANR 3, 25, 40; CPW; DA3; DAM NOV, POP; DLB 206; DLBY 1980; MTCW 1, 2; RGAL 4

**Lampedusa, Giuseppe (Tomasi) di**
...................... **TCLC 13**
See Tomasi di Lampedusa, Giuseppe
See also CA 164; EW 11; MTCW 2; RGWL 2, 3

**Lampman, Archibald** 1861-1899 ... **NCLC 25**
See also DLB 92; RGEL 2; TWA

**Lancaster, Bruce** 1896-1963 ............. **CLC 36**
See also CA 9-10; CANR 70; CAP 1; SATA 9

**Lanchester, John** 1962- ...................... **CLC 99**
See also CA 194; DLB 267

**Landau, Mark Alexandrovich**
See Aldanov, Mark (Alexandrovich)

**Landau-Aldanov, Mark Alexandrovich**
See Aldanov, Mark (Alexandrovich)

**Landis, Jerry**
See Simon, Paul (Frederick)

**Landis, John** 1950- ...................... **CLC 26**
See also CA 112; 122; CANR 128

**Landolfi, Tommaso** 1908-1979 .... **CLC 11, 49**
See also CA 127; 117; DLB 177; EWL 3

**Landon, Letitia Elizabeth**
1802-1838 ...................... **NCLC 15**
See also DLB 96

**Landor, Walter Savage**
1775-1864 ...................... **NCLC 14**
See also BRW 4; DLB 93, 107; RGEL 2

**Landwirth, Heinz** 1927-
See Lind, Jakov
See also CA 9-12R; CANR 7

**Lane, Patrick** 1939- ...................... **CLC 25**
See also CA 97-100; CANR 54; CP 7; DAM POET; DLB 53; INT CA-97-100

**Lang, Andrew** 1844-1912 ............... **TCLC 16**
See also CA 114; 137; CANR 85; CLR 101; DLB 98, 141, 184; FANT; MAICYA 1, 2; RGEL 2; SATA 16; WCH

**Lang, Fritz** 1890-1976 ............... **CLC 20, 103**
See also CA 77-80; 69-72; CANR 30

**Lange, John**
See Crichton, (John) Michael

**Langer, Elinor** 1939- ...................... **CLC 34**
See also CA 121

**Langland, William** 1332(?)-1400(?) ..... **LC 19**
See also BRW 1; DA; DAB; DAC; DAM MST, POET; DLB 146; RGEL 2; TEA; WLIT 3

**Langstaff, Launcelot**
See Irving, Washington

**Lanier, Sidney** 1842-1881 . **NCLC 6, 118; PC 50**
See also AMWS 1; DAM POET; DLB 64; DLBD 13; EXPP; MAICYA 1; PFS 14; RGAL 4; SATA 18

**Lanyer, Aemilia** 1569-1645 .... **LC 10, 30, 83; PC 60**
See also DLB 121

**Lao-Tzu**
See Lao Tzu

**Lao Tzu** c. 6th cent. B.C.-3rd cent.
B.C. ............................................. **CMLC 7**

**Lapine, James (Elliot)** 1949- ............. **CLC 39**
See also CA 123; 130; CANR 54, 128; INT
CA-130

**Larbaud, Valery (Nicolas)**
1881-1957 ............................ **TCLC 9**
See also CA 106; 152; EWL 3; GFL 1789
to the Present

**Lardner, Ring**
See Lardner, Ring(gold) W(ilmer)
See also BPFB 2; CDALB 1917-1929; DLB
11, 25, 86, 171; DLBD 16; RGAL 4;
RGSF 2

**Lardner, Ring W., Jr.**
See Lardner, Ring(gold) W(ilmer)

**Lardner, Ring(gold) W(ilmer)**
1885-1933 ............. **SSC 32; TCLC 2, 14**
See Lardner, Ring
See also AMW; CA 104; 131; MTCW 1, 2;
TUS

**Laredo, Betty**
See Codrescu, Andrei

**Larkin, Maia**
See Wojciechowska, Maia (Teresa)

**Larkin, Philip (Arthur)** 1922-1985 ... **CLC 3,
5, 8, 9, 13, 18, 33, 39, 64; PC 21**
See also BRWS 1; CA 5-8R; 117; CANR
24, 62; CDBLB 1960 to Present; DA3;
DAB; DAM MST, POET; DLB 27; EWL
3; MTCW 1, 2; PFS 3, 4, 12; RGEL 2

**La Roche, Sophie von**
1730-1807 .............................. **NCLC 121**
See also DLB 94

**La Rochefoucauld, Francois**
1613-1680 ............................ **LC 108**

**Larra (y Sanchez de Castro), Mariano Jose
de** 1809-1837 .................... **NCLC 17, 130**

**Larsen, Eric** 1941- ............................ **CLC 55**
See also CA 132

**Larsen, Nella** 1893(?)-1963 ....... **BLC 2; CLC
37; HR 3**
See also AFAW 1, 2; BW 1; CA 125; CANR
83; DAM MULT; DLB 51; FW; LATS
1:1; LMFS 2

**Larson, Charles R(aymond)** 1938- ... **CLC 31**
See also CA 53-56; CANR 4, 121

**Larson, Jonathan** 1961-1996 ............. **CLC 99**
See also AAYA 28; CA 156

**La Sale, Antoine de** c. 1386-1460(?) . **LC 104**
See also DLB 208

**Las Casas, Bartolome de**
1474-1566 ......................... **HLCS; LC 31**
See Casas, Bartolome de las
See also LAW

**Lasch, Christopher** 1932-1994 ........ **CLC 102**
See also CA 73-76; 144; CANR 25, 118;
DLB 246; MTCW 1, 2

**Lasker-Schueler, Else** 1869-1945 ... **TCLC 57**
See Lasker-Schuler, Else
See also CA 183; DLB 66, 124

**Lasker-Schuler, Else**
See Lasker-Schueler, Else
See also EWL 3

**Laski, Harold J(oseph)** 1893-1950 . **TCLC 79**
See also CA 188

**Latham, Jean Lee** 1902-1995 ............ **CLC 12**
See also AITN 1; BYA 1; CA 5-8R; CANR
7, 84; CLR 50; MAICYA 1, 2; SATA 2,
68; YAW

**Latham, Mavis**
See Clark, Mavis Thorpe

**Lathen, Emma** ..................................... **CLC 2**
See Hennissart, Martha; Latsis, Mary J(ane)
See also BPFB 2; CMW 4; DLB 306

**Lathrop, Francis**
See Leiber, Fritz (Reuter, Jr.)

**Latsis, Mary J(ane)** 1927-1997
See Lathen, Emma
See also CA 85-88; 162; CMW 4

**Lattany, Kristin**
See Lattany, Kristin (Elaine Eggleston)
Hunter

**Lattany, Kristin (Elaine Eggleston) Hunter**
1931- ............................................. **CLC 35**
See also AITN 1; BW 1; BYA 3; CA 13-
16R; CANR 13, 108; CLR 3; CN 7; DLB
33; INT CANR-13; MAICYA 1, 2; SAAS
10; SATA 12, 132; YAW

**Lattimore, Richmond (Alexander)**
1906-1984 ................................. **CLC 3**
See also CA 1-4R; 112; CANR 1

**Laughlin, James** 1914-1997 ............... **CLC 49**
See also CA 21-24R; 162; CAAS 22; CANR
9, 47; CP 7; DLB 48; DLBY 1996, 1997

**Laurence, (Jean) Margaret (Wemyss)**
1926-1987 . **CLC 3, 6, 13, 50, 62; SSC 7**
See also BYA 13; CA 5-8R; 121; CANR
33; DAC; DAM MST; DLB 53; EWL 3;
FW; MTCW 1, 2; NFS 11; RGEL 2;
RGSF 2; SATA-Obit 50; TCWW 2

**Laurent, Antoine** 1952- .................... **CLC 50**

**Lauscher, Hermann**
See Hesse, Hermann

**Lautreamont** 1846-1870 .. **NCLC 12; SSC 14**
See Lautreamont, Isidore Lucien Ducasse
See also GFL 1789 to the Present; RGWL
2, 3

**Lautreamont, Isidore Lucien Ducasse**
See Lautreamont
See also DLB 217

**Lavater, Johann Kaspar**
1741-1801 .............................. **NCLC 142**
See also DLB 97

**Laverty, Donald**
See Blish, James (Benjamin)

**Lavin, Mary** 1912-1996 . **CLC 4, 18, 99; SSC
4, 67**
See also CA 9-12R; 151; CANR 33; CN 7;
DLB 15; FW; MTCW 1; RGEL 2; RGSF
2

**Lavond, Paul Dennis**
See Kornbluth, C(yril) M.; Pohl, Frederik

**Lawler, Ray**
See Lawler, Raymond Evenor
See also DLB 289

**Lawler, Raymond Evenor** 1922- ....... **CLC 58**
See Lawler, Ray
See also CA 103; CD 5; RGEL 2

**Lawrence, D(avid) H(erbert Richards)**
1885-1930 ........... **PC 54; SSC 4, 19, 73;
TCLC 2, 9, 16, 33, 48, 61, 93; WLC**
See Chambers, Jessie
See also BPFB 2; BRW 7; BRWR 2; CA
104; 121; CANR 131; CDBLB 1914-
1945; DA; DA3; DAB; DAC; DAM MST,
NOV, POET; DLB 10, 19, 36, 98, 162,
195; EWL 3; EXPP; EXPS; LAIT 2, 3;
MTCW 1, 2; NFS 18; PFS 6; RGEL 2;
RGSF 2; SSFS 2, 6; TEA; WLIT 4; WP

**Lawrence, T(homas) E(dward)**
1888-1935 ................................. **TCLC 18**
See Dale, Colin
See also BRWS 2; CA 115; 167; DLB 195

**Lawrence of Arabia**
See Lawrence, T(homas) E(dward)

**Lawson, Henry (Archibald Hertzberg)**
1867-1922 ................ **SSC 18; TCLC 27**
See also CA 120; 181; DLB 230; RGEL 2;
RGSF 2

**Lawton, Dennis**
See Faust, Frederick (Schiller)

**Layamon** fl. c. 1200- ..................... **CMLC 10**
See Laȝamon
See also DLB 146; RGEL 2

**Laye, Camara** 1928-1980 ..... **BLC 2; CLC 4,
38**
See Camara Laye
See also AFW; BW 1; CA 85-88; 97-100;
CANR 25; DAM MULT; MTCW 1, 2;
WLIT 2

**Layton, Irving (Peter)** 1912- ....... **CLC 2, 15,
164**
See also CA 1-4R; CANR 2, 33, 43, 66,
129; CP 7; DAC; DAM MST, POET;
DLB 88; EWL 3; MTCW 1, 2; PFS 12;
RGEL 2

**Lazarus, Emma** 1849-1887 ...... **NCLC 8, 109**

**Lazarus, Felix**
See Cable, George Washington

**Lazarus, Henry**
See Slavitt, David R(ytman)

**Lea, Joan**
See Neufeld, John (Arthur)

**Leacock, Stephen (Butler)**
1869-1944 ................... **SSC 39; TCLC 2**
See also CA 104; 141; CANR 80; DAC;
DAM MST; DLB 92; EWL 3; MTCW 2;
RGEL 2; RGSF 2

**Lead, Jane Ward** 1623-1704 ............... **LC 72**
See also DLB 131

**Leapor, Mary** 1722-1746 ..................... **LC 80**
See also DLB 109

**Lear, Edward** 1812-1888 ................. **NCLC 3**
See also AAYA 48; BRW 5; CLR 1, 75;
DLB 32, 163, 166; MAICYA 1, 2; RGEL
2; SATA 18, 100; WCH; WP

**Lear, Norman (Milton)** 1922- .......... **CLC 12**
See also CA 73-76

**Leautaud, Paul** 1872-1956 ............. **TCLC 83**
See also CA 203; DLB 65; GFL 1789 to the
Present

**Leavis, F(rank) R(aymond)**
1895-1978 ................................. **CLC 24**
See also BRW 7; CA 21-24R; 77-80; CANR
44; DLB 242; EWL 3; MTCW 1, 2;
RGEL 2

**Leavitt, David** 1961- ......................... **CLC 34**
See also CA 116; 122; CANR 50, 62, 101;
CPW; DA3; DAM POP; DLB 130; GLL
1; INT CA-122; MTCW 2

**Leblanc, Maurice (Marie Emile)**
1864-1941 ................................. **TCLC 49**
See also CA 110; CMW 4

**Lebowitz, Fran(ces Ann)** 1951(?)- ... **CLC 11,
36**
See also CA 81-84; CANR 14, 60, 70; INT
CANR-14; MTCW 1

**Lebrecht, Peter**
See Tieck, (Johann) Ludwig

**le Carre, John** ............... **CLC 3, 5, 9, 15, 28**
See Cornwell, David (John Moore)
See also AAYA 42; BEST 89:4; BPFB 2;
BRWS 2; CDBLB 1960 to Present; CMW
4; CN 7; CPW; DLB 87; EWL 3; MSW;
MTCW 2; RGEL 2; TEA

**Le Clezio, J(ean) M(arie) G(ustave)**
1940- .................................... **CLC 31, 155**
See also CA 116; 128; CWW 2; DLB 83;
EWL 3; GFL 1789 to the Present; RGSF
2

**Leconte de Lisle, Charles-Marie-Rene**
1818-1894 ................................. **NCLC 29**
See also DLB 217; EW 6; GFL 1789 to the
Present

**Le Coq, Monsieur**
See Simenon, Georges (Jacques Christian)

**Leduc, Violette** 1907-1972 ................. **CLC 22**
See also CA 13-14; 33-36R; CANR 69;
CAP 1; EWL 3; GFL 1789 to the Present;
GLL 1

**Ledwidge, Francis** 1887(?)-1917 .... **TCLC 23**
See also CA 123; 203; DLB 20

**Lee, Andrea** 1953- ............... **BLC 2; CLC 36**
See also BW 1, 3; CA 125; CANR 82; DAM MULT

**Lee, Andrew**
See Auchincloss, Louis (Stanton)

**Lee, Chang-rae** 1965- ....................... **CLC 91**
See also CA 148; CANR 89; LATS 1:2

**Lee, Don L.** ........................................ **CLC 2**
See Madhubuti, Haki R.

**Lee, George W(ashington)**
1894-1976 ..................... **BLC 2; CLC 52**
See also BW 1; CA 125; CANR 83; DAM MULT; DLB 51

**Lee, (Nelle) Harper** 1926- . **CLC 12, 60, 194; WLC**
See also AAYA 13; AMWS 8; BPFB 2; BYA 3; CA 13-16R; CANR 51, 128; CDALB 1941-1968; CSW; DA; DA3; DAB; DAC; DAM MST, NOV; DLB 6; EXPN; LAIT 3; MTCW 1, 2; NFS 2; SATA 11; WYA; YAW

**Lee, Helen Elaine** 1959(?)- ............... **CLC 86**
See also CA 148

**Lee, John** ............................................ **CLC 70**

**Lee, Julian**
See Latham, Jean Lee

**Lee, Larry**
See Lee, Lawrence

**Lee, Laurie** 1914-1997 ..................... **CLC 90**
See also CA 77-80; 158; CANR 33, 73; CP 7; CPW; DAB; DAM POP; DLB 27; MTCW 1; RGEL 2

**Lee, Lawrence** 1941-1990 ................. **CLC 34**
See also CA 131; CANR 43

**Lee, Li-Young** 1957- ..... **CLC 164; PC 24**
See also CA 153; CANR 118; CP 7; DLB 165; LMFS 2; PFS 11, 15, 17

**Lee, Manfred B(ennington)**
1905-1971 .................................. **CLC 11**
See Queen, Ellery
See also CA 1-4R; 29-32R; CANR 2; CMW 4; DLB 137

**Lee, Nathaniel** 1645(?)-1692 ............. **LC 103**
See also DLB 80; RGEL 2

**Lee, Shelton Jackson** 1957(?)- .. **BLCS; CLC 105**
See Lee, Spike
See also BW 2, 3; CA 125; CANR 42; DAM MULT

**Lee, Spike**
See Lee, Shelton Jackson
See also AAYA 4, 29

**Lee, Stan** 1922- ................................ **CLC 17**
See also AAYA 5, 49; CA 108; 111; CANR 129; INT CA-111

**Lee, Tanith** 1947- ............................. **CLC 46**
See also AAYA 15; CA 37-40R; CANR 53, 102; DLB 261; FANT; SATA 8, 88, 134; SFW 4; SUFW 1, 2; YAW

**Lee, Vernon** ...................... **SSC 33; TCLC 5**
See Paget, Violet
See also DLB 57, 153, 156, 174, 178; GLL 1; SUFW 1

**Lee, William**
See Burroughs, William S(eward)
See also GLL 1

**Lee, Willy**
See Burroughs, William S(eward)
See also GLL 1

**Lee-Hamilton, Eugene (Jacob)**
1845-1907 ............................... **TCLC 22**
See also CA 117

**Leet, Judith** 1935- ............................. **CLC 11**
See also CA 187

**Le Fanu, Joseph Sheridan**
1814-1873 ............. **NCLC 9, 58; SSC 14**
See also CMW 4; DA3; DAM POP; DLB 21, 70, 159, 178; HGG; RGEL 2; RGSF 2; SUFW 1

**Leffland, Ella** 1931- .......................... **CLC 19**
See also CA 29-32R; CANR 35, 78, 82; DLBY 1984; INT CANR-35; SATA 65

**Leger, Alexis**
See Leger, (Marie-Rene Auguste) Alexis Saint-Leger

**Leger, (Marie-Rene Auguste) Alexis**
**Saint-Leger** 1887-1975 .. **CLC 4, 11, 46; PC 23**
See Perse, Saint-John; Saint-John Perse
See also CA 13-16R; 61-64; CANR 43; DAM POET; MTCW 1

**Leger, Saintleger**
See Leger, (Marie-Rene Auguste) Alexis Saint-Leger

**Le Guin, Ursula K(roeber)** 1929- ..... **CLC 8, 13, 22, 45, 71, 136; SSC 12, 69**
See also AAYA 9, 27; AITN 1; BPFB 2; BYA 5, 8, 11, 14; CA 21-24R; CANR 9, 32, 52, 74, 132; CDALB 1968-1988; CLR 3, 28, 91; CN 7; CPW; DA3; DAB; DAC; DAM MST, POP; DLB 8, 52, 256, 275; EXPS; FANT; FW; INT CANR-32; JRDA; LAIT 5; MAICYA 1, 2; MTCW 1, 2; NFS 6, 9; SATA 4, 52, 99, 149; SCFW; SFW 4; SSFS 2; SUFW 1, 2; WYA; YAW

**Lehmann, Rosamond (Nina)**
1901-1990 ................................... **CLC 5**
See also CA 77-80; 131; CANR 8, 73; DLB 15; MTCW 2; RGEL 2; RHW

**Leiber, Fritz (Reuter, Jr.)**
1910-1992 ................................ **CLC 25**
See also BPFB 2; CA 45-48; 139; CANR 2, 40, 86; DLB 8; FANT; HGG; MTCW 1, 2; SATA 45; SATA-Obit 73; SCFW 2; SFW 4; SUFW 1, 2

**Leibniz, Gottfried Wilhelm von**
1646-1716 .................................. **LC 35**
See also DLB 168

**Leimbach, Martha** 1963-
See Leimbach, Marti
See also CA 130

**Leimbach, Marti** ............................... **CLC 65**
See Leimbach, Martha

**Leino, Eino** ...................................... **TCLC 24**
See Lonnbohm, Armas Eino Leopold
See also EWL 3

**Leiris, Michel (Julien)** 1901-1990 ..... **CLC 61**
See also CA 119; 128; 132; EWL 3; GFL 1789 to the Present

**Leithauser, Brad** 1953- ..................... **CLC 27**
See also CA 107; CANR 27, 81; CP 7; DLB 120, 282

**le Jars de Gournay, Marie**
See de Gournay, Marie le Jars

**Lelchuk, Alan** 1938- ........................... **CLC 5**
See also CA 45-48; CAAS 20; CANR 1, 70; CN 7

**Lem, Stanislaw** 1921- ...... **CLC 8, 15, 40, 149**
See also CA 105; CAAS 1; CANR 32; CWW 2; MTCW 1; SCFW 2; SFW 4

**Lemann, Nancy (Elise)** 1956- ........... **CLC 39**
See also CA 118; 136; CANR 121

**Lemonnier, (Antoine Louis) Camille**
1844-1913 ............................... **TCLC 22**
See also CA 121

**Lenau, Nikolaus** 1802-1850 ........... **NCLC 16**

**L'Engle, Madeleine (Camp Franklin)**
1918- ....................................... **CLC 12**
See also AAYA 28; AITN 2; BPFB 2; BYA 2, 4, 5, 7; CA 1-4R; CANR 3, 21, 39, 66, 107; CLR 1, 14, 57; CPW; CWRI 5; DA3; DAM POP; DLB 52; JRDA; MAICYA 1, 2; MTCW 1, 2; SAAS 15; SATA 1, 27, 75, 128; SFW 4; WYA; YAW

**Lengyel, Jozsef** 1896-1975 .................. **CLC 7**
See also CA 85-88; 57-60; CANR 71; RGSF 2

**Lenin** 1870-1924
See Lenin, V. I.
See also CA 121; 168

**Lenin, V. I.** ..................................... **TCLC 67**
See Lenin

**Lennon, John (Ono)** 1940-1980 .. **CLC 12, 35**
See also CA 102; SATA 114

**Lennox, Charlotte Ramsay**
1729(?)-1804 .................... **NCLC 23, 134**
See also DLB 39; RGEL 2

**Lentricchia, Frank, (Jr.)** 1940- ......... **CLC 34**
See also CA 25-28R; CANR 19, 106; DLB 246

**Lenz, Gunter** ...................................... **CLC 65**

**Lenz, Jakob Michael Reinhold**
1751-1792 ................................. **LC 100**
See also DLB 94; RGWL 2, 3

**Lenz, Siegfried** 1926- .......... **CLC 27; SSC 33**
See also CA 89-92; CANR 80; CWW 2; DLB 75; EWL 3; RGSF 2; RGWL 2, 3

**Leon, David**
See Jacob, (Cyprien-)Max

**Leonard, Elmore (John, Jr.)** 1925- . **CLC 28, 34, 71, 120**
See also AAYA 22, 59; AITN 1; BEST 89:1, 90:4; BPFB 2; CA 81-84; CANR 12, 28, 53, 76, 96, 133; CMW 4; CN 7; CPW; DA3; DAM POP; DLB 173, 226; INT CANR-28; MSW; MTCW 1, 2; RGAL 4; TCWW 2

**Leonard, Hugh** ................................... **CLC 19**
See Byrne, John Keyes
See also CBD; CD 5; DFS 13; DLB 13

**Leonov, Leonid (Maximovich)**
1899-1994 ................................. **CLC 92**
See Leonov, Leonid Maksimovich
See also CA 129; CANR 74, 76; DAM NOV; EWL 3; MTCW 1, 2

**Leonov, Leonid Maksimovich**
See Leonov, Leonid (Maximovich)
See also DLB 272

**Leopardi, (Conte) Giacomo**
1798-1837 ........... **NCLC 22, 129; PC 37**
See also EW 5; RGWL 2, 3; WP

**Le Reveler**
See Artaud, Antonin (Marie Joseph)

**Lerman, Eleanor** 1952- ....................... **CLC 9**
See also CA 85-88; CANR 69, 124

**Lerman, Rhoda** 1936- ......................... **CLC 56**
See also CA 49-52; CANR 70

**Lermontov, Mikhail Iur'evich**
See Lermontov, Mikhail Yuryevich
See also DLB 205

**Lermontov, Mikhail Yuryevich**
1814-1841 ....... **NCLC 5, 47, 126; PC 18**
See Lermontov, Mikhail Iur'evich
See also EW 6; RGWL 2, 3; TWA

**Leroux, Gaston** 1868-1927 ............. **TCLC 25**
See also CA 108; 136; CANR 69; CMW 4; NFS 20; SATA 65

**Lesage, Alain-Rene** 1668-1747 ........ **LC 2, 28**
See also EW 3; GFL Beginnings to 1789; RGWL 2, 3

**Leskov, N(ikolai) S(emenovich)** 1831-1895
See Leskov, Nikolai (Semyonovich)

**Leskov, Nikolai (Semyonovich)**
1831-1895 ................. **NCLC 25; SSC 34**
See Leskov, Nikolai Semenovich

**Leskov, Nikolai Semenovich**
See Leskov, Nikolai (Semyonovich)
See also DLB 238

**Lesser, Milton**
See Marlowe, Stephen

**Lessing, Doris (May)** 1919- ... **CLC 1, 2, 3, 6, 10, 15, 22, 40, 94, 170; SSC 6, 61; WLCS**
See also AAYA 57; AFW; BRWS 1; CA 9-12R; CAAS 14; CANR 33, 54, 76, 122; CD 5; CDBLB 1960 to Present; CN 7;

DA; DA3; DAB; DAC; DAM MST, NOV;
DFS 20; DLB 15, 139; DLBY 1985; EWL
3; EXPS; FW; LAIT 4; MTCW 1, 2;
RGEL 2; RGSF 2; SFW 4; SSFS 1, 12,
20; TEA; WLIT 2, 4

**Lessing, Gotthold Ephraim** 1729-1781 . **LC 8**
See also CDWLB 2; DLB 97; EW 4; RGWL
2, 3

**Lester, Richard** 1932- ..................... **CLC 20**

**Levenson, Jay** .................................. **CLC 70**

**Lever, Charles (James)**
1806-1872 ............................... **NCLC 23**
See also DLB 21; RGEL 2

**Leverson, Ada Esther**
1862(?)-1933(?) ...................... **TCLC 18**
See Elaine
See also CA 117; 202; DLB 153; RGEL 2

**Levertov, Denise** 1923-1997 .. **CLC 1, 2, 3, 5,
8, 15, 28, 66; PC 11**
See also AMWS 3; CA 1-4R, 178; 163;
CAAE 178; CAAS 19; CANR 3, 29, 50,
108; CDALBS; CP 7; CWP; DAM POET;
DLB 5, 165; EWL 3; EXPP; FW; INT
CANR-29; MTCW 1, 2; PAB; PFS 7, 17;
RGAL 4; TUS; WP

**Levi, Carlo** 1902-1975 ................... **TCLC 125**
See also CA 65-68; 53-56; CANR 10; EWL
3; RGWL 2, 3

**Levi, Jonathan** ............................... **CLC 76**
See also CA 197

**Levi, Peter (Chad Tigar)**
1931-2000 ................................. **CLC 41**
See also CA 5-8R; 187; CANR 34, 80; CP
7; DLB 40

**Levi, Primo** 1919-1987 ...... **CLC 37, 50; SSC
12; TCLC 109**
See also CA 13-16R; 122; CANR 12, 33,
61, 70, 132; DLB 177, 299; EWL 3;
MTCW 1, 2; RGWL 2, 3

**Levin, Ira** 1929- .............................. **CLC 3, 6**
See also CA 21-24R; CANR 17, 44, 74;
CMW 4; CN 7; CPW; DA3; DAM POP;
HGG; MTCW 1, 2; SATA 66; SFW 4

**Levin, Meyer** 1905-1981 ...................... **CLC 7**
See also AITN 1; CA 9-12R; 104; CANR
15; DAM POP; DLB 9, 28; DLBY 1981;
SATA 21; SATA-Obit 27

**Levine, Norman** 1924- ....................... **CLC 54**
See also CA 73-76; CAAS 23; CANR 14,
70; DLB 88

**Levine, Philip** 1928- .. **CLC 2, 4, 5, 9, 14, 33,
118; PC 22**
See also AMWS 5; CA 9-12R; CANR 9,
37, 52, 116; CP 7; DAM POET; DLB 5;
EWL 3; PFS 8

**Levinson, Deirdre** 1931- .................... **CLC 49**
See also CA 73-76; CANR 70

**Levi-Strauss, Claude** 1908- ............... **CLC 38**
See also CA 1-4R; CANR 6, 32, 57; DLB
242; EWL 3; GFL 1789 to the Present;
MTCW 1, 2; TWA

**Levitin, Sonia (Wolff)** 1934- .............. **CLC 17**
See also AAYA 13, 48; CA 29-32R; CANR
14, 32, 79; CLR 53; JRDA; MAICYA 1,
2; SAAS 2; SATA 4, 68, 119, 131; SATA-
Essay 131; YAW

**Levon, O. U.**
See Kesey, Ken (Elton)

**Levy, Amy** 1861-1889 ...................... **NCLC 59**
See also DLB 156, 240

**Lewes, George Henry** 1817-1878 ... **NCLC 25**
See also DLB 55, 144

**Lewis, Alun** 1915-1944 ....... **SSC 40; TCLC 3**
See also BRW 7; CA 104; 188; DLB 20,
162; PAB; RGEL 2

**Lewis, C. Day**
See Day Lewis, C(ecil)

**Lewis, C(live) S(taples)** 1898-1963 .... **CLC 1,
3, 6, 14, 27, 124; WLC**
See also AAYA 3, 39; BPFB 2; BRWS 3;
BYA 15, 16; CA 81-84; CANR 33, 71,
132; CDBLB 1945-1960; CLR 3, 27;
CWRI 5; DA; DA3; DAB; DAC; DAM
MST, NOV, POP; DLB 15, 100, 160, 255;
EWL 3; FANT; JRDA; LMFS 2; MAI-
CYA 1; MTCW 1, 2; RGEL 2; SATA
13, 100; SCFW; SFW 4; SUFW 1; TEA;
WCH; WYA; YAW

**Lewis, Cecil Day**
See Day Lewis, C(ecil)

**Lewis, Janet** 1899-1998 ..................... **CLC 41**
See Winters, Janet Lewis
See also CA 9-12R; 172; CANR 29, 63;
CAP 1; CN 7; DLBY 1987; RHW;
TCWW 2

**Lewis, Matthew Gregory**
1775-1818 .......................... **NCLC 11, 62**
See also DLB 39, 158, 178; HGG; LMFS
1; RGEL 2; SUFW

**Lewis, (Harry) Sinclair** 1885-1951 . **TCLC 4,
13, 23, 39; WLC**
See also AMW; AMWC 1; BPFB 2; CA
104; 133; CANR 132; CDALB 1917-
1929; DA; DA3; DAB; DAC; DAM MST,
NOV; DLB 9, 102, 284; DLBD 1; EWL
3; LAIT 3; MTCW 1, 2; NFS 15, 19;
RGAL 4; TUS

**Lewis, (Percy) Wyndham**
1884(?)-1957 .. **SSC 34; TCLC 2, 9, 104**
See also BRW 7; CA 104; 157; DLB 15;
EWL 3; FANT; MTCW 2; RGEL 2

**Lewisohn, Ludwig** 1883-1955 .......... **TCLC 19**
See also CA 107; 203; DLB 4, 9, 28, 102

**Lewton, Val** 1904-1951 .................... **TCLC 76**
See also CA 199; IDFW 3, 4

**Leyner, Mark** 1956- ........................... **CLC 92**
See also CA 110; CANR 28, 53; DA3; DLB
292; MTCW 2

**Lezama Lima, Jose** 1910-1976 .... **CLC 4, 10,
101; HLCS 2**
See also CA 77-80; CANR 71; DAM
MULT; DLB 113, 283; EWL 3; HW 1, 2;
LAW; RGWL 2, 3

**L'Heureux, John (Clarke)** 1934- ...... **CLC 52**
See also CA 13-16R; CANR 23, 45, 88;
DLB 244

**Li Ch'ing-chao** 1081(?)-1141(?) .... **CMLC 71**

**Liddell, C. H.**
See Kuttner, Henry

**Lie, Jonas (Lauritz Idemil)**
1833-1908(?) ............................. **TCLC 5**
See also CA 115

**Lieber, Joel** 1937-1971 ....................... **CLC 6**
See also CA 73-76; 29-32R

**Lieber, Stanley Martin**
See Lee, Stan

**Lieberman, Laurence (James)**
1935- ..................................... **CLC 4, 36**
See also CA 17-20R; CANR 8, 36, 89; CP
7

**Lieh Tzu** fl. 7th cent. B.C.-5th cent.
B.C. ....................................... **CMLC 27**

**Lieksman, Anders**
See Haavikko, Paavo Juhani

**Li Fei-kan** 1904-
See Pa Chin
See also CA 105; TWA

**Lifton, Robert Jay** 1926- ................... **CLC 67**
See also CA 17-20R; CANR 27, 78; INT
CANR-27; SATA 66

**Lightfoot, Gordon** 1938- ................... **CLC 26**
See also CA 109

**Lightman, Alan P(aige)** 1948- ........... **CLC 81**
See also CA 141; CANR 63, 105

**Ligotti, Thomas (Robert)** 1953- ...... **CLC 44;
SSC 16**
See also CA 123; CANR 49; HGG; SUFW
2

**Li Ho** 791-817 ................................. **PC 13**

**Li Ju-chen** c. 1763-c. 1830 ........... **NCLC 137**

**Lilar, Francoise**
See Mallet-Joris, Francoise

**Liliencron, (Friedrich Adolf Axel) Detlev
von** 1844-1909 ........................ **TCLC 18**
See also CA 117

**Lille, Alain de**
See Alain de Lille

**Lilly, William** 1602-1681 .................... **LC 27**

**Lima, Jose Lezama**
See Lezama Lima, Jose

**Lima Barreto, Afonso Henrique de**
1881-1922 ............................... **TCLC 23**
See also CA 117; 181; LAW

**Lima Barreto, Afonso Henriques de**
See Lima Barreto, Afonso Henrique de

**Limonov, Edward** 1944- .................... **CLC 67**
See also CA 137

**Lin, Frank**
See Atherton, Gertrude (Franklin Horn)

**Lin, Yutang** 1895-1976 ................... **TCLC 149**
See also CA 45-48; 65-68; CANR 2; RGAL
4

**Lincoln, Abraham** 1809-1865 ......... **NCLC 18**
See also LAIT 2

**Lind, Jakov** ............... **CLC 1, 2, 4, 27, 82**
See Landwirth, Heinz
See also CAAS 4; DLB 299; EWL 3

**Lindbergh, Anne (Spencer) Morrow**
1906-2001 ............................... **CLC 82**
See also BPFB 2; CA 17-20R; 193; CANR
16, 73; DAM NOV; MTCW 1, 2; SATA
33; SATA-Obit 125; TUS

**Lindsay, David** 1878(?)-1945 .......... **TCLC 15**
See also CA 113; 187; DLB 255; FANT;
SFW 4; SUFW 1

**Lindsay, (Nicholas) Vachel**
1879-1931 ....... **PC 23; TCLC 17; WLC**
See also AMWS 1; CA 114; 135; CANR
79; CDALB 1865-1917; DA; DA3; DAC;
DAM MST, POET; DLB 54; EWL 3;
EXPP; RGAL 4; SATA 40; WP

**Linke-Poot**
See Doeblin, Alfred

**Linney, Romulus** 1930- ..................... **CLC 51**
See also CA 1-4R; CAD; CANR 40, 44,
79; CD 5; CSW; RGAL 4

**Linton, Eliza Lynn** 1822-1898 ....... **NCLC 41**
See also DLB 18

**Li Po** 701-763 ...................... **CMLC 2; PC 29**
See also PFS 20; WP

**Lipsius, Justus** 1547-1606 .................. **LC 16**

**Lipsyte, Robert (Michael)** 1938- ...... **CLC 21**
See also AAYA 7, 45; CA 17-20R; CANR
8, 57; CLR 23, 76; DA; DAC; DAM
MST, NOV; JRDA; LAIT 5; MAICYA 1,
2; SATA 5, 68, 113; WYA; YAW

**Lish, Gordon (Jay)** 1934- ... **CLC 45; SSC 18**
See also CA 113; 117; CANR 79; DLB 130;
INT CA-117

**Lispector, Clarice** 1925(?)-1977 ....... **CLC 43;
HLCS 2; SSC 34**
See also CA 139; 116; CANR 71; CDWLB
3; DLB 113; DNFS 1; EWL 3; FW; HW
2; LAW; RGSF 2; RGWL 2, 3; WLIT 1

**Littell, Robert** 1935(?)- ..................... **CLC 42**
See also CA 109; 112; CANR 64, 115;
CMW 4

**Little, Malcolm** 1925-1965
See Malcolm X
See also BW 1, 3; CA 125; 111; CANR 82;
DA; DA3; DAB; DAC; DAM MST,
MULT; MTCW 1, 2

**Littlewit, Humphrey Gent.**
See Lovecraft, H(oward) P(hillips)

**Litwos**
See Sienkiewicz, Henryk (Adam Alexander Pius)

**Liu, E.** 1857-1909 ........................... **TCLC 15**
See also CA 115; 190

**Lively, Penelope (Margaret)** 1933- .. **CLC 32, 50**
See also BPFB 2; CA 41-44R; CANR 29, 67, 79, 131; CLR 7; CN 7; CWRI 5; DAM NOV; DLB 14, 161, 207; FANT; JRDA; MAICYA 1, 2; MTCW 1, 2; SATA 7, 60, 101; TEA

**Livesay, Dorothy (Kathleen)**
1909-1996 ........................ **CLC 4, 15, 79**
See also AITN 2; CA 25-28R; CAAS 8; CANR 36, 67; DAC; DAM MST, POET; DLB 68; FW; MTCW 1; RGEL 2; TWA

**Livy** c. 59B.C.-c. 12 ....................... **CMLC 11**
See also AW 2; CDWLB 1; DLB 211; RGWL 2, 3

**Lizardi, Jose Joaquin Fernandez de**
1776-1827 ................................. **NCLC 30**
See also LAW

**Llewellyn, Richard**
See Llewellyn Lloyd, Richard Dafydd Vivian
See also DLB 15

**Llewellyn Lloyd, Richard Dafydd Vivian**
1906-1983 .............................. **CLC 7, 80**
See Llewellyn, Richard
See also CA 53-56; 111; CANR 7, 71; SATA 11; SATA-Obit 37

**Llosa, (Jorge) Mario (Pedro) Vargas**
See Vargas Llosa, (Jorge) Mario (Pedro)
See also RGWL 3

**Llosa, Mario Vargas**
See Vargas Llosa, (Jorge) Mario (Pedro)

**Lloyd, Manda**
See Mander, (Mary) Jane

**Lloyd Webber, Andrew** 1948-
See Webber, Andrew Lloyd
See also AAYA 1, 38; CA 116; 149; DAM DRAM; SATA 56

**Llull, Ramon** c. 1235-c. 1316 ........ **CMLC 12**

**Lobb, Ebenezer**
See Upward, Allen

**Locke, Alain (Le Roy)**
1886-1954 ........ **BLCS; HR 3; TCLC 43**
See also BW 1, 3; CA 106; 124; CANR 79; DLB 51; LMFS 2; RGAL 4

**Locke, John** 1632-1704 ................... **LC 7, 35**
See also DLB 31, 101, 213, 252; RGEL 2; WLIT 3

**Locke-Elliott, Sumner**
See Elliott, Sumner Locke

**Lockhart, John Gibson** 1794-1854 .. **NCLC 6**
See also DLB 110, 116, 144

**Lockridge, Ross (Franklin), Jr.**
1914-1948 .............................. **TCLC 111**
See also CA 108; 145; CANR 79; DLB 143; DLBY 1980; RGAL 4; RHW

**Lockwood, Robert**
See Johnson, Robert

**Lodge, David (John)** 1935- ....... **CLC 36, 141**
See also BEST 90:1; BRWS 4; CA 17-20R; CANR 19, 53, 92; CN 7; CPW; DAM POP; DLB 14, 194; EWL 3; INT CANR-19; MTCW 1, 2

**Lodge, Thomas** 1558-1625 .................. **LC 41**
See also DLB 172; RGEL 2

**Loewinsohn, Ron(ald William)**
1937- ...................................... **CLC 52**
See also CA 25-28R; CANR 71

**Logan, Jake**
See Smith, Martin Cruz

**Logan, John (Burton)** 1923-1987 ....... **CLC 5**
See also CA 77-80; 124; CANR 45; DLB 5

**Lo Kuan-chung** 1330(?)-1400(?) .......... **LC 12**

**Lombard, Nap**
See Johnson, Pamela Hansford

**Lombard, Peter** 1100(?)-1160(?) ... **CMLC 72**

**London, Jack** 1876-1916 .. **SSC 4, 49; TCLC 9, 15, 39; WLC**
See London, John Griffith
See also AAYA 13; AITN 2; AMW; BPFB 2; BYA 4, 13; CDALB 1865-1917; DLB 8, 12, 78, 212; EWL 3; EXPS; LAIT 3; NFS 8; RGAL 4; RGSF 2; SATA 18; SFW 4; SSFS 7; TCWW 2; TUS; WYA; YAW

**London, John Griffith** 1876-1916
See London, Jack
See also CA 110; 119; CANR 73; DA; DA3; DAB; DAC; DAM MST, NOV; JRDA; MAICYA 1, 2; MTCW 1, 2; NFS 19

**Long, Emmett**
See Leonard, Elmore (John, Jr.)

**Longbaugh, Harry**
See Goldman, William (W.)

**Longfellow, Henry Wadsworth**
1807-1882 .... **NCLC 2, 45, 101, 103; PC 30; WLCS**
See also AMW; AMWR 2; CDALB 1640-1865; CLR 99; DA; DA3; DAB; DAC; DAM MST, POET; DLB 1, 59, 235; EXPP; PAB; PFS 2, 7, 17; RGAL 4; SATA 19; TUS; WP

**Longinus** c. 1st cent. - .................. **CMLC 27**
See also AW 2; DLB 176

**Longley, Michael** 1939- ..................... **CLC 29**
See also BRWS 8; CA 102; CP 7; DLB 40

**Longus** fl. c. 2nd cent. - ................... **CMLC 7**

**Longway, A. Hugh**
See Lang, Andrew

**Lonnbohm, Armas Eino Leopold** 1878-1926
See Leino, Eino
See also CA 123

**Lonnrot, Elias** 1802-1884 ............... **NCLC 53**
See also EFS 1

**Lonsdale, Roger ed.** .......................... **CLC 65**

**Lopate, Phillip** 1943- ........................ **CLC 29**
See also CA 97-100; CANR 88; DLBY 1980; INT CA-97-100

**Lopez, Barry (Holstun)** 1945- ........... **CLC 70**
See also AAYA 9; ANW; CA 65-68; CANR 7, 23, 47, 68, 92; DLB 256, 275; INT CANR-7, -23; MTCW 1; RGAL 4; SATA 67

**Lopez Portillo (y Pacheco), Jose**
1920-2004 ................................... **CLC 46**
See also CA 129; 224; HW 1

**Lopez y Fuentes, Gregorio**
1897(?)-1966 ............................... **CLC 32**
See also CA 131; EWL 3; HW 1

**Lorca, Federico Garcia**
See Garcia Lorca, Federico
See also DFS 4; EW 11; PFS 20; RGWL 2, 3; WP

**Lord, Audre**
See Lorde, Audre (Geraldine)
See also EWL 3

**Lord, Bette Bao** 1938- ............ **AAL; CLC 23**
See also BEST 90:3; BPFB 2; CA 107; CANR 41, 79; INT CA-107; SATA 58

**Lord Auch**
See Bataille, Georges

**Lord Brooke**
See Greville, Fulke

**Lord Byron**
See Byron, George Gordon (Noel)

**Lorde, Audre (Geraldine)**
1934-1992 .. **BLC 2; CLC 18, 71; PC 12**
See Domini, Rey; Lord, Audre
See also AFAW 1, 2; BW 1, 3; CA 25-28R; 142; CANR 16, 26, 46, 82; DA3; DAM MULT, POET; DLB 41; FW; MTCW 1, 2; PFS 16; RGAL 4

**Lord Houghton**
See Milnes, Richard Monckton

**Lord Jeffrey**
See Jeffrey, Francis

**Loreaux, Nichol** ............................... **CLC 65**

**Lorenzini, Carlo** 1826-1890
See Collodi, Carlo
See also MAICYA 1, 2; SATA 29, 100

**Lorenzo, Heberto Padilla**
See Padilla (Lorenzo), Heberto

**Loris**
See Hofmannsthal, Hugo von

**Loti, Pierre** ..................................... **TCLC 11**
See Viaud, (Louis Marie) Julien
See also DLB 123; GFL 1789 to the Present

**Lou, Henri**
See Andreas-Salome, Lou

**Louie, David Wong** 1954- ................. **CLC 70**
See also CA 139; CANR 120

**Louis, Adrian C.** ................................. **NNAL**
See also CA 223

**Louis, Father M.**
See Merton, Thomas (James)

**Louise, Heidi**
See Erdrich, Louise

**Lovecraft, H(oward) P(hillips)**
1890-1937 ........ **SSC 3, 52; TCLC 4, 22**
See also AAYA 14; BPFB 2; CA 104; 133; CANR 106; DA3; DAM POP; HGG; MTCW 1, 2; RGAL 4; SCFW; SFW 4; SUFW

**Lovelace, Earl** 1935- .......................... **CLC 51**
See also BW 2; CA 77-80; CANR 41, 72, 114; CD 5; CDWLB 3; CN 7; DLB 125; EWL 3; MTCW 1

**Lovelace, Richard** 1618-1657 .............. **LC 24**
See also BRW 2; DLB 131; EXPP; PAB; RGEL 2

**Lowe, Pardee** 1904- .............................. **AAL**

**Lowell, Amy** 1874-1925 ... **PC 13; TCLC 1, 8**
See also AAYA 57; AMW; CA 104; 151; DAM POET; DLB 54, 140; EWL 3; EXPP; LMFS 2; MAWW; MTCW 2; RGAL 4; TUS

**Lowell, James Russell** 1819-1891 ... **NCLC 2, 90**
See also AMWS 1; CDALB 1640-1865; DLB 1, 11, 64, 79, 189, 235; RGAL 4

**Lowell, Robert (Traill Spence, Jr.)**
1917-1977 .... **CLC 1, 2, 3, 4, 5, 8, 9, 11, 15, 37, 124; PC 3; WLC**
See also AMW; AMWC 2; AMWR 2; CA 9-12R; 73-76; CABS 2; CANR 26, 60; CDALBS; DA; DA3; DAB; DAC; DAM MST, NOV; DLB 5, 169; EWL 3; MTCW 1, 2; PAB; PFS 6, 7; RGAL 4; WP

**Lowenthal, Michael (Francis)**
1969- ...................................... **CLC 119**
See also CA 150; CANR 115

**Lowndes, Marie Adelaide (Belloc)**
1868-1947 ................................. **TCLC 12**
See also CA 107; CMW 4; DLB 70; RHW

**Lowry, (Clarence) Malcolm**
1909-1957 ............. **SSC 31; TCLC 6, 40**
See also BPFB 2; BRWS 3; CA 105; 131; CANR 62, 105; CDBLB 1945-1960; DLB 15; EWL 3; MTCW 1, 2; RGEL 2

**Lowry, Mina Gertrude** 1882-1966
See Loy, Mina
See also CA 113

**Loxsmith, John**
See Brunner, John (Kilian Houston)

**Loy, Mina** ............................. **CLC 28; PC 16**
See Lowry, Mina Gertrude
See also DAM POET; DLB 4, 54; PFS 20

**Loyson-Bridet**
See Schwob, Marcel (Mayer Andre)

Lucan 39-65 .................................. CMLC 33
See also AW 2; DLB 211; EFS 2; RGWL 2, 3

Lucas, Craig 1951- ............................ CLC 64
See also CA 137; CAD; CANR 71, 109; CD 5; GLL 2

Lucas, E(dward) V(errall) 1868-1938 ................... TCLC 73
See also CA 176; DLB 98, 149, 153; SATA 20

Lucas, George 1944- ........................... CLC 16
See also AAYA 1, 23; CA 77-80; CANR 30; SATA 56

Lucas, Hans
See Godard, Jean-Luc

Lucas, Victoria
See Plath, Sylvia

Lucian c. 125-c. 180 ....................... CMLC 32
See also AW 2; DLB 176; RGWL 2, 3

Lucretius c. 94B.C.-c. 49B.C. ........... CMLC 48
See also AW 2; CDWLB 1; DLB 211; EFS 2; RGWL 2, 3

Ludlam, Charles 1943-1987 ........ CLC 46, 50
See also CA 85-88; 122; CAD; CANR 72, 86; DLB 266

Ludlum, Robert 1927-2001 ......... CLC 22, 43
See also AAYA 10, 59; BEST 89:1, 90:3; BPFB 2; CA 33-36R; 195; CANR 25, 41, 68, 105, 131; CMW 4; CPW; DA3; DAM NOV, POP; DLBY 1982; MSW; MTCW 1, 2; LAW

Ludwig, Ken ............................... CLC 60
See also CA 195; CAD

Ludwig, Otto 1813-1865 ................... NCLC 4
See also DLB 129

Lugones, Leopoldo 1874-1938 ........ HLCS 2; TCLC 15
See also CA 116; 131; CANR 104; DLB 283; EWL 3; HW 1; LAW

Lu Hsun ........................... SSC 20; TCLC 3
See Shu-Jen, Chou
See also EWL 3

Lukacs, George ........................... CLC 24
See Lukacs, Gyorgy (Szegeny von)

Lukacs, Gyorgy (Szegeny von) 1885-1971
See Lukacs, George
See also CA 101; 29-32R; CANR 62; CD-WLB 4; DLB 215, 242; EW 10; EWL 3; MTCW 2

Luke, Peter (Ambrose Cyprian) 1919-1995 ................... CLC 38
See also CA 81-84; 147; CANR 72; CBD; CD 5; DLB 13

Lunar, Dennis
See Mungo, Raymond

Lurie, Alison 1926- ..... CLC 4, 5, 18, 39, 175
See also BPFB 2; CA 1-4R; CANR 2, 17, 50, 88; CN 7; DLB 2; MTCW 1; SATA 46, 112

Lustig, Arnost 1926- ......................... CLC 56
See also AAYA 3; CA 69-72; CANR 47, 102; CWW 2; DLB 232, 299; EWL 3; SATA 56

Luther, Martin 1483-1546 ............... LC 9, 37
See also CDWLB 2; DLB 179; EW 2; RGWL 2, 3

Luxemburg, Rosa 1870(?)-1919 ..... TCLC 63
See also CA 118

Luzi, Mario 1914- ............................ CLC 13
See also CA 61-64; CANR 9, 70; CWW 2; DLB 128; EWL 3

L'vov, Arkady ............................... CLC 59

Lydgate, John c. 1370-1450(?) ............ LC 81
See also BRW 1; DLB 146; RGEL 2

Lyly, John 1554(?)-1606 ........... DC 7; LC 41
See also BRW 1; DAM DRAM; DLB 62, 167; RGEL 2

L'Ymagier
See Gourmont, Remy(-Marie-Charles) de

Lynch, B. Suarez
See Borges, Jorge Luis

Lynch, David (Keith) 1946- ...... CLC 66, 162
See also AAYA 55; CA 124; 129; CANR 111

Lynch, James
See Andreyev, Leonid (Nikolaevich)

Lyndsay, Sir David 1485-1555 ............. LC 20
See also RGEL 2

Lynn, Kenneth S(chuyler) 1923-2001 ........................... CLC 50
See also CA 1-4R; 196; CANR 3, 27, 65

Lynx
See West, Rebecca

Lyons, Marcus
See Blish, James (Benjamin)

Lyotard, Jean-Francois 1924-1998 ............................. TCLC 103
See also DLB 242; EWL 3

Lyre, Pinchbeck
See Sassoon, Siegfried (Lorraine)

Lytle, Andrew (Nelson) 1902-1995 ... CLC 22
See also CA 9-12R; 150; CANR 70; CN 7; CSW; DLB 6; DLBY 1995; RGAL 4; RHW

Lyttelton, George 1709-1773 ................. LC 10
See also RGEL 2

Lytton of Knebworth, Baron
See Bulwer-Lytton, Edward (George Earle Lytton)

Maas, Peter 1929-2001 ..................... CLC 29
See also CA 93-96; 201; INT CA-93-96; MTCW 2

Macaulay, Catherine 1731-1791 ......... LC 64
See also DLB 104

Macaulay, (Emilie) Rose 1881(?)-1958 ....................... TCLC 7, 44
See also CA 104; DLB 36; EWL 3; RGEL 2; RHW

Macaulay, Thomas Babington 1800-1859 ............................. NCLC 42
See also BRW 4; CDBLB 1832-1890; DLB 32, 55; RGEL 2

MacBeth, George (Mann) 1932-1992 ..................... CLC 2, 5, 9
See also CA 25-28R; 136; CANR 61, 66; DLB 40; MTCW 1; PFS 8; SATA 4; SATA-Obit 70

MacCaig, Norman (Alexander) 1910-1996 ........................... CLC 36
See also BRWS 6; CA 9-12R; CANR 3, 34; CP 7; DAB; DAM POET; DLB 27; EWL 3; RGEL 2

MacCarthy, Sir (Charles Otto) Desmond 1877-1952 ............................. TCLC 36
See also CA 167

MacDiarmid, Hugh .... CLC 2, 4, 11, 19, 63; PC 9
See Grieve, C(hristopher) M(urray)
See also CDBLB 1945-1960; DLB 20; EWL 3; RGEL 2

MacDonald, Anson
See Heinlein, Robert A(nson)

Macdonald, Cynthia 1928- ......... CLC 13, 19
See also CA 49-52; CANR 4, 44; DLB 105

MacDonald, George 1824-1905 ....... TCLC 9, 113
See also AAYA 57; BYA 5; CA 106; 137; CANR 80; CLR 67; DLB 18, 163, 178; FANT; MAICYA 1, 2; RGEL 2; SATA 33, 100; SFW 4; SUFW; WCH

Macdonald, John
See Millar, Kenneth

MacDonald, John D(ann) 1916-1986 .................... CLC 3, 27, 44
See also BPFB 2; CA 1-4R; 121; CANR 1, 19, 60; CMW 4; CPW; DAM NOV, POP; DLB 8, 306; DLBY 1986; MSW; MTCW 1, 2; SFW 4

Macdonald, John Ross
See Millar, Kenneth

Macdonald, Ross ..... CLC 1, 2, 3, 14, 34, 41
See Millar, Kenneth
See also AMWS 4; BPFB 2; DLBD 6; MSW; RGAL 4

MacDougal, John
See Blish, James (Benjamin)

MacDougal, John
See Blish, James (Benjamin)

MacDowell, John
See Parks, Tim(othy Harold)

MacEwen, Gwendolyn (Margaret) 1941-1987 ........................... CLC 13, 55
See also CA 9-12R; 124; CANR 7, 22; DLB 53, 251; SATA 50; SATA-Obit 55

Macha, Karel Hynek 1810-1846 .... NCLC 46

Machado (y Ruiz), Antonio 1875-1939 ................................. TCLC 3
See also CA 104; 174; DLB 108; EW 9; EWL 3; HW 2; RGWL 2, 3

Machado de Assis, Joaquim Maria 1839-1908 .... BLC 2; HLCS 2; SSC 24; TCLC 10
See also CA 107; 153; CANR 91; LAW; RGSF 2; RGWL 2, 3; TWA; WLIT 1

Machaut, Guillaume de c. 1300-1377 ............................. CMLC 64
See also DLB 208

Machen, Arthur ............. SSC 20; TCLC 4
See Jones, Arthur Llewellyn
See also CA 179; DLB 156, 178; RGEL 2; SUFW 1

Machiavelli, Niccolo 1469-1527 ... DC 16; LC 8, 36; WLCS
See also AAYA 58; DA; DAB; DAC; DAM MST; EW 2; LAIT 1; LMFS 1; NFS 9; RGWL 2, 3; TWA

MacInnes, Colin 1914-1976 .......... CLC 4, 23
See also CA 69-72; 65-68; CANR 21; DLB 14; MTCW 1, 2; RGEL 2; RHW

MacInnes, Helen (Clark) 1907-1985 ........................... CLC 27, 39
See also BPFB 2; CA 1-4R; 117; CANR 1, 28, 58; CMW 4; CPW; DAM POP; DLB 87; MSW; MTCW 1, 2; SATA 22; SATA-Obit 44

Mackay, Mary 1855-1924
See Corelli, Marie
See also CA 118; 177; FANT; RHW

Mackay, Shena 1944- ..................... CLC 195
See also CA 104; CANR 88; DLB 231

Mackenzie, Compton (Edward Montague) 1883-1972 .............. CLC 18; TCLC 116
See also CA 21-22; 37-40R; CAP 2; DLB 34, 100; RGEL 2

Mackenzie, Henry 1745-1831 ......... NCLC 41
See also DLB 39; RGEL 2

Mackey, Nathaniel (Ernest) 1947- ....... PC 49
See also CA 153; CANR 114; CP 7; DLB 169

MacKinnon, Catharine A. 1946- .... CLC 181
See also CA 128; 132; CANR 73; FW; MTCW 2

Mackintosh, Elizabeth 1896(?)-1952
See Tey, Josephine
See also CA 110; CMW 4

MacLaren, James
See Grieve, C(hristopher) M(urray)

Mac Laverty, Bernard 1942- ............ CLC 31
See also CA 116; 118; CANR 43, 88; CN 7; DLB 267; INT CA-118; RGSF 2

MacLean, Alistair (Stuart) 1922(?)-1987 ....... CLC 3, 13, 50, 63
See also CA 57-60; 121; CANR 28, 61; CMW 4; CPW; DAM POP; DLB 276; MTCW 1; SATA 23; SATA-Obit 50; TCWW 2

**Maclean, Norman (Fitzroy)**
1902-1990 .................... **CLC 78; SSC 13**
See also CA 102; 132; CANR 49; CPW;
DAM POP; DLB 206; TCWW 2

**MacLeish, Archibald** 1892-1982 ... **CLC 3, 8,
14, 68; PC 47**
See also AMW; CA 9-12R; 106; CAD;
CANR 33, 63; CDALBS; DAM POET;
DFS 15; DLB 4, 7, 45; DLBY 1982; EWL
3; EXPP; MTCW 1, 2; PAB; PFS 5;
RGAL 4; TUS

**MacLennan, (John) Hugh**
1907-1990 ........................ **CLC 2, 14, 92**
See also CA 5-8R; 142; CANR 33; DAC;
DAM MST; DLB 68; EWL 3; MTCW 1,
2; RGEL 2; TWA

**MacLeod, Alistair** 1936- ........... **CLC 56, 165**
See also CA 123; CCA 1; DAC; DAM
MST; DLB 60; MTCW 2; RGSF 2

**Macleod, Fiona**
See Sharp, William
See also RGEL 2; SUFW

**MacNeice, (Frederick) Louis**
1907-1963 .................... **CLC 1, 4, 10, 53**
See also BRW 7; CA 85-88; CANR 61;
DAB; DAM POET; DLB 10, 20; EWL 3;
MTCW 1, 2; RGEL 2

**MacNeill, Dand**
See Fraser, George MacDonald

**Macpherson, James** 1736-1796 ........... **LC 29**
See Ossian
See also BRWS 8; DLB 109; RGEL 2

**Macpherson, (Jean) Jay** 1931- ........ **CLC 14**
See also CA 5-8R; CANR 90; CP 7; CWP;
DLB 53

**Macrobius** fl. 430- .......................... **CMLC 48**

**MacShane, Frank** 1927-1999 ........... **CLC 39**
See also CA 9-12R; 186; CANR 3, 33; DLB
111

**Macumber, Mari**
See Sandoz, Mari(e Susette)

**Madach, Imre** 1823-1864 ............... **NCLC 19**

**Madden, (Jerry) David** 1933- ....... **CLC 5, 15**
See also CA 1-4R; CAAS 3; CANR 4, 45;
CN 7; CSW; DLB 6; MTCW 1

**Maddern, Al(an)**
See Ellison, Harlan (Jay)

**Madhubuti, Haki R.** 1942- ... **BLC 2; CLC 6,
73; PC 5**
See Lee, Don L.
See also BW 2, 3; CA 73-76; CANR 24,
51, 73; CP 7; CSW; DAM MULT, POET;
DLB 5, 41; DLBD 8; EWL 3; MTCW 2;
RGAL 4

**Madison, James** 1751-1836 .......... **NCLC 126**
See also DLB 37

**Maepenn, Hugh**
See Kuttner, Henry

**Maepenn, K. H.**
See Kuttner, Henry

**Maeterlinck, Maurice** 1862-1949 ..... **TCLC 3**
See also CA 104; 136; CANR 80; DAM
DRAM; DLB 192; EW 8; EWL 3; GFL
1789 to the Present; LMFS 2; RGWL 2,
3; SATA 66; TWA

**Maginn, William** 1794-1842 ............. **NCLC 8**
See also DLB 110, 159

**Mahapatra, Jayanta** 1928- ................ **CLC 33**
See also CA 73-76; CAAS 9; CANR 15,
33, 66, 87; CP 7; DAM MULT

**Mahfouz, Naguib (Abdel Aziz Al-Sabilgi)**
1911(?)- ...................... **CLC 153; SSC 66**
See Mahfuz, Najib (Abdel Aziz al-Sabilgi)
See also AAYA 49; BEST 89:2; CA 128;
CANR 55, 101; DA3; DAM NOV;
MTCW 1, 2; RGWL 2, 3; SSFS 9

**Mahfuz, Najib (Abdel Aziz al-Sabilgi)**
............................................. **CLC 52, 55**
See Mahfouz, Naguib (Abdel Aziz Al-
Sabilgi)
See also AFW; CWW 2; DLBY 1988; EWL
3; RGSF 2; WLIT 2

**Mahon, Derek** 1941- ............. **CLC 27; PC 60**
See also BRWS 6; CA 113; 128; CANR 88;
CP 7; DLB 40; EWL 3

**Maiakovskii, Vladimir**
See Mayakovski, Vladimir (Vladimirovich)
See also IDTP; RGWL 2, 3

**Mailer, Norman (Kingsley)** 1923- . **CLC 1, 2,
3, 4, 5, 8, 11, 14, 28, 39, 74, 111**
See also AAYA 31; AITN 2; AMW; AMWC
2; AMWR 2; BPFB 2; CA 9-12R; CABS
1; CANR 28, 74, 77, 130; CDALB 1968-
1988; CN 7; CPW; DA; DA3; DAB;
DAC; DAM MST, NOV, POP; DLB 2,
16, 28, 185, 278; DLBD 3; DLBY 1980,
1983; EWL 3; MTCW 1, 2; NFS 10;
RGAL 4; TUS

**Maillet, Antonine** 1929- ............. **CLC 54, 118**
See also CA 115; 120; CANR 46, 74, 77;
CCA 1; CWW 2; DAC; DLB 60; INT CA-
120; MTCW 2

**Mais, Roger** 1905-1955 ..................... **TCLC 8**
See also BW 1, 3; CA 105; 124; CANR 82;
CDWLB 3; DLB 125; EWL 3; MTCW 1;
RGEL 2

**Maistre, Joseph** 1753-1821 ............. **NCLC 37**
See also GFL 1789 to the Present

**Maitland, Frederic William**
1850-1906 ................................ **TCLC 65**

**Maitland, Sara (Louise)** 1950- ......... **CLC 49**
See also CA 69-72; CANR 13, 59; DLB
271; FW

**Major, Clarence** 1936- ... **BLC 2; CLC 3, 19,
48**
See also AFAW 2; BW 2, 3; CA 21-24R;
CAAS 6; CANR 13, 25, 53, 82; CN 7;
CP 7; CSW; DAM MULT; DLB 33; EWL
3; MSW

**Major, Kevin (Gerald)** 1949- ............ **CLC 26**
See also AAYA 16; CA 97-100; CANR 21,
38, 112; CLR 11; DAC; DLB 60; INT
CANR-21; JRDA; MAICYA 1, 2; MAIC-
YAS 1; SATA 32, 82, 134; WYA; YAW

**Maki, James**
See Ozu, Yasujiro

**Malabaila, Damiano**
See Levi, Primo

**Malamud, Bernard** 1914-1986 .. **CLC 1, 2, 3,
5, 8, 9, 11, 18, 27, 44, 78, 85; SSC 15;
TCLC 129; WLC**
See also AAYA 16; AMWS 1; BPFB 2;
BYA 15; CA 5-8R; 118; CABS 1; CANR
28, 62, 114; CDALB 1941-1968; CPW;
DA; DA3; DAB; DAC; DAM MST, NOV,
POP; DLB 2, 28, 152; DLBY 1980, 1986;
EWL 3; EXPS; LAIT 4; LATS 1:1;
MTCW 1, 2; NFS 4, 9; RGAL 4; RGSF
2; SSFS 8, 13, 16; TUS

**Malan, Herman**
See Bosman, Herman Charles; Bosman,
Herman Charles

**Malaparte, Curzio** 1898-1957 ........ **TCLC 52**
See also DLB 264

**Malcolm, Dan**
See Silverberg, Robert

**Malcolm X** .... **BLC 2; CLC 82, 117; WLCS**
See Little, Malcolm
See also LAIT 5; NCFS 3

**Malherbe, Francois de** 1555-1628 ......... **LC 5**
See also GFL Beginnings to 1789

**Mallarme, Stephane** 1842-1898 ...... **NCLC 4,
41; PC 4**
See also DAM POET; DLB 217; EW 7;
GFL 1789 to the Present; LMFS 2; RGWL
2, 3; TWA

**Mallet-Joris, Francoise** 1930- ........... **CLC 11**
See also CA 65-68; CANR 17; CWW 2;
DLB 83; EWL 3; GFL 1789 to the Present

**Malley, Ern**
See McAuley, James Phillip

**Mallon, Thomas** 1951- ..................... **CLC 172**
See also CA 110; CANR 29, 57, 92

**Mallowan, Agatha Christie**
See Christie, Agatha (Mary Clarissa)

**Maloff, Saul** 1922- ............................. **CLC 5**
See also CA 33-36R

**Malone, Louis**
See MacNeice, (Frederick) Louis

**Malone, Michael (Christopher)**
1942- ....................................... **CLC 43**
See also CA 77-80; CANR 14, 32, 57, 114

**Malory, Sir Thomas** 1410(?)-1471(?) . **LC 11,
88; WLCS**
See also BRW 1; BRWR 2; CDBLB Before
1660; DA; DAB; DAC; DAM MST; DLB
146; EFS 2; RGEL 2; SATA 59; SATA-
Brief 33; TEA; WLIT 3

**Malouf, (George Joseph) David**
1934- ................................... **CLC 28, 86**
See also CA 124; CANR 50, 76; CN 7; CP
7; DLB 289; EWL 3; MTCW 2

**Malraux, (Georges-)Andre**
1901-1976 .......... **CLC 1, 4, 9, 13, 15, 57**
See also BPFB 2; CA 21-22; 69-72; CANR
34, 58; CAP 2; DA3; DAM NOV; DLB
72; EW 12; EWL 3; GFL 1789 to the
Present; MTCW 1, 2; RGWL 2, 3; TWA

**Malthus, Thomas Robert**
1766-1834 ............................... **NCLC 145**
See also DLB 107, 158; RGEL 2

**Malzberg, Barry N(athaniel)** 1939- ... **CLC 7**
See also CA 61-64; CAAS 4; CANR 16;
CMW 4; DLB 8; SFW 4

**Mamet, David (Alan)** 1947- .. **CLC 9, 15, 34,
46, 91, 166; DC 4, 24**
See also AAYA 3; CA 81-84; CABS 3;
CANR 15, 41, 67, 72, 129; CD 5; DA3;
DAM DRAM; DFS 2, 3, 6, 12, 15; DLB
7; EWL 3; IDFW 4; MTCW 1, 2; RGAL
4

**Mamoulian, Rouben (Zachary)**
1897-1987 ................................ **CLC 16**
See also CA 25-28R; 124; CANR 85

**Mandelshtam, Osip**
See Mandelstam, Osip (Emilievich)
See also EW 10; EWL 3; RGWL 2, 3

**Mandelstam, Osip (Emilievich)**
1891(?)-1943(?) ........ **PC 14; TCLC 2, 6**
See Mandelshtam, Osip
See also CA 104; 150; MTCW 2; TWA

**Mander, (Mary) Jane** 1877-1949 ... **TCLC 31**
See also CA 162; RGEL 2

**Mandeville, Bernard** 1670-1733 .......... **LC 82**
See also DLB 101

**Mandeville, Sir John** fl. 1350- ...... **CMLC 19**
See also DLB 146

**Mandiargues, Andre Pieyre de** ....... **CLC 41**
See Pieyre de Mandiargues, Andre
See also DLB 83

**Mandrake, Ethel Belle**
See Thurman, Wallace (Henry)

**Mangan, James Clarence**
1803-1849 ............................... **NCLC 27**
See also RGEL 2

**Maniere, J.-E.**
See Giraudoux, Jean(-Hippolyte)

**Mankiewicz, Herman (Jacob)**
1897-1953 ............................... **TCLC 85**
See also CA 120; 169; DLB 26; IDFW 3, 4

**Manley, (Mary) Delariviere**
1672(?)-1724 ............................. **LC 1, 42**
See also DLB 39, 80; RGEL 2

**Mann, Abel**
See Creasey, John

**Mann, Emily** 1952- ................................. **DC 7**
  See also CA 130; CAD; CANR 55; CD 5;
  CWD; DLB 266
**Mann, (Luiz) Heinrich** 1871-1950 ... **TCLC 9**
  See also CA 106; 164, 181; DLB 66, 118;
  EW 8; EWL 3; RGWL 2, 3
**Mann, (Paul) Thomas** 1875-1955 ....... **SSC 5,
  70; TCLC 2, 8, 14, 21, 35, 44, 60;
  WLC**
  See also BPFB 2; CA 104; 128; CANR 133;
  CDWLB 2; DA; DA3; DAB; DAC; DAM
  MST, NOV; DLB 66; EW 9; EWL 3; GLL
  1; LATS 1:1; LMFS 1; MTCW 1, 2; NFS
  17; RGSF 2; RGWL 2, 3; SSFS 4, 9;
  TWA
**Mannheim, Karl** 1893-1947 ........... **TCLC 65**
  See also CA 204
**Manning, David**
  See Faust, Frederick (Schiller)
  See also TCWW 2
**Manning, Frederic** 1882-1935 ........ **TCLC 25**
  See also CA 124; 216; DLB 260
**Manning, Olivia** 1915-1980 .......... **CLC 5, 19**
  See also CA 5-8R; 101; CANR 29; EWL 3;
  FW; MTCW 1; RGEL 2
**Mano, D. Keith** 1942- ................... **CLC 2, 10**
  See also CA 25-28R; CAAS 6; CANR 26,
  57; DLB 6
**Mansfield, Katherine** . **SSC 9, 23, 38; TCLC
  2, 8, 39; WLC**
  See Beauchamp, Kathleen Mansfield
  See also BPFB 2; BRW 7; DAB; DLB 162;
  EWL 3; EXPS; FW; GLL 1; RGEL 2;
  RGSF 2; SSFS 2, 8, 10, 11; WWE 1
**Manso, Peter** 1940- ............................ **CLC 39**
  See also CA 29-32R; CANR 44
**Mantecon, Juan Jimenez**
  See Jimenez (Mantecon), Juan Ramon
**Mantel, Hilary (Mary)** 1952- .......... **CLC 144**
  See also CA 125; CANR 54, 101; CN 7;
  DLB 271; RHW
**Manton, Peter**
  See Creasey, John
**Man Without a Spleen, A**
  See Chekhov, Anton (Pavlovich)
**Manzoni, Alessandro** 1785-1873 ... **NCLC 29,
  98**
  See also EW 5; RGWL 2, 3; TWA
**Map, Walter** 1140-1209 ................. **CMLC 32**
**Mapu, Abraham (ben Jekutiel)**
  1808-1867 ................................ **NCLC 18**
**Mara, Sally**
  See Queneau, Raymond
**Maracle, Lee** 1950- ............................ **NNAL**
  See also CA 149
**Marat, Jean Paul** 1743-1793 ................ **LC 10**
**Marcel, Gabriel Honore** 1889-1973 . **CLC 15**
  See also CA 102; 45-48; EWL 3; MTCW 1,
  2
**March, William** 1893-1954 ............. **TCLC 96**
  See also CA 216
**Marchbanks, Samuel**
  See Davies, (William) Robertson
  See also CCA 1
**Marchi, Giacomo**
  See Bassani, Giorgio
**Marcus Aurelius**
  See Aurelius, Marcus
  See also AW 2
**Marguerite**
  See de Navarre, Marguerite
**Marguerite d'Angouleme**
  See de Navarre, Marguerite
  See also GFL Beginnings to 1789
**Marguerite de Navarre**
  See de Navarre, Marguerite
  See also RGWL 2, 3

**Margulies, Donald** 1954- .................. **CLC 76**
  See also AAYA 57; CA 200; DFS 13; DLB
  228
**Marie de France** c. 12th cent. - ..... **CMLC 8;
  PC 22**
  See also DLB 208; FW; RGWL 2, 3
**Marie de l'Incarnation** 1599-1672 ...... **LC 10**
**Marier, Captain Victor**
  See Griffith, D(avid Lewelyn) W(ark)
**Mariner, Scott**
  See Pohl, Frederik
**Marinetti, Filippo Tommaso**
  1876-1944 ................................ **TCLC 10**
  See also CA 107; DLB 114, 264; EW 9;
  EWL 3
**Marivaux, Pierre Carlet de Chamblain de**
  1688-1763 ............................ **DC 7; LC 4**
  See also GFL Beginnings to 1789; RGWL
  2, 3; TWA
**Markandaya, Kamala** .................. **CLC 8, 38**
  See Taylor, Kamala (Purnaiya)
  See also BYA 13; CN 7; EWL 3
**Markfield, Wallace** 1926-2002 ............ **CLC 8**
  See also CA 69-72; 208; CAAS 3; CN 7;
  DLB 2, 28; DLBY 2002
**Markham, Edwin** 1852-1940 .......... **TCLC 47**
  See also CA 160; DLB 54, 186; RGAL 4
**Markham, Robert**
  See Amis, Kingsley (William)
**Markoosie** ............................................. **NNAL**
  See Patsauq, Markoosie
  See also CLR 23; DAM MULT
**Marks, J**
  See Highwater, Jamake (Mamake)
**Marks, J.**
  See Highwater, Jamake (Mamake)
**Marks-Highwater, J**
  See Highwater, Jamake (Mamake)
**Marks-Highwater, J.**
  See Highwater, Jamake (Mamake)
**Markson, David M(errill)** 1927- ....... **CLC 67**
  See also CA 49-52; CANR 1, 91; CN 7
**Marlatt, Daphne (Buckle)** 1942- .... **CLC 168**
  See also CA 25-28R; CANR 17, 39; CN 7;
  CP 7; CWP; DLB 60; FW
**Marley, Bob** ................................... **CLC 17**
  See Marley, Robert Nesta
**Marley, Robert Nesta** 1945-1981
  See Marley, Bob
  See also CA 107; 103
**Marlowe, Christopher** 1564-1593 . **DC 1; LC
  22, 47; PC 57; WLC**
  See also BRW 1; BRWR 1; CDBLB Before
  1660; DA; DA3; DAB; DAC; DAM
  DRAM, MST; DFS 1, 5, 13; DLB 62;
  EXPP; LMFS 1; RGEL 2; TEA; WLIT 3
**Marlowe, Stephen** 1928- .................... **CLC 70**
  See Queen, Ellery
  See also CA 13-16R; CANR 6, 55; CMW
  4; SFW 4
**Marmion, Shakerley** 1603-1639 .......... **LC 89**
  See also DLB 58; RGEL 2
**Marmontel, Jean-Francois** 1723-1799 .. **LC 2**
**Maron, Monika** 1941- ..................... **CLC 165**
  See also CA 201
**Marquand, John P(hillips)**
  1893-1960 ............................ **CLC 2, 10**
  See also AMW; BPFB 2; CA 85-88; CANR
  73; CMW 4; DLB 9, 102; EWL 3; MTCW
  2; RGAL 4
**Marques, Rene** 1919-1979 .. **CLC 96; HLC 2**
  See also CA 97-100; 85-88; CANR 78;
  DAM MULT; DLB 305; EWL 3; HW 1,
  2; LAW; RGSF 2
**Marquez, Gabriel (Jose) Garcia**
  See Garcia Marquez, Gabriel (Jose)

**Marquis, Don(ald Robert Perry)**
  1878-1937 ................................ **TCLC 7**
  See also CA 104; 166; DLB 11, 25; RGAL
  4
**Marquis de Sade**
  See Sade, Donatien Alphonse Francois
**Marric, J. J.**
  See Creasey, John
  See also MSW
**Marryat, Frederick** 1792-1848 ........ **NCLC 3**
  See also DLB 21, 163; RGEL 2; WCH
**Marsden, James**
  See Creasey, John
**Marsh, Edward** 1872-1953 ............ **TCLC 99**
**Marsh, (Edith) Ngaio** 1895-1982 .. **CLC 7, 53**
  See also CA 9-12R; CANR 6, 58; CMW 4;
  CPW; DAM POP; DLB 77; MSW;
  MTCW 1, 2; RGEL 2; TEA
**Marshall, Garry** 1934- ...................... **CLC 17**
  See also AAYA 3; CA 111; SATA 60
**Marshall, Paule** 1929- .. **BLC 3; CLC 27, 72;
  SSC 3**
  See also AFAW 1, 2; AMWS 11; BPFB 2;
  BW 2, 3; CA 77-80; CANR 25, 73, 129;
  CN 7; DA3; DAM MULT; DLB 33, 157,
  227; EWL 3; LATS 1:2; MTCW 1, 2;
  RGAL 4; SSFS 15
**Marshallik**
  See Zangwill, Israel
**Marsten, Richard**
  See Hunter, Evan
**Marston, John** 1576-1634 .................... **LC 33**
  See also BRW 2; DAM DRAM; DLB 58,
  172; RGEL 2
**Martel, Yann** 1963- .......................... **CLC 192**
  See also CA 146; CANR 114
**Martha, Henry**
  See Harris, Mark
**Marti, Jose**
  See Marti (y Perez), Jose (Julian)
  See also DLB 290
**Marti (y Perez), Jose (Julian)**
  1853-1895 .................. **HLC 2; NCLC 63**
  See Marti, Jose
  See also DAM MULT; HW 2; LAW; RGWL
  2, 3; WLIT 1
**Martial** c. 40-c. 104 .......... **CMLC 35; PC 10**
  See also AW 2; CDWLB 1; DLB 211;
  RGWL 2, 3
**Martin, Ken**
  See Hubbard, L(afayette) Ron(ald)
**Martin, Richard**
  See Creasey, John
**Martin, Steve** 1945- .......................... **CLC 30**
  See also AAYA 53; CA 97-100; CANR 30,
  100; DFS 19; MTCW 1
**Martin, Valerie** 1948- ...................... **CLC 89**
  See also BEST 90:2; CA 85-88; CANR 49,
  89
**Martin, Violet Florence** 1862-1915 .. **SSC 56;
  TCLC 51**
**Martin, Webber**
  See Silverberg, Robert
**Martindale, Patrick Victor**
  See White, Patrick (Victor Martindale)
**Martin du Gard, Roger**
  1881-1958 ................................ **TCLC 24**
  See also CA 118; CANR 94; DLB 65; EWL
  3; GFL 1789 to the Present; RGWL 2, 3
**Martineau, Harriet** 1802-1876 ...... **NCLC 26,
  137**
  See also DLB 21, 55, 159, 163, 166, 190;
  FW; RGEL 2; YABC 2
**Martines, Julia**
  See O'Faolain, Julia
**Martinez, Enrique Gonzalez**
  See Gonzalez Martinez, Enrique
**Martinez, Jacinto Benavente y**
  See Benavente (y Martinez), Jacinto

**Martinez de la Rosa, Francisco de Paula**
1787-1862 ............................... **NCLC 102**
See also TWA

**Martinez Ruiz, Jose** 1873-1967
See Azorin; Ruiz, Jose Martinez
See also CA 93-96; HW 1

**Martinez Sierra, Gregorio**
1881-1947 ...................................... **TCLC 6**
See also CA 115; EWL 3

**Martinez Sierra, Maria (de la O'LeJarraga)**
1874-1974 ...................................... **TCLC 6**
See also CA 115; EWL 3

**Martinsen, Martin**
See Follett, Ken(neth Martin)

**Martinson, Harry (Edmund)**
1904-1978 ..................................... **CLC 14**
See also CA 77-80; CANR 34, 130; DLB
259; EWL 3

**Martyn, Edward** 1859-1923 ......... **TCLC 131**
See also CA 179; DLB 10; RGEL 2

**Marut, Ret**
See Traven, B.

**Marut, Robert**
See Traven, B.

**Marvell, Andrew** 1621-1678 .... **LC 4, 43; PC
10; WLC**
See also BRW 2; BRWR 2; CDBLB 1660-
1789; DA; DAB; DAC; DAM MST,
POET; DLB 131; EXPP; PFS 5; RGEL 2;
TEA; WP

**Marx, Karl (Heinrich)**
1818-1883 ........................... **NCLC 17, 114**
See also DLB 129; LATS 1:1; TWA

**Masaoka, Shiki** -1902 ...................... **TCLC 18**
See Masaoka, Tsunenori
See also RGWL 3

**Masaoka, Tsunenori** 1867-1902
See Masaoka, Shiki
See also CA 117; 191; TWA

**Masefield, John (Edward)**
1878-1967 .............................. **CLC 11, 47**
See also CA 19-20; 25-28R; CANR 33;
CAP 2; CDBLB 1890-1914; DAM POET;
DLB 10, 19, 153, 160; EWL 3; EXPP;
FANT; MTCW 1, 2; PFS 5; RGEL 2;
SATA 19

**Maso, Carole** 19(?)- .......................... **CLC 44**
See also CA 170; GLL 2; RGAL 4

**Mason, Bobbie Ann** 1940- ... **CLC 28, 43, 82,
154; SSC 4**
See also AAYA 5, 42; AMWS 8; BPFB 2;
CA 53-56; CANR 11, 31, 58, 83, 125;
CDALBS; CN 7; CSW; DA3; DLB 173;
DLBY 1987; EWL 3; EXPS; INT CANR-
31; MTCW 1, 2; NFS 4; RGAL 4; RGSF
2; SSFS 3, 8, 20; YAW

**Mason, Ernst**
See Pohl, Frederik

**Mason, Hunni B.**
See Sternheim, (William Adolf) Carl

**Mason, Lee W.**
See Malzberg, Barry N(athaniel)

**Mason, Nick** 1945- ........................... **CLC 35**

**Mason, Tally**
See Derleth, August (William)

**Mass, Anna** ........................................ **CLC 59**

**Mass, William**
See Gibson, William

**Massinger, Philip** 1583-1640 ................ **LC 70**
See also DLB 58; RGEL 2

**Master Lao**
See Lao Tzu

**Masters, Edgar Lee** 1868-1950 ...... **PC 1, 36;
TCLC 2, 25; WLCS**
See also AMWS 1; CA 104; 133; CDALB
1865-1917; DA; DAC; DAM MST,
POET; DLB 54; EWL 3; EXPP; MTCW
1, 2; RGAL 4; TUS; WP

**Masters, Hilary** 1928- ...................... **CLC 48**
See also CA 25-28R, 217; CAAE 217;
CANR 13, 47, 97; CN 7; DLB 244

**Mastrosimone, William** 19(?)- .......... **CLC 36**
See also CA 186; CAD; CD 5

**Mathe, Albert**
See Camus, Albert

**Mather, Cotton** 1663-1728 ................... **LC 38**
See also AMWS 2; CDALB 1640-1865;
DLB 24, 30, 140; RGAL 4; TUS

**Mather, Increase** 1639-1723 ................. **LC 38**
See also DLB 24

**Matheson, Richard (Burton)** 1926- .. **CLC 37**
See also AAYA 31; CA 97-100; CANR 88,
99; DLB 8, 44; HGG; INT CA-97-100;
SCFW 2; SFW 4; SUFW 2

**Mathews, Harry** 1930- ................. **CLC 6, 52**
See also CA 21-24R; CAAS 6; CANR 18,
40, 98; CN 7

**Mathews, John Joseph** 1894-1979 .. **CLC 84;
NNAL**
See also CA 19-20; 142; CANR 45; CAP 2;
DAM MULT; DLB 175

**Mathias, Roland (Glyn)** 1915- .......... **CLC 45**
See also CA 97-100; CANR 19, 41; CP 7;
DLB 27

**Matsuo Basho** 1644-1694 .......... **LC 62; PC 3**
See Basho, Matsuo
See also DAM POET; PFS 2, 7

**Mattheson, Rodney**
See Creasey, John

**Matthews, (James) Brander**
1852-1929 ...................................... **TCLC 95**
See also DLB 71, 78; DLBD 13

**Matthews, Greg** 1949- ...................... **CLC 45**
See also CA 135

**Matthews, William (Procter III)**
1942-1997 ...................................... **CLC 40**
See also AMWS 9; CA 29-32R; 162; CAAS
18; CANR 12, 57; CP 7; DLB 5

**Matthias, John (Edward)** 1941- ......... **CLC 9**
See also CA 33-36R; CANR 56; CP 7

**Matthiessen, F(rancis) O(tto)**
1902-1950 ...................................... **TCLC 100**
See also CA 185; DLB 63

**Matthiessen, Peter** 1927- ... **CLC 5, 7, 11, 32,
64**
See also AAYA 6, 40; AMWS 5; ANW;
BEST 90:4; BPFB 2; CA 9-12R; CANR
21, 50, 73, 100; CN 7; DA3; DAM NOV;
DLB 6, 173, 275; MTCW 1, 2; SATA 27

**Maturin, Charles Robert**
1780(?)-1824 ............................... **NCLC 6**
See also BRWS 8; DLB 178; HGG; LMFS
1; RGEL 2; SUFW

**Matute (Ausejo), Ana Maria** 1925- .. **CLC 11**
See also CA 89-92; CANR 129; CWW 2;
EWL 3; MTCW 1; RGSF 2

**Maugham, W. S.**
See Maugham, W(illiam) Somerset

**Maugham, W(illiam) Somerset**
1874-1965 .. **CLC 1, 11, 15, 67, 93; SSC
8; WLC**
See also AAYA 55; BPFB 2; BRW 6; CA
5-8R; 25-28R; CANR 40, 127; CDBLB
1914-1945; CMW 4; DA; DA3; DAB;
DAC; DAM DRAM, MST, NOV; DLB
10, 36, 77, 100, 162, 195; EWL 3; LAIT
3; MTCW 1, 2; RGEL 2; RGSF 2; SATA
54; SSFS 17

**Maugham, William Somerset**
See Maugham, W(illiam) Somerset

**Maupassant, (Henri Rene Albert) Guy de**
1850-1893 . **NCLC 1, 42, 83; SSC 1, 64;
WLC**
See also BYA 14; DA; DA3; DAB; DAC;
DAM MST; DLB 123; EW 7; EXPS; GFL

1789 to the Present; LAIT 2; LMFS 1;
RGSF 2; RGWL 2, 3; SSFS 4; SUFW;
TWA

**Maupin, Armistead (Jones, Jr.)**
1944- ............................................. **CLC 95**
See also CA 125; 130; CANR 58, 101;
CPW; DA3; DAM POP; DLB 278; GLL
1; INT CA-130; MTCW 2

**Maurhut, Richard**
See Traven, B.

**Mauriac, Claude** 1914-1996 ............... **CLC 9**
See also CA 89-92; 152; CWW 2; DLB 83;
EWL 3; GFL 1789 to the Present

**Mauriac, Francois (Charles)**
1885-1970 ........... **CLC 4, 9, 56; SSC 24**
See also CA 25-28; CAP 2; DLB 65; EW
10; EWL 3; GFL 1789 to the Present;
MTCW 1, 2; RGWL 2, 3; TWA

**Mavor, Osborne Henry** 1888-1951
See Bridie, James
See also CA 104

**Maxwell, William (Keepers, Jr.)**
1908-2000 ...................................... **CLC 19**
See also AMWS 8; CA 93-96; 189; CANR
54, 95; CN 7; DLB 218, 278; DLBY
1980; INT CA-93-96; SATA-Obit 128

**May, Elaine** 1932- ............................. **CLC 16**
See also CA 124; 142; CAD; CWD; DLB
44

**Mayakovski, Vladimir (Vladimirovich)**
1893-1930 ............................. **TCLC 4, 18**
See Maiakovskii, Vladimir; Mayakovsky,
Vladimir
See also CA 104; 158; EWL 3; MTCW 2;
SFW 4; TWA

**Mayakovsky, Vladimir**
See Mayakovski, Vladimir (Vladimirovich)
See also EW 11; WP

**Mayhew, Henry** 1812-1887 ............. **NCLC 31**
See also DLB 18, 55, 190

**Mayle, Peter** 1939(?)- ........................ **CLC 89**
See also CA 139; CANR 64, 109

**Maynard, Joyce** 1953- ....................... **CLC 23**
See also CA 111; 129; CANR 64

**Mayne, William (James Carter)**
1928- ............................................. **CLC 12**
See also AAYA 20; CA 9-12R; CANR 37,
80, 100; CLR 25; FANT; JRDA; MAI-
CYA 1, 2; MAICYAS 1; SAAS 11; SATA
6, 68, 122; SUFW 2; YAW

**Mayo, Jim**
See L'Amour, Louis (Dearborn)
See also TCWW 2

**Maysles, Albert** 1926- ....................... **CLC 16**
See also CA 29-32R

**Maysles, David** 1932-1987 ................. **CLC 16**
See also CA 191

**Mazer, Norma Fox** 1931- ................... **CLC 26**
See also AAYA 5, 36; BYA 1, 8; CA 69-72;
CANR 12, 32, 66, 129; CLR 23; JRDA;
MAICYA 1, 2; SAAS 1; SATA 24, 67,
105; WYA; YAW

**Mazzini, Guiseppe** 1805-1872 ........ **NCLC 34**

**McAlmon, Robert (Menzies)**
1895-1956 ...................................... **TCLC 97**
See also CA 107; 168; DLB 4, 45; DLBD
15; GLL 1

**McAuley, James Phillip** 1917-1976 .. **CLC 45**
See also CA 97-100; DLB 260; RGEL 2

**McBain, Ed**
See Hunter, Evan
See also MSW

**McBrien, William (Augustine)**
1930- ............................................. **CLC 44**
See also CA 107; CANR 90

**McCabe, Patrick** 1955- ................... **CLC 133**
See also BRWS 9; CA 130; CANR 50, 90;
CN 7; DLB 194

**McCaffrey, Anne (Inez)** 1926- .......... **CLC 17**
 See also AAYA 6, 34; AITN 2; BEST 89:2;
 BPFB 2; BYA 5; CA 25-28R, 227; CAAE
 227; CANR 15, 35, 55, 96; CLR 49;
 CPW; DA3; DAM NOV, POP; DLB 8;
 JRDA; MAICYA 1, 2; MTCW 1, 2; SAAS
 11; SATA 8, 70, 116, 152; SATA-Essay
 152; SFW 4; SUFW 2; WYA; YAW
**McCall, Nathan** 1955(?)- ................... **CLC 86**
 See also AAYA 59; BW 3; CA 146; CANR
 88
**McCann, Arthur**
 See Campbell, John W(ood, Jr.)
**McCann, Edson**
 See Pohl, Frederik
**McCarthy, Charles, Jr.** 1933-
 See McCarthy, Cormac
 See also CANR 42, 69, 101; CN 7; CPW;
 CSW; DA3; DAM POP; MTCW 2
**McCarthy, Cormac** .............. **CLC 4, 57, 101**
 See McCarthy, Charles, Jr.
 See also AAYA 41; AMWS 8; BPFB 2; CA
 13-16R; CANR 10; DLB 6, 143, 256;
 EWL 3; LATS 1:2; TCWW 2
**McCarthy, Mary (Therese)**
 1912-1989 .. **CLC 1, 3, 5, 14, 24, 39, 59;**
 **SSC 24**
 See also AMW; BPFB 2; CA 5-8R; 129;
 CANR 16, 50, 64; DA3; DLB 2; DLBY
 1981; EWL 3; FW; INT CANR-16;
 MAWW; MTCW 1, 2; RGAL 4; TUS
**McCartney, (James) Paul** 1942- . **CLC 12, 35**
 See also CA 146; CANR 111
**McCauley, Stephen (D.)** 1955- .......... **CLC 50**
 See also CA 141
**McClaren, Peter** ................................. **CLC 70**
**McClure, Michael (Thomas)** 1932- ... **CLC 6,**
 **10**
 See also BG 3; CA 21-24R; CAD; CANR
 17, 46, 77, 131; CD 5; CP 7; DLB 16;
 WP
**McCorkle, Jill (Collins)** 1958- .......... **CLC 51**
 See also CA 121; CANR 113; CSW; DLB
 234; DLBY 1987
**McCourt, Frank** 1930- ................... **CLC 109**
 See also AMWS 12; CA 157; CANR 97;
 NCFS 1
**McCourt, James** 1941- ...................... **CLC 5**
 See also CA 57-60; CANR 98
**McCourt, Malachy** 1931- ................ **CLC 119**
 See also SATA 126
**McCoy, Horace (Stanley)**
 1897-1955 ................................. **TCLC 28**
 See also AMWS 13; CA 108; 155; CMW 4;
 DLB 9
**McCrae, John** 1872-1918 ................ **TCLC 12**
 See also CA 109; DLB 92; PFS 5
**McCreigh, James**
 See Pohl, Frederik
**McCullers, (Lula) Carson (Smith)**
 1917-1967 .... **CLC 1, 4, 10, 12, 48, 100;**
 **SSC 9, 24; TCLC 155; WLC**
 See also AAYA 21; AMW; AMWC 2; BPFB
 2; CA 5-8R; 25-28R; CABS 1, 3; CANR
 18, 132; CDALB 1941-1968; DA; DA3;
 DAB; DAC; DAM MST, NOV; DFS 5,
 18; DLB 2, 7, 173, 228; EWL 3; EXPS;
 FW; GLL 1; LAIT 3, 4; MAWW; MTCW
 1, 2; NFS 6, 13; RGAL 4; RGSF 2; SATA
 27; SSFS 5; TUS; YAW
**McCulloch, John Tyler**
 See Burroughs, Edgar Rice
**McCullough, Colleen** 1938(?)- .. **CLC 27, 107**
 See also AAYA 36; BPFB 2; CA 81-84;
 CANR 17, 46, 67, 98; CPW; DA3; DAM
 NOV, POP; MTCW 1; RHW
**McCunn, Ruthanne Lum** 1946- .......... **AAL**
 See also CA 119; CANR 43, 96; LAIT 2;
 SATA 63

**McDermott, Alice** 1953- .................... **CLC 90**
 See also CA 109; CANR 40, 90, 126; DLB
 292
**McElroy, Joseph** 1930- .................. **CLC 5, 47**
 See also CA 17-20R; CN 7
**McEwan, Ian (Russell)** 1948- .... **CLC 13, 66,**
 **169**
 See also BEST 90:4; BRWS 4; CA 61-64;
 CANR 14, 41, 69, 87, 132; CN 7; DAM
 NOV; DLB 14, 194; HGG; MTCW 1, 2;
 RGSF 2; SUFW 2; TEA
**McFadden, David** 1940- .................... **CLC 48**
 See also CA 104; CP 7; DLB 60; INT CA-
 104
**McFarland, Dennis** 1950- .................. **CLC 65**
 See also CA 165; CANR 110
**McGahern, John** 1934- ... **CLC 5, 9, 48, 156;**
 **SSC 17**
 See also CA 17-20R; CANR 29, 68, 113;
 CN 7; DLB 14, 231; MTCW 1
**McGinley, Patrick (Anthony)** 1937- . **CLC 41**
 See also CA 120; 127; CANR 56; INT CA-
 127
**McGinley, Phyllis** 1905-1978 ............. **CLC 14**
 See also CA 9-12R; 77-80; CANR 19;
 CWRI 5; DLB 11, 48; PFS 9, 13; SATA
 2, 44; SATA-Obit 24
**McGinniss, Joe** 1942- ........................ **CLC 32**
 See also AITN 2; BEST 89:2; CA 25-28R;
 CANR 26, 70; CPW; DLB 185; INT
 CANR-26
**McGivern, Maureen Daly**
 See Daly, Maureen
**McGrath, Patrick** 1950- .................... **CLC 55**
 See also CA 136; CANR 65; CN 7; DLB
 231; HGG; SUFW 2
**McGrath, Thomas (Matthew)**
 1916-1990 ............................. **CLC 28, 59**
 See also AMWS 10; CA 9-12R; 132; CANR
 6, 33, 95; DAM POET; MTCW 1; SATA
 41; SATA-Obit 66
**McGuane, Thomas (Francis III)**
 1939- .................. **CLC 3, 7, 18, 45, 127**
 See also AITN 2; BPFB 2; CA 49-52;
 CANR 5, 24, 49, 94; CN 7; DLB 2, 212;
 DLBY 1980; EWL 3; INT CANR-24;
 MTCW 1; TCWW 2
**McGuckian, Medbh** 1950- ....... **CLC 48, 174;**
 **PC 27**
 See also BRWS 5; CA 143; CP 7; CWP;
 DAM POET; DLB 40
**McHale, Tom** 1942(?)-1982 ............. **CLC 3, 5**
 See also AITN 1; CA 77-80; 106
**McIlvanney, William** 1936- ............... **CLC 42**
 See also CA 25-28R; CANR 61; CMW 4;
 DLB 14, 207
**McIlwraith, Maureen Mollie Hunter**
 See Hunter, Mollie
 See also SATA 2
**McInerney, Jay** 1955- ............... **CLC 34, 112**
 See also AAYA 18; BPFB 2; CA 116; 123;
 CANR 45, 68, 116; CN 7; CPW; DA3;
 DAM POP; DLB 292; INT CA-123;
 MTCW 2
**McIntyre, Vonda N(eel)** 1948- .......... **CLC 18**
 See also CA 81-84; CANR 17, 34, 69;
 MTCW 1; SFW 4; YAW
**McKay, Claude** .......... **BLC 3; HR 3; PC 2;**
 **TCLC 7, 41; WLC**
 See McKay, Festus Claudius
 See also AFAW 1, 2; AMWS 10; DAB;
 DLB 4, 45, 51, 117; EWL 3; EXPP; GLL
 2; LAIT 3; LMFS 2; PAB; PFS 4; RGAL
 4; WP
**McKay, Festus Claudius** 1889-1948
 See McKay, Claude
 See also BW 1, 3; CA 104; 124; CANR 73;
 DA; DAC; DAM MST, MULT, NOV,
 POET; MTCW 1, 2; TUS

**McKuen, Rod** 1933- ....................... **CLC 1, 3**
 See also AITN 1; CA 41-44R; CANR 40
**McLoughlin, R. B.**
 See Mencken, H(enry) L(ouis)
**McLuhan, (Herbert) Marshall**
 1911-1980 ............................. **CLC 37, 83**
 See also CA 9-12R; 102; CANR 12, 34, 61;
 DLB 88; INT CANR-12; MTCW 1, 2
**McManus, Declan Patrick Aloysius**
 See Costello, Elvis
**McMillan, Terry (L.)** 1951- . **BLCS; CLC 50,**
 **61, 112**
 See also AAYA 21; AMWS 13; BPFB 2;
 BW 2, 3; CA 140; CANR 60, 104, 131;
 CPW; DA3; DAM MULT, NOV, POP;
 MTCW 2; RGAL 4; YAW
**McMurtry, Larry (Jeff)** 1936- .. **CLC 2, 3, 7,**
 **11, 27, 44, 127**
 See also AAYA 15; AITN 2; AMWS 5;
 BEST 89:2; BPFB 2; CA 5-8R; CANR
 19, 43, 64, 103; CDALB 1968-1988; CN
 7; CPW; CSW; DA3; DAM NOV, POP;
 DLB 2, 143, 256; DLBY 1980, 1987;
 EWL 3; MTCW 1, 2; RGAL 4; TCWW 2
**McNally, T. M.** 1961- ....................... **CLC 82**
**McNally, Terrence** 1939- .... **CLC 4, 7, 41, 91**
 See also AMWS 13; CA 45-48; CAD;
 CANR 2, 56, 116; CD 5; DA3; DAM
 DRAM; DFS 16, 19; DLB 7, 249; EWL
 3; GLL 1; MTCW 2
**McNamer, Deirdre** 1950- .................. **CLC 70**
**McNeal, Tom** ................................... **CLC 119**
**McNeile, Herman Cyril** 1888-1937
 See Sapper
 See also CA 184; CMW 4; DLB 77
**McNickle, (William) D'Arcy**
 1904-1977 ................... **CLC 89; NNAL**
 See also CA 9-12R; 85-88; CANR 5, 45;
 DAM MULT; DLB 175, 212; RGAL 4;
 SATA-Obit 22
**McPhee, John (Angus)** 1931- ........... **CLC 36**
 See also AMWS 3; ANW; BEST 90:1; CA
 65-68; CANR 20, 46, 64, 69, 121; CPW;
 DLB 185, 275; MTCW 1, 2; TUS
**McPherson, James Alan** 1943- . **BLCS; CLC**
 **19, 77**
 See also BW 1, 3; CA 25-28R; CAAS 17;
 CANR 24, 74; CN 7; CSW; DLB 38, 244;
 EWL 3; MTCW 1, 2; RGAL 4; RGSF 2
**McPherson, William (Alexander)**
 1933- ....................................... **CLC 34**
 See also CA 69-72; CANR 28; INT
 CANR-28
**McTaggart, J. McT. Ellis**
 See McTaggart, John McTaggart Ellis
**McTaggart, John McTaggart Ellis**
 1866-1925 ............................... **TCLC 105**
 See also CA 120; DLB 262
**Mead, George Herbert** 1863-1931 . **TCLC 89**
 See also CA 212; DLB 270
**Mead, Margaret** 1901-1978 ............... **CLC 37**
 See also AITN 1; CA 1-4R; 81-84; CANR
 4; DA3; FW; MTCW 1, 2; SATA-Obit 20
**Meaker, Marijane (Agnes)** 1927-
 See Kerr, M. E.
 See also CA 107; CANR 37, 63; INT CA-
 107; JRDA; MAICYA 1, 2; MAICYAS 1;
 MTCW 1; SATA 20, 61, 99; SATA-Essay
 111; YAW
**Medoff, Mark (Howard)** 1940- .... **CLC 6, 23**
 See also AITN 1; CA 53-56; CAD; CANR
 5; CD 5; DAM DRAM; DFS 4; DLB 7;
 INT CANR-5
**Medvedev, P. N.**
 See Bakhtin, Mikhail Mikhailovich
**Meged, Aharon**
 See Megged, Aharon
**Meged, Aron**
 See Megged, Aharon

**Megged, Aharon** 1920- ...................... **CLC 9**
  See also CA 49-52; CAAS 13; CANR 1;
  EWL 3

**Mehta, Gita** 1943- .......................... **CLC 179**
  See also CA 225; DNFS 2

**Mehta, Ved (Parkash)** 1934- ............. **CLC 37**
  See also CA 1-4R, 212; CAAE 212; CANR
  2, 23, 69; MTCW 1

**Melanchthon, Philipp** 1497-1560 ........ **LC 90**
  See also DLB 179

**Melanter**
  See Blackmore, R(ichard) D(oddridge)

**Meleager** c. 140B.C.-c. 70B.C. ...... **CMLC 53**

**Melies, Georges** 1861-1938 ............. **TCLC 81**

**Melikow, Loris**
  See Hofmannsthal, Hugo von

**Melmoth, Sebastian**
  See Wilde, Oscar (Fingal O'Flahertie Wills)

**Melo Neto, Joao Cabral de**
  See Cabral de Melo Neto, Joao
  See also CWW 2; EWL 3

**Meltzer, Milton** 1915- ...................... **CLC 26**
  See also AAYA 8, 45; BYA 2, 6; CA 13-
  16R; CANR 38, 92, 107; CLR 13; DLB
  61; JRDA; MAICYA 1, 2; SAAS 1; SATA
  1, 50, 80, 128; SATA-Essay 124; WYA;
  YAW

**Melville, Herman** 1819-1891 ..... **NCLC 3, 12,
  29, 45, 49, 91, 93, 123; SSC 1, 17, 46;
  WLC**
  See also AAYA 25; AMW; AMWR 1;
  CDALB 1640-1865; DA; DA3; DAB;
  DAC; DAM MST, NOV; DLB 3, 74, 250,
  254; EXPN; EXPS; LAIT 1, 2; NFS 7, 9;
  RGAL 4; RGSF 2; SATA 59; SSFS 3;
  TUS

**Members, Mark**
  See Powell, Anthony (Dymoke)

**Membreno, Alejandro** ...................... **CLC 59**

**Menander** c. 342B.C.-c. 293B.C. .... **CMLC 9,
  51; DC 3**
  See also AW 1; CDWLB 1; DAM DRAM;
  DLB 176; LMFS 1; RGWL 2, 3

**Menchu, Rigoberta** 1959- .. **CLC 160; HLCS
  2**
  See also CA 175; DNFS 1; WLIT 1

**Mencken, H(enry) L(ouis)**
  1880-1956 ................................ **TCLC 13**
  See also AMW; CA 105; 125; CDALB
  1917-1929; DLB 11, 29, 63, 137, 222;
  EWL 3; MTCW 1, 2; NCFS 4; RGAL 4;
  TUS

**Mendelsohn, Jane** 1965- .................... **CLC 99**
  See also CA 154; CANR 94

**Menton, Francisco de**
  See Chin, Frank (Chew, Jr.)

**Mercer, David** 1928-1980 .................... **CLC 5**
  See also CA 9-12R; 102; CANR 23; CBD;
  DAM DRAM; DLB 13; MTCW 1; RGEL
  2

**Merchant, Paul**
  See Ellison, Harlan (Jay)

**Meredith, George** 1828-1909 .. **PC 60; TCLC
  17, 43**
  See also CA 117; 153; CANR 80; CDBLB
  1832-1890; DAM POET; DLB 18, 35, 57,
  159; RGEL 2; TEA

**Meredith, William (Morris)** 1919- .... **CLC 4,
  13, 22, 55; PC 28**
  See also CA 9-12R; CAAS 14; CANR 6,
  40, 129; CP 7; DAM POET; DLB 5

**Merezhkovsky, Dmitrii Sergeevich**
  See Merezhkovsky, Dmitry Sergeyevich
  See also DLB 295

**Merezhkovsky, Dmitry Sergeyevich**
  See Merezhkovsky, Dmitry Sergeyevich
  See also EWL 3

**Merezhkovsky, Dmitry Sergeyevich**
  1865-1941 ................................ **TCLC 29**
  See Merezhkovsky, Dmitrii Sergeevich;
  Merezhkovsky, Dmitry Sergeevich
  See also CA 169

**Merimee, Prosper** 1803-1870 ... **NCLC 6, 65;
  SSC 7**
  See also DLB 119, 192; EW 6; EXPS; GFL
  1789 to the Present; RGSF 2; RGWL 2,
  3; SSFS 8; SUFW

**Merkin, Daphne** 1954- ...................... **CLC 44**
  See also CA 123

**Merleau-Ponty, Maurice**
  1908-1961 ................................ **TCLC 156**
  See also CA 114; 89-92; DLB 296; GFL
  1789 to the Present

**Merlin, Arthur**
  See Blish, James (Benjamin)

**Mernissi, Fatima** 1940- .................... **CLC 171**
  See also CA 152; FW

**Merrill, James (Ingram)** 1926-1995 .. **CLC 2,
  3, 6, 8, 13, 18, 34, 91; PC 28**
  See also AMWS 3; CA 13-16R; 147; CANR
  10, 49, 63, 108; DA3; DAM POET; DLB
  5, 165; DLBY 1985; EWL 3; INT CANR-
  10; MTCW 1, 2; PAB; RGAL 4

**Merriman, Alex**
  See Silverberg, Robert

**Merriman, Brian** 1747-1805 .......... **NCLC 70**

**Merritt, E. B.**
  See Waddington, Miriam

**Merton, Thomas (James)**
  1915-1968 . **CLC 1, 3, 11, 34, 83; PC 10**
  See also AMWS 8; CA 5-8R; 25-28R;
  CANR 22, 53, 111, 131; DA3; DLB 48;
  DLBY 1981; MTCW 1, 2

**Merwin, W(illiam) S(tanley)** 1927- ... **CLC 1,
  2, 3, 5, 8, 13, 18, 45, 88; PC 45**
  See also AMWS 3; CA 13-16R; CANR 15,
  51, 112; CP 7; DA3; DAM POET; DLB
  5, 169; EWL 3; INT CANR-15; MTCW
  1, 2; PAB; PFS 5, 15; RGAL 4

**Metcalf, John** 1938- ............ **CLC 37; SSC 43**
  See also CA 113; CN 7; DLB 60; RGSF 2;
  TWA

**Metcalf, Suzanne**
  See Baum, L(yman) Frank

**Mew, Charlotte (Mary)** 1870-1928 .. **TCLC 8**
  See also CA 105; 189; DLB 19, 135; RGEL
  2

**Mewshaw, Michael** 1943- ................... **CLC 9**
  See also CA 53-56; CANR 7, 47; DLBY
  1980

**Meyer, Conrad Ferdinand**
  1825-1898 ................................ **NCLC 81**
  See also DLB 129; EW; RGWL 2, 3

**Meyer, Gustav** 1868-1932
  See Meyrink, Gustav
  See also CA 117; 190

**Meyer, June**
  See Jordan, June (Meyer)

**Meyer, Lynn**
  See Slavitt, David R(ytman)

**Meyers, Jeffrey** 1939- ...................... **CLC 39**
  See also CA 73-76, 186; CAAE 186; CANR
  54, 102; DLB 111

**Meynell, Alice (Christina Gertrude
  Thompson)** 1847-1922 .............. **TCLC 6**
  See also CA 104; 177; DLB 19, 98; RGEL
  2

**Meyrink, Gustav** ........................... **TCLC 21**
  See Meyer, Gustav
  See also DLB 81; EWL 3

**Michaels, Leonard** 1933-2003 ..... **CLC 6, 25;
  SSC 16**
  See also CA 61-64; 216; CANR 21, 62, 119;
  CN 7; DLB 130; MTCW 1

**Michaux, Henri** 1899-1984 ........... **CLC 8, 19**
  See also CA 85-88; 114; DLB 258; EWL 3;
  GFL 1789 to the Present; RGWL 2, 3

**Micheaux, Oscar (Devereaux)**
  1884-1951 ................................ **TCLC 76**
  See also BW 3; CA 174; DLB 50; TCWW
  2

**Michelangelo** 1475-1564 .................... **LC 12**
  See also AAYA 43

**Michelet, Jules** 1798-1874 .............. **NCLC 31**
  See also EW 5; GFL 1789 to the Present

**Michels, Robert** 1876-1936 ............. **TCLC 88**
  See also CA 212

**Michener, James A(lbert)**
  1907(?)-1997 .. **CLC 1, 5, 11, 29, 60, 109**
  See also AAYA 27; AITN 1; BEST 90:1;
  BPFB 2; CA 5-8R; 161; CANR 21, 45,
  68; CN 7; CPW; DA3; DAM NOV, POP;
  DLB 6; MTCW 1, 2; RHW

**Mickiewicz, Adam** 1798-1855 . **NCLC 3, 101;
  PC 38**
  See also EW 5; RGWL 2, 3

**Middleton, (John) Christopher**
  1926- ........................................ **CLC 13**
  See also CA 13-16R; CANR 29, 54, 117;
  CP 7; DLB 40

**Middleton, Richard (Barham)**
  1882-1911 ................................ **TCLC 56**
  See also CA 187; DLB 156; HGG

**Middleton, Stanley** 1919- ............. **CLC 7, 38**
  See also CA 25-28R; CAAS 23; CANR 21,
  46, 81; CN 7; DLB 14

**Middleton, Thomas** 1580-1627 ...... **DC 5; LC
  33**
  See also BRW 2; DAM DRAM, MST; DFS
  18; DLB 58; RGEL 2

**Migueis, Jose Rodrigues** 1901-1980 . **CLC 10**
  See also DLB 287

**Mikszath, Kalman** 1847-1910 ........ **TCLC 31**
  See also CA 170

**Miles, Jack** ................................... **CLC 100**
  See also CA 200

**Miles, John Russiano**
  See Miles, Jack

**Miles, Josephine (Louise)**
  1911-1985 .............. **CLC 1, 2, 14, 34, 39**
  See also CA 1-4R; 116; CANR 2, 55; DAM
  POET; DLB 48

**Militant**
  See Sandburg, Carl (August)

**Mill, Harriet (Hardy) Taylor**
  1807-1858 ............................... **NCLC 102**
  See also FW

**Mill, John Stuart** 1806-1873 .... **NCLC 11, 58**
  See also CDBLB 1832-1890; DLB 55, 190,
  262; FW 1; RGEL 2; TEA

**Millar, Kenneth** 1915-1983 ............... **CLC 14**
  See Macdonald, Ross
  See also CA 9-12R; 110; CANR 16, 63,
  107; CMW 4; CPW; DA3; DAM POP;
  DLB 2, 226; DLBD 6; DLBY 1983;
  MTCW 1, 2

**Millay, E. Vincent**
  See Millay, Edna St. Vincent

**Millay, Edna St. Vincent** 1892-1950 .... **PC 6;
  TCLC 4, 49; WLCS**
  See Boyd, Nancy
  See also AMW; CA 104; 130; CDALB
  1917-1929; DA; DA3; DAB; DAC; DAM
  MST, POET; DLB 45, 249; EWL 3;
  EXPP; MAWW; MTCW 1, 2; PAB; PFS
  3, 17; RGAL 4; TUS; WP

**Miller, Arthur** 1915- ...... **CLC 1, 2, 6, 10, 15,
  26, 47, 78, 179; DC 1; WLC**
  See also AAYA 15; AITN 1; AMW; AMWC
  1; CA 1-4R; CABS 3; CAD; CANR 2,
  30, 54, 76, 132; CD 5; CDALB 1941-
  1968; DA; DA3; DAB; DAC; DAM
  DRAM, MST; DFS 1, 3, 8; DLB 7, 266;

EWL 3; LAIT 1, 4; LATS 1:2; MTCW 1, 2; RGAL 4; TUS; WYAS 1

**Miller, Henry (Valentine)**
1891-1980 .... **CLC 1, 2, 4, 9, 14, 43, 84; WLC**
See also AMW; BPFB 2; CA 9-12R; 97-100; CANR 33, 64; CDALB 1929-1941; DA; DA3; DAB; DAC; DAM MST, NOV; DLB 4, 9; DLBY 1980; EWL 3; MTCW 1, 2; RGAL 4; TUS

**Miller, Hugh** 1802-1856 ................ **NCLC 143**
See also DLB 190

**Miller, Jason** 1939(?)-2001 .................. **CLC 2**
See also AITN 1; CA 73-76; 197; CAD; CANR 130; DFS 12; DLB 7

**Miller, Sue** 1943- ................................. **CLC 44**
See also AMWS 12; BEST 90:3; CA 139; CANR 59, 91, 128; DA3; DAM POP; DLB 143

**Miller, Walter M(ichael, Jr.)**
1923-1996 ................................. **CLC 4, 30**
See also BPFB 2; CA 85-88; CANR 108; DLB 8; SCFW; SFW 4

**Millett, Kate** 1934- ........................... **CLC 67**
See also AITN 1; CA 73-76; CANR 32, 53, 76, 110; DA3; DLB 246; FW; GLL 1; MTCW 1, 2

**Millhauser, Steven (Lewis)** 1943- .... **CLC 21, 54, 109; SSC 57**
See also CA 110; 111; CANR 63, 114, 133; CN 7; DA3; DLB 2; FANT; INT CA-111; MTCW 2

**Millin, Sarah Gertrude** 1889-1968 ... **CLC 49**
See also CA 102; 93-96; DLB 225; EWL 3

**Milne, A(lan) A(lexander)**
1882-1956 ................................ **TCLC 6, 88**
See also BRWS 5; CA 104; 133; CLR 1, 26; CMW 4; CWRI 5; DA3; DAB; DAC; DAM MST; DLB 10, 77, 100, 160; FANT; MAICYA 1, 2; MTCW 1, 2; RGEL 2; SATA 100; WCH; YABC 1

**Milner, Ron(ald)** 1938-2004 ..... **BLC 3; CLC 56**
See also AITN 1; BW 1; CA 73-76; CAD; CANR 24, 81; CD 5; DAM MULT; DLB 38; MTCW 1

**Milnes, Richard Monckton**
1809-1885 ................................. **NCLC 61**
See also DLB 32, 184

**Milosz, Czeslaw** 1911- ...... **CLC 5, 11, 22, 31, 56, 82; PC 8; WLCS**
See also CA 81-84; CANR 23, 51, 91, 126; CDWLB 4; CWW 2; DA3; DAM MST, POET; DLB 215; EW 13; EWL 3; MTCW 1, 2; PFS 16; RGWL 2, 3

**Milton, John** 1608-1674 ..... **LC 9, 43, 92; PC 19, 29; WLC**
See also BRW 2; BRWR 2; CDBLB 1660-1789; DA; DA3; DAB; DAC; DAM MST, POET; DLB 131, 151, 281; EFS 1; EXPP; LAIT 1; PAB; PFS 3, 17; RGEL 2; TEA; WLIT 3; WP

**Min, Anchee** 1957- ............................. **CLC 86**
See also CA 146; CANR 94

**Minehaha, Cornelius**
See Wedekind, (Benjamin) Frank(lin)

**Miner, Valerie** 1947- .......................... **CLC 40**
See also CA 97-100; CANR 59; FW; GLL 2

**Minimo, Duca**
See D'Annunzio, Gabriele

**Minot, Susan** 1956- .................... **CLC 44, 159**
See also AMWS 6; CA 134; CANR 118; CN 7

**Minus, Ed** 1938- ................................ **CLC 39**
See also CA 185

**Mirabai** 1498(?)-1550(?) ...................... **PC 48**

**Miranda, Javier**
See Bioy Casares, Adolfo
See also CWW 2

**Mirbeau, Octave** 1848-1917 ........... **TCLC 55**
See also CA 216; DLB 123, 192; GFL 1789 to the Present

**Mirikitani, Janice** 1942- ...................... **AAL**
See also CA 211; RGAL 4

**Mirk, John** (?)-c. 1414 ...................... **LC 105**
See also DLB 146

**Miro (Ferrer), Gabriel (Francisco Victor)**
1879-1930 .................................. **TCLC 5**
See also CA 104; 185; EWL 3

**Misharin, Alexandr** ........................... **CLC 59**

**Mishima, Yukio** ... **CLC 2, 4, 6, 9, 27; DC 1; SSC 4**
See Hiraoka, Kimitake
See also AAYA 50; BPFB 2; GLL 1; MJW; MTCW 2; RGSF 2; RGWL 2, 3; SSFS 5, 12

**Mistral, Frederic** 1830-1914 ........... **TCLC 51**
See also CA 122; 213; GFL 1789 to the Present

**Mistral, Gabriela**
See Godoy Alcayaga, Lucila
See also DLB 283; DNFS 1; EWL 3; LAW; RGWL 2, 3; WP

**Mistry, Rohinton** 1952- ... **CLC 71, 196; SSC 73**
See also CA 141; CANR 86, 114; CCA 1; CN 7; DAC; SSFS 6

**Mitchell, Clyde**
See Ellison, Harlan (Jay)

**Mitchell, Emerson Blackhorse Barney**
1945- ........................................ **NNAL**
See also CA 45-48

**Mitchell, James Leslie** 1901-1935
See Gibbon, Lewis Grassic
See also CA 104; 188; DLB 15

**Mitchell, Joni** 1943- .......................... **CLC 12**
See also CA 112; CCA 1

**Mitchell, Joseph (Quincy)**
1908-1996 ................................. **CLC 98**
See also CA 77-80; 152; CANR 69; CN 7; CSW; DLB 185; DLBY 1996

**Mitchell, Margaret (Munnerlyn)**
1900-1949 ................................. **TCLC 11**
See also AAYA 23; BPFB 2; BYA 1; CA 109; 125; CANR 55, 94; CDALBS; DA3; DAM NOV, POP; DLB 9; LAIT 2; MTCW 1, 2; NFS 9; RGAL 4; RHW; TUS; WYAS 1; YAW

**Mitchell, Peggy**
See Mitchell, Margaret (Munnerlyn)

**Mitchell, S(ilas) Weir** 1829-1914 .... **TCLC 36**
See also CA 165; DLB 202; RGAL 4

**Mitchell, W(illiam) O(rmond)**
1914-1998 ................................. **CLC 25**
See also CA 77-80; 165; CANR 15, 43; CN 7; DAC; DAM MST; DLB 88

**Mitchell, William (Lendrum)**
1879-1936 ................................. **TCLC 81**
See also CA 213

**Mitford, Mary Russell** 1787-1855 ... **NCLC 4**
See also DLB 110, 116; RGEL 2

**Mitford, Nancy** 1904-1973 ................ **CLC 44**
See also CA 9-12R; DLB 191; RGEL 2

**Miyamoto, (Chujo) Yuriko**
1899-1951 ................................. **TCLC 37**
See Miyamoto Yuriko
See also CA 170, 174

**Miyamoto Yuriko**
See Miyamoto, (Chujo) Yuriko
See also DLB 180

**Miyazawa, Kenji** 1896-1933 ........... **TCLC 76**
See Miyazawa Kenji
See also CA 157; RGWL 3

**Miyazawa Kenji**
See Miyazawa, Kenji
See also EWL 3

**Mizoguchi, Kenji** 1898-1956 ........... **TCLC 72**
See also CA 167

**Mo, Timothy (Peter)** 1950(?)- ... **CLC 46, 134**
See also CA 117; CANR 128; CN 7; DLB 194; MTCW 1; WLIT 4; WWE 1

**Modarressi, Taghi (M.)** 1931-1997 ... **CLC 44**
See also CA 121; 134; INT CA-134

**Modiano, Patrick (Jean)** 1945- ......... **CLC 18**
See also CA 85-88; CANR 17, 40, 115; CWW 2; DLB 83, 299; EWL 3

**Mofolo, Thomas (Mokopu)**
1875(?)-1948 ............... **BLC 3; TCLC 22**
See also AFW; CA 121; 153; CANR 83; DAM MULT; DLB 225; EWL 3; MTCW 2; WLIT 2

**Mohr, Nicholasa** 1938- ........ **CLC 12; HLC 2**
See also AAYA 8, 46; CA 49-52; CANR 1, 32, 64; CLR 22; DAM MULT; DLB 145; HW 1, 2; JRDA; LAIT 5; LLW 1; MAICYA 2; MAICYAS 1; RGAL 4; SAAS 8; SATA 8, 97; SATA-Essay 113; WYA; YAW

**Moi, Toril** 1953- ................................. **CLC 172**
See also CA 154; CANR 102; FW

**Mojtabai, A(nn) G(race)** 1938- ..... **CLC 5, 9, 15, 29**
See also CA 85-88; CANR 88

**Moliere** 1622-1673 ..... **DC 13; LC 10, 28, 64; WLC**
See also DA; DA3; DAB; DAC; DAM DRAM, MST; DFS 13, 18, 20; DLB 268; EW 3; GFL Beginnings to 1789; LATS 1:1; RGWL 2, 3; TWA

**Molin, Charles**
See Mayne, William (James Carter)

**Molnar, Ferenc** 1878-1952 ............. **TCLC 20**
See also CA 109; 153; CANR 83; CDWLB 4; DAM DRAM; DLB 215; EWL 3; RGWL 2, 3

**Momaday, N(avarre) Scott** 1934- ...... **CLC 2, 19, 85, 95, 160; NNAL; PC 25; WLCS**
See also AAYA 11; AMWS 4; ANW; BPFB 2; BYA 12; CA 25-28R; CANR 14, 34, 68; CDALBS; CN 7; CPW; DA; DA3; DAB; DAC; DAM MST, MULT, NOV, POP; DLB 143, 175, 256; EWL 3; EXPP; INT CANR-14; LAIT 4; LATS 1:2; MTCW 1, 2; NFS 10; PFS 2, 11; RGAL 4; SATA 48; SATA-Brief 30; WP; YAW

**Monette, Paul** 1945-1995 ................... **CLC 82**
See also AMWS 10; CA 139; 147; CN 7; GLL 1

**Monroe, Harriet** 1860-1936 ............ **TCLC 12**
See also CA 109; 204; DLB 54, 91

**Monroe, Lyle**
See Heinlein, Robert A(nson)

**Montagu, Elizabeth** 1720-1800 ....... **NCLC 7, 117**
See also FW

**Montagu, Mary (Pierrepont) Wortley**
1689-1762 .................... **LC 9, 57; PC 16**
See also DLB 95, 101; RGEL 2

**Montagu, W. H.**
See Coleridge, Samuel Taylor

**Montague, John (Patrick)** 1929- ..... **CLC 13, 46**
See also CA 9-12R; CANR 9, 69, 121; CP 7; DLB 40; EWL 3; MTCW 1; PFS 12; RGEL 2

**Montaigne, Michel (Eyquem) de**
1533-1592 ................. **LC 8, 105; WLC**
See also DA; DAB; DAC; DAM MST; EW 2; GFL Beginnings to 1789; LMFS 1; RGWL 2, 3; TWA

**Montale, Eugenio** 1896-1981 ... **CLC 7, 9, 18;**
**PC 13**
See also CA 17-20R; 104; CANR 30; DLB
114; EW 11; EWL 3; MTCW 1; RGWL
2, 3; TWA

**Montesquieu, Charles-Louis de Secondat**
1689-1755 ................................ **LC 7, 69**
See also EW 3; GFL Beginnings to 1789;
TWA

**Montessori, Maria** 1870-1952 ...... **TCLC 103**
See also CA 115; 147

**Montgomery, (Robert) Bruce** 1921(?)-1978
See Crispin, Edmund
See also CA 179; 104; CMW 4

**Montgomery, L(ucy) M(aud)**
1874-1942 ........................ **TCLC 51, 140**
See also AAYA 12; BYA 1; CA 108; 137;
CLR 8, 91; DA3; DAC; DAM MST; DLB
92; DLBD 14; JRDA; MAICYA 1, 2;
MTCW 2; RGEL 2; SATA 100; TWA;
WCH; WYA; YABC 1

**Montgomery, Marion H., Jr.** 1925- .... **CLC 7**
See also AITN 1; CA 1-4R; CANR 3, 48;
CSW; DLB 6

**Montgomery, Max**
See Davenport, Guy (Mattison, Jr.)

**Montherlant, Henry (Milon) de**
1896-1972 .............................. **CLC 8, 19**
See also CA 85-88; 37-40R; DAM DRAM;
DLB 72; EW 11; EWL 3; GFL 1789 to
the Present; MTCW 1

**Monty Python**
See Chapman, Graham; Cleese, John
(Marwood); Gilliam, Terry (Vance); Idle,
Eric; Jones, Terence Graham Parry; Palin,
Michael (Edward)
See also AAYA 7

**Moodie, Susanna (Strickland)**
1803-1885 ........................ **NCLC 14, 113**
See also DLB 99

**Moody, Hiram (F. III)** 1961-
See Moody, Rick
See also CA 138; CANR 64, 112

**Moody, Minerva**
See Alcott, Louisa May

**Moody, Rick** ...................................... **CLC 147**
See Moody, Hiram (F. III)

**Moody, William Vaughan**
1869-1910 ................................ **TCLC 105**
See also CA 110; 178; DLB 7, 54; RGAL 4

**Mooney, Edward** 1951-
See Mooney, Ted
See also CA 130

**Mooney, Ted** .................................. **CLC 25**
See Mooney, Edward

**Moorcock, Michael (John)** 1939- ...... **CLC 5,**
**27, 58**
See Bradbury, Edward P.
See also AAYA 26; CA 45-48; CAAS 5;
CANR 2, 17, 38, 64, 122; CN 7; DLB 14,
231, 261; FANT; MTCW 1, 2; SATA 93;
SCFW 2; SFW 4; SUFW 1, 2

**Moore, Brian** 1921-1999 ... **CLC 1, 3, 5, 7, 8,**
**19, 32, 90**
See Bryan, Michael
See also BRWS 9; CA 1-4R; 174; CANR 1,
25, 42, 63; CCA 1; CN 7; DAB; DAC;
DAM MST; DLB 251; EWL 3; FANT;
MTCW 1, 2; RGEL 2

**Moore, Edward**
See Muir, Edwin
See also RGEL 2

**Moore, G. E.** 1873-1958 ................. **TCLC 89**
See also DLB 262

**Moore, George Augustus**
1852-1933 .................. **SSC 19; TCLC 7**
See also BRW 6; CA 104; 177; DLB 10,
18, 57, 135; EWL 3; RGEL 2; RGSF 2

**Moore, Lorrie** ....................... **CLC 39, 45, 68**
See Moore, Marie Lorena
See also AMWS 10; DLB 234; SSFS 19

**Moore, Marianne (Craig)**
1887-1972 .... **CLC 1, 2, 4, 8, 10, 13, 19,**
**47; PC 4, 49; WLCS**
See also AMW; CA 1-4R; 33-36R; CANR
3, 61; CDALB 1929-1941; DA; DA3;
DAB; DAC; DAM MST, POET; DLB 45;
DLBD 7; EWL 3; EXPP; MAWW;
MTCW 1, 2; PAB; PFS 14, 17; RGAL 4;
SATA 20; TUS; WP

**Moore, Marie Lorena** 1957- ........... **CLC 165**
See Moore, Lorrie
See also CA 116; CANR 39, 83; CN 7; DLB
234

**Moore, Thomas** 1779-1852 ....... **NCLC 6, 110**
See also DLB 96, 144; RGEL 2

**Moorhouse, Frank** 1938- .................... **SSC 40**
See also CA 118; CANR 92; CN 7; DLB
289; RGSF 2

**Mora, Pat(ricia)** 1942- ........................ **HLC 2**
See also AMWS 13; CA 129; CANR 57,
81, 112; CLR 58; DAM MULT; DLB 209;
HW 1, 2; LLW 1; MAICYA 2; SATA 92,
134

**Moraga, Cherrie** 1952- ...... **CLC 126; DC 22**
See also CA 131; CANR 66; DAM MULT;
DLB 82, 249; FW; GLL 1; HW 1, 2; LLW
1

**Morand, Paul** 1888-1976 .... **CLC 41; SSC 22**
See also CA 184; 69-72; DLB 65; EWL 3

**Morante, Elsa** 1918-1985 .............. **CLC 8, 47**
See also CA 85-88; 117; CANR 35; DLB
177; EWL 3; MTCW 1, 2; RGWL 2, 3

**Moravia, Alberto** ........ **CLC 2, 7, 11, 27, 46;**
**SSC 26**
See Pincherle, Alberto
See also DLB 177; EW 12; EWL 3; MTCW
2; RGSF 2; RGWL 2, 3

**More, Hannah** 1745-1833 ...... **NCLC 27, 141**
See also DLB 107, 109, 116, 158; RGEL 2

**More, Henry** 1614-1687 ........................ **LC 9**
See also DLB 126, 252

**More, Sir Thomas** 1478(?)-1535 .... **LC 10, 32**
See also BRWC 1; BRWS 7; DLB 136, 281;
LMFS 1; RGEL 2; TEA

**Moreas, Jean** ................................... **TCLC 18**
See Papadiamantopoulos, Johannes
See also GFL 1789 to the Present

**Moreton, Andrew Esq.**
See Defoe, Daniel

**Morgan, Berry** 1919-2002 .................. **CLC 6**
See also CA 49-52; 208; DLB 6

**Morgan, Claire**
See Highsmith, (Mary) Patricia
See also GLL 1

**Morgan, Edwin (George)** 1920- ....... **CLC 31**
See also BRWS 9; CA 5-8R; CANR 3, 43,
90; CP 7; DLB 27

**Morgan, (George) Frederick**
1922-2004 ................................ **CLC 23**
See also CA 17-20R; 224; CANR 21; CP 7

**Morgan, Harriet**
See Mencken, H(enry) L(ouis)

**Morgan, Jane**
See Cooper, James Fenimore

**Morgan, Janet** 1945- ........................ **CLC 39**
See also CA 65-68

**Morgan, Lady** 1776(?)-1859 ........... **NCLC 29**
See also DLB 116, 158; RGEL 2

**Morgan, Robin (Evonne)** 1941- .......... **CLC 2**
See also CA 69-72; CANR 29, 68; FW;
GLL 2; MTCW 1; SATA 80

**Morgan, Scott**
See Kuttner, Henry

**Morgan, Seth** 1949(?)-1990 .............. **CLC 65**
See also CA 185; 132

**Morgenstern, Christian (Otto Josef**
**Wolfgang)** 1871-1914 ............... **TCLC 8**
See also CA 105; 191; EWL 3

**Morgenstern, S.**
See Goldman, William (W.)

**Mori, Rintaro**
See Mori Ogai
See also CA 110

**Moricz, Zsigmond** 1879-1942 ........ **TCLC 33**
See also CA 165; DLB 215; EWL 3

**Morike, Eduard (Friedrich)**
1804-1875 ................................ **NCLC 10**
See also DLB 133; RGWL 2, 3

**Mori Ogai** 1862-1922 ..................... **TCLC 14**
See Ogai
See also CA 164; DLB 180; EWL 3; RGWL
3; TWA

**Moritz, Karl Philipp** 1756-1793 ........... **LC 2**
See also DLB 94

**Morland, Peter Henry**
See Faust, Frederick (Schiller)

**Morley, Christopher (Darlington)**
1890-1957 ................................ **TCLC 87**
See also CA 112; 213; DLB 9; RGAL 4

**Morren, Theophil**
See Hofmannsthal, Hugo von

**Morris, Bill** 1952- .............................. **CLC 76**
See also CA 225

**Morris, Julian**
See West, Morris L(anglo)

**Morris, Steveland Judkins** 1950(?)-
See Wonder, Stevie
See also CA 111

**Morris, William** 1834-1896 . **NCLC 4; PC 55**
See also BRW 5; CDBLB 1832-1890; DLB
18, 35, 57, 156, 178, 184; FANT; RGEL
2; SFW 4; SUFW

**Morris, Wright** 1910-1998 .. **CLC 1, 3, 7, 18,**
**37; TCLC 107**
See also AMW; CA 9-12R; 167; CANR 21,
81; CN 7; DLB 2, 206, 218; DLBY 1981;
EWL 3; MTCW 1, 2; RGAL 4; TCWW 2

**Morrison, Arthur** 1863-1945 ............ **SSC 40;**
**TCLC 72**
See also CA 120; 157; CMW 4; DLB 70,
135, 197; RGEL 2

**Morrison, Chloe Anthony Wofford**
See Morrison, Toni

**Morrison, James Douglas** 1943-1971
See Morrison, Jim
See also CA 73-76; CANR 40

**Morrison, Jim** ................................... **CLC 17**
See Morrison, James Douglas

**Morrison, Toni** 1931- ..... **BLC 3; CLC 4, 10,**
**22, 55, 81, 87, 173, 194**
See also AAYA 1, 22; AFAW 1, 2; AMWC
1; AMWS 3; BPFB 2; BW 2, 3; CA 29-
32R; CANR 27, 42, 67, 113, 124; CDALB
1968-1988; CLR 99; CN 7; CPW; DA;
DA3; DAB; DAC; DAM MST, MULT,
NOV, POP; DLB 6, 33, 143; DLBY 1981;
EWL 3; EXPN; FW; LAIT 2, 4; LATS
1:2; LMFS 2; MAWW; MTCW 1, 2; NFS
1, 6, 8, 14; RGAL 4; RHW; SATA 57,
144; SSFS 5; TUS; YAW

**Morrison, Van** 1945- ........................ **CLC 21**
See also CA 116; 168

**Morrissy, Mary** 1957- ....................... **CLC 99**
See also CA 205; DLB 267

**Mortimer, John (Clifford)** 1923- ..... **CLC 28,**
**43**
See also CA 13-16R; CANR 21, 69, 109;
CD 5; CDBLB 1960 to Present; CMW 4;
CN 7; CPW; DA3; DAM DRAM, POP;
DLB 13, 245, 271; INT CANR-21; MSW;
MTCW 1, 2; RGEL 2

**Mortimer, Penelope (Ruth)**
1918-1999 ..................................... **CLC 5**
See also CA 57-60; 187; CANR 45, 88; CN 7

**Mortimer, Sir John**
See Mortimer, John (Clifford)

**Morton, Anthony**
See Creasey, John

**Morton, Thomas** 1579(?)-1647(?) ........ **LC 72**
See also DLB 24; RGEL 2

**Mosca, Gaetano** 1858-1941 ............. **TCLC 75**

**Moses, Daniel David** 1952- ................. **NNAL**
See also CA 186

**Mosher, Howard Frank** 1943- ......... **CLC 62**
See also CA 139; CANR 65, 115

**Mosley, Nicholas** 1923- ................ **CLC 43, 70**
See also CA 69-72; CANR 41, 60, 108; CN 7; DLB 14, 207

**Mosley, Walter** 1952- .... **BLCS; CLC 97, 184**
See also AAYA 57; AMWS 13; BPFB 2; BW 2; CA 142; CANR 57, 92; CMW 4; CPW; DA3; DAM MULT, POP; DLB 306; MSW; MTCW 2

**Moss, Howard** 1922-1987 . **CLC 7, 14, 45, 50**
See also CA 1-4R; 123; CANR 1, 44; DAM POET; DLB 5

**Mossgiel, Rab**
See Burns, Robert

**Motion, Andrew (Peter)** 1952- ......... **CLC 47**
See also BRWS 7; CA 146; CANR 90; CP 7; DLB 40

**Motley, Willard (Francis)**
1909-1965 ................................... **CLC 18**
See also BW 1; CA 117; 106; CANR 88; DLB 76, 143

**Motoori, Norinaga** 1730-1801 ........ **NCLC 45**

**Mott, Michael (Charles Alston)**
1930- ...................................... **CLC 15, 34**
See also CA 5-8R; CAAS 7; CANR 7, 29

**Mountain Wolf Woman** 1884-1960 . **CLC 92; NNAL**
See also CA 144; CANR 90

**Moure, Erin** 1955- ............................. **CLC 88**
See also CA 113; CP 7; CWP; DLB 60

**Mourning Dove** 1885(?)-1936 ............. **NNAL**
See also CA 144; CANR 90; DAM MULT; DLB 175, 221

**Mowat, Farley (McGill)** 1921- ......... **CLC 26**
See also AAYA 1, 50; BYA 2; CA 1-4R; CANR 4, 24, 42, 68, 108; CLR 20; CPW; DAC; DAM MST; DLB 68; INT CANR-24; JRDA; MAICYA 1, 2; MTCW 1, 2; SATA 3, 55; YAW

**Mowatt, Anna Cora** 1819-1870 ..... **NCLC 74**
See also RGAL 4

**Moyers, Bill** 1934- ............................. **CLC 74**
See also AITN 2; CA 61-64; CANR 31, 52

**Mphahlele, Es'kia**
See Mphahlele, Ezekiel
See also AFW; CDWLB 3; DLB 125, 225; RGSF 2; SSFS 11

**Mphahlele, Ezekiel** 1919- ... **BLC 3; CLC 25, 133**
See Mphahlele, Es'kia
See also BW 2, 3; CA 81-84; CANR 26, 76; CN 7; DA3; DAM MULT; EWL 3; MTCW 2; SATA 119

**Mqhayi, S(amuel) E(dward) K(rune Loliwe)**
1875-1945 ................... **BLC 3; TCLC 25**
See also CA 153; CANR 87; DAM MULT

**Mrozek, Slawomir** 1930- ............... **CLC 3, 13**
See also CA 13-16R; CAAS 10; CANR 29; CDWLB 4; CWW 2; DLB 232; EWL 3; MTCW 1

**Mrs. Belloc-Lowndes**
See Lowndes, Marie Adelaide (Belloc)

**Mrs. Fairstar**
See Horne, Richard Henry Hengist

**M'Taggart, John M'Taggart Ellis**
See McTaggart, John McTaggart Ellis

**Mtwa, Percy** (?)- ................................ **CLC 47**

**Mueller, Lisel** 1924- ........ **CLC 13, 51; PC 33**
See also CA 93-96; CP 7; DLB 105; PFS 9, 13

**Muggeridge, Malcolm (Thomas)**
1903-1990 .............................. **TCLC 120**
See also AITN 1; CA 101; CANR 33, 63; MTCW 1, 2

**Muhammad** 570-632 .......................... **WLCS**
See also DA; DAB; DAC; DAM MST

**Muir, Edwin** 1887-1959 . **PC 49; TCLC 2, 87**
See Moore, Edward
See also BRWS 6; CA 104; 193; DLB 20, 100, 191; EWL 3; RGEL 2

**Muir, John** 1838-1914 ..................... **TCLC 28**
See also AMWS 9; ANW; CA 165; DLB 186, 275

**Mujica Lainez, Manuel** 1910-1984 ... **CLC 31**
See Lainez, Manuel Mujica
See also CA 81-84; 112; CANR 32; EWL 3; HW 1

**Mukherjee, Bharati** 1940- ..... **AAL; CLC 53, 115; SSC 38**
See also AAYA 46; BEST 89:2; CA 107; CANR 45, 72, 128; CN 7; DAM NOV; DLB 60, 218; DNFS 1, 2; EWL 3; FW; MTCW 1, 2; RGAL 4; RGSF 2; SSFS 7; TUS; WWE 1

**Muldoon, Paul** 1951- .......... **CLC 32, 72, 166**
See also BRWS 4; CA 113; 129; CANR 52, 91; CP 7; DAM POET; DLB 40; INT CA-129; PFS 7

**Mulisch, Harry (Kurt Victor)**
1927- ...................................... **CLC 42**
See also CA 9-12R; CANR 6, 26, 56, 110; CWW 2; DLB 299; EWL 3

**Mull, Martin** 1943- ......................... **CLC 17**
See also CA 105

**Muller, Wilhelm** ............................ **NCLC 73**

**Mulock, Dinah Maria**
See Craik, Dinah Maria (Mulock)
See also RGEL 2

**Munday, Anthony** 1560-1633 ............... **LC 87**
See also DLB 62, 172; RGEL 2

**Munford, Robert** 1737(?)-1783 ............. **LC 5**
See also DLB 31

**Mungo, Raymond** 1946- .................... **CLC 72**
See also CA 49-52; CANR 2

**Munro, Alice** 1931- .... **CLC 6, 10, 19, 50, 95; SSC 3; WLCS**
See also AITN 2; BPFB 2; CA 33-36R; CANR 33, 53, 75, 114; CCA 1; CN 7; DA3; DAC; DAM MST, NOV; DLB 53; EWL 3; MTCW 1, 2; RGEL 2; RGSF 2; SATA 29; SSFS 5, 13, 19; WWE 1

**Munro, H(ector) H(ugh)** 1870-1916 .... **WLC**
See Saki
See also AAYA 56; CA 104; 130; CANR 104; CDBLB 1890-1914; DA; DA3; DAB; DAC; DAM MST, NOV; DLB 34, 162; EXPS; MTCW 1, 2; RGEL 2; SSFS 15

**Murakami, Haruki** 1949- ............... **CLC 150**
See Murakami Haruki
See also CA 165; CANR 102; MJW; RGWL 3; SFW 4

**Murakami Haruki**
See Murakami, Haruki
See also CWW 2; DLB 182; EWL 3

**Murasaki, Lady**
See Murasaki Shikibu

**Murasaki Shikibu** 978(?)-1026(?) ... **CMLC 1**
See also EFS 2; LATS 1:1; RGWL 2, 3

**Murdoch, (Jean) Iris** 1919-1999 ... **CLC 1, 2, 3, 4, 6, 8, 11, 15, 22, 31, 51**
See also BRWS 1; CA 13-16R; 179; CANR 8, 43, 68, 103; CDBLB 1960 to Present;

CN 7; CWD; DA3; DAB; DAC; DAM MST, NOV; DLB 14, 194, 233; EWL 3; INT CANR-8; MTCW 1, 2; NFS 18; RGEL 2; TEA; WLIT 4

**Murfree, Mary Noailles** 1850-1922 .. **SSC 22; TCLC 135**
See also CA 122; 176; DLB 12, 74; RGAL 4

**Murnau, Friedrich Wilhelm**
See Plumpe, Friedrich Wilhelm

**Murphy, Richard** 1927- .................... **CLC 41**
See also BRWS 5; CA 29-32R; CP 7; DLB 40; EWL 3

**Murphy, Sylvia** 1937- ....................... **CLC 34**
See also CA 121

**Murphy, Thomas (Bernard)** 1935- ... **CLC 51**
See also CA 101

**Murray, Albert L.** 1916- .................... **CLC 73**
See also BW 2; CA 49-52; CANR 26, 52, 78; CSW; DLB 38

**Murray, James Augustus Henry**
1837-1915 .............................. **TCLC 117**

**Murray, Judith Sargent**
1751-1820 ................................ **NCLC 63**
See also DLB 37, 200

**Murray, Les(lie Allan)** 1938- ............ **CLC 40**
See also BRWS 7; CA 21-24R; CANR 11, 27, 56, 103; CP 7; DAM POET; DLB 289; DLBY 2001; EWL 3; RGEL 2

**Murry, J. Middleton**
See Murry, John Middleton

**Murry, John Middleton**
1889-1957 ................................ **TCLC 16**
See also CA 118; 217; DLB 149

**Musgrave, Susan** 1951- ............... **CLC 13, 54**
See also CA 69-72; CANR 45, 84; CCA 1; CP 7; CWP

**Musil, Robert (Edler von)**
1880-1942 ........... **SSC 18; TCLC 12, 68**
See also CA 109; CANR 55, 84; CDWLB 2; DLB 81, 124; EW 9; EWL 3; MTCW 2; RGSF 2; RGWL 2, 3

**Muske, Carol** ............................... **CLC 90**
See Muske-Dukes, Carol (Anne)

**Muske-Dukes, Carol (Anne)** 1945-
See Muske, Carol
See also CA 65-68; 203; CAAE 203; CANR 32, 70; CWP

**Musset, (Louis Charles) Alfred de**
1810-1857 .................................. **NCLC 7**
See also DLB 192, 217; EW 6; GFL 1789 to the Present; RGWL 2, 3; TWA

**Mussolini, Benito (Amilcare Andrea)**
1883-1945 ................................ **TCLC 96**
See also CA 116

**Mutanabbi, Al-**
See al-Mutanabbi, Ahmad ibn al-Husayn Abu al-Tayyib al-Jufi al-Kindi

**My Brother's Brother**
See Chekhov, Anton (Pavlovich)

**Myers, L(eopold) H(amilton)**
1881-1944 ................................ **TCLC 59**
See also CA 157; DLB 15; EWL 3; RGEL 2

**Myers, Walter Dean** 1937- .. **BLC 3; CLC 35**
See also AAYA 4, 23; BW 2; BYA 6, 8, 11; CA 33-36R; CANR 20, 42, 67, 108; CLR 4, 16, 35; DAM MULT, NOV; DLB 33; INT CANR-20; JRDA; LAIT 5; MAICYA 1, 2; MAICYAS 1; MTCW 2; SAAS 2; SATA 41, 71, 109; SATA-Brief 27; WYA; YAW

**Myers, Walter M.**
See Myers, Walter Dean

**Myles, Symon**
See Follett, Ken(neth Martin)

**Nabokov, Vladimir (Vladimirovich)**
1899-1977 ....... **CLC 1, 2, 3, 6, 8, 11, 15,
23, 44, 46, 64; SSC 11; TCLC 108;
WLC**
See also AAYA 45; AMW; AMWC 1;
AMWR 1; BPFB 2; CA 5-8R; 69-72;
CANR 20, 102; CDALB 1941-1968; DA;
DA3; DAB; DAC; DAM MST, NOV;
DLB 2, 244, 278; DLBD 3; DLBY 1980,
1991; EWL 3; EXPS; LATS 1:2; MTCW
1, 2; NCFS 4; NFS 9; RGAL 4; RGSF 2;
SSFS 6, 15; TUS
**Naevius** c. 265B.C.-201B.C. ........... **CMLC 37**
See also DLB 211
**Nagai, Kafu** ............................................ **TCLC 51**
See Nagai, Sokichi
See also DLB 180
**Nagai, Sokichi** 1879-1959
See Nagai, Kafu
See also CA 117
**Nagy, Laszlo** 1925-1978 ...................... **CLC 7**
See also CA 129; 112
**Naidu, Sarojini** 1879-1949 .............. **TCLC 80**
See also EWL 3; RGEL 2
**Naipaul, Shiva(dhar Srinivasa)**
1945-1985 ....... **CLC 32, 39; TCLC 153**
See also CA 110; 112; 116; CANR 33;
DA3; DAM NOV; DLB 157; DLBY 1985;
EWL 3; MTCW 1, 2
**Naipaul, V(idiadhar) S(urajprasad)**
1932- ........ **CLC 4, 7, 9, 13, 18, 37, 105;
SSC 38**
See also BPFB 2; BRWS 1; CA 1-4R;
CANR 1, 33, 51, 91, 126; CDBLB 1960
to Present; CDWLB 3; CN 7; DA3; DAB;
DAC; DAM MST, NOV; DLB 125, 204,
207; DLBY 1985, 2001; EWL 3; LATS
1:2; MTCW 1, 2; RGEL 2; RGSF 2;
TWA; WLIT 4; WWE 1
**Nakos, Lilika** 1903(?)-1989 ............... **CLC 29**
**Napoleon**
See Yamamoto, Hisaye
**Narayan, R(asipuram) K(rishnaswami)**
1906-2001 . **CLC 7, 28, 47, 121; SSC 25**
See also BPFB 2; CA 81-84; 196; CANR
33, 61, 112; CN 7; DA3; DAM NOV;
DNFS 1; EWL 3; MTCW 1, 2; RGEL 2;
RGSF 2; SATA 62; SSFS 5; WWE 1
**Nash, (Frediric) Ogden** 1902-1971 . **CLC 23;
PC 21; TCLC 109**
See also CA 13-14; 29-32R; CANR 34, 61;
CAP 1; DAM POET; DLB 11; MAICYA
1, 2; MTCW 1, 2; RGAL 4; SATA 2, 46;
WP
**Nashe, Thomas** 1567-1601(?) ......... **LC 41, 89**
See also DLB 167; RGEL 2
**Nathan, Daniel**
See Dannay, Frederic
**Nathan, George Jean** 1882-1958 .... **TCLC 18**
See Hatteras, Owen
See also CA 114; 169; DLB 137
**Natsume, Kinnosuke**
See Natsume, Soseki
**Natsume, Soseki** 1867-1916 ........ **TCLC 2, 10**
See Natsume Soseki; Soseki
See also CA 104; 195; RGWL 2, 3; TWA
**Natsume Soseki**
See Natsume, Soseki
See also DLB 180; EWL 3
**Natti, (Mary) Lee** 1919-
See Kingman, Lee
See also CA 5-8R; CANR 2
**Navarre, Marguerite de**
See de Navarre, Marguerite
**Naylor, Gloria** 1950- ..... **BLC 3; CLC 28, 52,
156; WLCS**
See also AAYA 6, 39; AFAW 1, 2; AMWS
8; BW 2, 3; CA 107; CANR 27, 51, 74,
130; CN 7; CPW; DA; DA3; DAC; DAM

MST, MULT, NOV, POP; DLB 173; EWL
3; FW; MTCW 1, 2; NFS 4, 7; RGAL 4;
TUS
**Neff, Debra** ..................................... **CLC 59**
**Neihardt, John Gneisenau**
1881-1973 ................................. **CLC 32**
See also CA 13-14; CANR 65; CAP 1; DLB
9, 54, 256; LAIT 2
**Nekrasov, Nikolai Alekseevich**
1821-1878 ................................ **NCLC 11**
See also DLB 277
**Nelligan, Emile** 1879-1941 ............. **TCLC 14**
See also CA 114; 204; DLB 92; EWL 3
**Nelson, Willie** 1933- .......................... **CLC 17**
See also CA 107; CANR 114
**Nemerov, Howard (Stanley)**
1920-1991 ........ **CLC 2, 6, 9, 36; PC 24;
TCLC 124**
See also AMW; CA 1-4R; 134; CABS 2;
CANR 1, 27, 53; DAM POET; DLB 5, 6;
DLBY 1983; EWL 3; INT CANR-27;
MTCW 1, 2; PFS 10, 14; RGAL 4
**Neruda, Pablo** 1904-1973 .. **CLC 1, 2, 5, 7, 9,
28, 62; HLC 2; PC 4; WLC**
See also CA 19-20; 45-48; CANR 131; CAP
2; DA; DA3; DAB; DAC; DAM MST,
MULT, POET; DLB 283; DNFS 2; EWL
3; HW 1; LAW; MTCW 1, 2; PFS 11;
RGWL 2, 3; TWA; WLIT 1; WP
**Nerval, Gerard de** 1808-1855 ... **NCLC 1, 67;
PC 13; SSC 18**
See also DLB 217; EW 6; GFL 1789 to the
Present; RGSF 2; RGWL 2, 3
**Nervo, (Jose) Amado (Ruiz de)**
1870-1919 ................ **HLCS 2; TCLC 11**
See also CA 109; 131; DLB 290; EWL 3;
HW 1; LAW
**Nesbit, Malcolm**
See Chester, Alfred
**Nessi, Pio Baroja y**
See Baroja (y Nessi), Pio
**Nestroy, Johann** 1801-1862 ........... **NCLC 42**
See also DLB 133; RGWL 2, 3
**Netterville, Luke**
See O'Grady, Standish (James)
**Neufeld, John (Arthur)** 1938- ........... **CLC 17**
See also AAYA 11; CA 25-28R; CANR 11,
37, 56; CLR 52; MAICYA 1, 2; SAAS 3;
SATA 6, 81, 131; SATA-Essay 131; YAW
**Neumann, Alfred** 1895-1952 ......... **TCLC 100**
See also CA 183; DLB 56
**Neumann, Ferenc**
See Molnar, Ferenc
**Neville, Emily Cheney** 1919- ............. **CLC 12**
See also BYA 2; CA 5-8R; CANR 3, 37,
85; JRDA; MAICYA 1, 2; SAAS 2; SATA
1; YAW
**Newbound, Bernard Slade** 1930-
See Slade, Bernard
See also CA 81-84; CANR 49; CD 5; DAM
DRAM
**Newby, P(ercy) H(oward)**
1918-1997 ............................ **CLC 2, 13**
See also CA 5-8R; 161; CANR 32, 67; CN
7; DAM NOV; DLB 15; MTCW 1; RGEL
2
**Newcastle**
See Cavendish, Margaret Lucas
**Newlove, Donald** 1928- ...................... **CLC 6**
See also CA 29-32R; CANR 25
**Newlove, John (Herbert)** 1938- ........ **CLC 14**
See also CA 21-24R; CANR 9, 25; CP 7
**Newman, Charles** 1938- .................. **CLC 2, 8**
See also CA 21-24R; CANR 84; CN 7
**Newman, Edwin (Harold)** 1919- ...... **CLC 14**
See also AITN 1; CA 69-72; CANR 5

**Newman, John Henry** 1801-1890 . **NCLC 38,
99**
See also BRWS 7; DLB 18, 32, 55; RGEL
2
**Newton, (Sir) Isaac** 1642-1727 ...... **LC 35, 53**
See also DLB 252
**Newton, Suzanne** 1936- ...................... **CLC 35**
See also BYA 7; CA 41-44R; CANR 14;
JRDA; SATA 5, 77
**New York Dept. of Ed.** .................... **CLC 70**
**Nexo, Martin Andersen**
1869-1954 ................................. **TCLC 43**
See also CA 202; DLB 214; EWL 3
**Nezval, Vitezslav** 1900-1958 .......... **TCLC 44**
See also CA 123; CDWLB 4; DLB 215;
EWL 3
**Ng, Fae Myenne** 1957(?)- ................. **CLC 81**
See also BYA 11; CA 146
**Ngema, Mbongeni** 1955- .................. **CLC 57**
See also BW 2; CA 143; CANR 84; CD 5
**Ngugi, James T(hiong'o)** . **CLC 3, 7, 13, 182**
See Ngugi wa Thiong'o
**Ngugi wa Thiong'o**
See Ngugi wa Thiong'o
See also DLB 125; EWL 3
**Ngugi wa Thiong'o** 1938- ... **BLC 3; CLC 36,
182**
See Ngugi, James T(hiong'o); Ngugi wa
Thiong'o
See also AFW; BRWS 8; BW 2; CA 81-84;
CANR 27, 58; CDWLB 3; DAM MULT,
NOV; DNFS 2; MTCW 1, 2; RGEL 2;
WWE 1
**Niatum, Duane** 1938- ......................... **NNAL**
See also CA 41-44R; CANR 21, 45, 83;
DLB 175
**Nichol, B(arrie) P(hillip)** 1944-1988 . **CLC 18**
See also CA 53-56; DLB 53; SATA 66
**Nicholas of Cusa** 1401-1464 ................ **LC 80**
See also DLB 115
**Nichols, John (Treadwell)** 1940- ....... **CLC 38**
See also AMWS 13; CA 9-12R, 190; CAAE
190; CAAS 2; CANR 6, 70, 121; DLBY
1982; LATS 1:2; TCWW 2
**Nichols, Leigh**
See Koontz, Dean R(ay)
**Nichols, Peter (Richard)** 1927- .... **CLC 5, 36,
65**
See also CA 104; CANR 33, 86; CBD; CD
5; DLB 13, 245; MTCW 1
**Nicholson, Linda ed.** ......................... **CLC 65**
**Ni Chuilleanain, Eilean** 1942- ............. **PC 34**
See also CA 126; CANR 53, 83; CP 7;
CWP; DLB 40
**Nicolas, F. R. E.**
See Freeling, Nicolas
**Niedecker, Lorine** 1903-1970 ..... **CLC 10, 42;
PC 42**
See also CA 25-28; CAP 2; DAM POET;
DLB 48
**Nietzsche, Friedrich (Wilhelm)**
1844-1900 ................... **TCLC 10, 18, 55**
See also CA 107; 121; CDWLB 2; DLB
129; EW 7; RGWL 2, 3; TWA
**Nievo, Ippolito** 1831-1861 .............. **NCLC 22**
**Nightingale, Anne Redmon** 1943-
See Redmon, Anne
See also CA 103
**Nightingale, Florence** 1820-1910 ... **TCLC 85**
See also CA 188; DLB 166
**Nijo Yoshimoto** 1320-1388 ............ **CMLC 49**
See also DLB 203
**Nik. T. O.**
See Annensky, Innokenty (Fyodorovich)
**Nin, Anais** 1903-1977 ..... **CLC 1, 4, 8, 11, 14,
60, 127; SSC 10**
See also AITN 2; AMWS 10; BPFB 2; CA
13-16R; 69-72; CANR 22, 53; DAM

NOV, POP; DLB 2, 4, 152; EWL 3; GLL 2; MAWW; MTCW 1, 2; RGAL 4; RGSF 2

**Nisbet, Robert A(lexander)**
    1913-1996 ............................. **TCLC 117**
    See also CA 25-28R; 153; CANR 17; INT CANR-17

**Nishida, Kitaro** 1870-1945 ............. **TCLC 83**

**Nishiwaki, Junzaburo**
    See Nishiwaki, Junzaburo
    See also CA 194

**Nishiwaki, Junzaburo** 1894-1982 ........ **PC 15**
    See Nishiwaki, Junzaburo; Nishiwaki Junzaburo
    See also CA 194; 107; MJW; RGWL 3

**Nishiwaki Junzaburo**
    See Nishiwaki, Junzaburo
    See also EWL 3

**Nissenson, Hugh** 1933- .................... **CLC 4, 9**
    See also CA 17-20R; CANR 27, 108; CN 7; DLB 28

**Nister, Der**
    See Der Nister
    See also EWL 3

**Niven, Larry** ................................... **CLC 8**
    See Niven, Laurence Van Cott
    See also AAYA 27; BPFB 2; BYA 10; DLB 8; SCFW 2

**Niven, Laurence Van Cott** 1938-
    See Niven, Larry
    See also CA 21-24R, 207; CAAE 207; CAAS 12; CANR 14, 44, 66, 113; CPW; DAM POP; MTCW 1, 2; SATA 95; SFW 4

**Nixon, Agnes Eckhardt** 1927- ........... **CLC 21**
    See also CA 110

**Nizan, Paul** 1905-1940 .................... **TCLC 40**
    See also CA 161; DLB 72; EWL 3; GFL 1789 to the Present

**Nkosi, Lewis** 1936- ............. **BLC 3; CLC 45**
    See also BW 1, 3; CA 65-68; CANR 27, 81; CBD; CD 5; DAM MULT; DLB 157, 225; WWE 1

**Nodier, (Jean) Charles (Emmanuel)**
    1780-1844 ............................... **NCLC 19**
    See also DLB 119; GFL 1789 to the Present

**Noguchi, Yone** 1875-1947 ............... **TCLC 80**

**Nolan, Christopher** 1965- .................. **CLC 58**
    See also CA 111; CANR 88

**Noon, Jeff** 1957- ................................ **CLC 91**
    See also CA 148; CANR 83; DLB 267; SFW 4

**Norden, Charles**
    See Durrell, Lawrence (George)

**Nordhoff, Charles Bernard**
    1887-1947 ............................... **TCLC 23**
    See also CA 108; 211; DLB 9; LAIT 1; RHW 1; SATA 23

**Norfolk, Lawrence** 1963- .................. **CLC 76**
    See also CA 144; CANR 85; CN 7; DLB 267

**Norman, Marsha** 1947- . **CLC 28, 186; DC 8**
    See also CA 105; CABS 3; CAD; CANR 41, 131; CD 5; CSW; CWD; DAM DRAM; DFS 2; DLB 266; DLBY 1984; FW

**Normyx**
    See Douglas, (George) Norman

**Norris, (Benjamin) Frank(lin, Jr.)**
    1870-1902 ........ **SSC 28; TCLC 24, 155**
    See also AAYA 57; AMW; AMWC 2; BPFB 2; CA 110; 160; CDALB 1865-1917; DLB 12, 71, 186; LMFS 2; NFS 12; RGAL 4; TCWW 2; TUS

**Norris, Leslie** 1921- ......................... **CLC 14**
    See also CA 11-12; CANR 14, 117; CAP 1; CP 7; DLB 27, 256

**North, Andrew**
    See Norton, Andre

**North, Anthony**
    See Koontz, Dean R(ay)

**North, Captain George**
    See Stevenson, Robert Louis (Balfour)

**North, Captain George**
    See Stevenson, Robert Louis (Balfour)

**North, Milou**
    See Erdrich, Louise

**Northrup, B. A.**
    See Hubbard, L(afayette) Ron(ald)

**North Staffs**
    See Hulme, T(homas) E(rnest)

**Northup, Solomon** 1808-1863 ...... **NCLC 105**

**Norton, Alice Mary**
    See Norton, Andre
    See also MAICYA 1; SATA 1, 43

**Norton, Andre** 1912- .......................... **CLC 12**
    See Norton, Alice Mary
    See also AAYA 14; BPFB 2; BYA 4, 10, 12; CA 1-4R; CANR 68; CLR 50; DLB 8, 52; JRDA; MAICYA 2; MTCW 1; SATA 91; SUFW 1, 2; YAW

**Norton, Caroline** 1808-1877 ......... **NCLC 47**
    See also DLB 21, 159, 199

**Norway, Nevil Shute** 1899-1960
    See Shute, Nevil
    See also CA 102; 93-96; CANR 85; MTCW 2

**Norwid, Cyprian Kamil**
    1821-1883 ............................... **NCLC 17**
    See also RGWL 3

**Nosille, Nabrah**
    See Ellison, Harlan (Jay)

**Nossack, Hans Erich** 1901-1978 ......... **CLC 6**
    See also CA 93-96; 85-88; DLB 69; EWL 3

**Nostradamus** 1503-1566 ...................... **LC 27**

**Nosu, Chuji**
    See Ozu, Yasujiro

**Notenburg, Eleanora (Genrikhovna) von**
    See Guro, Elena (Genrikhovna)

**Nova, Craig** 1945- ............................ **CLC 7, 31**
    See also CA 45-48; CANR 2, 53, 127

**Novak, Joseph**
    See Kosinski, Jerzy (Nikodem)

**Novalis** 1772-1801 ............................ **NCLC 13**
    See also CDWLB 2; DLB 90; EW 5; RGWL 2, 3

**Novick, Peter** 1934- .......................... **CLC 164**
    See also CA 188

**Novis, Emile**
    See Weil, Simone (Adolphine)

**Nowlan, Alden (Albert)** 1933-1983 ... **CLC 15**
    See also CA 9-12R; CANR 5; DAC; DAM MST; DLB 53; PFS 12

**Noyes, Alfred** 1880-1958 ...... **PC 27; TCLC 7**
    See also CA 104; 188; DLB 20; EXPP; FANT; PFS 4; RGEL 2

**Nugent, Richard Bruce** 1906(?)-1987 ... **HR 3**
    See also BW 1; CA 125; DLB 51; GLL 2

**Nunn, Kem** ................................... **CLC 34**
    See also CA 159

**Nwapa, Flora (Nwanzuruaha)**
    1931-1993 ................... **BLCS; CLC 133**
    See also BW 2; CA 143; CANR 83; CD-WLB 3; CWRI 5; DLB 125; EWL 3; WLIT 2

**Nye, Robert** 1939- .......................... **CLC 13, 42**
    See also CA 33-36R; CANR 29, 67, 107; CN 7; CP 7; CWRI 5; DAM NOV; DLB 14, 271; FANT; HGG; MTCW 1; RHW; SATA 6

**Nyro, Laura** 1947-1997 .................... **CLC 17**
    See also CA 194

**Oates, Joyce Carol** 1938- .. **CLC 1, 2, 3, 6, 9, 11, 15, 19, 33, 52, 108, 134; SSC 6, 70; WLC**
    See also AAYA 15, 52; AITN 1; AMWS 2; BEST 89:2; BPFB 2; BYA 11; CA 5-8R;

CANR 25, 45, 74, 113, 129; CDALB 1968-1988; CN 7; CP 7; CPW; CWP; DA; DA3; DAB; DAC; DAM MST, NOV, POP; DLB 2, 5, 130; DLBY 1981; EWL 3; EXPS; FW; HGG; INT CANR-25; LAIT 4; MAWW; MTCW 1, 2; NFS 8; RGAL 4; RGSF 2; SSFS 17; SUFW 2; TUS

**O'Brian, E. G.**
    See Clarke, Arthur C(harles)

**O'Brian, Patrick** 1914-2000 ........... **CLC 152**
    See also AAYA 55; CA 144; 187; CANR 74; CPW; MTCW 2; RHW

**O'Brien, Darcy** 1939-1998 ................. **CLC 11**
    See also CA 21-24R; 167; CANR 8, 59

**O'Brien, Edna** 1936- ..... **CLC 3, 5, 8, 13, 36, 65, 116; SSC 10**
    See also BRWS 5; CA 1-4R; CANR 6, 41, 65, 102; CDBLB 1960 to Present; CN 7; DA3; DAM NOV; DLB 14, 231; EWL 3; FW; MTCW 1, 2; RGSF 2; WLIT 4

**O'Brien, Fitz-James** 1828-1862 ..... **NCLC 21**
    See also DLB 74; RGAL 4; SUFW

**O'Brien, Flann** .......... **CLC 1, 4, 5, 7, 10, 47**
    See O Nuallain, Brian
    See also BRWS 2; DLB 231; EWL 3; RGEL 2

**O'Brien, Richard** 1942- ..................... **CLC 17**
    See also CA 124

**O'Brien, (William) Tim(othy)** 1946- . **CLC 7, 19, 40, 103; SSC 74**
    See also AAYA 16; AMWS 5; CA 85-88; CANR 40, 58, 133; CDALBS; CN 7; CPW; DA3; DAM POP; DLB 152; DLBD 9; DLBY 1980; LATS 1:2; MTCW 2; RGAL 4; SSFS 5, 15

**Obstfelder, Sigbjoern** 1866-1900 .... **TCLC 23**
    See also CA 123

**O'Casey, Sean** 1880-1964 .... **CLC 1, 5, 9, 11, 15, 88; DC 12; WLCS**
    See also BRW 7; CA 89-92; CANR 62; CBD; CDBLB 1914-1945; DA3; DAB; DAC; DAM DRAM, MST; DFS 19; DLB 10; EWL 3; MTCW 1, 2; RGEL 2; TEA; WLIT 4

**O'Cathasaigh, Sean**
    See O'Casey, Sean

**Occom, Samson** 1723-1792 .... **LC 60; NNAL**
    See also DLB 175

**Ochs, Phil(ip David)** 1940-1976 ........ **CLC 17**
    See also CA 185; 65-68

**O'Connor, Edwin (Greene)**
    1918-1968 ............................... **CLC 14**
    See also CA 93-96; 25-28R

**O'Connor, (Mary) Flannery**
    1925-1964 .... **CLC 1, 2, 3, 6, 10, 13, 15, 21, 66, 104; SSC 1, 23, 61; TCLC 132; WLC**
    See also AAYA 7; AMW; AMWR 2; BPFB 3; BYA 16; CA 1-4R; CANR 3, 41; CDALB 1941-1968; DA; DA3; DAB; DAC; DAM MST, NOV; DLB 2, 152; DLBD 12; DLBY 1980; EWL 3; EXPS; LAIT 5; MAWW; MTCW 1, 2; NFS 3; RGAL 4; RGSF 2; SSFS 2, 7, 10, 19; TUS

**O'Connor, Frank** ................. **CLC 23; SSC 5**
    See O'Donovan, Michael Francis
    See also DLB 162; EWL 3; RGSF 2; SSFS 5

**O'Dell, Scott** 1898-1989 .................... **CLC 30**
    See also AAYA 3, 44; BPFB 3; BYA 1, 2, 3, 5; CA 61-64; 129; CANR 12, 30, 112; CLR 1, 16; DLB 52; JRDA; MAICYA 1, 2; SATA 12, 60, 134; WYA; YAW

**Odets, Clifford** 1906-1963 ..... **CLC 2, 28, 98; DC 6**
    See also AMWS 2; CA 85-88; CAD; CANR 62; DAM DRAM; DFS 3, 17, 20; DLB 7, 26; EWL 3; MTCW 1, 2; RGAL 4; TUS

**O'Doherty, Brian** 1928- ................... **CLC 76**
See also CA 105; CANR 108

**O'Donnell, K. M.**
See Malzberg, Barry N(athaniel)

**O'Donnell, Lawrence**
See Kuttner, Henry

**O'Donovan, Michael Francis**
1903-1966 ................................. **CLC 14**
See O'Connor, Frank
See also CA 93-96; CANR 84

**Oe, Kenzaburo** 1935- .. **CLC 10, 36, 86, 187;**
**SSC 20**
See Oe Kenzaburo
See also CA 97-100; CANR 36, 50, 74, 126;
DA3; DAM NOV; DLB 182; DLBY 1994;
LATS 1:2; MJW; MTCW 1, 2; RGSF 2;
RGWL 2, 3

**Oe Kenzaburo**
See Oe, Kenzaburo
See also CWW 2; EWL 3

**O'Faolain, Julia** 1932- .... **CLC 6, 19, 47, 108**
See also CA 81-84; CAAS 2; CANR 12,
61; CN 7; DLB 14, 231; FW; MTCW 1;
RHW

**O'Faolain, Sean** 1900-1991 ...... **CLC 1, 7, 14,**
**32, 70; SSC 13; TCLC 143**
See also CA 61-64; 134; CANR 12, 66;
DLB 15, 162; MTCW 1, 2; RGEL 2;
RGSF 2

**O'Flaherty, Liam** 1896-1984 ....... **CLC 5, 34;**
**SSC 6**
See also CA 101; 113; CANR 35; DLB 36,
162; DLBY 1984; MTCW 1, 2; RGEL 2;
RGSF 2; SSFS 5, 20

**Ogai**
See Mori Ogai
See also MJW

**Ogilvy, Gavin**
See Barrie, J(ames) M(atthew)

**O'Grady, Standish (James)**
1846-1928 ................................. **TCLC 5**
See also CA 104; 157

**O'Grady, Timothy** 1951- ................... **CLC 59**
See also CA 138

**O'Hara, Frank** 1926-1966 ....... **CLC 2, 5, 13,**
**78; PC 45**
See also CA 9-12R; 25-28R; CANR 33;
DA3; DAM POET; DLB 5, 16, 193; EWL
3; MTCW 1, 2; PFS 8; 12; RGAL 4; WP

**O'Hara, John (Henry)** 1905-1970 . **CLC 1, 2,**
**3, 6, 11, 42; SSC 15**
See also AMW; BPFB 3; CA 5-8R; 25-28R;
CANR 31, 60; CDALB 1929-1941; DAM
NOV; DLB 9, 86; DLBD 2; EWL 3;
MTCW 1, 2; NFS 11; RGAL 4; RGSF 2

**O Hehir, Diana** 1922- ....................... **CLC 41**
See also CA 93-96

**Ohiyesa**
See Eastman, Charles A(lexander)

**Okada, John** 1923-1971 ......................... **AAL**
See also BYA 14; CA 212

**Okigbo, Christopher (Ifenayichukwu)**
1932-1967 .... **BLC 3; CLC 25, 84; PC 7**
See also AFW; BW 1, 3; CA 77-80; CANR
74; CDWLB 3; DAM MULT, POET; DLB
125; EWL 3; MTCW 1, 2; RGEL 2

**Okri, Ben** 1959- ................................. **CLC 87**
See also AFW; BRWS 5; BW 2, 3; CA 130;
138; CANR 65, 128; CN 7; DLB 157,
231; EWL 3; INT CA-138; MTCW 2;
RGSF 2; SSFS 20; WLIT 2; WWE 1

**Olds, Sharon** 1942- .. **CLC 32, 39, 85; PC 22**
See also AMWS 10; CA 101; CANR 18,
41, 66, 98; CP 7; CPW; CWP; DAM
POET; DLB 120; MTCW 2; PFS 17

**Oldstyle, Jonathan**
See Irving, Washington

**Olesha, Iurii**
See Olesha, Yuri (Karlovich)
See also RGWL 2

**Olesha, Iurii Karlovich**
See Olesha, Yuri (Karlovich)
See also DLB 272

**Olesha, Yuri (Karlovich)** 1899-1960 . **CLC 8;**
**SSC 69; TCLC 136**
See Olesha, Iurii; Olesha, Iurii Karlovich;
Olesha, Yury Karlovich
See also CA 85-88; EW 11; RGWL 3

**Olesha, Yury Karlovich**
See Olesha, Yuri (Karlovich)
See also EWL 3

**Oliphant, Mrs.**
See Oliphant, Margaret (Oliphant Wilson)
See also SUFW

**Oliphant, Laurence** 1829(?)-1888 .. **NCLC 47**
See also DLB 18, 166

**Oliphant, Margaret (Oliphant Wilson)**
1828-1897 ........... **NCLC 11, 61; SSC 25**
See Oliphant, Mrs.
See also DLB 18, 159, 190; HGG; RGEL
2; RGSF 2

**Oliver, Mary** 1935- ............... **CLC 19, 34, 98**
See also AMWS 7; CA 21-24R; CANR 9,
43, 84, 92; CP 7; CWP; DLB 5, 193;
EWL 3; PFS 15

**Olivier, Laurence (Kerr)** 1907-1989 . **CLC 20**
See also CA 111; 150; 129

**Olsen, Tillie** 1912- ... **CLC 4, 13, 114; SSC 11**
See also AAYA 51; AMWS 13; BYA 11;
CA 1-4R; CANR 1, 43, 74, 132;
CDALBS; CN 7; DA; DA3; DAB; DAC;
DAM MST; DLB 28, 206; DLBY 1980;
EWL 3; EXPS; FW; MTCW 1, 2; RGAL
4; RGSF 2; SSFS 1; TUS

**Olson, Charles (John)** 1910-1970 .. **CLC 1, 2,**
**5, 6, 9, 11, 29; PC 19**
See also AMWS 2; CA 13-16; 25-28R;
CABS 2; CANR 35, 61; CAP 1; DAM
POET; DLB 5, 16, 193; EWL 3; MTCW
1, 2; RGAL 4; WP

**Olson, Toby** 1937- ............................. **CLC 28**
See also CA 65-68; CANR 9, 31, 84; CP 7

**Olyesha, Yuri**
See Olesha, Yuri (Karlovich)

**Olympiodorus of Thebes** c. 375-c.
430 ......................................... **CMLC 59**

**Omar Khayyam**
See Khayyam, Omar
See also RGWL 2, 3

**Ondaatje, (Philip) Michael** 1943- .... **CLC 14,**
**29, 51, 76, 180; PC 28**
See also CA 77-80; CANR 42, 74, 109, 133;
CN 7; CP 7; DA3; DAB; DAC; DAM
MST; DLB 60; EWL 3; LATS 1:2; LMFS
2; MTCW 2; PFS 8, 19; TWA; WWE 1

**Oneal, Elizabeth** 1934-
See Oneal, Zibby
See also CA 106; CANR 28, 84; MAICYA
1, 2; SATA 30, 82; YAW

**Oneal, Zibby** .................................... **CLC 30**
See Oneal, Elizabeth
See also AAYA 5, 41; BYA 13; CLR 13;
JRDA; WYA

**O'Neill, Eugene (Gladstone)**
1888-1953 ... **DC 20; TCLC 1, 6, 27, 49;**
**WLC**
See also AAYA 54; AITN 1; AMW; AMWC
1; CA 110; 132; CAD; CANR 131;
CDALB 1929-1941; DA; DA3; DAB;
DAC; DAM DRAM, MST; DFS 2, 4, 5,
6, 9, 11, 12, 16, 20; DLB 7; EWL 3; LAIT
3; LMFS 2; MTCW 1, 2; RGAL 4; TUS

**Onetti, Juan Carlos** 1909-1994 ... **CLC 7, 10;**
**HLCS 2; SSC 23; TCLC 131**
See also CA 85-88; 145; CANR 32, 63; CD-
WLB 3; CWW 2; DAM MULT, NOV;

DLB 113; EWL 3; HW 1, 2; LAW;
MTCW 1, 2; RGSF 2

**O Nuallain, Brian** 1911-1966
See O'Brien, Flann
See also CA 21-22; 25-28R; CAP 2; DLB
231; FANT; TEA

**Ophuls, Max** 1902-1957 .................. **TCLC 79**
See also CA 113

**Opie, Amelia** 1769-1853 ................. **NCLC 65**
See also DLB 116, 159; RGEL 2

**Oppen, George** 1908-1984 ..... **CLC 7, 13, 34;**
**PC 35; TCLC 107**
See also CA 13-16R; 113; CANR 8, 82;
DLB 5, 165

**Oppenheim, E(dward) Phillips**
1866-1946 ................................. **TCLC 45**
See also CA 111; 202; CMW 4; DLB 70

**Opuls, Max**
See Ophuls, Max

**Orage, A(lfred) R(ichard)**
1873-1934 ............................... **TCLC 157**
See also CA 122

**Origen** c. 185-c. 254 ....................... **CMLC 19**

**Orlovitz, Gil** 1918-1973 ..................... **CLC 22**
See also CA 77-80; 45-48; DLB 2, 5

**Orris**
See Ingelow, Jean

**Ortega y Gasset, Jose** 1883-1955 ...... **HLC 2;**
**TCLC 9**
See also CA 106; 130; DAM MULT; EW 9;
EWL 3; HW 1, 2; MTCW 1, 2

**Ortese, Anna Maria** 1914-1998 ........ **CLC 89**
See also DLB 177; EWL 3

**Ortiz, Simon J(oseph)** 1941- ........... **CLC 45;**
**NNAL; PC 17**
See also AMWS 4; CA 134; CANR 69, 118;
CP 7; DAM MULT, POET; DLB 120,
175, 256; EXPP; PFS 4, 16; RGAL 4

**Orton, Joe** ...... **CLC 4, 13, 43; DC 3; TCLC**
**157**
See Orton, John Kingsley
See also BRWS 5; CBD; CDBLB 1960 to
Present; DFS 3, 6; DLB 13; GLL 1;
MTCW 2; RGEL 2; TEA; WLIT 4

**Orton, John Kingsley** 1933-1967
See Orton, Joe
See also CA 85-88; CANR 35, 66; DAM
DRAM; MTCW 1, 2

**Orwell, George** ...... **SSC 68; TCLC 2, 6, 15,**
**31, 51, 128, 129; WLC**
See Blair, Eric (Arthur)
See also BPFB 3; BRW 7; BYA 5; CDBLB
1945-1960; CLR 68; DAB; DLB 15, 98,
195, 255; EWL 3; EXPN; LAIT 4, 5;
LATS 1:1; NFS 3, 7; RGEL 2; SCFW 2;
SFW 4; SSFS 4; TEA; WLIT 4; YAW

**Osborne, David**
See Silverberg, Robert

**Osborne, George**
See Silverberg, Robert

**Osborne, John (James)** 1929-1994 .... **CLC 1,**
**2, 5, 11, 45; TCLC 153; WLC**
See also BRWS 1; CA 13-16R; 147; CANR
21, 56; CDBLB 1945-1960; DA; DAB;
DAC; DAM DRAM, MST; DFS 4, 19;
DLB 13; EWL 3; MTCW 1, 2; RGEL 2

**Osborne, Lawrence** 1958- ................. **CLC 50**
See also CA 189

**Osbourne, Lloyd** 1868-1947 .......... **TCLC 93**

**Osgood, Frances Sargent**
1811-1850 ............................... **NCLC 141**
See also DLB 250

**Oshima, Nagisa** 1932- ....................... **CLC 20**
See also CA 116; 121; CANR 78

**Oskison, John Milton**
1874-1947 ................... **NNAL; TCLC 35**
See also CA 144; CANR 84; DAM MULT;
DLB 175

**Ossian** c. 3rd cent. - ....................... **CMLC 28**
See Macpherson, James
**Ossoli, Sarah Margaret (Fuller)**
1810-1850 ............................ **NCLC 5, 50**
See Fuller, Margaret; Fuller, Sarah Margaret
See also CDALB 1640-1865; FW; LMFS 1;
SATA 25
**Ostriker, Alicia (Suskin)** 1937- ....... **CLC 132**
See also CA 25-28R; CAAS 24; CANR 10,
30, 62, 99; CWP; DLB 120; EXPP; PFS
19
**Ostrovsky, Aleksandr Nikolaevich**
See Ostrovsky, Alexander
See also DLB 277
**Ostrovsky, Alexander** 1823-1886 .. **NCLC 30,
57**
See Ostrovsky, Aleksandr Nikolaevich
**Otero, Blas de** 1916-1979 ................. **CLC 11**
See also CA 89-92; DLB 134; EWL 3
**O'Trigger, Sir Lucius**
See Horne, Richard Henry Hengist
**Otto, Rudolf** 1869-1937 ................... **TCLC 85**
**Otto, Whitney** 1955- ....................... **CLC 70**
See also CA 140; CANR 120
**Otway, Thomas** 1652-1685 ... **DC 24; LC 106**
See also DAM DRAM; DLB 80; RGEL 2
**Ouida** ............................................. **TCLC 43**
See De la Ramee, Marie Louise (Ouida)
See also DLB 18, 156; RGEL 2
**Ouologuem, Yambo** 1940- ............... **CLC 146**
See also CA 111; 176
**Ousmane, Sembene** 1923- ... **BLC 3; CLC 66**
See Sembene, Ousmane
See also BW 1, 3; CA 117; 125; CANR 81;
CWW 2; MTCW 1
**Ovid** 43B.C.-17 ....................... **CMLC 7; PC 2**
See also AW 2; CDWLB 1; DA3; DAM
POET; DLB 211; RGWL 2, 3; WP
**Owen, Hugh**
See Faust, Frederick (Schiller)
**Owen, Wilfred (Edward Salter)**
1893-1918 ... **PC 19; TCLC 5, 27; WLC**
See also BRW 6; CA 104; 141; CDBLB
1914-1945; DA; DAB; DAC; DAM MST,
POET; DLB 20; EWL 3; EXPP; MTCW
2; PFS 10; RGEL 2; WLIT 4
**Owens, Louis (Dean)** 1948-2002 ........ **NNAL**
See also CA 137, 179; 207; CAAE 179;
CAAS 24; CANR 71
**Owens, Rochelle** 1936- ....................... **CLC 8**
See also CA 17-20R; CAAS 2; CAD;
CANR 39; CD 5; CP 7; CWD; CWP
**Oz, Amos** 1939- ...... **CLC 5, 8, 11, 27, 33, 54;
SSC 66**
See also CA 53-56; CANR 27, 47, 65, 113;
CWW 2; DAM NOV; EWL 3; MTCW 1,
2; RGSF 2; RGWL 3
**Ozick, Cynthia** 1928- ....... **CLC 3, 7, 28, 62,
155; SSC 15, 60**
See also AMWS 5; BEST 90:1; CA 17-20R;
CANR 23, 58, 116; CN 7; CPW; DA3;
DAM NOV, POP; DLB 28, 152, 299;
DLBY 1982; EWL 3; EXPS; INT CANR-
23; MTCW 1, 2; RGAL 4; RGSF 2; SSFS
3, 12
**Ozu, Yasujiro** 1903-1963 ................... **CLC 16**
See also CA 112
**Pabst, G. W.** 1885-1967 ................. **TCLC 127**
**Pacheco, C.**
See Pessoa, Fernando (Antonio Nogueira)
**Pacheco, Jose Emilio** 1939- ................. **HLC 2**
See also CA 111; 131; CANR 65; CWW 2;
DAM MULT; DLB 290; EWL 3; HW 1,
2; RGSF 2
**Pa Chin** ........................................... **CLC 18**
See Li Fei-kan
See also EWL 3

**Pack, Robert** 1929- ............................ **CLC 13**
See also CA 1-4R; CANR 3, 44, 82; CP 7;
DLB 5; SATA 118
**Padgett, Lewis**
See Kuttner, Henry
**Padilla (Lorenzo), Heberto**
1932-2000 ...................................... **CLC 38**
See also AITN 1; CA 123; 131; 189; CWW
2; EWL 3; HW 1
**Page, James Patrick** 1944-
See Page, Jimmy
See also CA 204
**Page, Jimmy** 1944- ............................ **CLC 12**
See Page, James Patrick
**Page, Louise** 1955- ............................ **CLC 40**
See also CA 140; CANR 76; CBD; CD 5;
CWD; DLB 233
**Page, P(atricia) K(athleen)** 1916- ...... **CLC 7,
18; PC 12**
See Cape, Judith
See also CA 53-56; CANR 4, 22, 65; CP 7;
DAC; DAM MST; DLB 68; MTCW 1;
RGEL 2
**Page, Stanton**
See Fuller, Henry Blake
**Page, Stanton**
See Fuller, Henry Blake
**Page, Thomas Nelson** 1853-1922 ....... **SSC 23**
See also CA 118; 177; DLB 12, 78; DLBD
13; RGAL 4
**Pagels, Elaine Hiesey** 1943- ............ **CLC 104**
See also CA 45-48; CANR 2, 24, 51; FW;
NCFS 4
**Paget, Violet** 1856-1935
See Lee, Vernon
See also CA 104; 166; GLL 1; HGG
**Paget-Lowe, Henry**
See Lovecraft, H(oward) P(hillips)
**Paglia, Camille (Anna)** 1947- .......... **CLC 68**
See also CA 140; CANR 72; CPW; FW;
GLL 2; MTCW 2
**Paige, Richard**
See Koontz, Dean R(ay)
**Paine, Thomas** 1737-1809 ............... **NCLC 62**
See also AMWS 1; CDALB 1640-1865;
DLB 31, 43, 73, 158; LAIT 1; RGAL 4;
RGEL 2; TUS
**Pakenham, Antonia**
See Fraser, Antonia (Pakenham)
**Palamas, Costis**
See Palamas, Kostes
**Palamas, Kostes** 1859-1943 ............. **TCLC 5**
See Palamas, Kostis
See also CA 105; 190; RGWL 2, 3
**Palamas, Kostis**
See Palamas, Kostes
See also EWL 3
**Palazzeschi, Aldo** 1885-1974 ............. **CLC 11**
See also CA 89-92; 53-56; DLB 114, 264;
EWL 3
**Pales Matos, Luis** 1898-1959 ........... **HLCS 2**
See Pales Matos, Luis
See also DLB 290; HW 1; LAW
**Paley, Grace** 1922- .. **CLC 4, 6, 37, 140; SSC
8**
See also AMWS 6; CA 25-28R; CANR 13,
46, 74, 118; CN 7; CPW; DA3; DAM
POP; DLB 28, 218; EWL 3; EXPS; FW;
INT CANR-13; MAWW; MTCW 1, 2;
RGAL 4; RGSF 2; SSFS 3, 20
**Palin, Michael (Edward)** 1943- ........ **CLC 21**
See Monty Python
See also CA 107; CANR 35, 109; SATA 67
**Palliser, Charles** 1947- ...................... **CLC 65**
See also CA 136; CANR 76; CN 7
**Palma, Ricardo** 1833-1919 ............. **TCLC 29**
See also CA 168; LAW
**Pamuk, Orhan** 1952- ....................... **CLC 185**
See also CA 142; CANR 75, 127; CWW 2

**Pancake, Breece Dexter** 1952-1979
See Pancake, Breece D'J
See also CA 123; 109
**Pancake, Breece D'J** ......... **CLC 29; SSC 61**
See Pancake, Breece Dexter
See also DLB 130
**Panchenko, Nikolai** ...................... **CLC 59**
**Pankhurst, Emmeline (Goulden)**
1858-1928 .............................. **TCLC 100**
See also CA 116; FW
**Panko, Rudy**
See Gogol, Nikolai (Vasilyevich)
**Papadiamantis, Alexandros**
1851-1911 ................................. **TCLC 29**
See also CA 168; EWL 3
**Papadiamantopoulos, Johannes** 1856-1910
See Moreas, Jean
See also CA 117
**Papini, Giovanni** 1881-1956 ........... **TCLC 22**
See also CA 121; 180; DLB 264
**Paracelsus** 1493-1541 ............................ **LC 14**
See also DLB 179
**Parasol, Peter**
See Stevens, Wallace
**Pardo Bazan, Emilia** 1851-1921 ........ **SSC 30**
See also EWL 3; FW; RGSF 2; RGWL 2, 3
**Pareto, Vilfredo** 1848-1923 ............. **TCLC 69**
See also CA 175
**Paretsky, Sara** 1947- ....................... **CLC 135**
See also AAYA 30; BEST 90:3; CA 125;
129; CANR 59, 95; CMW 4; CPW; DA3;
DAM POP; DLB 306; INT CA-129;
MSW; RGAL 4
**Parfenie, Maria**
See Codrescu, Andrei
**Parini, Jay (Lee)** 1948- .............. **CLC 54, 133**
See also CA 97-100; CAAS 16; CANR 32,
87
**Park, Jordan**
See Kornbluth, C(yril) M.; Pohl, Frederik
**Park, Robert E(zra)** 1864-1944 ..... **TCLC 73**
See also CA 122; 165
**Parker, Bert**
See Ellison, Harlan (Jay)
**Parker, Dorothy (Rothschild)**
1893-1967 . **CLC 15, 68; PC 28; SSC 2;
TCLC 143**
See also AMWS 9; CA 19-20; 25-28R; CAP
2; DA3; DAM POET; DLB 11, 45, 86;
EXPP; FW; MAWW; MTCW 1, 2; PFS
18; RGAL 4; RGSF 2; TUS
**Parker, Robert B(rown)** 1932- ......... **CLC 27**
See also AAYA 28; BEST 89:4; BPFB 3;
CA 49-52; CANR 1, 26, 52, 89, 128;
CMW 4; CPW; DAM NOV, POP; DLB
306; INT CANR-26; MSW; MTCW 1
**Parkin, Frank** 1940- .......................... **CLC 43**
See also CA 147
**Parkman, Francis, Jr.** 1823-1893 .. **NCLC 12**
See also AMWS 2; DLB 1, 30, 183, 186,
235; RGAL 4
**Parks, Gordon (Alexander Buchanan)**
1912- ......................... **BLC 3; CLC 1, 16**
See also AAYA 36; AITN 2; BW 2, 3; CA
41-44R; CANR 26, 66; DA3; DAM
MULT; DLB 33; MTCW 2; SATA 8, 108
**Parks, Suzan-Lori** 1964(?)- ................. **DC 23**
See also AAYA 55; CA 201; CAD; CD 5;
CWD; RGAL 4
**Parks, Tim(othy Harold)** 1954- ...... **CLC 147**
See also CA 126; 131; CANR 77; DLB 231;
INT CA-131
**Parmenides** c. 515B.C.-c.
450B.C. ...................................... **CMLC 22**
See also DLB 176
**Parnell, Thomas** 1679-1718 ................... **LC 3**
See also DLB 95; RGEL 2
**Parr, Catherine** c. 1513(?)-1548 .......... **LC 86**
See also DLB 136

**Parra, Nicanor** 1914- ... **CLC 2, 102; HLC 2; PC 39**
See also CA 85-88; CANR 32; CWW 2; DAM MULT; DLB 283; EWL 3; HW 1; LAW; MTCW 1

**Parra Sanojo, Ana Teresa de la**
1890-1936 .................................. **HLCS 2**
See de la Parra, (Ana) Teresa (Sonojo)
See also LAW

**Parrish, Mary Frances**
See Fisher, M(ary) F(rances) K(ennedy)

**Parshchikov, Aleksei** 1954- .............. **CLC 59**
See Parshchikov, Aleksei Maksimovich

**Parshchikov, Aleksei Maksimovich**
See Parshchikov, Aleksei
See also DLB 285

**Parson, Professor**
See Coleridge, Samuel Taylor

**Parson Lot**
See Kingsley, Charles

**Parton, Sara Payson Willis**
1811-1872 .................................. **NCLC 86**
See also DLB 43, 74, 239

**Partridge, Anthony**
See Oppenheim, E(dward) Phillips

**Pascal, Blaise** 1623-1662 ...................... **LC 35**
See also DLB 268; EW 3; GFL Beginnings to 1789; RGWL 2, 3; TWA

**Pascoli, Giovanni** 1855-1912 .......... **TCLC 45**
See also CA 170; EW 7; EWL 3

**Pasolini, Pier Paolo** 1922-1975 .. **CLC 20, 37, 106; PC 17**
See also CA 93-96; 61-64; CANR 63; DLB 128, 177; EWL 3; MTCW 1; RGWL 2, 3

**Pasquini**
See Silone, Ignazio

**Pastan, Linda (Olenik)** 1932- .......... **CLC 27**
See also CA 61-64; CANR 18, 40, 61, 113; CP 7; CSW; CWP; DAM POET; DLB 5; PFS 8

**Pasternak, Boris (Leonidovich)**
1890-1960 ...... **CLC 7, 10, 18, 63; PC 6; SSC 31; WLC**
See also BPFB 3; CA 127; 116; DA; DA3; DAB; DAC; DAM MST, NOV, POET; DLB 302; EW 10; MTCW 1, 2; RGSF 2; RGWL 2, 3; TWA; WP

**Patchen, Kenneth** 1911-1972 .... **CLC 1, 2, 18**
See also BG 3; CA 1-4R; 33-36R; CANR 3, 35; DAM POET; DLB 16, 48; EWL 3; MTCW 1; RGAL 4

**Pater, Walter (Horatio)** 1839-1894 . **NCLC 7, 90**
See also BRW 5; CDBLB 1832-1890; DLB 57, 156; RGEL 2; TEA

**Paterson, A(ndrew) B(arton)**
1864-1941 .................................. **TCLC 32**
See also CA 155; DLB 230; RGEL 2; SATA 97

**Paterson, Banjo**
See Paterson, A(ndrew) B(arton)

**Paterson, Katherine (Womeldorf)**
1932- .................................. **CLC 12, 30**
See also AAYA 1, 31; BYA 1, 2, 7; CA 21-24R; CANR 28, 59, 111; CLR 7, 50; CWRI 5; DLB 52; JRDA; LAIT 4; MAICYA 1, 2; MAICYAS 1; MTCW 1; SATA 13, 53, 92, 133; WYA; YAW

**Patmore, Coventry Kersey Dighton**
1823-1896 .................... **NCLC 9; PC 59**
See also DLB 35, 98; RGEL 2; TEA

**Paton, Alan (Stewart)** 1903-1988 ...... **CLC 4, 10, 25, 55, 106; WLC**
See also AAYA 26; AFW; BPFB 3; BRWS 2; BYA 1; CA 13-16; 125; CANR 22; CAP 1; DA; DA3; DAB; DAC; DAM MST, NOV; DLB 225; DLBD 17; EWL 3; EXPN; LAIT 4; MTCW 1, 2; NFS 3,
12; RGEL 2; SATA 11; SATA-Obit 56; TWA; WLIT 2; WWE 1

**Paton Walsh, Gillian** 1937- .............. **CLC 35**
See Paton Walsh, Jill; Walsh, Jill Paton
See also AAYA 11; CANR 38, 83; CLR 2, 65; DLB 161; JRDA; MAICYA 1, 2; SAAS 3; SATA 4, 72, 109; YAW

**Paton Walsh, Jill**
See Paton Walsh, Gillian
See also AAYA 47; BYA 1, 8

**Patterson, (Horace) Orlando (Lloyd)**
1940- .................................. **BLCS**
See also BW 1; CA 65-68; CANR 27, 84; CN 7

**Patton, George S(mith), Jr.**
1885-1945 .................................. **TCLC 79**
See also CA 189

**Paulding, James Kirke** 1778-1860 ... **NCLC 2**
See also DLB 3, 59, 74, 250; RGAL 4

**Paulin, Thomas Neilson** 1949-
See Paulin, Tom
See also CA 123; 128; CANR 98; CP 7

**Paulin, Tom** .............................. **CLC 37, 177**
See Paulin, Thomas Neilson
See also DLB 40

**Pausanias** c. 1st cent. - .................. **CMLC 36**

**Paustovsky, Konstantin (Georgievich)**
1892-1968 .................................. **CLC 40**
See also CA 93-96; 25-28R; DLB 272; EWL 3

**Pavese, Cesare** 1908-1950 .... **PC 13; SSC 19; TCLC 3**
See also CA 104; 169; DLB 128, 177; EW 12; EWL 3; PFS 20; RGSF 2; RGWL 2, 3; TWA

**Pavic, Milorad** 1929- .......................... **CLC 60**
See also CA 136; CDWLB 4; CWW 2; DLB 181; EWL 3; RGWL 3

**Pavlov, Ivan Petrovich** 1849-1936 . **TCLC 91**
See also CA 118; 180

**Pavlova, Karolina Karlovna**
1807-1893 .............................. **NCLC 138**
See also DLB 205

**Payne, Alan**
See Jakes, John (William)

**Paz, Gil**
See Lugones, Leopoldo

**Paz, Octavio** 1914-1998 . **CLC 3, 4, 6, 10, 19, 51, 65, 119; HLC 2; PC 1, 48; WLC**
See also AAYA 50; CA 73-76; 165; CANR 32, 65, 104; CWW 2; DA; DA3; DAB; DAC; DAM MST, MULT, POET; DLB 290; DLBY 1990, 1998; DNFS 1; EWL 3; HW 1, 2; LAW; LAWS 1; MTCW 1, 2; PFS 18; RGWL 2, 3; SSFS 13; TWA; WLIT 1

**p'Bitek, Okot** 1931-1982 .... **BLC 3; CLC 96; TCLC 149**
See also AFW; BW 2, 3; CA 124; 107; CANR 82; DAM MULT; DLB 125; EWL 3; MTCW 1, 2; RGEL 2; WLIT 2

**Peacock, Molly** 1947- ........................ **CLC 60**
See also CA 103; CAAS 21; CANR 52, 84; CP 7; CWP; DLB 120, 282

**Peacock, Thomas Love**
1785-1866 .............................. **NCLC 22**
See also BRW 4; DLB 96, 116; RGEL 2; RGSF 2

**Peake, Mervyn** 1911-1968 ............. **CLC 7, 54**
See also CA 5-8R; 25-28R; CANR 3; DLB 15, 160, 255; FANT; MTCW 1; RGEL 2; SATA 23; SFW 4

**Pearce, Philippa**
See Christie, Philippa
See also CA 5-8R; CANR 4, 109; CWRI 5; FANT; MAICYA 2

**Pearl, Eric**
See Elman, Richard (Martin)

**Pearson, T(homas) R(eid)** 1956- ....... **CLC 39**
See also CA 120; 130; CANR 97; CSW; INT CA-130

**Peck, Dale** 1967- .............................. **CLC 81**
See also CA 146; CANR 72, 127; GLL 2

**Peck, John (Frederick)** 1941- ............ **CLC 3**
See also CA 49-52; CANR 3, 100; CP 7

**Peck, Richard (Wayne)** 1934- ........... **CLC 21**
See also AAYA 1, 24; BYA 1, 6, 8, 11; CA 85-88; CANR 19, 38, 129; CLR 15; INT CANR-19; JRDA; MAICYA 1, 2; SAAS 2; SATA 18, 55, 97; SATA-Essay 110; WYA; YAW

**Peck, Robert Newton** 1928- .............. **CLC 17**
See also AAYA 3, 43; BYA 1, 6; CA 81-84, 182; CAAE 182; CANR 31, 63, 127; CLR 45; DA; DAC; DAM MST; JRDA; LAIT 3; MAICYA 1, 2; SAAS 1; SATA 21, 62, 111; SATA-Essay 108; WYA; YAW

**Peckinpah, (David) Sam(uel)**
1925-1984 .................................. **CLC 20**
See also CA 109; 114; CANR 82

**Pedersen, Knut** 1859-1952
See Hamsun, Knut
See also CA 104; 119; CANR 63; MTCW 1, 2

**Peeslake, Gaffer**
See Durrell, Lawrence (George)

**Peguy, Charles (Pierre)**
1873-1914 .................................. **TCLC 10**
See also CA 107; 193; DLB 258; EWL 3; GFL 1789 to the Present

**Peirce, Charles Sanders**
1839-1914 .................................. **TCLC 81**
See also CA 194; DLB 270

**Pellicer, Carlos** 1900(?)-1977 ......... **HLCS 2**
See also CA 153; 69-72; DLB 290; EWL 3; HW 1

**Pena, Ramon del Valle y**
See Valle-Inclan, Ramon (Maria) del

**Pendennis, Arthur Esquir**
See Thackeray, William Makepeace

**Penn, William** 1644-1718 .................... **LC 25**
See also DLB 24

**PEPECE**
See Prado (Calvo), Pedro

**Pepys, Samuel** 1633-1703 ... **LC 11, 58; WLC**
See also BRW 2; CDBLB 1660-1789; DA; DA3; DAB; DAC; DAM MST; DLB 101, 213; NCFS 4; RGEL 2; TEA; WLIT 3

**Percy, Thomas** 1729-1811 .............. **NCLC 95**
See also DLB 104

**Percy, Walker** 1916-1990 ....... **CLC 2, 3, 6, 8, 14, 18, 47, 65**
See also AMWS 3; BPFB 3; CA 1-4R; 131; CANR 1, 23, 64; CPW; CSW; DA3; DAM NOV, POP; DLB 2; DLBY 1980, 1990; EWL 3; MTCW 1, 2; RGAL 4; TUS

**Percy, William Alexander**
1885-1942 .................................. **TCLC 84**
See also CA 163; MTCW 2

**Perec, Georges** 1936-1982 ......... **CLC 56, 116**
See also CA 141; DLB 83, 299; EWL 3; GFL 1789 to the Present; RGWL 3

**Pereda (y Sanchez de Porrua), Jose Maria de** 1833-1906 ......................... **TCLC 16**
See also CA 117

**Pereda y Porrua, Jose Maria de**
See Pereda (y Sanchez de Porrua), Jose Maria de

**Peregoy, George Weems**
See Mencken, H(enry) L(ouis)

**Perelman, S(idney) J(oseph)**
1904-1979 .. **CLC 3, 5, 9, 15, 23, 44, 49; SSC 32**
See also AITN 1, 2; BPFB 3; CA 73-76; 89-92; CANR 18; DAM DRAM; DLB 11, 44; MTCW 1, 2; RGAL 4

**Peret, Benjamin** 1899-1959 .... **PC 33; TCLC 20**
See also CA 117; 186; GFL 1789 to the Present

**Peretz, Isaac Leib** 1851(?)-1915
See Peretz, Isaac Loeb
See also CA 201

**Peretz, Isaac Loeb** 1851(?)-1915 ...... **SSC 26; TCLC 16**
See Peretz, Isaac Leib
See also CA 109

**Peretz, Yitzkhok Leibush**
See Peretz, Isaac Loeb

**Perez Galdos, Benito** 1843-1920 ..... **HLCS 2; TCLC 27**
See Galdos, Benito Perez
See also CA 125; 153; EWL 3; HW 1; RGWL 2, 3

**Peri Rossi, Cristina** 1941- .. **CLC 156; HLCS 2**
See also CA 131; CANR 59, 81; CWW 2; DLB 145, 290; EWL 3; HW 1, 2

**Perlata**
See Peret, Benjamin

**Perloff, Marjorie G(abrielle)** 1931- ............................... **CLC 137**
See also CA 57-60; CANR 7, 22, 49, 104

**Perrault, Charles** 1628-1703 ........... **LC 2, 56**
See also BYA 4; CLR 79; DLB 268; GFL Beginnings to 1789; MAICYA 1, 2; RGWL 2, 3; SATA 25; WCH

**Perry, Anne** 1938- ........................... **CLC 126**
See also CA 101; CANR 22, 50, 84; CMW 4; CN 7; CPW; DLB 276

**Perry, Brighton**
See Sherwood, Robert E(mmet)

**Perse, St.-John**
See Leger, (Marie-Rene Auguste) Alexis Saint-Leger

**Perse, Saint-John**
See Leger, (Marie-Rene Auguste) Alexis Saint-Leger
See also DLB 258; RGWL 3

**Perutz, Leo(pold)** 1882-1957 ......... **TCLC 60**
See also CA 147; DLB 81

**Peseenz, Tulio F.**
See Lopez y Fuentes, Gregorio

**Pesetsky, Bette** 1932- ......................... **CLC 28**
See also CA 133; DLB 130

**Peshkov, Alexei Maximovich** 1868-1936
See Gorky, Maxim
See also CA 105; 141; CANR 83; DA; DAC; DAM DRAM, MST, NOV; MTCW 2

**Pessoa, Fernando (Antonio Nogueira)** 1888-1935 ..... **HLC 2; PC 20; TCLC 27**
See also CA 125; 183; DAM MULT; DLB 287; EW 10; EWL 3; RGWL 2, 3; WP

**Peterkin, Julia Mood** 1880-1961 ...... **CLC 31**
See also CA 102; DLB 9

**Peters, Joan K(aren)** 1945- ............... **CLC 39**
See also CA 158; CANR 109

**Peters, Robert L(ouis)** 1924- ............... **CLC 7**
See also CA 13-16R; CAAS 8; CP 7; DLB 105

**Petofi, Sandor** 1823-1849 ................ **NCLC 21**
See also RGWL 2, 3

**Petrakis, Harry Mark** 1923- ............... **CLC 3**
See also CA 9-12R; CANR 4, 30, 85; CN 7

**Petrarch** 1304-1374 ............ **CMLC 20; PC 8**
See also DA3; DAM POET; EW 2; LMFS 1; RGWL 2. 3

**Petronius** c. 20-66 ........................... **CMLC 34**
See also AW 2; CDWLB 1; DLB 211; RGWL 2, 3

**Petrov, Evgeny** ............................... **TCLC 21**
See Kataev, Evgeny Petrovich

**Petry, Ann (Lane)** 1908-1997 .. **CLC 1, 7, 18; TCLC 112**
See also AFAW 1, 2; BPFB 3; BW 1, 3; BYA 2; CA 5-8R; 157; CAAS 6; CANR 4, 46; CLR 12; CN 7; DLB 76; EWL 3; JRDA; LAIT 1; MAICYA 1, 2; MAIC-YAS 1; MTCW 1; RGAL 4; SATA 5; SATA-Obit 94; TUS

**Petursson, Halligrimur** 1614-1674 ........ **LC 8**

**Peychinovich**
See Vazov, Ivan (Minchov)

**Phaedrus** c. 15B.C.-c. 50 ............... **CMLC 25**
See also DLB 211

**Phelps (Ward), Elizabeth Stuart**
See Phelps, Elizabeth Stuart
See also FW

**Phelps, Elizabeth Stuart** 1844-1911 ............................... **TCLC 113**
See Phelps (Ward), Elizabeth Stuart
See also DLB 74

**Philips, Katherine** 1632-1664 . **LC 30; PC 40**
See also DLB 131; RGEL 2

**Philipson, Morris H.** 1926- .............. **CLC 53**
See also CA 1-4R; CANR 4

**Phillips, Caryl** 1958- ............. **BLCS; CLC 96**
See also BRWS 5; BW 2; CA 141; CANR 63, 104; CBD; CD 5; CN 7; DA3; DAM MULT; DLB 157; EWL 3; MTCW 2; WLIT 4; WWE 1

**Phillips, David Graham** 1867-1911 ........................... **TCLC 44**
See also CA 108; 176; DLB 9, 12, 303; RGAL 4

**Phillips, Jack**
See Sandburg, Carl (August)

**Phillips, Jayne Anne** 1952- ........ **CLC 15, 33, 139; SSC 16**
See also AAYA 57; BPFB 3; CA 101; CANR 24, 50, 96; CN 7; CSW; DLBY 1980; INT CANR-24; MTCW 1, 2; RGAL 4; RGSF 2; SSFS 4

**Phillips, Richard**
See Dick, Philip K(indred)

**Phillips, Robert (Schaeffer)** 1938- .... **CLC 28**
See also CA 17-20R; CAAS 13; CANR 8; DLB 105

**Phillips, Ward**
See Lovecraft, H(oward) P(hillips)

**Philostratus, Flavius** c. 179-c. 244 .................................... **CMLC 62**

**Piccolo, Lucio** 1901-1969 ................. **CLC 13**
See also CA 97-100; DLB 114; EWL 3

**Pickthall, Marjorie L(owry) C(hristie)** 1883-1922 ........................... **TCLC 21**
See also CA 107; DLB 92

**Pico della Mirandola, Giovanni** 1463-1494 ....................................... **LC 15**
See also LMFS 1

**Piercy, Marge** 1936- .... **CLC 3, 6, 14, 18, 27, 62, 128; PC 29**
See also BPFB 3; CA 21-24R, 187; CAAE 187; CAAS 1; CANR 13, 43, 66, 111; CN 7; CP 7; CWP; DLB 120, 227; EXPP; FW; MTCW 1, 2; PFS 9; SFW 4

**Piers, Robert**
See Anthony, Piers

**Pieyre de Mandiargues, Andre** 1909-1991
See Mandiargues, Andre Pieyre de
See also CA 103; 136; CANR 22, 82; EWL 3; GFL 1789 to the Present

**Pilnyak, Boris** 1894-1938 . **SSC 48; TCLC 23**
See Vogau, Boris Andreyevich
See also EWL 3

**Pinchback, Eugene**
See Toomer, Jean

**Pincherle, Alberto** 1907-1990 ...... **CLC 11, 18**
See Moravia, Alberto
See also CA 25-28R; 132; CANR 33, 63; DAM NOV; MTCW 1

**Pinckney, Darryl** 1953- ..................... **CLC 76**
See also BW 2, 3; CA 143; CANR 79

**Pindar** 518(?)B.C.-438(?)B.C. ....... **CMLC 12; PC 19**
See also AW 1; CDWLB 1; DLB 176; RGWL 2

**Pineda, Cecile** 1942- ........................... **CLC 39**
See also CA 118; DLB 209

**Pinero, Arthur Wing** 1855-1934 .... **TCLC 32**
See also CA 110; 153; DAM DRAM; DLB 10; RGEL 2

**Pinero, Miguel (Antonio Gomez)** 1946-1988 ............................... **CLC 4, 55**
See also CA 61-64; 125; CAD; CANR 29, 90; DLB 266; HW 1; LLW 1

**Pinget, Robert** 1919-1997 ....... **CLC 7, 13, 37**
See also CA 85-88; 160; CWW 2; DLB 83; EWL 3; GFL 1789 to the Present

**Pink Floyd**
See Barrett, (Roger) Syd; Gilmour, David; Mason, Nick; Waters, Roger; Wright, Rick

**Pinkney, Edward** 1802-1828 .......... **NCLC 31**
See also DLB 248

**Pinkwater, Daniel**
See Pinkwater, Daniel Manus

**Pinkwater, Daniel Manus** 1941- ....... **CLC 35**
See also AAYA 1, 46; BYA 9; CA 29-32R; CANR 12, 38, 89; CLR 4; CSW; FANT; JRDA; MAICYA 1, 2; SAAS 3; SATA 8, 46, 76, 114; SFW 4; YAW

**Pinkwater, Manus**
See Pinkwater, Daniel Manus

**Pinsky, Robert** 1940- ....... **CLC 9, 19, 38, 94, 121; PC 27**
See also AMWS 6; CA 29-32R; CAAS 4; CANR 58, 97; CP 7; DA3; DAM POET; DLBY 1982, 1998; MTCW 2; PFS 18; RGAL 4

**Pinta, Harold**
See Pinter, Harold

**Pinter, Harold** 1930- .. **CLC 1, 3, 6, 9, 11, 15, 27, 58, 73; DC 15; WLC**
See also BRWR 1; BRWS 1; CA 5-8R; CANR 33, 65, 112; CBD; CD 5; CDBLB 1960 to Present; DA; DA3; DAB; DAC; DAM DRAM, MST; DFS 3, 5, 7, 14; DLB 13; EWL 3; IDFW 3, 4; LMFS 2; MTCW 1, 2; RGEL 2; TEA

**Piozzi, Hester Lynch (Thrale)** 1741-1821 ............................... **NCLC 57**
See also DLB 104, 142

**Pirandello, Luigi** 1867-1936 .. **DC 5; SSC 22; TCLC 4, 29; WLC**
See also CA 104; 153; CANR 103; DA; DA3; DAB; DAC; DAM DRAM, MST; DFS 4, 9; DLB 264; EW 8; EWL 3; MTCW 2; RGSF 2; RGWL 2, 3

**Pirsig, Robert M(aynard)** 1928- ... **CLC 4, 6, 73**
See also CA 53-56; CANR 42, 74; CPW 1; DA3; DAM POP; MTCW 1, 2; SATA 39

**Pisarev, Dmitrii Ivanovich**
See Pisarev, Dmitry Ivanovich
See also DLB 277

**Pisarev, Dmitry Ivanovich** 1840-1868 ............................... **NCLC 25**
See Pisarev, Dmitrii Ivanovich

**Pix, Mary (Griffith)** 1666-1709 ............. **LC 8**
See also DLB 80

**Pixerecourt, (Rene Charles) Guilbert de** 1773-1844 ............................... **NCLC 39**
See also DLB 192; GFL 1789 to the Present

**Plaatje, Sol(omon) T(shekisho)** 1878-1932 ................. **BLCS; TCLC 73**
See also BW 2, 3; CA 141; CANR 79; DLB 125, 225

**Plaidy, Jean**
See Hibbert, Eleanor Alice Burford

**Planche, James Robinson**
1796-1880 .................................. **NCLC 42**
See also RGEL 2

**Plant, Robert** 1948- ........................... **CLC 12**

**Plante, David (Robert)** 1940- . **CLC 7, 23, 38**
See also CA 37-40R; CANR 12, 36, 58, 82;
CN 7; DAM NOV; DLBY 1983; INT
CANR-12; MTCW 1

**Plath, Sylvia** 1932-1963 ..... **CLC 1, 2, 3, 5, 9,
11, 14, 17, 50, 51, 62, 111; PC 1, 37;
WLC**
See also AAYA 13; AMWR 2; AMWS 1;
BPFB 3; CA 19-20; CANR 34, 101; CAP
2; CDALB 1941-1968; DA; DA3; DAB;
DAC; DAM MST, POET; DLB 5, 6, 152;
EWL 3; EXPN; EXPP; FW; LAIT 4;
MAWW; MTCW 1, 2; NFS 1; PAB; PFS
1, 15; RGAL 4; SATA 96; TUS; WP;
YAW

**Plato** c. 428B.C.-347B.C. ... **CMLC 8; WLCS**
See also AW 1; CDWLB 1; DA; DA3;
DAB; DAC; DAM MST; DLB 176; LAIT
1; LATS 1:1; RGWL 2, 3

**Platonov, Andrei**
See Klimentov, Andrei Platonovich

**Platonov, Andrei Platonovich**
See Klimentov, Andrei Platonovich
See also DLB 272

**Platonov, Andrey Platonovich**
See Klimentov, Andrei Platonovich
See also EWL 3

**Platt, Kin** 1911- ................................. **CLC 26**
See also AAYA 11; CA 17-20R; CANR 11;
JRDA; SAAS 17; SATA 21, 86; WYA

**Plautus** c. 254B.C.-c. 184B.C. ...... **CMLC 24;
DC 6**
See also AW 1; CDWLB 1; DLB 211;
RGWL 2, 3

**Plick et Plock**
See Simenon, Georges (Jacques Christian)

**Plieksans, Janis**
See Rainis, Janis

**Plimpton, George (Ames)**
1927-2003 ................................. **CLC 36**
See also AITN 1; CA 21-24R; 224; CANR
32, 70, 103, 133; DLB 185, 241; MTCW
1, 2; SATA 10; SATA-Obit 150

**Pliny the Elder** c. 23-79 ................ **CMLC 23**
See also DLB 211

**Pliny the Younger** c. 61-c. 112 ...... **CMLC 62**
See also AW 2; DLB 211

**Plomer, William Charles Franklin**
1903-1973 ............................ **CLC 4, 8**
See also AFW; CA 21-22; CANR 34; CAP
2; DLB 20, 162, 191, 225; EWL 3;
MTCW 1; RGEL 2; RGSF 2; SATA 24

**Plotinus** 204-270 ............................ **CMLC 46**
See also CDWLB 1; DLB 176

**Plowman, Piers**
See Kavanagh, Patrick (Joseph)

**Plum, J.**
See Wodehouse, P(elham) G(renville)

**Plumly, Stanley (Ross)** 1939- ........... **CLC 33**
See also CA 108; 110; CANR 97; CP 7;
DLB 5, 193; INT CA-110

**Plumpe, Friedrich Wilhelm**
1888-1931 ................................. **TCLC 53**
See also CA 112

**Plutarch** c. 46-c. 120 ...................... **CMLC 60**
See also AW 2; CDWLB 1; DLB 176;
RGWL 2, 3; TWA

**Po Chu-i** 772-846 ........................... **CMLC 24**

**Podhoretz, Norman** 1930- .............. **CLC 189**
See also AMWS 8; CA 9-12R; CANR 7, 78

**Poe, Edgar Allan** 1809-1849 ..... **NCLC 1, 16,
55, 78, 94, 97, 117; PC 1, 54; SSC 1,
22, 34, 35, 54; WLC**
See also AAYA 14; AMW; AMWC 1;
AMWR 2; BPFB 3; BYA 5, 11; CDALB

1640-1865; CMW 4; DA; DA3; DAB;
DAC; DAM MST, POET; DLB 3, 59, 73,
74, 248, 254; EXPP; EXPS; HGG; LAIT
2; LATS 1:1; LMFS 1; MSW; PAB; PFS
1, 3, 9; RGAL 4; RGSF 2; SATA 23;
SCFW 2; SFW 4; SSFS 2, 4, 7, 8, 16;
SUFW; TUS; WP; WYA

**Poet of Titchfield Street, The**
See Pound, Ezra (Weston Loomis)

**Pohl, Frederik** 1919- ........... **CLC 18; SSC 25**
See also AAYA 24; CA 61-64, 188; CAAE
188; CAAS 1; CANR 11, 37, 81; CN 7;
DLB 8; INT CANR-11; MTCW 1, 2;
SATA 24; SCFW 2; SFW 4

**Poirier, Louis** 1910-
See Gracq, Julien
See also CA 122; 126

**Poitier, Sidney** 1927- ......................... **CLC 26**
See also BW 1; CA 117; CANR 94

**Pokagon, Simon** 1830-1899 ............... **NNAL**
See also DAM MULT

**Polanski, Roman** 1933- ........... **CLC 16, 178**
See also CA 77-80

**Poliakoff, Stephen** 1952- ................... **CLC 38**
See also CA 106; CANR 116; CBD; CD 5;
DLB 13

**Police, The**
See Copeland, Stewart (Armstrong); Summers, Andrew James

**Polidori, John William** 1795-1821 . **NCLC 51**
See also DLB 116; HGG

**Pollitt, Katha** 1949- ................... **CLC 28, 122**
See also CA 120; 122; CANR 66, 108;
MTCW 1, 2

**Pollock, (Mary) Sharon** 1936- .......... **CLC 50**
See also CA 141; CANR 132; CD 5; CWD;
DAC; DAM DRAM, MST; DFS 3; DLB
60; FW

**Pollock, Sharon** 1936- ......................... **DC 20**

**Polo, Marco** 1254-1324 ................. **CMLC 15**

**Polonsky, Abraham (Lincoln)**
1910-1999 ................................. **CLC 92**
See also CA 104; 187; DLB 26; INT CA-
104

**Polybius** c. 200B.C.-c. 118B.C. ...... **CMLC 17**
See also AW 1; DLB 176; RGWL 2, 3

**Pomerance, Bernard** 1940- ................ **CLC 13**
See also CA 101; CAD; CANR 49; CD 5;
DAM DRAM; DFS 9; LAIT 2

**Ponge, Francis** 1899-1988 ............ **CLC 6, 18**
See also CA 85-88; 126; CANR 40, 86;
DAM POET; DLBY 2002; EWL 3; GFL
1789 to the Present; RGWL 2, 3

**Poniatowska, Elena** 1933- . **CLC 140; HLC 2**
See also CA 101; CANR 32, 66, 107; CD-
WLB 3; CWW 2; DAM MULT; DLB 113;
EWL 3; HW 1, 2; LAWS 1; WLIT 1

**Pontoppidan, Henrik** 1857-1943 .... **TCLC 29**
See also CA 170; DLB 300

**Ponty, Maurice Merleau**
See Merleau-Ponty, Maurice

**Poole, Josephine** ................................. **CLC 17**
See Helyar, Jane Penelope Josephine
See also SAAS 2; SATA 5

**Popa, Vasko** 1922-1991 ..................... **CLC 19**
See also CA 112; 148; CDWLB 4; DLB
181; EWL 3; RGWL 2, 3

**Pope, Alexander** 1688-1744 ...... **LC 3, 58, 60,
64; PC 26; WLC**
See also BRW 3; BRWC 1; BRWR 1; CD-
BLB 1660-1789; DA; DA3; DAB; DAC;
DAM MST, POET; DLB 95, 101, 213;
EXPP; PAB; PFS 12; RGEL 2; WLIT 3;
WP

**Popov, Evgenii Anatol'evich**
See Popov, Yevgeny
See also DLB 285

**Popov, Yevgeny** ................................. **CLC 59**
See Popov, Evgenii Anatol'evich

**Poquelin, Jean-Baptiste**
See Moliere

**Porphyry** c. 233-c. 305 .................. **CMLC 71**

**Porter, Connie (Rose)** 1959(?)- ......... **CLC 70**
See also BW 2, 3; CA 142; CANR 90, 109;
SATA 81, 129

**Porter, Gene(va Grace) Stratton** .. **TCLC 21**
See Stratton-Porter, Gene(va Grace)
See also BPFB 3; CA 112; CWRI 5; RHW

**Porter, Katherine Anne** 1890-1980 ... **CLC 1,
3, 7, 10, 13, 15, 27, 101; SSC 4, 31, 43**
See also AAYA 42; AITN 2; AMW; BPFB
3; CA 1-4R; 101; CANR 1, 65; CDALBS;
DA; DA3; DAB; DAC; DAM MST, NOV;
DLB 4, 9, 102; DLBD 12; DLBY 1980;
EWL 3; EXPS; LAIT 3; MAWW; MTCW
1, 2; NFS 14; RGAL 4; RGSF 2; SATA
39; SATA-Obit 23; SSFS 1, 8, 11, 16;
TUS

**Porter, Peter (Neville Frederick)**
1929- ..................................... **CLC 5, 13, 33**
See also CA 85-88; CP 7; DLB 40, 289;
WWE 1

**Porter, William Sydney** 1862-1910
See Henry, O.
See also CA 104; 131; CDALB 1865-1917;
DA; DA3; DAB; DAC; DAM MST; DLB
12, 78, 79; MTCW 1, 2; TUS; YABC 2

**Portillo (y Pacheco), Jose Lopez**
See Lopez Portillo (y Pacheco), Jose

**Portillo Trambley, Estela** 1927-1998 .. **HLC 2**
See Trambley, Estela Portillo
See also CANR 32; DAM MULT; DLB
209; HW 1

**Posey, Alexander (Lawrence)**
1873-1908 ................................. **NNAL**
See also CA 144; CANR 80; DAM MULT;
DLB 175

**Posse, Abel** ................................. **CLC 70**

**Post, Melville Davisson**
1869-1930 ................................. **TCLC 39**
See also CA 110; 202; CMW 4

**Potok, Chaim** 1929-2002 ... **CLC 2, 7, 14, 26,
112**
See also AAYA 15, 50; AITN 1, 2; BPFB 3;
BYA 1; CA 17-20R; 208; CANR 19, 35,
64, 98; CLR 92; CN 7; DA3; DAM NOV;
DLB 28, 152; EXPN; INT CANR-19;
LAIT 4; MTCW 1, 2; NFS 4; SATA 33,
106; SATA-Obit 134; TUS; YAW

**Potok, Herbert Harold** -2002
See Potok, Chaim

**Potok, Herman Harold**
See Potok, Chaim

**Potter, Dennis (Christopher George)**
1935-1994 ................................. **CLC 58, 86, 123**
See also CA 107; 145; CANR 33, 61; CBD;
DLB 233; MTCW 1

**Pound, Ezra (Weston Loomis)**
1885-1972 .. **CLC 1, 2, 3, 4, 5, 7, 10, 13,
18, 34, 48, 50, 112; PC 4; WLC**
See also AAYA 47; AMW; AMWR 1; CA
5-8R; 37-40R; CANR 40; CDALB 1917-
1929; DA; DA3; DAB; DAC; DAM MST,
POET; DLB 4, 45, 63; DLBD 15; EFS 2;
EWL 3; EXPP; LMFS 2; MTCW 1, 2;
PAB; PFS 2, 8, 16; RGAL 4; TUS; WP

**Povod, Reinaldo** 1959-1994 ............... **CLC 44**
See also CA 136; 146; CANR 83

**Powell, Adam Clayton, Jr.**
1908-1972 ................... **BLC 3; CLC 89**
See also BW 1, 3; CA 102; 33-36R; CANR
86; DAM MULT

**Powell, Anthony (Dymoke)**
1905-2000 ........... **CLC 1, 3, 7, 9, 10, 31**
See also BRW 7; CA 1-4R; 189; CANR 1,
32, 62, 107; CDBLB 1945-1960; CN 7;
DLB 15; EWL 3; MTCW 1, 2; RGEL 2;
TEA

**Powell, Dawn** 1896(?)-1965 .............. **CLC 66**
See also CA 5-8R; CANR 121; DLBY 1997

**Powell, Padgett** 1952- ..................... **CLC 34**
See also CA 126; CANR 63, 101; CSW;
DLB 234; DLBY 01

**Powell, (Oval) Talmage** 1920-2000
See Queen, Ellery
See also CA 5-8R; CANR 2, 80

**Power, Susan** 1961- ........................... **CLC 91**
See also BYA 14; CA 160; NFS 11

**Powers, J(ames) F(arl)** 1917-1999 ..... **CLC 1,
4, 8, 57; SSC 4**
See also CA 1-4R; 181; CANR 2, 61; CN
7; DLB 130; MTCW 1; RGAL 4; RGSF
2

**Powers, John J(ames)** 1945-
See Powers, John R.
See also CA 69-72

**Powers, John R.** ............................... **CLC 66**
See Powers, John J(ames)

**Powers, Richard (S.)** 1957- .............. **CLC 93**
See also AMWS 9; BPFB 3; CA 148;
CANR 80; CN 7

**Pownall, David** 1938- ........................ **CLC 10**
See also CA 89-92, 180; CAAS 18; CANR
49, 101; CBD; CD 5; CN 7; DLB 14

**Powys, John Cowper** 1872-1963 ... **CLC 7, 9,
15, 46, 125**
See also CA 85-88; CANR 106; DLB 15,
255; EWL 3; FANT; MTCW 1, 2; RGEL
2; SUFW

**Powys, T(heodore) F(rancis)**
1875-1953 ..................................... **TCLC 9**
See also BRWS 8; CA 106; 189; DLB 36,
162; EWL 3; FANT; RGEL 2; SUFW

**Prado (Calvo), Pedro** 1886-1952 ... **TCLC 75**
See also CA 131; DLB 283; HW 1; LAW

**Prager, Emily** 1952- ........................ **CLC 56**
See also CA 204

**Pratchett, Terry** 1948- ..................... **CLC 197**
See also AAYA 19, 54; BPFB 3; CA 143;
CANR 87, 126; CLR 64; CN 7; CPW;
CWRI 5; FANT; SATA 82, 139; SFW 4;
SUFW 2

**Pratolini, Vasco** 1913-1991 .......... **TCLC 124**
See also CA 211; DLB 177; EWL 3; RGWL
2, 3

**Pratt, E(dwin) J(ohn)** 1883(?)-1964 . **CLC 19**
See also CA 141; 93-96; CANR 77; DAC;
DAM POET; DLB 92; EWL 3; RGEL 2;
TWA

**Premchand** ...................................... **TCLC 21**
See Srivastava, Dhanpat Rai
See also EWL 3

**Preseren, France** 1800-1849 ......... **NCLC 127**
See also CDWLB 4; DLB 147

**Preussler, Otfried** 1923- ..................... **CLC 17**
See also CA 77-80; SATA 24

**Prevert, Jacques (Henri Marie)**
1900-1977 ..................................... **CLC 15**
See also CA 77-80; 69-72; CANR 29, 61;
DLB 258; EWL 3; GFL 1789 to the
Present; IDFW 3, 4; MTCW 1; RGWL 2,
3; SATA-Obit 30

**Prevost, (Antoine Francois)**
1697-1763 ......................................... **LC 1**
See also EW 4; GFL Beginnings to 1789;
RGWL 2, 3

**Price, (Edward) Reynolds** 1933- ... **CLC 3, 6,
13, 43, 50, 63; SSC 22**
See also AMWS 6; CA 1-4R; CANR 1, 37,
57, 87, 128; CN 7; CSW; DAM NOV;
DLB 2, 218, 278; EWL 3; INT CANR-
37; NFS 18

**Price, Richard** 1949- ..................... **CLC 6, 12**
See also CA 49-52; CANR 3; DLBY 1981

**Prichard, Katharine Susannah**
1883-1969 ..................................... **CLC 46**
See also CA 11-12; CANR 33; CAP 1; DLB
260; MTCW 1; RGEL 2; RGSF 2; SATA
66

**Priestley, J(ohn) B(oynton)**
1894-1984 ..................... **CLC 2, 5, 9, 34**
See also BRW 7; CA 9-12R; 113; CANR
33; CDBLB 1914-1945; DA3; DAM
DRAM, NOV; DLB 10, 34, 77, 100, 139;
DLBY 1984; EWL 3; MTCW 1, 2; RGEL
2; SFW 4

**Prince** 1958- ...................................... **CLC 35**
See also CA 213

**Prince, F(rank) T(empleton)**
1912-2003 ..................................... **CLC 22**
See also CA 101; 219; CANR 43, 79; CP 7;
DLB 20

**Prince Kropotkin**
See Kropotkin, Peter (Aleksieevich)

**Prior, Matthew** 1664-1721 ..................... **LC 4**
See also DLB 95; RGEL 2

**Prishvin, Mikhail** 1873-1954 ......... **TCLC 75**
See Prishvin, Mikhail Mikhailovich

**Prishvin, Mikhail Mikhailovich**
See Prishvin, Mikhail
See also DLB 272; EWL 3

**Pritchard, William H(arrison)**
1932- ......................................... **CLC 34**
See also CA 65-68; CANR 23, 95; DLB
111

**Pritchett, V(ictor) S(awdon)**
1900-1997 ... **CLC 5, 13, 15, 41; SSC 14**
See also BPFB 3; BRWS 3; CA 61-64; 157;
CANR 31, 63; CN 7; DA3; DAM NOV;
DLB 15, 139; EWL 3; MTCW 1, 2;
RGEL 2; RGSF 2; TEA

**Private 19022**
See Manning, Frederic

**Probst, Mark** 1925- ........................... **CLC 59**
See also CA 130

**Prokosch, Frederic** 1908-1989 ...... **CLC 4, 48**
See also CA 73-76; 128; CANR 82; DLB
48; MTCW 2

**Propertius, Sextus** c. 50B.C.-c.
16B.C. ....................................... **CMLC 32**
See also AW 2; CDWLB 1; DLB 211;
RGWL 2, 3

**Prophet, The**
See Dreiser, Theodore (Herman Albert)

**Prose, Francine** 1947- ........................ **CLC 45**
See also CA 109; 112; CANR 46, 95, 132;
DLB 234; SATA 101, 149

**Proudhon**
See Cunha, Euclides (Rodrigues Pimenta)
da

**Proulx, Annie**
See Proulx, E(dna) Annie

**Proulx, E(dna) Annie** 1935- ...... **CLC 81, 158**
See also AMWS 7; BPFB 3; CA 145;
CANR 65, 110; CN 7; CPW 1; DA3;
DAM POP; MTCW 2; SSFS 18

**Proust, (Valentin-Louis-George-Eugene)
Marcel** 1871-1922 ..... **SSC 75; TCLC 7,
13, 33; WLC**
See also AAYA 58; BPFB 3; CA 104; 120;
CANR 110; DA; DA3; DAB; DAC; DAM
MST, NOV; DLB 65; EW 8; EWL 3; GFL
1789 to the Present; MTCW 1, 2; RGWL
2, 3; TWA

**Prowler, Harley**
See Masters, Edgar Lee

**Prus, Boleslaw** 1845-1912 .............. **TCLC 48**
See also RGWL 2, 3

**Pryor, Richard (Franklin Lenox Thomas)**
1940- ......................................... **CLC 26**
See also CA 122; 152

**Przybyszewski, Stanislaw**
1868-1927 ................................. **TCLC 36**
See also CA 160; DLB 66; EWL 3

**Pteleon**
See Grieve, C(hristopher) M(urray)
See also DAM POET

**Puckett, Lute**
See Masters, Edgar Lee

**Puig, Manuel** 1932-1990 .... **CLC 3, 5, 10, 28,
65, 133; HLC 2**
See also BPFB 3; CA 45-48; CANR 2, 32,
63; CDWLB 3; DA3; DAM MULT; DLB
113; DNFS 1; EWL 3; GLL 1; HW 1, 2;
LAW; MTCW 1, 2; RGWL 2, 3; TWA;
WLIT 1

**Pulitzer, Joseph** 1847-1911 ............. **TCLC 76**
See also CA 114; DLB 23

**Purchas, Samuel** 1577(?)-1626 ............. **LC 70**
See also DLB 151

**Purdy, A(lfred) W(ellington)**
1918-2000 ................... **CLC 3, 6, 14, 50**
See also CA 81-84; 189; CAAS 17; CANR
42, 66; CP 7; DAC; DAM MST, POET;
DLB 88; PFS 5; RGEL 2

**Purdy, James (Amos)** 1923- .... **CLC 2, 4, 10,
28, 52**
See also AMWS 7; CA 33-36R; CAAS 1;
CANR 19, 51, 132; CN 7; DLB 2, 218;
EWL 3; INT CANR-19; MTCW 1; RGAL
4

**Pure, Simon**
See Swinnerton, Frank Arthur

**Pushkin, Aleksandr Sergeevich**
See Pushkin, Alexander (Sergeyevich)
See also DLB 205

**Pushkin, Alexander (Sergeyevich)**
1799-1837 ....... **NCLC 3, 27, 83; PC 10;
SSC 27, 55; WLC**
See Pushkin, Aleksandr Sergeevich
See also DA; DA3; DAB; DAC; DAM
DRAM, MST, POET; EW 5; EXPS; RGSF
2; RGWL 2, 3; SATA 61; SSFS 9; TWA

**P'u Sung-ling** 1640-1715 ....... **LC 49; SSC 31**

**Putnam, Arthur Lee**
See Alger, Horatio, Jr.

**Puzo, Mario** 1920-1999 ........ **CLC 1, 2, 6, 36,
107**
See also BPFB 3; CA 65-68; 185; CANR 4,
42, 65, 99, 131; CN 7; CPW; DA3; DAM
NOV, POP; DLB 6; MTCW 1, 2; NFS 16;
RGAL 4

**Pygge, Edward**
See Barnes, Julian (Patrick)

**Pyle, Ernest Taylor** 1900-1945
See Pyle, Ernie
See also CA 115; 160

**Pyle, Ernie** ...................................... **TCLC 75**
See Pyle, Ernest Taylor
See also DLB 29; MTCW 2

**Pyle, Howard** 1853-1911 ................. **TCLC 81**
See also AAYA 57; BYA 2, 4; CA 109; 137;
CLR 22; DLB 42, 188; DLBD 13; LAIT
1; MAICYA 1, 2; SATA 16, 100; WCH;
YAW

**Pym, Barbara (Mary Crampton)**
1913-1980 ............... **CLC 13, 19, 37, 111**
See also BPFB 3; BRWS 2; CA 13-14; 97-
100; CANR 13, 34; CAP 1; DLB 14, 207;
DLBY 1987; EWL 3; MTCW 1, 2; RGEL
2; TEA

**Pynchon, Thomas (Ruggles, Jr.)**
1937- ...... **CLC 2, 3, 6, 9, 11, 18, 33, 62,
72, 123, 192; SSC 14; WLC**
See also AMWS 2; BEST 90:2; BPFB 3;
CA 17-20R; CANR 22, 46, 73; CN 7;
CPW 1; DA; DA3; DAB; DAC; DAM
MST, NOV, POP; DLB 2, 173; EWL 3;
MTCW 1, 2; RGAL 4; SFW 4; TUS

**Pythagoras** c. 582B.C.-c. 507B.C. . **CMLC 22**
See also DLB 176

**Q**
See Quiller-Couch, Sir Arthur (Thomas)

**Qian, Chongzhu**
See Ch'ien, Chung-shu

**Qian, Sima** 145B.C.-c. 89B.C. ....... **CMLC 72**

**Qian Zhongshu**
See Ch'ien, Chung-shu
See also CWW 2

**Qroll**
See Dagerman, Stig (Halvard)

**Quarrington, Paul (Lewis)** 1953- ..... **CLC 65**
See also CA 129; CANR 62, 95

**Quasimodo, Salvatore** 1901-1968 .... **CLC 10; PC 47**
See also CA 13-16; 25-28R; CAP 1; DLB 114; EW 12; EWL 3; MTCW 1; RGWL 2, 3

**Quatermass, Martin**
See Carpenter, John (Howard)

**Quay, Stephen** 1947- ......................... **CLC 95**
See also CA 189

**Quay, Timothy** 1947- ........................ **CLC 95**
See also CA 189

**Queen, Ellery** ............................... **CLC 3, 11**
See Dannay, Frederic; Davidson, Avram (James); Deming, Richard; Fairman, Paul W.; Flora, Fletcher; Hoch, Edward D(entinger); Kane, Henry; Lee, Manfred B(ennington); Marlowe, Stephen; Powell, (Oval) Talmage; Sheldon, Walter J(ames); Sturgeon, Theodore (Hamilton); Tracy, Don(ald Fiske); Vance, John Holbrook
See also BPFB 3; CMW 4; MSW; RGAL 4

**Queen, Ellery, Jr.**
See Dannay, Frederic; Lee, Manfred B(ennington)

**Queneau, Raymond** 1903-1976 ..... **CLC 2, 5, 10, 42**
See also CA 77-80; 69-72; CANR 32; DLB 72, 258; EW 12; EWL 3; GFL 1789 to the Present; MTCW 1, 2; RGWL 2, 3

**Quevedo, Francisco de** 1580-1645 ....... **LC 23**

**Quiller-Couch, Sir Arthur (Thomas)** 1863-1944 ......................... **TCLC 53**
See also CA 118; 166; DLB 135, 153, 190; HGG; RGEL 2; SUFW 1

**Quin, Ann (Marie)** 1936-1973 ............. **CLC 6**
See also CA 9-12R; 45-48; DLB 14, 231

**Quincey, Thomas de**
See De Quincey, Thomas

**Quindlen, Anna** 1953- ...................... **CLC 191**
See also AAYA 35; CA 138; CANR 73, 126; DA3; DLB 292; MTCW 2

**Quinn, Martin**
See Smith, Martin Cruz

**Quinn, Peter** 1947- ............................ **CLC 91**
See also CA 197

**Quinn, Simon**
See Smith, Martin Cruz

**Quintana, Leroy V.** 1944- ...... **HLC 2; PC 36**
See also CA 131; CANR 65; DAM MULT; DLB 82; HW 1, 2

**Quiroga, Horacio (Sylvestre)** 1878-1937 ................. **HLC 2; TCLC 20**
See also CA 117; 131; DAM MULT; EWL 3; HW 1; LAW; MTCW 1; RGSF 2; WLIT 1

**Quoirez, Francoise** 1935- ................... **CLC 9**
See Sagan, Francoise
See also CA 49-52; CANR 6, 39, 73; MTCW 1, 2; TWA

**Raabe, Wilhelm (Karl)** 1831-1910 . **TCLC 45**
See also CA 167; DLB 129

**Rabe, David (William)** 1940- .. **CLC 4, 8, 33; DC 16**
See also CA 85-88; CABS 3; CAD; CANR 59, 129; CD 5; DAM DRAM; DFS 3, 8, 13; DLB 7, 228; EWL 3

**Rabelais, Francois** 1494-1553 ........ **LC 5, 60; WLC**
See also DA; DAB; DAC; DAM MST; EW 2; GFL Beginnings to 1789; LMFS 1; RGWL 2, 3; TWA

**Rabinovitch, Sholem** 1859-1916
See Aleichem, Sholom
See also CA 104

**Rabinyan, Dorit** 1972- ..................... **CLC 119**
See also CA 170

**Rachilde**
See Vallette, Marguerite Eymery; Vallette, Marguerite Eymery
See also EWL 3

**Racine, Jean** 1639-1699 ...................... **LC 28**
See also DA3; DAB; DAM MST; DLB 268; EW 3; GFL Beginnings to 1789; LMFS 1; RGWL 2, 3; TWA

**Radcliffe, Ann (Ward)** 1764-1823 ... **NCLC 6, 55, 106**
See also DLB 39, 178; HGG; LMFS 1; RGEL 2; SUFW; WLIT 3

**Radclyffe-Hall, Marguerite**
See Hall, (Marguerite) Radclyffe

**Radiguet, Raymond** 1903-1923 ...... **TCLC 29**
See also CA 162; DLB 65; EWL 3; GFL 1789 to the Present; RGWL 2, 3

**Radnoti, Miklos** 1909-1944 ............. **TCLC 16**
See also CA 118; 212; CDWLB 4; DLB 215; EWL 3; RGWL 2, 3

**Rado, James** 1939- ............................. **CLC 17**
See also CA 105

**Radvanyi, Netty** 1900-1983
See Seghers, Anna
See also CA 85-88; 110; CANR 82

**Rae, Ben**
See Griffiths, Trevor

**Raeburn, John (Hay)** 1941- .............. **CLC 34**
See also CA 57-60

**Ragni, Gerome** 1942-1991 ................ **CLC 17**
See also CA 105; 134

**Rahv, Philip** ...................................... **CLC 24**
See Greenberg, Ivan
See also DLB 137

**Raimund, Ferdinand Jakob** 1790-1836 ................................ **NCLC 69**
See also DLB 90

**Raine, Craig (Anthony)** 1944- .. **CLC 32, 103**
See also CA 108; CANR 29, 51, 103; CP 7; DLB 40; PFS 7

**Raine, Kathleen (Jessie)** 1908-2003 .. **CLC 7, 45**
See also CA 85-88; 218; CANR 46, 109; CP 7; DLB 20; EWL 3; MTCW 1; RGEL 2

**Rainis, Janis** 1865-1929 ................. **TCLC 29**
See also CA 170; CDWLB 4; DLB 220; EWL 3

**Rakosi, Carl** ...................................... **CLC 47**
See Rawley, Callman
See also CAAS 5; CP 7; DLB 193

**Ralegh, Sir Walter**
See Raleigh, Sir Walter
See also BRW 1; RGEL 2; WP

**Raleigh, Richard**
See Lovecraft, H(oward) P(hillips)

**Raleigh, Sir Walter** 1554(?)-1618 ....... **LC 31, 39; PC 31**
See Ralegh, Sir Walter
See also CDBLB Before 1660; DLB 172; EXPP; PFS 14; TEA

**Rallentando, H. P.**
See Sayers, Dorothy L(eigh)

**Ramal, Walter**
See de la Mare, Walter (John)

**Ramana Maharshi** 1879-1950 ........ **TCLC 84**

**Ramoacn y Cajal, Santiago** 1852-1934 ................................ **TCLC 93**

**Ramon, Juan**
See Jimenez (Mantecon), Juan Ramon

**Ramos, Graciliano** 1892-1953 ........ **TCLC 32**
See also CA 167; EWL 3; HW 2; LAW; WLIT 1

**Rampersad, Arnold** 1941- ................. **CLC 44**
See also BW 2, 3; CA 127; 133; CANR 81; DLB 111; INT CA-133

**Rampling, Anne**
See Rice, Anne
See also GLL 2

**Ramsay, Allan** 1686(?)-1758 ................ **LC 29**
See also DLB 95; RGEL 2

**Ramsay, Jay**
See Campbell, (John) Ramsey

**Ramuz, Charles-Ferdinand** 1878-1947 ................................ **TCLC 33**
See also CA 165; EWL 3

**Rand, Ayn** 1905-1982 ...... **CLC 3, 30, 44, 79; WLC**
See also AAYA 10; AMWS 4; BPFB 3; BYA 12; CA 13-16R; 105; CANR 27, 73; CDALBS; CPW; DA; DA3; DAC; DAM MST, NOV, POP; DLB 227, 279; MTCW 1, 2; NFS 10, 16; RGAL 4; SFW 4; TUS; YAW

**Randall, Dudley (Felker)** 1914-2000 . **BLC 3; CLC 1, 135**
See also BW 1, 3; CA 25-28R; 189; CANR 23, 82; DAM MULT; DLB 41; PFS 5

**Randall, Robert**
See Silverberg, Robert

**Ranger, Ken**
See Creasey, John

**Rank, Otto** 1884-1939 .................. **TCLC 115**

**Ransom, John Crowe** 1888-1974 .. **CLC 2, 4, 5, 11, 24**
See also AMW; CA 5-8R; 49-52; CANR 6, 34; CDALBS; DA3; DAM POET; DLB 45, 63; EWL 3; EXPP; MTCW 1, 2; RGAL 4; TUS

**Rao, Raja** 1909- ........................... **CLC 25, 56**
See also CA 73-76; CANR 51; CN 7; DAM NOV; EWL 3; MTCW 1, 2; RGEL 2; RGSF 2

**Raphael, Frederic (Michael)** 1931- ... **CLC 2, 14**
See also CA 1-4R; CANR 1, 86; CN 7; DLB 14

**Ratcliffe, James P.**
See Mencken, H(enry) L(ouis)

**Rathbone, Julian** 1935- ................. **CLC 41**
See also CA 101; CANR 34, 73

**Rattigan, Terence (Mervyn)** 1911-1977 ....................... **CLC 7; DC 18**
See also BRWS 7; CA 85-88; 73-76; CBD; CDBLB 1945-1960; DAM DRAM; DFS 8; DLB 13; IDFW 3, 4; MTCW 1, 2; RGEL 2

**Ratushinskaya, Irina** 1954- .............. **CLC 54**
See also CA 129; CANR 68; CWW 2

**Raven, Simon (Arthur Noel)** 1927-2001 ................................ **CLC 14**
See also CA 81-84; 197; CANR 86; CN 7; DLB 271

**Ravenna, Michael**
See Welty, Eudora (Alice)

**Rawley, Callman** 1903-2002
See Rakosi, Carl
See also CA 21-24R; CANR 12, 32, 91

**Rawlings, Marjorie Kinnan** 1896-1953 ................................ **TCLC 4**
See also AAYA 20; AMWS 10; ANW; BPFB 3; BYA 3; CA 104; 137; CANR 74; CLR 63; DLB 9, 22, 102; DLBD 17;

JRDA; MAICYA 1, 2; MTCW 2; RGAL
4; SATA 100; WCH; YABC 1; YAW

**Ray, Satyajit** 1921-1992 ............. **CLC 16, 76**
See also CA 114; 137; DAM MULT

**Read, Herbert Edward** 1893-1968 ..... **CLC 4**
See also BRW 6; CA 85-88; 25-28R; DLB
20, 149; EWL 3; PAB; RGEL 2

**Read, Piers Paul** 1941- ........... **CLC 4, 10, 25**
See also CA 21-24R; CANR 38, 86; CN 7;
DLB 14; SATA 21

**Reade, Charles** 1814-1884 .......... **NCLC 2, 74**
See also DLB 21; RGEL 2

**Reade, Hamish**
See Gray, Simon (James Holliday)

**Reading, Peter** 1946- ........................ **CLC 47**
See also BRWS 8; CA 103; CANR 46, 96;
CP 7; DLB 40

**Reaney, James** 1926- ........................ **CLC 13**
See also CA 41-44R; CAAS 15; CANR 42;
CD 5; CP 7; DAC; DAM MST; DLB 68;
RGEL 2; SATA 43

**Rebreanu, Liviu** 1885-1944 ............ **TCLC 28**
See also CA 165; DLB 220; EWL 3

**Rechy, John (Francisco)** 1934- ...... **CLC 1, 7,
14, 18, 107; HLC 2**
See also CA 5-8R, 195; CAAE 195; CAAS
4; CANR 6, 32, 64; CN 7; DAM MULT;
DLB 122, 278; DLBY 1982; HW 1, 2;
INT CANR-6; LLW 1; RGAL 4

**Redcam, Tom** 1870-1933 ................ **TCLC 25**

**Reddin, Keith** .................................... **CLC 67**
See also CAD

**Redgrove, Peter (William)**
1932-2003 ......................... **CLC 6, 41**
See also BRWS 6; CA 1-4R; 217; CANR 3,
39, 77; CP 7; DLB 40

**Redmon, Anne** ............................... **CLC 22**
See Nightingale, Anne Redmon
See also DLBY 1986

**Reed, Eliot**
See Ambler, Eric

**Reed, Ishmael** 1938- ..... **BLC 3; CLC 2, 3, 5,
6, 13, 32, 60, 174**
See also AFAW 1, 2; AMWS 10; BPFB 3;
BW 2, 3; CA 21-24R; CANR 25, 48, 74,
128; CN 7; CP 7; CSW; DA3; DAM
MULT; DLB 2, 5, 33, 169, 227; DLBD 8;
EWL 3; LMFS 2; MSW; MTCW 1, 2;
PFS 6; RGAL 4; TCWW 2

**Reed, John (Silas)** 1887-1920 .......... **TCLC 9**
See also CA 106; 195; TUS

**Reed, Lou** .......................................... **CLC 21**
See Firbank, Louis

**Reese, Lizette Woodworth** 1856-1935 . **PC 29**
See also CA 180; DLB 54

**Reeve, Clara** 1729-1807 ................. **NCLC 19**
See also DLB 39; RGEL 2

**Reich, Wilhelm** 1897-1957 ............. **TCLC 57**
See also CA 199

**Reid, Christopher (John)** 1949- ....... **CLC 33**
See also CA 140; CANR 89; CP 7; DLB
40; EWL 3

**Reid, Desmond**
See Moorcock, Michael (John)

**Reid Banks, Lynne** 1929-
See Banks, Lynne Reid
See also AAYA 49; CA 1-4R; CANR 6, 22,
38, 87; CLR 24; CN 7; JRDA; MAICYA
1, 2; SATA 22, 75, 111; YAW

**Reilly, William K.**
See Creasey, John

**Reiner, Max**
See Caldwell, (Janet Miriam) Taylor
(Holland)

**Reis, Ricardo**
See Pessoa, Fernando (Antonio Nogueira)

**Reizenstein, Elmer Leopold**
See Rice, Elmer (Leopold)
See also EWL 3

**Remarque, Erich Maria** 1898-1970 . **CLC 21**
See also AAYA 27; BPFB 3; CA 77-80; 29-
32R; CDWLB 2; DA; DA3; DAB; DAC;
DAM MST, NOV; DLB 56; EWL 3;
EXPN; LAIT 3; MTCW 1, 2; NFS 4;
RGWL 2, 3

**Remington, Frederic** 1861-1909 ..... **TCLC 89**
See also CA 108; 169; DLB 12, 186, 188;
SATA 41

**Remizov, A.**
See Remizov, Aleksei (Mikhailovich)

**Remizov, A. M.**
See Remizov, Aleksei (Mikhailovich)

**Remizov, Aleksei (Mikhailovich)**
1877-1957 ........................... **TCLC 27**
See Remizov, Alexey Mikhaylovich
See also CA 125; 133; DLB 295

**Remizov, Alexey Mikhaylovich**
See Remizov, Aleksei (Mikhailovich)
See also EWL 3

**Renan, Joseph Ernest** 1823-1892 . **NCLC 26,
145**
See also GFL 1789 to the Present

**Renard, Jules(-Pierre)** 1864-1910 .. **TCLC 17**
See also CA 117; 202; GFL 1789 to the
Present

**Renault, Mary** ........................ **CLC 3, 11, 17**
See Challans, Mary
See also BPFB 3; BYA 2; DLBY 1983;
EWL 3; GLL 1; LAIT 1; MTCW 2; RGEL
2; RHW

**Rendell, Ruth (Barbara)** 1930- .. **CLC 28, 48**
See Vine, Barbara
See also BPFB 3; BRWS 9; CA 109; CANR
32, 52, 74, 127; CN 7; CPW; DAM POP;
DLB 87, 276; INT CANR-32; MSW;
MTCW 1, 2

**Renoir, Jean** 1894-1979 .................... **CLC 20**
See also CA 129; 85-88

**Resnais, Alain** 1922- .......................... **CLC 16**

**Revard, Carter (Curtis)** 1931- ........... **NNAL**
See also CA 144; CANR 81; PFS 5

**Reverdy, Pierre** 1889-1960 ............... **CLC 53**
See also CA 97-100; 89-92; DLB 258; EWL
3; GFL 1789 to the Present

**Rexroth, Kenneth** 1905-1982 .... **CLC 1, 2, 6,
11, 22, 49, 112; PC 20**
See also BG 3; CA 5-8R; 107; CANR 14,
34, 63; CDALB 1941-1968; DAM POET;
DLB 16, 48, 165, 212; DLBY 1982; EWL
3; INT CANR-14; MTCW 1, 2; RGAL 4

**Reyes, Alfonso** 1889-1959 .... **HLCS 2; TCLC
33**
See also CA 131; EWL 3; HW 1; LAW

**Reyes y Basoalto, Ricardo Eliecer Neftali**
See Neruda, Pablo

**Reymont, Wladyslaw (Stanislaw)**
1868(?)-1925 ............................ **TCLC 5**
See also CA 104; EWL 3

**Reynolds, Jonathan** 1942- ............. **CLC 6, 38**
See also CA 65-68; CANR 28

**Reynolds, Joshua** 1723-1792 ................ **LC 15**
See also DLB 104

**Reynolds, Michael S(hane)**
1937-2000 .................................. **CLC 44**
See also CA 65-68; 189; CANR 9, 89, 97

**Reznikoff, Charles** 1894-1976 ............ **CLC 9**
See also CA 33-36; 61-64; CAP 2; DLB 28,
45; WP

**Rezzori (d'Arezzo), Gregor von**
1914-1998 .................................. **CLC 25**
See also CA 122; 136; 167

**Rhine, Richard**
See Silverstein, Alvin; Silverstein, Virginia
B(arbara Opshelor)

**Rhodes, Eugene Manlove**
1869-1934 ................................ **TCLC 53**
See also CA 198; DLB 256

**R'hoone, Lord**
See Balzac, Honore de

**Rhys, Jean** 1894(?)-1979 ...... **CLC 2, 4, 6, 14,
19, 51, 124; SSC 21, 76**
See also BRWS 2; CA 25-28R; 85-88;
CANR 35, 62; CDBLB 1945-1960; CD-
WLB 3; DA3; DAM NOV; DLB 36, 117,
162; DNFS 2; EWL 3; LATS 1:1; MTCW
1, 2; RGEL 2; RGSF 2; RHW; TEA;
WWE 1

**Ribeiro, Darcy** 1922-1997 ................. **CLC 34**
See also CA 33-36R; 156; EWL 3

**Ribeiro, Joao Ubaldo (Osorio Pimentel)**
1941- ..................................... **CLC 10, 67**
See also CA 81-84; CWW 2; EWL 3

**Ribman, Ronald (Burt)** 1932- ............ **CLC 7**
See also CA 21-24R; CAD; CANR 46, 80;
CD 5

**Ricci, Nino (Pio)** 1959- ...................... **CLC 70**
See also CA 137; CANR 130; CCA 1

**Rice, Anne** 1941- ....................... **CLC 41, 128**
See Rampling, Anne
See also AAYA 9, 53; AMWS 7; BEST
89:2; BPFB 3; CA 65-68; CANR 12, 36,
53, 74, 100, 133; CN 7; CPW; CSW;
DA3; DAM POP; DLB 292; GLL 2;
HGG; MTCW 2; SUFW 2; YAW

**Rice, Elmer (Leopold)** 1892-1967 ...... **CLC 7,
49**
See Reizenstein, Elmer Leopold
See also CA 21-22; 25-28R; CAP 2; DAM
DRAM; DFS 12; DLB 4, 7; MTCW 1, 2;
RGAL 4

**Rice, Tim(othy Miles Bindon)**
1944- ............................................. **CLC 21**
See also CA 103; CANR 46; DFS 7

**Rich, Adrienne (Cecile)** 1929- ... **CLC 3, 6, 7,
11, 18, 36, 73, 76, 125; PC 5**
See also AMWR 2; AMWS 1; CA 9-12R;
CANR 20, 53, 74, 128; CDALBS; CP 7;
CSW; CWP; DA3; DAM POET; DLB 5,
67; EWL 3; EXPP; FW; MAWW; MTCW
1, 2; PAB; PFS 15; RGAL 4; WP

**Rich, Barbara**
See Graves, Robert (von Ranke)

**Rich, Robert**
See Trumbo, Dalton

**Richard, Keith** ................................... **CLC 17**
See Richards, Keith

**Richards, David Adams** 1950- .......... **CLC 59**
See also CA 93-96; CANR 60, 110; DAC;
DLB 53

**Richards, I(vor) A(rmstrong)**
1893-1979 .............................. **CLC 14, 24**
See also BRWS 2; CA 41-44R; 89-92;
CANR 34, 74; DLB 27; EWL 3; MTCW
2; RGEL 2

**Richards, Keith** 1943-
See Richard, Keith
See also CA 107; CANR 77

**Richardson, Anne**
See Roiphe, Anne (Richardson)

**Richardson, Dorothy Miller**
1873-1957 ................................... **TCLC 3**
See also CA 104; 192; DLB 36; EWL 3;
FW; RGEL 2

**Richardson (Robertson), Ethel Florence
Lindesay** 1870-1946
See Richardson, Henry Handel
See also CA 105; 190; DLB 230; RHW

**Richardson, Henry Handel** ............ **TCLC 4**
See Richardson (Robertson), Ethel Florence
Lindesay
See also DLB 197; EWL 3; RGEL 2; RGSF
2

**Richardson, John** 1796-1852 .......... **NCLC 55**
See also CCA 1; DAC; DLB 99

**Richardson, Samuel** 1689-1761 ...... **LC 1, 44; WLC**
See also BRW 3; CDBLB 1660-1789; DA; DAB; DAC; DAM MST, NOV; DLB 39; RGEL 2; TEA; WLIT 3

**Richardson, Willis** 1889-1977 ............... **HR 3**
See also BW 1; CA 124; DLB 51; SATA 60

**Richler, Mordecai** 1931-2001 .... **CLC 3, 5, 9, 13, 18, 46, 70, 185**
See also AITN 1; CA 65-68; 201; CANR 31, 62, 111; CCA 1; CLR 17; CWRI 5; DAC; DAM MST, NOV; DLB 53; EWL 3; MAICYA 1, 2; MTCW 1, 2; RGEL 2; SATA 44, 98; SATA-Brief 27; TWA

**Richter, Conrad (Michael)** 1890-1968 .................................. **CLC 30**
See also AAYA 21; BYA 2; CA 5-8R; 25-28R; CANR 23; DLB 9, 212; LAIT 1; MTCW 1, 2; RGAL 4; SATA 3; TCWW 2; TUS; YAW

**Ricostranza, Tom**
See Ellis, Trey

**Riddell, Charlotte** 1832-1906 ......... **TCLC 40**
See Riddell, Mrs. J. H.
See also CA 165; DLB 156

**Riddell, Mrs. J. H.**
See Riddell, Charlotte
See also HGG; SUFW

**Ridge, John Rollin** 1827-1867 ...... **NCLC 82; NNAL**
See also CA 144; DAM MULT; DLB 175

**Ridgeway, Jason**
See Marlowe, Stephen

**Ridgway, Keith** 1965- ....................... **CLC 119**
See also CA 172

**Riding, Laura** .................................. **CLC 3, 7**
See Jackson, Laura (Riding)
See also RGAL 4

**Riefenstahl, Berta Helene Amalia** 1902-2003
See Riefenstahl, Leni
See also CA 108; 220

**Riefenstahl, Leni** ........................ **CLC 16, 190**
See Riefenstahl, Berta Helene Amalia

**Riffe, Ernest**
See Bergman, (Ernst) Ingmar

**Riggs, (Rolla) Lynn** 1899-1954 ................... **NNAL; TCLC 56**
See also CA 144; DAM MULT; DLB 175

**Riis, Jacob A(ugust)** 1849-1914 ..... **TCLC 80**
See also CA 113; 168; DLB 23

**Riley, James Whitcomb** 1849-1916 .... **PC 48; TCLC 51**
See also CA 118; 137; DAM POET; MAICYA 1, 2; RGAL 4; SATA 17

**Riley, Tex**
See Creasey, John

**Rilke, Rainer Maria** 1875-1926 ........... **PC 2; TCLC 1, 6, 19**
See also CA 104; 132; CANR 62, 99; CD-WLB 2; DA3; DAM POET; DLB 81; EW 9; EWL 3; MTCW 1, 2; PFS 19; RGWL 2, 3; TWA; WP

**Rimbaud, (Jean Nicolas) Arthur** 1854-1891 ... **NCLC 4, 35, 82; PC 3, 57; WLC**
See also DA; DA3; DAB; DAC; DAM MST, POET; DLB 217; EW 7; GFL 1789 to the Present; LMFS 2; RGWL 2, 3; TWA; WP

**Rinehart, Mary Roberts** 1876-1958 ................................. **TCLC 52**
See also BPFB 3; CA 108; 166; RGAL 4; RHW

**Ringmaster, The**
See Mencken, H(enry) L(ouis)

**Ringwood, Gwen(dolyn Margaret) Pharis** 1910-1984 ................................. **CLC 48**
See also CA 148; 112; DLB 88

**Rio, Michel** 1945(?)- ............................. **CLC 43**
See also CA 201

**Rios, Alberto (Alvaro)** 1952- ............... **PC 57**
See also AMWS 4; CA 113; CANR 34, 79; CP 7; DLB 122; HW 2; PFS 11

**Ritsos, Giannes**
See Ritsos, Yannis

**Ritsos, Yannis** 1909-1990 ........ **CLC 6, 13, 31**
See also CA 77-80; 133; CANR 39, 61; EW 12; EWL 3; MTCW 1; RGWL 2, 3

**Ritter, Erika** 1948(?)- .......................... **CLC 52**
See also CD 5; CWD

**Rivera, Jose Eustasio** 1889-1928 ... **TCLC 35**
See also CA 162; EWL 3; HW 1, 2; LAW

**Rivera, Tomas** 1935-1984 .................. **HLCS 2**
See also CA 49-52; CANR 32; DLB 82; HW 1; LLW 1; RGAL 4; SSFS 15; TCWW 2; WLIT 1

**Rivers, Conrad Kent** 1933-1968 ......... **CLC 1**
See also BW 1; CA 85-88; DLB 41

**Rivers, Elfrida**
See Bradley, Marion Zimmer
See also GLL 1

**Riverside, John**
See Heinlein, Robert A(nson)

**Rizal, Jose** 1861-1896 ..................... **NCLC 27**

**Roa Bastos, Augusto (Antonio)** 1917- ............................. **CLC 45; HLC 2**
See also CA 131; CWW 2; DAM MULT; DLB 113; EWL 3; HW 1; LAW; RGSF 2; WLIT 1

**Robbe-Grillet, Alain** 1922- .... **CLC 1, 2, 4, 6, 8, 10, 14, 43, 128**
See also BPFB 3; CA 9-12R; CANR 33, 65, 115; CWW 2; DLB 83; EW 13; EWL 3; GFL 1789 to the Present; IDFW 3, 4; MTCW 1, 2; RGWL 2, 3; SSFS 15

**Robbins, Harold** 1916-1997 ............... **CLC 5**
See also BPFB 3; CA 73-76; 162; CANR 26, 54, 112; DA3; DAM NOV; MTCW 1, 2

**Robbins, Thomas Eugene** 1936-
See Robbins, Tom
See also CA 81-84; CANR 29, 59, 95; CN 7; CPW; CSW; DA3; DAM NOV, POP; MTCW 1, 2

**Robbins, Tom** ........................ **CLC 9, 32, 64**
See Robbins, Thomas Eugene
See also AAYA 32; AMWS 10; BEST 90:3; BPFB 3; DLBY 1980; MTCW 2

**Robbins, Trina** 1938- ......................... **CLC 21**
See also CA 128

**Roberts, Charles G(eorge) D(ouglas)** 1860-1943 ................................. **TCLC 8**
See also CA 105; 188; CLR 33; CWRI 5; DLB 92; RGEL 2; RGSF 2; SATA 88; SATA-Brief 29

**Roberts, Elizabeth Madox** 1886-1941 ............................... **TCLC 68**
See also CA 111; 166; CLR 100; CWRI 5; DLB 9, 54, 102; RGAL 4; RHW; SATA 33; SATA-Brief 27; WCH

**Roberts, Kate** 1891-1985 .................. **CLC 15**
See also CA 107; 116

**Roberts, Keith (John Kingston)** 1935-2000 ................................. **CLC 14**
See also CA 25-28R; CANR 46; DLB 261; SFW 4

**Roberts, Kenneth (Lewis)** 1885-1957 ................................. **TCLC 23**
See also CA 109; 199; DLB 9; RGAL 4; RHW

**Roberts, Michele (Brigitte)** 1949- .... **CLC 48, 178**
See also CA 115; CANR 58, 120; CN 7; DLB 231; FW

**Robertson, Ellis**
See Ellison, Harlan (Jay); Silverberg, Robert

**Robertson, Thomas William** 1829-1871 ................................. **NCLC 35**
See Robertson, Tom
See also DAM DRAM

**Robertson, Tom**
See Robertson, Thomas William
See also RGEL 2

**Robeson, Kenneth**
See Dent, Lester

**Robinson, Edwin Arlington** 1869-1935 ......... **PC 1, 35; TCLC 5, 101**
See also AMW; CA 104; 133; CDALB 1865-1917; DA; DAC; DAM MST, POET; DLB 54; EWL 3; EXPP; MTCW 1, 2; PAB; PFS 4; RGAL 4; WP

**Robinson, Henry Crabb** 1775-1867 ................................. **NCLC 15**
See also DLB 107

**Robinson, Jill** 1936- ......................... **CLC 10**
See also CA 102; CANR 120; INT CA-102

**Robinson, Kim Stanley** 1952- ........... **CLC 34**
See also AAYA 26; CA 126; CANR 113; CN 7; SATA 109; SCFW 2; SFW 4

**Robinson, Lloyd**
See Silverberg, Robert

**Robinson, Marilynne** 1944- ...... **CLC 25, 180**
See also CA 116; CANR 80; CN 7; DLB 206

**Robinson, Mary** 1758-1800 .......... **NCLC 142**
See also DLB 158; FW

**Robinson, Smokey** ........................... **CLC 21**
See Robinson, William, Jr.

**Robinson, William, Jr.** 1940-
See Robinson, Smokey
See also CA 116

**Robison, Mary** 1949- .................. **CLC 42, 98**
See also CA 113; 116; CANR 87; CN 7; DLB 130; INT CA-116; RGSF 2

**Rochester**
See Wilmot, John
See also RGEL 2

**Rod, Edouard** 1857-1910 ............... **TCLC 52**

**Roddenberry, Eugene Wesley** 1921-1991
See Roddenberry, Gene
See also CA 110; 135; CANR 37; SATA 45; SATA-Obit 69

**Roddenberry, Gene** ........................... **CLC 17**
See Roddenberry, Eugene Wesley
See also AAYA 5; SATA-Obit 69

**Rodgers, Mary** 1931- ......................... **CLC 12**
See also BYA 5; CA 49-52; CANR 8, 55, 90; CLR 20; CWRI 5; INT CANR-8; JRDA; MAICYA 1, 2; SATA 8, 130

**Rodgers, W(illiam) R(obert)** 1909-1969 ................................. **CLC 7**
See also CA 85-88; DLB 20; RGEL 2

**Rodman, Eric**
See Silverberg, Robert

**Rodman, Howard** 1920(?)-1985 ........ **CLC 65**
See also CA 118

**Rodman, Maia**
See Wojciechowska, Maia (Teresa)

**Rodo, Jose Enrique** 1871(?)-1917 .... **HLCS 2**
See also CA 178; EWL 3; HW 2; LAW

**Rodolph, Utto**
See Ouologuem, Yambo

**Rodriguez, Claudio** 1934-1999 ......... **CLC 10**
See also CA 188; DLB 134

**Rodriguez, Richard** 1944- .... **CLC 155; HLC 2**
See also CA 110; CANR 66, 116; DAM MULT; DLB 82, 256; HW 1, 2; LAIT 5; LLW 1; NCFS 3; WLIT 1

**Roelvaag, O(le) E(dvart)** 1876-1931
See Rolvaag, O(le) E(dvart)
See also CA 117; 171

**Roethke, Theodore (Huebner)**
1908-1963 ......... **CLC 1, 3, 8, 11, 19, 46, 101; PC 15**
See also AMW; CA 81-84; CABS 2; CDALB 1941-1968; DA3; DAM POET; DLB 5, 206; EWL 3; EXPP; MTCW 1, 2; PAB; PFS 3; RGAL 4; WP

**Rogers, Carl R(ansom)**
1902-1987 ............................. **TCLC 125**
See also CA 1-4R; 121; CANR 1, 18; MTCW 1

**Rogers, Samuel** 1763-1855 ............ **NCLC 69**
See also DLB 93; RGEL 2

**Rogers, Thomas Hunton** 1927- ......... **CLC 57**
See also CA 89-92; INT CA-89-92

**Rogers, Will(iam Penn Adair)**
1879-1935 .............. **NNAL; TCLC 8, 71**
See also CA 105; 144; DA3; DAM MULT; DLB 11; MTCW 2

**Rogin, Gilbert** 1929- ......................... **CLC 18**
See also CA 65-68; CANR 15

**Rohan, Koda**
See Koda Shigeyuki

**Rohlfs, Anna Katharine Green**
See Green, Anna Katharine

**Rohmer, Eric** .................................... **CLC 16**
See Scherer, Jean-Marie Maurice

**Rohmer, Sax** ................................... **TCLC 28**
See Ward, Arthur Henry Sarsfield
See also DLB 70; MSW; SUFW

**Roiphe, Anne (Richardson)** 1935- .. **CLC 3, 9**
See also CA 89-92; CANR 45, 73; DLBY 1980; INT CA-89-92

**Rojas, Fernando de** 1475-1541 ... **HLCS 1, 2; LC 23**
See also DLB 286; RGWL 2, 3

**Rojas, Gonzalo** 1917- ......................... **HLCS 2**
See also CA 178; HW 2; LAWS 1

**Roland, Marie-Jeanne** 1754-1793 ....... **LC 98**

**Rolfe, Frederick (William Serafino Austin Lewis Mary)** 1860-1913 ......... **TCLC 12**
See Al Siddik
See also CA 107; 210; DLB 34, 156; RGEL 2

**Rolland, Romain** 1866-1944 .......... **TCLC 23**
See also CA 118; 197; DLB 65, 284; EWL 3; GFL 1789 to the Present; RGWL 2, 3

**Rolle, Richard** c. 1300-c. 1349 ...... **CMLC 21**
See also DLB 146; LMFS 1; RGEL 2

**Rolvaag, O(le) E(dvart)** ................. **TCLC 17**
See Roelvaag, O(le) E(dvart)
See also DLB 9, 212; NFS 5; RGAL 4

**Romain Arnaud, Saint**
See Aragon, Louis

**Romains, Jules** 1885-1972 .................. **CLC 7**
See also CA 85-88; CANR 34; DLB 65; EWL 3; GFL 1789 to the Present; MTCW 1

**Romero, Jose Ruben** 1890-1952 .... **TCLC 14**
See also CA 114; 131; EWL 3; HW 1; LAW

**Ronsard, Pierre de** 1524-1585 . **LC 6, 54; PC 11**
See also EW 2; GFL Beginnings to 1789; RGWL 2, 3; TWA

**Rooke, Leon** 1934- ...................... **CLC 25, 34**
See also CA 25-28R; CANR 23, 53; CCA 1; CPW; DAM POP

**Roosevelt, Franklin Delano**
1882-1945 ................................. **TCLC 93**
See also CA 116; 173; LAIT 3

**Roosevelt, Theodore** 1858-1919 ..... **TCLC 69**
See also CA 115; 170; DLB 47, 186, 275

**Roper, William** 1498-1578 ................... **LC 10**

**Roquelaure, A. N.**
See Rice, Anne

**Rosa, Joao Guimaraes** 1908-1967 ... **CLC 23; HLCS 1**
See Guimaraes Rosa, Joao
See also CA 89-92; DLB 113; EWL 3; WLIT 1

**Rose, Wendy** 1948- . **CLC 85; NNAL; PC 13**
See also CA 53-56; CANR 5, 51; CWP; DAM MULT; DLB 175; PFS 13; RGAL 4; SATA 12

**Rosen, R. D.**
See Rosen, Richard (Dean)

**Rosen, Richard (Dean)** 1949- ........... **CLC 39**
See also CA 77-80; CANR 62, 120; CMW 4; INT CANR-30

**Rosenberg, Isaac** 1890-1918 .......... **TCLC 12**
See also BRW 6; CA 107; 188; DLB 20, 216; EWL 3; PAB; RGEL 2

**Rosenblatt, Joe** ................................ **CLC 15**
See Rosenblatt, Joseph

**Rosenblatt, Joseph** 1933-
See Rosenblatt, Joe
See also CA 89-92; CP 7; INT CA-89-92

**Rosenfeld, Samuel**
See Tzara, Tristan

**Rosenstock, Sami**
See Tzara, Tristan

**Rosenstock, Samuel**
See Tzara, Tristan

**Rosenthal, M(acha) L(ouis)**
1917-1996 ................................. **CLC 28**
See also CA 1-4R; 152; CAAS 6; CANR 4, 51; CP 7; DLB 5; SATA 59

**Ross, Barnaby**
See Dannay, Frederic

**Ross, Bernard L.**
See Follett, Ken(neth Martin)

**Ross, J. H.**
See Lawrence, T(homas) E(dward)

**Ross, John Hume**
See Lawrence, T(homas) E(dward)

**Ross, Martin** 1862-1915
See Martin, Violet Florence
See also DLB 135; GLL 2; RGEL 2; RGSF 2

**Ross, (James) Sinclair** 1908-1996 ... **CLC 13; SSC 24**
See also CA 73-76; CANR 81; CN 7; DAC; DAM MST; DLB 88; RGEL 2; RGSF 2; TCWW 2

**Rossetti, Christina (Georgina)**
1830-1894 ......... **NCLC 2, 50, 66; PC 7; WLC**
See also AAYA 51; BRW 5; BYA 4; DA; DA3; DAB; DAC; DAM MST, POET; DLB 35, 163, 240; EXPP; LATS 1:1; MAICYA 1, 2; PFS 10, 14; RGEL 2; SATA 20; TEA; WCH

**Rossetti, Dante Gabriel** 1828-1882 . **NCLC 4, 77; PC 44; WLC**
See also AAYA 51; BRW 5; CDBLB 1832-1890; DA; DAB; DAC; DAM MST, POET; DLB 35; EXPP; RGEL 2; TEA

**Rossi, Cristina Peri**
See Peri Rossi, Cristina

**Rossi, Jean-Baptiste** 1931-2003
See Japrisot, Sebastien
See also CA 201; 215

**Rossner, Judith (Perelman)** 1935- . **CLC 6, 9, 29**
See also AITN 2; BEST 90:3; BPFB 3; CA 17-20R; CANR 18, 51, 73; CN 7; DLB 6; INT CANR-18; MTCW 1, 2

**Rostand, Edmond (Eugene Alexis)**
1868-1918 .............. **DC 10; TCLC 6, 37**
See also CA 104; 126; DA; DA3; DAB; DAC; DAM DRAM, MST; DFS 1; DLB 192; LAIT 1; MTCW 1; RGWL 2, 3; TWA

**Roth, Henry** 1906-1995 ..... **CLC 2, 6, 11, 104**
See also AMWS 9; CA 11-12; 149; CANR 38, 63; CAP 1; CN 7; DA3; DLB 28; EWL 3; MTCW 1, 2; RGAL 4

**Roth, (Moses) Joseph** 1894-1939 ... **TCLC 33**
See also CA 160; DLB 85; EWL 3; RGWL 2, 3

**Roth, Philip (Milton)** 1933- ... **CLC 1, 2, 3, 4, 6, 9, 15, 22, 31, 47, 66, 86, 119; SSC 26; WLC**
See also AMWR 2; AMWS 3; BEST 90:3; BPFB 3; CA 1-4R; CANR 1, 22, 36, 55, 89, 132; CDALB 1968-1988; CN 7; CPW 1; DA; DA3; DAB; DAC; DAM MST, NOV, POP; DLB 2, 28, 173; DLBY 1982; EWL 3; MTCW 1, 2; RGAL 4; RGSF 2; SSFS 12, 18; TUS

**Rothenberg, Jerome** 1931- ........... **CLC 6, 57**
See also CA 45-48; CANR 1, 106; CP 7; DLB 5, 193

**Rotter, Pat ed.** ................................... **CLC 65**

**Roumain, Jacques (Jean Baptiste)**
1907-1944 .................... **BLC 3; TCLC 19**
See also BW 1; CA 117; 125; DAM MULT; EWL 3

**Rourke, Constance Mayfield**
1885-1941 ................................. **TCLC 12**
See also CA 107; 200; YABC 1

**Rousseau, Jean-Baptiste** 1671-1741 ...... **LC 9**

**Rousseau, Jean-Jacques** 1712-1778 .... **LC 14, 36; WLC**
See also DA; DA3; DAB; DAC; DAM MST; EW 4; GFL Beginnings to 1789; LMFS 1; RGWL 2, 3; TWA

**Roussel, Raymond** 1877-1933 ........ **TCLC 20**
See also CA 117; 201; EWL 3; GFL 1789 to the Present

**Rovit, Earl (Herbert)** 1927- ................ **CLC 7**
See also CA 5-8R; CANR 12

**Rowe, Elizabeth Singer** 1674-1737 ..... **LC 44**
See also DLB 39, 95

**Rowe, Nicholas** 1674-1718 ................... **LC 8**
See also DLB 84; RGEL 2

**Rowlandson, Mary** 1637(?)-1678 ......... **LC 66**
See also DLB 24, 200; RGAL 4

**Rowley, Ames Dorrance**
See Lovecraft, H(oward) P(hillips)

**Rowley, William** 1585(?)-1626 ........... **LC 100**
See also DLB 58; RGEL 2

**Rowling, J(oanne) K(athleen)**
1966- ..................................... **CLC 137**
See also AAYA 34; BYA 11, 13, 14; CA 173; CANR 128; CLR 66, 80; MAICYA 2; SATA 109; SUFW 2

**Rowson, Susanna Haswell**
1762(?)-1824 ................... **NCLC 5, 69**
See also DLB 37, 200; RGAL 4

**Roy, Arundhati** 1960(?)- ................. **CLC 109**
See also CA 163; CANR 90, 126; DLBY 1997; EWL 3; LATS 1:2; WWE 1

**Roy, Gabrielle** 1909-1983 ........... **CLC 10, 14**
See also CA 53-56; 110; CANR 5, 61; CCA 1; DAB; DAC; DAM MST; DLB 68; EWL 3; MTCW 1; RGWL 2, 3; SATA 104

**Royko, Mike** 1932-1997 .................. **CLC 109**
See also CA 89-92; 157; CANR 26, 111; CPW

**Rozanov, Vasilii Vasil'evich**
See Rozanov, Vassili
See also DLB 295

**Rozanov, Vasily Vasilyevich**
See Rozanov, Vassili
See also EWL 3

**Rozanov, Vassili** 1856-1919 ........... **TCLC 104**
See Rozanov, Vasilii Vasil'evich; Rozanov, Vasily Vasilyevich

**Rozewicz, Tadeusz** 1921- ...... **CLC 9, 23, 139**
See also CA 108; CANR 36, 66; CWW 2;
DA3; DAM POET; DLB 232; EWL 3;
MTCW 1, 2; RGWL 3

**Ruark, Gibbons** 1941- ...................... **CLC 3**
See also CA 33-36R; CAAS 23; CANR 14,
31, 57; DLB 120

**Rubens, Bernice (Ruth)** 1923- .... **CLC 19, 31**
See also CA 25-28R; CANR 33, 65, 128;
CN 7; DLB 14, 207; MTCW 1

**Rubin, Harold**
See Robbins, Harold

**Rudkin, (James) David** 1936- .......... **CLC 14**
See also CA 89-92; CBD; CD 5; DLB 13

**Rudnik, Raphael** 1933- ..................... **CLC 7**
See also CA 29-32R

**Ruffian, M.**
See Hasek, Jaroslav (Matej Frantisek)

**Ruiz, Jose Martinez** ...................... **CLC 11**
See Martinez Ruiz, Jose

**Ruiz, Juan** c. 1283-c. 1350 ........... **CMLC 66**

**Rukeyser, Muriel** 1913-1980 . **CLC 6, 10, 15,
27; PC 12**
See also AMWS 6; CA 5-8R; 93-96; CANR
26, 60; DA3; DAM POET; DLB 48; EWL
3; FW; GLL 2; MTCW 1, 2; PFS 10;
RGAL 4; SATA-Obit 22

**Rule, Jane (Vance)** 1931- .................. **CLC 27**
See also CA 25-28R; CAAS 18; CANR 12,
87; CN 7; DLB 60; FW

**Rulfo, Juan** 1918-1986 .. **CLC 8, 80; HLC 2;
SSC 25**
See also CA 85-88; 118; CANR 26; CD-
WLB 3; DAM MULT; DLB 113; EWL 3;
HW 1, 2; LAW; MTCW 1, 2; RGSF 2;
RGWL 2, 3; WLIT 1

**Rumi, Jalal al-Din** 1207-1273 ...... **CMLC 20;
PC 45**
See also RGWL 2, 3; WP

**Runeberg, Johan** 1804-1877 ........... **NCLC 41**

**Runyon, (Alfred) Damon**
1884(?)-1946 ...................... **TCLC 10**
See also CA 107; 165; DLB 11, 86, 171;
MTCW 2; RGAL 4

**Rush, Norman** 1933- ........................ **CLC 44**
See also CA 121; 126; CANR 130; INT CA-
126

**Rushdie, (Ahmed) Salman** 1947- .... **CLC 23,
31, 55, 100, 191; WLCS**
See also BEST 89:3; BPFB 3; BRWS 4;
CA 108; 111; CANR 33, 56, 108, 133;
CN 7; CPW 1; DA3; DAB; DAC; DAM
MST, NOV, POP; DLB 194; EWL 3;
FANT; INT CA-111; LATS 1:2; LMFS 2;
MTCW 1, 2; RGEL 2; RGSF 2; TEA;
WLIT 4; WWE 1

**Rushforth, Peter (Scott)** 1945- .......... **CLC 19**
See also CA 101

**Ruskin, John** 1819-1900 ................ **TCLC 63**
See also BRW 5; BYA 5; CA 114; 129; CD-
BLB 1832-1890; DLB 55, 163, 190;
RGEL 2; SATA 24; TEA; WCH

**Russ, Joanna** 1937- ........................... **CLC 15**
See also BPFB 3; CA 5-28R; CANR 11,
31, 65; CN 7; DLB 8; FW; GLL 1;
MTCW 1; SCFW 2; SFW 4

**Russ, Richard Patrick**
See O'Brian, Patrick

**Russell, George William** 1867-1935
See A.E.; Baker, Jean H.
See also BRWS 8; CA 104; 153; CDBLB
1890-1914; DAM POET; EWL 3; RGEL
2

**Russell, Jeffrey Burton** 1934- .......... **CLC 70**
See also CA 25-28R; CANR 11, 28, 52

**Russell, (Henry) Ken(neth Alfred)**
1927- ........................................ **CLC 16**
See also CA 105

**Russell, William Martin** 1947-
See Russell, Willy
See also CA 164; CANR 107

**Russell, Willy** ........................... **CLC 60**
See Russell, William Martin
See also CBD; CD 5; DLB 233

**Russo, Richard** 1949- ...................... **CLC 181**
See also AMWS 12; CA 127; 133; CANR
87, 114

**Rutherford, Mark** ...................... **TCLC 25**
See White, William Hale
See also DLB 18; RGEL 2

**Ruyslinck, Ward** ........................... **CLC 14**
See Belser, Reimond Karel Maria de

**Ryan, Cornelius (John)** 1920-1974 ..... **CLC 7**
See also CA 69-72; 53-56; CANR 38

**Ryan, Michael** 1946- ........................ **CLC 65**
See also CA 49-52; CANR 109; DLBY
1982

**Ryan, Tim**
See Dent, Lester

**Rybakov, Anatoli (Naumovich)**
1911-1998 ............................ **CLC 23, 53**
See Rybakov, Anatolii (Naumovich)
See also CA 126; 135; 172; SATA 79;
SATA-Obit 108

**Rybakov, Anatolii (Naumovich)**
See Rybakov, Anatoli (Naumovich)
See also DLB 302

**Ryder, Jonathan**
See Ludlum, Robert

**Ryga, George** 1932-1987 ................... **CLC 14**
See also CA 101; 124; CANR 43, 90; CCA
1; DAC; DAM MST; DLB 60

**S. H.**
See Hartmann, Sadakichi

**S. S.**
See Sassoon, Siegfried (Lorraine)

**Sa'adawi, al- Nawal**
See El Saadawi, Nawal
See also AFW; EWL 3

**Saadawi, Nawal El**
See El Saadawi, Nawal
See also WLIT 2

**Saba, Umberto** 1883-1957 ............. **TCLC 33**
See also CA 144; CANR 79; DLB 114;
EWL 3; RGWL 2, 3

**Sabatini, Rafael** 1875-1950 ............. **TCLC 47**
See also BPFB 3; CA 162; RHW

**Sabato, Ernesto (R.)** 1911- ........ **CLC 10, 23;
HLC 2**
See also CA 97-100; CANR 32, 65; CD-
WLB 3; CWW 2; DAM MULT; DLB 145;
EWL 3; HW 1, 2; LAW; MTCW 1, 2

**Sa-Carneiro, Mario de** 1890-1916 . **TCLC 83**
See also DLB 287; EWL 3

**Sacastru, Martin**
See Bioy Casares, Adolfo
See also CWW 2

**Sacher-Masoch, Leopold von**
1836(?)-1895 ........................... **NCLC 31**

**Sachs, Hans** 1494-1576 ...................... **LC 95**
See also CDWLB 2; DLB 179; RGWL 2, 3

**Sachs, Marilyn (Stickle)** 1927- ......... **CLC 35**
See also AAYA 2; BYA 6; CA 17-20R;
CANR 13, 47; CLR 2; JRDA; MAICYA
1, 2; SAAS 2; SATA 3, 68; SATA-Essay
110; WYA; YAW

**Sachs, Nelly** 1891-1970 ............... **CLC 14, 98**
See also CA 17-18; 25-28R; CANR 87;
CAP 2; EWL 3; MTCW 2; PFS 20;
RGWL 2, 3

**Sackler, Howard (Oliver)**
1929-1982 ............................ **CLC 14**
See also CA 61-64; 108; CAD; CANR 30;
DFS 15; DLB 7

**Sacks, Oliver (Wolf)** 1933- ............... **CLC 67**
See also CA 53-56; CANR 28, 50, 76;
CPW; DA3; INT CANR-28; MTCW 1, 2

**Sackville, Thomas** 1536-1608 ............... **LC 98**
See also DAM DRAM; DLB 62, 132;
RGEL 2

**Sadakichi**
See Hartmann, Sadakichi

**Sa'dawi, Nawal al-**
See El Saadawi, Nawal
See also CWW 2

**Sade, Donatien Alphonse Francois**
1740-1814 ............................ **NCLC 3, 47**
See also EW 4; GFL Beginnings to 1789;
RGWL 2, 3

**Sade, Marquis de**
See Sade, Donatien Alphonse Francois

**Sadoff, Ira** 1945- ................................ **CLC 9**
See also CA 53-56; CANR 5, 21, 109; DLB
120

**Saetone**
See Camus, Albert

**Safire, William** 1929- ...................... **CLC 10**
See also CA 17-20R; CANR 31, 54, 91

**Sagan, Carl (Edward)** 1934-1996 .... **CLC 30,
112**
See also AAYA 2; CA 25-28R; 155; CANR
11, 36, 74; CPW; DA3; MTCW 1, 2;
SATA 58; SATA-Obit 94

**Sagan, Francoise** ............ **CLC 3, 6, 9, 17, 36**
See Quoirez, Francoise
See also CWW 2; DLB 83; EWL 3; GFL
1789 to the Present; MTCW 2

**Sahgal, Nayantara (Pandit)** 1927- .... **CLC 41**
See also CA 9-12R; CANR 11, 88; CN 7

**Said, Edward W.** 1935-2003 ........... **CLC 123**
See also CA 21-24R; 220; CANR 45, 74,
107, 131; DLB 67; MTCW 2

**Saint, H(arry) F.** 1941- ...................... **CLC 50**
See also CA 127

**St. Aubin de Teran, Lisa** 1953-
See Teran, Lisa St. Aubin de
See also CA 118; 126; CN 7; INT CA-126

**Saint Birgitta of Sweden** c.
1303-1373 .............................. **CMLC 24**

**Sainte-Beuve, Charles Augustin**
1804-1869 ................................. **NCLC 5**
See also DLB 217; EW 6; GFL 1789 to the
Present

**Saint-Exupery, Antoine (Jean Baptiste
Marie Roger) de** 1900-1944 .... **TCLC 2,
56; WLC**
See also BPFB 3; BYA 3; CA 108; 132;
CLR 10; DA3; DAM NOV; DLB 72; EW
12; EWL 3; GFL 1789 to the Present;
LAIT 3; MAICYA 1, 2; MTCW 1, 2;
RGWL 2, 3; SATA 20; TWA

**St. John, David**
See Hunt, E(verette) Howard, (Jr.)

**St. John, J. Hector**
See Crevecoeur, Michel Guillaume Jean de

**Saint-John Perse**
See Leger, (Marie-Rene Auguste) Alexis
Saint-Leger
See also EW 10; EWL 3; GFL 1789 to the
Present; RGWL 2

**Saintsbury, George (Edward Bateman)**
1845-1933 ................................ **TCLC 31**
See also CA 160; DLB 57, 149

**Sait Faik** ...................................... **TCLC 23**
See Abasiyanik, Sait Faik

**Saki** ................................... **SSC 12; TCLC 3**
See Munro, H(ector) H(ugh)
See also BRWS 6; BYA 11; LAIT 2; MTCW
2; RGEL 2; SSFS 1; SUFW

**Sala, George Augustus** 1828-1895 . **NCLC 46**

**Saladin** 1138-1193 ........................ **CMLC 38**

**Salama, Hannu** 1936- ...................... **CLC 18**
See also EWL 3

**Salamanca, J(ack) R(ichard)** 1922- .. **CLC 4,
15**
See also CA 25-28R, 193; CAAE 193

**Salas, Floyd Francis** 1931- ................. **HLC 2**
    See also CA 119; CAAS 27; CANR 44, 75, 93; DAM MULT; DLB 82; HW 1, 2; MTCW 2
**Sale, J. Kirkpatrick**
    See Sale, Kirkpatrick
**Sale, Kirkpatrick** 1937- .................... **CLC 68**
    See also CA 13-16R; CANR 10
**Salinas, Luis Omar** 1937- ... **CLC 90; HLC 2**
    See also AMWS 13; CA 131; CANR 81; DAM MULT; DLB 82; HW 1, 2
**Salinas (y Serrano), Pedro**
    1891(?)-1951 ........................... **TCLC 17**
    See also CA 117; DLB 134; EWL 3
**Salinger, J(erome) D(avid)** 1919- .. **CLC 1, 3, 8, 12, 55, 56, 138; SSC 2, 28, 65; WLC**
    See also AAYA 2, 36; AMW; AMWC 1; BPFB 3; CA 5-8R; CANR 39, 129; CDALB 1941-1968; CLR 18; CN 7; CPW 1; DA; DA3; DAB; DAC; DAM MST, NOV, POP; DLB 2, 102, 173; EWL 3; EXPN; LAIT 4; MAICYA 1, 2; MTCW 1, 2; NFS 1; RGAL 4; RGSF 2; SATA 67; SSFS 17; TUS; WYA; YAW
**Salisbury, John**
    See Caute, (John) David
**Sallust** c. 86B.C.-35B.C. ................ **CMLC 68**
    See also AW 2; CDWLB 1; DLB 211; RGWL 2, 3
**Salter, James** 1925- .. **CLC 7, 52, 59; SSC 58**
    See also AMWS 9; CA 73-76; CANR 107; DLB 130
**Saltus, Edgar (Everton)** 1855-1921 . **TCLC 8**
    See also CA 105; DLB 202; RGAL 4
**Saltykov, Mikhail Evgrafovich**
    1826-1889 ................................. **NCLC 16**
    See also DLB 238:
**Saltykov-Shchedrin, N.**
    See Saltykov, Mikhail Evgrafovich
**Samarakis, Andonis**
    See Samarakis, Antonis
    See also EWL 3
**Samarakis, Antonis** 1919-2003 .......... **CLC 5**
    See also CA 25-28R; 224; CAAS 16; CANR 36
**Sanchez, Florencio** 1875-1910 ........ **TCLC 37**
    See also CA 153; DLB 305; EWL 3; HW 1; LAW
**Sanchez, Luis Rafael** 1936- .............. **CLC 23**
    See also CA 128; DLB 305; EWL 3; HW 1; WLIT 1
**Sanchez, Sonia** 1934- .... **BLC 3; CLC 5, 116; PC 9**
    See also BW 2, 3; CA 33-36R; CANR 24, 49, 74, 115; CLR 18; CP 7; CSW; CWP; DA3; DAM MULT; DLB 41; DLBD 8; EWL 3; MAICYA 1, 2; MTCW 1, 2; SATA 22, 136; WP
**Sancho, Ignatius** 1729-1780 ................. **LC 84**
**Sand, George** 1804-1876 ..... **NCLC 2, 42, 57; WLC**
    See also DA; DA3; DAB; DAC; DAM MST, NOV; DLB 119, 192; EW 6; FW; GFL 1789 to the Present; RGWL 2, 3; TWA
**Sandburg, Carl (August)** 1878-1967 . **CLC 1, 4, 10, 15, 35; PC 2, 41; WLC**
    See also AAYA 24; AMW; BYA 1, 3; CA 5-8R; 25-28R; CANR 35; CDALB 1865-1917; CLR 67; DA; DA3; DAB; DAC; DAM MST, POET; DLB 17, 54, 284; EWL 3; EXPP; LAIT 2; MAICYA 1, 2; MTCW 1, 2; PAB; PFS 3, 6, 12; RGAL 4; SATA 8; TUS; WCH; WP; WYA
**Sandburg, Charles**
    See Sandburg, Carl (August)
**Sandburg, Charles A.**
    See Sandburg, Carl (August)

**Sanders, (James) Ed(ward)** 1939- .... **CLC 53**
    See Sanders, Edward
    See also BG 3; CA 13-16R; CAAS 21; CANR 13, 44, 78; CP 7; DAM POET; DLB 16, 244
**Sanders, Edward**
    See Sanders, (James) Ed(ward)
    See also DLB 244
**Sanders, Lawrence** 1920-1998 .......... **CLC 41**
    See also BEST 89:4; BPFB 3; CA 81-84; 165; CANR 33, 62; CMW 4; CPW; DA3; DAM POP; MTCW 1
**Sanders, Noah**
    See Blount, Roy (Alton), Jr.
**Sanders, Winston P.**
    See Anderson, Poul (William)
**Sandoz, Mari(e Susette)** 1900-1966 .. **CLC 28**
    See also CA 1-4R; 25-28R; CANR 17, 64; DLB 9, 212; LAIT 2; MTCW 1, 2; SATA 5; TCWW 2
**Sandys, George** 1578-1644 .................... **LC 80**
    See also DLB 24, 121
**Saner, Reg(inald Anthony)** 1931- ....... **CLC 9**
    See also CA 65-68; CP 7
**Sankara** 788-820 ............................ **CMLC 32**
**Sannazaro, Jacopo** 1456(?)-1530 .......... **LC 8**
    See also RGWL 2, 3
**Sansom, William** 1912-1976 . **CLC 2, 6; SSC 21**
    See also CA 5-8R; 65-68; CANR 42; DAM NOV; DLB 139; EWL 3; MTCW 1; RGEL 2; RGSF 2
**Santayana, George** 1863-1952 ........ **TCLC 40**
    See also AMW; CA 115; 194; DLB 54, 71, 246, 270; DLBD 13; EWL 3; RGAL 4; TUS
**Santiago, Danny** ............................... **CLC 33**
    See James, Daniel (Lewis)
    See also DLB 122
**Santmyer, Helen Hooven**
    1895-1986 .............. **CLC 33; TCLC 133**
    See also CA 1-4R; 118; CANR 15, 33; DLBY 1984; MTCW 1; RHW
**Santoka, Taneda** 1882-1940 ........... **TCLC 72**
**Santos, Bienvenido N(uqui)**
    1911-1996 ... **AAL; CLC 22; TCLC 156**
    See also CA 101; 151; CANR 19, 46; DAM MULT; EWL; RGAL 4; SSFS 19
**Sapir, Edward** 1884-1939 ............. **TCLC 108**
    See also CA 211; DLB 92
**Sapper** .................................. **TCLC 44**
    See McNeile, Herman Cyril
**Sapphire**
    See Sapphire, Brenda
**Sapphire, Brenda** 1950- .................... **CLC 99**
**Sappho** fl. 6th cent. B.C.- ... **CMLC 3, 67; PC 5**
    See also CDWLB 1; DA3; DAM POET; DLB 176; PFS 20; RGWL 2, 3; WP
**Saramago, Jose** 1922- ..... **CLC 119; HLCS 1**
    See also CA 153; CANR 96; CWW 2; DLB 287; EWL 3; LATS 1:2
**Sarduy, Severo** 1937-1993 .......... **CLC 6, 97; HLCS 2**
    See also CA 89-92; 142; CANR 58, 81; CWW 2; DLB 113; EWL 3; HW 1, 2; LAW
**Sargeson, Frank** 1903-1982 ............. **CLC 31**
    See also CA 25-28R; 106; CANR 38, 79; EWL 3; GLL 2; RGEL 2; RGSF 2; SSFS 20
**Sarmiento, Domingo Faustino**
    1811-1888 ................................ **HLCS 2**
    See also LAW; WLIT 1
**Sarmiento, Felix Ruben Garcia**
    See Dario, Ruben

**Saro-Wiwa, Ken(ule Beeson)**
    1941-1995 ................................. **CLC 114**
    See also BW 2; CA 142; 150; CANR 60; DLB 157
**Saroyan, William** 1908-1981 ... **CLC 1, 8, 10, 29, 34, 56; SSC 21; TCLC 137; WLC**
    See also CA 5-8R; 103; CAD; CANR 30; CDALBS; DA; DA3; DAB; DAC; DAM DRAM, MST, NOV; DFS 17; DLB 7, 9, 86; DLBY 1981; EWL 3; LAIT 4; MTCW 1, 2; RGAL 4; RGSF 2; SATA 23; SATA-Obit 24; SSFS 14; TUS
**Sarraute, Nathalie** 1900-1999 .... **CLC 1, 2, 4, 8, 10, 31, 80; TCLC 145**
    See also BPFB 3; CA 9-12R; 187; CANR 23, 66; CWW 2; DLB 83; EW 12; EWL 3; GFL 1789 to the Present; MTCW 1, 2; RGWL 2, 3
**Sarton, (Eleanor) May** 1912-1995 ..... **CLC 4, 14, 49, 91; PC 39; TCLC 120**
    See also AMWS 8; CA 1-4R; 149; CANR 1, 34, 55, 116; CN 7; CP 7; DAM POET; DLB 48; DLBY 1981; EWL 3; FW; INT CANR-34; MTCW 1, 2; RGAL 4; SATA 36; SATA-Obit 86; TUS
**Sartre, Jean-Paul** 1905-1980 . **CLC 1, 4, 7, 9, 13, 18, 24, 44, 50, 52; DC 3; SSC 32; WLC**
    See also CA 9-12R; 97-100; CANR 21; DA; DA3; DAB; DAC; DAM DRAM, MST, NOV; DFS 5; DLB 72, 296; EW 12; EWL 3; GFL 1789 to the Present; LMFS 2; MTCW 1, 2; RGSF 2; RGWL 2, 3; SSFS 9; TWA
**Sassoon, Siegfried (Lorraine)**
    1886-1967 .............. **CLC 36, 130; PC 12**
    See also BRW 6; CA 104; 25-28R; CANR 36; DAB; DAM MST, NOV, POET; DLB 20, 191; DLBD 18; EWL 3; MTCW 1, 2; PAB; RGEL 2; TEA
**Satterfield, Charles**
    See Pohl, Frederik
**Satyremont**
    See Peret, Benjamin
**Saul, John (W. III)** 1942- ................. **CLC 46**
    See also AAYA 10; BEST 90:4; CA 81-84; CANR 16, 40, 81; CPW; DAM NOV, POP; HGG; SATA 98
**Saunders, Caleb**
    See Heinlein, Robert A(nson)
**Saura (Atares), Carlos** 1932-1998 .... **CLC 20**
    See also CA 114; 131; CANR 79; HW 1
**Sauser, Frederic Louis**
    See Sauser-Hall, Frederic
**Sauser-Hall, Frederic** 1887-1961 ...... **CLC 18**
    See Cendrars, Blaise
    See also CA 102; 93-96; CANR 36, 62; MTCW 1
**Saussure, Ferdinand de**
    1857-1913 ................................ **TCLC 49**
    See also DLB 242
**Savage, Catharine**
    See Brosman, Catharine Savage
**Savage, Richard** 1697(?)-1743 ............. **LC 96**
    See also DLB 95; RGEL 2
**Savage, Thomas** 1915-2003 ............... **CLC 40**
    See also CA 126; 132; 218; CAAS 15; CN 7; INT CA-132; SATA-Obit 147; TCWW 2
**Savan, Glenn** 1953-2003 .................... **CLC 50**
    See also CA 225
**Sax, Robert**
    See Johnson, Robert
**Saxo Grammaticus** c. 1150-c.
    1222 ......................................... **CMLC 58**
**Saxton, Robert**
    See Johnson, Robert

**Sayers, Dorothy L(eigh)** 1893-1957 . **SSC 71; TCLC 2, 15**
See also BPFB 3; BRWS 3; CA 104; 119; CANR 60; CDBLB 1914-1945; CMW 4; DAM POP; DLB 10, 36, 77, 100; MSW; MTCW 1, 2; RGEL 2; SSFS 12; TEA

**Sayers, Valerie** 1952- ................. **CLC 50, 122**
See also CA 134; CANR 61; CSW

**Sayles, John (Thomas)** 1950- . **CLC 7, 10, 14**
See also CA 57-60; CANR 41, 84; DLB 44

**Scammell, Michael** 1935- .................. **CLC 34**
See also CA 156

**Scannell, Vernon** 1922- .................... **CLC 49**
See also CA 5-8R; CANR 8, 24, 57; CP 7; CWRI 5; DLB 27; SATA 59

**Scarlett, Susan**
See Streatfeild, (Mary) Noel

**Scarron** 1847-1910
See Mikszath, Kalman

**Schaeffer, Susan Fromberg** 1941- ..... **CLC 6, 11, 22**
See also CA 49-52; CANR 18, 65; CN 7; DLB 28, 299; MTCW 1, 2; SATA 22

**Schama, Simon (Michael)** 1945- ..... **CLC 150**
See also BEST 89:4; CA 105; CANR 39, 91

**Schary, Jill**
See Robinson, Jill

**Schell, Jonathan** 1943- ...................... **CLC 35**
See also CA 73-76; CANR 12, 117

**Schelling, Friedrich Wilhelm Joseph von** 1775-1854 ................................. **NCLC 30**
See also DLB 90

**Scherer, Jean-Marie Maurice** 1920-
See Rohmer, Eric
See also CA 110

**Schevill, James (Erwin)** 1920- ........... **CLC 7**
See also CA 5-8R; CAAS 12; CAD; CD 5

**Schiller, Friedrich von** 1759-1805 ...... **DC 12; NCLC 39, 69**
See also CDWLB 2; DAM DRAM; DLB 94; EW 5; RGWL 2, 3; TWA

**Schisgal, Murray (Joseph)** 1926- ....... **CLC 6**
See also CA 21-24R; CAD; CANR 48, 86; CD 5

**Schlee, Ann** 1934- .......................... **CLC 35**
See also CA 101; CANR 29, 88; SATA 44; SATA-Brief 36

**Schlegel, August Wilhelm von** 1767-1845 ......................... **NCLC 15, 142**
See also DLB 94; RGWL 2, 3

**Schlegel, Friedrich** 1772-1829 ........ **NCLC 45**
See also DLB 90; EW 5; RGWL 2, 3; TWA

**Schlegel, Johann Elias (von)** 1719(?)-1749 ..................................... **LC 5**

**Schleiermacher, Friedrich** 1768-1834 ............................... **NCLC 107**
See also DLB 90

**Schlesinger, Arthur M(eier), Jr.** 1917- ............................................. **CLC 84**
See also AITN 1; CA 1-4R; CANR 1, 28, 58, 105; DLB 17; INT CANR-28; MTCW 1, 2; SATA 61

**Schlink, Bernhard** 1944- ................. **CLC 174**
See also CA 163; CANR 116

**Schmidt, Arno (Otto)** 1914-1979 ...... **CLC 56**
See also CA 128; 109; DLB 69; EWL 3

**Schmitz, Aron Hector** 1861-1928
See Svevo, Italo
See also CA 104; 122; MTCW 1

**Schnackenberg, Gjertrud (Cecelia)** 1953- ............................. **CLC 40; PC 45**
See also CA 116; CANR 100; CP 7; CWP; DLB 120, 282; PFS 13

**Schneider, Leonard Alfred** 1925-1966
See Bruce, Lenny
See also CA 89-92

**Schnitzler, Arthur** 1862-1931 ..... **DC 17; SSC 15, 61; TCLC 4**
See also CA 104; CDWLB 2; DLB 81, 118; EW 8; EWL 3; RGSF 2; RGWL 2, 3

**Schoenberg, Arnold Franz Walter** 1874-1951 ................................... **TCLC 75**
See also CA 109; 188

**Schonberg, Arnold**
See Schoenberg, Arnold Franz Walter

**Schopenhauer, Arthur** 1788-1860 .. **NCLC 51**
See also DLB 90; EW 5

**Schor, Sandra (M.)** 1932(?)-1990 ..... **CLC 65**
See also CA 132

**Schorer, Mark** 1908-1977 ................... **CLC 9**
See also CA 5-8R; 73-76; CANR 7; DLB 103

**Schrader, Paul (Joseph)** 1946- .......... **CLC 26**
See also CA 37-40R; CANR 41; DLB 44

**Schreber, Daniel** 1842-1911 .......... **TCLC 123**

**Schreiner, Olive (Emilie Albertina)** 1855-1920 ................................... **TCLC 9**
See also AFW; BRWS 2; CA 105; 154; DLB 18, 156, 190, 225; EWL 3; FW; RGEL 2; TWA; WLIT 2; WWE 1

**Schulberg, Budd (Wilson)** 1914- .. **CLC 7, 48**
See also BPFB 3; CA 25-28R; CANR 19, 87; CN 7; DLB 6, 26, 28; DLBY 1981, 2001

**Schulman, Arnold**
See Trumbo, Dalton

**Schulz, Bruno** 1892-1942 .. **SSC 13; TCLC 5, 51**
See also CA 115; 123; CANR 86; CDWLB 4; DLB 215; EWL 3; MTCW 2; RGSF 2; RGWL 2, 3

**Schulz, Charles M(onroe)** 1922-2000 ................................... **CLC 12**
See also AAYA 39; CA 9-12R; 187; CANR 6, 132; INT CANR-6; SATA 10; SATA-Obit 118

**Schumacher, E(rnst) F(riedrich)** 1911-1977 ................................... **CLC 80**
See also CA 81-84; 73-76; CANR 34, 85

**Schumann, Robert** 1810-1856 ...... **NCLC 143**

**Schuyler, George Samuel** 1895-1977 .... **HR 3**
See also BW 2; CA 81-84; 73-76; CANR 42; DLB 29, 51

**Schuyler, James Marcus** 1923-1991 .. **CLC 5, 23**
See also CA 101; 134; DAM POET; DLB 5, 169; EWL 3; INT CA-101; WP

**Schwartz, Delmore (David)** 1913-1966 ... **CLC 2, 4, 10, 45, 87; PC 8**
See also AMWS 2; CA 17-18; 25-28R; CANR 35; CAP 2; DLB 28, 48; EWL 3; MTCW 1, 2; PAB; RGAL 4; TUS

**Schwartz, Ernst**
See Ozu, Yasujiro

**Schwartz, John Burnham** 1965- ....... **CLC 59**
See also CA 132; CANR 116

**Schwartz, Lynne Sharon** 1939- ........ **CLC 31**
See also CA 103; CANR 44, 89; DLB 218; MTCW 2

**Schwartz, Muriel A.**
See Eliot, T(homas) S(tearns)

**Schwarz-Bart, Andre** 1928- ........... **CLC 2, 4**
See also CA 89-92; CANR 109; DLB 299

**Schwarz-Bart, Simone** 1938- . **BLCS; CLC 7**
See also BW 2; CA 97-100; CANR 117; EWL 3

**Schwerner, Armand** 1927-1999 ........... **PC 42**
See also CA 9-12R; 179; CANR 50, 85; CP 7; DLB 165

**Schwitters, Kurt (Hermann Edward Karl Julius)** 1887-1948 ................... **TCLC 95**
See also CA 158

**Schwob, Marcel (Mayer Andre)** 1867-1905 .............................. **TCLC 20**
See also CA 117; 168; DLB 123; GFL 1789 to the Present

**Sciascia, Leonardo** 1921-1989 .. **CLC 8, 9, 41**
See also CA 85-88; 130; CANR 35; DLB 177; EWL 3; MTCW 1; RGWL 2, 3

**Scoppettone, Sandra** 1936- .............. **CLC 26**
See Early, Jack
See also AAYA 11; BYA 8; CA 5-8R; CANR 41, 73; GLL 1; MAICYA 2; MAICYAS 1; SATA 9, 92; WYA; YAW

**Scorsese, Martin** 1942- ............... **CLC 20, 89**
See also AAYA 38; CA 110; 114; CANR 46, 85

**Scotland, Jay**
See Jakes, John (William)

**Scott, Duncan Campbell** 1862-1947 ................................. **TCLC 6**
See also CA 104; 153; DAC; DLB 92; RGEL 2

**Scott, Evelyn** 1893-1963 ................... **CLC 43**
See also CA 104; 112; CANR 64; DLB 9, 48; RHW

**Scott, F(rancis) R(eginald)** 1899-1985 ................................ **CLC 22**
See also CA 101; 114; CANR 87; DLB 88; INT CA-101; RGEL 2

**Scott, Frank**
See Scott, F(rancis) R(eginald)

**Scott, Joan** ............................................ **CLC 65**

**Scott, Joanna** 1960- ........................... **CLC 50**
See also CA 126; CANR 53, 92

**Scott, Paul (Mark)** 1920-1978 ...... **CLC 9, 60**
See also BRWS 1; CA 81-84; 77-80; CANR 33; DLB 14, 207; EWL 3; MTCW 1; RGEL 2; RHW; WWE 1

**Scott, Ridley** 1937- .......................... **CLC 183**
See also AAYA 13, 43

**Scott, Sarah** 1723-1795 ........................ **LC 44**
See also DLB 39

**Scott, Sir Walter** 1771-1832 .... **NCLC 15, 69, 110; PC 13; SSC 32; WLC**
See also AAYA 22; BRW 4; BYA 2; CD-BLB 1789-1832; DA; DAB; DAC; DAM MST, NOV, POET; DLB 93, 107, 116, 144, 159; HGG; LAIT 1; RGEL 2; RGSF 2; SSFS 10; SUFW 1; TEA; WLIT 3; YABC 2

**Scribe, (Augustin) Eugene** 1791-1861 . **DC 5; NCLC 16**
See also DAM DRAM; DLB 192; GFL 1789 to the Present; RGWL 2, 3

**Scrum, R.**
See Crumb, R(obert)

**Scudery, Georges de** 1601-1667 .......... **LC 75**
See also GFL Beginnings to 1789

**Scudery, Madeleine de** 1607-1701 .. **LC 2, 58**
See also DLB 268; GFL Beginnings to 1789

**Scum**
See Crumb, R(obert)

**Scumbag, Little Bobby**
See Crumb, R(obert)

**Seabrook, John**
See Hubbard, L(afayette) Ron(ald)

**Seacole, Mary Jane Grant** 1805-1881 .............................. **NCLC 147**
See also DLB 166

**Sealy, I(rwin) Allan** 1951- ............... **CLC 55**
See also CA 136; CN 7

**Search, Alexander**
See Pessoa, Fernando (Antonio Nogueira)

**Sebald, W(infried) G(eorg)** 1944-2001 ............................ **CLC 194**
See also BRWS 8; CA 159; 202; CANR 98

**Sebastian, Lee**
See Silverberg, Robert

**Sebastian Owl**
See Thompson, Hunter S(tockton)

**Sebestyen, Igen**
  See Sebestyen, Ouida
**Sebestyen, Ouida** 1924- ...................... CLC 30
  See also AAYA 8; BYA 7; CA 107; CANR
  40, 114; CLR 17; JRDA; MAICYA 1, 2;
  SAAS 10; SATA 39, 140; WYA; YAW
**Sebold, Alice** 1963(?)- ...................... CLC 193
  See also AAYA 56; CA 203
**Second Duke of Buckingham**
  See Villiers, George
**Secundus, H. Scriblerus**
  See Fielding, Henry
**Sedges, John**
  See Buck, Pearl S(ydenstricker)
**Sedgwick, Catharine Maria**
  1789-1867 .......................... NCLC 19, 98
  See also DLB 1, 74, 183, 239, 243, 254;
  RGAL 4
**Seelye, John (Douglas)** 1931- .............. CLC 7
  See also CA 97-100; CANR 70; INT CA-
  97-100; TCWW 2
**Seferiades, Giorgos Stylianou** 1900-1971
  See Seferis, George
  See also CA 5-8R; 33-36R; CANR 5, 36;
  MTCW 1
**Seferis, George** ...................... CLC 5, 11
  See Seferiades, Giorgos Stylianou
  See also EW 12; EWL 3; RGWL 2, 3
**Segal, Erich (Wolf)** 1937- .............. CLC 3, 10
  See also BEST 89:1; BPFB 3; CA 25-28R;
  CANR 20, 36, 65, 113; CPW; DAM POP;
  DLBY 1986; INT CANR-20; MTCW 1
**Seger, Bob** 1945- ................................. CLC 35
**Seghers, Anna** ...................... CLC 7
  See Radvanyi, Netty
  See also CDWLB 2; DLB 69; EWL 3
**Seidel, Frederick (Lewis)** 1936- ........ CLC 18
  See also CA 13-16R; CANR 8, 99; CP 7;
  DLBY 1984
**Seifert, Jaroslav** 1901-1986 . CLC 34, 44, 93;
  PC 47
  See also CA 127; CDWLB 4; DLB 215;
  EWL 3; MTCW 1, 2
**Sei Shonagon** c. 966-1017(?) ........... CMLC 6
**Sejour, Victor** 1817-1874 ...................... DC 10
  See also DLB 50
**Sejour Marcou et Ferrand, Juan Victor**
  See Sejour, Victor
**Selby, Hubert, Jr.** 1928-2004 ..... CLC 1, 2, 4,
  8; SSC 20
  See also CA 13-16R; 226; CANR 33, 85;
  CN 7; DLB 2, 227
**Selzer, Richard** 1928- ...................... CLC 74
  See also CA 65-68; CANR 14, 106
**Sembene, Ousmane**
  See Ousmane, Sembene
  See also AFW; EWL 3; WLIT 2
**Senancour, Etienne Pivert de**
  1770-1846 ................................. NCLC 16
  See also DLB 119; GFL 1789 to the Present
**Sender, Ramon (Jose)** 1902-1982 ...... CLC 8;
  HLC 2; TCLC 136
  See also CA 5-8R; 105; CANR 8; DAM
  MULT; EWL 3; HW 1; MTCW 1; RGWL
  2, 3
**Seneca, Lucius Annaeus** c. 4B.C.-c.
  65 ...................................... CMLC 6; DC 5
  See also AW 2; CDWLB 1; DAM DRAM;
  DLB 211; RGWL 2, 3; TWA
**Senghor, Leopold Sedar** 1906-2001 ... BLC 3;
  CLC 54, 130; PC 25
  See also AFW; BW 2; CA 116; 125; 203;
  CANR 47, 74; CWW 2; DAM MULT,
  POET; DNFS 2; EWL 3; GFL 1789 to the
  Present; MTCW 1, 2; TWA
**Senna, Danzy** 1970- ......................... CLC 119
  See also CA 169; CANR 130

**Serling, (Edward) Rod(man)**
  1924-1975 ................................... CLC 30
  See also AAYA 14; AITN 1; CA 162; 57-
  60; DLB 26; SFW 4
**Serna, Ramon Gomez de la**
  See Gomez de la Serna, Ramon
**Serpieres**
  See Guillevic, (Eugene)
**Service, Robert**
  See Service, Robert W(illiam)
  See also BYA 4; DAB; DLB 92
**Service, Robert W(illiam)**
  1874(?)-1958 ................ TCLC 15; WLC
  See Service, Robert
  See also CA 115; 140; CANR 84; DA;
  DAC; DAM MST, POET; PFS 10; RGEL
  2; SATA 20
**Seth, Vikram** 1952- ..................... CLC 43, 90
  See also CA 121; 127; CANR 50, 74, 131;
  CN 7; CP 7; DA3; DAM MULT; DLB
  120, 271, 282; EWL 3; INT CA-127;
  MTCW 2; WWE 1
**Seton, Cynthia Propper** 1926-1982 .. CLC 27
  See also CA 5-8R; 108; CANR 7
**Seton, Ernest (Evan) Thompson**
  1860-1946 ................................... TCLC 31
  See also ANW; BYA 3; CA 109; 204; CLR
  59; DLB 92; DLBD 13; JRDA; SATA 18
**Seton-Thompson, Ernest**
  See Seton, Ernest (Evan) Thompson
**Settle, Mary Lee** 1918- ................ CLC 19, 61
  See also BPFB 3; CA 89-92; CAAS 1;
  CANR 44, 87, 126; CN 7; CSW; DLB 6;
  INT CA-89-92
**Seuphor, Michel**
  See Arp, Jean
**Sevigne, Marie (de Rabutin-Chantal)**
  1626-1696 ..................................... LC 11
  See Sevigne, Marie de Rabutin Chantal
  See also GFL Beginnings to 1789; TWA
**Sevigne, Marie de Rabutin Chantal**
  See Sevigne, Marie (de Rabutin-Chantal)
  See also DLB 268
**Sewall, Samuel** 1652-1730 ................... LC 38
  See also DLB 24; RGAL 4
**Sexton, Anne (Harvey)** 1928-1974 ..... CLC 2,
  4, 6, 8, 10, 15, 53, 123; PC 2; WLC
  See also AMWS 2; CA 1-4R; 53-56; CABS
  2; CANR 3, 36; CDALB 1941-1968; DA;
  DA3; DAB; DAC; DAM MST, POET;
  DLB 5, 169; EWL 3; EXPP; FW;
  MAWW; MTCW 1, 2; PAB; PFS 4, 14;
  RGAL 4; SATA 10; TUS
**Shaara, Jeff** 1952- ........................... CLC 119
  See also CA 163; CANR 109
**Shaara, Michael (Joseph, Jr.)**
  1929-1988 ................................... CLC 15
  See also AITN 1; BPFB 3; CA 102; 125;
  CANR 52, 85; DAM POP; DLBY 1983
**Shackleton, C. C.**
  See Aldiss, Brian W(ilson)
**Shacochis, Bob** ................................. CLC 39
  See Shacochis, Robert G.
**Shacochis, Robert G.** 1951-
  See Shacochis, Bob
  See also CA 119; 124; CANR 100; INT CA-
  124
**Shaffer, Anthony (Joshua)**
  1926-2001 ................................... CLC 19
  See also CA 110; 116; 200; CBD; CD 5;
  DAM DRAM; DFS 13; DLB 13
**Shaffer, Peter (Levin)** 1926- .. CLC 5, 14, 18,
  37, 60; DC 7
  See also BRWS 1; CA 25-28R; CANR 25,
  47, 74, 118; CBD; CD 5; CDBLB 1960 to
  Present; DA3; DAB; DAM DRAM, MST;
  DFS 5, 13; DLB 13, 233; EWL 3; MTCW
  1, 2; RGEL 2; TEA

**Shakespeare, William** 1564-1616 ......... WLC
  See also AAYA 35; BRW 1; CDBLB Before
  1660; DA; DA3; DAB; DAC; DAM
  DRAM, MST, POET; DFS 20; DLB 62,
  172, 263; EXPP; LAIT 1; LATS 1:1;
  LMFS 1; PAB; PFS 1, 2, 3, 4, 5, 8, 9;
  RGEL 2; TEA; WLIT 3; WP; WS; WYA
**Shakey, Bernard**
  See Young, Neil
**Shalamov, Varlam (Tikhonovich)**
  1907-1982 ................................... CLC 18
  See also CA 129; 105; DLB 302; RGSF 2
**Shamloo, Ahmad**
  See Shamlu, Ahmad
**Shamlou, Ahmad**
  See Shamlu, Ahmad
**Shamlu, Ahmad** 1925-2000 .............. CLC 10
  See also CA 216; CWW 2
**Shammas, Anton** 1951- ..................... CLC 55
  See also CA 199
**Shange, Ntozake** 1948- ... BLC 3; CLC 8, 25,
  38, 74, 126; DC 3
  See also AAYA 9; AFAW 1, 2; BW 2; CA
  85-88; CABS 3; CAD; CANR 27, 48, 74,
  131; CD 5; CP 7; CWD; CWP; DA3;
  DAM DRAM, MULT; DFS 2, 11; DLB
  38, 249; FW; LAIT 5; MTCW 1, 2; NFS
  11; RGAL 4; YAW
**Shanley, John Patrick** 1950- ............. CLC 75
  See also CA 128; 133; CAD; CANR 83;
  CD 5
**Shapcott, Thomas W(illiam)** 1935- .. CLC 38
  See also CA 69-72; CANR 49, 83, 103; CP
  7; DLB 289
**Shapiro, Jane** 1942- ........................... CLC 76
  See also CA 196
**Shapiro, Karl (Jay)** 1913-2000 ...... CLC 4, 8,
  15, 53; PC 25
  See also AMWS 2; CA 1-4R; 188; CAAS
  6; CANR 1, 36, 66; CP 7; DLB 48; EWL
  3; EXPP; MTCW 1, 2; PFS 3; RGAL 4
**Sharp, William** 1855-1905 ............. TCLC 39
  See Macleod, Fiona
  See also CA 160; DLB 156; RGEL 2
**Sharpe, Thomas Ridley** 1928-
  See Sharpe, Tom
  See also CA 114; 122; CANR 85; INT CA-
  122
**Sharpe, Tom** ...................................... CLC 36
  See Sharpe, Thomas Ridley
  See also CN 7; DLB 14, 231
**Shatrov, Mikhail** .............................. CLC 59
**Shaw, Bernard**
  See Shaw, George Bernard
  See also DLB 190
**Shaw, G. Bernard**
  See Shaw, George Bernard
**Shaw, George Bernard** 1856-1950 ..... DC 23;
  TCLC 3, 9, 21, 45; WLC
  See Shaw, Bernard
  See also BRW 6; BRWC 1; BRWR 2; CA
  104; 128; CDBLB 1914-1945; DA; DA3;
  DAB; DAC; DAM DRAM, MST; DFS 1,
  3, 6, 11, 19; DLB 10, 57; EWL 3; LAIT
  3; LATS 1:1; MTCW 1, 2; RGEL 2; TEA;
  WLIT 4
**Shaw, Henry Wheeler** 1818-1885 .. NCLC 15
  See also DLB 11; RGAL 4
**Shaw, Irwin** 1913-1984 ............. CLC 7, 23, 34
  See also AITN 1; BPFB 3; CA 13-16R; 112;
  CANR 21; CDALB 1941-1968; CPW;
  DAM DRAM, POP; DLB 6, 102; DLBY
  1984; MTCW 1, 21
**Shaw, Robert** 1927-1978 ...................... CLC 5
  See also AITN 1; CA 1-4R; 81-84; CANR
  4; DLB 13, 14

**Shaw, T. E.**
See Lawrence, T(homas) E(dward)

**Shawn, Wallace** 1943- ...................... **CLC 41**
See also CA 112; CAD; CD 5; DLB 266

**Shchedrin, N.**
See Saltykov, Mikhail Evgrafovich

**Shea, Lisa** 1953- ................................ **CLC 86**
See also CA 147

**Sheed, Wilfrid (John Joseph)** 1930- . **CLC 2, 4, 10, 53**
See also CA 65-68; CANR 30, 66; CN 7; DLB 6; MTCW 1, 2

**Sheehy, Gail** 1937- ........................... **CLC 171**
See also CA 49-52; CANR 1, 33, 55, 92; CPW; MTCW 1

**Sheldon, Alice Hastings Bradley**
1915(?)-1987
See Tiptree, James, Jr.
See also CA 108; 122; CANR 34; INT CA-108; MTCW 1

**Sheldon, John**
See Bloch, Robert (Albert)

**Sheldon, Walter J(ames)** 1917-1996
See Queen, Ellery
See also AITN 1; CA 25-28R; CANR 10

**Shelley, Mary Wollstonecraft (Godwin)**
1797-1851 ...... **NCLC 14, 59, 103; WLC**
See also AAYA 20; BPFB 3; BRW 3; BRWC 2; BRWS 3; BYA 5; CDBLB 1789-1832; DA; DA3; DAB; DAC; DAM MST, NOV; DLB 110, 116, 159, 178; EXPN; HGG; LAIT 1; LMFS 1, 2; NFS 1; RGEL 2; SATA 29; SCFW; SFW 4; TEA; WLIT 3

**Shelley, Percy Bysshe** 1792-1822 .. **NCLC 18, 93, 143; PC 14; WLC**
See also BRW 4; BRWR 1; CDBLB 1789-1832; DA; DA3; DAB; DAC; DAM MST, POET; DLB 96, 110, 158; EXPP; LMFS 1; PAB; PFS 2; RGEL 2; TEA; WLIT 3; WP

**Shepard, Jim** 1956- ........................... **CLC 36**
See also CA 137; CANR 59, 104; SATA 90

**Shepard, Lucius** 1947- ...................... **CLC 34**
See also CA 128; 141; CANR 81, 124; HGG; SCFW 2; SFW 4; SUFW 2

**Shepard, Sam** 1943- .... **CLC 4, 6, 17, 34, 41, 44, 169; DC 5**
See also AAYA 1, 58; AMWS 3; CA 69-72; CABS 3; CAD; CANR 22, 120; CD 5; DA3; DAM DRAM; DFS 3, 6, 7, 14; DLB 7, 212; EWL 3; IDFW 3, 4; MTCW 1, 2; RGAL 4

**Shepherd, Michael**
See Ludlum, Robert

**Sherburne, Zoa (Lillian Morin)**
1912-1995 .................................. **CLC 30**
See also AAYA 13; CA 1-4R; 176; CANR 3, 37; MAICYA 1, 2; SAAS 18; SATA 3; YAW

**Sheridan, Frances** 1724-1766 ................ **LC 7**
See also DLB 39, 84

**Sheridan, Richard Brinsley**
1751-1816 .... **DC 1; NCLC 5, 91; WLC**
See also BRW 3; CDBLB 1660-1789; DA; DAB; DAC; DAM DRAM, MST; DFS 15; DLB 89; WLIT 3

**Sherman, Jonathan Marc** ............... **CLC 55**

**Sherman, Martin** 1941(?)- ............... **CLC 19**
See also CA 116; 123; CAD; CANR 86; CD 5; DFS 20; DLB 228; GLL 1; IDTP

**Sherwin, Judith Johnson**
See Johnson, Judith (Emlyn)
See also CANR 85; CP 7; CWP

**Sherwood, Frances** 1940- ................ **CLC 81**
See also CA 146, 220; CAAE 220

**Sherwood, Robert E(mmet)**
1896-1955 .................................. **TCLC 3**
See also CA 104; 153; CANR 86; DAM DRAM; DFS 11, 15, 17; DLB 7, 26, 249; IDFW 3, 4; RGAL 4

**Shestov, Lev** 1866-1938 ................. **TCLC 56**

**Shevchenko, Taras** 1814-1861 ........ **NCLC 54**

**Shiel, M(atthew) P(hipps)**
1865-1947 .................................... **TCLC 8**
See Holmes, Gordon
See also CA 106; 160; DLB 153; HGG; MTCW 2; SFW 4; SUFW

**Shields, Carol (Ann)** 1935-2003 ...... **CLC 91, 113, 193**
See also AMWS 7; CA 81-84; 218; CANR 51, 74, 98, 133; CCA 1; CN 7; CPW; DA3; DAC; MTCW 2

**Shields, David (Jonathan)** 1956- ...... **CLC 97**
See also CA 124; CANR 48, 99, 112

**Shiga, Naoya** 1883-1971 ..... **CLC 33; SSC 23**
See Shiga Naoya
See also CA 101; 33-36R; MJW; RGWL 3

**Shiga Naoya**
See Shiga, Naoya
See also DLB 180; EWL 3; RGWL 3

**Shilts, Randy** 1951-1994 ................... **CLC 85**
See also AAYA 19; CA 115; 127; 144; CANR 45; DA3; GLL 1; INT CA-127; MTCW 2

**Shimazaki, Haruki** 1872-1943
See Shimazaki Toson
See also CA 105; 134; CANR 84; RGWL 3

**Shimazaki Toson** .............................. **TCLC 5**
See Shimazaki, Haruki
See also DLB 180; EWL 3

**Shirley, James** 1596-1666 ................... **LC 96**
See also DLB 58; RGEL 2

**Sholokhov, Mikhail (Aleksandrovich)**
1905-1984 .............................. **CLC 7, 15**
See also CA 101; 112; DLB 272; EWL 3; MTCW 1, 2; RGWL 2, 3; SATA-Obit 36

**Shone, Patric**
See Hanley, James

**Showalter, Elaine** 1941- .................. **CLC 169**
See also CA 57-60; CANR 58, 106; DLB 67; FW; GLL 2

**Shreve, Susan**
See Shreve, Susan Richards

**Shreve, Susan Richards** 1939- .......... **CLC 23**
See also CA 49-52; CAAS 5; CANR 5, 38, 69, 100; MAICYA 1, 2; SATA 46, 95, 152; SATA-Brief 41

**Shue, Larry** 1946-1985 ..................... **CLC 52**
See also CA 145; 117; DAM DRAM; DFS 7

**Shu-Jen, Chou** 1881-1936
See Lu Hsun
See also CA 104

**Shulman, Alix Kates** 1932- .......... **CLC 2, 10**
See also CA 29-32R; CANR 43; FW; SATA 7

**Shuster, Joe** 1914-1992 ..................... **CLC 21**
See also AAYA 50

**Shute, Nevil** ..................................... **CLC 30**
See Norway, Nevil Shute
See also BPFB 3; DLB 255; NFS 9; RHW; SFW 4

**Shuttle, Penelope (Diane)** 1947- ......... **CLC 7**
See also CA 93-96; CANR 39, 84, 92, 108; CP 7; CWP; DLB 14, 40

**Shvarts, Elena** 1948- ........................... **PC 50**
See also CA 147

**Sidhwa, Bapsy (N.)** 1938- ............... **CLC 168**
See also CA 108; CANR 25, 57; CN 7; FW

**Sidney, Mary** 1561-1621 ............. **LC 19, 39**
See Sidney Herbert, Mary

**Sidney, Sir Philip** 1554-1586 . **LC 19, 39; PC 32**
See also BRW 1; BRWR 2; CDBLB Before 1660; DA; DA3; DAB; DAC; DAM MST, POET; DLB 167; EXPP; PAB; RGEL 2; TEA; WP

**Sidney Herbert, Mary**
See Sidney, Mary
See also DLB 167

**Siegel, Jerome** 1914-1996 ................. **CLC 21**
See Siegel, Jerry
See also CA 116; 169; 151

**Siegel, Jerry**
See Siegel, Jerome
See also AAYA 50

**Sienkiewicz, Henryk (Adam Alexander Pius)**
1846-1916 .................................. **TCLC 3**
See also CA 104; 134; CANR 84; EWL 3; RGSF 2; RGWL 2, 3

**Sierra, Gregorio Martinez**
See Martinez Sierra, Gregorio

**Sierra, Maria (de la O'LeJarraga) Martinez**
See Martinez Sierra, Maria (de la O'LeJarraga)

**Sigal, Clancy** 1926- ........................... **CLC 7**
See also CA 1-4R; CANR 85; CN 7

**Siger of Brabant** 1240(?)-1284(?) . **CMLC 69**
See also DLB 115

**Sigourney, Lydia H.**
See Sigourney, Lydia Howard (Huntley)
See also DLB 73, 183

**Sigourney, Lydia Howard (Huntley)**
1791-1865 ........................... **NCLC 21, 87**
See Sigourney, Lydia H.; Sigourney, Lydia Huntley
See also DLB 1

**Sigourney, Lydia Huntley**
See Sigourney, Lydia Howard (Huntley)
See also DLB 42, 239, 243

**Siguenza y Gongora, Carlos de**
1645-1700 ........................... **HLCS 2; LC 8**
See also LAW

**Sigurjonsson, Johann**
See Sigurjonsson, Johann

**Sigurjonsson, Johann** 1880-1919 ... **TCLC 27**
See also CA 170; DLB 293; EWL 3

**Sikelianos, Angelos** 1884-1951 ........... **PC 29; TCLC 39**
See also EWL 3; RGWL 2, 3

**Silkin, Jon** 1930-1997 ............... **CLC 2, 6, 43**
See also CA 5-8R; CAAS 5; CANR 89; CP 7; DLB 27

**Silko, Leslie (Marmon)** 1948- .... **CLC 23, 74, 114; NNAL; SSC 37, 66; WLCS**
See also AAYA 14; AMWS 4; ANW; BYA 12; CA 115; 122; CANR 45, 65, 118; CN 7; CP 7; CPW 1; CWP; DA; DA3; DAC; DAM MST, MULT, POP; DLB 143, 175, 256, 275; EWL 3; EXPP; EXPS; LAIT 4; MTCW 4; NFS 4; PFS 9, 16; RGAL 4; RGSF 2; SSFS 4, 8, 10, 11

**Sillanpaa, Frans Eemil** 1888-1964 ... **CLC 19**
See also CA 129; 93-96; EWL 3; MTCW 1

**Sillitoe, Alan** 1928- .. **CLC 1, 3, 6, 10, 19, 57, 148**
See also AITN 1; BRWS 5; CA 9-12R, 191; CAAE 191; CAAS 2; CANR 8, 26, 55; CDBLB 1960 to Present; CN 7; DLB 14, 139; EWL 3; MTCW 1, 2; RGEL 2; RGSF 2; SATA 61

**Silone, Ignazio** 1900-1978 ................... **CLC 4**
See also CA 25-28; 81-84; CANR 34; CAP 2; DLB 264; EW 12; EWL 3; MTCW 1; RGSF 2; RGWL 2, 3

**Silone, Ignazione**
See Silone, Ignazio

**Silver, Joan Micklin** 1935- ............... **CLC 20**
See also CA 114; 121; INT CA-121

**Silver, Nicholas**
See Faust, Frederick (Schiller)
See also TCWW 2

**Silverberg, Robert** 1935- ............ **CLC 7, 140**
See also AAYA 24; BPFB 3; BYA 7, 9; CA 1-4R, 186; CAAE 186; CAAS 3; CANR 1, 20, 36, 85; CLR 59; CN 7; CPW; DAM POP; DLB 8; INT CANR-20; MAICYA 1, 2; MTCW 1, 2; SATA 13, 91; SATA-Essay 104; SCFW 2; SFW 4; SUFW 2

**Silverstein, Alvin** 1933- .................... **CLC 17**
See also CA 49-52; CANR 2; CLR 25; JRDA; MAICYA 1, 2; SATA 8, 69, 124

**Silverstein, Shel(don Allan)**
1932-1999 ................................ **PC 49**
See also AAYA 40; BW 3; CA 107; 179; CANR 47, 74, 81; CLR 5, 96; CWRI 5; JRDA; MAICYA 1, 2; MTCW 2; SATA 33, 92; SATA-Brief 27; SATA-Obit 116

**Silverstein, Virginia B(arbara Opshelor)**
1937- ........................................ **CLC 17**
See also CA 49-52; CANR 2; CLR 25; JRDA; MAICYA 1, 2; SATA 8, 69, 124

**Sim, Georges**
See Simenon, Georges (Jacques Christian)

**Simak, Clifford D(onald)** 1904-1988 . **CLC 1, 55**
See also CA 1-4R; 125; CANR 1, 35; DLB 8; MTCW 1; SATA-Obit 56; SFW 4

**Simenon, Georges (Jacques Christian)**
1903-1989 ............ **CLC 1, 2, 3, 8, 18, 47**
See also BPFB 3; CA 85-88; 129; CANR 35; CMW 4; DA3; DAM POP; DLB 72; DLBY 1989; EW 12; EWL 3; GFL 1789 to the Present; MSW; MTCW 1, 2; RGWL 2, 3

**Simic, Charles** 1938- .... **CLC 6, 9, 22, 49, 68, 130**
See also AMWS 8; CA 29-32R; CAAS 4; CANR 12, 33, 52, 61, 96; CP 7; DA3; DAM POET; DLB 105; MTCW 2; PFS 7; RGAL 4; WP

**Simmel, Georg** 1858-1918 ............... **TCLC 64**
See also CA 157; DLB 296

**Simmons, Charles (Paul)** 1924- ........ **CLC 57**
See also CA 89-92; INT CA-89-92

**Simmons, Dan** 1948- ........................ **CLC 44**
See also AAYA 16, 54; CA 138; CANR 53, 81, 126; CPW; DAM POP; HGG; SUFW 2

**Simmons, James (Stewart Alexander)**
1933- ........................................ **CLC 43**
See also CA 105; CAAS 21; CP 7; DLB 40

**Simms, William Gilmore**
1806-1870 .................................. **NCLC 3**
See also DLB 3, 30, 59, 73, 248, 254; RGAL 4

**Simon, Carly** 1945- ........................ **CLC 26**
See also CA 105

**Simon, Claude (Eugene Henri)**
1913-1984 .................... **CLC 4, 9, 15, 39**
See also CA 89-92; CANR 33, 117; CWW 2; DAM NOV; DLB 83; EW 13; EWL 3; GFL 1789 to the Present; MTCW 1

**Simon, Myles**
See Follett, Ken(neth Martin)

**Simon, (Marvin) Neil** 1927- ... **CLC 6, 11, 31, 39, 70; DC 14**
See also AAYA 32; AITN 1; AMWS 4; CA 21-24R; CANR 26, 54, 87, 126; CD 5; DA3; DAM DRAM; DFS 2, 6, 12, 18; DLB 7, 266; LAIT 4; MTCW 1, 2; RGAL 4; TUS

**Simon, Paul (Frederick)** 1941(?)- ..... **CLC 17**
See also CA 116; 153

**Simonon, Paul** 1956(?)- ...................... **CLC 30**

**Simonson, Rick** ed. ........................... **CLC 70**

**Simpson, Harriette**
See Arnow, Harriette (Louisa) Simpson

**Simpson, Louis (Aston Marantz)**
1923- ..................... **CLC 4, 7, 9, 32, 149**
See also AMWS 9; CA 1-4R; CAAS 4; CANR 1, 61; CP 7; DAM POET; DLB 5; MTCW 1, 2; PFS 7, 11, 14; RGAL 4

**Simpson, Mona (Elizabeth)** 1957- ... **CLC 44, 146**
See also CA 122; 135; CANR 68, 103; CN 7; EWL 3

**Simpson, N(orman) F(rederick)**
1919- ........................................ **CLC 29**
See also CA 13-16R; CBD; DLB 13; RGEL 2

**Sinclair, Andrew (Annandale)** 1935- . **CLC 2, 14**
See also CA 9-12R; CAAS 5; CANR 14, 38, 91; CN 7; DLB 14; FANT; MTCW 1

**Sinclair, Emil**
See Hesse, Hermann

**Sinclair, Iain** 1943- ........................... **CLC 76**
See also CA 132; CANR 81; CP 7; HGG

**Sinclair, Iain MacGregor**
See Sinclair, Iain

**Sinclair, Irene**
See Griffith, D(avid Lewelyn) W(ark)

**Sinclair, Mary Amelia St. Clair** 1865(?)-1946
See Sinclair, May
See also CA 104; HGG; RHW

**Sinclair, May** ............................... **TCLC 3, 11**
See Sinclair, Mary Amelia St. Clair
See also CA 166; DLB 36, 135; EWL 3; RGEL 2; SUFW

**Sinclair, Roy**
See Griffith, D(avid Lewelyn) W(ark)

**Sinclair, Upton (Beall)** 1878-1968 ..... **CLC 1, 11, 15, 63; WLC**
See also AMWS 5; BPFB 3; BYA 2; CA 5-8R; 25-28R; CANR 7; CDALB 1929-1941; DA; DA3; DAB; DAC; DAM MST, NOV; DLB 9; EWL 3; INT CANR-7; LAIT 3; MTCW 1, 2; NFS 6; RGAL 4; SATA 9; TUS; YAW

**Singe, (Edmund) J(ohn) M(illington)**
1871-1909 ...................................... **WLC**

**Singer, Isaac**
See Singer, Isaac Bashevis

**Singer, Isaac Bashevis** 1904-1991 .. **CLC 1, 3, 6, 9, 11, 15, 23, 38, 69, 111; SSC 3, 53; WLC**
See also AAYA 32; AITN 1, 2; AMW; AMWR 2; BPFB 3; BYA 1, 4; CA 1-4R; 134; CANR 1, 39, 106; CDALB 1941-1968; CLR 1; CWRI 5; DA; DA3; DAB; DAC; DAM MST, NOV; DLB 6, 28, 52, 278; DLBY 1991; EWL 3; EXPS; HGG; JRDA; LAIT 3; MAICYA 1, 2; MTCW 1, 2; RGAL 4; RGSF 2; SATA 3, 27; SATA-Obit 68; SSFS 2, 12, 16; TUS; TWA

**Singer, Israel Joshua** 1893-1944 .... **TCLC 33**
See also CA 169; EWL 3

**Singh, Khushwant** 1915- .................... **CLC 11**
See also CA 9-12R; CAAS 9; CANR 6, 84; CN 7; EWL 3; RGEL 2

**Singleton, Ann**
See Benedict, Ruth (Fulton)

**Singleton, John** 1968(?)- .................... **CLC 156**
See also AAYA 50; BW 2, 3; CA 138; CANR 67, 82; DAM MULT

**Siniavskii, Andrei**
See Sinyavsky, Andrei (Donatevich)
See also CWW 2

**Sinjohn, John**
See Galsworthy, John

**Sinyavsky, Andrei (Donatevich)**
1925-1997 ...................................... **CLC 8**
See Siniavskii, Andrei; Sinyavsky, Andrey Donatovich; Tertz, Abram
See also CA 85-88; 159

**Sinyavsky, Andrey Donatovich**
See Sinyavsky, Andrei (Donatevich)
See also EWL 3

**Sirin, V.**
See Nabokov, Vladimir (Vladimirovich)

**Sissman, L(ouis) E(dward)**
1928-1976 ............................... **CLC 9, 18**
See also CA 21-24R; 65-68; CANR 13; DLB 5

**Sisson, C(harles) H(ubert)**
1914-2003 ...................................... **CLC 8**
See also CA 1-4R; 220; CAAS 3; CANR 3, 48, 84; CP 7; DLB 27

**Sitting Bull** 1831(?)-1890 .................... **NNAL**
See also DA3; DAM MULT

**Sitwell, Dame Edith** 1887-1964 ..... **CLC 2, 9, 67; PC 3**
See also BRW 7; CA 9-12R; CANR 35; CDBLB 1945-1960; DAM POET; DLB 20; EWL 3; MTCW 1, 2; RGEL 2; TEA

**Siwaarmill, H. P.**
See Sharp, William

**Sjoewall, Maj** 1935- ........................... **CLC 7**
See Sjowall, Maj
See also CA 65-68; CANR 73

**Sjowall, Maj**
See Sjoewall, Maj
See also BPFB 3; CMW 4; MSW

**Skelton, John** 1460(?)-1529 ..... **LC 71; PC 25**
See also BRW 1; DLB 136; RGEL 2

**Skelton, Robin** 1925-1997 ................. **CLC 13**
See Zuk, Georges
See also AITN 2; CA 5-8R; 160; CAAS 5; CANR 28, 89; CCA 1; CP 7; DLB 27, 53

**Skolimowski, Jerzy** 1938- .................. **CLC 20**
See also CA 128

**Skram, Amalie (Bertha)**
1847-1905 ............................... **TCLC 25**
See also CA 165

**Skvorecky, Josef (Vaclav)** 1924- ...... **CLC 15, 39, 69, 152**
See also CA 61-64; CAAS 1; CANR 10, 34, 63, 108; CDWLB 4; CWW 2; DA3; DAC; DAM NOV; DLB 232; EWL 3; MTCW 1, 2

**Slade, Bernard** .......................... **CLC 11, 46**
See Newbound, Bernard Slade
See also CAAS 9; CCA 1; DLB 53

**Slaughter, Carolyn** 1946- .................... **CLC 56**
See also CA 85-88; CANR 85; CN 7

**Slaughter, Frank G(ill)** 1908-2001 ... **CLC 29**
See also AITN 2; CA 5-8R; 197; CANR 5, 85; INT CANR-5; RHW

**Slavitt, David R(ytman)** 1935- ...... **CLC 5, 14**
See also CA 21-24R; CAAS 3; CANR 41, 83; CP 7; DLB 5, 6

**Slesinger, Tess** 1905-1945 ............... **TCLC 10**
See also CA 107; 199; DLB 102

**Slessor, Kenneth** 1901-1971 ............. **CLC 14**
See also CA 102; 89-92; DLB 260; RGEL 2

**Slowacki, Juliusz** 1809-1849 .......... **NCLC 15**
See also RGWL 3

**Smart, Christopher** 1722-1771 . **LC 3; PC 13**
See also DAM POET; DLB 109; RGEL 2

**Smart, Elizabeth** 1913-1986 ............. **CLC 54**
See also CA 81-84; 118; DLB 88

**Smiley, Jane (Graves)** 1949- ...... **CLC 53, 76, 144**
See also AMWS 6; BPFB 3; CA 104; CANR 30, 50, 74, 96; CN 7; CPW 1; DA3; DAM POP; DLB 227, 234; EWL 3; INT CANR-30; SSFS 19

**Smith, A(rthur) J(ames) M(arshall)**
1902-1980 ...................................... **CLC 15**
See also CA 1-4R; 102; CANR 4; DAC; DLB 88; RGEL 2

**Smith, Adam** 1723(?)-1790 .................. **LC 36**
See also DLB 104, 252; RGEL 2

**Smith, Alexander** 1829-1867 .......... **NCLC 59**
See also DLB 32, 55

**Smith, Anna Deavere** 1950- .............. **CLC 86**
See also CA 133; CANR 103; CD 5; DFS 2

**Smith, Betty (Wehner)** 1904-1972 .... **CLC 19**
See also BPFB 3; BYA 3; CA 5-8R; 33-36R; DLBY 1982; LAIT 3; RGAL 4; SATA 6

**Smith, Charlotte (Turner)**
1749-1806 ........................ **NCLC 23, 115**
See also DLB 39, 109; RGEL 2; TEA

**Smith, Clark Ashton** 1893-1961 ....... **CLC 43**
See also CA 143; CANR 81; FANT; HGG; MTCW 2; SCFW 2; SFW 4; SUFW

**Smith, Dave** ........................... **CLC 22, 42**
See Smith, David (Jeddie)
See also CAAS 7; DLB 5

**Smith, David (Jeddie)** 1942-
See Smith, Dave
See also CA 49-52; CANR 1, 59, 120; CP 7; CSW; DAM POET

**Smith, Florence Margaret** 1902-1971
See Smith, Stevie
See also CA 17-18; 29-32R; CANR 35; CAP 2; DAM POET; MTCW 1, 2; TEA

**Smith, Iain Crichton** 1928-1998 ....... **CLC 64**
See also BRWS 9; CA 21-24R; 171; CN 7; CP 7; DLB 40, 139; RGSF 2

**Smith, John** 1580(?)-1631 .................. **LC 9**
See also DLB 24, 30; TUS

**Smith, Johnston**
See Crane, Stephen (Townley)

**Smith, Joseph, Jr.** 1805-1844 ......... **NCLC 53**

**Smith, Lee** 1944- ........................... **CLC 25, 73**
See also CA 114; 119; CANR 46, 118; CSW; DLB 143; DLBY 1983; EWL 3; INT CA-119; RGAL 4

**Smith, Martin**
See Smith, Martin Cruz

**Smith, Martin Cruz** 1942- .. **CLC 25; NNAL**
See also BEST 89:4; BPFB 3; CA 85-88; CANR 6, 23, 43, 65, 119; CMW 4; CPW; DAM MULT, POP; HGG; INT CANR-23; MTCW 2; RGAL 4

**Smith, Patti** 1946- ............................ **CLC 12**
See also CA 93-96; CANR 63

**Smith, Pauline (Urmson)**
1882-1959 ................................. **TCLC 25**
See also DLB 225; EWL 3

**Smith, Rosamond**
See Oates, Joyce Carol

**Smith, Sheila Kaye**
See Kaye-Smith, Sheila

**Smith, Stevie** .... **CLC 3, 8, 25, 44; PC 12**
See Smith, Florence Margaret
See also BRWS 2; DLB 20; EWL 3; MTCW 2; PAB; PFS 3; RGEL 2

**Smith, Wilbur (Addison)** 1933- ........ **CLC 33**
See also CA 13-16R; CANR 7, 46, 66; CPW; MTCW 1, 2

**Smith, William Jay** 1918- ................... **CLC 6**
See also AMWS 13; CA 5-8R; CANR 44, 106; CP 7; CSW; CWRI 5; DLB 5; MAICYA 1, 2; SAAS 22; SATA 2, 68

**Smith, Woodrow Wilson**
See Kuttner, Henry

**Smith, Zadie** 1976- ......................... **CLC 158**
See also AAYA 50; CA 193

**Smolenskin, Peretz** 1842-1885 ....... **NCLC 30**

**Smollett, Tobias (George)** 1721-1771 ... **LC 2, 46**
See also BRW 3; CDBLB 1660-1789; DLB 39, 104; RGEL 2; TEA

**Snodgrass, W(illiam) D(e Witt)**
1926- ..................... **CLC 2, 6, 10, 18, 68**
See also AMWS 6; CA 1-4R; CANR 6, 36, 65, 85; CP 7; DAM POET; DLB 5; MTCW 1, 2; RGAL 4

**Snorri Sturluson** 1179-1241 .......... **CMLC 56**
See also RGWL 2, 3

**Snow, C(harles) P(ercy)** 1905-1980 ... **CLC 1, 4, 6, 9, 13, 19**
See also BRW 7; CA 5-8R; 101; CANR 28; CDBLB 1945-1960; DAM NOV; DLB 15, 77; DLBD 17; EWL 3; MTCW 1, 2; RGEL 2; TEA

**Snow, Frances Compton**
See Adams, Henry (Brooks)

**Snyder, Gary (Sherman)** 1930- . **CLC 1, 2, 5, 9, 32, 120; PC 21**
See also AMWS 8; ANW; BG 3; CA 17-20R; CANR 30, 60, 125; CP 7; DA3; DAM POET; DLB 5, 16, 165, 212, 237, 275; EWL 3; MTCW 2; PFS 9, 19; RGAL 4; WP

**Snyder, Zilpha Keatley** 1927- ........... **CLC 17**
See also AAYA 15; BYA 1; CA 9-12R; CANR 38; CLR 31; JRDA; MAICYA 1, 2; SAAS 2; SATA 1, 28, 75, 110; SATA-Essay 112; YAW

**Soares, Bernardo**
See Pessoa, Fernando (Antonio Nogueira)

**Sobh, A.**
See Shamlu, Ahmad

**Sobh, Alef**
See Shamlu, Ahmad

**Sobol, Joshua** 1939- ........................... **CLC 60**
See Sobol, Yehoshua
See also CA 200

**Sobol, Yehoshua** 1939-
See Sobol, Joshua
See also CWW 2

**Socrates** 470B.C.-399B.C. .............. **CMLC 27**

**Soderberg, Hjalmar** 1869-1941 ...... **TCLC 39**
See also DLB 259; EWL 3; RGSF 2

**Soderbergh, Steven** 1963- ............... **CLC 154**
See also AAYA 43

**Sodergran, Edith (Irene)** 1892-1923
See Soedergran, Edith (Irene)
See also CA 202; DLB 259; EW 11; EWL 3; RGWL 2, 3

**Soedergran, Edith (Irene)**
1892-1923 ................................. **TCLC 31**
See Sodergran, Edith (Irene)

**Softly, Edgar**
See Lovecraft, H(oward) P(hillips)

**Softly, Edward**
See Lovecraft, H(oward) P(hillips)

**Sokolov, Alexander V(sevolodovich)** 1943-
See Sokolov, Sasha
See also CA 73-76

**Sokolov, Raymond** 1941- .................... **CLC 7**
See also CA 85-88

**Sokolov, Sasha** ................................. **CLC 59**
See Sokolov, Alexander V(sevolodovich)
See also CWW 2; DLB 285; EWL 3; RGWL 2, 3

**Solo, Jay**
See Ellison, Harlan (Jay)

**Sologub, Fyodor** ............................... **TCLC 9**
See Teternikov, Fyodor Kuzmich
See also EWL 3

**Solomons, Ikey Esquir**
See Thackeray, William Makepeace

**Solomos, Dionysios** 1798-1857 ....... **NCLC 15**

**Solwoska, Mara**
See French, Marilyn

**Solzhenitsyn, Aleksandr I(sayevich)**
1918- .. **CLC 1, 2, 4, 7, 9, 10, 18, 26, 34, 78, 134; SSC 32; WLC**
See Solzhenitsyn, Aleksandr Isaevich
See also AAYA 49; AITN 1; BPFB 3; CA 69-72; CANR 40, 65, 116; DA; DA3; DAB; DAC; DAM MST, NOV; DLB 302; EW 13; EXPS; LAIT 4; MTCW 1, 2; NFS 6; RGSF 2; RGWL 2, 3; SSFS 9; TWA

**Solzhenitsyn, Aleksandr Isaevich**
See Solzhenitsyn, Aleksandr I(sayevich)
See also CWW 2; EWL 3

**Somers, Jane**
See Lessing, Doris (May)

**Somerville, Edith Oenone**
1858-1949 ................. **SSC 56; TCLC 51**
See also CA 196; DLB 135; RGEL 2; RGSF 2

**Somerville & Ross**
See Martin, Violet Florence; Somerville, Edith Oenone

**Sommer, Scott** 1951- ......................... **CLC 25**
See also CA 106

**Sommers, Christina Hoff** 1950- ...... **CLC 197**
See also CA 153; CANR 95

**Sondheim, Stephen (Joshua)** 1930- . **CLC 30, 39, 147; DC 22**
See also AAYA 11; CA 103; CANR 47, 67, 125; DAM DRAM; LAIT 4

**Sone, Monica** 1919- .............................. **AAL**

**Song, Cathy** 1955- ..................... **AAL; PC 21**
See also CA 154; CANR 118; CWP; DLB 169; EXPP; FW; PFS 5

**Sontag, Susan** 1933- .... **CLC 1, 2, 10, 13, 31, 105, 195**
See also AMWS 3; CA 17-20R; CANR 25, 51, 74, 97; CN 7; CPW; DA3; DAM POP; DLB 2, 67; EWL 3; MAWW; MTCW 1, 2; RGAL 4; RHW; SSFS 10

**Sophocles** 496(?)B.C.-406(?)B.C. .... **CMLC 2, 47, 51; DC 1; WLCS**
See also AW 1; CDWLB 1; DA; DA3; DAB; DAC; DAM DRAM, MST; DFS 1, 4, 8; DLB 176; LAIT 1; LATS 1:1; LMFS 1; RGWL 2, 3; TWA

**Sordello** 1189-1269 ......................... **CMLC 15**

**Sorel, Georges** 1847-1922 .............. **TCLC 91**
See also CA 118; 188

**Sorel, Julia**
See Drexler, Rosalyn

**Sorokin, Vladimir** ............................. **CLC 59**
See Sorokin, Vladimir Georgievich

**Sorokin, Vladimir Georgievich**
See Sorokin, Vladimir
See also DLB 285

**Sorrentino, Gilbert** 1929- .. **CLC 3, 7, 14, 22, 40**
See also CA 77-80; CANR 14, 33, 115; CN 7; CP 7; DLB 5, 173; DLBY 1980; INT CANR-14

**Soseki**
See Natsume, Soseki
See also MJW

**Soto, Gary** 1952- ... **CLC 32, 80; HLC 2; PC 28**
See also AAYA 10, 37; BYA 11; CA 119; 125; CANR 50, 74, 107; CLR 38; CP 7; DAM MULT; DLB 82; EWL 3; EXPP; HW 1, 2; INT CA-125; JRDA; LLW 1; MAICYA 2; MAICYAS 1; MTCW 2; PFS 7; RGAL 4; SATA 80, 120; WYA; YAW

**Soupault, Philippe** 1897-1990 ......... **CLC 68**
See also CA 116; 147; 131; EWL 3; GFL 1789 to the Present; LMFS 2

**Souster, (Holmes) Raymond** 1921- .... **CLC 5, 14**
See also CA 13-16R; CAAS 14; CANR 13, 29, 53; CP 7; DA3; DAC; DAM POET; DLB 88; RGEL 2; SATA 63

**Southern, Terry** 1924(?)-1995 ............. **CLC 7**
See also AMWS 11; BPFB 3; CA 1-4R; 150; CANR 1, 55, 107; CN 7; DLB 2; IDFW 3, 4

**Southerne, Thomas** 1660-1746 ........... **LC 99**
See also DLB 80; RGEL 2

**Southey, Robert** 1774-1843 ........ **NCLC 8, 97**
See also BRW 4; DLB 93, 107, 142; RGEL 2; SATA 54

**Southwell, Robert** 1561(?)-1595 ........ **LC 108**
See also DLB 167; RGEL 2; TEA

**Southworth, Emma Dorothy Eliza Nevitte**
1819-1899 ................................. **NCLC 26**
See also DLB 239

**Souza, Ernest**
See Scott, Evelyn

**Soyinka, Wole** 1934- .. **BLC 3; CLC 3, 5, 14,
36, 44, 179; DC 2; WLC**
See also AFW; BW 2, 3; CA 13-16R;
CANR 27, 39, 82; CD 5; CDWLB 3; CN
7; CP 7; DA; DA3; DAB; DAC; DAM
DRAM, MST, MULT; DFS 10; DLB 125;
EWL 3; MTCW 1, 2; RGEL 2; TWA;
WLIT 2; WWE 1

**Spackman, W(illiam) M(ode)**
1905-1990 .................................. **CLC 46**
See also CA 81-84; 132

**Spacks, Barry (Bernard)** 1931- ........ **CLC 14**
See also CA 154; CANR 33, 109; CP 7;
DLB 105

**Spanidou, Irini** 1946- .......................... **CLC 44**
See also CA 185

**Spark, Muriel (Sarah)** 1918- ..... **CLC 2, 3, 5,
8, 13, 18, 40, 94; SSC 10**
See also BRWS 1; CA 5-8R; CANR 12, 36,
76, 89, 131; CDBLB 1945-1960; CN 7;
CP 7; DA3; DAB; DAC; DAM MST,
NOV; DLB 15, 139; EWL 3; FW; INT
CANR-12; LAIT 4; MTCW 1, 2; RGEL
2; TEA; WLIT 4; YAW

**Spaulding, Douglas**
See Bradbury, Ray (Douglas)

**Spaulding, Leonard**
See Bradbury, Ray (Douglas)

**Speght, Rachel** 1597-c. 1630 ................ **LC 97**
See also DLB 126

**Spelman, Elizabeth** ........................... **CLC 65**

**Spence, J. A. D.**
See Eliot, T(homas) S(tearns)

**Spencer, Anne** 1882-1975 ...................... **HR 3**
See also BW 2; CA 161; DLB 51, 54

**Spencer, Elizabeth** 1921- .... **CLC 22; SSC 57**
See also CA 13-16R; CANR 32, 65, 87; CN
7; CSW; DLB 6, 218; EWL 3; MTCW 1;
RGAL 4; SATA 14

**Spencer, Leonard G.**
See Silverberg, Robert

**Spencer, Scott** 1945- ........................... **CLC 30**
See also CA 113; CANR 51; DLBY 1986

**Spender, Stephen (Harold)**
1909-1995 .......... **CLC 1, 2, 5, 10, 41, 91**
See also BRWS 2; CA 9-12R; 149; CANR
31, 54; CDBLB 1945-1960; CP 7; DA3;
DAM POET; DLB 20; EWL 3; MTCW 1,
2; PAB; RGEL 2; TEA

**Spengler, Oswald (Arnold Gottfried)**
1880-1936 ................................. **TCLC 25**
See also CA 118; 189

**Spenser, Edmund** 1552(?)-1599 ..... **LC 5, 39;
PC 8, 42; WLC**
See also BRW 1; CDBLB Before 1660; DA;
DA3; DAB; DAC; DAM MST, POET;
DLB 167; EFS 2; EXPP; PAB; RGEL 2;
TEA; WLIT 3; WP

**Spicer, Jack** 1925-1965 ........... **CLC 8, 18, 72**
See also BG 3; CA 85-88; DAM POET;
DLB 5, 16, 193; GLL 1; WP

**Spiegelman, Art** 1948- ............... **CLC 76, 178**
See also AAYA 10, 46; CA 125; CANR 41,
55, 74, 124; DLB 299; MTCW 2; SATA
109; YAW

**Spielberg, Peter** 1929- ......................... **CLC 6**
See also CA 5-8R; CANR 4, 48; DLBY
1981

**Spielberg, Steven** 1947- ............ **CLC 20, 188**
See also AAYA 8, 24; CA 77-80; CANR
32; SATA 32

**Spillane, Frank Morrison** 1918-
See Spillane, Mickey
See also CA 25-28R; CANR 28, 63, 125;
DA3; MTCW 1, 2; SATA 66

**Spillane, Mickey** ......................... **CLC 3, 13**
See Spillane, Frank Morrison
See also BPFB 3; CMW 4; DLB 226;
MSW; MTCW 2

**Spinoza, Benedictus de** 1632-1677 .. **LC 9, 58**

**Spinrad, Norman (Richard)** 1940- ... **CLC 46**
See also BPFB 3; CA 37-40R; CAAS 19;
CANR 20, 91; DLB 8; INT CANR-20;
SFW 4

**Spitteler, Carl (Friedrich Georg)**
1845-1924 ................................. **TCLC 12**
See also CA 109; DLB 129; EWL 3

**Spivack, Kathleen (Romola Drucker)**
1938- ............................................. **CLC 6**
See also CA 49-52

**Spoto, Donald** 1941- ........................... **CLC 39**
See also CA 65-68; CANR 11, 57, 93

**Springsteen, Bruce (F.)** 1949- ........... **CLC 17**
See also CA 111

**Spurling, (Susan) Hilary** 1940- ......... **CLC 34**
See also CA 104; CANR 25, 52, 94

**Spyker, John Howland**
See Elman, Richard (Martin)

**Squared, A.**
See Abbott, Edwin A.

**Squires, (James) Radcliffe**
1917-1993 ................................. **CLC 51**
See also CA 1-4R; 140; CANR 6, 21

**Srivastava, Dhanpat Rai** 1880(?)-1936
See Premchand
See also CA 118; 197

**Stacy, Donald**
See Pohl, Frederik

**Stael**
See Stael-Holstein, Anne Louise Germaine
Necker
See also EW 5; RGWL 2, 3

**Stael, Germaine de**
See Stael-Holstein, Anne Louise Germaine
Necker
See also DLB 119, 192; FW; GFL 1789 to
the Present; TWA

**Stael-Holstein, Anne Louise Germaine**
**Necker** 1766-1817 ............... **NCLC 3, 91**
See also Stael; Stael, Germaine de

**Stafford, Jean** 1915-1979 .. **CLC 4, 7, 19, 68;
SSC 26**
See also CA 1-4R; 85-88; CANR 3, 65;
DLB 2, 173; MTCW 1, 2; RGAL 4; RGSF
2; SATA-Obit 22; TCWW 2; TUS

**Stafford, William (Edgar)**
1914-1993 ........................... **CLC 4, 7, 29**
See also AMWS 11; CA 5-8R; 142; CAAS
3; CANR 5, 22; DAM POET; DLB 5,
206; EXPP; INT CANR-22; PFS 2, 8, 16;
RGAL 4; WP

**Stagnelius, Eric Johan** 1793-1823 . **NCLC 61**

**Staines, Trevor**
See Brunner, John (Kilian Houston)

**Stairs, Gordon**
See Austin, Mary (Hunter)
See also TCWW 2

**Stalin, Joseph** 1879-1953 ................ **TCLC 92**

**Stampa, Gaspara** c. 1524-1554 ........... **PC 43**
See also RGWL 2, 3

**Stampflinger, K. A.**
See Benjamin, Walter

**Stancykowna**
See Szymborska, Wislawa

**Standing Bear, Luther**
1868(?)-1939(?) ........................... **NNAL**
See also CA 113; 144; DAM MULT

**Stannard, Martin** 1947- .................... **CLC 44**
See also CA 142; DLB 155

**Stanton, Elizabeth Cady**
1815-1902 ................................. **TCLC 73**
See also CA 171; DLB 79; FW

**Stanton, Maura** 1946- .......................... **CLC 9**
See also CA 89-92; CANR 15, 123; DLB
120

**Stanton, Schuyler**
See Baum, L(yman) Frank

**Stapledon, (William) Olaf**
1886-1950 ................................. **TCLC 22**
See also CA 111; 162; DLB 15, 255; SFW
4

**Starbuck, George (Edwin)**
1931-1996 ................................. **CLC 53**
See also CA 21-24R; 153; CANR 23; DAM
POET

**Stark, Richard**
See Westlake, Donald E(dwin)

**Staunton, Schuyler**
See Baum, L(yman) Frank

**Stead, Christina (Ellen)** 1902-1983 ... **CLC 2,
5, 8, 32, 80**
See also BRWS 4; CA 13-16R; 109; CANR
33, 40; DLB 260; EWL 3; FW; MTCW 1,
2; RGEL 2; RGSF 2; WWE 1

**Stead, William Thomas**
1849-1912 ................................. **TCLC 48**
See also CA 167

**Stebnitsky, M.**
See Leskov, Nikolai (Semyonovich)

**Steele, Sir Richard** 1672-1729 ............. **LC 18**
See also BRW 3; CDBLB 1660-1789; DLB
84, 101; RGEL 2; WLIT 3

**Steele, Timothy (Reid)** 1948- ........... **CLC 45**
See also CA 93-96; CANR 16, 50, 92; CP
7; DLB 120, 282

**Steffens, (Joseph) Lincoln**
1866-1936 ................................. **TCLC 20**
See also CA 117; 198; DLB 303

**Stegner, Wallace (Earle)** 1909-1993 .. **CLC 9,
49, 81; SSC 27**
See also AITN 1; AMWS 4; ANW; BEST
90:3; BPFB 3; CA 1-4R; 141; CAAS 9;
CANR 1, 21, 46; DAM NOV; DLB 9,
206, 275; DLBY 1993; EWL 3; MTCW
1, 2; RGAL 4; TCWW 2; TUS

**Stein, Gertrude** 1874-1946 .... **DC 19; PC 18;
SSC 42; TCLC 1, 6, 28, 48; WLC**
See also AMW; AMWC 2; CA 104; 132;
CANR 108; CDALB 1917-1929; DA;
DA3; DAB; DAC; DAM MST, NOV,
POET; DLB 4, 54, 86, 228; DLBD 15;
EWL 3; EXPS; GLL 1; MAWW; MTCW
1, 2; NCFS 4; RGAL 4; RGSF 2; SSFS 5;
TUS; WP

**Steinbeck, John (Ernst)** 1902-1968 ... **CLC 1,
5, 9, 13, 21, 34, 45, 75, 124; SSC 11,
37; TCLC 135; WLC**
See also AAYA 12; AMW; BPFB 3; BYA 2,
3, 13; CA 1-4R; 25-28R; CANR 1, 35;
CDALB 1929-1941; DA; DA3; DAB;
DAC; DAM DRAM, MST, NOV; DLB 7,
9, 212, 275; DLBD 2; EWL 3; EXPS;
LAIT 3; MTCW 1, 2; NFS 1, 5, 7, 17,
19; RGAL 4; RGSF 2; RHW; SATA 9;
SSFS 3, 6; TCWW 2; TUS; WYA; YAW

**Steinem, Gloria** 1934- ......................... **CLC 63**
See also CA 53-56; CANR 28, 51; DLB
246; FW; MTCW 1, 2

**Steiner, George** 1929- ......................... **CLC 24**
See also CA 73-76; CANR 31, 67, 108;
DAM NOV; DLB 67, 299; EWL 3;
MTCW 1, 2; SATA 62

**Steiner, K. Leslie**
See Delany, Samuel R(ay), Jr.

**Steiner, Rudolf** 1861-1925 ............. **TCLC 13**
See also CA 107

**Stendhal** 1783-1842 .. **NCLC 23, 46; SSC 27; WLC**
See also DA; DA3; DAB; DAC; DAM MST, NOV; DLB 119; EW 5; GFL 1789 to the Present; RGWL 2, 3; TWA

**Stephen, Adeline Virginia**
See Woolf, (Adeline) Virginia

**Stephen, Sir Leslie** 1832-1904 ........ **TCLC 23**
See also BRW 5; CA 123; DLB 57, 144, 190

**Stephen, Sir Leslie**
See Stephen, Sir Leslie

**Stephen, Virginia**
See Woolf, (Adeline) Virginia

**Stephens, James** 1882(?)-1950 .......... **SSC 50; TCLC 4**
See also CA 104; 192; DLB 19, 153, 162; EWL 3; FANT; RGEL 2; SUFW

**Stephens, Reed**
See Donaldson, Stephen R(eeder)

**Steptoe, Lydia**
See Barnes, Djuna
See also GLL 1

**Sterchi, Beat** 1949- ............................. **CLC 65**
See also CA 203

**Sterling, Brett**
See Bradbury, Ray (Douglas); Hamilton, Edmond

**Sterling, Bruce** 1954- ........................ **CLC 72**
See also CA 119; CANR 44; SCFW 2; SFW 4

**Sterling, George** 1869-1926 ........... **TCLC 20**
See also CA 117; 165; DLB 54

**Stern, Gerald** 1925- .................. **CLC 40, 100**
See also AMWS 9; CA 81-84; CANR 28, 94; CP 7; DLB 105; RGAL 4

**Stern, Richard (Gustave)** 1928- ... **CLC 4, 39**
See also CA 1-4R; CANR 1, 25, 52, 120; CN 7; DLB 218; DLBY 1987; INT CANR-25

**Sternberg, Josef von** 1894-1969 ....... **CLC 20**
See also CA 81-84

**Sterne, Laurence** 1713-1768 .......... **LC 2, 48; WLC**
See also BRW 3; BRWC 1; CDBLB 1660-1789; DA; DAB; DAC; DAM MST, NOV; DLB 39; RGEL 2; TEA

**Sternheim, (William Adolf) Carl** 1878-1942 ................................. **TCLC 8**
See also CA 105; 193; DLB 56, 118; EWL 3; RGWL 2, 3

**Stevens, Mark** 1951- ......................... **CLC 34**
See also CA 122

**Stevens, Wallace** 1879-1955 . **PC 6; TCLC 3, 12, 45; WLC**
See also AMW; AMWR 1; CA 104; 124; CDALB 1929-1941; DA; DA3; DAB; DAC; DAM MST, POET; DLB 54; EWL 3; EXPP; MTCW 1, 2; PAB; PFS 13, 16; RGAL 4; TUS; WP

**Stevenson, Anne (Katharine)** 1933- .. **CLC 7, 33**
See also BRWS 6; CA 17-20R; CAAS 9; CANR 9, 33, 123; CP 7; CWP; DLB 40; MTCW 1; RHW

**Stevenson, Robert Louis (Balfour)** 1850-1894 ...... **NCLC 5, 14, 63; SSC 11, 51; WLC**
See also AAYA 24; BPFB 3; BRW 5; BRWC 1; BRWR 1; BYA 1, 2, 4, 13; CD-BLB 1890-1914; CLR 10, 11; DA; DA3; DAB; DAC; DAM MST, NOV; DLB 18, 57, 141, 156, 174; DLBD 13; HGG; JRDA; LAIT 1, 3; MAICYA 1, 2; NFS 11, 20; RGEL 2; RGSF 2; SATA 100; SUFW; TEA; WCH; WLIT 4; WYA; YABC 2; YAW

**Stewart, J(ohn) I(nnes) M(ackintosh)** 1906-1994 ........................ **CLC 7, 14, 32**
See Innes, Michael
See also CA 85-88; 147; CAAS 3; CANR 47; CMW 4; MTCW 1, 2

**Stewart, Mary (Florence Elinor)** 1916- .............................. **CLC 7, 35, 117**
See also AAYA 29; BPFB 3; CA 1-4R; CANR 1, 59, 130; CMW 4; CPW; DAB; FANT; RHW; SATA 12; YAW

**Stewart, Mary Rainbow**
See Stewart, Mary (Florence Elinor)

**Stifle, June**
See Campbell, Maria

**Stifter, Adalbert** 1805-1868 .. **NCLC 41; SSC 28**
See also CDWLB 2; DLB 133; RGSF 2; RGWL 2, 3

**Still, James** 1906-2001 ...................... **CLC 49**
See also CA 65-68; 195; CAAS 17; CANR 10, 26; CSW; DLB 9; DLBY 01; SATA 29; SATA-Obit 127

**Sting** 1951-
See Sumner, Gordon Matthew
See also CA 167

**Stirling, Arthur**
See Sinclair, Upton (Beall)

**Stitt, Milan** 1941- ............................. **CLC 29**
See also CA 69-72

**Stockton, Francis Richard** 1834-1902
See Stockton, Frank R.
See also CA 108; 137; MAICYA 1, 2; SATA 44; SFW 4

**Stockton, Frank R.** ....................... **TCLC 47**
See Stockton, Francis Richard
See also BYA 4, 13; DLB 42, 74; DLBD 13; EXPS; SATA-Brief 32; SSFS 3; SUFW; WCH

**Stoddard, Charles**
See Kuttner, Henry

**Stoker, Abraham** 1847-1912
See Stoker, Bram
See also CA 105; 150; DA; DA3; DAC; DAM MST, NOV; HGG; SATA 29

**Stoker, Bram** . **SSC 62; TCLC 8, 144; WLC**
See Stoker, Abraham
See also AAYA 23; BPFB 3; BRWS 3; BYA 5; CDBLB 1890-1914; DAB; DLB 304; LATS 1:1; NFS 18; RGEL 2; SUFW; TEA; WLIT 4

**Stolz, Mary (Slattery)** 1920- ............ **CLC 12**
See also AAYA 8; AITN 1; CA 5-8R; CANR 13, 41, 112; JRDA; MAICYA 1, 2; SAAS 3; SATA 10, 71, 133; YAW

**Stone, Irving** 1903-1989 ...................... **CLC 7**
See also AITN 1; BPFB 3; CA 1-4R; 129; CAAS 3; CANR 1, 23; CPW; DA3; DAM POP; INT CANR-23; MTCW 1, 2; RHW; SATA 3; SATA-Obit 64

**Stone, Oliver (William)** 1946- .......... **CLC 73**
See also AAYA 15; CA 110; CANR 55, 125

**Stone, Robert (Anthony)** 1937- ... **CLC 5, 23, 42, 175**
See also AMWS 5; BPFB 3; CA 85-88; CANR 23, 66, 95; CN 7; DLB 152; EWL 3; INT CANR-23; MTCW 1

**Stone, Ruth** 1915- ............................ **PC 53**
See also CA 45-48; CANR 2, 91; CP 7; CSW; DLB 105; PFS 19

**Stone, Zachary**
See Follett, Ken(neth Martin)

**Stoppard, Tom** 1937- ... **CLC 1, 3, 4, 5, 8, 15, 29, 34, 63, 91; DC 6; WLC**
See also BRWC 1; BRWR 2; BRWS 1; CA 81-84; CANR 39, 67, 125; CBD; CD 5; CDBLB 1960 to Present; DA; DA3; DAB; DAC; DAM DRAM, MST; DFS 2, 5, 8, 11, 13, 16; DLB 13, 233; DLBY 1985; EWL 3; LATS 1:2; MTCW 1, 2; RGEL 2; TEA; WLIT 4

**Storey, David (Malcolm)** 1933- . **CLC 2, 4, 5, 8**
See also BRWS 1; CA 81-84; CANR 36; CBD; CD 5; CN 7; DAM DRAM; DLB 13, 14, 207, 245; EWL 3; MTCW 1; RGEL 2

**Storm, Hyemeyohsts** 1935- ... **CLC 3; NNAL**
See also CA 81-84; CANR 45; DAM MULT

**Storm, (Hans) Theodor (Woldsen)** 1817-1888 ................... **NCLC 1; SSC 27**
See also CDWLB 2; DLB 129; EW; RGSF 2; RGWL 2, 3

**Storni, Alfonsina** 1892-1938 . **HLC 2; PC 33; TCLC 5**
See also CA 104; 131; DAM MULT; DLB 283; HW 1; LAW

**Stoughton, William** 1631-1701 ........... **LC 38**
See also DLB 24

**Stout, Rex (Todhunter)** 1886-1975 ..... **CLC 3**
See also AITN 2; BPFB 3; CA 61-64; CANR 71; CMW 4; DLB 306; MSW; RGAL 4

**Stow, (Julian) Randolph** 1935- ... **CLC 23, 48**
See also CA 13-16R; CANR 33; CN 7; DLB 260; MTCW 1; RGEL 2

**Stowe, Harriet (Elizabeth) Beecher** 1811-1896 ........ **NCLC 3, 50, 133; WLC**
See also AAYA 53; AMWS 1; CDALB 1865-1917; DA; DA3; DAB; DAC; DAM MST, NOV; DLB 1, 12, 42, 74, 189, 239, 243; EXPN; JRDA; LAIT 2; MAICYA 1, 2; NFS 6; RGAL 4; TUS; YABC 1

**Strabo** c. 64B.C.-c. 25 .................... **CMLC 37**
See also DLB 176

**Strachey, (Giles) Lytton** 1880-1932 ............................... **TCLC 12**
See also BRWS 2; CA 110; 178; DLB 149; DLBD 10; EWL 3; MTCW 2; NCFS 4

**Stramm, August** 1874-1915 ................. **PC 50**
See also CA 195; EWL 3

**Strand, Mark** 1934- .......... **CLC 6, 18, 41, 71**
See also AMWS 4; CA 21-24R; CANR 40, 65, 100; CP 7; DAM POET; DLB 5; EWL 3; PAB; PFS 9, 18; RGAL 4; SATA 41

**Stratton-Porter, Gene(va Grace)** 1863-1924
See Porter, Gene(va Grace) Stratton
See also ANW; CA 137; CLR 87; DLB 221; DLBD 14; MAICYA 1, 2; SATA 15

**Straub, Peter (Francis)** 1943- ... **CLC 28, 107**
See also BEST 89:1; BPFB 3; CA 85-88; CANR 28, 65, 109; CPW; DAM POP; DLBY 1984; HGG; MTCW 1, 2; SUFW 2

**Strauss, Botho** 1944- ......................... **CLC 22**
See also CA 157; CWW 2; DLB 124

**Strauss, Leo** 1899-1973 ................. **TCLC 141**
See also CA 101; 45-48; CANR 122

**Streatfeild, (Mary) Noel** 1897(?)-1986 ............................. **CLC 21**
See also CA 81-84; 120; CANR 31; CLR 17, 83; CWRI 5; DLB 160; MAICYA 1, 2; SATA 20; SATA-Obit 48

**Stribling, T(homas) S(igismund)** 1881-1965 ................................. **CLC 23**
See also CA 189; 107; CMW 4; DLB 9; RGAL 4

**Strindberg, (Johan) August** 1849-1912 ... **DC 18; TCLC 1, 8, 21, 47; WLC**
See also CA 104; 135; DA; DA3; DAB; DAC; DAM DRAM, MST; DFS 4, 9; DLB 259; EW 7; EWL 3; IDTP; LMFS 2; MTCW 2; RGWL 2, 3; TWA

**Stringer, Arthur** 1874-1950 ........... **TCLC 37**
See also CA 161; DLB 92

**Stringer, David**
See Roberts, Keith (John Kingston)

Stroheim, Erich von 1885-1957 ..... **TCLC 71**
Strugatskii, Arkadii (Natanovich)
    1925-1991 ......................... **CLC 27**
    See Strugatsky, Arkadii Natanovich
    See also CA 106; 135; SFW 4
Strugatskii, Boris (Natanovich)
    1933- ................................... **CLC 27**
    See Strugatsky, Boris (Natanovich)
    See also CA 106; SFW 4
Strugatsky, Arkadii Natanovich
    See Strugatskii, Arkadii (Natanovich)
    See also DLB 302
Strugatsky, Boris (Natanovich)
    See Strugatskii, Boris (Natanovich)
    See also DLB 302
Strummer, Joe 1953(?)- .................... **CLC 30**
Strunk, William, Jr. 1869-1946 ...... **TCLC 92**
    See also CA 118; 164; NCFS 5
Stryk, Lucien 1924- ............................. **PC 27**
    See also CA 13-16R; CANR 10, 28, 55,
    110; CP 7
Stuart, Don A.
    See Campbell, John W(ood, Jr.)
Stuart, Ian
    See MacLean, Alistair (Stuart)
Stuart, Jesse (Hilton) 1906-1984 ... **CLC 1, 8,
    11, 14, 34; SSC 31**
    See also CA 5-8R; 112; CANR 31; DLB 9,
    48, 102; DLBY 1984; SATA 2; SATA-
    Obit 36
Stubblefield, Sally
    See Trumbo, Dalton
Sturgeon, Theodore (Hamilton)
    1918-1985 ............................. **CLC 22, 39**
    See Queen, Ellery
    See also AAYA 51; BPFB 3; BYA 9, 10;
    CA 81-84; 116; CANR 32, 103; DLB 8;
    DLBY 1985; HGG; MTCW 1, 2; SCFW;
    SFW 4; SUFW
Sturges, Preston 1898-1959 ............ **TCLC 48**
    See also CA 114; 149; DLB 26
Styron, William 1925- .... **CLC 1, 3, 5, 11, 15,
    60; SSC 25**
    See also AMW; AMWC 2; BEST 90:4;
    BPFB 3; CA 5-8R; CANR 6, 33, 74, 126;
    CDALB 1968-1988; CN 7; CPW; CSW;
    DA3; DAM NOV, POP; DLB 2, 143, 299;
    DLBY 1980; EWL 3; INT CANR-6;
    LAIT 2; MTCW 1, 2; NCFS 1; RGAL 4;
    RHW; TUS
Su, Chien 1884-1918
    See Su Man-shu
    See also CA 123
Suarez Lynch, B.
    See Bioy Casares, Adolfo; Borges, Jorge
    Luis
Suassuna, Ariano Vilar 1927- .......... **HLCS 1**
    See also CA 178; HW 2; LAW
Suckert, Kurt Erich
    See Malaparte, Curzio
Suckling, Sir John 1609-1642 . **LC 75; PC 30**
    See also BRW 2; DAM POET; DLB 58,
    126; EXPP; PAB; RGEL 2
Suckow, Ruth 1892-1960 .................... **SSC 18**
    See also CA 193; 113; DLB 9, 102; RGAL
    4; TCWW 2
Sudermann, Hermann 1857-1928 .. **TCLC 15**
    See also CA 107; 201; DLB 118
Sue, Eugene 1804-1857 .................... **NCLC 1**
    See also DLB 119
Sueskind, Patrick 1949- ........... **CLC 44, 182**
    See Suskind, Patrick
Suetonius c. 70-c. 130 .................... **CMLC 60**
    See also AW 2; DLB 211; RGWL 2, 3
Sukenick, Ronald 1932-2004 ..... **CLC 3, 4, 6,
    48**
    See also CA 25-28R, 209; CAAE 209;
    CAAS 8; CANR 32, 89; CN 7; DLB 173;
    DLBY 1981

Suknaski, Andrew 1942- ................... **CLC 19**
    See also CA 101; CP 7; DLB 53
Sullivan, Vernon
    See Vian, Boris
Sully Prudhomme, Rene-Francois-Armand
    1839-1907 ............................. **TCLC 31**
    See also GFL 1789 to the Present
Su Man-shu ...................................... **TCLC 24**
    See Su, Chien
    See also EWL 3
Sumarokov, Aleksandr Petrovich
    1717-1777 .............................. **LC 104**
    See also DLB 150
Summerforest, Ivy B.
    See Kirkup, James
Summers, Andrew James 1942- ....... **CLC 26**
Summers, Andy
    See Summers, Andrew James
Summers, Hollis (Spurgeon, Jr.)
    1916- ................................... **CLC 10**
    See also CA 5-8R; CANR 3; DLB 6
Summers, (Alphonsus Joseph-Mary
    Augustus) Montague
    1880-1948 ............................. **TCLC 16**
    See also CA 118; 163
Sumner, Gordon Matthew .............. **CLC 26**
    See Police, The; Sting
Sun Tzu c. 400B.C.-c. 320B.C. ...... **CMLC 56**
Surrey, Henry Howard 1517-1574 ...... **PC 59**
    See also BRW 1; RGEL 2
Surtees, Robert Smith 1805-1864 .. **NCLC 14**
    See also DLB 21; RGEL 2
Susann, Jacqueline 1921-1974 ........... **CLC 3**
    See also AITN 1; BPFB 3; CA 65-68; 53-
    56; MTCW 1, 2
Su Shi
    See Su Shih
    See also RGWL 2, 3
Su Shih 1036-1101 ......................... **CMLC 15**
    See Su Shi
Suskind, Patrick .............................. **CLC 182**
    See Sueskind, Patrick
    See also BPFB 3; CA 145; CWW 2
Sutcliff, Rosemary 1920-1992 ........... **CLC 26**
    See also AAYA 10; BYA 1, 4; CA 5-8R;
    139; CANR 37; CLR 1, 37; CPW; DAB;
    DAC; DAM MST, POP; JRDA; LATS
    1:1; MAICYA 1, 2; MAICYAS 1; RHW;
    SATA 6, 44, 78; SATA-Obit 73; WYA;
    YAW
Sutro, Alfred 1863-1933 .................... **TCLC 6**
    See also CA 105; 185; DLB 10; RGEL 2
Sutton, Henry
    See Slavitt, David R(ytman)
Suzuki, D. T.
    See Suzuki, Daisetz Teitaro
Suzuki, Daisetz T.
    See Suzuki, Daisetz Teitaro
Suzuki, Daisetz Teitaro
    1870-1966 ............................. **TCLC 109**
    See also CA 121; 111; MTCW 1, 2
Suzuki, Teitaro
    See Suzuki, Daisetz Teitaro
Svevo, Italo ................. **SSC 25; TCLC 2, 35**
    See Schmitz, Aron Hector
    See also DLB 264; EW 8; EWL 3; RGWL
    2, 3
Swados, Elizabeth (A.) 1951- ............ **CLC 12**
    See also CA 97-100; CANR 49; INT CA-
    97-100
Swados, Harvey 1920-1972 ................ **CLC 5**
    See also CA 5-8R; 37-40R; CANR 6; DLB
    2
Swan, Gladys 1934- .......................... **CLC 69**
    See also CA 101; CANR 17, 39
Swanson, Logan
    See Matheson, Richard (Burton)

Swarthout, Glendon (Fred)
    1918-1992 ............................. **CLC 35**
    See also AAYA 55; CA 1-4R; 139; CANR
    1, 47; LAIT 5; SATA 26; TCWW 2; YAW
Swedenborg, Emanuel 1688-1772 ..... **LC 105**
Sweet, Sarah C.
    See Jewett, (Theodora) Sarah Orne
Swenson, May 1919-1989 ...... **CLC 4, 14, 61,
    106; PC 14**
    See also AMWS 4; CA 5-8R; 130; CANR
    36, 61, 131; DA; DAB; DAC; DAM MST,
    POET; DLB 5; EXPP; GLL 2; MTCW 1,
    2; PFS 16; SATA 15; WP
Swift, Augustus
    See Lovecraft, H(oward) P(hillips)
Swift, Graham (Colin) 1949- ...... **CLC 41, 88**
    See also BRWC 2; BRWS 5; CA 117; 122;
    CANR 46, 71, 128; CN 7; DLB 194;
    MTCW 2; NFS 18; RGSF 2
Swift, Jonathan 1667-1745 ..... **LC 1, 42, 101;
    PC 9; WLC**
    See also AAYA 41; BRW 3; BRWC 1;
    BRWR 1; BYA 5, 14; CDBLB 1660-1789;
    CLR 53; DA; DA3; DAB; DAC; DAM
    MST, NOV, POET; DLB 39, 95, 101;
    EXPN; LAIT 1; NFS 6; RGEL 2; SATA
    19; TEA; WCH; WLIT 3
Swinburne, Algernon Charles
    1837-1909 ... **PC 24; TCLC 8, 36; WLC**
    See also BRW 5; CA 105; 140; CDBLB
    1832-1890; DA; DA3; DAB; DAC; DAM
    MST, POET; DLB 35, 57; PAB; RGEL 2;
    TEA
Swinfen, Ann ..................................... **CLC 34**
    See also CA 202
Swinnerton, Frank Arthur
    1884-1982 ............................. **CLC 31**
    See also CA 108; DLB 34
Swithen, John
    See King, Stephen (Edwin)
Sylvia
    See Ashton-Warner, Sylvia (Constance)
Symmes, Robert Edward
    See Duncan, Robert (Edward)
Symonds, John Addington
    1840-1893 ............................. **NCLC 34**
    See also DLB 57, 144
Symons, Arthur 1865-1945 ............. **TCLC 11**
    See also CA 107; 189; DLB 19, 57, 149;
    RGEL 2
Symons, Julian (Gustave)
    1912-1994 ........................ **CLC 2, 14, 32**
    See also CA 49-52; 147; CAAS 3; CANR
    3, 33, 59; CMW 4; DLB 87, 155; DLBY
    1992; MSW; MTCW 1
Synge, (Edmund) J(ohn) M(illington)
    1871-1909 ..................... **DC 2; TCLC 6, 37**
    See also BRW 6; BRWR 1; CA 104; 141;
    CDBLB 1890-1914; DAM DRAM; DFS
    18; DLB 10, 19; EWL 3; RGEL 2; TEA;
    WLIT 4
Syruc, J.
    See Milosz, Czeslaw
Szirtes, George 1948- ........... **CLC 46; PC 51**
    See also CA 109; CANR 27, 61, 117; CP 7
Szymborska, Wislawa 1923- ... **CLC 99, 190;
    PC 44**
    See also CA 154; CANR 91, 133; CDWLB
    4; CWP; CWW 2; DA3; DLB 232; DLBY
    1996; EWL 3; MTCW 2; PFS 15; RGWL
    3
T. O., Nik
    See Annensky, Innokenty (Fyodorovich)
Tabori, George 1914- .......................... **CLC 19**
    See also CA 49-52; CANR 4, 69; CBD; CD
    5; DLB 245
Tacitus c. 55-c. 117 ........................ **CMLC 56**
    See also AW 2; CDWLB 1; DLB 211;
    RGWL 2, 3

**Tagore, Rabindranath** 1861-1941 ......... **PC 8; SSC 48; TCLC 3, 53**
See also CA 104; 120; DA3; DAM DRAM, POET; EWL 3; MTCW 1, 2; PFS 18; RGEL 2; RGSF 2; RGWL 2, 3; TWA

**Taine, Hippolyte Adolphe**
1828-1893 .................... **NCLC 15**
See also EW 7; GFL 1789 to the Present

**Talayesva, Don C.** 1890-(?) ................ **NNAL**

**Talese, Gay** 1932- ................................ **CLC 37**
See also AITN 1; CA 1-4R; CANR 9, 58; DLB 185; INT CANR-9; MTCW 1, 2

**Tallent, Elizabeth (Ann)** 1954- .......... **CLC 45**
See also CA 117; CANR 72; DLB 130

**Tallmountain, Mary** 1918-1997 ......... **NNAL**
See also CA 146; 161; DLB 193

**Tally, Ted** 1952- ................................ **CLC 42**
See also CA 120; 124; CAD; CANR 125; CD 5; INT CA-124

**Talvik, Heiti** 1904-1947 ................ **TCLC 87**
See also EWL 3

**Tamayo y Baus, Manuel**
1829-1898 ..................... **NCLC 1**

**Tammsaare, A(nton) H(ansen)**
1878-1940 ..................... **TCLC 27**
See also CA 164; CDWLB 4; DLB 220; EWL 3

**Tam'si, Tchicaya U**
See Tchicaya, Gerald Felix

**Tan, Amy (Ruth)** 1952- . **AAL; CLC 59, 120, 151**
See also AAYA 9, 48; AMWS 10; BEST 89:3; BPFB 3; CA 136; CANR 54, 105, 132; CDALBS; CN 7; CPW 1; DA3; DAM MULT, NOV, POP; DLB 173; EXPN; FW; LAIT 3, 5; MTCW 2; NFS 1, 13, 16; RGAL 4; SATA 75; SSFS 9; YAW

**Tandem, Felix**
See Spitteler, Carl (Friedrich Georg)

**Tanizaki, Jun'ichiro** 1886-1965 ... **CLC 8, 14, 28; SSC 21**
See Tanizaki Jun'ichiro
See also CA 93-96; 25-28R; MJW; MTCW 2; RGSF 2; RGWL 2

**Tanizaki Jun'ichiro**
See Tanizaki, Jun'ichiro
See also DLB 180; EWL 3

**Tanner, William**
See Amis, Kingsley (William)

**Tao Lao**
See Storni, Alfonsina

**Tapahonso, Luci** 1953- ....................... **NNAL**
See also CA 145; CANR 72, 127; DLB 175

**Tarantino, Quentin (Jerome)**
1963- ........................................ **CLC 125**
See also AAYA 58; CA 171; CANR 125

**Tarassoff, Lev**
See Troyat, Henri

**Tarbell, Ida M(inerva)** 1857-1944 . **TCLC 40**
See also CA 122; 181; DLB 47

**Tarkington, (Newton) Booth**
1869-1946 ................................ **TCLC 9**
See also BPFB 3; BYA 3; CA 110; 143; CWRI 5; DLB 9, 102; MTCW 2; RGAL 4; SATA 17

**Tarkovskii, Andrei Arsen'evich**
See Tarkovsky, Andrei (Arsenyevich)

**Tarkovsky, Andrei (Arsenyevich)**
1932-1986 .................................. **CLC 75**
See also CA 127

**Tartt, Donna** 1963- ............................ **CLC 76**
See also AAYA 56; CA 142

**Tasso, Torquato** 1544-1595 ............. **LC 5, 94**
See also EFS 2; EW 2; RGWL 2, 3

**Tate, (John Orley) Allen** 1899-1979 .. **CLC 2, 4, 6, 9, 11, 14, 24; PC 50**
See also AMW; CA 5-8R; 85-88; CANR 32, 108; DLB 4, 45, 63; DLBD 17; EWL 3; MTCW 1, 2; RGAL 4; RHW

**Tate, Ellalice**
See Hibbert, Eleanor Alice Burford

**Tate, James (Vincent)** 1943- ..... **CLC 2, 6, 25**
See also CA 21-24R; CANR 29, 57, 114; CP 7; DLB 5, 169; EWL 3; PFS 10, 15; RGAL 4; WP

**Tauler, Johannes** c. 1300-1361 ...... **CMLC 37**
See also DLB 179; LMFS 1

**Tavel, Ronald** 1940- ............................ **CLC 6**
See also CA 21-24R; CAD; CANR 33; CD 5

**Taviani, Paolo** 1931- ........................... **CLC 70**
See also CA 153

**Taylor, Bayard** 1825-1878 .............. **NCLC 89**
See also DLB 3, 189, 250, 254; RGAL 4

**Taylor, C(ecil) P(hilip)** 1929-1981 .... **CLC 27**
See also CA 25-28R; 105; CANR 47; CBD

**Taylor, Edward** 1642(?)-1729 .............. **LC 11**
See also AMW; DA; DAB; DAC; DAM MST, POET; DLB 24; EXPP; RGAL 4; TUS

**Taylor, Eleanor Ross** 1920- ................ **CLC 5**
See also CA 81-84; CANR 70

**Taylor, Elizabeth** 1932-1975 ..... **CLC 2, 4, 29**
See also CA 13-16R; CANR 9, 70; DLB 139; MTCW 1; RGEL 2; SATA 13

**Taylor, Frederick Winslow**
1856-1915 ................................ **TCLC 76**
See also CA 188

**Taylor, Henry (Splawn)** 1942- ......... **CLC 44**
See also CA 33-36R; CAAS 7; CANR 31; CP 7; DLB 5; PFS 10

**Taylor, Kamala (Purnaiya)** 1924-2004
See Markandaya, Kamala
See also CA 77-80; 227; NFS 13

**Taylor, Mildred D(elois)** 1943- ......... **CLC 21**
See also AAYA 10, 47; BW 1; BYA 3, 8; CA 85-88; CANR 25, 115; CLR 9, 59, 90; CSW; DLB 52; JRDA; LAIT 3; MAI-CYA 1, 2; SAAS 5; SATA 135; WYA; YAW

**Taylor, Peter (Hillsman)** 1917-1994 .. **CLC 1, 4, 18, 37, 44, 50, 71; SSC 10**
See also AMWS 5; BPFB 3; CA 13-16R; 147; CANR 9, 50; CSW; DLB 218, 278; DLBY 1981, 1994; EWL 3; EXPS; INT CANR-9; MTCW 1, 2; RGSF 2; SSFS 9; TUS

**Taylor, Robert Lewis** 1912-1998 ....... **CLC 14**
See also CA 1-4R; 170; CANR 3, 64; SATA 10

**Tchekhov, Anton**
See Chekhov, Anton (Pavlovich)

**Tchicaya, Gerald Felix** 1931-1988 .. **CLC 101**
See Tchicaya U Tam'si
See also CA 129; 125; CANR 81

**Tchicaya U Tam'si**
See Tchicaya, Gerald Felix
See also EWL 3

**Teasdale, Sara** 1884-1933 .... **PC 31; TCLC 4**
See also CA 104; 163; DLB 45; GLL 1; PFS 14; RGAL 4; SATA 32; TUS

**Tecumseh** 1768-1813 ........................... **NNAL**
See also DAM MULT

**Tegner, Esaias** 1782-1846 ................ **NCLC 2**

**Teilhard de Chardin, (Marie Joseph) Pierre**
1881-1955 .................................. **TCLC 9**
See also CA 105; 210; GFL 1789 to the Present

**Temple, Ann**
See Mortimer, Penelope (Ruth)

**Tennant, Emma (Christina)** 1937- .. **CLC 13, 52**
See also BRWS 9; CA 65-68; CAAS 9; CANR 10, 38, 59, 88; CN 7; DLB 14; EWL 3; SFW 4

**Tenneshaw, S. M.**
See Silverberg, Robert

**Tenney, Tabitha Gilman**
1762-1837 ............................. **NCLC 122**
See also DLB 37, 200

**Tennyson, Alfred** 1809-1892 ... **NCLC 30, 65, 115; PC 6; WLC**
See also AAYA 50; BRW 4; CDBLB 1832-1890; DA; DA3; DAB; DAC; DAM MST, POET; DLB 32; EXPP; PAB; PFS 1, 2, 4, 11, 15, 19; RGEL 2; TEA; WLIT 4; WP

**Teran, Lisa St. Aubin de** ..................... **CLC 36**
See St. Aubin de Teran, Lisa

**Terence** c. 184B.C.-c. 159B.C. ...... **CMLC 14; DC 7**
See also AW 1; CDWLB 1; DLB 211; RGWL 2, 3; TWA

**Teresa de Jesus, St.** 1515-1582 ........... **LC 18**

**Terkel, Louis** 1912-
See Terkel, Studs
See also CA 57-60; CANR 18, 45, 67, 132; DA3; MTCW 1, 2

**Terkel, Studs** .................................... **CLC 38**
See Terkel, Louis
See also AAYA 32; AITN 1; MTCW 2; TUS

**Terry, C. V.**
See Slaughter, Frank G(ill)

**Terry, Megan** 1932- .............. **CLC 19; DC 13**
See also CA 77-80; CABS 3; CAD; CANR 43; CD 5; CWD; DFS 18; DLB 7, 249; GLL 2

**Tertullian** c. 155-c. 245 ................. **CMLC 29**

**Tertz, Abram**
See Sinyavsky, Andrei (Donatevich)
See also RGSF 2

**Tesich, Steve** 1943(?)-1996 .......... **CLC 40, 69**
See also CA 105; 152; CAD; DLBY 1983

**Tesla, Nikola** 1856-1943 ................. **TCLC 88**

**Teternikov, Fyodor Kuzmich** 1863-1927
See Sologub, Fyodor
See also CA 104

**Tevis, Walter** 1928-1984 ................... **CLC 42**
See also CA 113; SFW 4

**Tey, Josephine** ................................. **TCLC 14**
See Mackintosh, Elizabeth
See also DLB 77; MSW

**Thackeray, William Makepeace**
1811-1863 .... **NCLC 5, 14, 22, 43; WLC**
See also BRW 5; BRWC 2; CDBLB 1832-1890; DA; DA3; DAB; DAC; DAM MST, NOV; DLB 21, 55, 159, 163; NFS 13; RGEL 2; SATA 23; TEA; WLIT 3

**Thakura, Ravindranatha**
See Tagore, Rabindranath

**Thames, C. H.**
See Marlowe, Stephen

**Tharoor, Shashi** 1956- ...................... **CLC 70**
See also CA 141; CANR 91; CN 7

**Thelwell, Michael Miles** 1939- .......... **CLC 22**
See also BW 2; CA 101

**Theobald, Lewis, Jr.**
See Lovecraft, H(oward) P(hillips)

**Theocritus** c. 310B.C.- ................... **CMLC 45**
See also AW 1; DLB 176; RGWL 2, 3

**Theodorescu, Ion N.** 1880-1967
See Arghezi, Tudor
See also CA 116

**Theriault, Yves** 1915-1983 ................ **CLC 79**
See also CA 102; CCA 1; DAC; DAM MST; DLB 88; EWL 3

**Theroux, Alexander (Louis)** 1939- .... **CLC 2, 25**
See also CA 85-88; CANR 20, 63; CN 7

**Theroux, Paul (Edward)** 1941- ..... **CLC 5, 8, 11, 15, 28, 46**
See also AAYA 28; AMWS 8; BEST 89:4; BPFB 3; CA 33-36R; CANR 20, 45, 74, 133; CDALBS; CN 7; CPW 1; DA3; DAM POP; DLB 2, 218; EWL 3; HGG; MTCW 1, 2; RGAL 4; SATA 44, 109; TUS

**Thesen, Sharon** 1946- ........................ **CLC 56**
See also CA 163; CANR 125; CP 7; CWP

**Thespis** fl. 6th cent. B.C.- ............... **CMLC 51**
See also LMFS 1

**Thevenin, Denis**
See Duhamel, Georges

**Thibault, Jacques Anatole Francois** 1844-1924
See France, Anatole
See also CA 106; 127; DA3; DAM NOV; MTCW 1, 2; TWA

**Thiele, Colin (Milton)** 1920- ............. **CLC 17**
See also CA 29-32R; CANR 12, 28, 53, 105; CLR 27; DLB 289; MAICYA 1, 2; SAAS 2; SATA 14, 72, 125; YAW

**Thistlethwaite, Bel**
See Wetherald, Agnes Ethelwyn

**Thomas, Audrey (Callahan)** 1935- .... **CLC 7, 13, 37, 107; SSC 20**
See also AITN 2; CA 21-24R; CAAS 19; CANR 36, 58; CN 7; DLB 60; MTCW 1; RGSF 2

**Thomas, Augustus** 1857-1934 ......... **TCLC 97**

**Thomas, D(onald) M(ichael)** 1935- . **CLC 13, 22, 31, 132**
See also BPFB 3; BRWS 4; CA 61-64; CAAS 11; CANR 17, 45, 75; CDBLB 1960 to Present; CN 7; CP 7; DA3; DLB 40, 207, 299; HGG; INT CANR-17; MTCW 1, 2; SFW 4

**Thomas, Dylan (Marlais)** 1914-1953 .... **PC 2, 52; SSC 3, 44; TCLC 1, 8, 45, 105; WLC**
See also AAYA 45; BRWS 1; CA 104; 120; CANR 65; CDBLB 1945-1960; DA; DA3; DAB; DAC; DAM DRAM, MST, POET; DLB 13, 20, 139; EWL 3; EXPP; LAIT 3; MTCW 1, 2; PAB; PFS 1, 3, 8; RGEL 2; RGSF 2; SATA 60; TEA; WLIT 4; WP

**Thomas, (Philip) Edward** 1878-1917 . **PC 53; TCLC 10**
See also BRW 6; BRWS 3; CA 106; 153; DAM POET; DLB 19, 98, 156, 216; EWL 3; PAB; RGEL 2

**Thomas, Joyce Carol** 1938- ............. **CLC 35**
See also AAYA 12, 54; BW 2, 3; CA 113; 116; CANR 48, 114; CLR 19; DLB 33; INT CA-116; JRDA; MAICYA 1, 2; MTCW 1, 2; SAAS 7; SATA 40, 78, 123, 137; SATA-Essay 137; WYA; YAW

**Thomas, Lewis** 1913-1993 ................. **CLC 35**
See also ANW; CA 85-88; 143; CANR 38, 60; DLB 275; MTCW 1, 2

**Thomas, M. Carey** 1857-1935 ....... **TCLC 89**
See also FW

**Thomas, Paul**
See Mann, (Paul) Thomas

**Thomas, Piri** 1928- ............. **CLC 17; HLCS 2**
See also CA 73-76; HW 1; LLW 1

**Thomas, R(onald) S(tuart)** 1913-2000 ........................ **CLC 6, 13, 48**
See also CA 89-92; 189; CAAS 4; CANR 30; CDBLB 1960 to Present; CP 7; DAB; DAM POET; DLB 27; EWL 3; MTCW 1; RGEL 2

**Thomas, Ross (Elmore)** 1926-1995 .. **CLC 39**
See also CA 33-36R; 150; CANR 22, 63; CMW 4

**Thompson, Francis (Joseph)** 1859-1907 ................................... **TCLC 4**
See also BRW 5; CA 104; 189; CDBLB 1890-1914; DLB 19; RGEL 2; TEA

**Thompson, Francis Clegg**
See Mencken, H(enry) L(ouis)

**Thompson, Hunter S(tockton)** 1937(?)- ..................... **CLC 9, 17, 40, 104**
See also AAYA 45; BEST 89:1; BPFB 3; CA 17-20R; CANR 23, 46, 74, 77, 111, 133; CPW; CSW; DA3; DAM POP; DLB 185; MTCW 1, 2; TUS

**Thompson, James Myers**
See Thompson, Jim (Myers)

**Thompson, Jim (Myers)** 1906-1977(?) ............................. **CLC 69**
See also BPFB 3; CA 140; CMW 4; CPW; DLB 226; MSW

**Thompson, Judith** ............................ **CLC 39**
See also CWD

**Thomson, James** 1700-1748 .... **LC 16, 29, 40**
See also BRWS 3; DAM POET; DLB 95; RGEL 2

**Thomson, James** 1834-1882 ........... **NCLC 18**
See also DAM POET; DLB 35; RGEL 2

**Thoreau, Henry David** 1817-1862 .. **NCLC 7, 21, 61, 138; PC 30; WLC**
See also AAYA 42; AMW; ANW; BYA 3; CDALB 1640-1865; DA; DA3; DAB; DAC; DAM MST; DLB 1, 183, 223, 270, 298; LAIT 2; LMFS 1; NCFS 3; RGAL 4; TUS

**Thorndike, E. L.**
See Thorndike, Edward L(ee)

**Thorndike, Edward L(ee)** 1874-1949 ............................... **TCLC 107**
See also CA 121

**Thornton, Hall**
See Silverberg, Robert

**Thorpe, Adam** 1956- ....................... **CLC 176**
See also CA 129; CANR 92; DLB 231

**Thubron, Colin (Gerald Dryden)** 1939- ......................................... **CLC 163**
See also CA 25-28R; CANR 12, 29, 59, 95; CN 7; DLB 204, 231

**Thucydides** c. 455B.C.-c. 395B.C. . **CMLC 17**
See also AW 1; DLB 176; RGWL 2, 3

**Thumboo, Edwin Nadason** 1933- ........ **PC 30**
See also CA 194

**Thurber, James (Grover)** 1894-1961 .. **CLC 5, 11, 25, 125; SSC 1, 47**
See also AAYA 56; AMWS 1; BPFB 3; BYA 5; CA 73-76; CANR 17, 39; CDALB 1929-1941; CWRI 5; DA; DAB; DAC; DAM DRAM, MST, NOV; DLB 4, 11, 22, 102; EWL 3; EXPS; FANT; LAIT 3; MAICYA 1, 2; MTCW 1, 2; RGAL 4; RGSF 2; SATA 13; SSFS 1, 10, 19; SUFW; TUS

**Thurman, Wallace (Henry)** 1902-1934 ......... **BLC 3; HR 3; TCLC 6**
See also BW 1, 3; CA 104; 124; CANR 81; DAM MULT; DLB 51

**Tibullus** c. 54B.C.-c. 18B.C. .......... **CMLC 36**
See also AW 2; DLB 211; RGWL 2, 3

**Ticheburn, Cheviot**
See Ainsworth, William Harrison

**Tieck, (Johann) Ludwig** 1773-1853 ............. **NCLC 5, 46; SSC 31**
See also CDWLB 2; DLB 90; EW 5; IDTP; RGSF 2; RGWL 2, 3; SUFW

**Tiger, Derry**
See Ellison, Harlan (Jay)

**Tilghman, Christopher** 1946- ........... **CLC 65**
See also CA 159; CSW; DLB 244

**Tillich, Paul (Johannes)** 1886-1965 ................................ **CLC 131**
See also CA 5-8R; 25-28R; CANR 33; MTCW 1, 2

**Tillinghast, Richard (Williford)** 1940- ........................................ **CLC 29**
See also CA 29-32R; CAAS 23; CANR 26, 51, 96; CP 7; CSW

**Timrod, Henry** 1828-1867 ............. **NCLC 25**
See also DLB 3, 248; RGAL 4

**Tindall, Gillian (Elizabeth)** 1938- ...... **CLC 7**
See also CA 21-24R; CANR 11, 65, 107; CN 7

**Tiptree, James, Jr.** ...................... **CLC 48, 50**
See Sheldon, Alice Hastings Bradley
See also DLB 8; SCFW 2; SFW 4

**Tirone Smith, Mary-Ann** 1944- ........ **CLC 39**
See also CA 118; 136; CANR 113; SATA 143

**Tirso de Molina** 1580(?)-1648 ........... **DC 13; HLCS 2; LC 73**
See also RGWL 2, 3

**Titmarsh, Michael Angelo**
See Thackeray, William Makepeace

**Tocqueville, Alexis (Charles Henri Maurice Clerel Comte) de** 1805-1859 .. **NCLC 7, 63**
See also EW 6; GFL 1789 to the Present; TWA

**Toer, Pramoedya Ananta** 1925- ...... **CLC 186**
See also CA 197; RGWL 3

**Toffler, Alvin** 1928- ........................... **CLC 168**
See also CA 13-16R; CANR 15, 46, 67; CPW; DAM POP; MTCW 1, 2

**Toibin, Colm**
See Toibin, Colm
See also DLB 271

**Toibin, Colm** 1955- .......................... **CLC 162**
See Toibin, Colm
See also CA 142; CANR 81

**Tolkien, J(ohn) R(onald) R(euel)** 1892-1973 ... **CLC 1, 2, 3, 8, 12, 38; TCLC 137; WLC**
See also AAYA 10; AITN 1; BPFB 3; BRWC 2; BRWS 2; CA 17-18; 45-48; CANR 36; CAP 2; CDBLB 1914-1945; CLR 56; CPW 1; CWRI 5; DA; DA3; DAB; DAC; DAM MST, NOV, POP; DLB 15, 160, 255; EFS 2; EWL 3; FANT; JRDA; LAIT 1; LATS 1:2; LMFS 2; MAICYA 1, 2; MTCW 1, 2; NFS 8; RGEL 2; SATA 2, 32, 100; SATA-Obit 24; SFW 4; SUFW; TEA; WCH; WYA; YAW

**Toller, Ernst** 1893-1939 ................... **TCLC 10**
See also CA 107; 186; DLB 124; EWL 3; RGWL 2, 3

**Tolson, M. B.**
See Tolson, Melvin B(eaunorus)

**Tolson, Melvin B(eaunorus)** 1898(?)-1966 ........ **BLC 3; CLC 36, 105**
See also AFAW 1, 2; BW 1, 3; CA 124; 89-92; CANR 80; DAM MULT, POET; DLB 48, 76; RGAL 4

**Tolstoi, Aleksei Nikolaevich**
See Tolstoy, Alexey Nikolaevich

**Tolstoi, Lev**
See Tolstoy, Leo (Nikolaevich)
See also RGSF 2; RGWL 2, 3

**Tolstoy, Aleksei Nikolaevich**
See Tolstoy, Alexey Nikolaevich
See also DLB 272

**Tolstoy, Alexey Nikolaevich** 1882-1945 ................................ **TCLC 18**
See Tolstoy, Aleksei Nikolaevich
See also CA 107; 158; EWL 3; SFW 4

**Tolstoy, Leo (Nikolaevich)** 1828-1910 . **SSC 9, 30, 45, 54; TCLC 4, 11, 17, 28, 44, 79; WLC**
See Tolstoi, Lev
See also AAYA 56; CA 104; 123; DA; DA3; DAB; DAC; DAM MST, NOV; DLB 238;

EFS 2; EW 7; EXPS; IDTP; LAIT 2; LATS 1:1; LMFS 1; NFS 10; SATA 26; SSFS 5; TWA

**Tolstoy, Count Leo**
See Tolstoy, Leo (Nikolaevich)

**Tomalin, Claire** 1933- ..................... **CLC 166**
See also CA 89-92; CANR 52, 88; DLB 155

**Tomasi di Lampedusa, Giuseppe** 1896-1957
See Lampedusa, Giuseppe (Tomasi) di
See also CA 111; DLB 177; EWL 3

**Tomlin, Lily** ....................... **CLC 17**
See Tomlin, Mary Jean

**Tomlin, Mary Jean** 1939(?)-
See Tomlin, Lily
See also CA 117

**Tomline, F. Latour**
See Gilbert, W(illiam) S(chwenck)

**Tomlinson, (Alfred) Charles** 1927- .... **CLC 2, 4, 6, 13, 45; PC 17**
See also CA 5-8R; CANR 33; CP 7; DAM POET; DLB 40

**Tomlinson, H(enry) M(ajor)** 1873-1958 ............................... **TCLC 71**
See also CA 118; 161; DLB 36, 100, 195

**Tonna, Charlotte Elizabeth** 1790-1846 .............................. **NCLC 135**
See also DLB 163

**Tonson, Jacob** fl. 1655(?)-1736 ............ **LC 86**
See also DLB 170

**Toole, John Kennedy** 1937-1969 ..... **CLC 19, 64**
See also BPFB 3; CA 104; DLBY 1981; MTCW 2

**Toomer, Eugene**
See Toomer, Jean

**Toomer, Eugene Pinchback**
See Toomer, Jean

**Toomer, Jean** 1894-1967 .. **BLC 3; CLC 1, 4, 13, 22; HR 3; PC 7; SSC 1, 45; WLCS**
See also AFAW 1, 2; AMWS 3, 9; BW 1; CA 85-88; CDALB 1917-1929; DA3; DAM MULT; DLB 45, 51; EWL 3; EXPP; EXPS; LMFS 2; MTCW 1, 2; NFS 11; RGAL 4; RGSF 2; SSFS 5

**Toomer, Nathan Jean**
See Toomer, Jean

**Toomer, Nathan Pinchback**
See Toomer, Jean

**Torley, Luke**
See Blish, James (Benjamin)

**Tornimparte, Alessandra**
See Ginzburg, Natalia

**Torre, Raoul della**
See Mencken, H(enry) L(ouis)

**Torrence, Ridgely** 1874-1950 ......... **TCLC 97**
See also DLB 54, 249

**Torrey, E(dwin) Fuller** 1937- ........... **CLC 34**
See also CA 119; CANR 71

**Torsvan, Ben Traven**
See Traven, B.

**Torsvan, Benno Traven**
See Traven, B.

**Torsvan, Berick Traven**
See Traven, B.

**Torsvan, Berwick Traven**
See Traven, B.

**Torsvan, Bruno Traven**
See Traven, B.

**Torsvan, Traven**
See Traven, B.

**Tourneur, Cyril** 1575(?)-1626 ............. **LC 66**
See also BRW 2; DAM DRAM; DLB 58; RGEL 2

**Tournier, Michel (Edouard)** 1924- .... **CLC 6, 23, 36, 95**
See also CA 49-52; CANR 3, 36, 74; CWW 2; DLB 83; EWL 3; GFL 1789 to the Present; MTCW 1, 2; SATA 23

**Tournimparte, Alessandra**
See Ginzburg, Natalia

**Towers, Ivar**
See Kornbluth, C(yril) M.

**Towne, Robert (Burton)** 1936(?)- ..... **CLC 87**
See also CA 108; DLB 44; IDFW 3, 4

**Townsend, Sue** ...................... **CLC 61**
See Townsend, Susan Lilian
See also AAYA 28; CA 119; 127; CANR 65, 107; CBD; CD 5; CPW; CWD; DAB; DAC; DAM MST; DLB 271; INT CA-127; SATA 55, 93; SATA-Brief 48; YAW

**Townsend, Susan Lilian** 1946-
See Townsend, Sue

**Townshend, Pete**
See Townshend, Peter (Dennis Blandford)

**Townshend, Peter (Dennis Blandford)** 1945- ...................... **CLC 17, 42**
See also CA 107

**Tozzi, Federigo** 1883-1920 ............. **TCLC 31**
See also CA 160; CANR 110; DLB 264; EWL 3

**Tracy, Don(ald Fiske)** 1905-1970(?)
See Queen, Ellery
See also CA 1-4R; 176; CANR 2

**Trafford, F. G.**
See Riddell, Charlotte

**Traherne, Thomas** 1637(?)-1674 .......... **LC 99**
See also BRW 2; DLB 131; PAB; RGEL 2

**Traill, Catharine Parr** 1802-1899 .. **NCLC 31**
See also DLB 99

**Trakl, Georg** 1887-1914 ....... **PC 20; TCLC 5**
See also CA 104; 165; EW 10; EWL 3; LMFS 2; MTCW 2; RGWL 2, 3

**Tranquilli, Secondino**
See Silone, Ignazio

**Transtroemer, Tomas Gosta**
See Transtromer, Tomas (Goesta)

**Transtromer, Tomas (Gosta)**
See Transtromer, Tomas (Goesta)
See also CWW 2

**Transtromer, Tomas (Goesta)** 1931- .................................. **CLC 52, 65**
See Transtromer, Tomas (Gosta)
See also CA 117; 129; CAAS 17; CANR 115; DAM POET; DLB 257; EWL 3; PFS 21

**Transtromer, Tomas Gosta**
See Transtromer, Tomas (Goesta)

**Traven, B.** 1882(?)-1969 ................ **CLC 8, 11**
See also CA 19-20; 25-28R; CAP 2; DLB 9, 56; EWL 3; MTCW 1; RGAL 4

**Trediakovsky, Vasilii Kirillovich** 1703-1769 ............................... **LC 68**
See also DLB 150

**Treitel, Jonathan** 1959- ...................... **CLC 70**
See also CA 210; DLB 267

**Trelawny, Edward John** 1792-1881 ............................... **NCLC 85**
See also DLB 110, 116, 144

**Tremain, Rose** 1943- .......................... **CLC 42**
See also CA 97-100; CANR 44, 95; CN 7; DLB 14, 271; RGSF 2; RHW

**Tremblay, Michel** 1942- ........... **CLC 29, 102**
See also CA 116; 128; CCA 1; CWW 2; DAC; DAM MST; DLB 60; EWL 3; GLL 1; MTCW 1, 2

**Trevanian** ......................... **CLC 29**
See Whitaker, Rod(ney)

**Trevor, Glen**
See Hilton, James

**Trevor, William** .. **CLC 7, 9, 14, 25, 71, 116; SSC 21, 58**
See Cox, William Trevor
See also BRWS 4; CBD; CD 5; CN 7; DLB 14, 139; EWL 3; LATS 1:2; MTCW 2; RGEL 2; RGSF 2; SSFS 10

**Trifonov, Iurii (Valentinovich)**
See Trifonov, Yuri (Valentinovich)
See also DLB 302; RGWL 2, 3

**Trifonov, Yuri (Valentinovich)** 1925-1981 ................................. **CLC 45**
See Trifonov, Iurii (Valentinovich); Trifonov, Yury Valentinovich
See also CA 126; 103; MTCW 1

**Trifonov, Yury Valentinovich**
See Trifonov, Yuri (Valentinovich)
See also EWL 3

**Trilling, Diana (Rubin)** 1905-1996 . **CLC 129**
See also CA 5-8R; 154; CANR 10, 46; INT CANR-10; MTCW 1, 2

**Trilling, Lionel** 1905-1975 ..... **CLC 9, 11, 24; SSC 75**
See also AMWS 3; CA 9-12R; 61-64; CANR 10, 105; DLB 28, 63; EWL 3; INT CANR-10; MTCW 1, 2; RGAL 4; TUS

**Trimball, W. H.**
See Mencken, H(enry) L(ouis)

**Tristan**
See Gomez de la Serna, Ramon

**Tristram**
See Housman, A(lfred) E(dward)

**Trogdon, William (Lewis)** 1939-
See Heat-Moon, William Least
See also CA 115; 119; CANR 47, 89; CPW; INT CA-119

**Trollope, Anthony** 1815-1882 .... **NCLC 6, 33, 101; SSC 28; WLC**
See also BRW 5; CDBLB 1832-1890; DA; DA3; DAB; DAC; DAM MST, NOV; DLB 21, 57, 159; RGEL 2; RGSF 2; SATA 22

**Trollope, Frances** 1779-1863 .......... **NCLC 30**
See also DLB 21, 166

**Trollope, Joanna** 1943- .................... **CLC 186**
See also CA 101; CANR 58, 95; CPW; DLB 207; RHW

**Trotsky, Leon** 1879-1940 ............... **TCLC 22**
See also CA 118; 167

**Trotter (Cockburn), Catharine** 1679-1749 ...................................... **LC 8**
See also DLB 84, 252

**Trotter, Wilfred** 1872-1939 ............ **TCLC 97**

**Trout, Kilgore**
See Farmer, Philip Jose

**Trow, George W. S.** 1943- ................ **CLC 52**
See also CA 126; CANR 91

**Troyat, Henri** 1911- ........................ **CLC 23**
See also CA 45-48; CANR 2, 33, 67, 117; GFL 1789 to the Present; MTCW 1

**Trudeau, G(arretson) B(eekman)** 1948-
See Trudeau, Garry B.
See also CA 81-84; CANR 31; SATA 35

**Trudeau, Garry B.** ........................... **CLC 12**
See Trudeau, G(arretson) B(eekman)
See also AAYA 10; AITN 2

**Truffaut, Francois** 1932-1984 ... **CLC 20, 101**
See also CA 81-84; 113; CANR 34

**Trumbo, Dalton** 1905-1976 ............... **CLC 19**
See also CA 21-24R; 69-72; CANR 10; DLB 26; IDFW 3, 4; YAW

**Trumbull, John** 1750-1831 .............. **NCLC 30**
See also DLB 31; RGAL 4

**Trundlett, Helen B.**
See Eliot, T(homas) S(tearns)

**Truth, Sojourner** 1797(?)-1883 ...... **NCLC 94**
See also DLB 239; FW; LAIT 2

**Tryon, Thomas** 1926-1991 ............. **CLC 3, 11**
See also AITN 1; BPFB 3; CA 29-32R; 135;
CANR 32, 77; CPW; DA3; DAM POP;
HGG; MTCW 1
**Tryon, Tom**
See Tryon, Thomas
**Ts'ao Hsueh-ch'in** 1715(?)-1763 ............ **LC 1**
**Tsushima, Shuji** 1909-1948
See Dazai Osamu
See also CA 107
**Tsvetaeva (Efron), Marina (Ivanovna)**
1892-1941 ............... **PC 14; TCLC 7, 35**
See also CA 104; 128; CANR 73; DLB 295;
EW 11; MTCW 1, 2; RGWL 2, 3
**Tuck, Lily** 1938- .................................... **CLC 70**
See also CA 139; CANR 90
**Tu Fu** 712-770 ......................................... **PC 9**
See Du Fu
See also DAM MULT; TWA; WP
**Tunis, John R(oberts)** 1889-1975 ..... **CLC 12**
See also BYA 1; CA 61-64; CANR 62; DLB
22, 171; JRDA; MAICYA 1, 2; SATA 37;
SATA-Brief 30; YAW
**Tuohy, Frank** ........................................... **CLC 37**
See Tuohy, John Francis
See also DLB 14, 139
**Tuohy, John Francis** 1925-
See Tuohy, Frank
See also CA 5-8R; 178; CANR 3, 47; CN 7
**Turco, Lewis (Putnam)** 1934- ..... **CLC 11, 63**
See also CA 13-16R; CAAS 22; CANR 24,
51; CP 7; DLBY 1984
**Turgenev, Ivan (Sergeevich)**
1818-1883 ..... **DC 7; NCLC 21, 37, 122;**
**SSC 7, 57; WLC**
See also AAYA 58; DA; DAB; DAC; DAM
MST, NOV; DLB 238, 284; EW
6; LATS 1:1; NFS 16; RGSF 2; RGWL 2,
3; TWA
**Turgot, Anne-Robert-Jacques**
1727-1781 ...................................... **LC 26**
**Turner, Frederick** 1943- .................... **CLC 48**
See also CA 73-76, 227; CAAE 227; CAAS
10; CANR 12, 30, 56; DLB 40, 282
**Turton, James**
See Crace, Jim
**Tutu, Desmond M(pilo)** 1931- .. **BLC 3; CLC 80**
See also BW 1, 3; CA 125; CANR 67, 81;
DAM MULT
**Tutuola, Amos** 1920-1997 ..... **BLC 3; CLC 5, 14, 29**
See also AFW; BW 2, 3; CA 9-12R; 159;
CANR 27, 66; CDWLB 3; CN 7; DA3;
DAM MULT; DLB 125; DNFS 2; EWL
3; MTCW 1, 2; RGEL 2; WLIT 2
**Twain, Mark** .. **SSC 34; TCLC 6, 12, 19, 36, 48, 59; WLC**
See Clemens, Samuel Langhorne
See also AAYA 20; AMW; AMWC 1; BPFB
3; BYA 2, 3, 11, 14; CLR 58, 60, 66; DLB
11; EXPN; EXPS; FANT; LAIT 2; NCFS
4; NFS 1, 6; RGAL 4; RGSF 2; SFW 4;
SSFS 1, 7; SUFW; TUS; WCH; WYA;
YAW
**Tyler, Anne** 1941- . **CLC 7, 11, 18, 28, 44, 59, 103**
See also AAYA 18; AMWS 4; BEST 89:1;
BPFB 3; BYA 12; CA 9-12R; CANR 11,
33, 53, 109, 132; CDALBS; CN 7; CPW;
CSW; DAM NOV, POP; DLB 6, 143;
DLBY 1982; EWL 3; EXPN; LATS 1:2;
MAWW; MTCW 1, 2; NFS 2, 7, 10;
RGAL 4; SATA 7, 90; SSFS 17; TUS;
YAW
**Tyler, Royall** 1757-1826 .................... **NCLC 3**
See also DLB 37; RGAL 4
**Tynan, Katharine** 1861-1931 ........... **TCLC 3**
See also CA 104; 167; DLB 153, 240; FW

**Tyndale, William** c. 1484-1536 .......... **LC 103**
See also DLB 132
**Tyutchev, Fyodor** 1803-1873 .......... **NCLC 34**
**Tzara, Tristan** 1896-1963 ..... **CLC 47; PC 27**
See also CA 153; 89-92; DAM POET; EWL
3; MTCW 2
**Uchida, Yoshiko** 1921-1992 ................... **AAL**
See also AAYA 16; BYA 2, 3; CA 13-16R;
139; CANR 6, 22, 47, 61; CDALBS; CLR
6, 56; CWRI 5; JRDA; MAICYA 1, 2;
MTCW 1, 2; SAAS 1; SATA 1, 53; SATA-
Obit 72
**Udall, Nicholas** 1504-1556 ................... **LC 84**
See also DLB 62; RGEL 2
**Ueda Akinari** 1734-1809 ............... **NCLC 131**
**Uhry, Alfred** 1936- ............................... **CLC 55**
See also CA 127; 133; CAD; CANR 112;
CD 5; CSW; DA3; DAM DRAM, POP;
DFS 11, 15; INT CA-133
**Ulf, Haerved**
See Strindberg, (Johan) August
**Ulf, Harved**
See Strindberg, (Johan) August
**Ulibarri, Sabine R(eyes)**
1919-2003 ................... **CLC 83; HLCS 2**
See also CA 131; 214; CANR 81; DAM
MULT; DLB 82; HW 1, 2; RGSF 2
**Unamuno (y Jugo), Miguel de**
1864-1936 .. **HLC 2; SSC 11, 69; TCLC 2, 9, 148**
See also CA 104; 131; CANR 81; DAM
MULT, NOV; DLB 108; EW 8; EWL 3;
HW 1, 2; MTCW 1, 2; RGSF 2; RGWL
2, 3; SSFS 20; TWA
**Uncle Shelby**
See Silverstein, Shel(don Allan)
**Undercliffe, Errol**
See Campbell, (John) Ramsey
**Underwood, Miles**
See Glassco, John
**Undset, Sigrid** 1882-1949 ..... **TCLC 3; WLC**
See also CA 104; 129; DA; DA3; DAB;
DAC; DAM MST, NOV; DLB 293; EW
9; EWL 3; FW; MTCW 1, 2; RGWL 2, 3
**Ungaretti, Giuseppe** 1888-1970 ... **CLC 7, 11, 15; PC 57**
See also CA 19-20; 25-28R; CAP 2; DLB
114; EW 10; EWL 3; PFS 20; RGWL 2,
3
**Unger, Douglas** 1952- ......................... **CLC 34**
See also CA 130; CANR 94
**Unsworth, Barry (Forster)** 1930- .... **CLC 76, 127**
See also BRWS 7; CA 25-28R; CANR 30,
54, 125; CN 7; DLB 194
**Updike, John (Hoyer)** 1932- . **CLC 1, 2, 3, 5, 7, 9, 13, 15, 23, 34, 43, 70, 139; SSC 13, 27; WLC**
See also AAYA 36; AMW; AMWC 1;
AMWR 1; BPFB 3; BYA 12; CA 1-4R;
CABS 1; CANR 4, 33, 51, 94, 133;
CDALB 1968-1988; CN 7; CP 7; CPW 1;
DA; DA3; DAB; DAC; DAM MST, NOV,
POET, POP; DLB 2, 5, 143, 218, 227;
DLBD 3; DLBY 1980, 1982, 1997; EWL
3; EXPP; HGG; MTCW 1, 2; NFS 12;
RGAL 4; RGSF 2; SSFS 3, 19; TUS
**Upshaw, Margaret Mitchell**
See Mitchell, Margaret (Munnerlyn)
**Upton, Mark**
See Sanders, Lawrence
**Upward, Allen** 1863-1926 .............. **TCLC 85**
See also CA 117; 187; DLB 36
**Urdang, Constance (Henriette)**
1922-1996 ................................. **CLC 47**
See also CA 21-24R; CANR 9, 24; CP 7;
CWP
**Uriel, Henry**
See Faust, Frederick (Schiller)

**Uris, Leon (Marcus)** 1924-2003 ... **CLC 7, 32**
See also AITN 1, 2; BEST 89:2; BPFB 3;
CA 1-4R; 217; CANR 1, 40, 65, 123; CN
7; CPW 1; DA3; DAM NOV, POP;
MTCW 1, 2; SATA 49; SATA-Obit 146
**Urista (Heredia), Alberto (Baltazar)**
1947- ............................. **HLCS 1; PC 34**
See Alurista
See also CA 45-48, 182; CANR 2, 32; HW
1
**Urmuz**
See Codrescu, Andrei
**Urquhart, Guy**
See McAlmon, Robert (Menzies)
**Urquhart, Jane** 1949- ....................... **CLC 90**
See also CA 113; CANR 32, 68, 116; CCA
1; DAC
**Usigli, Rodolfo** 1905-1979 ................ **HLCS 1**
See also CA 131; DLB 305; EWL 3; HW 1;
LAW
**Ustinov, Peter (Alexander)**
1921-2004 ..................................... **CLC 1**
See also AITN 1; CA 13-16R; 225; CANR
25, 51; CBD; CD 5; DLB 13; MTCW 2
**U Tam'si, Gerald Felix Tchicaya**
See Tchicaya, Gerald Felix
**U Tam'si, Tchicaya**
See Tchicaya, Gerald Felix
**Vachss, Andrew (Henry)** 1942- ....... **CLC 106**
See also CA 118, 214; CAAE 214; CANR
44, 95; CMW 4
**Vachss, Andrew H.**
See Vachss, Andrew (Henry)
**Vaculik, Ludvik** 1926- ......................... **CLC 7**
See also CA 53-56; CANR 72; CWW 2;
DLB 232; EWL 3
**Vaihinger, Hans** 1852-1933 ............. **TCLC 71**
See also CA 116; 166
**Valdez, Luis (Miguel)** 1940- ..... **CLC 84; DC 10; HLC 2**
See also CA 101; CAD; CANR 32, 81; CD
5; DAM MULT; DFS 5; DLB 122; EWL
3; HW 1; LAIT 4; LLW 1
**Valenzuela, Luisa** 1938- ........... **CLC 31, 104; HLCS 2; SSC 14**
See also CA 101; CANR 32, 65, 123; CD-
WLB 3; CWW 2; DAM MULT; DLB 113;
EWL 3; FW; HW 1, 2; LAW; RGSF 2;
RGWL 3
**Valera y Alcala-Galiano, Juan**
1824-1905 ................................. **TCLC 10**
See also CA 106
**Valerius Maximus** fl. 20- .............. **CMLC 64**
See also DLB 211
**Valery, (Ambroise) Paul (Toussaint Jules)**
1871-1945 ................ **PC 9; TCLC 4, 15**
See also CA 104; 122; DA3; DAM POET;
DLB 258; EW 8; EWL 3; GFL 1789 to
the Present; MTCW 1, 2; RGWL 2, 3;
TWA
**Valle-Inclan, Ramon (Maria) del**
1866-1936 ..................... **HLC 2; TCLC 5**
See also CA 106; 153; CANR 80; DAM
MULT; DLB 134; EW 8; EWL 3; HW 2;
RGSF 2; RGWL 2, 3
**Vallejo, Antonio Buero**
See Buero Vallejo, Antonio
**Vallejo, Cesar (Abraham)**
1892-1938 .............. **HLC 2; TCLC 3, 56**
See also CA 105; 153; DAM MULT; DLB
290; EWL 3; HW 1; LAW; RGWL 2, 3
**Valles, Jules** 1832-1885 .................... **NCLC 71**
See also DLB 123; GFL 1789 to the Present
**Vallette, Marguerite Eymery**
1860-1953 ............................... **TCLC 67**
See Rachilde
See also CA 182; DLB 123, 192
**Valle Y Pena, Ramon del**
See Valle-Inclan, Ramon (Maria) del

**Van Ash, Cay** 1918-1994 .................. **CLC 34**
See also CA 220

**Vanbrugh, Sir John** 1664-1726 ........... **LC 21**
See also BRW 2; DAM DRAM; DLB 80;
IDTP; RGEL 2

**Van Campen, Karl**
See Campbell, John W(ood, Jr.)

**Vance, Gerald**
See Silverberg, Robert

**Vance, Jack** ........................................ **CLC 35**
See Vance, John Holbrook
See also DLB 8; FANT; SCFW 2; SFW 4;
SUFW 1, 2

**Vance, John Holbrook** 1916-
See Queen, Ellery; Vance, Jack
See also CA 29-32R; CANR 17, 65; CMW
4; MTCW 1

**Van Den Bogarde, Derek Jules Gaspard
Ulric Niven** 1921-1999 ............. **CLC 14**
See Bogarde, Dirk
See also CA 77-80; 179

**Vandenburgh, Jane** .......................... **CLC 59**
See also CA 168

**Vanderhaeghe, Guy** 1951- ................. **CLC 41**
See also BPFB 3; CA 113; CANR 72

**van der Post, Laurens (Jan)**
1906-1996 ...................................... **CLC 5**
See also AFW; CA 5-8R; 155; CANR 35;
CN 7; DLB 204; RGEL 2

**van de Wetering, Janwillem** 1931- ... **CLC 47**
See also CA 49-52; CANR 4, 62, 90; CMW
4

**Van Dine, S. S.** ............................... **TCLC 23**
See Wright, Willard Huntington
See also DLB 306; MSW

**Van Doren, Carl (Clinton)**
1885-1950 .................................... **TCLC 18**
See also CA 111; 168

**Van Doren, Mark** 1894-1972 ........ **CLC 6, 10**
See also CA 1-4R; 37-40R; CANR 3; DLB
45, 284; MTCW 1, 2; RGAL 4

**Van Druten, John (William)**
1901-1957 ...................................... **TCLC 2**
See also CA 104; 161; DLB 10; RGAL 4

**Van Duyn, Mona (Jane)** 1921- ...... **CLC 3, 7,
63, 116**
See also CA 9-12R; CANR 7, 38, 60, 116;
CP 7; CWP; DAM POET; DLB 5; PFS
20

**Van Dyne, Edith**
See Baum, L(yman) Frank

**van Itallie, Jean-Claude** 1936- ........... **CLC 3**
See also CA 45-48; CAAS 2; CAD; CANR
1, 48; CD 5; DLB 7

**Van Loot, Cornelius Obenchain**
See Roberts, Kenneth (Lewis)

**van Ostaijen, Paul** 1896-1928 ........ **TCLC 33**
See also CA 163

**Van Peebles, Melvin** 1932- ........... **CLC 2, 20**
See also BW 2, 3; CA 85-88; CANR 27,
67, 82; DAM MULT

**van Schendel, Arthur(-Francois-Emile)**
1874-1946 .................................. **TCLC 56**
See also EWL 3

**Vansittart, Peter** 1920- ...................... **CLC 42**
See also CA 1-4R; CANR 3, 49, 90; CN 7;
RHW

**Van Vechten, Carl** 1880-1964 ... **CLC 33; HR
3**
See also AMWS 2; CA 183; 89-92; DLB 4,
9, 51; RGAL 4

**van Vogt, A(lfred) E(lton)** 1912-2000 . **CLC 1**
See also BPFB 3; BYA 13, 14; CA 21-24R;
190; CANR 28; DLB 8, 251; SATA 14;
SATA-Obit 124; SCFW; SFW 4

**Vara, Madeleine**
See Jackson, Laura (Riding)

**Varda, Agnes** 1928- ........................... **CLC 16**
See also CA 116; 122

**Vargas Llosa, (Jorge) Mario (Pedro)**
1939- .... **CLC 3, 6, 9, 10, 15, 31, 42, 85,
181; HLC 2**
See Llosa, (Jorge) Mario (Pedro) Vargas
See also BPFB 3; CA 73-76; CANR 18, 32,
42, 67, 116; CDWLB 3; CWW 2; DA;
DA3; DAB; DAC; DAM MST, MULT,
NOV; DLB 145; DNFS 2; EWL 3; HW 1,
2; LAIT 5; LATS 1:2; LAW; LAWS 1;
MTCW 1, 2; RGWL 2; SSFS 14; TWA;
WLIT 1

**Varnhagen von Ense, Rahel**
1771-1833 ................................. **NCLC 130**
See also DLB 90

**Vasiliu, George**
See Bacovia, George

**Vasiliu, Gheorghe**
See Bacovia, George
See also CA 123; 189

**Vassa, Gustavus**
See Equiano, Olaudah

**Vassilikos, Vassilis** 1933- ................ **CLC 4, 8**
See also CA 81-84; CANR 75; EWL 3

**Vaughan, Henry** 1621-1695 ................. **LC 27**
See also BRW 2; DLB 131; PAB; RGEL 2

**Vaughn, Stephanie** ........................... **CLC 62**

**Vazov, Ivan (Minchov)** 1850-1921 . **TCLC 25**
See also CA 121; 167; CDWLB 4; DLB
147

**Veblen, Thorstein B(unde)**
1857-1929 .................................... **TCLC 31**
See also AMWS 1; CA 115; 165; DLB 246

**Vega, Lope de** 1562-1635 .... **HLCS 2; LC 23**
See also EW 2; RGWL 2, 3

**Vendler, Helen (Hennessy)** 1933- .... **CLC 138**
See also CA 41-44R; CANR 25, 72; MTCW
1, 2

**Venison, Alfred**
See Pound, Ezra (Weston Loomis)

**Ventsel, Elena Sergeevna** 1907-2002
See Grekova, I.
See also CA 154

**Verdi, Marie de**
See Mencken, H(enry) L(ouis)

**Verdu, Matilde**
See Cela, Camilo Jose

**Verga, Giovanni (Carmelo)**
1840-1922 .................. **SSC 21; TCLC 3**
See also CA 104; 123; CANR 101; EW 7;
EWL 3; RGSF 2; RGWL 2, 3

**Vergil** 70B.C.-19B.C. ... **CMLC 9, 40; PC 12;
WLCS**
See Virgil
See also AW 2; DA; DA3; DAB; DAC;
DAM MST, POET; EFS 1; LMFS 1

**Vergil, Polydore** c. 1470-1555 ........... **LC 108**
See also DLB 132

**Verhaeren, Emile (Adolphe Gustave)**
1855-1916 ................................. **TCLC 12**
See also CA 109; EWL 3; GFL 1789 to the
Present

**Verlaine, Paul (Marie)** 1844-1896 .. **NCLC 2,
51; PC 2, 32**
See also DAM POET; DLB 217; EW 7;
GFL 1789 to the Present; LMFS 2; RGWL
2, 3; TWA

**Verne, Jules (Gabriel)** 1828-1905 ... **TCLC 6,
52**
See also AAYA 16; BYA 4; CA 110; 131;
CLR 88; DA3; DLB 123; GFL 1789 to
the Present; JRDA; LAIT 2; LMFS 2;
MAICYA 1, 2; RGWL 2, 3; SATA 21;
SCFW; SFW 4; TWA; WCH

**Verus, Marcus Annius**
See Aurelius, Marcus

**Very, Jones** 1813-1880 ...................... **NCLC 9**
See also DLB 1, 243; RGAL 4

**Vesaas, Tarjei** 1897-1970 .................. **CLC 48**
See also CA 190; 29-32R; DLB 297; EW
11; EWL 3; RGWL 3

**Vialis, Gaston**
See Simenon, Georges (Jacques Christian)

**Vian, Boris** 1920-1959(?) .................. **TCLC 9**
See also CA 106; 164; CANR 111; DLB
72; EWL 3; GFL 1789 to the Present;
MTCW 2; RGWL 2, 3

**Viaud, (Louis Marie) Julien** 1850-1923
See Loti, Pierre
See also CA 107

**Vicar, Henry**
See Felsen, Henry Gregor

**Vicente, Gil** 1465-c. 1536 .................... **LC 99**
See also DLB 287; RGWL 2, 3

**Vicker, Angus**
See Felsen, Henry Gregor

**Vidal, (Eugene Luther) Gore** 1925- .. **CLC 2,
4, 6, 8, 10, 22, 33, 72, 142**
See Box, Edgar
See also AITN 1; AMWS 4; BEST 90:2;
BPFB 3; CA 5-8R; CAD; CANR 13, 45,
65, 100, 132; CD 5; CDALBS; CN 7;
CPW; DA3; DAM NOV, POP; DFS 2;
DLB 6, 152; EWL 3; INT CANR-13;
MTCW 1, 2; RGAL 4; RHW; TUS

**Viereck, Peter (Robert Edwin)**
1916- ............................. **CLC 4; PC 27**
See also CA 1-4R; CANR 1, 47; CP 7; DLB
5; PFS 9, 14

**Vigny, Alfred (Victor) de**
1797-1863 ............. **NCLC 7, 102; PC 26**
See also DAM POET; DLB 119, 192, 217;
EW 5; GFL 1789 to the Present; RGWL
2, 3

**Vilakazi, Benedict Wallet**
1906-1947 .................................. **TCLC 37**
See also CA 168

**Villa, Jose Garcia** 1914-1997 .... **AAL; PC 22**
See also CA 25-28R; CANR 12, 118; EWL
3; EXPP

**Villa, Jose Garcia** 1914-1997
See Villa, Jose Garcia

**Villarreal, Jose Antonio** 1924- ........... **HLC 2**
See also CA 133; CANR 93; DAM MULT;
DLB 82; HW 1; LAIT 4; RGAL 4

**Villaurrutia, Xavier** 1903-1950 ...... **TCLC 80**
See also CA 192; EWL 3; HW 1; LAW

**Villaverde, Cirilo** 1812-1894 ........ **NCLC 121**
See also LAW

**Villehardouin, Geoffroi de**
1150(?)-1218(?) ....................... **CMLC 38**

**Villiers, George** 1628-1687 ................ **LC 107**
See also DLB 80; RGEL 2

**Villiers de l'Isle Adam, Jean Marie Mathias
Philippe Auguste** 1838-1889 ... **NCLC 3;
SSC 14**
See also DLB 123, 192; GFL 1789 to the
Present; RGSF 2

**Villon, Francois** 1431-1463(?) . **LC 62; PC 13**
See also DLB 208; EW 2; RGWL 2, 3;
TWA

**Vine, Barbara** ..................................... **CLC 50**
See Rendell, Ruth (Barbara)
See also BEST 90:4

**Vinge, Joan (Carol) D(ennison)**
1948- ............................. **CLC 30; SSC 24**
See also AAYA 32; BPFB 3; CA 93-96;
CANR 72; SATA 36, 113; SFW 4; YAW

**Viola, Herman J(oseph)** 1938- .......... **CLC 70**
See also CA 61-64; CANR 8, 23, 48, 91;
SATA 126

**Violis, G.**
See Simenon, Georges (Jacques Christian)

**Viramontes, Helena Maria** 1954- .... **HLCS 2**
See also CA 159; DLB 122; HW 2; LLW 1

**Virgil**
See Vergil
See also CDWLB 1; DLB 211; LAIT 1;
RGWL 2, 3; WP

**Visconti, Luchino** 1906-1976 ............. **CLC 16**
See also CA 81-84; 65-68; CANR 39

**Vitry, Jacques de**
See Jacques de Vitry

**Vittorini, Elio** 1908-1966 .......... **CLC 6, 9, 14**
See also CA 133; 25-28R; DLB 264; EW
12; EWL 3; RGWL 2, 3

**Vivekananda, Swami** 1863-1902 .... **TCLC 88**

**Vizenor, Gerald Robert** 1934- ....... **CLC 103;
NNAL**
See also CA 13-16R, 205; CAAE 205;
CAAS 22; CANR 5, 21, 44, 67; DAM
MULT; DLB 175, 227; MTCW 2; TCWW
2

**Vizinczey, Stephen** 1933- ................... **CLC 40**
See also CA 128; CCA 1; INT CA-128

**Vliet, R(ussell) G(ordon)**
1929-1984 ................................. **CLC 22**
See also CA 37-40R; 112; CANR 18

**Vogau, Boris Andreyevich** 1894-1938
See Pilnyak, Boris
See also CA 123; 218

**Vogel, Paula A(nne)** 1951- ... **CLC 76; DC 19**
See also CA 108; CAD; CANR 119; CD 5;
CWD; DFS 14; RGAL 4

**Voigt, Cynthia** 1942- .......................... **CLC 30**
See also AAYA 3, 30; BYA 1, 3, 6, 7, 8;
CA 106; CANR 18, 37, 40, 94; CLR 13,
48; INT CANR-18; JRDA; LAIT 5; MAI-
CYA 1, 2; MAICYAS 1; SATA 48, 79,
116; SATA-Brief 33; WYA; YAW

**Voigt, Ellen Bryant** 1943- .................. **CLC 54**
See also CA 69-72; CANR 11, 29, 55, 115;
CP 7; CSW; CWP; DLB 120

**Voinovich, Vladimir (Nikolaevich)**
1932- ............................. **CLC 10, 49, 147**
See also CA 81-84; CAAS 12; CANR 33,
67; CWW 2; DLB 302; MTCW 1

**Vollmann, William T.** 1959- ............... **CLC 89**
See also CA 134; CANR 67, 116; CPW;
DA3; DAM NOV, POP; MTCW 2

**Voloshinov, V. N.**
See Bakhtin, Mikhail Mikhailovich

**Voltaire** 1694-1778 ......... **LC 14, 79; SSC 12;
WLC**
See also BYA 13; DA; DA3; DAB; DAC;
DAM DRAM, MST; EW 4; GFL Begin-
nings to 1789; LATS 1:1; LMFS 1; NFS
7; RGWL 2, 3; TWA

**von Aschendrof, Baron Ignatz**
See Ford, Ford Madox

**von Chamisso, Adelbert**
See Chamisso, Adelbert von

**von Daeniken, Erich** 1935- ............... **CLC 30**
See also AITN 1; CA 37-40R; CANR 17,
44

**von Daniken, Erich**
See von Daeniken, Erich

**von Hartmann, Eduard**
1842-1906 ................................. **TCLC 96**

**von Hayek, Friedrich August**
See Hayek, F(riedrich) A(ugust von)

**von Heidenstam, (Carl Gustaf) Verner**
See Heidenstam, (Carl Gustaf) Verner von

**von Heyse, Paul (Johann Ludwig)**
See Heyse, Paul (Johann Ludwig von)

**von Hofmannsthal, Hugo**
See Hofmannsthal, Hugo von

**von Horvath, Odon**
See von Horvath, Odon

**von Horvath, Odon**
See von Horvath, Odon

**von Horvath, Odon** 1901-1938 ....... **TCLC 45**
See von Horvath, Oedoen
See also CA 118; 194; DLB 85, 124; RGWL
2, 3

**von Horvath, Oedoen**
See von Horvath, Odon
See also CA 184

**von Kleist, Heinrich**
See Kleist, Heinrich von

**von Liliencron, (Friedrich Adolf Axel)
Detlev**
See Liliencron, (Friedrich Adolf Axel) De-
tlev von

**Vonnegut, Kurt, Jr.** 1922- . **CLC 1, 2, 3, 4, 5,
8, 12, 22, 40, 60, 111; SSC 8; WLC**
See also AAYA 6, 44; AITN 1; AMWS 2;
BEST 90:4; BPFB 3; BYA 3, 14; CA
1-4R; CANR 1, 25, 49, 75, 92; CDALB
1968-1988; CN 7; CPW 1; DA; DA3;
DAB; DAC; DAM MST, NOV, POP;
DLB 2, 8, 152; DLBD 3; DLBY 1980;
EWL 3; EXPN; EXPS; LAIT 4; LMFS 2;
MTCW 1, 2; NFS 3; RGAL 4; SCFW;
SFW 4; SSFS 5; TUS; YAW

**Von Rachen, Kurt**
See Hubbard, L(afayette) Ron(ald)

**von Rezzori (d'Arezzo), Gregor**
See Rezzori (d'Arezzo), Gregor von

**von Sternberg, Josef**
See Sternberg, Josef von

**Vorster, Gordon** 1924- ....................... **CLC 34**
See also CA 133

**Vosce, Trudie**
See Ozick, Cynthia

**Voznesensky, Andrei (Andreievich)**
1933- ............................. **CLC 1, 15, 57**
See Voznesensky, Andrey
See also CA 89-92; CANR 37; CWW 2;
DAM POET; MTCW 1

**Voznesensky, Andrey**
See Voznesensky, Andrei (Andreievich)
See also EWL 3

**Wace, Robert** c. 1100-c. 1175 ........ **CMLC 55**
See also DLB 146

**Waddington, Miriam** 1917-2004 ....... **CLC 28**
See also CA 21-24R; 225; CANR 12, 30;
CCA 1; CP 7; DLB 68

**Wagman, Fredrica** 1937- ..................... **CLC 7**
See also CA 97-100; INT CA-97-100

**Wagner, Linda W.**
See Wagner-Martin, Linda (C.)

**Wagner, Linda Welshimer**
See Wagner-Martin, Linda (C.)

**Wagner, Richard** 1813-1883 ..... **NCLC 9, 119**
See also DLB 129; EW 6

**Wagner-Martin, Linda (C.)** 1936- .... **CLC 50**
See also CA 159

**Wagoner, David (Russell)** 1926- .... **CLC 3, 5,
15; PC 33**
See also AMWS 9; CA 1-4R; CAAS 3;
CANR 2, 71; CN 7; CP 7; DLB 5, 256;
SATA 14; TCWW 2

**Wah, Fred(erick James)** 1939- ......... **CLC 44**
See also CA 107; 141; CP 7; DLB 60

**Wahloo, Per** 1926-1975 ....................... **CLC 7**
See also BPFB 3; CA 61-64; CANR 73;
CMW 4; MSW

**Wahloo, Peter**
See Wahloo, Per

**Wain, John (Barrington)** 1925-1994 . **CLC 2,
11, 15, 46**
See also CA 5-8R; 145; CAAS 4; CANR
23, 54; CDBLB 1960 to Present; DLB 15,
27, 139, 155; EWL 3; MTCW 1, 2

**Wajda, Andrzej** 1926- ........................ **CLC 16**
See also CA 102

**Wakefield, Dan** 1932- .......................... **CLC 7**
See also CA 21-24R, 211; CAAE 211;
CAAS 7; CN 7

**Wakefield, Herbert Russell**
1888-1965 ............................... **TCLC 120**
See also CA 5-8R; CANR 77; HGG; SUFW

**Wakoski, Diane** 1937- ...... **CLC 2, 4, 7, 9, 11,
40; PC 15**
See also CA 13-16R, 216; CAAE 216;
CAAS 1; CANR 9, 60, 106; CP 7; CWP;
DAM POET; DLB 5; INT CANR-9;
MTCW 2

**Wakoski-Sherbell, Diane**
See Wakoski, Diane

**Walcott, Derek (Alton)** 1930- ... **BLC 3; CLC
2, 4, 9, 14, 25, 42, 67, 76, 160; DC 7;
PC 46**
See also BW 2; CA 89-92; CANR 26, 47,
75, 80, 130; CBD; CD 5; CDWLB 3; CP
7; DA3; DAB; DAC; DAM MST, MULT,
POET; DLB 117; DLBY 1981; DNFS 1;
EFS 1; EWL 3; LMFS 2; MTCW 1, 2;
PFS 6; RGEL 2; TWA; WWE 1

**Waldman, Anne (Lesley)** 1945- .......... **CLC 7**
See also BG 3; CA 37-40R; CAAS 17;
CANR 34, 69, 116; CP 7; CWP; DLB 16

**Waldo, E. Hunter**
See Sturgeon, Theodore (Hamilton)

**Waldo, Edward Hamilton**
See Sturgeon, Theodore (Hamilton)

**Walker, Alice (Malsenior)** 1944- ........ **BLC 3;
CLC 5, 6, 9, 19, 27, 46, 58, 103, 167;
PC 30; SSC 5; WLCS**
See also AAYA 3, 33; AFAW 1, 2; AMWS
3; BEST 89:4; BPFB 3; BW 2, 3; CA 37-
40R; CANR 9, 27, 49, 66, 82, 131;
CDALB 1968-1988; CN 7; CPW; CSW;
DA; DA3; DAB; DAC; DAM MST,
MULT, NOV, POET, POP; DLB 6, 33,
143; EWL 3; EXPN; EXPS; FW; INT
CANR-27; LAIT 3; MAWW; MTCW 1,
2; NFS 5; RGAL 4; RGSF 2; SATA 31;
SSFS 2, 11; TUS; YAW

**Walker, David Harry** 1911-1992 ...... **CLC 14**
See also CA 1-4R; 137; CANR 1; CWRI 5;
SATA 8; SATA-Obit 71

**Walker, Edward Joseph** 1934-2004
See Walker, Ted
See also CA 21-24R; 226; CANR 12, 28,
53; CP 7

**Walker, George F.** 1947- ............. **CLC 44, 61**
See also CA 103; CANR 21, 43, 59; CD 5;
DAB; DAC; DAM MST; DLB 60

**Walker, Joseph A.** 1935- ................... **CLC 19**
See also BW 1, 3; CA 89-92; CAD; CANR
26; CD 5; DAM DRAM, MST; DFS 12;
DLB 38

**Walker, Margaret (Abigail)**
1915-1998 ........ **BLC; CLC 1, 6; PC 20;
TCLC 129**
See also AFAW 1, 2; BW 2, 3; CA 73-76;
172; CANR 26, 54, 76; CN 7; CP 7;
CSW; DAM MULT; DLB 76, 152; EXPP;
FW; MTCW 1, 2; RGAL 4; RHW

**Walker, Ted** ........................................ **CLC 13**
See Walker, Edward Joseph
See also DLB 40

**Wallace, David Foster** 1962- ... **CLC 50, 114;
SSC 68**
See also AAYA 50; AMWS 10; CA 132;
CANR 59, 133; DA3; MTCW 2

**Wallace, Dexter**
See Masters, Edgar Lee

**Wallace, (Richard Horatio) Edgar**
1875-1932 ................................. **TCLC 57**
See also CA 115; 218; CMW 4; DLB 70;
MSW; RGEL 2

**Wallace, Irving** 1916-1990 ............ **CLC 7, 13**
See also AITN 1; BPFB 3; CA 1-4R; 132;
CAAS 1; CANR 1, 27; CPW; DAM NOV,
POP; INT CANR-27; MTCW 1, 2

**Wallant, Edward Lewis** 1926-1962 ... **CLC 5, 10**
See also CA 1-4R; CANR 22; DLB 2, 28, 143, 299; EWL 3; MTCW 1, 2; RGAL 4

**Wallas, Graham** 1858-1932 ........... **TCLC 91**

**Waller, Edmund** 1606-1687 ................. **LC 86**
See also BRW 2; DAM POET; DLB 126; PAB; RGEL 2

**Walley, Byron**
See Card, Orson Scott

**Walpole, Horace** 1717-1797 ............. **LC 2, 49**
See also BRW 3; DLB 39, 104, 213; HGG; LMFS 1; RGEL 2; SUFW 1; TEA

**Walpole, Hugh (Seymour)**
1884-1941 .................................. **TCLC 5**
See also CA 104; 165; DLB 34; HGG; MTCW 2; RGEL 2; RHW

**Walrond, Eric (Derwent)** 1898-1966 .... **HR 3**
See also BW 1; CA 125; DLB 51

**Walser, Martin** 1927- ................. **CLC 27, 183**
See also CA 57-60; CANR 8, 46; CWW 2; DLB 75, 124; EWL 3

**Walser, Robert** 1878-1956 ..... **SSC 20; TCLC 18**
See also CA 118; 165; CANR 100; DLB 66; EWL 3

**Walsh, Gillian Paton**
See Paton Walsh, Gillian

**Walsh, Jill Paton** ............................... **CLC 35**
See Paton Walsh, Gillian
See also CLR 2, 65; WYA

**Walter, Villiam Christian**
See Andersen, Hans Christian

**Walters, Anna L(ee)** 1946- ................. **NNAL**
See also CA 73-76

**Walther von der Vogelweide** c. 1170-1228 ........................... **CMLC 56**

**Walton, Izaak** 1593-1683 ..................... **LC 72**
See also BRW 2; CDBLB Before 1660; DLB 151, 213; RGEL 2

**Wambaugh, Joseph (Aloysius), Jr.** 1937- ......................................... **CLC 3, 18**
See also AITN 1; BEST 89:3; BPFB 3; CA 33-36R; CANR 42, 65, 115; CMW 4; CPW 1; DA3; DAM NOV, POP; DLB 6; DLBY 1983; MSW; MTCW 1, 2

**Wang Wei** 699(?)-761(?) ...................... **PC 18**
See also TWA

**Warburton, William** 1698-1779 ........... **LC 97**
See also DLB 104

**Ward, Arthur Henry Sarsfield** 1883-1959
See Rohmer, Sax
See also CA 108; 173; CMW 4; HGG

**Ward, Douglas Turner** 1930- ........... **CLC 19**
See also BW 1; CA 81-84; CAD; CANR 27; CD 5; DLB 7, 38

**Ward, E. D.**
See Lucas, E(dward) V(errall)

**Ward, Mrs. Humphry** 1851-1920
See Ward, Mary Augusta
See also RGEL 2

**Ward, Mary Augusta** 1851-1920 ... **TCLC 55**
See Ward, Mrs. Humphry
See also DLB 18

**Ward, Peter**
See Faust, Frederick (Schiller)

**Warhol, Andy** 1928(?)-1987 ............. **CLC 20**
See also AAYA 12; BEST 89:4; CA 89-92; 121; CANR 34

**Warner, Francis (Robert le Plastrier)** 1937- ......................................... **CLC 14**
See also CA 53-56; CANR 11

**Warner, Marina** 1946- ....................... **CLC 59**
See also CA 65-68; CANR 21, 55, 118; CN 7; DLB 194

**Warner, Rex (Ernest)** 1905-1986 ...... **CLC 45**
See also CA 89-92; 119; DLB 15; RGEL 2; RHW

**Warner, Susan (Bogert)** 1819-1885 ........................ **NCLC 31, 146**
See also DLB 3, 42, 239, 250, 254

**Warner, Sylvia (Constance) Ashton**
See Ashton-Warner, Sylvia (Constance)

**Warner, Sylvia Townsend** 1893-1978 .. **CLC 7, 19; SSC 23; TCLC 131**
See also BRWS 7; CA 61-64; 77-80; CANR 16, 60, 104; DLB 34, 139; EWL 3; FANT; FW; MTCW 1, 2; RGEL 2; RGSF 2; RHW

**Warren, Mercy Otis** 1728-1814 ..... **NCLC 13**
See also DLB 31, 200; RGAL 4; TUS

**Warren, Robert Penn** 1905-1989 .. **CLC 1, 4, 6, 8, 10, 13, 18, 39, 53, 59; PC 37; SSC 4, 58; WLC**
See also AITN 1; AMW; AMWC 2; BPFB 3; BYA 1; CA 13-16R; 129; CANR 10, 47; CDALB 1968-1988; DA; DA3; DAB; DAC; DAM MST, NOV, POET; DLB 2, 48, 152; DLBY 1980, 1989; EWL 3; INT CANR-10; MTCW 1, 2; NFS 13; RGAL 4; RGSF 2; RHW; SATA 46; SATA-Obit 63; SSFS 8; TUS

**Warrigal, Jack**
See Furphy, Joseph

**Warshofsky, Isaac**
See Singer, Isaac Bashevis

**Warton, Joseph** 1722-1800 ........... **NCLC 118**
See also DLB 104, 109; RGEL 2

**Warton, Thomas** 1728-1790 ......... **LC 15, 82**
See also DAM POET; DLB 104, 109; RGEL 2

**Waruk, Kona**
See Harris, (Theodore) Wilson

**Warung, Price** ............................... **TCLC 45**
See Astley, William
See also DLB 230; RGEL 2

**Warwick, Jarvis**
See Garner, Hugh
See also CCA 1

**Washington, Alex**
See Harris, Mark

**Washington, Booker T(aliaferro)** 1856-1915 ................... **BLC 3; TCLC 10**
See also BW 1; CA 114; 125; DA3; DAM MULT; LAIT 2; RGAL 4; SATA 28

**Washington, George** 1732-1799 .......... **LC 25**
See also DLB 31

**Wassermann, (Karl) Jakob** 1873-1934 .................................. **TCLC 6**
See also CA 104; 163; DLB 66; EWL 3

**Wasserstein, Wendy** 1950- ... **CLC 32, 59, 90, 183; DC 4**
See also CA 121; 129; CABS 3; CAD; CANR 53, 75, 128; CD 5; CWD; DA3; DAM DRAM; DFS 5, 17; DLB 228; EWL 3; FW; INT CA-129; MTCW 2; SATA 94

**Waterhouse, Keith (Spencer)** 1929- . **CLC 47**
See also CA 5-8R; CANR 38, 67, 109; CBD; CN 7; DLB 13, 15; MTCW 1, 2

**Waters, Frank (Joseph)** 1902-1995 .. **CLC 88**
See also CA 5-8R; 149; CAAS 13; CANR 3, 18, 63, 121; DLB 212; DLBY 1986; RGAL 4; TCWW 2

**Waters, Mary C.** ............................... **CLC 70**

**Waters, Roger** 1944- ........................ **CLC 35**

**Watkins, Frances Ellen**
See Harper, Frances Ellen Watkins

**Watkins, Gerrold**
See Malzberg, Barry N(athaniel)

**Watkins, Gloria Jean** 1952(?)- .......... **CLC 94**
See also BW 2; CA 143; CANR 87, 126; DLB 246; MTCW 2; SATA 115

**Watkins, Paul** 1964- ......................... **CLC 55**
See also CA 132; CANR 62, 98

**Watkins, Vernon Phillips** 1906-1967 ........................... **CLC 43**
See also CA 9-10; 25-28R; CAP 1; DLB 20; EWL 3; RGEL 2

**Watson, Irving S.**
See Mencken, H(enry) L(ouis)

**Watson, John H.**
See Farmer, Philip Jose

**Watson, Richard F.**
See Silverberg, Robert

**Watts, Ephraim**
See Horne, Richard Henry Hengist

**Watts, Isaac** 1674-1748 ....................... **LC 98**
See also DLB 95; RGEL 2; SATA 52

**Waugh, Auberon (Alexander)** 1939-2001 ................................. **CLC 7**
See also CA 45-48; 192; CANR 6, 22, 92; DLB 14, 194

**Waugh, Evelyn (Arthur St. John)** 1903-1966 .. **CLC 1, 3, 8, 13, 19, 27, 44, 107; SSC 41; WLC**
See also BPFB 3; BRW 7; CA 85-88; 25-28R; CANR 22; CDBLB 1914-1945; DA; DA3; DAB; DAC; DAM MST, NOV, POP; DLB 15, 162, 195; EWL 3; MTCW 1, 2; NFS 13, 17; RGEL 2; RGSF 2; TEA; WLIT 4

**Waugh, Harriet** 1944- ......................... **CLC 6**
See also CA 85-88; CANR 22

**Ways, C. R.**
See Blount, Roy (Alton), Jr.

**Waystaff, Simon**
See Swift, Jonathan

**Webb, Beatrice (Martha Potter)** 1858-1943 ................................. **TCLC 22**
See also CA 117; 162; DLB 190; FW

**Webb, Charles (Richard)** 1939- ......... **CLC 7**
See also CA 25-28R; CANR 114

**Webb, Frank J.** ............................... **NCLC 143**
See also DLB 50

**Webb, James H(enry), Jr.** 1946- ...... **CLC 22**
See also CA 81-84

**Webb, Mary Gladys (Meredith)** 1881-1927 ................................. **TCLC 24**
See also CA 182; 123; DLB 34; FW

**Webb, Mrs. Sidney**
See Webb, Beatrice (Martha Potter)

**Webb, Phyllis** 1927- ........................... **CLC 18**
See also CA 104; CANR 23; CCA 1; CP 7; CWP; DLB 53

**Webb, Sidney (James)** 1859-1947 .. **TCLC 22**
See also CA 117; 163; DLB 190

**Webber, Andrew Lloyd** ................... **CLC 21**
See Lloyd Webber, Andrew
See also DFS 7

**Weber, Lenora Mattingly** 1895-1971 ................................. **CLC 12**
See also CA 19-20; 29-32R; CAP 1; SATA 2; SATA-Obit 26

**Weber, Max** 1864-1920 ................... **TCLC 69**
See also CA 109; 189; DLB 296

**Webster, John** 1580(?)-1634(?) ...... **DC 2; LC 33, 84; WLC**
See also BRW 2; CDBLB Before 1660; DA; DAB; DAC; DAM DRAM, MST; DFS 17, 19; DLB 58; IDTP; RGEL 2; WLIT 3

**Webster, Noah** 1758-1843 ............... **NCLC 30**
See also DLB 1, 37, 42, 43, 73, 243

**Wedekind, (Benjamin) Frank(lin)** 1864-1918 ................................. **TCLC 7**
See also CA 104; 153; CANR 121, 122; CDWLB 2; DAM DRAM; DLB 118; EW 8; EWL 3; LMFS 2; RGWL 2, 3

**Wehr, Demaris** ............................... **CLC 65**

**Weidman, Jerome** 1913-1998 ............. **CLC 7**
See also AITN 2; CA 1-4R; 171; CAD; CANR 1; DLB 28

**Weil, Simone (Adolphine)**
1909-1943 .................................. **TCLC 23**
See also CA 117; 159; EW 12; EWL 3; FW;
GFL 1789 to the Present; MTCW 2

**Weininger, Otto** 1880-1903 ............. **TCLC 84**

**Weinstein, Nathan**
See West, Nathanael

**Weinstein, Nathan von Wallenstein**
See West, Nathanael

**Weir, Peter (Lindsay)** 1944- .............. **CLC 20**
See also CA 113; 123

**Weiss, Peter (Ulrich)** 1916-1982 .. **CLC 3, 15,**
**51; TCLC 152**
See also CA 45-48; 106; CANR 3; DAM
DRAM; DFS 3; DLB 69, 124; EWL 3;
RGWL 2, 3

**Weiss, Theodore (Russell)**
1916-2003 ........................... **CLC 3, 8, 14**
See also CA 9-12R; 189; 216; CAAE 189;
CAAS 2; CANR 46, 94; CP 7; DLB 5

**Welch, (Maurice) Denton**
1915-1948 ............................... **TCLC 22**
See also BRWS 8, 9; CA 121; 148; RGEL
2

**Welch, James (Phillip)** 1940-2003 ..... **CLC 6,**
**14, 52; NNAL**
See also CA 85-88; 219; CANR 42, 66, 107;
CN 7; CP 7; CPW; DAM MULT, POP;
DLB 175, 256; LATS 1:1; RGAL 4;
TCWW 2

**Weldon, Fay** 1931- . **CLC 6, 9, 11, 19, 36, 59,**
**122**
See also BRWS 4; CA 21-24R; CANR 16,
46, 63, 97; CDBLB 1960 to Present; CN
7; CPW; DAM POP; DLB 14, 194; EWL
3; FW; HGG; INT CANR-16; MTCW 1,
2; RGEL 2; RGSF 2

**Wellek, Rene** 1903-1995 ................... **CLC 28**
See also CA 5-8R; 150; CAAS 7; CANR 8;
DLB 63; EWL 3; INT CANR-8

**Weller, Michael** 1942- .............. **CLC 10, 53**
See also CA 85-88; CAD; CD 5

**Weller, Paul** 1958- .............................. **CLC 26**

**Wellershoff, Dieter** 1925- ................... **CLC 46**
See also CA 89-92; CANR 16, 37

**Welles, (George) Orson** 1915-1985 .. **CLC 20,**
**80**
See also AAYA 40; CA 93-96; 117

**Wellman, John McDowell** 1945-
See Wellman, Mac
See also CA 166; CD 5

**Wellman, Mac** ...................................... **CLC 65**
See Wellman, John McDowell; Wellman,
John McDowell
See also CAD; RGAL 4

**Wellman, Manly Wade** 1903-1986 ... **CLC 49**
See also CA 1-4R; 118; CANR 6, 16, 44;
FANT; SATA 6; SATA-Obit 47; SFW 4;
SUFW

**Wells, Carolyn** 1869(?)-1942 ......... **TCLC 35**
See also CA 113; 185; CMW 4; DLB 11

**Wells, H(erbert) G(eorge)** 1866-1946 . **SSC 6,**
**70; TCLC 6, 12, 19, 133; WLC**
See also AAYA 18; BPFB 3; BRW 6; CA
110; 121; CDBLB 1914-1945; CLR 64;
DA; DA3; DAB; DAC; DAM MST, NOV;
DLB 34, 70, 156, 178; EWL 3; EXPS;
HGG; LAIT 3; LMFS 2; MTCW 1, 2;
NFS 17, 20; RGEL 2; RGSF 2; SATA 20;
SCFW; SFW 4; SSFS 3; SUFW; TEA;
WCH; WLIT 4; YAW

**Wells, Rosemary** 1943- ...................... **CLC 12**
See also AAYA 13; BYA 7, 8; CA 85-88;
CANR 48, 120; CLR 16, 69; CWRI 5;
MAICYA 1, 2; SAAS 1; SATA 18, 69,
114; YAW

**Wells-Barnett, Ida B(ell)**
1862-1931 ............................. **TCLC 125**
See also CA 182; DLB 23, 221

**Welsh, Irvine** 1958- ......................... **CLC 144**
See also CA 173; DLB 271

**Welty, Eudora (Alice)** 1909-2001 .. **CLC 1, 2,**
**5, 14, 22, 33, 105; SSC 1, 27, 51; WLC**
See also AAYA 48; AMW; AMWR 1; BPFB
3; CA 9-12R; 199; CABS 1; CANR 32,
65, 128; CDALB 1941-1968; CN 7; CSW;
DA; DA3; DAB; DAC; DAM MST, NOV;
DLB 2, 102, 143; DLBD 12; DLBY 1987,
2001; EWL 3; EXPS; HGG; LAIT 3;
MAWW; MTCW 1, 2; NFS 13, 15; RGAL
4; RGSF 2; RHW; SSFS 2, 10; TUS

**Wen I-to** 1899-1946 ......................... **TCLC 28**
See also EWL 3

**Wentworth, Robert**
See Hamilton, Edmond

**Werfel, Franz (Viktor)** 1890-1945 ... **TCLC 8**
See also CA 104; 161; DLB 81, 124; EWL
3; RGWL 2, 3

**Wergeland, Henrik Arnold**
1808-1845 .................................. **NCLC 5**

**Wersba, Barbara** 1932- ..................... **CLC 30**
See also AAYA 2, 30; BYA 6, 12, 13; CA
29-32R, 182; CAAE 182; CANR 16, 38;
CLR 3, 78; DLB 52; JRDA; MAICYA 1,
2; SAAS 2; SATA 1, 58; SATA-Essay 103;
WYA; YAW

**Wertmueller, Lina** 1928- .................. **CLC 16**
See also CA 97-100; CANR 39, 78

**Wescott, Glenway** 1901-1987 .. **CLC 13; SSC**
**35**
See also CA 13-16R; 121; CANR 23, 70;
DLB 4, 9, 102; RGAL 4

**Wesker, Arnold** 1932- ............... **CLC 3, 5, 42**
See also CA 1-4R; CAAS 7; CANR 1, 33;
CBD; CD 5; CDBLB 1960 to Present;
DAB; DAM DRAM; DLB 13; EWL 3;
MTCW 1; RGEL 2; TEA

**Wesley, John** 1703-1791 ...................... **LC 88**
See also DLB 104

**Wesley, Richard (Errol)** 1945- ........... **CLC 7**
See also BW 1; CA 57-60; CAD; CANR
27; CD 5; DLB 38

**Wessel, Johan Herman** 1742-1785 ........ **LC 7**
See also DLB 300

**West, Anthony (Panther)**
1914-1987 ................................. **CLC 50**
See also CA 45-48; 124; CANR 3, 19; DLB
15

**West, C. P.**
See Wodehouse, P(elham) G(renville)

**West, Cornel (Ronald)** 1953- .... **BLCS; CLC**
**134**
See also CA 144; CANR 91; DLB 246

**West, Delno C(loyde), Jr.** 1936- ........ **CLC 70**
See also CA 57-60

**West, Dorothy** 1907-1998 .. **HR 3; TCLC 108**
See also BW 2; CA 143; 169; DLB 76

**West, (Mary) Jessamyn** 1902-1984 ... **CLC 7,**
**17**
See also CA 9-12R; 112; CANR 27; DLB
6; DLBY 1984; MTCW 1, 2; RGAL 4;
RHW; SATA-Obit 37; TCWW 2; TUS;
YAW

**West, Morris**
See West, Morris L(anglo)
See also DLB 289

**West, Morris L(anglo)** 1916-1999 ..... **CLC 6,**
**33**
See West, Morris
See also BPFB 3; CA 5-8R; 187; CANR
24, 49, 64; CN 7; CPW; MTCW 1, 2

**West, Nathanael** 1903-1940 ... **SSC 16; TCLC**
**1, 14, 44**
See also AMW; AMWR 2; BPFB 3; CA
104; 125; CDALB 1929-1941; DA3; DLB
4, 9, 28; EWL 3; MTCW 1, 2; NFS 16;
RGAL 4; TUS

**West, Owen**
See Koontz, Dean R(ay)

**West, Paul** 1930- ......................... **CLC 7, 14, 96**
See also CA 13-16R; CAAS 7; CANR 22,
53, 76, 89; CN 7; DLB 14; INT CANR-
22; MTCW 2

**West, Rebecca** 1892-1983 ... **CLC 7, 9, 31, 50**
See also BPFB 3; BRWS 3; CA 5-8R; 109;
CANR 19; DLB 36; DLBY 1983; EWL
3; FW; MTCW 1, 2; NCFS 4; RGEL 2;
TEA

**Westall, Robert (Atkinson)**
1929-1993 ................................. **CLC 17**
See also AAYA 12; BYA 2, 6, 7, 8, 9, 15;
CA 69-72; 141; CANR 18, 68; CLR 13;
FANT; JRDA; MAICYA 1, 2; MAICYAS
1; SAAS 2; SATA 23, 69; SATA-Obit 75;
WYA; YAW

**Westermarck, Edward** 1862-1939 . **TCLC 87**

**Westlake, Donald E(dwin)** 1933- . **CLC 7, 33**
See also BPFB 3; CA 17-20R; CAAS 13;
CANR 16, 44, 65, 94; CMW 4; CPW;
DAM POP; INT CANR-16; MSW;
MTCW 2

**Westmacott, Mary**
See Christie, Agatha (Mary Clarissa)

**Weston, Allen**
See Norton, Andre

**Wetcheek, J. L.**
See Feuchtwanger, Lion

**Wetering, Janwillem van de**
See van de Wetering, Janwillem

**Wetherald, Agnes Ethelwyn**
1857-1940 ................................. **TCLC 81**
See also CA 202; DLB 99

**Wetherell, Elizabeth**
See Warner, Susan (Bogert)

**Whale, James** 1889-1957 ................. **TCLC 63**

**Whalen, Philip (Glenn)** 1923-2002 .... **CLC 6,**
**29**
See also BG 3; CA 9-12R; 209; CANR 5,
39; CP 7; DLB 16; WP

**Wharton, Edith (Newbold Jones)**
1862-1937 ... **SSC 6; TCLC 3, 9, 27, 53,**
**129, 149; WLC**
See also AAYA 25; AMW; AMWC 2;
AMWR 1; BPFB 3; CA 104; 132; CDALB
1865-1917; DA; DA3; DAB; DAC; DAM
MST, NOV; DLB 4, 9, 12, 78, 189; DLBD
13; EWL 3; EXPS; HGG; LAIT 2, 3;
LATS 1:1; MAWW; MTCW 1, 2; NFS 5,
11, 15, 20; RGAL 4; RGSF 2; RHW;
SSFS 6, 7; SUFW; TUS

**Wharton, James**
See Mencken, H(enry) L(ouis)

**Wharton, William (a pseudonym)** . **CLC 18,**
**37**
See also CA 93-96; DLBY 1980; INT CA-
93-96

**Wheatley (Peters), Phillis**
1753(?)-1784 ... **BLC 3; LC 3, 50; PC 3;**
**WLC**
See also AFAW 1, 2; CDALB 1640-1865;
DA; DA3; DAC; DAM MST, MULT,
POET; DLB 31, 50; EXPP; PFS 13;
RGAL 4

**Wheelock, John Hall** 1886-1978 ....... **CLC 14**
See also CA 13-16R; 77-80; CANR 14;
DLB 45

**Whim-Wham**
See Curnow, (Thomas) Allen (Monro)

**White, Babington**
See Braddon, Mary Elizabeth

**White, E(lwyn) B(rooks)**
1899-1985 ...................... **CLC 10, 34, 39**
See also AITN 2; AMWS 1; CA 13-16R;
116; CANR 16, 37; CDALBS; CLR 1, 21;
CPW; DA3; DAM POP; DLB 11, 22;

EWL 3; FANT; MAICYA 1, 2; MTCW 1, 2; NCFS 5; RGAL 4; SATA 2, 29, 100; SATA-Obit 44; TUS

**White, Edmund (Valentine III)**
1940- ................................ **CLC 27, 110**
See also AAYA 7; CA 45-48; CANR 3, 19, 36, 62, 107, 133; CN 7; DA3; DAM POP; DLB 227; MTCW 1, 2

**White, Hayden V.** 1928- ................ **CLC 148**
See also CA 128; DLB 246

**White, Patrick (Victor Martindale)**
1912-1990 ... **CLC 3, 4, 5, 7, 9, 18, 65, 69; SSC 39**
See also BRWS 1; CA 81-84; 132; CANR 43; DLB 260; EWL 3; MTCW 1; RGEL 2; RGSF 2; RHW; TWA; WWE 1

**White, Phyllis Dorothy James** 1920-
See James, P. D.
See also CA 21-24R; CANR 17, 43, 65, 112; CMW 4; CN 7; CPW; DA3; DAM POP; MTCW 1, 2; TEA

**White, T(erence) H(anbury)**
1906-1964 ................................ **CLC 30**
See also AAYA 22; BPFB 3; BYA 4, 5; CA 73-76; CANR 37; DLB 160; FANT; JRDA; LAIT 1; MAICYA 1, 2; RGEL 2; SATA 12; SUFW 1; YAW

**White, Terence de Vere** 1912-1994 ... **CLC 49**
See also CA 49-52; 145; CANR 3

**White, Walter**
See White, Walter F(rancis)

**White, Walter F(rancis)** 1893-1955 ... **BLC 3; HR 3; TCLC 15**
See also BW 1; CA 115; 124; DAM MULT; DLB 51

**White, William Hale** 1831-1913
See Rutherford, Mark
See also CA 121; 189

**Whitehead, Alfred North**
1861-1947 ................................ **TCLC 97**
See also CA 117; 165; DLB 100, 262

**Whitehead, E(dward) A(nthony)**
1933- ..................................... **CLC 5**
See also CA 65-68; CANR 58, 118; CBD; CD 5

**Whitehead, Ted**
See Whitehead, E(dward) A(nthony)

**Whiteman, Roberta J. Hill** 1947- ...... **NNAL**
See also CA 146

**Whitemore, Hugh (John)** 1936- ....... **CLC 37**
See also CA 132; CANR 77; CBD; CD 5; INT CA-132

**Whitman, Sarah Helen (Power)**
1803-1878 ................................ **NCLC 19**
See also DLB 1, 243

**Whitman, Walt(er)** 1819-1892 .. **NCLC 4, 31, 81; PC 3; WLC**
See also AAYA 42; AMW; AMWR 1; CDALB 1640-1865; DA; DA3; DAB; DAC; DAM MST, POET; DLB 3, 64, 224, 250; EXPP; LAIT 2; LMFS 1; PAB; PFS 2, 3, 13; RGAL 4; SATA 20; TUS; WP; WYAS 1

**Whitney, Phyllis A(yame)** 1903- ....... **CLC 42**
See also AAYA 36; AITN 2; BEST 90:3; CA 1-4R; CANR 3, 25, 38, 60; CLR 59; CMW 4; CPW; DA3; DAM POP; JRDA; MAICYA 1, 2; MTCW 2; RHW; SATA 1, 30; YAW

**Whittemore, (Edward) Reed, Jr.**
1919- ..................................... **CLC 4**
See also CA 9-12R, 219; CAAE 219; CAAS 8; CANR 4, 119; CP 7; DLB 5

**Whittier, John Greenleaf**
1807-1892 ................................ **NCLC 8, 59**
See also AMWS 1; DLB 1, 243; RGAL 4

**Whittlebot, Hernia**
See Coward, Noel (Peirce)

**Wicker, Thomas Grey** 1926-
See Wicker, Tom
See also CA 65-68; CANR 21, 46

**Wicker, Tom** ................................ **CLC 7**
See Wicker, Thomas Grey

**Wideman, John Edgar** 1941- ... **BLC 3; CLC 5, 34, 36, 67, 122; SSC 62**
See also AFAW 1, 2; AMWS 10; BPFB 4; BW 2, 3; CA 85-88; CANR 14, 42, 67, 109; CN 7; DAM MULT; DLB 33, 143; MTCW 2; RGAL 4; RGSF 2; SSFS 6, 12

**Wiebe, Rudy (Henry)** 1934- .. **CLC 6, 11, 14, 138**
See also CA 37-40R; CANR 42, 67, 123; CN 7; DAC; DAM MST; DLB 60; RHW

**Wieland, Christoph Martin**
1733-1813 ................................ **NCLC 17**
See also DLB 97; EW 4; LMFS 1; RGWL 2, 3

**Wiene, Robert** 1881-1938 ............... **TCLC 56**

**Wieners, John** 1934- ...................... **CLC 7**
See also BG 3; CA 13-16R; CP 7; DLB 16; WP

**Wiesel, Elie(zer)** 1928- ....... **CLC 3, 5, 11, 37, 165; WLCS**
See also AAYA 7, 54; AITN 1; CA 5-8R; CAAS 4; CANR 8, 40, 65, 125; CDALBS; CWW 2; DA; DA3; DAB; DAC; DAM MST, NOV; DLB 83, 299; DLBY 1987; EWL 3; INT CANR-8; LAIT 4; MTCW 1, 2; NCFS 4; NFS 4; RGWL 3; SATA 56; YAW

**Wiggins, Marianne** 1947- ................. **CLC 57**
See also BEST 89:3; CA 130; CANR 60

**Wigglesworth, Michael** 1631-1705 .... **LC 106**
See also DLB 24; RGAL 4

**Wiggs, Susan** ................................ **CLC 70**
See also CA 201

**Wight, James Alfred** 1916-1995
See Herriot, James
See also CA 77-80; SATA 55; SATA-Brief 44

**Wilbur, Richard (Purdy)** 1921- ..... **CLC 3, 6, 9, 14, 53, 110; PC 51**
See also AMWS 3; CA 1-4R; CABS 2; CANR 2, 29, 76, 93; CDALBS; CP 7; DA; DAB; DAC; DAM MST, POET; DLB 5, 169; EWL 3; EXPP; INT CANR-29; MTCW 1, 2; PAB; PFS 11, 12, 16; RGAL 4; SATA 9, 108; WP

**Wild, Peter** 1940- ............................ **CLC 14**
See also CA 37-40R; CP 7; DLB 5

**Wilde, Oscar (Fingal O'Flahertie Wills)**
1854(?)-1900 ..... **DC 17; SSC 11; TCLC 1, 8, 23, 41; WLC**
See also AAYA 49; BRW 5; BRWC 1, 2; BRWR 2; BYA 15; CA 104; 119; CANR 112; CDBLB 1890-1914; DA; DA3; DAB; DAC; DAM DRAM, MST, NOV; DFS 4, 8, 9; DLB 10, 19, 34, 57, 141, 156, 190; EXPS; FANT; LATS 1:1; NFS 20; RGEL 2; RGSF 2; SATA 24; SSFS 7; SUFW; TEA; WCH; WLIT 4

**Wilder, Billy** ................................ **CLC 20**
See Wilder, Samuel
See also DLB 26

**Wilder, Samuel** 1906-2002
See Wilder, Billy
See also CA 89-92; 205

**Wilder, Stephen**
See Marlowe, Stephen

**Wilder, Thornton (Niven)**
1897-1975 .. **CLC 1, 5, 6, 10, 15, 35, 82; DC 1, 24; WLC**
See also AAYA 29; AITN 2; AMW; CA 13-16R; 61-64; CAD; CANR 40, 132; CDALBS; DA; DA3; DAB; DAC; DAM DRAM, MST, NOV; DFS 1, 4, 16; DLB 4, 7, 9, 228; DLBY 1997; EWL 3; LAIT 3; MTCW 1, 2; RGAL 4; RHW; WYAS 1

**Wilding, Michael** 1942- ...... **CLC 73; SSC 50**
See also CA 104; CANR 24, 49, 106; CN 7; RGSF 2

**Wiley, Richard** 1944- ...................... **CLC 44**
See also CA 121; 129; CANR 71

**Wilhelm, Kate** ................................ **CLC 7**
See Wilhelm, Katie (Gertrude)
See also AAYA 20; BYA 16; CAAS 5; DLB 8; INT CANR-17; SCFW 2

**Wilhelm, Katie (Gertrude)** 1928-
See Wilhelm, Kate
See also CA 37-40R; CANR 17, 36, 60, 94; MTCW 1; SFW 4

**Wilkins, Mary**
See Freeman, Mary E(leanor) Wilkins

**Willard, Nancy** 1936- .................... **CLC 7, 37**
See also BYA 5; CA 89-92; CANR 10, 39, 68, 107; CLR 5; CWP; CWRI 5; DLB 5, 52; FANT; MAICYA 1, 2; MTCW 1; SATA 37, 71, 127; SATA-Brief 30; SUFW 2

**William of Malmesbury** c. 1090B.C.-c. 1140B.C. ................................ **CMLC 57**

**William of Ockham** 1290-1349 ..... **CMLC 32**

**Williams, Ben Ames** 1889-1953 ..... **TCLC 89**
See also CA 183; DLB 102

**Williams, C(harles) K(enneth)**
1936- ............................ **CLC 33, 56, 148**
See also CA 37-40R; CAAS 26; CANR 57, 106; CP 7; DAM POET; DLB 5

**Williams, Charles**
See Collier, James Lincoln

**Williams, Charles (Walter Stansby)**
1886-1945 ........................... **TCLC 1, 11**
See also BRWS 9; CA 104; 163; DLB 100, 153, 255; FANT; RGEL 2; SUFW 1

**Williams, Ella Gwendolen Rees**
See Rhys, Jean

**Williams, (George) Emlyn**
1905-1987 ................................ **CLC 15**
See also CA 104; 123; CANR 36; DAM DRAM; DLB 10, 77; IDTP; MTCW 1

**Williams, Hank** 1923-1953 ............. **TCLC 81**
See Williams, Hiram King

**Williams, Helen Maria**
1761-1827 ................................ **NCLC 135**
See also DLB 158

**Williams, Hiram Hank**
See Williams, Hank

**Williams, Hiram King**
See Williams, Hank
See also CA 188

**Williams, Hugo (Mordaunt)** 1942- ... **CLC 42**
See also CA 17-20R; CANR 45, 119; CP 7; DLB 40

**Williams, J. Walker**
See Wodehouse, P(elham) G(renville)

**Williams, John A(lfred)** 1925- . **BLC 3; CLC 5, 13**
See also AFAW 2; BW 2, 3; CA 53-56, 195; CAAE 195; CAAS 3; CANR 6, 26, 51, 118; CN 7; CSW; DAM MULT; DLB 2, 33; EWL 3; INT CANR-6; RGAL 4; SFW 4

**Williams, Jonathan (Chamberlain)**
1929- ..................................... **CLC 13**
See also CA 9-12R; CAAS 12; CANR 8, 108; CP 7; DLB 5

**Williams, Joy** 1944- ......................... **CLC 31**
See also CA 41-44R; CANR 22, 48, 97

**Williams, Norman** 1952- .................. **CLC 39**
See also CA 118

**Williams, Sherley Anne** 1944-1999 ... **BLC 3; CLC 89**
See also AFAW 2; BW 2, 3; CA 73-76; 185; CANR 25, 82; DAM MULT, POET; DLB 41; INT CANR-25; SATA 78; SATA-Obit 116

**Williams, Shirley**
    See Williams, Sherley Anne
**Williams, Tennessee** 1911-1983 . **CLC 1, 2, 5, 7, 8, 11, 15, 19, 30, 39, 45, 71, 111; DC 4; WLC**
    See also AAYA 31; AITN 1, 2; AMW; AMWC 1; CA 5-8R; 108; CABS 3; CAD; CANR 31, 132; CDALB 1941-1968; DA; DA3; DAB; DAC; DAM DRAM, MST; DFS 17; DLB 7; DLBD 4; DLBY 1983; EWL 3; GLL 1; LAIT 4; LATS 1:2; MTCW 1, 2; RGAL 4; TUS
**Williams, Thomas (Alonzo)**
    1926-1990 ............................ **CLC 14**
    See also CA 1-4R; 132; CANR 2
**Williams, William C.**
    See Williams, William Carlos
**Williams, William Carlos**
    1883-1963 .... **CLC 1, 2, 5, 9, 13, 22, 42, 67; PC 7; SSC 31**
    See also AAYA 46; AMW; AMWR 1; CA 89-92; CANR 34; CDALB 1917-1929; DA; DA3; DAB; DAC; DAM MST, POET; DLB 4, 16, 54, 86; EWL 3; EXPP; MTCW 1, 2; NCFS 4; PAB; PFS 1, 6, 11; RGAL 4; RGSF 2; TUS; WP
**Williamson, David (Keith)** 1942- ..... **CLC 56**
    See also CA 103; CANR 41; CD 5; DLB 289
**Williamson, Ellen Douglas** 1905-1984
    See Douglas, Ellen
    See also CA 17-20R; 114; CANR 39
**Williamson, Jack** ............................... **CLC 29**
    See Williamson, John Stewart
    See also CAAS 8; DLB 8; SCFW 2
**Williamson, John Stewart** 1908-
    See Williamson, Jack
    See also CA 17-20R; CANR 23, 70; SFW 4
**Willie, Frederick**
    See Lovecraft, H(oward) P(hillips)
**Willingham, Calder (Baynard, Jr.)**
    1922-1995 ............................... **CLC 5, 51**
    See also CA 5-8R; 147; CANR 3; CSW; DLB 2, 44; IDFW 3, 4; MTCW 1
**Willis, Charles**
    See Clarke, Arthur C(harles)
**Willy**
    See Colette, (Sidonie-Gabrielle)
**Willy, Colette**
    See Colette, (Sidonie-Gabrielle)
    See also GLL 1
**Wilmot, John** 1647-1680 ..................... **LC 75**
    See Rochester
    See also BRW 2; DLB 131; PAB
**Wilson, A(ndrew) N(orman)** 1950- .. **CLC 33**
    See also BRWS 6; CA 112; 122; CN 7; DLB 14, 155, 194; MTCW 2
**Wilson, Angus (Frank Johnstone)**
    1913-1991 . **CLC 2, 3, 5, 25, 34; SSC 21**
    See also BRWS 1; CA 5-8R; 134; CANR 21; DLB 15, 139, 155; EWL 3; MTCW 1, 2; RGEL 2; RGSF 2
**Wilson, August** 1945- ... **BLC 3; CLC 39, 50, 63, 118; DC 2; WLCS**
    See also AAYA 16; AFAW 2; AMWS 8; BW 2, 3; CA 115; 122; CAD; CANR 42, 54, 76, 128; CD 5; DA; DA3; DAB; DAC; DAM DRAM, MST, MULT; DFS 3, 7, 15, 17; DLB 228; EWL 3; LAIT 4; LATS 1:2; MTCW 1, 2; RGAL 4
**Wilson, Brian** 1942- ........................... **CLC 12**
**Wilson, Colin** 1931- ......................... **CLC 3, 14**
    See also CA 1-4R; CAAS 5; CANR 1, 22, 33, 77; CMW 4; CN 7; DLB 14, 194; HGG; MTCW 1; SFW 4
**Wilson, Dirk**
    See Pohl, Frederik

**Wilson, Edmund** 1895-1972 .. **CLC 1, 2, 3, 8, 24**
    See also AMW; CA 1-4R; 37-40R; CANR 1, 46, 110; DLB 63; EWL 3; MTCW 1, 2; RGAL 4; TUS
**Wilson, Ethel Davis (Bryant)**
    1888(?)-1980 ............................... **CLC 13**
    See also CA 102; DAC; DAM POET; DLB 68; MTCW 1; RGEL 2
**Wilson, Harriet**
    See Wilson, Harriet E. Adams
    See also DLB 239
**Wilson, Harriet E.**
    See Wilson, Harriet E. Adams
    See also DLB 243
**Wilson, Harriet E. Adams**
    1827(?)-1863(?) ......... **BLC 3; NCLC 78**
    See Wilson, Harriet; Wilson, Harriet E.
    See also DAM MULT; DLB 50
**Wilson, John** 1785-1854 ................... **NCLC 5**
**Wilson, John (Anthony) Burgess** 1917-1993
    See Burgess, Anthony
    See also CA 1-4R; 143; CANR 2, 46; DA3; DAC; DAM NOV; MTCW 1, 2; NFS 15; TEA
**Wilson, Lanford** 1937- .. **CLC 7, 14, 36, 197; DC 19**
    See also CA 17-20R; CABS 3; CAD; CANR 45, 96; CD 5; DAM DRAM; DFS 4, 9, 12, 16, 20; DLB 7; EWL 3; TUS
**Wilson, Robert M.** 1941- ................. **CLC 7, 9**
    See also CA 49-52; CAD; CANR 2, 41; CD 5; MTCW 1
**Wilson, Robert McLiam** 1964- ......... **CLC 59**
    See also CA 132; DLB 267
**Wilson, Sloan** 1920-2003 ................... **CLC 32**
    See also CA 1-4R; 216; CANR 1, 44; CN 7
**Wilson, Snoo** 1948- ........................... **CLC 33**
    See also CA 69-72; CBD; CD 5
**Wilson, William S(mith)** 1932- ......... **CLC 49**
    See also CA 81-84
**Wilson, (Thomas) Woodrow**
    1856-1924 ............................... **TCLC 79**
    See also CA 166; DLB 47
**Wilson and Warnke eds.** ................. **CLC 65**
**Winchilsea, Anne (Kingsmill) Finch**
    1661-1720
    See Finch, Anne
    See also RGEL 2
**Windham, Basil**
    See Wodehouse, P(elham) G(renville)
**Wingrove, David (John)** 1954- ......... **CLC 68**
    See also CA 133; SFW 4
**Winnemucca, Sarah** 1844-1891 .... **NCLC 79; NNAL**
    See also DAM MULT; DLB 175; RGAL 4
**Winstanley, Gerrard** 1609-1676 .......... **LC 52**
**Wintergreen, Jane**
    See Duncan, Sara Jeannette
**Winters, Janet Lewis** ........................ **CLC 41**
    See Lewis, Janet
    See also DLBY 1987
**Winters, (Arthur) Yvor** 1900-1968 .... **CLC 4, 8, 32**
    See also AMWS 2; CA 11-12; 25-28R; CAP 1; DLB 48; EWL 3; MTCW 1; RGAL 4
**Winterson, Jeanette** 1959- ........ **CLC 64, 158**
    See also BRWS 4; CA 136; CANR 58, 116; CN 7; CPW; DA3; DAM POP; DLB 207, 261; FANT; FW; GLL 1; MTCW 2; RHW
**Winthrop, John** 1588-1649 .......... **LC 31, 107**
    See also DLB 24, 30
**Wirth, Louis** 1897-1952 ................. **TCLC 92**
    See also CA 210
**Wiseman, Frederick** 1930- ............... **CLC 20**
    See also CA 159
**Wister, Owen** 1860-1938 ................ **TCLC 21**
    See also BPFB 3; CA 108; 162; DLB 9, 78, 186; RGAL 4; SATA 62; TCWW 2

**Wither, George** 1588-1667 ................... **LC 96**
    See also DLB 121; RGEL 2
**Witkacy**
    See Witkiewicz, Stanislaw Ignacy
**Witkiewicz, Stanislaw Ignacy**
    1885-1939 ................................. **TCLC 8**
    See also CA 105; 162; CDWLB 4; DLB 215; EW 10; EWL 3; RGWL 2, 3; SFW 4
**Wittgenstein, Ludwig (Josef Johann)**
    1889-1951 ................................. **TCLC 59**
    See also CA 113; 164; DLB 262; MTCW 2
**Wittig, Monique** 1935(?)-2003 .......... **CLC 22**
    See also CA 116; 135; 212; CWW 2; DLB 83; EWL 3; FW; GLL 1
**Wittlin, Jozef** 1896-1976 ................... **CLC 25**
    See also CA 49-52; 65-68; CANR 3; EWL 3
**Wodehouse, P(elham) G(renville)**
    1881-1975 . **CLC 1, 2, 5, 10, 22; SSC 2; TCLC 108**
    See also AITN 2; BRWS 3; CA 45-48; 57-60; CANR 3, 33; CDBLB 1914-1945; CPW 1; DA3; DAB; DAC; DAM NOV; DLB 34, 162; EWL 3; MTCW 1, 2; RGEL 2; RGSF 2; SATA 22; SSFS 10
**Woiwode, L.**
    See Woiwode, Larry (Alfred)
**Woiwode, Larry (Alfred)** 1941- ... **CLC 6, 10**
    See also CA 73-76; CANR 16, 94; CN 7; DLB 6; INT CANR-16
**Wojciechowska, Maia (Teresa)**
    1927-2002 ............................... **CLC 26**
    See also AAYA 8, 46; BYA 3; CA 9-12R; 183; 209; CAAE 183; CANR 4, 41; CLR 1; JRDA; MAICYA 1, 2; SAAS 1; SATA 1, 28, 83; SATA-Essay 104; SATA-Obit 134; YAW
**Wojtyla, Karol**
    See John Paul II, Pope
**Wolf, Christa** 1929- ....... **CLC 14, 29, 58, 150**
    See also CA 85-88; CANR 45, 123; CD-WLB 2; CWW 2; DLB 75; EWL 3; FW; MTCW 1; RGWL 2, 3; SSFS 14
**Wolf, Naomi** 1962- ........................... **CLC 157**
    See also CA 141; CANR 110; FW
**Wolfe, Gene (Rodman)** 1931- ............. **CLC 25**
    See also AAYA 35; CA 57-60; CAAS 9; CANR 6, 32, 60; CPW; DAM POP; DLB 8; FANT; MTCW 2; SATA 118; SCFW 2; SFW 4; SUFW 2
**Wolfe, George C.** 1954- ........ **BLCS; CLC 49**
    See also CA 149; CAD; CD 5
**Wolfe, Thomas (Clayton)**
    1900-1938 ...... **SSC 33; TCLC 4, 13, 29, 61; WLC**
    See also AMW; BPFB 3; CA 104; 132; CANR 102; CDALB 1929-1941; DA; DA3; DAB; DAC; DAM MST, NOV; DLB 9, 102, 229; DLBD 2, 16; DLBY 1985, 1997; EWL 3; MTCW 1, 2; NFS 18; RGAL 4; TUS
**Wolfe, Thomas Kennerly, Jr.**
    1931- ................................... **CLC 147**
    See Wolfe, Tom
    See also CA 13-16R; CANR 9, 33, 70, 104; DA3; DAM POP; DLB 185; EWL 3; INT CANR-9; MTCW 1, 2; SSFS 18; TUS
**Wolfe, Tom** .............. **CLC 1, 2, 9, 15, 35, 51**
    See Wolfe, Thomas Kennerly, Jr.
    See also AAYA 8; AITN 2; AMWS 3; BEST 89:1; BPFB 3; CN 7; CPW; CSW; DLB 152; LAIT 5; RGAL 4
**Wolff, Geoffrey (Ansell)** 1937- .......... **CLC 41**
    See also CA 29-32R; CANR 29, 43, 78
**Wolff, Sonia**
    See Levitin, Sonia (Wolff)
**Wolff, Tobias (Jonathan Ansell)**
    1945- ............ **CLC 39, 64, 172; SSC 63**
    See also AAYA 16; AMWS 7; BEST 90:2; BYA 12; CA 114; 117; CAAS 22; CANR

Author Index

54, 76, 96; CN 7; CSW; DA3; DLB 130; EWL 3; INT CA-117; MTCW 2; RGAL 4; RGSF 2; SSFS 4, 11

**Wolfram von Eschenbach** c. 1170-c. 1220 .......................................... **CMLC 5**
See Eschenbach, Wolfram von
See also CDWLB 2; DLB 138; EW 1; RGWL 2

**Wolitzer, Hilma** 1930- ....................... **CLC 17**
See also CA 65-68; CANR 18, 40; INT CANR-18; SATA 31; YAW

**Wollstonecraft, Mary** 1759-1797 .... **LC 5, 50, 90**
See also BRWS 3; CDBLB 1789-1832; DLB 39, 104, 158, 252; FW; LAIT 1; RGEL 2; TEA; WLIT 3

**Wonder, Stevie** ............................... **CLC 12**
See Morris, Steveland Judkins

**Wong, Jade Snow** 1922- ................... **CLC 17**
See also CA 109; CANR 91; SATA 112

**Woodberry, George Edward** 1855-1930 ................................... **TCLC 73**
See also CA 165; DLB 71, 103

**Woodcott, Keith**
See Brunner, John (Kilian Houston)

**Woodruff, Robert W.**
See Mencken, H(enry) L(ouis)

**Woolf, (Adeline) Virginia** 1882-1941 . **SSC 7; TCLC 1, 5, 20, 43, 56, 101, 123, 128; WLC**
See also AAYA 44; BPFB 3; BRW 7; BRWC 2; BRWR 1; CA 104; 130; CANR 64, 132; CDBLB 1914-1945; DA; DA3; DAB; DAC; DAM MST, NOV; DLB 36, 100, 162; DLBD 2; EWL 3; EXPS; FW; LAIT 3; LATS 1:1; LMFS 1; MTCW 1, 2; NCFS 2; NFS 8, 12; RGEL 2; RGSF 2; SSFS 4, 12; TEA; WLIT 4

**Woollcott, Alexander (Humphreys)** 1887-1943 ................................... **TCLC 5**
See also CA 105; 161; DLB 29

**Woolrich, Cornell** ............................ **CLC 77**
See Hopley-Woolrich, Cornell George
See also MSW

**Woolson, Constance Fenimore** 1840-1894 ................................... **NCLC 82**
See also DLB 12, 74, 189, 221; RGAL 4

**Wordsworth, Dorothy** 1771-1855 . **NCLC 25, 138**
See also DLB 107

**Wordsworth, William** 1770-1850 .. **NCLC 12, 38, 111; PC 4; WLC**
See also BRW 4; BRWC 1; CDBLB 1789-1832; DA; DA3; DAB; DAC; DAM MST, POET; DLB 93, 107; EXPP; LATS 1:1; LMFS 1; PAB; PFS 2; RGEL 2; TEA; WLIT 3; WP

**Wotton, Sir Henry** 1568-1639 ............. **LC 68**
See also DLB 121; RGEL 2

**Wouk, Herman** 1915- ............ **CLC 1, 9, 38**
See also BPFB 2, 3; CA 5-8R; CANR 6, 33, 67; CDALBS; CN 7; CPW; DA3; DAM NOV, POP; DLBY 1982; INT CANR-6; LAIT 4; MTCW 1, 2; NFS 7; TUS

**Wright, Charles (Penzel, Jr.)** 1935- .. **CLC 6, 13, 28, 119, 146**
See also AMWS 5; CA 29-32R; CAAS 7; CANR 23, 36, 62, 88; CP 7; DLB 165; DLBY 1982; EWL 3; MTCW 1, 2; PFS 10

**Wright, Charles Stevenson** 1932- ..... **BLC 3; CLC 49**
See also BW 1; CA 9-12R; CANR 26; CN 7; DAM MULT, POET; DLB 33

**Wright, Frances** 1795-1852 ............ **NCLC 74**
See also DLB 73

**Wright, Frank Lloyd** 1867-1959 .... **TCLC 95**
See also AAYA 33; CA 174

**Wright, Jack R.**
See Harris, Mark

**Wright, James (Arlington)** 1927-1980 ....... **CLC 3, 5, 10, 28; PC 36**
See also AITN 2; AMWS 3; CA 49-52; 97-100; CANR 4, 34, 64; CDALBS; DAM POET; DLB 5, 169; EWL 3; EXPP; MTCW 1, 2; PFS 7, 8; RGAL 4; TUS; WP

**Wright, Judith (Arundell)** 1915-2000 ................ **CLC 11, 53; PC 14**
See also CA 13-16R; 188; CANR 31, 76, 93; CP 7; CWP; DLB 260; EWL 3; MTCW 1, 2; PFS 8; RGEL 2; SATA 14; SATA-Obit 121

**Wright, L(aurali) R.** 1939- ................ **CLC 44**
See also CA 138; CMW 4

**Wright, Richard (Nathaniel)** 1908-1960 ... **BLC 3; CLC 1, 3, 4, 9, 14, 21, 48, 74; SSC 2; TCLC 136; WLC**
See also AAYA 5, 42; AFAW 1, 2; AMW; BPFB 3; BW 1; BYA 2; CA 108; CANR 64; CDALB 1929-1941; DA; DA3; DAB; DAC; DAM MST, MULT, NOV; DLB 76, 102; DLBD 2; EWL 3; EXPN; LAIT 3, 4; MTCW 1, 2; NCFS 1; NFS 1, 7; RGAL 4; RGSF 2; SSFS 3, 9, 15, 20; TUS; YAW

**Wright, Richard B(ruce)** 1937- .......... **CLC 6**
See also CA 85-88; CANR 120; DLB 53

**Wright, Rick** 1945- ............................ **CLC 35**

**Wright, Rowland**
See Wells, Carolyn

**Wright, Stephen** 1946- ....................... **CLC 33**

**Wright, Willard Huntington** 1888-1939
See Van Dine, S. S.
See also CA 115; 189; CMW 4; DLBD 16

**Wright, William** 1930- ...................... **CLC 44**
See also CA 53-56; CANR 7, 23

**Wroth, Lady Mary** 1587-1653(?) ....... **LC 30; PC 38**
See also DLB 121

**Wu Ch'eng-en** 1500(?)-1582(?) ............. **LC 7**

**Wu Ching-tzu** 1701-1754 ...................... **LC 2**

**Wulfstan** c. 10th cent. -1023 .......... **CMLC 59**

**Wurlitzer, Rudolph** 1938(?)- .... **CLC 2, 4, 15**
See also CA 85-88; CN 7; DLB 173

**Wyatt, Sir Thomas** c. 1503-1542 . **LC 70; PC 27**
See also BRW 1; DLB 132; EXPP; RGEL 2; TEA

**Wycherley, William** 1640-1716 ....... **LC 8, 21, 102**
See also BRW 2; CDBLB 1660-1789; DAM DRAM; DLB 80; RGEL 2

**Wyclif, John** c. 1330-1384 ............. **CMLC 70**
See also DLB 146

**Wylie, Elinor (Morton Hoyt)** 1885-1928 .................... **PC 23; TCLC 8**
See also AMWS 1; CA 105; 162; DLB 9, 45; EXPP; RGAL 4

**Wylie, Philip (Gordon)** 1902-1971 ... **CLC 43**
See also CA 21-22; 33-36R; CAP 2; DLB 9; SFW 4

**Wyndham, John** ............................... **CLC 19**
See Harris, John (Wyndham Parkes Lucas) Beynon
See also DLB 255; SCFW 2

**Wyss, Johann David Von** 1743-1818 ................................ **NCLC 10**
See also CLR 92; JRDA; MAICYA 1, 2; SATA 29; SATA-Brief 27

**Xenophon** c. 430B.C.-c. 354B.C. ... **CMLC 17**
See also AW 1; DLB 176; RGWL 2, 3

**Xingjian, Gao** 1940-
See Gao Xingjian
See also CA 193; RGWL 3

**Yakamochi** 718-785 ........... **CMLC 45; PC 48**

**Yakumo Koizumi**
See Hearn, (Patricio) Lafcadio (Tessima Carlos)

**Yamada, Mitsuye (May)** 1923- ........... **PC 44**
See also CA 77-80

**Yamamoto, Hisaye** 1921- ......... **AAL; SSC 34**
See also CA 214; DAM MULT; LAIT 4; SSFS 14

**Yamauchi, Wakako** 1924- ...................... **AAL**
See also CA 214

**Yanez, Jose Donoso**
See Donoso (Yanez), Jose

**Yanovsky, Basile S.**
See Yanovsky, V(assily) S(emenovich)

**Yanovsky, V(assily) S(emenovich)** 1906-1989 ............................. **CLC 2, 18**
See also CA 97-100; 129

**Yates, Richard** 1926-1992 ......... **CLC 7, 8, 23**
See also AMWS 11; CA 5-8R; 139; CANR 10, 43; DLB 2, 234; DLBY 1981, 1992; INT CANR-10

**Yeats, W. B.**
See Yeats, William Butler

**Yeats, William Butler** 1865-1939 . **PC 20, 51; TCLC 1, 11, 18, 31, 93, 116; WLC**
See also AAYA 48; BRW 6; BRWR 1; CA 104; 127; CANR 45; CDBLB 1890-1914; DA; DA3; DAB; DAC; DAM DRAM, MST, POET; DLB 10, 19, 98, 156; EWL 3; EXPP; MTCW 1, 2; NCFS 3; PAB; PFS 1, 2, 5, 7, 13, 15; RGEL 2; TEA; WLIT 4; WP

**Yehoshua, A(braham) B.** 1936- .. **CLC 13, 31**
See also CA 33-36R; CANR 43, 90; CWW 2; EWL 3; RGSF 2; RGWL 3

**Yellow Bird**
See Ridge, John Rollin

**Yep, Laurence Michael** 1948- .......... **CLC 35**
See also AAYA 5, 31; BYA 7; CA 49-52; CANR 1, 46, 92; CLR 3, 17, 54; DLB 52; FANT; JRDA; MAICYA 1, 2; MAICYAS 1; SATA 7, 69, 123; WYA; YAW

**Yerby, Frank G(arvin)** 1916-1991 ..... **BLC 3; CLC 1, 7, 22**
See also BPFB 3; BW 1, 3; CA 9-12R; 136; CANR 16, 52; DAM MULT; DLB 76; INT CANR-16; MTCW 1; RGAL 4; RHW

**Yesenin, Sergei Alexandrovich**
See Esenin, Sergei (Alexandrovich)

**Yesenin, Sergey**
See Esenin, Sergei (Alexandrovich)
See also EWL 3

**Yevtushenko, Yevgeny (Alexandrovich)** 1933- ...... **CLC 1, 3, 13, 26, 51, 126; PC 40**
See Evtushenko, Evgenii Aleksandrovich
See also CA 81-84; CANR 33, 54; DAM POET; EWL 3; MTCW 1

**Yezierska, Anzia** 1885(?)-1970 .......... **CLC 46**
See also CA 126; 89-92; DLB 28, 221; FW; MTCW 1; RGAL 4; SSFS 15

**Yglesias, Helen** 1915- .................... **CLC 7, 22**
See also CA 37-40R; CAAS 20; CANR 15, 65, 95; CN 7; INT CANR-15; MTCW 1

**Yokomitsu, Riichi** 1898-1947 .......... **TCLC 47**
See also CA 170; EWL 3

**Yonge, Charlotte (Mary)** 1823-1901 ................................. **TCLC 48**
See also CA 109; 163; DLB 18, 163; RGEL 2; SATA 17; WCH

**York, Jeremy**
See Creasey, John

**York, Simon**
See Heinlein, Robert A(nson)

**Yorke, Henry Vincent** 1905-1974 ..... **CLC 13**
See Green, Henry
See also CA 85-88; 49-52

**Yosano Akiko** 1878-1942 .... **PC 11; TCLC 59**
  See also CA 161; EWL 3; RGWL 3

**Yoshimoto, Banana** ........................... **CLC 84**
  See Yoshimoto, Mahoko
  See also AAYA 50; NFS 7

**Yoshimoto, Mahoko** 1964-
  See Yoshimoto, Banana
  See also CA 144; CANR 98; SSFS 16

**Young, Al(bert James)** 1939- ... **BLC 3; CLC 19**
  See also BW 2, 3; CA 29-32R; CANR 26, 65, 109; CN 7; CP 7; DAM MULT; DLB 33

**Young, Andrew (John)** 1885-1971 ...... **CLC 5**
  See also CA 5-8R; CANR 7, 29; RGEL 2

**Young, Collier**
  See Bloch, Robert (Albert)

**Young, Edward** 1683-1765 .............. **LC 3, 40**
  See also DLB 95; RGEL 2

**Young, Marguerite (Vivian)** 1909-1995 .................................. **CLC 82**
  See also CA 13-16; 150; CAP 1; CN 7

**Young, Neil** 1945- ............................... **CLC 17**
  See also CA 110; CCA 1

**Young Bear, Ray A.** 1950- ... **CLC 94; NNAL**
  See also CA 146; DAM MULT; DLB 175

**Yourcenar, Marguerite** 1903-1987 ... **CLC 19, 38, 50, 87**
  See also BPFB 3; CA 69-72; CANR 23, 60, 93; DAM NOV; DLB 72; DLBY 1988; EW 12; EWL 3; GFL 1789 to the Present; GLL 1; MTCW 1, 2; RGWL 2, 3

**Yuan, Chu** 340(?)B.C.-278(?)B.C. . **CMLC 36**

**Yurick, Sol** 1925- .................................. **CLC 6**
  See also CA 13-16R; CANR 25; CN 7

**Zabolotsky, Nikolai Alekseevich** 1903-1958 ............................... **TCLC 52**
  See Zabolotsky, Nikolay Alekseevich
  See also CA 116; 164

**Zabolotsky, Nikolay Alekseevich**
  See Zabolotsky, Nikolai Alekseevich
  See also EWL 3

**Zagajewski, Adam** 1945- ..................... **PC 27**
  See also CA 186; DLB 232; EWL 3

**Zalygin, Sergei** -2000 ........................ **CLC 59**

**Zalygin, Sergei (Pavlovich)** 1913-2000 ............................... **CLC 59**
  See also DLB 302

**Zamiatin, Evgenii**
  See Zamyatin, Evgeny Ivanovich
  See also RGSF 2; RGWL 2, 3

**Zamiatin, Evgenii Ivanovich**
  See Zamyatin, Evgeny Ivanovich
  See also DLB 272

**Zamiatin, Yevgenii**
  See Zamyatin, Evgeny Ivanovich

**Zamora, Bernice (B. Ortiz)** 1938- .. **CLC 89; HLC 2**
  See also CA 151; CANR 80; DAM MULT; DLB 82; HW 1, 2

**Zamyatin, Evgeny Ivanovich** 1884-1937 ........................... **TCLC 8, 37**
  See Zamiatin, Evgenii; Zamiatin, Evgenii Ivanovich; Zamyatin, Yevgeny Ivanovich
  See also CA 105; 166; EW 10; SFW 4

**Zamyatin, Yevgeny Ivanovich**
  See Zamyatin, Evgeny Ivanovich
  See also EWL 3

**Zangwill, Israel** 1864-1926 ... **SSC 44; TCLC 16**
  See also CA 109; 167; CMW 4; DLB 10, 135, 197; RGEL 2

**Zappa, Francis Vincent, Jr.** 1940-1993
  See Zappa, Frank
  See also CA 108; 143; CANR 57

**Zappa, Frank** .................................... **CLC 17**
  See Zappa, Francis Vincent, Jr.

**Zaturenska, Marya** 1902-1982 ..... **CLC 6, 11**
  See also CA 13-16R; 105; CANR 22

**Zayas y Sotomayor, Maria de** 1590-c. 1661 ......................................... **LC 102**
  See also RGSF 2

**Zeami** 1363-1443 ....................... **DC 7; LC 86**
  See also DLB 203; RGWL 2, 3

**Zelazny, Roger (Joseph)** 1937-1995 . **CLC 21**
  See also AAYA 7; BPFB 3; CA 21-24R; 148; CANR 26, 60; CN 7; DLB 8; FANT; MTCW 1, 2; SATA 57; SATA-Brief 39; SCFW; SFW 4; SUFW 1, 2

**Zhang Ailing** 1920(?)-1995
  See Chang, Eileen
  See also CWW 2; RGSF 2

**Zhdanov, Andrei Alexandrovich** 1896-1948 ................................. **TCLC 18**
  See also CA 117; 167

**Zhukovsky, Vasilii Andreevich**
  See Zhukovsky, Vasily (Andreevich)
  See also DLB 205

**Zhukovsky, Vasily (Andreevich)** 1783-1852 ................................. **NCLC 35**
  See Zhukovsky, Vasilii Andreevich

**Ziegenhagen, Eric** ........................... **CLC 55**

**Zimmer, Jill Schary**
  See Robinson, Jill

**Zimmerman, Robert**
  See Dylan, Bob

**Zindel, Paul** 1936-2003 ...... **CLC 6, 26; DC 5**
  See also AAYA 2, 37; BYA 2, 3, 8, 11, 14; CA 73-76; 213; CAD; CANR 31, 65, 108; CD 5; CDALBS; CLR 3, 45, 85; DA; DA3; DAB; DAC; DAM DRAM, MST, NOV; DFS 12; DLB 7, 52; JRDA; LAIT 5; MAICYA 1, 2; MTCW 1, 2; NFS 14; SATA 16, 58, 102; SATA-Obit 142; WYA; YAW

**Zinov'Ev, A. A.**
  See Zinoviev, Alexander (Aleksandrovich)

**Zinov'ev, Aleksandr (Aleksandrovich)**
  See Zinoviev, Alexander (Aleksandrovich)
  See also DLB 302

**Zinoviev, Alexander (Aleksandrovich)** 1922- ................................... **CLC 19**
  See Zinov'ev, Aleksandr (Aleksandrovich)
  See also CA 116; 133; CAAS 10

**Zizek, Slavoj** 1949- ........................... **CLC 188**
  See also CA 201

**Zoilus**
  See Lovecraft, H(oward) P(hillips)

**Zola, Emile (Edouard Charles Antoine)** 1840-1902 ...... **TCLC 1, 6, 21, 41; WLC**
  See also CA 104; 138; DA; DA3; DAB; DAC; DAM MST, NOV; DLB 123; EW 7; GFL 1789 to the Present; IDTP; LMFS 1, 2; RGWL 2; TWA

**Zoline, Pamela** 1941- ......................... **CLC 62**
  See also CA 161; SFW 4

**Zoroaster** 628(?)B.C.-551(?)B.C. ... **CMLC 40**

**Zorrilla y Moral, Jose** 1817-1893 .... **NCLC 6**

**Zoshchenko, Mikhail (Mikhailovich)** 1895-1958 ................. **SSC 15; TCLC 15**
  See also CA 115; 160; EWL 3; RGSF 2; RGWL 3

**Zuckmayer, Carl** 1896-1977 ............. **CLC 18**
  See also CA 69-72; DLB 56, 124; EWL 3; RGWL 2, 3

**Zuk, Georges**
  See Skelton, Robin
  See also CCA 1

**Zukofsky, Louis** 1904-1978 ... **CLC 1, 2, 4, 7, 11, 18; PC 11**
  See also AMWS 3; CA 9-12R; 77-80; CANR 39; DAM POET; DLB 5, 165; EWL 3; MTCW 1; RGAL 4

**Zweig, Paul** 1935-1984 ............... **CLC 34, 42**
  See also CA 85-88; 113

**Zweig, Stefan** 1881-1942 ................. **TCLC 17**
  See also CA 112; 170; DLB 81, 118; EWL 3

**Zwingli, Huldreich** 1484-1531 ............. **LC 37**
  See also DLB 179

# Literary Criticism Series
# Cumulative Topic Index

This index lists all topic entries in Gale's *Classical and Medieval Literature Criticism* (CMLC), *Contemporary Literary Criticism* (CLC), *Drama Criticism* (DC), *Literature Criticism from 1400 to 1800* (LC), *Nineteenth-Century Literature Criticism* (NCLC), *Short Story Criticism* (SSC), and *Twentieth-Century Literary Criticism* (TCLC). The index also lists topic entries in the Gale Critical Companion Collection, which includes the following publications: *The Beat Generation* (BG), and *Harlem Renaissance* (HR).

**Abbey Theatre in the Irish Literary Renaissance** TCLC 154: 1-114
origins and development, 2-14
major figures, 14-30
plays and controversies, 30-59
artistic vision and significance, 59-114

**Abolitionist Literature of Cuba and Brazil, Nineteenth-Century** NCLC 132: 1-94
overviews, 2-11
origins and development, 11-23
sociopolitical concerns, 23-39
poetry, 39-47
prose, 47-93

**Aborigine in Nineteenth-Century Australian Literature, The** NCLC 120: 1-88
overviews, 2-27
representations of the Aborigine in Australian literature, 27-58
Aboriginal myth, literature, and oral tradition, 58-88

**Aesopic Fable, The** LC 51: 1-100
the British Aesopic Fable, 1-54
the Aesopic tradition in non-English-speaking cultures, 55-66
political uses of the Aesopic fable, 67-88
the evolution of the Aesopic fable, 89-99

**African-American Folklore and Literature** TCLC 126: 1-67
African-American folk tradition, 1-16
representative writers, 16-34
hallmark works, 35-48
the study of African-American literature and folklore, 48-64

**Age of Johnson** LC 15: 1-87
Johnson's London, 3-15
aesthetics of neoclassicism, 15-36
"age of prose and reason," 36-45
clubmen and bluestockings, 45-56
printing technology, 56-62
periodicals: "a map of busy life," 62-74
transition, 74-86

**Age of Spenser** LC 39: 1-70
overviews and general studies, 2-21
literary style, 22-34
poets and the crown, 34-70

**AIDS in Literature** CLC 81: 365-416

**Alcohol and Literature** TCLC 70: 1-58
overview, 2-8
fiction, 8-48
poetry and drama, 48-58

**American Abolitionism** NCLC 44: 1-73
overviews and general studies, 2-26
abolitionist ideals, 26-46
the literature of abolitionism, 46-72

**American Autobiography** TCLC 86: 1-115
overviews and general studies, 3-36
American authors and autobiography, 36-82
African-American autobiography, 82-114

**American Black Humor Fiction** TCLC 54: 1-85
characteristics of black humor, 2-13
origins and development, 13-38
black humor distinguished from related literary trends, 38-60
black humor and society, 60-75
black humor reconsidered, 75-83

**American Civil War in Literature** NCLC 32: 1-109
overviews and general studies, 2-20
regional perspectives, 20-54
fiction popular during the war, 54-79
the historical novel, 79-108

**American Frontier in Literature** NCLC 28: 1-103
definitions, 2-12
development, 12-17
nonfiction writing about the frontier, 17-30
frontier fiction, 30-45
frontier protagonists, 45-66
portrayals of Native Americans, 66-86
feminist readings, 86-98
twentieth-century reaction against frontier literature, 98-100

**American Humor Writing** NCLC 52: 1-59
overviews and general studies, 2-12
the Old Southwest, 12-42
broader impacts, 42-5
women humorists, 45-58

**American Novel of Manners** TCLC 130: 1-42
history of the Novel of Manners in America, 4-10
representative writers, 10-18
relevancy of the Novel of Manners, 18-24

hallmark works in the Novel of Manners, 24-36
Novel of Manners and other media, 36-40

**American Mercury, The** TCLC 74: 1-80

**American Popular Song, Golden Age of** TCLC 42: 1-49
background and major figures, 2-34
the lyrics of popular songs, 34-47

**American Proletarian Literature** TCLC 54: 86-175
overviews and general studies, 87-95
American proletarian literature and the American Communist Party, 95-111
ideology and literary merit, 111-17
novels, 117-36
Gastonia, 136-48
drama, 148-54
journalism, 154-9
proletarian literature in the United States, 159-74

**American Realism** NCLC 120: 89-246
overviews, 91-112
background and sources, 112-72
social issues, 172-223
women and realism, 223-45

**American Renaissance** SSC 64: 46-193
overviews and general studies, 47-103
major authors of short fiction, 103-92

**American Romanticism** NCLC 44: 74-138
overviews and general studies, 74-84
sociopolitical influences, 84-104
Romanticism and the American frontier, 104-15
thematic concerns, 115-37

**American Western Literature** TCLC 46: 1-100
definition and development of American Western literature, 2-7
characteristics of the Western novel, 8-23
Westerns as history and fiction, 23-34
critical reception of American Western literature, 34-41
the Western hero, 41-73
women in Western fiction, 73-91
later Western fiction, 91-9

**American Writers in Paris** TCLC 98: 1-156
overviews and general studies, 2-155

**Anarchism** NCLC 84: 1-97
overviews and general studies, 2-23
the French anarchist tradition, 23-56
Anglo-American anarchism, 56-68
anarchism: incidents and issues, 68-97

**Animals in Literature** TCLC 106: 1-120
overviews and general studies, 2-8
animals in American literature, 8-45
animals in Canadian literature, 45-57
animals in European literature, 57-100
animals in Latin American literature, 100-06
animals in women's literature, 106-20

**Antebellum South, Literature of the** NCLC 112:1-188
overviews, 4-55
culture of the Old South, 55-68
antebellum fiction: pastoral and heroic romance, 68-120
role of women: a subdued rebellion, 120-59
slavery and the slave narrative, 159-85

**The Apocalyptic Movement** TCLC 106: 121-69

**Aristotle** CMLC 31:1-397
philosophy, 3-100
poetics, 101-219
rhetoric, 220-301
science, 302-397

**Art and Literature** TCLC 54: 176-248
overviews and general studies, 176-93
definitions, 193-219
influence of visual arts on literature, 219-31
spatial form in literature, 231-47

**Arthurian Literature** CMLC 10: 1-127
historical context and literary beginnings, 2-27
development of the legend through Malory, 27-64
development of the legend from Malory to the Victorian Age, 65-81
themes and motifs, 81-95
principal characters, 95-125

**Arthurian Revival** NCLC 36: 1-77
overviews and general studies, 2-12
Tennyson and his influence, 12-43
other leading figures, 43-73
the Arthurian legend in the visual arts, 73-6

**Australian Cultural Identity in Nineteenth-Century Literature** NCLC 124: 1-164
overviews and general studies, 4-22
poetry, 22-67
fiction, 67-135
role of women writers, 135-64

**Australian Literature** TCLC 50: 1-94
origins and development, 2-21
characteristics of Australian literature, 21-33
historical and critical perspectives, 33-41
poetry, 41-58
fiction, 58-76
drama, 76-82
Aboriginal literature, 82-91

**Beat Generation, The** BG 1:1-562
the Beat Generation: an overview, 1-137
primary sources, 3-32
overviews and general studies, 32-47
Beat Generation as a social phenomenon, 47-65
drugs, inspiration, and the Beat Generation, 65-92
religion and the Beat Generation, 92-124
women of the Beat Generation, 124-36
Beat "scene": East and West, 139-259
primary sources, 141-77
Beat scene in the East, 177-218
Beat scene in the West, 218-59
Beat Generation publishing: periodicals, small presses, and censorship, 261-349

primary sources, 263-74
overview, 274-88
Beat periodicals: "little magazines," 288-311
Beat publishing: small presses, 311-24
Beat battles with censorship, 324-49
performing arts and the Beat Generation, 351-417
primary sources, 353-58
Beats and film, 358-81
Beats and music, 381-415
visual arts and the Beat Generation, 419-91
primary sources, 421-24
critical commentary, 424-90

**Beat Generation, Literature of the** TCLC 42: 50-102
overviews and general studies, 51-9
the Beat generation as a social phenomenon, 59-62
development, 62-5
Beat literature, 66-96
influence, 97-100

**The Bell Curve Controversy** CLC 91: 281-330

**Bildungsroman in Nineteenth-Century Literature** NCLC 20: 92-168
surveys, 93-113
in Germany, 113-40
in England, 140-56
female *Bildungsroman,* 156-67

**Bloomsbury Group** TCLC 34: 1-73
history and major figures, 2-13
definitions, 13-7
influences, 17-27
thought, 27-40
prose, 40-52
and literary criticism, 52-4
political ideals, 54-61
response to, 61-71

**The Bloomsbury Group** TCLC 138: 1-59
representative members of the Bloomsbury Group, 9-24
literary relevance of the Bloomsbury Group, 24-36
Bloomsbury's hallmark works, 36-48
other modernists studied with the Bloomsbury Group, 48-54

**The Blues in Literature** TCLC 82: 1-71

**Bly, Robert, *Iron John: A Book about Men and Men's Work*** CLC 70: 414-62

**The Book of J** CLC 65: 289-311

**Brazilian Literature** TCLC 134: 1-126
overviews and general studies, 3-33
Brazilian poetry, 33-48
contemporary Brazilian writing, 48-76
culture, politics, and race in Brazilian writing, 76-100
modernism and postmodernism in Brazil, 100-25

**British Ephemeral Literature** LC 59: 1-70
overviews and general studies, 1-9
broadside ballads, 10-40
chapbooks, jestbooks, pamphlets, and newspapers, 40-69

**Buddhism and Literature** TCLC 70: 59-164
eastern literature, 60-113
western literature, 113-63

**The *Bulletin* and the Rise of Australian Literary Nationalism** NCLC 116: 1-121
overviews, 3-32
legend of the nineties, 32-55
*Bulletin* style, 55-71
Australian literary nationalism, 71-98
myth of the bush, 98-120

**Businessman in American Literature** TCLC 26: 1-48

portrayal of the businessman, 1-32
themes and techniques in business fiction, 32-47

**The Calendar** LC 55: 1-92
overviews and general studies, 2-19
measuring time, 19-28
calendars and culture, 28-60
calendar reform, 60-92

**Captivity Narratives** LC 82: 71-172
overviews, 72-107
captivity narratives and Puritanism, 108-34
captivity narratives and Native Americans, 134-49
influence on American literature, 149-72

**Caribbean Literature** TCLC 138: 60-135
overviews and general studies, 61-9
ethnic and national identity, 69-107
expatriate Caribbean literature, 107-23
literary histoiography, 123-35

**Catholicism in Nineteenth-Century American Literature** NCLC 64: 1-58
overviews, 3-14
polemical literature, 14-46
Catholicism in literature, 47-57

**Celtic Mythology** CMLC 26: 1-111
overviews and general studies, 2-22
Celtic myth as literature and history, 22-48
Celtic religion: Druids and divinities, 48-80
Fionn MacCuhaill and the Fenian cycle, 80-111

**Celtic Twilight See Irish Literary Renaissance**

**Censorship and Contemporary World Literature** CLC 194: 1-80
overviews and general studies, 2-19
notorious cases, 19-59
censorship in the global context, 59-79

**Censorship in Twentieth-Century Literature** TCLC 154: 115-238
overviews and general studies, 117-25
censorship and obscenity trials, 125-61
censorship and sexual politics, 161-81
censorship and war, 181-207
political censorship and the state, 207-28
censorship and the writer, 228-38

**Chartist Movement and Literature, The** NCLC 60: 1-84
overview: nineteenth-century working-class fiction, 2-19
Chartist fiction and poetry, 19-73
the Chartist press, 73-84

**Chicago Renaissance, The** TCLC 154: 239-341
overviews and general studies, 240-60
definitions and growth, 260-82
the language debate, 282-318
major authors, 318-40

**Child Labor in Nineteenth-Century Literature** NCLC 108: 1-133
overviews, 3-10
climbing boys and chimney sweeps, 10-16
the international traffic in children, 16-45
critics and reformers, 45-82
fictional representations of child laborers, 83-132

**Children's Literature, Nineteenth-Century** NCLC 52: 60-135
overviews and general studies, 61-72
moral tales, 72-89
fairy tales and fantasy, 90-119
making men/making women, 119-34

**Christianity in Twentieth-Century Literature** TCLC 110: 1-79
overviews and general studies, 2-31
Christianity in twentieth-century fiction, 31-78

**Chronicle Plays** LC 89: 1-106
development of the genre, 2-33
historiography and literature, 33-56
genre and performance, 56-88
politics and ideology, 88-106

**The City and Literature** TCLC 90: 1-124
overviews and general studies, 2-9
the city in American literature, 9-86
the city in European literature, 86-124

**Civic Critics, Russian** NCLC 20: 402-46
principal figures and background, 402-9
and Russian Nihilism, 410-6
aesthetic and critical views, 416-45

**The Cockney School** NCLC 68: 1-64
overview, 2-7
*Blackwood's Magazine* and the contemporary critical response, 7-24
the political and social import of the Cockneys and their critics, 24-63

**Colonial America: The Intellectual Background** LC 25: 1-98
overviews and general studies, 2-17
philosophy and politics, 17-31
early religious influences in Colonial America, 31-60
consequences of the Revolution, 60-78
religious influences in post-revolutionary America, 78-87
colonial literary genres, 87-97

**Colonialism in Victorian English Literature** NCLC 56: 1-77
overviews and general studies, 2-34
colonialism and gender, 34-51
monsters and the occult, 51-76

**Columbus, Christopher, Books on the Quincentennial of His Arrival in the New World** CLC 70: 329-60

**Comic Books** TCLC 66: 1-139
historical and critical perspectives, 2-48
superheroes, 48-67
underground comix, 67-88
comic books and society, 88-122
adult comics and graphic novels, 122-36

**Comedy of Manners** LC 92: 1-75
overviews, 2-21
comedy of manners and society, 21-47
comedy of manners and women, 47-74

**Commedia dell'Arte** LC 83: 1-147
overviews, 2-7
origins and development, 7-23
characters and actors, 23-45
performance, 45-62
texts and authors, 62-100
influence in Europe, 100-46

**Connecticut Wits** NCLC 48: 1-95
overviews and general studies, 2-40
major works, 40-76
intellectual context, 76-95

**Contemporary Feminist Criticism** CLC 180: 1-103
overviews and general studies, 2–59
modern French feminist theory, 59-102

**Contemporary Gay and Lesbian Literature** CLC 171: 1-130
overviews and general studies, 2-43
contemporary gay literature, 44-95
lesbianism in contemporary literature, 95-129

**Contemporary Southern Literature** CLC 167: 1-132
criticism, 2-131

**Crime in Literature** TCLC 54: 249-307
evolution of the criminal figure in literature, 250-61
crime and society, 261-77

literary perspectives on crime and punishment, 277-88
writings by criminals, 288-306

**Crime-Mystery-Detective Stories** SSC 59:89-226
overviews and general studies, 90-140
origins and early masters of the crime-mystery-detective story, 140-73
hard-boiled crime-mystery-detective fiction, 173-209
diversity in the crime-mystery-detective story, 210-25

**The Crusades** CMLC 38: 1-144
history of the Crusades, 3-60
literature of the Crusades, 60-116
the Crusades and the people: attitudes and influences, 116-44

**Cyberpunk** TCLC 106: 170-366
overviews and general studies, 171-88
feminism and cyberpunk, 188-230
history and cyberpunk, 230-70
sexuality and cyberpunk, 270-98
social issues and cyberpunk, 299-366

**Cyberpunk Short Fiction** SSC 60: 44-108
overviews and general studies, 46-78
major writers of cyberpunk fiction, 78-81
sexuality and cyberpunk fiction, 81-97
additional pieces, 97-108

**Czechoslovakian Literature of the Twentieth Century** TCLC 42:103-96
through World War II, 104-35
de-Stalinization, the Prague Spring, and contemporary literature, 135-72
Slovak literature, 172-85
Czech science fiction, 185-93

**Dadaism** TCLC 46: 101-71
background and major figures, 102-16
definitions, 116-26
manifestos and commentary by Dadaists, 126-40
theater and film, 140-58
nature and characteristics of Dadaist writing, 158-70

**Danish Literature See Twentieth-Century Danish Literature**

**Darwinism and Literature** NCLC 32: 110-206
background, 110-31
direct responses to Darwin, 131-71
collateral effects of Darwinism, 171-205

**Death in American Literature** NCLC 92: 1-170
overviews and general studies, 2-32
death in the works of Emily Dickinson, 32-72
death in the works of Herman Melville, 72-101
death in the works of Edgar Allan Poe, 101-43
death in the works of Walt Whitman, 143-70

**Death in Nineteenth-Century British Literature** NCLC 68: 65-142
overviews and general studies, 66-92
responses to death, 92-102
feminist perspectives, 103-17
striving for immortality, 117-41

**Death in Literature** TCLC 78:1-183
fiction, 2-115
poetry, 115-46
drama, 146-81

**Deconstruction** TCLC 138: 136-256
overviews and general studies, 137-83
deconstruction and literature, 183-221
deconstruction in philosophy and history, 221-56

**de Man, Paul, Wartime Journalism of** CLC 55: 382-424

**Detective Fiction, Nineteenth-Century** NCLC 36: 78-148
origins of the genre, 79-100
history of nineteenth-century detective fiction, 101-33
significance of nineteenth-century detective fiction, 133-46

**Detective Fiction, Twentieth-Century** TCLC 38: 1-96
genesis and history of the detective story, 3-22
defining detective fiction, 22-32
evolution and varieties, 32-77
the appeal of detective fiction, 77-90

**Detective Story See Crime-Mystery-Detective Stories**

**Dime Novels** NCLC 84: 98-168
overviews and general studies, 99-123
popular characters, 123-39
major figures and influences, 139-52
socio-political concerns, 152-167

**Disease and Literature** TCLC 66: 140-283
overviews and general studies, 141-65
disease in nineteenth-century literature, 165-81
tuberculosis and literature, 181-94
women and disease in literature, 194-221
plague literature, 221-53
AIDS in literature, 253-82

**El Dorado, The Legend of See Legend of El Dorado, The**

**The Double in Nineteenth-Century Literature** NCLC 40: 1-95
genesis and development of the theme, 2-15
the double and Romanticism, 16-27
sociological views, 27-52
psychological interpretations, 52-87
philosophical considerations, 87-95

**Dramatic Realism** NCLC 44: 139-202
overviews and general studies, 140-50
origins and definitions, 150-66
impact and influence, 166-93
realist drama and tragedy, 193-201

**Drugs and Literature** TCLC 78: 184-282
overviews and general studies, 185-201
pre-twentieth-century literature, 201-42
twentieth-century literature, 242-82

**Dystopias in Contemporary Literature** CLC 168: 1-91
overviews and general studies, 2-52
dystopian views in Margaret Atwood's *The Handmaid's Tale* (1985), 52-71
feminist readings of dystopias, 71-90

**Eastern Mythology** CMLC 26: 112-92
heroes and kings, 113-51
cross-cultural perspective, 151-69
relations to history and society, 169-92

**Ecocriticism and Nineteenth-Century Literature** NCLC 140: 1-168
overviews, 3-20
American literature: Romantics and Realists, 20-76
American explorers and naturalists, 76-123
English literature: Romantics and Victorians, 123-67

**Ecofeminism and Nineteenth-Century Literature** NCLC 136: 1-110
overviews, 2-24
the local landscape, 24-72
travel writing, 72-109

**Eighteenth-Century British Periodicals** LC 63: 1-123
rise of periodicals, 2-31

impact and influence of periodicals, 31-64
periodicals and society, 64-122

**Eighteenth-Century Travel Narratives** LC 77: 252-355
overviews and general studies, 254-79
eighteenth-century European travel narratives, 279-334
non-European eighteenth-century travel narratives, 334-55

**Electronic "Books": Hypertext and Hyperfiction** CLC 86: 367-404
books vs. CD-ROMS, 367-76
hypertext and hyperfiction, 376-95
implications for publishing, libraries, and the public, 395-403

**Eliot, T. S., Centenary of Birth** CLC 55: 345-75

**Elizabethan Drama** LC 22: 140-240
origins and influences, 142-67
characteristics and conventions, 167-83
theatrical production, 184-200
histories, 200-12
comedy, 213-20
tragedy, 220-30

**Elizabethan Prose Fiction** LC 41: 1-70
overviews and general studies, 1-15
origins and influences, 15-43
style and structure, 43-69

**The Emergence of the Short Story in the Nineteenth Century** NCLC 140: 169-279
overviews, 171-74
the American short story, 174-214
the short story in Great Britain and Ireland, 214-235
stories by women in English, 235-45
the short story in France and Russia, 245-66
the Latin American short story, 266-77

**Enclosure of the English Common** NCLC 88: 1-57
overviews and general studies, 1-12
early reaction to enclosure, 12-23
nineteenth-century reaction to enclosure, 23-56

**The Encyclopedists** LC 26: 172-253
overviews and general studies, 173-210
intellectual background, 210-32
views on esthetics, 232-41
views on women, 241-52

**English Abolitionist Literature of the Nineteenth Century** NCLC 136: 111-235
overview, 112-35
origins and development, 135-42
poetry, 142-58
prose, 158-80
sociopolitical concerns, 180-95
English abolitionist literature and feminism, 195-233

**English Caroline Literature** LC 13: 221-307
background, 222-41
evolution and varieties, 241-62
the Cavalier mode, 262-75
court and society, 275-91
politics and religion, 291-306

**English Decadent Literature of the 1890s** NCLC 28: 104-200
fin de siècle: the Decadent period, 105-19
definitions, 120-37
major figures: "the tragic generation," 137-50
French literature and English literary Decadence, 150-7
themes, 157-61
poetry, 161-82
periodicals, 182-96

**English Essay, Rise of the** LC 18: 238-308
definitions and origins, 236-54

influence on the essay, 254-69
historical background, 269-78
the essay in the seventeenth century, 279-93
the essay in the eighteenth century, 293-307

**English Mystery Cycle Dramas** LC 34: 1-88
overviews and general studies, 1-27
the nature of dramatic performances, 27-42
the medieval worldview and the mystery cycles, 43-67
the doctrine of repentance and the mystery cycles, 67-76
the fall from grace in the mystery cycles, 76-88

**The English Realist Novel, 1740-1771** LC 51: 102-98
overviews and general studies, 103-22
from Romanticism to Realism, 123-58
women and the novel, 159-175
the novel and other literary forms, 176-197

**English Revolution, Literature of the** LC 43: 1-58
overviews and general studies, 2-24
pamphlets of the English Revolution, 24-38
political sermons of the English Revolution, 38-48
poetry of the English Revolution, 48-57

**English Romantic Hellenism** NCLC 68: 143-250
overviews and general studies, 144-69
historical development of English Romantic Hellenism, 169-91
influence of Greek mythology on the Romantics, 191-229
influence of Greek literature, art, and culture on the Romantics, 229-50

**English Romantic Poetry** NCLC 28: 201-327
overviews and reputation, 202-37
major subjects and themes, 237-67
forms of Romantic poetry, 267-78
politics, society, and Romantic poetry, 278-99
philosophy, religion, and Romantic poetry, 299-324

**The Epistolary Novel** LC 59: 71-170
overviews and general studies, 72-96
women and the Epistolary novel, 96-138
principal figures: Britain, 138-53
principal figures: France, 153-69

**Espionage Literature** TCLC 50: 95-159
overviews and general studies, 96-113
espionage fiction/formula fiction, 113-26
spies in fact and fiction, 126-38
the female spy, 138-44
social and psychological perspectives, 144-58

**European Debates on the Conquest of the Americas** LC 67: 1-129
overviews and general studies, 3-56
major Spanish figures, 56-98
English perceptions of Native Americans, 98-129

**European Romanticism** NCLC 36: 149-284
definitions, 149-77
origins of the movement, 177-82
Romantic theory, 182-200
themes and techniques, 200-23
Romanticism in Germany, 223-39
Romanticism in France, 240-61
Romanticism in Italy, 261-4
Romanticism in Spain, 264-8
impact and legacy, 268-82

**Exile in Literature** TCLC 122: 1-129
overviews and general studies, 2-33
exile in fiction, 33-92
German literature in exile, 92-129

**Existentialism and Literature** TCLC 42: 197-268
overviews and definitions, 198-209
history and influences, 209-19
Existentialism critiqued and defended, 220-35
philosophical and religious perspectives, 235-41
Existentialist fiction and drama, 241-67

**Ezra Pound Controversy** TCLC 150: 1-132
politics of Ezra Pound, 3-42
anti-semitism of Ezra Pound, 42-57
the Bollingen Award controversy, 57-76
Pound's later writing, 76-104
criticism of *The Pisan Cantos,* 104-32

**Familiar Essay** NCLC 48: 96-211
definitions and origins, 97-130
overview of the genre, 130-43
elements of form and style, 143-59
elements of content, 159-73
the Cockneys: Hazlitt, Lamb, and Hunt, 173-91
status of the genre, 191-210

**Fantasy in Contemporary Literature** CLC 193: 137-250
overviews and general studies, 139-57
language, form, and theory, 157-91
major writers, 191-230
women writers and fantasy, 230-50

**Fashion in Nineteenth-Century Literature** NCLC 128: 104-93
overviews and general studies, 105-38
fashion and American literature, 138-46
fashion and English literature, 146-74
fashion and French literature, 174-92

**The Faust Legend** LC 47: 1-117

**Fear in Literature** TCLC 74: 81-258
overviews and general studies, 81
pre-twentieth-century literature, 123
twentieth-century literature, 182

**Feminism in the 1990s: Commentary on Works by Naomi Wolf, Susan Faludi, and Camille Paglia** CLC 76: 377-415

**Feminist Criticism** See Contemporary Feminist Criticism

**Feminist Criticism in 1990** CLC 65: 312-60

**Fifteenth-Century English Literature** LC 17: 248-334
background, 249-72
poetry, 272-315
drama, 315-23
prose, 323-33

**Fifteenth-Century Spanish Poetry** LC 100:82-173
overviews and general studies, 83-101
the Cancioneros, 101-57
major figures, 157-72

**Film and Literature** TCLC 38: 97-226
overviews and general studies, 97-119
film and theater, 119-34
film and the novel, 134-45
the art of the screenplay, 145-66
genre literature/genre film, 167-79
the writer and the film industry, 179-90
authors on film adaptations of their works, 190-200
fiction into film: comparative essays, 200-23

**Finance and Money as Represented in Nineteenth-Century Literature** NCLC 76: 1-69
historical perspectives, 2-20
the image of money, 20-37
the dangers of money, 37-50
women and money, 50-69

**Folklore and Literature** TCLC 86: 116-293
  overviews and general studies, 118-144
  Native American literature, 144-67
  African-American literature, 167-238
  folklore and the American West, 238-57
  modern and postmodern literature, 257-91

**Food in Literature** TCLC 114: 1-133
  food and children's literature, 2-14
  food as a literary device, 14-32
  rituals involving food, 33-45
  food and social and ethnic identity, 45-90
  women's relationship with food, 91-132

**Food in Nineteenth-Century Literature**
NCLC 108: 134-288
  overviews, 136-74
  food and social class, 174-85
  food and gender, 185-219
  food and love, 219-31
  food and sex, 231-48
  eating disorders, 248-70
  vegetarians, carnivores, and cannibals, 270-87

**French Drama in the Age of Louis XIV** LC
28: 94-185
  overview, 95-127
  tragedy, 127-46
  comedy, 146-66
  tragicomedy, 166-84

**French Enlightenment** LC 14: 81-145
  the question of definition, 82-9
  le siècle des lumières, 89-94
  women and the salons, 94-105
  censorship, 105-15
  the philosophy of reason, 115-31
  influence and legacy, 131-44

**French New Novel** TCLC 98: 158-234
  overviews and general studies, 158-92
  influences, 192-213
  themes, 213-33

**French Realism** NCLC 52: 136-216
  origins and definitions, 137-70
  issues and influence, 170-98
  realism and representation, 198-215

**French Revolution and English Literature**
NCLC 40: 96-195
  history and theory, 96-123
  romantic poetry, 123-50
  the novel, 150-81
  drama, 181-92
  children's literature, 192-5

**French Symbolist Poetry** NCLC 144: 1-107
  overviews, 2-14
  Symbolist aesthetics, 14-47
  the Symbolist lyric, 47-60
  history and influence, 60-105

**Futurism, Italian** TCLC 42: 269-354
  principles and formative influences, 271-9
  manifestos, 279-88
  literature, 288-303
  theater, 303-19
  art, 320-30
  music, 330-6
  architecture, 336-9
  and politics, 339-46
  reputation and significance, 346-51

**Gaelic Revival See Irish Literary Renaissance**

**Gates, Henry Louis, Jr., and African-American Literary Criticism** CLC 65: 361-405

**Gay and Lesbian Literature** CLC 76: 416-39

**Gay and Lesbian Literature See also Contemporary Gay and Lesbian Literature**

**German Exile Literature** TCLC 30: 1-58
  the writer and the Nazi state, 1-10
  definition of, 10-4

  life in exile, 14-32
  surveys, 32-50
  Austrian literature in exile, 50-2
  German publishing in the United States, 52-7

**German Expressionism** TCLC 34: 74-160
  history and major figures, 76-85
  aesthetic theories, 85-109
  drama, 109-26
  poetry, 126-38
  film, 138-42
  painting, 142-7
  music, 147-53
  and politics, 153-8

**The Ghost Story** SSC 58: 1-142
  overviews and general studies, 1-21
  the ghost story in American literature, 21-49
  the ghost story in Asian literature, 49-53
  the ghost story in European and English literature, 54-89
  major figures, 89-141

**The Gilded Age** NCLC 84: 169-271
  popular themes, 170-90
  Realism, 190-208
  Aestheticism, 208-26
  socio-political concerns, 226-70

***Glasnost* and Contemporary Soviet Literature** CLC 59: 355-97

**Gothic Drama** NCLC 132: 95-198
  overviews, 97-125
  sociopolitical contexts, 125-58
  Gothic playwrights, 158-97

**Gothic Novel** NCLC 28: 328-402
  development and major works, 328-34
  definitions, 334-50
  themes and techniques, 350-78
  in America, 378-85
  in Scotland, 385-91
  influence and legacy, 391-400

**The Governess in Nineteenth-Century Literature** NCLC 104: 1-131
  overviews and general studies, 3-28
  social roles and economic conditions, 28-86
  fictional governesses, 86-131

**The Grail Theme in Twentieth-Century Literature** TCLC 142: 1-89
  overviews and general studies, 2-20
  major works, 20-89

**Graphic Narratives** CLC 86: 405-32
  history and overviews, 406-21
  the "Classics Illustrated" series, 421-2
  reviews of recent works, 422-32

**Graphic Novels** CLC 177: 163-299
  overviews and general studies, 165-198
  critical readings of major works, 198-286
  reviews of recent graphic novels, 286-299

**Graveyard Poets** LC 67: 131-212
  origins and development, 131-52
  major figures, 152-75
  major works, 175-212

**Greek Historiography** CMLC 17: 1-49

**Greek Mythology** CMLC 26: 193-320
  overviews and general studies, 194-209
  origins and development of Greek mythology, 209-29
  cosmogonies and divinities in Greek mythology, 229-54
  heroes and heroines in Greek mythology, 254-80
  women in Greek mythology, 280-320

**Greek Theater** CMLC 51: 1-58
  criticism, 2-58

**Hard-Boiled Fiction** TCLC 118: 1-109
  overviews and general studies, 2-39

  major authors, 39-76
  women and hard-boiled fiction, 76-109

**The Harlem Renaissance** HR 1: 1-563
  overviews and general studies of the Harlem Renaissance, 1-137
    primary sources, 3-12
    overviews, 12-38
    background and sources of the Harlem Renaissance, 38-56
    the New Negro aesthetic, 56-91
    patrons, promoters, and the New York Public Library, 91-121
    women of the Harlem Renaissance, 121-37
  social, economic, and political factors that influenced the Harlem Renaissance, 139-240
    primary sources, 141-53
    overviews, 153-87
    social and economic factors, 187-213
    Black intellectual and political thought, 213-40
  publishing and periodicals during the Harlem Renaissance, 243-339
    primary sources, 246-52
    overviews, 252-68
    African American writers and mainstream publishers, 268-91
    anthologies: *The New Negro* and others, 291-309
    African American periodicals and the Harlem Renaissance, 309-39
  performing arts during the Harlem Renaissance, 341-465
    primary sources, 343-48
    overviews, 348-64
    drama of the Harlem Renaissance, 364-92
    influence of music on Harlem Renaissance writing, 437-65
  visual arts during the Harlem Renaissance, 467-563
    primary sources, 470-71
    overviews, 471-517
    painters, 517-36
    sculptors, 536-58
    photographers, 558-63

**Harlem Renaissance** TCLC 26: 49-125
  principal issues and figures, 50-67
  the literature and its audience, 67-74
  theme and technique in poetry, fiction, and drama, 74-115
  and American society, 115-21
  achievement and influence, 121-2

**Havel, Václav, Playwright and President** CLC 65: 406-63

**Heroic Drama** LC 91: 249-373
  definitions and overviews, 251-78
  politics and heroic drama, 278-303
  early plays: Dryden and Orrery, 303-51
  later plays: Lee and Otway, 351-73

**Historical Fiction, Nineteenth-Century** NCLC 48: 212-307
  definitions and characteristics, 213-36
  Victorian historical fiction, 236-65
  American historical fiction, 265-88
  realism in historical fiction, 288-306

**Hollywood and Literature** TCLC 118: 110-251
  overviews and general studies, 111-20
  adaptations, 120-65
  socio-historical and cultural impact, 165-206
  theater and hollywood, 206-51

**Holocaust and the Atomic Bomb: Fifty Years Later** CLC 91: 331-82
  the Holocaust remembered, 333-52
  Anne Frank revisited, 352-62

the atomic bomb and American memory, 362-81

**Holocaust Denial Literature** TCLC 58: 1-110
overviews and general studies, 1-30
Robert Faurisson and Noam Chomsky, 30-52
Holocaust denial literature in America, 52-71
library access to Holocaust denial literature, 72-5
the authenticity of Anne Frank's diary, 76-90
David Irving and the "normalization" of Hitler, 90-109

**Holocaust, Literature of the** TCLC 42: 355-450
historical overview, 357-61
critical overview, 361-70
diaries and memoirs, 370-95
novels and short stories, 395-425
poetry, 425-41
drama, 441-8

**Homosexuality in Nineteenth-Century Literature** NCLC 56: 78-182
defining homosexuality, 80-111
Greek love, 111-44
trial and danger, 144-81

**Humors Comedy** LC 85: 194-324
overviews, 195-251
major figures: Ben Jonson, 251-93
major figures: William Shakespeare, 293-324

**Hungarian Literature of the Twentieth Century** TCLC 26: 126-88
surveys of, 126-47
*Nyugat* and early twentieth-century literature, 147-56
mid-century literature, 156-68
and politics, 168-78
since the 1956 revolt, 178-87

**Hysteria in Nineteenth-Century Literature** NCLC 64: 59-184
the history of hysteria, 60-75
the gender of hysteria, 75-103
hysteria and women's narratives, 103-57
hysteria in nineteenth-century poetry, 157-83

**Image of the Noble Savage in Literature** LC 79: 136-252
overviews and development, 136-76
the Noble Savage in the New World, 176-221
Rousseau and the French Enlightenment's view of the noble savage, 221-51

**Imagism** TCLC 74: 259-454
history and development, 260
major figures, 288
sources and influences, 352
Imagism and other movements, 397
influence and legacy, 431

**Immigrants in Nineteenth-Century Literature, Representation of** NCLC 112: 188-298
overview, 189-99
immigrants in America, 199-223
immigrants and labor, 223-60
immigrants in England, 260-97

**Incest in Nineteenth-Century American Literature** NCLC 76: 70-141
overview, 71-88
the concern for social order, 88-117
authority and authorship, 117-40

**Incest in Victorian Literature** NCLC 92: 172-318
overviews and general studies, 173-85
novels, 185-276
plays, 276-84
poetry, 284-318

**Indian Literature in English** TCLC 54: 308-406
overview, 309-13
origins and major figures, 313-25
the Indo-English novel, 325-55
Indo-English poetry, 355-67
Indo-English drama, 367-72
critical perspectives on Indo-English literature, 372-80
modern Indo-English literature, 380-9
Indo-English authors on their work, 389-404

**The Industrial Revolution in Literature** NCLC 56: 183-273
historical and cultural perspectives, 184-201
contemporary reactions to the machine, 201-21
themes and symbols in literature, 221-73

**The Irish Famine as Represented in Nineteenth-Century Literature** NCLC 64: 185-261
overviews and general studies, 187-98
historical background, 198-212
famine novels, 212-34
famine poetry, 234-44
famine letters and eye-witness accounts, 245-61

**Irish Literary Renaissance** TCLC 46: 172-287
overview, 173-83
development and major figures, 184-202
influence of Irish folklore and mythology, 202-22
Irish poetry, 222-34
Irish drama and the Abbey Theatre, 234-56
Irish fiction, 256-86

**Irish Nationalism and Literature** NCLC 44: 203-73
the Celtic element in literature, 203-19
anti-Irish sentiment and the Celtic response, 219-34
literary ideals in Ireland, 234-45
literary expressions, 245-73

**Irish Novel, The** NCLC 80: 1-130
overviews and general studies, 3-9
principal figures, 9-22
peasant and middle class Irish novelists, 22-76
aristocratic Irish and Anglo-Irish novelists, 76-129

**Israeli Literature** TCLC 94: 1-137
overviews and general studies, 2-18
Israeli fiction, 18-33
Israeli poetry, 33-62
Israeli drama, 62-91
women and Israeli literature, 91-112
Arab characters in Israeli literature, 112-36

**Italian Futurism** See Futurism, Italian

**Italian Humanism** LC 12: 205-77
origins and early development, 206-18
revival of classical letters, 218-23
humanism and other philosophies, 224-39
humanism and humanists, 239-46
the plastic arts, 246-57
achievement and significance, 258-76

**Italian Romanticism** NCLC 60: 85-145
origins and overviews, 86-101
Italian Romantic theory, 101-25
the language of Romanticism, 125-45

**Jacobean Drama** LC 33: 1-37
the Jacobean worldview: an era of transition, 2-14
the moral vision of Jacobean drama, 14-22
Jacobean tragedy, 22-3
the Jacobean masque, 23-36

**Jazz and Literature** TCLC 102: 3-124

**Jewish-American Fiction** TCLC 62: 1-181
overviews and general studies, 2-24
major figures, 24-48
Jewish writers and American life, 48-78
Jewish characters in American fiction, 78-108
themes in Jewish-American fiction, 108-43
Jewish-American women writers, 143-59
the Holocaust and Jewish-American fiction, 159-81

**Jews in Literature** TCLC 118: 252-417
overviews and general studies, 253-97
representing the Jew in literature, 297-351
the Holocaust in literature, 351-416

**Journals of Lewis and Clark, The** NCLC 100: 1-88
overviews and general studies, 4-30
journal-keeping methods, 30-46
Fort Mandan, 46-51
the Clark journal, 51-65
the journals as literary texts, 65-87

**Kabuki** LC 73: 118-232
overviews and general studies, 120-40
the development of Kabuki, 140-65
major works, 165-95
Kabuki and society, 195-231

**Kit-Kat Club, The** LC 71: 66-112
overviews and general studies, 67-88
major figures, 88-107
attacks on the Kit-Kat Club, 107-12

**Knickerbocker Group, The** NCLC 56: 274-341
overviews and general studies, 276-314
Knickerbocker periodicals, 314-26
writers and artists, 326-40

*Künstlerroman* TCLC 150: 133-260
overviews and general studies, 135-51
major works, 151-212
feminism in the *Künstlerroman*, 212-49
minority *Künstlerroman*, 249-59

**Lake Poets, The** NCLC 52: 217-304
characteristics of the Lake Poets and their works, 218-27
literary influences and collaborations, 227-66
defining and developing Romantic ideals, 266-84
embracing Conservatism, 284-303

**Language Poets** TCLC 126: 66-172
overviews and general studies, 67-122
selected major figures in language poetry, 122-72

**Larkin, Philip, Controversy** CLC 81: 417-64

**Latin American Literature, Twentieth-Century** TCLC 58: 111-98
historical and critical perspectives, 112-36
the novel, 136-45
the short story, 145-9
drama, 149-60
poetry, 160-7
the writer and society, 167-86
Native Americans in Latin American literature, 186-97

**Law and Literature** TCLC 126: 173-347
overviews and general studies, 174-253
fiction critiquing the law, 253-88
literary responses to the law, 289-346

**Legend of El Dorado, The** LC 74: 248-350
overviews, 249-308
major explorations for El Dorado, 308-50

**The Levellers** LC 51: 200-312
overviews and general studies, 201-29
principal figures, 230-86
religion, political philosophy, and pamphleteering, 287-311

**Literary Criticism in the Nineteenth Century, American** NCLC 128: 1-103
  overviews and general studies, 2-44
  the trancendentalists, 44-65
  "young America," 65-71
  James Russell Lowell, 71-9
  Edgar Allan Poe, 79-97
  Walt Whitman, 97-102

**Literary Expressionism** TCLC 142: 90-185
  overviews and general studies, 91-138
  themes in literary expressionism, 138-61
  expressionism in Germany, 161-84

**Literary Marketplace, The Nineteenth-Century** NCLC 128: 194-368
  overviews and general studies, 197-228
  British literary marketplace, 228-66
  French literary marketplace, 266-82
  American literary marketplace, 282-323
  Women in the literary marketplace, 323-67

**Literary Prizes** TCLC 122: 130-203
  overviews and general studies, 131-34
  the Nobel Prize in Literature, 135-83
  the Pulitzer Prize, 183-203

**Literature and Millenial Lists** CLC 119: 431-67
  The Modern Library list, 433
  The Waterstone list, 438-439

**Literature in Response to the September 11 Attacks** CLC 174: 1-46
  Major works about September 11, 2001, 2-22
  Critical, artistic, and journalistic responses, 22-45

**Literature of the American Cowboy** NCLC 96: 1-60
  overview, 3-20
  cowboy fiction, 20-36
  cowboy poetry and songs, 36-59

**Literature of the California Gold Rush** NCLC 92: 320-85
  overviews and general studies, 322-24
  early California Gold Rush fiction, 324-44
  Gold Rush folklore and legend, 344-51
  the rise of Western local color, 351-60
  social relations and social change, 360-385

**Living Theatre, The** DC 16: 154-214

**Luddism in Nineteenth-Century Literature** NCLC 140: 280-365
  overviews, 281-322
  the literary response, 322-65

**Madness in Nineteenth-Century Literature** NCLC 76: 142-284
  overview, 143-54
  autobiography, 154-68
  poetry, 168-215
  fiction, 215-83

**Madness in Twentieth-Century Literature** TCLC 50: 160-225
  overviews and general studies, 161-71
  madness and the creative process, 171-86
  suicide, 186-91
  madness in American literature, 191-207
  madness in German literature, 207-13
  madness and feminist artists, 213-24

**Magic Realism** TCLC 110: 80-327
  overviews and general studies, 81-94
  magic realism in African literature, 95-110
  magic realism in American literature, 110-32
  magic realism in Canadian literature, 132-46
  magic realism in European literature, 146-66
  magic realism in Asian literature, 166-79
  magic realism in Latin-American literature, 179-223

  magic realism in Israeli literature and the novels of Salman Rushdie, 223-38
  magic realism in literature written by women, 239-326

**The Martin Marprelate Tracts** LC 101: 165-240
  criticism, 166-240

**Marxist Criticism** TCLC 134: 127-57
  overviews and general studies, 128-67
  Marxist interpretations, 167-209
  cultural and literary Marxist theory, 209-49
  Marxism and feminist critical theory, 250-56

**The Masque** LC 63: 124-265
  development of the masque, 125-62
  sources and structure, 162-220
  race and gender in the masque, 221-64

**Medical Writing** LC 55: 93-195
  colonial America, 94-110
  enlightenment, 110-24
  medieval writing, 124-40
  sexuality, 140-83
  vernacular, 185-95

**Memoirs of Trauma** CLC 109: 419-466
  overview, 420
  criticism, 429

**Metafiction** TCLC 130: 43-228
  overviews and general studies, 44-85
  Spanish metafiction, 85-117
  studies of metafictional authors and works, 118-228

**Metaphysical Poets** LC 24: 356-439
  early definitions, 358-67
  surveys and overviews, 367-92
  cultural and social influences, 392-406
  stylistic and thematic variations, 407-38

**Missionaries in the Nineteenth-Century, Literature of** NCLC 112: 299-392
  history and development, 300-16
  uses of ethnography, 316-31
  sociopolitical concerns, 331-82
  David Livingstone, 382-91

**Modern Essay, The** TCLC 58: 199-273
  overview, 200-7
  the essay in the early twentieth century, 207-19
  characteristics of the modern essay, 219-32
  modern essayists, 232-45
  the essay as a literary genre, 245-73

**Modern French Literature** TCLC 122: 205-359
  overviews and general studies, 207-43
  French theater, 243-77
  gender issues and French women writers, 277-315
  ideology and politics, 315-24
  modern French poetry, 324-41
  resistance literature, 341-58

**Modern Irish Literature** TCLC 102: 125-321
  overview, 129-44
  dramas, 144-70
  fiction, 170-247
  poetry, 247-321

**Modern Japanese Literature** TCLC 66: 284-389
  poetry, 285-305
  drama, 305-29
  fiction, 329-61
  western influences, 361-87

**Modernism** TCLC 70: 165-275
  definitions, 166-184
  Modernism and earlier influences, 184-200
  stylistic and thematic traits, 200-229
  poetry and drama, 229-242
  redefining Modernism, 242-275

**Muckraking Movement in American Journalism** TCLC 34: 161-242
  development, principles, and major figures, 162-70
  publications, 170-9
  social and political ideas, 179-86
  targets, 186-208
  fiction, 208-19
  decline, 219-29
  impact and accomplishments, 229-40

**Multiculturalism** CLC 189: 167-254
  overviews and general studies, 168-93
  the effects of multiculturalism on global literature, 193-213
  multicultural themes in specific contemporary works, 213-53

**Multiculturalism in Literature and Education** CLC 70: 361-413

**Music and Modern Literature** TCLC 62: 182-329
  overviews and general studies, 182-211
  musical form/literary form, 211-32
  music in literature, 232-50
  the influence of music on literature, 250-73
  literature and popular music, 273-303
  jazz and poetry, 303-28

**Mystery Story** See Crime-Mystery-Detective Stories

**Native American Literature** CLC 76: 440-76

**Natural School, Russian** NCLC 24: 205-40
  history and characteristics, 205-25
  contemporary criticism, 225-40

**Naturalism** NCLC 36: 285-382
  definitions and theories, 286-305
  critical debates on Naturalism, 305-16
  Naturalism in theater, 316-32
  European Naturalism, 332-61
  American Naturalism, 361-72
  the legacy of Naturalism, 372-81

**Negritude** TCLC 50: 226-361
  origins and evolution, 227-56
  definitions, 256-91
  Negritude in literature, 291-343
  Negritude reconsidered, 343-58

**New Criticism** TCLC 34: 243-318
  development and ideas, 244-70
  debate and defense, 270-99
  influence and legacy, 299-315

TCLC 146: 1–108
  overviews and general studies, 3–19
  defining New Criticism, 19–28
  place in history, 28–51
  poetry and New Criticism, 51–78
  major authors, 78–108

**New South, Literature of the** NCLC 116: 122-240
  overviews, 124-66
  the novel in the New South, 166-209
  myth of the Old South in the New, 209-39

**The New World in Renaissance Literature** LC 31: 1-51
  overview, 1-18
  utopia vs. terror, 18-31
  explorers and Native Americans, 31-51

**New York Intellectuals and *Partisan Review*** TCLC 30: 117-98
  development and major figures, 118-28
  influence of Judaism, 128-39
  *Partisan Review,* 139-57
  literary philosophy and practice, 157-75
  political philosophy, 175-87
  achievement and significance, 187-97

***The New Yorker*** TCLC 58: 274-357
  overviews and general studies, 274-95
  major figures, 295-304
  *New Yorker* style, 304-33

Topic Index

fiction, journalism, and humor at *The New
    Yorker,* 333-48
the new *New Yorker,* 348-56

**Newgate Novel** NCLC 24: 166-204
development of Newgate literature, 166-73
*Newgate Calendar,* 173-7
Newgate fiction, 177-95
Newgate drama, 195-204

**New Zealand Literature** TCLC 134: 258-368
overviews and general studies, 260-300
Maori literature, 300-22
New Zealand drama, 322-32
New Zealand fiction, 332-51
New Zealand poetry, 351-67

**Nigerian Literature of the Twentieth Century**
TCLC 30: 199-265
surveys of, 199-227
English language and African life, 227-45
politics and the Nigerian writer, 245-54
Nigerian writers and society, 255-62

**Nihilism and Literature** TCLC 110: 328-93
overviews and general studies, 328-44
European and Russian nihilism, 344-73
nihilism in the works of Albert Camus,
    Franz Kafka, and John Barth, 373-92

**Nineteenth-Century Captivity Narratives**
NCLC 80:131-218
overview, 132-37
the political significance of captivity narra-
    tives, 137-67
images of gender, 167-96
moral instruction, 197-217

**Nineteenth-Century Euro-American Literary
Representations of Native Americans** NCLC
104: 132-264
overviews and general studies, 134-53
Native American history, 153-72
the Indians of the Northeast, 172-93
the Indians of the Southeast, 193-212
the Indians of the West, 212-27
Indian-hater fiction, 227-43
the Indian as exhibit, 243-63

**Nineteenth-Century Native American Autobi-
ography** NCLC 64: 262-389
overview, 263-8
problems of authorship, 268-81
the evolution of Native American autobiog-
    raphy, 281-304
political issues, 304-15
gender and autobiography, 316-62
autobiographical works during the turn of
    the century, 362-88

**Nineteenth-Century Pornography** NCLC 144:
108-202
nineteenth-century pornographers, 110-64
pornography and literature, 164-91
pornography and censorship, 191-201

**Noh Drama** LC 103: 189-270
overviews, 190-94
origins and development, 194-214
structure, 214-28
types of plays, 228-45
masks in Noh drama, 245-57
Noh drama and the audience, 257-69

**Norse Mythology** CMLC 26: 321-85
history and mythological tradition, 322-44
Eddic poetry, 344-74
Norse mythology and other traditions,
    374-85

**Northern Humanism** LC 16: 281-356
background, 282-305
precursor of the Reformation, 305-14
the Brethren of the Common Life, the De-
    votio Moderna, and education, 314-40
the impact of printing, 340-56

**Novel of Manners, The** NCLC 56: 342-96
social and political order, 343-53

domestic order, 353-73
depictions of gender, 373-83
the American novel of manners, 383-95

**Novels of the Ming and Early Ch'ing Dynas-
ties** LC 76: 213-356
overviews and historical development,
    214-45
major works—overview, 245-85
genre studies, 285-325
cultural and social themes, 325-55

**Nuclear Literature: Writings and Criticism
in the Nuclear Age** TCLC 46: 288-390
overviews and general studies, 290-301
fiction, 301-35
poetry, 335-8
nuclear war in Russo-Japanese literature,
    338-55
nuclear war and women writers, 355-67
the nuclear referent and literary criticism,
    367-88

**Occultism in Modern Literature** TCLC 50:
362-406
influence of occultism on literature, 363-72
occultism, literature, and society, 372-87
fiction, 387-96
drama, 396-405

**Opium and the Nineteenth-Century Literary
Imagination** NCLC 20:250-301
original sources, 250-62
historical background, 262-71
and literary society, 271-9
and literary creativity, 279-300

**Orientalism** NCLC 96: 149-364
overviews and general studies, 150-98
Orientalism and imperialism, 198-229
Orientalism and gender, 229-59
Orientalism and the nineteenth-century
    novel, 259-321
Orientalism in nineteenth-century poetry,
    321-63

**The Oxford Movement** NCLC 72: 1-197
overviews and general studies, 2-24
background, 24-59
and education, 59-69
religious responses, 69-128
literary aspects, 128-178
political implications, 178-196

**The Parnassian Movement** NCLC 72: 198-
241
overviews and general studies, 199-231
and epic form, 231-38
and positivism, 238-41

**Pastoral Literature of the English Renais-
sance** LC 59: 171-282
overviews and general studies, 172-214
principal figures of the Elizabethan period,
    214-33
principal figures of the later Renaissance,
    233-50
pastoral drama, 250-81

**Periodicals, Nineteenth-Century American**
NCLC 132: 199-374
overviews, chronology, and development,
    200-41
literary periodicals, 241-83
regional periodicals, 283-317
women's magazines and gender issues,
    317-47
minority periodicals, 347-72

**Periodicals, Nineteenth-Century British**
NCLC 24: 100-65
overviews and general studies, 100-30
in the Romantic Age, 130-41
in the Victorian era, 142-54
and the reviewer, 154-64

**Picaresque Literature of the Sixteenth and
Seventeenth Centuries** LC 78: 223-355

context and development, 224-71
genre, 271-98
the picaro, 299-326
the picara, 326-53

**Plath, Sylvia, and the Nature of Biography**
CLC 86: 433-62
the nature of biography, 433-52
reviews of *The Silent Woman,* 452-61

**Political Theory from the 15th to the 18th
Century** LC 36: 1-55
overview, 1-26
natural law, 26-42
empiricism, 42-55

**Polish Romanticism** NCLC 52: 305-71
overviews and general studies, 306-26
major figures, 326-40
Polish Romantic drama, 340-62
influences, 362-71

**Politics and Literature** TCLC 94: 138-61
overviews and general studies, 139-96
Europe, 196-226
Latin America, 226-48
Africa and the Caribbean, 248-60

**Popular Literature** TCLC 70: 279-382
overviews and general studies, 280-324
"formula" fiction, 324-336
readers of popular literature, 336-351
evolution of popular literature, 351-382

**The Portrayal of Jews in Nineteenth-Century
English Literature** NCLC 72: 242-368
overviews and general studies, 244-77
Anglo-Jewish novels, 277-303
depictions by non-Jewish writers, 303-44
Hebraism versus Hellenism, 344-67

**The Portrayal of Mormonism** NCLC 96: 61-
148
overview, 63-72
early Mormon literature, 72-100
Mormon periodicals and journals, 100-10
women writers, 110-22
Mormonism and nineteenth-century litera-
    ture, 122-42
Mormon poetry, 142-47

**Post-apartheid Literature** CLC 187: 284-382
overviews and general studies, 286-318
the post-apartheid novel, 318-65
post-apartheid drama, 365-81

**Postcolonial African Literature** TCLC 146:
110-239
overviews and general studies, 111–45
ideology and theory, 145–62
postcolonial testimonial literature, 162–99
major authors, 199–239

**Postcolonialism** TCLC 114: 134-239
overviews and general studies, 135-153
African postcolonial writing, 153-72
Asian/Pacific literature, 172-78
postcolonial literary theory, 178-213
postcolonial women's writing, 213-38

**Postmodernism** TCLC 90:125-307
overview, 126-166
criticism, 166-224
fiction, 224-282
poetry, 282-300
drama, 300-307

**Pre-Raphaelite Movement** NCLC 20: 302-401
overview, 302-4
genesis, 304-12
*Germ* and *Oxford and Cambridge Maga-
    zine,* 312-20
Robert Buchanan and the "Fleshly School
    of Poetry," 320-31
satires and parodies, 331-4
surveys, 334-51
aesthetics, 351-75
sister arts of poetry and painting, 375-94
influence, 394-9

**Pre-romanticism** LC 40: 1-56
　overviews and general studies, 2-14
　defining the period, 14-23
　new directions in poetry and prose, 23-45
　the focus on the self, 45-56

**Pre-Socratic Philosophy** CMLC 22: 1-56
　overviews and general studies, 3-24
　the Ionians and the Pythagoreans, 25-35
　Heraclitus, the Eleatics, and the Atomists,
　　36-47
　the Sophists, 47-55

**Prison in Nineteenth-Century Literature,
The** NCLC 116: 241-357
　overview, 242-60
　romantic prison, 260-78
　domestic prison, 278-316
　America as prison, 316-24
　physical prisons and prison authors, 324-56

**Protestant Hagiography and Martyrology** LC
84: 106-217
　overview, 106-37
　John Foxe's *Book of Martyrs,* 137-97
　martyrology and the feminine perspective,
　　198-216

**Protestant Reformation, Literature of the** LC
37: 1-83
　overviews and general studies, 1-49
　humanism and scholasticism, 49-69
　the reformation and literature, 69-82

**Psychoanalysis and Literature** TCLC 38: 227-
338
　overviews and general studies, 227-46
　Freud on literature, 246-51
　psychoanalytic views of the literary pro-
　　cess, 251-61
　psychoanalytic theories of response to
　　literature, 261-88
　psychoanalysis and literary criticism, 288-
　　312
　psychoanalysis as literature/literature as
　　psychoanalysis, 313-34

**The Quarrel between the Ancients and the
Moderns** LC 63: 266-381
　overviews and general studies, 267-301
　Renaissance origins, 301-32
　Quarrel between the Ancients and the
　　Moderns in France, 332-58
　Battle of the Books in England, 358-80

**Racism in Literature** TCLC 138: 257-373
　overviews and general studies, 257-326
　racism and literature by and about African
　　Americans, 292-326
　theme of racism in literature, 326-773

**Rap Music** CLC 76: 477-50

**Reader-Response Criticism** TCLC 146: 240–
357
　overviews and general studies, 241–88
　critical approaches to reader response, 288–
　　342
　reader-response interpretation, 342–57

**Realism in Short Fiction** SSC 63: 128-57
　overviews and general studies, 129-37
　realist short fiction in France, 137-62
　realist short fiction in Russia, 162-215
　realist short fiction in England, 215-31
　realist short fiction in the United States,
　　231-56

**Regionalism and Local Color in Short Fic-
tion** SSC 65: 160-289
　overviews and general studies, 163-205
　regionalism/local color fiction of the west,
　　205-42
　regionalism/local color fiction of the mid-
　　west, 242-57
　regionalism/local color fiction of the south,
　　257-88

**Renaissance Natural Philosophy** LC 27:
201-87
　cosmology, 201-28
　astrology, 228-54
　magic, 254-86

**Representations of the Devil in Nineteenth-
Century Literature** NCLC 100: 89-223
　overviews and general studies, 90-115
　the Devil in American fiction, 116-43
　English Romanticism: the satanic school,
　　143-89
　Luciferian discourse in European literature,
　　189-222

**Restoration Drama** LC 21: 184-275
　general overviews and general studies, 185-
　　230
　Jeremy Collier stage controversy, 230-9
　other critical interpretations, 240-75

**Revenge Tragedy** LC 71: 113-242
　overviews and general studies, 113-51
　Elizabethan attitudes toward revenge,
　　151-88
　the morality of revenge, 188-216
　reminders and remembrance, 217-41

**Revising the Literary Canon** CLC 81: 465-
509

**Revising the Literary Canon** TCLC 114:
240-84
　overviews and general studies, 241-85
　canon change in American literature, 285-
　　339
　gender and the literary canon, 339-59
　minority and third-world literature and the
　　canon, 359-84

**Revolutionary Astronomers** LC 51: 314-65
　overviews and general studies, 316-25
　principal figures, 325-51
　Revolutionary astronomical models, 352-64

**Robin Hood, Legend of** LC 19: 205-58
　origins and development of the Robin Hood
　　legend, 206-20
　representations of Robin Hood, 220-44
　Robin Hood as hero, 244-56

**Romantic Literary Criticism** NCLC 144: 203-
357
　background and overviews, 205-30
　literary reviews, 230-38
　the German Romantics, 238-81
　Wordsworth and Coleridge, 281-326
　variations on Romantic critical theory,
　　326-56

**Rushdie, Salman,** *Satanic Verses* **Controversy**
CLC 55: 214-63; 59:404-56

**Russian Nihilism** NCLC 28: 403-47
　definitions and overviews, 404-17
　women and Nihilism, 417-27
　literature as reform: the Civic Critics,
　　427-33
　Nihilism and the Russian novel: Turgenev
　　and Dostoevsky, 433-47

**Russian Thaw** TCLC 26: 189-247
　literary history of the period, 190-206
　theoretical debate of socialist realism,
　　206-11
　*Novy Mir,* 211-7
　*Literary Moscow,* 217-24
　Pasternak, *Zhivago,* and the Nobel prize,
　　224-7
　poetry of liberation, 228-31
　Brodsky trial and the end of the Thaw,
　　231-6
　achievement and influence, 236-46

**Salem Witch Trials** LC 38: 1-145
　overviews and general studies, 2-30
　historical background, 30-65
　judicial background, 65-78

　the search for causes, 78-115
　the role of women in the trials, 115-44

**Salinger, J. D., Controversy Surrounding** *In
Search of J. D. Salinger* CLC 55: 325-44

**Samizdat Literature** TCLC 150: 261-342
　overviews and general studies, 262-64
　history and development, 264-309
　politics and Samizdat, 309-22
　voices of Samizdat, 322-42

**Sanitation Reform, Nineteenth-Century**
NCLC 124: 165-257
　overviews and general studies, 166
　primary texts, 186-89
　social context, 189-221
　public health in literature, 221-56

**Science and Modern Literature** TCLC 90:
308-419
　overviews and general studies, 295-333
　fiction, 333-95
　poetry, 395-405
　drama, 405-19

**Science in Nineteenth-Century Literature**
NCLC 100: 224-366
　overviews and general studies, 225-65
　major figures, 265-336
　sociopolitical concerns, 336-65

**Science Fiction, Nineteenth-Century** NCLC
24: 241-306
　background, 242-50
　definitions of the genre, 251-56
　representative works and writers, 256-75
　themes and conventions, 276-305

**Scottish Chaucerians** LC 20: 363-412

**Scottish Poetry, Eighteenth-Century** LC 29:
95-167
　overviews and general studies, 96-114
　the Scottish Augustans, 114-28
　the Scots Vernacular Revival, 132-63
　Scottish poetry after Burns, 163-66

**Sea in Literature, The** TCLC 82: 72-191
　drama, 73-9
　poetry, 79-119
　fiction, 119-91

**Sea in Nineteenth-Century English and
American Literature, The** NCLC 104: 265-
362
　overviews and general studies, 267-306
　major figures in American sea fiction—
　　Cooper and Melville, 306-29
　American sea poetry and short stories,
　　329-45
　English sea literature, 345-61

**Sensation Novel, The** NCLC 80: 219-330
　overviews and general studies, 221-46
　principal figures, 246-62
　nineteenth-century reaction, 262-91
　feminist criticism, 291-329

**Sentimental Novel, The** NCLC 60: 146-245
　overviews and general studies, 147-58
　the politics of domestic fiction, 158-79
　a literature of resistance and repression,
　　179-212
　the reception of sentimental fiction, 213-44

**September 11 Attacks See Literature in
Response to the September 11 Attacks**

**Sex and Literature** TCLC 82: 192-434
　overviews and general studies, 193-216
　drama, 216-63
　poetry, 263-87
　fiction, 287-431

**Sherlock Holmes Centenary** TCLC 26: 248-
310
　Doyle's life and the composition of the
　　Holmes stories, 248-59
　life and character of Holmes, 259-78
　method, 278-79

Topic Index

Holmes and the Victorian world, 279-92
Sherlockian scholarship, 292-301
Doyle and the development of the detective story, 301-07
Holmes's continuing popularity, 307-09

**Short Science Fiction, Golden Age of, 1938-1950** SSC 73: 1-145
overviews and general studies, 3-48
publishing history of Golden Age Short Science Fiction, 48-65
major Golden Age Short Science Fiction authors and editors
Isaac Asimov, 65-77
Ray Bradbury, 77-92
John W. Campbell, 92-106
Arthur C. Clarke, 106-15
Robert A. Heinlein, 115-29
Damon Knight, 129-40
Frederik Pohl, 141-43

**Short-Short Fiction** SSC 61: 311-36
overviews and general studies, 312-19
major short-short fiction writers, 319-35

**The Silver Fork Novel** NCLC 88: 58-140
criticism, 59-139

**Slave Narratives, American** NCLC 20: 1-91
background, 2-9
overviews and general studies, 9-24
contemporary responses, 24-7
language, theme, and technique, 27-70
historical authenticity, 70-5
antecedents, 75-83
role in development of Black American literature, 83-8

**The Slave Trade in British and American Literature** LC 59: 283-369
overviews and general studies, 284-91
depictions by white writers, 291-331
depictions by former slaves, 331-67

**Social Conduct Literature** LC 55: 196-298
overviews and general studies, 196-223
prescriptive ideology in other literary forms, 223-38
role of the press, 238-63
impact of conduct literature, 263-87
conduct literature and the perception of women, 287-96
women writing for women, 296-98

**Social Protest Literature Outside England, Nineteenth-Century** NCLC 124: 258-350
overviews and general studies, 259-72
oppression revealed, 272-306
literature to incite or prevent reform, 306-50

**Socialism** NCLC 88: 141-237
origins, 142-54
French socialism, 154-83
Anglo-American socialism, 183-205
Socialist-Feminism, 205-36

**Southern Gothic Literature** TCLC 142: 186-270
overviews and general studies, 187-97
major authors in southern Gothic literature, 197-230
structure and technique in southern Gothic literature, 230-50
themes in southern Gothic literature, 250-70

**Southern Literature See Contemporary Southern Literature**

**Southern Literature of the Reconstruction** NCLC 108: 289-369
overview, 290-91
reconstruction literature: the consequences of war, 291-321
old south to new: continuities in southern culture, 321-68

**Spanish Civil War Literature** TCLC 26: 311-85

topics in, 312-33
British and American literature, 333-59
French literature, 359-62
Spanish literature, 362-73
German literature, 373-75
political idealism and war literature, 375-83

**Spanish Golden Age Literature** LC 23: 262-332
overviews and general studies, 263-81
verse drama, 281-304
prose fiction, 304-19
lyric poetry, 319-31

**Sparta in Literature** CMLC 70: 145-271
overviews, 147-61
Spartan poetry, 161-72
the Spartan myth, 172-200
historical background, 200-27
Spartan society and culture, 227-69

**Spasmodic School of Poetry** NCLC 24: 307-52
history and major figures, 307-21
the Spasmodics on poetry, 321-7
*Firmilian* and critical disfavor, 327-39
theme and technique, 339-47
influence, 347-51

**Sports in Literature** TCLC 86: 294-445
overviews and general studies, 295-324
major writers and works, 324-402
sports, literature, and social issues, 402-45

**Steinbeck, John, Fiftieth Anniversary of *The Grapes of Wrath*** CLC 59: 311-54

**Sturm und Drang** NCLC 40: 196-276
definitions, 197-238
poetry and poetics, 238-58
drama, 258-75

**Supernatural Fiction in the Nineteenth Century** NCLC 32: 207-87
major figures and influences, 208-35
the Victorian ghost story, 236-54
the influence of science and occultism, 254-66
supernatural fiction and society, 266-86

**Supernatural Fiction, Modern** TCLC 30: 59-116
evolution and varieties, 60-74
"decline" of the ghost story, 74-86
as a literary genre, 86-92
technique, 92-101
nature and appeal, 101-15

**Surrealism** TCLC 30: 334-406
history and formative influences, 335-43
manifestos, 343-54
philosophic, aesthetic, and political principles, 354-75
poetry, 375-81
novel, 381-6
drama, 386-92
film, 392-8
painting and sculpture, 398-403
achievement, 403-5

**Symbolism, Russian** TCLC 30: 266-333
doctrines and major figures, 267-92
theories, 293-8
and French Symbolism, 298-310
themes in poetry, 310-4
theater, 314-20
and the fine arts, 320-32

**Symbolist Movement, French** NCLC 20: 169-249
background and characteristics, 170-86
principles, 186-91
attacked and defended, 191-7
influences and predecessors, 197-211
and Decadence, 211-6
theater, 216-26
prose, 226-33
decline and influence, 233-47

**Television and Literature** TCLC 78: 283-426
television and literacy, 283-98
reading vs. watching, 298-341
adaptations, 341-62
literary genres and television, 362-90
television genres and literature, 390-410
children's literature/children's television, 410-25

**Theater of the Absurd** TCLC 38: 339-415
"The Theater of the Absurd," 340-7
major plays and playwrights, 347-58
and the concept of the absurd, 358-86
theatrical techniques, 386-94
predecessors of, 394-402
influence of, 402-13

**Tin Pan Alley See American Popular Song, Golden Age of**

**Tobacco Culture** LC 55: 299-366
social and economic attitudes toward tobacco, 299-344
tobacco trade between the old world and the new world, 344-55
tobacco smuggling in Great Britain, 355-66

**Transcendentalism, American** NCLC 24: 1-99
overviews and general studies, 3-23
contemporary documents, 23-41
theological aspects of, 42-52
and social issues, 52-74
literature of, 74-96

**Travel Writing in the Nineteenth Century** NCLC 44: 274-392
the European grand tour, 275-303
the Orient, 303-47
North America, 347-91

**Travel Writing in the Twentieth Century** TCLC 30: 407-56
conventions and traditions, 407-27
and fiction writing, 427-43
comparative essays on travel writers, 443-54

**Tristan and Isolde Legend** CMLC 42: 311-404

**Troubadours** CMLC 66: 244-383
overviews, 245-91
politics, economics, history, and the troubadours, 291-344
troubadours and women, 344-82

**True-Crime Literature** CLC 99: 333-433
history and analysis, 334-407
reviews of true-crime publications, 407-23
writing instruction, 424-29
author profiles, 429-33

**Twentieth-Century Danish Literature** TCLC 142: 271-344
major works, 272-84
major authors, 284-344

***Ulysses* and the Process of Textual Reconstruction** TCLC 26: 386-416
evaluations of the new *Ulysses*, 386-94
editorial principles and procedures, 394-401
theoretical issues, 401-16

**Utilitarianism** NCLC 84: 272-340
J. S. Mill's Utilitarianism: liberty, equality, justice, 273-313
Jeremy Bentham's Utilitarianism: the science of happiness, 313-39

**Utopianism** NCLC 88: 238-346
overviews: Utopian literature, 239-59
Utopianism in American literature, 259-99
Utopianism in British literature, 299-311
Utopianism and Feminism, 311-45

**Utopian Literature, Nineteenth-Century** NCLC 24: 353-473
definitions, 354-74
overviews and general studies, 374-88

theory, 388-408
communities, 409-26
fiction, 426-53
women and fiction, 454-71

**Utopian Literature, Renaissance** LC 32: 1-63
overviews and general studies, 2-25
classical background, 25-33
utopia and the social contract, 33-9
origins in mythology, 39-48
utopia and the Renaissance country house,
48-52
influence of millenarianism, 52-62

**Vampire in Literature** TCLC 46: 391-454
origins and evolution, 392-412
social and psychological perspectives,
413-44
vampire fiction and science fiction, 445-53

**Vernacular Bibles** LC 67: 214-388
overviews and general studies, 215-59
the English Bible, 259-355
the German Bible, 355-88

**Victorian Autobiography** NCLC 40: 277-363
development and major characteristics,
278-88
themes and techniques, 289-313
the autobiographical tendency in Victorian
prose and poetry, 313-47
Victorian women's autobiographies, 347-62

**Victorian Critical Theory** NCLC 136: 236-
379
overviews and general studies, 237-86
Matthew Arnold, 286-324
Walter Pater and aestheticism, 324-36
other Victorian critics, 336-78

**Victorian Fantasy Literature** NCLC 60: 246-
384
overviews and general studies, 247-91
major figures, 292-366
women in Victorian fantasy literature,
366-83

**Victorian Hellenism** NCLC 68: 251-376
overviews and general studies, 252-78
the meanings of Hellenism, 278-335
the literary influence, 335-75

**Victorian Illustrated Fiction** NCLC 120: 247-
356
overviews and development, 128-76
technical and material aspects of book illustration, 276-84
Charles Dickens and his illustrators, 284-
320

William Makepeace Thackeray, 320-31
George Eliot and Frederic Leighton, 331-51
Lewis Carroll and John Tenniel, 351-56

**Victorian Novel** NCLC 32: 288-454
development and major characteristics,
290-310
themes and techniques, 310-58
social criticism in the Victorian novel,
359-97
urban and rural life in the Victorian novel,
397-406
women in the Victorian novel, 406-25
Mudie's Circulating Library, 425-34
the late-Victorian novel, 434-51

**Vietnamese Literature** TCLC 102: 322-386

**Vietnam War in Literature and Film** CLC
91: 383-437
overview, 384-8
prose, 388-412
film and drama, 412-24
poetry, 424-35

**Violence in Literature** TCLC 98: 235-358
overviews and general studies, 236-74
violence in the works of modern authors,
274-358

**Vorticism** TCLC 62: 330-426
Wyndham Lewis and Vorticism, 330-8
characteristics and principles of Vorticism,
338-65
Lewis and Pound, 365-82
Vorticist writing, 382-416
Vorticist painting, 416-26

**Well-Made Play, The** NCLC 80: 331-370
overviews and general studies, 332-45
Scribe's style, 345-56
the influence of the well-made play, 356-69

**Women's Autobiography, Nineteenth Cen-
tury** NCLC 76: 285-368
overviews and general studies, 287-300
autobiographies concerned with religious
and political issues, 300-15
autobiographies by women of color, 315-38
autobiographies by women pioneers,
338-51
autobiographies by women of letters,
351-68

**Women's Diaries, Nineteenth-Century** NCLC
48: 308-54
overview, 308-13
diary as history, 314-25
sociology of diaries, 325-34

diaries as psychological scholarship, 334-43
diary as autobiography, 343-8
diary as literature, 348-53

**Women in Modern Literature** TCLC 94: 262-
425
overviews and general studies, 263-86
American literature, 286-304
other national literatures, 304-33
fiction, 333-94
poetry, 394-407
drama, 407-24

**Women Writers, Seventeenth-Century** LC 30:
2-58
overview, 2-15
women and education, 15-9
women and autobiography, 19-31
women's diaries, 31-9
early feminists, 39-58

**World War I Literature** TCLC 34: 392-486
overview, 393-403
English, 403-27
German, 427-50
American, 450-66
French, 466-74
and modern history, 474-82

**World War I Short Fiction** SSC 71: 187-347
overviews and general studies, 187-206
female short fiction writers of World War I,
206-36
Central Powers
Czechoslovakian writers of short fiction,
236-44
German writers of short fiction, 244-61
Entente/Allied Alliance
Australian writers of short fiction, 261-73
English writers of short fiction, 273-305
French writers of short fiction, 305-11
Associated Power: American writers of
short fiction, 311-46

**Yellow Journalism** NCLC 36: 383-456
overviews and general studies, 384-96
major figures, 396-413

**Yiddish Literature** TCLC 130: 229-364
overviews and general studies, 230-54
major authors, 254-305
Yiddish literature in America, 305-34
Yiddish and Judaism, 334-64

**Young Playwrights Festival**
1988 CLC 55: 376-81
1989 CLC 59: 398-403
1990 CLC 65: 444-8

**Topic Index**

# *CLC* Cumulative Nationality Index

## ALBANIAN

Kadare, Ismail **52, 190**

## ALGERIAN

Althusser, Louis **106**
Camus, Albert **1, 2, 4, 9, 11, 14, 32, 63, 69, 124**
Cardinal, Marie **189**
Cixous, Hélène **92**
Cohen-Solal, Annie **50**
Djebar, Assia **182**

## AMERICAN

Abbey, Edward **36, 59**
Abbott, Lee K(ittredge) **48**
Abish, Walter **22**
Abrams, M(eyer) H(oward) **24**
Acker, Kathy **45, 111**
Adams, Alice (Boyd) **6, 13, 46**
Addams, Charles (Samuel) **30**
Adler, C(arole) S(chwerdtfeger) **35**
Adler, Renata **8, 31**
Ai **4, 14, 69**
Aiken, Conrad (Potter) **1, 3, 5, 10, 52**
Albee, Edward (Franklin III) **1, 2, 3, 5, 9, 11, 13, 25, 53, 86, 113**
Alexander, Lloyd (Chudley) **35**
Alexie, Sherman (Joseph Jr.) **96, 154**
Algren, Nelson **4, 10, 33**
Allen, Edward **59**
Allen, Paula Gunn **84**
Allen, Woody **16, 52, 195**
Allison, Dorothy E. **78, 153**
Alta **19**
Alter, Robert B(ernard) **34**
Alther, Lisa **7, 41**
Altman, Robert **16, 116**
Alvarez, Julia **93**
Ambrose, Stephen E(dward) **145**
Ammons, A(rchie) R(andolph) **2, 3, 5, 8, 9, 25, 57, 108**
L'Amour, Louis (Dearborn) **25, 55**
Anaya, Rudolfo A(lfonso) **23, 148**
Anderson, Jon (Victor) **9**
Anderson, Poul (William) **15**
Anderson, Robert (Woodruff) **23**
Angell, Roger **26**
Angelou, Maya **12, 35, 64, 77, 155**
Anthony, Piers **35**
Apple, Max (Isaac) **9, 33**
Appleman, Philip (Dean) **51**
Archer, Jules **12**
Arendt, Hannah **66, 98**
Arnow, Harriette (Louisa) Simpson **2, 7, 18**
Arrick, Fran **30**
Arzner, Dorothy **98**
Ashbery, John (Lawrence) **2, 3, 4, 6, 9, 13, 15, 25, 41, 77, 125**
Asimov, Isaac **1, 3, 9, 19, 26, 76, 92**
Attaway, William (Alexander) **92**
Auchincloss, Louis (Stanton) **4, 6, 9, 18, 45**

Auden, W(ystan) H(ugh) **1, 2, 3, 4, 6, 9, 11, 14, 43, 123**
Auel, Jean M(arie) **31, 107**
Auster, Paul **47, 131**
Bach, Richard (David) **14**
Badanes, Jerome **59**
Baker, Elliott **8**
Baker, Nicholson **61, 165**
Baker, Russell (Wayne) **31**
Bakshi, Ralph **26**
Baldwin, James (Arthur) **1, 2, 3, 4, 5, 8, 13, 15, 17, 42, 50, 67, 90, 127**
Bambara, Toni Cade **19, 88**
Banks, Russell **37, 72, 187**
Baraka, Amiri **1, 2, 3, 5, 10, 14, 33, 115**
Barber, Benjamin R. **141**
Barbera, Jack (Vincent) **44**
Barnard, Mary (Ethel) **48**
Barnes, Djuna **3, 4, 8, 11, 29, 127**
Barondess, Sue K(aufman) **8**
Barrett, Andrea **150**
Barrett, William (Christopher) **27**
Barth, John (Simmons) **1, 2, 3, 5, 7, 9, 10, 14, 27, 51, 89**
Barthelme, Donald **1, 2, 3, 5, 6, 8, 13, 23, 46, 59, 115**
Barthelme, Frederick **36, 117**
Barzun, Jacques (Martin) **51, 145**
Bass, Rick **79, 143**
Baumbach, Jonathan **6, 23**
Bausch, Richard (Carl) **51**
Baxter, Charles (Morley) **45, 78**
Beagle, Peter S(oyer) **7, 104**
Beattie, Ann **8, 13, 18, 40, 63, 146**
Becker, Walter **26**
Beecher, John **6**
Begiebing, Robert J(ohn) **70**
Behrman, S(amuel) N(athaniel) **40**
Belitt, Ben **22**
Bell, Madison Smartt **41, 102**
Bell, Marvin (Hartley) **8, 31**
Bellow, Saul **1, 2, 3, 6, 8, 10, 13, 15, 25, 33, 34, 63, 79**
Benary-Isbert, Margot **12**
Benchley, Peter (Bradford) **4, 8**
Benedikt, Michael **4, 14**
Benford, Gregory (Albert) **52**
Bennett, Jay **35**
Benson, Jackson J. **34**
Benson, Sally **17**
Bentley, Eric (Russell) **24**
Berendt, John (Lawrence) **86**
Berger, Melvin H. **12**
Berger, Thomas (Louis) **3, 5, 8, 11, 18, 38**
Bergstein, Eleanor **4**
Bernard, April **59**
Bernstein, Charles **142,**
Berriault, Gina **54, 109**
Berrigan, Daniel **4**
Berry, Chuck **17**
Berry, Wendell (Erdman) **4, 6, 8, 27, 46**
Berryman, John **1, 2, 3, 4, 6, 8, 10, 13, 25, 62**

Bessie, Alvah **23**
Bettelheim, Bruno **79**
Betts, Doris (Waugh) **3, 6, 28**
Bidart, Frank **33**
Birkerts, Sven **116**
Bishop, Elizabeth **1, 4, 9, 13, 15, 32**
Bishop, John **10**
Blackburn, Paul **9, 43**
Blackmur, R(ichard) P(almer) **2, 24**
Blaise, Clark **29**
Blatty, William Peter **2**
Blessing, Lee **54**
Blish, James (Benjamin) **14**
Bloch, Robert (Albert) **33**
Bloom, Harold **24, 103**
Blount, Roy (Alton) Jr. **38**
Blume, Judy (Sussman) **12, 30**
Bly, Robert (Elwood) **1, 2, 5, 10, 15, 38, 128**
Bochco, Steven **35**
Bogan, Louise **4, 39, 46, 93**
Bogosian, Eric **45, 141**
Bograd, Larry **35**
Bonham, Frank **12**
Bontemps, Arna(ud Wendell) **1, 18**
Booth, Philip **23**
Booth, Wayne C(layson) **24**
Bottoms, David **53**
Bourjaily, Vance (Nye) **8, 62**
Bova, Ben(jamin William) **45**
Bowers, Edgar **9**
Bowles, Jane (Sydney) **3, 68**
Bowles, Paul (Frederick) **1, 2, 19, 53**
Boyle, Kay **1, 5, 19, 58, 121**
Boyle, T(homas) Coraghessan **36, 55, 90**
Bradbury, Ray (Douglas) **1, 3, 10, 15, 42, 98**
Bradley, David (Henry) Jr. **23, 118**
Bradley, John Ed(mund Jr.) **55**
Bradley, Marion Zimmer **30**
Bradshaw, John **70**
Brady, Joan **86**
Brammer, William **31**
Brancato, Robin F(idler) **35**
Brand, Millen **7**
Branden, Barbara **44**
Branley, Franklyn M(ansfield) **21**
Brautigan, Richard (Gary) **1, 3, 5, 9, 12, 34, 42**
Braverman, Kate **67**
Brennan, Maeve **5**
Bridgers, Sue Ellen **26**
Brin, David **34**
Brodkey, Harold (Roy) **56**
Brodsky, Joseph **4, 6, 13, 36, 100**
Brodsky, Michael (Mark) **19**
Bromell, Henry **5**
Broner, E(sther) M(asserman) **19**
Bronk, William (M.) **10**
Brooks, Cleanth **24, 86, 110**
Brooks, Gwendolyn (Elizabeth) **1, 2, 4, 5, 15, 49, 125**
Brooks, Mel **12**
Brooks, Peter **34**
Brooks, Van Wyck **29**

Brosman, Catharine Savage **9**
Broughton, T(homas) Alan **19**
Broumas, Olga **10, 73**
Brown, Claude **30**
Brown, Dee (Alexander) **18, 47**
Brown, Rita Mae **18, 43, 79**
Brown, Rosellen **32, 170**
Brown, Sterling Allen **1, 23, 59**
Brown, (William) Larry **73**
Brownmiller, Susan **159**
Browne, (Clyde) Jackson **21**
Browning, Tod **16**
Bruccoli, Matthew J(oseph) **34**
Bruce, Lenny **21**
Bryan, C(ourtlandt) D(ixon) B(arnes) **29**
Buchwald, Art(hur) **33**
Buck, Pearl S(ydenstricker) **7, 11, 18, 127**
Buckley, Christopher **165**
Buckley, William F(rank) Jr. **7, 18, 37**
Buechner, (Carl) Frederick **2, 4, 6, 9**
Bukowski, Charles **2, 5, 9, 41, 82, 108**
Bullins, Ed **1, 5, 7**
Burke, Kenneth (Duva) **2, 24**
Burnshaw, Stanley **3, 13, 44**
Burr, Anne **6**
Burroughs, William S(eward) **1, 2, 5, 15, 22, 42, 75, 109**
Busch, Frederick **7, 10, 18, 47, 166**
Bush, Ronald **34**
Butler, Octavia E(stelle) **38, 121**
Butler, Robert Olen (Jr.) **81, 162**
Byars, Betsy (Cromer) **35**
Byrne, David **26**
Cage, John (Milton Jr.) **41**
Cain, James M(allahan) **3, 11, 28**
Caldwell, Erskine (Preston) **1, 8, 14, 50, 60**
Caldwell, (Janet Miriam) Taylor (Holland) **2, 28, 39**
Calisher, Hortense **2, 4, 8, 38, 134**
Cameron, Carey **59**
Cameron, Peter **44**
Campbell, John W(ood Jr.) **32**
Campbell, Joseph **69**
Campion, Jane **95**
Canby, Vincent **13**
Canin, Ethan **55**
Capote, Truman **1, 3, 8, 13, 19, 34, 38, 58**
Capra, Frank **16**
Caputo, Philip **32**
Card, Orson Scott **44, 47, 50**
Carey, Ernestine Gilbreth **17**
Carlisle, Henry (Coffin) **33**
Carlson, Ron(ald F.) **54**
Carpenter, Don(ald Richard) **41**
Carpenter, John **161**
Carr, Caleb **86**
Carr, John Dickson **3**
Carr, Virginia Spencer **34**
Carroll, James P. **38**
Carroll, Jim **35, 143**
Carruth, Hayden **4, 7, 10, 18, 84**
Carson, Rachel Louise **71**
Carver, Raymond **22, 36, 53, 55, 126**
Casey, John (Dudley) **59**
Casey, Michael **2**
Casey, Warren (Peter) **12**
Cassavetes, John **20**
Cassill, R(onald) V(erlin) **4, 23**
Cassity, (Allen) Turner **6, 42**
Castaneda, Carlos (Cesar Aranha) **12, 119**
Castedo, Elena **65**
Castillo, Ana (Hernandez Del) **151**
Catton, (Charles) Bruce **35**
Caunitz, William J. **34**
Chabon, Michael **55, 149**
Chappell, Fred (Davis) **40, 78, 162**
Charyn, Jerome **5, 8, 18**
Chase, Mary Ellen **2**
Chayefsky, Paddy **23**
Cheever, John **3, 7, 8, 11, 15, 25, 64**
Cheever, Susan **18, 48**
Cheney, Lynne V. **70**

Chester, Alfred **49**
Childress, Alice **12, 15, 86, 96**
Chin, Frank (Chew Jr.) **135**
Choi, Susan **119**
Chomsky, (Avram) Noam **132**
Chute, Carolyn **39**
Ciardi, John (Anthony) **10, 40, 44, 129**
Cimino, Michael **16**
Cisneros, Sandra **69, 118, 193**
Clampitt, Amy **32**
Clancy, Tom **45, 112**
Clark, Eleanor **5, 19**
Clark, Walter Van Tilburg **28**
Clarke, Shirley **16**
Clavell, James (duMaresq) **6, 25, 87**
Cleaver, (Leroy) Eldridge **30, 119**
Clifton, (Thelma) Lucille **19, 66, 162**
Coburn, D(onald) L(ee) **10**
Codrescu, Andrei **46, 121**
Coen, Ethan **108**
Coen, Joel **108**
Cohen, Arthur A(llen) **7, 31**
Coles, Robert (Martin) **108**
Collier, Christopher **30**
Collier, James Lincoln **30**
Collins, Linda **44**
Colter, Cyrus **58**
Colum, Padraic **28**
Colwin, Laurie (E.) **5, 13, 23, 84**
Condon, Richard (Thomas) **4, 6, 8, 10, 45, 100**
Connell, Evan S(helby) Jr. **4, 6, 45**
Connelly, Marc(us Cook) **7**
Conroy, (Donald) Pat(rick) **30, 74**
Cook, Robin **14**
Cooke, Elizabeth **55**
Cook-Lynn, Elizabeth **93**
Cooper, J(oan) California **56**
Coover, Robert (Lowell) **3, 7, 15, 32, 46, 87, 161**
Coppola, Francis Ford **16, 126**
Corcoran, Barbara (Asenath) **17**
Corman, Cid **9**
Cormier, Robert (Edmund) **12, 30**
Corn, Alfred (DeWitt III) **33**
Cornwell, Patricia (Daniels) **155**
Corso, (Nunzio) Gregory **1, 11**
Costain, Thomas B(ertram) **30**
Cowley, Malcolm **39**
Cozzens, James Gould **1, 4, 11, 92**
Crane, R(onald) S(almon) **27**
Crase, Douglas **58**
Creeley, Robert (White) **1, 2, 4, 8, 11, 15, 36, 78**
Crews, Harry (Eugene) **6, 23, 49**
Crichton, (John) Michael **2, 6, 54, 90**
Cristofer, Michael **28**
Cronenberg, David **143**
Crow Dog, Mary (Ellen) **93**
Crowley, John **57**
Crumb, R(obert) **17**
Cryer, Gretchen (Kiger) **21**
Cudlip, David R(ockwell) **34**
Cummings, E(dward) E(stlin) **1, 3, 8, 12, 15, 68**
Cunningham, J(ames) V(incent) **3, 31**
Cunningham, Julia (Woolfolk) **12**
Cunningham, Michael **34**
Currie, Ellen **44**
Dacey, Philip **51**
Dahlberg, Edward **1, 7, 14**
Daitch, Susan **103**
Daly, Elizabeth **52**
Daly, Mary **173**
Daly, Maureen **17**
Dannay, Frederic **11**
Danvers, Dennis **70**
Danziger, Paula **21**
Davenport, Guy (Mattison Jr.) **6, 14, 38**
Davidson, Donald (Grady) **2, 13, 19**
Davidson, Sara **9**
Davis, Angela (Yvonne) **77**

Davis, H(arold) L(enoir) **49**
Davison, Peter (Hubert) **28**
Dawson, Fielding **6**
Deer, Sandra **45**
Delany, Samuel R(ay) Jr. **8, 14, 38, 141**
Delbanco, Nicholas (Franklin) **6, 13, 167**
DeLillo, Don **8, 10, 13, 27, 39, 54, 76, 143**
Deloria, Vine (Victor) Jr. **21, 122**
Del Vecchio, John M(ichael) **29**
de Man, Paul (Adolph Michel) **55**
DeMarinis, Rick **54**
Demby, William **53**
Denby, Edwin (Orr) **48**
De Palma, Brian (Russell) **20**
Deren, Maya **16, 102**
Derleth, August (William) **31**
Deutsch, Babette **18**
De Vries, Peter **1, 2, 3, 7, 10, 28, 46**
Dexter, Pete **34, 55**
Diamond, Neil **30**
Dick, Philip K(indred) **10, 30, 72**
Dickey, James (Lafayette) **1, 2, 4, 7, 10, 15, 47, 109**
Dickey, William **3, 28**
Dickinson, Charles **49**
Didion, Joan **1, 3, 8, 14, 32, 129**
Dillard, Annie **9, 60, 115**
Dillard, R(ichard) H(enry) W(ilde) **5**
Disch, Thomas M(ichael) **7, 36**
Dixon, Stephen **52**
Dobyns, Stephen **37**
Doctorow, E(dgar) L(aurence) **6, 11, 15, 18, 37, 44, 65, 113**
Dodson, Owen (Vincent) **79**
Doerr, Harriet **34**
Donaldson, Stephen R(eeder) **46, 138**
Donleavy, J(ames) P(atrick) **1, 4, 6, 10, 45**
Donovan, John **35**
Doolittle, Hilda **3, 8, 14, 31, 34, 73**
Dorn, Edward (Merton) **10, 18**
Dorris, Michael (Anthony) **109**
Dos Passos, John (Roderigo) **1, 4, 8, 11, 15, 25, 34, 82**
Doty, Mark **176**
Douglas, Ellen **73**
Dove, Rita (Frances) **50, 81**
Dowell, Coleman **60**
Drexler, Rosalyn **2, 6**
Drury, Allen (Stuart) **37**
Duberman, Martin (Bauml) **8**
Dubie, Norman (Evans) **36**
Du Bois, W(illiam) E(dward) B(urghardt) **1, 2, 13, 64, 96**
Dubus, André **13, 36, 97**
Duffy, Bruce **50**
Dugan, Alan **2, 6**
Dumas, Henry L. **6, 62**
Duncan, Lois **26**
Duncan, Robert (Edward) **1, 2, 4, 7, 15, 41, 55**
Dunn, Katherine (Karen) **71**
Dunn, Stephen (Elliott) **36**
Dunne, John Gregory **28**
Durang, Christopher (Ferdinand) **27, 38**
Durban, (Rosa) Pam **39**
Dworkin, Andrea **43, 123**
Dwyer, Thomas A. **114**
Dybek, Stuart **114**
Dylan, Bob **3, 4, 6, 12, 77**
Eastlake, William (Derry) **8**
Eberhart, Richard (Ghormley) **3, 11, 19, 56**
Eberstadt, Fernanda **39**
Eckert, Allan W. **17**
Edel, (Joseph) Leon **29, 34**
Edgerton, Clyde (Carlyle) **39**
Edmonds, Walter D(umaux) **35**
Edson, Russell **13**
Edwards, Gus **43**
Ehle, John (Marsden Jr.) **27**
Ehrenreich, Barbara **110**
Eigner, Larry **9**
Eiseley, Loren Corey **7**

Eisenstadt, Jill **50**
Eliade, Mircea **19**
Eliot, T(homas) S(tearns) **1, 2, 3, 6, 9, 10, 13, 15, 24, 34, 41, 55, 57, 113**
Elkin, Stanley L(awrence) **4, 6, 9, 14, 27, 51, 91**
Elledge, Scott **34**
Elliott, George P(aul) **2**
Ellis, Bret Easton **39, 71, 117**
Ellison, Harlan (Jay) **1, 13, 42, 139**
Ellison, Ralph (Waldo) **1, 3, 11, 54, 86, 114**
Ellmann, Lucy (Elizabeth) **61**
Ellmann, Richard (David) **50**
Elman, Richard (Martin) **19**
L'Engle, Madeleine (Camp Franklin) **12**
Ephron, Nora **17, 31**
Epstein, Daniel Mark **7**
Epstein, Jacob **19**
Epstein, Joseph **39**
Epstein, Leslie **27**
Erdman, Paul E(mil) **25**
Erdrich, Louise **39, 54, 120, 176**
Erickson, Steve **64**
Eshleman, Clayton **7**
Estleman, Loren D. **48**
Eugenides, Jeffrey **81**
Everett, Percival L. **57**
Everson, William (Oliver) **1, 5, 14**
Exley, Frederick (Earl) **6, 11**
Ezekiel, Tish O'Dowd **34**
Fagen, Donald **26**
Fair, Ronald L. **18**
Faludi, Susan **140**
Fante, John (Thomas) **60**
Farina, Richard **9**
Farley, Walter (Lorimer) **17**
Farmer, Philip José **1, 19**
Farrell, James T(homas) **1, 4, 8, 11, 66**
Fast, Howard (Melvin) **23, 131**
Faulkner, William (Cuthbert) **1, 3, 6, 8, 9, 11, 14, 18, 28, 52, 68**
Fauset, Jessie Redmon **19, 54**
Faust, Irvin **8**
Fearing, Kenneth (Flexner) **51**
Federman, Raymond **6, 47**
Feiffer, Jules (Ralph) **2, 8, 64**
Feinberg, David B. **59**
Feldman, Irving (Mordecai) **7**
Felsen, Henry Gregor **17**
Ferber, Edna **18, 93**
Ferlinghetti, Lawrence (Monsanto) **2, 6, 10, 27, 111**
Ferrigno, Robert **65**
Fiedler, Leslie A(aron) **4, 13, 24**
Field, Andrew **44**
Fierstein, Harvey (Forbes) **33**
Fish, Stanley Eugene **142**
Fisher, M(ary) F(rances) K(ennedy) **76, 87**
Fisher, Vardis (Alvero) **7**
Fitzgerald, Robert (Stuart) **39**
Flanagan, Thomas (James Bonner) **25, 52**
Fleming, Thomas (James) **37**
Foote, Horton **51, 91**
Foote, Shelby **75**
Forbes, Esther **12**
Forché, Carolyn (Louise) **25, 83, 86**
Ford, John **16**
Ford, Richard **46, 99**
Foreman, Richard **50**
Forman, James Douglas **21**
Fornés, María Irene **39, 61, 187**
Forrest, Leon (Richard) **4**
Fosse, Bob **20**
Fox, Paula **2, 8, 121**
Fox, William Price (Jr.) **22**
Francis, Robert (Churchill) **15**
Frank, Elizabeth **39**
Fraze, Candida (Merrill) **50**
Frazier, Ian **46**
Freeman, Judith **55**
French, Albert **86**
French, Marilyn **10, 18, 60, 177**

Friedan, Betty (Naomi) **74**
Friedman, B(ernard) H(arper) **7**
Friedman, Bruce Jay **3, 5, 56**
Frost, Robert (Lee) **1, 3, 4, 9, 10, 13, 15, 26, 34, 44**
Frye, (Herman) Northrop **24, 70**
Fuchs, Daniel **34**
Fuchs, Daniel **8, 22**
Fukuyama, Francis **131**
Fuller, Charles (H. Jr.) **25**
Fulton, Alice **52**
Fuson, Robert H(enderson) **70**
Fussell, Paul **74**
Gaddis, William **1, 3, 6, 8, 10, 19, 43, 86**
Gaines, Ernest J(ames) **3, 11, 18, 86, 181**
Gaitskill, Mary **69**
Gallagher, Tess **18, 63**
Gallant, Roy A(rthur) **17**
Gallico, Paul (William) **2**
Galvin, James **38**
Gann, Ernest Kellogg **23**
Garcia, Cristina **76**
Gardner, Herb(ert) **44**
Gardner, John (Champlin) Jr. **2, 3, 5, 7, 8, 10, 18, 28, 34**
Garrett, George (Palmer) **3, 11, 51**
Garrigue, Jean **2, 8**
Gass, William H(oward) **1, 2, 8, 11, 15, 39, 132**
Gates, Henry Louis Jr. **65**
Gay, Peter (Jack) **158**
Gaye, Marvin (Pentz Jr.) **26**
Gelbart, Larry (Simon) **21, 61**
Gelber, Jack **1, 6, 14, 79**
Gellhorn, Martha (Ellis) **14, 60**
Gent, Peter **29**
George, Jean Craighead **35**
Gertler, T. **134**
Ghiselin, Brewster **23**
Gibbons, Kaye **50, 88, 145**
Gibson, William **23**
Gibson, William (Ford) **39, 63**
Gifford, Barry (Colby) **34**
Gilbreth, Frank B(unker) Jr. **17**
Gilchrist, Ellen (Louise) **34, 48, 143**
Giles, Molly **39**
Gilliam, Terry (Vance) **21, 141**
Gilroy, Frank D(aniel) **2**
Gilstrap, John **99**
Ginsberg, Allen **1, 2, 3, 4, 6, 13, 36, 69, 109**
Giovanni, Nikki **2, 4, 19, 64, 117**
Glasser, Ronald J. **37**
Gleick, James (W.) **147**
Glück, Louise (Elisabeth) **7, 22, 44, 81, 160**
Godwin, Gail (Kathleen) **5, 8, 22, 31, 69, 125**
Goines, Donald **80**
Gold, Herbert **4, 7, 14, 42, 152**
Goldbarth, Albert **5, 38**
Goldman, Francisco **76**
Goldman, William (W.) **1, 48**
Goldsberry, Steven **34**
Goodman, Paul **1, 2, 4, 7**
Gordon, Caroline **6, 13, 29, 83**
Gordon, Mary (Catherine) **13, 22, 128**
Gordon, Sol **26**
Gordone, Charles **1, 4**
Gould, Lois **4, 10**
Gould, Stephen Jay **163**
Goyen, (Charles) William **5, 8, 14, 40**
Grafton, Sue **163**
Graham, Jorie **48, 118**
Grau, Shirley Ann **4, 9, 146**
Graver, Elizabeth **70**
Gray, Amlin **29**
Gray, Francine du Plessix **22, 153**
Gray, Spalding **49, 112**
Grayson, Richard (A.) **38**
Greeley, Andrew M(oran) **28**
Green, Hannah **3**
Green, Julien **3, 11, 77**
Green, Paul (Eliot) **25**

Greenberg, Joanne (Goldenberg) **7, 30**
Greenberg, Richard **57**
Greenblatt, Stephen J(ay) **70**
Greene, Bette **30**
Greene, Gael **8**
Gregor, Arthur **9**
Griffin, John Howard **68**
Griffin, Peter **39**
Grisham, John **84**
Grumbach, Doris (Isaac) **13, 22, 64**
Grunwald, Lisa **44**
Guare, John **8, 14, 29, 67**
Gubar, Susan (David) **145**
Guest, Barbara **34**
Guest, Judith (Ann) **8, 30**
Guild, Nicholas M. **33**
Gunn, Bill **5**
Gurganus, Allan **70**
Gurney, A(lbert) R(amsdell) Jr. **32, 50, 54**
Gustafson, James M(oody) **100**
Guterson, David **91**
Guthrie, A(lfred) B(ertram) Jr. **23**
Guy, Rosa (Cuthbert) **26**
Hacker, Marilyn **5, 9, 23, 72, 91**
Hagedorn, Jessica (Tarahata) **185**
Hailey, Elizabeth Forsythe **40**
Haines, John (Meade) **58**
Haldeman, Joe (William) **61**
Haley, Alex(ander Murray Palmer) **8, 12, 76**
Hall, Donald (Andrew Jr.) **1, 13, 37, 59, 151**
Halpern, Daniel **14**
Hamill, Pete **10**
Hamilton, Edmond **1**
Hamilton, Jane **179**
Hamilton, Virginia (Esther) **26**
Hammett, (Samuel) Dashiell **3, 5, 10, 19, 47**
Hamner, Earl (Henry) Jr. **12**
Hannah, Barry **23, 38, 90**
Hansberry, Lorraine (Vivian) **17, 62**
Hansen, Joseph **38**
Hanson, Kenneth O(stlin) **13**
Hardwick, Elizabeth (Bruce) **13**
Harjo, Joy **83**
Harlan, Louis R(udolph) **34**
Harling, Robert **53**
Harmon, William (Ruth) **38**
Harper, Michael S(teven) **7, 22**
Harris, MacDonald **9**
Harris, Mark **19**
Harrison, Barbara Grizzuti **144**
Harrison, Harry (Max) **42**
Harrison, James (Thomas) **6, 14, 33, 66, 143**
Harrison, Kathryn **70, 151**
Harriss, Will(ard Irvin) **34**
Hart, Moss **66**
Hartman, Geoffrey H. **27**
Haruf, Kent **34**
Hass, Robert **18, 39, 99**
Haviaras, Stratis **33**
Hawkes, John (Clendennin Burne Jr.) **1, 2, 3, 4, 7, 9, 14, 15, 27, 49**
Hayden, Robert E(arl) **5, 9, 14, 37**
Hayman, Ronald **44**
H. D. **3, 8, 14, 31, 34, 73**
Hearne, Vicki **56**
Hearon, Shelby **63**
Hecht, Anthony (Evan) **8, 13, 19**
Hecht, Ben **8**
Heifner, Jack **11**
Heilbrun, Carolyn G(old) **25, 173**
Heinemann, Larry (Curtiss) **50**
Heinlein, Robert A(nson) **1, 3, 8, 14, 26, 55**
Heller, Joseph **1, 3, 5, 8, 11, 36, 63**
Hellman, Lillian (Florence) **2, 4, 8, 14, 18, 34, 44, 52**
Helprin, Mark **7, 10, 22, 32**
Hemingway, Ernest (Miller) **1, 3, 6, 8, 10, 13, 19, 30, 34, 39, 41, 44, 50, 61, 80**
Hempel, Amy **39**
Henley, Beth **23**
Hentoff, Nat(han Irving) **26**
Herbert, Frank (Patrick) **12, 23, 35, 44, 85**

Herbst, Josephine (Frey) **34**
Herlihy, James Leo **6**
Herrmann, Dorothy **44**
Hersey, John (Richard) **1, 2, 7, 9, 40, 81, 97**
L'Heureux, John (Clarke) **52**
Heyen, William **13, 18**
Higgins, George V(incent) **4, 7, 10, 18**
Highsmith, (Mary) Patricia **2, 4, 14, 42, 102**
Highwater, Jamake (Mamake) **12**
Hijuelos, Oscar **65**
Hill, George Roy **26**
Hillerman, Tony **62, 170**
Himes, Chester (Bomar) **2, 4, 7, 18, 58, 108**
Hinton, S(usan) E(loise) **30, 111**
Hirsch, Edward **31, 50**
Hirsch, E(ric) D(onald) Jr. **79**
Hoagland, Edward **28**
Hoban, Russell (Conwell) **7, 25**
Hobson, Laura Z(ametkin) **7, 25**
Hochman, Sandra **3, 8**
Hoffman, Alice **51**
Hoffman, Daniel (Gerard) **6, 13, 23**
Hoffman, Eva **182**
Hoffman, Stanley **5**
Hoffman, William **141**
Hoffman, William M(oses) **40**
Hogan, Linda **73**
Holland, Isabelle **21**
Hollander, John **2, 5, 8, 14**
Holleran, Andrew **38**
Holmes, John Clellon **56**
Honig, Edwin **33**
Horgan, Paul (George Vincent
    O'Shaughnessy) **9, 53**
Horovitz, Israel (Arthur) **56**
Horwitz, Julius **14**
Hougan, Carolyn **34**
Howard, Maureen **5, 14, 46, 151**
Howard, Richard **7, 10, 47**
Howe, Fanny (Quincy) **47**
Howe, Irving **85**
Howe, Susan **72, 152**
Howe, Tina **48**
Howes, Barbara **15**
Hubbard, L(afayette) Ron(ald) **43**
Huddle, David **49**
Hughart, Barry **39**
Hughes, (James) Langston **1, 5, 10, 15, 35,
    44, 108**
Hugo, Richard F(ranklin) **6, 18, 32**
Humphrey, William **45**
Humphreys, Josephine **34, 57**
Hunt, E(verette) Howard (Jr.) **3**
Hunt, Marsha **70**
Hunter, Evan **11, 31**
Hunter, Kristin (Eggleston) **35**
Hurston, Zora Neale **7, 30, 61**
Huston, John (Marcellus) **20**
Hustvedt, Siri **76**
Huxley, Aldous (Leonard) **1, 3, 4, 5, 8, 11,
    18, 35, 79**
Hwang, David Henry **55**
Hyde, Margaret O(ldroyd) **21**
Hynes, James **65**
Ian, Janis **21**
Ignatow, David **4, 7, 14, 40**
Ingalls, Rachel (Holmes) **42**
Inge, William (Motter) **1, 8, 19**
Innaurato, Albert (F.) **21, 60**
Irving, John (Winslow) **13, 23, 38, 112, 175**
Isaacs, Susan **32**
Isler, Alan (David) **91**
Ivask, Ivar Vidrik **14**
Jackson, Jesse **12**
Jackson, Shirley **11, 60, 87**
Jacobs, Jim **12**
Jacobsen, Josephine **48, 102**
Jakes, John (William) **29**
Jameson, Fredric (R.) **142**
Janowitz, Tama **43, 145**
Jarrell, Randall **1, 2, 6, 9, 13, 49**
Jeffers, (John) Robinson **2, 3, 11, 15, 54**

Jen, Gish **70**
Jennings, Waylon **21**
Jensen, Laura (Linnea) **37**
Jin, Xuefei **109**
Joel, Billy **26**
Johnson, Charles (Richard) **7, 51, 65, 163**
Johnson, Denis **52, 160**
Johnson, Diane **5, 13, 48**
Johnson, Joyce **58**
Johnson, Judith (Emlyn) **7, 15**
Jones, Edward P. **76**
Jones, Gayl **6, 9, 131**
Jones, James **1, 3, 10, 39**
Jones, LeRoi **1, 2, 3, 5, 10, 14**
Jones, Louis B. **65**
Jones, Madison (Percy Jr.) **4**
Jones, Nettie (Pearl) **34**
Jones, Preston **10**
Jones, Robert F(rancis) **7**
Jones, Thom (Douglas) **81**
Jong, Erica **4, 6, 8, 18, 83**
Jordan, June **5, 11, 23, 114**
Jordan, Pat(rick M.) **37**
Just, Ward (Swift) **4, 27**
Justice, Donald (Rodney) **6, 19, 102**
Kadohata, Cynthia **59, 122**
Kahn, Roger **30**
Kaletski, Alexander **39**
Kallman, Chester (Simon) **2**
Kaminsky, Stuart M(elvin) **59**
Kanin, Garson **22**
Kantor, MacKinlay **7**
Kaplan, David Michael **50**
Kaplan, James **59**
Karl, Frederick R(obert) **34**
Karr, Mary **188**
Katz, Steve **47**
Kauffman, Janet **42**
Kaufman, Bob (Garnell) **49**
Kaufman, George S. **38**
Kaufman, Sue **3, 8**
Kazan, Elia **6, 16, 63**
Kazin, Alfred **34, 38, 119**
Keaton, Buster **20**
Keene, Donald **34**
Keillor, Garrison **40, 115**
Kellerman, Jonathan **44**
Kelley, William Melvin **22**
Kellogg, Marjorie **2**
Kemelman, Harry **2**
Kennedy, Adrienne (Lita) **66**
Kennedy, William **6, 28, 34, 53**
Kennedy, X. J. **8, 42**
Kenny, Maurice (Francis) **87**
Kerouac, Jack **1, 2, 3, 5, 14, 29, 61**
Kerr, Jean **22**
Kerr, M. E. **12, 35**
Kerr, Robert **55**
Kerrigan, (Thomas) Anthony **4, 6**
Kesey, Ken (Elton) **1, 3, 6, 11, 46, 64**
Kesselring, Joseph (Otto) **45**
Kessler, Jascha (Frederick) **4**
Kettelkamp, Larry (Dale) **12**
Keyes, Daniel **80**
Kherdian, David **6, 9**
Kienzle, William X(avier) **25**
Killens, John Oliver **10**
Kincaid, Jamaica **43, 68, 137**
King, Martin Luther Jr. **83**
King, Stephen (Edwin) **12, 26, 37, 61, 113**
King, Thomas **89, 171**
Kingman, Lee **17**
Kingsley, Sidney **44**
Kingsolver, Barbara **55, 81, 130**
Kingston, Maxine (Ting Ting) Hong **12, 19,
    58, 121**
Kinnell, Galway **1, 2, 3, 5, 13, 29, 129**
Kirkwood, James **9**
Kissinger, Henry A(lfred) **137**
Kizer, Carolyn (Ashley) **15, 39, 80**
Klappert, Peter **57**
Klein, Joe **154**

Klein, Norma **30**
Klein, T(heodore) E(ibon) D(onald) **34**
Knapp, Caroline **99**
Knebel, Fletcher **14**
Knight, Etheridge **40**
Knowles, John **1, 4, 10, 26**
Koch, Kenneth **5, 8, 44**
Komunyakaa, Yusef **86, 94**
Koontz, Dean R(ay) **78**
Kopit, Arthur (Lee) **1, 18, 33**
Kosinski, Jerzy (Nikodem) **1, 2, 3, 6, 10, 15,
    53, 70**
Kostelanetz, Richard (Cory) **28**
Kotlowitz, Robert **4**
Kotzwinkle, William **5, 14, 35**
Kozol, Jonathan **17**
Kozoll, Michael **35**
Kramer, Kathryn **34**
Kramer, Larry **42**
Kristofferson, Kris **26**
Krumgold, Joseph (Quincy) **12**
Krutch, Joseph Wood **24**
Kubrick, Stanley **16**
Kumin, Maxine (Winokur) **5, 13, 28, 164**
Kunitz, Stanley (Jasspon) **6, 11, 14, 148**
Kushner, Tony **81**
Kuzma, Greg **7**
Lancaster, Bruce **36**
Landis, John **26**
Langer, Elinor **34**
Lapine, James (Elliot) **39**
Larsen, Eric **55**
Larsen, Nella **37**
Larson, Charles R(aymond) **31**
Lasch, Christopher **102**
Latham, Jean Lee **12**
Lattimore, Richmond (Alexander) **3**
Laughlin, James **49**
Lear, Norman (Milton) **12**
Leavitt, David **34**
Lebowitz, Fran(ces Ann) **11, 36**
Lee, Andrea **36**
Lee, Chang-rae **91**
Lee, Don L. **2**
Lee, George W(ashington) **52**
Lee, Helen Elaine **86**
Lee, Lawrence **34**
Lee, Manfred B(ennington) **11**
Lee, (Nelle) Harper **12, 60, 194**
Lee, Shelton Jackson **105**
Lee, Stan **17**
Leet, Judith **11**
Leffland, Ella **19**
Le Guin, Ursula K(roeber) **8, 13, 22, 45, 71,
    136**
Leiber, Fritz (Reuter Jr.) **25**
Leimbach, Marti **65**
Leithauser, Brad **27**
Lelchuk, Alan **5**
Lemann, Nancy **39**
Lentricchia, Frank (Jr.) **34**
Leonard, Elmore (John Jr.) **28, 34, 71, 120**
Lerman, Eleanor **9**
Lerman, Rhoda **56**
Lester, Richard **20**
Levertov, Denise **1, 2, 3, 5, 8, 15, 28, 66**
Levi, Jonathan **76**
Levin, Ira **3, 6**
Levin, Meyer **7**
Levine, Philip **2, 4, 5, 9, 14, 33, 118**
Levinson, Deirdre **49**
Levitin, Sonia (Wolff) **17**
Lewis, Janet **41**
Leyner, Mark **92**
Lieber, Joel **6**
Lieberman, Laurence (James) **4, 36**
Lifton, Robert Jay **67**
Lightman, Alan P(aige) **81**
Ligotti, Thomas (Robert) **44**
Lindbergh, Anne (Spencer) Morrow **82**
Linney, Romulus **51**
Lipsyte, Robert (Michael) **21**

Lish, Gordon (Jay) **45**
Littell, Robert **42**
Loewinsohn, Ron(ald William) **52**
Logan, John (Burton) **5**
Lopate, Phillip **29**
Lopez, Barry (Holstun) **70**
Lord, Bette Bao **23**
Lorde, Audre (Geraldine) **18, 71**
Louie, David Wong **70**
Lowell, Robert (Traill Spence Jr.) **1, 2, 3, 4, 5, 8, 9, 11, 15, 37, 124**
Loy, Mina **28**
Lucas, Craig **64**
Lucas, George **16**
Ludlam, Charles **46, 50**
Ludlum, Robert **22, 43**
Ludwig, Ken **60**
Lurie, Alison **4, 5, 18, 39, 175**
Lynch, David (K.) **66, 162**
Lynn, Kenneth S(chuyler) **50**
Lytle, Andrew (Nelson) **22**
Maas, Peter **29**
Macdonald, Cynthia **13, 19**
MacDonald, John D(ann) **3, 27, 44**
MacInnes, Helen (Clark) **27, 39**
Maclean, Norman (Fitzroy) **78**
MacKinnon, Catherine **181**
MacLeish, Archibald **3, 8, 14, 68**
MacShane, Frank **39**
Madden, (Jerry) David **5, 15**
Madhubuti, Haki R. **6, 73**
Mailer, Norman **1, 2, 3, 4, 5, 8, 11, 14, 28, 39, 74, 111**
Major, Clarence **3, 19, 48**
Malamud, Bernard **1, 2, 3, 5, 8, 9, 11, 18, 27, 44, 78, 85**
Malcolm X **82, 117**
Mallon, Thomas **172**
Maloff, Saul **5**
Malone, Michael (Christopher) **43**
Malzberg, Barry N(athaniel) **7**
Mamet, David (Alan) **9, 15, 34, 46, 91, 166**
Mamoulian, Rouben (Zachary) **16**
Mano, D. Keith **2, 10**
Manso, Peter **39**
Margulies, Donald **76**
Markfield, Wallace **8**
Markson, David M(errill) **67**
Marlowe, Stephen **70**
Marquand, John P(hillips) **2, 10**
Marqués, René **96**
Marshall, Garry **17**
Marshall, Paule **27, 72**
Martin, Steve **30**
Martin, Valerie **89**
Maso, Carole **44**
Mason, Bobbie Ann **28, 43, 82, 154**
Masters, Hilary **48**
Mastrosimone, William **36**
Matheson, Richard (Burton) **37**
Mathews, Harry **6, 52**
Mathews, John Joseph **84**
Matthews, William (Procter III) **40**
Matthias, John (Edward) **9**
Matthiessen, Peter **5, 7, 11, 32, 64**
Maupin, Armistead (Jones Jr.) **95**
Maxwell, William (Keepers Jr.) **19**
May, Elaine **16**
Maynard, Joyce **23**
Maysles, Albert **16**
Maysles, David **16**
Mazer, Norma Fox **26**
McBrien, William (Augustine) **44**
McCaffrey, Anne (Inez) **17**
McCall, Nathan **86**
McCarthy, Mary (Therese) **1, 3, 5, 14, 24, 39, 59**
McCauley, Stephen (D.) **50**
McClure, Michael (Thomas) **6, 10**
McCorkle, Jill (Collins) **51**
McCourt, James **5**
McCourt, Malachy **119**

McCullers, (Lula) Carson (Smith) **1, 4, 10, 12, 48, 100**
McDermott, Alice **90**
McElroy, Joseph **5, 47**
McFarland, Dennis **65**
McGinley, Phyllis **14**
McGinniss, Joe **32**
McGrath, Thomas (Matthew) **28, 59**
McGuane, Thomas (Francis III) **3, 7, 18, 45, 127**
McHale, Tom **3, 5**
McInerney, Jay **34, 112**
McIntyre, Vonda N(eel) **18**
McKuen, Rod **1, 3**
McMillan, Terry (L.) **50, 61, 112**
McMurtry, Larry (Jeff) **2, 3, 7, 11, 27, 44, 127**
McNally, Terrence **4, 7, 41, 91**
McNally, T. M. **82**
McNamer, Deirdre **70**
McNeal, Tom **119**
McNickle, (William) D'Arcy **89**
McPhee, John (Angus) **36**
McPherson, James Alan **19, 77**
McPherson, William (Alexander) **34**
Mead, Margaret **37**
Medoff, Mark (Howard) **6, 23**
Mehta, Ved (Parkash) **37**
Meltzer, Milton **26**
Mendelsohn, Jane **99**
Meredith, William (Morris) **4, 13, 22, 55**
Merkin, Daphne **44**
Merrill, James (Ingram) **2, 3, 6, 8, 13, 18, 34, 91**
Merton, Thomas **1, 3, 11, 34, 83**
Merwin, W(illiam) S(tanley) **1, 2, 3, 5, 8, 13, 18, 45, 88**
Mewshaw, Michael **9**
Meyers, Jeffrey **39**
Michaels, Leonard **6, 25**
Michener, James A(lbert) **1, 5, 11, 29, 60, 109**
Miles, Jack **100**
Miles, Josephine (Louise) **1, 2, 14, 34, 39**
Millar, Kenneth **14**
Miller, Arthur **1, 2, 6, 10, 15, 26, 47, 78, 179**
Miller, Henry (Valentine) **1, 2, 4, 9, 14, 43, 84**
Miller, Jason **2**
Miller, Sue **44**
Miller, Walter M(ichael Jr.) **4, 30**
Millett, Kate **67**
Millhauser, Steven (Lewis) **21, 54, 109**
Milner, Ron(ald) **56**
Miner, Valerie **40**
Minot, Susan **44, 159**
Minus, Ed **39**
Mitchell, Joseph (Quincy) **98**
Modarressi, Taghi (M.) **44**
Mohr, Nicholasa **12**
Mojtabai, A(nn) G(race) **5, 9, 15, 29**
Momaday, N(avarre) Scott **2, 19, 85, 95, 160**
Monette, Paul **82**
Montague, John (Patrick) **13, 46**
Montgomery, Marion H. Jr. **7**
Moody, Rick **147**
Mooney, Ted **25**
Moore, Lorrie **39, 45, 68, 165**
Moore, Marianne (Craig) **1, 2, 4, 8, 10, 13, 19, 47**
Moraga, Cherrie **126**
Morgan, Berry **6**
Morgan, (George) Frederick **23**
Morgan, Robin (Evonne) **2**
Morgan, Seth **65**
Morris, Bill **76**
Morris, Wright **1, 3, 7, 18, 37**
Morrison, Jim **17**
Morrison, Toni **4, 10, 22, 55, 81, 87, 173, 194**
Mosher, Howard Frank **62**
Mosley, Walter **97**

Moss, Howard **7, 14, 45, 50**
Motley, Willard (Francis) **18**
Mountain Wolf Woman **92**
Moyers, Bill **74**
Mueller, Lisel **13, 51**
Mull, Martin **17**
Mungo, Raymond **72**
Murphy, Sylvia **34**
Murray, Albert L. **73**
Muske, Carol **90**
Myers, Walter Dean **35**
Nabokov, Vladimir (Vladimirovich) **1, 2, 3, 6, 8, 11, 15, 23, 44, 46, 64**
Nash, (Fredric) Ogden **23**
Naylor, Gloria **28, 52, 156**
Neihardt, John Gneisenau **32**
Nelson, Willie **17**
Nemerov, Howard (Stanley) **2, 6, 9, 36**
Neufeld, John (Arthur) **17**
Neville, Emily Cheney **12**
Newlove, Donald **6**
Newman, Charles **2, 8**
Newman, Edwin (Harold) **14**
Newton, Suzanne **35**
Nichols, John (Treadwell) **38**
Niedecker, Lorine **10, 42**
Nin, Anaïs **1, 4, 8, 11, 14, 60, 127**
Nissenson, Hugh **4, 9**
Nixon, Agnes Eckhardt **21**
Norman, Marsha **28, 186**
Norton, Andre **12**
Nova, Craig **7, 31**
Nunn, Kem **34**
Nyro, Laura **17**
Oates, Joyce Carol **1, 2, 3, 6, 9, 11, 15, 19, 33, 52, 108, 134**
O'Brien, Darcy **11**
O'Brien, (William) Tim(othy) **7, 19, 40, 103**
Ochs, Phil(ip David) **17**
O'Connor, Edwin (Greene) **14**
O'Connor, (Mary) Flannery **1, 2, 3, 6, 10, 13, 15, 21, 66, 104**
O'Dell, Scott **30**
Odets, Clifford **2, 28, 98**
O'Donovan, Michael John **14**
O'Grady, Timothy **59**
O'Hara, Frank **2, 5, 13, 78**
O'Hara, John (Henry) **1, 2, 3, 6, 11, 42**
O Hehir, Diana **41**
Olds, Sharon **32, 39, 85**
Oliver, Mary **19, 34, 98**
Olsen, Tillie **4, 13, 114**
Olson, Charles (John) **1, 2, 5, 6, 9, 11, 29**
Olson, Toby **28**
Oppen, George **7, 13, 34**
Orlovitz, Gil **22**
Ortiz, Simon J(oseph) **45**
Ostriker, Alicia (Suskin) **132**
Otto, Whitney **70**
Owens, Rochelle **8**
Ozick, Cynthia **3, 7, 28, 62, 155**
Pack, Robert **13**
Pagels, Elaine Hiesey **104**
Paglia, Camille (Anna) **68**
Paley, Grace **4, 6, 37, 140**
Palliser, Charles **65**
Pancake, Breece D'J **29**
Paretsky, Sara **135**
Parini, Jay (Lee) **54, 133**
Parker, Dorothy (Rothschild) **15, 68**
Parker, Robert B(rown) **27**
Parks, Gordon (Alexander Buchanan) **1, 16**
Pastan, Linda (Olenik) **27**
Patchen, Kenneth **1, 2, 18**
Paterson, Katherine (Womeldorf) **12, 30**
Peacock, Molly **60**
Pearson, T(homas) R(eid) **39**
Peck, John (Frederick) **3**
Peck, Richard (Wayne) **21**
Peck, Robert Newton **17**
Peckinpah, (David) Sam(uel) **20**
Percy, Walker **2, 3, 6, 8, 14, 18, 47, 65**

Perelman, S(idney) J(oseph) **3, 5, 9, 15, 23, 44, 49**
Perloff, Marjorie G(abrielle) **137**
Pesetsky, Bette **28**
Peterkin, Julia Mood **31**
Peters, Joan K(aren) **39**
Peters, Robert L(ouis) **7**
Petrakis, Harry Mark **3**
Petry, Ann (Lane) **1, 7, 18**
Philipson, Morris H. **53**
Phillips, Jayne Anne **15, 33, 139**
Phillips, Robert (Schaeffer) **28**
Piercy, Marge **3, 6, 14, 18, 27, 62, 128**
Pinckney, Darryl **76**
Pineda, Cecile **39**
Pinkwater, Daniel Manus **35**
Pinsky, Robert **9, 19, 38, 94, 121**
Pirsig, Robert M(aynard) **4, 6, 73**
Plante, David (Robert) **7, 23, 38**
Plath, Sylvia **1, 2, 3, 5, 9, 11, 14, 17, 50, 51, 62, 111**
Platt, Kin **26**
Plimpton, George (Ames) **36**
Plumly, Stanley (Ross) **33**
Podhoretz, Norman **189**
Pohl, Frederik **18**
Poitier, Sidney **26**
Pollitt, Katha **28, 122**
Polonsky, Abraham (Lincoln) **92**
Pomerance, Bernard **13**
Porter, Connie (Rose) **70**
Porter, Katherine Anne **1, 3, 7, 10, 13, 15, 27, 101**
Potok, Chaim **2, 7, 14, 26, 112**
Pound, Ezra (Weston Loomis) **1, 2, 3, 4, 5, 7, 10, 13, 18, 34, 48, 50, 112**
Povod, Reinaldo **44**
Powell, Adam Clayton Jr. **89**
Powell, Dawn **66**
Powell, Padgett **34**
Power, Susan **91**
Powers, J(ames) F(arl) **1, 4, 8, 57**
Powers, John R. **66**
Powers, Richard (S.) **93**
Prager, Emily **56**
Price, (Edward) Reynolds **3, 6, 13, 43, 50, 63**
Price, Richard **6, 12**
Prince **35**
Pritchard, William H(arrison) **34**
Probst, Mark **59**
Prokosch, Frederic **4, 48**
Prose, Francine **45**
Proulx, E(dna) Annie **81, 158**
Pryor, Richard (Franklin Lenox Thomas) **26**
Purdy, James (Amos) **2, 4, 10, 28, 52**
Puzo, Mario **1, 2, 6, 36, 107**
Pynchon, Thomas (Ruggles Jr.) **2, 3, 6, 9, 11, 18, 33, 62, 72, 123, 192**
Quay, Stephen **95**
Quay, Timothy **95**
Queen, Ellery **3, 11**
Quindlen, Anna **191**
Quinn, Peter **91**
Rabe, David (William) **4, 8, 33**
Rado, James **17**
Raeburn, John (Hay) **34**
Ragni, Gerome **17**
Rahv, Philip **24**
Rakosi, Carl **47**
Rampersad, Arnold **44**
Rand, Ayn **3, 30, 44, 79**
Randall, Dudley (Felker) **1, 135**
Ransom, John Crowe **2, 4, 5, 11, 24**
Raphael, Frederic (Michael) **2, 14**
Rechy, John (Francisco) **1, 7, 14, 18, 107**
Reddin, Keith **67**
Redmon, Anne **22**
Reed, Ishmael **2, 3, 5, 6, 13, 32, 60, 174**
Reed, Lou **21**
Remarque, Erich Maria **21**
Rexroth, Kenneth **1, 2, 6, 11, 22, 49, 112**

Reynolds, Jonathan **6, 38**
Reynolds, Michael S(hane) **44**
Reznikoff, Charles **9**
Ribman, Ronald (Burt) **7**
Rice, Anne **41, 128**
Rice, Elmer (Leopold) **7, 49**
Rich, Adrienne (Cecile) **3, 6, 7, 11, 18, 36, 73, 76, 125**
Richter, Conrad (Michael) **30**
Riding, Laura **3, 7**
Ringwood, Gwen(dolyn Margaret) Pharis **48**
Rivers, Conrad Kent **1**
Robbins, Harold **5**
Robbins, Trina **21**
Robinson, Jill **10**
Robinson, Kim Stanley **34**
Robinson, Marilynne **25, 180**
Robinson, Smokey **21**
Robison, Mary **42, 98**
Roddenberry, Gene **17**
Rodgers, Mary **12**
Rodman, Howard **65**
Rodriguez, Richard **155**
Roethke, Theodore (Huebner) **1, 3, 8, 11, 19, 46, 101**
Rogers, Thomas Hunton **57**
Rogin, Gilbert **18**
Roiphe, Anne (Richardson) **3, 9**
Rooke, Leon **25, 34**
Rose, Wendy **85**
Rosen, Richard (Dean) **39**
Rosenthal, M(acha) L(ouis) **28**
Rossner, Judith (Perelman) **6, 9, 29**
Roth, Henry **2, 6, 11, 104**
Roth, Philip (Milton) **1, 2, 3, 4, 6, 9, 15, 22, 31, 47, 66, 86, 119**
Rothenberg, Jerome **6, 57**
Rovit, Earl (Herbert) **7**
Royko, Mike **109**
Ruark, Gibbons **3**
Rudnik, Raphael **7**
Rukeyser, Muriel **6, 10, 15, 27**
Rule, Jane (Vance) **27**
Rush, Norman **44**
Russ, Joanna **15**
Russell, Jeffrey Burton **70**
Russo, Richard **181**
Ryan, Cornelius (John) **7**
Ryan, Michael **65**
Sachs, Marilyn (Stickle) **35**
Sackler, Howard (Oliver) **14**
Sadoff, Ira **9**
Safire, William **10**
Sagan, Carl (Edward) **30, 112**
Said, Edward W. **123**
Saint, H(arry) F. **50**
Salamanca, J(ack) R(ichard) **4, 15**
Sale, Kirkpatrick **68**
Salinas, Luis Omar **90**
Salinger, J(erome) D(avid) **1, 3, 8, 12, 55, 56, 138**
Salter, James **7, 52, 59**
Sanchez, Sonia **5, 116**
Sandburg, Carl (August) **1, 4, 10, 15, 35**
Sanders, (James) Ed(ward) **53**
Sanders, Lawrence **41**
Sandoz, Mari(e Susette) **28**
Saner, Reg(inald Anthony) **9**
Santiago, Danny **33**
Santmyer, Helen Hooven **33**
Santos, Bienvenido N(uqui) **22**
Sapphire, Brenda **99**
Saroyan, William **1, 8, 10, 29, 34, 56**
Sarton, (Eleanor) May **4, 14, 49, 91**
Saul, John (W. III) **46**
Savage, Thomas **40**
Savan, Glenn **50**
Sayers, Valerie **50, 122**
Sayles, John (Thomas) **7, 10, 14**
Schaeffer, Susan Fromberg **6, 11, 22**
Schell, Jonathan **35**
Schevill, James (Erwin) **7**

Schisgal, Murray (Joseph) **6**
Schlesinger, Arthur M(eier) Jr. **84**
Schnackenberg, Gjertrud (Cecelia) **40**
Schor, Sandra (M.) **65**
Schorer, Mark **9**
Schrader, Paul (Joseph) **26**
Schulberg, Budd (Wilson) **7, 48**
Schulz, Charles M(onroe) **12**
Schuyler, James Marcus **5, 23**
Schwartz, Delmore (David) **2, 4, 10, 45, 87**
Schwartz, John Burnham **59**
Schwartz, Lynne Sharon **31**
Scoppettone, Sandra **26**
Scorsese, Martin **20, 89**
Scott, Evelyn **43**
Scott, Joanna **50**
Sebestyen, Ouida **30**
Sebold, Alice **193**
Seelye, John (Douglas) **7**
Segal, Erich (Wolf) **3, 10**
Seger, Bob **35**
Seidel, Frederick (Lewis) **18**
Selby, Hubert Jr. **1, 2, 4, 8**
Selzer, Richard **74**
Serling, (Edward) Rod(man) **30**
Seton, Cynthia Propper **27**
Settle, Mary Lee **19, 61**
Sexton, Anne (Harvey) **2, 4, 6, 8, 10, 15, 53, 123**
Shaara, Michael (Joseph Jr.) **15**
Shacochis, Bob **39**
Shange, Ntozake **8, 25, 38, 74, 126**
Shanley, John Patrick **75**
Shapiro, Jane **76**
Shapiro, Karl (Jay) **4, 8, 15, 53**
Shaw, Irwin **7, 23, 34**
Shawn, Wallace **41**
Shea, Lisa **86**
Sheed, Wilfrid (John Joseph) **2, 4, 10, 53**
Sheehy, Gail **171**
Shepard, Jim **36**
Shepard, Lucius **34**
Shepard, Sam **4, 6, 17, 34, 41, 44, 169**
Sherburne, Zoa (Lillian Morin) **30**
Sherman, Jonathan Marc **55**
Sherman, Martin **19**
Shields, David **97**
Shilts, Randy **85**
Showalter, Elaine **169**
Shreve, Susan Richards **23**
Shue, Larry **52**
Shulman, Alix Kates **2, 10**
Shuster, Joe **21**
Sidhwa, Bapsi **168**
Siegel, Jerome **21**
Sigal, Clancy **7**
Silko, Leslie (Marmon) **23, 74, 114**
Silver, Joan Micklin **20**
Silverberg, Robert **7, 140**
Silverstein, Alvin **17**
Silverstein, Virginia B(arbara Opshelor) **17**
Simak, Clifford D(onald) **1, 55**
Simic, Charles **6, 9, 22, 49, 68, 130**
Simmons, Charles (Paul) **57**
Simmons, Dan **44**
Simon, Carly **26**
Simon, (Marvin) Neil **6, 11, 31, 39, 70**
Simon, Paul (Frederick) **17**
Simpson, Louis (Aston Marantz) **4, 7, 9, 32, 149**
Simpson, Mona (Elizabeth) **44, 146**
Sinclair, Upton (Beall) **1, 11, 15, 63**
Singer, Isaac Bashevis **1, 3, 6, 9, 11, 15, 23, 38, 69, 111**
Singleton, John **156**
Sissman, L(ouis) E(dward) **9, 18**
Slaughter, Frank G(ill) **29**
Slavitt, David R(ytman) **5, 14**
Smiley, Jane (Graves) **53, 76, 144**
Smith, Anna Deavere **86**
Smith, Betty (Wehner) **19**
Smith, Clark Ashton **43**

Smith, Dave **22, 42**
Smith, Lee **25, 73**
Smith, Martin Cruz **25**
Smith, Mary-Ann Tirone **39**
Smith, Patti **12**
Smith, William Jay **6**
Snodgrass, W(illiam) D(e Witt) **2, 6, 10, 18, 68**
Snyder, Gary (Sherman) **1, 2, 5, 9, 32, 120**
Snyder, Zilpha Keatley **17**
Soderbergh, Steven **154**
Sokolov, Raymond **7**
Sommer, Scott **25**
Sondheim, Stephen (Joshua) **30, 39, 147**
Sontag, Susan **1, 2, 10, 13, 31, 105, 195**
Sorrentino, Gilbert **3, 7, 14, 22, 40**
Soto, Gary **32, 80**
Southern, Terry **7**
Spackman, W(illiam) M(ode) **46**
Spacks, Barry (Bernard) **14**
Spanidou, Irini **44**
Spencer, Elizabeth **22**
Spencer, Scott **30**
Spicer, Jack **8, 18, 72**
Spiegelman, Art **76, 178**
Spielberg, Peter **6**
Spielberg, Steven **20, 188**
Spinrad, Norman (Richard) **46**
Spivack, Kathleen (Romola Drucker) **6**
Spoto, Donald **39**
Springsteen, Bruce (F.) **17**
Squires, (James) Radcliffe **51**
Stafford, Jean **4, 7, 19, 68**
Stafford, William (Edgar) **4, 7, 29**
Stanton, Maura **9**
Starbuck, George (Edwin) **53**
Steele, Timothy (Reid) **45**
Stegner, Wallace (Earle) **9, 49, 81**
Steinbeck, John (Ernst) **1, 5, 9, 13, 21, 34, 45, 75, 124**
Steinem, Gloria **63**
Steiner, George **24**
Sterling, Bruce **72**
Stern, Gerald **40, 100**
Stern, Richard (Gustave) **4, 39**
Sternberg, Josef von **20**
Stevens, Mark **34**
Stevenson, Anne (Katharine) **7, 33**
Still, James **49**
Stitt, Milan **29**
Stolz, Mary (Slattery) **12**
Stone, Irving **7**
Stone, Oliver (William) **73**
Stone, Robert (Anthony) **5, 23, 42, 175s**
Storm, Hyemeyohsts **3**
Stout, Rex (Todhunter) **3**
Strand, Mark **6, 18, 41, 71**
Straub, Peter (Francis) **28, 107**
Stribling, T(homas) S(igismund) **23**
Stuart, Jesse (Hilton) **1, 8, 11, 14, 34**
Sturgeon, Theodore (Hamilton) **22, 39**
Styron, William **1, 3, 5, 11, 15, 60**
Sukenick, Ronald **3, 4, 6, 48**
Summers, Hollis (Spurgeon Jr.) **10**
Susann, Jacqueline **3**
Swados, Elizabeth (A.) **12**
Swados, Harvey **5**
Swan, Gladys **69**
Swarthout, Glendon (Fred) **35**
Swenson, May **4, 14, 61, 106**
Talese, Gay **37**
Tallent, Elizabeth (Ann) **45**
Tally, Ted **42**
Tan, Amy (Ruth) **59, 120, 151**
Tartt, Donna **76**
Tate, James (Vincent) **2, 6, 25**
Tate, (John Orley) Allen **2, 4, 6, 9, 11, 14, 24**
Tavel, Ronald **6**
Taylor, Eleanor Ross **5**
Taylor, Henry (Splawn) **44**
Taylor, Mildred D(elois) **21**

Taylor, Peter (Hillsman) **1, 4, 18, 37, 44, 50, 71**
Taylor, Robert Lewis **14**
Terkel, Studs **38**
Terry, Megan **19**
Tesich, Steve **40, 69**
Tevis, Walter **42**
Theroux, Alexander (Louis) **2, 25**
Theroux, Paul (Edward) **5, 8, 11, 15, 28, 46, 159**
Thomas, Audrey (Callahan) **7, 13, 37, 107**
Thomas, Joyce Carol **35**
Thomas, Lewis **35**
Thomas, Piri **17**
Thomas, Ross (Elmore) **39**
Thompson, Hunter S(tockton) **9, 17, 40, 104**
Thompson, Jim (Myers) **69**
Thurber, James (Grover) **5, 11, 25, 125**
Tilghman, Christopher **65**
Tillich, Paul (Johannes) **131**
Tillinghast, Richard (Williford) **29**
Toffler, Alvin
Tolson, Melvin B(eaunorus) **36, 105**
Tomlin, Lily **17**
Toole, John Kennedy **19, 64**
Toomer, Jean **1, 4, 13, 22**
Torrey, E(dwin) Fuller **34**
Towne, Robert (Burton) **87**
Traven, B. **8, 11**
Trevanian **29**
Trilling, Diana (Rubin) **129**
Trilling, Lionel **9, 11, 24**
Trow, George W. S. **52**
Trudeau, Garry B. **12**
Trumbo, Dalton **19**
Tryon, Thomas **3, 11**
Tuck, Lily **70**
Tunis, John R(oberts) **12**
Turco, Lewis (Putnam) **11, 63**
Turner, Frederick **48**
Tyler, Anne **7, 11, 18, 28, 44, 59, 103**
Uhry, Alfred **55**
Ulibarrí, Sabine R(eyes) **83**
Unger, Douglas **34**
Updike, John (Hoyer) **1, 2, 3, 5, 7, 9, 13, 15, 23, 34, 43, 70, 139**
Urdang, Constance (Henriette) **47**
Uris, Leon (Marcus) **7, 32**
Vachss, Andrew (Henry) **106**
Valdez, Luis (Miguel) **84**
Van Ash, Cay **34**
Vandenburgh, Jane **59**
Van Doren, Mark **6, 10**
Van Duyn, Mona (Jane) **3, 7, 63, 116**
Van Peebles, Melvin **2, 20**
Van Vechten, Carl **33**
Vaughn, Stephanie **62**
Vendler, Helen (Hennessy) **138**
Vidal, Gore **2, 4, 6, 8, 10, 22, 33, 72, 142**
Viereck, Peter (Robert Edwin) **4**
Vinge, Joan (Carol) D(ennison) **30**
Viola, Herman J(oseph) **70**
Vizenor, Gerald Robert **103**
Vliet, R(ussell) G(ordon) **22**
Vogel, Paula A(nne) **76**
Voigt, Cynthia **30**
Voigt, Ellen Bryant **54**
Vollmann, William T. **89**
Vonnegut, Kurt Jr. **1, 2, 3, 4, 5, 8, 12, 22, 40, 60, 111**
Wagman, Fredrica **7**
Wagner-Martin, Linda (C.) **50**
Wagoner, David (Russell) **3, 5, 15**
Wakefield, Dan **7**
Wakoski, Diane **2, 4, 7, 9, 11, 40**
Waldman, Anne (Lesley) **7**
Walker, Alice (Malsenior) **5, 6, 9, 19, 27, 46, 58, 103, 167**
Walker, Joseph A. **19**
Walker, Margaret (Abigail) **1, 6**
Wallace, David Foster **50, 114**
Wallace, Irving **7, 13**

Wallant, Edward Lewis **5, 10**
Wambaugh, Joseph (Aloysius Jr.) **3, 18**
Ward, Douglas Turner **19**
Warhol, Andy **20**
Warren, Robert Penn **1, 4, 6, 8, 10, 13, 18, 39, 53, 59**
Wasserstein, Wendy **32, 59, 90**
Waters, Frank (Joseph) **88**
Watkins, Paul **55**
Webb, Charles (Richard) **7**
Webb, James H(enry) Jr. **22**
Weber, Lenora Mattingly **12**
Weidman, Jerome **7**
Weiss, Theodore (Russell) **3, 8, 14**
Welch, James **6, 14, 52**
Wellek, Rene **28**
Weller, Michael **10, 53**
Welles, (George) Orson **20, 80**
Wellman, Mac **65**
Wellman, Manly Wade **49**
Wells, Rosemary **12**
Welty, Eudora **1, 2, 5, 14, 22, 33, 105**
Wersba, Barbara **30**
Wescott, Glenway **13**
Wesley, Richard (Errol) **7**
West, Cornel (Ronald) **134**
West, Delno C(loyde) Jr. **70**
West, (Mary) Jessamyn **7, 17**
West, Paul **7, 14, 96**
Westlake, Donald E(dwin) **7, 33**
Whalen, Philip **6, 29**
Wharton, William (a pseudonym) **18, 37**
Wheelock, John Hall **14**
White, Edmund (Valentine III) **27, 110**
White, E(lwyn) B(rooks) **10, 34, 39**
White, Hayden V. **148**
Whitney, Phyllis A(yame) **42**
Whittemore, (Edward) Reed (Jr.) **4**
Wicker, Tom **7**
Wideman, John Edgar **5, 34, 36, 67, 122**
Wieners, John **7**
Wiesel, Elie(zer) **3, 5, 11, 37, 165**
Wiggins, Marianne **57**
Wilbur, Richard (Purdy) **3, 6, 9, 14, 53, 110**
Wild, Peter **14**
Wilder, Billy **20**
Wilder, Thornton (Niven) **1, 5, 6, 10, 15, 35, 82**
Wiley, Richard **44**
Willard, Nancy **7, 37**
Williams, C(harles) K(enneth) **33, 56, 148**
Williams, John A(lfred) **5, 13**
Williams, Jonathan (Chamberlain) **13**
Williams, Joy **31**
Williams, Norman **39**
Williams, Sherley Anne **89**
Williams, Tennessee **1, 2, 5, 7, 8, 11, 15, 19, 30, 39, 45, 71, 111**
Williams, Thomas (Alonzo) **14**
Williams, William Carlos **1, 2, 5, 9, 13, 22, 42, 67**
Willingham, Calder (Baynard Jr.) **5, 51**
Wilson, August **39, 50, 63, 118**
Wilson, Brian **12**
Wilson, Edmund **1, 2, 3, 8, 24**
Wilson, Lanford **7, 14, 36**
Wilson, Robert M. **7, 9**
Wilson, Sloan **32**
Wilson, William S(mith) **49**
Winters, (Arthur) Yvor **4, 8, 32**
Winters, Janet Lewis **41**
Wiseman, Frederick **20**
Wodehouse, P(elham) G(renville) **1, 2, 5, 10, 22**
Woiwode, Larry (Alfred) **6, 10**
Wojciechowska, Maia (Teresa) **26**
Wolf, Naomi **157**
Wolfe, Gene (Rodman) **25**
Wolfe, George C. **49**
Wolfe, Thomas Kennerly Jr. **147**
Wolff, Geoffrey (Ansell) **41**
Wolff, Tobias (Jonathan Ansell) **39, 64, 172**

*Nationality Index*

Wolitzer, Hilma 17
Wonder, Stevie 12
Wong, Jade Snow 17
Woolrich, Cornell 77
Wouk, Herman 1, 9, 38
Wright, Charles (Penzel Jr.) 6, 13, 28, 119, 146
Wright, Charles Stevenson 49
Wright, James (Arlington) 3, 5, 10, 28
Wright, Richard (Nathaniel) 1, 3, 4, 9, 14, 21, 48, 74
Wright, Stephen 33
Wright, William 44
Wurlitzer, Rudolph 2, 4, 15
Wylie, Philip (Gordon) 43
Yates, Richard 7, 8, 23
Yep, Laurence Michael 35
Yerby, Frank G(arvin) 1, 7, 22
Yglesias, Helen 7, 22
Young, Al(bert James) 19
Young, Marguerite (Vivian) 82
Young Bear, Ray A. 94
Yurick, Sol 6
Zamora, Bernice (B. Ortiz) 89
Zappa, Frank 17
Zaturenska, Marya 6, 11
Zelazny, Roger (Joseph) 21
Ziegenhagen, Eric 55
Zindel, Paul 6, 26
Zoline, Pamela 62
Zukofsky, Louis 1, 2, 4, 7, 11, 18
Zweig, Paul 34, 42

**ANGOLAN**

Wellman, Manly Wade 49

**ANTIGUAN**

Edwards, Gus 43
Kincaid, Jamaica 43, 68, 137

**ARGENTINIAN**

Bioy Casares, Adolfo 4, 8, 13, 88
Borges, Jorge Luis 1, 2, 3, 4, 6, 8, 9, 10, 13, 19, 44, 48, 83
Cortázar, Julio 2, 3, 5, 10, 13, 15, 33, 34, 92
Costantini, Humberto 49
Dorfman, Ariel 48, 77, 189
Guevara, Che 87
Guevara (Serna), Ernesto 87
Mujica Lainez, Manuel 31
Puig, Manuel 3, 5, 10, 28, 65, 133
Sabato, Ernesto (R.) 10, 23
Valenzuela, Luisa 31, 104

**ARMENIAN**

Mamoulian, Rouben (Zachary) 16

**AUSTRALIAN**

Anderson, Jessica (Margaret) Queale 37
Astley, Thea (Beatrice May) 41
Brinsmead, H(esba) F(ay) 21
Buckley, Vincent (Thomas) 57
Buzo, Alexander (John) 61
Carey, Peter 40, 55, 96
Clark, Mavis Thorpe 12
Clavell, James (duMaresq) 6, 25, 87
Conway, Jill K(er) 152
Courtenay, Bryce 59
Davison, Frank Dalby 15
Elliott, Sumner Locke 38
FitzGerald, Robert D(avid) 19
Greer, Germaine 131
Grenville, Kate 61
Hall, Rodney 51
Hazzard, Shirley 18
Hope, A(lec) D(erwent) 3, 51
Hospital, Janette Turner 42, 145
Jolley, (Monica) Elizabeth 46
Jones, Rod 50

Keneally, Thomas (Michael) 5, 8, 10, 14, 19, 27, 43, 117
Koch, C(hristopher) J(ohn) 42
Lawler, Raymond Evenor 58
Malouf, (George Joseph) David 28, 86
Matthews, Greg 45
McAuley, James Phillip 45
McCullough, Colleen 27, 107
Murray, Les(lie Allan) 40
Porter, Peter (Neville Frederick) 5, 13, 33
Prichard, Katharine Susannah 46
Shapcott, Thomas W(illiam) 38
Slessor, Kenneth 14
Stead, Christina (Ellen) 2, 5, 8, 32, 80
Stow, (Julian) Randolph 23, 48
Thiele, Colin (Milton) 17
Weir, Peter (Lindsay) 20
West, Morris L(anglo) 6, 33
White, Patrick (Victor Martindale) 3, 4, 5, 7, 9, 18, 65, 69
Wilding, Michael 73
Williamson, David (Keith) 56
Wright, Judith (Arundell) 11, 53

**AUSTRIAN**

Adamson, Joy(-Friederike Victoria) 17
Bachmann, Ingeborg 69
Bernhard, Thomas 3, 32, 61
Bettelheim, Bruno 79
Frankl, Viktor E(mil) 93
Gregor, Arthur 9
Handke, Peter 5, 8, 10, 15, 38, 134
Hochwaelder, Fritz 36
Jelinek, Elfriede 169
Jandl, Ernst 34
Lang, Fritz 20, 103
Lind, Jakov 1, 2, 4, 27, 82
Perloff, Marjorie G(abrielle) 137
Sternberg, Josef von 20
Wellek, Rene 28
Wilder, Billy 20

**BARBADIAN**

Brathwaite, Edward (Kamau) 11
Clarke, Austin C(hesterfield) 8, 53
Kennedy, Adrienne (Lita) 66
Lamming, George (William) 2, 4, 66, 144

**BELGIAN**

Crommelynck, Fernand 75
Ghelderode, Michel de 6, 11
Lévi-Strauss, Claude 38
Mallet-Joris, Françoise 11
Michaux, Henri 8, 19
Sarton, (Eleanor) May 4, 14, 49, 91
Simenon, Georges (Jacques Christian) 1, 2, 3, 8, 18, 47
van Itallie, Jean-Claude 3
Yourcenar, Marguerite 19, 38, 50, 87

**BOTSWANAN**

Head, Bessie 25, 67

**BRAZILIAN**

Amado, Jorge 13, 40, 106
Boff, Leonardo (Genezio Darci) 70
Cabral de Melo Neto, João 76
Castaneda, Carlos (Cesar Aranha) 12, 119
Dourado, (Waldomiro Freitas) Autran 23, 60
Drummond de Andrade, Carlos 18
Lispector, Clarice 43
Ribeiro, Darcy 34
Ribeiro, Joao Ubaldo (Osorio Pimentel) 10, 67
Rosa, João Guimarães 23

**BULGARIAN**

Belcheva, Elisaveta Lyubomirova 10
Canetti, Elias 3, 14, 25, 75, 86
Kristeva, Julia 77, 140

**CAMEROONIAN**

Beti, Mongo 27

**CANADIAN**

Acorn, Milton 15
Aquin, Hubert 15
Atwood, Margaret (Eleanor) 2, 3, 4, 8, 13, 15, 25, 44, 84, 135
Avison, Margaret 2, 4, 97
Barfoot, Joan 18
Berton, Pierre (Francis Demarigny) 104
Birney, (Alfred) Earle 1, 4, 6, 11
Bissett, Bill 18
Blais, Marie-Claire 2, 4, 6, 13, 22
Blaise, Clark 29
Bowering, George 15, 47
Bowering, Marilyn R(uthe) 32
Brand, Dionne 192
Brossard, Nicole 115, 169
Buckler, Ernest 13
Buell, John (Edward) 10
Callaghan, Morley Edward 3, 14, 41, 65
Campbell, Maria 85
Carrier, Roch 13, 78
Carson, Anne 185
Child, Philip 19, 68
Chislett, (Margaret) Anne 34
Clarke, Austin C(hesterfield) 8, 53
Cohen, Leonard (Norman) 3, 38
Cohen, Matt(hew) 19
Coles, Don 46
Cook, Michael 58
Cooper, Douglas 86
Coupland, Douglas 85, 133
Craven, Margaret 17
Cronenberg, David 143
Davies, (William) Robertson 2, 7, 13, 25, 42, 75, 91
de la Roche, Mazo 14
Donnell, David 34
Ducharme, Rejean 74
Dudek, Louis 11, 19
Egoyan, Atom 151
Engel, Marian 36
Everson, R(onald) G(ilmour) 27
Faludy, George 42
Ferron, Jacques 94
Finch, Robert (Duer Claydon) 18
Findley, Timothy 27, 102
Fraser, Sylvia 64
Frye, (Herman) Northrop 24, 70
Gallant, Mavis 7, 18, 38, 172
Garner, Hugh 13
Gibson, William (Ford) 39, 63, 186, 192
Gilmour, David 35
Glassco, John 9
Gotlieb, Phyllis Fay (Bloom) 18
Govier, Katherine 51
Gunnars, Kristjana 69
Gustafson, Ralph (Barker) 36
Haig-Brown, Roderick (Langmere) 21
Hailey, Arthur 5
Harris, Christie (Lucy) Irwin 12
Hébert, Anne 4, 13, 29
Highway, Tomson 92
Hillis, Rick 66
Hine, (William) Daryl 15
Hodgins, Jack 23
Hood, Hugh (John Blagdon) 15, 28
Hyde, Anthony 42
Jacobsen, Josephine 48, 102
Jiles, Paulette 13, 58
Johnston, George (Benson) 51
Jones, D(ouglas) G(ordon) 10
Kelly, M(ilton) T(errence) 55
King, Thomas 89
Kinsella, W(illiam) P(atrick) 27, 43, 166
Klein, A(braham) M(oses) 19
Kogawa, Joy Nozomi 78, 129
Krizanc, John 57
Kroetsch, Robert 5, 23, 57, 132

Kroker, Arthur (W.) **77**
Lane, Patrick **25**
Laurence, (Jean) Margaret (Wemyss) **3, 6, 13, 50, 62**
Layton, Irving (Peter) **2, 15, 164**
Levine, Norman **54**
Lightfoot, Gordon **26**
Livesay, Dorothy (Kathleen) **4, 15, 79**
MacEwen, Gwendolyn (Margaret) **13, 55**
MacLennan, (John) Hugh **2, 14, 92**
MacLeod, Alistair **56, 165**
Macpherson, (Jean) Jay **14**
Maillet, Antonine **54, 118**
Major, Kevin (Gerald) **26**
Marlatt, Daphne **168**
Martel, Yann **192**
McFadden, David **48**
McLuhan, (Herbert) Marshall **37, 83**
Metcalf, John **37**
Mistry, Rohinton **71**
Mitchell, Joni **12**
Mitchell, W(illiam) O(rmond) **25**
Moore, Brian **1, 3, 5, 7, 8, 19, 32, 90**
Morgan, Janet **39**
Moure, Erin **88**
Mowat, Farley (McGill) **26**
Mukherjee, Bharati **53, 115**
Munro, Alice **6, 10, 19, 50, 95**
Musgrave, Susan **13, 54**
Newlove, John (Herbert) **14**
Nichol, B(arrie) P(hillip) **18**
Nowlan, Alden (Albert) **15**
Ondaatje, (Philip) Michael **14, 29, 51, 76, 180**
Page, P(atricia) K(athleen) **7, 18**
Pollock, (Mary) Sharon **50**
Pratt, E(dwin) J(ohn) **19**
Purdy, A(lfred) W(ellington) **3, 6, 14, 50**
Quarrington, Paul (Lewis) **65**
Reaney, James **13**
Ricci, Nino **70**
Richards, David Adams **59**
Richler, Mordecai **3, 5, 9, 13, 18, 46, 70, 185**
Ringwood, Gwen(dolyn Margaret) Pharis **48**
Ritter, Erika **52**
Rooke, Leon **25, 34**
Rosenblatt, Joe **15**
Ross, (James) Sinclair **13**
Roy, Gabrielle **10, 14**
Rule, Jane (Vance) **27**
Ryga, George **14**
Scott, F(rancis) R(eginald) **22**
Shields, Carol **91, 113, 193**
Skelton, Robin **13**
Škvorecký, Josef (Vaclav) **15, 39, 69, 152**
Slade, Bernard **11, 46**
Smart, Elizabeth **54**
Smith, A(rthur) J(ames) M(arshall) **15**
Souster, (Holmes) Raymond **5, 14**
Suknaski, Andrew **19**
Theriault, Yves **79**
Thesen, Sharon **56**
Thomas, Audrey (Callahan) **7, 13, 37, 107**
Thompson, Judith **39**
Tremblay, Michel **29, 102**
Urquhart, Jane **90**
Vanderhaeghe, Guy **41**
van Vogt, A(lfred) E(lton) **1**
Vizinczey, Stephen **40**
Waddington, Miriam **28**
Wah, Fred(erick James) **44**
Walker, David Harry **14**
Walker, George F. **44, 61**
Webb, Phyllis **18**
Wiebe, Rudy (Henry) **6, 11, 14, 138**
Wilson, Ethel Davis (Bryant) **13**
Wright, L(aurali) R. **44**
Wright, Richard B(ruce) **6**
Young, Neil **17**

**CHILEAN**

Alegria, Fernando **57**
Allende, Isabel **39, 57, 97, 170**
Donoso (Yañez), José **4, 8, 11, 32, 99**
Dorfman, Ariel **48, 77**
Neruda, Pablo **1, 2, 5, 7, 9, 28, 62**
Parra, Nicanor **2, 102**

**CHINESE**

Chang, Jung **71**
Ch'ien, Chung-shu **22**
Ding Ling **68**
Lord, Bette Bao **23**
Mo, Timothy (Peter) **46, 134**
Pa Chin **18**
Peake, Mervyn **7, 54**
Wong, Jade Snow **17**

**COLOMBIAN**

García Márquez, Gabriel (Jose) **2, 3, 8, 10, 15, 27, 47, 55, 68, 170**

**CONGOLESE**

Tchicaya, Gerald Felix **101**

**CROATION**

Drakulic, Slavenka **173**

**CUBAN**

Arenas, Reinaldo **41**
Cabrera Infante, G(uillermo) **5, 25, 45, 120**
Calvino, Italo **5, 8, 11, 22, 33, 39, 73**
Carpentier (y Valmont), Alejo **8, 11, 38, 110**
Fornés, María Irene **39, 61**
Garcia, Cristina **76**
Guevara, Che **87**
Guillén, Nicolás (Cristobal) **48, 79**
Lezama Lima, José **4, 10, 101**
Padilla (Lorenzo), Heberto **38**
Sarduy, Severo **6, 97**

**CZECH**

Forman, Milos **164**
Friedlander, Saul **90**
Havel, Václav **25, 58, 65, 123**
Holub, Miroslav **4**
Hrabal, Bohumil **13, 67**
Klima, Ivan **56, 172**
Kohout, Pavel **13**
Kundera, Milan **4, 9, 19, 32, 68, 115, 135**
Lustig, Arnost **56**
Seifert, Jaroslav **34, 44, 93**
Škvorecký, Josef (Vaclav) **15, 39, 69, 152**
Vaculik, Ludvik **7**

**DANISH**

Abell, Kjeld **15**
Bodker, Cecil **21**
Dreyer, Carl Theodor **16**
Hoeg, Peter **95, 156**

**DOMINICAN REPUBLIC**

Alvarez, Julia **93**

**DUTCH**

Bernhard, Thomas **3, 32, 61**
Buruma, Ian **163**
de Hartog, Jan **19**
Mulisch, Harry **42**
Ruyslinck, Ward **14**
van de Wetering, Janwillem **47**

**EGYPTIAN**

Chedid, Andree **47**
Mahfouz, Naguïb (Abdel Azīz Al-Sabilgi) **153**

**ENGLISH**

Ackroyd, Peter **34, 52, 140**
Adams, Douglas (Noel) **27, 60**
Adams, Richard (George) **4, 5, 18**
Adcock, Fleur **41**
Aickman, Robert (Fordyce) **57**
Aiken, Joan (Delano) **35**
Aldington, Richard **49**
Aldiss, Brian W(ilson) **5, 14, 40**
Allingham, Margery (Louise) **19**
Almedingen, E. M. **12**
Alvarez, A(lfred) **5, 13**
Ambler, Eric **4, 6, 9**
Amis, Kingsley (William) **1, 2, 3, 5, 8, 13, 40, 44, 129**
Amis, Martin (Louis) **4, 9, 38, 62, 101**
Anderson, Lindsay (Gordon) **20**
Anthony, Piers **35**
Archer, Jeffrey (Howard) **28**
Arden, John **6, 13, 15**
Armatrading, Joan **17**
Arthur, Ruth M(abel) **12**
Arundel, Honor (Morfydd) **17**
Atkinson, Kate **99**
Auden, W(ystan) H(ugh) **1, 2, 3, 4, 6, 9, 11, 14, 43, 123**
Ayckbourn, Alan **5, 8, 18, 33, 74**
Ayrton, Michael **7**
Bagnold, Enid **25**
Bailey, Paul **45**
Bainbridge, Beryl (Margaret) **4, 5, 8, 10, 14, 18, 22, 62, 130**
Ballard, J(ames) G(raham) **3, 6, 14, 36, 137**
Banks, Lynne Reid **23**
Barker, Clive **52**
Barker, George Granville **8, 48**
Barker, Howard **37**
Barker, Pat(ricia) **32, 94, 146**
Barnes, Julian (Patrick) **42, 141**
Barnes, Peter **5, 56**
Barrett, (Roger) Syd **35**
Bates, H(erbert) E(rnest) **46**
Beer, Patricia **58**
Bennett, Alan **45, 77**
Berger, John (Peter) **2, 19**
Berkoff, Steven **56**
Bermant, Chaim (Icyk) **40**
Betjeman, John **2, 6, 10, 34, 43**
Billington, (Lady) Rachel (Mary) **43**
Binyon, T(imothy) J(ohn) **34**
Blunden, Edmund (Charles) **2, 56**
Bolt, Robert (Oxton) **14**
Bond, Edward **4, 6, 13, 23**
Booth, Martin **13**
Bowen, Elizabeth (Dorothea Cole) **1, 3, 6, 11, 15, 22, 118**
Bowie, David **17**
Boyd, William **28, 53, 70**
Bradbury, Malcolm (Stanley) **32, 61**
Bragg, Melvyn **10**
Braine, John (Gerard) **1, 3, 41**
Brenton, Howard **31**
Brittain, Vera (Mary) **23**
Brooke-Rose, Christine **40**
Brookner, Anita **32, 34, 51, 136**
Brophy, Brigid (Antonia) **6, 11, 29, 105**
Brunner, John (Kilian Houston) **8, 10**
Bunting, Basil **10, 39, 47**
Burgess, Anthony **1, 2, 4, 5, 8, 10, 13, 15, 22, 40, 62, 81, 94**
Byatt, A(ntonia) S(usan Drabble) **19, 65, 136**
Caldwell, (Janet Miriam) Taylor (Holland) **2, 28, 39**
Campbell, (John) Ramsey **42**
Carter, Angela (Olive) **5, 41, 76**
Causley, Charles (Stanley) **7**
Caute, (John) David **29**
Chambers, Aidan **35**
Chaplin, Charles Spencer **16**
Chapman, Graham **21**
Chatwin, (Charles) Bruce **28, 57, 59**
Chitty, Thomas Willes **11**

Christie, Agatha (Mary Clarissa) **1, 6, 8, 12, 39, 48, 110**
Churchill, Caryl **31, 55, 157**
Clark, (Robert) Brian **29**
Clarke, Arthur C(harles) **1, 4, 13, 18, 35, 136**
Cleese, John (Marwood) **21**
Colegate, Isabel **36**
Comfort, Alex(ander) **7**
Compton-Burnett, I(vy) **1, 3, 10, 15, 34**
Cooney, Ray **62**
Copeland, Stewart (Armstrong) **26**
Cornwell, David (John Moore) **9, 15**
Costello, Elvis **21**
Coward, Noël (Peirce) **1, 9, 29, 51**
Crace, Jim **157**
Creasey, John **11**
Crispin, Edmund **22**
Dabydeen, David **34**
D'Aguiar, Fred **145**
Dahl, Roald **1, 6, 18, 79**
Daryush, Elizabeth **6, 19**
Davie, Donald (Alfred) **5, 8, 10, 31**
Davies, Rhys **23**
Day Lewis, C(ecil) **1, 6, 10**
Deighton, Len **4, 7, 22, 46**
Delaney, Shelagh **29**
Dennis, Nigel (Forbes) **8**
Dickinson, Peter (Malcolm) **12, 35**
Drabble, Margaret **2, 3, 5, 8, 10, 22, 53, 129**
Duffy, Maureen **37**
du Maurier, Daphne **6, 11, 59**
Durrell, Lawrence (George) **1, 4, 6, 8, 13, 27, 41**
Dyer, Geoff **149**
Eagleton, Terence (Francis) **63, 132**
Edgar, David **42**
Edwards, G(erald) B(asil) **25**
Eliot, T(homas) S(tearns) **1, 2, 3, 6, 9, 10, 13, 15, 24, 34, 41, 55, 57, 113**
Elliott, Janice **47**
Ellis, A. E. **7**
Ellis, Alice Thomas **40**
Empson, William **3, 8, 19, 33, 34**
Enright, D(ennis) J(oseph) **4, 8, 31**
Ewart, Gavin (Buchanan) **13, 46**
Fairbairns, Zoe (Ann) **32**
Farrell, J(ames) G(ordon) **6**
Feinstein, Elaine **36**
Fenton, James Martin **32**
Ferguson, Niall **134**
Fielding, Helen **146**
Figes, Eva **31**
Fisher, Roy **25**
Fitzgerald, Penelope **19, 51, 61, 143**
Fleming, Ian (Lancaster) **3, 30**
Follett, Ken(neth Martin) **18**
Forester, C(ecil) S(cott) **35**
Forster, E(dward) M(organ) **1, 2, 3, 4, 9, 10, 13, 15, 22, 45, 77**
Forster, Margaret **149**
Forsyth, Frederick **2, 5, 36**
Fowles, John (Robert) **1, 2, 3, 4, 6, 9, 10, 15, 33, 87**
Francis, Dick **2, 22, 42, 102**
Fraser, George MacDonald **7**
Frayn, Michael **3, 7, 31, 47, 176**
Freeling, Nicolas **38**
Fry, Christopher **2, 10, 14**
Fugard, Sheila **48**
Fuller, John (Leopold) **62**
Fuller, Roy (Broadbent) **4, 28**
Gaiman, Neil **195**
Gardam, Jane (Mary) **43**
Gardner, John (Edmund) **30**
Garfield, Leon **12**
Garner, Alan **17**
Garnett, David **3**
Gascoyne, David (Emery) **45**
Gee, Maggie (Mary) **57**
Gerhardie, William Alexander **5**
Gilliatt, Penelope (Ann Douglass) **2, 10, 13, 53**

Glanville, Brian (Lester) **6**
Glendinning, Victoria **50**
Gloag, Julian **40**
Godden, (Margaret) Rumer **53**
Golding, William (Gerald) **1, 2, 3, 8, 10, 17, 27, 58, 81**
Graham, Winston (Mawdsley) **23**
Graves, Richard Perceval **44**
Graves, Robert (von Ranke) **1, 2, 6, 11, 39, 44, 45**
Gray, Simon (James Holliday) **9, 14, 36**
Green, Henry **2, 13, 97**
Greenaway, Peter **159**
Greene, Graham (Henry) **1, 3, 6, 9, 14, 18, 27, 37, 70, 72, 125**
Griffiths, Trevor **13, 52**
Grigson, Geoffrey (Edward Harvey) **7, 39**
Gunn, Thom(son William) **3, 6, 18, 32, 81**
Haig-Brown, Roderick (Langmere) **21**
Hailey, Arthur **5**
Hall, Rodney **51**
Hamburger, Michael (Peter Leopold) **5, 14**
Hamilton, Ian **191**
Hamilton, (Anthony Walter) Patrick **51**
Hampton, Christopher (James) **4**
Hare, David **29, 58, 136**
Harris, (Theodore) Wilson **25, 159**
Harrison, Tony **43, 129**
Hartley, L(eslie) P(oles) **2, 22**
Harwood, Ronald **32**
Hastings, Selina **44**
Hawking, Stephen W(illiam) **63, 105**
Headon, (Nicky) Topper **30**
Heppenstall, (John) Rayner **10**
Hibbert, Eleanor Alice Burford **7**
Hill, Geoffrey (William) **5, 8, 18, 45**
Hill, Susan (Elizabeth) **4, 113**
Hinde, Thomas **6, 11**
Hitchcock, Alfred (Joseph) **16**
Hitchens, Christopher **157**
Hocking, Mary (Eunice) **13**
Holden, Ursula **18**
Holdstock, Robert P. **39**
Hollinghurst, Alan **55, 91**
Hooker, (Peter) Jeremy **43**
Hopkins, John (Richard) **4**
Household, Geoffrey (Edward West) **11**
Howard, Elizabeth Jane **7, 29**
Hughes, David (John) **48**
Hughes, Richard (Arthur Warren) **1, 11**
Hughes, Ted **2, 4, 9, 14, 37, 119**
Huxley, Aldous (Leonard) **1, 3, 4, 5, 8, 11, 18, 35, 79**
Idle, Eric **21**
Ingalls, Rachel (Holmes) **42**
Isherwood, Christopher (William Bradshaw) **1, 9, 11, 14, 44**
Ishiguro, Kazuo **27, 56, 59, 110**
Jacobson, Dan **4, 14**
Jagger, Mick **17**
James, C(yril) L(ionel) R(obert) **33**
James, P. D. **18, 46, 122**
Jellicoe, (Patricia) Ann **27**
Jennings, Elizabeth (Joan) **5, 14, 131**
Jhabvala, Ruth Prawer **4, 8, 29, 94, 138**
Johnson, B(ryan) S(tanley William) **6, 9**
Johnson, Pamela Hansford **1, 7, 27**
Johnson, Paul (Bede) **147**
Jolley, (Monica) Elizabeth **46**
Jones, David (Michael) **2, 4, 7, 13, 42**
Jones, Diana Wynne **26**
Jones, Mervyn **10, 52**
Jones, Mick **30**
Josipovici, Gabriel (David) **6, 43, 153**
Kavan, Anna **5, 13, 82**
Kaye, M(ary) M(argaret) **28**
Keates, Jonathan **34**
King, Francis (Henry) **8, 53, 145**
Kirkup, James **1**
Koestler, Arthur **1, 3, 6, 8, 15, 33**
Kops, Bernard **4**
Kureishi, Hanif **64, 135**

Lanchester, John **99**
Larkin, Philip (Arthur) **3, 5, 8, 9, 13, 18, 33, 39, 64**
Leavis, F(rank) R(aymond) **24**
Lee, Laurie **90**
Lee, Tanith **46**
Lehmann, Rosamond (Nina) **5**
Lennon, John (Ono) **12, 35**
Lessing, Doris (May) **1, 2, 3, 6, 10, 15, 22, 40, 94, 170**
Levertov, Denise **1, 2, 3, 5, 8, 15, 28, 66**
Levi, Peter (Chad Tigar) **41**
Lewis, C(live) S(taples) **1, 3, 6, 14, 27, 124**
Lively, Penelope (Margaret) **32, 50**
Lodge, David (John) **36, 141**
Loy, Mina **28**
Luke, Peter (Ambrose Cyprian) **38**
MacInnes, Colin **4, 23**
Mackenzie, Compton (Edward Montague) **18**
Macpherson, (Jean) Jay **14**
Maitland, Sara (Louise) **49**
Manning, Olivia **5, 19**
Mantel, Hilary (Mary) **144**
Masefield, John (Edward) **11, 47**
Mason, Nick **35**
Maugham, W(illiam) Somerset **1, 11, 15, 67, 93**
Mayle, Peter **89**
Mayne, William (James Carter) **12**
McEwan, Ian (Russell) **13, 66, 169**
McGrath, Patrick **55**
Mercer, David **5**
Middleton, Christopher **13**
Middleton, Stanley **7, 38**
Mitford, Nancy **44**
Mo, Timothy (Peter) **46, 134**
Moorcock, Michael (John) **5, 27, 58**
Mortimer, John (Clifford) **28, 43**
Mortimer, Penelope (Ruth) **5**
Mosley, Nicholas **43, 70**
Motion, Andrew (Peter) **47**
Mott, Michael (Charles Alston) **15, 34**
Murdoch, (Jean) Iris **1, 2, 3, 4, 6, 8, 11, 15, 22, 31, 51**
Naipaul, V(idiadhar) S(urajprasad) **4, 7, 9, 13, 18, 37, 105**
Newby, P(ercy) H(oward) **2, 13**
Nichols, Peter (Richard) **5, 36, 65**
Noon, Jeff **91**
Norfolk, Lawrence **76**
Nye, Robert **13, 42**
O'Brien, Richard **17**
O'Faolain, Julia **6, 19, 47, 108**
Olivier, Laurence (Kerr) **20**
Orton, Joe **4, 13, 43**
Osborne, John (James) **1, 2, 5, 11, 45**
Osborne, Lawrence **50**
Page, Jimmy **12**
Page, Louise **40**
Page, P(atricia) K(athleen) **7, 18**
Palin, Michael (Edward) **21**
Parkin, Frank **43**
Parks, Tim(othy Harold) **147**
Paton Walsh, Gillian **35**
Paulin, Tom **37, 177**
Peake, Mervyn **7, 54**
Perry, Anne **126**
Phillips, Caryl **96**
Pinter, Harold **1, 3, 6, 9, 11, 15, 27, 58, 73**
Plant, Robert **12**
Poliakoff, Stephen **38**
Potter, Dennis (Christopher George) **58, 86, 123**
Powell, Anthony (Dymoke) **1, 3, 7, 9, 10, 31**
Pownall, David **10**
Powys, John Cowper **7, 9, 15, 46, 125**
Priestley, J(ohn) B(oynton) **2, 5, 9, 34**
Prince, F(rank) T(empleton) **22**
Pritchett, V(ictor) S(awdon) **5, 13, 15, 41**
Pym, Barbara (Mary Crampton) **13, 19, 37, 111**
Quin, Ann (Marie) **6**

Raine, Craig (Anthony) **32, 103**
Raine, Kathleen (Jessie) **7, 45**
Rathbone, Julian **41**
Rattigan, Terence (Mervyn) **7**
Raven, Simon (Arthur Noel) **14**
Read, Herbert Edward **4**
Read, Piers Paul **4, 10, 25**
Reading, Peter **47**
Redgrove, Peter (William) **6, 41**
Reid, Christopher (John) **33**
Rendell, Ruth (Barbara) **28, 48**
Rhys, Jean **2, 4, 6, 14, 19, 51, 124**
Rice, Tim(othy Miles Bindon) **21**
Richard, Keith **17**
Richards, I(vor) A(rmstrong) **14, 24**
Roberts, Keith (John Kingston) **14**
Roberts, Michele (Brigitte) **48, 178**
Rowling, J(oanne) K(athleen) **137**
Rudkin, (James) David **14**
Rushdie, (Ahmed) Salman **23, 31, 55, 100, 191**
Rushforth, Peter (Scott) **19**
Russell, (Henry) Ken(neth Alfred) **16**
Russell, William Martin **60**
Sacks, Oliver (Wolf) **67**
Sansom, William **2, 6**
Sassoon, Siegfried (Lorraine) **36, 130**
Scammell, Michael **34**
Scannell, Vernon **49**
Schama, Simon (Michael) **150**
Schlee, Ann **35**
Schumacher, E(rnst) F(riedrich) **80**
Scott, Paul (Mark) **9, 60**
Shaffer, Anthony (Joshua) **19**
Shaffer, Peter (Levin) **5, 14, 18, 37, 60**
Sharpe, Tom **36**
Shaw, Robert **5**
Sheed, Wilfrid (John Joseph) **2, 4, 10, 53**
Shute, Nevil **30**
Shuttle, Penelope (Diane) **7**
Silkin, Jon **2, 6, 43**
Sillitoe, Alan **1, 3, 6, 10, 19, 57, 148**
Simonon, Paul **30**
Simpson, N(orman) F(rederick) **29**
Sinclair, Andrew (Annandale) **2, 14**
Sinclair, Iain **76**
Sisson, C(harles) H(ubert) **8**
Sitwell, Edith **2, 9, 67**
Slaughter, Carolyn **56**
Smith, Stevie **3, 8, 25, 44**
Smith, Zadie **158**
Snow, C(harles) P(ercy) **1, 4, 6, 9, 13, 19**
Spender, Stephen (Harold) **1, 2, 5, 10, 41, 91**
Spurling, Hilary **34**
Stannard, Martin **44**
Stewart, J(ohn) I(nnes) M(ackintosh) **7, 14, 32**
Stewart, Mary (Florence Elinor) **7, 35, 117**
Stoppard, Tom **1, 3, 4, 5, 8, 15, 29, 34, 63, 91**
Storey, David (Malcolm) **2, 4, 5, 8**
Streatfeild, (Mary) Noel **21**
Strummer, Joe **30**
Summers, Andrew James **26**
Sumner, Gordon Matthew **26**
Sutcliff, Rosemary **26**
Swift, Graham (Colin) **41, 88**
Swinfen, Ann **34**
Swinnerton, Frank Arthur **31**
Symons, Julian (Gustave) **2, 14, 32**
Szirtes, George **46**
Taylor, Elizabeth **2, 4, 29**
Tennant, Emma (Christina) **13, 52**
Teran, Lisa St. Aubin de **36**
Thomas, D(onald) M(ichael) **13, 22, 31, 132**
Thorpe, Adam **176**
Thubron, Colin (Gerald Dryden) **163**
Tindall, Gillian (Elizabeth) **7**
Tolkien, J(ohn) R(onald) R(euel) **1, 2, 3, 8, 12, 38**
Tomalin, Claire **166**
Tomlinson, (Alfred) Charles **2, 4, 6, 13, 45**

Townshend, Peter (Dennis Blandford) **17, 42**
Treitel, Jonathan **70**
Tremain, Rose **42**
Trollope, Joanna **186**
Tuohy, Frank **37**
Turner, Frederick **48**
Unsworth, Barry (Forster) **76, 127**
Ustinov, Peter (Alexander) **1**
Van Den Bogarde, Derek Jules Gaspard Ulric Niven
Vansittart, Peter **42**
Wain, John (Barrington) **2, 11, 15, 46**
Walker, Ted **13**
Walsh, Jill Paton **35**
Warner, Francis (Robert le Plastrier) **14**
Warner, Marina **59**
Warner, Rex (Ernest) **45**
Warner, Sylvia Townsend **7, 19**
Waterhouse, Keith (Spencer) **47**
Waters, Roger **35**
Waugh, Auberon (Alexander) **7**
Waugh, Evelyn (Arthur St. John) **1, 3, 8, 13, 19, 27, 44, 107**
Waugh, Harriet **6**
Webber, Andrew Lloyd **21**
Weldon, Fay **6, 9, 11, 19, 36, 59, 122**
Weller, Paul **26**
Wesker, Arnold **3, 5, 42**
West, Anthony (Panther) **50**
West, Paul **7, 14, 96**
West, Rebecca **7, 9, 31, 50**
Westall, Robert (Atkinson) **17**
White, Patrick (Victor Martindale) **3, 4, 5, 7, 9, 18, 65, 69**
White, T(erence) H(anbury) **30**
Whitehead, E(dward) A(nthony) **5**
Whitemore, Hugh (John) **37**
Wilding, Michael **73**
Williams, Hugo **42**
Wilson, A(ndrew) N(orman) **33**
Wilson, Angus (Frank Johnstone) **2, 3, 5, 25, 34**
Wilson, Colin **3, 14**
Wilson, Snoo **33**
Wingrove, David (John) **68**
Winterson, Jeanette **64, 158**
Wodehouse, P(elham) G(renville) **1, 2, 5, 10, 22**
Wright, Rick **35**
Yorke, Henry Vincent **13**
Young, Andrew (John) **5**

**ESTONIAN**

Ivask, Ivar Vidrik **14**

**FIJI ISLANDER**

Prichard, Katharine Susannah **46**

**FILIPINO**

Santos, Bienvenido N(uqui) **22**

**FINNISH**

Haavikko, Paavo Juhani **18, 34**
Salama, Hannu **18**
Sillanpaa, Frans Eemil **19**

**FRENCH**

Adamov, Arthur **4, 25**
Anouilh, Jean (Marie Lucien Pierre) **1, 3, 8, 13, 40, 50**
Aragon, Louis **3, 22**
Arp, Jean **5**
Audiberti, Jacques **38**
Aymé, Marcel (Andre) **11**
Barthes, Roland (Gérard) **24, 83**
Barzun, Jacques (Martin) **51, 145**
Bataille, Georges **29**
Baudrillard, Jean **60**

Beauvoir, Simone (Lucie Ernestine Marie Bertrand) de **1, 2, 4, 8, 14, 31, 44, 50, 71, 124**
Beckett, Samuel (Barclay) **1, 2, 3, 4, 6, 9, 10, 11, 14, 18, 29, 57, 59, 83**
Ben Jelloun, Tahar **180**
Blanchot, Maurice **135**
Bonnefoy, Yves **9, 15, 58**
Bresson, Robert **16**
Breton, André **2, 9, 15, 54**
Butor, Michel (Marie François) **1, 3, 8, 11, 15, 161**
Camus, Albert **1, 2, 4, 9, 11, 14, 32, 63, 69, 124**
Carrere, Emmanuel **89**
Cayrol, Jean **11**
Chabrol, Claude **16**
Char, René(-émile) **9, 11, 14, 55**
Chedid, Andree **47**
Cixous, Hélène **92**
Clair, Rene **20**
Cocteau, Jean (Maurice Eugène Clément) **1, 8, 15, 16, 43**
Cousteau, Jacques-Yves **30**
del Castillo, Michel **38**
Derrida, Jacques **24, 87**
Destouches, Louis-Ferdinand **9, 15**
Duhamel, Georges **8**
Duras, Marguerite **3, 6, 11, 20, 34, 40, 68, 100**
Ernaux, Annie **88**
Federman, Raymond **6, 47**
Foucault, Michel **31, 34, 69**
Fournier, Pierre **11**
Francis, Claude **50**
Gallo, Max Louis **95**
Gao Xingjian **167**
Gary, Romain **25**
Gascar, Pierre **11**
Genet, Jean **1, 2, 5, 10, 14, 44, 46**
Giono, Jean **4, 11**
Godard, Jean-Luc **20**
Goldmann, Lucien **24**
Gontier, Fernande **50**
Gray, Francine du Plessix **22, 153**
Green, Julien **3, 11, 77**
Guillevic, (Eugene) **33**
Houellebecq, Michel **179**
Ionesco, Eugène **1, 4, 6, 9, 11, 15, 41, 86**
Irigarary, Luce **164**
Japrisot, Sebastien **90**
Josipovici, Gabriel (David) **6, 43, 153**
Jouve, Pierre Jean **47**
Kristeva, Julia **77, 140**
Lacan, Jacques (Marie Emile) **75**
Laurent, Antoine **50**
Le Clézio, J(ean) M(arie) G(ustave) **31, 155**
Leduc, Violette **22**
Leger, (Marie-Rene Auguste) Alexis Saint-Leger **4, 11, 46**
Leiris, Michel (Julien) **61**
Lévi-Strauss, Claude **38**
Mallet-Joris, Françoise **11**
Malraux, (Georges-)André **1, 4, 9, 13, 15, 57**
Mandiargues, Andre Pieyre de **41**
Marcel, Gabriel Honore **15**
Mauriac, Claude **9**
Mauriac, François (Charles) **4, 9, 56**
Merton, Thomas **1, 3, 11, 34, 83**
Modiano, Patrick (Jean) **18**
Montherlant, Henry (Milon) de **8, 19**
Morand, Paul **41**
Nin, Anaïs **1, 4, 8, 11, 14, 60, 127**
Perec, Georges **56, 116**
Pinget, Robert **7, 13, 37**
Polanski, Roman **16, 17mech**
Ponge, Francis **6, 18**
Poniatowska, Elena **140**
Prévert, Jacques (Henri Marie) **15**
Queneau, Raymond **2, 5, 10, 42**
Quoirez, Francoise **9**
Renoir, Jean **20**

Resnais, Alain **16**
Reverdy, Pierre **53**
Rio, Michel **43**
Robbe-Grillet, Alain **1, 2, 4, 6, 8, 10, 14, 43, 128**
Rohmer, Eric **16**
Romains, Jules **7**
Sachs, Nelly **14, 98**
Sarraute, Nathalie **1, 2, 4, 8, 10, 31, 80**
Sartre, Jean-Paul **1, 4, 7, 9, 13, 18, 24, 44, 50, 52**
Sauser-Hall, Frederic **18**
Schwarz-Bart, André **2, 4**
Schwarz-Bart, Simone **7**
Simenon, Georges (Jacques Christian) **1, 2, 3, 8, 18, 47**
Simon, Claude **4, 9, 15, 39**
Soupault, Philippe **68**
Steiner, George **24**
Tournier, Michel (édouard) **6, 23, 36, 95**
Troyat, Henri **23**
Truffaut, Francois **20, 101**
Tuck, Lily **70**
Tzara, Tristan **47**
Varda, Agnes **16**
Wittig, Monique **22**
Yourcenar, Marguerite **19, 38, 50, 87**

## FRENCH GUINEAN

Damas, Leon-Gontran **84**

## GERMAN

Amichai, Yehuda **9, 22, 57, 116**
Arendt, Hannah **66, 98**
Arp, Jean **5**
Becker, Jurek **7, 19**
Benary-Isbert, Margot **12**
Bienek, Horst **7, 11**
Boell, Heinrich (Theodor) **2, 3, 6, 9, 11, 15, 27, 32, 72**
Buchheim, Lothar-Guenther **6**
Bukowski, Charles **2, 5, 9, 41, 82, 108**
Eich, Guenter **15**
Ende, Michael (Andreas Helmuth) **31**
Enzensberger, Hans Magnus **43**
Fassbinder, Rainer Werner **20**
Figes, Eva **31**
Grass, Guenter (Wilhelm) **1, 2, 4, 6, 11, 15, 22, 32, 49, 88**
Habermas, Juergen **104**
Hamburger, Michael (Peter Leopold) **5, 14**
Handke, Peter **5, 8, 10, 15, 38, 134**
Heidegger, Martin **24**
Hein, Christoph **154**
Herzog, Werner **16**
Hesse, Hermann **1, 2, 3, 6, 11, 17, 25, 69**
Heym, Stefan **41**
Hildesheimer, Wolfgang **49**
Hochhuth, Rolf **4, 11, 18**
Hofmann, Gert **54**
Jhabvala, Ruth Prawer **4, 8, 29, 94, 138**
Johnson, Uwe **5, 10, 15, 40**
Juenger, Ernst **125**
Kirsch, Sarah **176**
Kissinger, Henry A(lfred) **137**
Kroetz, Franz Xaver **41**
Kunze, Reiner **10**
Lenz, Siegfried **27**
Levitin, Sonia (Wolff) **17**
Maron, Monika **165**
Mueller, Lisel **13, 51**
Nossack, Hans Erich **6**
Preussler, Otfried **17**
Remarque, Erich Maria **21**
Riefenstahl, Leni **16, 190**
Sachs, Nelly **14, 98**
Schlink, Bernhard **174**
Schmidt, Arno (Otto) **56**
Schumacher, E(rnst) F(riedrich) **80**
Sebald, W. G. **194**
Seghers, Anna **7**

Strauss, Botho **22**
Süskind, Patrick **44, 182**
Tillich, Paul (Johannes) **131**
Walser, Martin **27**
Weiss, Peter (Ulrich) **3, 15, 51**
Wellershoff, Dieter **46**
Wolf, Christa **14, 29, 58, 150**
Zuckmayer, Carl **18**

## GHANIAN

Aidoo, Ama Ata **177**
Armah, Ayi Kwei **5, 33, 136**

## GREEK

Broumas, Olga **10, 73**
Elytis, Odysseus **15, 49, 100**
Haviaras, Stratis **33**
Karapanou, Margarita **13**
Nakos, Lilika **29**
Ritsos, Yannis **6, 13, 31**
Samarakis, Antonis **5**
Seferis, George **5, 11**
Spanidou, Irini **44**
Vassilikos, Vassilis **4, 8**

## GUADELOUPEAN

Condé, Maryse **52, 92**
Schwarz-Bart, Simone **7**

## GUATEMALAN

Asturias, Miguel Ángel **3, 8, 13**

## GUINEAN

Laye, Camara **4, 38**

## GUYANESE

Dabydeen, David **34**
Harris, (Theodore) Wilson **25**

## HAITIAN

Danticat, Edwidge **94, 139**

## HUNGARIAN

Faludy, George **42**
Koestler, Arthur **1, 3, 6, 8, 15, 33**
Konrád, György **4, 10, 73**
Lengyel, József **7**
Lukacs, George **24**
Nagy, Laszlo **7**
Szirtes, George **46**
Tabori, George **19**
Vizinczey, Stephen **40**

## ICELANDIC

Gunnars, Kristjana **69**

## INDIAN

Alexander, Meena **121**
Ali, Ahmed **69**
Anand, Mulk Raj **23, 93**
Das, Kamala **191**
Desai, Anita **19, 37, 97, 175**
Ezekiel, Nissim **61**
Ghosh, Amitav **44, 153**
Mahapatra, Jayanta **33**
Mehta, Gita **179**
Mehta, Ved (Parkash) **37**
Mistry, Rohinton **71**
Mukherjee, Bharati **53, 115**
Narayan, R(asipuram) K(rishnaswami) **7, 28, 47, 121**
Rao, Raja **25, 56**
Ray, Satyajit **16, 76**
Rushdie, (Ahmed) Salman **23, 31, 55, 100**
Sahgal, Nayantara (Pandit) **41**
Sealy, I(rwin) Allan **55**
Seth, Vikram **43, 90**
Singh, Khushwant **11**

Tharoor, Shashi **70**
White, T(erence) H(anbury) **30**

## INDONESIAN

Lee, Li-Young **164**
Pramoedya Ananta Toer **186**

## IRANIAN

Modarressi, Taghi (M.) **44**
Shamlu, Ahmad **10**

## IRISH

Banville, John **46, 118**
Beckett, Samuel (Barclay) **1, 2, 3, 4, 6, 9, 10, 11, 14, 18, 29, 57, 59, 83**
Behan, Brendan **1, 8, 11, 15, 79**
Binchy, Maeve **153**
Blackwood, Caroline **6, 9, 100**
Boland, Eavan (Aisling) **40, 67, 113**
Bowen, Elizabeth (Dorothea Cole) **1, 3, 6, 11, 15, 22, 118**
Boyle, Patrick **19**
Brennan, Maeve **5**
Brown, Christy **63**
Carroll, Paul Vincent **10**
Clarke, Austin **6, 9**
Colum, Padraic **28**
Day Lewis, C(ecil) **1, 6, 10**
Dillon, Eilis **17**
Donleavy, J(ames) P(atrick) **1, 4, 6, 10, 45**
Doyle, Roddy **81, 178**
Durcan, Paul **43, 70**
Friel, Brian **5, 42, 59, 115**
Gébler, Carlo (Ernest) **39**
Hanley, James **3, 5, 8, 13**
Hart, Josephine **70**
Heaney, Seamus (Justin) **5, 7, 14, 25, 37, 74, 91, 171**
Johnston, Jennifer (Prudence) **7, 150**
Jordan, Neil (Patrick) **110**
Kavanagh, Patrick (Joseph) **22**
Keane, Molly **31**
Kiely, Benedict **23, 43**
Kinsella, Thomas **4, 19, 138**
Lavin, Mary **4, 18, 99**
Leonard, Hugh **19**
Longley, Michael **29**
Mac Laverty, Bernard **31**
MacNeice, (Frederick) Louis **1, 4, 10, 53**
Mahon, Derek **27**
McCabe, Patrick **133**
McGahern, John **5, 9, 48, 156**
McGinley, Patrick (Anthony) **41**
McGuckian, Medbh **48, 174**
Montague, John (Patrick) **13, 46**
Moore, Brian **1, 3, 5, 7, 8, 19, 32, 90**
Morrison, Van **21**
Morrissy, Mary **99**
Muldoon, Paul **32, 72, 166**
Murphy, Richard **41**
Murphy, Thomas (Bernard) **51**
Nolan, Christopher **58**
O'Brian, Patrick **152**
O'Brien, Edna **3, 5, 8, 13, 36, 65, 116**
O'Casey, Sean **1, 5, 9, 11, 15, 88**
O'Doherty, Brian **76**
O'Faolain, Julia **6, 19, 47, 108**
O'Faolain, Sean **1, 7, 14, 32, 70**
O'Flaherty, Liam **5, 34**
Paulin, Tom **37**
Rodgers, W(illiam) R(obert) **7**
Simmons, James (Stewart Alexander) **43**
Toibin, Colm **162**
Trevor, William **7, 9, 14, 25, 71, 116**
White, Terence de Vere **49**
Wilson, Robert McLiam **59**

## ISRAELI

Agnon, S(hmuel) Y(osef Halevi) **4, 8, 14**
Amichai, Yehuda **9, 22, 57, 116**
Appelfeld, Aharon **23, 47**

Bakshi, Ralph **26**
Friedlander, Saul **90**
Grossman, David **67**
Kaniuk, Yoram **19**
Levin, Meyer **7**
Megged, Aharon **9**
Oz, Amos **5, 8, 11, 27, 33, 54**
Shammas, Anton **55**
Sobol, Joshua **60**
Yehoshua, A(braham) B. **13, 31**

**ITALIAN**

Antonioni, Michelangelo **20, 144**
Bacchelli, Riccardo **19**
Bassani, Giorgio **9**
Bertolucci, Bernardo **16, 157**
Bufalino, Gesualdo **74**
Buzzati, Dino **36**
Calasso, Roberto **81**
Calvino, Italo **5, 8, 11, 22, 33, 39, 73**
De Sica, Vittorio **20**
Eco, Umberto **28, 60, 142**
Fallaci, Oriana **11, 110**
Fellini, Federico **16, 85**
Fo, Dario **32, 109**
Gadda, Carlo Emilio **11**
Ginzburg, Natalia **5, 11, 54, 70**
Giovene, Andrea **7**
Landolfi, Tommaso **11, 49**
Levi, Primo **37, 50**
Luzi, Mario **13**
Montale, Eugenio **7, 9, 18**
Morante, Elsa **8, 47**
Moravia, Alberto **2, 7, 11, 27, 46**
Ortese, Anna Maria **89**
Palazzeschi, Aldo **11**
Pasolini, Pier Paolo **20, 37, 106**
Piccolo, Lucio **13**
Pincherle, Alberto **11, 18**
Quasimodo, Salvatore **10**
Ricci, Nino **70**
Sciascia, Leonardo **8, 9, 41**
Silone, Ignazio **4**
Ungaretti, Giuseppe **7, 11, 15**
Visconti, Luchino **16**
Vittorini, Elio **6, 9, 14**
Wertmueller, Lina **16**

**JAMAICAN**

Bennett, Louise (Simone) **28**
Cliff, Jimmy **21**
Cliff, Michelle **120**
Marley, Bob **17**
Thelwell, Michael Miles **22**

**JAPANESE**

Abe, Kōbō **8, 22, 53, 81**
Enchi, Fumiko (Ueda) **31**
Endō, Shūsaku **7, 14, 19, 54, 99**
Ibuse, Masuji **22**
Ichikawa, Kon **20**
Ishiguro, Kazuo **27, 56, 59, 110**
Kawabata, Yasunari **2, 5, 9, 18, 107**
Kurosawa, Akira **16, 119**
Murakami, Haruki
Ōe, Kenzaburo **10, 36, 86, 187**
Oshima, Nagisa **20**
Ozu, Yasujiro **16**
Shiga, Naoya **33**
Tanizaki, Jun'ichirō **8, 14, 28**
Whitney, Phyllis A(yame) **42**
Yoshimoto, Banana **84**

**KENYAN**

Ngugi, James T(hiong'o) **3, 7, 13**
Ngũgĩ wa Thiong'o **36, 182**

**MALIAN**

Ouologuem, Yambo **146**

**MARTINICAN**

Césaire, Aimé (Fernand) **19, 32, 112**
Fanon, Frantz **74**
Glissant, Edouard **10, 68**

**MEXICAN**

Arreola, Juan José **147**
Castellanos, Rosario **66**
Esquivel, Laura **141**
Fuentes, Carlos **3, 8, 10, 13, 22, 41, 60, 113**
Ibarguengoitia, Jorge **37**
Lopez Portillo (y Pacheco), Jose **46**
Lopez y Fuentes, Gregorio **32**
Paz, Octavio **3, 4, 6, 10, 19, 51, 65, 119**
Poniatowska, Elena **140**
Rulfo, Juan **8, 80**

**MOROCCAN**

Arrabal, Fernando **2, 9, 18, 58**
Mernissi, Fatima **171**

**NEW ZEALANDER**

Adcock, Fleur **41**
Ashton-Warner, Sylvia (Constance) **19**
Baxter, James K(eir) **14**
Campion, Jane **95**
Gee, Maurice (Gough) **29**
Grace, Patricia Frances **56**
Hilliard, Noel (Harvey) **15**
Hulme, Keri **39, 130**
Ihimaera, Witi **46**
Marsh, (Edith) Ngaio **7, 53**
Sargeson, Frank **31**

**NICARAGUAN**

Alegria, Claribel **75**
Cardenal, Ernesto **31, 161**

**NIGERIAN**

Achebe, (Albert) Chinua(lumogu) **1, 3, 5, 7, 11, 26, 51, 75, 127, 152**
Clark Bekedermo, J(ohnson) P(epper) **38**
Ekwensi, Cyprian (Odiatu Duaka) **4**
Emecheta, (Florence Onye) Buchi **14, 48, 128**
Nwapa, Flora **133**
Okigbo, Christopher (Ifenayichukwu) **25, 84**
Okri, Ben **87**
Saro-Wiwa, Ken(ule Beeson) **114**
Soyinka, Wole **3, 5, 14, 36, 44, 179**
Tutuola, Amos **5, 14, 29**

**NORTHERN IRISH**

Deane, Seamus (Francis) **122**
Simmons, James (Stewart Alexander) **43**
Wilson, Robert McLiam **59**

**NORWEGIAN**

Friis-Baastad, Babbis Ellinor **12**
Heyerdahl, Thor **26**
Moi, Toril **172**
Vesaas, Tarjei **48**

**PAKISTANI**

Ali, Ahmed **69**
Ali, Tariq **173**
Ghose, Zulfikar **42**

**PARAGUAYAN**

Roa Bastos, Augusto (Antonio) **45**

**PERUVIAN**

Allende, Isabel **39, 57, 97**
Arguedas, José María **10, 18**
Goldemberg, Isaac **52**
Vargas Llosa, (Jorge) Mario (Pedro) **3, 6, 9, 10, 15, 31, 42, 85, 181**

**POLISH**

Agnon, S(hmuel) Y(osef Halevi) **4, 8, 14**
Becker, Jurek **7, 19**
Bermant, Chaim (Icyk) **40**
Bienek, Horst **7, 11**
Brandys, Kazimierz **62**
Dabrowska, Maria (Szumska) **15**
Gombrowicz, Witold **4, 7, 11, 49**
Herbert, Zbigniew **9, 43**
John Paul II, Pope **128**
Kieslowski, Krzysztof **120**
Konwicki, Tadeusz **8, 28, 54, 117**
Kosinski, Jerzy (Nikodem) **1, 2, 3, 6, 10, 15, 53, 70**
Lem, Stanislaw **8, 15, 40, 149**
Milosz, Czeslaw **5, 11, 22, 31, 56, 82**
Mrozek, Slawomir **3, 13**
Rozewicz, Tadeusz **9, 23, 139**
Singer, Isaac Bashevis **1, 3, 6, 9, 11, 15, 23, 38, 69, 111**
Skolimowski, Jerzy **20**
Szymborska, Wislawa **99, 190**
Wajda, Andrzej **16**
Wittlin, Jozef **25**
Wojciechowska, Maia (Teresa) **26**

**PORTUGUESE**

Migueis, Jose Rodrigues **10**
Saramago, José **119**

**PUERTO RICAN**

Ferré, Rosario **139**
Marqués, René **96**
Piñero, Miguel (Antonio Gomez) **4, 55**
Sánchez, Luis Rafael **23**

**ROMANIAN**

Celan, Paul **10, 19, 53, 82**
Cioran, E(mil) M. **64**
Codrescu, Andrei **46, 121**
Ionesco, Eugène **1, 4, 6, 9, 11, 15, 41, 86**
Rezzori (d'Arezzo), Gregor von **25**
Tzara, Tristan **47**
Wiesel, Elie(zer) **3, 5, 11, 37**

**RUSSIAN**

Aitmatov, Chingiz (Torekulovich) **71**
Akhmadulina, Bella Akhatovna **53**
Akhmatova, Anna **11, 25, 64, 126**
Aksyonov, Vassily (Pavlovich) **22, 37, 101**
Aleshkovsky, Yuz **44**
Almedingen, E. M. **12**
Asimov, Isaac **1, 3, 9, 19, 26, 76, 92**
Bakhtin, Mikhail Mikhailovich **83**
Bitov, Andrei (Georgievich) **57**
Brodsky, Joseph **4, 6, 13, 36, 100**
Deren, Maya **16, 102**
Ehrenburg, Ilya (Grigoryevich) **18, 34, 62**
Eliade, Mircea **19**
Gary, Romain **25**
Goldberg, Anatol **34**
Grade, Chaim **10**
Grossman, Vasily (Semenovich) **41**
Iskander, Fazil **47**
Kabakov, Sasha **59**
Kaletski, Alexander **39**
Krotkov, Yuri **19**
Leonov, Leonid (Maximovich) **92**
Limonov, Edward **67**
Nabokov, Vladimir (Vladimirovich) **1, 2, 3, 6, 8, 11, 15, 23, 44, 46, 64**
Olesha, Yuri (Karlovich) **8**
Pasternak, Boris (Leonidovich) **7, 10, 18, 63**
Paustovsky, Konstantin (Georgievich) **40**
Rahv, Philip **24**
Rand, Ayn **3, 30, 44, 79**
Ratushinskaya, Irina **54**
Rybakov, Anatoli (Naumovich) **23, 53**
Sarraute, Nathalie **1, 2, 4, 8, 10, 31, 80**
Shalamov, Varlam (Tikhonovich) **18**

Nationality Index

Shatrov, Mikhail **59**
Sholokhov, Mikhail (Aleksandrovich) **7, 15**
Sinyavsky, Andrei (Donatevich) **8**
Solzhenitsyn, Aleksandr I(sayevich) **1, 2, 4, 7, 9, 10, 18, 26, 34, 78, 134**
Strugatskii, Arkadii (Natanovich) **27**
Strugatskii, Boris (Natanovich) **27**
Tarkovsky, Andrei (Arsenyevich) **75**
Trifonov, Yuri (Valentinovich) **45**
Troyat, Henri **23**
Voinovich, Vladimir (Nikolaevich) **10, 49, 147**
Voznesensky, Andrei (Andreievich) **1, 15, 57**
Yanovsky, V(assily) S(emenovich) **2, 18**
Yevtushenko, Yevgeny (Alexandrovich) **1, 3, 13, 26, 51, 126**
Yezierska, Anzia **46**
Zaturenska, Marya **6, 11**
Zinoviev, Alexander (Aleksandrovich) **19**

**SALVADORAN**

Alegria, Claribel **75**
Argueta, Manlio **31**

**SCOTTISH**

Banks, Iain M(enzies) **34**
Brown, George Mackay **5, 48, 100**
Cronin, A(rchibald) J(oseph) **32**
Dunn, Douglas (Eaglesham) **6, 40**
Graham, W(illiam) S(idney) **29**
Gray, Alasdair (James) **41**
Grieve, C(hristopher) M(urray) **11, 19**
Hunter, Mollie **21**
Jenkins, (John) Robin **52**
Kelman, James **58, 86**
Kennedy, A. L. **188**
Laing, R(onald) D(avid) **95**
MacBeth, George (Mann) **2, 5, 9**
MacCaig, Norman (Alexander) **36**
MacInnes, Helen (Clark) **27, 39**
MacLean, Alistair (Stuart) **3, 13, 50, 63**
Mackay, Shena **195**
McIlvanney, William **42**
Morgan, Edwin (George) **31**
Smith, Iain Crichton **64**
Spark, Muriel (Sarah) **2, 3, 5, 8, 13, 18, 40, 94**
Taylor, C(ecil) P(hilip) **27**
Walker, David Harry **14**
Welsh, Irvine **144**
Young, Andrew (John) **5**

**SENEGALESE**

Ousmane, Sembene **66**
Senghor, Léopold Sédar **54, 130**

**SLOVENIAN**

Žižek, Slavoj **188**

**SOMALIAN**

Farah, Nuruddin **53, 137**

**SOUTH AFRICAN**

Abrahams, Peter (Henry) **4**
Breytenbach, Breyten **23, 37, 126**
Brink, André (Philippus) **18, 36, 106**
Brutus, Dennis **43**

Coetzee, J(ohn) M(ichael) **23, 33, 66, 117, 161, 162**
Courtenay, Bryce **59**
Fugard, (Harold) Athol **5, 9, 14, 25, 40, 80**
Fugard, Sheila **48**
Gordimer, Nadine **3, 5, 7, 10, 18, 33, 51, 70, 123, 160, 161**
Harwood, Ronald **32**
Head, Bessie **25, 67**
Hope, Christopher (David Tully) **52**
Kunene, Mazisi (Raymond) **85**
La Guma, (Justin) Alex(ander) **19**
Millin, Sarah Gertrude **49**
Mphahlele, Ezekiel **25, 133**
Mtwa, Percy **47**
Ngema, Mbongeni **57**
Nkosi, Lewis **45**
Paton, Alan (Stewart) **4, 10, 25, 55, 106**
Plomer, William Charles Franklin **4, 8**
Prince, F(rank) T(empleton) **22**
Smith, Wilbur (Addison) **33**
Tolkien, J(ohn) R(onald) R(euel) **1, 2, 3, 8, 12, 38**
Tutu, Desmond M(pilo) **80**
van der Post, Laurens (Jan) **5**
Vorster, Gordon **34**

**SPANISH**

Alberti, Rafael **7**
Alfau, Felipe **66**
Almodovar, Pedro **114**
Alonso, Damaso **14**
Arrabal, Fernando **2, 9, 18, 58**
Benet, Juan **28**
Buero Vallejo, Antonio **15, 46, 139**
Bunuel, Luis **16, 80**
Casona, Alejandro **49**
Castedo, Elena **65**
Cela, Camilo José **4, 13, 59, 122**
Cernuda (y Bidón), Luis **54**
del Castillo, Michel **38**
Delibes, Miguel **8, 18**
Espriu, Salvador **9**
Gironella, José María **11**
Gomez de la Serna, Ramon **9**
Goytisolo, Juan **5, 10, 23, 133**
Guillén, Jorge **11**
Matute (Ausejo), Ana María **11**
Otero, Blas de **11**
Rodriguez, Claudio **10**
Ruiz, Jose Martinez **11**
Saura (Atares), Carlos **20**
Sender, Ramón (José) **8**

**SRI LANKAN**

Gunesekera, Romesh **91**

**ST. LUCIAN**

Walcott, Derek (Alton) **2, 4, 9, 14, 25, 42, 67, 76, 160**

**SWEDISH**

Beckman, Gunnel **26**
Bergman, (Ernst) Ingmar **16, 72**
Ekeloef, (Bengt) Gunnar **27**
Johnson, Eyvind (Olof Verner) **14**
Lagerkvist, Paer (Fabian) **7, 10, 13, 54**
Martinson, Harry (Edmund) **14**
Sjoewall, Maj **7**

Transtroemer, Tomas (Goesta) **52, 65**
Wahlöö, Per **7**
Weiss, Peter (Ulrich) **3, 15, 51**

**SWISS**

Canetti, Elias **3, 14, 25, 75, 86**
Duerrenmatt, Friedrich **1, 4, 8, 11, 15, 43, 102**
Frisch, Max (Rudolf) **3, 9, 14, 18, 32, 44**
Hesse, Hermann **1, 2, 3, 6, 11, 17, 25, 69**
King, Francis (Henry) **8, 53, 145**
Kung, Hans **130**
Pinget, Robert **7, 13, 37**
Sauser-Hall, Frederic **18**
Sterchi, Beat **65**
von Daeniken, Erich **30**

**TRINIDADIAN**

Guy, Rosa (Cuthbert) **26**
James, C(yril) L(ionel) R(obert) **33**
Lovelace, Earl **51**
Naipaul, Shiva(dhar Srinivasa) **32, 39**
Naipaul, V(idiadhar) S(urajprasad) **4, 7, 9, 13, 18, 37, 105**
Rampersad, Arnold **44**

**TURKISH**

Hikmet, Nazim **40**
Kemal, Yashar **14, 29**
Pamuk, Orhan **185**
Seferis, George **5, 11**

**UGANDAN**

p'Bitek, Okot **96**

**URUGUAYAN**

Galeano, Eduardo (Hughes) **72**
Onetti, Juan Carlos **7, 10**
Peri Rossi, Cristina **156**

**WELSH**

Abse, Dannie **7, 29**
Arundel, Honor (Morfydd) **17**
Clarke, Gillian **61**
Dahl, Roald **1, 6, 18, 79**
Davies, Rhys **23**
Francis, Dick **2, 22, 42, 102**
Hughes, Richard (Arthur Warren) **1, 11**
Humphreys, Emyr Owen **47**
Jones, David (Michael) **2, 4, 7, 13, 42**
Jones, Terence Graham Parry **21**
Levinson, Deirdre **49**
Llewellyn Lloyd, Richard Dafydd Vivian **7, 80**
Mathias, Roland (Glyn) **45**
Norris, Leslie **14**
Roberts, Kate **15**
Rubens, Bernice (Ruth) **19, 31**
Thomas, R(onald) S(tuart) **6, 13, 48**
Watkins, Vernon Phillips **43**
Williams, (George) Emlyn **15**

**YUGOSLAVIAN**

Andrić, Ivo **8**
Cosic, Dobrica **14**
Kiš, Danilo **57**
Krlěa, Miroslav **8, 114**
Pavic, Milorad **60**
Popa, Vasko **19**
Simic, Charles **6, 9, 22, 49, 68, 130**
Tesich, Steve **40, 69**

# *CLC*-195 Title Index

*An Advent Calendar* (Mackay) **195**:243, 263, 266-68, 276

*Adventures in the Dream Trade* (Gaiman) **195**:193

"The Aesthetics of Silence" (Sontag) **195**:287, 294, 298, 344

*Against Interpretation* (Sontag) **195**:294-95, 298, 303, 306, 308, 313, 316, 319, 324, 333, 335, 341-43, 346-47, 353

"Against Interpretation" (Sontag) **195**:285, 287, 322, 333, 336

*AIDS and Its Metaphors* (Sontag) **195**:289-91, 298, 300, 303, 320, 348, 350, 352, 360

*Alice* (Allen) **195**:19-23, 32, 36, 54, 87, 93, 129, 131

*Alice in Bed* (Sontag) **195**:301, 303, 311

"All Purpose Folk Song" (Gaiman) **195**:197

"All the Pubs in Soho" (Mackay) **195**:245-47

*American Gods* (Gaiman) **195**:186-89, 192-93, 196, 204, 206-7, 209, 226-27, 229, 232-33

*Angels and Visitations* (Gaiman) **195**:230

*Annie Hall* (Allen) **195**:5, 8, 10, 13-18, 25, 32, 36-37, 49-51, 58, 65, 89, 93-94, 107-8, 110, 120, 128-32, 134, 143, 148, 150, 152-53, 155, 165

*Another Woman* (Allen) **195**:22, 29, 33, 51, 69, 87, 106, 120, 129

*Anything Else* (Allen) **195**:150-51, 165

"Art of Humor" (Allen) **195**:117

*The Artist's Widow* (Mackay) **195**:268-72, 274, 278-80

"August" (Gaiman) **195**:238

*Bananas* (Allen) **195**:4-9, 11, 17, 28, 36, 59, 84, 110, 129, 132

"Barbarians" (Mackay) **195**:272

"Bay Wolf" (Gaiman) **195**:230

*The Benefactor* (Sontag) **195**:293, 303, 305-7, 310-11, 325, 344-47

*Black Orchid* (Gaiman) **195**:173, 227, 234, 236

*Books of Magic* (Gaiman) **195**:173, 187, 194, 206, 236

*A Bowl of Cherries* (Mackay) **195**:263-64, 274, 277, 279-80

*Brief Lives* (Gaiman)
    See *The Sandman: Brief Lives*

*Broadway Danny Rose* (Allen) **195**:25, 37, 49, 59, 85, 92, 106, 120-21, 143-44, 148-51, 160, 162

*Brother Carl* (Sontag) **195**:303

*Bullets over Broadway* (Allen) **195**:51, 54-56, 60, 75, 78, 80, 83, 85-87, 89, 92-95, 98, 100-101, 106-7, 120, 152, 155-58, 161-62

"Calliope" (Gaiman) **195**:174, 205, 219-20

"Cardboard City" (Mackay) **195**:247

*Celebrity* (Allen) **195**:103-5, 119-20, 162, 165

"A Century of Cinema" (Sontag) **195**:343, 354

"Cerements" (Gaiman) **195**:222

"Chivalry" (Gaiman) **195**:231

"Cloud-Cuckoo-Land" (Mackay) **195**:252-53

*The Collected Prose of Woody Allen* (Allen) **195**:116

"Convergence" (Gaiman) **195**:222-23

"Conversations with Helmholtz" (Allen) **195**:114

*Conversations with Susan Sontag* (Sontag) **195**:323, 333

*Coraline* (Gaiman) **195**:187, 191-93, 199-200, 204, 206-8, 210, 226, 232-34

"Crazy Hair" (Gaiman) **195**:193

*Crimes and Misdemeanors* (Allen) **195**:23, 27, 29, 32-33, 44-45, 52, 54-55, 60, 80, 86-87, 92, 106-8, 110, 120, 128-29, 141, 143, 150, 153, 159-60, 162

"Crossing the Border" (Mackay) **195**:273

*The Curse of the Jade Scorpion* (Allen) **195**:134-37, 140-42, 165

"The Daughter of Owls" (Gaiman) **195**:230

*The Day I Swapped My Dad for Two Goldfish* (Gaiman) **195**:189, 204, 210, 228, 233-34

"The Day of the Gecko" (Mackay) **195**:272-73

*Death: The High Cost of Living* (Gaiman) **195**:174, 206, 210, 227, 233-34

*Death: The Time of Your Life* (Gaiman) **195**:174, 234

"Death and Venice" (Gaiman) **195**:230

"Death by Art Deco" (Mackay) **195**:273, 278

"Death" (Gaiman) **195**:208

*Death Kit* (Sontag) **195**:292, 303, 307-8, 310-11, 325, 347

"Debriefing" (Sontag) **195**:309

*Deconstructing Harry* (Allen) **195**:76, 81-85, 87-92, 105-12, 119-20, 152, 155, 158-60, 162

"Demons and Dreams" (Sontag) **195**:347

"The Discovery and Use of the Fake Ink Blot" (Allen) **195**:132

*The Doll's House* (Gaiman)
    See *The Sandman: The Doll's House*

"Don't Ask Jack" (Gaiman) **195**:230

*Don't Drink the Water* (Allen) **195**:56

*Don't Panic* (Gaiman) **195**:207

"DQ" (Sontag) **195**:341

*Dream Country* (Gaiman)
    See *The Sandman: Dream Country*

*The Dream Hunters* (Gaiman)
    See *The Sandman: The Dream Hunters*

"A Dream of a Thousand Cats" (Gaiman) **195**:215-16, 223, 229-30, 238

*Dreams of Dead Women's Handbags* (Mackay) **195**:245, 247, 263-64, 273

*Duet for Cannibals* (Sontag) **195**:303

*Dunedin* (Mackay) **195**:247-51, 253-54, 257-59, 261, 263-64, 270, 272, 274, 277

*Dust Falls on Eugene Schlumberger* (Mackay) **195**:250, 263, 280

"The Early Essays" (Allen) **195**:117

*Endless Nights* (Gaiman)
    See *The Sandman: Endless Nights*

*Everyone Says I Love You* (Allen) **195**:74-79, 85, 87, 89, 91, 110, 120, 130

*Everything You Always Wanted to Know about Sex but Were Afraid to Ask* (Allen) **195**:59, 105, 117, 129

*Fables and Reflections* (Gaiman)
    See *The Sandman: Fables and Reflections*

"Fabrizio's: Criticism and Response" (Allen) **195**:114

"Fascinating Fascism" (Sontag) **195**:284, 298, 326

"Fear of Falling" (Gaiman) **195**:219, 229

"Fifteen Portraits of Despair" (Gaiman) **195**:208, 230

*Firefly Motel* (Mackay) **195**:277

*The Front* (Allen) **195**:32

*A Game of You* (Gaiman)
    See *The Sandman: A Game of You*

*Getting Even* (Allen) **195**:8, 113-16

*Ghastly beyond Belief* (Gaiman) **195**:190, 227

"Glass" (Mackay) **195**:253

"God (A Play)" (Allen) **195**:132-33

"The Golden Boy" (Gaiman) **195**:216, 230

"The Goldfish Bowl and Other Stories" (Gaiman) **195**:191

*Good Omens* (Gaiman) **195**:173, 187, 191, 193, 195-96, 209, 228-29

"The Gossage-Vardebedian Papers" (Allen) **195**:114, 132

*Green Lantern/Superman: Legend of the Green Flame* (Gaiman) **195**:236

*Hannah and Her Sisters* (Allen) **195**:20-21, 24, 27, 36, 38-39, 44, 55, 62, 64-66, 79-81, 84-85, 94, 106-7, 111, 120, 129, 141, 149, 152, 157, 159

*Harlequin Valentine* (Gaiman) **195**:233

"The Heart of a Star" (Gaiman) **195**:226

*Heligoland* (Mackay) **195**:279-81

*The High Cost of Living* (Gaiman)
    See *Death: The High Cost of Living*

"Hob's Leviathan" (Gaiman) **195**:230

*Hollywood Ending* (Allen) **195**:134, 138-42, 151, 165

"The Hunt" (Gaiman) **195**:223

*Husbands and Wives* (Allen) **195**:38-39, 41-46, 50-52, 56, 68, 78, 80, 83-85, 89, 91-92, 94, 109, 119-20, 129, 152-56, 158-59, 162

*I, etcetera* (Sontag) **195**:293, 303, 307, 309, 325, 340

"The Idea of Europe (One More Elegy)" (Sontag) **195**:354

"If the Impressionists Had Been Dentists: A Fantasy Exploring the Transposition of Temperament" (Allen) **195**:117

*Illness as Metaphor* (Sontag) **195**:288-91, 298, 303, 309, 352, 360

*In America* (Sontag) **195**:311, 327, 329-30, 333-41, 346

"The Index of Embarrassment" (Mackay) **195**:272, 278

*Interiors* (Allen) **195**:5, 17, 25-28, 33, 51, 69, 80, 87, 93, 124, 126-30, 141, 152

"Introduction" (Gaiman) **195**:230

*The Kindly Ones* (Gaiman) **195**:194, 215, 217, 230

"The Kugelmass Episode" (Allen) **195**:116

"The Last Sand Dance" (Mackay) **195**:273

*The Last Temptation* (Gaiman) **195**:233

*The Laughing Academy* (Mackay) **195**:252-53

"A Letter to Borges" (Sontag) **195**:342

"Lexicon for Available Light" (Sontag) **195**:342

*Illness as Metaphor* (Sontag) **195**:342

"Looking for the Girl" (Gaiman) **195**:231

*Love and Death* (Allen) **195**:12-13, 26, 28, 47, 84, 110, 121, 129, 141

"Man with a Pain" (Sontag) **195**:307

*Manhattan* (Allen) **195**:22, 25, 36-37, 46-47, 49-50, 52, 68, 75, 81, 84, 91, 93, 106-8, 110, 120, 129, 132, 150, 152-56, 162, 165

*Manhattan Murder Mystery* (Allen) **195**:47-49, 51, 54, 56, 78, 83, 85, 89, 92, 94, 106, 129, 165

"Match Wits with Inspector Ford" (Allen) **195**:132

"Men of Good Fortune" (Gaiman) **195**:181-82

"The Metterling Lists" (Allen) **195**:114

"Midsummer Night's Dream" (Gaiman) **195**:220-21

"A Midsummer Night's Dream" (Gaiman) **195**:180-85, 194, 229

*A Midsummer Night's Sex Comedy* (Allen) **195**:27, 33, 56, 126

*Mighty Aphrodite* (Allen) **195**:57-60, 78-79, 83, 85, 89, 91, 106-7, 124, 129

*Miracleman: The Golden Age* (Gaiman) **195**:173, 227, 234

*Mirror Mask* (Gaiman) **195**:204, 227, 233

"The Most Beautiful Dress in the World" (Mackay) **195**:246

"Mr. Big" (Allen) **195**:115, 132

*Mr. Punch* (Gaiman)
See *The Tragical Comedy or Comical Tragedy of Mr. Punch*

*Murder Mysteries* (Gaiman) **195**:233

"Murder Mysteries" (Gaiman) **195**:227

*Music Upstairs* (Mackay) **195**:250, 263, 276, 279-80

"My Philosophy" (Allen) **195**:113

*Neil Gaiman's Midnight Days* (Gaiman) **195**:236

*Neverwhere* (Gaiman) **195**:187, 192-93, 203, 206, 210, 226, 231, 233

*New York Stories* (Allen) **195**:19, 52, 84, 92

"Nicholas Was" (Gaiman) **195**:230

*The Nightclub Years* (Allen) **195**:113, 130

"Notes on 'Camp'" (Sontag) **195**:284-85, 287, 298, 308, 322, 335, 344

*Now We Are Sick* (Gaiman) **195**:227

*Oedipus Wrecks* (Allen) **195**:159

"Oedipus Wrecks" (Allen) **195**:52, 54, 137

*The Official Hitchhiker's Guide to the Galaxy Companion* (Gaiman) **195**:227

*Old Crow* (Mackay) **195**:263, 276

*Old Saybrook* (Allen) **195**:142

*On Photography* (Sontag) **195**:288, 298, 302-3, 309, 313, 315-16, 318, 326, 335, 341-42, 358-60, 362

"On Roland Barthes" (Sontag)
See "Writing Itself: On Roland Barthes"

"On Style" (Sontag) **195**:287, 322-23, 326

"On the Peninsula" (Gaiman) **195**:230

"One Culture and the New Sensibility" (Sontag) **195**:322, 325

"One Life, Furnished in Early Moorcock" (Gaiman) **195**:231

*Only the End of the World Again* (Gaiman) **195**:233

"Only the End of the World Again" (Gaiman) **195**:230

*The Orchard on Fire* (Mackay) **195**:260-62, 264-66, 271-72, 277-80

*Outrageous: Tales of the Old Testament* (Gaiman) **195**:227

"A Pair of Spoons" (Mackay) **195**:252-53

"A Parliament of Rooks" (Gaiman) **195**:214, 223

"Perpetual Spinach" (Mackay) **195**:246-47

"Pilgrimage" (Sontag) **195**:305-6

*Play It Again, Sam* (Allen) **195**:4, 6, 9-10, 12-13, 16, 60, 109-10

"The Pornographic Imagination" (Sontag) **195**:324-25, 344

"the Pornographic Imagination" (Sontag) **195**:298

*Preludes and Nocturnes* (Gaiman)
See *The Sandman: Preludes and Nocturnes*

*Princess Mononoke* (Gaiman) **195**:178, 194, 196-97, 206

"Project for a Trip to China" (Sontag) **195**:293, 297, 306

*Promised Lands* (Sontag) **195**:303-4

*The Purple Rose of Cairo* (Allen) **195**:6, 25, 29, 31-32, 49, 56, 83-84, 106, 111, 120, 129-30, 132-33

*Radio Days* (Allen) **195**:27, 29, 32-33, 36-38, 47, 75, 83-85, 92, 106, 108, 132, 159

"Ramadan" (Gaiman) **195**:194, 238

*Redhill Rococo* (Mackay) **195**:243-44, 246, 263, 279-80

*Regarding the Pain of Others* (Sontag) **195**:355, 358-60, 362

"Retribution" (Allen) **195**:117

*Riverside Drive* (Allen) **195**:142-43

*The Sandman: A Game of You* (Gaiman) **195**:195, 215, 229, 238

*The Sandman: Book of Dreams* (Gaiman) **195**:178, 212

*The Sandman: Brief Lives* (Gaiman) **195**:194-95, 229

*The Sandman: Dream Country* (Gaiman) **195**:229

*The Sandman: Endless Nights* (Gaiman) **195**:201-2, 204, 208-9, 230, 234, 238

*The Sandman: Fables and Reflections* (Gaiman) **195**:219, 229

*The Sandman: Preludes and Nocturnes* (Gaiman) **195**:171, 228

*The Sandman: Season of Mists* (Gaiman) **195**:195, 215, 229

*The Sandman: The Doll's House* (Gaiman) **195**:171, 215, 222, 229, 237

*The Sandman: The Dream Hunters* (Gaiman) **195**:178-79, 230, 234, 238

*The Sandman: The Wake* (Gaiman) **195**:195, 230

*The Sandman: World's End* (Gaiman) **195**:222, 230

*The Sandman* (Gaiman) **195**:171-78, 180, 187-89, 192-95, 201-2, 204-12, 214-25, 227-28, 230, 234-35, 237-39

*The Sandman Special* (Gaiman) **195**:228-29

*Season of Mists* (Gaiman)
See *The Sandman: Season of Mists*

"Selections from the Allen Notebooks" (Allen) **195**:116

*September* (Allen) **195**:27, 29, 33, 46, 69, 93, 120, 129

*Shadows and Fog* (Allen) **195**:23-24, 33-34, 52-54, 56, 78, 87, 106, 111, 158, 160

"The Shallowest Man" (Allen) **195**:117

"Shinty" (Mackay) **195**:252

"Shoggoth's Old Peculiar" (Gaiman) **195**:230

*Side Effects* (Allen) **195**:115-17

*Signal to Noise* (Gaiman) **195**:173, 227, 234-36, 239

"A Silver Summer" (Mackay) **195**:278

"Singleness" (Sontag) **195**:343342

*1602* (Gaiman) **195**:205, 227

"Slang Origins" (Allen) **195**:132

*Sleeper* (Allen) **195**:5, 25, 47, 84, 110, 129-30, 132

*Small Time Crooks* (Allen) **195**:123-24, 134

*Smoke and Mirrors* (Gaiman) **195**:191, 203, 230, 233

"Snow, Glass, Apples" (Gaiman) **195**:227, 230

"Soft Places" (Gaiman) **195**:223

"The Song of Orpheus" (Gaiman) **195**:229

"The Sound of Her Wings" (Gaiman) **195**:229

"Spring Bulletin" (Allen) **195**:115

*Stardust* (Gaiman) **195**:178-79, 187, 189, 192, 194, 203, 206, 231, 233

*Stardust Memories* (Allen) **195**:13, 27-28, 30, 32-33, 50-51, 57, 84, 106, 109-10, 119-20, 129, 150, 152, 155-56, 162

*Styles of Radical Will* (Sontag) **195**:297, 303, 313, 315-16, 318-19, 324, 340, 342

*A Susan Sontag Reader* (Sontag) **195**:287-88, 303

*Sweet and Lowdown* (Allen) **195**:120-21, 123, 152, 162

*Take the Money and Run* (Allen) **195**:4-10, 27, 110, 129, 132

"Tales in the Sand" (Gaiman) **195**:222, 229

"Tastings" (Gaiman) **195**:231

"Tea and Corpses" (Gaiman) **195**:197

"The Tea Song" (Gaiman) **195**:197

"The Tempest" (Gaiman) **195**:183-84, 194

"'There' and 'Here'" (Sontag) **195**:355

"The Thirty First of October" (Mackay) **195**:246

"Thirty Years Later . . ." (Sontag) **195**:343

*The Time of Your Life* (Gaiman)
See *Death: The Time of Your Life*

*Toddler on the Run* (Mackay) **195**:263, 279

*The Tragical Comedy or Comical Tragedy of Mr. Punch* (Gaiman) **195**:173, 227, 234, 236, 239

*Trip to Hanoi* (Sontag) **195**:296-98

"Trip to Hanoi" (Sontag) **195**:303, 326

"Trouser Ladies" (Mackay) **195**:272, 278

"A Twenties Memory" (Allen) **195**:115

"24 Hours" (Gaiman) **195**:217, 219-20

*Under the Sign of Saturn* (Sontag) **195**:284-85, 297, 303, 308, 324, 342

*Unguided Tour* (Sontag) **195**:303

"Unguided Tour" (Sontag) **195**:293, 309

*Violent Cases* (Gaiman) **195**:173, 227, 233-36, 239

"Violets and Strawberries in the Snow" (Mackay) **195**:245

"Viva Vargas" (Allen) **195**:8

*The Volcano Lover* (Sontag) **195**:301, 303, 305, 308-13, 315, 320, 327, 329-30, 334, 336, 341, 353

"Waiting for Godot in Sarajevo" (Sontag) **195**:342

*The Wake* (Gaiman)
See *The Sandman: The Wake*

"The Way We Live Now" (Sontag) **195**:299-300, 309, 329, 335, 348, 350-51

"We Can Get Them for You Wholesale" (Gaiman) **195**:231

"What I've Tasted of Desire" (Gaiman) **195**:209

"What's Happening in America" (Sontag) **195**:287-88, 326

*What's New, Pussycat?* (Allen) **195**:4

"Where the Carpet Ends" (Mackay) **195**:246

*Where the Stress Falls* (Sontag) **195**:341-43, 353

"The Whore of Mensa" (Allen) **195**:115, 132

*Without Feathers* (Allen) **195**:115-17, 132-34

*The Wolves in the Walls* (Gaiman) **195**:204, 207, 210, 227, 233-34

*World's End* (Gaiman)
See *The Sandman: World's End*

*The World's Smallest Unicorn* (Mackay) **195**:273

"The World's Smallest Unicorn" (Mackay) **195**:278

*Writer's Block* (Allen) **195**:142

"Writing Itself: On Roland Barthes" (Sontag) **195**:303, 322, 341-42

*Zelig* (Allen) **195**:27-29, 32-33, 46, 84, 106, 110, 120, 141, 160

ISBN 0-7876-7965-8

90000